MORTGAGES AND
REAL ESTATE FINANCE

CONTEMPORARY LEGAL EDUCATION SERIES

CASES AND MATERIALS ON

Mortgages and Real Estate Finance

JAMES COOPER-HILL

Senior Counsel, Coldwell Banker Commercial Real Estate Services
Adjunct Professor of Law, University of Houston

MARTIN J. GREENBERG

Member of Wisconsin Bar
Adjunct Professor of Law, Marquette University

THE MICHIE COMPANY
Law Publishers
CHARLOTTESVILLE, VIRGINIA

Preface

The new attorney first venturing into practice will likely be called upon by peers to provide counsel in the purchasing and financing of residential real estate. Assuming that basic first year property courses touch on real estate acquisition and finance only lightly, if at all, a course for second or third year students in real estate finance is desirable to provide some background for an area of the law likely to be encountered in the early years of one's practice. Such a course should not be too heavily academic for it is a subject most conducive to a practical approach.

Both of the authors of this book have background as full-time law school professors as well as having spent considerable years in the private practice of law involving real estate transactions. The common ground for our undertaking the compiling of this book was agreement that a pragmatic approach would best serve law students. Interspersed among the case opinions are text and note material designed to have the student consider the subject matter from the point of view of an attorney dealing with such a problem for a client. Text was often prepared from the perspective of instructing a new lawyer how to do something as well as providing an academic approach to educating a student.

The final chapter in the book, "Obtaining a Mortgage Loan," is designed to orient the student to the real world of loan applications, percentage point loan fees, getting the commitment and ultimately closing the transaction. This chapter should provide needed information to the novice, either lawyer or student. In teaching the course one may wish to take the last chapter out of order and cover this material immediately after the introductory chapter. This would be an acceptable alternative to using the book in the order in which it was assembled. The chapter on government involvement is designed to demonstrate to the student that financing real estate does not always involve just the borrower and the lender; often it involves the government's regulation, permission or even participation.

As a suitable conclusion to a course using this book we would recommend the professor demonstrate a real estate closing for the class using typical participants in a closing: real estate brokers, loan officers, title company closers and, of course, a buyer and a seller. A mock closing can be done using the forms found in chapters one and ten. A closing, mock or real, can be video taped, if such equipment is available, and shown to students who are also furnished copies of all the documents used in the closing. Having used this format to conclude a course covering the material of this book we feel that the students not only can have the entire course material brought together for them in a brief hour; they also can have the experience of attending what is for most of them their first real estate closing.

Changes in the national economy in recent years have brought about many changes in the area of real estate finance which have resulted in new law. New cases are being handed down with such frequency that it is easy to envision areas which are going to need updated lectures in this course to modify our comments or those of courts reported in the cases. Areas where litigation is pending, such as "due-on" clauses, or where litigation is likely, such as the defense of "clogging" to the enforcement of a convertible mortgage, warrant close scrutiny by professors so that the text can be supplemented by lecture. Because these changes in the law will likely stimulate the production of a second edition, we welcome the comments and criticisms of faculty and students as to how we can improve our book.

Acknowledgments

Acknowledgment of assistance and expression of appreciation is somewhat a private matter which becomes public in print. Those who expect to find themselves mentioned here should read on while for others continued reading is optional.

One observation made of other's acknowledgments: if the author's spouse is not mentioned last she usually only precedes old dog Rover who sat quietly at his master's feet while the manuscript was prepared. To deviate from that precedent let me express my great appreciation to my wife, Jane Cooper-Hill, a lawyer and scholar, who read the manuscript and offered many suggestions. Some of what appears is at her suggestion; more importantly some material that does not appear is absent for the same reason. Her help and patience is much appreciated. Others deserve thanks for their contributions to the development of this book: John Hetland first interested me in legal writing by giving me the opportunity to contribute to his CALIFORNIA REAL ESTATE SECURED TRANSACTIONS, portions of which are reproduced in Chapter 3 with his kind permission; Norman George, recently acting Dean of the University of Dayton School of Law, always had a word of encouragement for me. William C. Cooper of the California Bar and David A. Barnette of the West Virginia Bar each co-authored articles with me on subjects which were helpful in assembling portions of the book. Several students did cite checking and tedious hours of photocopying of case material and they deserve special thanks: Harriet Turney, Sandra Smith, William Sudela and the Varsity Team from the University of Dayton School of Law: Nancy Heckard, Kathryn Lamme, Mary Silverberg, Gene Silverblatt and Greg Todd. All these students contributed with research and suggestions along the way. Jane Roberts assembled and typed the footnotes in the final hours of manuscript preparation. My thanks to all these people for their efforts without which my task would have been more difficult. The final responsibility, however, is the author's and whatever errors exist are mine.

Houston, Texas
February 1982

All of us have certain priorities in life. Family has always been of a major importance in my life. While my wife, Bev, did not contribute to the writing or editing of this book, her encouragement and support were key to the completion of this book.

Thanks, Bev, for your continued kindness and understanding.

Thanks also to Kari and Steven, my children, who have shared their father's time with this project.

Marquette University Law School and especially Dean Robert Boden and Dean Charles Mentkowski have been part and parcel of this project from its commencement. Thank you, Deans, and Marquette University Law School for your faith in me and for your committing your resources to assist in the completion of this book

O. K. Johnson, Jr., Senior Vice-President of Milwaukee Western Bank, has lent me his years of experience in creating some of the more practical aspects of this book. Thanks, O. K., for sharing your wisdom.

Finally, Marquette Law School graduates, Attorneys Henry Pinekenstein and Nicholas J. Wood's time, research, suggestions, and continued input over the last several years have been essential to the completion of this project. Thank you, Henry and Nick, for your dedicated efforts.

Milwaukee, Wisconsin
February 1982

Summary Table of Contents

Table of Contents

Table of Cases

Principal cases are those with page references in italics.

Chapter 1

MORTGAGES: PAST AND PRESENT

Neither a borrower, nor a lender be;
for loan oft loses both itself and friend,
and borrowing dulls the edge of husbandry.

Shakespeare, *Hamlet,* Act I, Scene III

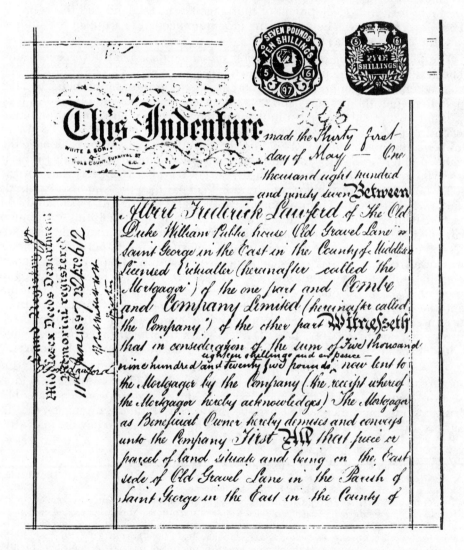

Illustration 1

Nineteenth Century English Mortgage

A. INTRODUCTION

The origin of the use of real property by English speaking people as security for a loan is lost in history.[1] It even precedes the Battle of Hastings in 1066, which changed much of English real property law. Some knowledge of that early law is desirable for the student of the modern mortgage; learning how we arrived at our present status may be helpful in understanding that status. A detailed description of the evolution of the mortgage is better left to scholars of history and the law, as it has already been set forth quite well.[2] Osborne, in his thorough volume on mortgages,[3] can provide the reader with more than adequate detail on the history and development of mortgage law in England and this country. Therefore, history will be kept to the minimum needed to acquaint the student with the basis for today's formats.

The *fee simple subject to a condition subsequent* is a fruitful place to begin. The grantor held a *right of entry* which was also known as a *power of termination.* When the condition subsequent occurred, the grantor, or his heirs, had the right to reenter the property and take title. Most textbook examples of this type of grant involve either the continued maintenance of a church or a prohibition against the sale of alcohol on the land. A typical grant might read: "To *A* and his heirs, but if alcohol is ever sold on the land then the Grantor shall have the right to enter upon the land and terminate the estate of *A*." All this is a bit wearying to the jaded second or third year law student. However, consider the following grant: "To *A*, but if the Grantor shall pay to *A* the sum of 100 pounds on Law Day, then the Grantor shall have the right to enter upon the land and terminate the estate of *A*."[4] Here is where a bit of history is helpful. At common law when a landowner mortgaged his property, the lender took title and possession until the mortgage was paid in full. Amortization with periodic payments was unheard of. The borrower had but one opportunity to satisfy the obligation and that opportunity lasted only one day, Law Day.[5] If the borrower failed to repay the loan on the one day specified, then the lender simply retained the land and the borrower lost all rights.[6] This is far from the various foreclosure practices used in the United States today,[7] but it is a short journey from the forfeitures that occurred on Law Day to post-foreclosure redemption and anti-deficiency statutes that give considerable rights to defaulting borrowers.

The strangeness of modern mortgage practice to law students probably is due in part to the inconsistencies with basic contract law. The loss of land held as security upon the default by the borrower seems straightforward enough. The basic contract ingredients appear to be there: consideration, mutuality, etc. To suggest that the defaulting borrower should have the right to pay the loan after

---

[1] Wigmore, The Pledge Idea, 10 Harv. L. Rev. 321 (1897).

[2] *See* Hazeltine, The Gage of Land in Medieval England, 17 Harv. L. Rev. 549 (1904); Chaplin, The Story of Mortgage Law, 4 Harv. L. Rev. 1 (1890).

[3] G. Osborne, Mortgages (2d ed. 1970). This volume has been revised into an excellent edition which has a more modern approach and deletes some of the history. The earlier second edition has a very detailed history and students wishing more background should look to the second edition. The later revision is G. Osborne, G. Nelson & D. Whitman, Real Estate Finance Law (1979).

[4] Law Day as used here means the day on which the mortgage was payable and should not be confused with Law Day in the United States which is a day set aside to honor the law and falls on May 1.

[5] G. Osborne, Secured Transactions 217 (1967); G. Osborne, G. Nelson & D. Whitman, Real Estate Finance Law 7 (1979).

[6] *Id.*

[7] *See* Chapter 5 *infra* on Foreclosure.

foreclosure on the land,[8] or to prevent the lender from collecting all the debt [9] if the land value is insufficient, is contrary to all that was learned in Contracts I. However, the course that allows the borrower these apparently extraordinary rights was a logical one traveled through the Courts of Equity.

Being given but one day, and one day only, on which to pay one's debt or alternatively lose one's land seems harsh, particularly when one considers that the lender might hide in the woods all day in order to avoid receiving payment and thus keep the borrower's land.[10] Allowing the borrower a little more time in which to pay and not lose the land hardly violates the contract excessively. After all, the lender bargained for one of two things: either to keep the land, or to have his money repaid.[11] Extending the day of payment a short period still allows the lender the benefit of his bargain. Thus, the first sign of equitable redemption appeared in England.[12]

If the land had increased in value during the time the loan was unpaid, should the borrower or the lender benefit from that increase? Do not forget that the lender had possession of the land during the loan term and was able to keep all the rents and profits generated by the land. One way to insure that the lender is not unjustly enriched from the land's increased value would be to put the land up for sale and pay the lender from the proceeds. Any excess above the loan could be paid to the borrower. That idea gave birth to foreclosure by sale [13] and is reasonable enough. However, allowing the borrower to return [14] with cash in hand even after the foreclosure sale seems contrary to both logic and law. In order to protect borrowers in difficult times from losing their land, the concept of statutory redemption was conceived. Finally, in order to protect the borrower from losing both his money *and* his land the law developed anti-deficiency legislation which prevented the lender from entering too low a bid at the foreclosure sale and later suing for the balance of the debt, thus collecting both money and land.[15]

B. SECURED VERSUS UNSECURED

The most basic step in learning mortgage law is to understand the nature of security. A creditor who has no security, who has no legal interest in the debtor's property, must seek to collect that debt from any source available. When a borrower defaults in repaying an obligation the lender's remedy generally would be to sue the borrower, obtain a judgment for the debt (plus attorney's fees and court costs when appropriate), and search for property of the debtor to have sold in order to satisfy the judgment. The property might be anything of value which the borrower owns that has not been labeled "exempt" by statute. Likewise, the judgment creditor with no security must scramble with all the other unsecured creditors in looking for the debtor's property. Whoever arrives first can grab virtually anything the debtor owns to the exclusion of a second arriving creditor.

---

[8] *See* Chapter 6 *infra* on Redemption.

[9] *See* Chapter 7 *infra* on Depression Legislation, particularly the section on anti-deficiency statutes.

[10] G. Osborne, G. Nelson & D. Whitman, Real Estate Finance Law 7 (1979).

[11] This is the basic concept for both anti-deficiency statutes and Connecticut style strict foreclosure. *See* North End Bank & Trust Co. v. Mandell, 155 A. 80, 81 (Conn. 1931); Bergin v. Robbins, 146 A. 724, 726 (Conn. 1929).

[12] G. Osborne, Mortgages § 6 (2d ed. 1970).

[13] *See generally* Chapter 6 *infra* on Redemption. *See also* G. Osborne, Mortgages § 7 (2d ed. 1970).

[14] Less than 1% of foreclosed mortgages are redeemed, however.

[15] *See* Chapter 7 *infra* on Depression Legislation.

If one has a security interest in a specific item of property owned by the debtor, speed ceases to be as important. The creditor may look first to the particular item used as security for the loan to the exclusion of all other creditors. The security item may be sold and the proceeds used to satisfy the secured obligation. In the event there are excess proceeds, the general rule is that the excess goes to the borrower who owned the item.

A borrower may use the same item of property as security for more than one loan. In that case, the first lender has the better right to be repaid in the event of default and foreclosure sale. What money remains after satisfying the first obligation may then be used to satisfy the second obligation. This is called priority and is dealt with in Chapter 4.

TYLER v. WRIGHT

Supreme Judicial Court of Maine
122 Me. 558, 119 A. 583 (1923)

PER CURIAM. This is a real action to obtain possession of certain lands. The demandant claims under a mortgage given her by Charles R. Foote in his lifetime. The defendants are the heirs at law of said Foote. By way of brief statement the defendants alleged that the mortgage was not intended to secure, and did not secure, any valid legal obligation or indebtedness, and was never executed by Foote for that purpose; that there was no valid legal consideration for said mortgage; and that said mortgage was never delivered by Foote to the plaintiff. Briefly, the defendants invoke the familiar legal principle that it is essential to the validity of a mortgage, and to the right of the mortgagee to enforce it, that it should be supported by a valid consideration (27 Cyc. 1049); or, to state the principle in more quaint form, since a conveyance cannot be a mortgage unless given to secure the performance of an obligation, the existence of an obligation to be secured is an essential element, without which the mortgage instrument is but a shadow without substance (19 R. C. L. 294).

The case was tried before a jury, and at the conclusion of the testimony the presiding justice directed a verdict for the defendants. Upon plaintiff's exception to this ruling the case comes before us.

It is a well-established and familiar rule of procedure in this state that the court may properly instruct the jury to return a verdict for either party when it is apparent that a contrary verdict would not be allowed to stand. *Wellington v. Corinna*, 104 Me. 252, 71 Atl. 889.

We are to examine the report, therefore, in order to test the question whether upon the same a verdict for the plaintiff could be sustained. It is the opinion of the court that such verdict could not stand, and that the presiding justice was correct in his determination, upon the law involved and the testimony given in the case, to rule as he did.

Exceptions overruled.

C. FORMS OF MORTGAGES

In the United States today there are two general forms of mortgages when real property is the item used as security for a loan. These two forms are called a mortgage and a deed of trust. The deed of trust is a three-party form in which a trustee has the security interest for the benefit of the lender. The trustee is given the power to sell the property for the benefit of the lender in case of default. It has been accurately stated that a deed of trust is nothing more than a mortgage with a power of sale.[16] The two different forms of mortgage may cause some confusion, particularly in the granting language. The language used in a mortgage appears to convey the property to the lender. Further on in the mortgage, language is found that indicates the conveyance is void if the borrower pays the loan. How different is this from the common law mortgage which provided for repayment and reentry on the land?

The deed of trust may be more readily understood. It clearly states that the property in question is being transferred to the trustee to secure the repayment of a certain sum of money, plus the performance of other obligations which will become important to the reader later. The "fine print" of the deed of trust sets forth the many rights which are vested in the trustee, the most important of which is the power to sell the property and use the sale proceeds to satisfy the loan for which the land was security.

One thing that the two forms have in common is that they are always accompanied by a note or some other form of written obligation. A promissory note spells out the nature of the debt; the mortgage spells out the nature of the security for the payment of the debt. Without a debt the mortgage ceases to exist.[17]

Following this section are several forms in use at the present time. The forms identified by the letters FNMA are those prepared and distributed by the Federal National Mortgage Association, an organization which buys mortgages from lenders.[18] These forms are by no means the only ones used today but they are frequently used and are typical of mortgages or deeds of trust found in any part of the United States. There is considerable variety in the types of note forms used today, depending on which of many ways the interest is charged by the lender and the time for either repaying or renegotiating the loan.[19] Variable interest rates and renegotiable loans have made substantial inroads into an area where interest rates were once fixed at the time the loan was made and remained constant for the entire loan term; twenty, twenty-five, or thirty years. Because of the changes in the lending market today, forms for some of these alternatives are also included.

A passing acquaintance with these forms is likely to make many of the subsequent cases more readable. Reference back to the forms after reading each new section of the book will undoubtedly assist the student in assimilating the concepts of mortgage law.

---

[16] "[F]or all practical purposes, a mortgage which contains a power of sale is similar in legal effect and economic functions as [sic] the deed of trust." H. Miller & M. Starr, Current Law of California Real Estate § 3:1, p. 315 (1975).

[17] Tyler v. Wright, 122 Me. 558, 559, 119 A. 583, 584 (1923), *supra* p. 4.

[18] The Federal National Mortgage Association (FNMA) commonly called "Fanny Mae" is discussed in Chapter 9 *infra*, along with the Government National Mortgage Association (GNMA) called "Ginnie Mae" and the Federal Home Loan Mortgage Corporation (FHLMC) called "Freddie Mac."

[19] Variable interest rate loans, renegotiable interest rate loans, graduated payment loans and other alternative mortgage forms are discussed in Chapter 2 *infra*.

MORTGAGE

THIS MORTGAGE is made this............................day of........................., 19...., between the Mortgagor, ...(herein "Borrower"), and the Mortgagee, ..., a corporation organized and existing under the laws of....................................., whose address is............................. ....(herein "Lender").

WHEREAS, Borrower is indebted to Lender in the principal sum of............................ ....Dollars, which indebtedness is evidenced by Borrower's note dated...........................(herein "Note"), providing for monthly installments of principal and interest, with the balance of the indebtedness, if not sooner paid, due and payable on.......................... ....;

To SECURE to Lender (a) the repayment of the indebtedness evidenced by the Note, with interest thereon, the payment of all other sums, with interest thereon, advanced in accordance herewith to protect the security of this Mortgage, and the performance of the covenants and agreements of Borrower herein contained, and (b) the repayment of any future advances, with interest thereon, made to Borrower by Lender pursuant to paragraph 21 hereof (herein "Future Advances"), Borrower does hereby mortgage, grant and convey to Lender the following described property located in the County of....................................., State of New York:

which has the address of...,..................................,
                             [Street]   [City]
..............................(herein "Property Address");
    [State and Zip Code]

TOGETHER with all the improvements now or hereafter erected on the property, and all easements, rights, appurtenances, rents, royalties, mineral, oil and gas rights and profits, water, water rights, and water stock, and all fixtures now or hereafter attached to the property, and all right, title and interest of Borrower in and to the land lying in the streets and roads in front of and adjoining the property, all of which, including replacements and additions thereto, shall be deemed to be and remain a part of the property covered by this Mortgage; and all of the foregoing, together with said property (or the leasehold estate if this Mortgage is on a leasehold) are herein referred to as the "Property".

Borrower covenants that Borrower is lawfully seised of the estate hereby conveyed and has the right to mortgage, grant and convey the Property, that the Property is unencumbered, and that Borrower will warrant and defend generally the title to the Property against all claims and demands, subject to any declarations, easements or restrictions listed in a schedule of exceptions to coverage in any title insurance policy insuring Lender's interest in the Property.

NEW YORK—1 to 4 Family—6/75—**FNMA/FHLMC UNIFORM INSTRUMENT**

Illustration 2

FNMA/FHLMC Mortgage

UNIFORM COVENANTS. Borrower and Lender covenant and agree as follows:

1. Payment of Principal and Interest. Borrower shall promptly pay when due the principal of and interest on the indebtedness evidenced by the Note, prepayment and late charges as provided in the Note, and the principal of and interest on any Future Advances secured by this Mortgage.

2. Funds for Taxes and Insurance. Subject to applicable law or to a written waiver by Lender, Borrower shall pay to Lender on the day monthly installments of principal and interest are payable under the Note, until the Note is paid in full, a sum (herein "Funds") equal to one-twelfth of the yearly taxes and assessments which may attain priority over this Mortgage, and ground rents on the Property, if any, plus one-twelfth of yearly premium installments for hazard insurance, plus one-twelfth of yearly premium installments for mortgage insurance, if any, all as reasonably estimated initially and from time to time by Lender on the basis of assessments and bills and reasonable estimates thereof.

The Funds shall be held in an institution the deposits or accounts of which are insured or guaranteed by a Federal or state agency (including Lender if Lender is such an institution). Lender shall apply the Funds to pay said taxes, assessments, insurance premiums and ground rents. Lender may not charge for so holding and applying the Funds, analyzing said account, or verifying and compiling said assessments and bills, unless Lender pays Borrower interest on the Funds and applicable law permits Lender to make such a charge. Borrower and Lender may agree in writing at the time of execution of this Mortgage that interest on the Funds shall be paid to Borrower, and unless such agreement is made or applicable law requires such interest to be paid, Lender shall not be required to pay Borrower any interest or earnings on the Funds. Lender shall give to Borrower, without charge, an annual accounting of the Funds showing credits and debits to the Funds and the purpose for which each debit to the Funds was made. The Funds are pledged as additional security for the sums secured by this Mortgage.

If the amount of the Funds held by Lender, together with the future monthly installments of Funds payable prior to the due dates of taxes, assessments, insurance premiums and ground rents, shall exceed the amount required to pay said taxes, assessments, insurance premiums and ground rents as they fall due, such excess shall be, at Borrower's option, either promptly repaid to Borrower or credited to Borrower on monthly installments of Funds. If the amount of the Funds held by Lender shall not be sufficient to pay taxes, assessments, insurance premiums and ground rents as they fall due, Borrower shall pay to Lender any amount necessary to make up the deficiency within 30 days from the date notice is mailed by Lender to Borrower requesting payment thereof.

Upon payment in full of all sums secured by this Mortgage, Lender shall promptly refund to Borrower any Funds held by Lender. If under paragraph 18 hereof the Property is sold or the Property is otherwise acquired by Lender, Lender shall apply, no later than immediately prior to the sale of the Property or its acquisition by Lender, any Funds held by Lender at the time of application as a credit against the sums secured by this Mortgage.

3. Application of Payments. Unless applicable law provides otherwise, all payments received by Lender under the Note and paragraphs 1 and 2 hereof shall be applied by Lender first in payment of amounts payable to Lender by Borrower under paragraph 2 hereof, then to interest payable on the Note, then to the principal of the Note, and then to interest and principal on any Future Advances.

4. Charges; Liens. Borrower shall pay all taxes, assessments and other charges, fines and impositions attributable to the Property which may attain a priority over this Mortgage, and leasehold payments or ground rents, if any, in the manner provided under paragraph 2 hereof or, if not paid in such manner, by Borrower making payment, when due, directly to the payee thereof. Borrower shall promptly furnish to Lender all notices of amounts due under this paragraph, and in the event Borrower shall make payment directly, Borrower shall promptly furnish to Lender receipts evidencing such payments. Borrower shall promptly discharge any lien which has priority over this Mortgage; provided, that Borrower shall not be required to discharge any such lien so long as Borrower shall agree in writing to the payment of the obligation secured by such lien in a manner acceptable to Lender, or shall in good faith contest such lien by, or defend enforcement of such lien in, legal proceedings which operate to prevent the enforcement of the lien or forfeiture of the Property or any part thereof.

5. Hazard Insurance. Borrower shall keep the improvements now existing or hereafter erected on the Property insured against loss by fire, hazards included within the term "extended coverage", and such other hazards as Lender may require and in such amounts and for such periods as Lender may require; provided, that Lender shall not require that the amount of such coverage exceed that amount of coverage required to pay the sums secured by this Mortgage.

The insurance carrier providing the insurance shall be chosen by Borrower subject to approval by Lender; provided, that such approval shall not be unreasonably withheld. All premiums on insurance policies shall be paid in the manner provided under paragraph 2 hereof or, if not paid in such manner, by Borrower making payment, when due, directly to the insurance carrier.

All insurance policies and renewals thereof shall be in form acceptable to Lender and shall include a standard mortgage clause in favor of and in form acceptable to Lender. Lender shall have the right to hold the policies and renewals thereof, and Borrower shall promptly furnish to Lender all renewal notices and all receipts of paid premiums. In the event of loss, Borrower shall give prompt notice to the insurance carrier and Lender. Lender may make proof of loss if not made promptly by Borrower.

Unless Lender and Borrower otherwise agree in writing, insurance proceeds shall be applied to restoration or repair of the Property damaged, provided such restoration or repair is economically feasible and the security of this Mortgage is not thereby impaired. If such restoration or repair is not economically feasible or if the security of this Mortgage would be impaired, the insurance proceeds shall be applied to the sums secured by this Mortgage, with the excess, if any, paid to Borrower. If the Property is abandoned by Borrower, or if Borrower fails to respond to Lender within 30 days from the date notice is mailed by Lender to Borrower that the insurance carrier offers to settle a claim for insurance benefits, Lender is authorized to collect and apply the insurance proceeds at Lender's option either to restoration or repair of the Property or to the sums secured by this Mortgage.

Unless Lender and Borrower otherwise agree in writing, any such application of proceeds to principal shall not extend or postpone the due date of the monthly installments referred to in paragraphs 1 and 2 hereof or change the amount of such installments. If under paragraph 18 hereof the Property is acquired by Lender, all right, title and interest of Borrower in and to any insurance policies and in and to the proceeds thereof resulting from damage to the Property prior to the sale or acquisition shall pass to Lender to the extent of the sums secured by this Mortgage immediately prior to such sale or acquisition.

6. Preservation and Maintenance of Property; Leaseholds; Condominiums; Planned Unit Developments. Borrower shall keep the Property in good repair and shall not commit waste or permit impairment or deterioration of the Property and shall comply with the provisions of any lease if this Mortgage is on a leasehold. If this Mortgage is on a unit in a condominium or a planned unit development, Borrower shall perform all of Borrower's obligations under the declaration or covenants creating or governing the condominium or planned unit development, the by-laws and regulations of the condominium or planned unit development, and constituent documents. If a condominium or planned unit development rider is executed by Borrower and recorded together with this Mortgage, the covenants and agreements of such rider shall be incorporated into and shall amend and supplement the covenants and agreements of this Mortgage as if the rider were a part hereof.

7. Protection of Lender's Security. If Borrower fails to perform the covenants and agreements contained in this Mortgage, or if any action or proceeding is commenced which materially affects Lender's interest in the Property, including, but not limited to, eminent domain, insolvency, code enforcement, or arrangements or proceedings involving a bankrupt or decedent, then Lender at Lender's option, upon notice to Borrower, may make such appearances, disburse such sums and take such action as is necessary to protect Lender's interest, including, but not limited to, disbursement of reasonable attorney's fees and entry upon the Property to make repairs. If Lender required mortgage insurance as a condition of making the loan secured by this Mortgage, Borrower shall pay the premiums required to maintain such insurance in effect until such time as the requirement for such insurance terminates in accordance with Borrower's and Lender's written agreement or applicable law. Borrower shall pay the amount of all mortgage insurance premiums in the manner provided under paragraph 2 hereof.

Any amounts disbursed by Lender pursuant to this paragraph 7, with interest thereon, shall become additional indebtedness of Borrower secured by this Mortgage. Unless Borrower and Lender agree to other terms of payment, such amounts shall be payable upon notice from Lender to Borrower requesting payment thereof, and shall bear interest from the date of disbursement at the rate payable from time to time on outstanding principal under the Note unless payment of interest at such rate would be contrary to applicable law, in which event such amounts shall bear interest at the highest rate permissible under applicable law. Nothing contained in this paragraph 7 shall require Lender to incur any expense or take any action hereunder.

8. Inspection. Lender may make or cause to be made reasonable entries upon and inspections of the Property, provided that Lender shall give Borrower notice prior to any such inspection specifying reasonable cause therefor related to Lender's interest in the Property.

9. Condemnation. The proceeds of any award or claim for damages, direct or consequential, in connection with any condemnation or other taking of the Property, or part thereof, or for conveyance in lieu of condemnation, are hereby assigned and shall be paid to Lender.

In the event of a total taking of the Property, the proceeds shall be applied to the sums secured by this Mortgage, with the excess, if any, paid to Borrower. In the event of a partial taking of the Property, unless Borrower and Lender otherwise agree in writing, there shall be applied to the sums secured by this Mortgage such proportion of the proceeds as is equal to that proportion which the amount of the sums secured by this Mortgage immediately prior to the date of taking bears to the fair market value of the Property immediately prior to the date of taking, with the balance of the proceeds paid to Borrower.

If the Property is abandoned by Borrower, or if, after notice by Lender to Borrower that the condemnor offers to make an award or settle a claim for damages, Borrower fails to respond to Lender within 30 days after the date such notice is mailed, Lender is authorized to collect and apply the proceeds, at Lender's option, either to restoration or repair of the Property or to the sums secured by this Mortgage.

Unless Lender and Borrower otherwise agree in writing, any such application of proceeds to principal shall not extend or postpone the due date of the monthly installments referred to in paragraphs 1 and 2 hereof or change the amount of such installments.

10. Borrower Not Released. Extension of the time for payment or modification of amortization of the sums secured by this Mortgage granted by Lender to any successor in interest of Borrower shall not operate to release, in any manner, the liability of the original Borrower and Borrower's successors in interest. Lender shall not be required to commence proceedings against such successor or refuse to extend time for payment or otherwise modify amortization of the sums secured by this Mortgage by reason of any demand made by the original Borrower and Borrower's successors in interest.

11. Forbearance by Lender Not a Waiver. Any forbearance by Lender in exercising any right or remedy hereunder, or otherwise afforded by applicable law, shall not be a waiver of or preclude the exercise of any such right or remedy. The procurement of insurance or the payment of taxes or other liens or charges by Lender shall not be a waiver of Lender's right to accelerate the maturity of the indebtedness secured by this Mortgage.

12. Remedies Cumulative. All remedies provided in this Mortgage are distinct and cumulative to any other right or remedy under this Mortgage or afforded by law or equity, and may be exercised concurrently, independently or successively.

13. Successors and Assigns Bound; Joint and Several Liability; Captions. The covenants and agreements herein contained shall bind, and the rights hereunder shall inure to, the respective successors and assigns of Lender and Borrower, subject to the provisions of paragraph 17 hereof. All covenants and agreements of Borrower shall be joint and several. The captions and headings of the paragraphs of this Mortgage are for convenience only and are not to be used to interpret or define the provisions hereof.

14. Notice. Except for any notice required under applicable law to be given in another manner, (a) any notice to Borrower provided for in this Mortgage shall be given by mailing such notice by certified mail addressed to Borrower at the Property Address or at such other address as Borrower may designate by notice to Lender as provided herein, and (b) any notice to Lender shall be given by certified mail, return receipt requested, to Lender's address stated herein or to such other address as Lender may designate by notice to Borrower as provided herein. Any notice provided for in this Mortgage shall be deemed to have been given to Borrower or Lender when given in the manner designated herein.

15. Uniform Mortgage; Governing Law; Severability. This form of mortgage combines uniform covenants for national use and non-uniform covenants with limited variations by jurisdiction to constitute a uniform security instrument covering real property. This Mortgage shall be governed by the law of the jurisdiction in which the Property is located. In the event that any provision or clause of this Mortgage or the Note conflicts with applicable law, such conflict shall not affect other provisions of this Mortgage or the Note which can be given effect without the conflicting provision, and to this end the provisions of the Mortgage and the Note are declared to be severable.

16. Borrower's Copy. Borrower shall be furnished a conformed copy of the Note and of this Mortgage at the time of execution or after recordation hereof.

17. Transfer of the Property; Assumption. If all or any part of the Property or an interest therein is sold or transferred by Borrower without Lender's prior written consent, excluding (a) the creation of a lien or encumbrance subordinate to this Mortgage, (b) the creation of a purchase money security interest for household appliances, (c) a transfer by devise, descent or by operation of law upon the death of a joint tenant or (d) the grant of any leasehold interest of three years or less not containing an option to purchase, Lender may, at Lender's option, declare all the sums secured by this Mortgage to be immediately due and payable. Lender shall have waived such option to accelerate if, prior to the sale or transfer, Lender and the person to whom the Property is to be sold or transferred reach agreement in writing that the credit of such person is satisfactory to Lender and that the interest payable on the sums secured by this Mortgage shall be at such rate as Lender shall request. If Lender has waived the option to accelerate provided in this paragraph 17, and if Borrower's successor in interest has executed a written assumption agreement accepted in writing by Lender, Lender shall release Borrower from all obligations under this Mortgage and the Note.

If Lender exercises such option to accelerate, Lender shall mail Borrower notice of acceleration in accordance with paragraph 14 hereof. Such notice shall provide a period of not less than 30 days from the date the notice is mailed within which Borrower may pay the sums declared due. If Borrower fails to pay such sums prior to the expiration of such period, Lender may, without further notice or demand on Borrower, invoke any remedies permitted by paragraph 18 hereof.

NON-UNIFORM COVENANTS. Borrower and Lender further covenant and agree as follows:

18. Acceleration; Remedies. Except as provided in paragraph 17 hereof, upon Borrower's breach of any covenant or agreement of Borrower in this Mortgage, including the covenants to pay when due any sums secured by this Mortgage, Lender prior to acceleration shall mail notice to Borrower as provided in paragraph 14 hereof specifying: (1) the breach; (2) the action required to cure such breach; (3) a date, not less than 30 days from the date the notice is mailed to Borrower, by which such breach must be cured; and (4) that failure to cure such breach on or before the date specified in the notice may result in acceleration of the sums secured by this Mortgage, foreclosure by judicial proceeding and sale of the Property. The notice shall further inform Borrower of the right to reinstate after acceleration and the right to assert in the foreclosure proceeding the non-existence of a default or any other defense of Borrower to accelera ion and foreclosure. If the breach is not cured on or before the date specified in the notice, Lender at Lender's option may declare all of the sums secured by this Mortgage to be immediately due and payable without further demand and may foreclose this Mortgage by judicial proceeding. Lender shall be entitled to collect in such proceeding all costs allowed by applicable law.

19. Borrower's Right to Reinstate. Notwithstanding Lender's acceleration of the sums secured by this Mortgage, Borrower shall have the right to have any proceedings begun by Lender to enforce this Mortgage discontinued at any time prior to entry of a judgment enforcing this Mortgage if: (a) Borrower pays Lender all sums which would be then due under this Mortgage, the Note and notes securing Future Advances, if any, had no acceleration occurred; (b) Borrower cures all breaches of any other covenants or agreements of Borrower contained in this Mortgage; (c) Borrower pays all reasonable expenses incurred by Lender in enforcing the covenants and agreements of Borrower contained in this Mortgage and in enforcing Lender's remedies as provided in paragraph 18 hereof, including, but not limited to, reasonable attorney's fees; and (d) Borrower takes such action as Lender may reasonably require to assure that the lien of this Mortgage, Lender's interest in the Property and Borrower's obligation to pay the sums secured by this Mortgage shall continue unimpaired. Upon such payment and cure by Borrower, this Mortgage and the obligations secured hereby shall remain in full force and effect as if no acceleration had occurred.

20. Assignment of Rents; Appointment of Receiver; Lender in Possession. As additional security hereunder, Borrower hereby assigns to Lender the rents of the Property, provided that Borrower shall, prior to acceleration under paragraph 18 hereof or abandonment of the Property, have the right to collect and retain such rents as they become due and payable.

Upon acceleration under paragraph 18 hereof or abandonment of the Property, Lender, in person, by agent or by judicially appointed receiver, shall be entitled to enter upon, take possession of and manage the Property and to collect the rents of the Property including those past due. All rents collected by Lender or the receiver shall be applied first to payment of the costs of management of the Property and collection of rents, including, but not limited to, receiver's fees, premiums on receiver's bonds and reasonable attorney's fees, and then to the sums secured by this Mortgage. Lender and the receiver shall be liable to account only for those rents actually received.

21. Future Advances. Upon request of Borrower, Lender, at Lender's option prior to release of this Mortgage, may make Future Advances to Borrower. Such Future Advances, with interest thereon, shall be secured by this Mortgage when evidenced by promissory notes stating that said notes are secured hereby. At no time shall the principal amount of the indebtedness secured by this Mortgage, not including the sums advanced in accordance herewith to protect the security of this Mortgage, exceed the original amount of the Note plus US $. . . . .

22. Release. Upon payment of all sums secured by this Mortgage, Lender shall discharge this Mortgage without charge to Borrower. Borrower shall pay all costs of recordation, if any.

23. Lien Law. Borrower will receive advances hereunder subject to the trust fund provisions of Section 13 of the Lien Law.

IN WITNESS WHEREOF, Borrower has executed this Mortgage.

Witnesses:

. . . .
                                                                                                                                                                    —Borrower

. . . .
                                                                                                                                                                    —Borrower

STATE OF NEW YORK, ... County ss:

On this . . . . day of . . . . , 19 . . . . , before me personally came . . . .
. . . . to me known and known to me to be the individual(s) described in and who executed the foregoing instrument, and . . he . . duly acknowledged to me that . . he . . executed the same.

. . . .
                                        Notary Public

──────────── (Space Below This Line Reserved For Lender and Recorder) ────────────

NOTICE Prepared by the State Bar of Texas for use by Lawyers only.
To select the proper form, fill in blank spaces, strike out form provisions or insert special terms constitutes the practice of law. No "standard form" can meet all requirements.

REAL ESTATE LIEN NOTE

$ .... , Texas, ...

For value received, I, We, or either of us, as principals, promise to pay to the order of ....

....

....

in the City of..County, Texas, the sum of

.... Dollars ($ ....),

in legal and lawful money of the United States of America, with interest thereon from date hereof until

maturity at the rate of .... per cent (............ %) per annum; the interest payable

.... ; matured unpaid principal and interest shall bear interest at the rate of ten per

cent (10%) per annum from date of maturity until paid.

This note is due and payable as follows, to-wit:

It is expressly provided that upon default in the punctual payment of this note or any part thereof, principal or interest, as the same shall become due and payable, the entire indebtedness secured by the hereinafter mentioned lien shall be matured, at the option of the holder; and in the event default is made in the prompt payment of this note when due or declared due, and the same is placed in the hands of an attorney for collection, or suit is brought on same, or the same is collected through Probate, Bankruptcy or other judicial proceedings, then the makers agree and promise to pay ten per cent (10%) additional on the amount of principal and interest then owing, as attorney's fees.

Each maker, surety and endorser of this note expressly waives all notices, demands for payment, presentations for payment, notices of intention to accelerate the maturity, protest and notice of protest, as to this note and as to each, every and all installments hereof.

Payment hereof is secured by

Illustration 3
Texas Real Estate Lien Note

ADJUSTABLE RATE NOTE

**NOTICE TO BORROWER: THIS NOTE CONTAINS A PROVISION ALLOW-
ING FOR CHANGES IN THE INTEREST RATE. INCREASES IN THE
INTEREST RATE WILL RESULT IN HIGHER PAYMENTS. DECREASES
IN THE INTEREST RATE WILL RESULT IN LOWER PAYMENTS.**

HOUSTON ,HARRIS COUNTY, TEXAS

........................., 19..... ....,.....................

City   *State*

....

Property Address   *City*   *State*   *Zip Code*

1. BORROWER'S PROMISE TO PAY

In return for a loan that I have received, I promise to pay U.S. $.................. (this amount will be
called "principal"), plus interest, to the order of the Lender. The Lender is ....
..............:..

I understand that the Lender may transfer this Note. The Lender or anyone who takes this Note by transfer and
who is entitled to receive payments under this Note will be called the "Note Holder".

2. INTEREST

Interest will be charged on that part of outstanding principal which has not been paid. Interest will be charged
beginning on the date I receive principal and continuing until the full amount of principal I receive has been paid.

Beginning on the date of this Note, I will pay interest at a yearly rate of ....% (the "Initial Interest Rate"). The interest rate that I will pay will change in accordance with Section 4 of this Note until my loan is paid.
Interest rate changes may occur on the 1st . day of the month beginning on ....,
19..... and on that day of the month every .TWELVE.......... months thereafter. Each date on which the rate
of interest may change will be called a "Change Date".

3. PAYMENTS

(A) Time and Place of Payments

I will pay principal and interest by making payments every month. I will make my monthly payments on the
.1st day of each month beginning on ....,19...... I will make these payments
until I have paid all of the principal and interest and any other charges, described below, that I may owe under this
Note. I will pay all sums that I owe under this Note no later than ....,.....
(the "final payment date").

I will make my monthly payments at ....,.......
....or at a different place if required by the Note Holder.

(B) Borrower's Payments Before They Are Due

I have the right to make payments of principal at any time before they are due. A payment of principal only is
known as a "prepayment". When I make a prepayment, I will tell the Note Holder in writing that I am doing so. I may
make a full prepayment or a partial prepayment without paying any penalty. The Note Holder will use all of my
prepayments to reduce the amount of principal that I owe under this Note. If I make a partial prepayment, there will be
no delays in the due dates of my monthly payments unless the Note Holder agrees in writing to those delays. My partial
prepayment will reduce the amount of my monthly payments after the first Change Date following my partial prepayment. However, any reduction due to my partial prepayment may be offset by an interest rate increase.

(C) Amount of Monthly Payments

My initial monthly payments will be in the amount of U.S. $.................... If the interest rate
that I pay changes, the amount of my monthly payments will change. Increases in the interest rate will result in higher
payments (unless my prepayments since the last Change Date offset the increases in my monthly payments). Decreases
in the interest rate will result in lower payments. The amount of my monthly payments will always be sufficient to repay
my loan in full in substantially equal payments by the final payment date. In setting the monthly payment amount on
each Change Date, the Note Holder will assume that the Note interest rate will not change again prior to the final payment date.

4. INTEREST RATE CHANGES

(A) The Index

Any changes in the interest rate will be based on changes in an interest rate index which will be called the
"Index". The Index is the: [*Check one box to indicate Index.*]

(1) ☒* "Contract Interest Rate, Purchase of Previously Occupied Homes, National Average for all Major
Types of Lenders" published by the Federal Home Loan Bank Board.

(2) ☐* ....
....

If the Index ceases to be made available by the publisher, or by any successor to the publisher, the Note
Holder will set the Note interest rate by using a comparable index.

TEXAS—ADJUSTABLE RATE LOAN NOTE—6/81—FHLMC UNIFORM INSTRUMENT

Illustration 4
Variable Interest Rate Note

(B) Setting the New Interest Rate

To set the new interest rate, the Note Holder will determine the change between the Base Index figure and the Current Index figure. The Base Index figure is .... The Current Index figure is the most recent Index figure available ⁻.45⁻... days prior to each Change Date. If the amount of the change is less than one-eighth of one percentage point, the change will be rounded to zero. If the amount of the change is one-eighth of one percentage point or more, the Note Holder will round the amount of the change to the nearest one-eighth of one percentage point.

If the Current Index figure is larger than the Base Index figure, the Note Holder will add the rounded amount of the change to the Initial Interest Rate. If the Current Index figure is smaller than the Base Index figure, the Note Holder will subtract the rounded amount of the change from the Initial Interest Rate. The result of this addition or subtraction will be the preliminary rate. If there is no change between the Base Index figure and the Current Index figure after rounding, the Initial Interest Rate will be the preliminary rate.

[Check one box to indicate whether there is any maximum limit on interest rate changes; if no box is checked, there will be no maximum limit on changes.]

(1)   ☒ If this box is checked, there will be no maximum limit on changes in the interest rate up or down. The preliminary rate will be the new interest rate.

(2)   ☐ If this box is checked, the interest rate will not be changed by more than .... percentage points on any Change Date. The Note Holder will adjust the preliminary rate so that the change in the interest rate will not be more than that limit. The new interest rate will equal the figure that results from this adjustment of the preliminary rate.

(C) Effective Date of Changes

Each new interest rate will become effective on the next Change Date. If my monthly payment changes as a result of a change in the interest rate, my monthly payment will change as of the first monthly payment date after the Change Date.

(D) Notice to Borrower

The Note Holder will mail me a notice by first class mail at least thirty and no more than forty-five days before each Change Date if the interest rate is to change. The notice will advise me of:

(i)   the new interest rate on my loan;

(ii)   the amount of my new monthly payment; and

(iii) any additional matters which the Note Holder is required to disclose.

5. BORROWER'S FAILURE TO PAY AS REQUIRED

(A) Late Charge for Overdue Payments

If the Note Holder has not received the full amount of any of my monthly payments by the end of 15th.. calendar days after the date it is due, I will pay a late charge to the Note Holder. The amount of the charge will be ....5⁻..% of my overdue payment of principal and interest. I will pay this late charge only once on any late payment.

(B) Notice from Note Holder

If I do not pay the full amount of each monthly payment on time, the Note Holder may send me a written notice telling me that if I do not pay the overdue amount by a certain date I will be in default. That date must be at least 30 days after the date on which the notice is mailed to me.

(C) Default

If I do not pay the overdue amount by the date stated in the notice described in (B) above, I will be in default. If I am in default, the Note Holder may require me to pay immediately the full amount of principal which has not been paid and all the interest that I owe on that amount.

Even if, at a time when I am in default, the Note Holder does not require me to pay immediately in full as described above, the Note Holder will still have the right to do so if I am in default at a later time.

(D) Payment of Note Holder's Costs and Expenses

If the Note Holder has required me to pay immediately in full as described above, the Note Holder will have the right to be paid back by me for all its reasonable costs and expenses to the extent not prohibited by applicable law. Those expenses may include, for example, reasonable attorneys' fees.

6. WAIVERS

Anyone who signs this Note to transfer it to someone else (known as an "endorser") waives certain rights. Those rights are (A) the right to require the Note Holder to demand payment of amounts due (known as "presentment") and (B) the right to require the Note Holder to give notice that amounts due have not been paid (known as "notice of dishonor").

7. GIVING OF NOTICES

Except for the notice provided in Section 4(D), any notice that must be given to me under this Note will be given by mailing it by certified mail. All notices will be addressed to me at the Property Address above. Notices will be mailed to me at a different address if I give the Note Holder a notice of my different address.

Any notice that must be given to the Note Holder under this Note will be given by mailing it by certified mail to the Note Holder at the address stated in Section 3(A) above. Notices will be mailed to the Note Holder at a different address if I am given a notice of that different address.

8. RESPONSIBILITY OF PERSONS UNDER THIS NOTE

If more than one person signs this Note, each of us is fully and personally obligated to pay the full amount owed and to keep all of the promises made in this Note. Any guarantor, surety, or endorser of this Note is also obligated to do these things. The Note Holder may enforce its rights under this Note against each of us individually or against all of us together. This means that any one of us may be required to pay all of the amounts owed under this Note.

Any person who takes over my rights or obligations under this Note will have all of my rights and must keep all of my promises made in this Note. Any person who takes over the rights or obligations of a guarantor, surety, or endorser of this Note is also obligated to keep all of the promises made in this Note.

* If more than one box is checked or if no box is checked, and Lender and Borrower do not otherwise agree in writing, the first Index named will apply.

9. LOAN CHARGES

It could be that this loan is subject to a law which sets maximum loan charges and that law is interpreted so that the interest or other loan charges collected or to be collected in connection with this loan would exceed permitted limits. If this is the case, then: (A) any such loan charge shall be reduced by the amount necessary to reduce the charge to the permitted limit; and (B) any sums already collected from me which exceeded permitted limits will be refunded to me. The Note Holder may choose to make this refund by reducing the principal I owe under this Note or by making a direct payment to me. If a refund reduces principal, the reduction will be treated as a partial prepayment.

10. THIS NOTE SECURED BY A DEED OF TRUST

In addition to the protections given to the Note Holder under this Note, a Deed of Trust, dated ...., 19 .... protects the Note Holder from possible losses which might result if I do not keep the promises which I make in this Note. That Deed of Trust describes how and under what conditions I may be required to make immediate payment in full of all amounts that I owe under this Note. One of those conditions relates to any transfer of the property covered by the Deed of Trust. In that regard, the Deed of Trust provides in paragraph 17:

17. Transfer of the Property; Assumption. If all or any part of the Property or an interest therein is sold or transferred by Borrower without Lender's prior written consent, excluding (a) the creation of a lien or encumbrance subordinate to this Deed of Trust, (b) the creation of a purchase money security interest for household appliances, (c) a transfer by devise, descent or by operation of law upon the death of a joint tenant or (d) the grant of any leasehold interest of three years or less not containing an option to purchase, Lender may, at Lender's option, declare all the sums secured by this Deed of Trust to be immediately due and payable. Lender shall have waived such option to accelerate if, prior to the sale or transfer, Lender and the person to whom the Property is to be sold or transferred reach agreement in writing that the credit of such person is satisfactory to Lender and that the interest payable on the sums secured by this Deed of Trust shall be at such rate as Lender shall request. If Lender has waived the option to accelerate provided in this paragraph 17, and if Borrower's successor in interest has executed a written assumption agreement accepted in writing by Lender, Lender shall release Borrower from all obligations under this Deed of Trust and the Note.

If Lender exercises such option to accelerate, Lender shall mail Borrower notice of acceleration in accordance with paragraph 14 hereof. Such notice shall provide a period of not less than 30 days from the date the notice is mailed within which Borrower may pay the sums declared due. If Borrower fails to pay such sums prior to the expiration of such period, Lender may, without further notice or demand on Borrower, invoke any remedies permitted by paragraph 18 hereof.

An Adjustable Rate Loan Rider supplements the Deed of Trust and provides:

If there is a transfer of the Property subject to paragraph 17 of the Security Instrument, Lender may require (1) an increase in the current Note interest rate, or (2) an increase in (or removal of) the limit on the amount of any one interest rate change (if there is a limit), or (3) a change in the Base Index figure, or all of these, as a condition of Lender's waiving the option to accelerate provided in paragraph 17.

.... (Seal)
Borrower

.... (Seal)
Borrower

.... (Seal)
Borrower
(Sign Original Only)

NOTES

1. The mortgage form shown in Illustration 2 is one of the most common forms used. It is a form adopted for use by the Federal National Mortgage Association, commonly called "Fanny Mae," which buys mortgages from institutional lenders. See Chapter 9 on government involvement in mortgages. The other initials on the form, FHLMC, stand for Federal Home Loan Mortgage Corporation, another mortgage buyer. FHLMC is commonly called "Freddie Mac."

The form contains seventeen uniform covenants and six that are not uniform in all states. In addition to these Fanny Mae covenants, lenders sometimes will insert additional covenants of their own. *See Covenants in a Mortgage infra* p. 208.

2. The Real Estate Lien Note shown in Illustration 3 is fairly straightforward. It is the *indicia* of indebtedness. A deed of trust or a mortgage, such as Illustration 2, is the document which creates the security interest in the borrower's real property.

3. Illustration 5 is a variable interest rate note. It is used when the lender retains the right to shift the interest rate, both up and down, depending on factors in the economy which are spelled out in the note.

4. The FNMA mortgage form in Illustration 2 is also used in a deed of trust form which differs only in that it adds a trustee to hold title for security purposes; the covenants are the same regardless of the form.

Chapter 2

LESS OBVIOUS TYPES OF MORTGAGES

We're alone, you and I, we're alive and secure but in a bank or the church we can never feel sure.

Jacques Brel and Eric Blau, "Alone" from *Jacques Brel Is Alive and Well and Living in Paris* *

A written document which transfers an interest in a parcel of real property to secure the performance of an obligation is a legal mortgage. However, should a mortgage fail because of some flaw, then it likely will give rise to an equitable mortgage. That is, an equitable mortgage results even though the attempt at creation of a legal mortgage fails. An error preventing a legal description from "closing" is one example of a flaw which is fatal to a legal mortgage but which creates an equitable mortgage. Typically, a promise to execute a mortgage gives rise to an equitable mortgage if breached. Likewise, if the clear intent of the parties was to create a mortgage but traditional mortgage documents were not executed, and instead the transaction took another form, then an equitable mortgage will be recognized. The use of such transactional camouflage is not uncommon. A mortgage may take a form so well disguised that the casual observer may not realize a mortgage has in fact been created. Of these forms, a deed absolute with a right to redeem or option to repurchase has been one source of litigation. A landowner may wish to borrow money using her land for security but wish to conceal the transaction from the rest of the world. Instead of executing a mortgage, the borrower executes a deed absolute and transfers title to the lender with the option to repurchase (sometimes the *requirement* to repurchase). During the time the "loan" is outstanding it appears to the world that the borrower does not own the land, but rather that the lender does. This permits the borrower to transact business without fear of creditors seeking recourse against the subject property.[1] This transaction also permits the lender some advantages. He can avoid imposing usurious interest rates by providing for a price differential upon resale which will appear as profit from the transaction rather than interest. Profits, unlike interest payments, are not subject to the usury limitations. Another aspect favorable to the lender is that profits generated by subsequent resale, if the property was held for the requisite period, will be considered a long-term capital gain and be given favorable tax treatment. Simply charging interest will result in ordinary income which is taxed at a higher rate.

There are other factors which may influence the parties' decision to disguise a mortgage. While the reasons for entering into a disguised transaction are many,

---

* Copyright © 1959 Editions Musicales Tutti Paris, France. All rights for the United States controlled by N. S. Justinian Music, Inc.

[1] Since the public records in the Recorder's Office would show only a deed absolute, it would appear that the borrower has no interest in the property subject to execution by judgment creditors. If a legal mortgage form is used the borrower would still show in the public records as the vested owner, thus making the property susceptible to execution. Of course, any execution would be subject to the state's statutes on homestead and exemption from execution. The removal from the public records of the borrower's name as an owner simply eliminates execution unless a judgment creditor indulges in some tedious post-judgment discovery.

15

most of them favor the lender: avoidance of foreclosure procedures, avoidance of the borrower's equity of redemption, and the ability to obtain a forfeiture. The borrower's motivation may be to avoid the possibility of a deficiency judgment. Both parties may wish to use a form to allow a loan which otherwise might be illegal. The illegality may stem from usurious interest or from governmental regulations prohibiting some types of loans.[2] Finally, the lender may simply wish to fool the borrower into believing that a "mortgage" has not been created, even though a "security interest" has been. The latter seems unlikely today in light of a trend toward protecting the consumer and the requirement that the parties' intent is needed to give effect to an equitable mortgage.[3] When a mortgage is not in legal form but is disguised, an equitable mortgage will arise which will require that the parties treat the transaction as a mortgage rather than whatever the face of the documents would indicate.

All equitable mortgages create equitable liens, but not all equitable liens arise out of equitable mortgages. Equitable lien is a more generic label which refers to the equitable lienor's right to satisfy a debt from a specific fund or property. Unlike an equitable mortgage, an equitable lien need not attach to property. Liens on construction funds which arise in equity are not equitable mortgages, but rather are liens on a specific fund which arose from a real estate financing situation. The area of subordination is one in which equitable liens or mortgages, or both, may arise; in the event a subordination agreement is not upheld or if priority is bifurcated after a misapplication of construction loan funds, equity may create a lien.[4] Mistake as to the effect of subordination can result in an equitable lien to prevent unjust enrichment.[5]

There is not uniform agreement on whether a security interest is created by the execution of a land installment contract. It may be difficult to see how the vendor is said to have a security interest if he retained record title after entering into an installment contract. But if the doctrine of equitable conversion is applied, the vendor's interest is converted into personalty while the vendee's interest is realty. Then the vendor's interest is evidenced by his holding record title, which does not change during the executory period of the contract, for the purpose of securing the performance of an obligation — payment of the purchase price.

It is important to distinguish between the two basic types of real estate contracts and observe the differences in available remedies for breach in each case. One type of contract is used primarily to bring the buyer and seller together, obtain a writing so as to comply with the Statute of Frauds, and to provide a basis for the payment of the broker's commission. This contract, usually a brief printed form furnished by the broker, requires only the completion of blank spaces by the insertion of names, dates, and price. It is designed to remain executory for a short period of time, thirty to ninety days usually, while the buyer obtains institutional financing and the seller makes arrangements to move elsewhere. While there may be a provision for the seller to carry back a purchase money mortgage as part of the sale price, the majority of transactions are "all cash to seller." Possession generally remains with the seller during the

---

[2] National banks and federally chartered savings and loan associations must secure their loans with a senior lien. *See* 12 C.F.R. § 545.6-1.

[3] *Compare* Coast Bank v. Minderhout, 61 Cal. 2d 311, 392 P.2d 265 (1964) *with* Tahoe Bank v. Phillips, 4 Cal. 3d 11, 480 P.2d 320 (1971). Intent of the parties seems less important than whether the document in question is reasonably susceptible to being construed as a mortgage.

[4] *See* Middlebrook-Anderson v. Southwest Sav. & Loan Ass'n, 18 Cal. App. 3d 1023 (Cal. App. 1971).

[5] *See* Jones v. Sacramento Sav. & Loan Ass'n, 248 Cal. App. 2d 522 (Cal. App. 1967).

executory period of the contract. Such contracts are known by different names in various jurisdictions; deposit receipt, binder, and earnest money contract are all commonly used terms. The essential element is that such contracts are for the purpose of merchandising the property. These contracts will be referred to as marketing contracts.

Other contracts for the sale of real property provide for a long executory period, years rather than a few months, and transfer possession of the property upon execution of the contract; these are security contracts. The purpose of a security contract is to secure the performance of an obligation: payment of the purchase price. Such contracts are called installment contracts, land contracts, contracts of sale, and by some writers, security contracts.[6]

If in fact the land installment contract is a security document, the ramifications are obvious. Foreclosure by prescribed methods other than forfeiture is required. There is a division of authority on whether the payments made during the executory period of a security contract can be treated as rent and forfeited upon default by the vendee. Some states have treated installment land contracts as security documents by statute[7] while others have set forth particular foreclosure requirements for security contracts.[8]

Increasing inflation in both the purchase price of homes and the cost of borrowing has necessitated inventiveness by the conveyancing bar. Many alternative forms of financing the purchase of real property can be seen today. Security contracts are among the most frequent and popular, notwithstanding the myriad of problems inherent to both vendor and vendee. Other alternative forms, some sanctioned by government regulatory bodies, have appeared and are testing the market. Variable interest rates and reverse annuity mortgages are now authorized for federally chartered savings and loans. Wrap-a-round mortgages, a form of second mortgage advantageous to both vendor and vendee, appear to have a healthy future while interest rates soar.

A. EQUITABLE MORTGAGES

1. PROMISE TO GIVE A MORTGAGE

SLEETH v. SAMPSON

Court of Appeals of New York
237 N.Y.S. 69, 142 N.E. 355 (1923)

Cardozo, J. The action is brought for the specific performance of an oral agreement to execute a mortgage upon land as security for a loan.

Ernest P. Sampson was the owner of a farm in the county of Onondaga. He died December 5, 1921, intestate, leaving his mother, the defendant Cornelia A. Sampson, and two nephews, the defendants Shepard, his sole heirs at law. Letters of administration were granted to the mother.

Sampson, according to the testimony, asked the plaintiff on November 15, 1921, for a loan of $100. Plaintiff responded that he had already loaned enough without security. The existing indebtedness was figured at about $1,200. Sampson offered to give security in the shape of a mortgage on the farm if

---

[6] *See* J. Hetland, California Real Estate Secured Transactions 100 (1970).
[7] *See* Cal. Civ. Code § 2953.1, *infra* at p. 61.
[8] *See* Ohio Rev. Stat. § 5313.07 (1970).

plaintiff would make the loan. Some money was then handed to the borrower, though exactly how much the witness who overheard the conversation was unable to state. Thereupon Sampson produced the deed under which the farm had been conveyed to him in 1904, and an abstract of title, saying at the same time: "You look these over, and see what you can do, and we will go down to the lawyer's in a few days and draw this up." Nothing more was said or done. Upon Sampson's death a few weeks later this action was brought against those succeeding to his title.

An estate or interest in real property (other than a lease for a term not exceeding one year) cannot be created, granted, or assigned "unless by act or operation of law, or by a deed or conveyance in writing." Real Property Law (Consol. Laws, c. 50), § 242. A contract "for the sale, of any real property, or an interest therein," is void unless the contract, or some note or memorandum thereof, expressing the consideration, is in writing, subscribed by the grantor Real Property Law, § 259. A mortgage is a conveyance of an interest in real property within the meaning of section 242. *Bogert v. Bliss,* 148 N.Y. 194, 199, 42 N. E. 582, 51 Am. St. Rep. 684. A contract to give a mortgage is a contract for the sale of an interest in real property within the meaning of section 259. No doubt the word "sale," when applied to such a transaction, is inexact and inappropriate. Our present statute comes to us by descent from the English statute (29 Car. II, c. 3, § 4), which speaks of "any contract or sale of lands, tenements or hereditaments or any interest in or concerning them." The change of phraseology has not worked a change of meaning. One who promises to make another the owner of a lien or charge upon land promises to make him the owner of an interest in land, and this is equivalent in effect to a promise to sell him such an interest. The meaning is fixed by an unbroken series of decisions.

The question remains whether there have been acts of part performance sufficient to relieve from the production of a writing. To be thus effective they must be of such a nature as to be "unintelligible or at least extraordinary," unless related to a contract to convey an interest in land. *Burns v. McCormick,* 233 N. Y. 230, 232, 135 N. E. 273. The payment of money is not enough, unless followed by other acts, as, for example, possession or improvements. *Russell v. Briggs,* 165 N. Y. 500, 505, 59 N. E. 303, 53 L. R. A. 556; Williston, Contracts, § 494. We see no distinction in this respect between a payment for an absolute conveyance and a payment for a mortgage. *Matter of Whitting, Ex parte Hall,* 10 Ch. Div. 615; *Bloomfield State Bank v. Miller,* 55 Neb. 243, 255, 75 N. W. 569, 444 L. R. A. 387, 70 Am. St. Rep. 381. A different holding would open wide the door to the entry of the evils against which the statute is directed. Any one who had made a loan would be free to transmute it into a loan with a lien upon the land. The danger is emphasized in this case where the bulk of the indebtedness was antecedent to the promise. Dicta in *Sprague v. Cochran,* 144 N. Y. 104, 38 N. E. 1000, and *Smith v. Smith,* 125 N. Y. 224, 26 N. E. 259, may seem to suggest that the doctrine of part performance has been extended more liberally to contracts to mortgage than to contracts to sell. They lose their significance when read in relation to the subject-matter of the controversy. In the one case a mortgage had actually been given, and the court gave relief against an erroneous description. In the other the lender had gone into possession and had put improvements on the land. We conclude that payment without more does not obviate the necessity for a writing.

. . . Equitable mortgages by the deposit of title deeds have long been recognised in England. . . . Even in England, however, the deposit must have been made for the purpose of creating a present or immediate security, and not merely as a preliminary step to the preparation of a mortgage which will be security thereafter. *Norris v. Wilkinson,* 12 Ves. Jr. 192; *Ex parte Bulteel,* 2 Cox Ch. 243. We find no suggestion here of the existence of a purpose to create a present lien. "You look these over, and see what you can do, and we will go down to the lawyer's in a few days and draw this up." Far from suggesting a present lien, the implication is that something more, either through an additional loan or in some other way, is to be done by the lender. At best, the case is within the rule that acts merely ancillary or preliminary to performance are not acts of part performance within the equitable doctrine. The delivery of abstracts, putting a deed in the hands of a solicitor to prepare a conveyance, even the preparation of the conveyance, if not followed by the signing, these and like acts have been held to be inadequate. *Nibert v. Baghurst,* 47 N. J. Eq. 201, 205, 20 Atl. 252; *Brown v. Drew,* 67 N. H. 569, 42 Atl. 177; Williston, Contracts, § 494, p. 962.

The judgment should be affirmed, with costs.

HISCOCK, C. J., and HOGAN, POUND, MCLAUGHLIN, CRANE, and ANDREWS, JJ., concur.

Judgment affirmed.

OWENS v. CONTINENTAL SUPPLY CO.

United States Court of Appeals
71 F.2d 862 (10th Cir. 1934)

MCDERMOTT, CIRCUIT JUDGE.

For a valuable consideration, appellant executed and delivered to appellee his negotiable promissory notes for $33,787.39, which are due and unpaid. Appellant transmitted the notes to appellee with a letter, describing them fully, and providing:

Payment of said notes is secured by a lien on my riverbed leases in Sections 5 and 17, Township 18 North, Range 7 East, Creek County, Oklahoma, such lien to be evidenced at a later date by regular form mortgage. I am arranging now to discharge two small items which are secured by chattel mortgage and conditional sales contract, both of which are of record, but upon payment of such items the mortgage and conditional sales contract will be released, whereupon the mortgage, to be executed to you, will be a first and prior lien. Pending the execution of such mortgage, there is one other item of approximately $500 adjustment of which can and will be made without payment by issuance of credit memorandum in the adjustment of accounts and claims due me.

Unless unforeseen delays develop, these items can be disposed of in sufficient time to permit the execution of the above mentioned mortgage to your company on January 15th, 1932. In the meantime no liens or encumbrances will be created that might take priority over the mortgage to be executed to your company.

Yours very truly,   O. O. Owens.

Appellee brought its bill to foreclose the lien on the riverbed leases, and for judgment on the notes. The bill alleged a more detailed and definite description of the leases set forth in the letter.

In answer, appellant alleged that he executed the notes in order to secure further credit for supplies and with the oral understanding and agreement that he would not be required to pay them according to their tenor, but might pay them at his convenience. That it was not intended that the agreement to execute a mortgage should create a lien on the property therein described.

No motion for judgment notwithstanding the answer was interposed. Without objection, the trial court heard the conflicting stories of the oral negotiations leading up to the execution of the notes and the lien, the great preponderance of which supports the decree below.

The errors assigned and specified are objectionably indefinite. The principal ones are founded upon the assumption that appellant's version of the oral negotiations was found by the trial court to be true. But the trial court found otherwise, and we concur. Another error specified is that there was no evidence to identify the "river-bed leases in sections 5 and 17, township 18 north, range 7 east, Creek County, Oklahoma." The bill identified them more specifically and that allegation, being undenied, stands admitted. Equity Rule 30 (28 USCA § 723). The last error assigned is that appellant only agreed to execute a mortgage, but did not carry out his agreement. The letter clearly creates a present charge or lien upon the property described. It recites "Payment of said notes is secured by a lien . . . such lien to be evidenced at a later date by regular form mortgage." Can such a present lien be divested by appellant's failure to carry out his agreement to execute a formal mortgage evidencing such lien?

Clearly not. Equity treats that as done which ought to be done. A valid agreement to execute a mortgage will be enforced in equity against the maker or third persons who have notice thereof or who are volunteers. "It is an equitable mortgage," said Justice McLean in *King v. Thompson,* 9 Pet. 221, "and in a court of chancery, is as binding on the parties as if a mortgage in form, had been duly executed." *In Re Strand Music Hall Co.,* 3 De Gex, J. & S. 147, Lord Justice Turner held that where the parties, by their agreement, intend to create a charge upon property, equity will give effect to their intention, notwithstanding any mistake which may have occurred in the attempt to effect it. Story, in his work on Equity Jurisprudence, early laid down the same rule. Vol. II, § 1231. This rule has been uniformly followed in the courts of the United States. . . . The Oklahoma Supreme Court, in an elaborate opinion, has followed this general rule. *Carter v. Sapulpa & I. R. Co.,* 49 Okl. 471, 153 P. 853, 855.

The errors assigned are without merit. Because we have discussed them, it must not be assumed that we hold, even inferentially, that a defense was pleaded by the answer, or that the evidence offered in support thereof was admissible.

The decree is affirmed.

NOTES

1. A promise to give a mortgage must be specifically enforceable to serve as the basis for an equitable mortgage. It also must create a present interest in the subject land rather than the possibility of an interest arising in the future. *See* G. Osborne, Mortgages 41 (2d ed. 1970).

2. A transfer within the four-month period immediately prior to the filing of a petition in bankruptcy may or may not be held a mortgage depending on the facts giving rise to the transfer. *See White v. Barnard,* 29 F.2d 510 (1st Cir. 1928).

3. A promise to give a mortgage accompanied by a defective document will result in an equitable mortgage, even where the mortgagor does not hold title to the subject property at the time the promise is made or the defective mortgage executed. The doctrine of after-acquired title applies to mortgagors. *See Beck v. Brooks,* 224 Kan. 300, 580 P.2d 882 (1978).

2. DEFECT IN EXECUTION OR DESCRIPTION

SPRAGUE v. COCHRAN

Court of Appeals of New York
144 N.Y.S. 104, 38 N.E. 1000 (1894)

O'BRIEN, J. Before reaching the real question in this case, it is necessary to clear away some complications resulting from the practice adopted. The action was begun in September, 1887, to foreclose a mortgage. The complaint alleged that on the 9th of February, 1876, the defendant delivered his personal bond to one Antoinette Appley to secure the payment of $3,000 on the 1st of June, 1881, with annual interest, and, as collateral to this bond, a mortgage upon certain lands described, which was duly recorded; that this bond and mortgage had been assigned to the plaintiff, and that neither the principal nor the interest, nor any part thereof, had ever been paid; and the usual judgment on foreclosure actions was demanded. The answer, in substance, was that at the time of the loan, and the delivery of the bond and mortgage, the defendant and the mortgagor, Mrs. Appley, were partners in business, she having succeeded her husband, who had been a member of the firm for several years prior to his death, in 1875; that the money advanced by her was for the purpose of paying debts of the firm of which she was a member, and of the old firm of which her husband had been a member, and which in some form were a charge upon property which she took under his will; that upon an accounting, concerning the partnership affairs, between her and the defendant, there was due to the firm and to the defendant more than sufficient to pay and satisfy the mortgage; and that the assignment to the plaintiff was without consideration, and subject to this equity. In July, 1887, the defendant brought an action against Mrs. Appley, the mortgagor, and others, to which the plaintiff was subsequently made a party, to settle the partnership affairs, including the bond and mortgage in question. The complaint set forth various complicated transactions, not necessary to specify, and among them the execution and delivery of the bond and mortgage for the purpose substantially as alleged in the answer in this case, and asked that it be adjudged to be a partnership debt. Subsequently, this action was consolidated with the partnership action, and referred for trial. The referee took proofs at length, very little of which appear in the record, and made and filed his report, in which he held that the plaintiff was entitled to foreclose the mortgage, and made numerous findings of fact and law concerning the rights of the parties in the partnership action. It will not be necessary to refer to these findings, except so far as they relate to the mortgage in question, and as to these facts there was no dispute. It appears that the husband of the mortgagor and the defendant's former partner had effected an insurance upon his life for $3,000, payable to his wife at death, and that upon his death, in 1875, or soon after, that sum was paid to her upon the policy; that the defendant requested her to loan it to him, offering to secure the payment, with interest, by a mortgage on all his interests in real estate; that she consented to make the loan on this security, and paid over the money to him; that he gave the bond referred to, and procured a mortgage which both parties supposed covered the land intended to be included therein, but, by mistake of the scrivener who drew the paper, a portion of the land, of considerable value, constituting a substantial part of the security upon the faith of which the mortgagor advanced the money, was omitted from the description of the property conveyed. The mistake was not discovered until after the commencement of both the actions in question. The referee, in his report, directed that the description of the lands contained in the mortgage be amended so as to include the omitted parcel, which was a lot containing about 70 acres in lot No. 27 of "great lot No. 4 of the Hardenburgh patent." The complaint in the action for the partnership accounting, as I understand it, alleged, in substance, that this land was embraced in the mortgage. After this report of the referee, the plaintiff applied to the special term for leave to amend the complaint in the foreclosure suit by inserting an allegation that this land was intended by both parties to be mortgaged as security for the debt, and both supposed it had been, but by mutual mistake had been omitted from the description, and asking relief to the effect that the instrument be reformed by amending the description of the property in the mortgage, so as to cover it, and enforced accordingly. This motion was granted upon terms and upon the condition that the defendant should be allowed to amend his answer by interposing the statute of limitations as a defense. The pleadings were amended accordingly; the defendant alleging that more than 10 years had elapsed since the cause of action had accrued up to the time of the commencement of the foreclosure suit. Judgment was then entered upon the report, and the defendant in this action, who was plaintiff in the other action, appealed to the general term from the order allowing the amendment, and also from that portion of the judgment which decreed a reformation of the mortgage; and that court reversed the judgment, so far as appealed from, on the ground that the statute of limitations was a defense, and also reversed the order allowing the pleadings to be amended, upon what ground or for what reason does not appear.

The order is not reviewable here, since the application to amend was addressed to the discretion of the court below, and it would seem to be clear that, when it was reversed, the amendment to the pleadings which it authorized fell with it. This would leave the parties in the same position as they were in before any amendment was made. The testimony was all taken in the defendant's action to settle and close up the partnership affairs, and all the facts in relation to the mortgage came out without any objection, and then the parties entered into a stipulation before the referee that he should decide both cases in one report, upon the evidence thus taken; and there is but one report and one judgment, and that in the accounting case. The broad allegations of the complaint in the accounting case, which drew into that action every question concerning the mortgage, supplemented by the stipulation, left the pleadings in the foreclosure case without any important function to perform in the litigation. The pleadings in the two actions and the stipulation, when read together, furnished a sufficient basis for the referee to find all the facts, and to draw from them such legal conclusions as were necessary in order to adjust the rights of the parties. When both actions were submitted to the referee, it was evidently the intention that he should decide every question arising upon the evidence, so far as it became necessary to a complete adjustment of all the rights of the parties, without regard to any nice questions of pleading or procedure. The questions concerning the plaintiff's right to have the mortgage reformed were attached to the case subsequently, but have again disappeared by the reversal of the order which introduced that element into the controversy. Even if that feature of the case still remained, the statute of limitations would probably be a sufficient answer to it. Code, § 388; *Bruce v. Tilson,* 25 N. Y. 194; *Peters v. Delaplaine,* 49 N. Y. 365. So that the only question now is whether, upon the findings, the mortgage must be considered in equity as covering the omitted parcel which both parties intended should be included, and which they supposed all the time had been embraced in the description of the lands pledged as security for the debt; in other words, whether, as to that parcel, that was not in fact an equitable mortgage, which the plaintiff could foreclose for the satisfaction of his debt in the same action, and by the same procedure, that the other property was sought to be applied.

There can be no doubt upon the authorities that where one party advances money to another upon the faith of a verbal agreement by the latter to secure its payment by a mortgage upon certain lands, but which is never executed, or which, if executed, is so defective or informal, as to fail in effectuating the purpose of its execution, equity will impress upon the land intended to be mortgaged a lien in favor of the creditor who advanced the money for the security and satisfaction of his debt. This lien attaches upon the payment of the money, and unless there is a waiver of it, express or implied, remains and may be enforced so long as the debt itself may be enforced; and no waiver can be implied from the act of the creditor in receiving a mortgage which, by reason of fraud, inadvertence, or mistake, is not effectual to secure a specific lien on the lands, or any part of them, nor is this lien merged in any such instrument subsequently executed. Some of these cases hold that the lien of the party who has advanced money under such circumstances is analogous to that of the vendor of real estate for the unpaid purchase money. The vendor's lien rests solely upon the doctrine of equity that it would be inequitable for the vendee, who has received the legal title without payment of the purchase money, to hold the estate discharged from the claim of the seller for its price, and it is certainly difficult to see any just distinction between the two cases. In one case a party receives the title to real property without paying for it, with or without an agreement that his vendor shall be secured in the payment of the purchase price by a lien upon it by way of mortgage or otherwise. In the other case the party advances money under an agreement that its payment shall be secured by mortgage upon specific real estate, but which agreement has never been perfected. The right of the vendor and that of the person who has advanced the money are not essentially different, and each would seem to commend itself with equal force to the conscience of a court of equity. The doctrine of equitable mortgages is not limited to written instruments intended as mortgages, but which, by reason of formal defects, cannot have such operation without the aid of the court, but also to a very great variety of transactions to which equity attaches that character. It is not necessary that such transactions or agreements as to lands should be in writing, in order to take them out of the operation of the statute of frauds, for two reasons: First, because they are completely executed by at least one of the parties, and are no longer executory; and, secondly, because the statute by its own terms does not affect the power which courts of equity have always exercised to compel specific performance of such agreements. 2 Rev. St. p. 135, § 10; *Smith v. Smith,* supra; *Beardsley v. Duntley,* 69 N. Y. 577.

Assuming, as I think we must, that an equitable lien attached to all the lands intended to be embraced in the mortgage in this case, at the moment of the payment of the money, in favor of Mrs. Appley, what has since occurred to change the situation or to disturb the lien? It has not been discharged by payment. It has not, as we have seen, been waived nor merged, and therefore must have existed at the time of the commencement of this action. If this is so, then an action to compel the specific performance of the verbal agreement to give a mortgage, or to reform the defective one given, was not necessary, since the plaintiff could proceed to foreclose the existing lien by an application of the property, under the judgment of the court, to the satisfaction of the debt. It is no doubt true that such actions are necessary in most cases, for the reason that a mere lien in equity is a somewhat precarious security to the creditor, liable to be defeated at any time by the intervention of the claims of innocent third parties, who may have dealt with the owner and the land upon the faith of his record title, and in ignorance of the equitable lien. In order to preserve and protect the lien against the rights of such parties, it is necessary, generally, to make it a matter of record, and that cannot be done except by means of a proper action for that purpose. But in this case, as presented, no such question arises. The controversy is between the original parties, who have rested during a long series of years upon the situation as it existed when the money was advanced and the mortgage given, until the loan has more than doubled by the accumulation of unpaid interest, both supposing that the parcel in question had been pledged with the rest for its payment. The case is therefore, as it seems to us, a peculiarly proper one for the application of the equitable doctrine referred to, and we think that the result of the trial before the referee was correct upon principle and authority. The whole doctrine of equitable mortgages is founded upon that cardinal maxim of equity which regards that as done which has been agreed to be done and ought to have been done. In order to apply this maxim according to its true meaning, the court will treat the subject-matter, as to collateral conse-quences and incidents, in the same manner as if the final acts contemplated by the parties had been executed exactly as they ought to have been, and not as the parties might have executed them, always regarding the substance, and not the form, of the transaction. Story, Eq. Jur. §§ 64g, 156. It follows that the judgment of the general term should be reversed, and that entered upon the report of the referee affirmed, with costs in all courts, and the appeal from the order involving the right to amend the pleadings should be dismissed. All concur. Judgment accordingly.

NOTES

1. An incomplete or vague description, while resulting in the failure of a legal mort-gage, may provide the basis for an equitable mortgage. An agreement referring to "a 107 acre parcel known as THE WOODS" was held not inadequate to provide such notice as to give an equitable mortgage effect where the agreement also provided a promise to execute a mortgage. See Prell v. Trustees of Baird & Warner Mortgage & Realty Investors, 386 N.E.2d 1221 (Ind. App. 1979).

2. The omission of the entire description has been held a fatal defect in a mortgage not correctable by a judicially created equitable mortgage. See Air Flow Heating & Air Condi-tioning, Inc. v. Baker, 326 So. 2d 449 (Fla. App. 1976).

3. Technical errors in the signatures of mortgagors, witnesses or notaries may not be fatal defects and may give rise to equitable mortgages. Even if the mortgagor neglects to sign the mortgage, Martin v. Nixon, 92 Mo. 26, 4 S.W. 503 (1886), or the financial interest of the notary public attaching the acknowledgment, Harney v. Montgomery, 29 Wyo. 362, 213 P. 378 (1923), an equitable mortgage may still give the parties intent effect.

4. Expired notary commissions may be cured by statute when a mortgage is executed and the notary acknowledgment affixed after the notary's commission expires. See Ohio Rev. Code § 147.12, which provides that an act performed after the expiration of the notary's commission is as valid as an act performed during the term of the commission.

B. EQUITABLE LIENS

PHELPS v. T. O. MAHAFFEY, INC.

District Court of Appeals of Florida
156 So. 2d 900 (1963)

Smith, Chief Judge.
The appellant, Otis Phelps, as plaintiff, filed his second amended complaint in chancery against the defendants, appellees here, seeking foreclosure of an

alleged statutory mechanic's lien in one count and foreclosure of an alleged equitable lien in another count. After the defendants filed answers generally denying the facts alleged in the plaintiff's complaint, the cause proceeded to final hearing. At the conclusion of the plaintiff's case, both defendants moved for a decree in their favor. The court entered its findings of fact and law and subsequently entered a final decree in favor of the defendants. The court denied plaintiff's motions for rehearing and for modification of the final decree, and the plaintiff brings this appeal.

By entering the final decree at the conclusion of the plaintiff's case, the court necessarily found that the plaintiff had failed to prove the essential facts necessary to entitle the plaintiff to any of the relief which he sought. The facts leading to the instant litigation are as follows: In the Fall of 1960, Mr. T. O. Mahaffey, the President of the defendant corporation which bears his name, told the plaintiff that he, Mahaffey, and another person were planning to build a warehouse and do some paving. . . . Mr. Mahaffey introduced Phelps to Mr. Ruke. Mr. Mahaffey said: "We [Ruke and Mahaffey] are planning to do some paving and build a warehouse." Phelps testified that Mr. Mahaffey told him and Mr. Ruke to "talk it over and whatever settlement we made was up to us." Mr. Mahaffey then left Phelps and Ruke at the site discussing the job. Mr. Ruke designated the area to be paved and told the plaintiff to start immediately at $1.50 per yard for approximately 4,100 yards. After beginning the work, the plaintiff became concerned as to who would pay him, since that part of the contract had not been discussed. The plaintiff questioned Mr. Mahaffey, who replied that if the plaintiff had been told to go ahead that he, Mr. Mahaffey, would stand behind him and see that everything was taken care of. About a month later, on partial completion of the work, the plaintiff mailed a bill to Mr. Mahaffey, whereupon Mr. Mahaffey stated that he would accept responsibility for only one-sixth of the bill. Mr. Ruke disclaimed all responsibility. Mr. Mahaffey gave the plaintiff approximately one-half of the amount of the bill on condition that he pay back a substantial part when Phelps was paid in full by Ruke. Plaintiff admits that Ruke never told the plaintiff that he, Ruke, would pay the plaintiff. There was no written agreement or lease between Mahaffey and Ruke.

The paved surface was adjacent to a freight-truck terminal and warehouse owned by Mahaffey and constructed for the principal use of Ruke, all located on the real property owned by Mahaffey.

Ruke moved into the major portion of the building prior to completion, with the understanding that Mahaffey was to complete the warehouse and that Mahaffey and Ruke were then to agree upon the amount of rent per month after they found out how much the warehouse was going to cost Mr. Mahaffey. Ruke paid Mahaffey rent beginning at the middle of November until January, when Ruke moved from the premises. Ruke's discussions with Mahaffey included not only the construction and use of the building, but the use of a paved area around the building. Mr. Mahaffey, called by plaintiff as an adverse witness, testified that his agreement with Ruke was that if any paving was to be done, the paving would be Ruke's responsibility. He explained his subsequent agreement to pay one-sixth of the payment as follows: he, Mahaffey, increased the size of the warehouse by one-sixth over that size requested by Ruke, so Mahaffey felt the increase was his obligation. Mr. Mahaffey did not deny that he made the statement in his prior deposition that in discussing the matter with Ruke, he had stated to Ruke that he, Mahaffey, would handle the paving. In arriving at the amount of rent subsequently paid by Ruke to Mahaffey, the cost of paving was not considered as a factor. The contemplated lease between Mahaffey and Ruke never materialized. Ruke vacated the premises in January, and Mahaffey rented the premises to another tenant. After completion of the work, the plaintiff filed a claim of lien and within one year thereafter instituted this action for foreclosure thereof.

In its findings of fact and law, the court found: (1) that the plaintiff failed to prove the eixstence of a contract between himself and Mahaffey, either for the construction of the improvements or for the payment of the same; (2) that the plaintiff failed to prove the existence of a lease between Mahaffey and Ruke by which Mahaffey became obligated to Ruke to provide and pay for any paving; (3) that Ruke was a tenant at will for only a portion of the time while the work was in progress and that he did not have any interest in the land upon which a lien could attach; and, (4) that the plaintiff failed to file a notice of the pendency of this action as required by § 84.21, Florida Statutes, F.S.A. These findings of fact are substantiated by the record. The finding that there was no contract between Phelps and Mahaffey precludes the privity of contract necessary to establish the statutory lien. *Lee v. Sas,* Fla.1951, 53 So.2d 114. The finding that there was no lease between Mahaffey and Ruke removes the case at bar from the decisions granting a contractor a lien against the owner under certain circumstances where the contractor contracted with a lessee of the owner. Such a case is *Tom Joyce Realty Corp. v. Popkin,* Fla.App.1959, 111 So.2d 707. The finding that the plaintiff failed to file a notice of the pendency of the action within one year after he had filed his claim of lien bars the action and discharges the property from the lien. *Stilley v. Post,* Fla.App.1963, 148 So.2d 569. These findings sustain the decree of the trial court entered in favor of the defendants insofar as it relates to the count seeking foreclosure of the alleged statutory mechanic's lien.

. . . .

The question remains as to whether or not the plaintiff proved all of the facts necessary to establish his right to an equitable lien on the property of the corporate defendant. An equitable lien is based upon the fundamental maxim of equity that no one shall be unjustly enriched at the expense of another. Such a lien may be implied and declared out of general considerations of right and justice. *Scott v. Kirtley,* 1934, 113 Fla. 637, 152 So. 721, 93 A.L.R. 661. Equitable liens are necessarily based on the doctrine of estoppel and often arise in cases where a party innocently and in good faith makes improvements on the property of another. *Jones v. Carpenter,* 1925, 90 Fla. 407, 106 So. 127, 43 A.L.R. 1409. Although the type of work done is entirely different, the basic principles justifying an equitable lien in the instant case are substantially the same as those in *Dewing v. Davis,* Fla.App.1960, 117 So.2d 747. There, the court (Judge Kanner) explained the factors distinguishing the granting of an equitable lien in that case from those requiring denial of an equitable lien in the companion case of *Dewing v. Nelson & Company,* Fla.App. 1960, 117 So.2d 744. The same distinguishing facts are applicable here.

Where a plaintiff claimed, but in fact did not have, a statutory lien, such a claim does not bar his suit for an equitable lien. *Palmer v. Edwards,* Fla.1951, 51 So.2d 495; *Green v. Putnam,* Fla.1957, 93 So.2d 378; *Tremont Company v. Paasche,* Fla.1955, 81 So.2d 489; and *Ross v. Gerung,* Fla.1954, 69 So.2d 650. The case at bar is not one in which the claimant had a statutory lien and, having failed to institute an action to enforce the same, subsequently endeavored to establish an equitable lien which was denied on the ground that equitable liens become necessary only on account of the absence of an adequate remedy provided by law, as was the case in *Kimbrell v. Fink,* Fla.1955, 78 So.2d 96; *Blanton v. Young,*

Fla.1955, 80 So.2d 351; *Wood v. Wilson,* Fla.1955, 84 So.2d 32; and *Rood Company v. Luber,* Fla.1956, 91 So.2d 629. The court's determination that the plaintiff did not have a statutory lien removes from our consideration the question pursued by the appellee; that is, whether an equitable lien may be allowed where a statutory lien once available had been lost by failure to perfect the same. The court found that there was no statutory lien. Likewise, there is no question of laches because this action was instituted within one year from the time of the filing of the claim of lien, and this would have complied with the requirements for a statutory lien *had one existed.* Thus, the principles of law announced in the *Kimbrell, Blanton, Wood* and *Rood* decisions are not applicable.

The plaintiff introduced evidence to establish the reasonable value of the work done and the materials furnished in placing the paving upon the corporate defendant's property. Cf. *Ross v. Gerung,* supra. While acting for this corporate defendant, Mr. Mahaffey purchased the property for the corporation during the negotiations by the parties. He approached the plaintiff with the statement that he and another person were planning to build a warehouse and do some paving. He introduced Mr. Phelps to Mr. Ruke. During the course of the work, he reassured Mr. Phelps with the statement: "Well, if you were told to do it, go ahead. I will stand behind you and see that everything is taken care of." The plaintiff's evidence is sufficient to justify the conclusion that Mr. Mahaffey's actions, together with his failure to advise Mr. Phelps of the ownership of the property and of Ruke's interest — or lack of interest, misled Mr. Phelps, who innocently and in good faith improved the corporation's property, enhancing its value and making it suitable for the contemplated use. Mr. Mahaffey received and accepted the benefits of the improvements. The relations of the parties, and the circumstances of their dealings, are sufficient to establish a prima facie case on plaintiff's part for an equitable lien upon general consideration of right and justice. The facts here establish more than a moral obligation alone, as was the circumstance in *Hullum v. Bre-Lew Corporation,* Fla.1957, 93 So.2d 727.

That part of the final decree in favor of the corporate defendant is reversed for further proceedings in order that that defendant may offer evidence in its defense to the same extent as if its motion had not been made and granted.

The decree is affirmed in part and reversed in part.

SHANNON, J. and McNATT, JOHN M., ASSOCIATE JUDGE, concur.

SWINERTON & WALBERG CO. v. UNION BANK

California District Court of Appeals
25 Cal. App. 3d 259, 101 Cal. Rptr. 665 (1972)

FLEMING, J. — Union Bank (Bank) appeals a portion of a judgment imposing an equitable lien in favor of Swinerton & Walberg Co. (Swinerton) on funds held by Bank in a construction loan disbursement account.

Facts

In February 1964 James and Audrey Casey (Casey) contracted with Swinerton, a building contractor, for the construction of a 78-unit apartment building on Casey's property in Redondo Beach at a price of $785,000. To finance construction and related expenses Casey in March 1964 borrowed $892,000 from Bank, signing a promissory note secured in part by a trust deed on the property.

Casey and Bank entered into a building loan agreement pursuant to which the

$892,000 loan was deposited with Bank in a construction loan disbursement account. At Bank's request Casey deposited an additional $37,700 in the account to make a total of $929,700. $186,000 was to be disbursed for purposes other than construction, and $3,700 was to be held in the account for unforeseen expenses. The balance of $740,000 was to be disbursed as construction progressed to Swinerton (who was named in the agreement as the contractor), but $74,000 of that amount would be withheld until a title insurance company on completion of construction guaranteed that no mechanics' liens were outstanding against the property. The building loan agreement provided that if Casey should default on any obligation to Bank, the latter could apply funds in the construction loan disbursement account against Casey's obligation, and it recited "that nothing contained in this agreement shall be construed to vest in any contractor . . . any interest in or claim upon the funds so set aside in this agreement." As contractor, Swinerton signed a declaration in the building loan agreement that it accepted the agreements, conditions, and provisions of the loan agreement, and that these would control inconsistent provisions in its building contract with Casey.

Construction began in March 1964 and was completed in January 1965. Casey ordered extras amounting to $5,000, thereby raising the contract price to $790,000. During the construction period Bank disbursed $666,000 to Swinerton.

In March 1965 Casey defaulted on obligations to both Swinerton and Bank, and Swinerton recorded a mechanics' lien for $150,932.93 against Casey's property. On 16 September 1965 Swinerton offered to release its mechanics' lien, the only lien outstanding, if Bank would disburse the withheld amount of $74,000 on deposit in the construction loan account. Bank refused. In November 1966 Bank foreclosed its trust deed on the Casey property, buying in the property on the foreclosure sale for $810,000 and thereby wiping out Swinerton's mechanics' lien, a result Swinerton did not challenge.

Bank never sought to press its claim under the building loan agreement to apply undisbursed construction funds to Casey's defaulted obligation to Bank, and $104,472.68 remains undisbursed in the construction loan account. Swinerton instituted the present action against Casey and Bank for breach of contract and for imposition of an equitable lien against funds on deposit in the construction loan account.

Trial Court's Determination

The trial court found: Swinerton was induced to construct the apartment building by Casey and Bank; Swinerton was induced to rely on, and did rely on, the construction loan disbursement fund for payment; Swinerton, in signing the building loan agreement, did not intend to give up its rights to an equitable lien against undisbursed construction funds; Swinerton completed the construction called for by its contract in a workmanlike manner, and the reasonable value of construction exceeded $740,000; Bank had no reason to refuse to disburse $74,000 to Swinerton after Swinerton offered to release its mechanics' lien on 16 September 1965.

The trial court concluded that Casey was indebted to Swinerton for $124,000 [$790,000 contract price, less $666,000 construction loan disbursement]; Swinerton had no contractual rights against Bank; Swinerton was entitled to $74,000 plus interest from 16 September 1965 from Bank; and Swinerton's recovery against Bank was to be credited against Casey's debt to Swinerton.

Bank contends (1) as a general contractor Swinerton could not assert an equitable lien upon construction funds, (2) Swinerton waived any claim he might have had to an equitable lien, and (3) pre-judgment interest was improperly imposed on the equitable lien.

Equitable Lien

Bank argues that a general contractor may not assert an equitable lien, and it insists that this conclusion is compelled by *Gordon Bldg. Corp. v. Gibraltar Sav. & Loan Assn.,* 247 Cal.App.2d 1, 4, 10 [55 Cal.Rptr. 884]. We disagree. In *Gordon* a general contractor, sued by a subcontractor for money due for labor and materials, cross-complained against a lender, in part to impose an equitable lien on construction loan proceeds held by the lender on the construction project on which the contractor had worked. The lender's demurrer was sustained without leave to amend, and judgment of dismissal was affirmed on appeal, because two allegations essential to the imposition of an equitable lien were missing from the general contractor's cross-complaint against the lender: an allegation that the general contractor directly supplied labor or materials to the construction project, and an allegation that the general contractor justifiably relied on the construction loan proceeds. Since the general contractor had made "several futile attempts to allege sufficient facts" to state a cause of action, the demurrer was properly sustained without leave to amend.

Gordon does state: "It would be a novel theory that the general contractor should accede to the benefit of loan proceeds heretofore considered to constitute a trust for the payment of liens and claims established by subcontractors and materialmen. Indeed, the demonstrated attitude of the law has been to implement the existing statutory scheme protecting subcontractors by methods calculated to forestall the misapplication or diversion of construction funds by the entrepreneurs of the project, including owner, builder, and the general contractor or whatever combinations thereof may exist in an individual case." (247 Cal.App.2d at p. 9.) That language, however, was used to support the court's conclusion that under the circumstances of the case the general contractor's complaint did not state a cause of action based on a *third-party beneficiary theory,* i.e., a contract theory of recovery. Since recovery in the present case is not grounded on contract but rather on equitable considerations arising out of estoppel and unjust enrichment, its disposition is not controlled by the foregoing language from *Gordon.* Significantly, the latter case did not declare that a general contractor, entirely unrelated to the owner and builder, could never assert an equitable lien against construction loan proceeds.

Bank next argues that all cases in which equitable liens have been upheld involve subcontractors and not general contractors, and from this it concludes that a general contractor can never become entitled to an equitable lien against construction loan funds. Yet the fact that all other cases recognizing equitable liens have involved subcontractors, even if true, does not by itself preclude imposition of an equitable lien against construction loan funds on behalf of a general contractor. The lender of construction funds stands in the same approximate relationship to a subcontractor as it does to a general contractor who is wholly independent from the borrower. In both instances the position of the lender is that summarized in the following language: "Where the lender has received the benefit of the claimant's performance, and therefore a more valuable security for its note, it is not justified in withholding or appropriating to any other use money originally intended to be used to pay for such performance and relied upon by the claimant in rendering its performance." *(Miller v. Mountain View Sav. & Loan Assn.,* 238 Cal.App.2d 644, 661 [48 Cal.Rptr.

278], paraphrasing the court's statement in *Pacific Ready Cut Homes v. Title I. & T. Co.,* 216 Cal. 447, 452 [14 P.2d 510].)

Here, Swinerton performed its work and completed the construction of the apartment building (work whose reasonable value exceeded $740,000) but received only $666,000. Bank obtained the benefit of that performance by foreclosing on its trust deed and selling the apartment building for $810,000. It is equally clear that Swinerton was induced by the creation of the building construction loan fund to supply work, labor, and materials for the project and that in rendering its performance it relied on the fund for payment. Indeed, since Bank had acquired a first lien on the property to protect its construction loan, Swinerton could look to little else for security. The only contractual obstacle to Swinerton's right to the undisbursed construction loan funds was the existence of its own mechanics' lien against the property, a lien which on 16 September 1965 it offered to release if Bank would disburse $74,000 from the remaining construction loan funds. Bank refused the offer. Under these circumstances — full performance by the contractor and reliance by the contractor on the fund for payment — we think Swinerton became entitled to the $74,000 withheld in the construction loan disbursement account for payment of construction costs.

There are no statutory impediments to this conclusion, for the events with which we are concerned took place in 1964 and 1965. A 1967 addition to former Code of Civil Procedure section 1190.1, subdivision (n) (now Civ. Code, § 3264) provides: "The rights of all persons furnishing labor, services, equipment, or materials for any work of improvement, with respect to any fund for payment of construction costs, are governed exclusively by this article, and no such person may assert any legal or equitable right with respect to such fund, other than a right created by direct written contract between such person and the person holding the fund, except pursuant to the provisions of this article."

Bank argues that this provision shows legislative opposition to the imposition of equitable liens against construction funds. We do not read such a broad meaning into that section (see Lefcoe and Schaffer, *Construction Lending and the Equitable Lien,* 40 So.Cal.L.Rev. 439, 459, fn. 4), but in any event that section does not apply retrospectively. The Legislature specifically provided that the addition to former Code of Civil Procedure section 1190.1, subdivision (n) (now Civ. Code, § 3264), "shall not apply to any work of improvement commenced prior to [8 November 1967]." (Stats. 1967, ch. 789, § 4.)

Finally, Bank argues that the equitable lien was designed to aid only those who are entitled to a stop notice but fail to properly perfect it, that general contractors are not entitled to stop notices (former Code Civ. Proc., § 1190.1, subd. (h), now Civ. Code, § 3159), and that because a general contractor's equitable rights should not exceed his legal rights, a general contractor is not entitled to an equitable lien. Bank's major premise is incorrect: The equitable lien is wholly independent of the statutory mechanics' lien and stop notice remedies (Goulden and Dent, *More on Mechanics' Liens, Stop Notices, and the Like,* 54 Cal. L. Rev. 179, 190; see *Smith v. Anglo-California Trust Co.,* 205 Cal. 496, 502 [271 P. 898]), and therefore does not depend on the availability to the claimant of the statutory stop notice remedy.

We conclude that in 1965 a general contractor could claim an equitable lien on construction loan proceeds, and that in this case the general contractor became entitled to such a lien. . . .

The judgment is affirmed.

ROTH, P.J., and COMPTON, J., concurred.

SMITH v. SMITH

Court of Appeals of New York
125 N.Y. 224, 26 N.E. 259 (1891)

O'BRIEN, J. The plaintiff sought by this action to compel the defendant, who is his wife, to convey to him certain real estate, of which she holds the title, or to have a lien in his favor declared thereon. The courts below have held that he was entitled to the lien, but not to the conveyance, and as there is no appeal, except by the defendant, it is only necessary to examine the grounds upon which the right to such lien was based. In the year 1863, the plaintiff was the owner of the real estate described in the complaint, and concerning which the relief was demanded. On the 21st of September, in that year, he conveyed it through a third party to the defendant, who has ever since held the title, though the plaintiff has managed it, and collected the rents, and applied what was not expended in the payment of taxes, insurance, and necessary repairs, to the support of the family. The consideration expressed in the deed is $25, but it is quite evident that it was a voluntary transfer of the property by the husband to the wife, without consideration, and for the purpose of better securing its benefits to the family. The parties to this action have ever since resided upon the property as husband and wife, renting such portions of it as were not necessary for their own use. It was found by the special term upon sufficient evidence that in the spring of 1879, the plaintiff informed the defendant, his wife, that he had some money in the bank, drawing only three and a half per cent. interest, and that by using it in building a block on a portion of the premises, he could realize a larger income from this money. The defendant replied that it would be a good thing; that he could go on and build there, and that "if he got any ways distressed in any shape or manner, he had a right to sell the block; that it was at his disposal at any time." The plaintiff replied that it was all right, and that he would go on and build it. It is also found that, relying upon this arrangement, the plaintiff, with his own means, and at an expense of $4,500, constructed a brick block upon a portion of the land, which enhanced its value to the extent of the sum so expended, and that the management of the property ever since by the plaintiff, the collection and receipt of the rents, and the disposition made by him of the same, was with the defendant's knowledge and consent. It was held that the plaintiff was entitled to have a lien declared upon the land for the sum so expended by him, with interest thereon from March 1, 1887, the date when the plaintiff ceased to collect the rents, in consequence, apparently, of some disagreement between the parties. We think that the judgment is correct. It would be contrary to equity to permit the defendant, under the circumstances, to hold the property, without subjecting it as security, in some form, to the expenditures made upon it, with her knowledge and consent. She was informed by her husband that he had money invested at low interest, which could be used in improving the property in such way as to yield a much larger income to him. From what was said, she is chargeable with knowledge of his intentions to expend the money only for the purpose of making a more profitable investment, and with this knowledge on her part, she permitted him to erect the building. Unless the transaction gave him some claim or lien upon the property he had, of course, no investment at all after he drew the money from the bank, and used it in the construction of the block. The defendant had no right to understand from what was said that her husband intended to make a gift of the money to her by expending it upon the property. What was said and done amounted to an assent

on the part of the wife, that in case the husband used the money in constructing
the block on the land, of which she was the owner, his money would, at least, be
as safe to him as it was before. Her remark that he had the right to dispose of
the block at any time, in case he became in any way distressed, has no point or
significance, unless it is construed as an assent on her part that he was to have
a lien, and consequently a right to sell, in virtue of the expenditure which he
contemplated making upon the property. The transaction was in substance an
agreement on her part to give such a lien, in case the expediture was made. Upon
the findings made by the trial court, the plaintiff, acting in good faith, and in
reliance upon this promise, expended his money, and the defendant has the full
benefit thereof, so that, in equity, she ought to pay for the same. We do not
conceive it to be necessary to quote at length from the elementary books upon
equity jurisprudence, or from the adjudged cases, the language in which the
principles are expressed that sustain the judgment in this case. A citation of these
authorities is sufficient. 1 Story, Eq.Jur. § 388; 2 Story, Eq. Jur. § 1237; 3 Pom.
Eq. Jur. 233; *King's Heirs v. Thompson,* 9 Pet. 204; *Chase v. Peck,* 21 N. Y. 581;
Freeman v. Freeman, 43 N. Y. 34; *Hale v. Bank,* 49 N. Y. 627; *Husted v.
Ingraham,* 75 N. Y. 255; *Perry v. Board,* 102 N. Y. 99, 6 N. E. Rep. 116.

It is urged in support of this appeal that the husband cannot invoke the power
of a court of equity for the purpose of obtaining relief, until he first does equity,
by accounting to her for the rents received by him, and which were used for the
support of the family, an obligation which the law imposes upon the husband
alone. That point was not specifically raised at the trial, and for that reason alone,
should not now prevail to reverse the judgment. It does not appear, however,
what sum, if any, remained of the rent after the payment of taxes, insurance,
repairs, and interest on the $4,500. That balance, whatever it was, is all that can
be said to have been used by the husband for the payment of family expenses.
It was the income of property that formerly belonged to the husband, and which
he deeded to the wife without consideration, and it was accepted by her,
evidently, with the tacit understanding on both sides that the income should be
used as it had been before, and as it actually was used to some extent, for the
benefit of the family. This is apparent from the conduct of the parties; for the
husband, notwithstanding the conveyance, continued to manage the property
and collect and use the rents as if the transfer had never been made, and in this,
so far as appears, the wife acquiesced. The wife, having assented to the disposition which her husband made of the rents, cannot now change her position, and
ask him to account to her therefor. His application of some part of the rents to
the support of the family was not, under all the circumstances, inequitable as
against his wife, but her refusal to give him a lien or security for the money
expended in building upon the property was. This favorite maxim of equity does
not, as it seems to us, apply to this case. An agreement to give a lien upon land
to secure money to be expended in improving it, followed by an actual
expenditure of the money, and the improvement contemplated, is so far performed that equity does not regard the statute of frauds as a defense to an action
to enforce the agreement. *Freeman v. Freeman,* supra; *Burdick v. Jackson,* 7
Hun, 488; Pom. Spec. Perf. § 30. We think that the judgment is based upon
correct principles, and that it should be affirmed, with costs. All concur, except
RUGER, C. J., and FINCH, J., dissenting.

JONES v. SACRAMENTO SAVINGS & LOAN ASS'N

California District Court of Appeals
248 Cal. App. 2d 522, 56 Cal. Rptr. 741 (1967)

FRIEDMAN, J. — The 13 lots involved in this quiet title action are part of a residential subdivision in Yuba County. These lots were successively the subject of a set of purchase money trust deeds and a set of construction money trust deeds. Sacramento Savings and Loan Association was the lender of construction funds. The suit represents a title contest between plaintiff Jones, who had bought the purchase money notes and bid in the properties at his trustee's sales, and Sacramento Savings, which purchased at sales held by its own trustee. Neither party bid at the other's sales.

The trial court sustained Jones' claim of title and denied that of Sacramento Savings. The latter appeals from the judgment. . . .

The earlier group of trust deeds secured purchase money loans of $806.45 per lot. All were recorded August 21, 1959. All contained subordination provisions, the effect of which is now in dispute.[1] Yuba County Title Company was designated as trustee.

Somewhat over a year later the owners took out construction loans aggregating $143,900 and approximating $11,000 to $12,000 a lot. The owners gave Sacramento Savings instalment notes with principal and interest payable at the rate of $86 per month. These notes included a due-on-sale clause, giving the holder an option to accelerate maturity upon any sale by the borrower.[2]

Before making the construction loans Sacramento Savings issued escrow instructions to Yuba County Title Company, stating: "Please secure subordination." The title company refused to issue insurance covering the Sacramento Savings trust deeds unless it received additional subordination agreements from the trustee of the purchase money trust deeds. Sacramento Savings then withdrew the escrow from Yuba County Title Company and another title company became the escrow depositary. Sacramento Savings then made the construction loans and its deeds of trust were recorded. No subordination agreements were executed, other than those contained in the purchase money trust deeds.

---

[1] The printed trust deeds contained the following subordination agreement:

By the acceptance of this deed of trust: The beneficiary hereby authorizes and instructs the trustee, on demand of the Trustor, or their [sic] successor in interest, without notice, demand or further instruction, to subordinate the priority of this trust deed to a construction or improvement loan or a permanent loan on said property so long as the loan is extended by a conventional financial institution and the amount of said loan is at least three times the amount of the note which this trust deed is given to secure.

A typewritten addendum declared:

Notwithstanding the language contained in said Subordination Agreement, it is understood that any such deed of trust must be extended by a licensed bank, savings and loan association, insurance company, or the Federal National Mortgage Association and provided said loan has a maturity of not less than fifteen years.

A construction loan as referred to in said Subordination Agreement shall be considered prior to this deed of trust only should there be a permanent take-out committed by a licensed bank, savings and loan association, insurance company or the Federal National Mortgage Association.

[2] The acceleration clause declared:

If the trustor shall sell, convey or alienate the property described in the deed of trust securing this note, or any part thereof, or any interest therein, or shall be divested of his title, or any interest therein, in any manner or way, whether voluntary or involuntary, any indebtedness or obligation secured thereby, irrespective of the maturity dates expressed in any note evidencing the same, at the option of the beneficiary hereof, and without demand or notice, shall immediately become due and payable.

Homes were built on the 13 lots. Both the purchase money loans and the construction loans became delinquent. Jones bought up the defaulted purchase money notes and commenced the sale of individual parcels. The parties have effectually stipulated that Jones' proceedings complied with Civil Code section 2924, in that notices of default were properly recorded and notices of the trustee's sales given. At sales held in August and September 1961, Jones bid in three of the lots. At trustee's sales held in February and April 1962 he bid in three more lots.

In the meantime Sacramento Savings' trustee commenced sale proceedings under the construction money trust deeds. In Novermber 1961 it caused notices of default to be recorded against 11 of the lots. In May 1962 Sacramento Savings bid in these 11 lots at a sale held by its own trustee. Six of these were the lots which had already been sold to Jones at sales held by his own trustee. The other five had not yet been foreclosed by Jones, and as to these the sales to Sacramento Savings preceded the sales to Jones under the purchase money trust deeds. The remaining two lots were the subject of sales to Jones in April 1962 and to Sacramento Savings in November 1962. Not only did the timing of the various trustee's sales overlap; so did recordation of notices of default and notices of sale. Neither party chose to bid at any of the other's sales. Neither chose to exercise a junior lienor's right to reinstate the senior loan after the latter had become delinquent. (See Civ. Code, § 2924c.) Each, apparently, relied upon the assumption that its own trust deeds had superiority.

Sacramento Savings asserts priority of its construction money trust deeds on the theory that the subordination provision of the earlier trust deeds (fn. 1, *supra)* operated automatically for the benefit of the construction lender, requiring no separate subordination document. It also claims equitable seniority, urging that equity will impose a subordinating lien to carry out the parties' intent, although their contract language may fall short, citing *Coast Bank v. Minderhout,* 61 Cal.2d 311, 313-314 [38 Cal.Rptr. 505, 392 P.2d 265].

Whatever their merit in an appropriate case, these claims are not dispositive here. A lender may agree to subordinate his lien to a later encumbrance upon specified conditions; in order to achieve priority, the later encumbrance must substantially respond to these conditions. (*Collins v. Home Savings & Loan Assn.,* 205 Cal.App.2d 86, 95 [22 Cal. Rptr. 817]; Comment, 52 Cal.L.Rev. 157, 166-167; California Land Security and Development (Cont. Ed. Bar) pp. 132-138; see also *Bank of America v. Hirsch Mercantile Co.,* 64 Cal.App.2d 175, 183 [148 P.2d 110].) The construction loans of Sacramento Savings departed substantially from the subordination conditions of the purchase money trust deeds. As printed, the latter permitted subordination either to a construction or permanent loan. The typewritten addendum qualified these alternatives, requiring that the construction loan be accompanied by a "permanent take-out" commitment and that any "permanent" loan have a maturity of not less that 15 years.

Although the term "take-out" does not seem to have received judicial definition, the transaction of that name is a common feature of residential subdivision financing. The term refers to the permanent secured loan which the ultimate home buyer floats to finance his purchase of the dwelling and which supersedes or "takes out" the interim construction loan secured by the subdivision developer. (California Land Security and Development (Cont. Ed. Bar), *supra,* pp. 552-553; see, e.g., *Magna Development Co. v. Reed,* 228 Cal.App.2d 230, 236 [39 Cal.Rptr. 284].) The commitment in turn is a statement from a lending institution (or, in the case of Federal National Mortgage Association, a loan buyer) that financing to a specified amount will be available to qualified home buyers. No permanent take-out commitment was supplied here.

The notes taken by Sacramento Savings were payable at the rate of $86 per month, including interest, but could be called, at the holder's option, upon the developer's sale of the property. Thus the very objective of the subdivider's borrowing, construction of a house and sale to a home buyer, would permit acceleration of the note. The due-on-sale clause gave the construction lender a wide range of options. It might elect to continue the subdivider as its primary obligor; or, if a home buyer of satisfactory credit appeared, permit the latter to assume the "construction" loan; or choose to exercise the power of sale conferred by its deed of trust, putting the subordinate lienholder under economic pressure to bid in the property. A construction loan accompanied by such options fell far short of supplying the "permanent" or 15-year financing demanded by the purchase-money lienholder as a condition of subordination.

There is no reason why priority of a later lienholder should not be made to depend upon compliance with these conditions. They represent a means by which the purchase money lienholder protects himself against the subdivider's default after the construction loan is made. A take-out commitment or, in the alternative, a long-term loan will assure the availability of consumer financing despite the property developer's insolvency. Either device tends to enhance the property's value, promote its marketability and avoid distress sale if the subdivider encounters financial trouble. The interim financing supplied by Sacramento Savings and Loan Association did not supply this protection. Consequently it failed to achieve superiority over the earlier lien of the purchase money trust deeds.

There is no claim that any of the trustees' sales produced bids exceeding the secured debt. The sales to Jones in enforcement of the senior liens wiped out the junior liens of Sacramento Savings. (*Call v. Thunderbird Mortgage Co.,* 58 Cal.2d 542, 548 [25 Cal.Rptr. 265, 375 P.2d 169]; *Sohn v. California Pac. Title Ins. Co.,* 124 Cal.App.2d 757, 767 [269 P.2d 223]; *Barr Lumber Co. v. Shaffer,* 108 Cal.App.2d 14, 16-23 [238 P.2d 99].) In those cases where Jones' trustee was the first to give notices and hold sales, the subsequent sales conveyed no title to Sacramento Savings and succeeded only in clouding Jones' title. (*Metropolis etc. Sav. Bank v. Barnet,* 165 Cal. 449, 455 [132 P. 833].) Where Sacramento Savings' trustee was the first to give notices and hold sales, Sacramento Savings purchased title subordinate to the senior liens of the purchase money trust deeds. (*Penziner v. West American Finance Co.,* 10 Cal.2d 160, 180 [74 P.2d 252]; *Streiff v. Darlington,* 9 Cal.2d 42, 45 [68 P.2d 728].) It is immaterial that in some cases the junior lienholder was the first to give notice and hold sales. (*Martin v. Hildebrand,* 190 Cal. 369, 372 [212 P. 618]; *Woods v. Kellerman,* 3 Cal.App. 422, 425 [89 P. 358]; see also *Carpenter v. Smallpage,* 220 Cal. 129, 132 [29 P.2d 841, 30 P.2d 995]; 34 Cal. Jur.2d, Mortgages, § 463, p. 141.)

Sacramento Savings charges Jones with unclean hands. It points out that equity's denial of relief extends not only to outright fraud, but to any kind of unconscionable conduct on a plaintiff's part. The evidence indicates that Jones bought up the purchase money notes (of the face amount of $806.45 each) at a discount, knowing that the value of the lots securing them had been enhanced by the construction of homes financed by Sacramento Savings. Presumably Jones was also aware that he was buying deeds of trust burdened by subordination provisions.

There is nothing unconscionable in such conduct. Neither party lacked notice of any step taken by the other. Whatever of value Jones might gain is attributable: (a) to the disingenuous draftsmanship of Sacramento Savings, which sought subordination of the purchase money liens by supplying the form but not the substance of long-term financing; (b) to Jones' willingness to gamble on continued superiority of the purchase money liens; (c) to Sacramento Savings' expenditure of construction money in the face of recorded purchase money liens and its misplaced reliance on the subordinating effect of its own loan papers; (d) to Sacramento Savings' unwillingness to reinstate the defaulted purchase money loans (Civ. Code, § 2924c) or to bid in at the ensuing sales. Jones did nothing to prevent these latter steps. Had Sacramento Savings chosen to take either action, it could have protected its own large investment in these lots and limited Jones' profit to the difference between the unpaid purchase money notes and the discounted price paid for them by Jones.

Nevertheless, Sacramento Savings seeks an equitable lien premised upon the doctrine of unjust enrichment, pointing out that a decree for the plaintiff will present him with the financial benefit of expensive improvements constructed with its money. It assigns trial court error in the denial of its motion to amend pleadings and in the rejection of its request for findings permitting imposition of such a lien. It cites the following text statement: "The general doctrine, that equity will create a lien on property where this is necessary to accomplish justice, is not confined to situations involving defective mortgages, but extends to any case where the parties attempt to make property security for an obligation. [Citations.] In some cases the lien is created as a desirable remedy though the parties did not in fact intend to make the property security for an obligation; e.g. where the object is to prevent unjust enrichment. [Citations.]" (1 Witkin, Summary of Cal. Law (1960) p. 707.)

We have concluded that Sacramento Savings is entitled to an equitable lien on the properties in Jones' hands. Nonconflicting evidence demonstrates and this court finds that both the then owner and the lender intended that the construction loan be secured by first liens; that the savings and loan association advanced construction funds of $143,900 in reliance, however erroneous, on expected first liens; that the loan funds were actually applied to the construction of improvements having a value far exceeding that of the land; that Jones, buyer of liens on the land, was aware of the improvements financed by the lending institution when he bought these liens. Since he paid a discounted price for the purchase money notes, his investment is but a fraction of the value of the improved properties. He would be unjustly enriched were he permitted to hold or sell the properties without making restitution for the improvements built at the expense of the savings and loan association.

A general doctrine of equity permits imposition of an equitable lien where the claimant's expenditure has benefited another's property under circumstances entitling the claimant to restitution. (*McColgan v. Bank of California Assn.*, 208 Cal. 329, 338 [281 P. 381, 65 A.L.R. 1075]; *Stockwell v. Mutual Life Ins. Co.*, 140 Cal. 198, 202-203 [73 P. 833, 98 Am.St. Rep. 25]; *Ohio Electric Car Co. v. Duffet*, 48 Cal.App. 674, 678 [192 P. 298]; Rest., Restitution, § 161, com. a; *ibid.*, § 170; 4 Pomeroy's Equity Jurisprudence (5th ed.) § 1235, pp. 696-699; 3 Pomeroy's Equity Jurisprudence (5th ed.) § 390, p. 67; Comment, 17 Cal.L.Rev. 411.) A specific application of the doctrine occurs when a lender advances money which benefits the land of another in mistaken reliance upon an imperfect mortgage or lien upon that land. (*Estate of Pitts*, 218 Cal. 184, 189 [22 P.2d 694]; *Smith v. Anglo-California Trust Co.*, 205 Cal. 496, 502-504 [271 P. 898]; *Beckwith v. Sheldon*, 168 Cal. 742, 746-747 [145 P. 97, Ann. Cas. 1916A 963]; see 17

Cal.L.Rev. at pp. 412-413.) The present circumstances fit both the general doctrine and the specific rule with nicety.

It is necessary that the lien claimant's money be spent upon the expected security of the property against which the lien is sought. *(A-1 Door & Materials Co. v. Fresno Guar. Sav. & Loan Assn.,* 61 Cal.2d 728, 732 [40 Cal.Rptr. 85, 394 P.2d 829].) The evidence permits no question but that such reliance existed here.

A quiet title suit aimed at terminating claims upon real estate is in one sense a strict foreclosure. *(Petersen v. Ridenour,* 135 Cal.App.2d 720, 728 [287 P.2d 848].) Equitable principles apply in a quiet title action and, in the absence of a breach of duty, the court may protect against forfeiture. *(Gonzalez v. Hirose,* 33 Cal.2d 213, 217 [200 P.2d 793].) There is a distinction between a constructive trust arising from the property owner's wrongdoing and an equitable lien imposed to prevent his unjust enrichment. The former may call for sale of the property and distribution of its proceeds. Equity imposes a lien here not to vindicate a wrong but to prevent unjust enrichment. The objective may be accomplished by a decree impressing the lien but without demanding an immediate sale. *(Gonzalez v. Hirose, supra,* 33 Cal.2d at p. 217; *Warner Bros. Co. v. Freud,* 138 Cal. 651, 654-656 [72 P. 345]; *Petersen v. Ridenour, supra,* 135 Cal.App.2d at p. 728; Rest., Restitution, § 161, com. b.) Equitable liens in favor of Sacramento Savings should be paid off at such times and under such circumstances as will avoid undue hardship on Jones. . . .

. . . .

The judgment is reversed and the cause remanded with directions to enter judgment and to take such other proceedings not inconsistent with this opinion as may be necessary or appropriate.

PIERCE, P. J., and REGAN, J., concurred.

NOTES

1. Could the court have given title to Sacramento Savings and given Jones a lien just as easily as it did the opposite? The equities seem close to equal and the enrichment does not seem unjust in light of Sacramento Savings shopping for a title company to undertake the risk. What basis did the court use to justify the result? For a more detailed treatment of the equitable lien in this case see J. HETLAND, CALIFORNIA REAL ESTATE SECURED TRANSACTIONS 213 (1970).

2. Compare the enrichment of the parties giving rise to a lien in *Jones v. Sacramento Savings & Loan Ass'n* with *Smith v. Smith, supra.* Note the difference in the positions of the two parties requesting an equitable lien. Should the results be the same? Does the arms length nature of the *Jones* case suggest a different result in the *Smith* case, where the prospective lienor was the husband of the vestee?

3. *Swinerton & Walberg v. Union Bank, supra,* involves a lien on a fund rather than on specific realty. Does the concept of unjust enrichment enter into the picture, or is the bank in fact attempting to simply keep its own money? Can a comparison be made between this case and the other two cases in this section?

4. While equitable mortgages arising from an attempt at creating a mortgage which fails for a defect, or even a promise to give a mortgage which is accompanied by a specific form, may provide the terms of the equitable mortgage, what terms are to be provided in a judicially created equitable lien? The court in the *Jones* case clearly does not want Jones unduly burdened by repayment of the equitable obligation at an inconvenient time, but it does not spell out the terms or conditions of a repayment schedule. Had the appellate court been more specific, Jones might have been burdened; while here the matter is remanded back to the trial court which can ascertain a reasonable payment schedule for Jones consistent with his needs, as well as that of the savings and loan. Notice finally that the savings and loan does not get the benefit of its bargain by also receiving interest, but is saved only from "unjustly enriching" Jones by repayment of principal.

C. DISGUISED MORTGAGES

Of all the categories in this chapter disguised mortgages is probably the most accurate. It can be debated that a disguised mortgage in fact creates a legal mortgage inasmuch as there is a transfer for the purpose of securing performance of an obligation. However, it is also felt that disguised mortgages being in other than the usual form create an equitable mortgage.[9] The difference of opinion is academic, for if a disguised form is used and ultimately held to be a mortgage, it is immaterial whether it is legal or equitable.

Of the various forms possible it appears that a deed absolute is a form available everywhere, although it is questionable in Pennsylvania. Other forms such as sale and lease-back may be more commonplace today, but still have the same potential for litigation. According to one source, the negative covenant which appeared as allowing banks great flexibility in deciding after the fact whether an obligation is secured or unsecured have fallen into disuse.[10]

COAST BANK v. MINDERHOUT

Supreme Court of California
61 Cal. 2d 311, 392 P.2d 265 (1964)

TRAYNOR, J. — Defendants appeal from a judgment foreclosing an equitable mortgage on certain real property in San Luis Obispo County. The trial court overruled defendants' general demurrer and upon defendants' failure to answer the complaint decreed foreclosure and ordered a sale of the property. (See Code Civ. Proc., § 585, subd. 4.)

From January 18 to November 12, 1957, plaintiff bank made several loans to Burton and Donald Enright, who executed a promissory note for the full amount of the indebtedness. In a separate instrument dated January 18, 1957,[1] the

---

[9] *See* Coast Bank v. Minderhout, fn. 3, *supra. See also* G. Osborne, G. Nelson & D. Whitman, Real Estate Finance Law 110 (1979).

[10] *See* G. Osborne, G. Nelson & D. Whitman, Real Estate Finance Law 113 (1979).

[1] "AGREEMENT NOT TO ENCUMBER OR TRANSFER PROPERTY

"(For use with Property Improvement Loan)

"In consideration of any loan or advance made by Bank of Belmont Shore (hereinafter referred to as 'Bank') to the undersigned, either jointly or severally, the undersigned (hereinafter referred to as 'Borrower' whether one or more), jointly and severally promise and agree that until all such loans and advances and all other indebtedness or liabilities to the Bank shall have been paid in full, or until 21 years following the death of the last survivor of the undersigned, whichever shall first occur, they will pay all taxes, assessments and charges of every kind, imposed or levied, or which may be imposed or levied upon the hereinafter described real property prior to the time when any of such taxes, assessments or charges shall become delinquent and will not, without the consent in writing of Bank, first had and obtained, create or permit any lien or other encumbrances (other than those presently existing and/or securing the payment of loans and advances made to them by Bank) to exist on said real property, and will not transfer, sell, hypothecate, assign, or in any manner whatever dispose of said real property, or any interest therein or any portion thereof, which real property is situated in *San Luis Obispo* County, California. . . . [Description omitted.]

"It is further agreed and understood that if default be made in the performance of any of the terms hereof, or of any Instrument executed by Borrower in connection herewith, or in the payment of any indebtedness or liabilities now or hereafter owing to Bank, Bank may, at its election, in addition to all other remedies and rights which it may have by law, declare the entire remaining unpaid principal and interest of any obligations or indebtedness then remaining unpaid to the Bank due and payable forthwith.

"It is further agreed and understood that Bank may, in its discretion, and is hereby authorized by Borrower, to cause this instrument to be recorded at such time and in such places as Bank may, in its discretion elect."

Enrights agreed that they would not transfer or encumber without plaintiff's consent certain real property owned by them until all of their indebtedness was paid. If the Enrights defaulted, plaintiff could declare all remaining indebtedness due forthwith. Plaintiff immediately recorded the instrument as authorized therein. In November 1958, while part of the indebtedness was still unpaid, the Enrights conveyed the property to defendants without plaintiff's knowledge or consent. Defendants concede that they had not only constructive but actual knowledge of the terms of the agreement. Plaintiff apparently elected to accelerate the due date, but was unable to collect the unpaid balance. It then brought this action to foreclose the equitable mortgage that it claims the instrument created.

"[E]very express executory agreement in writing, whereby the contracting party sufficiently indicates an intention to make some particular property, real or personal, or fund, therein described or identified, a security for a debt or other obligation . . . creates an equitable lien upon the property so indicated, which is enforceable against the property in the hands not only of the original contractor, but of his . . . purchasers or encumbrancers with notice." (4 Pomeroy, Equity Jurisprudence (5th ed. Symons) § 1235.) Thus, a promise to give a mortgage or a trust deed on particular property as security for a debt will be specifically enforced by granting an equitable mortgage. An agreement that particular property is security for a debt also gives rise to an equitable mortgage even though it does not constitute a legal mortgage. If a mortgage or trust deed is defectively executed, for example, an equitable mortgage will be recognized. Specific mention of a security interest is unnecessary if it otherwise appears that the parties intended to create such an interest.

Defendants contend that the instrument did not create an equitable mortgage because it does not show on its face that the parties intended to make the property security for the indebtedness. They suggest that the parties intended to protect the lender in another manner than by giving it a security interest in the property and point out that the parties must have been familiar with the usual methods of creating a legal mortgage or trust deed on real property. In their view, plaintiff simply extended unsecured credit to the Enrights as property owners while retaining the power to withdraw the credit by accelerating the due date of the indebtedness if the Enrights breached their agreement not to convey or encumber the property. They invoke cases from other jurisdictions holding that comparable instruments do not create security interests.

In the present case, however, plaintiff pleaded and defendants admitted by demurring and failing to answer that the parties intended to create a security interest in the property. Accordingly, the question presented is not what meaning appears from the face of the instrument alone, but whether the pleaded meaning is one to which the instrument is reasonably susceptible. (*Richards v. Farmers' & Merchants' Bank,* 7 Cal.App. 387, 395 [94 P. 393]; see 2 Witkin, Cal. Procedure, pp. 1231-1232.) It is essentially the question that would be presented had defendants denied that the parties intended to create a security interest and plaintiff had offered extrinsic evidence to prove that they did. Such evidence would be admissible to interpret the instrument, but not to give it a meaning to which it is not reasonably susceptible.

The instrument restricts the rights of the Enrights in dealing with their property for plaintiff's benefit; it describes itself as "For use with Property Improvement Loan," it specifically sets forth the property it covers, and it authorizes plaintiff to record it. These provisions afford some indication that the parties intended to create a security interest and are clearly sufficient to support the pleaded meaning.

Defendants contend that even if the instrument created an equitable mortgage, it cannot be given effect because it contains an invalid restraint on alienation. The provision that the Enrights would not transfer the property without plaintiff's consent is a restraint on alienation. (*Fritz v. Gilbert,* 8 Cal.2d 68, 71 [63 P.2d 291]; *Prey v. Stanley,* 110 Cal. 423, 426 [42 P. 908]; *Murray v. Green,* 64 Cal. 363, 367 [28 P. 118].) A restraint created by contract is governed by the rules that govern a restraint in a conveyance (*Prey v. Stanley, supra,* 110 Cal. 423, 427), and it has frequently been stated that any restraint on alienation is invalid.

The view that the common-law rule against restraints on alienation prohibits all such restraints has been forcefully criticized on the ground that it loses sight of the purposes of the rule and needlessly invalidates reasonable restraints designed to protect justifiable interests of the parties.

The protection of several such interests has been recognized as justifying reasonable restraints on alienation. Spendthrift trusts are permitted because of the settlor's interest in protecting potentially improvident beneficiaries. . . . A restraint on alienation in an executory land contract has been upheld because of the vendor's interest in the upkeep of the property and in the character and integrity of the purchaser. *In the present case it was not unreasonable for plaintiff to condition its continued extension of credit to the Enrights on their retaining their interest in the property that stood as security for the debt.* Accordingly, plaintiff validly provided that it might accelerate the due date if the Enrights encumbered or transferred the property. [Emphasis added.]

Whether the promise not to transfer or encumber the property would be directly enforcible by injunction, specific performance or an action for damages is another question. It is open to doubt whether such a promise would be a reasonable restraint when, as in this case, plaintiff had the additional protection of a security interest and the right to declare the entire debt due in the event of default. It is unnecessary, however, to decide this question now. Plaintiff is seeking not to enforce the Enrights' promise not to transfer the property but only to foreclose its security interest. The creation of that interest was a separate lawful object of the agreement.

The judgment is affirmed.

Gibson, C. J., Schauer, J., McComb, J., Peters, J., Tobriner J., and Peek, J., concurred.

WINTERS v. EARL

Court of Chancery of New Jersey
52 N.J. Eq. 52, 28 A. 15 (1893)

Van Fleet, V. C. The object of this suit is to have a deed absolute on its face declared to be a mortgage. The principle is well established that if a debtor makes a conveyance, absolute on its face, to his creditor as a security for a debt, the deed will be considered in equity to be a mortgage, and the fact that it was executed as a security, and not as an unconditional conveyance, may be established by parol evidence. *Phillips v. Hulsizer,* 20 N. J. Eq. 308, and the cases there cited. Any legal means of proof may be used to establish the fact that the deed was executed as a security. In the absence of a written defeasance, the evidence in such cases usually consists of the declarations of the grantee; the relations subsisting between the parties at the time the deed was executed; the retention by the grantor, subsequent to the execution of the deed, of the possession of the land, and the exercise of dominion over it in making improvements and repairs, paying taxes, and the like; the value of the property compared with the consideration actually paid or allowed; an understanding that the consideration should be repaid; and the payment of interest on it subsequent to the date of the deed. *Sweet v. Parker,* 22 N. J. Eq. 453. The burden of proof is, of course, on the party claiming that the deed is not what it purports to be on its face, and, in order to prevail, his proof must outweigh that of his adversary.

The deed in question was made by the complainant to the defendant on the 8th day of June, 1889, and conveyed about eight acres of rough land, with a small house, the whole being then worth not much over $500. The complainant was a laborer, who occasionally drank to excess, and the defendant was the proprietor of a saloon and restaurant. When the deed was made, the land was in process of foreclosure. The person who was prosecuting the foreclosure suit had purchased the mortgage for the purpose of foreclosing it. He wanted to get rid of the complainant as a neighbor, and he foreclosed the mortgage in order that he might buy the land at the foreclosure sale, and then expel the complainant from it. The complainant knew that this was the purpose of the foreclosure, and, as was natural, desired, with strong desire, to defeat it. Through a third person he applied to the defendant for help. This person testifies that he asked the defendant, on behalf of the complainant, to furnish the money required to take up the mortgage, and that the defendant, after two or three interviews, promised to furnish sufficient money to help the complainant "out of the scrape." The complainant says that, when the deed was made, it was distinctly understood between the defendant and himself that the deed was to stand as a security, the same as a mortgage, and that, when he repaid the defendant the money advanced to take up the mortgage, he was to have his property back, and that the defendant said all he wanted in the mean time was the interest on his money. The complainant further says that when he signed the deed the defendant promised to give him "articles" to show that he held the deed as a security, but that the defendant has never performed his promise. The defendant, on the contrary, denies that the deed was executed as a security, but he admits that he made a promise to reconvey. When first asked to state the bargain under which the deed was made, the defendant said: "There was no bargain, only that he didn't want Mr. French to have the property." (Mr. French was the complainant in the foreclosure suit.) Subsequently, the defendant said he told the complainant, when the deed was executed, that whenever he wanted to sell the property he would give him the first chance to buy, and that the complainant replied he would give as much as anybody. This is the position in which the evidence of the parties themselves puts the case. The evidence of the complainant shows that the deed was executed as a security, while the defendant says it was executed as an unconditional conveyance, and that the only right the complainant retained rested on a parol promise that he might repurchase the property, provided he would pay as much as any other person.

But there is other evidence tending to show the real character of the deed. Two different persons applied to the defendant, about a year after the execution of the deed, to purchase the land. To the first he said that he could not sell then, because the complainant had a right to redeem the land, but he would let the applicant know when the complaint's right to redeem had expired. . . . The other applicant made an offer of $500 for the property. The defendant had paid $366. He declined this offer, saying that he had promised to hold the property for the complainant, and he was going to do it. At the time the deed was made, a tenant was in possession of the land under a letting for three years, at an annual rent of $48. After the delivery of the deed the complainant remained on the land with the tenant, and collected the rent, up to spring of 1892. He also paid the taxes on the property, and paid to the defendant the interest of $366, in annual payments, for three years. The first payment was made June 9, 1890, (the deed was delivered, it will be remembered, June 8, 1889,) the second payment was made June 19, 1891, and the third, June 7, 1892. For the first payment the defendant gave the complainant a receipt in which he stated that he had received from the complainant $21.96, "in full for one year's interest." The complainant also, during the three years succeeding the delivery of the deed, made permanent improvements on the property. He had a well dug; also, a ditch made, at a cost of $15 besides his own labor. He put windows in the house, and also new boards on one of its sides. He removed rocks and stones from the garden, and built a stone fence, which added, as seems to be undisputed, at least, $50 to the value of the property. He also planted currant bushes and fruit trees. These improvements added, as the proofs show, at least $100 to the value of the property.

These facts corroborate the truth of the complainant's evidence, and go very far to prove that the defendant's story cannot be true.... In my opinion, the decided weight of the evidence on the point in dispute is with the complainant. All the material undisputed facts of the case lead to the conclusion that the deed was executed as a security, and it must consequently be declared to be a mortgage.

KOCH v. WASSON

Supreme Court of Iowa
161 N.W.2d 173 (1968)

BECKER, JUSTICE.

Plaintiffs bring action in three counts to recover title to and possession of 218 acres of Washington County farm land conveyed by them to defendants in February 1961. In Count I plaintiffs allege they conveyed legal title to the land to defendants and received back an option agreement allowing them to repurchase the property on stated terms, all as a part of a security transaction. They pray the deed be construed as a mortgage, title to the real estate be quieted in them subject to a lien in favor of defendants, in an amount to be computed and determined by the court and for general equitable relief.

....

The trial court found against plaintiffs on the first two counts but in their favor on the third count, ordered plaintiffs to pay $6,200 (the option price), $1,340.30 (the 1961 to 1964 taxes), the costs of the improvements placed on the real estate by defendants, ordered defendants to pay all taxes for years 1965 through 1967, awarded crops and income for the crop years to and including 1967 to defendants, allowed defendants to file supplemental claim for costs of improvements to the farm (which was not done), ordered defendants to present to the clerk current abstract of title and deed to plaintiffs and, on approval thereof, defendants were to get the sums provided for and plaintiffs were to get the property. Possession was to be seasonally delivered after the crops were harvested.

Defendants contend the deed, regular on its face, conveyed title to them: the plaintiffs failed to exercise their option properly and the property now belongs to defendants.... We find the contract between the parties was a security transaction.... We therefore remand, modify and affirm.

I. Early in February, 1961, Elmer Koch was indebted to his brother-in-law in the sum of $2,800 and had other debts he desired to pay. He sought a $5000 loan from defendant Jasper Wasson. Koch insists he eventually got the $5000 as a loan. Wasson equally insists he did not make a loan but told Koch he would buy the farm for $5000 and actually did buy the farm for that sum.

On February 17, 1961, the parties met in the office of Louis J. Kehoe, also defendants' attorney. At that time a warranty deed from the Kochs to the Wassons was prepared and executed and the Kochs got their $4250., part of which was paid directly to their creditors. An option to purchase was also prepared and executed. The latter instrument provided the Kochs should have the option to repurchase the land by paying $5000, plus $300 per year, plus taxes accrued or paid by sellers, plus reimbursement for improvements. . . . Upon payment of the stipulated sums defendants were to deliver abstract of title, showing good title in them, and warranty deed transferring the property to plaintiffs.

Both Mr. and Mrs. Koch said they wanted to have the option agreement examined by their attorney but Mr. Neuzil said: "Well now, it is either this or nothing.", and the matter would have to be concluded that day or the Wassons didn't want to go ahead with it. Mr. Wasson stated he did not remember such a request.

Defendants took possession of the farm immediately.

Plaintiffs both testified they intended to negotiate a loan with the deed as security and thought they had done so. Defendants testified the $300, added to the principal for each year the option remained unexercised, represented 6% interest on $5000 and during the period from February 17, 1961 to March 1, 1965 they regarded the Kochs as owing them, the Wassons, $5000. Mr. Wasson also testified on redirect examination, "My understanding of P-3 (the option agreement) was to receive $5000 plus $300 a year, plus taxes, plus improvements if the option was exercised. If the option was not exercised, the farm was to be mine. My understanding as to when the farm should be mine was March 1, 1965." Mrs. Wasson also testified she regarded the Kochs as owing $5000, and if it was not repaid by March, 1965 then the farm was to be theirs (Wassons). This testimony is inconsistent with the theory that the February 17, 1961 deed was intended to convey unconditional title at the time of delivery and is consistent with the argument that the deed was, in fact, a security instrument.

II. The problem raised by Count I is succinctly stated in *Brown v. Hermance,* 233 Iowa 510, 514, 10 N.W.2d 66, 68, "The only real issue is whether appellant had a mere option to purchase the property from appellee or whether appellee took title as security for a loan for part of the purchase price."

The basic general rule controlling our review was clearly stated as early as 1865 in *Trucks v. Lindsey,* 18 Iowa 504.

A conveyance absolute on its face may, by proper evidence, be shown to be but a mortgage, and parol testimony is admissible and competent to establish such fact. . . .

It is a rule of equity that the right to redeem attaches necessarily and conclusively to every grant made as a security. In other words, equity forbids an irredeemable mortgage.

More recent decisions couch the rule against denial of redemption rights in the following terms, "It is the rule that where the mortgagor deeds the property to the mortgagee, the deed is presumed to be but a continuation of the security and the right of redemption is presumed to continue. This right is a favorite of equity and the transfer will operate as a bar only when it clearly appears both parties intended an absolute sale." *Swartz v. Stone,* 243 Iowa 128, 132, 49 N.W.2d 475, 477.

Under a variety of circumstances we have adhered to the above principles. One of the leading Iowa cases in this field, oft relied upon by debtors seeking to redeem their property, is *Guttenfelder v. Iebsen,* 230 Iowa 1080, 1084, 300 N.W. 299, 301, where we said: "To summarize the law applicable to this case, such a transaction as appellants seek to enforce will be closely scrutinized and upheld only where it is perfectly fair, based upon adequate consideration and it clearly and unmistakably appears that an absolute sale and not a transfer for security only was within the contemplation of the parties. In arriving at the intention of the contracting parties, courts look behind the form of the instruments to the real relationship between the parties. *Fort v. Colby,* 165 Iowa 95, 121, 144 N.W. 393. The instruments must be read in the light of the surrounding circumstances and the practical construction which the parties themselves placed thereon. *McGuire v. Halloran,* 182 Iowa 209, 219, 160 N.W. 363, 165 N.W. 405; *McRobert v. Bridget,* 168 Iowa 28, 32, 149 N.W. 906; *Keeline v. Clark,* 132 Iowa 360, 364, 106 N.W. 257."

III. In *Guttenfelder* there was a creditor-debtor, mortgagor-mortgagee relationship present at the inception of the questioned transaction. This is an important factor but not a necessary element to the application of the principle. It is enough if the creditor-debtor relationship is created by the transaction itself. In *Harrington v. Foley,* 108 Iowa 287, 79 N.W. 64, the plaintiff furnished the money to help defendant redeem her land. No prior creditor-debtor relationship existed between the parties.

. . . .

In *Fort v. Colby,* supra, this court held at page 102, 144 N.W. at page 395: "It is a further well-established rule that, where a conveyance absolute upon its face is accompanied by a contract or agreement, by which the grantee undertakes to reconvey the land to the grantor on specified conditions, and the terms of such agreement or the circumstances under which it was made renders it doubtful whether a mortgage or conditional sale was intended, the courts will hold it to be a mortgage. (Cases cited.)" *Brown v. Hermance,* supra; *Greene v. Bride & Son Const. Co.,* 252 Iowa 220, 106 N.W.2d 603, *Collins v. Isaacson,* Iowa, 158 N.W.2d 14, 18.

IV. The farm in question was worth a great deal more than the $5000 advanced by defendant. Except for the testimony of Mrs. Wasson, who said the farm was worth just what they paid for it, the lowest estimate of the 1961 value of the property was $12,000. . . .

Inadequacy of consideration is a strong circumstance tending to show the transaction was intended to be a mortgage. *Greene v. Bride & Son Const. Co.,* 252 Iowa 220, 106 N.W.2d 603 and cases therein cited.

V. Retention of possession by the grantor is considered a circumstance consistent with the claim of creditor-debtor relationship and inconsistent with the theory of absolute conveyance. *Guttenfelder v. Iebsen,* supra. But such a circumstance, or the converse relinquishment of possession by the grantor, is not conclusive. In *Fort v. Colby,* supra, we said at page 130 of 165 Iowa, at page 406 of 144 N.W.: "Indeed, it is not at all an unusual circumstance that a deed given as a mortgage is accompanied or followed by a surrender of possession or by a lease to the grantor." Cf: *McGuire v. Halloran,* 182 Iowa 209, 165 N.W. 405, *Keeline v. Clark,* supra.

We have often said each case must be considered on the totality of its own facts. *Brown v. Hermance,* supra. So it is here. The testimonies of both the Kochs and the Wassons indicate a security transaction was intended when the instrument was signed in 1961. The straitened circumstances of the Kochs, the inadequacy of consideration, the execution and delivery of an option to repurchase, unavailability of legal advice for the grantor, (*Koob v. Zoller,* 231 Iowa 1106, 1110 and citations, 3 N.W.2d 130) are all classic circumstances pointing to a debtor-creditor relationship. The courts look behind the form of the instrument to the real relationship between the parties. *Collins v. Isaacson,* Iowa, 158 N.W.2d 14, 18.

Once such relationship has been established the rights of the parties are those fixed by law and not what the parties conceive them to be. The right of redemption is presumed to continue and, as before indicated, a transfer, absolute on its face, will operate to bar redemption only when it appears both parties intended an absolute sale. *Swartz v. Stone,* 243 Iowa 128, 49 N.W.2d 475.

We have said the grantor in a case such as this carries the burden to show by clear and convincing evidence that the deed was intended to be something other than what it purports to be. *Brown v. Hermance,* supra. The evidence here meets the standard.

. . . .

Since this controversy involves farm land, possession should be retained by defendants until the 1968 crops are seasonably harvested. At that time defendants shall surrender possession to plaintiffs. Upon determination of the amount due from plaintiffs to defendants, plaintiffs shall be given a reasonable time, to be fixed by the court, to pay such sum. Defendants shall be ordered to convey legal title to the property in question to plaintiffs, deed and abstract of title continued as contemplated to be delivered upon payment into court of the amount due. If defendants fail to execute the deed as ordered, the court shall proceed as authorized by Iowa Code, 1966, sections 624.29 et seq. Costs of this action are assessed to defendants.

For further proceedings not inconsistent with this opinion this case must be and is:

Modified and Remanded.

All Justices concur.

GILLILAND v. PORT AUTHORITY

Supreme Court of Minnesota
270 N.W.2d 743 (1978)

PER CURIAM.

Twenty-two tenants and former tenants of the Capri Hotel in St. Paul seek to enjoin construction activity at the Capri and to halt threatened evictions until their claims to relocation assistance under the Minnesota Uniform Relocation Act ("M.U.R.A."), Minn.St. 117.50, et seq., can be judicially determined. They appeal from the order of the Ramsey County District Court of January 25, 1978, denying their motion for injunctive relief. . . .

The tenants, predominantly older persons, age 60 and over, and disabled persons, had rented furnished rooms in the Capri Hotel on a month-to-month basis over periods of several years. On July 15, 1977, they received written notice from the C. G. Rein Company, the owner of the building, that it would begin major renovation of the Capri, now called Seventh Place Residence. The notice stated that the rental agreements for the specific rooms then occupied would not be renewed after August 31, 1977, but residents would be permitted to stay on after September 1, 1977, if they agreed to move to other rooms as the renovation work progressed. Appellants continued to pay monthly rent and received no further communication until the "notice to vacate" of November 30, 1977. This notice announced that renovation and construction would commence immediately and that tenants must vacate within 30 days.

. . . .

On January 17, 1978, the motion for a temporary injunction was heard. . . . The trial court weighed the relative harms to the parties, found both to be serious, and accordingly turned to a consideration of the tenants' likelihood of success on the merits. In the memorandum accompanying its order, the court stated:

> . . . The plaintiffs contend that Minnesota Statute 117.50 requires relocation benefits to the plaintiffs by virtue of the fact that the Capri Hotel was an "acquisition" within the meaning of Minnesota Statute 117.54, Subd. 4. [sic].
> Minnesota Statute 117.50 through .56 is a portion of the eminent domain statute of this state. This statute requires relocation benefits for any displaced person whose property is acquired by a public body which has the power of eminent domain. The plaintiffs contend that since the renovation of the Capri Hotel is being financed by industrial revenue bonds of the Port Authority that there is an acquisition within the meaning of this statute.
>
> An examination of Minnesota law relative to this case is necessary. Under Minnesota law a sale and a leaseback will be treated as a mortgage where it appears that the conveyance was for security for a debt or for the performance of an act. The case of *Land O Lakes Dairy Company v. Wadena County,* 229 Minn. 263, 39 N.W.2d 164 (1949), is very illustrative of this situation. In the *Land O Lakes* case the dairy company entered into an agreement with the United States Government whereby the company acquired land and erected a building thereon. The company conveyed title to the U.S. Government for a purchase price to be determined in a manner provided by the contract with the provision that title would revert to the company upon the payment of the purchase price and other conditions. The question before the Court in the *Land O Lakes* case was the duty of the dairy company to pay real estate taxes. The Minnesota Court held that under the circumstances the arrangement with the dairy company and the United States Government was a sale and a leaseback, and in effect a mortgage, and therefore the dairy company was subject to Minnesota taxes.
>
> . . . .
>
> [Here the court referred to other instances of Port Authority financing.]
>
> It therefore appears to this Court that the plaintiffs have almost no likelihood of success for a permanent injunction in this case.

The determination of whether the transaction involved here constituted an "acquisition" within the meaning of Minn.St. 117.50 cannot be made simply by finding that the Port Authority did not exercise its power of eminent domain. Minn.St. 117.50, subd. 4, defines "acquisition" as follows:

> "Acquisition" includes:
> (a) acquisition by eminent domain;
> (b) acquisition by negotiation;
> (c) programs of areawide systematic housing code enforcement, and
> (d) demolition.

We are concerned only with transactions included in clause (b) but must give consideration to the entire subdivision since clauses (c) and (d) describe acts outside the usual meaning of "acquisition".

Webster's Third New International Dictionary (1976) p. 18 defines "to acquire" as "to come into possession, control, or power of disposal," and Black's Law Dictionary (Rev. 4 ed.) defines "acquisition" as "[t]he act of becoming the owner of certain property . . . ." In *Clarno v. Gamble-Robinson Co.,* 190 Minn. 256, 259, 251 N.W. 268, 269 (1933), we construed the term "acquire" in an automobile insurance policy to mean "to get as one's own." The United States Supreme Court has stated, in reference to the revenue acts, that "[t]he word 'acquired' is not a term of art in the law of property but one in common use. The plain import of the word is 'obtained as one's own'." *Helvering v. San Joaquin Fruit & Investment Co.,* 297 U.S. 496, 499, 56 S.Ct. 569, 570, 80 L.Ed. 824, 826 (1936). That the word "acquisition" as used in Minn.St. 117.50, subd. 4(b), is to have the meaning adopted by these authorities is supported by its use in reference to eminent domain. When that power is exercised, the governmental body obtains full right to use the property as its own, consistent with the purposes for which the power is granted. See *Buck v. City of Winona,* 271 Minn. 145, 135 N.W.2d 190 (1965).

When "acquisition" is given its common meaning, it becomes clear that the transaction involved in this case was not an "acquisition by negotiation." C. G. Rein/C. G. Rein Construction Co., the defendant-owner of the Capri, secured financing for the hotel renovation through the issuance of industrial revenue bonds by the Port Authority of the City of St. Paul. The Port Authority obtained fee simple title to the hotel, and the owners received the bond sale proceeds. The Port Authority contemporaneously leased the hotel back to its former owners under a 30-year lease. At the end of the lease period, fee simple title will revert to Rein upon payment of $1.00. This sale and leaseback arrangement gave the Port Authority no power to possess the hotel or to use it for its own purposes. The authority secured only such rights over the property as were necessary to protect the interests of the bond holders.

It is well established that the sale portion of a sale and leaseback cannot be considered a separate transaction for tax purposes. *Land O'Lakes Dairy Co. v. County of Wadena,* 229 Minn. 263, 39 N.W.2d 164, affirmed, 338 U.S. 897, 70 S.Ct. 251, 94 L.Ed. 552 (1949); 26 U.S.C.A., § 103(b)(2). We have held that similar transactions where a deed and a contract for deed or an option to purchase are simultaneously exchanged are forms of financing and constitute equitable mortgages. *Albright v. Henry,* 285 Minn. 452, 174 N.W.2d 106 (1970); *Gagne v. Hoban,* 280 Minn. 475, 159 N.W.2d 896 (1968). The exchange of a deed and a long-term lease must be treated in the same manner, especially when title to the property reverts to the lessee upon payment of a nominal sum at the expiration of the lease term. The transaction is purely a financing arrangement and the title simply provides security. To break the transaction into two separate parts, a sale and a lease, would be to distort its real nature and to ignore the intent of the parties.

Had the state legislature intended to provide relocation assistance to persons displaced by private, government-financed rehabilitation projects it could have done so. M.U.R.A. expressly grants assistance where voluntary private rehabilitation results from a systematic program of housing code enforcement. Minn.St. 117.50, 117.52. The Uniform Relocation Assistance and Real Property Acquisition Policies Act of 1970, 42 U.S.C.A., § 4601, et seq., M.U.R.A.'s Federal counterpart, provides assistance to those displaced by Federally financed state projects, 42 U.S.C.A., § 4630. These provisions were adequate models for the expression of an intent to afford assistance where governmental financing results in displacement. From the legislature's failure to include such a provision in the statute we conclude that relocation assistance is not available where the governmental action causing displacement is solely the financing of a private rehabilitation project.

Affirmed.

NOTES

1. When a lease form was used to finance a transaction so as to avoid the usury limitations, it has been held that the substance rather than the form determines the nature of the transaction. The court also said that the parties cannot convert a mortgage into a lease by merely labeling it a lease. *Standard Leasing Corp. v. Schmidt Aviation, Inc.,* 264 Ark. 851, 576 S.W.2d 181 (1979).

2. One motivation for disguising a mortgage is to avoid the mortgagor's right to redeem. This reason for a disguised mortgage may be of no value since it has been held that the right cannot be waived in advance. *Kawauchi v. Tabata,* 49 Hawaii 160, 431 P.2d 221 (1966).

3. Unclean hands may bar a "grantor" in a disguised mortgage if the motivation was to defraud creditors. *Benton v. Benton,* 215 Kan. 875, 528 P.2d 1244 (1974).

4. The usual situation with a deed absolute form used to disguise a mortgage results in the "grantee" alleging the validity of the deed, while the "grantor" alleges it was in fact a mortgage. *Robinson v. Durston,* 83 Nev. 337, 432 P.2d 75 (1966). However, for an unusual situation compare *Down v. Ziegler,* 13 Ariz. App. 387, 477 P.2d 261 (1971), where the "grantees" alleged a mortgage in order to escape personal liability of a potential deficiency judgment.

5. The intent of the parties may not be easy to ascertain; even when a quitclaim or other deed in lieu of foreclosure has been delivered, there may be a finding that such deed was merely additional security. *Bearss v. Ford,* 108 Ill. 16 (1883).

SALE—LEASEBACK TRANSACTION

1. Introduction—Definition

The sale-leaseback transaction typically involves a sale of real estate by an owner-user to an investor and a simultaneous leaseback of the real estate by the investor to the owner-user. The leaseback is probably for a term at least equal to the amortizable period of the investor's mortgage and the rent payments geared to cover debt service, plus a reasonable return to investor on invested capital. The sale-leaseback is really a financing technique, more particularly a substitute for refinancing.

2. Advantages to Seller-Lessee

a. The capital tied up in the property is freed for other purposes such as operating capital, debt retirement, expansion, or other investment.

b. This type of transaction may improve a company's credit position, *i.e.,* by replacing on the balance sheet fixed assets (the real estate) with current assets (cash); by creating liquidity which enhances the company's borrowing position. However, the new accounting rules of the Financial Accounting Standards Board now require for financial reporting purposes that the conventional sale-leaseback of land and buildings be shown as a debt obligation if: (a) the lease term (including bargain renewals and economically compelled renewals) extends for 75% or more of the estimated useful life of the buildings, or (b) the present value (at the commencement of the lease term) of the future base rental payments equals 90% or more of the fair market value of the property. *See* Financial Accounting Standards Board, *Statement of Financial Accounting* Standards No. 13, Accounting for Leases § 7 (Nov. 1976).

c. This type of transaction accomplishes the equivalent of mortgage refinancing except that it may produce more cash to the seller in that if the entire purchase price is taken up-front, that amount presumably will be greater than the amount obtainable through refinancing, given loan to value ratios for the particular type of property.

d. The seller's mortgage payments are deductible except to the extent of principal amortization. Further, that portion of the initial cost attributable to land is not depreciable. However, the seller-lessee's rental payments are fully deductible for income tax purposes.

e. The position of the seller-lessee is generally more desirable than that of the ordinary tenant. By entering into the sale-leaseback transaction, the seller-lessee retains the real property improvements that may have been built or adapted to suit its own particular requirements. The lessee also obtains certainty of tenure commensurate with the life of the lease.

3. Advantages to Buyer-Lessor

On the other hand, this type of transaction has its advantages to the buyer-lessor:

1. The mortgage obtained to finance the property will probably be fully amortized by the rent payments to be made by the seller-lessee. Furthermore, the rental payment should produce a satisfactory return to the buyer-lessor on his investment with all or part of such return sheltered due to the availability of the depreciation deduction to the buyer-lessor.

2. This type of transaction is usually considered "safe" due to the credit standing of the seller-lessee ("banking the lease").

3. If the lease is structured, as it is commonly done, on a triple net basis, the buyer-lessor will have a relatively carefree investment.

4. Mortgage financing may be more readily obtainable and the buyer-lessor may be able to obtain a higher debt-equity ratio due to the credit standing of the seller-lessee.

4. Disadvantages to Seller-Lessee

The sale-leaseback transaction also has its disadvantages to the seller-lessee:

1. The seller-lessee is bound by the lease term and its obligation to pay rent continues even under adverse business conditions or periods of economic decline.

2. The seller-lessee loses the benefit of any future increment or appreciation in the value of the real estate.

3. The seller-lessee may lose its right to occupy the premises at the termination of the lease unless renewal options or a recapture provision is part of the lease agreement.

4. The seller-lessee may realize a gain, and therefore incur a tax liability on sale, if the purchase price is in excess of the seller's adjusted basis.

5. If the seller-lessee is in need of or desires improvements for expansion, he must either incur the cost therefore or have the buyer-lessor finance such improvements, which should result in an increase in the rental.

5. Disadvantages to Buyer-Lessor

On the other hand, there may be disadvantages to the buyer-lessor:

1. The buyer-lessor takes the risk that the seller-lessee may suffer financial reverses which could result in a default in payment of the prescribed rental. Furthermore, the buyer-lessor is not a protected or preferred creditor.

2. If the seller-lessee decides not to exercise its renewal options, the buyer-lessor may be forced with re-rental of a property that has only a very special use for a limited market.

6. Tax Ramifications

a. Sale-Leaseback-Exchange

Section 1031 of the IRC provides that no loss or gain is recognized if property held for productive use in a trade, business, or for investment is exchanged solely for property of a like kind for the same use. The words "like kind" include the exchange of a leasehold of a fee with thirty years or more to run for real estate. Treas. Reg. § 1.1031(c)-1 (exchange of fee interest for a lease interest). Therefore, if real estate is sold for less than its basis, and as part of the same transaction leased back for a period of thirty years or more, the leasehold is an asset of "like kind," received by the seller, so that the loss on the sale is not recognized. If there was a gain on the sale, the gain would be recognized to the seller-owner only to the extent of any cash or other boot received. However, in *Jordan Marsh Co. v. Commissioner,* 269 F.2d 453 (2d Cir. 1959), the Second Circuit found that a sale had taken place despite the fact that the property was leased back to the seller for a period of thirty years and three days, with an option to renew for an additional thirty years on the basis that both the sale price and rent reserved in the lease truly reflected current market values.

In *City Investing Co.,* 38 T.C. 1 (1961), *non-acq.* 1963-2 C.B. 6, the Tax Court passed upon a sale and leaseback wherein the sale price and rental terms accurately reflected market values. The leaseback carried an original term of twenty-one years, with renewal provisions aggregating two hundred and four years. Nevertheless, the court allowed the loss deduction, relying heavily upon the fact that the seller was in the process of liquidating all of its investments, which the court thought significant in justifying the loss deduction. There is now a respectable body of opinion to the effect that where a sale and leaseback is the result of an arms length transaction, accurately reflects current market values with respect to both the sale price and rent reserved, the transaction will be treated as a "sale" and not an "exchange" if the lease bears an initial term of less than thirty years, even though options to renew are continued in the lease.

b. Sale-Leaseback Between Related Parties

If the sale-leaseback transaction involves related parties (such as members of a family, a corporation in which 50% of the stock is owned by such individual, affiliated corporations and certain trusts — *see* IRC § 267) the loss realized on the sale of the property may be automatically disallowed.

If the property sold for the purposes of leaseback consists of depreciable property, the gain realized will be treated as ordinary rather than capital gain if the sale is made directly or indirectly between a husband and wife or between a stockholder and his corporation, if more than than 80% of the outstanding stock is owned by the stockholder, his spouse, minor children or grandchildren. *See* IRC § 1239.

7. Equitable Mortgages and Adverse Consequences

In many cases, the seller-lessee is unwilling to give up the reversionary interest in the property. It therefore negotiates for the right to recapture the real estate at one or more times during or at the end of the term of the lease by means of repurchase options.

Unless the two parties proceed with great care, they may find that because of the repurchase options, they have so structured a transaction that the Internal Revenue Service or the courts consider to be an equitable mortgage, rather than a true conveyance and a true lease. *See Paul W. Frenzel,* 22 CCH T.C. Memo. 1391 (1963); *Ministers Life & Casualty Union v. Franklin Park Towers Corp.,* 39 N.W.2d 207 (1976); *In re Atlantic Times Inc.,* 259 F. Supp. 820 (1966); *Sun Oil Co. v. Commissioner,* 562 F.2d 258 (3d Cir. 1977).

The seller-lessee must guard against the possibility that the transaction will be characterized as a loan rather than a sale (in which event the lessee will be denied the right to treat his monthly payments as tax deductible rent). At the outset, the question will turn in some measure upon whether the parties intended a sale or mere financing devices (with the transfer of title serving as security for repayment of the loan). *See Helvering v. F. & R. Lazarus & Co.,* 308 U.S. 252 (1939); *Judson Mills,* 11 T.C. 25 (1948). In passing upon this issue, the courts have been influenced by various aspects of the sale and lease, among them the following:

1. whether the lease term is exceedingly long and in excess of the useful life of the improvements;
2. whether the sale price and rent reserved are in excess of the current fair market value of comparable properties and leases;
3. upon whom the risk of loss of the property is placed (who has taken the risk of the investment and bears the burden of ownership) and;
4. whether the seller-lessee is given an option to repurchase the property, and if so, on what economic terms.

See Frank Lyons Co. v. United States, 435 U.S. 561, *rev'g* 536 F.2d 746 (8th Cir. 1976).

The consequences of having a sale and leaseback treated as a mortgage or financing transaction, instead of a sale, are quite far reaching, and include the following:

1. There should be no gain or loss recognized to the "seller-lessee."
2. The rental payments made under the lease will not be deductible as rent. They will be classified as mortgage payments and deductible only to the extent they reflect interest on the mortgage loan.
3. The rental payments received by the "purchaser-lessor" will not be fully taxable rent, but treated as mortgage repayments and only taxable to the extent they reflect an interest factor.
4. The "purchaser-lessor," being classified as a lender, and not as an owner, will be denied the right to the depreciation deduction. The "seller-lessee," in turn, will continue to be entitled to the depreciation deduction.

D. INSTALLMENT LAND CONTRACTS (SECURITY CONTRACTS)

A land contract is a transfer and conveyance of equitable title to buyer (vendee) with the seller (vendor) holding legal title as security for the fulfillment of the land contract obligations.

Upon execution of the land contract, the vendee becomes the owner of the real estate subject only to the vendor's lien on such real estate for the balance due from the vendee on the purchase price. The vendor holds legal title as trustee for the vendee; his interest is therefore equivalent to a mortgagee's interest which is in the nature of personal property. As equitable owner, the vendee may sell, lease, or encumber the real estate subject to the rights of the vendor, unless the land contract provides to the contrary. The vendee is responsible for the payment of real estate taxes and may take the deductions for income tax purposes commonly associated with real estate, including the depreciation deduction.

A money judgment granted and docketed in a court of proper jurisdiction against the vendee, is a lien on his interest in the real estate described in such contract. With respect to a vendor, where, because of an unpaid purchase balance, the vendor has an interest in personalty, equivalent to a mortgagee's interest, the vendor's interest may be dealt with by a judgment creditor as personal property, and that interest may be reached by proper procedure. But, since the vendor has alienated himself from title to the land, and such title is in the vendee from the date of the contract, the real estate cannot be levied against to reach the vendor's interest in the personalty. It is possible for the vendee to purchase with a shoe-string down payment; that is, the down payment or equity required under such financing is usually less than that required for conventional financing, *i.e.*, the so-called shoe-string down payment. Likewise, there is greater flexibility in structuring the terms of a land installment contract: extended amortization, smaller monthly payments, less than market interest rates, and leverage. Land contract financing is characterized by no front-end expenses. There are no closing costs such as points, discount fees, appraisal costs, and surveys. Nor is there any necessity for mortgage insurance in the transfer of equitable title to the real estate.

Land contract financing may make it possible to obtain conventional financing without further investment of capital ("mortgaging out"). Land contract financing is often characterized by a balloon payment of the balance of the principal within three to five years after the execution of the land contract. For instance, vendor sells a parcel for $42,000 on the following terms: $4,200 in cash at the execution of the land contract, the remainder of $37,800 at 9% interest per annum paid in equal monthly installments of principal, and an interest of $330.26 commencing October 1, 1976. However, the entire unpaid principal balance is due and payable on the fifth anniversary of such land contract. Although the monthly payments referred to above reflect a twenty-five year amortization, on October 1, 1981 a balloon payment for the unpaid principal balance of $35,430 will be due and payable. In the balloon payment example above, vendee, in order to make the deal, was required to take a 10% equity position. At the time of the balloon payment, vendee will be required to refinance the land contract, probably through conventional financing. It is assumed for the purposes of this example that the vendee's lender is willing to make a mortgage loan equal to 80% of the appraised value of the real estate at the time of refinancing. Presuming that the real estate appreciates at the rate of 2% per annum on a compounded basis, the value of the real estate at the time of refinancing will be $46,370. His lender then would be willing to make a mortgage loan in the amount of $37,096 (80% of $46,370 — appraised value). The mortgage loan available then would be sufficient to pay off the land contract balance, *i.e.*, $35,430, while also providing the vendee with additional dollars for closing costs and pocket cash. As can be seen from the above example, the vendee is permitted to refinance the subject property without the necessity of additional equity dollars by virtue of amortization and appreciation. Therefore, in essence, through the land contract, vendee has achieved a partial mortgaging out by virtue of the refinancing process.

Pricing Structure — Time Value Theory of Money. It should be further understood that the sophisticated land contract vendor has, in the determination of his sale price for the subject real estate, considered the time value theory of money. The basic premise of the theory is that the right to receive a dollar today is more valuable by some measurable amount than the right to receive a dollar at some future date. This is because he can invest the dollar now and by the indefinite future date he should have accumulated some amount greater than one dollar (that dollar plus the interest earned on that dollar). This theory is important in land contract financing especially where such financing is characterized by a balloon payment. In other words, the vendor is really not receiving the full purchase price at the time of the execution of the land contract but at some future date. Therefore the sales price should be adjusted to reflect the diminution of the value of that dollar received at the balloon payment date rather than at the execution of the land contract.

Income Tax Advantage to Vendor — Installment Sale. The vendor may be motivated to enter into a land contract for the purposes of taking advantage of the installment sale provision of § 453 of the Internal Revenue Code. This is especially true where the purchase price far exceeds the vendor's adjusted basis in the real estate and where the vendor may experience a substantial capital gain on sale. By utilization of the provisions of IRC § 453, the vendor is able to spread the taxable income from the sale over a period of years. The advantages of this approach are quite clear:

1. The tax cost of the gain is matched to the collections as the taxpayer does not have to pay out cash for taxes before actually receiving the payments in which his gain is included.

2. To the extent that the taxpayer can defer the payment of the tax, he has the use of the tax money at no interest cost for the period of deferral.

3. Since the gain is spread over a number of years, it may be subject to lower marginal tax rates, especially if the income is reported in years of declining earning power, than if the entire gain were reported in one year. In attempting to utilize IRC § 453, a careful installment sale analysis should be undertaken to insure that the payments received in the year of sale including non-cash payments (mortgage in excess of basis) are well within the statutory limitation.

SEBASTIAN v. FLOYD

Supreme Court of Kentucky
585 S.W.2d 381 (1979)

Aker, Justice.

This case presents the question whether a clause in an installment land sale contract providing for forfeiture of the buyer's payments upon the buyer's default may be enforced by the seller.

The movant, Jean Sebastian, contracted on November 8, 1974, to buy a house and lot situated in Covington, Kentucky, from Perl and Zona Floyd, respondents in this motion for review. Sebastian paid $3,800.00 down and was to pay the balance of the $10,900.00 purchase price, plus taxes, insurance, and interest at the rate of 8½% per annum, in monthly installments of $120.00. A forfeiture clause in the contract provided that if Sebastian failed to make any monthly payment and remained in default for 60 days, the Floyds could terminate the contract and retain all payments previously made as rent and liquidated damages.

During the next 21 months, Sebastian missed seven installments. Including her down payment, she paid the Floyds a total of $5,480.00, rather than the

$6,320.00 which was called for by the terms of the contract. Of this amount, $4,300.00, or nearly 40% of the contract price, had been applied against the principal.

The Floyds brought suit in the Kenton Circuit Court against Sebastian in August, 1976, seeking a judgment of $700.00 plus compensation for payments for taxes and insurance, and seeking enforcement of the forfeiture clause. Sebastian admitted by her answer that she was in default but asked the court not to enforce the forfeiture clause. Sebastian counterclaimed for all payments made pursuant to the contract. On advice of counsel, Sebastian ceased to make payments after the institution of this law suit.

The case was referred to a master commissioner for hearing. The commissioner recommended termination of the land sale contract and enforcement of the forfeiture clause. The Kenton Circuit Court entered a judgment adopting the commissioner's recommendations. On appeal, the Court of Appeals affirmed. We granted discretionary review to consider the validity of the forfeiture clause. We reverse.

When a typical installment land contract is used as the means of financing the purchase of property, legal title to the property remains in the seller until the buyer has paid the entire contract price or some agreed-upon portion thereof, at which time the seller tenders a deed to the buyer. However, equitable title passes to the buyer when the contract is entered. The seller holds nothing but the bare legal title, as security for the payment of the purchase price. *Henkenberns v. Hauck,* 314 Ky. 631, 236 S.W.2d 703 (1951).

There is no practical distinction between the land sale contract and a purchase money mortgage, in which the seller conveys legal title to the buyer but retains a lien on the property to secure payment. The significant feature of each device is the seller's financing the buyer's purchase of the property, using the property as collateral for the loan.

Where the purchaser of property has given a mortgage and subsequently defaults on his payments, his entire interest in the property is not forfeited. The mortgagor has the right to redeem the property by paying the full debt plus interest and expenses incurred by the creditor due to default. In order to cut off the mortgagor's right to redeem, the mortgagee must request a court to sell the property at public auction. See Lewis, Reeves, How the Doctrine of Equitable Conversion Affects Land Sale Contract Forfeitures, 3 Real Estate Law Journal 249, 253 (1974). See also KRS 426.005, 426.525. From the proceeds of the sale, the mortgagee recovers the amount owed him on the mortgage, as well as the expenses of bringing suit; the mortgagor is entitled to the balance, if any.

The modern trend is for courts to treat land sale contracts as analogous to conventional mortgages, thus requiring a seller to seek a judicial sale of the property upon the buyer's default. It was stated in *Skendzel v. Marshall,* 261 Ind. 226, 301 N.E.2d 641, 648 (1973):

> A conditional land contract in effect creates a vendor's lien in the property to secure the unpaid balance owed under the contract. This lien is closely analogous to a mortgage — in fact, the vendor is commonly referred to as an "equitable mortgagee." . . . In view of this characterization of the vendor as a lienholder, it is only logical that such a lien be enforced through foreclosure proceedings.

See also *H & L Land Company, Inc. v. Warner,* Fla.App., 258 So.2d 293 (1972). We are of the opinion that a rule treating the seller's interest as a lien will best protect the interests of both buyer and seller. Ordinarily, the seller will receive the balance due on the contract, plus expenses, thus fulfilling the expectations he had when he agreed to sell his land. In addition, the buyer's equity in the property will be protected.

This holding comports with our decision in *Real Estate and Mortgage Co. of Louisville v. Duke*, 251 Ky. 385, 65 S.W.2d 81 (1933), wherein it was stated at page 82 of 65 S.W.2d:

> The forfeiture clause was intended simply as a security for the payment of the purchase price. In these circumstances the forfeiture provided for by the contract will be disregarded . . . .

Respondents contend the preponderance of Kentucky cases permits enforcement of forfeiture clauses in land sale contracts. However, installment land contracts were not involved in two of the cases cited in respondents' brief. In *Ward Real Estate v. Childers*, 223 Ky. 302, 3 S.W.2d 601 (1928), and *Graves v. Winer*, Ky., 351 S.W.2d 193 (1961), this court permitted retention by the sellers of "earnest money" deposited pursuant to an executory deposit receipt agreement. The ordinary short-term real estate contract presents a situation very different from the case at bar. Such an agreement generally provides that in the event the buyer fails to perform the contract, the seller may retain the down payment (usually no more than ten per cent of the contract price) as liquidated damages. In *Ward,* supra, and *Graves,* supra, the sum specified as liquidated damages clearly bore a reasonable relation to the actual damages suffered by the seller, which damages would be difficult to ascertain. *Robert F. Simmons and Associates v. Urban Renewal and Community Development Agency of Louisville*, Ky., 497 S.W.2d 705 (1973). Our holding therefore has no bearing on the typical earnest money deposit.

Respondents also cite *Maschinot v. Moore,* 275 Ky. 36, 120 S.W.2d 750 (1938). Their reliance on that case is misplaced, however, because there the court dealt with the question whether the vendor could maintain an action in ejectment against the vendee under a land sale contract; the court did not address the issue of the enforceability of a forfeiture clause such as that in the instant case.

In *Miles v. Proffitt*, Ky., 266 S.W.2d 333 (1954), we held that a party to an installment land sale contract who had advanced money in part performance and then failed to make further payments was not entitled to recover any of the money so advanced. The court relied on *Kravitz v. Grimm,* 273 Ky. 18, 115 S.W.2d 368 (1938), as authority for its holding in *Miles.* To the extent *Miles* and *Kravitz* uphold the validity of forfeiture clauses in installment land sale contracts, they are overruled. The seller's remedy for breach of the contract is to obtain a judicial sale of the property.

The judgment of the trial court and the opinion of the Court of Appeals are reversed and the case remanded for further proceedings consistent with this opinion.

All concur except STERNBERG, J., who did not sit.

GOFF v. GRAHAM

Court of Appeals of Indiana
156 Ind. App. 324, 306 N.E.2d 758 (1974)

SULLIVAN, PRESIDING JUDGE.

Defendants-appellants George Wesley Goff and Patricia Anne Goff, d/b/a Mid-Town Realty Co. (Goff) (purchaser) appeal from a judgment awarding damages and which had the effect of cancellation of a Conditional Sales Contract for Real Estate. The findings of the Court specifically found that defendants had breached the contract. The judgment did not specifically restore permanent possession to the vendor nor did it decree that the contract was terminated and cancelled. The parties, however, have acquiesced in a construction of the judgment which terminates the contract, e. g., defendants have waived any claim to specific performance of the contract by vendor.

On May 31, 1971, Goff purchased five parcels of real estate from Harley and Florence Graham (vendor) by virtue of five sales contracts which were identical in all respects except for the legal descriptions of the property and the consideration to be paid therefor. The parties throughout the proceedings below and in their briefs herein refer to the sales agreement as being a single contract. Since neither party has argued that the contracts must be considered individually, for the purposes of this opinion we shall consider the five separate agreements as one contract. The properties were investment properties containing some thirty rental units. At the time of the sale, all of the apartments were occupied by tenants. The contract contained the following pertinent provisions:

2. Taxes and Insurance.

a. Taxes. Purchaser shall pay the taxes on the Real Estate beginning with the installment payable by the first Monday in November, 1971, and all installments of taxes payable thereafter.

b. Assessments. Purchaser shall pay all assessments for municipal or other public improvements becoming a lien after this date.

c. Insurance. Purchaser shall keep the improvements on said real estate insured under fire and extended coverage policies and pay the premiums on such insurance policies as they become due. Such insurance shall be obtained from companies approved by Vendor and in an amount not less than the balance of the purchase price due hereunder, or to the full extent of their insurable value, if that is less. Such policy or policies shall be issued in the names of Vendor and Purchaser, as their respective interests may appear, and shall be delivered to and retained by Vendor during the continuance of this agreement.

. . . .

Insurance is to be prorated as of the 1st day of the month following the date of execution and delivery of the conditional sales contract. Purchaser is to keep property in good repair, and to maintain said properties in accordance with the laws of the State of Indiana and City of Indpls.

. . . .

7. Use of the Real Estate by Purchaser; Vendor's Right of Inspection; Purchaser's Responsibility for Injuries.

a. Use. The Real Estate shall not be rented, leased or occupied by persons other than Purchaser, nor shall any of the improvements now or hereafter placed thereon be changed, remodeled, or altered in any way unless Purchaser shall first obtain the written consent of Vendor. No additional improvements shall be placed on the Real Estate by Purchaser unless written consent of Vendor shall have been first obtained. Purchaser shall use the Real Estate and the improvements thereon carefully, and shall keep the same in good repair at his expense. Purchaser shall not commit waste on the Real Estate. In his occupancy of the Real Estate, Purchaser shall comply with all laws, ordinances, and regulations of any governmental authority having jurisdiction thereof.

. . . .

8. Vendor's Remedies on Purchaser's Default.

Time shall be of the essence of this agreement. If Purchaser fails to pay any installment of the purchase price or interest thereon, or any installment of taxes on the Real Estate, or assessment for a public improvement, or any premium of insurance, as the same becomes due, and if such failure continues for a period of sixty (60) days; or if Purchaser fails to perform or observe any other condition or term of this agreement and such default continues for a period of sixty (60) days after written notice thereof is given to Purchaser; then Vendor may, at his option:

a. Cancel this agreement and take possession of the Real Estate, and remove Purchaser therefrom, or those holding or claiming under him, without any demand.

b. Declare the entire unpaid balance of this contract immediately due and payable, and in such event, Vendor may pursue whatever remedies, legal or equitable, are available to collect the entire unpaid balance of the purchase price.

c. Exercise any other remedies available at law, or in equity.

The remedies herein provided shall be cumulative and not exclusive. Failure of Vendor to exercise any remedy at any time shall not operate as a waiver of the right of Vendor to exercise any remedy for the same or any subsequent default at any time thereafter. In the event of Vendor's cancellation after default by Purchaser, all rights and demands of Purchaser under this contract and in and to the Real Estate shall cease and terminate and Purchaser shall have no further right, title or interest, legal or equitable, in or to the Real Estate and Vendor shall have the right to retain all amounts theretofore paid by Purchaser as agreed payment for Purchaser's possession of the Real Estate prior to default. Such retention shall not bar Vendor's right to recover damages for unlawful detention of the real estate after default, for any failure to pay taxes or insurance, for failure to maintain the Real Estate at any time, for waste committed thereon or for any other damages suffered by Vendor, including reasonable attorney's fees incurred by Vendor in enforcing any right hereunder or in removing any encumbrance on the Real Estate made or suffered by Purchaser.

. . . .

On the date the contract was executed, vendor delivered to purchaser copies of premium renewal notices for insurance policies which vendor had procured during his possession. The notices revealed that premiums for continuation of insurance on the various parcels were due June 8, 1971, July 11, 1971, July 29, 1971, February 14, 1972 and February 27, 1972.

On July 7, 1971 purchaser paid the first contract installment which was due July 1. However, purchaser did not obtain his own insurance coverage for the subject properties nor did he pay the premiums on the vendor's policies as they became due; neither did he make any payments in connection with contractually required pro-ration of premiums which had been prepaid by vendor.

After the purchaser failed to make the second contract payment due August 1, relations between the parties became strained. Graham demanded that Goff pay the insurance premiums since some of the properties were at that time uninsured. Several heated arguments ensued and in the middle of August, the purchaser was sent a letter demanding payment of the insurance and the August 1 contract installment. He was instructed that upon failure to do so he was to surrender possession of the buildings on August 27.

Various tenants testified that during the month of August, purchaser began removing furniture from the apartments, selling some and taking the rest to his home and to other investment properties he owned nearby.

. . . .

Purchaser failed to make the third contract payment which was due September 1. On September 2, 1971, vendor filed suit for cancellation of the contract, seeking damages and the appointment of a receiver for the properties.

At the time the suit was filed, purchaser had not obtained new insurance upon the properties, had not paid any of the insurance renewal premiums due in June or July, had not tendered any sort of pro-rated refund of the pre-paid insurance premiums, and he had failed to make the second and third contract payments. Furniture had been removed from the apartments and the properties to a degree had begun to deteriorate.

Purchaser testified that during the period of June 1 to September 2, he collected a total of $6,352.99 in rent while making the one installment payment of $562.62.

The Marion County Division of Public Health cited one of the apartment buildings on September 8, 1971 for inadequate rubbish containers, accumulation of trash and improper storage of a refrigerator.

After a hearing, the parties on September 15, 1971 stipulated and the court so ordered that the contract could continue under the following conditions:

1. Purchaser would make the August 1 and September 1 payments by October 1.
2. Purchaser would obtain fire and liability insurance by October 1.
3. Purchaser would make the October 1 payment on October 15.

If the above requirements were not complied with, it was stipulated and ordered that a receiver would be appointed.

Purchaser filed a counter-claim for breach of contract on September 24, 1971, seeking $32,451.00 in damages. . . .

Purchaser failed to make the three payments as called for by the stipulation and failed to insure the properties. A receiver was appointed by the court on October 18.

The receiver discovered that many utility payments were delinquent and shut-offs had occurred or were threatened. Many of [the] apartments were vacant. Former tenants testified that they had moved because purchaser had refused to make needed repairs or had not called pest exterminators when they were needed. There was testimony that after the receiver was appointed, purchaser had encouraged tenants to move out of the subject property and into apartments owned by purchaser nearby. Purchaser continued to remove furniture, knowingly allowed a bootlegging operation to operate in one apartment and permitted a "poker parlor" to operate all night long on week-ends.

On January 25, 1972, the trial court discharged the receiver and returned temporary possession of the apartments to vendor. The trial court entered a judgment in favor of vendor on June 30, 1972. The court awarded damages of $1686.00, the sum representing the contract payments due on August 1, September 1 and October 1; and awarded $2500.00 to Graham for damages to the property.

. . . .

The final question to be answered in this portion of our discussion is whether, having established an actionable breach on September 2, 1971, vendor was entitled to a cancellation of the contract rather than mere compensatory damages for the breach.

As stated in *Faylor v. Brice* (1893), 7 Ind.App. 551, 553, 34 N.E. 833:

While forfeitures are never favored in law, yet when by a reasonable construction, it appears that the contracting parties agreed that a forfeiture should take place, upon the failure of one of the parties to the contract to comply with a material part thereof, courts will decree a forfeiture.

Our determination thus depends upon whether the breach is a material one, going to the heart of the contract. Whether such a total breach exists is to be determined under the facts of the case, and whether the breach is material is itself a question of fact, to be decided by the trier of fact. See 6 Williston on Contracts, § 841 (3rd Ed.). As we have noted, it is not our function to reweigh the evidence in reviewing the trial court's findings of fact.

The Restatement of Contracts § 275 succinctly summarizes the considerations used in determining the materiality of a breach:

(a) The extent to which the injured party will obtain the substantial benefit which he could have reasonably anticipated;

(b) The extent to which the injured party may be adequately compensated in damages for lack of complete performance;

(c) The extent to which the party failing to perform has already partly performed or made preparations for performance;

(d) The greater or less hardship on the party failing to perform in terminating the contract;

(e) The wilful, negligent or innocent behavior of the party failing to perform;

(f) The greater or less uncertainty that the party failing to perform will perform the remainder of the contract.

Most recently our Supreme Court in *Skendzel v. Marshall* (1973), Ind., 301 N.E.2d 641 dealt with the reluctance of the courts to permit forfeitures under land contracts. In quoting from Pomeroy, Equity Jurisprudence, § 433 (5th ed. 1941), the court said:

The test which determines whether equity will or will not interfere in such cases *is the fact whether compensation can or cannot be adequately made for a breach of the obligation which is thus secured. If the penalty is to secure the mere payment of money, compensation can always be made, and a court of equity will relieve the debtor party upon his paying the principal and interest. . . .*

[The granting of relief in such circumstances is based on the ground that it is wholly against conscience to say that because a man has stipulated for a penalty in case of his omission to do a particular act — *the real object of the parties being the performance of the act* — if he omits to do the act, he shall suffer a loss which is *wholly disproportionate to the injury sustained by the other party*.] Pomeroy, Equity Jurisprudence, § 433, 5th Edition (1941). (Emphasis added.)

Justice Hunter, speaking for the court, proceeded to hold:

A conditional land contract in effect creates a vendor's lien in the property to secure the unpaid balance owed under the contract. This lien is closely analogous to a mortgage — in fact, the vendor is commonly referred to as an "equitable mortgagee." *D. S. B. Johnston Land Co. v. Whipple, supra* [60 N.D. 334, 234 N.W. 59]; *Harris v. Halverson, supra* [192 Wis. 71, 211 N.W. 295]. In view of this characterization of the vendor as a lienholder, it is only logical that such a lien be enforced through foreclosure proceedings. Such a lien "has all the incidents of a mortgage" (*D. S. B. Johnston Land Co. v. Whipple, supra,* at 61, [of 234 N.W.]), one of which is the right to foreclose.

With reference to factual situations similar to that before us, however, the court acknowledged the propriety of cancellation or forfeiture:

This is not to suggest that a forfeiture is an inappropriate remedy for the breach of *all* land contracts. In the case of an abandoning, absconding vendee, forfeiture is a logical and equitable remedy. Forfeiture would also be appropriate where the vendee has paid a minimal amount on the contract at the time of default and seeks to retain possession while the vendor is paying taxes, insurance, and other upkeep in order to preserve the premises. Of course, in this latter situation, the vendee will have acquired very little, if any, equity in the property. However, a court of equity must always approach forfeitures with great caution, being forever aware of the possibility of inequitable dispossession of property and exorbitant monetary loss. We are persuaded that forfeiture may only be appropriate under circumstances in which it is found to be consonant with notions of fairness and justice under the law.

From the evidence adduced at trial, the court could reasonably have found that purchaser's failure to insure the properties was wilful and constituted a material breach. While purchaser's breach was not contemporaneous with the commencement of performance, it was preceded only by his down payment, and thus in no sense had substantial performance occurred.

Under the circumstances, there existed great uncertainty that purchaser would perform his continuing obligations under the contract: On September 2, 1971, purchaser had paid no insurance, and was two months in arrears in contract payments, having belatedly paid the first installment. By the time of the trial court's decision on June 30, 1972, the situation had deteriorated further. Evidence indicated that purchaser had committed waste and deliberately neglected the properties, as heretofore set out. Such activities did not auger well for the future performance of the contract over its twenty-year course. We do not thus have before us the harsh forfeiture condemned in *Skendzel v. Marshall, supra.*

The facts were sufficient for the trial court to find that vendor was entitled to bring an action for cancellation on September 2, 1971.

. . . .

The court awarded damages in the amount of $4186.00, of which $1686.00 was denominated as attributable to unpaid contract payments. The other $2500.00 was apparently intended as compensation for waste committed upon the property by purchaser and the loss of income resulting from tenants who moved away or were moved by purchaser, many of which empty apartments were not immediately rentable when the vendor regained possession.

With respect to the $2500.00 portion of the judgment, although the evidence was sufficient to prove that these damages existed, there was no evidence from which the trial court could fix a compensatory amount attributable to such damages.

The well established appellate rule, however, is that a judgment will be upheld if it may be sustained upon any theory. *See Devine v. Grace Construction & Supply* (1962), 243 Ind. 98, 181 N.E.2d 862; *Ross v. Review Bd. of Indiana Employment Security Division* (1962), 243 Ind. 61, 182 N.E.2d 585; *Hatcher v. Smith* (1972 Ind.App.), 283 N.E.2d 582.

Purchaser testified that in the period of June 1 — September 2, he collected rent in the amount of approximately $6350.00. He received this amount as a direct consequence of Graham's performance under the contract, that is, because of vendor's relinquishment to purchaser of the possession and income-producing use of the property.

Under the facts of this case, the trial court would have been justified in awarding money to vendor as restitution after the contract was cancelled. See Restatement of Contracts § 347. One of the alternative methods of evaluating the plaintiff's performance for which restitution is to be made is by measuring the extent to which the defendant was enriched by such performance.

Restitution clearly implies a restoration of the status quo. *See Grissom v. Moran* (1973 Ind.App.), 292 N.E.2d 627. Restoration of the status quo requires not only a consideration of the rental income collected by purchaser as a result of vendor's performance of the contract, but as well a consideration of the benefits derived by the vendor under the contract. The record in this respect discloses that vendor received:

Down Payment	$1950.00
June Installment contract payment	562.62
July, Aug. and Sept. contract payments reflected in judgment	1686.00
Damages awarded by judgment	2500.00
Total	$6698.62

The $6698.62 benefit derived by vendor by virtue of the contract as supplemented by the judgment entered is not excessive in light of the benefit derived by purchaser under the contract. There is evidence of probative value to support the award of $4186.00 in damages under a restitution theory.

Judgment affirmed.

BUCHANAN and WHITE, JJ., concur.

California Civil Code

§ 2953.1 "Real property security instrument;" "subordination clause;" "subordination agreement"

As used in this section:

(a) "Real property security instrument" shall include any mortgage or trust deed or land contract in or on real property.

(b) "Subordination clause" shall mean a clause in a real property security instrument whereby the holder of the security interest under such instrument agrees that upon the occurrence of conditions or circumstances specified therein his security interest will become subordinate to or he will execute an agreement subordinating his interest to the lien of another real property security instrument which would otherwise be of lower priority than his lien or security interest.

(c) "Subordination agreement" shall mean a separate agreement or instrument whereby the holder of the security interest under a real property security instrument agrees that (1) his existing security interest is subordinate to, or (2) upon the occurrence of conditions or circumstances specified in such separate agreement his security interest will become subordinate to, or (3) he will execute an agreement subordinating his interest to, the lien of another real property security instrument which would otherwise be of lower priority than his lien or security interest.

(Added by Stats. 1963, c. 1861, p. 3841, § 1, operative Jan. 2, 1964.)

NOTES

1. The California legislature has classified a land contract as a security instrument, *see* Cal. Civ. Code § 2953.1, *supra*. Professor Hetland has long differentiated between the earnest money contract, which he calls a marketing contract, and the installment land contract, which he calls a security contract. The difference between the two is not merely nomenclature, but the availability of remedies and, perhaps more importantly, the rights of the vendee-mortgagor. *See* J. HETLAND, CALIFORNIA REAL ESTATE SECURED TRANSACTIONS 100 *et seq.* (1970).

2. The courts in California slowly evolved the status of a defaulting vendee in a land installment contract. The culmination of the California doctrine came in the case of *MacFadden v. Walker*, 5 Cal. 3d 809, 488 P.2d 1353 (1971), a case on which Professor

Hetland was *amicus curiae*. The *MacFadden* case held that a willfully defaulting vendee in a land installment contract was entitled to reinstatement and specific performance on the contract. The court also precluded the use of forfeiture as a remedy for the vendor in such a case.

The *MacFadden* case was the concluding case in a series that began with *Barkis v. Scott*, 34 Cal. 2d 116, 208 P.2d 367 (1949). In the *Barkis* case the court granted what appears to be an equity of redemption to a vendee provided the default was neither "willful nor grossly negligent." *Barkis* was followed shortly afterwards by *Baffa v. Johnson*, 35 Cal. 2d 36, 216 P.2d 13 (1950), which is important in the series because of the *dicta* suggesting no retention of earnest money beyond the damages calculated by the difference between the contract price and the value at the time of breach. *Freedman v. The Rector*, 37 Cal. 2d 16, 230 P.2d 629 (1951), clearly established the nonavailability of forfeiture of earnest money, in the event of a willfully defaulting vendee. *Ward v. Union Bond & Trust Co.*, 243 F.2d 476 (9th Cir. 1957), prognosticated what the California court would do if it encountered a willfully defaulting vendee in an installment contract who wished to reinstate and complete the contract. Citing *Barkis, supra,* and *Freedman, supra,* the court allowed reinstatement. This position was ultimately confirmed by the court in *MacFadden v. Walker.*

3. For a good statement of the remedies available upon default by a vendee, see *Honey v. Henry's Franchise Leasing Corp. of America,* 64 Cal. 2d 801, 415 P.2d 833 (1966). Why is the vendor given the election of remedies?

4. Courts have not uniformly held land installment contracts to be security instruments as in *Sebastian v. Floyd, supra*. In a similar situation the Supreme Court of Wyoming held that an installment contract did not establish either a security interest or an equitable mortgage. *Barker v. Johnson,* 591 P.2d 886 (1979). However, the holding is based on a lack of evidence that the parties intended the creation of a security instrument or equitable mortgage. Which argument is more appealing, the Kentucky court's or the Wyoming court's? Should the parties' intent control in a land contract as it does in other disguised or equitable mortgage cases? If not, why not?

5. Forfeiture is permitted in some jurisdictions and disallowed in others. *Weyher v. Peterson,* 16 Utah 2d 278, 399 P.2d 438 (1955); *but see Krentz v. Johnson,* 36 Ill. App. 3d 142, 343 N.E.2d 165 (1976).

DRAFTING A LAND INSTALLMENT CONTRACT

1. Provision for a Deed

a. Deliver to vendee, upon full performance of land contract obligation, a deed.

b. *Exception Clause.* Under a land contract, the vendee is customarily in possession for a number of years before the deed is executed. He is thus in a position to make and suffer liens and other encumbrances upon the property. The vendor in his deed naturally does not want to warrant that the title is free from such liens. Therefore, the following clause is recommended: "Except any liens or encumbrances created or suffered to be created by the acts or defaults of the grantee."

2. Proof of Title

a. Proof of merchantability or marketability of title ought to be procured prior to the execution of the land contract. The new offer to purchase form (Rev. 1-19-77) recognizes the validity of the aforementioned statement and provides as follows: "If this offer provides for a land contract, the same evidence of title shall be furnished prior to the execution of the land contract."

b. Title binder should insure vendee's interest under land contract.

c. Exceptions to insurability (Schedule B of Title Binder).

1. "No liability is assumed for loss or damage by the title insurer occasioned by a rejection of the land contract pursuant to any provisions of the Federal Bankruptcy Act."

Presumably this exception applied to § 70(b) of the Bankruptcy Act which indicates that the trustee shall assume or reject any executory contract within sixty days after adjudication. Some federal district courts have applied this section to land contracts which would leave the vendee with a claim for damages instead of an interest in real estate.

The Bankruptcy Reform Act of 1978, which became effective on October 1, 1979, appears to have somewhat resolved the problem in favor of the land contract vendee. Where the vendee is in possession, the trustee's right to reject the contract will be subject to the vendee's right to obtain title by completing payments under the contract (Bankruptcy Reform Act of 1978, § 365(i)). Where the vendee is not in possession, the trustee will be able to reject the contract and leave the vendee with a claim for damages for breach. While the vendee in this latter situation will have a lien on the contract property to the extent of prior payments under the contract, he will have the status of an unsecured creditor for purposes of recovering other damages.

2. "Title insurer will not insure performance under the land contract."

3. Prepayment (Preservation of Installment Sale Status)

A major motive of many vendors in accepting land contract financing is to stagger the purchase price over time, and thus limit the tax consequences which would result from recognizing the entire capital gain from sale in a single tax year. The following clause is recommended to limit the vendee's right to prepay the land contract:

> Purchaser shall not prepay or offer to prepay the amount of this land contract or any part thereof during the calendar year of 1977. Purchaser further agrees to indemnify vendor against any additional Federal income tax or interest thereon which vendor becomes obligated to pay by virtue of such prepayment or offer to prepay during the calendar year of 1977.

4. Underlying Mortgage (Due-On-Sale Clause)

a. Representing Vendee

As a condition to the closing, written evidence should be obtained from the underlying mortgagee that it consents to the transfer of equitable title to the vendee, and that the land contract transaction does not constitute a default or result in the acceleration of the principal amount due the mortgagee. In turn, the mortgagee may require, as a condition to providing the written consent to the transaction, the vendee's execution of a document(s) which will bind the vendee to assume and agree to pay the underlying mortgage in the event of the nonpayment of the mortgage debt by the vendor.

The following clause is recommended:

> It is understood that the property is presently encumbered by a mortgage given by Seller to the First Wisconsin National Bank of Milwaukee. Said mortgage has a principal balance of $29,950.30 as of October 31, 1975. As a condition precedent to the consummation of this transaction, Seller shall obtain appropriate evidence from said Mortgagee, that the conveyance by Seller to Buyer of an equitable interest in the real estate shall not constitute an event of default or result in the acceleration of the principal amount due said Mort-

gagee. In the event said Mortgagee requires Buyer to assume the existent mortgage, Buyer shall execute such documents as may be necessary to effectuate the same.

b. Representing Vendor

If the above clause is required, the vendor should obtain credit report information on the vendee to establish the credentials of the vendee and to qualify him with the mortgagee. In addition, the vendor will not want to make any warranty regarding the acceleration of the mortgage loan by the mortgagee; he will want the risk of such acceleration to rest exclusively with the vendee. Therefore, the vendee will generally want, within a reasonable time after the notice of acceleration, to obtain a replacement first mortgage in an attempt to refinance the property. In the event such replacement first mortgage is less than the principal balance due and owing on the land contract, the vendor should contractually agree to cover the difference in the form of secondary financing on terms acceptable to the vendee.

5. Restriction on Assignability or Sale of Vendee's Interest ("Stacking Prohibition")

A provision similar to the Due-on-Sale Clause in a mortgage note should be provided in the land contract to limit the vendee's right to assign or transfer his interest in the land contract without first obtaining the vendor's prior consent. The following clauses are recommended:

Purchaser shall not, except upon first obtaining the written consent of Vendor, sell, convey, transfer, assign or further encumber financially Purchaser's interest, legal or equitable, in this land contract and in the premises for the breach of which restriction this land contract shall, at the option of Vendor, mature and become due and payable in full, at once, without notice, notice being hereby expressly waived.

Purchaser agrees not to convey (by deed, option, assignment, lease,' or otherwise) any or all of his interest in the premises, or in this Land Contract (or if Purchaser or any successor is a partnership, joint venture, or corporation, not to cumulatively transfer or permit the cumulative transfer of more than 25% of the ownership thereof) without the consent of Vendor, provided however, that this prohibition shall not apply to conveyances by Purchaser to members of his immediate family. Such consent shall (unless the conveyance would violate the provisions of any underlying encumbrance) not be unreasonably withheld if Vendor is furnished with the proposed successor's true, complete, and current financial statement and his recordable agreement to be bound by this Land Contract, and to assume all of the obligations and covenants on the part of the Purchaser to be performed herein. The basis of giving or withholding consent shall be the financial ability of the transferee and the continuation of competent management. In the event of any violation of this provision, Vendor shall have the following options:

(a) Charge a 1% transfer fee;
(b) Increase the interest to the default rate;
(c) Declare the Land Contract balance due and payable; and
(d) Declare the transfer null and void.

All of the provisions hereof shall apply to subsequent transfers. The foregoing options are not to be mutually exclusive, and any or all of the foregoing which are not inconsistent may be exercised by Vendor at any time. A delay in exercising such options shall not be deemed a waiver of Vendor's right to exercise the same, nor shall a delay be deemed to constitute laches on the part of Vendor. Consent given to any transfer shall not release any Purchaser or his predecessor from liabilities due hereunder and Vendor may deal with any assignee or transferee as to his interest in this Land Contract as with Purchaser, without in any way discharging or limiting the liability of the Purchaser hereunder.

Additionally, if there is an underlying mortgage on the property, the vendee's assignment or transfer of the land contract will also require the consent of the underlying mortgagee.

6. Land Contract Interest Rate

If there is an underlying mortgage affecting the property transferred by land contract, the mortgage note may reserve the right to "bump" (escalate) the mortgage interest rate if equitable title is transferred. If this is the case, the land contract should contain an escalator clause effective in the event the underlying mortgagee escalates the mortgage interest rate either because of such land contract transfer or in the normal course of events, during the term of the mortgage.

The following clause is recommended:

Purchaser agrees that in the event there is an escalation of the interest rate on the underlying mortgage as a result of this land contract or during the term of said mortgage, then the Purchaser agrees that there shall be a similar escalation in the interest rate of this land contract, but in no event shall such interest rate exceed 9.5% per annum during the terms of this land contract.

7. Evidence by Seller of Payment to His Mortgagee

When there is an underlying mortgage, the vendee should also be concerned that the vendor is making the required payments under the mortgage and complying with the covenants and provisions of such mortgage and mortgage note. The vendee may be better able to protect his position in one of two ways. As part of the land contract, he might require the vendor to provide him, on or before the 10th day of each calendar month, appropriate evidence that the vendor has complied with the monthly payment terms of said first mortgage and mortgage note for the said month (including principal and interest and tax and insurance escrow payments, if required). The vendee may further request of the mortgagee a copy of any notice of default under the mortgage given to the mortgagor or a written notification as to the nonpayment of any mortgage installment.

To the extent the vendor does or does not make those payments required under the mortgage the vendee's investment becomes a risk. Therefore, the vendee should require that he be permitted, in the event of default of such payments, to make payments directly to the holder of the first mortgage and then be entitled to a credit on the land contract for the amount paid thereunder. In the alternative, the land contract might require a bifurcated payment: the vendee directly makes the payment to the underlying mortgagee for the total mortgage amount on a monthly payment basis. The excess, *i.e.,* the difference between the land contract payment and mortgage payment is paid directly to the land contract vendor. Obviously, such payments made on said first mortgage directly by the vendee will be credited against the land contract balance as applicable.

8. Prepayment Penalty

The vendor's mortgage or note may also contain a prepayment penalty. If the vendee is given an unfettered right to prepay, his liquidation of the outstanding land contract balance may result in a penalty being incurred by the land contract vendor. If the vendor has such a prepayment penalty provision in his mortgage, he may want to include in the land contract a provision requiring the vendee to reimburse him for the actual amount paid by the vendor to said mortgagee by reason of said provision. In turn, however, the vendee will want the land contract to include his right to negotiate directly with said mortgagee to obtain consent to prepayment or to compromise, reduce, or obtain a waiver of said prepayment penalty.

9. Recapture of Equity by Vendor

Often a vendor will want to recapture some or all of the remaining equity he has under the land contract prior to the time of the balloon payment by the vendee. A question arises as to how this might be accomplished, given the nature of the vendor's interest. Although considered risky by some lenders, a vendor may be able to convince his lender to take an assignment of his vendor's interest without discount for the purpose of producing the cash desired. The lender will take an assignment of the vendor's interest under the land contract, thereafter notifying the vendee that payments to be made under said land contract are to be paid directly to the lender. In order to perfect such an assignment, the lender will want to record the assignment of the vendor's interest, indicating therein that such assignment is for collateral purposes. Further, because the vendor's interest is in the nature of personal property, the lender will also want to undertake a UCC filing in order to perfect the assignment. In some instances the lender will prefer to place a mortgage on the vendor's interest, but such a mortgage is only a security interest in personalty and not a security interest in the real estate.

The question arises as to whether it is ever possible for a lender who extends money to a vendor in a situation involving recapture of equity to take a security interest, i.e., a mortgage, in the vendee's interest in the real estate as additional security for the extension of such recapture money to the vendor. The answer may be "yes" if the land contract contains a so-called further encumbrance clause. Such a clause will read somewhat as follows:

"The Vendee's interest shall be subject to and subordinate to any mortgage or mortgages now on said real estate or that the vendor of said real estate may hereafter and at any time elect to place on said real estate, and to all advances already made or that may hereafter be made on account of said mortgages to the full extent of the principal sum secured thereby and interest thereon, provided that the mortgage balance at any time shall not exceed the then remaining principal balance due on said land contract. The payments hereunder shall not be greater than the payments required on said land contract and the vendee agrees upon request to execute any documents that counsel for the vendor may deem necessary to accomplish that end, and in default thereof, the vendor is hereby empowered to execute such documents in the name of the vendee and as the act and deed of said vendee, and this authority is hereby declared to be coupled with an interest and to be irrevocable."

By consenting to such a clause, the vendee in essence is agreeing to a further encumbering of his interest in the real estate by virtue of a power of attorney granted to the vendor, making the land contract subordinate to a future mortgage given by the vendor. This type of clause, if encountered, ought to be seriously questioned and objected to by the vendee's attorney.

10. Conclusion

Although the land contract has been generally regarded as a means to convey title to real estate, it is perhaps a more important means to create financing for the real estate transaction. The installment land contract has experienced a remarkable growth in popularity not only because of the increasing reliance on installment credit in all sectors of the American economy but also because of the tightening money market and the rigidity of terms imposed by the conventional mortgage lender. In many instances, the land contract may be the only means by which a particular property can be readily marketed. The land contract is exceedingly easy to work with because it is, by its very nature, highly flexible. Consequently, there is much room for negotiation as to its precise terms. This aspect of the land contract may increase the market for a particular property by making the property more readily available to a greater variety of potential buyers. Even granting that the resurgence of the land contract may be reflective of an accelerated demand for low equity financing on the part of buyers, its popularity also is reflective of the desire on the part of the sellers to limit the income tax impact upon the sale of real estate. Regardless of the motivation, the land contract has become a useful and attractive tool in the financing of the real estate transaction and therefore, as a financing device, should be thoroughly understood by the practitioner.

E. ALTERNATIVE MORTGAGE SYSTEMS FOR RESIDENTIAL PROPERTY

1. THE PROBLEM

The buying and selling of residential property has changed very little in the past forty years. The conventional fixed rate, fixed payment mortgage has been effectively used as the primary financing tool in real estate purchase and development. However, since the mid-1960's the American economy has been beset by a changing economic and financial situation which has led to serious questions regarding the adequacy of the standard fixed payment mortgage (SFPM) in an inflationary economy. Because of the inflated price of existing housing and the cost of financing new housing, prospective homeowners have found themselves trapped in a financial bind; either they must continue to rent in order to solve their housing needs, thereby foregoing any equity accrual obtained in an ownership interest, or they must "buy down" to a house which although inadequate to meet future needs nevertheless gives them a chance to build up an equity position enabling them to purchase an adequate home in the future. Lenders have also been hard hit by economic reality, finding that the growth of rising interest rates induced by a rapid inflation and uneven real economic growth has forced them to operate under restrictive credit policies, thereby reducing the amount of funds available for home mortgage lending.

Within the past ten years the financial community has undergone a "soul searching" analysis of its dependence upon conventional financing and has undertaken the job of adjusting to perceived defects in the present system. New instruments, such as the variable rate mortgage, the graduated payment mortgage, the reverse annuity mortgage, and the FLIP mortgage, are being explored to determine whether the credit crunch of today's economy can be alleviated. Unlike the SFPM, these new instruments look to the financial needs and prospects of the individual borrower, tailoring the type of housing desired to the borrower's particular ability to pay. Old precepts such as the requirement of a ten to twenty percent downpayment on any home are being cast to the winds by insurance techniques and alternative financial arrangements. While at first sight this would seem to increase the probability of default and foreclosure, such consequences are seen as secondary to considerations of practical development and growth necessary to maintain a healthy financial community.

The current reevaluation of home financing techniques derives its impetus from two factors. The first of these factors is the problem of high interest rates charged to new borrowers. Loans given by savings and loan associations, which originate approximately fifty percent of all home mortgage arrangements, are most often in the twenty to thirty year category while savings deposits are typically a more short term investment. This discrepancy creates an imbalance which constricts an S&L's lending abilities. When the economy fluctuates, this "lending long, borrowing short" quality impedes the amount of loans a lender can give out. The reason is that during periods of rapid inflation the capacity to attract new savings is reduced while at the same time revenue generated by mortgage interest payments fails to increase at the same rate that the economy inflates. The result is a potentially crippling cash flow problem. At times the situation leads to a savings outflow, while due to an inflated money supply the demand for housing is increasing.

Compounding the problem, S&L's are also faced with a situation called "disintermediation," which occurs when depositors take their money out of savings accounts and put it into higher yield investments, or simply do not deposit it into savings accounts in the first place. In order to remain competitive for the savers' dollar, lenders must raise the interest paid to savings depositors, thereby increasing the discrepancy between mortgage yield and interest expense. Attempts to rectify this discrepancy have taken the form of increased interest rates on new mortgages, thereby generating a "subsidy" paid to existing borrowers by the new borrowers.

The second factor which has generated the current controversy regarding the adequacy of present financing techniques is the high cost of housing. As of December, 1978, the average sales price of a new one-family home in the United States has increased to $67,600 compared to $44,200 in 1976. With housing costs inflating between one and two percent per month, depending upon the area, many potential borrowers are being priced out of the housing market either because they lack the required down payment or because they cannot afford the monthly payments. Compounding this problem is the fact that some lenders attempt to estimate the future rate of inflation and pass on potential cost escalations in the form of inflation premiums, even though no accurate measure of long term inflation is currently available.

The long run problem faced by the home mortgage industry is to gain an increased base for revenue and retain competitiveness in the savings market without placing the entire burden of the current cost of money onto new mortgages. From the borrowers' standpoint, the problems that must be overcome are high initial monthly payments and an inability to afford the kind of house that meets their longer term income expectations. Given these considerations, the lending industry is attempting to make their mortgages more palatable through various financing formulas.

2. ALTERNATE MORTGAGE FORMS

a. Variable Rate Mortgage Plan (VRM)

1. Interest rate raised or lowered over life of loan in accord with variation of some other financial indicator or rate, such as the Federal Reserve Discount Rate or Prime Rate.

2. Most lenders are subject to one or more restrictions on the use of a VRM. The restrictions include:

(a) Limiting the number of rate adjustments which can be made within a given period;

(b) Requiring the Lender to give the Borrower advance notice of any rate change (with the Borrower having the right to prepay, without a prepayment charge, within a specified period of notification of any increase);

(c) Providing for rate reductions on the same formula as rate increases;

(d) Limiting the amount of any change in rate.

In essence then, a VRM is a mortgage with a flexible interest rate that can be adjusted up or down in direct correlation with the formula which measures the cost of funds to lending institutions.

b. Flexible Payment Mortgage Loan

Borrower and lender negotiate the payment scheduled based on borrower's financial ability to pay. However, each such payment would at least cover interest due on that payment and the loan would be on a fully amortized basis by the end of some specified term. See Wis. Adm. Code S-L § 18.011(2)(b). Sanctioned by the Housing and Community Development Act of 1977.

c. Roll-Over Mortgage (ROM)

The interest rate on the mortgage is set for a specified term, such as 3 or 5 years, and then totally renegotiated at *current mortgage loan rates.*

d. Reverse Annuity Mortgage

Reverse annuity mortgage (RAM) is not a financing device in the strict sense of the term. It is rather, a method which enables homeowners who own their homes free and clear of mortgage encumbrances to utilize their equity built up over time to subsidize their present income. The RAM financing device is a means by which homeowners may convert the equity in their home into a stream of income or into a single lump sum payment. Under this arrangement, the lender pays the homeowner a fixed annuity based on a percentage of the value of the property. The annuitant would not be required to repay the loan until sale or upon his demise, at which time the loan would be paid through the probate process. Reverse annuity mortgage is designed to be a 10-year annuity tool. If the annuitant were to die prior to the maturity of the annuity the proceeds of the estate could be used to pay the lender for the money extended. If the annuitant lived beyond the 10-year period, he could sell the home, or assuming he wished to remain, either a new RAM could be issued based upon the current appreciated value of the home or a sale-leaseback agreement could be drawn up to enable him to live in the home for the rest of his life.

e. Deferred Interest Mortgage

Under a deferred interest mortgage arrangement, the borrower receives a lower initial interest rate than one obtainable under a conventional mortgage, resulting then in a lower initial monthly payment. In return for this arrangement the lender receives the deferred interest plus a fee upon re-sale of the home. This type of mortgage is meant as a short term financing tool and is geared toward homeowners who do not expect to live in the home for more than five years. In the event the house is not sold within five years, the mortgage is refinanced as a conventional loan with the deferred interest and fee coming from the borrower's equity in the home.

f. Step-Rate Mortgage

The interest rates are scheduled to increase at a predetermined rate and at predetermined intervals.

g. Price Level Adjusted Mortgage (PLAM)

In a PLAM mortgage the lender charges the contract stated interest rate but the principal balance of the loan is adjusted periodically in accordance with some index of inflation, such as the Consumer Price Index.

h. Split-Rate Mortgage

A recent inovation has been the offering of a split rate mortgage. The purpose of said mortgage is to make the initial cash requirement more affordable for the mortgagor by financing the loan origination fee, *i.e.,* the points. On a 90% mortgage, the points are financed by paying a higher rate of interest for the first 18 months of the mortgage loan and thereafter the principal and interest is adjusted to the commitment rate. In essence, then, a borrower is paying those points on a monthly payment basis rather than required to obtain the additional cash necessary to pay points to the extent of 1% to 2% of the mortgage amount at the time of closing.

FOR VALUE RECEIVED, We, the undersigned, the Promisors and Mortgagors, jointly and severally promise and agree as follows:

To pay to the order of SECURITY SAVINGS AND LOAN ASSOCIATION, Promisee and Mortgagee, a Wisconsin corporation, hereinafter called the Association, its successors and assigns, at its offices at Milwaukee, Wisconsin, or at such other place as may be designated by the holder of this mortgage note, the principal sum of _____ Dollars ($_____) and such additional sums as may be subsequently advanced hereon to the Promisors and Mortgagors by the Association, together with interest at the rate of _____ per cent (_____ %) per annum until _____, 19_____, and _____ _____ per cent (_____%) per annum for the remaining term of the loan, or until the loan shall have been fully paid, subject, to the provisions hereinafter set forth. Such principal and interest shall be due and payable in monthly installments of _____ _____ Dollars ($_____) per month, until _____ _____, 19 _____, and _____ Dollars ($ _____) per month thereafter, subject to the provisions hereinafter set forth. Payments shall be due on the first day of each and every month, commencing _____, 19_____. Notwithstanding any other provisions in this note or the mortgage given as collateral security therefor, the entire sum due hereon, including any additional advances, shall be paid within the time prescribed by law.

i. Graduated Payment Mortgage (GPM)

The graduated payment mortgage has recently been introduced in real estate financing in order to offset in part the difficulties encountered by young homebuyers in financing their first homestead purchase. The GPM concept is based upon the assumption that a family's income will increase over time and therefore the amount of income available to make payments on a home will also increase. Consequently, although a GPM uses the same interest owed as in a conventional mortgage, the monthly payments start out at a low level and gradually increase until they rise above the level at which a standard mortgage would have been written.

Implicit within this device is the fact that initial monthly payments are not sufficient to amortize the loan. In effect, the mortgagor is borrowing the difference between his payments and the current interest, and paying off these amounts in later years.

The GPM mortgage plan has three definite effects:

a. It qualifies more potential homebuyers for conventional loans;
b. It qualifies buyers to enter the housing market sooner;
c. It qualifies buyers to purchase more house and amenities.

Effect of Lower P&I Payment on Mortgagor's Purchasing Power *

Annual Income	1st Year Mo. Cash Payment		House Price Qualification	
	GPM	STD	GPM	STD
$12,000.00	117.00	167.01	23,300	17,438
15,000.00	180.41	250.69	34,471	26,250
20,000.00	306.82	375.83	49,683	41,578
25,000.00	408.46	470.19	61,153	53,940

* *Assumes:* 9¼%, 30 year loan
      25% Housing Expense-to-Income Ratio
      5-year Supplementary Period
      6% Annual Income Growth Rate

Delayed GPM plans are tailored to the borrower to relate monthly mortgage payments to expected increases in future income. Mortgagors can select different plans including payment rate increases at 2.5, 5.0 and 7.5 graduations over five years before leveling off, or two different annual payment rate increases, 2.5 and 3.0 graduations, over 10 years before leveling off. For example, for a standard 3-year, 8½%, $35,000.00 mortgage loan, monthly payments would be at $269.00. Under one of the GPM options, borrower would only have to pay $203.00 a month during the first year, $217.00 during the second year, and so on. Payments would level off at $291.00 at the beginning of the sixth year. It should be noted that the Housing and Community Development Act of 1977 has given authorization to the use by federal lenders of GPM instruments as part of their mortgage loan documentation.

j. FLIP Mortgage

A FLIP mortgage is a graduated payment mortgage which has the effect of reducing a homebuyer's monthly mortgage payments. The reduction in monthly payments is accomplished by using the homebuyer's down payment to fund a pledged savings account. Funds are drawn from the account each month to supplement the buyer's mortgage payment. The pledged account serves as additional collateral for the lender. Reduction in the homebuyer's out-of-pocket monthly mortgage payment is accomplished through supplementary payments taken monthly by the lender from the interest-bearing pledged account funded from the homebuyer's down payment. This pledged account is deposited with the lender at the time the mortgage is created. Each succeeding year, the monthly supplementary payments are reduced. Responsive to an individual homebuyer's requirements and capabilities, the FLIP mortgage takes into consideration the cost of the home, the cash available for down payment, the family income, mortgage terms and potential for income growth. The effects are dramatic.

First, monthly mortgage payments can be reduced an average of 20 to 30 percent the first year. Second, the required qualifying income to make the purchase is also reduced. For example, a family making a 10% down payment on a $41,000.00 home with a 30-year mortgage at 9% would normally have to earn $17,000.00 annually to qualify. But with the FLIP mortgage, the family needs only to make $13,400.00 per year, or 21% less.

The reason for this is by using the FLIP mortgage, monthly payments the first year would be $220.20, the second year $238.72, the third year $258.45, the fourth year $279.50, the fifth year $301.94, and then $325.87 the sixth year and for the remainder of the 30-year mortgage.

In this example, approximately $3,600.00 of the $4,100.00 down payment would be deposited in a pledged savings account; the remaining $500.00 of the down payment would go towards the $41,000.00 purchase price, leaving a mortgage of $40,500.00. The funds in the pledged savings account would earn interest and this interest coupled with withdrawals of principal from the pledged savings account would be used to supplement the homebuyer's monthly payments.

The monthly payment schedule for this FLIP mortgage incorporating the pledged savings account would break down in the following manner:

Monthly Payment Schedule

Year	Homebuyer's Mo. Pmt.	Mo. Principal Drawn From Pledged Savings Acct.	Mo. Interest Drawn From Pledged Savings Acct.	Mo. Payment Received By Lender
1	$220.20	$92.33	$13.34	$325.87
2	238.72	78.30	8.85	325.87
3	258.45	62.25	5.17	325.87
4	279.50	43.99	2.38	325.87
5	301.94	23.32	0.61	325.87
6	325.87	0.00	0.00	325.87

By comparison, using this example, monthly payments with a conventional mortgage would be $297.00; with the FLIP mortgage, first year payments are approximately $220.00 per month, resulting in a $77.00 reduction (about 25%).

Yet throughout the supplemental payment period, the lender receives full monthly payments providing full amortization. Moreover, this reduction in monthly payments is achieved while utilizing the lender's conventional underwriting standard of allowing 25% of gross annual income to be used for housing expenses.

k. Shared Appreciation Mortgage

This is but another in an apparently endless stream of alternative forms designed to allow the public to continue buying, and financing, homes in a market where money is in short supply and interest rates are high. This form, dubbed "SAM" by its originators, allows borrowers a lower interest rate, which means the payments are less than the borrower would pay at the prevailing rate. For example, if the borrower obtained a conventional mortgage at 13% on a principal sum of $50,000, the monthly principal and interest payment would be $553. However, if the borrower obtains a SAM the rate is reduced to 9½% and the payments are $420 per month. This also means that the buyer will need less income to qualify for a loan on a SAM than on a conventional loan.

The price for the reduced rate and payments is that the homeowner-borrower will share the appreciation with the lender when the house is sold. If the borrower does not sell within ten years of obtaining a SAM, then the house must be either sold or refinanced at the end of ten years. In either case the lender collects a percentage, up to 40%, of the increase in value of the home.

l. Buy Down

This alternative is not really a different form of mortgage, but rather a means to obtain a mortgage at a lower rate of interest by paying the lender a higher amount of points at the commencement of the loan. Points are a loan origination fee which lenders charge for placing the loan. One point equals one percent of the principal of the loan when placed. A Buy Down program will enable a borrower to obtain a short-term loan, one or two years, and reduce the monthly payments and the interest rate by paying additional "points" in the beginning. For example, a $50,000 mortgage for two years at 16.5% would generate $16,500 in interest in two years. The same loan at 13% would generate $13,000. A borrower could reduce the rate from 16.5% to 13% by paying a 7% fee. The payments will be reduced more than if the $3,500 (the 7% fee) had been used to reduce the principal amount of the loan. Borrowing on a Buy Down for a short term is a means of reducing payments for a short term while hoping that the rates will decline before it is time to obtain new financing. The lender takes no risk, having been paid at the commencement of the loan.

JACKSON, GRADUATED-PAYMENT MORTGAGES HELP HOME BUYERS — AT A COST, The Wall Street Journal, August 20, 1980 *

Always reluctant to admit that one of their creations has gone the slightest bit sour, federal officials still refer to graduated-payment mortgages by their formal initials — GPMs. But on Wall Street traders irreverently call them "Gyp 'Ems," and home buyers have cause to feel the traders are right.

With graduated-payment mortgages, which the Federal Housing Administration began insuring in 1977, payments are much lower at first than for traditional level-payment mortgages. Then they rise gradually and level off after a few

---

* The Wall Street Journal, August 20, 1980. Reprinted by permission from The Wall Street Journal.

years. The idea is to put home ownership within reach of young people who might otherwise be forced by spiraling housing prices and high interest rates to remain renters. The mortgages have proven popular. The FHA has insured 220,000 of the loans, which at times have accounted for roughly one-third of all FHA single-family mortgage originations.

But insurance companies, pension funds and other mortgage investors aren't so delighted with "Gyp 'Ems." Because of the complexities and uncertain return of GPMs, they have been demanding deeper discounts on GPMs than for level-payment loans. Result: consumers lured by the GPM's seductively low initial payments are getting less of a good deal than they might have hoped.

Higher yields for GPMs have persisted so long that the Federal National Mortgage Association, the government-spawned company that buys more mortgages than anybody else, recently gave up paying a better price than private investors. "We can't argue with the market; not for too long, anyway," says Fannie Mae's chief economist, Peter Treadway.

And yesterday the FHA, proud parent of the graduated-payment mortgage, also gave formal recognition to its higher cost by announcing that lenders will be allowed for the first time to charge a higher nominal interest rate for GPMs than for level-payment mortgages. Effective today, the maximum rate for an FHA level-payment mortgage is 12%, but for a GPM it is 12½%.

Until today the FHA ceiling had been 11½% on both types of mortgages, but this didn't mean the consumer escaped paying the higher cost of a GPM. The higher yields demanded by the people who actually put up the money were simply translated into "discount points," a one-time fee that someone had to pay to reduce the amount of principal and increase the yield to the investor. One point is 1% of a loan's face value.

Before today's increase, two to three more points had to be paid to get a GPM than to get a level-payment FHA loan. On a $50,000 loan, that's $1,000 to $1,500 more cash someone had to put into the deal, up front, when the buyer wanted a graduated-payment mortgage. Federal rules require the seller to pay anything over one point. And in the current housing market, some desperate sellers reluctantly have done so.

But more often the seller finds a way to work the points into a higher selling price for the house. This raises either the buyer's down payment or the amount of the loan, or both.

How much more the buyer pays depends on the deal. But unless he or she put up more cash at the sale, the monthly payments were roughly $15 to $20 higher on a $50,000, 30-year GPM than they would have been if investors priced such loans the same as level-payment mortgages. With the FHA's action yesterday, the higher cost of GPMs becomes plain. Consider the $50,000, 30-year loan.

At 12% interest, the initial monthly payment for principal and interest would be $395.69 on the most popular form of GPM, rising each year to $568.06 a month in the sixth and later years. But the extra half a percentage point in interest that the FHA is allowing means an extra $16 to $23 a month in payments. At 12½% interest, the same loan carries payments of $411.79 a month to start, rising to $591.18 in the sixth and subsequent years.

That's still about $100 a month less to start than the $512.50 required for a comparable level-payment loan. So many consumers may still find GPMs a good deal, or at least the only one they can afford. But after five years the payments on a 12½% GPM level off at $76.68 a month higher than for the comparable 12% level-payment loan. If investors didn't demand a better return on GPMs, the difference would be only $53.56.

Why the extra costs? Lewis Ranieri, head of Salomon Brothers's mortgage department, gives three reasons why higher yields are needed to attract reluctant investors to GPMs:

* The complex structure of the mortgages creates "an accounting nightmare" that frightens away some institutions.

* The low payments in the early years don't cover the interest, which means the lender actually increases the amount of the loan for a while. For some investors this means paying taxes on income that won't be realized for years.

* The return is uncertain. Since GPMs have been around fewer than three years, there isn't any way to tell whether their average life will be longer or shorter than ordinary FHA mortgages. The quicker the repayment, the smaller the discount demanded by investors and the lower the cost to the consumer.

Nobody can be sure whether the relatively higher cost for graduated-payment mortgages will persist. The gap between GPMs and level-payment mortgages is much higher than what it was and that difference is less than the four or five discount points previously. Some, however, suspect it may widen as federal officials swamp the mortgage market with new types of mortgage paper. Already headed for the market, or being considered, are a more liberal GPM and a hybrid mortgage combining graduated payments and an adjustable interest rate.

Chapter 3

PRIORITY

> But many that are first shall be last; and the last shall be first.
>
> *Matthew* 19:30

In the absence of an agreement or a contrary code provision, priority of liens is determined by chronology. Prior in time is senior in interest. This is important in the event of a default resulting in sale of the subject property to satisfy the obligation. If the foreclosure sale price is greater than the total amount of liens, then all lienors can be paid from the sale proceeds. If the amount of liens exceeds the sale price, then the funds are distributed, generally, in order of priority. It is at that point that disputes regarding priority arise.

If the law were always that priority is determined by the chronological sequence of creation of liens, then there would be less to discuss or litigate. However there are three factors which can affect priority other than chronology: (1) statutes which affect priority, such as recording statutes and liens which are created by statute; (2) the character of the debt secured, such as purchase money; and (3) priority by contract generally called subordination agreements. It is with these three exceptions that this chapter is concerned.

A. RECORDING STATUTES

Each state has provided by statute for the recording of documents affecting or transferring title to real property so that these documents become a matter of public record. The office in which these documents are made public records may be known as the County Recorder's Office,[1] the Registrar of Deeds,[2] or some similar name. The purpose, however, is the same in all states, to provide a public record of real property transactions. This record will in many instances have an effect on the priority of encumbrances based on the time of recording *rather* than the time of creation. Other factors, such as notice, may enter into the effect that the recording statutes have on priority. Therefore, one must look to the recording statute of any given jurisdiction to determine what type of recording statute is employed, for there are differences in statutes which cause a difference in effect.

Earlier in this country it could be said that there were four types of recording statutes: (1) race; (2) notice; (3) race-notice (sometimes called notice-race); and, (4) grace period statutes.[3] It appears that there are no longer any grace period

---

[1] Many states designate a County Recorder and the duties of office. *See* Cal. Gov't Code §§ 24300 and 27201.

[2] Massachusetts refers to the Registry of Deeds. *See* Mass. Ann. Laws ch. 183, § 4. Other states designate the County Clerk as the recorder. *See* Tex. Civ. Stat. § 6591 (Vernon 1969).

[3] Delaware had a statute which stated: "If a deed concerning land or tenements is not recorded in the proper office within 15 days after the day of the sealing and delivery thereof, the deed shall not avail against a subsequent fair creditor, mortgagee or purchaser for a valuable consideration . . .". Del. Code Ann. tit. 25, § 153. However, this section was repealed in 1968. *See* 56 Del. Laws ch. 318 (1968). Pennsylvania, however, has a curious grace period for purchase money mortgages. It allows priority from the date of delivery to the mortgagee provided they are recorded within ten days; otherwise priority dates from the date of recording. *See* Pa. Stat. Ann. tit. 68, § 602 (Purdon Supp. 1976).

statutes. That leaves three types of statutes with similar and admittedly confusing names. A pure race recording statute affords priority, or gives effect to a document, based only on who arrives at the Recorder's Office first. It is literally a race to the court house. A notice statute only protects those persons recording documents who are *bona fide purchasers,* or the equivalent, in a mortgage transaction. That is, the statute protects only those who do not have notice of any defects. This type of statute might more appropriately be called a "no notice" statute. The hybrid type statute combines aspects of both notice and race statutes providing protection only to *bona fide purchasers* who record first. Examples of these three types of statutes follow.

1. RACE

General Laws of North Carolina
§ 47-18

(a) No (i) conveyance of land, or (ii) contract to convey, or (iii) option to convey, or (iv) lease of land for more than three years shall be valid to pass any property interest as against lien creditors or purchasers for a valuable consideration from the donor, bargainor or lessor but from the time of registration thereof in the county where the land lies, or if the land is located in more than one county, then in each county where any portion of the land lies to be effective as to the land in that county.

(b) This section shall not apply to contracts, leases or deeds executed prior to March 1, 1885, until January 1, 1886; and no purchase from any such donor, bargainor or lessor shall avail or pass title as against any unregistered deed executed prior to December 1, 1885, when the person holding or claiming under such unregistered deed shall be in actual possession and enjoyment of such land, either in person or by his tenant, at the time of the execution of such second deed, or when the person claiming under or taking such second deed had at the time of taking or purchasing under such deed actual or constructive notice of such unregistered deed, or the claim of the person holding or claiming thereunder. (Code, s. 1245; 1885, c. 147, s. 1; Rev., s. 980; C. S., s. 3309; 1959, c. 90; 1975, c. 507.)

Ohio Revised Code
§ 5301.23 (1970)

All mortgages properly executed shall be recorded in the office of the county recorder of the county in which the mortgaged premises are situated, and take effect from the time they are delivered to such recorder for record. If two or more mortgages are presented for record on the same day, they shall take effect in the order of presentation. The first mortgage presented must be the first recorded, and the first recorded shall have preference.

Note that the Ohio statute refers only to mortgages. There is a separate statute for deeds which is the hybrid race-notice type. Perhaps Ohio wished to require mortgagees to be diligent in getting the mortgage to the Recorder, but further wished only to protect bona fide purchasers in the transfer of title. *See* Ohio Rev. Code § 65301.25(A)(1970).

2. NOTICE

Annotated Laws of Massachusetts
Ch. 183, § 4 (Supp. 1976-77)

A conveyance of an estate in fee simple, fee tail or for life, or a lease for a term of seven years, or an assignment of rents or profits from an estate or lease, shall not be valid as against any person, except the grantor or lessor, his heirs and devisees and persons having actual notice of it, unless it, or an office copy as provided in section thirteen of chapter thirty-six, or, with respect to such a lease or an assignment of rents or profits, a notice of lease or a notice of assignment of rents or profits, as hereinafter defined, is recorded in the registry of deeds for the county or district in which the land to which it relates lies. A "notice of lease", as used in this section, shall mean an instrument in writing executed by all persons who are parties to the lease of which notice is given and shall contain the following information with reference to such lease: — the date of execution thereof and a description, in the form contained in such lease, of the premises demised, and the term of such lease, with the date of commencement of such term and all rights of extension or renewal. A "notice of assignment of rents or profits", as used in this section, shall mean an instrument in writing executed by the assignor and containing the following information: — a description of the premises, the rent or profits of which have been assigned, adequate to identify the premises, the name of assignee, and the rents and profits which have been assigned. A provision in a recorded mortgage assigning or conditionally assigning rents or profits or obligating the mortgagor to assign or conditionally assign existing or future rents or profits shall constitute a "notice of assignment of rents or profits".

3. RACE-NOTICE

Texas Civil Statutes
§ 6627 (Vernon Supp. 1980-81)

All bargains, sales and other conveyances whatever, of any land, tenements and hereditaments, whether they may be made for passing any estate of freehold of inheritance or for a term of years; and deeds of settlement upon marriage, whether land, money or other personal thing; and all deeds of trust and mortgages shall be void as to all creditors and subsequent purchasers for a valuable consideration without notice, unless they shall be acknowledged or proved and filed with the clerk, to be recorded as required by law; but the same as between the parties and their heirs, and as to all subsequent purchasers, with notice thereof or without valuable consideration, shall be valid and binding; provided, however, that the rights, duties, obligations, and priorities of debtors, secured parties and their heirs, successors, and assigns, and the rights and priorities of creditors and subsequent purchasers with respect to the goods or other collateral described in the financing statements or security agreements filed as financing statements or continuation statements filed for record pursuant to the Business & Commerce Code, shall be governed by that code. Amended by Acts 1975, 64th Leg., p. 944, ch. 353, § 14, eff. June 19, 1975.
Note that the Texas statute has been amended so as to bring it into conformity with provisions of the Uniform Commercial Code.

California Civil Code
§ 1214

Every conveyance of real property, other than a lease for a term not exceeding one year, is void as against any subsequent purchaser or mortgagee of the same property, or any part thereof, in good faith and for a valuable consideration, whose conveyance is first duly recorded, and as against any judgment affecting the title, unless such conveyance shall have been duly recorded prior to the record of notice of action. (Enacted 1872. As amended Stats. 1895, c. 48, p. 50, § 1.)

SECURITY LIFE INSURANCE CO. v. TRAVIS

District Court of Appeal of Florida
340 So. 2d 529 (1976)

PER CURIAM.

Security Life provided the financing for the construction of motels in various locations, including the one here involved which is located in Bradford County. Travis signed promissory notes, construction loan agreements, and a mortgage on the Bradford County property. Travis defaulted prior to the project being completed. Security instituted this action against Travis (Travis' widow and executrix) and nine materialmen. Four of the materialmen filed cross-claims against Security and Travis. Ultimately, a final judgment of foreclosure was entered, with a condition precedent that Security deposit into the registry of the court the sum of $46,113.28 which Security alleged that it had not disbursed pursuant to the terms of the construction loan agreement and was holding in escrow. A final judgment on cross-claims was subsequently entered in favor of the materialmen in the sum of $12,569.06, plus interest, costs, and attorney's fees.

The primary issue relates solely to the cross-claims of the materialmen. Security urges that the trial court erred in awarding the materialmen a lien superior to its recorded mortgage. We agree and reverse.

The subject mortgage was recorded prior to commencement of any construction and the subject construction loan agreement was executed prior to any materials being furnished by cross-claimants. As stated above the project had not been completed.

The judgment appealed is reversed.

RAWLS, ACTING C. J., and SMITH and MILLS, JJ., concur.

BANK OF CAVE CITY v. HILL

Supreme Court of Arkansas
266 Ark. 727, 587 S.W.2d 833 (1979)

FOGLEMAN, JUSTICE.

Appellant claims that its construction money mortgage has priority over the materialmen's liens of appellees Bobby Hill and White River Materials, Inc., and that the decree of the trial court to the contrary should be reversed. We agree with the chancery court and affirm.

The case was tried upon the following stipulation of facts:

I. Prince Construction and Metal Supply, Inc. purchased the property being the subject of this dispute on the 13th day of April, 1977, and on the same day verbally agreed with Bobby Hill to purchase a metal building to be placed on said real property.

II. That John E. Bryant & Sons Lumber Co., which is not a party to this proceeding, delivered material to the construction site on the 18th day of April, 1977.

III. That the Bank of Cave City agreed to loan the defendant, Prince Construction and Metal Supply, Inc. the sum of $12,000 to be used in the construction of a metal building on the aforementioned real property. On the same date, Prince Construction and Metal Supply, Inc. was advanced the sum of $8,500 by the Bank of Cave City, and in turn executed their promissory note and deed of trust securing the sum of $12,000 which was subsequently filed for record on the 25th day of April, 1977.

IV. That White River Materials, Inc. delivered certain materials in the sum of $1,354.64 on the 28th day of April, 1977.

V. On the 11th day of May, 1977, Bobby Hill delivered to the real property being the subject matter of this dispute, materials for erection and construction of a metal building.

VI. On the 31st day of May, 1977, White River Materials, Inc. delivered materials valued at $144.20 to the construction site.

VII. On the 6th day of June, 1977, the Bank of Cave City advanced the sum of $6,000 as an additional advance on the notes secured by the aforementioned deed of trust.

VIII. On the 8th day of August, 1977, White River Materials, Inc. served Prince Construction and Metal Supply, Inc. with a notice of materialman's lien.

IX. On the 11th day of August, 1977, plaintiff, Bobby Hill commenced this action by filing a complaint against Prince Construction and Metal Supply, Inc. and the Bank of Cave City, Cave City, Arkansas, seeking to establish a materialman's lien and to foreclose the same.

X. On the 18th day of August, 1977, White River Materials, Inc. filed suit seeking to foreclose its materialman's lien.

XI. On the 20th day of September, 1977, the Bank of Cave City, paid the sum of $1,875.38 to Bryant Lumber Co. for materials delivered to the construction site on April 18, 1977, to preclude the possibility of the filing of a lien by Bryant Lumber Co.

Appellant contends that a materialman who furnishes materials after the recording of a construction money mortgage is not entitled to priority over the lien of the mortgage. We have held to the contrary in *Planters Lumber Co. v. Jack Collier East Co.,* 234 Ark. 1091, 356 S.W.2d 631, where we said that the lien of such materialmen relates back to the commencement of the construction of the building. Appellant seeks to distinguish this case from that one by pointing out that the materialman who furnished material prior to the recording of the construction money mortgage, in that case, perfected his lien, while the John E. Bryant & Sons Lumber Company did not perfect its lien. Appellant says that, under the circumstances existing here, the liens of appellees cannot stand on the same footing as that of Bryant, because Bryant never perfected its lien.

Appellant's argument is not sound. In the *Planters* case the mortgagee also paid the claim of the claimant which had furnished material prior to the filing of the mortgage. The decision in that case did not turn upon the fact that the first material supplier had perfected its lien. The subsequent suppliers did not rely on that fact at all. They contended that their liens related back to the "commencement of the building" and that the date of delivery of the material of the first supplier to the lot on which the building was constructed was the "commencement of such building." We agreed, pointing out that when the materialman claiming a lien files his account with the circuit clerk, as provided by Ark. Stat. Ann. § 51-613 (Repl. 1971), his lien dates back to the "commencement of such building" and is superior to any lien on the property that may have been placed there "subsequent to the commencement of such building." We said that, in order for the construction money mortgage to have priority, it must have been executed before the "commencement of the building."

We consider our previous decision controlling here. The lender who proposes to lend construction money can determine whether its mortgage will have priority by an inspection of the premises. *Mark's Sheet Metal, Inc. v. Republic Mortgage Co.,* 242 Ark. 475, 414 S.W.2d 106; *Clark v. General Electric Co.,* 243 Ark. 399, 420 S.W.2d 830. Under the authority of these cases, such a mortgagee is charged with notice of whatever an inspection of the premises would have disclosed. Appellant concedes that the Bryant company had delivered materials to the construction site prior to the filing of its mortgage.

Appellant laments that "if the lower court is upheld most lending institutions will not make any advances over and above the original amount committed to in the construction mortgage, and second mortgages for the purpose of completing construction will be almost non-existent." It is interesting to note that the writer of the dissenting opinion in *Planters Lumber Co. v. Jack Collier East Co.,* supra, said: "I fear the economic repercussions which will flow from the majority opinion. Following the rule set down by the Court today, no individual or lending institution can safely loan money to further a building project after one nail has been driven which has been purchased on credit. A lender willing to make a construction loan and take a mortgage to secure it cannot gain security for his loan by searching the records to determine the extent of prior liens on a building project, ascertain the amount of work done and materials furnished, and then act on the basis of this information. If he advances money on a project upon which construction has already begun, his mortgage would be inferior to those who might subsequently furnish labor or material for the project . . ." The fears of today's appellant and yesteryear's dissenters are the same, but the latter plainly recognized the impact of the majority opinion. In the ensuing 17 years the General Assembly has not seen fit to change the law in respect to priority of liens, even though other substantial changes were made in 1979. The question is still one for legislative determination.

The judgment is affirmed.

We agree. HARRIS, C. J., and GEORGE ROSE SMITH and HICKMAN, JJ.

AMERICAN FEDERAL SAVINGS & LOAN ASS'N v. ORENSTEIN

Michigan Court of Appeals
81 Mich. App. 249, 265 N.W.2d 111 (1978)

R. B. BURNS, JUDGE.

We concur in the opinion of Judge Brown, except as to his discussion and resolution of the substantive issue. The reader is referred to Judge Brown's opinion for the facts in the instant case.

The trial court granted summary judgment because it found the subordination clause unambiguously subordinated Orenstein's mortgage to that of plaintiff. However, each party on appeal has presented reasonable interpretations of the same clause which are at variance with each other. If the clause is interpreted, as plaintiff suggests, as subordinating Orenstein's mortgage not only to the interests of the New York State Teacher's Retirement System and the General

Electric Pension Trust, but also to an unspecified, yet-to-be-incurred interest of $4,125,000, then one immediately encounters an obvious ambiguity. If Orenstein's mortgage is subordinate to three interests, why are only two numerals listed?

Judge Brown's argument that the ambiguity must be resolved against the drafter of the clause, Orenstein, rests on the premise that a title searcher is never chargeable with inquiry notice when an ambiguity is encountered. This is not the law.

It is the duty of a purchaser of real estate to investigate the title of his vendor, and to take notice of any adverse rights or equities of third persons which he has the means of discovering, and as to which he is put on inquiry. If he makes all the inquiry which due diligence requires, and still fails to discover the outstanding right, he is excused, but, if he fails to use due diligence, he is chargeable, as a matter of law, with notice of the facts which the inquiry would have disclosed.

. . . .

. . . The questions in such cases are: *First,* whether the facts were sufficient to put the party on inquiry; and, *second,* did he fail to exercise due diligence in making the inquiry? *Schweiss v. Woodruff,* 73 Mich. 473, 477-478, 41 N.W. 511, 512-513 (1889). (Emphasis in original.)

Cases in which a title defect would prevent a diligent title searcher from discovering the deed or recognizing its applicability must be distinguished from those in which the deed would have been discovered and a possible error revealed. *Schweiss v. Woodruff, supra* at 478-479, 41 N.W. at 513; see, *e.g., Savidge v. Seager,* 175 Mich. 47, 140 N.W. 951 (1913); *Van Slyck v. Skinner,* 41 Mich. 186, 1 N.W. 971 (1879). In *Patterson v. Miller,* 249 Mich. 89, 96, 227 N.W. 674, 677 (1929), the ambiguity contained in a subordination clause was so subtle that the Court indicated that a covenant would have had to have been read into the clause to give it the asserted meaning.

The ambiguity in the instant subordination clause was so obvious as to put a prudent person on inquiry notice. Whether plaintiff would have discovered that the Orenstein mortgage would be superior or inferior to its own is a fact which is in dispute. Summary judgment was therefore improper.

Reversed and remanded for trial.

BROWN, JUDGE, concurring in part and dissenting in part.

Defendant Orenstein appeals from a partial summary judgment of June 23, 1976, that Orenstein's mortgage was junior to that of plaintiff, and Orenstein appeals from the July 26, 1976, judgment of foreclosure, as well as the June 17, 1977, order making the judgment of foreclosure a final judgment pursuant to GCR 1963, 518.2.

Defendant Orenstein was given a mortgage on the subject property on March 10, 1972, to secure a loan of $1,300,000. The purpose of the loan was to supplement construction funds for the completion of an office building in Southfield, Michigan. Previously, a mortgage had been conveyed to a third party in the amount of $3,025,000 to provide funds for construction of the building, with an agreement for an additional loan of $1,100,000 upon attaining a certain percentage of tenants for the building. The other mortgagee, however, declined to consummate the additional $1,100,000 loan and the building owners eventually sought and obtained the loan from Orenstein in the amount of $1,300,000. Although the agreement was reached on March 10, 1972, the Orenstein mortgage was not recorded until November 20, 1973. The Orenstein mortgage contained the following emphasized subordination clause which is at the crux of the dispute before us:

> 12. This Mortgage and Assignment of Leases and Rentals is subject and subordinate in all respects to the following: (i) The lien of that certain mortgage given by Mortgagor by assignment to the New York State Teacher's Retirement System dated May 21, 1970, recorded at Liber 5508, page 167, Oakland County Records on May 22, 1970, and all obligations and indebtedness thereof up to the sum of Four Million One Hundred Twenty-Five Thousand and 00/100 Dollars ($4,125,000.00), exclusive of interest; *and all advances, obligations and indebtedness now or hereafter incurred up to the sum of $4,125,000.00, exclusive of interest,* and (ii) The terms and conditions of a land lease from the Trustees of General Electric Pension Trust fee holder granted to Mortgagor from said Trustees executed on May 21, 1970 and recorded on May 22, 1970, in Liber 5508, page 167, Oakland County Records. (Emphasis added.)

On November 28, 1973, a document purporting to discharge the Orenstein mortgage was recorded. Defendant Orenstein claims that the document is a forgery and for purposes of review of the summary judgment, we will assume this assertion is correct. On April 1, 1974, plaintiff recorded its mortgage securing a loan in the amount of $4,110,000. It is undisputed that, at that time, plaintiff had no actual knowledge of the existence of the Orenstein mortgage. On December 13, 1974, the Orenstein mortgage was re-recorded.

Plaintiff commenced this action on October 13, 1975, alleging default and requesting that the Orenstein mortgage be declared a nullity and that plaintiff's mortgage be foreclosed. Following the filing of counter-complaints and cross-complaints, plaintiff moved for a summary judgment that its mortgage has priority over the Orenstein mortgage based on the above-quoted subordination clause in the Orenstein mortgage. Defendant Orenstein seeks review of the summary judgment as well as the judgment of foreclosure and the confirmation of sale.

. . . .

II. Priorities of the Mortgages

The majority and I part company as to the substantive issue in this appeal, whether the subordination clause in the Orenstein mortgage gives plaintiff priority. I respectfully dissent.

Absent the subordination clause of Orenstein's mortgage, Orenstein's would have priority over plaintiff's as being the first mortgage recorded for purposes of constructive notice by virtue of M.C.L.A. § 565.25; M.S.A. § 26.543. The forged discharge does not entitle plaintiff to priority. *Ferguson v. Glassford,* 68 Mich. 36, 47, 35 N.W. 820 (1888). See also *Saginaw Building & Loan Assoc. v. Tennant,* 111 Mich. 515, 516, 69 N.W. 1118 (1897), 66 Am.Jur.2d, Records and Recording Laws, § 123, p. 415, *cf. Horvath v. National Mortgage Co.,* 238 Mich. 354, 360, 213 N.W. 202 (1927). However, if the subordination clause is read to afford plaintiff priority, Orenstein cannot prevail despite the earlier recorded mortgage. See generally, 59 C.J.S. Mortgages § 246, p. 315.

Defendant Orenstein argues on appeal that the trial judge should not have granted summary judgment because the subordination clause is ambiguous, thereby leaving fact questions to be resolved by further testimony. While such an argument might be appropriate if this case involved only a contract, we are dealing with constructive notice to the public at large as well as plaintiff. It does great violence to the recording statutes to hold that a party may on the one hand rely on the recording statutes for priority purposes, but on the other hand assert an ambiguity in the recorded document and bring in extrinsic evidence to explain such an ambiguity.

One important purpose of the recording statutes is to impart certainty so that parties can rely on the public record of outstanding property interests. *Atwood v. Bearss,* 47 Mich. 72, 73, 10 N.W. 112 (1881). In *Savidge v. Seager,* 175 Mich. 47, 55, 140 N.W. 951, 954 (1913), the Michigan Supreme Court indicated that it is impermissible to resort to extrinsic evidence to determine what property interests are protected by recording:

[T]he constructive notice imported by the record of an instrument is strictly limited to that which is set forth on its face . . . .

While *Savidge* was concerned with a property description, the same requirement of certainty should be required of any interest sought to be protected by recording. See also *Van Slyck v. Skinner,* 41 Mich. 186, 190, 1 N.W. 971 (1879). Nor should a different rule apply by virtue of the fact that this is a subordination clause. By statute, a recorded waiver of priority of a mortgage is "constructive notice thereof to all persons dealing with the mortgage". M.C.L.A. § 565.391; M.S.A. § 26.701. Even in a case arising prior to the effective date of this statute, the Michigan Supreme Court gave effect to a subordination clause in a recorded mortgage and held that it should be strictly construed against the party who drafted and recorded the subordination clause. See *Patterson v. Miller,* 249 Mich. 89, 96-97, 227 N.W. 674 (1929).

As a matter of constructive notice, the trial court properly considered and resolved the motion for summary judgment as to the priorities. No extrinsic evidence can be submitted to explain the import of a recorded document, *Savidge v. Seager, supra,* and the extent of constructive notice by virtue of a recorded document should be regarded as peculiarly one of law for a trial court to resolve from within the four corners of the recorded document. Defendant Orenstein's argument that the clause is ambiguous concedes the point that the clause can be interpreted to afford plaintiff protection; thus, construing the subordination clause against defendant Orenstein, *Patterson v. Miller, supra,* plaintiff is entitled to priority.

The inquiry notice on which the majority rests reversal raises entirely separate considerations. While the forged discharge cannot be considered for constructive notice purposes, I believe the majority holding in this case goes too far in failing to give due regard to the forged discharge for purposes of inquiry notice. I have no quarrel with the law quoted from *Schweiss v. Woodruff,* 73 Mich. 473, 477-478, 41 N.W. 511, 512-513 (1889). However, where a party such as plaintiff has searched the record and in reliance on a discharge contained therein has attained the status of a bona fide mortgagee without notice of defects in the title, it is incorrect to hold that the mortgagee must be charged with inquiry notice as to a more subtle defect earlier in time. As *Schweiss, supra,* points out, "If he makes all the inquiry which due diligence requires, and still fails to discover the outstanding right, he is excused".

For inquiry notice purposes, a mortgagee is fully entitled to rely on an apparently perfect legal title as shown by the records:

He will generally be justified in relying on an apparently perfect legal title in his mortgagor, as shown by the records. 59 C.J.S. Mortgages § 235, p. 305.

Ferguson v. Glassford, supra, 68 Mich. at 46-47, 35 N.W. at 827 indicates that this is the law in Michigan, stating that parties "have a right to look to the record for protection".

A similar statement of the law is found in 92 C.J.S. Vendor & Purchaser § 335, p. 250:

It is the duty of a purchaser of real estate to search the public records with respect to the title he plans to purchase *and he is entitled to rely on the record.* (Emphasis added).

In light of plaintiff having obtained title insurance following a search of the record, I cannot agree that plaintiff must be charged with inquiry notice as plaintiff might be if the forged discharge had not been filed. *Cf.* 92 C.J.S. Vendor & Purchaser § 326, p. 238.

Lastly, I dissent from the absence of meaningful instructions to the trial court on remand. The majority holds that plaintiff is chargeable with inquiry notice as a matter of law. The case should then be remanded for entry of judgment against plaintiff, or, trial of the secondary issue as to whether or not Orenstein's attorney had authority to sign and enter the discharge. I cannot agree with the last paragraph of the majority opinion, indicating on the one hand that plaintiff is chargeable with inquiry notice as a matter of law, and on the other hand, indicating that this is a fact question yet to be resolved.

NOTES

1. North Carolina and Louisiana are the only states now having pure race statutes. However, note the Ohio statute refers to mortgages only.

2. In *Security Life Insurance Co. v. Travis, supra,* the materialmen's liens are given a priority junior to the construction loan because they were recorded before any work actually commenced on the project. What type of recording statute do you think Florida has?

3. In *American Federal Savings & Loan Ass'n v. Orenstein, supra,* the recording of a subordination agreement was ambiguous. The court found that the ambiguity was so obvious as to put a person on inquiry notice. Does this mean that the substance of the agreement, making it ambiguous, superceded the effect of the recording statute?

4. The use of an "after-acquired" property clause to achieve priority of lien rights on property subsequently acquired does not always work. In *Pro-Vid-All Mills, Inc. v. Cargill, Inc.,* 142 N.W.2d 290 (Minn. 1966), an action to determine the priority of two chattel mortgages of flocks of turkeys, the court held that a lien of a mortgage upon a flock of turkeys for funds used to purchase supplies and feed was superior to liens in earlier chattel mortgages with after-acquired property clauses.

B. PURCHASE MONEY MORTGAGES

Purchase money mortgages have traditionally been given priority over other types of liens. The theory behind this practice is that the vendor who carries back a purchase money mortgage as part of the sale transaction is entitled to priority, even though there may have been in existence a lien caused by the grantee which would attach to the subject land. For example, if the grantee had an outstanding judgment which had been recorded prior to the grantee purchasing (or owning) any real property, that judgment would become a lien on any property later acquired by the judgment debtor. When the judgment debtor becomes a grantee, the previous judgment lien attaches automatically and instantly on the property acquired. However, if the judgment debtor buys land on credit and the vendor carries back a *purchase money mortgage,* the vendor's lien will be superior to the prior existing judgment lien.

More than one theory has been advanced as the basis for special treatment of purchase money mortgages. Osborne states:

The most venerable and frequently stated explanation is that of transitory seizin. The idea is that title shot into the grantee and out of him again into the purchase money mortgagee so fleetingly *quasi uno flattu,* in one breath, as it were — that no other interest had time to fasten itself to it: the grantee-mortgagor must be regarded as a mere conduit.[4]

However, Osborne acknowledges that a better view is that title passed to the grantee with the vendor's lien already attached.[5]

The character of the debt as purchase money is easily determined where the vendor carries back a purchase money mortgage. However, is it still purchase money if a third party lendor, such as a savings and loan, advances most of the purchase price secured by a mortgage? What if a lender advances funds for the construction of improvements on property purchased for cash?

The character of the debt as purchase money may become critical as to priority when the subject property is overencumbered. It may also become of even greater importance if there is anti-deficiency legislation which prohibits a deficiency judgment when the debt has been purchase money. *See generally* Chapter 7, *infra,* and the cases characterizing debts as purchase money or otherwise to determine the availability of a deficiency judgment. The same criteria may be employed to characterize the debt for the purpose of determining priority.

Purdon's Pennsylvania Statutes Annotated
Title 68, § 602 (Supp. 1976)

Time from which liens have priority

Liens against real property shall have priority over each other on the following basis:

(1) Purchase money mortgages, from the time they are delivered to the mortgagee, if they are recorded within thirty days after their date; otherwise, from the time they are left for record.

(2) Other mortgages and defeasible deeds in the nature of mortgages, from the time they are left for record.

(3) Verdicts for a specific sum of money, from the time they are recorded by the court.

(4) Adverse judgments, orders and decrees, from the time they are rendered.

(5) Amicable judgments, from the time the instruments on which they are entered are left for entry.

(6) Writs which when issued and indexed by the prothonotary create liens against real property, from the time they are issued.

(7) Other instruments which when entered or filed and indexed in the prothonotary's office create liens against real property, from the time they are left for entry or filing. 1951, June 28, P.L. 927, § 2.

MARTIN v. FIRST NATIONAL BANK

Supreme Court of Alabama
279 Ala. 303, 184 So. 2d 815 (1966)

Hardwood, Justice.

This is an appeal from a decree of the Circuit Court of Macon County, In Equity, in a declaratory action, holding that certain advances made to appellant's

---

[4] G. Osborne, Mortgages 390 (1970).
[5] G. Osborne, Mortgages 391 (1970).

husband by the appellee were secured by a mortgage executed to appellee bank by the appellant and her husband.

The appellant, Colie Lee Martin, and her husband, Hughie Martin, purchased a tract of land in Macon County containing 80 acres from one Francis Thompson and wife on October 5, 1956, for the sum of $7,000. Title to said property was taken in the name of appellant and her husband as joint tenants with the right of survivorship. On the same date appellant and her husband executed a mortgage on said lands to the appellee to secure a loan of $2,000, said loan being evidenced by their promissory note of even date, due one year after date, with interest. The appellant and her husband occupied the property as their home from the date of the purchase until the date of her husband's death on February 6, 1963. The appellant and her minor children were still occupying said property as their homestead at the time of trial of this suit.

The note for $2,000 and the mortgage securing the same were signed by both appellant and her husband. The mortgage contains an "advance clause," set out in the consideration clause of the mortgage, as follows:

> Now, therefore, in consideration of the premises and of said indebtedness and in order to secure the prompt payment of the same according to the terms and stipulations contained in said note, *and to secure any other amount that the mortgagee or his assigns may advance to the mortgagor before the payment in full of said mortgage indebtedness,* the said mortgagors, Hughie Martin and Colie Lee Martin, husband and wife, hereby grant, bargain, sell . . . (Emphasis ours.)

The first paragraph of the mortgage describing the parties thereto refers to "Hughie Martin and Colie Lee Martin, husband and wife, hereinafter called *mortgagor* . . ." (Emphasis ours.) Throughout the mortgage the word "mortgagor," the singular, is used in referring to both mortgagors, except in two places, one being the granting clause and the other pertaining to the payment of taxes on the property.

In paragraph five of the mortgage, a defeasance clause, it is provided that the mortgage shall be subject to foreclosure if the mortgagor fails to pay the note "and advances, if any." Paragraph six provides for the application of proceeds of sale of the mortgaged premises to the debt "including advances."

Paragraph nine is as follows:

> Unless contrary intention is indicated by the context, words used herein in the masculine gender include the feminine and the neuter, *the singular includes the plural and the plural the singular.* (Emphasis ours.)

The terms of the mortgage also provide that the mortgagor waives all "right of homestead and personal property exemption" provided under the Constitution and laws of the State of Alabama and of any other state.

The lower court found that the $2,000 borrowed from the appellee by the appellant and her husband was applied on the payment of the purchase price of the property in question.

It appears that approximately one year after the execution of the original note and mortgage the appellant and her husband made a payment to the appellee of $400 on principal and a renewal note for $1,600, due in one year from date, was executed. This note was signed by both husband and wife. Approximately one year later appellant and her husband paid $200 on principal and executed a renewal note in the amount of $1,400, due one year later. This note was also signed by both husband and wife. Some six months later a payment of $1,000 was paid on principal which was noted on the $1,400 note, leaving a balance of $400. Upon the arrival of the due date of this second renewal note, another renewal note was given to appellee to secure the $400 indebtedness then outstanding. This note was not submitted into evidence, however, the president of the appellee bank testified that it was executed by both husband and wife. Upon the due date of this third renewal note a payment of $300 was made leaving an outstanding balance of $100, and the appellant's husband executed a renewal note for $100 due one year from date. The appellant did not sign this note. Approximately one month later the appellant's husband executed a note for $2,000, payable one year from date. The appellee advanced the appellant's husband $1,900 in cash and applied $100 to the last note executed by appellant's husband. The appellant did not sign this note. Approximately one year later the appellant's husband paid $1,000 on principal on the last mentioned note and executed a renewal note for $1,000. The appellant's husband died before the due date of the last note.

Each of the renewal notes mentioned above were marked "Ext. Mtge. Real Estate." The appellee bank retained possession of the original note and mortgage throughout these transactions.

The appellant's bill for a declaratory judgment alleges in part that she was under opinion and impression that the mortgage on the property had been paid in full; that the appellee was claiming the sum of $1,000 due on the mortgage; that the basis of said claim was an advance or extension given her husband secured by a note which she did not sign; that she had no knowledge of such transaction prior to her notification by the appellee that it was claiming under an extension of said mortgage; that she had not executed any instrument extending the mortgage on the homestead; and that said transaction was done without her knowledge. The prayer for relief asked that the lower court declare that the transaction between her husband and the appellee bank be declared not an extension of the mortgage on the homestead; that the original mortgage had been satisfied prior to the advancement in question which was made to her husband; and that any indebtedness is against her husband's estate and is not an indebtedness secured by the mortgage referred to in these proceedings.

The trial court found that the advance of $1,900 made by the appellee bank to appellant's husband on a note executed by him alone was and is secured by the mortgage executed by appellant and her husband on October 5, 1956; that the original indebtedness secured had not been paid in full at the time of the said advance of $1,900, the sum of $100 remaining unpaid; and that there was now due appellee bank the sum of $1,000 plus interest, which indebtedness was then in default.

The appellant has argued six assignments of error.

Assignment of error No. 1 is based upon the trial court's holding that the original mortgage was a purchase-money mortgage and therefore superior to any homestead rights of the appellant.

The appellant insists that a purchase-money mortgage can only be given to a vendor as a substitute for his vendor's lien and therefore a mortgage given to a third party, who advances the purchase price to the vendee, cannot be a purchase-money mortgage as the third party has no vendor's lien for which a mortgage can be substituted.

The fact that a mortgage is made to a person other than the vendor does not alone prevent its being a purchase-money mortgage. A mortgage on land executed to secure the purchase money by a purchaser of the land executed contemporaneously with the acquisition of the legal title thereto, or afterward, but as a part of the same transaction, is a purchase-money mortgage. 36 Am.Jur., Mortgages, Section 15; 59 C.J.S. Mortgages § 168; *Lipps v. Lipps,* (Ohio App.), 87 N.E.2d 823, 827; *Hill v. Hill,* 185 Kan. 389, 345 P.2d 1015; *Wermes v. McCowan,* 286 Ill. App. 381, 3 N.E.2d 720. In the case of *Birmingham Building & Loan Association v. Boggs,* 116 Ala. 587, 22 So. 852, it was held that a mortgage given to a party, other than the vendor, who loaned money to the vendee to be applied to the purchase price as part of one transaction, was superior to a mechanic's or material-man's lien. In *Russell v. Stockton,* 199 Ala. 48, 74 So. 225, the mortgagee who advanced part of the purchase price was held to have a lien superior to the vendor's lien where that was found to be the intention of the parties. In *Cates v. White,* 252 Ala. 422, 41 So.2d 401, a mortgage given to a party, other than the vendor, who advanced the purchase price, was held to be a purchase-money mortgage given contemporaneously with the purchase and to be superior to a homestead exemption claim.

Section 627, Title 7, Code of Alabama 1940, provides in part that the provisions of the chapter containing such section do not prevent any lien attaching to the homestead in favor of "any vendor for unpaid purchase money, or so as to affect any deed, mortgage, or lien on such homestead, lawfully executed or created."

It is apparent therefore that a lien secured by a mortgage which is lawfully executed or created is superior to a claim of homestead exemption. The constitutional and statutory provisions, requiring separate voluntary acknowledgment by the wife, are for the benefit of the wife. *Leonard v. Whitman,* 249 Ala. 205, 30 So.2d 241. The purpose of the statutory provision requiring voluntary signature and assent is to safeguard the wife from duress of the husband. *Weatherwax v. Heflin,* 244 Ala. 210, 12 So.2d 554.

Even if this mortgage had not been executed to secure the mortgagee's advancement of part of the purchase price and contemporaneously with the purchase of the property in question, the appellant fails to demonstrate why, considering the terms of this mortgage, this encumbrance would not be superior to her claim of homestead exemption in as much as it appears she voluntarily signed the original note and mortgage. Assignment of error No. 1 is without merit.

. . . .

The evidence was ample to support the finding and conclusions of the court below, and the legal principles above set forth dispose in substance of these last two assignments.

Affirmed.

Livingston, C. J., and Simpson and Merrill, JJ., concur.

C. SUBORDINATION AND RELEASE

Subordination of one's mortgage allows a mortgagee to achieve a position of seniority to which the document involved would not otherwise be entitled. One court said: "[T]o subordinate is to lose position — to give up a better for a worse status." [6] A frequent reason for the use of subordination is to purchase unimproved land for development when the purchase price is paid partially, if not entirely, in the form of a note. The motivation to a seller is probably found

---

[6] Connell v. Zaid, 268 Cal. App. 2d 788, 792 (1969).

in an inflated price, a desire to share in the profits of the development, or simply wanting to be rid of a parcel that has been difficult to sell. While not always the case, it is not unusual to find low down payments coupled with the subordination agreement. The potential for abuse by the vendee is obvious to the sophisticated vendor, but in cases where agricultural land has become developable and *ad valorem* taxes have forced the property into the marketplace, a vendor may be susceptible to entering into a subordination agreement. Problems, usually in the form of reluctance to proceed, can arise at any stage of the transaction: when the marketing contract has been signed but the transaction has not yet closed; after the closing but before the vendor is requested to make the subordination agreement effective; or, after the entire transaction has been completed and the vendor is not satisfied with the results.

HILL, SUBORDINATION AGREEMENTS AND RELEASE CLAUSES in J. HETLAND, CALIFORNIA REAL ESTATE SECURED TRANSACTIONS 203, 205-06 (1970)*

In real property transactions [a subordination agreement] often occurs when a developer purchases raw land, giving back a purchase-money deed of trust to the seller, and thereafter having to give a first lien to a construction lender to obtain funds for development. The vendor is requested to accept as a portion, if not all, of the purchase price a note from the purchaser secured by a deed of trust on the property. This arrangement allows the purchaser to finance only the price of the unimproved land. In order to finance the improvements (including cost of preparation for construction of improvements such as engineering studies, subdivision maps, and surveys) and to finance off-site improvements (e.g., curbs, gutters, streets), the purchaser-developer must obtain third party financing.

As long as the purchase-money deed of trust held by the vendor is in existence, it will be senior to a subsequently acquired construction loan, unless the purchaser and vendor enter into a subordination agreement. Because most institutional lenders are not allowed to make loans that are secured by other than a first deed of trust (and those legally able usually will not), a subordination agreement becomes necessary for the development of the property. . . .

Once an institutional loan is made, all funds disbursed, and the vendor's purchase-money lien subordinated to junior status, the property may be overencumbered. The usual inducement to the vendor to enter into such an arrangement is a higher purchase price than could be obtained for cash. The rationalization for participating in a plan that makes the vendor a quasi-joint-venturer with the developer is that the property, once developed, will increase in value, making the security adequate protection for both the senior construction loan and the vendor's junior purchase-money lien.

Subordination agreements arise in each of the following situations:

(1) The executory agreement (as in the contract to sell), before any conveyance;

(2) The fully executed agreement, after conveyance and recordation of both the junior and the senior encumbrances and complete disbursement of funds under the advanced loan; and

---

* Reprinted by permission of John R. Hetland and the University of California.

(3) The partially executory agreement, after conveyance and recordation of the purchase-money deed of trust but before recordation of the subsequent encumbrance to which the vendor has agreed to subordinate his interest.

Less common than the typical subordination situation that arises in purchase and sale of property is subordination of a lessor's fee interest to the lessee, in order to allow the lessee to obtain financing for improvements on the property.

1. SPECIFICITY AND FAIRNESS

HANDY v. GORDON

Supreme Court of California
65 Cal. 2d 578, 422 P.2d 329 (1967)

TRAYNOR, CHIEF JUSTICE.

Plaintiff appeals from a judgment for defendants entered after the trial court granted a motion for judgment on the pleadings. Plaintiff contends that his complaint states a cause of action for specific performance of a contract to sell land and that therefore the trial court erred in granting the defendants' motion. (See *MacIsaac v. Pozzo* (1945) 26 Cal.2d 809, 815-816, 161 P.2d 449.)

The complaint alleges that on January 21, 1964, the parties entered into a written contract in which defendants agreed to sell certain real property to plaintiff. The contract was set forth in escrow instructions that described the property as approximately 320 acres known as the Gordon Ranch and excepted about three acres that included the sellers' home. The purchase price was $1,500,100. The instructions stated that $300,000 was paid to the sellers outside of escrow and that an additional $100 was deposited with the escrow company. The buyer agreed to execute a note secured by a deed of trust for the balance of $1,200,000 plus interest of 2 percent per year. The note was to be paid in annual installments of $120,000 or more beginning three years after the close of the escrow, and any unpaid balance was to become due 10 years after the escrow closed. The sellers agreed to subordinate their trust deed to other trust deeds securing loans to be obtained by the buyer for construction and permanent financing.

The buyer was given the right to obtain a zoning modification and to withdraw from the contract if he did not approve geological, engineering, and zoning reports. At the close of the escrow the legal description was to be approved by the parties and was to show title vested in plaintiff C. Jon Handy or nominee.

The complaint alleged that the recital of the $300,000 payment was a sham and was included in the instructions at the sellers' request to win a bet. The true consideration was $1,200,100, which plaintiff alleged was fair and reasonable and was substantially higher than the prices at which comparable property in the locality was selling.

After defendants sought to rescind the contract on April 2, 1964, plaintiff brought this action for specific performance. The court granted the defendants' motion for a judgment on the pleadings on the ground that the agreement was too uncertain to be enforced because the subordination clause lacked essential terms.

Plaintiff contends that the trial court erred in holding that the subordination clause lacked essential terms. He points out that the clause specified that the construction and financing loans should be in the maximum amounts of $10,000 and $52,000 per lot, should have maximum interest rates of 7 percent and 6.6

percent, and should mature in not more than 6 and 35 years respectively. Although the contract does not specify the number of lots into which the land is to be divided, plaintiff contends that the number of lots was not left to future agreement of the parties but was properly left to his discretion as the developer of the contemplated subdivision. No problem of indefiniteness is presented under plaintiff's view of the contract. It sets forth all the terms defendants deemed essential to protect their interests and leaves to the business judgment and good faith of plaintiff the working out with lenders, builders, and home buyers of the details to make the venture a success.

Defendants contend that whether or not the trial court erred in finding that the contract is too indefinite to enforce, its ruling must be sustained on the ground that it appears from the complaint as a matter of law that the contract "is not, as to [them], just as reasonable." (Civ.Code, § 3391, subd. 2.) We agree with defendants' contention.

Although the parties to a contract of sale containing a subordination clause may delegate to the vendee or third party lenders power to determine the details of subordinating loans, an enforceable subordination clause must contain terms that will define and minimize the risk that the subordinating liens will impair or destroy the seller's security. (*Stockwell v. Lindeman,* 229 Cal.App.2d 750, 758, 40 Cal.Rptr. 555; *Magna Development Co. v. Reed,* 228 Cal.App.2d 230, 236, 39 Cal.Rptr. 284; *Burrow v. Timmsen,* 223 Cal.App.2d 283, 289-290, 35 Cal.Rptr. 668, 100 A.L.R.2d 544; *Roven v. Miller,* 168 Cal.App.2d 391, 398, 335 P.2d 1035.) Such terms may include limits on the use to which the proceeds may be put to insure that their use will improve the value of the land, maximum amounts so that the loans will not exceed the contemplated value of the improvements they finance, requirements that the loans do not exceed some specified percentage of the construction costs or value of the property as improved, specified amounts per square foot of construction, or other limits designed to protect the security. Without some such terms, however, the seller is forced to rely entirely on the buyer's good faith and ability as a developer to insure that he will not lose both his land and the purchase price. Even if we were to assume that a contract of sale contemplating subdivision by the vendee is sufficiently different from the usual land sale contract to take it out of the operation of the antideficiency legislation (Code Civ.Proc. § 580b; see Hetland, Real Property, 53 Cal.L.Rev. 151, 161-162), the personal liability alone of the vendee would not constitute sufficient protection to the vendor to permit specific performance. (Civ.Code, § 3391, subd. 2; *Klein v. Markarin,* 175 Cal. 37, 41, 165 P. 3; *Quan v. Kraseman,* 84 Cal.App.2d 550, 551, 191 P.2d 16; see Rest., Contracts, § 373.)

The contract alleged in the complaint does not afford defendants any additional protection. Although the proceeds of the subordinating loans are to be used primarily for construction and refinancing, any funds that are not needed for these purposes may be disbursed to plaintiff. The absence of restrictions on plaintiff's use of these funds leaves defendants without assurance that all of the proceeds of the loans will be used to improve the land that represents their security. Because the limits on the loans are expressed as absolutes, they provide no assurance that the amounts of the loans will not exceed the value the improvements add to the security. Moreover, the limits are maximums per lot, and plaintiff has unrestricted discretion in determining the size of each lot. Thus defendants are not assured that the total amount of the subordinating loans will be kept low enough to enable them to protect themselves by bidding on the property if the senior liens are foreclosed. Finally defendants did not receive a down payment that would effectively cushion their position, and the first payment of principal is deferred until three years after the close of escrow.

Thus, the contract leaves defendants with nothing but plaintiff's good faith and business judgment to insure them that they will ever receive anything for conveying their land. Such a contract is not as to them "just and reasonable" within the meaning of Civil Code, section 3391.

The judgment is affirmed.

McCOMBS, PETERS, TOBRINER, MOSK, BURKE & SULLIVAN JJ. concur.

RIVERS v. RICE

Supreme Court of Georgia
283 Ga. 819, 213 S.E.2d 678 (1975)

JORDAN, JUSTICE.

Mrs. Eugene Clark Rivers appeals from the denial of an interlocutory injunction and the vacating of a temporary restraining order.

On January 30, 1970, Mrs. Rivers sold certain real property to Davro, Inc., for $65,000, and Davro executed a note and security deed to Mrs. Rivers. This security deed recited that: "Grantee [Mrs. Rivers] herein agrees to subordinate all of her rights, title, interests and claims herein and hereunder, to any security deed hereafter given by grantor herein (or its successors in title or assigns) to any bank, savings and loan association, insurance company, or real estate investment trust, for the purpose of grantor herein (or its successors in title or assigns) to make a construction loan and/or a permanent loan; such construction loan and/or permanent loan shall be on such terms and in such amounts as the lender and borrower shall agree upon; provided, however, that grantee herein will subordinate to only one such prior lender at any one time. Grantee will execute a subordination agreement in accordance with the form agreed to by the parties hereto in writing this date."

On December 3, 1970, Robert F. Rice and David F. Rice assumed the indebtedness of Davro, and Mrs. Rivers executed a subordination agreement consenting that her security deed be subordinated to a security deed to be executed by the Rices to Great American Mortgage Investors to secure a loan of $647,000. The consideration of this agreement was recited as $1.00 and the consummation of the described loan in reliance upon the agreement.

On September 27, 1971, Mrs. Rivers executed a "Modification of Subordination Agreement," which recited that: On December 3, 1970, she agreed to subordinate her interest in property described in a security deed from the Rices to Great American, securing an indebtedness of $647,000, to the interest of Great American; since the execution of such document, the Rices have received a commitment from Scott Hudgens Realty and Mortgage, Inc., to make a permanent loan of $750,000, such commitment being based upon a similar commitment to Scott Hudgens from Midwest Federal Savings and Loan Association; and in reliance on such commitment, Great American has agreed to advance an additional $103,000 to the Rices, provided Mrs. Rivers agrees to subordinate to such additional amount. In consideration of $1.00, the consummation of the modification of the former loan, and the making of a permanent loan by either Scott Hudgens or Midwest, Mrs. Rivers waived and subordinated her rights in her security deed as against the temporary and permanent loan in the amount of $750,000.

On January 3, 1972, Mrs. Rivers executed another subordination agreement which recited the Davro security deed in her favor; and that the Rices have succeeded to the interest of Davro in the property and have applied for a loan from Scott Hudgens. In consideration of $1.00 and the consummation of the loan from Scott Hudgens, Mrs. Rivers subordinated her security deed as against the loan to be made by Scott Hudgens, and agreed that the subordination would operate to the benefit of the successors and assigns of Scott Hudgens, including, but not limited to, Midwest Federal Savings & Loan Association of Minneapolis.

On January 20, 1972, the Rices executed a security deed to Scott Hudgens to secure an indebtedness of $750,000, and this deed was transferred and assigned to Midwest.

On January 24, 1972, the security deed from the Rices to Great American was canceled of record.

Thereafter the Rices defaulted on their obligations under the security deed assigned to Midwest. Midwest advertised the property for sale as a first lien holder.

Mrs. Rivers then filed suit seeking to enjoin the sale of the realty unless notice was given to all prospective purchasers of her senior and superior lien thereon. The matter was submitted at the interlocutory hearing on the pleadings and documentary evidence. The trial court denied the interlocutory injunction and vacated the temporary restraining order, from which order Mrs. Rivers filed this appeal.

This question presented is whether Mrs. Rivers' first security deed was subordinated to the second security deed of Midwest Federal Savings and Loan Association which Midwest was attempting to foreclose.

Counsel for Mrs. Rivers have separately analyzed the three subordination agreements executed by her and pointed out defects and discrepancies in these agreements. Counsel argues that none of the agreements constitute a valid and enforceable contract by Mrs. Rivers to subordinate her security deed to the later security deed of Midwest, under the requirements of Code § 20-107.

In order to determine the intention of the parties we must construe together the obligation of Mrs. Rivers in her security deed to subordinate her lien to the subsequent maker of a construction or permanent loan and the three subordination agreements she executed.

Despite the defects and discrepancies pointed out by counsel for Mrs. Rivers, it is obvious that the three subordination agreements executed by her were intended to fulfill her obligation in her security deed to waive her prior lien in favor of the maker of a construction or permanent loan.

It is not necessary that an agreement to subordinate a security deed to a construction or permanent loan for the improvement of the property set forth with particularity the terms of the loan. *Ideal Realty Co. v. Reese,* 122 Ga.App. 707(1d), 178 S.E.2d 564.

Construing the subordination agreements together, it is plain that Mrs. Rivers agreed to subordinate her lien to the lien of Midwest, and this constituted the essential "terms of the contract" under Code § 20-107.

There was sufficient consideration for the subordination agreement. In *Mitchell·v. West End Park Co.,* 171 Ga. 878(1b), 156 S.E. 888, it was held: "A senior grantee in a security deed has an unquestionable right to waive his priority of lien thereunder in favor of a junior security deed. Such senior grantee may waive his lien in favor of a person who advances money to the vendor therein to enable him to improve the property thereby conveyed, the enhanced value of the property being sufficient consideration to sustain such waiver."

The trial judge was authorized to find that Mrs. Rivers had subordinated her lien to that of Midwest by valid contracts, and did not err in refusing to enjoin Midwest from proceeding with the foreclosure of its security deed.

Judgment affirmed.

All the Justices concur.

NOTES

1. *Handy v. Gordon, supra,* was very much a landmark decision. The California courts had vacillated for a decade and a half between enforceability and unenforceability. Several earlier cases held that a subordination agreement was material to the essence of the contract and thus if unenforceable invalidated the entire agreement. *Magna Development Co. v. Reed,* 228 Cal. App. 2d 230 (1964); *Conley v. Fate,* 227 Cal. App. 2d 418 (1964); *Kessler v. Sapp,* 169 Cal. App. 2d 818 (1959); *Roven v. Miller,* 168 Cal. App. 2d 391, 335 P.2d 1035 (1959); *Gould v. Callan,* 127 Cal. App. 2d 1, 273 P.2d 93 (1954). However, these cases were followed by a series of cases in which the subordination agreement failed to include some terms and conditions which would appear to render it sufficiently vague to be unenforceable. The California courts held the agreements enforceable notwithstanding this apparent vagueness. *Simmons v. Dryer,* 216 Cal. App. 2d 733 (1963); *Stockwell v. Lindeman,* 229 Cal. App. 2d 750 (1964); *Cummins v. Gates,* 235 Cal. App. 2d 532 (1965).

2. Since *Handy v. Gordon, supra,* the California courts have continued to hold unfairness as a basis for unenforceability in an executory subordination agreement, whether the unfairness arose from the vendor's lack of sophistication due to age (an eighty-year-old vendor) in *Loeb v. Wilson,* 253 Cal. App. 2d 383 (1967); or lack of communication (non-English speaking vendor) in *Butcher v. Dauz,* 57 Cal. App. 2d 524 (1967). Lack of specificity likewise continues to be a basis for refusing to enforce a subordination agreement which lacks essential terms. The ultimate in vagueness can be found in an agreement which stated only: "Seller to subordinate to a Construction Loan." *Krasley v. Superior Court,* 101 Cal. App. 3d 425 (1980).

2. SUBORDINATION: EFFECT ON INTERVENING LIENS

OLD STONE MORTGAGE & REALTY TRUST v. NEW GEORGIA PLUMBING, INC.

Court of Appeals of Georgia
140 Ga. App. 686, 231 S.E.2d 785 (1976)

CLARK, JUDGE.

The principal question presented for decision in this appeal is whether plaintiff's materialman's lien is entitled to priority over the deeds to secure debt of certain lenders.

In November, 1971, Accent Development Corporation ("Owner") borrowed $270,000 from two of its stockholders, First American Investment Corporation and Fidelity Capital Corporation ("Seed Lenders"), to acquire nine acres of land in Dekalb County, Georgia. As security for the loan, Owner gave a debt deed to Seed Lenders. This instrument was recorded on November 18, 1971. Thereafter, Cousins Mortgage and Equity Investments, a real estate investment trust, lent Owner $1,900,000 to finance the construction of an apartment complex on the newly acquired property.

On November 14, 1972, the plaintiff, New Georgia Plumbing, Inc., entered into a contract with Accent Construction Company, Inc., the general contractor, to install plumbing for the apartments.

Plaintiff fulfilled its obligations under the contract in late October or early November of 1973. Shortly thereafter, Owner borrowed $1,920,000 from Investment Mortgage Company ("Permanent Lender") to pay off the construction loan obtained from Cousins Mortgage and Equity Investments. A deed to secure debt was given to Permanent Lender by Owner as security. Before making the loan, Permanent Lender required Seed Lender to subordinate the prior deed to secure debt to Permanent Lender's security deed. Accordingly, Seed Lender executed a subordination agreement in favor of Permanent Lender. Permanent Lender's deed to secure debt and the subordination agreement were recorded on November 19, 1973. Thereafter, the deed to secure debt was transferred to Old Stone Mortgage & Realty Trust which, in turn, transferred it to Old Stone Bank.

Prior to closing the permanent loan, Seed Lenders and Permanent Lender had actual knowledge that plaintiff was the plumbing subcontractor for the apartment project and that plaintiff claimed money was due it for work performed and materials furnished. Moreover, Seed Lenders and Permanent Lender knew that Owner had been facing large construction cost overruns.

On December 17, 1973, plaintiff recorded its claim of lien. Thereafter, on October 18, 1974, plaintiff brought suit against Contractor to recover the amount of its claim and on December 11, 1974, obtained judgment thereon by default.

On December 3, 1974, Seed Lenders foreclosed on the property in question pursuant to the first security deed. The property was sold to Seed Lenders subject to Permanent Lender's deed to secure debt to which the foreclosed loan deed had been subordinated by agreement between the two security deed grantees.

On November 27, 1974, plaintiff brought this action against Owner, Contractor, Permanent Lender, Seed Lenders, Old Stone Mortgage & Realty Trust, Old Stone Bank, Cousins Mortgage Equity and Investments, Pioneer National Title Insurance Company and William R. Nelson, a principal stockholder in Accent Development Corporation. The complaint was couched in five counts. Count one demanded the sum of $67,154.73 against defendants, jointly and severally, for work performed and material furnished by plaintiff. Counts two and five pursued remedies for alleged fraudulent conduct. Counts three and four sought the foreclosure of plaintiff's materialman's lien and a declaration that its lien is entitled to priority over the deeds to secure debt which had been granted to Seed Lenders and Permanent Lender.

Following discovery, plaintiff moved for summary judgment. Five of the nine defendants, Seed Lenders, Old Stone Mortgage & Realty Trust, Old Stone Bank, and Pioneer National Title Insurance Company also moved for summary judgment. The trial court granted plaintiff's motion with regard to counts three and four of the complaint and denied the motions of defendants. The court ruled that plaintiff's materialmen's lien is entitled to priority over the deeds to secure debt of the lenders. This appeal followed.

1. A contractor's lien attaches from the time work is commenced or material is furnished under the contract. *Guaranty Investment and Loan Co. v. Athens Engineering Co.,* 152 Ga. 596, 598(6), 110 S.E. 873; *Loudon v. Blandford & Garrard,* 56 Ga. 150, 154(5). "The record of the lien ... within three months from the date when the material was furnished, and the institution of a suit within one year from that date, merely preserve the lien and the right to establish it against the property." *Davis v. Stone,* 48 Ga.App. 532, 533, 173 S.E. 454. Thus, where title to real property is conveyed to a lender by a duly recorded deed to secure debt, and the lender takes the deed with actual notice of a materialman's

claim of lien upon the property, the title acquired by the lender is inferior to the lien, provided that the lien is subsequently perfected within the time prescribed by law. *Oglethorpe Savings & Trust Co. v. Morgan,* 149 Ga. 787, 102 S.E. 528; *Picklesimer v. Smith,* 164 Ga. 600, 139 S.E. 72. Inasmuch as Permanent Lender had actual knowledge of plaintiff's claim of lien prior to taking the deed to secure debt, the lien is entitled to priority over the security instrument, provided it was properly preserved.

Was plaintiff's materialman's lien properly preserved? In order to preserve a materialman's lien, it is essential to show that (1) the plaintiff completed his contract, (2) the plaintiff filed for record his claim of lien within three months after completion of the contract, and (3) the plaintiff brought suit to recover the amount of his claim within 12 months after the debt became due. Code § 67-2002.

The evidence shows that plaintiff completed the contract in late October or early November of 1973. Plaintiff's president testified that plaintiff was working on the project as of October 26, 1973. Plaintiff filed for record its claim of lien on December 17, 1973 and commenced suit to recover the amount of its claim on October 18, 1974. Clearly, plaintiff took the necessary steps to preserve and enforce its lien within the time limitations prescribed by the statute.

Defendants point out that plaintiff billed Contractor in August of 1973 for the balance due under the contract and that plaintiff did not bring this action against Owner until November 27, 1974. Thus, defendants argue, a genuine issue of fact exists as to whether plaintiff timely perfected its lien. We disagree.

That plaintiff billed the Contractor in August cannot alter the fact that the debt became due when the last materials were furnished, and labor was performed, under the contract. *Dixie Lime & Stone Company v. Ryder Truck Rental, Inc.,* 140 Ga.App. 188, 230 S.E.2d 322. Moreover, plaintiff was not required to commence suit against Owner within the time specified in Code § 67-2002(3). Under the circumstances of this case, plaintiff was only required to bring timely suit against Contractor for the amount of his claim. *Lombard v. Trustees, Etc.,* 73 Ga. 322; *Jordan Co. v. Adkins,* 105 Ga.App. 157, 123 S.E.2d 731. The record shows that plaintiff commenced suit against the Contractor within twelve months after the "debt became due." *Dixie Lime & Stone Co. v. Ryder Truck Rental, Inc.,* supra.

2. Is plaintiff's materialman's lien entitled to priority over the security deed which Owner gave to Seed Lenders?

While the issue has not heretofore been decided in Georgia, it is the rule in other jurisdictions that "One who subordinates a first lien to a third lien makes his lien inferior to both the second and the third liens." 51 Am.Jur.2d Liens, § 55; *Ladner v. Hogue Lumber & Supply Co.,* 229 Miss. 505, 91 So.2d 545. Thus, where a first mortgagee subordinated his interest to a second mortgagee, the prior mortgage was necessarily inferior to an intervening materialman's lien: "It cannot be questioned that things equal to the same thing are equal to each other, and it is equally true that if B is inferior to A and C is inferior to B, C is also necessarily inferior to A." *Dunlop v. Teagle,* 101 Fla. 721, 135 So. 132, 134 (1931). This rule is especially applicable where, as here, the grantees of the prior security deed had actual knowledge of the intervening materialman's claim of lien and impliedly consent to the improvement of the real estate. See also *Williams v. Brewton,* 170 Ga. 164, 152 S.E. 441.

Permanent Lender's deed to secure debt is inferior to plaintiff's materialman's lien. In view of the subordination agreement, Seed Lenders' deed to secure debt is inferior to Permanent Lender's deed to secure debt. Accordingly, Seed

Lenders' deed to secure debt is necessarily inferior to plaintiff's materialman's lien.

3. Defendants assert plaintiff's claim of lien was dissolved by an affidavit from owner which stated that outstanding bills for labor and materials had been paid. This assertion is not meritorious. "There is no provision of law for one who improves real estate while the legal title or its equivalent is in him to relieve another from a lien on the property by the making of an affidavit as is authorized under Code Ann. § 67-2001(2)." *Builders Supply Co., Inc. v. Thomas,* 118 Ga.App. 830(1a), 166 S.E.2d 33. Thus, the sworn statement of an owner that "the agreed price or reasonable value of work done has been paid" cannot dissolve a materialman's lien.

4. Since plaintiff's materialman's lien is entitled to priority over the deeds to secure debt of Permanent Lender and Seed Lenders, the trial court did not err in granting partial summary judgment to plaintiff and in denying the defendants' motions for summary judgment.

Judgment affirmed.

BELL, C.J., and STOLZ, J., concur.

NATIONAL BANK v. EQUITY INVESTORS

Supreme Court of Washington
83 Wash. 2d 435, 518 P.2d 1072 (1974)

HUNTER, ASSOCIATE JUSTICE.

This is a second review by this court on the issue of lien priorities of various parties resulting from the construction of an apartment complex. Our disposition of the first appeal was in *National Bank of Washington v. Equity Investors,* 81 Wash. 2d 886, 506 P.2d 20 (1973). We again state the facts for a more complete understanding of the background of the second appeal.

In 1968 a group of four Boeing Company engineers, hereinafter referred to as the "MacDonald group" or "MacDonald," owned two parcels of land in south Seattle and set in motion a scheme for the construction of a large apartment complex. They obtained some initial capital backing, and eventually signed a real estate contract to sell the two parcels to a developer, Equity Investors, on December 30, 1968.

Shortly thereafter, a construction loan was obtained from the respondent, National Bank of Washington, hereinafter referred to as the "Bank." The Bank's construction loan was secured by a deed of trust recorded on May 19, 1969. At this point, the parties to the real estate contract decided that the contract for sale should be terminated, and the property passed to Equity Investors subject to a deed of trust designating MacDonald as beneficiary. MacDonald's deed of trust was recorded on May 15, 1969, but in order to facilitate the loan for Equity Investors from the Bank, MacDonald agreed that its otherwise prior interest would be subordinated to the security interest of the Bank. On May 26, 1969, the petitioner, Columbia Wood Products, Inc., hereinafter referred to as "Columbia," commenced delivering lumber to the construction project. Its materialman's lien was thereafter duly perfected.

As construction on the project progressed, it became clear to the parties that the construction loan by the Bank would be insufficient to complete the project due to substantial cost overruns. Consequently, lien foreclosure suits resulted, and the cases were consolidated for trial in the Superior Court for King County. The three cases with which we are concerned in this second review involved the following: foreclosure of the deed of trust lien by the Bank, the construction lender; foreclosure of the purchase money deed of trust of the MacDonald group, which deed of trust lien had been subordinated by agreement to the deed of trust lien of the Bank; and the foreclosure of the materialman's lien of Columbia.

On October 22, 1971, the trial court determined the lien priorities of the three parties, among others, to be as follows: First, the deed of trust lien of the Bank securing the construction loan; second, the deed of trust lien of MacDonald, securing the balance of the purchase price of property; and third, the materialman's lien of Columbia, which waived its right to foreclose at the trial after the trial court's determination that its lien was inferior to the Bank and MacDonald.

After the judgment was entered by the trial court on October 22, 1971, a number of parties, including the petitioner Columbia, appealed to this court. In its appeal, Columbia assigned error to the priority of the Bank lien, but did not assign error to the priority of the MacDonald lien. On that appeal Columbia contended that notwithstanding the fact that the Bank had duly recorded its deed of trust lien prior to the time that Columbia commenced to deliver materials, its materialman's lien attached as of May 26, 1969, and was superior to the lien of the Bank for all advances made after that date. It argued that under the Bank's loan agreement with the developer, advances made by the Bank were voluntary or optional and the lien for same attached as of the date of the advance instead of the date of the recording of the deed of trust. We agreed with the reasoning of Columbia in our decision in *National Bank of Washington v. Equity Investors, supra,* where we stated on page 927, 506 P.2d on page 44:

> In conclusion, then, and to summarize: We find that advances by the bank under its construction loan agreement with Equity Investors were optional in law rather than obligatory, and hold that Columbia Wood Products' materialman's lien is superior to the bank's lien for later advances and, accordingly, reverse.

A petition for rehearing filed by the Bank was denied on June 14, 1973, and this court sent the remittitur to the Superior Court for King County.

Shortly thereafter, the petitioner Columbia filed a motion with the trial court for an award of attorneys' fees and entry of judgment in its favor against the Bank. The Bank moved for a denial of Columbia's motion and for the setting of a trial on a number of issues involved in Columbia's claim, other than the issue of lien priority determined by this court in the first appeal. Columbia filed an additional motion asking the court to enforce a lien on funds held by the Bank in the amount of its judgment, or in the alternative to vacate the foreclosure sale held on February 18, 1972, where the Bank and General Mortgage Investments were the successful bidders for the sum of $1,883,712.33. At a hearing held on July 2, 1973, where all parties were represented except the respondent MacDonald, the trial court rendered an oral decision denying the Bank's motion and determined that Columbia was entitled to recover the amount of its judgment claim from the proceeds of the foreclosure sale. The matter was continued to July 12, 1973, for the purpose of determining the amount of attorneys' fees to be allowed Columbia.

Subsequently, the respondent MacDonald filed a motion with the trial court asking it to enter a judgment giving to MacDonald an amount equal to its judgment on foreclosure *prior* to the judgment claim by Columbia. On July 12, 1973, the trial court ruled that after the payment of the earlier advances to the Bank, MacDonald was entitled to be paid the first proceeds of the foreclosure sale in an amount equal to the MacDonald claim; next, Columbia was to receive an amount equal to its claim, less the amount to be paid to MacDonald; and the Bank was to receive the remaining sale proceeds. In addition, the trial court ruled that Columbia was entitled to an award of attorneys' fees in the sum of $4,410.17 for the original trial, $10,000 for the first appeal, and $10,000 in the event of a further appeal. Columbia's failure to assign error to the priority of the MacDonald lien in the first appeal was evidently controlling in the trial court's decision.

On August 22, 1973, the trial court entered findings of fact and conclusions of law with respect to its oral decisions, and entered an order denying the Bank's motion for a trial on issues relating to Columbia's lien. On August 23, 1973, Columbia made application with this court for a writ of prohibition and stay of proceedings, contending that the distribution of the proceeds by the trial court was contrary to a fair interpretation of the Supreme Court's opinion in the earlier appeal. In response, this court entered a stay order and the petitioner Columbia posted a bond in the amount of $10,000 to protect MacDonald from damages that it might suffer by reason of the stay. On September 13, 1973, the trial court entered a partial judgment on remand and order pursuant to the first Supreme Court opinion.

Columbia contends that the trial court failed to carry out the directions of this court in the decision of this case on the first appeal by determining that MacDonald rather than Columbia was entitled to the first proceeds of the foreclosure sale. MacDonald, on the other hand, . . . contends that Columbia's failure to appeal the trial court's ruling in the first trial, that MacDonald was prior to Columbia in lien priorities, now prevents Columbia from asserting priority over the MacDonald group. MacDonald submits that the decision of this court placing Columbia ahead of the Bank in participating in the foreclosure sale proceeds did not affect MacDonald's priority as to Columbia. We must agree with the contention made by Columbia.

To untangle this web, we first examine the subordination agreement between MacDonald and the Bank. The pertinent language provides:

> In consideration of benefits to "subordinator" from "owner" receipt and sufficiency of which hereby acknowledged, and to induce "lender" to advance funds under its mortgage and all agreements in connection therewith, the "subordinator" does hereby unconditionally subordinate the lien of his mortgage identified in Paragraph 1 above to the lien of "lender's" mortgage, identified in Paragraph 2 above, and all advances or charges made or accruing thereunder, including any extension or renewal thereof.

This language is unconditional, broad and comprehensive. There is no way that MacDonald, by this subordination agreement, can be placed in a more favorable position than the Bank in the sharing of the proceeds of the foreclosure sale. Furthermore, MacDonald is bound by the result of any determination by the Bank in the exercise of its option to pay the materialman, as the loan advancements are made.

Had the Bank determined to pay Columbia for the materials as they were furnished, it would have resulted in MacDonald becoming inferior to Columbia in the payment of its lien claim, to which it would have been bound under its subordination agreement. By the same token, the Bank's bypassing of Columbia for payment of materials as they were furnished, resulting in our placing Columbia ahead of the Bank because of its unjust enrichment, again results in Columbia coming ahead of MacDonald as a result of the Bank's action, to which MacDonald is bound under its subordination agreement. The basis upon which we directed Columbia to share in the foreclosure proceeds ahead of the Bank is stated on pages 899-900 of our opinion, 506 P.2d on pages 29, 30:

> Thus, we are adhering to what we perceive to be the weight of authority embodied in the rule that, where the advances of promised loan moneys are, under an agreement to lend money, largely optional, that is, where the time and the amount of the moneys to be advanced are largely discretionary in the lender, the legal effect of such provisions is to bring the transaction under the rule for optional advances rather than the rule governing mandatory advances for the purpose of determining lien priorities. Optional advances under a construction loan agreement attach when the advances are actually made. Any liens attaching prior to an optional advance would thus be superior to it, and attaching afterwards, junior to it. . . .
>
> A contrary rule on that point would allow a lender, having power to allocate the loan moneys in such a way as to insure that those whose work, materials and efforts serve to enhance the value of the security, to sit idly by and watch his security grow, while at the same time potentially leaving the materialmen, subcontractors and workmen in the position of doing their work and supplying materials for little or nothing. The rule here contended for by lender would lead to an inevitable unjust enrichment, enabling the lender to withhold or apply the loan money as he saw fit, all the while knowing that putative lien claimants were furnishing valuable materials and doing valuable work to the enhancement of his security. The bank here had the option of withholding its advances on the loan from the borrower, and the right to apply the money to the account of Columbia Wood Products in payment of the lumber that company was delivering to the construction project.

(Citations omitted.) *National Bank of Washington v. Equity Investors,* 81 Wash. 2d 886, 506 P.2d 20 (1973).

We again state our conclusion in *National Bank of Washington v. Equity Investors, supra,* 81 Wash.2d on page 927, 506 P.2d on page 44:

> In conclusion, then, and to summarize: We find that advances by the bank under its construction loan agreement with Equity Investors were optional in law rather than obligatory, and hold that Columbia Wood Products' materialman's lien is superior to the bank's lien for later advances and, accordingly, reverse.

It is clear that we intended Columbia's lien claim for materials furnished to be satisfied in full from the proceeds of the foreclosure sale prior to the Bank's lien claim for later advances in order to nullify the Bank's unjust enrichment at the expense of Columbia. MacDonald, therefore, cannot be permitted to take advantage of the Bank's unjust enrichment and to thwart the direction of this court that Columbia be paid in full from the proceeds of the foreclosure sale. The trial court by its judgment, in effect, erroneously paid MacDonald's claim not from the proceeds of the foreclosure sale, but from the amount of foreclosure sale proceeds which we directed to be paid to Columbia. If MacDonald, on the basis of its asserted priority, was to be paid at all, it should have been from the proceeds of the foreclosure sale ahead of Columbia, but this cannot be permitted since such a disposition would be putting MacDonald in a more favorable position than the Bank in violation of the subordination agreement.

. . . .

The judgment of the trial court in determining MacDonald's lien prior to Columbia is reversed with directions that Columbia's lien in the amount determined by the trial court, together with costs and the modification of attorneys' fees on appeal to $5,000 for each appeal, be satisfied from the proceeds of the foreclosure sale consistent with this opinion.

The bond posted by Columbia pending this review is quashed and the sureties thereon are exonerated.

HALE, C. J., HAMILTON, STAFFORD and WRIGHT, JJ., and RYAN and LEVEQUE, JJ., PRO TEM.

WILLIAMS v. AMERICAN BANKERS LIFE ASSURANCE CO.

Florida District Court of Appeals
379 So. 2d 119 (1980)

CHAPPELL, BILL G., ASSOCIATE JUDGE.

Appellee, American Bankers Life Assurance Company of Florida, held a first mortgage in the original amount of $500,000, and Development International Corporation of Florida held a second mortgage in the original amount of $125,000 on real property owned by Maule Industries, Inc. Then, on August 6, 1974, Appellee obtained a third mortgage in the amount of $239,530.74 on the subject property relying upon a Subordination Agreement dated July 11, 1974 from Development International Corporation of Florida yielding priority of the second mortgage to a "new mortgage" in the amount of $700,000. On August 15, 1974, American Bankers recorded a Mortgage Consolidation and Extension Agreement which consolidated and extended the first and third mortgages to form a single lien of $700,000. Prior to executing the Subordination Agreement, Development International Corporation of Florida had made a collateral assignment of the second mortgage to Security Mortgage Investors securing all obligations of Development International Corporation to Security Mortgage Investors. This assignment was dated April 5, 1974 and recorded April 25, 1974. On April 15, 1975, pursuant to a Stipulation of Settlement in a lawsuit filed in Osceola County, Security Mortgage Investors executed a General Release to Development International Corporation and assigned the second mortgage to appellants herein. This appeal is from a final judgment of foreclosure in which the Court below ruled that the Mortgage Consolidation and Extension Agreement and the first and third mortgages of appellee, consolidated and extended by said Agreement, together constituted a first lien upon the subject property.

Obviously, the trial court found the subordination agreement to be binding, and with this we do not agree. When collateral is duly assigned as security for a debt, the assignee creditor acquires the title of the security which the assignor cannot abridge, the latter enjoying merely an equity of redemption. *Travelers Insurance Company v. Tallahassee Bank and Trust Co.,* 133 So.2d 463 (Fla. 1st DCA 1961).

If nothing is left to be redeemed, the assignor's rights therein would be terminated. Since Security Mortgage Investors, the assignee, was not a party to the Subordination Agreement, it cannot be bound thereby. *Roberts v. Harkins,* 292 So.2d 603 (Fla. 2nd DCA 1974).

A mortgage that is assigned as collateral security may be foreclosed by the assignee, *Gables Racing Assoc., Inc. v. Persky,* 116 Fla. 77, 156 So. 392 (1934), but the original mortgagee may intervene in the suit for the purpose of showing that the assignment was made as collateral security only. *Torreyson v. Dutton,* 145 Fla. 169, 198 So. 796 (1940). Here, it appears that the debt secured by the mortgage was in default, and as part of an agreement releasing the debtor of its obligations, Security Mortgage Investors assigned the mortgage to appellants, leaving nothing for Development International Corporation of Florida to redeem. Appellants, as assignees of the mortgage, may foreclose the mortgage in a proceeding brought in their own names. *Smith v. Kleiser,* 91 Fla. 84, 107 So. 262 (1926).

Appellants further contend that the Mortgage Consolidation and Extension Agreement extinguishes the first and third mortgages and creates a new mortgage inferior to their second mortgage. We see nothing in the Agreement indicating an intention to extinguish these mortgages. *Federal Land Bank of Columbia v. Godwin,* 136 So. 513 (Fla.1931), aff'd. as mod., 107 Fla. 537, 145 So. 883 (1932). Nor do we see any indication that a new debt is being substituted for the old. *Murphy v. Green,* 102 Fla. 102, 135 So. 531 (1931); *Taines v. Capital City First Nat. Bank,* 344 So.2d 273 (Fla. 1st DCA 1977). In fact, the language describes the consolidated mortgage as *two* mortgages taken together and the consolidated note as *two* notes taken together. It is our opinion that this agreement merely changes the mode of payment without discharging the mortgages or depriving the holder of the security afforded thereby. *Marden v. The Elks Club,* 138 Fla. 707, 190 So. 40 (1939).

In view of our holding the Subordination Agreement ineffective as to the appellants herein, we must further point out that the third mortgage cannot be elevated to the same priority of that held by the first mortgage. In accordance with the general rule, the three mortgages herein rank in the priority of their acquisition.

Accordingly, the order appealed is reversed and the cause is remanded with directions for further proceedings to establish the amounts due the parties on each of the mortgages consistent with the views herein expressed.

Reversed and remanded with directions.

NOTES

1. There might be a different result if the senior lienor had agreed to subordinate to a junior lienor conditioned upon no intervening lienors being elevated. *See Colorado National Bank v. F. E. Biegert,* 165 Colo. 78, 438 P.2d 506 (1968).

2. The Supreme Court of Georgia subsequently affirmed the holding of the Georgia Court of Appeals. *See Old Stone Mortgage & Realty Trust v. New Georgia Plumbing, Inc.,* 239 Ga. 345, 236 S.E.2d 592 (1977).

3. MISAPPLICATION OF FUNDS

MIDDLEBROOK-ANDERSON CO. v. SOUTHWEST SAVINGS & LOAN ASS'N

California District Court of Appeals
18 Cal. App. 3d 1027 (1971)

GABBERT, ASSOCIATE JUSTICE.

The plaintiffs appeal from a judgment of dismissal entered after defendants' general and special demurrers were sustained without leave to amend in this complicated land development action. Plaintiffs are two California corporations, doing business as Middlebrook-Anderson Co., a partnership, hereinafter referred to as "seller".

The seller owned real property consisting of 28 lots in Orange County. It entered into a land sale contract with certain developers, hereinafter referred to as "buyers", who are not before us in this action. An escrow at a bank was opened between seller and the buyers; the instructions specified the sale price to be $365,000, which was to be partially paid by a purchase money deed of trust in the amount of $169,500. This deed was to be second and junior to a construction loan to be obtained at some later time by the buyers.

During a period of several months buyers negotiated for a construction loan from defendant Southwest Savings and Loan Association, hereinafter referred to as "lender". Defendant Western Escrow Company was the escrow agent for the buyers and the lender. The buyers represented to the seller that the bank escrow would have to be revised to provide for a purchase money deed of trust in favor of seller in the sum of $69,500 and to allow the lender to obtain priority over seller's deed of trust by priority of recording. The bank escrow between seller and buyers was amended accordingly.

After these terms were agreed to by the seller and the buyers, the construction loan was consummated. Western Escrow prepared 28 deeds of trust in favor of lender, with Western named as trustee, each in the amount of $52,300. A deed of trust in favor of seller in the amount of $69,500, expressly stating it was junior to the lender's deeds of trust, was also prepared. These 29 trust deeds were recorded on April 22, 1966. Three days later, to repair the distortion caused by the $100,000 reduction in the apparent size of the purchase money loan, the $69,500 deed was reconveyed and 28 new ones prepared and recorded, each in the amount of $6,053.

The third amended complaint alleges the lender disbursed $1,464,400 into a construction loan account, and allowed the buyers to use $300,000 of this for purposes other than for construction improvements. When the loan funds ran out in November 1966, the buyers abandoned the unfinished apartment houses on the property. In the same month, Western Escrow gave notice of default and election to sell under lender's trust deeds. Seller tendered payment of the due principal, interest, and late charges to cure the default, but Western and lender demanded in excess of $50,000, in addition, to repay lender for sums it claimed it had expended for repairs caused by vandalism on the property and completion of the construction. Lender purchased the property at a series of foreclosure sales in April and May 1967, remained in possession and collected rents for a period of time, and then sold the properties to members of the public not parties to this action.

This litigation was commenced by a complaint filed before the foreclosure sales were complete. After plaintiffs' third amended complaint, attempting to state seven different causes of action against Southwest Savings and Loan and Western Escrow was filed, the trial court sustained defendant's general demurrers to the complaint on grounds of failure to state a cause of action, and 44 special demurrers on grounds of uncertainty.

Plaintiffs' causes of action are based essentially on the failure of lender to limit the use of the loan funds to construction purposes. The theories of recovery and remedies sought in the respective numbered causes of action are:

(1) a restoration of the priority of seller's trust deeds;

(2) damages for rendering seller's trust deeds valueless by foreclosure on lender's first trust deeds;

(3) either restoration of priority or money damages based on lender's knowingly permitting the use of $300,000 for nonconstruction purposes;

(4) either restoration of priority or damages based on seller's status as a third party beneficiary of the construction loan contract between lender and the buyers . . . .

. . . .

The pleadings allege an original contract existed between the seller and buyers; the escrow at the bank was solely between seller and buyers; the sellers were to receive a purchase money trust deed which would be junior to a construction loan that was to be negotiated. Thereafter negotiations with the lender by the buyers resulted in a commitment by the lender to the buyers on the condition, as represented by the buyers to the seller, that the lender would make a construction loan and would require documents to show the buyers had made a greater cash investment in the property than originally contemplated and would require subordination of seller's trust deed by priority of recording rather than through a formal subordination agreement.

The complaint further alleges the buyers represented to the seller the funds received from the lender would be used exclusively for construction of improvements on the property and, based on these representations, the seller agreed to the terms. The buyers then entered into the escrow with Western Escrow which, acting as agent for the buyers and the lender, received a copy of the escrow instructions between the seller and buyers. [Emphasis added.]

The seller alleges the lender had knowledge of the second trust deeds taken by the seller and had a duty to inquire of the seller as to the terms and conditions under which the seller agreed to accept a junior lien. The complaint further alleges the lender voluntarily undertook to control disbursements from the construction loan fund and that the seller did not attempt to follow the progress of the construction or status of disbursements because it relied on such control by the lender, who knew and intended that seller so rely.

The seller continues that the lender owed a duty to seller because of lender's conduct which induced the seller to "subordinate" its lien, because of lender's voluntary assumption of control of disbursements and because of the lender's knowledge of the security interest of the seller and knowledge that the seller would subordinate its lien on condition the loan funds were to be used only for construction improvements. Seller alleges the lender disbursed $300,000 in funds which were not for construction purposes, in wanton, reckless disregard of the security interest of seller.

The complaint also alleges that by reason of these improper disbursements the construction of the project was not completed and the market value of the property did not increase through the construction of improvements to a sufficient extent to support the security interests of both seller and lender. The value of seller's security interest in the property was thus diminished to the extent of the alleged wrongful disbursements. The seller finally contends that at the time of the commencement of the case the unpaid balance on the trust deeds in favor of sellers was in the sum of $141,250.23, plus interest.

All of plaintiffs' causes of action depend upon a conclusion that seller's agreement to take a second trust deed constituted a subordination agreement or an agreement in the nature of a subordination agreement. Lender, on the other hand, claims seller got what it bargained for — a second trust deed — and thus had no prior lien to subordinate. Lender would thus conclude no priority existed which could be restored, the seller could not state any cause of action, and the trial court correctly sustained the demurrers.

As we state below, we conclude that the duties owed by a lender to a seller under a formal subordination agreement do not differ from the duties owed by a lender to a seller when the lender obtains priority over the seller under an agreement by the seller to record after the lender. We thus conclude that, in part, the complaint is sufficient to withstand defendants' general demurrers.

Subordination is, strictly speaking, a status, not an agreement or form of litigation. It refers to the establishment of priority between different existing encumbrances on the same parcel of property, by some means other than the basic priority involved in the concept of "first in time, first in priority", or the automatic priority accorded purchase money liens. (See Laseher, Vol. 1, San Fernando Valley Law Rev., p. 2, "Subordination Clauses in Court: Is California Unfair to Unfairness?")

By statute, a purchase money deed of trust is prior to other liens on real property. (Civil Code, § 2898.) But banks and savings and loan institutions may not lend money on the security of real property unless they hold first liens. (Fin.Code, §§ 1413 subd. (d), 7102 subd. (a), 1560.) The two common methods of arranging for the commercial lender to hold the first lien include: (1) an express subordination agreement in which the seller agrees to make his lien junior to the lender's; (2) recording the lender's trust deed before the seller's.

Both methods of giving a lender a prior lien, whether by express subordination agreement or by priority of recording, are used to obtain a quicker sale and a higher price for the land. A reading of the commentators suggests lending institutions may prefer the latter method over written subordination agreements because of the reluctance of courts to enforce express written agreements which are deemed to be unfair to the seller. (See *Handy v. Gordon,* 65 Cal.2d 578, 55 Cal.Reptr. 769, 422 P.2d 329.) This latter type of subordination situation has been referred to as "automatic subordination".

On the basis of the allegations in the complaint, the project in the case at bench would appear to be a typical automatic subordination arrangement as found in *Miller v. Citizens Sav. & Loan Assn., supra,* 248 Cal.App.2d 655, 56 Cal.Rptr. 844. As we interpret the pleadings, the subordination agreement shows the parties intended to enter into an arrangement of subordination whereby the seller relied upon the responsibility of the lender to make voucher payments only for construction purposes and the reliance of the seller was known to the lender.

The basic thrust of plaintiffs' complaint is that the automatic subordination should be voided because of the misapplication of a portion of the construction loan fund, in that the lender failed to comply with the conditions which occasioned plaintiffs' agreement to subordinate. This theory is supported by a number of cases and is endorsed by certain of the text writers mentioned herein.

In *Collins v. Home Sav. & Loan Assn., supra,* 205 Cal.App.2d 86, 22 Cal.Rptr. 817, the lender had exercised his power of sale, asserting priority based on the subordination agreement between plaintiff and the defaulting buyer. The agreement contained a limitation that the loan proceeds were to be used for construction purposes. The plaintiff seller sought a declaration that the agreement did not alter the priorities, in part, because the buyer had misused the loan funds. The trial court found that the lender had disbursed funds knowing that the buyer would use them for unauthorized purposes. Judgment was entered for the seller and against the lender for the principal amount of the purchase money note, plus interest, and the appellate court affirmed, stating in part:

> The trial court ... could properly infer that it would be rather incredible for respondents ... to have subordinated the lien of their purchase money deed of trust to those of other tremendously larger liens ... which would have made respondents' trust deed of questionable worth. ... [T]he trial court could, and presumably did, infer that the only reason for respondents' subordination of their lien was the expectation that if payments were advanced by appellant solely for construction purposes, the liens superior to their own would increase in value only as the property under development enjoyed a corresponding increase in value because of the accompanying progress in the work of construction." (205 Cal.App.2d at 98, 22 Cal.Rptr. at 824.)

The case of *Radunich v. Basso, supra,* 235 Cal.App.2d 826, 45 Cal.Rptr. 824, held the sellers' lien superior where the lender knew of the variance between the actual intended use for the loan proceeds and the use restriction in the subordination clause. The lender was thus on notice of a possible violation of the agreement and under a duty to ascertain the true facts from the seller. His failure to investigate was thus held to be negligence.

In *Miller v. Citizens Sav. & Loan Assn., supra,* 248 Cal.App.2d 655, 56 Cal.-Rptr. 844, the appellate court, in reversing the decision of the trial court granting a motion of defendant lender under Code of Civil Procedure, § 631.8, held that since the lender was aware of the limitations contained in the subordination arrangement, it could not claim priority for any monies advanced for purposes outside those permitted.

Respondents assert their non-liability on four grounds: (1) the lender had no duty to supervise the distribution of loan funds (*Gill v. Misson Sav. & Loan Assn., supra,* 236 Cal.App.2d 753, 46 Cal.Rptr. 456); (2) there was no privity of contract between lender and seller (*Matthews v. Hinton, supra,* 234 Cal.App.2d 736, 44 Cal.Rptr. 692); (3) since no "subordination agreement" was alleged, seller could have suffered no loss of priority; and (4) no public policy basis exists for imposing a duty on the lender *(Gill v. Mission Sav. & Loan Assn., supra).* Respondent cites two other cases in support of the asserted grounds: *Weiss v. Brentwood Sav. & Loan, supra,* 4 Cal.App.3d 738, 84 Cal.Rptr. 736, and *Spaziani v. Millar, supra,* 215 Cal.App.2d 667, 30 Cal.Rptr. 658.

In light of the facts set forth in the complaint, however, we find insufficient merit in these arguments to prevent a trial of the matter on the merits. We find compelling reasons to the contrary.

Gill involved an appeal from a judgment of dismissal upon an order sustaining a demurrer with leave to amend, no amendment having been filed. The issue was whether the lender owed a duty to the sellers to manage and supervise the distribution of loan funds so that these funds would be used solely for construction purposes. The court concluded that because of the lack of privity of contract and the fact that plaintiffs did not allege that defendant had voluntarily undertaken to supervise the distribution of the loan funds, the complaint for damages was properly demurrable.

In *Gill* the complaint was that the lender had acted negligently in failing to supervise and manage the loan funds. As stated by the court in *Gill,* "Nowhere in the first amended complaint does it appear that the defendant agreed with anyone to manage or supervise distribution of the loaned funds, assumed to do so, actually undertook such, or was required by statutory law or regulation to so manage and supervise. Nor is there any showing of a voluntarily assumed relationship between defendant and plaintiffs from which such an obligation might arise." (236 Cal.App.2d at 756-757, 46 Cal.Rptr. at 458.)

Such allegations do appear in the pleading in the case at bench. Moreover, the damage claim in the complaint in *Gill* rests on a different legal theory than the claim of loss of priority here involved. The former is grounded on traditional negligence concepts while the latter is based on principles of contract law. Underlying the latter theory, the lender's claim to priority flows from the agreement between the seller and the buyer. It is only as a result of the seller's waiver of his statutory right to a first lien that the lender achieves priority. Thus, the lender is a third party beneficiary in the seller-buyer agreement, but only to the extent that it abides by the conditions of subordination. If the lender does not comply with the seller's conditions it does not achieve priority. Since one condition to priority is the proper use of the construction loan funds, the priority of the construction loan lien does not vest until such time as the funds are applied to the construction purpose. (See C.E.B. California Real Estate Secured Transactions, § 5.13 at 215.) This latter theory was not before the *Gill* court. *Matthews v. Hinton, supra,* 234 Cal.App.2d 736, 44 Cal.Rptr. 692, involves the same problem as *Gill,* namely, the cross-complaint was seeking damages rather than a restoration of priority. Moreover, the court in *Matthews,* concluded that the transaction with the lender produced a new agreement which effectively eliminated any restrictions on the use of the loan proceeds. (See *Miller v. Citizens Sav. & Loan Assn., supra,* 248 Cal.App.2d 655, 663-664, n. 5, 56 Cal.Rptr. 844.) Finally, the parties in *Matthews,* were lessors, a lessee and a lender and, therefore, the case did not involve a purchase money second trust deed. For these reasons *Matthews* is distinguishable from the within action.

Lender contends since the case before us does not involve a "subordination agreement" there was no loss of priority and therefore as a matter of law plaintiffs may not have their lien declared to be prior to the construction loan lien. In support of this argument defendants rely on a treatise, Current Law of California Real Estate, Vol. 2, by Messrs. Miller and Starr. The same authors have restated their position in 13 U.C.L.A. L.Rev. 1298, 1301 to the effect that if the seller agrees in the deposit receipt agreement or the escrow instructions that the buyer may obtain a construction loan which will be recorded as a first trust deed and the seller's purchase money trust deed is made junior by virtue of the time of its recording, then a "true" subordination does not result. The problem, it is said, ". . . does not involve alteration of lien priority; that is, it does not involve the subordination of an earlier lien to a later lien, because by the execution of the purchase transaction the priorities are determined by the initial creation and recordation of the liens. Since the seller at no time has a 'prior' lien, he is not 'subordinating' his lien but merely agreeing to accept junior security. The problem, therefore, is primarily one of contract law between the buyer and the seller and not one of lien law between the seller and the lender." (p. 1301.)

In our view there is no justification, legal or otherwise, which would call for a different result whether the seller in a joint transaction records first and then agrees that his lien will be subordinated or whether he agrees that the lender may achieve priority through first recording. In C.E.B. California Real Estate Secured Transactions, *supra* § 5.16 at 217 the author expressly disagrees with the Miller and Starr position stating:

This author disagrees with Miller and Starr due to the prevailing policy of title companies of recording the subordinating lien before the subordinated deed of trust. [citation] ¶ In *Conley v. Fate* (1964) 227 Cal.App.2d 418, 38 CR [Cal.-Rptr.] 680, a seller agreed to accept a second deed of trust for a portion of the purchase price, and the court properly referred to this as being subordinate to the construction loan, and further referred to the pertinent portion of the deposit receipt as a subordination clause. ¶ In the event the vendor is required to finance partially the purchase of his property, through either a second deed of trust or a subordinated first deed of trust, there should be no difference in his status based on the time of recording of the two encumbrances. On some occasions the purchase-money deed of trust held by the vendor will be reconveyed and rerecorded immediately after recordation of the subordinating encumbrance. [citation]. Therefore, if the institutional lender is to finance a portion of the purchase price, the institutional lender should incur the same liabilities for misapplication of funds, whether the vendor holds a second deed of trust by virtue of reconveyance and rerecordation or a first subordinated by agreement without a change in the order of recording. But see *Spaziani v. Millar,* (1963) 215 Cal.App.2d 667, 30 CR [Cal.Rptr.] 658.

Respondent finds support for a result contrary to that which we have reached in *Spaziani v. Millar, supra,* 215 Cal.App.2d 667, 30 Cal.Rptr. 658, and in "Subordination Agreements in California", *supra,* Miller, Starr and Regalia, Vol. 13 U.C.L.A. L.Rev. 1298, 1309-312. *Spaziani* states:

> The deed of trust held by the defendant loan company was a first deed of trust; the deed of trust held by the plaintiff was a second deed of trust; by virtue of these facts the latter was subordinated to the first; and the purpose for which the first loan had been made bore no relationship to its priority. (p. 681, 30 Cal.Rptr. at p. 665.)

The result in *Spaziani* is approved in the law review article mentioned above, which reasons:

> The seller's lien is not usually recorded until title has passed to the buyer and the lien of the construction lender has been recorded; the seller at no time has a prior lien to be 'subordinated'. If the proceeds of the construction loan are not applied as required by the contract between the seller and the buyer, there is no failure of a condition of subordination, and the seller's recourse is limited to an action for breach of contract against the buyer or breach of instructions against the title company. The seller should have no recourse against the lender unless he can establish a contractual privity with the lender. (fn. omitted) (13 U.C.L.A. L.Rev. at 1309.)

While *Spaziani,* in all candor, must be considered closely on point, nevertheless there are certain distinguishing features which we think sufficient to permit us to reach a contrary position, and to allow the case before us to go to trial on the merits. The *Spaziani* court did not find a subordination agreement between the lender and the seller; the application of the rule as to the lender's duty to the seller was a conclusionary statement, made without citation of authority or reasoning to support it. Further, the loan involved was not a construction loan but was denominated a "purchase assistance" loan. *Spaziani* principally turned on the lack of duty on the lender to inform the buyer that the loan involved was not a construction loan. Nor has *Spaziani* been cited for its point that there was no subordination in a second trust deed situation. Additionally, even in *Spaziani* the non-suit as to the escrow company was reversed, so that relief was given the seller.

Although *Spaziani* is apparently the closest case on point, other analogous cases suggest a different result. *Conley v. Fate,* 227 Cal.App.2d 418, 38 Cal.Rptr. 680, refused to specifically enforce a land sale contract in which the seller promised to take a second trust deed junior to a construction loan. One of the reasons the court gave was the fact the contract contained no specification of the purpose and nature of the construction loan described, offering no protection to the seller's junior security. This concern for the seller's security indicates there should be no difference between formal subordination of a first trust deed and an agreement to take a second trust deed. Two commentators support this view and are critical of *Spaziani* and the law review article cited by defendants. (C.E.B. California Real Estate Secured Transactions, *supra,* § 5.16 at 217; Comment, "Subordination of Purchase-Money Security", 52 Cal.L.Rev. 157, 164-170.)

. . . .

It has been pointed out by many courts and commentators that as between the seller and the lender, the lender is by far in the better position to control the use of the loan proceeds and thereby prevent misappropriations by the developer. The lender can require documented evidence that expenses have been incurred and can corroborate this by on-site inspections. It is common for lenders to control disbursements, since they, too, have an interest in preventing misuse of loan proceeds (see 52 Cal.L.Rev. 157-158, n. 5). If the lender loses priority as a result of improper disbursements, it remains in a position to redeem the seller's purchase money lien and foreclose on the junior construction lien and thereby own the property for a price presumably less than the market value. Also, loan proceeds would be at least partially recouped by the improvements made. The seller, on the other hand, is normally not in a position to protect himself by redemption of the larger construction lien in the event the lender were to obtain priority. After redemption, the lender can obtain a deficiency judgment against the defaulting developer whereas the seller, holding a purchase money security interest, would be barred by Code of Civil Procedure, § 580b, if he tried to recover a deficiency judgment against the developer. (*Kistler v. Vasi,* 71 Cal.2d 261, 263-264, 78 Cal.Rptr. 170, 455 P.2d 106.) The lender is in a far better position to absorb any loss since such contingencies may be provided for in its profit and loss estimates. Finally, allocation of the loss to the lender would encourage the parties to provide for the various contingencies by contract.

An implied agreement in the instant case can and, in equity, should be spelled out from lender's alleged actual knowledge of the provisions of the seller's lien in general, and of the subordination therein in particular. In the superior position of a financial institution constantly engaged in professional construction lending, Southwestern had no reason to believe their trust deed conferred any lien to which the fee was subordinate other than to the extent of money spent for construction purposes. Its loan under the circumstances cannot be viewed other than as subject to the fair application of the construction funds. Accordingly, we conclude that such lien as the trust deed might have conferred on the lender should not be advanced or preferred over the seller.

Here, it is alleged the lender, with full knowledge of the subordinated lien of the seller, disbursed the funds without limitation. Its disinterest in the application of the funds not used for construction amounted to a failure to prevent the loss sustained by seller — who, in the vernacular of the market place, was "wiped out". The particular equities discussed above incline us to the conviction that the philosophy of fair dealing as expressed in *Handy v. Gordon, supra,* 65 Cal.2d 578, 55 Cal. Rptr. 769, 422 P.2d 329, is most appropriately invoked here.

We hold the actions of the parties here, if proved as alleged, did create a subordination agreement, and the lender's failure to protect seller's security interest gives seller a cause of action; the validity of the first, second, and third causes of action are supported by the cases.

. . . .

Thus since a subordination agreement is sufficiently alleged in the pleadings and supported in law, the first, second, third and fourth causes of action are valid and the judgment of dismissal should be reversed as to them. . . .

. . . .

The judgment is reversed in part and affirmed in part as set forth herein. KERRIGAN, ACTING P. J., and KAUFMAN, J., concur.

GRENADA READY-MIX CONCRETE v. WATKINS

United States District Court
453 F. Supp. 1298 (N.D. Miss. 1978)

I. Facts

Grenada, a Mississippi corporation, was in 1973 the owner of a 10-acre parcel of vacant, unimproved land which fronted U.S. Highway 8, and was located west of Grenada's city limits near the intersection of Highway 8 with Interstate 55.

This property, regarded as a prime location for commercial development, had been owned by Grenada for a number of years. Grenada was, in 1973, a wholly-owned corporation, of which Grady Green was president and his wife, Frances B. Green, secretary; together they owned all of the corporate stock. Green, then 60 years of age, had personally been extensively engaged in construction work of all kinds, commencing in the ready-mix concrete business after World War II. For the ensuing 32 years, his firm was continuously engaged in erecting various buildings as well as supplying concrete to the public. Among other structures, Green developed the Grady Green Shopping Center on old Highway 51 south of Grenada, and had built a shopping center at Kosciusko, composed of several free-standing units. Since 1973 Green has engaged in the development of still another shopping center adjoining the one in issue, which was proposed to be erected by Watkins, an individual who first did business as a corporation under the name of Watkins Investment Company and later as a partnership under the same name. Mrs. Green, a college graduate, kept Grenada's business records and her husband's other business operations under the supervision of an auditor. She routinely prepared financial statements and also served as an advisory member on the Board of Directors of the Grenada Bank. Mrs. Green was aware of, and participated in, most major decisions which were largely conceived and developed by her husband relative to the business carried on by their company.

(a) Nature of Project

In the spring months of 1973, Green was approached by Watkins' representatives, Joe Byrd and David Martindale, regarding the possibility of the development of Grenada's 10-acre unimproved parcel as a commercial shopping center. Martindale conducted the initial negotiations on behalf of Watkins and advised Green that the Watkins' organization was prepared to offer a ground lease of $25,000 annually for a 25-year term, with three optional extensions of five years each, subsequent to their acceptance of which Watkins would erect a shopping center with Magic Mart and a major grocery chain (later identified as Big Star) as the two principal or "anchor" tenants, leaving large and small mall spaces for speculative purposes. Martindale and Byrd represented that the shopping center improvements, estimated to contain approximately 96,000 square feet, would be erected at a cost of $1,125,000. They represented that *Grenada, as a condition for the lease, would be required to join in the construction loan to be secured from a lender, without personal liability upon Grenada or the Greens, but subjecting the latter's fee simple title to a first mortgage lien required by the lender.* [Emphasis added.]

. . . On July 9, Grenada entered a 25-year lease agreement beginning July 1, 1973, with Watkins.

The document provided that rent would be payable during the primary term at the rate of $2,083.34 per month, with the first month's rent commencing "upon the completion of the first building to be constructed on the above described property by the lessee (Watkins) or on January 1, 1974, in the event the first building had not been completed by that time." It was further provided that upon the request of Watkins, Grenada would execute "the necessary instrument or instruments subordinating its lien on the [leased property] to the lien of the security instrument to be executed -by [Watkins] for temporary construction money to construct improvements on the above described property and also the lien of the security instrument to be executed by [Watkins] for permanent financing of the entire project when construction is completed." . . .

. . . .

(c) Guaranty, the Mortgage Bankers

After completing the arrangements with Guaranty, Watkins executed his promissory note and deed of trust against the real property, subject to the ground lease between him and Grenada; Watkins then presented the deed of trust to Green and his wife for their joinder on behalf of Grenada. All three parties went to the law office of Attorney Fedric where the deed of trust was reviewed and approved by Fedric and signed by the Greens as Grenada's officers. The deed of trust specifically recited that Grenada joined in the instrument as fee owner "for the purpose of subordinating its interests and mortgaging the fee in the property owned by it, without, however, assuming or agreeing to any liability (other than its ownership in the fee) to the mortgagee." The deed of trust, of course, recited that it secured the payment by Watkins of a $1,125,000 loan from Guaranty, providing that in event of default in paying the indebtedness or any installment, Guaranty would be authorized to accelerate the maturity of the entire debt and cause the trustee named therein, Randall Travis, or his substitute, to foreclose the collateral, including the realty, the ground lease in favor of Watkins and all tenants' rentals derived thereunder, by proceedings conducted in accordance with Mississippi law. The deed of trust dated October 1, 1973, was promptly filed for record upon its execution.

Guaranty understood that Watkins would, through his own organization, construct the Grenada Shopping Center and would deal only with subcontractors. . . . Guaranty, however, required that the independent firm of Hart-Freeland-Roberts, architects and engineers of Nashville, assign one of its employees to make periodic inspections as to the percentage of completion on each occasion that Watkins might request a partial draw of funds to defray costs of construction.

(d) Advance of Funds During Progress of Work

The evidence shows without dispute that in accordance with long-established custom, Watkins, to obtain a drawdown, was required to furnish, and did furnish, to Guaranty four items or documents:

1. His voucher request.

2. His affidavit as project owner of items of work done.

3. A certificate executed by Don Petty for the architectural firm stating, after examining the job site on a specified date, the percentage of the job completed.

4. Owner's affidavit to Mississippi Valley Title Insurance Company that Watkins had fully paid all construction costs and the absence of any mechanics, materialmen or other claim costs for unpaid items, together with an attorney's up-date of search of land records showing the absence of filing of any liens by materialmen or laborers against the property.

Watkins proceeded to draw against the construction loan partial installments on the dates and in the amounts set forth below:

Date	Amount
10-5-73	$125,275
11-13-73	175,852

Date	Amount
12-12-73	$172,729
1-15-74	94,945
2-11-74	79,192
3-11-74	22,660
7-12-74	32,080
8-13-74	114,818
9-10-74	97,407
Total	$914,958

On the occasion of each drawdown, Watkins complied with Guaranty's requirements by executing the customary voucher request and owner's affidavit of job completion, obtaining from Petty a certificate of the percentage of completion, including materials in place and at the job site, and procuring title updates obtained by attorney Fedric and supplied through Mississippi Valley Title Insurance Company indicating the absence of any filed materialmen or laborers' liens.

On October 14, 1974, Guaranty made an additional advance, however, to Watkins for $175,157 without obtaining a title update search from attorney Fedric; yet on that date no liens by an unpaid claimant had actually been filed as provided by state law. The total of all draws, $1,090,115, left a balance of $34,885 in the Watkins' loan account, which sum Guaranty declined to disburse because of its awareness that Watkins had become involved in severe financial difficulties.

As of November 4, 1974, Tuttle, Guaranty's appraiser, stated that according to estimates on file, $101,618 additional funds were required to complete the project, thus causing an overdraw of $66,733. In addition, unpaid bills owed to materialmen and laborers on the Grenada Shopping Center amounted to not less than $130,000, according to Watkins' records. Additional outlays of at least $231,618 would be needed to complete the shopping center. On March 8, 1974, Magic Mart and the small mall area were 100% complete; on November 11, 1974, Big Star Grocery was 100% complete, with the remaining large mall on the latter date 97% complete. Thus, the value of the completed improvements, exclusive of land value, according to Petty's certificates, was $1,008,380. Since total additional funds of $231,618 were required to pay bills and to complete the project, it thus follows that the cost overran the loan by $114,998.

There was opinion evidence from Byrd, Martindale and Grady Green, experienced builders, that the shopping center could have been completed within Guaranty's loan of $1,125,000. There was contrary evidence from Travis, Freeland, as well as Watkins, that unprecedented escalating costs of materials and labor, during the inflationary period in 1973 and 1974, rendered it impossible to construct the 96,000 square foot shopping center, with proper finish, within the amount of the loan. Green readily conceded his awareness of inflationary costs of labor and materials occurring during this period. It is established by credible evidence that, as of November 1974, $1,008,380 advanced by Guaranty had been expended on the project, which was then incomplete and required additional outlays to make the entire cost of the shopping center project exceed the construction loan by $114,998. Although counsel for Grenada baldly asserts that Watkins' methods, by use of expensive airplane and helicopters, were wasteful, and this must have drained funds otherwise available for construction, there is no solid evidence that Watkins diverted funds advanced by Guaranty for construction at the Grenada job site. . . . Grenada offered no proof that Guaranty's construction funds were diverted from the project, and that Guaranty acquiesced therein. Contrariwise, we find it more reasonable to infer, and find as a fact, from the whole evidence that the total amount of Guaranty's loan, though expended upon the job, was inadequate to complete the shopping center as planned by Watkins, and this inadequacy of borrowed funds was solely attributable to increased costs of labor and materials, at an unanticipated high rate during 1973-74. This conclusion is supported by the fact that Watkins, with a successful track record as a commercial developer, simultaneously failed on many other commercial jobs, including various shopping centers similar to Grenada. The evidence fails to show any condition at Grenada which uniquely caused that project to fail for causes imposing liability upon anyone except the bankrupt Watkins.

The substantial evidence is to the effect that Guaranty's method of doing business in advancing temporary construction funds, pending permanent financing with a major institutional lender, was in keeping with the established custom of mortgage banking in the Mid-South area. Moreover, according to such custom, where the commercial developer did his own construction, it was neither customary nor necessary for formal construction contracts to be made, and constructions costs, in lieu of contracts, were estimated by experienced developers and made the basis upon which temporary financing would be granted by mortgage bankers. Also, in accordance with custom, experienced commercial developers frequently did not employ independent engineers and architects to draw plans and specifications but developed such within their own organization, in which eventuality the mortgage bankers customarily followed the same procedure of having a limited inspection of degree of completion verified by an independent firm of architects, such as Hart-Freeland-Roberts. Despite Grenada's contrary assertion, the established custom in the construction trade was for commercial builders to operate their construction jobs from a single bank account, or several such accounts, with separate records maintained on the cost allocated to each construction project. Separate check books were kept on each job under the direction of Watkins' office manager and controller. We find nothing sinister in Watkins' organization operating in that manner, or the absence of further "accounting" to Guaranty beyond the documentation required at each partial advance of loan funds. . . .

. . . .

(f) [This section recites details of the difficulties which arose on the construction project.]

. . . .

(g) Foreclosure Proceedings

On March 20, 1975, when Watkins was in substantial default upon his loan from Guaranty, the latter retained counsel at Jackson, Mississippi, to foreclose the deed of trust on Grenada's fee interest as landowner, as well as Watkins' leasehold interest. Before any proceedings were commenced, however, Green was notified in writing by such counsel that the amount of the outstanding debt, both principal and interest as of February 28, 1975, was $1,155,579.05, with interest accruing daily at the rate of $338.75. A copy of this communication was sent to attorney Fedric; Green was invited to contact Guaranty's counsel. Neither Green nor his attorney responded to the letter.

Fedric advised Green that there was nothing Grenada could do to forestall the foreclosure unless it elected to assume or pay off Guaranty's indebtedness. Grenada thereupon discharged Fedric as its attorney and sought other legal counsel. Charles E. Gibson, Jackson attorney, was substituted as trustee in the deed of trust in the place of Randall Travis and directed by Guaranty to proceed with foreclosure in accordance with the provisions of the trust deed. Gibson notified both mortgagors — Watkins as well as Grenada — that foreclosure was iminent. Beginning September 3, 1975, Gibson, as substituted trustee, advertised notice of sale in the *Daily Sentinel Star,* a local newspaper published in Grenada County, for three consecutive weeks, and posted notice of sale on the bulletin board at the Grenada County courthouse, with sale set for September 25, 1975.

. . . The only bid at the foreclosure sale was one made by Guaranty, the mortgagee, which had the right under the deed of trust to become the purchaser at sale. Subsequently, Guaranty sold the property to Sevenprop for substantial value; and Sevenprop, upon taking immediate possession, made substantial repairs and additional improvements, unaware of any controversy existing between Grenada, Guaranty, or Watkins.

. . . .

II. Law

Admittedly, this court has diversity jurisdiction under 28 U.S.C. § 1332, and the substantive law of Mississippi, since that jurisdiction represents the center of gravity of most contacts in this case, must govern the rights and obligations of all parties herein. It is familiar teaching that in a case of first impression, or where state law is unsettled, as to controlling principles, the federal courts must determine what would be the position taken by the Mississippi Supreme Court.

. . . .

4. No Action Against Guaranty

The remaining issue in the case relates to whether Grenada has a cause of action against Guaranty. This emerges as the dominant legal question for us to decide under the particular facts and circumstances of this case. Since Mississippi has no case in point, it becomes necessary that we examine relevant decisions of the State Supreme Court as well as the state of the law in other jurisdictions on facts analogous to those here presented.

Mississippi has had a long-standing statutory policy of protecting any person who furnishes material or labor in the erection of any structure, through a procedure for binding funds in the hands of the owner where the contractor or master workman fails to pay for the material used, or labor performed, in such construction; this binding is accomplished by the unpaid materialman or mechanic giving written notice to the owner of his outstanding claim. Miss. Code Ann. § 85-7-181 (1972) (This statute first appeared in the Mississippi Code of 1880.). The unpaid claimant is thereby granted a statutory method for insuring the collection of his claim, so long as funds remain in the owner's hands — and such claim has priority over any balance due the general contractor. Moreover, this priority position is further protected against subsequent purchasers or encumbrancers for value when the unpaid materialman or laborer files his claim upon the lis pendens record maintained in the office of the chancery clerk of the county where the improved realty is located. § 85-7-197. These statutory rights did not exist at common law, and without them, materialmen and laborers would merely be general creditors of the contractor. *Chancellor v. Melvin,* 211 Miss. 590, 52 So.2d 360 (1951). The sections have been strictly construed. For example, the right to acquire such liens extends only to persons engaged by the original contractor, and not to those supplying materials or labor at the request of a subcontractor. *Monroe Banking & Trust Co. v. Allen,* 286 F.Supp. 201 (N.D.Miss.1968); *Lake v. Brannin,* 90 Miss. 737, 44 So. 65 (1907). See 53

Am.Jur.2d, *Mechnic's Liens* § 168 at 683-85 (1970). Mississippi cases have clearly settled the conditions for priority of claims as between mortgage lenders of construction funds and materialmen or laborers engaged by the owner or his contractor. The maxim that first in time of recording primes the lender's deed of trust or mortgage does not necessarily control when a subsequent lien is asserted by a materialman or laborer. The landmark decision in this field is *First National Bank of Greenville v. Virden,* 208 Miss. 679, 45 So.2d 268 (1950), which squarely presented the issue of priority between the lien of a statutory claimant for material and the mortgage lien of a bank advancing funds to Hilliard, the property owner, to erect thereon two houses. The bank placed the loan in a suspense account for release to Hilliard at intervals, but did not supervise the expenditures, made no request of Hilliard for paid invoices, and simply accepted the borrower's word that the funds were going into the construction. The bank held a deed of trust for $11,200, which was recorded August 9, 1947, and had no notice of the materialman's claim for $4,307.18. The court, upon the sale of the houses, awarded the bank priority for $7,315.76, the amount of the advances by the bank shown to have been used to purchase the lots and construct the houses, but granted priority to the materialman for its entire claim of $4,307.18. In so holding, the Court said:

> The mortgagee, in a case such as this, should advance the proceeds with reasonable diligence in order that the *holders of statutory liens* may not be unjustly defeated in their claims. It is simple justice that such mortgagee [nevertheless] shall have preference *only to the extent that its funds actually went into the construction.* 45 So.2d 270-271. (Our emphasis).

This holding was followed in *Deposit Guaranty Bank & Trust Co. v. J. F. Weaver Lbr. Co.,* 215 Miss. 183, 60 So.2d 598 (1952).

The "simple justice" rule, above alluded to, was qualified for the benefit of construction lenders in *Wortman & Mann, Inc. v. Frierson Building Supply Co.,* 184 So.2d 857 (Miss. 1966), when the Court held: "It is only necessary for the mortgagee to show reasonable diligence to see that [its] funds are used in the construction of the building." at 860. The Court in *Wortman and Mann* found that the title company required the furnishing of an owner's affidavit that he did not owe for materials and labor at the time of any advance, and attorneys made regular trips to the chancery clerk's office to ascertain if any claimant had perfected his claim by filing notice thereof, and ruled that the construction lender's lien was prior to that of materialmen who had omitted filing claims on the lis pendens record or the instituting of suit until after the mortgage lender disbursed all funds to its borrower, Alton W. Ivey.

It is well established law in Mississippi that the construction lender will be protected in the priority of its recorded mortgage against an unpaid materialman or laborer where the former exercises reasonable diligence to see that the funds are actually used to defray construction costs, *Southern Life Ins. Co. v. Pollard Appliance Co.,* 247 Miss. 211, 150 So.2d 416 (1963), but loses that priority, to the extent that loaned funds are diverted from the work, when failing to discharge its duty in disbursing loan proceeds, *Cook v. Citizens Savings & Loan Ass'n,* 346 So.2d 370 (Miss.1977). The "reasonable standard of care" test was only recently applied by the State Supreme Court in *North American Mortgage Investors v. Mississippi Hardware Co., Inc.,* 360 So.2d 1203 (Miss.1978).

Grenada contends that, although it is neither a materialman nor laborer, it is entitled to the especial protection of the courts since it subordinated its fee interest in the land to a construction lender's mortgage for the sole purpose of having a commercial shopping center erected on the subordinated property by its ground lessee, Watkins. Grenada urges that it is entitled to priority over Guaranty's mortgage lien on two alternative grounds: (1) that the understanding of the parties — Grenada in executing a ground lease to Watkins and in agreeing to subordinate its fee simple title to a construction loan, Watkins in representing that he would erect on the leased premises a commercial shopping center, and Guaranty, the mortgage banker, in agreeing to advance $1,125,000 to construct the shopping center — created an implied contractual duty on the part of Guaranty to Grenada for the successful fruition of the project; and that Guaranty's failure to maintain adequate safeguards to insure that periodic advances of construction funds to Watkins were used only for the project, constituted negligent breach of such duty causing Grenada not only to lose its valuable real estate but to be deprived of the longterm benefits accruing from the 25-year ground lease; and (2) that Grenada's relationship to the project, i.e., subordinating landowner vis-a-vis a mortgage lender dealing with a commercial developer, over neither of which Grenada had supervision or control, calls for the imposition of equitable duties on the construction lender to avoid manifest injury to Grenada. Finding both of these contentions to be without merit, we will undertake to give such discussion as may be proper in view of the fact that this issue is one of first impression in Mississippi.

As for any duty based upon contract, it should be pointed out initially that neither the ground lease nor the deed of trust which Grenada signed contained any protective clauses to insure that the loan proceeds would be used for the construction of the shopping center, nor did they contain any safeguards or restrictions on the manner of distribution or expenditure of the advances. Indeed, the documents which Grenada signed, after consulting with its own attorney, neither specified the size of the shopping center, nor the nature or quality of the buildings to be contained therein. Furthermore, these documents did not require that the shopping center structures be designed by an architect whose plans and specifications would form the basis for Guaranty's advances and which would be subject to Grenada's approval. The only conclusion which we can reasonably draw from these notable omissions is that Grenada was primarily concerned with obtaining a 25-year ground lease producing an annual rent of $25,000, or 10% of the net investment in the real estate which Green in 1973 valued at $250,000; Grenada and its officers obviously regarded Watkins as not only a person of large net worth, capable of meeting his financial commitments but also as an experienced shopping center developer in whom they had full confidence. There can be no other explanation for Grenada's omission of specific standard protective clauses designed to assure it, as the landowner, that Watkins' representations, through the use of borrowed money, would be carried out in an arms-length transaction between an owner of a valuable piece of unencumbered real estate and its lessee-developer.

The general rule throughout the United States is that where a landowner agrees to subordinate his fee interest to a mortgage lien for the purposes of obtaining a construction loan, without an express covenant from the mortgagee (or lessee-developer) to the landowner, to see to the application of the sums advanced, possible diversion of funds by the mortgagor-developer is a risk assumed by the landowner, unless the latter is able to demonstrate fraud or collusion between the mortgagor-developer and the mortgagee. *Gill v. Mission Savings & Loan Ass'n,* 236 Cal.App.2d 753, 46 Cal.Rptr. 456 (D.C.App.1965); *Iowa Loan & Trust Co. v. Plewe,* 202 Iowa 70, 209 N.W. 399 (1926); *Cambridge Acceptance Corp. v. Hockstein,* 102 N.J.Super. 435, 246 A.2d 138 (1968); *Kennedy v. Betts,* 33 Md.App. 258, 364 A.2d 74 (Md.Ct.Spec.App.1976); *Forest,*

Inc. of Knoxville v. Guaranty Mortgage Co., Inc., 534 S.W.2d 853 (Tenn.Ct.App.1975); *Drobnick v. Western Federal Savings & Loan Ass'n,* 479 P.2d 393 (Colo.Ct.App.1970). The obvious rationale for this rule is that when parties see fit to enter into contractual arrangements, their rights and obligations are to be measured by the terms thereof, without help or assistance from courts in adding to the agreement clauses which it would have been wise or useful to have employed in the first instance.

In the case sub judice, there is, as previously found, an absence of any proof of fraud or collusion between Guaranty, Travis or Watkins. Moreover, there was no express contractual duty upon Guaranty to erect safeguards of any kind for the release of funds to Watkins in the construction of the shopping center. Of course, had Watkins used none of the loan funds at the Grenada site and had Guaranty been aware of such diversion, that would constitute fraud or collusion justifying a court in invalidating both the ground lease and the subordination executed by the landowner. The evidence in this case compels an entirely different conclusion for, as we have already found, all of the funds advanced to Watkins were used in the shopping center, even though they proved to be insufficient to complete the project.

Grenada, despite the absence of any express contractual provision, nevertheless argues that there was an implied duty on the part of Guaranty to establish proper safeguards to assure that the construction funds would go into the project; in advancing this argument, Grenada necessarily assumes that a substantial part of the loan funds were diverted to other purposes. In support of this contention, Grenada asserts not only the rationale of the Mississippi mechanics' lien decisions, see, e. g., *Cook v. Citizens Savings & Loan Association, supra; First Nat'l Bank of Greenville v. Virden, supra,* but also seeks comfort in decisions from other jurisdictions which have specifically addressed the issue of whether, and if so, to what extent a duty is owed by a construction lender to an injured subordinating landowner. As to the latter, Grenada places particular reliance upon *Middlebrook-Anderson Co. v. Southwest S.&L. Ass'n,* 18 Cal.App.3d 1023, 96 Cal.Rptr. 338, wherein the California Court departed from the generally established rule in recognizing that equity will raise an implied agreement in proper circumstances for the benefit of a subordinating landowner. Grenada refers specifically to the following language of the California Court in describing the basis for and nature of the duties arising from such agreement:

> [A]s between the seller and the lender, the lender is in by far the better position to control the use of the loan proceeds and thereby prevent misappropriations by the developer. The lender can require documented evidence that expenses have been incurred and can corroborate this by on site inspection. . . . Here, it is alleged the lender, with full knowledge of the subordinated lien of the seller, disbursed the funds *without limitation.* Its disinterest in the application of the *funds not used for the construction* amounted to a failure to prevent the loss sustained by the seller — who, in the vernacular of the market place, was "wiped out."

96 Cal.Rptr. at 346-47. (Emphasis added). Thus, by comparison with our foregoing analysis of Mississippi cases, it is readily apparent that the rationale of the above quoted California decision is congruent with the "simple justice" rule first announced in *Virden* by the Mississippi Supreme Court in connection with mechanics' and materialmen's liens, i. e., when the lender fails to use reasonable diligence to insure that loan funds are used for the construction for which the

loan is made, such lender will be preferred *only* to the extent that such funds actually go into the construction.

This conclusion is buttressed by the fact that the Court in *Middlebrook* also stated:

> An implied agreement in the instant case can and, in equity, should be spelled out from the lender's alleged actual knowledge of the provisions of the seller's lien in general, and of the subordination therein in particular. In the superior position of a financial institution constantly engaged in professional construction lending [it] had no reason to believe [its] trust deed conferred any lien to which the fee was subordinate *other than to the extent of money spent for construction purposes.*

96 Cal.Rptr. at 347. (Emphasis added). Thus, even under *Middlebrook's* acknowledgment of an implied contractual duty upon the mortgage-lender to supervise the expenditure of money lent, the subordinating landowner is granted only the degree of priority accorded an unpaid materialman in Mississippi and therefore is entitled to recover only those amounts advanced which were diverted from the construction project.

In our opinion, the Mississippi Supreme Court, if faced with the question before us, would adopt the majority rule prevailing in the United States to the effect that, absent express clauses in the loan documents directing or restricting the use of construction funds to a particular project, the subordinating landowner bears the risk of diversion by a developer who obtains a mortgage to finance improvements, unless the landowner can show fraud, collusion or other inequitable conduct participated in by the mortgagee and the mortgagor-developer. We hold to this view because the Mississippi Court, since *Wortman & Mann* was decided in 1966, has consistently followed what may fairly be regarded as a conservative view in supporting the priority of mortgagees who exercise ordinary care in the disbursement of their funds, even against the claims of unpaid materialmen or laborers — claimants who stand upon a much higher plane than would the subordinated landowner who contributes no materials or efforts to the construction job, and who has at his disposal a means for protecting his interests in any commercial venture by insisting upon the inclusion of protective language in the documents comprising the agreement. Secondly, the *Middlebrook* case, upon which plaintiff principally relies, is based upon a California statute, and the Court's analysis thereof, which makes subordinating agreements that contain no restrictive clauses unenforceable. See *Middlebrook, supra,* 96 Cal.Rptr. at 347. There is no such statutory counterpart in Mississippi to justify judicial invalidation of an otherwise valid contractual provision.

Even assuming that Mississippi would adopt the view that under some circumstances an implied duty would be placed upon a construction lender, with knowledge of the owner's subordination, to adopt proper safeguards to insure that the funds went into a construction project, the overwhelming proof in this case is that Guaranty exercised ordinary care in the disbursement of funds to Watkins by the adoption of the methods heretofore discussed: requiring a certificate of inspection by an independent firm of architects; requiring an owner's affidavit stating the degree of completion of the various phases of each aspect of the project; obtaining an affidavit from the title company that all construction costs had been paid; and having an attorney regularly search the records to ascertain the existence of any materialmen or mechanics' liens on file at the time of each advance. It is significant to note that such actions are not only clearly sufficient to constitute reasonable diligence on the part of the mortgagee in Mississippi where the statutorily favored liens of unpaid materialmen and laborers are involved, see, e. g., *North American Mortgage Investors, supra,* but also would be, under the *Middlebrook* decision, determinative of the issue of whether the mortgagee has complied with the equitable duty imposed therein for the subordinating landowner's benefit. See 96 Cal.Rptr. at 346-47.

Therefore, if the evidence conclusively showed compliance with the above noted procedures with respect to every advance, then Grenada would clearly be entitled to no relief under either theory.

Grenada contends, however, that by analogizing its position to that of an unpaid materialman who gives the statutorily required notice of his claim, Green placed Guaranty on notice that there were outstanding, unpaid materialmen and laborers in July 1974, thus requiring Guaranty to make certain that any subsequent advances went to pay such creditors. Additionally, the record does show that Guaranty's later advance of $175,157 was made without previously obtaining an attorney's updated title certificate; however, as of the date of that advance, no materialman or mechanic's lien had been filed so that examination of the land records would have revealed no additional facts that Guaranty, in the exercise of ordinary care, could have ascertained. Moreover, even if Grenada, as subordinating landowner, is placed in a position analogous to that of an unpaid materialman in Mississippi by virtue of (1) oral notice to Guaranty's representative in July 1974 of the existence of unpaid, but unfiled, claims; and (2) Guaranty's failure to do anything but advance the full amount, under the settled principles of Mississippi law relative to materialmen's liens, as well as under *Middlebrook,* Guaranty would be denied priority *only* to the extent that amounts advanced did not actually go into the construction project. See *Virden, supra; Middlebrook,* 96 Cal.Rptr. at 347.

From the preponderance of credible evidence presented at trial, we have found that as of November 4, 1974, the value of the completed improvements on Grenada's land was $1,008,380, and that there were outstanding claims of $130,000 which were subsequently paid by Guaranty. The record further shows that by November 1974 Guaranty had advanced $1,090,115, which amount is $48,265 less than the value of the completed improvements, plus the total of unpaid claims existing at that time; in other words, as we have found in part I(d) of this opinion, Grenada totally failed to show that any funds advanced by Guaranty were diverted by Watkins from the Grenada project, and that the cost overrun of $114,998 resulted from an unexpectedly high rate of inflation in prices for materials and labor. Thus, even if Guaranty's action after oral notice from Green constitutes negligence, Grenada has no claim for relief since no diversion was shown.

. . . .

For the foregoing reasons we are of the opinion that Grenada has no claim for relief and its complaint should be dismissed with prejudice.

Let an order be entered accordingly.

STARR v. MOOSLIN

California District Court of Appeals
14 Cal. App. 3d 988 (1971)

HERNDON, ACTING P. J. —

Statement of the Case

Defendant and appellant Carl J. Mooslin, an attorney at law, appeals from the judgment awarding plaintiff damages in this action for legal malpractice. Plaintiff Elena Starr charged that as the result of defendant's negligence in representing her in a transaction involving a sale of real property, she suffered damages in the sum of $50,000. The judgment against defendant in the amount of $42,000 was entered upon the verdict of a jury. Defendant also appeals from the order denying his motion for judgment notwithstanding the verdict.

Statement of the Facts

Plaintiff, a woman in her eighties, was the owner of real property located at 355 South Alvarado Street, Los Angeles. Defendant, a practicing attorney and engaged in the general practice of law, had handled various legal matters for plaintiff over a period of approximately 10 years.

Some time in the year 1965 plaintiff decided that she would offer her property for sale. Thereafter she received offers from Lucius Foster and William Cooper. Plaintiff discussed some of these offers with the defendant. On January 4, 1966, plaintiff and defendant met with Foster and Cooper at defendant's law office. At this meeting the parties negotiated further with respect to the purchase and sale of the property but no agreement was reached. Foster stated that he would not be participating in the transaction as a principal but that a Mr. Robert Fisher, "an experienced builder and developer" whom he represented, would offer $60,000 for the property, $10,000 to be paid in cash at the close of escrow with the balance to be evidenced by a $50,000 promissory note secured by a deed of trust. The offer further provided that the purchase money deed of trust would be subordinated at a later date to a $275,000 construction loan. The money for construction purposes would be borrowed in installments, the first to be in the amount of $30,000. Foster further stated that Fisher would be willing to provide additional security by way of a deed of trust on other real property owned by him.

On the following day, January 5, 1966, Mrs. Starr decided that she would accept the offer as presented by Foster on behalf of Fisher. After calling Foster and informing him of her decision, she called defendant and requested that he appear at the City National Bank in Beverly Hills at the time appointed to represent her in the opening of the escrow for the purpose of effectuating the sale.

In response to plaintiff's request, defendant went to the City National Bank and, after verifying the terms of the sale with the parties present, proceeded to dictate the escrow instructions to an employee of the bank using a printed form.

The escrow instructions thus prepared provided for a total purchase price of $63,000 of which $10,000 was to be paid in cash and the balance to be evidenced by a $50,000 promissory note payable to plaintiff secured by a purchase money deed of trust. Further provision was made for the delivery to Foster of a note in the amount of $3,000 to cover his broker's commission. Fisher and Cooper and/or their nominee were named as purchasers. By a subsequent amendment to these instructions the purchase price was reduced to $60,000 and the provision for the promissory note in payment of Foster's commission was eliminated.

The instructions further provided that the buyer would execute and place in escrow a deed of trust as additional security in favor of the seller on real property located at Roseland and LaBrea, Los Angeles, California, the legal description of said property to be furnished at a later date. Beneath the foregoing provisions the following language as dictated by defendant was typewritten into the instructions:

The following is stated as a matter of record only with which the escrow holder is not to be concerned: (1) Seller agrees to subordinate on demand, to a 1st trust deed, not to exceed $275,000.00, bearing interest at not more than 7.5% per annum, for not more than 30 years. Seller agrees to subordinate forthwith to $30,000.00, the same being a portion of the above referred to $275,000.00 loan, and will execute upon demand any additional subordination agreement in order to enable Buyer to refinance or to increase the encumbrance to be placed upon the land provided the same shall not exceed in total $275,000.00 represented by a single 1st trust deed.

The escrow instructions thus prepared by defendant were signed by plaintiff as seller and by Fisher and Cooper as buyers and were deposited with City National Bank as escrow agent. By an amendment to the instructions Fisher alone was designated as the buyer and plaintiff's deed to Fisher as grantee was thereafter deposited in escrow.

Within a few days thereafter Fisher made arrangements to borrow $30,000 from Irving and Matilda Scham and Ben and Eva Solomon. This loan was to be evidenced by a promissory note secured by a first deed of trust on the property which plaintiff had agreed to sell to Fisher. On January 18, 1966, Fisher and the parties from whom he was borrowing the $30,000 opened an escrow at LaCienega Escrow Company for the purpose of effectuating that loan. Fisher deposited therein his promissory note and the lenders deposited the $30,000.

On the following day, January 19, 1966, Fisher deposited in the original escrow at City National Bank his promissory note in the amount of $50,000 payable to plaintiff and the two deeds of trust on the subject property, one of which was security for the $30,000 and the other was to secure plaintiff's $50,000 note. Plaintiff's deed of trust contained on its face the following provision: "This deed of trust is second and subject to a first deed of trust to record concurrently."

On January 24, 1966, the LaCienega Escrow Company paid out $10,150 to the City National Bank for plaintiff's account, $18,265 to Robert Fisher, $300 to Lucius Foster, and $1,285 to other persons not involved in this case.

According to the testimony of the employee of City National Bank who handled the escrow for that institution, the instruments deposited therein were recorded pursuant to the oral direction of defendant and the escrow was thereupon closed. As a result of these procedures plaintiff's $50,000 purchase money deed of trust and the $300,000 deed of trust held by the Schams and Solomons were recorded concurrently. Plaintiff's deed of trust was thereby subordinated.

Subsequently, Fisher failed to make the payments on the Scham-Solomon note. Fisher's default resulted in foreclosure proceedings instituted by the Schams and the Solomons. At the trustee's sale the property was purchased by the beneficiaries. Plaintiff was unable to bid at the sale because of her lack of sufficient funds. The purchasers at the foreclosure sale thereafter brought an unlawful detainer action against Mrs. Starr to obtain possession. Mrs. Starr filed an answer and cross-complaint naming as cross-defendants Fisher, Cooper, Foster, the Schams, the Solomons, and others, and charging said cross-defendants with fraud and conspiracy to deprive her of her property. This litigation was terminated by a settlement whereby Mrs. Starr repurchased her property for $32,500.

Immediately thereafter plaintiff resold the property for $57,500 of which $32,500 was paid to the buyers at the foreclosure sale. Plaintiff received $1,500 in cash and a promissory note in the amount of $14,035 secured by a deed of trust on the subject property. Approximately $800 was expended in escrow expenses and $8,167 was paid over to Mr. J. J. Brandlin as compensation for his legal services.

Thereafter the instant action against defendant was filed by Mrs. Starr. Her complaint alleges that defendant, as an attorney, undertook to represent her and to act as her attorney in consummating the sale of her property. It is further alleged in substance that defendant negligently performed his duties in that he failed to use that degree of learning, skill and judgment ordinarily used by lawyers of good standing and practicing in the same locality under similar circumstances and as a proximate result of such negligence plaintiff was damaged in the sum of $50,000.

At the trial oral and documentary evidence was introduced proving the facts as above recited. It is to be observed that except for the opinions of the expert witnesses hereinafter summarized, the evidence was virtually uncontradicted. On cross-examination by counsel for plaintiff, defendant testified that he was acquainted with subordination agreements and recognized that such agreements ordinarily provided that the proceeds from secured loans would be used to improve the real property. Defendant did not research the applicable law prior to preparing the escrow instructions in this case. At the time of this transaction it was defendant's understanding that it was probably the law that if plaintiff and the buyer entered into a subordination agreement which provided that the buyer was to use the $30,000 to improve the property and if the lenders of the $30,000 had notice thereof and plaintiff did not waive her rights under the subordination agreement and if the $30,000 was not so used, the subordination would not be effective and plaintiff's trust deed would retain its priority. Notwithstanding his uncertainty on the subject, however, defendant did not research the law and the escrow instructions as prepared by him did not contain such provisions.

Plaintiff's Expert Witness

Plaintiff called Dennis G. Harkavy, an attorney at law, as an expert witness. The qualifications of this witness as indicated by his testimony are unquestioned. Over defendant's objection, made solely on the ground that expert testimony is inadmissible to prove negligence in a legal malpractice suit, the witness was permitted to state his opinion in response to a hypothetical question whether or not, on the basis of the facts assumed, defendant had exercised that degree of learning, care and skill ordinarily possessed by attorneys in good standing practicing in the Los Angeles area at about this time and under similar circumstances. The witness answered: "In my opinion the requisite skill of a general practitioner was not employed in drawing these instructions." The witness thereafter stated at length the reasons for his opinion and pointed out in detail the several respects in which he considered the escrow instructions deficient.

Defendant's Expert Witnesses

Near the end of the trial on a Friday afternoon, counsel for defendant called as his last witness an escrow officer employed by a local title company. This witness was asked to examine the escrow instructions and then to state his opinion as to whether or not under those instructions an escrow officer could properly record a $30,000 deed of trust ahead of the $50,000 deed of trust referred to therein. The trial court sustained plaintiff's objection to this question on the ground that qualifications of the witness to testify as an expert on the subject had not been sufficiently indicated. Defendant does not question the correctness of this ruling. Defense counsel then asked that the trial be continued to the following Monday to enable him to secure a qualified witness. The understanding upon which defendant's request was granted is indicated by the following colloquy between court and counsel:

THE COURT: The record will show the absence of the members of the jury and the presence of counsel. I think the record should also show that before I dismissed the jury for the day, counsel favored me with a conference at the side bench from which I got the impression that the defense case so far as proof is concerned is ready to rest with one exception; that the defense proposes to offer, given time, to produce a witness, evidence by some qualified witness that the custom and usage among reputable escrow holders in Los Angeles County in early 1966 was such that the defendant might reasonably have relied upon such escrow holder, presumably the escrow holder referred to at the City National Bank, to prevent the recordation of the $30,000 encumbrance in such a manner that it would take priority over the $50,000 purchase price trust deed. Is that the request you made? MR. KIRWAN: Correct, your Honor. THE COURT: Now, will your proof embrace anything else? MR. KIRWAN: Well, I think it would have to follow with the questions from my client as to whether he knew that custom from his experience in handling escrows and he relied on that, but that is the gist of it. THE COURT: All right. On the representation by Mr. Kirwan that he desires to make such proof and because of the hour and my disposition not to have argument commence today, I did continue the matter until Monday at 9:30, solely for the receipt of that evidence, and I did promise Mr. Brandlin that we would clearly delineate the area to be covered since Mr. Brandlin has indicated he had no rebuttal to the case thus far presented. Did I understand you correctly? MR. BRANDLIN: Yes, your Honor. THE COURT: Now, then, Mr. Brandlin, you have the area in mind. Mr. Kirwan may or may not have such proof, but you are forewarned.

On the following Monday defense counsel called two expert witnesses, attorney David Sefman and the Honorable Alfred Gitelson, a judge of the superior court. The rulings of the trial court permitted each of these witnesses to testify to his extensive experience in relation to the handling of escrows in similar transactions. Each of these witnesses was permitted over plaintiff's objections to testify to his opinion that in conformity with prevailing custom and practice among escrow agencies, a reasonably careful escrow holder would not have recorded the deeds of trust as was done in the instant case but would have required something more in the way of authorization than was required by the City National Bank in this case.

Each of defendant's expert witnesses was permitted to testify to his opinion that an attorney engaged in the general practice of law in the community exercising reasonable care could properly rely upon the custom and usage prevailing among escrow holders concerning which the witnesses previously had testified. Judge Gitelson testified as follows: "Q. Now, in respect to the custom with which you are familiar, do you have an opinion as to whether in the custom that prevailed at that time the escrow holder would have, in following that custom, recorded any documents relating to a $30,000 that is mentioned in that language? A. I do. Q. What is that opinion? [Objection interposed. Question rephrased.] Q. In the escrow instructions which I read to you, that portion from them, would they in the custom and usage that then prevailed, would an escrow officer record any documents relating to the $30,000 as mentioned in there that would give that $30,000 any priority in respect to the monies referred to in the escrow instructions? A. He would not."

The witness thereafter testified at some length in giving his reasons for that opinion. The essence of his testimony was that in recording the deeds of trust, the City National Bank had transgressed against the established custom and practice of escrow holders upon which defendant had reasonably relied. On the basis of the testimony of the two experts called by him, defense counsel argued in the trial court that the conceded deficiencies in the escrow instructions were not the proximate cause of plaintiff's damages.

. . . .

The inadequacy of the escrow instructions to afford plaintiff the protection which the circumstances of the transaction involved in this case obviously required is undeniable and virtually conceded. No lawyer with knowledge of the most elementary rules of law governing such transactions would have failed to insist upon more adequate provisions to insure that all of the proceeds of the $30,000 loan, which was to be given security prior to that of his client's purchase money lien, would be used to improve the property.

The teachings of hindsight were not necessary to prove that it was negligent and hazardous to fail to provide such protection. This truth is emphasized by the fact that there was no requirement that the construction loan would be obtained from an institutional lender which could be relied upon to see that the proceeds of the loan were properly used to improve the real property. Moreover, it is an apparent fact that defendant made no inquiry or investigation for the purpose of ascertaining the reliability, financial or otherwise, of the purchaser or the value of the other property which he had promised to encumber as additional security.

In these circumstances it is understandable that defendant and his trial counsel based their defense entirely upon the contention that it was not the conceded deficiencies in the escrow instructions prepared by defendant, but rather it was the mistake or misconduct of the City National Bank as escrow agent, which constituted the proximate cause of plaintiff's loss. The only possible basis upon which defendant could claim freedom from negligence was his contention that he had justifiably relied upon an asserted custom and practice among escrow agents which the City National Bank violated when it delivered the two deeds of trust for recordation. This contention necessarily implies that defendant contemplated the taking of further unspecified steps to protect his client's interests prior to the closing of the escrow.

Since the trial court submitted the issue of defendant's negligence to the jury upon legally correct instructions, we need not decide the arguable contention that defendant was guilty of negligence as a matter of law. The trial court permitted defendant to introduce the only expert testimony which would have been consistent with the theory of his defense.

. . . .

The trial court's instructions clearly advised the jury that plaintiff could not recover unless she had proved by a preponderance of the evidence that defendant's negligence was a proximate cause of her injury. Defendant's argument fails to recognize that an attorney's negligence need not be the *sole* cause of the client's loss in order to subject him to liability. That is to say, where there is causation in fact it need not be the sole proximate cause. (*Modica v. Crist*, 129 Cal.App.2d 144, 146 [276 P.2d 614]; *Ishmael v. Millington, supra*, 241 Cal.App.2d 520, 529; *Lysick v. Walcom, supra*, 258 Cal.App.2d 136, 153, fn. 7.)

Conclusion

We reject appellant's additional assignments of error deeming them not sufficiently substantial to merit further discussion. The contention that the trial court erred in denying defendant's motions for a directed verdict, for a new trial, and for judgment notwithstanding the verdict is predicated upon the assignments of error which we have rejected as unmeritorious. It is unquestioned and unquestionable that the implied findings of the jury upon the issues of negligence, proximate cause, and damages are supported by substantial evidence.

The judgment and the order denying defendant's motion for judgment notwithstanding the verdict are affirmed.

Compton, J., concurred.

Fleming, J. — I concur in the opinion but find an additional basis for defendant's liability, viz., his negligence in allowing his client to be defrauded and swindled out of her property.

Under the purported sale of plaintiff's real property for $60,000, the purchaser put up nothing and used the seller's own property as security to borrow $30,000, out of which he paid $10,000 to the seller and pocketed the balance of $20,000 for his own use. When the transaction is stripped of its documentary window dressing, it becomes readily apparent that plaintiff was relieved of assets of a value of $20,000. Such a transaction amounts to elementary fraud, for protection against which persons employ lawyers to provide them with advice and counsel. If a lawyer fails to provide advice and counsel of sufficient quality to enable his client to protect herself against such an obvious swindle, he may be held liable for the ensuing loss.

The foregoing covers the bare-faced swindle. The more genteel, dressed-up version concocted by the buyer and his agents was only slightly less rapacious. Under this version the buyer agreed to put up $10,000, and the seller agreed to subordinate the unpaid balance of the purchase price, $50,000, to a $275,000 construction loan. Even if it should turn out that the lien ahead of plaintiff represented moneys actually expended in improving the property, plaintiff's security would remain wholly vulnerable to a complete wipe-out if any mild deflation in real estate values occurred, for her security interest would have been subordinated to 82 percent of the total amount put into the venture, and the entire loan of $275,000 would have to be repaid before she could realize anything on her security. Under such a deal plaintiff would be saddled with the primary risk of speculative loss and wholly excluded from any hope of speculative gain. These terms are so one-sided and so unfair as to be only slightly less fraudulent than the bald fraud which actually took place. (Cf. *Handy v. Gordon*, 65 Cal.2d 578 [55 Cal. Rptr. 769, 422 P.2d 329, 26 A.L.R.3d 848].) Here again, a lawyer who has been employed to represent the interests of the seller is required to provide advice and counsel which will enable his client to protect herself against such imposition, and if he does not adequately do this he may become liable for losses suffered by his client as a result of his negligence.

Needless to say, these considerations have special application to the case at bench, where the client was an 80-year-old, semi-literate widow of limited means and limited business experience. In representing such clients lawyers are required to exercise extra caution, for these clients are not equipped to protect themselves.

A petition for a rehearing was denied March 2, 1971, and appellant's petition for a hearing by the Supreme Court was denied April 29, 1971. Peters, J., was of the opinion that the petition should be granted.

NOTES

1. The general rule is that the subordinating party runs the risk that construction funds will be diverted unless there is an express contract or proof of collusion between the mortgagor and the subsequent lienor, typically the construction lender. This is true

whether damages are sought as in *Grenada, supra,* or a rearrangement of priorities as in *Middlebrook-Anderson, supra. See Kennedy v. Betts,* 33 Md. App. 258, 364 A.2d 74 (1976).

2. Note the position of the parties in *Grenada Ready-Mix v. Watkins, supra.* The plaintiff was not a purchase money mortgagee, but rather a lessor who joined in a mortgage for construction but not in the note. The court refers to this as subordination. Is it really subordination, or merely a willingness to subject one's property to a lien in order to have improvements constructed?

3. *Middlebrook-Anderson v. Southwest Savings & Loan Ass'n, supra,* important for its departure from the general rule, is equally important in resolving the dispute over the difference between a purchase money second mortgage and a subordinated first mortgage. Can you see why it would have made a difference in the result if the court had found the two different in substance rather than in form only?

4. The attorney for the injured subordinating party may be liable for not taking adequate precautions to avoid misuse of funds. Mooslin could have used several different controls on the disbursal of funds to protect Mrs. Starr, but did not do so. What sort of control would you suggest? Does this case make you think you will avoid handling even *simple* real estate transactions?

5. A gross misuse of funds may give rise to a fraud action against the builder if the other remedies appear inappropriate. In one case, by using substandard materials, the builder pocketed about half of the construction funds which were meant for the project. An appraiser at the trial testified that the kitchen equipment was so unique that he had photographed it, having never seen such equipment except in boats and house trailers. *See Joanco Projects, Inc. v. Nixon & Tierney Construction Co.,* 248 Cal. App. 2d 821, 57 Cal. Rptr. 48 (1967).

4. RELEASE CLAUSES*

Release clauses are found in nearly every real estate transaction involving incremental development of unimproved property. Typically, a developer will have executed a purchase money mortgage as part of the purchase price, subject to some smaller parcels being released from the mortgage upon the payment of a certain amount of funds to the mortgagee. As the developer sells off parcels of land from the subject property, a portion of the proceeds of sale are used to partially satisfy the encumbrance represented by the vendor's purchase money mortgage. In return for this partial payment, the mortgagee releases from the purchase money mortgage the smaller parcel sold by the mortgagor. In other instances the purchaser-mortgagor enters into an agreement with the vendor-mortgagee whereby the vendor agrees to release from the mortgage a portion of the subject property after the mortgagor has reduced the principal balance on the purchase money mortgage by an agreed amount. There are several methods for determining the property to be released and several pitfalls which both the mortgagor and the mortgagee will want to avoid.

The best and most specific method of determining the property to be released is the use of a survey and map attached to the marketing contract. Often, however, a marketing contract will be executed in haste providing for release without first having had a survey made. It is generally impossible to delay execution of a marketing contract until completion of a survey. In the absence of a survey map, the parties will resort to other means to identify the property which is to be released from the mortgage at a later date.

While there may be more justification for requiring less specificity in a release clause than in a subordination agreement, since a release clause could be clarified

* Portions of this section originally appeared in Subordination Agreements & Release Clauses, in California Real Estate Secured Transactions 221-28 and are reprinted here by permission of John R. Hetland and the University of California.

with greater ease, it is still dangerous for the parties to enter into a release agreement without sufficient specificity.

Developers may proffer a release price per acre without specific acreage being designated. Often the inducement is an inflated price for the purchase of a large parcel of land within which there is great disparity in value among different portions. Using a simple per-acre release price, a purchaser may take title to the entire parcel with little or no down payment. After payment of the prescribed per-acre price for release, the purchaser may request release of the choice acreage, which may have a value far in excess of the release price. Once the choice acreage is released, the mortgagor can default in the payments on the purchase money mortgage leaving the vendor-mortgagee to foreclose. If the jurisdiction prohibits deficiency judgments, the vendor is likely to end up with a portion of the land back, having lost the best portion for an inadequate release payment. For this reason the drafter of any release clause must make certain that the land to be released is designated with sufficient specificity; and, that the price per acre for release is not less than the value per acre of the best portion of the subject property.

LAWRENCE v. SHUTT

California District Court of Appeals
269 Cal. App. 2d 753 (1969)

FOGG, J. pro tem. — This appeal concerns the issues of the validity of a release clause in a purchase money deed of trust, and if invalid, whether or not rescission of the entire sales transaction was justified. The action was brought by plaintiffs Marvin E. Lawrence, Beverlie A. Lawrence, and Marvin E. Lawrence Company (Lawrence) and S. V. Hunsaker & Sons, Inc. (Hunsaker) for specific performance of the release clause, for a declaration of the rights and obligations of the parties under the release clause, and to quiet title to the property as to which the release was demanded . . . Roy V. Shutt and Winifred Shutt (Shutt), sellers of the property and beneficiaries under the deed of trust, answered the complaint by denying the validity of the release clause, counterclaimed for rescission of the transaction of sale, and sought to set aside the conveyance to Lawrence. After a court trial, judgment was entered in favor of the Shutts rescinding the agreement of sale and declaring the grant deeds and deeds of trust to be void, ordering the grant deeds and deeds of trust to be cancelled, declaring the Shutts to be the owners of said property, and further ordering the Shutts to restore to plaintiffs the $250,000 paid by the latter under said agreement.

. . . This appeal is from the judgment.

In March 1963, the Shutts were the owners of 1,280 acres of land situated, for the most part, in Riverside County at the boundary between Riverside and San Bernardino Counties. Except for the Shutt residence and accompanying farm structures, the property is unimproved. Access from County Line Road, a public road, can only be had from the east, and there are no public or improved roads on the property. The land is very hilly and rough except for the most easterly 80 acres.

By escrow instructions, dated March 15, 1963 and March 22, 1963, the Shutts agreed to sell the 1,280 acres to Dr. Gerald Rutten for the total sum of $1,175,000 of which $250,000 was to be in cash and the balance of $925,000 to be evidenced by a promissory note secured by a first deed of trust. In these instructions, Rutten reserved the right to assign his interest in said transaction without further approval of the seller. The instructions also contained a provision which later was incorporated in the deeds of trust and which provided for the manner in which parcels of the real property would be released from the lien of the deed of trust. This clause was drafted in its entirety by the attorney for the Shutts. It was subsequently revised so as to break down the property from two to three sectors for release purposes. The three sectors became the "80-acre parcel" having a release price of $5,000 per acre; that portion of the 1,200-acre parcel lying in Section 15, Township 2 South, Range 2 West, S.B.B. & M. (containing 240 acres) having a release price of $2,000 per acre; and the remainder of the 1,200-acre parcel (960 acres) having a release price of $1,000 per acre.

. . . .

On March 20, 1964, Rutten sold, assigned and transferred all right, title, and interest in the escrow to Marvin E. Lawrence for agreed cash payments totaling $65,000 and a trust deed to be given at close of escrow for the balance of the purchase price . . . .

On June 24, 1964, the escrow holder forwarded to the Shutts a map and legal description of two parcels, totaling 143.5 acres, which the buyers had requested to be excluded from the deed of trust pursuant to the release clause. The Shutts refused to release the parcels requested and, on August 13, 1964, the escrow closed and the various grant deeds and trust deed were recorded. On the same morning, plaintiffs commenced this action and attached the proceeds of the escrow as well as the bank accounts of the Shutts. Plaintiffs also demanded a partial reconveyance of the two parcels previously requested to be omitted from the trust deed; however, this request was refused by the Shutts. From August 13, 1964, the two parcels for which releases were sought were owned by S. V. Hunsaker & Sons, Inc., and Marvin E. Lawrence, joint venturers doing business under the firm name of S.V.H. & L.C. Development Co., which joint venture became effective July 10, 1964. The $250,000 down payment which was eventually received by the Shutts was paid by Hunsaker.

Some three or four months before the escrow was to close, the Shutts began expressing dissatisfaction with the release clause. They changed counsel twice prior to the close of escrow, and again following the close of escrow. Just prior to close of escrow, the Shutts, through their then counsel, indicated their belief that the release clause was unenforceable in its present form as contended by the buyers, and that it was their interpretation that the property first eligible for release was the 80-acre parcel. However, they did not specifically object to the closing of escrow.

. . . .

[The Shutts served a Notice of Rescission after the escrow closed and later refused to comply with a release request on the grounds that it did not comply with the provisions of the release clause.]

During the entire period from the close of escrow to date of judgment, the Shutts denied Lawrence's ownership and interfered with his access, use and development of the property. Lawrence sought and obtained a temporary injunction against further interference and harassment by the Shutts, with access to and use of said property by Lawrence, his agents, employees and representatives. Ultimately, Mr. Shutt was incarcerated three days for contempt of this court order.

The Shutts also refused to accept interest on the deed of trust and continued to pay real property taxes after the close of escrow.

In its findings of fact, the trial court found, in pertinent part, as follows:

19. At the time of entering into the escrow instructions defendant SHUTT believed that property would be released from the provisions of the Deed of

Trust in such a manner that the property in the "80 acre parcel" would first be released, and that thereafter generally rectangular shape parcels of 40 acres or more, each proceeding from one boundary of the property parallel to adjacent boundaries towards the center of the property, would be released; and defendants would not have agreed to a provision for partial release and would not have agreed to the provisions for the purchase relative to payment of interest only on the promissory note secured by the Deed of Trust for a period of three (3) years, but for such relief.

20. The property for which plaintiffs sought a release, described in Exhibit "H" and attached to plaintiffs' complaint, did not conform to the requirements for release in that parcel "B" thereof is smaller than 40 acres; to wit, 6.5 acres.

21. Release of the parcels as requested by plaintiffs would not leave reasonable access to portions of the 1200 acre parcel.

22. Release of the parcels requested by plaintiffs would depreciate the value of the remaining portion of the subject property and cause it to be of less value than the balance due upon the note secured by the Deed of Trust.

23. Plaintiffs asserted in open court that they had the unrestricted right to seek releases that wind around in any fashion they wanted, and that after they had taken the part that was suitable for development they could leave defendants with the hilltops with no security at all for the purchase price; and that they had the right to select for release a piece of property that merely touches a parcel previously released, and that they would stand or fall on that interpretation of the "release clause". ·

24. Interpreted in the manner advanced by plaintiffs herein, the provisions of the escrow instructions and the Deed of Trust relating to partial release would not be just or reasonable to defendants and the consideration to defendants for the entire transaction under such interpretation would be inadequate.

25. The manner in which the plaintiffs would exercise the purported "release clause" is unreasonable and arbitrary and so threatens to destroy defendants' security interest in the property as to amount to the total failure of consideration.

26. The manner in which the plaintiffs seek to have property released from the trust deed described in the First Amended Complaint is inequitable, unfair, harsh, unjust, oppressive and, if carried out, would impose an undue hardship on the defendants.

27. The provisions in the escrow instructions and in the Deed of Trust for the release of portions of the property from the lien or charge of the Deed of Trust are so vague and indefinite and uncertain that the Court is unable to determine the manner in which parcels of the property, if any, should be released.

28. The parties to the escrow instructions had no agreement between them as to any special meaning to be given to the language of the agreement applicable to releases of portions of the property from the Deed of Trust; nor did defendants have any such agreement with plaintiffs, or either of them.

29. The provisions in the escrow instructions and in the Deed of Trust for the release of portions of the property from the lien or charge of the Deed of Trust are so vague and indefinite and uncertain as to be unenforceable and to render the entire sale transaction void and of no force and effect. . . .

Plaintiffs' contentions upon appeal may be summarized as follows:

1. This release clause which gives to the buyers the right to select acreage for release is specifically enforceable in equity.

(a) It is not uncertain nor indefinite, nor does it constitute merely an agreement to agree.

(b) It is not unjust nor unreasonable.

2. Even if this release clause is unenforceable, it was error to declare the conveyance itself invalid.

3. The unilateral misunderstanding of the Shutts as to the meaning of the release clause will not justify rescission of the entire transaction based upon unilateral mistake.

4. A release clause is not an agreement for the sale of real property within the statute of frauds.

5. The rescission was defective in that the Shutts failed to join an indispensable party — Dr. Rutten.

6. The rescission was defective because the property sought to be released was owned by a bona fide purchaser — Hunsaker.

In support of the judgment, defendants argue that:

1. This release clause is void because it is indefinite and uncertain.

2. If not void, the release clause is so indefinite and uncertain that it will not support an action for specific performance.

3. If not void, the release clause is not specifically enforceable because it is not just and reasonable and is not supported by adequate consideration.

4. The release clause is an integral part of the transaction and its invalidity renders the entire transaction void.

5. The Shutts are entitled to rescission of the entire transaction based upon unilateral mistake.

6. Hunsaker is not a bona fide purchaser.

7. Rutten is not an indispensable party.

Initially, plaintiffs maintain the trial court erred in determining that the provisions of the escrow instructions and the deed of trust calling for the release of portions of the property were so vague, indefinite and uncertain as to be unenforceable and hence rendered the entire sale transaction void and of no force or effect.

. . . .

It is well settled that courts will give written agreements, if reasonably possible, a construction which will result in their being enforceable contracts. "That a greater degree or amount of certainty is required in the terms of an agreement which is to be specifically executed in equity than is necessary in a contract which is the basis of an action at law for damages" has often been declared.

In order for a court of equity to decree that an obligation is specifically enforceable the terms of the contract must be complete and certain in all particulars essential to its enforcement. The agreement must not only contain all the material terms but also express each in a reasonably definite manner. (*Spellman v. Dixon,* 256 Cal.App.2d 1, 3 [63 Cal.Rptr. 668]; *Magna Dev. Co. v. Reed, supra.*) These principles have been repeatedly applied to deny specific performance of agreements which are incomplete, indefinite or uncertain with respect to the terms of payment of deferred balances or the terms of encumbrances representing such deferred balances. Recently these principles have been applied in denying specific performance to subordination agreements when the subordination provisions have been found uncertain and incapable of ascertainment by reference to an objective standard. (*Handy v. Gordon,* 65 Cal.2d 578 [55 Cal.Rptr. 769, 422 P.2d 329]; *Spellman v. Dixon, supra,* 256 Cal.App.2d 1; *Stockwell v. Lindeman,* 229 Cal.App.2d 750 [40 Cal.Rptr. 555]; *Magna Dev. Co. v. Reed, supra; Gould v. Callan,* 127 Cal.App.2d 1 [273 P.2d 93].)

As stated by the Supreme Court in *Handy v. Gordon, supra,* at p. 581:

. . . an enforceable subordination clause must contain terms that will define and minimize the risk that the subordinating liens will impair or destroy the seller's security. [Cases cited.] Such terms may include limits on the use to which the proceeds may be put to insure that their use will improve the value of the land, maximum amounts so that the loans will not exceed the contemplated value of the improvements they finance, requirements that the loans do not exceed some specified percentage of the construction cost or value of the property as improved, specified amounts per square foot of construction, or other limits designed to protect the security. Without some such terms, however, the seller is forced to rely entirely on the buyer's good faith and ability as a developer to insure that he will not lose both his land and the purchase price.

In the instant case the trial court was clearly, and with good reason, concerned about the ambiguity of the operation of the release clause. Plaintiffs had asserted in open court that the word "contiguous," as used in the release clause, gave them the unrestricted "right to select for release a piece of property that merely touches" and hence they could take that portion of the property suitable for development and leave defendants with the hills and gullies. Plaintiffs argued below and argue here that the word "contiguous" is fundamentally certain in meaning and that, therefore, the agreement is not void for indefiniteness and uncertainty. Plaintiffs cite *Ganiats Constr., Inc. v. Hesse,* 180 Cal.App.2d 377, 385 [4 Cal.Rptr. 706], wherein the court said that " 'contiguous' realty need have only a minimum common boundary with the adjacent property" as authority for the proposition that the word "contiguous" is fundamentally certain in meaning. However, in *Ganiats* the appellate court also said (pp. 384-385) in considering an option giving the optionee the right to purchase 10 acres of property and thereafter upon certain terms and conditions the "next contiguous thirty (30) acres;" thereafter upon further terms and conditions the "next contiguous seventy (70) acres" and the "next contiguous one hundred twenty (120) acres:"

The reference to the acreage in the designation "the next contiguous thirty acres" is not in itself a self-sufficient description. An acre is "[a] quantity of land containing 160 square rods of land, in whatever shape." (Black's Law Dictionary (4th ed., 1951), p. 42.) An acre can be a circular, square, triangular, irregular, broad or narrow strip of land. Indeed, an acre is not a concrete form; it is a term of quantity and it can be applied to land in all manner of patterns.

As we shall point out *infra* in more detail, the crucial term "next contiguous thirty acres" does not in itself specify the area covered by the option. In the first place the contiguity of *one acre* "next" to the westerly boundary would literally suffice to fulfill the definition, leaving open and unspecified the location of the remaining acreage. Even if we place all the 30 acres as close to the westerly boundary as possible: that is, the maximum number of acres adjacent to the westerly line, the remaining acres of the area may still take various forms or shapes, and the location of the easterly boundary remains indefinite.

In the case at bench the release clause was even more indefinite and uncertain; it provided only that any parcel of property no smaller than a certain number of acres released must be contiguous to that previously released.

While plaintiffs may be technically correct in asserting that the word "contiguous" is certain in meaning, it is apparent that the word, as used in this release clause, renders the release clause uncertain and unreasonable in equity on the ground that the provision placed the sellers in a position where they could be deprived of all the choice land without adequate protection that they would ever be compensated by the buyer for the remainder. (See *Handy v. Gordon, supra,* 65 Cal.2d 578, 581; cf. *Magna Dev. Co. v. Reed, supra,* 228 Cal.App.2d

230, 243-244.) The fact that the release clause is not sufficiently certain for specific performance does not, however, require us to invalidate the entire agreement. (See *Norris v. Lilly,* 147 Cal. 754, 756-757 [82 P. 425, 109 Am.St.Rep. 188]; *Schomaker v. Osborne,* 250 Cal.App.2d 887, 893 [58 Cal.Rptr. 827]; *Brooks v. Allard,* 244 Cal.App.2d 283, 290-291 [53 Cal.Rptr. 82]; *Leider v. Evans,* 209 Cal.App.2d 696, 699-701 [26 Cal.Rptr. 123].)

Defendants' reliance upon *Spellman v. Dixon, supra,* 256 Cal.App.2d 1, and *Magna Dev. Co. v. Reed, supra,* 228 Cal.App.2d 230, for the proposition that the uncertainty of the release clause renders the entire transaction void is misplaced for the reason that in the instant case the escrow had closed, the grant deeds and trust deed were recorded, and thus the agreement had been executed. Defendants concede and the trial court found, that the escrow properly closed. The sale was thus complete at that moment. Since the property sold was described with detailed certainty, the agreement to convey the realty was not incomplete. (See *Carlson v. Richardson,* 267 Cal.App.2d 204 [72 Cal.Rptr. 769]; *Calvi v. Bittner,* 198 Cal.App.2d 312, 321 [17 Cal.Rptr. 850].)

The plaintiffs here, unlike the plaintiffs in *Spellman* and *Magna,* were not attempting to have the court decree that a contract existed, but were merely attempting to enforce the release clause provision. While the uncertainty of the release clause precludes specific performance of the provision, the contract was nevertheless certain enough to bind defendants to the obligation. (*Schomaker v. Osborne, supra,* 250 Cal.App.2d 887, 893; *Eastwood Homes, Inc. v. Hudson,* 161 Cal.App.2d 532, 540 [327 P.2d 29].) " 'The law does not favor but leans against the destruction of contracts because of uncertainty; and it will, if feasible, so construe agreements as to carry into effect the reasonable intentions of the parties if that can be ascertained.' " (*California Lettuce Growers, Inc. v. Union Sugar Co.,* 45 Cal.2d 474, 481 [289 P.2d 785, 49 A.L.R.2d 496], quoted in *Ontario Downs, Inc. v. Lauppe,* 192 Cal.App.2d 697, 703 [13 Cal.Rptr. 782].)

In the case under review, the defendants contended, and the trial court concluded, that the unilateral misunderstanding of the defendants as to the meaning of the release clause justified rescission of the entire transaction based upon unilateral mistake. The "mistake" which the trial court relied upon in decreeing rescission was the alleged belief of defendant Roy V. Shutt that the releases would first be in the 80-acre parcel and that the parcels to be released would be perpendicular parcels, parallel in shape and working from one boundary to the other.

Rescission of a contract for mistake, like reformation, is usually founded upon either mutual mistake of the parties or a mistake by one induced or contributed to by the other's fraud. (*California Trust Co. v. Cohn,* 214 Cal. 619, 626 [7 P.2d 297]; *Taylor v. Taylor,* 66 Cal.App.2d 390, 398 [152 P.2d 480]; 33 Cal.Jur.2d. p. 318, § 4.) It is clear, however, that a court, under its equitable power, does have the right to rescind a contract for the purely unilateral mistake of one contracting party not induced or contributed to by the other party. . . .

. . . .

In the case at bench the record reflects that three or four months prior to the scheduled close of escrow, the defendants expressed dissatisfaction with the release clause. They retained new counsel at this time and subsequently again changed counsel. Just before the close of escrow, the defendants, through their then counsel, indicated their dissatisfaction with the terms of the release clause as drafted by their prior counsel, but raised no objection to the close of escrow. It is thus "clear" that defendants had notice of sufficient facts to put them on inquiry as to the meaning of the word "contiguous," or as to the configuration of the parcels to be released and the area from which they would be released. Nevertheless they failed to make reasonable inquiry, or any inquiry, and were hence guilty of neglect of a legal duty. Consequently, the mistake which the defendants entertained was not a mistake of fact within the meaning of the law. (*Mesmer v. White, supra,* 121 Cal.App.2d 665, 674; *Roller v. California Pac. Title Ins. Co., supra,* 92 Cal.App.2d 149; *Taylor v. Taylor, supra,* 66 Cal.App.2d 390.)

In addition to the fact that defendants were guilty of neglect of a legal duty and thus not entitled to rescission, the record reflects that rescission was also improper for the reason that enforcement of the contract (without the release clause) would not impose an oppressive burden on the defendants, while rescission of the contract would impose substantial hardship on the plaintiffs. (Cf. *M. F. Kemper Constr. Co. v. City of Los Angeles,* 37 Cal.2d 696, 701 [235 P.2d 7].)

In the case under review, there is no evidence that the original price for the land was not fair. Moreover, there is no evidence which would support an inference that enforcement of this contract (without the release clause) at the present time would be oppressive to the defendants. On the other hand, there is substantial evidence which convinces this court that rescission as ordered by the trial court would impose great hardship on the plaintiffs.

Defendants urge that the release clause is an integral part of the transaction and that its invalidity renders the entire transaction void and rescindable. However, it is obvious that this release clause was designed for the benefit of the plaintiffs as the buyers, and the Shutts as sellers would not be prejudiced by the enforcement of the contract without the release clause. Also, even assuming the executory release clause is an integral part of this transaction, the defendants are not in a position to assert its invalidity because they created the ambiguity or uncertainty which invalidates the clause. They, therefore, are estopped to assert this contention upon general principles of equity.

Plaintiffs have not sought rescission in the event the release clause was invalidated. Moreover, in their opening brief they have indicated a willingness to retain title to this property without the benefit of the release clause in the event it is held unenforceable. In order to obviate any concern that plaintiffs might, at retrial, ask leave to amend to rescind this transaction, we hold that they are estopped to change their remedy to rescission by their original election to seek specific performance of this release clause. Plaintiffs have clearly manifested an intention to pursue one of two inconsistent remedies, and such a change obviously would operate to defendants' prejudice in view of the lapse of time.

The judgment is reversed and the case remanded for further proceedings in conformity with this opinion.

KERRIGAN, ACTING P. J., and TAMURA, J., concurred.

YACKEY v. PACIFICA DEVELOPMENT CO.

California District Court of Appeals
99 Cal. App. 3d 776 (1979)

STANIFORTH, ACTING PRESIDING JUSTICE.

Plaintiffs George F. Yackey and Alma H. Yackey brought this action to recover money damages for breach of contract (escrow instructions) against the Pacifica Development Company (partnership) and its co-partners William R. Swann and Edward Gessin.

Upon trial, the court found the release clause in the escrow agreement so uncertain as to render the entire agreement void, unenforceable and upon that sole basis gave judgment for defendants. Yackey appeals.

I

Mr. and Mrs. Yackey agreed to sell to the partnership 375 acres of real property located in Fallbrook, California. When the buyers refused to perform the agreement, according to the terms of the escrow agreement, the Yackeys filed this suit for damages for breach of contract. The partnership denied the essential allegations of the complaint and set up affirmative defenses including allegations of fraud in the inducement. The partnership also cross-complained against Mr. Yackey, seeking damages for fraud.

At trial, the defendants abandoned their cross-complaint and rested their whole case upon the premise that the escrow instructions, more particularly the release clause contained therein, were so uncertain as to render the entire contract unenforceable. The trial court after making specific findings in favor of the Yackeys on the existence of the contract, its breach by defendants and $70,785.40 damages, and against the partnership in its fraud contention, concluded "[t]he release clause set forth in the escrow instructions . . . was so uncertain as to render the entire agreement void and unenforcible [sic] both in equity and in law." And that "[b]ut for [such] invalidity . . . defendants would have been in breach of contract and plaintiffs would have been entitled to damages" totalling $70,785.40. Judgment was thereupon entered in favor of defendants on the complaint and for plaintiffs (cross-defendants) on the cross-complaint. The Yackeys appeal; defendants have not appealed the adverse ruling on their cross-complaint.

II

The Yackeys owned 375 acres of real property, unplanted, undeveloped, consisting of brushlands, canyons and rolling hills.

In April 1975, . . . Swann was introduced [to] the property. Partner Swann was an experienced builder and developer. He had built roughly 5,000 units and put together eight to ten subdivisions. Swann met the Yackeys at the property and discussed the physical characteristics of the land at that time. Thereafter, Swann instructed [his agent] to make an offer on the property. Yackey, against his lawyer's advice, agreed to accept the Swann offer. Swann selected the escrow company — one which he frequently used — to handle the sale and Swann telephoned the information to the escrow officer which was in fact used in preparation of the escrow instructions.

By the terms of the escrow instructions, so dictated by Swann, $750,000 was to be paid for the 375 acres, $150,000 to be paid at close of escrow and the balance, $600,000, to be paid in the form of a promissory note secured by a purchase money trust deed.

Swann directed the escrow officer to include in the instructions a provision for the following release clause to be included in the trust deed:

> Provided the trustor is not then in default hereunder or with respect to the payments due on note secured hereby, at his request, a partial reconveyance may be had and will be given from the lien or amount to apply on the principal of said note based on the rate of $2500.00 for each acre to be so reconveyed.

These escrow instructions were dated April 30, 1975, and provided that the sale was to close "on or before 120" days from that date. Escrow did not close within the 120-day period and thereafter several attempts were made to find a means whereby the date for closing could be extended and at the same time to allow the Swann-Pacifica to commence their development of the property. These efforts proved fruitless, and finally, by letter dated December 2, 1975, Swann's attorney stated that Yackeys' last offer was unacceptable and Swann had no counterproposal to submit at that time. On that date, the attorney for the Yackeys wrote Swann's attorney to announce that the Yackeys considered Mr. Swann to be in breach of the contract. He had, in fact, not performed any of the terms specified to be performed in the escrow agreement.

III

The trial court concluded the release clause was uncertain and that uncertainty rendered the whole agreement void upon the reasoning expressed in *White Point Co. v. Herrington,* 268 Cal.App.2d 458, 466, 73 Cal.Rptr. 885, 889, where it was said:

In recent years subordination agreements have frequently been reviewed by appellate courts with respect to the issues of uncertainty, materiality and fairness. Where the subordination provisions have been found uncertain and incapable of ascertainment by reference to an objective standard, the contracts have been deemed void for the uncertainty of a material provision [citations].

In *White Point Co. v. Herrington, supra,* 268 Cal.App.2d 458, 73 Cal.Rptr. 885, the parties, with numerous terms as yet unresolved, including the trust deed obligation and others relating to the financing of the security in the event of future development, disregarded the escrow officer's advice that they first consult a lawyer to resolve the uncertainties, caused the escrow instructions to be prepared and signed. Among the matters which remained unresolved were the terms of contemplated release clause. The instructions, after providing for a trust deed note, simply stated that the note was to have a release clause providing for partial releases of $3,000 per acre. (*Id.,* at p. 462, fn. 1, 73 Cal.Rptr. 885.) The buyers thereafter deposited the proposed form of release clause in escrow; it was never approved by the sellers. Thus, *White Point, supra,* is a classic example of an agreement to agree. Upon such factual base, the reasoning and the conclusion of the *White Point* court is sound contract law.

However, the *White Point* rule does not fit this case. If we assume for purposes of discussion the release clause is uncertain, yet such fact does not render the entire contract ipso facto void; only where the terms of such clauses are to be determined at a later date and by mutual consent of the buyer and seller — in effect an agreement to agree — will the contract be deemed void from its inception. (*Stockwell v. Lindeman,* 229 Cal.App.2d 750, 40 Cal.Rptr. 555; *Woodworth v. Redwood Empire Sav. & Loan Assn.,* 22 Cal.App.3d 347, 99 Cal.Rptr. 373.) However, as was said in *Schomaker v. Osborne,* 250 Cal.App.2d 887, 893, 58 Cal.Rptr. 827, 830:

The necessity of future agreement on limited phases of the transaction does not prevent birth of a binding contract upon acceptance since, if the parties cannot agree on these phases, each may force the other to accept the determination of a court of equity.

And in *Eldridge v. Burns,* 76 Cal.App.3d 396, 425, 142 Cal.Rptr. 845, it was held a release clause will not be deemed uncertain merely because the parties delegate to the buyer or to the third party lender the right to determine the property to be released or the power to detail terms of construction in permanent loans.

Similarly, if such determination is reserved by or given to the seller, a contract is not thereby rendered unenforceable for uncertainty. (*Ontario Downs, Inc. v.*

Lauppe, 192 Cal.App.2d 697, 13 Cal.Rptr. 782.) Where, however, such delegation is made to the buyer and it does not contain terms that will sufficiently protect the *seller's* security from undue risk, the clause and/or the entire contract may be vulnerable to the claim that it is not, *as to the seller,* just and reasonable. (*Handy v. Gordon,* 65 Cal.2d 578, 55 Cal.Rptr. 769, 422 P.2d 329; *Eldridge v. Burns, supra,* 76 Cal.App.3d 396, 142 Cal.Rptr. 845.)

Further, the claim of unfairness may be asserted only in an action for specific performance. It is not available to the party defendants here in an action for damages for breach of contract. It may be asserted only as a defense and only by the person as to whom the contract is unjust and unreasonable. In this instance it would be the Yackeys who would have the right to claim that the provision for release was unjust. (Civ.Code, § 3391, subd. 2; *Dessert Seed Co. v. Garbus,* 66 Cal.App.2d 838, 153 P.2d 184.)

Finally, if there is an uncertainty or unfairness in the release clause (and if we assume further such clause is not an agreement to agree at a future time) it *may not* be asserted by the party who was responsible for such uncertainty or unfairness. In this case the defendants were responsible for the precise language of the release clause. (*Lawrence v. Shutt,* 269 Cal.App.2d 749, 766, 75 Cal.Rptr. 533; *Woodworth v. Redwood Empire Sav. & Loan Assn., supra,* 22 Cal.App.3d 347, 99 Cal.Rptr. 373.)

In *Handy v. Gordon, supra,* 65 Cal.2d 578, 55 Cal.Rptr. 769, 422 P.2d 329, the Supreme Court upheld a trial court's refusal to grant specific performance. The Supreme Court said: "[T]he contract leaves defendants with nothing but plaintiff's good faith and business judgment to insure them that they will ever receive anything for conveying their land. Such a contract is not as to them 'just and reasonable' within the meaning of Civil Code section 3391." (*Id.,* at p. 582, 55 Cal.Rptr. at p. 771, 422 P.2d at p. 331.)

The foregoing case authorities compel our conclusion that if the release clause here were in fact uncertain, that fact will not, in and of itself, render the entire contract void or voidable. Only when the provision contemplates that the actual terms of the clause to be included in the deed of trust will be determined at a future date, and by mutual agreement of the parties, would the entire contract be deemed void from its inception. The sales escrow agreement here contained no such agreement. *To the contrary, the precise wording of the actual release clause to be so included was set forth in hac verba in the instructions.*

Finally, and of great significance is the form of action here. This is not an action for specific performance by the buyers but rather an action by the seller for damages. A greater degree of certainty is required in terms of the agreement which is sought to be specifically enforced in equity than is necessary in a contract which forms the basis of an action for damages. (*Lawrence v. Shutt, supra,* 269 Cal.App.2d 749, 761, 75 Cal.Rptr. 533; *Boyd v. Bevilacqua,* 247 Cal.App.2d 272, 287-288, 55 Cal.Rptr. 610; *Janssen v. Davis,* 219 Cal. 783, 787, 29 P.2d 196; *Eastwood Homes Inc. v. Hudson,* 161 Cal.App.2d 532, 540, 327, P.2d 29.)

IV

The discussions thus far have been based upon the premise of an uncertain release clause. This is not the fact here. The release clause language here is clear, unambiguous. It provides in simple terms that for each $2,500 paid on the principal balance on the promissory note, one acre of the conveyed land be released from the lien of deed of trust securing the note.

The partnership does not suggest the clause was intended to have any other than its plain, clear meaning. Rather, they contend uncertainty arises *from what remains unstated* in the clause. They argue from *White Point Co. v. Herrington, supra,* the lack of the further refinement in the language would allow the buyers to select choice portions of land for release and leave the seller's security including only the desirable [*sic*] parts. Here the record is absent any evidence which would suggest that these buyers would seek to obtain releases of portions of the best portions of the property and allow the unusable portions to remain. What the defendants seek to do is to make a contract uncertain, which on its face is free and clear from any ambiguity; they wish to speculate upon their own future inequitable approach to obtaining releases. The case of *Simmons v. Dryer,* 216 Cal.App.2d 733, 743, 31 Cal.Rptr. 199, 206, disposes adversely of such contention. The "buyers were not free to act arbitrarily."

V

We conclude that the escrow agreement here was not void. It did not contain an agreement to agree in the future. The particular release clause is certain but perhaps unfair, or capable of being used unfairly as to the seller. However, such potential unfairness to the seller does not render the entire contract void for uncertainty. Based upon these factual-legal conclusions, the judgment must be reversed and the matter remanded to the trial court with instructions to enter judgment in favor of the Yackeys and for the amount of damages found by the trial court, to wit, the sum of $70,785.40 — if such sum is legally the correct measure of damage.

We conclude that the measure of damages determined by the trial court adequately placed Yackeys in the position they would have been had defendants performed the contract.

The judgment is reversed and remanded with directions to the trial court to enter judgment for plaintiff for the sum of $70,785.40.

WIENER and FOCHT (San Diego Superior Court Judge sitting under assignment by the Chairman of the Judicial Council), JJ., concur.

NOTES

1. Note that in *Lawrence v. Shutt* while the release clause is too uncertain to allow specific performance, the court nevertheless does not allow rescission of the entire transaction. Compare that position with the situation in *White Point Co. v. Herrington,* 268 Cal. App. 2d 458 (1968) which was litigated when the entire transaction was still executory. The release provision called for simply ". . . partial releases at $3,000.00 per acre." The court of appeals reversed a judgment for specific performance on the basis that lack of specificity was unfair to the vendor. Would the court have allowed rescission in *White Point Co. v. Herrington* if the sale was completed and only the release clause was executory?

2. *Lawrence v. Shutt; White Point Co. v. Herrington;* and *Yackey v. Pacifica Development Co.* all cite to *Handy v. Gordon, supra.* Is it safe to assume that the law of subordination agreements is always equally applicable to release clauses? If not, why not?

3. If a map of the subject property exists at the time the marketing contract is entered into, then reference can be made to specific lots or parcels and the price of each. If the map does not subdivide the land into smaller parcels, then reference to the map and a description of the dimensions of any acreage to be released would be needed in order to avoid a charge of lack of specificity. Reference to earlier government surveys may not be adequate, due to the inaccuracy of the early surveys and subsequent destruction of monuments. *See Hellman v. Los Angeles,* 125 Cal. 383 (1899).

4. Not all problems arising from disagreements over release clauses lead to suits for specific performance. When more land has been released than the contract provisions would justify and the mortgagee becomes the purchaser at a foreclosure sale after default,

an action for reformation would be the appropriate remedy. *See Vilkin v. Sommer*, 260 Cal. App. 2d 687 (1968).

5. What happens when the mortgage contains both a release clause and a due-on-sale clause? In one such case the court held that the due-on clause was inapplicable to those portions of the property controlled by the release provisions. The court did not hold that the release clause superseded the due-on, but that the due-on was inapplicable only to those portions where release was possible. *Williams Construction Co. v. Standard-Pacific Corp.*, 254 Cal. App. 2d 442 (1967). However, could the mortgagor have sold portions subject to being released without having made the necessary payments and seeking release? It seems likely that a sale of the area to be released without seeking release would trigger the due-on.

Chapter 4

THE OBLIGATION

Ah, take the Cash, and let the Credit go. . . .

RUBÁIYÁT OF OMAR KHAYYAM

A. NECESSITY FOR AN UNDERLYING OBLIGATION

While a debt may exist either secured or unsecured, it has long been held that no mortgage can exist without an underlying obligation. If the obligation is the payment of a debt in money, once the debt is paid the security interest in the subject of the mortgage is released. That the security interest cannot stand alone without obligation is so well settled that little comment is necessary. What is of paramount importance, and thus productive of litigation, is the nature and extent of the obligation, as well as the time and manner of performance.

What is the effect of additional debts incurred by the mortgagor? Do they become secured, or are they new and unsecured debts? What is the effect of conduct by the mortgagor which accelerates the due date of the obligation? What rights and duties exist *vis-à-vis* the mortgagor and mortgagee when payments on the debt are not timely made, either late or early? These are questions which borrowers and lenders, as well as their counsel, must ask and answer in order to participate in the modern world of finance of real property and its development.

B. VARIATION OF THE OBLIGATION

The cases which follow demonstrate that simply borrowing a sum of money from a lender does not necessarily determine the amount of the debt, the time for payment, or all circumstances in which the lender may look to the security for satisfaction of the debt. Lenders utilize forms which allow borrowers to receive additional sums of money after the first loan, using the same security without a change in priority and modifying only the amount of the debt. Construction loans are an example of an instance when a lender would find it commercially feasible to obtain the security only once, while advancing funds to the borrower on many occasions during the course of construction.

Efforts by lenders to have the opportunity to be either secured or unsecured, whichever is most advantageous, have taken different forms. The equitable lien of the *Coast Bank* mortgage is but one example. Another is the use of clauses in the mortgage document securing other obligations of the same borrower. These are considered *infra* in the sections on Future Advances and Dragnet clauses.

The consequences of acceleration, a rapidly changing area of the law, are dealt with in the acceleration section by comparing various "due-on" clauses: sale, encumbrance or default. The time of payment and the additional payment which a lender may require if the payment is either early or late, in the form of pre-payment penalty or late charges, is considered in the section Time of Payment.

IN RE JEFFREY TOWERS, INC.

Supreme Court, Westchester County, New York
57 Misc. 2d 46, 291 N.Y.S.2d 41 (1968)

JOSEPH F. GAGLIARDI, JUSTICE.

This is a petition to compel satisfaction of a mortgage dated October 29, 1965, in return for payment of the sum of $225,000. with interest in the sum of $3,712.50, on premises consisting of approximately 5 acres off Central Park Avenue in Yonkers, New York. The mortgagees do not contest that this is the amount due on the bond secured by this purchase money mortgage which was part of the price of the sale of the land to petitioner's predecessor in title but they do insist that they are entitled to keep the mortgage open of record to secure other promises made by the mortgagor in the mortgage agreement to benefit eight adjacent acres of land which the seller-mortgagees had retained. Those promises are (1) to install a 12-inch sewer main from Central Park Avenue across the petitioner's property to service the mortgagees' property before October 29, 1967, with provisions permitting the mortgagees to construct the sewer at the mortgagor's expense upon default and for a $20,000. surety bond to secure completion by October 29, 1973; (2) to construct a 561.18 foot "Alternate Driveway" from Young Avenue across petitioner's property to service the mortgagees' property by October 29, 1968, with similar rights to complete the driveway at mortgagor's expense; (3) to consent to any applications for variances, changes of zone or special exception uses affecting the mortgagees' retained parcel; and (4) to complete a 292-family apartment house. The foregoing promises were included in "RIDER B CONSTITUTING PART OF THE MORTGAGE DATED OCTOBER 29, 1965, BETWEEN TWIN TOWERS, INC., [petitioner's predecessor in title], MORTGAGOR, AND IRMA STRAUS AND LILLIAN ROMM, MORTGAGEE."

Petitioner relies on an express prepayment clause in the mortgage. In addition, it replies that the other promises were part of a collateral agreement dated October 29, 1965, which (1) stipulated the termination of the mortgagees' driveway easement when Morrow Avenue becomes a public street; and (2) prevented the mortgagees from seeking any zoning relief until October 29, 1968. Furthermore, it urges that it expressed readiness to construct the sewer but the City of Yonkers denied it a permit to do so because of the mortgagees having failed, despite request, to file an application for a sewer permit.

The initial question is whether a mortgage can secure the performance of unliquidated engagements such as these promises to build a road and sewer. A mortgage has been defined as "any conveyance of land intended by the parties at the time of making it to be a security for the payment of money, *or the doing of some prescribed act*" (*Burnett v. Wright,* 135 N.Y. 543, 547, 32 N.E. 253, 254) (emphasis added). This definition which can be found in modern treatises (See, e. g., 38 N.Y.Jur., Mortgages and Deeds of Trust, § 1; 2 Rasch, Real Property Law & Practice, § 1681) admits the possibility of such an unusual purpose although it does not obviate the problems which would be caused by it.

There are recorded cases of mortgages securing promises to provide support in stated instalments for the mortgagee's lifetime (See, e. g., *De Clow v. Haverkamp,* 198 App.Div. 83, 189 N.Y.S. 617 [4th Dept., 1921]) although such a promise must be expressly adopted in the mortgage (*Castelli v. Walton Lake Country Club,* 112 N.Y.S.2d 179 [Eager, J., Sup.Ct., Orange Co., 1952]). So, too, a mortgage was employed to secure a promise to purchase all of the gasoline sold at a garage premises from the mortgagee in *Blakeley v. Agency of Canadian Car*

& *Foundry Co.*, 73 N.Y.S.2d 573 [Sup.Ct., N.Y.Co., 1947]. There, the court refused to compel satisfaction of the mortgage even when the principal amount was paid because of the open promise to purchase gasoline for an unexpired term. In addition, Section 1921 of the Real Property Actions and Proceedings Law which authorizes this proceeding to compel discharge of a mortgage states that the satisfaction piece must certify "that the mortgage has been paid or *otherwise satisfied and discharged*" (emphasis added). The Court concludes that in the absence of defects such as illegality, unliquidated promises in the nature of those presented in this case may be secured by a mortgage. It follows, therefore, that such promises must be fulfilled to entitle petitioner to a discharge of the mortgage.

That brings the Court to the intention of the parties. The prepayment clause is contained in Rider "A" to the mortgage and reads as follows:

> Any owner of the mortgaged premises may at any time after January 1, 1966 pay the said sum of $500,000 and accrued interest thereon upon giving to the holder hereof and of the accompanying note 10 days prior written notice of such prepayment.

With respect to the "Alternate Driveway," petitioner notes that that promise is related to an instrument executed in conjunction with the deed and mortgage, which conveys easements to the mortgagees for the benefit of their remaining parcel over the paths of the proposed "Alternate Driveway" and the proposed sewer connection. Petitioner properly urges that the promises in the mortgage are incidental to and subject to the provisions of the grant of easement. In other words, the promises in the mortgage should be enforced only insofar as they fulfill the interests of the mortgagees in protecting their remaining parcel. Otherwise, there would be no purpose in enforcing those promises except to oppress the owners of the mortgaged property.

In this connection, petitioner relies upon the provision of the "Alternate Driveway" easement which maintains it as "a covenant running with the land until such time as all of Morrow Avenue shall have been opened, laid out and improved as a public street of the City of Yonkers and accepted for dedication or declared by the City of Yonkers as such public street . . . ." Petitioner exhibits a copy of Special Ordinance No. 121-1967 (dated April 11, 1967) which declares Morrow Avenue as a public street. It insists that the need for the "Alternate Driveway" over its property has been obviated by that ordinance so that the driveway easement and promise to pave it are fulfilled and terminated. But the mortgagees contend that Morrow Avenue was at the time of the transaction a mere "paper street" proposed to furnish access to their remaining parcel which has not been paved to this day. They argue that the quoted language could not have been meant to wipe out the "Alternate Driveway" until Morrow Avenue was a serviceable public street, in fact, as well as in law.

The issue is whether the disjunctive phrase "or declared by the City of Yonkers as such public street" is intended as an alternative to all the other phrases including the street having been "opened, laid out and improved" as well as "accepted for dedication." The Court deems the meaning of the language to be clear. Morrow Avenue may be either "accepted for dedication" or "declared" as a city street by the City of Yonkers but in any event, it must also be "improved" as such. This not being the case, the easement and the mortgage securing the mortgagees' rights to a paved "Alternate Driveway" are not terminated. Therefore, the mortgage securing that right cannot now be discharged of record. The "Alternate Driveway" must be built or Morrow Avenue must be properly paved.

The same reasoning applies to petitioner's obligation to build a sewer connection. Of course, in this connection, the mortgagees cannot unreasonably prevent performance by the mortgagor (*Jones v. Dodge,* 137 App.Div. 853, 122 N.Y.S. 815). Hence, improper refusal by the mortgagees to apply for a permit to do the sewer work would excuse its necessity.

Moreover, the Court doubts that the promise to consent to zoning applications is enforceable by the mortgage or may hinder its satisfaction. The reason is that the promises to do work are readily translatable into money, albeit without precision. But the value of a consent to a zoning application (which might not even influence the zoning authority) is of such speculative monetary value that it cannot be enforced as a mortgage lien. It would be impossible for the Court in the event of foreclosure to fix the amount of the lien and direct the disposition of proceeds of a foreclosure sale (See, Real Prop.Actions & Proc.Law, § 1351).

A final consideration is petitioner's right of prepayment of the principal and interest. Under the instrument, it is clear that this right is unfettered so that petitioner by making tender of the principal and interest stops the further accrual of interest. Thus, the mortgage lien can only remain to secure the performance of the unliquidated obligations. Petitioner is entitled to have this reduction of the lien established of record. Therefore, the petition is granted to the extent that upon payment of $225,000, with interest in the sum of $3,712.50, the mortgagees must deliver an instrument in recordable form certifying that the principal and interest stated in the mortgage have been paid. The form of the instrument shall be determined in the judgment herein.

The petition is otherwise denied.

NOTES

1. In a later case the court is clear in linking a mortgage to a debt.

For our purpose on this review, a mortgage may be defined as a conveyance of an estate or interest in land by way of pledge as security for payment of a debt, and it becomes void upon payment. 1 Jones on Mortgages (8th ed.) p. 21, § 17. In order to constitute a valid mortgage, it is not necessary that the instrument itself should contain a description of the debt, payment of which is intended to be secured, nor is it essential that there be a note or other obligation separate from the mortgage itself evidencing the indebtedness, *but it is necessary that there be a debt to be discharged;* that this indebtedness be recited in the mortgage; and the nature and amount of the indebtedness secured by the mortgage must be so expressed that subsequent purchasers and attaching creditors need not look beyond the mortgage itself to ascertain both the existence and amount of the debt. 1 Jones on Mortgages (8th ed.) p. 538, § 425. [Emphasis added.]

Smith v. Haertel, 125 Colo. 348, 244 P.2d 377 (1952).

2. West's Annotated California Civil Code:

§ 2941. Satisfaction of mortgage or deed of trust; obligation to issue certificate of discharge or to reconvey; recordation; damages; fee

(a) When any mortgage has been satisfied, the mortgagee or the assignee of the mortgagee shall execute a certificate of the discharge thereof, as provided in Section 2939, and shall record or cause to be recorded, except as provided in subdivision (c), such certificate in the office of the county recorder in which the mortgage is recorded. The mortgagee shall then deliver, upon the written request of the mortgagor or the mortgagor's heirs, successors, or assignees, as the case may be, the original note and mortgage to the person making such request.

(b) When the obligation secured by any deed of trust has been satisfied, the beneficiary or the assignee of the beneficiary shall execute and deliver to the trustee the original note and deed of trust and a request for a full reconveyance to be executed by the trustee. The trustee shall execute and shall record or cause to be recorded, except as provided in subdivision (c), such full reconveyance in the office of the county recorder in which the deed of trust is recorded. The trustee shall then deliver, upon the written request of the trustor or the trustor's heirs, successors, or assignees, as the case may be, the original note and deed of trust to the person making such request.

(c) The mortgagee or trustee shall not record or cause to be recorded such certificate of discharge or full reconveyance where (1) the mortgagee or trustee has received written instructions to the contrary from the mortgagor or trustor, or the owner of the land, as the case may be, or from the owner of the obligation secured by the deed of trust, his agent or escrow, or (2) such certificate of discharge or full reconveyance is to be delivered to the mortgagor or trustor, or the owner of the land, as the case may be, through an escrow to which such mortgagor, trustor, or owner is a party.

(d) The violation by a beneficiary, trustee, or mortgagee, or assignee thereof, of any provision of this section shall make the beneficiary, trustee, or mortgagee, or assignee thereof, liable to the trustor or mortgagor, or the owner of the land, as the case may be, or such person's grantees or heirs, for all damages which any of such persons may sustain by reason of such violation, and shall also forfeit to any of such persons the sum of three hundred dollars ($300).

(e) The trustee, beneficiary or mortgagee may charge a fee to the trustor or mortgagor, or the owner of the land, as the case may be, for all services rendered in connection with the preparation, execution or recordation of a full reconveyance, or request for a full reconveyance, or certificate of discharge of a mortgage. Such fee may be made payable in advance of the performance of any services required by this section. (Amended by Stats.1978, c. 509, p. 1657, § 1.)

§ 2941.5. Obligation to execute certificate of discharge, satisfaction, or request for reconveyance; penalty

Every person who violates Section 2941 is guilty of a misdemeanor punishable by fine of not less than twenty-five dollars ($25) nor more than two hundred dollars ($200), or by imprisonment in the county jail for not to exceed six months, or by both such fine and imprisonment.

(Added by Stats.1946, 1st Ex.Sess., c. 58, p. 82, § 2.)

3. Notice that California makes it a misdemeanor to fail to execute a deed of reconveyance (the form of mortgage release used in a deed of trust). Why would a lender refuse to reconvey if the obligation had been satisfied? Perhaps there is a difference of opinion between the borrower and lender as to what obligation was secured and what was unsecured. See the "dragnet" cases that follow.

1. DRAGNETS

BLOOM v. FIRST VERMONT BANK & TRUST CO.

Supreme Court of Vermont
133 Vt. 407, 340 A.2d 78 (1975)

On April 22, 1964, defendant Theodor Kaufman acquired the premises in question from the American Radiator and Standard Sanitary Corporation. Kaufman that day gave defendant First Vermont Bank and Trust Company a $100,000 note secured by a mortgage on the Giant Store premises. The mortgage deed held by the bank contained a so-called "debt accrual" clause and covered, in addition to the $100,000 note,

all other notes, debts, sums of money and liabilities which are now due or which hereafter may become due from the said mortgagor to the said Vermont Bank and Trust Company, its successors and/or assigns, however specified, and whether direct or indirect, including without limitation, any present existing and future liabilities of the mortgagor by reason of being or becoming a maker, endorser, guarantor or surety on the obligations of any other party, person, or persons or evidences of indebtedness to this mortgagee.

Kaufman's attorney subsequently wrote First Vermont on May 13, 1964, and, pursuant to another clause of the mortgage deed, requested permission for Kaufman to convey a portion of the Giant Store premises to his partner Alfred H. Bloom, plaintiff herein. The bank granted its consent and on September 22, 1964, Kaufman conveyed one-half of the Giant Store premises to Bloom.

In early 1973, Kaufman telephoned an officer at First Vermont and requested a $100,000 personal line of credit on an unsecured basis. Kaufman was informed that the bank would require a loan application and financial statement from him. These requirements were satisfied, a $100,000 line of credit was approved by the bank, and a demand note in that amount was executed by Kaufman on February 5, 1973.

Kaufman subsequently suffered financial reversals and on June 1, 1973, he and Bloom entered into a contract to sell the Giant Store premises to Evans Product Company for $165,000. A dispute then arose between Bloom and First Vermont as to the extent of the latter's interest in the Giant Store premises as security for the second $100,000 note which Kaufman had executed on February 5, 1973. It was agreed, however, that the sale of the Giant Store premises be consummated. Bloom, Kaufman, and First Vermont entered into an agreement under which $51,326.32 from the proceeds of the sale, representing the principal sum due and owing from Kaufman to Vermont on the second $100,000 note, was placed in escrow "pending judicial determination of the validity of the bank's mortgage lien to secure the payment of said note balance as claimed by said bank." The first $100,000 note was discharged on the day of closing on the Giant Store premises.

This action, instituted pursuant to the escrow agreement by plaintiff Bloom in Windham Superior Court, was tried to the court and resulted in a judgment in Bloom's favor for the full amount of the escrow deposit, plus interest. This appeal by First Vermont followed.

The parties here have directed considerable attention to the sufficiency of the bank's notice of Bloom's intervening interest in the Giant Store premises and to the effect of this notice on the priority of the claimed interests. But these issues cannot be reached without first ascertaining the nature of the claimed interests themselves.

Bloom's interest in the proceeds from the sale of property of which he was co-owner is patent. The bank's legal interest, on the other hand, is less apparent. It is argued here that this interest springs from the original mortgage deed and its so-called "debt accrual" clause. The 1973 demand note, First Vermont contends, is secured by the Giant Store premises under that clause.

Although this Court has not yet had occasion to address the particular point here in question, we are in agreement with the Supreme Court of Ohio that a prerequisite to the mortgagee's secured position under accrual clauses of this nature is a showing that the subsequent "advance" was intended by the parties to be secured by the prior mortgage. *Second National Bank of Warren v. Boyle,* 155 Ohio St. 482, 99 N.E.2d 474 (1951). The court below found that "the defendant Bank and defendant Kaufman intended that the second loan of $100,000 to defendant Kaufman on 5 February 1973 be an unsecured loan." The parties were free to contract on this basis so long as the requirements of 8 V.S.A. § 1205 were met (as they were here), and the finding of the lower court that they did so is amply supported by the evidence.

It is undisputed that Kaufman's request was for an unsecured line of credit, that the loan officer in charge recommended approval of the loan to the bank's discount committee as an unsecured loan, and that the minutes of the discount committee meeting disclose that Kaufman's request was granted for an "unsecured short term line of credit in the amount of $100,000." Moreover, the $100,000 note signed by Kaufman on February 5 was clearly a demand note and, in contrast to the earlier $100,000 note executed in 1964 and secured by the mortgage in question, no mention was made of any collateral to be pledged.

First Vermont's challenge to the lower court's finding is based primarily on the testimony of the recommending loan officer who testified below that in reporting verbally to the discount committee, "I discussed a mortgage loan balance on the existing mortgage" and who rather self-servingly characterized the 1973 loan as "an unsecured loan with additional collateral under the accrued clause of the mortgage." These statements scarcely justify a conclusion here that the finding of the lower court was "clearly erroneous." V.R.C.P. 52(a).

The bank has simply failed to sustain its burden of establishing that the money advanced after the mortgage was executed was intended by the parties to be secured thereby. Absent such a showing, its claim to the escrowed funds as against plaintiff Bloom must necessarily fail. This conclusion renders any further inquiry into the issue of notice unnecessary.

Judgment affirmed.

ESTES v. REPUBLIC NATIONAL BANK

Supreme Court of Texas
462 S.W.2d 273 (1970)

SMITH, JUSTICE.

The Respondent sued the Petitioners seeking judgment on a series of promissory notes aggregating the sum of approximately $600,000.00. One of the notes, dated April 17, 1961, is in the sum of $30,000.00. Simultaneously with the execution of this note, Petitioner Burnett Estes, executed a deed of trust on 396 acres of land situated in Denton County, Texas. After the execution and delivery of the $30,000.00 note and deed of trust to the bank, Estes conveyed the land to Everett & Company and that Company later conveyed the land to Petitioner Dan Gibbs, subject to the payment of the $30,000.00 note. Thereafter, Gibbs' tender of payment of the balance due on the $30,000.00 note and demand for a release of the deed of trust was rejected by the bank. This suit followed. The bank sought recovery from Estes of the balance due on all indebtedness and the foreclosure of the deed of trust lien in accordance with its terms. Estes and Gibbs defended on the ground that the bank, through its authorized agent, orally agreed that the deed of trust was to secure the payment of the $30,000.00 note only and that when such note was paid the land described in the deed of trust was to be free of all indebtedness due the bank. Estes further pleaded that by accident or mutual mistake a "dragnet" clause remained in the printed form of the deed of trust, whereas the true agreement was that when the $30,000.00 note was repaid the land would be released. Evidence offered to establish this alleged agreement was excluded upon objection. At the close of all the evidence, the Court instructed the jury to return a verdict in favor of the bank for the total sum sued for and, thereafter, judgment was entered that the bank recover of Estes the sum of $600,000.00 and for the foreclosure of the deed of trust lien. The Court of Civil Appeals affirmed. 450 S.W.2d 397. We affirm.

The principal question presented for our decision is whether parol evidence is admissible to establish that the true intention of the parties was to provide in the deed of trust that the lien therein afforded was to secure payment of the $30,000.00 note only, rather than to secure all indebtedness in accordance with the "dragnet" clause which provided that:

This Deed of Trust shall secure, in addition to the said Note, [$30,000.00] all funds hereafter advanced by Beneficiary to or for the benefit of Grantors, as contemplated by any covenant or provision herein contained or for any other purpose, *and all other indebtedness, of whatever kind or character, owing or which may hereafter become owing by Grantors to Beneficiary,* whether such indebtedness is evidenced by note, open account, over-draft, endorsement, surety agreement, guaranty, or otherwise, *it being contemplated that Grantors may hereafter become indebted to Beneficiary in further sum or sums.* (Emphasis added.)

The deed of trust further provided that Estes would not sell all or any portion of the mortgaged property unless the purchaser shall either:

(a) expressly agree to assume the payment of the indebtedness hereby secured or (b) expressly agree that the title and rights of such purchaser are and shall remain subject to all and every the terms of this Deed of Trust for the complete fulfillment of all obligations of the Grantors hereunder, and unless, also, the deed shall expressly set forth the said agreement of the purchaser. . . .

It is admitted that Estes, both before and after the $30,000.00 transaction, had entered into many loan agreements by executing promissory notes payable to the bank. Some of the notes, if not all, were renewals of notes dated prior to the execution of the critical note and deed of trust. Petitioners wished to establish that when Estes executed that note and deed of trust, the true agreement was that it would be entirely separate and isolated from his other obligations to the bank. This of course is inconsistent with the terms of the "dragnet" clause in the deed of trust quoted above, and testimony at variance with that clause was excluded.

The law presumes that a written agreement correctly embodies the parties' intentions, and is an accurate expression of the agreement the parties reached in prior oral negotiations. While it is true that parol evidence is admissible to show that the writing, because of a mutual mistake, incorrectly reflects the true agreement, and that the equitable remedy of reformation is available to correct such a mutual mistake in the written instrument, reformation is unavailable unless the party claiming mistake presents "clear, exact, and satisfactory evidence," *Sun Oil Co. v. Bennett,* 125 Tex. 540, 84 S.W.2d 447 (1935) that he is entitled to it. There are two basic requirements which must be met before the remedy of reformation is granted: first, the party claiming the relief must show what the parties' true agreement was, and second, he must show that the instrument incorrectly reflects that agreement because of a mutual mistake. . . . The dual elements underlying the remedy of reformation were more clearly stated in *Sun Oil Co. v. Bennett, supra:*

The party seeking reformation must of course prove what the true agreement was, but his case is not made by proof that there was an agreement which is at variance with the writing. *He must go further and establish the fact that the terms or provisions of the writing which differ from the true agreement made were placed in the instrument by mutual mistake.* 84 S.W.2d at 451 (emphasis added).

The evidence of mutual mistake in this case, developed by bills of exception, does not meet that rather stringent requirement. Estes' answers to two questions posed to him do tend to establish that he and George Verner, the bank officer with whom he dealt when the $30,000 note was executed, did agree that the farm would be released once that note was paid off. Estes was asked: "Your understanding . . . with Mr. Verner, was that it would be an isolated transaction, and secured by just the one note." Estes answered, "Yes, sir." Then Estes was asked, "And did — he agree to that?" The answer was, "Yes, sir, he did." Other testimony by Estes reveals that he was under the impression that his stated goal of making the $30,000 loan an isolated transaction would be accomplished by inserting in the note a clause allowing prepayment without penalty. . . . Estes' testimony amounts to no evidence of a mutual mistake regarding the existence or nonexistence of the "dragnet" clause in the deed of trust. Assuming without deciding that Estes met the first requirement set out in *Sun Oil Co.* by adducing proof of the parties' true agreement, he failed to satisfy the second, that of adducing evidence that the challenged terms in the writing were placed there by mutual mistake.

It is plain that Estes cannot adduce proof on the vital second element, because according to his own testimony he failed to read the deed of trust or note before signing them. While a party's failure to read an instrument before signing is not always a bar to that party's suit for reformation to correct a mutual mistake, 3 Corbin on Contracts § 607; 81 A.L.R.2d 7, the general rule is that in the absence of a showing of fraud or imposition, a party's failure to read an instrument before signing it is not a ground for avoiding it.

We hold that the "dragnet" clause in the deed of trust lien clearly and unambiguously stated the parties' will that the land would stand as security not only for the instant $30,000 loan, but also for "all other indebtedness, of whatever kind or character, owing . . . by Grantors to Beneficiary." Parol evidence was inadmissible to vary the meaning of that clause.

. . . .

Accordingly, the judgments of the trial court and the Court of Civil Appeals are affirmed.

NOTES

1. *Dragnet or Anaconda Clauses.* A dragnet or anaconda clause provides that the mortgage shall stand as security for any other indebtedness that the mortgagor may incur, whether or not related to the original loan running from the mortgagor to the mortgagee. *See Capocasa v. First National Bank,* 36 Wis. 2d 714 (1967).

A typical example of a dragnet/anaconda clause is:

> To secure payment of any or all extensions or renewals and successive extensions or renewals of the Note above described, or of the indebtedness represented by the same, and of any other indebtedness represented by the same, and of any other indebtedness at any other time arising from the mortgagor to the mortgagee, whether represented by notes, drafts, open accounts or otherwise.

2. Several dragnet cases have turned upon the intent of the parties without getting to the issue of the validity of such a provision. *See Gates v. Crocker-Anglo National Bank,* 257 Cal. App. 2d 857 (1968); *Carlson v. Oppenheim,* 334 Mass. 462, 136 N.E.2d 205 (1956).

3. The language below is from a bank's deed of trust form followed by language from the same bank's Mastercharge Agreement.

TRUST DEED (With Assignment of Rents and Incorporating Recorded Provisions)

This Deed of Trust dated _____, 19_____, between
_____
herein called Trustor, and CROCKER CUSTODY CORPORATION, herein called
Trustee and CROCKER NATIONAL BANK herein called Beneficiary, whose address
is above, Witnesseth that:

1. Trustor, to secure payment and performance of Trustor's Note (herein called this
Note) of this date for $_____ principal, with interest, payable to Beneficiary, and all:
(a) moneys paid by or becoming due to Beneficiary or Trustee hereunder, (b) future
borrowings from Beneficiary by Trustor when evidenced by a note or writing reciting
that it is secured hereby, (c) other borrowings and indebtedness now or hereafter owing
to Beneficiary from Trustor (except such as may require a disclosure under The
Consumer Credit Protections Act and is evidenced by a note or writing that does not
recite that it is secured hereby), (d) agreements, covenants, and obligations of Trustor
contained herein or in any present of future assignment, agreement, or undertaking
by Trustor in connection with or for futher securing indebtedness now or hereafter
secured hereby or to supplement or amend this Deed of Trust or any instrument
secured hereby, and (e) extensions and renewals of this Note and said other sums,
borrowings, obligations and agreements: hereby irrevocably Grants, Transfers and
Assigns to Trustee in Trust With Power of Sale that certain real property situate in the
_____ County of _____, State of California, commonly known as
_____and
described as follows:

MASTER CHARGE

Not secured credit. Your Master Charge account is <u>not</u> secured credit. We have no
security interest for the account, regardless of any other agreement you may have with
us.

Does the disclaimer in the Mastercharge Agreement conflict with the language from the
deed of trust? Could a borrower assert that a debt incurred with the use of a Mastercharge
card was indeed secured if the deed of trust containing the dragnet preceded the
Mastercharge debt?

3. In the Crocker Bank forms above, note the disclaimer in the Mastercharge
Agreement. Does this conflict with the "dragnet" contained in the Crocker deed of trust?
Could a borrower assert that a debt incurred with the use of a Mastercharge card was
indeed secured if the deed of trust containing the dragnet preceded the Mastercharge
debt?

4. A borrower might wish to rely on the dragnet in the deed of trust to avoid payment
of the Mastercharge debt if the security on the prior obligation had already been sold at
a foreclosure sale, particularly in a state with anti-deficiency legislation. See section on
anti-deficiency *infra*. However, the lender might just as easily want to rely on the dragnet
in the event the borrower has sought a discharge in bankruptcy. Why, then, would the
lender preclude itself from this option by using a disclaimer such as contained in the
Crocker Bank Mastercharge Agreement? Could the lack of a disclaimer allow a borrower
to attack such an option held by the lender as void for ambiguity or lack of mutuality?

2. FUTURE ADVANCES

PIKE v. TUTTLE

California District Court of Appeals
18 Cal. App. 3d 746, 96 Cal. Rptr. 403 (1971)

GARGANO, J. — Appellant appeals from a judgment, after court trial, awarding respondent $4,000 on a promissory note, together with accrued interest and attorney's fees. The facts are undisputed.

In 1958 Ray Pike loaned $54,562 to Russell M. Edson and Anna E. Edson for the purchase of a nursing home. The loan was evidenced by a promissory note calling for $250 monthly payments on principal, payable on the tenth day of each month, and monthly interest payments on the unpaid balance at the rate of 8 percent per annum, and was secured by a first deed of trust against the nursing home. The deed of trust, hereafter referred to as the Pike-Edson trust deed, provided for additional loans, and in this respect contained the following provision:

> . . . any additional sums and interest thereon which may hereafter be loaned to the Trustor or his successors or assigns by the Beneficiary, and the performance of each agreement herein contained. Additional loans hereafter made and interest thereon shall be secured by this Deed of Trust only if made to the Trustor while he is the owner of record of his present interest in said property, or to his successors or assigns while they are the owners of record thereof, and shall be evidenced by a promissory note reciting that it is secured by this Deed of Trust.

In September 1960 the Edsons sold the nursing home to Dr. William P. Tuttle subject to the Pike-Edson trust deed, and Tuttle assumed the obligation to make the payments. He also gave the Edsons a second trust deed on the nursing home to secure the balance of the unpaid purchase price. Dr. Tuttle made the monthly payments on the Edsons' note as they became due, and by September 12, 1963, had reduced the amount of unpaid principal on that note to $23,750; these payments were recorded by Pike in a payment book and a portion of a page of that book is reproduced in the margin for illustrative purposes.[1]

---

[1] The following is an excerpt from Pike's payment book which illustrates the manner in which he treated the new loan and all payments made thereafter:

| Sept 12 | Sept 10 | 410.00 | 160.00 | 250.00 | 23,750.00 | RHP. |
| | New added loan | Sept 10 '63 | | = | 4,000.00 | RHP. |

Date of Payment	Date Due	Amount Paid	Credited on		Bal. of Prin. Unpaid	To Whom Paid
			Int.	Prin.		
New balance Sept 10th '63				=	27,750.00	RHP.
Oct 10	Oct 10	435.00	185.00	250.00	27,500.00	RHP.
Nov 12	Nov 10	433.34	183.34	250.00	27,250.00	RHP.
Dec 10	Dec 10	431.67	181.67	250.00	27,000.00	RHP.
Jan 10 '64	Jan 10	430.00	180.00	250.00	26,750.00	RHP.
Feb 11	Feb 10	428.34	178.34	250.00	26,500.00	RHP.
Mar 10	Mar 10	426.67	176.67	250.00	26,250.00	RHP.
Apr 12	Apr 10	425.00	175.00	250.00	26,000.00	RHP.
May 9	May 10	423.33	173.33	250.00	25,750.00	RHP.
June 10	June 10	421.66	171.66	250.00	25,500.00	RHP.
July 11	July 10	420.00	170.00	250.00	25,250.00	RHP.
Aug 10	Aug 10	418.50	168.50	250.00	25,000.00	RHP.

In September 1963 Pike loaned Tuttle $4,000, and the latter signed a promissory note for that amount. This note, like Edsons' note, called for $250 monthly payments on principal, payable on the tenth day of each month, monthly interest payments on the unpaid balance at the rate of 8 percent per annum and stated that it was secured by the Pike-Edson trust deed; in his payment book Pike designated the loan as a "new added loan" and added the $4,000 to the $23,750 balance which was then owing on the note signed by the Edsons; also the words "added loan" were written across the face of the second note. Thereafter Dr. Tuttle made a single payment of $250 per month toward principal plus monthly interest payments of 8 percent per annum on the combined balance; the monthly payments continued until July 9, 1965.

In January 1965 Ray Pike died, and his widow was appointed executrix of his estate. In August Tuttle defaulted on all his obligations, and the Edsons foreclosed on their second deed of trust and took possession of the property. They then paid off the first loan and received a reconveyance from Pike's executrix, after taking the position that all payments made by Tuttle for the period from October 1963 to July 1965 inured to the benefit of the first loan only. When Tuttle also refused to pay the $4,000 loan, contending that the loan was discharged by the first sixteen $250 payments he made to Pike, the widow instituted this action in the court below, and the cause proceeded to trial before the judge sitting without a jury.

The court inter alia found that the Pike-Edson trust deed was a purchase money deed of trust as to the Edson loan but not as to the $4,000 loan Pike made to Tuttle; that the $4,000 loan was authorized by the Pike-Edson deed of trust but because Pike knew that Tuttle had given the Edsons a second deed of trust, the resulting lien was a third lien against the nursing home; that the principal payments on the $4,000 note were exactly the same and were due on the same date as the principal payments on the Edson note; that during the period from October 1963 to July 1965 Tuttle made a single monthly principal payment of $250 per month and that neither he nor Pike informed the other as to the manner the payment was to be applied; that no payments were made by Tuttle on the $4,000 note and that after the Edsons foreclosed they paid off the first deed of trust without reference to the second loan. The court concluded that the $250 per month payments made by Tuttle to Pike during the period in question were applied to reduce the balance on the Edson note, that because the second loan was not secured by a purchase money mortgage, section 580b of the Code of Civil Procedure was inapplicable and that Pike's executrix was entitled to recover the amount of the loan from Tuttle, together with accrued interest at the

Date of Payment	Date Due	Amount Paid	Credited on		Bal. of Prin. Unpaid	To Whom Paid
			Int.	Prin.		
Sept 10	Sept 10	416.67	166.67	250.00	24,750.00	RHP.
Oct 10	Oct 10	415.00	165.00	250.00	24,500.00	RHP.
Nov 10	Nov 10	413.34	163.34	250.00	24,250.00	RHP.
Dec 10	Dec 10	411.67	161.67	250.00	24,000.00	RHP.
Jan 10 '65	Jan 10	410.00	160.00	250.00	23,750.00	RHP.
Feb 10	Feb 10	408.33	158.34	250.00	23,500.00	C.W.
March 10	March 10	406.67	156.67	250.00	23,250.00	C.W.
April 10	April 9	405.00	155.00	250.00	23,000.00	C.W.
May 10	May 10	403.33	153.33	250.00	22,750.00	C.W.
June 10	June 10	401.67	151.67	250.00	22,500.00	C.W.
July 9	July 10	400.00	150.00	250.00	22,250.00	C.W.

rate of 8 percent, and reasonable attorney's fees in the amount of $390. This appeal followed.

The court properly found that although the $4,000 loan was authorized by the Pike-Edson deed of trust, the resulting lien was a third lien and subordinate to the trust deed Tuttle gave the Edsons on the nursing home; Pike knew that Tuttle had given the Edsons a second trust deed, and it is the rule that if the mortgagee is not bound to make advances, as was true in this case, priority is determined by the circumstances existing at the time the advance is made, and if at that time the mortgagee has actual notice of other liens, the other liens have priority. (*Imhoff v. Title Ins. & Trust Co.,* 113 Cal.App.2d 139 [247 P.2d 851].) The court also correctly found that the Edsons' foreclosure of their second trust deed eliminated Pike's security on the $4,000 loan, and that because the loan was not made in connection with the purchase of the nursing home, Tuttle was personally liable for the debt unless it had been extinguished.

The crucial question is this: Does Civil Code section 1479 compel the presumption, as appellant contends, that the monthly payments Tuttle made to Pike during the period from October 10, 1963, to July 9, 1965, were applied toward the extinction of the $4,000 loan, since that obligation was earliest in date of maturity and was secured by the more precarious lien? [2]

Contrary to the implications which necessarily follow from the trial court's finding that neither Pike nor Tuttle indicated to the other the manner in which the $250 payments were to be applied, the evidence leads to the inescapable conclusion that the men treated the two loans as one debt and intended to discharge the combined obligation over the same period of time through the payment of a single monthly installment of $250 each month. Both notes were purportedly secured by the same trust deed, and neither contained a precise maturity date; each was dischargeable through the payment of monthly installments and, significantly, these installments, as well as the interest rate and date of payment were exactly the same. The words "additional loan" were written across the face of the Pike-Tuttle note, and Pike designated that loan as a "new added loan" in his payment book; he also added the amount of the loan to the Pike-Edson note balance, raising that balance to $27,750. Tuttle not only testified that a single monthly payment of $250 on both notes was contemplated, but he made one such monthly payment without variation or interruption for a period of 22 months; yet he also made a monthly interest payment on the combined reduced balance of both notes.

Nevertheless, the trial judge correctly concluded that Civil Code section 1479 was inapplicable, and we affirm the judgment. This is not a situation where both the debtor and creditor failed to direct the application of a payment as contemplated by section 1479, so as to bring into play the presumptions articulated there. It is a case where the parties unequivocally indicated their intentions but were thwarted in the realization of those intentions because of the intervening rights of a third party. What the debtor and creditor intended to accomplish is

---

[2] Under Civil Code section 1479, if a debtor who owes two or more obligations to the same creditor and makes payment on one obligation without specifying the manner in which payment is to be applied, the election may be made by the creditor. But if neither party makes such application, the performance must be applied to the extinction of the obligations in the following order:

1. Of interest due at the time of performance.
2. Of principal due at that time.
3. Of the obligation earliest in date of maturity.
4. Of an obligation not secured by a lien or collateral undertaking.
5. Of an obligation secured by a lien or collateral undertaking.

undeniable, but they failed to exercise properly their power of application. As we have demonstrated, Ray Pike and Dr. Tuttle undoubtedly believed that the two loans were in effect one obligation secured by the same security and that the combined obligation could be discharged through a single monthly payment. But Tuttle had given the Edsons a second trust deed and had assumed their obligation to make the payments on the Pike-Edson loan. Therefore, despite the intention of the parties, the loans remained different in nature and in legal effect were secured by entirely different liens and could not be discharged as a single obligation in the manner attempted.

Under these circumstances, we must resort to the common law to resolve the dilemma. It is settled that where none of the rules prescribed by the statute cover or apply to the particular situation, application of a payment will be made on common law principles. (*Bank of America v. Kelsey,* 6 Cal.App.2d 346 [44 P.2d 617]; *Murdock v. Clarke,* 88 Cal. 384 [26 P. 601].) Payment will be applied in the manner most consonant with justice and equity; therefore, under the prevailing rule where neither the creditor nor the debtor has made application of a payment, the court will apply it to a debt existing at the time of payment and to the relief of one secondarily liable thereon rather than apply it on a *"subsequently incurred debt."* [Italics added.] (70 C.J.S., § 76, p. 281.)

Because Dr. Tuttle failed to exercise properly his power of application, and because he gave no other directions as to the manner in which he wanted the payments applied, Pike could not have applied the payments to the extinction of the $4,000 loan even if he had wanted to; under the common law rule, he would have been required to apply the payments to the Pike-Edson note Tuttle had assumed. As the Restatement of Contracts, section 389, states:

> When a debtor having power to direct the application of a payment fails *properly* to exercise the power, the creditor *cannot* apply the payment . . . (e) to the exclusion of a claim, failure to discharge which, with the money then paid, will, as the creditor knows or has reason to know, violate a duty owed by the debtor to a third person, whether that duty arises from a fiduciary relation or from a contract. [Italics added.]

To relieve Tuttle of the burden of payment of a just debt by presuming that as to him the payments were applied to discharge that debt, when he gave Pike no such direction and when it would have been impossible for Pike himself to do so, would be patently inconsistent and would lend our approval to the perpetration of an injustice.

The judgment is affirmed.

STONE, P. J., and BROWN (G.A.), J., concurred.

Providing for Future Advances. Where a mortgagor and a mortgagee expect future advances to be made by the mortgagee to the mortgagor they can, in most states, avoid executing a new security for each new advance by entering into a mortgage covering future advances. Some courts have ruled that this type of mortgage, when given in good faith, has priority as against holders of subsequent interests in the real estate. Where this rule is followed, the mortgagee is in a better position than if he takes back a new mortgage every time he makes an advance, since, under those circumstances, he would not be protected against parties who acquired intervening interests in the property. In some instances, however, the courts have regarded a mortgage covering future advances as void as against holders of subsequent interests in the property, especially where the mortgagee had no obligation to make the future advances.

Some statutes provide that any additional advance made to a borrower, where the mortgage note provides for such additional advances, shall not exceed the amount specified in the mortgage. See FNMA form below for an example.

OPEN-END MORTGAGE

THIS MORTGAGE is made this   day of   19 between the Mortgagor,
          (herein "Borrower") and the Mortgagee, Citizens Federal Savings and Loan Association of Dayton, an association organized and existing under the laws of The United States of America, whose address is 110 North Main Street, Dayton, Ohio 45402 (herein "Lender").

WHEREAS, Borrower is indebted to Lender in the principal sum of   Dollars, which indebtedness is evidenced by Borrower's note dated   (herein "Note"), providing for monthly installments of principal and interest, with the balance of the indebtedness, if not sooner paid, due and payable on

TO SECURE to LENDER (a) the repayment of the indebtedness evidenced by the Note, with interest thereon, the payment of all other sums, with interest thereon, advanced in accordance herewith to protect the security of this Mortgage, and the performance of the convenants and agreements of Borrower herein contained and (b) the repayment of any future advances, with interest thereon, made to Borrower by Lender pursuant to paragraph 21 hereof (herein "Future Advances"), Borrower does hereby mortgage, grant and convey to Lender the following described property located in the County of   , State of Ohio:

* * *

21. Future Advances. Upon request of Borrower, Lender, at Lender's option prior to release of this Mortgage, may make Future Advances to Borrower. Such Future Advances, with interest thereon, shall be secured by this Mortgage when evidenced by promissory notes stating that said notes are secured hereby. At no time shall the principal amount of the indebtedness secured by this Mortgage, not including sums advanced in accordance herewith to protect the security of this Mortgage, exceed the original amount of the Note plus US $—0—.

Illustration 5

Portions of F.N.M.A. Open End Mortgage Showing
Future Advance Clause

NOTE

In the Federal National Mortgage Association form above, the lender has the right to make future advances secured by the original mortgage with the priority for the later debt dating back to the original note and mortgage. However, subsequent lienors are put on notice by the form that future advances will never exceed the original amount of the debt, thus limiting the amount that can be secured with a future advance. Any amount advanced beyond that would require new security or a change in priority; otherwise the amount in excess of the original debt will remain unsecured.

3. ESCROWS — IMPOUND OR RESERVE ACCOUNTS

Payment of Taxes and Insurance. Example:

We further covenant and agree, to pay to the Mortgagee additional monthly installments sufficient reasonably to anticipate the payment of taxes, special assessments, hazard insurance premiums and similar items that shall accrue against or in connection with the mortgaged real estate, and further agree that such payments may be held by the Mortgagee and commingled with other such funds or its own funds, and the Mortgagee may pay such items as charged or billed, without further inquiry, from such payments or its own funds, nor shall the Mortgagee pay any interest to the Mortgagor on such funds. If the installments so paid by us are insufficient to pay said items as they become due, we promise to pay the difference upon demand.

Such an escrow provision is generally non-negotiable if the mortgagee is a savings and loan association. A bank, however, may be willing to eliminate the clause if the mortgagor is a good customer and has sufficient funds available in a savings account to pay the taxes and insurance. Since no interest is paid on the escrowed funds, negotiating to eliminate the clause is generally advisable.

Maine Revised Statutes Annotated (1980)

§ 429. Residential mortgage escrow accounts

1. Definition. For purposes of this section, an "escrow account" means any account established by agreement between a mortgagor and a financial institution acting as a mortgagee under which the mortgagor pays to the institution or its assignee sums to be used to pay taxes.

2. Payment of interest or taxes. If a financial institution maintains an escrow account in connection with a first purchase money mortgage on a dwelling of 4 or fewer living units located in this State, the financial institution shall:

A. Pay the mortgagor quarterly dividends or interest on the account at a rate at least ½ the highest annual interest rate paid on regular savings accounts at that institution. The dividends or interest paid under this section may not be reduced by any charge for service or maintenance of the account; or

B. To the extent of the account, pay the taxes for which the account is maintained directly to the appropriate taxing authority when the taxes are due.

3. Computing and crediting interest. Under subsection 2, paragraph A, interest shall be computed on the daily balances in the account from the date of receipt to the date of disbursement, and shall be credited to the account as of the last business day of each quarter of a calendar or fiscal year. If the account is closed or discontinued before the last business day of a quarter of a calendar or fiscal year, interest shall be computed and credited as of the day the account is closed or discontinued. For purposes of this section, the financial institution may take into account debit balances resulting from advances, and may elect to compute interest on the basis of the actual number of days in each quarter and year or on the basis of a 30-day month and a 360-day year. At least once a year, the financial institution shall give the mortgagor a statement showing the interest credited on the account during the period which the statement covers.

Added by 1979, c. 426.

DERENCO, INC. v. BENJAMIN FRANKLIN FEDERAL SAVINGS & LOAN ASS'N

Supreme Court of Oregon
281 Or. 533, 577 P.2d 477 (1978)

Borrower brought suit, on behalf of itself and others, to obtain an accounting of profits allegedly realized by Federally chartered savings and loan association on funds in reserve accounts established to pay taxes and insurance premiums on mortgaged residences. The Circuit Court, Multnomah County, Pat Dooley, J., certified the suit as a class action and ordered an accounting. Both sides sought review to secure a final determination of controlling issues before entertaining statements of claim from class members, and the Supreme Court, Holman, J., held that: (1) the type of state regulation sought to be imposed was not preempted by federal law; (2) there was no necessity for exclusive use of federal decisional law in interpreting the parties' relationship and their resultant obligations; (3) in view of the fact that the plaintiff class consisted of borrowers who were unfamiliar with banking practices and where the borrowers were not informed of defendant's use of money deposited with it for payment of taxes and insurance premiums and defendant did not provide in the contract for its use of the money and the contract was drawn by defendant and was one of adhesion, the borrowers were entitled to recover income derived from defendant's investment of funds deposited to pay taxes and insurance premiums on their mortgaged dwellings; (4) the borrowers could not recover with respect to deposits for insurance that were not required by defendant; (5) the trial court's award of income equal to the amount paid by defendant on passbook savings accounts was proper; (6) the named plaintiff was sufficiently representative of the class to adequately and fairly protect the interests of all class members, and (7) it was proper that the proceeding continue as a class action.

Decree affirmed as modified and remanded.

HOLMAN, JUSTICE.

This is an interlocutory appeal accepted by this court under ORS 13.400. Plaintiff, Derenco, Inc., filed suit upon behalf of itself and others for an accounting of profits. The suit was certified by the trial court as a class action. The court found for plaintiff and ordered an accounting. Both sides seek review to secure a final determination of controlling issues before entertaining statements of claim from class members under ORS 13.260(2) and proceeding to judgment under ORS 13.380.

Defendant is a federally chartered savings and loan association engaged in making loans on single family dwellings. This suit, brought upon behalf of borrowers from defendant, claimed entitlement to the income derived from defendant's investment by funds deposited with it by borrowers for the payment of taxes and insurance premiums on their dwellings. With each month's payment of interest and principal on his loan, each borrower also deposited one-twelfth of the amount estimated to be required annually for taxes and insurance premiums. At the end of the period of accumulation, defendant used the deposits to pay the taxes and insurance premiums. During the period of accumulation defendant used the funds as its own, and it is reimbursement for this use which is in question here.

Plaintiff instituted this suit in July of 1974. We are concerned with the period commencing six years prior to that time. Not all of the security instruments used by defendant during the relevant period had the same provisions for prepayment of taxes and insurance premiums. The "conventional" mortgage form, used by defendant until February 1, 1972, contained the following language:

> ... The monies so deposited by Mortgagors *shall be credited to a reserve account,* and Mortgagee is herewith *authorized to charge against said account as a withdrawal sufficient amounts to pay accruing taxes and insurance premiums* when due to the full extent of said account, if necessary. If there should be insufficient sums in said account to pay said taxes and insurance premiums when due, Mortgagor shall, upon demand, pay to Mortgagee an amount necessary to satisfy said deficiency. . . . (Emphasis added.)

On February 1, 1972, there were inserted into the conventional mortgage form set forth above the words emphasized in the following excerpt:

> ... The monies so deposited by Mortgagors shall be credited to a *non-interest bearing* reserve account, and Mortgagee is herewith authorized . . . .

The trial judge required an accounting by defendant on the reserve accounts established through both of these forms on the theory that defendant was the borrowers' agent.[1]

In addition, a third form was required by the Federal Housing Administration (FHA) on loans which it insured, which form contained the following language:

> [S]uch sums to be held by the Beneficiary *in trust to pay* said ground rents, *premiums, taxes* and special assessments, before the same become delinquent . . . . (Emphasis added.)

The trial judge required an accounting on reserve accounts established through this form on the theory that the instrument created a trust relationship.[2]

On the question of the appropriate remedy, the trial judge held that because the exact amount of earnings enjoyed by defendant for its own purposes as a result of its use of the reserve accounts could not be ascertained, and because defendant had incurred some expense in administering the account and in investing the funds, it was equitable for defendant to pay interest on the reserve account funds at the same rate as that which defendant paid to depositors on ordinary demand savings accounts during the same period of time.

We will first consider an issue of consequence which may obviate all other problems, depending upon how it is decided. Defendant contends that the relevant federal law in this area has a preemptive effect and that the state is therefore precluded from regulating defendant's activities via enforcement of the common law . . . .

. . . .

We conclude that the type of state regulation sought to be imposed here is not preempted on any of the bases discussed. The present tendency of the United States Supreme Court appears to be to accommodate, if possible, both federal and state law. There is no substantial conflict or interference between the trial court's holding in the case and the regulation of federal associations by Congress

---

[1] Restatement (Second) of Agency § 388 states the rule requiring an agent to account to his principal for any profits derived from activities conducted for the principal's benefit.

[2] Defendant used a fourth security instrument on mortgages made by it and sold to the Federal Home Loan Mortgage Corporation. The trial court determined that this instrument created a mere debtor-creditor relationship, and that defendant owed no accounting duty to borrowers under it. The correctness of this ruling is not challenged on appeal.

and the Board. Neither do we believe the field has been entirely occupied. Congress is always capable of saying if it intends to occupy the field exclusively and so are federal regulators.

It is our belief that federal law should not and will not be held to occupy the field to the exclusion of state common law in the absence of more compelling reasons than those which exist here. Federally chartered institutions doing business within the state should comply with the business usages and ethics required of others engaged in similar businesses within the state unless such usages and ethics actually conflict or interfere with federal purposes or unless Congress or the federal regulatory body unmistakably indicates otherwise....

. . . .

An important aspect in the consideration of the surrounding circumstances is the purpose of the deposits. There is no substantial controversy in this regard. The deposits were for the purpose of protecting the security of defendant's mortgages from unpaid taxes and uncompensated loss of the improvements by fire or other disaster. In the absence of other evidence, it would be reasonable for us to assume that defendant should have whatever interest in the money that was necessary to accomplish the purpose of the deposits. Beneficial interest in the money by defendant during its period of accumulation was unnecessary to the security of its mortgages. However, there is no doubt that defendant had the unexpressed intention to have such interest. Insofar as the value of its use of the money might exceed the expense of administering the accounts and making payments, defendant would receive a gratuitous windfall. It results in the borrowers' paying defendant for the use of the money they have secured from it, while defendant is paying nothing for the use of the money it has obtained from borrowers for a purpose which can be fully accomplished without defendant's beneficial use thereof. At the time of the making of the contract there would have been no reason for the borrowers to assume, in the absence of their being otherwise informed, that defendant would have any interest other than that which was necessary to accomplish the purpose of the deposits.

Defendant contends that part of the *quid pro quo* for the use of the money is the benefit which borrowers derived from having their homes protected by the budgeted monthly amount against non-payment of taxes and risk of casualty loss. This is only argument from hindsight to justify what has occurred. The real reason for the deposits, at least in the case of all taxes and some insurance premiums, is that defendant required such deposits for its own protection rather than out of any sense of concern for the borrowers.[3]

There is another aspect of the matter which we consider to be important. We infer from the evidence that loans were required to be transacted on defendant's security forms. Ambiguous contracts are usually construed against the party who drafts them. Silence on the subject of a right which the drafter later contends he has is usually fatal to his contention unless such right is one which necessarily results from the other terms of the contract. In the present situation a beneficial interest in defendant in the money does not necessarily result from the written terms of the contract. Construction against the drafter of the contract is particularly appropriate in a situation like the present where the contract is one of adhesion with the borrowers' having no opportunity to negotiate its terms. We therefore reject the arguments that the borrowers were equally responsible for

---

[3] The Board's regulations required the deposits if loans were close to the actual value of the property.

the omission of any provisions concerning the use of the money and that, since the parties contracted for reserve accounts without providing for payment of interest or earnings, the agreement is conclusive of defendant's right to use the funds without reimbursement.[4] The borrowers were in no position to question or negotiate the terms of the contract.

Defendant contends, however, that there is reason in the present situation for the borrowers to know of defendant's purposed use of the money due to the general knowledge which people possess of banks and similar institutions making their profits by loaning funds deposited with them. Defendant depends on the following language from 1 Restatement (Second) of Trusts § 12, comment *l.*, at 41-42:

> If money is deposited in a bank for a special purpose, the bank is not a trustee or bailee of the money unless it is the clear understanding of the parties that the money deposited is not to be used by the bank for its own purposes.
> . . . .
> Where the deposit is in escrow, that is where the money is to be paid to a third person on the happening of a designated event and in the meantime the depositor has no right to withdraw the money, it depends upon the manifestation of the intention of the parties whether the bank may use as its own the money deposited or whether the money shall be held in trust. Such a deposit ordinarily indicates an intention that the bank may use the money as its own, the bank undertaking to pay to the third person the amount of the deposit on the happening of the designated event.

V Scott on Trusts § 524 at 3669 (3d ed 1967) is not so sure of the result:

> [O]ne circumstance of great importance is custom in the business of banking. It has sometimes been held that a custom is so well established and well known that the courts will take judicial notice of it. In many cases, however, the courts have acquired evidence of custom; and the amount of evidence and the character of the evidence offered have so varied that it is not unnatural perhaps that the decisions have shown a wide divergence in determining the character of the relation created. Moreover a custom may be one not known to the person whose rights are involved, and one not so well established and generally known that he is chargeable with notice of it; in which case, in spite of the existence of the custom, he will not be bound by it. Banking customs, however, are becoming better established and better known, and will doubtless play an increasing part in determining the results reached by the courts. (Footnote omitted.)

There is no evidence in this case of a uniform custom among lenders as to how, and for whose benefit, any earnings on funds representing prepayments are handled. To the contrary, there is evidence that some savings and loan associations do give borrowers, while the money is being accumulated, the benefit of any earnings from use of the deposits made for taxes and insurance premiums. This is accomplished by use of the "capitalization" method of administering reserve accounts. Under it, whenever a borrower makes a payment, the entire amount, including that portion attributable to taxes and insurance premiums, is credited to interest and debt. When the time comes for payment of the taxes and insurance premiums, the account is charged with these amounts. In this manner the

---

[4] For cases agreeing with defendant's contention but which fail to consider who drew the contract or to examine its adhesion nature, see Cale v. American National Bank, 37 Ohio Misc. 56, 66 Ohio Op.2d 122, 124 (C.P. Cuyahoga Cty. 1973); Brooks v. Valley National Bank, 113 Ariz. 169, 548 P.2d 1166, 1171 (1976).

purpose of the deposit, security for the lender, is accomplished and the borrower is given the benefit of the use of the funds.[5]

In addition, the concepts that persons who borrow money on their homes have knowledge of banking practices and that those who make reserve deposits are even aware of the beneficial use of such deposits are highly suspect. It is questionable whether homeowners would look at funds deposited with a savings and loan association or a bank for the payment of taxes and insurance premiums on premises put up as security for a loan in the same manner as they would look at money deposited in such institutions on which they were being paid interest. When a depositor is paid interest, it would seem to us probable that he realizes that the lending institution must have the use of the money in order to pay him the interest.[6] However, when he is not paid interest nor told that deposited funds will be put to the institution's use, but instead is told that they will be put into a reserve account, we believe it is doubtful that he would expect the money to be used for the benefit of such institution.

It would seem to us reasonable for a depositor to assume, in the usual situation in which money is deposited in a checking account or, at the request of the depositor, deposited for a special purpose, that the funds will be used by the bank in order that it be paid for its service. However, the deposits in question here were not established for the convenience of the depositor, as is the usual case, but were established at the insistence of defendant for its protection and for a purpose which had nothing to do with defendant's having a beneficial interest in the money.

From the testimony of defendant's officer in charge of loans and from the small value of the beneficial use of the deposits for each loan, we infer that the instances in which the beneficial use of the money even occurred to borrowers were isolated and infrequent.[7] Defendant's officer testified that the instances in which any information was requested by borrowers concerning income from their deposits were limited to three or four oral inquiries a year and to two or three written inquiries every five years. These inquiries were apparently limited to whether interest was paid, and the responses thereto were that interest was not paid. Considering that the borrowers who are affected by this opinion are in the many thousands, it would appear that the number of people who were knowledgeable enough to ask anything about the deposits at all is inconsequential. It could be argued that the balance did not inquire because they knew of the custom of loaning institutions making use of such deposits and they assented to it. However, because of the lack of evidence establishing such a custom and because of the other evidence, we believe the inference of the borrowers' lack of awareness of the subject of the beneficial use of the deposits is a fair one.[8]

For the reasons given, despite the following language from V Scott on Trusts

---

[5] It also obviates the expense of maintaining two or more accounts for each borrower.

[6] "Where the bank undertakes to pay interest on the deposit, it is clearly the intention of the parties that the bank should have the use of the money, ..." V Scott on Trusts § 530 at 3685 (3d ed 1967).

[7] Defendant accumulated deposits for taxes payable on Oregon real estate of approximately $18,000,000 annually. In addition, it made loans on property in southern Washington.

[8] It is both interesting and revealing to see how defendant's right to use the funds was treated for internal accounting purposes by defendant. According to the testimony of defendant's officer, the funds were designated as ". . . advance payments *on borrow* for taxes and insurance . . . ." (Emphasis added.) Thus, the funds were labeled for accounting purposes as prepayments which were borrowed by defendant.

§ 530 at 3684-685 (3d ed 1967), it is our conclusion that justice and fair dealing require a recovery by borrowers:

> The question in each case is a question of the intention of the depositor and the bank. *Usually the intention is not expressed in words and frequently the matter is not even in the minds of the parties. The courts in such cases have to struggle with the question what the parties would have thought if they had considered the matter.* In most cases a depositor surely would not expect a bank to segregate the money deposited nor would the bank expect to do so. It is believed that the cases which hold that a debt is intended show a more realistic attitude on the part of the courts, and that in many of the cases at least in which the courts have said that a trust was intended they have gone counter to the real intention of the parties. . . . The mere fact that a deposit is made for a special purpose is not a sufficient reason, unless there is an understanding that the money deposited should not be used as a part of the general assets of the bank.
>
> It would seem that the presumption is that when a bank receives money it is intended that the bank should use the money; and the burden is on the depositor to show that the understanding was different. The mere fact that the money deposited is not an ordinary general deposit, and is not subject to withdrawal by check of the depositor, is insufficient to rebut the presumption and to show an intention to make the deposit special. . . . (Emphasis added; footnote omitted.)

In summation, because (1) the class consists of persons unfamiliar with banking practices (homeowners); (2) borrowers were not informed of defendant's use of the deposits; (3) defendant did not provide in the contract for its use of the money; (4) the contract was drawn by defendant and is one of adhesion; (5) the purpose of the particular deposits is limited to protecting defendant's security interest; and (6) no uniform practice exists concerning the use of the kind of deposits in question, it is our conclusion that the borrowers were entitled to any income from the use of the funds during the period of accumulation. The borrowers being so entitled, they would be deprived of what was justly theirs and defendant would be unjustly enriched were defendant permitted to keep the proceeds of the use of the funds.

We realize that this is the first case in the United States by a court of last resort which has held after trial that borrowers have a right to recover in a case of this kind. There have been two decisions of courts of last resort which have upheld a complaint in a similar case as against an attack by demurrer. They are *Buchanan v. Brentwood Federal Savings & Loan Assn.,* 457 Pa. 135, 320 A.2d 117, 127 (1974), and *Carpenter v. Suffolk Franklin Savings Bank,* 362 Mass. 770, 291 N.E.2d 609 (1973). There are a considerable number of cases which have held to the contrary for various reasons. Most of them can be distinguished upon the facts; with any that cannot be so distinguished, we disagree. Most of the cases which hold for the defendant do so upon the basis of custom, upon the absence of any provision in the agreement that the borrower will receive any recompense, or upon a particular wording of the security agreement which is different from the ones here involved.

. . . .

Another problem is the computation of the amount of the borrowers' recovery. There is no way to determine exactly the amount of defendant's earnings on the deposits since the money from the deposits was commingled with defendant's other funds for investment. There is evidence from which defendant's earnings from its direct loans on real property can be determined as well as evidence from which its yield on its portfolio of other investments can be ascertained. There is, however, no way to determine the amount of money from the deposits which was in each type of investment. Of course, funds for taxes had to be available at taxpaying time and this meant that sufficient investments in short term securities had to be maintained for this purpose. These yields can vary from other investments.

The cost of servicing the accounts of deposited funds as of June 30, 1975, was estimated by defendant to be $4.87 per tax account and $4.58 per insurance account. The testimony was that this expense had steadily diminished through the years because of the gradually increased use of computers and that it was impossible to reconstruct the expense of maintaining the accounts for past years. Defendant also produced testimony that approximately one million dollars a year was advanced by it to make up deficiencies for borrowers in their tax accounts so that the three per cent tax discount for early payment could be secured. However, the expense of the advancement of these funds was computed in the average cost of servicing the accounts.

In addition to the servicing cost there was the expense of the investment and handling of the funds so that they would generate income. On top of all of this, defendant is required by the Board to maintain a reserve from accumulated profits which has to be a percentage of total savings accounts. As such accounts increase, profits have to be generated to maintain additional reserves so that the Board will permit defendant to continue to operate. This is also, in a way, an expense of doing business.

The trial judge looked at this complicated computation problem and resolved it with rough justice. He awarded income from the accounts to plaintiffs equal to the interest that was paid by defendant on ordinary pass book savings accounts. This is eminently sensible. The defendant is a mutual association. The total cost of all operations, including the maintenance of the reserve accounts as well as their investment, has necessarily been deducted from income before payment of such pass book interest. The deposits in question were completely commingled with defendant's other invested funds. The costs of servicing the accounts and investing the funds were not capable of being isolated as separate components of defendant's total expenses. It is true that the Board, and not defendant, sets the rates for pass book savings accounts. However, these rates are presumably set by the Board with a view to allowing defendant to pay expenses, to maintain the necessary reserves, and thus to perform the functions for which it was created. Lack of availability of evidence from which one can be completely accurate about computation of earnings does not prevent borrowers from prevailing when recovery is otherwise proper.

The decree requiring defendant to account is affirmed as modified, and the case is remanded to the trial court for an accounting in conformance with this opinion.

NOTES

1. Some state legislatures require mortgage lending institutions requiring escrow accounts to pay interest thereon. In *Jamaica Savings Bank v. Attorney General*, 390 F. Supp. 1357 (N.Y. 1975), a savings bank attacked the constitutionality of a New York statute requiring financial lending institutions to pay interest on so-called mortgage escrow accounts. The United States Supreme Court, 423 U.S. 802 (1975), affirmed the trial court's decision that the statutory approach was constitutional.

2. *Court Challenges.* It should be noted that escrow account requirements have been challenged as violating the Truth in Lending Act, as restraints of trade, and tie-in arrangements prohibited by the Sherman-Clayton Act. The case of *Sears v. First Federal Savings & Loan Ass'n,* 275 N.E.2d 300 (Ill. 1971) established that by virtue of the escrow provisions in a mortgage note there is no trust relationship created between the lender and the mortgagor, and by virtue of no trust relationship the mortgagor is not entitled to accounting of profits earned. However, the Supreme Court of Arkansas in *Tucker v. Pulaski Federal Savings & Loan Ass'n,* 481 S.W.2d 725 (Ark. 1972), ruled that a mortgage lender is entitled to retain profits realized from investing escrow funds. The court held that an escrow account is in essence a service to the mortgagor, freeing him from the responsibility of making the payments for real estate taxes and insurance premiums. The court also stated that the mortgage lender is entitled to insure itself, and that insurance premiums and taxes will be paid timely. Since the administration of a mortgage escrow account is time-consuming and required clerical attention, the court implied that the escrow agent, *i.e.,* the mortgage lender, is entitled to the use of the escrowed funds without penalty. In *Carpenter v. Suffolk Franklin Savings Bank,* 291 N.E.2d 609 (Mass. 1973), the court held that where a mortgagor pays funds to a lending institution with the expressed intention that the funds be held for a particular purpose, for example, the payment of real estate taxes and/or insurance premiums, the funds then are deemed to be held for the particular purpose, therefore creating a fiduciary or trust relationship.

4. ACCELERATION OR DUE-ON CLAUSES

Consent Required to Transfer. Example:

It is expressly understood and agreed that the Mortgage Note shall become due and payable forthwith at the option of the Mortgagee if, at any time during the loan, the Mortgagor shall sell, convey or transfer said mortgaged premises, or if either legal or equitable title shall vest in any other person than the Mortgagor in any manner and for any reason whatsoever, unless the consent in writing of the Mortgagee herein, or its successors or assigns, is first obtained. In the event of the approval by the Mortgagee of any such transfer of title, the Mortgagee may make a service charge of one percent of the original amount of the mortgage loan, which if not paid will be added to the unpaid balance of the mortgage loan.

HILL, "DUE-ON" CLAUSES: A TREND TOWARD EQUITABLE ENFORCEMENT, 2 University of Dayton Law Review 215-20 (1977)

Contemporary lenders presently utilize at least two types of clauses in a security instrument (mortgage or deed of trust) to generate additional income. Due-on-sale clauses accelerate the balance of the obligation upon the sale or transfer of the subject property, and due-on-encumbrance clauses accelerate the balance of the obligation upon the placing of an additional burden or encumbrance on the property. Such acceleration allows adjustment of interest to current rates whenever encumbered property is sold. In a second type of clause, prepayment penalty, lenders charge a penalty for early payment of a loan prior to its maturity date. Because of these kinds of limitations on the mortgagor, it can be said that these provisions are restraints on alienation, although permissible ones in most jurisdictions.

California courts and other courts across the country have had difficulty balancing the need for acceleration clauses in an inflationary economy with the traditional prohibition against restraints on alienation. This article analyzes the cases which have dealt with acceleration clauses and the solutions which have been formulated.

I. Historical Background

Restraints on alienation of land were imposed at common law by feudal lords with appropriate sanctions such as forfeiture or fine imposed for violation. While land was held tenurially and feudal incidents were due the lords, harsh penalties were needed to preserve the land in the hands of those familiar to the lords and, even more important, to prevent lands upon which the lords were dependent from falling into the hands of strangers or enemies. Certain transfers were absolutely prohibited, while other alienations of the fee were permitted, but only after payment of a fine to the lord.

A present day restraint on the transfer of encumbered land, imposed by a lender, is not unlike the restraint imposed by feudal lords who retained an interest in the land which for practical purposes served as security for the satisfaction of an obligation, although not a debt in the modern sense of the word. The oath of fealty has been replaced today by the financial statement and credit application; however, the desire to maintain the stability of the lord's relationship to the one obligated remains unchanged. Just as the lords were concerned about the performance of feudal incidents, so are modern lenders concerned that the payment of the debt be made promptly and that waste not be allowed to occur on the encumbered land.

In feudal times restraints on alienation, however, became repugnant to the concept of fee simple. In 1290 the Statute Quia Emptores was enacted bringing about a drastic change in the law regarding transfer of land. This statute allowed "freemen" to transfer land without payment of a fine to their lords and was the first step in disallowing restraints on alienation. While it has been urged that repugnancy alone is not sufficient to forbid restraints, the rule against restraints on alienation continues to exist today. Exceptions to the rule prohibiting restraints have so eroded the rule, however, that the precise status of restraints in particular circumstances may be impossible to determine. Justification for a restraint may occur, according to the *Restatement of Property,* due either to its social utility or because it is insignificant.

Because they may be considered restraints on alienation, acceleration clauses have not been used frequently until relatively recent times. An 1823 Louisiana case provides the earliest mention of a sanction imposed upon mortgagors in the United States. It involved a doctrine known as the *pact de non alienando.* While there has been some commentary on this doctrine, it does not appear to have been used outside Louisiana.

. . . .

III. The Coast Bank *Decision*

The earliest appellate decision to consider a clause permitting acceleration upon transfer of the subject property occurred in California in 1964. That case, *Coast Bank v. Minderhout,* became the leading case in the United States and continues so today. While *Coast Bank* has been followed in several jurisdictions as authority for the proposition that a lender could accelerate the due date of an obligation, the case did not arise out of a conventional mortgage or deed of trust utilizing a due-on-sale clause. Rather, *Coast Bank* involved an equitable mortgage on certain real property created by the recordation of a document entitled "An Agreement Not to Encumber or Transfer Property." Similar documents had been held not to create security interests in several other jurisdictions at that time. The type of instrument in *Coast Bank* was commonly used in California where certain lenders are prohibited from lending funds which would create a junior lien. By utilizing "An Agreement Not to Encumber or Transfer Property" rather than a conventional deed of trust, California lenders are able to place loans which could be construed as either a secured interest or an unsecured interest so as not to violate the prohibition against a junior security. The advantage to the lender in such a situation is obvious. In the event of a foreclosure by the senior lienor on the property in question or in the event the subject property appears overencumbered, the lender holding the "Agreement Not to Encumber or Transfer Property" may treat the debt as unsecured; and in the event of a bankruptcy by the mortgagor, the junior lender may treat the debt as secured, although in a junior position. The supreme court in *Coast Bank* found that the provisions of the instrument afforded some indication that the parties intended to create a security interest in the property and allowed foreclosure of the equitable mortgage. While *Coast Bank* did not present a clear-cut case involving a due-on-sale clause, it did allow the court to consider the issue of whether such an instrument created an unlawful restraint on alienation. The court mentioned several justifiable and reasonable restraints on alienation which have been permitted: spendthrift trusts, leases for a term of years terminable upon alienation, life estates terminable upon alienation, corporate restrictions on transfers of shares, and restraints on alienation in executory land contracts. The court held:

> In the present case it was not unreasonable for plaintiff [Coast Bank] to condition its continued extention of credit to the Enrights on their interest in the property that stood as security for the debt. Accordingly, plaintiff validly provided that it might accelerate the due date if the Enrights encumbered or transferred the property.

The language of Justice Traynor, who wrote the decision, is significant. He did *not* determine that due-on-sale clauses were reasonable; instead, he held simply that requiring the borrower's retention of an interest in the subject property was "not unreasonable." Subsequent decisions interpreting *Coast Bank,* however, have assumed that the case provided blanket approval for the use of due-on-sale clauses.

a. Due-On-Sale Clauses

MALOUFF v. MIDLAND FEDERAL SAVINGS & LOAN ASS'N

Supreme Court of Colorado
181 Colo. 294, 509 P.2d 1240 (1973)

LEE, JUSTICE. . . . The principal issue concerns the validity of the acceleration clause contained in a deed of trust, a matter of first impression in Colorado. The clause in controversy, sometimes designated as a "due on sale" clause, provides as follows:

> The said party of the first part [Borrower] further covenants and agrees:

> Not to alienate nor to encumber to the prejudice of the Association said real estate nor to commit, permit, or suffer any waste, impairment, or depreciation of said property and, in the event of any sale or transfer of title to the property herein described, such purchaser or new owner shall be deemed to have assumed and agreed to pay the indebtedness owing the Association hereunder, whether or not the instrument evidencing such sale or transfer expressly so provides, *and at any time after such sale or transfer, without limiting the*

foregoing, the Association may, at its option, declare all of the remainder of the indebtedness immediately due and collectible, whether or not any default exists; this covenant shall run with said land and remain in full force and effect until said indebtedness is liquidated and the Association may, without notice to party of the first part, deal with such new owner or owners with reference to the debt secured hereby in the same manner as with the party of the first part, without in any way altering or discharging the party of the first part's liability hereunder upon the indebtedness hereby secured. (Emphasis added.)

We are primarily concerned with the italicized portion of the above provision, which was specifically challenged by appellee, Virginia A. Malouff, and which was declared to be void by the trial court as an invalid restraint on alienation. We reverse the judgment.

I

The facts are essentially without basic dispute. In 1966 the subject property, a duplex located at 2170-72 Broadmoor Circle in Colorado Springs, was encumbered by a deed of trust from the owner, Gordon Price, to the use and benefit of appellant, Midland Federal Savings and Loan Association (Midland). The indebtedness secured thereby was in the principal sum of $33,000 bearing interest at 7% per annum, payable in monthly installments of $233.25. In May of 1971 appellee (Malouff) contracted to purchase the duplex for $57,000, by a cash payment of $27,000 and the assumption of the Midland encumbrance balance which was approximately $30,000. Malouff applied to Midland for permission to assume the loan. Midland agreed not to accelerate the indebtedness if Malouff would comply with Midland's assumption requirements, which included the execution of an Assumption and Modification Agreement. This provided that in consideration of Midland's permitting Malouff to assume the existing loan and agreeing not to exercise its acceleration privilege contained in the trust deed, the unpaid loan balance would bear interest at the increased rate of 8% and the monthly payments would thereby be increased to $254.29.

At the sale closing on July 9, 1971, Malouff's regular attorney could not be present. However, she was represented by his associate, who had previously examined the closing documents. Malouff signed the required assumption agreement. She testified that its terms were not read or explained to her. This was disputed by the testimony of the closing agent. In any event, the sale was closed and title to the duplex was transferred *subject to* the Midland trust deed. The closing documents were left with the agent for recording and appropriate distribution.

The next day, Malouff examined her copy of the assumption agreement and, upon reconsideration of its terms, she called the real estate agent and instructed that the papers not be delivered to Midland until her regular attorney had an opportunity to examine them.

After inspecting Midland's assumption agreement, Malouff's attorney informed Midland that his client would not agree to the higher 8% interest rate. The closing agent was then instructed by the attorney to record the deed. This was done. Thereafter, Malouff tendered to Midland monthly payments at the 7% rate, as originally provided in the note and deed of trust. The tendered payments were refused by Midland. Midland elected to accelerate the indebtedness and demanded payment in full by September 1, 1971. To this demand Malouff responded by commencing this action.

II

Malouff's complaint, brought in her behalf individually and as a representative of a class, sought relief under three claims. The first claim requested a preliminary and permanent injunction enjoining Midland from foreclosing its trust deed, and for a declaration that Malouff was legally entitled to assume the Midland loan.

... The third claim related to the class action and sought injunctive relief for those members of the class, similar to Malouff, who were not permitted to assume the existing loan but were required to pay increased interest to Midland on assumption, and for return of the increased interest paid.

After an evidentiary hearing, the court preliminarily enjoined Midland from foreclosing against Malouff, thus maintaining the status quo pending final determination of the merits. Malouff filed a motion for summary judgment. It was stipulated thereafter that all the facts necessary for the court to enter final judgment on the claims between Malouff and Midland were before the court, as shown by the evidence and exhibits at the hearing on prelininary injunction and as contained in the affidavits filed on behalf of Midland, and, therefore, no further evidentiary hearing was necessary. The trial court on February 29 entered extensive findings of fact, conclusions of law and final judgment in favor of Malouff, holding the acceleration clause invalid as an unlawful restraint on alienation, and, further, that it was too vague and uncertain to be enforceable; that the specific terms of the clause requiring assumption of the indebtedness on sale by a purchaser were unenforceable and void; and that plaintiff was entitled to proceed under the class action to obtain final declaratory and injunctive relief.

III

The common law doctrine of restraints on alienation is a part of the law in Colorado. C.R.S.1963, 135-1-1. As declared in *Atchison v. Englewood,* 170 Colo. 295, 463 P.2d 297, public policy demands that property interests be freely alienable and that restraints which withdraw property from the stream of commerce are invalid. In determining what restraints are invalid, some legal scholars have declared that all restraints on alienation are invalid unless they fall within certain recognized categories of exceptions. This view was adopted and followed by the trial court, which held that the due-on-sale clause here involved did not fall within one of the exceptions and it was an invalid restraint.

In contrast to this rigid approach, is the view that holds a restraint on alienation may or may not be invalid, depending upon the reasonableness of the restraint. As suggested in *Atchison v. Englewood, supra,* the rule against restraints on alienation relates to *unreasonable restraints.* In discussing this problem, Mr. Justice Traynor in *Coast Bank v. Minderhout,* 61 Cal.2d 311, 38 Cal.Rptr. 505, 392 P.2d 265, observed:

> The view that the common-law rule against restraints on alienation prohibits all such restraints has been forcefully criticized on the ground that it loses sight of the purposes of the rule and needlessly invalidates reasonable restraints designed to protect justifiable interests of the parties.
>
> . . . .
>
> We subscribe to the view that the question of the invalidity of a restraint depends upon its reasonableness in view of the justifiable interests of the parties.

Coast Bank, supra, considered a landmark decision in the area of due-on-sale clauses, upheld generally the validity of such a clause and in effect rejected the view that such a clause in a security instrument is per se an invalid restraint. Following *Coast Bank, supra,* numerous decisions have upheld the validity of such provisions in various circumstances. *Jones v. Sacramento Savings and Loan Association,* 248 Cal.App.2d 522, 56 Cal.Rptr. 741. . . .

We hold the due-on-sale clause here to be a reasonable restraint on alienation. The question then remains what conditions may be imposed on an assuming purchaser in return for non-exercise of the clause? In *Cherry v. Home Savings & Loan Association, supra,* an analogous situation to that in the present case was considered. It was there held to be a justifiable interest of the lender to protect itself against a rise in the interest rate and to permit an acceleration of the indebtedness on sale where the purchaser will not agree to pay an increased interest rate on assumption of the loan. The restraint on alienation by the election to exercise the due-on-sale clause under these circumstances was held to be a reasonable one and enforceable. The court stated:

> Secondly, loan agreements frequently permit a borrower to pay off a loan before it is due. When interest rates are high, a lender runs the risk they will drop and that the borrower will refinance his debt elsewhere at a lower rate and pay off the loan, leaving the lender with money to loan but at a less favorable interest rate. On the other hand, when money is loaned at low interest, the lender risks losing the benefit of a later increase in rates. As one protection against the foregoing contingency, a due-on-sale clause is employed permitting acceleration of the due date by the lender so that he may take advantage of rising interest rates in the event his borrower transfers the security. This is merely one example of ways taken to minimize risks by sensible lenders.
>
> There is no inequity visible from such a provision. . . .

Shalit, supra, Stith, supra, People's Savings Assn., supra, and *Gunther v. White, supra,* all specifically upheld the right to accelerate where a purchaser refused to pay an increased interest rate, as in *Cherry, supra.*

IV

Among the matters in evidence before the trial court was the affidavit of Marvin W. Buckles, Executive Vice President of Midland, which set forth the rationale with respect to the requirement by Midland of an increased interest rate on assumption of an outstanding loan, when the rate provided in the note is below the current market rate. This evidence, not in dispute, demonstrated that the imbalance between the loan demand and the money supply, arising out of an inflationary economy, required that Midland, as well as similar lending institutions, adopt measures which would protect the borrowers as well as the lenders from the hazards of long-term loans (20-30 years) at fixed interest rates. We quote from this affidavit:

> . . . As of November 30, 1971, Midland held 60,388 deposit accounts. Midland used these deposit accounts to make home loans. Midland must make loans at reasonable rates to its borrowers, but it also has the responsibility to give its depositors a reasonable rate of return on their deposits. A reasonable rate of return on dollars invested in home loans is an interest rate which is comparable to the current rate of return in the lending industry. Midland is willing to deal with the original borrower on a long term basis, but not with any other party without having an opportunity to consider the substituted borrower and current interest rates. . . .
>
> . . . The two primary ways that Midland may make the interest rate adjust-

ments essential for it to protect its depositors against inflation are by making variable interest rate loans or by employing a "due-on-sale" clause to adjust interest rates on assumptions of existing loans when circumstances warrant an adjustment. Midland has chosen the latter method to enable its depositors to combat inflation. The variable interest rate option may reflect the trend in the industry, but the "due on sale" provision is probably the most advantageous procedure to the borrowing public. Under this method, the interest rate is fixed between Midland and its original borrower. Unlike the variable interest rate loan, the original borrower is able to retain the advantage of his original interest rate for as long as he has the loan, even though current interest rates may have risen substantially. If the original borrower sells the property during the life of the loan, the purchaser is then able to assume the loan at no higher rate than the then current market interest rate and probably at a slightly lower rate than the market.

If lenders were unable to make some form of interest rate adjustments on long-term loans, they would have to make only short-term loans amoritized over periods of less than ten years. Original borrowers then would not be able to pay off their home purchases without having to refinance their indebtedness one or more times in the process. Short-term loans would also increase monthly payments and make the obtaining of such loans prohibitive to many people.

We do not consider the motive of Midland in seeking to protect itself and the borrower from the effects of inflationary or deflationary conditions in the money market to be improper or unlawful. Both parties have the benefit of their original bargain during their continued creditor-debtor relationship. However, when the property is sold to a purchaser who desires to assume the existing loan, economic consideration may reasonably justify the lender in raising the interest rate to or approaching one equal to the current market rate. We view the condition imposed for the non-exercise of the acceleration clause under such circumstances to be a reasonable protection of a justifiable interest and the operative effect of the clause does not therefore constitute an invalid restraint on alienation.

The issue of Midland's action under its due-on-sale clause here does not involve inequitable or unconscionable conduct. Malouff does not contend, and the record does not justify any inference, that Midland attempted to raise the interest rate beyond the current market rate then existing. According to the affidavit, the Midland policy was to raise the interest half way between that required by the note and the current interest rate at the time of the sale. Nothing suggests that was not the case here. Were there an effort to extract an excessive interest rate unrelated to the current rate, then the result might be otherwise. A court of equity may relieve a borrower from the effect of a due-on-sale clause where the exercise thereof is the result of some unconscionable or inequitable conduct of the lender. *Tucker v. Pulaski*, Ark., 481 S.W.2d 725; *Clark v. Lachenmeier*, 237 So.2d 583 (Fla.App., 1970); *Gunther v. White*, Tenn., 489 S.W.2d 529.

V

The trial court also erred in concluding that the due-on-sale clause was too vague and uncertain to be enforceable. This conclusion was based upon the language of the acceleration clause, which stated: "At any time after such sale or transfer, without limiting the foregoing, the Association may, at its option, declare all of the remainder of the indebtedness immediately due and collectible;

.... Malouff's contention was that this open-ended provision authorized an election to accelerate at any time, even years in the future. We do not agree. The prevailing rule is that under an ordinary acceleration clause in a mortgage or trust deed, the obligee has a reasonable time after the default or the event which gives rise to the right to accelerate in which to elect to declare the indebtedness due. *Lovell v. Goss,* 45 Colo. 304, 101 P. 72; *Washburn v. Williams,* 10 Colo.App. 153, 50 P. 223; 55 Am.Jur.2d Mortgages § 384. Accordingly, where, as here, no definite time is specified by which the election to accelerate must be exercised, such election to do so must be made within a reasonable time. Here, the election to accelerate was made by Midland within a month after notice of Malouff's refusal to tender the payments required by the Assumption and Modification Agreement. Of course, each case must be considered on its own facts, and, certainly, an election to accelerate a year or years in the future, as hypothesized by Malouff, could not be considered reasonable under ordinary circumstances.

VI

Finally, it is unnecessary to discuss the trial court's additional conclusion that the clause requiring assumption by the purchaser of the unpaid indebtedness on sale of the premises was unenforceable and void. This is so for the reason that the conclusion was predicated upon the assumed invalidity of the acceleration clause as an unlawful restraint on alienation. Having found the clause to be a reasonable restraint, and therefore valid, the agreement to forbear the exercise of that right to accelerate constituted adequate consideration for Malouff's undertaking to assume the unpaid indebtedness and to pay the increased interest rate.

Discussion of the additional issue of whether the trial court correctly ruled the third claim for relief to be a proper class action is also academic in view of our ruling that Malouff's claim for injunctive relief is without merit.

The judgment is reversed and the cause remanded with directions to vacate the injunction and to dismiss the first and third claims for relief.

PRINGLE, C. J., and DAY, J., dissent.

BAKER v. LOVE'S PARK SAVINGS & LOAN ASS'N

Supreme Court of Illinois
61 Ill. 2d 119, 333 N.E.2d 1 (1975)

RYAN, J.

The plaintiffs, Richard E. Baker and Laurie J. Baker, executed a promissory note dated March 5, 1967, payable to the defendant, Loves Park Savings and Loan Association. The note was for $15,700 with interest at 6 percent per annum and provided for monthly installment payments of $102. The note was secured by a mortgage on property improved with a single-family residence owned by the plaintiffs. Section A(8)(d) of the mortgage provides:

A. THE MORTGAGOR COVENANTS DURING THE TERM OF THIS MORTGAGE:

....

(8) Not to suffer or permit without the written permission or consent of the mortgagee being first had and obtained:

....

(d) A sale, assignment or transfer of any right, title or interest in and to said property or any portion thereof. . . .

The note provides:

> We further agree that upon any default upon this obligation, or the instrument securing it, interest at the rate of one per cent (1%) per annum above the original rate provided herein on the unpaid balance of this indebtedness may be charged for the period of such default. Upon any default under this obligation, or the instrument securing it, at the option of the holder of this note, the unpaid balance of this note, and any advances made under it, or the instrument securing it, together with interest, shall become due and payable, time being the essence of this contract. . . .

On March 14, 1970, without securing mortgagee's consent, the plaintiffs entered into an agreement for warranty deed contracting to convey the property covered by the mortgage to Alfred G. Wilson and Linda L. Wilson. The contract provides that the purchasers are to pay to the plaintiffs $102 per month, which amount includes interest at the rate of 6 percent per annum on the unpaid balance of the purchase price. The plaintiffs deposited an executed warranty deed in escrow to be delivered to the purchasers upon completion of the contract. The agreement provides that the purchasers are to have immediate possession.

The defendant learned of this transaction and on March 26, 1970, informed the plaintiffs by letter that it would not recognize the sale and that it would thereafter charge the additional 1 percent interest provided in the note increasing the monthly payments to $109.

The plaintiffs have refused to consent to the payment of the increased interest and have continued to make payments of $102 per month to the defendant. The defendant has added to the unpaid balance of the note the additional 1 percent per month interest.

Plaintiffs brought this action in the circuit court of Winnebago County seeking a declaration that section A(8)(d) of the mortgage and the corresponding provision of the note are unlawful and unenforceable. . . .

. . . The circuit court of Winnebago County . . . allowed the plaintiffs' motion for summary judgment on Count I, finding that section A(8)(d) of the mortgage constitutes an unlawful restraint on alienation.

The appellate court reversed the judgment and remanded the cause to the circuit court with directions that it determine whether the restraint on alienation is reasonable under the circumstances involved in this case. (21 Ill.App.3d 42, 314 N.E.2d 306.) We granted plaintiffs' petition for leave to appeal.

The power of alienation of real property, since an early date of the English common law, has been thought to be socially and economically desirable and is now regarded as an attribute of ownership. (Schnebly, Restraints Upon the Alienation of Legal Interests: I, 44 Yale L.J. 961 (1935).) From this early concept the rule against restraints on alienation has developed, although not always logically or consistently. It is not necessary in this opinion to develop the historical evolvement of the law relating to restraints nor to discuss the reasons therefor or the exceptions thereto. The subject has been extensively covered by writers in this field. See generally 6 R. Powell, The Law of Real Property, ch. 77; Bernhard, The Minority Doctrine Concerning Direct Restraints on Alienation, 57 Mich.L.Rev. 1173 (1959); L. Simes and A. Smith, The Law of Future Interests, secs. 1111, 1114, 1131, 1161 (2d ed. 1956); Browder, Restraints on the Alienation of Condominium Units (The Right of First Refusal), 1970 U.Ill.L.F. 231.

This court in *Gale v. York Center Community Cooperative, Inc.,* 21 Ill.2d 86,

171 N.E.2d 30, has recently summarized the law in this State relating to restraints as follows:

> Thus, as a general rule, restraints on alienation are void . . . . Such a restraint may be sustained, however, when it is reasonably designed to attain or encourage accepted social or economic ends.
>
> . . . .
>
> [I]t would appear that the crucial inquiry should be directed at the utility of the restraint as compared with the injurious consequences that will flow from its enforcement. If accepted social and economic considerations dictate that a partial restraint is reasonably necessary for their fulfillment, such a restraint should be sustained. . . . In short, the law of property, like other areas of the law, is not a mathematical science but takes shape at the direction of social and economic forces in an everchanging society, and decisions should be made to turn on these considerations. 21 Ill.2d 86, 92-93, 171 N.E.2d 30, 33.

The provision in the mortgage restricting the sale, or transfer of the property described without the written consent of the mortgagee constitutes a restraint on the alienation of the property. The fact that the mortgage permits such a transfer of interest with the consent of the mortgagee does not remove the restraint. (See 4 Restatement of Property, sec. 406, comment *h* at p. 2404 (1944); Comment, Debtor-Selection Provisions Found in Trust Deeds and the Extent of Their Enforceability in the Courts, 35 S.Cal.L.Rev. 475 (1962).) The defendant contends, however, that if the consent-to-sale clause in the mortgage constitutes a restraint, it was designed to encourage and attain an accepted social or economic goal and thus constitutes a reasonable restraint and should be upheld.

In applying the reasonableness test of *Gale* and not the rigid common law proscription of restraints on alienation, we look to the underlying purpose of the restraint. If the restraint is "reasonably designed to attain or encourage accepted social or economic ends," it may be sustained.

We see little difference in the end to be promoted by the restraint contained in the mortgage in this case from the end which is recognized as a legitimate object of protection by a restraint contained in a contract for sale of land. Section 416 of the Restatement of the Law of Property states that a restraint imposed by a vendor on the interest of a vendee under a contract for sale of land is valid. The restraint is imposed primarily for the protection of the security interest of the vendor. "The reasonableness of this form of protection of the vendor is sufficient to overcome the considerations otherwise favoring unrestricted freedom of alienation." (4 Restatement of Property, sec. 416, Comment a, at 2449 (1944).) Also, in *Coast Bank v. Minderhout* (1964), 61 Cal.2d 311, 38 Cal.Rptr. 505, 392 P.2d 265, it was held not to be unreasonable for a lender to condition the continued extension of credit to the debtors on their retaining their interest in the property that stood as security for the debt.

The extension of credit by a lender to a debtor involves more than a mere reliance on the property mortgaged as security for the obligation. Involved in each transaction is also the appraisal of the personal integrity of the borrower. It seems to be completely justifiable for the protection of the security interest of the lender to prohibit the alienation, without the consent of the lender, of property which stands as security for the debt to a person whose personal and financial qualities are unknown to and were never considered by the lender in making the loan.

Thus we conclude that the restraint contained in the mortgage in this case is permissible because it is a reasonable restraint, that is, one for which sound and convincing reason exists. (See Volkmer, The Application of the Restraints on Alienation Doctrine to Real Property Security Interests, 58 Iowa L.Rev. 747, 764 (1973).) It is a restraint imposed for the purpose of protecting the security interest of the lender, a recognized valid purpose for which a restraint may be imposed.

. . . .

Since stability of real estate titles is of paramount importance it is necessary that the court follow a policy in construing restraints on alienation which will produce a reasonable degree of certainty. An attorney, in construing a restraint in a chain of title, should be able to reasonably predict the effect of the restraint and whether it will or will not be enforced. (57 Mich.L.Rev. 1173, 1186-87; Manning, The Development of Restraints on Alienation Since Gray, 48 Harv. L. Rev. 373, 405 (1935).) We feel that in cases involving consent to sell restraints, judging the reasonableness of the same under the circumstances in each case would not promote the desired stability of titles and would in fact make it extremely difficult to predict whether a restraint will or will not be upheld.

We realize that in other fields of the law the test of reasonableness has been applied without difficulty on a case by case basis. However, where land titles are involved, more certainty and greater predictability are required. For this reason it is more appropriate to judge the reasonableness of this restraint by the purpose sought to be obtained.

Although the validity of the restraint is not to be determined under the circumstances of each case we consider that a court may relieve a borrower from unconscionable or inequitable conduct of the lender. The charge of the additional 1 percent interest is not unreasonable and in this case does not constitute unconscionable or inequitable conduct on the part of the lender. . . . [I]n this opinion we remand the case to the trial court for a hearing on the pleaded issue of waiver. We also consider that other traditional equitable defenses may be raised by a mortgagor. Also, the mortgagor should not be precluded from litigating the question of whether the required consent to transfer, when requested, has been unreasonably withheld.

The promissory note provides that upon any default upon the note or the instrument securing it, interest at the rate of 1 percent per annum above the original rate provided in the note may be charged on the unpaid balance of the note for the period of such default. The plaintiff challenges this provision contending it constitutes a penalty and is therefore unenforceable. This contention does not involve the question of usury. The note was executed in May, 1967, and provided for interest at the rate of 6 percent. The additional 1 percent interest does not violate the statutory maximum. Ill.Rev.Stat. 1965, ch. 74, pars. 4, 5.

It is generally held that the maker of a note may stipulate to pay a higher interest rate after maturity and the additional amount will not be considered a penalty but will be considered liquidated damages. (See Annot., 12 A.L.R. 367 (1921); Annot., 28 A.L.R.3d 449 (1969); 45 Am.Jur.2d Interest sec. 65 (1969).) Early cases in this State permitted the enforcement of stipulations for the payment of increased interest after maturity although the total amount of interest charged after maturity exceeded the maximum amount authorized by statute. The rationale of these cases is that the additional interest charge is not a penalty but is considered as liquidated damages accruing day to day for the duration of the default and which the obligor may relieve himself of at any time. (*Bane v. Gridley,* 67 Ill. 388; *Walker v. Abt,* 83 Ill. 226.) In 1879 the General Assembly enacted a law which prohibited contracting for the payment of a rate or interest in excess of the lawful rate by reason of nonpayment at maturity. . . .

The charge of the additional 1 percent interest may be triggered by any default upon the note or the mortgage. In addition to the covenant not to sell the property without the consent of the mortgagee, the mortgage contains several other covenants, such as: to pay taxes, to keep the improvements insured, not to commit waste, etc. A breach of any one of these covenants may bring about the increased interest charge. We do not consider this increase to be a penalty. (See 55 Am.Jur. 2d Mortgages sec. 371 (1971).) Instead, . . . we view this as a provision for liquidated damages for a breach of the covenant. The increase in the interest rate is not unreasonable. The additional charge is not for a fixed amount and does not relate back to be computed from a time prior to the breach. Rather it is computed at the stipulated rate only from the date of default and is charged only for the duration of the default. It would appear that actual damages for a breach of any of these covenants would be uncertain and difficult to ascertain or prove. Under these circumstances it would seem appropriate that the parties should agree on an increase in the interest rate as liquidated damages for a breach of a covenant in the mortgage. See Annot., 41 A.L.R. 979 (1926).

. . . .

Appellate court affirmed as modified; circuit court reversed and cause remanded, with directions.

WELLENKAMP v. BANK OF AMERICA

Supreme Court of California
21 Cal. 3d 943, 582 P.2d 970 (1978)

MANUEL, JUSTICE.

We address today the question whether enforcement of a due-on clause, contained in a deed of trust securing real property upon an outright sale of that property, constitutes an unreasonable restraint on alienation in violation of California law.

In July 1973, Birdie, Fred and Dorothy Mans (Mans) purchased a parcel of real property in Riverside County which they financed by a loan from defendant Bank of America in the amount of $19,100 (at 8 percent interest per annum) giving the bank their promissory note secured by a deed of trust. The deed of trust contained the standard due-on clause which provided that if the trustor (the Mans) "sells, conveys, alienates . . . said property or any part thereof, or any interest therein . . . or become divested of [his] title or any interest therein . . . in any manner or way, whether voluntarily or involuntarily, . . . Beneficiary shall have the right at its option, to declare said note . . . secured hereby . . . immediately due and payable without notice. . . ." The Mans' deed of trust named defendant Continental Auxiliary Company as trustee.

In July 1975, plaintiff Cynthia Wellenkamp purchased the property from the Mans. She paid the Mans the amount of their equity in the property, that is, the difference between the total selling price to plaintiff and the balance outstanding on the Mans' loan, and agreed with the Mans to assume the balance of their loan from defendant. A grant deed, transferring title to plaintiff was recorded on July 10, 1975. Defendant bank (hereinafter defendant) was given prompt notice of the transfer of title to plaintiff as well as her check for the July payment on the Mans' loan. Defendant thereupon returned this check to plaintiff with a letter notifying her of its right to accelerate upon transfer of the property by the Mans. The letter offered to waive defendant's right to accelerate in return for plaintiff's agreement to assume the Mans' loan at an increased rate of interest (from the original 8 percent to 9¼ percent per annum). A printed assumption agreement was enclosed with defendant's letter for plaintiff's signature.

Upon plaintiff's failure to accede to defendant's demand that the interest on the loan be raised to the then current rate, defendant filed a notice of default and election to sell under the deed of trust.

Plaintiff then filed the present action in which she sought an injunction against enforcement of the due-on clause, and a declaration that exercise of such a clause, without any showing that defendant's security had been impaired as a result of the sale of the property to plaintiff, constituted an unreasonable restraint on alienation in violation of California law.

After the superior court granted plaintiff's motion for a preliminary injunction restraining defendant's foreclosure sale of the property, defendant demurred to plaintiff's complaint on the ground that it failed to state facts sufficient to constitute a cause of action for declaratory relief because automatic enforcement of the due-on clause after transfer of the property in an outright sale is valid under California law, and therefore, plaintiff could not prevail on the merits. After a hearing the superior court sustained the general demurrer, without leave to amend, and entered a judgment dismissing plaintiff's complaint. This appeal follows.

. . . .

We next had occasion to determine whether a given restraint was unreasonable within the meaning of *Coast Bank* in *La Sala v. American Sav. and Loan Assn.* (1971) 5 Cal.3d 864, 97 Cal.Rptr. 849, 489 P.2d 1113. The restraint involved in *La Sala* was a due-on clause which provided for acceleration of the maturity of the loan upon encumbrance of the subject property. In determining whether enforcement of this clause constituted an unreasonable restraint on alienation, we considered not only whether the restraint was necessary to prevent impairment to the lender's security, but also the effect that enforcement of the restraint would have on alienation. We concluded that enforcement of a due-on clause upon encumbrance of the subject property involved a significant restraint on alienation such as to preclude enforcement of the clause unless the lender could show that enforcement was reasonably necessary to protect its security.

Three years later, in *Tucker v. Lassen Sav. & Loan Assn.* (1974) 12 Cal.3d 629, 116 Cal.Rptr. 633, 526 P.2d 1169, we confronted the question whether automatic enforcement of a due-on clause upon the sale of the subject property by installment contract constituted an unreasonable restraint against alienation. Examining the principles developed in *La Sala* we recognized that a direct relationship exists between the *justification* for enforcement of a particular restraint on the one hand, and the *quantum of restraint,* the actual practical effect upon alienation which would result from enforcement on the other. Thus, the greater the quantum of restraint that results from the enforcement of a given clause, the greater must be the justification for that enforcement. Applying this test in *Tucker v. Lassen Sav. & Loan Assn., supra,* 12 Cal.3d 629, 116 Cal.Rptr. 633, 526 P.2d 1169, we concluded that enforcement of a due-on clause upon sale of the property by installment contract involved a high quantum of restraint requiring a significant showing that enforcement was necessary to protect the lender's security.

We now proceed to apply the principles set forth in *La Sala* and *Tucker* to the case at bench which presents the issue, stated at the outset of this opinion, whether a due-on clause contained in a promissory note or deed of trust may be automatically enforced upon an outright sale of the property securing the loan.

We first discuss the *quantum of restraint* imposed by enforcement of the due-on clause after transfer of the property by outright sale, for if as defendant contends, automatic exercise of the clause in these circumstances results in little, if any, restraint on alienation, we need not reach the question whether there exists justification sufficient to warrant enforcement.

Although we suggested in *dicta* in both *Tucker* and *La Sala* that the restraint on alienation resulting from acceleration after an outright sale appeared to be de minimis, we indicated in those decisions that by the term "outright" sale we were referring to transactions wherein the seller/trustor received full payment from the buyer, usually through new financing of the purchase (an "all cash to seller" sale). We reasoned that the restraint on alienation was slight in such cases because the seller received payment sufficient to discharge the balance of the loan secured by the deed of trust, whereas in cases involving junior encumbrances or installment land contracts, the seller normally received only a fraction of the balance outstanding on the loan.

We do not here so restrict the meaning of the term "outright sale," but instead, and in accordance with actual real estate parlance, we refer by that term to any sale by the trustor of property wherein legal title (and usually possession) is transferred.

Outright sales of real property commonly involve different types of financing arrangements depending upon the circumstances existing at the time of sale. Thus, when new financing is available and economically feasible, a buyer will be able to arrange to pay the seller the purchase price in full, in an "all cash to seller" arrangement. When, however, new financing is unavailable or is economically unfeasible, the buyer may arrange, as did plaintiff herein, to pay the seller only the amount of the seller's equity in the property, agreeing to assume or take "subject to" the existing deed of trust, in a "cash to loan" arrangement.

The availability of new financing often depends upon general economic conditions. In times of inflation, when money is "tight" and funds available for real estate loans are in short supply, new financing may be difficult, if not impossible to obtain. The same result may occur when interest rates and the transactional costs of obtaining new financing are high, making it economically unfeasible for the buyer to acquire a new loan. When economic conditions are such that new financing is either unavailable or economically unfeasible, the seller and buyer will normally agree to a form of financing arrangement wherein the buyer will assume the seller's loan. In such circumstances, if the lender is unwilling to permit assumption of the existing loan, and instead elects to enforce the due-on clause, transfer of the property may be prohibited entirely, because the buyer will be unable to substitute a new loan for the loan being called due, and the seller will not receive an amount from the buyer sufficient to discharge that loan, particularly when the balance due is substantial. (See 1 Miller & Starr, Current Law of Cal. Real Estate, pt. 1 (1975 ed.) § 3:65, pp. 435-436.) Even when the lender is willing to waive its option to accelerate in return for the assumption of the existing loan at an increased interest rate, an inhibitory effect on transfer may still result. The buyer, faced with the lender's demand for increased interest, may insist that the seller lower the purchase price. The seller would then be forced to choose between lowering the purchase price and absorbing the loss with the resulting reduction in his equity interest, or refusing to go through with the sale at all. In either event, the result in terms of a restraint on alienation is clear. (See Note, *Judicial Treatment of the Due-On-Sale Clause: The Case for Adopting*

Standards of Reasonableness and Unconscionability (1975) 27 Stan.L.Rev. 1109, 1113.)

It is against this effect on alienation that we must measure the factors advanced in justification. In *Tucker* we held that a restraint on alienation could be justified only when a legitimate interest of the lender was threatened. We indicated that such interests, which pertain to protection against impairment to the lender's security, included preservation of the security from waste or depreciation and protection against the "moral risks" of having to resort to the security upon default by an uncreditworthy buyer. (See Hetland, *Real Property and Real Property Security: The Well Being of the Law* (1965) 53 Cal.L.Rev. 151, 170; see also Cal. Real Estate Secured Transactions (Cont.Ed.Bar 1970) § 4.56, p. 184.)

Defendant contends that the risk of waste and default is significant in an outright sale because both possession and legal title to the property are transferred thereby eliminating any incentive or ability that the seller/trustor would have to avoid realization of these risks by action of the buyer. Although we have previously distinguished on this basis both the junior encumbrance, where neither possession nor legal title was transferred (*La Sala*) and the installment land contract, where possession but not legal title was transferred (*Tucker*), we are now convinced that, although the original borrower/seller no longer retains an interest in the property after transfer of legal title in an outright sale involving no secondary financing by the seller (see fn. 5, *ante*) this fact does not necessarily increase the risk to the lender that waste or default will occur. Thus the buyer in an outright sale, in order to pay off the seller's equity, may make a large down payment on the property, thereby creating an equity interest in the property *in him* which is sufficient to provide an adequate incentive not to commit waste or permit the property to depreciate. Moreover, the buyer in such an outright sale may be at least as good, if not a better credit risk than the original borrower/seller. We therefore conclude that although circumstances may arise in which the interests of the lender may justify the enforcement of a due-on clause in the event of an outright sale, the mere fact of sale is not in itself sufficient to warrant enforcement of the clause, and the restraint on alienation resulting therefrom, in the absence of a showing by the lender that such circumstances exist.

We furthermore reject defendant's contention that the lender's interest in maintaining its loan portfolio at current interest rates justifies the restraint imposed by exercise of a due-on clause upon transfer of title in an outright sale. Although we recognize that lenders face increasing costs of doing business and must pay increasing amounts to depositors for the use of their funds in making long-term real estate loans as a result of inflation and a competitive money market, we believe that exercise of the due-on clause to protect against this kind of business risk would not further the purpose for which the due-on clause was legitimately designed, namely to protect against impairment to the lender's security that is shown to result from a transfer of title. Economic risks such as those caused by an inflationary economy are among the general risks inherent in every lending transaction. They are neither unforeseeable nor unforeseen. Lenders who provide funds for long-term real estate loans should and do, as a matter of business necessity, take into account their projections of future economic conditions when they initially determine the rate of payment and the interest on these long-term loans. (See Note, *Judicial Treatment of the Due-On-Sale Clause: The Case for Adopting Standards of Reasonableness and Unconscionability, supra,* 27 Stan.L.Rev. at p. 1117.) Unfortunately, these projections occasionally prove to be inaccurate. We believe, however, that it would be unjust to place the burden of the lender's mistaken economic projections on property owners exercising their right to freely alienate their property through the automatic enforcement of a due-on clause by the lender. As we stated in *La Sala*, ". . . a restraint on alienation cannot be found reasonable merely because it is commercially beneficial to the restrainor. Otherwise one could justify any restraint on alienation upon the ground that the lender could exact a valuable consideration in return for its waiver, and that sensible lenders find such devices profitable." (5 Cal.3d at pp. 880-881, fn. 17, 97 Cal.Rptr. at p. 860, 489 P.2d at p. 1124.)

For the foregoing reasons, we hold that a due-on clause contained in a promissory note or deed of trust cannot be enforced upon the occurrence of an outright sale unless the lender can demonstrate that enforcement is reasonably necessary to protect against impairment to its security or the risk of default. We therefore disapprove *Hellbaum v. Lytton Sav. & Loan Assn., supra,* 274 Cal.App.2d 456, 79 Cal.Rptr. 9 and *Cherry v. Home Sav. & Loan Assn., supra,* 276 Cal.App.2d 574, 81 Cal.Rptr. 135, and overrule to the extent inconsistent with this opinion the case of *Coast Bank v. Minderhout, supra,* 61 Cal.2d 311, 38 Cal.Rptr. 505, 392 P.2d 265.

The judgment is reversed.

BIRD, C. J., and TOBRINER, MOSK, RICHARDSON and NEWMAN, J. J., concur.
[The dissent of Justice Clark is omitted.]

NOTES

1. *Coast Bank v. Minderhout, supra* set the trend for other states to follow. *See People's Savings Ass'n v. Standard Industries, Inc.,* 22 Ohio App. 2d 35, 257 N.E.2d 406 (1970). Both *Malouff v. Midland, supra* and *Baker v. Loves Park, supra* rely on a broad interpretation of *Coast Bank* as the rationale for decision.

2. A new trend was starting in California with *Tucker v. Lassen Savings & Loan Ass'n,* 12 Cal. 3d 629, 526 P.2d 1169 (1974), preceding the *Wellenkamp* case. *See also Clark v. Lachenmeier,* 237 So. 2d 583 (Fla. App. 1970); *Stockman v. Burke,* 305 So. 2d 89 (Fla. App. 1970); *Baltimore Life Insurance v. Harn,* 15 Ariz. App. 78, 486 P.2d 190 (1971), *petition for review denied,* 108 Ariz. 192, 494 P.2d 1322 (1972); and *Mutual Federal Savings & Loan Ass'n v. Wisconsin Wire Works,* 58 Wis. 2d 112, 205 N.W.2d 762 (1973). These jurisdictions seem more likely to follow *Wellenkamp* than those which approve due-on-sale clauses without reference to *Coast Bank.* Two lines of authority now seem probable: equitable enforcement, as in *Wellenkamp;* and strict enforcement, as in *Shalit v. Investors Savings & Loan Ass'n,* 101 N.J. Super. 283, 244 A.2d 151 (1968); *Walker Bank & Trust Co. v. Neilson,* 26 Utah 2d 383, 490 P.2d 328 (1971); and *Gunther v. White,* 489 S.W.2d 529 (Tenn. 1973). Ohio, Illinois, and Colorado, all of which relied on *Coast Bank,* could fall into either line of authority.

3. The most recent decisions have held for automatic or strict enforcement. *See Occidental Savings & Loan Ass'n v. Venco Partnership,* 293 N.W.2d 843 (Neb. 1980), and *Tierce v. APS Co.,* 345 So. 2d 300 (Ala. 1980).

4. The issue of enforceability of due-on-sale clauses may ultimately be decided based on federal preemption, at least when the lender is a federally chartered savings and loan. The case of *Glendale Federal Savings & Loan Ass'n v. Fox,* 481 F. Supp. 616 (C.D. Cal. 1979) was decided in favor of the savings and loan based on federal preemption. The case is not based on any restraint on alienation, as are many due-on cases, but rather on what restrictions the state could impose on a lender in light of the regulations established by the Federal Home Loan Bank Board. Because regulations had been promulgated in the Code of Federal Regulations prohibiting automatic enforcement in four limited circumstances, the court held that the area of the law had been preempted by the federal government. The State Real Estate Commission had sought to impose some different restrictions as a condition to approval of loan documents to be used in financing a subdivision. At the time of this writing the case is on appeal in the Ninth Circuit.

5. While due-on-sale litigation started with *Coast Bank, supra,* it should be noted that *Wellenkamp* overrules *Coast Bank* where inconsistent. Are the two cases inconsistent, or is the court simply avoiding further litigation to resolve any potential disputes as to the meaning of *Coast Bank*? If the two are not inconsistent, then *Coast Bank* is still good law but can only be construed in light of *Wellenkamp.*

b. Due-On-Encumbrance Clause

A second type of acceleration clause is commonly referred to as a due-on-encumbrance clause. The provisions of this clause are activated when the mortgagor creates a lien or encumbrance subordinate to the mortgage, such as a second mortgage. The lender's position is that any additional debt service reduces the "cushion," *i.e.,* the amount of income generated from the property in excess of the debt service on the first mortgage. In the case of a residential mortgage, the additional financing lessens the credit status of the borrower. In addition, to the extent that the owner is able to reduce his equity investment to a very low figure by the use of secondary financing (so-called milking), his incentive to maintain the property is reduced.

Borrowers should seek to change the wording of the due-on-encumbrance clause to provide that the loan may be accelerated only when the creation of the encumbrance, or subsequent events (*e.g.,* a default under the second mortgage), would unreasonably impair the security of the first mortgage. The borrower may seek to except from the due-on-encumbrance clause secondary loans which, together with the first mortgage, do not exceed a fixed loan-to-value ratio, for example, eighty percent of the then market value of the property. This would assure the original mortgagee that a sufficient equity cushion remains to protect the first mortgagee's security.

LA SALA v. AMERICAN SAVINGS & LOAN ASS'N

Supreme Court of California
5 Cal. 3d 864, 97 Cal. Rptr. 849, 489 P.2d 1113 (1971)

TOBRINER, J. — Plaintiffs Frank La Sala, Grace La Sala, and Dorothy Iford brought a class action against American Savings & Loan Association, (hereinafter "American") alleging that a provision in American's form of trust deed, which permits American to accelerate if the borrower executes a junior encumbrance on the secured property, constituted an invalid restraint upon alienation. . . .

American utilizes a form deed of trust which contains, on the reverse side in fine print, a clause stating: "Should Trustor sell, convey, transfer, dispose of or further encumber said property, or any part thereof, or any interest therein, or agree to do so without the written consent of Beneficiary being first obtained, then Beneficiary shall have the right, at its option, to declare all sums secured hereby forthwith due and payable." We shall refer to this clause as a "due-on-encumbrance" provision; we thereby distinguish it from clauses which provide for acceleration only upon the sale, but not upon the encumbering of secured property.

On August 13, 1958, plaintiff Dorothy Iford and her late husband borrowed $9,500, at 6.6 percent interest, from American, and executed a promissory note and a trust deed which included the due-on-encumbrance provision. On November 20, 1963, Frank and Grace La Sala, the other named plaintiffs, borrowed $20,700 from American at 6 percent interest; they also executed a note and a trust deed with the due-on-encumbrance clause.

On June 9, 1969, the La Salas borrowed $3,800 from Fred D. Hudkins, and executed a note and second deed of trust; Statewide Home Mortgage Co. acted as loan broker. On June 11, 1969, Iford borrowed $2,500 from Edward and June Ulrich, and also gave a note and second trust deed; Lanco Mortgage Co. acted as broker. About July 7 of 1969 both Iford and La Salas received a form letter from American notifying them of American's right to accelerate. The letter to La Salas offered to waive American's right to accelerate in return for a payment of $150 and an increase in the rate of interest on the first deed of trust from 6 to 9 percent. The letter to Iford was identical in form, but asked a waiver fee of $50 and an increase in interest to 8.75 percent.

Plaintiffs then filed the present action for declaratory relief "for themselves and all other persons similarly situated." . . .

Although American's due-on-encumbrance clause is not per se an illegal restraint upon alienation, the enforcement of that clause unlawfully restrains alienation whenever the borrower's execution of a junior encumbrance does not endanger the lender's security.

Defendants finally contend that American's due-on-encumbrance clause is valid as a matter of law, and that a declaration by this court to that effect would serve in practical effect as a declaratory judgment in the class action and thus obviate the need for further proceedings. (*See Fairchild v. Bank of America* (1961) 192 Cal.App.2d 252, 261-262 [13 Cal.Rptr. 491].) We conclude, however, that whether the enforcement of the due-on-encumbrance clause unlawfully restrains alienation turns upon whether such enforcement is reasonably necessary to protect the lender's security — an issue which cannot be resolved merely by examination of the pleadings and declarations now before us.

We initially summarize the California law on restraints on alienation. Civil Code section 711 states simply that "Conditions restraining alienation, when repugnant to the interest created, are void." Until 1964, California courts interpreted this provision as invalidating not only absolute restraints on alienation, but also restraints partial as to persons or duration. Most other states had, by statute or court decision, adopted a similar position; Kentucky alone upheld a minority view approving restraints of reasonable duration.

Our decision in *Coast Bank v. Minderhout* (1964) 61 Cal.2d 311 [38 Cal.Rptr. 505, 392 P.2d 265], represented a radical break with the common law tradition. (Comment (1965) 12 U.C.L.A. L. Rev. 954, 961.) In *Coast Bank* the bank sought to enforce an agreement which provided that the borrower "will not, without the consent in writing of Bank . . . create or permit any lien or other encumbrances (other than those presently existing and/or securing the payment of loans and advances made to them by Bank) to exist on said real property, and will not transfer, sell, hypothecate, assign, or in any manner whatever dispose of said real property, or any interest therein . . . ." The agreement further provided that upon default the bank at its election, could accelerate the debt. The borrowers sold the property without the bank's consent. The bank elected to accelerate and brought an action to foreclose; defendants demurred, alleging that the provision was a restraint on alienation.

Our opinion explained that prior cases had stated that any restraint on alienation was invalid; we noted that this absolutist position succumbed to the criticism "that it loses sight of the purposes of the rule and needlessly invalidates reasonable restraints designed to protect justifiable interests of the parties." (61 Cal.2d at p. 316.) We observed also that statutes or judicial decisions had upheld reasonable restraints upon spendthrift trusts, assignments of leases, life estates, corporate shares, and executory land contracts. Resolving that only unreasonable restraints on alienation were invalid, we concluded that "In the present case it was not unreasonable for plaintiff to condition its continued extension of credit to [borrowers] on their retaining their interest in the property that stood as security for the debt. Accordingly, plaintiff validly provided that it might accelerate the due date if the [borrowers] encumbered or transferred the property." (61 Cal.2d at p. 317.)

Following *Coast Bank,* three published Court of Appeal decisions have held that due-on-sale clauses in trust deeds do not constitute unlawful restraints on alienation. (*Jones v. Sacramento Sav. & Loan Assn.* (1967) 248 Cal.App.2d 522, 527, fn. 3 [56 Cal.Rptr. 741]; *Hellbaum v. Lytton Sav. & Loan Assn.* (1969) 274 Cal.App.2d 456, 458 [79 Cal.Rptr. 9]; *Cherry v. Home Sav. & Loan Assn.* (1969) 276 Cal.App.2d 574, 578-579 [81 Cal.Rptr. 135]. Although *Hellbaum* and *Cherry* assert that due-on-encumbrance provisions are also valid, none of the Court of Appeal opinions set forth trust deeds which expressly restricted future encumbrances, and in each case the act triggering acceleration was a sale, not an encumbering, of the subject property.

Thus, although California cases have clearly held a due-on-sale clause valid, the language in such cases respecting due-on-encumbrance provisions is, as plaintiffs point out, entirely dictum. We must now inquire into the basis upon which the cases have approved the due-on-sale clause to determine whether those reasons apply in full measure to restraints against future encumbrances.

Coast Bank, as we have seen, spoke of the borrowers "retaining their interest in the property that stood as security for the debt." (61 Cal.2d at p. 317.) *Hellbaum,* in similar language, noted the creditor's interest "in maintaining the direct responsibility of the parties on whose credit the loan was made." (274 Cal.App.2d 456, 458.) *Cherry v. Home Sav. & Loan Assn.* discusses this reasoning in greater detail: "Lenders run the risk that security may depreciate in value, or be totally destroyed. This risk of loss is reduced in the lender's viewpoint if the borrower is known to be conscientious, experienced and able. . . . If a borrower were able to sell the security without concern for the debt, he may take the proceeds of the sale, leaving for parts unknown, and the new owner of the property might permit it to run down and depreciate." (276 Cal.App.2d at pp. 578-579.)

The reasoning of these cases, while justifying enforcement of due-on-sale provisions clearly does not apply with equal force to restraints against future encumbrances. A sale of the property usually divests the vendor of any interest in that property, and involves the transfer of possession, with responsibility for maintenance and upkeep, to the vendee. A junior encumbrance, on the other hand, does not terminate the borrower's interests in the property, and rarely involves a transfer of possession. A junior lien does, of course, create a possibility of future foreclosure and thus of future transfer of possession. But the risk of future foreclosure — a risk which reaches fruition in only a minority of cases — cannot justify an endowment to a lender of an uncontrolled discretion to accelerate upon the making of a junior encumbrance. A right to accelerate when foreclosure occurs, or looms imminent, would fully protect the lender.

Defendants argue that whenever a borrower takes out a second lien, his very conduct demonstrates that he has become financially irresponsible or at least a poor credit risk. Such an assertion, however, is an overgeneralization, a proposition true of some borrowers but not of others. Moreover, American does not claim a right to accelerate merely upon learning that the borrower has encountered economic adversity. In light of these considerations we find no justification in American's arbitrary seizure of the making of a second lien, a fact not necessarily indicative of declining credit ability, as a basis for acceleration.

We recognize, however, as defendants point out, that instances may occur when the institution of a second lien does endanger the security of the first lien. In some cases the giving of a possessory security interest, e.g., a conveyance to a mortgagee in possession, would pose the same dangers of waste and depreciation as would an outright sale. In other cases a second lien may be employed as a guise to effect a sale of the property. In still others a bona fide second loan may still leave the borrower with little or no equity in the property.

We conclude, then, in instances in which the borrower's subsequent conduct endangers the lender's security, the enforcement of the due-on-encumbrance clause may be reasonably necessary to protect the lender's interests. In many other instances, however, the clause serves no such purpose. In fact, American itself recognizes that enforcement of such a provision cannot invariably be sustained as reasonably necessary to protect the primary security. When a borrower takes out a secondary loan American itself maintains that it does not elect automatically to accelerate, but examines the circumstances of the transaction. If its security is safe, American states that it then waives its right to accelerate, as it eventually did for both La Salas and Iford.

Yet defendants claim, in essence, that the lender should retain an *absolute* discretion to determine whether the transaction calls for enforcement of the due-on-encumbrance clause. Such an uncontrolled power, however, creates too serious a potential of abuse. Even when the lender's security has not been exposed to danger, the lender, by threatening to accelerate, could compel the borrower to pay a fee or give other valuable consideration for the waiver. The Attorney General, as amicus curiae, charges that as a matter of practice American requires waiver fees whenever a borrower makes a junior encumbrance. Defendants deny this charge yet seek from us a declaration that a lender enjoys an unconditional right to enforce the due-on-encumbrance clause and, as a necessary corrolary the unconditional right to obtain from a borrower whatever consideration it can exact for the waiver, however inequitable such exaction may be.

In view of these factors we cannot rule upon the validity of a due-on-encumbrance clause in the abstract. Indeed, we note that it is not so much that clause itself as the lender's application of it that will effect an invalid restraint on the alienation of property. In those few instances previously discussed, in which the enforcement of that provision is reasonably necessary to avert danger to the lender's security, the restraint on alienation remains lawful under the principles established in *Coast Bank v. Minderhout* (1964) 61 Cal.2d 311, 317 [38 Cal.Rptr. 505, 392 P.2d 265]. When such enforcement is not reasonably necessary to protect the security, the lender's use of the clause to exact collateral benefits must be held an unlawful restraint on alienation.

The circumstances of American's enforcement of the due-on-encumbrance clause against the plaintiffs, who sue as a class, are not before us on this appeal. We do not know in which instances the execution of the secondary loan signaled an imminent transfer of possession to the junior lender, in which cases the making of the junior encumbrance overencumbered the property, or what other circumstances might have led American to believe its security was in danger; neither do we know whether in fact American exercises its right to accelerate under that clause only when its security is impaired. We therefore do not render a declaration fixing the rights of the parties respecting the enforcement of the due-on-encumbrance clause; such relief must await a trial on the merits in the superior court.

Our determination in this opinion that a due-on-encumbrance clause may be enforced only when necessary to protect the lender's security, however, does raise doubts as to whether it is desirable to continue this litigation in its class format. In the trial court, defendants had contended that American's due-on-encumbrance clause was valid on its face and could be enforced in the discretion of the lender, thus posing an important issue of law common to all members of plaintiff class. We have, however, determined that the clause may be enforced only when required to protect American's security. Anticipating this holding, defendants now argue that the need to inquire into the circumstances of American's enforcement, or threatened enforcement, of this clause against each borrower creates individual issues which far predominate over any remaining common issues.

As we have noted, we lack the requisite information as to the proportion of cases in which enforcement was clearly needed to protect the lender's security, those in which it plainly served no such purpose and those in which the matter will be in dispute. Nor do we know whether each class member must be considered individually, or whether they can be aggregated into a few subclasses sharing most issues of law and fact in common. Our lack of knowledge of such relevant data primarily results from the fact that the trial court has not held a hearing on the matter of continuing this case as a class action, and the parties have not submitted declarations on that issue.

We therefore conclude that any attempt on our part to determine whether individual or common issues will predominate in the future course of this litigation would be premature. Plaintiffs may wish to redefine the class they seek to represent. The parties, or the court, may find it feasible to subdivide the class into subclasses sharing common characteristics. In many instances the parties may be able to agree to the propriety of enforcement of the due-on-encumbrance clause. Finally, when, and if, it becomes necessary for the trial court to determine whether this suit should be continued as a class action, that court can have the assistance, which we lack, of declarations by the parties directed to that specific issue and prepared in the light of the principles set forth in this opinion.

4. Conclusion

The specific issue raised by this appeal is whether the superior court erred in dismissing the action on behalf of the class, without notice to its members, upon the ground that the named plaintiffs were no longer qualified to represent the class. We have concluded that the court did err and that its judgment dismissing the action on behalf of the class must be reversed. Our recent cases have recognized that the suit on behalf of the class is a valuable medium of litigation; we have accorded it a flexible, if careful, application. Defendants have also urged that we affirm the dismissal for numerous reasons besides that considered by the superior court; we have examined each such reason and found it insufficient to justify affirmance of the judgment.

Following our ruling upholding reasonable restraints on alienation, we have distinguished the due-on-sale from the due-on-encumbrance clauses; we have concluded that the lender may insist upon the automatic performance of the due-on-sale clause because such a provision is necessary to the lender's security. We have decided, however, that the power lodged in the lender by the due-on-encumbrance clause can claim no such mechanical justification. We sustain it only in the case of a trial court's finding that it is reasonably necessary to the protection of the lender's security; to repose an absolute power in the creditor to enforce the clause under any and all circumstances could lead to an abusive application of it and in some cases an arbitrary exaction of a *quid pro quo* from debtors.

The judgment of the superior court dismissing the action on behalf of the class is reversed, and the cause remanded to that court for further proceedings in accord with the views expressed in this opinion.

WRIGHT, C. J., PETERS, J., MOSK, J., BURKE, J., and SULLIVAN, J., concurred.

McCOMB, J. — I dissent. I would affirm the judgment for the reasons expressed by Mr. Justice Thompson in the opinion prepared by him for the Court of Appeal in *La Sala v. American Sav. & Loan Ass.* (Cal.App.) 91 Cal.Rptr. 238.

NOTES

1. Due-on-sale and due-on-encumbrance clauses may be of greater importance because of their absence. Without a due-on-sale clause in the mortgage, the lender is unable to compel payment in full upon the transfer of the property. This allows a mortgagor to sell encumbered property subject to the existing mortgage, which may give the mortgagor a great selling advantage in a time of rapidly escalating interest rates. This is discussed later along with a variation of taking subject to known as a wrap-around. *See* Chapter 8.

2. A statutory approach has also been used in regulating due-on-sale clauses. See the New Mexico statute that follows:

Laws of New Mexico
Senate Bill 195, ch. 45 (1979)
RELATING TO REAL ESTATE; PROHIBITING THE USE OF CERTAIN PROVISIONS IN MORTGAGES OR DEEDS OF TRUST RELATING TO REAL PROPERTY; PROVIDING PROCEDURES; DECLARING AN EMERGENCY.

BE IT ENACTED BY THE LEGISLATURE OF THE STATE OF NEW MEXICO:

Section 1. PURPOSE. — The legislature finds that clauses in mortgages and deeds of trust by way of mortgage of real estate on residential property consisting of not more than four housing units, which:

A. allow the mortgagee or similar party to accelerate payments upon a transfer of the property by the mortgagor may constitute an unreasonable restraint upon alienation, to the detriment of the public welfare; and

B. allow the mortgagee or similar party to increase the interest thereon if the property is transferred may constitute an unreasonable restraint upon alienation to the detriment of the public welfare.

Section 2. UNENFORCEABLE PROVISIONS. —

A. A provision in a mortgage instrument or a deed of trust by way of mortgage of real estate, securing an interest in residential property consisting of not more than four housing units, which permits:

(1) an acceleration of the payment of an indebtedness due in the event of a transfer of all or any part of the mortgagor's interest to another party by any means is unenforceable unless the security interest is substantially impaired; or

(2) an increase in the rate of interest on the indebtedness in the event of the transfer of all or any part of the mortgagor's interest to another party by any means is unenforceable unless the security interest is substantially impaired.

B. The provisions of this section shall not apply to a mortgage entered into between a bona fide employer as mortgagee and an employee and the employee's spouse if he is married.

Section 3. SECURITY — SAFEGUARD. — Any creditor or mortgagee who feels the security interest is endangered by the transfer of the real estate to another party may proceed by foreclosure; provided that the creditor or mortgagee shall, as a condition to such foreclosure, prove that the security interest in the property would be substantially impaired.

Section 4. MORTGAGE TRANSFER FEE OR ASSUMPTION FEE. — Nothing in this act shall prevent a mortgagee or creditor from charging a fee to transfer a mortgage or deed of trust by way of mortgage of real estate from one party to another; provided that such fee is reasonable and in no event exceeds one-half of one percent of the unpaid principle balance of the mortgage or deed of trust at the time of the transfer.

Section 5. SEVERABILITY. — If any part or application of this act is held invalid, the remainder, or its application to other situations or persons, shall not be affected.

Section 6. EMERGENCY. — It is necessary for the public peace, health and safety that this act take effect immediately.

3. The latest FNMA mortgage and deed of trust forms exclude a due-on-encumbrance clause by specifically providing that a junior lien shall not be the basis for acceleration of the debt. See the excerpt from the FNMA form that follows:

> **17. Transfer of the Property; Assumption.** If all or any part of the Property or an interest therein is sold or transferred by Borrower without Lender's prior written consent, excluding (a) the creation of a lien or encumbrance subordinate to this Mortgage, (b) the creation of a purchase money security interest for household appliances, (c) a transfer by devise, descent or by operation of law upon the death of a joint tenant or (d) the grant of any leasehold interest of three years or less not containing an option to purchase, Lender may, at Lender's option, declare all the sums secured by this Mortgage to be immediately due and payable. Lender shall have waived such option to accelerate if, prior to the sale or transfer, Lender and the person to whom the Property is to be sold or transferred reach agreement in writing that the credit of such person is satisfactory to Lender and that the interest payable on the sums secured by this Mortgage shall be at such rate as Lender shall request. If Lender has waived the option to accelerate provided in this paragraph 17 and if Borrower's successor in interest has executed a written assumption agreement accepted in writing by Lender, Lender shall release Borrower from all obligations under this Mortgage and the Note.

This provision coincides with the requirements of 12 C.F.R. § 545.8-3(g) which spells out the limitations on the exercise of a due-on-sale clause. Does this regulation make the *La Sala* case merely of academic interest at this point? Why might *La Sala* still be of importance?

NIXON v. BUCKEYE BUILDING & LOAN CO.

Ohio Court of Appeals
18 Ohio L. Abs. 261 (1934)

BARNES, J.

The above entitled cause is now being determined on proceedings in error from the judgment of the Court of Common Pleas of Franklin County, Ohio.

Parties will be referred to as they appeared in the trial court, inverse to their order here.

Plaintiff in its petition sought personal judgment against John W. Fought and wife, Gertrude Fought, Donald M. Clump and Charles E. Nixon, in the sum of $10,837.93 and foreclosure of a real estate mortgage securing note for the above amount.

The original note and mortgage was executed by John W. Fought and Gertrude Fought on November 22, 1928. The note, a copy of which is attached to the petition, called for the principal sum of $11,000.00. By the terms of the note and also mortgage the loan was to be repaid in monthly installments of $110.00 each and provision was contained in both instruments that failure to pay taxes and assessments or other charges levied on the real estate described, or failure to keep buildings on real estate in good and proper repair and insured against fire and windstorm, or it any three of the monthly payments became due and remained unpaid, then the note, at the option of the company, would become due and payable in full and the mortgage enforceable. Said note and mortgage also contained the further acceleration clause that the company, at its option, might declare the note due and payable and the mortgage enforceable should a change occur in the ownership of the real estate, or any part thereof, without the express written consent of the company.

There was a further acceleration clause that the company at any time after one year from the date of the note and mortgage, at its option and upon thirty days' written notice might declare the note due and payable and enforce the mortgage.

On or about January 27, 1931, the Foughts conveyed said real estate to the defendant Donald M. Clump, and, as a part of the consideration for the transfer, the grantee Clump assumed and agreed to pay the note and mortgage above referred to.

On February 2, 1931 the defendant Clump, on a printed blank furnished by the defendant company, executed an application for transfer of loan, wherein, in consideration of such transfer, the said Clump agreed to pay said note and comply with all the terms of the note and mortgage. On the same day the plaintiff company, in writing and in the same instrument, granted the application.

On July 9, 1931, Clump conveyed the mortgaged premises to Charles E. Nixon, subject to the mortgage held by the plaintiff company. On July 10, 1931, Nixon made application for a transfer of loan, in which he recited that he had purchased the real estate and in this separate instrument assumed and agreed to pay said mortgage loan and to comply with all terms and conditions provided the company consented to the transfer. The plaintiff company, on the same day, and on the same blank, executed its consent and approval.

The application for transfer of loan contained the further specific provisions to pay at once all interest and delinquent payments on said loan.

At the time of the sale and conveyance of the premises from Clump to Nixon there was a default in the payment of interest and also more than three monthly payments on the principal were then due and payable. The June payment of taxes had not been paid.

All defendants, except Nixon, were in default for pleading.

The defendant Nixon filed an answer and also cross-petition.

The answer admitted "that on or about the 10th day of July, 1931, he assumed and agreed in writing to pay the note described in the first cause of action of the petition. Further answering this defendant for want of knowledge denies each and every allegation in the petition not heretofore specifically admitted to be true."

The cross-petition charged fraud against the defendant Clump and prayed that Clump be required to return the consideration received from Nixon, at the same time Nixon tendering back his deed covering the mortgaged premises. It was also set out in the cross-petition that he had paid to the loan company the delinquent interest amounting to $336.62 and prayed that the loan company be required to repay this amount. The cross-petition contains no specific allegations of fraud on the part of the loan company, nor does it state against the Loan Company any knowledge of fraud upon the part of Clump. The defendant Nixon caused summons to be issued against the Loan Company and also Clump, but the sheriff's return shows that Clump was not served. The defendant Clump filed no pleading and therefore is not in court and no orders could be taken or made against him under the cross-petition.

The loan company was served with notice and thereafter filed demurrer, which latter was sustained and the cross-petition dismissed as to the plaintiff loan company.

We are in accord with the trial court on this branch of the case. We are unable to find that the cross-petition states sufficient facts to entitle the defendant Nixon to any affirmative relief against the loan company.

Thereafter jury was waived and the case tried to the court on the pleadings and the evidence.

Personal judgment was entered against the defendants the Foughts, Clump and Nixon.

This is the final order from which Nixon alone prosecutes error in this court. The only defendant in error named is the Buckeye State Building & Loan Company.

Opinion

By BARNES, J.

Aside from the claimed error in sustaining demurrer to the cross-petition, the remaining error is buttressed around the contention that the separate signed agreement to pay on the part of Nixon was without consideration, and that by reason thereof no personal judgment should be entered against him. We think that the defendant Nixon's answer in the admission that he assumed and agreed, in writing, to pay the note removes as an issue in the case the question of consideration. In our judgment the legal effect of the words "assumed and agreed" is the admission of an act binding in law.

Consideration is an element necessary in every contract. If there was the absence of consideration in the so-called "Application for Transfer of Loan," then it could not be said that he assumed and agreed to pay it. If he desired to raise the issue he should so plead.

The general denial following only traverses such allegations of the petition as are not admitted.

Even if we accept the theory of counsel for plaintiff in error that the question of consideration is an issue, we then agree with the finding of the trial court that consideration was shown.

It is the theory of counsel for Nixon that the loan company in merely giving its written consent to the transfer of the mortgaged premises from Clump still had the right by reason of default in principal to foreclose immediately; that by reason thereof the loan company gave up nothing and did not in the slightest extent alter any of its rights or remedies; that by executing the written consent for transfer they would take away the option of declaring an acceleration by reason of that fact, yet with defaults in payment of principal and interest, the right remains.

One answer to this contention is that the defendant Nixon in his application for transfer of loan agreed to pay *at once all* delinquencies and taxes and that he failed to do so. The words "pay at once" would mean contemporaneously with the execution of his agreement. It becomes apparent that had he complied with the terms of his agreement there would have been no delinquencies as to taxes and principal. He did pay the delinquent interest and thereby removed one of the elements through which the loan company might exercise its option of declaring an acceleration. We are unable to look with favor on this contention when it is apparent that the defendant Nixon is basing much of his contention on a default which he had agreed to pay.

Had he removed the default by making payments, as he had agreed to do, it is further urged that the company still had the option to declare the note due after a period of one year. This particular paragraph reads as follows:

> At any time after one year from date the whole amount of principal and interest then unpaid on this note shall become due and payable at the option of said company and upon at least thirty days prior written notice being given by mail sent to the last known address of each of the undersigned, and the mortgage or other security given to secure the payment of this debt may then be enforced.

The undersigned referred to is John W. Fought and Gertrude Fought. No provision is contained in the note or mortgage for notice to the grantees of Fought, and if vital or important in the determination of the instant case, there might be a very serious question as to whether or not this provision for acceleration would apply where the loan company had given its written consent to the transfer. Some of the language of the application for transfer may be broad enough to include the above clause, but if so the defendant Nixon would then be bound by his separate agreement and not necessarily through this clause in the original note.

In any event, the loan company could not commence suit on the note or foreclosure of the mortgage until after the expiration of the thirty days, as required in the quoted clause.

As a further reason for our conclusion, we would call attention to the fact that under the accelerating clauses of the note and mortgage certain affirmative acts were required in order to render the note due and payable and the mortgage enforceable. In each and every instance where provision is made for acceleration we find the words "at the option of said company." Under this situation the note was not rendered due and payable nor the mortgage enforceable merely by reason of the defaults, but it was necessary for the loan company to so declare.

It has been determined that the bringing of suit is a sufficient declaration of the exercise of the option. In the instant case the plaintiff pleads that it exercises its option. In support of this theory we make reference to the case of *Weinberg v. Naher et,* (Washington), 99 Pacific, 736.

> Syllabus 1. Where a mortgage note stipulates that, on default in payment of interest, the whole debt shall become due at the option of the holder, the debt does not become due unless the option is exercised by affirmative act brought to the notice of the mortgagor.
> Syllabus 2. Where a mortgage note stipulates that, on default in the payment of interest, the whole debt shall become due at the option of the holder, a tender of the overdue interest before the exercise of the option cuts off the right to the option, though the holder has a reasonable time in which to exercise the right.
> . . . .

Applying the above principles of law to the instant case, we hold that the note was not due and payable nor the mortgage enforceable until the loan company exercised its option by reason of certain defaults. The option was not exercised by reason of the note being more than one year old. So far as the evidence discloses there was no exercise of the option until the bringing of the suit, and this was some nine months after Nixon had become the owner of the mortgaged premises. At any period within the nine months he had the privilege of clearing up all defaults as per his agreement.

As heretofore stated, we think the agreement is supported by a consideration. On the part of the building and loan they agreed to the transfer of ownership. On the part of Nixon he agreed to pay up all delinquencies and comply with the terms of the note and mortgage.

Finding no prejudicial error, the judgment of the lower court will be affirmed and costs awarded against the plaintiff in error, Nixon. Exceptions will be allowed.

HORNBECK, PJ, AND KUNKLE, J, concur.

NOTE

The obvious reason that a debt is accelerated upon default in payment of an installment is to allow the lender to sue on the entire debt as soon as it becomes a collection problem rather than force the lender into multiple litigation for each payment as it becomes due, or to wait until the final installment is due at which time the borrower may be dead, insolvent or out of the jurisdiction.

C. TIME OF PAYMENT

Prepayment Provision. Example:

The Note may be prepaid in part or in full at any time with interest to date of payment, provided that when the aggregate of the principal payments made during the preceding twelve-month period exceeds twenty percent of the original amount of the loan; the Mortgagee may charge ninety days interest on that part of the prepayment which exceeds twenty percent of said original amount. If the Note is to be prepaid in full, thirty days written notice of such intention shall be given to the Mortgagee.

See Wis. Stat. § 215.21(11); Wis. Stat. § 422.208.

Federal Home Loan Mortgage Corporation (FHLMC) Provision. Example:

The undersigned shall have the right to prepay the principal amount outstanding in whole or in part, provided that the holder hereof may require that any partial prepayments shall be made on the date monthly installments are due and shall be in the amount of that part of one or more installments which would be applicable to principal. Any partial prepayment shall be applied against the principal amount outstanding and shall not extend or postpone the due date of any subsequent monthly installments or change the amount of such installments, unless the holder hereof shall otherwise agree in writing. If, within five years from the date of this Note, the undersigned makes any prepayments in any twelve month period beginning with the date of this Note or anniversary dates thereof ("loan year") with money lent to the undersigned by a lender other than the holder hereof, the undersigned shall pay the holder hereof (a) during each of the first three loan years 4.00 percent of the amount by which the sum of prepayments made in any such loan year exceeds 20 percent of the original principal amount of this Note and (b) during the fourth and fifth loan years 3.00 percent of the amount by which the sum of prepayments made in any such loan year exceeds 20 percent of the original principal amount of this Note.

Minnesota Statutes Annotated (Supp. 1980)

§ 48.154 Prepayment, extension of terms

The borrower may repay the entire balance or any portion of the balance of an installment loan in advance without penalty. An installment loan contract may provide that the parties, before or after default, may agree in writing to an extension of all or part of the unpaid installments and collect as an extension fee a finance charge not exceeding that rate agreed to in the original loan contract. No such extension shall be permitted to cause repayment of a loan to exceed those maturities set down in section 48.153. One day's finance charge shall mean an amount equal to $1/365$ of the per annum rate provided for in an installment loan.

Amended by Laws 1976, c. 196, § 3, eff. July 1, 1976.

Vernon's Annotated Missouri Statutes (Supp. 1980)

§ 408.036. Prepayment penalty by lender prohibited, when — maximum permitted

No prepayment penalty shall be charged or exacted by a lender on any promissory note or other evidence of debt secured by residential real estate when the full principal balance thereof is paid after five years from the origination date and prior to maturity; in no event shall any prepayment penalty exceed two percent of the balance at the time of prepayment.

Amended by Laws 1979, p. —, S.B.No.305, § 1.

KNIGHTSBRIDGE ESTATES TRUST v. BYRNE

House of Lords
[1940] A.C. 613

VISCOUNT MAUGHAM. My Lords, this appeal raises the question whether the appellants, who are mortgagors, are entitled to redeem on the usual notice a mortgage dated November 6, 1931, made between the appellants of the one part and the respondents (who are trustees of the Royal Lover Friendly Society) of the other part, notwithstanding a provision in the mortgage for repayment of the loan of £310,000 by eighty half-yearly instalments. It was not in dispute before your Lordships that on the true construction of the mortgage the appellants were not entitled to pay off the loan otherwise than by the instalments and at the times provided in the mortgage, so that the appellants would not be entitled to the free enjoyment of their property for forty years except by a voluntary concession from the respondents.

My Lords, loans made to limited companies on the security of their assets are in general very different from loans made to individuals. Companies may be wound up, in which event their debts have, if possible, to be paid, but they do not die. To the knowledge of both the company and the lender the loan is intended in most cases to be of the nature of a permanent investment. The former can only in the rarest of circumstances be at the mercy of the latter. There is no likelihood of oppression being exerted against the company. Considerations such as these make it manifest that clauses in debentures issued by companies making them irredeemable or redeemable only after long periods of time or on contingencies ought to be given validity. It may be conceded that the ground for excluding the rule in equity is stronger in the case of a series of debentures issued in one of the usual forms than in the case of mortgages of land to an individual; but some of the reasons still remain. It is difficult to see any real unfairness in a normal commercial agreement between a company and (for example) an insurance society for a loan to the former on the security of its real estate for a very prolonged term of years. Both parties may be equally desirous that the mortgage may have the quality of permanence. There is a great deal to be said in such a case for freedom of contract.

It is right on the question of hardship to take into account the circumstances in which the mortgage was entered into, the great experience of the solicitors on both sides, and the care with which the negotiations were conducted. The appellants executed the mortgage with their eyes wide open. In such a case, the Court in these days must be slow to interfere with a contract deliberately entered into. I must come to the conclusion that the appellants' claim to redeem contrary to the terms of the mortgage must fail.

For these reasons I am of opinion that the appeal should be dismissed with costs.

LAZZARESCHI v. SAN FRANCISCO FEDERAL SAVINGS & LOAN ASS'N

California District Court of Appeals
22 Cal. App. 3d 303 (1971)

DEVINE, P.J. — Plaintiff appeals from a summary judgment. . . .

On February 21, 1967, Frank A. Marshall borrowed $300,000 from defendant San Francisco Federal Savings and Loan Association, for which he executed a promissory note secured by a deed of trust on property used for commercial purposes. The second defendant is the trustee. In the note Marshall reserved the right to prepay in whole or in part at any time prior to maturity the $300,000 obligation. This privilege, however, was subject to a prepayment fee provision which provided for the following: "Privilege is reserved to make additional payments on the principal of this indebtedness at any time without penalty, except that as to any such payments made which exceed twenty percentum (20%) of the original principal amount of this loan during any successive twelve (12) month period beginning with the date of this promissory note, the undersigned agree to pay, as consideration for the acceptance of such prepayment, six (6) months advance interest on that part of the aggregate amount of all prepayments in excess of such twenty percentum (20%). The privilege of paying amounts not in excess of said twenty percentum (20%) of the original principal sum without consideration shall be noncumulative, if not exercised. The undersigned agree that such six (6) months advance interest shall be due and payable whether said prepayment is voluntary or involuntary, including any prepayment effected by the exercise of any acceleration clause provided for herein."

On November 17, 1967, plaintiff purchased the real property securing San Francisco Federal's loan from a court-appointed receiver, in the Contra Costa County divorce proceedings of Frank A. Marshall. The purchase price was $570,000. In order to consummate the purchase, plaintiff had to procure new financing. Immediately before the close of escrow, San Francisco Federal submitted a demand in the sum of $9,130.02, which constituted the prepayment fee computed in accordance with the provisions of the note. This sum was in addition to the price and other payments, including accrued interest, which plaintiff had agreed to pay for the real property. Plaintiff paid and defendants received the amount demanded, but plaintiff noted in the buyer's instructions that it did so under protest.

In his declaration, Mr. Lazzareschi, president of plaintiff corporation, avers that it was necessary for him to pay the money in order to close the escrow, "otherwise said judicial sale would have failed." Plaintiff also declares that the interest rate of defendants' loan was then 7¾ percent, substantially less than that which defendants could obtain by a new loan of the recovered funds; wherefore defendants actually profited from the early prepayment rather than being prejudiced thereby. On the basis of these circumstances, plaintiff alleges in its complaint that the amount of the prepayment charge bears no reasonable relationship to any damage allegedly sustained by the defendants by virtue of the prepayment. Plaintiff also alleges that the prepayment fee constitutes an unreasonable restraint on alienation.

Standing of Plaintiff to Sue

Respondents contend that the obligation to pay the amount required as a condition for prepayment of the loan was that of the maker of the note, Frank A. Marshall, and that plaintiff need not have made this payment but could simply have declined to go ahead with its purchase when demand for payment of the sum was made. But for purposes of reviewing the summary judgment, we regard plaintiff as a legitimate subrogee. According to the declaration which was made by Mr. Lazzareschi, the demand was made at the last minute before the closing of the escrow, plaintiff had been obliged to procure new and additional financing, defendants knew that the mere interjection of the demand would suspend the close of the escrow, and an adjudication by a court as to the duty to make the payment would take such time that the sale could not have been concluded. The sale was involuntary as to Marshall, wherefore he may have been indifferent to the success of the sale.

If plaintiff had withdrawn when it first was confronted with the demand, it might have suffered loss of expenses theretofore incurred (this at least is inferable from the Lazzareschi declaration, and inferences are to be drawn liberally in favor of the party who opposes a motion for summary judgment). Besides, it is inferable that a desirable result in a judicial proceeding would have been aborted, that is, the obtaining of funds for the payment of Mr. Marshall's past due debts to his wife. Although some of the inferences which we have referred to might not be drawn by a judge in a full-fledged trial, they are relevant for present purposes. Plaintiff presently has standing in the lawsuit and in this appeal. On the other hand, plaintiff has no better rights than those of its subrogor, and in considering the merits of the appeal, we must regard the contract as that of Frank A. Marshall.

The Subject of Penalty

Appellant cites *Freedman v. The Rector,* 37 Cal.2d 16 [230 P.2d 629], for the principle that damages imposed must bear a reasonable relationship to the injury caused. But the *Freedman* case and all of those which have been based on it are concerned with breach of a contract in some manner. In the instant case, there has been no breach. The borrower had the option, clearly spelled out in the promissory note, of making one or more prepayments. He, by the action of the receiver, availed himself of the option. This is not a situation of liquidated damages. Although the word "penalty" is used, and perhaps properly so in that a charge is made which is equivalent to unearned interest, there is no penalty in the sense of retribution for breach of an agreement, nor is there provision for liquidated damages because of ascertaining what the damages for such breach may be. Nor is the case one in which there is forfeiture for a default which, under appropriate circumstances, may be relieved under Civil Code section 3275, as in *Barkins v. Scott,* 34 Cal.2d 116 [208 P.2d 467], *Baffa v. Johnson,* 35 Cal.2d 36 [216 P.2d 13], and *Holiday Inns of America v. Knight,* 70 Cal.2d 327 [74 Cal.Rptr. 722, 450 P.2d 42]. Indeed, in the case before us there is the opposite of default, that is, a payment made before the promissor was obligated to make it.

Prepayment charges have been upheld against accusations of usury in *French v. Mortgage Guarantee Co.,* 16 Cal.2d 26 [104 P.2d 655, 130 A.L.R. 67]; *Grall v. San Diego Bldg. & Loan Assn.,* 127 Cal.App. 250 [15 P.2d 797]; and *McCarty v. Mellinkoff,* 118 Cal.App. 11 [4 P.2d 595]. But the usury laws do not now apply to building and loan associations (Cal. Const., art. XX, § 22), so that attack on prepayment charges as usurious is not possible.

There are indications that an extortionate charge for prepayment would not be supported in judicial proceedings and that on one theory or another, yet undetermined, a person forced to sustain such a charge might have a remedy. Suggestions to this effect are found in a student note, *Secured Real Estate Loan Prepayment and the Prepayment Penalty,* 51 California Law Review 923-938; California Real Estate Secured Transactions (Cont.Ed. Bar) sections 4.69-4.78, pages 193-202. There is dictum to this effect in *Hellbaum v. Lytton Sav. & Loan Assn.,* 274 Cal.App.2d 456 [79 Cal.Rptr. 9]. In *Hellbaum,* there was sustained a demand for assumption of the debt by buyers, where the original borrower had agreed that the whole debt would become due on sale. A profitable sale, it was alleged (this was a dismissal case), had failed because of the lender's demand. The dictum referred to follows a statement that the complaint contains no allegation that the fees proposed to be exacted had no reasonable relation to the justifiable interests of the lender, and is put thus: "Perhaps a fact question could have been presented as to whether in effect the restraint was unreasonable (see Civ. Co., § 711)." The Continuing Education of the Bar treatise, section 4.72, page 196, comments on the *Hellbaum* dictum: "However, it is entirely possible that a court, examining a prepayment charge so exorbitant as to shock the judicial conscience and entirely incompatible with customs of the trade, will reject the freedom of contract analysis and declare it an invalid penalty.

For the purpose of this appeal, we shall assume that palpably exorbitant charges would be subject to defeat by judicial decision. We proceed to examine the contract, the promissory note, in the present case. It is necessary, however, to examine it not as an isolated transaction, but as a transaction existing with a multitude of others which the lender must enter in order to stay in business. The case is not like that of *Freedman v. The Rector, supra,* or of *Freedman's* progeny. These are distinguishable not only because they involve defaults, as said above, but also because in ascertaining whether the nondefaulting party had really suffered loss and if so, how much, consideration need be given only to the circumstances of the particular sale or lease or other bargained for transaction and, perhaps, occasionally to contemporary economic patterns. But we are dealing with a 20-year loan. The lender cannot recall the funds in the absence of default or sale of the property (the due-on-sale clause is valid: *Coast Bank v.*

Minderhout, 61 Cal.2d 311 [38 Cal.Rptr. 505, 392 P.2d 264]). If interest rates increase sharply, the lender has no option to renegotiate the loan. Of course, if a prepayment is made at the borrower's choice (sometimes made for him as in this receiver's case, but chargeable to him) when interest rates have increased, the lender may gain from the repayment. But in the whole portfolio there may be many loans which will not be repaid although some of the borrowers have become well able to repay. The borrowers can use the money more advantageously. On the other hand, if interest rates decline, borrowers will be able to refinance at lower rates, and if there were not adequate charge for repayment, they could discharge the note, giving the original lender funds which could be put out only at a lower rate. In *Cherry v. Home Sav. & Loan Assn.,* 276 Cal.App.2d 574, 579 [81 Cal.Rptr. 135], this fact of economic life was recognized in a due-on-sale case. Thus, unlike the *Freedman* type of case, the loan situation calls for attention to economic forces over a period which may be long — here, 20 years.

But even prescinding from the variables which are built into a loan which may run for as long as 20 years, we observe that there would be difficulty in deciding upon the advantage, if any, to the lender by early repayment. There is, of course, the matter of expense in all of the activities which lead to the decision to make the loan on a particular basis. Moreover, there is the matter of possible loss of time between repayment of the funds and placing them on loan anew. It would be impossible to trace the exact funds from one loan to another. The repaid monies surely would be used, but until the expiration of such time as would ordinarily be necessary to complete the new loan or loans (not identifiable), the funds, as part of the loanable resources of the lending institution, must remain in competition, as it were, with other resources of the lender and with the resources of similar institutions, awaiting settlement upon an acceptable borrower.

Here again, we do not foreclose inquiry into possible exorbitancy, but merely point out that a prepayment case does not fall into a simple calculation at any one point of time of the difference between the interest rate on the repaid loan and that which might be available to the lending institution on a new loan of about the same size made to a new borrower.

. . . . .

We observe that the author of the student note referred to above states that the penalty terms in prepayment option agreements are often moderate, and in support of this statement says: "A typical penalty clause calls for six months' unearned interest on prepayments exceeding 20% of the original principal in any calendar year." (51 Cal.L.Rev. 925, fn. 14.) These are the exact terms of the subject promissory note.

We do not find the terms of the loan to be shocking to the judicial conscience. In this state there is no usury law applying to building and loan associations, and there is no statute forbidding or regulating prepayment charges. The borrower who signs such a note as the subject one and who becomes possessed of sufficient funds to make substantial payments above the periodic ones which he is required to make, may pay the whole note without any penalty in not more than five years. This is because of the deduction of 20 percent per year from the original principal, as described above. But if the borrower, as in this case, obtains funds with which to pay the entire amount, the rate of interest is not a shocking one. In this case, the charge of $9,130.02 was 3.0403 percent of the original loan of $300,000. It was 3.0883 percent of the unpaid principal of $295,726.05. (Six months' interest on the unpaid principal would have been a higher amount than

$9,130.02 because of the provision in the note that 20 percent of the original loan, that is, $60,000, shall be deducted for computing the prepayment charged.) In the absence of any statute or authorized regulation, and in the absence of any evidence produced by declaration of plaintiff in opposition to the motion for summary judgment or suggested by plaintiff as appellant in its briefs, we know of no means by which a court could come to the conclusion that the charge which appellant agreed to pay was exorbitant or out of line with that customarily provided in loan agreements. Indeed, plaintiff does not in its complaint or in its declaration in opposition to the motion for summary judgment, make the point that the charge exceeds that which is usual. Plaintiff's theory of excessiveness is that the charge bears no reasonable relationship to any damage sustained by virtue of the prepayment because of respondents' ability to lend the funds anew at a higher rate, a subject discussed above.

The Subject of Restraint on Alienation

Plaintiff contends that because the loan was secured by a deed of trust which could not be lifted without satisfying the promissory note, it partakes of the nature of a restraint on alienation in violation of section 711 of the Civil Code. But it has been held that reasonable restraints made in protection of justifiable interests of the parties are sustainable. (*Coast Bank v. Minderhout,* 61 Cal.2d 311, 316-317 [38 Cal.Rptr. 505, 392 P.2d 265].) The *Coast Bank* case involved a due-on-sale provision, but it was pointed out in the opinion that several other kinds of restraints on alienation are recognized as lawful. The prepayment charge by no means constitutes an absolute restraint and because we do not regard it as an exorbitant burden, as pointed out above, and because there are legitimate interests of the lender to be protected, as also discussed, we do not discern an unlawful restraint on alienation.

Conclusion

Finally, we remark that the control of charges, if it be desirable, is better accomplished by statute or by regulation authorized by statute than by *ad hoc* decisions of the courts. Legislative committees and an administrative officer charged with regulating an industry have better sources of gathering information and assessing its value than do courts in isolated cases. Besides, institutions which lend vast sums of money should be informed, not by judgments after the facts on a case-to-case basis, but by laws or regulations which are in existence in advance of the undertaking to execute loans, of the validity or invalidity of terms that are commonly used. Otherwise, the lending institutions themselves may be the object of lawsuits in which a penalty is demanded, as in the third cause of action in the present case in which plaintiff seeks punitive damages.

The judgment is affirmed.

ROGERS v. WILLIAMSBURGH SAVINGS BANK

District Court, Suffolk County
79 Misc. 2d 852, 361 N.Y.S.2d 702 (1974)

ANNE F. MEAD, JUDGE.
This is a motion to dismiss the complaint on grounds that a defense is based upon documentary evidence, under CPLR § 3211(a)(1), and that the complaint fails to state a cause of action, under CPLR § 3211(a)(7).

Plaintiffs were owners and occupants of a single family residence located at 6 Kejaro Court, Centereach. Defendant held a mortgage on it dated October 27, 1971 securing $23,700.00. They found buyers for the premises who wished to purchase the property subject to the existing mortgage. On their behalf, plaintiffs' attorney requested that defendant mortgagee either consent to a transfer subject to the existing mortgage or alternatively that they pay the balance of the principal due and have defendant waive the prepayment fee. Defendant consented neither to a sale subject to the existing mortgage, nor to waiver of the prepayment fee.

Plaintiffs' complaint is based on Real Property Law § 254 — a labelled "Right of election of mortgagee in certain cases." Plaintiffs sue for refund of the prepayments fee of $1,185.00 plus $500.00 attorney's fees, totalling $1,685.00.

The statute in question, RPL § 254-a, became effective May 29, 1972 and recently was amended effective April 1, 1974. (Laws 1974, ch. 119, § 5.) However, defendant's motion papers dated September 5, 1974 cite the statute as Exhibit A-1 without the pertinent changes. RPL § 254-a presently is as follows (new matter italicized):

§ 254-a. — Right of election of mortgagee in certain cases

If a bond or note, or the mortgage on real property, improved by a one *to six* family residence occupied by the owner, securing the payment of same contains (1) a provision whereby the mortgagee retains the right to accelerate the due date for payment of the balance of principal upon a transfer or sale of such real property or by alienation of title of such real property due to an act or operation of law, and (2) a provision for payment of any charge, however denominated in the nature of a prepayment fee and if a mortgagor sells or transfers his property or if title to the mortgaged property is transferred by act or operation of law and the *purchaser requests permission to assume the mortgage or take the mortgaged premises subject to the mortgage, but the* mortgagee does not consent to *such request* and thereby necessitates prepayment of the mortgage, the mortgagee shall not levy a prepayment fee; provided, however, that the provisions of this section shall not apply to the extent such provisions are inconsistent with any federal law or regulation. (RPL § 254-a, as amended, L.1974, ch. 119, § 5.) . . . [If] legislation is addressed to a legitimate end and the measures taken are reasonable and appropriate to that end, it may not be stricken as unconstitutional, even though it may interfere with rights established by existing contracts. (*Home Bldg. & Loan Ass'n v. Blaisdell,* 290 U.S. 398, 438, 54 S.Ct. 231, 78 L.Ed. 413); *Matter of People [Title & Mtg. Guar. Co.],* 264 N.Y. 69, 83, 190 N.E. 153, 157; *East New York Savings Bank v. Hahn,* 293 N.Y. 622, 627, 59 N.E.2d 625, 626.)

The Commercial Rent Law (L.1945, ch. 3, as amd.) providing for rent regulation and "emergency rent" was held constitutional as applied to leases predating the law. The law was designed to prevent unjust, unreasonable and oppressive rentals accruing after passage of the law. The Court stated "the evils denounced in the statute flowed, not merely from leases which might thereafter be executed, but even more directly from leases already made, and those evils could not be remedied by regulation purely prospective in their application, although the regulations adopted were only retroactive in that they applied to future payments of rent under pre-existing leases." (*Twentieth Century Associates, Inc. v. Waldman,* 294 N.Y. 571, 581, 63 N.E.2d 177, 180.) Likewise, in the present situation, the legislative intent that the statute in question apply to pre-existing mortgages is clear, as demonstrated herein. To deny applicability of the statute to cases involving pre-existing mortgages would be to emasculate the statute and to frustrate the benevolent purpose for which the Legislature enacted it.

Furthermore, in this type of situation, judicial inquiry into the validity of grounds for exercising the State's police power so as to impair pre-existing contracts is authorized.

> When the legislative choice of a remedy is challenged on the ground that it transcends the limits placed by the Constitution ... and that it impairs the obligation of a contract ... the legislative finding that a threatening public emergency exists is not conclusive. Judicial inquiry is not precluded ... but upon such an inquiry the legislative findings are entitled to great weight and the legislative remedy will not be stricken down unless its invalidity is clearly established. (*East New York Sav. Bank v. Hahn*, 293 N.Y. 622, 627, 59 N.E.2d 625, 626.)

Therefore the court will take notice of the fact that due to the present rampant inflation the cost of housing has soared to unprecedented heights, mortgage interest rates have never been higher, and construction money has never been so expensive. "Too often, mortgage money cannot be obtained at any price ... The situation is worst in large cities and, thanks to the crazy-quilt patterns of state mortgage laws, the populous Northeast .... Concentration on the free-standing single-family house may well be over." (Time, October 28, 1974, pp. 88, 92.) Thus the court feels that the validity of the grounds for exercising the State's police power so as to impair pre-existing contracts is indeed authorized.

The class of buyers and sellers of single family homes is much more significant, larger and deserving of protection than a class of dancing students for which retroactive application of a statute to dancing class contracts was upheld. "To assume that the Legislature intended to except from the statutory protection ... contracts executed prior to its effective date ... overlooks the obvious legislative intent to afford protection to the public .... So tested, this statute is not constitutionally invalid since it was intended to curb economic wrongs against consumers who relied on the franchise name." *(Totten v. Saionz*, 38 A.D.2d 630, 631, 327 N.Y.S.2d 55, 57.)

It is the court's opinion that RPL § 254-a as amended is a statute addressed to the legitimate end of aiding certain classes of consumers and as such it is indeed constitutional. Upon approving the law, Governor Wilson stated that the statute would "assist banking consumers by ... enlarging prepayment rights of home loan borrowers."

> This bill will assist banking consumers by: ... limiting penalty charges in connection with late payments of installments on mortgages .... Existing law guarantees mortgagors the right to prepay mortgages ... only after three years have passed from the date the mortgage was made. This bill establishes a statutory prepayment right for mortgagors on one to six family owner occupied residences .... These provisions will significantly reduce the cost to a home owner who, because of a change in his employment or because of some other reason, is forced to sell his property within three years of the date of its purchase... (L.1974, ch. 119, memo p. A-209.)

Significantly, the statutes involving prepayment penalties have accompanied other important consumer-oriented legislation: e. g. the original statute, General Obligations Law § 5-501(3)(b) was part of the usury law, and was passed in conjunction with the statute allowing the Banking Board to prescribe the rate of interest. The statute as amended April 1, 1974 was passed in conjunction with new laws granting the Banking Board power to prescribe the minimum rate of interest on mortgage escrow accounts and mandating mortgage investing institutions to pay interest on deposits in escrow. (L.1974, ch. 119) Thus it is clear that the state has a legitimate and compelling concern for the general welfare of its people in enacting consumer-oriented legislation of this type, and the state's sovereign right to promote the general welfare of its citizens is paramount to any rights under contracts between individuals. (*Farrell v. Drew,* 19 N.Y.2d 486, 281 N.Y.S.2d 1, 227 N.E.2d 824.)

The legislative history of the statute in question indicates beyond a doubt that the rule precluding prepayment penalties was designed to apply to mortgages already in existence and not merely to mortgages made subsequent to the effective date of the statute. In 1968 the prepayment penalty prohibition first appeared as a new section (3)(b) to GOL § 5-501, in conjunction with the amended laws on usury, and the prescription of the rate of interest by the banking board. (L.1968, ch. 349, § 1) This statute was never repealed but was amended to confine the prepayment penalty to loans made subsequent to April 1, 1974 and prepaid during the first year of the loan if the loan contract expressly provided for the penalty. (L.1974, ch. 119, § 3) The previous rule had limited the penalty to loans prepaid only after three years.

Significantly, the Legislature did not limit application of the original law to loans made subsequent to the effective date of the statute, but instead clearly stated that the statute should apply only to loans made on or before September 1, 1971, the date on which the Banking Board's authority to prescribe a maximum interest rate would cease. (L.1968, ch. 349, § 13)

RPL § 254-a was enacted in 1972 and was designed to protect home owners from the double liability of being required to pay both the balance of the principal and also a prepayment fee upon transfer of the property when the mortgagee rejects a request to take subject to or assume the mortgage. (L.1972, ch. 421) The statute became effective May 29, 1972, and was later amended, effective April 1, 1974. (L.1974, ch. 119, § 5) Nothing in the statute as it previously existed or as amended limits its application to mortgages dated subsequent to the effective date of the statute. In fact the inference that mortgages dated *before* the effective date of the statute are subject to it is clear: the Legislature deliberately excepted mortgages dated before the date of enactment of the two preceding companion laws (GOL § 5-501, and Banking Law § 293-a) to RPL § 254-a, but placed no such limitations on RPL § 254-a. (See L.1974, ch. 119, §§ 3, 4, 5, 7)

Therefore the court holds that RPL § 254-a does indeed apply to the facts of this case, and also is *constitutional* as applied, because it is a valid exercise of the state's power to promote the general welfare of its citizens.

Defendant's third argument is that before it can be charged with denying permission for a subject to transfer, a legitimate and firmed-up request must have been submitted. Because "the proposed or actual transfer facts were never relayed to the defendant," defendant argues that its consent to a valid request was never solicited. In support of this contention defendant cites certain documentary evidence, i. e. the sales contract (Defendant's Exhibit D) and plaintiffs' letter of January 21, 1974 (Defendant's Exhibit C) from which it infers that a transfer subject to the mortgage was never seriously contemplated. Defendant argues that the spirit of plaintiffs' letter is not one of request, but rather one of desiring avoidance of the prepayment fee.

The letter in question is as follows:

Please be advised that the above captioned premises are about to be conveyed. Since we are in a position to sell the premises subject to your existing mortgage, with the purchaser assuming same, or satisfying your mortgage, kindly advise the undersigned whether you would waive the prepayment penalty in consideration of the mortgagor satisfying your loan. Would you also please advise as to the amounts necessary to satisfy the existing mortgage, as well as that necessary if selling same subject to your existing mortgage. . . .

Defendant's Exhibit E makes clear the reasons for the request. It is a letter from plaintiffs' attorney to defendant's attorney dated June 26, 1974 a month after the closing.

> . . . The fact of the matter is that the Rogers would very well have sold the property to the purchasers subject to the existing mortgage and held a very small second mortgage. It certainly would have been to their advantage in view of the fact that they would have saved the $1,000.00 prepayment penalty. In addition, it would have been to the advantage of the purchasers in view of the fact that they would have saved on the interest rate as well as some of the various closing costs. . . .

Defendant's argument cannot stand because it is apparent from the letter of request (quoted above) that the request was legitimate and that it in fact inquired into what terms defendant would require. Also, Defendant's Exhibit A is a letter dated January 25, 1974, four days after the request, which indicates that defendant in fact flatly refused the request for permission to transfer subject to the *existing* mortgage, and required instead that a Modification Agreement and a higher rate of interest would be charged if defendant's committee approved the purchasers. The pertinent section of the letter is as follows:

> In reply to your letter of January 21st and our phone conversation regarding sale subject to the existing mortgage, please be advised the mortgage agreement contains clause numbered 9d which states mortgage cannot be sold subject to without the Bank's consent. To submit this mortgage to our committee for approval, I would require the following: . . . Mortgage interest rate would be the prevailing rate of interest at the time of closing, which is 8½% at the present time. A Modification Agreement would have to be drawn. The legal fee for drawing this Agreement is $150.00.

In effect defendant, in the above letter, denied consent to any proposed transfer subject to the *existing* mortgage, and instead held out the possibility of a Modification Agreement. After a flat denial of consent to the proposed subject-to transfer, defendant cannot now be heard to complain that the request was not legitimate in that no transfer facts were presented. Had defendant not flatly denied the request, transfer facts would in all probability have evolved.

RPL § 254-a contains no requirement that a request for permission to take the mortgaged premises subject to the mortgage be accompanied by details and transfer facts, and the court will not read such language into the statute. The court will not inquire into the "spirit" of the request. Where a request to transfer subject to the existing mortgage is flatly denied, there is no duty to subsequently submit to mortgagee details of the proposed transaction. Thus the court finds defendant's argument without foundation.

For the reasons stated above, defendant's motion to dismiss the complaint is in all respects denied.

Motion costs to plaintiff.

NOTES

1. Before the passage of the statute referred to in *Rogers v. Williamsburgh,* New York had judicially approved the concept of prepayment penalty if the payment was voluntary.

"Here the prepayment was voluntary and the amount of interest paid . . . did not exceed the interest that would have been earned had the debt continued to its maturity date." *Redmon v. Ninth Federal Savings Bank,* 147 N.Y.S.2d 702 (Sup. Ct. 1955).

2. Since the federal government has impliedly permitted lenders under its jurisdiction to assess a prepayment penalty by providing a limit, is it likely that any court will rule against a lender if the penalty is within the C.F.R. limits?

3. 12 C.F.R. § 545.6-12:

Loan payments.

(a) *Payments on monthly installment loans and flexible payment loans.* Payments on all monthly installment loans and flexible payment loans, other than construction loans, loans to finance substantial alteration, repair or improvement, insured loans, and guaranteed loans may be repayable upon terms acceptable to the insuring or guaranteeing agency. The Board hereby approves for use by any Federal association a loan plan whereby payments on any monthly installment loan or flexible payment loan which includes construction may begin not later than 36 months after the date of the first advance, but not later than 18 months if the loan is secured by real estate consisting solely of one or more homes or combination of home and business property; interest shall be payable at least semiannually until regular periodic payments become due.

(b) *Loan payments and prepayments.* Payments on the principal indebtedness of all loans on real estate security shall be applied directly to the reduction of such indebtedness, but prepayments made on an installment loan may be reapplied from time to time in whole or in part by a Federal association to offset payments which subsequently accrue under the loan contract. Each borrower from Federal associations on a loan secured by a home or combination of home and business property shall have the right to prepay the loan without penalty unless the loan contract makes express provision for a prepayment penalty. The prepayment penalty for a loan secured by a home which is occupied or to be occupied in whole or in part by a borrower shall not be more than 6 months' advance interest on that part of the aggregate amount of all prepayments made on such loan in any 12-month period which exceeds 20 percent of the original principal amount of the loan.

4. *Economic Effect.* Such prepayment penalty clauses provide the mortgagor with a limited right to prepay his mortgage without incurring a prepayment penalty. *Example:*

Smith purchases a four-family apartment building for $90,000 on January 3, 1977. He obtains a $72,000 mortgage from a savings and loan association at 9 percent interest per annum with a 30-year amortization. The mortgage note contains a prepayment penalty clause. On January 3, 1980, Smith sells the property for $107,000. On January 3, 1980, Smith's principal balance on his mortgage is $70,380. Applying the prepayment provision, Smith may prepay, without penalty, 20 percent of $72,000 or $14,400. This amount is subtracted from the principal balance due and owing on January 3, 1980 ($70,380 - $14,400 = $55,980). The stated interest of 9 percent is applied to $55,980 to determine annualized interest (9% X $55,980 = $5,038). The daily interest rate is approximately $13.80 ($5,038/365). Therefore, the prepayment penalty, representing 90 days interest, is approximately $1,242 ($13.80 X 90).

In determining whether a mortgagor should prepay and refinance his mortgage loan, the amount of the prepayment penalty is an important consideration. In some circumstances, the penalty might exceed the interest savings anticipated by refinancing a mortgage at a reduced interest rate. Since a prepayment penalty is deductible as interest, its tax effect should also be considered.

5. *No Prepayment Penalty on Condemnation Unless Specifically Provided So in Mortgage Instrument.* An insurance company held a mortgage on real property that was condemned by DeKalb County, Georgia. The mortgage provided a "privilege to prepay in full or in part beginning the fifth year at 5 percent penalty declining one-half of one percent." The condemnation took place during the first five years of the mortgage term so that, technically, the mortgagor did not yet have the right to prepay the loan. The lender nevertheless sought to collect the prepayment penalty but the Supreme Court of

Georgia ruled against it. *DeKalb County v. United Family Insurance Co.*, 219 S.E.2d 707 (Ga. 1976).

The insurance company made two arguments in support of its claim to the prepayment premium. First, it said denial of the premium would impair its contract rights. But the court pointed out that the right of prepayment technically did not exist at the time of condemnation, and so the prepayment premium could not be considered part of the "price" for the sale of the lender's security interest in the real estate. If the mortgage had specifically provided that the premium would be payable at any time in the event of condemnation, the court implied the result might have been different.

The lender also argued that the prepayment premium was part of the just and adequate compensation to which it was entitled. But the court said that the lender, in fact, suffered no economic loss because it was in a position to reinvest the funds repaid it as a result of the condemnation. A lender that wishes to protect its right to a prepayment premium in the event a mortgage is prepaid other than by the voluntary act of the borrower (*e.g.*, condemnation or destruction by fire or casualty) should provide so specifically in the mortgage instrument.

6. *Practical Exceptions.* It would be wise, and might be possible, to negotiate a mortgage note clause which provides that a prepayment penalty will not be charged or will decelerate in amount as the mortgage term increases, if:

a. The Mortgagor refinances with the Mortgagee;
b. The Buyer finances with the Seller's Mortgagee;
c. The interest is escalated and the Mortgagor pays in full;
d. Extenuating circumstances exist, *i.e.*, job transfer.

Challenged in Some Jurisdictions on the Following Grounds.

a. The standard attack on clauses imposing a prepayment penalty has been that the penalty is a usurious exaction. The standard judicial response has been that the sum exacted is not interest, but an agreed upon payment for exercising the privilege of repaying before the end of the loan term.

b. Prepayment penalty is a forfeiture disproportionate to the harm caused to the Mortgagee from prepayment and an offensive partial restraint on alienation ("locked-in loan"). Since the mortgage lender has received the balance of the funds advanced, it will be able to reloan the funds at a higher interest rate.

Therefore, the only real harm to the mortgage is the additional administrative cost of processing the loan termination.

Effect on Mortgage Payments. If the mortgage is silent on the point, partial prepayments are credited against the final payments to be made by the borrower. The borrower continues to make the same monthly payments, but since the principal outstanding has been reduced, a smaller percentage is allocated to interest and a larger percentage to amortization. Therefore, prepayment has the effect of reducing the amortization period of the loan. If the borrower wishes to reduce his monthly payments, this must be agreed to either in the mortgage instrument or at the time of prepayment.

Failure to Make Monthly Installment Payments Timely.

1. *Grace Period.* A period of time allowed after the payment due date before a late charge may be exacted.
2. *Late Charges.*

GARRETT v. COAST & SOUTHERN FEDERAL SAVINGS & LOAN ASS'N

Supreme Court of California
19 Cal. 3d 731, 511 P.2d 1197 (1973)

WRIGHT, C. J. — Plaintiffs in a class action appeal from an order of dismissal entered after the court sustained, without leave to amend, defendant's demurrer on the ground that the complaint failed to state a cause of action.

. . . .

Plaintiffs allege that they are or were obligors under promissory notes secured by deeds of trust in favor of defendant savings and loan association; that each of them has been assessed by reason of his failure to have made timely install-ment payments, certain sums designated as late charges; and that each such charge is a percentage of the unpaid principal balance of the loan obligation for the period during which payment was in default. Plaintiffs seek to recover sums paid in satisfaction of the charges, contending that they constitute assessments which cannot qualify as liquidated damages and thus are void under Civil Code section 1670.[1] For the reasons hereinafter stated we hold that plaintiffs have stated a cause of action and reverse the order of dismissal.

Plaintiffs' action is brought on behalf of themselves and other similarly situated obligors who within the applicable period of limitations (Code Civ. Proc., § 382) have paid late charges to defendant. They allege that of approximately 32,000 obligors some 5,000 have paid late charges totaling $1,900,000 during the four-year period immediately preceding the filing of the complaint. The promis-sory note signed by each obligor allegedly includes the following or similar provisions: "The undersigned further agrees that in the event that payments of either principal or interest on this note becomes in default, the holder may, without notice, charge additional interest at the rate of two (2%) per cent per annum on the unpaid principal balance of this note from the date unpaid interest started to accrue until the close of the business day upon which payment curing the default is received."

In order to evaluate the legality of a provision for late charges we must deter-mine its true function and character. If it is as plaintiffs contend a stipulation for ascertaining damages in anticipation of breach its validity must be tested against sections 1670 and 1671. Defendant seeks to avoid the question of damages by maintaining that the lending agreement, to the extent that it requires the payment of the additional interest, merely gives a borrower an option of alterna-tive performance of his obligation. If he makes timely payments, interest con-tinues at the contract rate; if, however, the borrower elects not to make such payments, interest charges for the loan are to be increased during the period of optional delinquency. In justification of such a construction of the provision defendant refers us to *Walsh v. Glendale Fed. Sav. & Loan Assn.* (1969) 1 Cal. App.3d 578, 585 [81 Cal.Rptr. 804] which relied inter alia on our decisions in *Finger v. McCaughey* (1896) 114 Cal. 64, 66 [45 P. 1004] and *Thompson v. Gorner* (1894) 104 Cal. 168 [37 P. 900]. (See also *O'Connor v. Richmond Sav. & Loan Assn.* (1968) 262 Cal.App.2d 523, 530 [68 Cal.Rptr. 882].)

The *Thompson* and *Finger* cases essentially involved obligations on promis-sory notes which included provisions that the loan was to bear one rate of interest if paid at maturity and a higher rate if not paid when the obligation became due. An additional provision in the note in *Thompson,* not relevant to the disposition of the case, related to an increased interest rate if any installment of interest was not paid as it became due.

In *Thompson* we held that a clause in a promissory note providing for a higher rate of interest if the "principal or interest is not paid as it becomes due" is not to be treated as a penalty, but as a contract to pay such higher rate upon and

---

[1] Civil Code section 1670 provides: "Every contract by which the amount of damage to be paid, or other compensation to be made, for a breach of an obligation, is determined in anticipation thereof, is to that extent void, except as expressly provided in the next section." Section 1671 defines and authorizes a liquidation of damages, stating, "The parties to a contract may agree therein upon an amount which shall be presumed to be the amount of damage sustained by a breach thereof, when, from the nature of the case, it would be impracticable or extremely difficult to fix the actual damage."

Unless otherwise herein provided all statutory references are to sections of the Civil Code.

commencing with the happening of one of the contingencies specified in the note, to wit, the failure to make payment of any sum when due.

In *Finger* the promissory note contained a provision that in the event of default at maturity a higher interest rate would apply than if the obligation had been paid when it became due. Unlike *Thompson,* however, the higher rate was to predate the default and relate back to the full term of the note. The court in *Finger* did not distinguish *Thompson* on the differing factual circumstances and rested its holding on *Thompson* in concluding that the amount so assessed was not a penalty within the meaning of section 1670.

Neither *Finger,* and certainly not *Thompson,* stand for the proposition, as defendant would have us hold, that upon a default in the payment of an install-ment of a note a higher interest rate may be assessed against the *whole of the unpaid balance of the principal* of the note whether or not in default. *Thompson* held only that amounts *in default* may bear a higher interest rate from the date of the default, and *Finger* further held that amounts in default may bear a higher *and retroactive* interest rate. *Thompson* and *Finger* incorrectly have been held to stand for the proposition that "It is the rule in this state that late-charge interest is not in the nature of a penalty, and is valid" in cases where increased interest charges are assessed against the unpaid balance of the principal whether or not in default. (*Walsh v. Glendale Fed. Sav. & Loan Assn., supra,* 1 Cal.App.3d 578, 585; *O'Connor v. Richmond Sav. & Loan Assn., supra,* 262 Cal.App.2d 523, 530.) Thus defendant's argument that a borrower in default is merely exercising a valid option to elect a different performance under the lending contract does find some support in the foregoing line of cases.

The mere fact that an agreement may be construed, if in fact it can be, to vest in one party an option to perform in a manner which, if it were not so construed, would result in a penalty does not validate the agreement. To so hold would be to condone a result which, although directly prohibited by the Legislature, may nevertheless be indirectly accomplished through the imagination of inventive minds. Accordingly, a borrower on an installment note cannot legally agree to forfeit what is clearly a penalty in exchange for the right to exercise an option to default in making a timely payment of an installment. Otherwise the legislative declarations of sections 1670 and 1671 would be completely frustrated. We have consistently ignored form and sought out the substance of arrangements which purport to legitimate penalties and forfeitures. (See *Caplan v. Schroeder* (1961) 56 Cal.2d 515, 519-521 [15 Cal.Rptr. 145, 364 P.2d 321]; *Freedman v. The Rector* (1951) 37 Cal.2d 16, 21-23 [230 P.2d 629, 31 A.L.R.2d 1].)

Thompson is not to the contrary. It did not involve a question of penalty. There the full amount of the note was in default and the parties contracted for an increased rate beginning with the moment of default on sums which became payable to the lender. No penalty was assessed as the borrower at the moment of default owed only what he had contracted to pay had there been no default, the principal amount plus accrued interest. If those amounts were not then paid the parties agreed that interest at the higher rate would accrue.

In *Finger,* although it purports to rely on *Thompson,* the question of a penalty was nevertheless involved. Because the increased interest rate was made retroac-tive the borrower, at the moment of default, became obligated for a sum *in addition* to what he had contracted to pay under the terms of the promissory note had there been no default. The validity of the provision, accordingly, should have been controlled by applicable statutory provisions relating to liq-uidated damages. We conclude that the *Finger* extension of the *Thompson* holding was unwarranted, and to that extent it is overruled. For similar reasons we disapprove both *Walsh v. Glendale Fed. Sav. & Loan Assn., supra,* 1 Cal.App.3d 578 and *O'Connor v. Richmond Sav. & Loan Assn., supra,* 262 Cal.App.2d 523 to the extent that they are inconsistent with our views herein.

We recognize, of course, the validity of provisions varying the acceptable performance under a contract upon the happening of a contingency. We cannot, however, so subvert the substance of a contract to form that we lose sight of the bargained-for performance. Thus when it is manifest that a contract expressed to be performed in the alternative is in fact a contract contemplating but a single, definite performance with an additional charge contingent on the breach of that performance, the provision cannot escape examination in light of pertinent rules relative to the liquidation of damages. (*Paolilli v. Piscitelli* (1923) 45 R.I. 354, 359 [121 A. 531]; Williston on Contracts (3d ed.) § 781.)

In the instant case, the only reasonable interpretation of the clause providing for imposition of an increased interest rate is that the parties agreed upon the rate which should govern the contract and then, realizing that the borrowers might fail to make timely payment, they further agreed that such borrowers were to pay an additional sum as damages for their breach which sum was determined by applying the increased rate to the entire unpaid principal balance. Inasmuch as this increased interest charge is assessed only upon default, it is invalid unless it meets the requirements of section 1671. (§§ 1670, 1671; see also *In re Tastyeast, Inc.* (3d Cir. 1942) 126 F.2d 879, 882; *Conn. Mutual Life Ins. Co. v. Westerhoff* (1899) 58 Neb. 379, 382 [78 N.W. 724, 79 N.W. 731]; cf. Com. Code, § 2718; *Feary v. Aaron Burglar Alarm, Inc.* (1973) 32 Cal.App.3d 553 [108 Cal.Rptr. 242].)

Section 1671 authorizes the assessment of agreed-upon and anticipated damages only when the fixing of the actual damages which would be sustained upon a breach would be "impracticable" or "extremely difficult." Where, as here, the issue is presented on admitted facts it is one of law and must be examined from the position of the parties at the time the contract was entered into. (*Better Food Mkts. v. Amer. Dist. Teleg. Co., supra,* 40 Cal.2d 179, 184, 185, 186.) (5) The party seeking to rely on a liquidated damages clause bears the burden of proof. (*Id.* at p. 185.) Because of the posture of the case before us it is not necessary that we consider issues of "difficulty" or "impracticability."

"The validity of a clause for liquidated damages requires that the parties to contract 'agree therein upon an amount which shall be presumed to be that amount of damages sustained by a breach thereof . . . .' (Civ. Code, § 1671.) This amount must represent the result of a reasonable endeavor by the parties to estimate a fair average compensation for any loss that may be sustained. (*Dyer Bros. Golden West Iron Works v. Central Iron Works, supra.* 182 Cal. 588 [189 P. 445]; *Rice v. Schmid, supra,* 18 Cal.2d 382, 386 [115 P.2d 498, 138 A.L.R. 589]; Restatement, Contracts, § 339, p. 554.)" (*Better Food Mkts. v. Amer. Dist. Teleg. Co., supra,* 40 Cal.2d 179, 186-187.) It is abundantly apparent for the reasons which follow that the parties here have made no "reasonable endeavor . . . to estimate a fair average compensation for any loss that [might] be sustained" by the delinquency in the payment of an installment. They have, in fact, contracted for the imposition of an additional sum to be paid by the borrower under the guise of an interest charge for which, in the absence of a showing that the same bore a relationship to any loss which may be suffered, must be construed as a penalty.

The fundamental difference between interest and penalty charges is that interest is a measure of compensation to which an obligee is entitled while a penalty is punitive in character. (*United States v. Childs* (1924) 266 U.S. 304, 305 (69

L.ED. 299, 45 S.Ct. 110].) A penalty provision operates to compel performance of (*Biles v. Robey* (1934) 43 Ariz. 276. 286 [30 P.2d 841]) and usually becomes effective only in the event of default (*Lagorio v. Yerxa* (1929) 96 Cal.App. 111, 117 [273 P. 856]) upon which a forfeiture is compelled without regard to the actual damages sustained by the party aggrieved by the breach (*Better Foods Mkts. v. Amer. Dist. Teleg. Co., supra,* 40 Cal.2d 179). The characteristic feature of a penalty is its lack of proportional relation to the damages which may actually flow from failure to perform under a contract. (*Dyer Bros. I. Wks. v. Central I. Wks.* (1920) 182 Cal. 588, 592-593 [189 P. 445]; *Muldoon v. Lynch* (1885) 66 Cal. 536, 539 [6 P. 417].)

Late charges in home loan contracts are presumably imposed because borrowers fail to make timely payments of their obligations. Such charges serve a dual purpose: (1) they compensate the lender for its administrative expenses and the cost of money wrongfully withheld; and (2) they encourage the borrower to make timely future payments. Whether late charges represent a reasonable endeavor to estimate fair compensation depends upon the motivation and purpose in imposing such charges and their effect. If the sum extracted from the borrower is designed to exceed substantially the damages suffered by the lender, the provision for the additional sum, whatever its label, is an invalid attempt to impose a penalty inasmuch as its primary purpose is to compel prompt payment through the threat of imposition of charges bearing little or no relationship to the amount of the actual loss incurred by the lender. (*First American Title Ins. & Trust Co. v. Cook* (1970) 12 Cal.App.3d 592, 596-597 [90 Cal.Rptr. 645]; *Lagorio v. Yerxa, supra,* 96 Cal.App. 111, 117; cf. *Clermont v. Secured Investment Corp.* (1972) 25 Cal.App.3d 766, 769 [102 Cal.Rptr. 340].)

The contractual provision as alleged in the complaint in the instant case provides that in the event of a late payment a borrower is to be charged an additional amount equal to 2 percent per annum for the period of delinquency assessed against the *unpaid* principal balance of the loan obligation. We are concluded that a charge for the late payment of a loan installment which is measured against the unpaid balance of the loan must be deemed to be punitive in character. It is an attempt to coerce timely payment by a forfeiture which is not reasonably calculated to merely compensate the injured lender. We conclude, accordingly, that because the parties failed to make a reasonable endeavor to estimate a fair compensation for a loss which would be sustained on the default of an installment payment, the provision for late charges is void.

We do not hold herein that merely because the late charge provision is void and thus cannot be used in determining the lender's damages, the borrower escapes unscathed. He remains liable for the actual damages resulting from his default. The lender's charges could be fairly measured by the period of time the money was wrongfully withheld plus the administrative costs reasonably related to collecting and accounting for a late payment. (*See Farthing v. San Mateo Clinic* (1956) 143 Cal.App.2d 385 (299 P.2d 977].)

Moreover we do not hold that had the amount of the late charges been fixed as a measure of anticipated damages in the event of a default that the provision would necessarily have violated section 1670. As indicated, liquidated damages can be validly anticipated by the parties' reasonable endeavors to do so if "extremely difficult" or "impracticable" to fix. Although we conclude on the record before us that defendant failed in its burden of establishing extreme difficulty in anticipating and fixing damages for the breach of an installment payment, it is possible that on a proper showing defendant might have been able to establish the impracticability of prospectively fixing its actual damages resulting from a default in an installment payment.

The instant case suggests the impracticability under certain circumstances of fixing actual damages when the amount thereof may be small but the cost of ascertaining the same may well be in excess of a reasonable sum agreed to in advance by the parties as fair compensation. We could not hold as violative of section 1671 a provision for liquidated damages where it is established that the measure of actual damages would be a comparatively small amount and that it would be economically impracticable in each instance of a default to require a lender to prove to the satisfaction of the borrower the actual damages by accounting procedures. If the test of impracticability is met the court should give effect to a liquidated damages provision resulting from the reasonable endeavors of the parties to fix a fair compensation.

For the reasons stated the complaint is not vulnerable to defendant's demurrer on the ground asserted. The order of dismissal is reversed and the cause remanded to the trial court with directions to overrule the demurrer and to allow a reasonable time within which to answer or otherwise plead.

McComb, J., Tobriner, J., Mosk, J., Burke, J., Sullivan, J., and Files, J., concurred.

NOTES

1. California has limited by statute the percentage that can be assessed as a late charge. *See* California Bus. & Prof. Code § 10242.5 (West). However, the limitation is not applicable to any "[l]oan secured directly or collaterally by a first trust deed, the principal of which is Sixteen Thousand Dollars ($16,000) or more, or to a bona fide loan secured directly or collaterally by any lien junior thereto, the principal of which is Eight Thousand Dollars ($8,000) or more." While there may be many junior liens (home improvement loans, swimming pool loans, etc.) of less than $8,000, how many first mortgages on residences are for less than $16,000? For practical purposes this restriction renders the statutory limitation virtually ineffective. This further creates a gray area between the limit of loans of less than $16,000 and the over-reaching by the lender in *Garrett*. The legislature has gone through the motions of creating a limitation while in fact still leaving it to the courts to decide the validity of late charges on a case by case method.

2. If borrowers have discovered that late charges, a substantial source of income to lenders ($1,900,000 in four years in the *Garrett* case), are subject to class action litigation, is further litigation for returned check charges unlikely? Could the maker of a check returned "for insufficient funds" make the same argument against a $5.00 charge that was made in *Garrett*?

3. Late charges have been attacked as being usurious in several jurisdictions. Where lenders have been exempt from usury limits, the courts have construed late charges as additional interest. *See Walsh v. Glendale Federal Savings & Loan Ass'n*, 1 Cal. App. 3d 578, 81 Cal. Rptr. 804 (1969); and *O'Connor v. Richmond Savings & Loan Ass'n*, 262 Cal. App. 2d 523, 68 Cal. Rptr. 882 (1968). The same jurisdiction had construed late charges as not being interest when the lender was not exempt from usury limits. *See First American Title Insurance & Trust Co. v. Cook*, 12 Cal. App. 3d 592, 90 Cal. Rptr. (1970). In states where lenders are not exempt from usury limits, courts have held late charges to be interest capable of being usurious. *See Foster v. Universal C.I.T. Credit Corp.*, 231 Ark. 230, 330 S.W.2d 288 (1959) and *Consolidated Loans Inc. v. Smith*, 190 So. 2d 522 (La. 1966).

4. Usury is generally made up of the following four elements: agreement to lend money or its equivalent, or to forebear to require repayment for a period of time; the borrower's obligation to repay absolutely and not contingently; the exaction of a greater compensation for making the loan, or agreeing to forebear, than is allowed by the applicable State Constitution or usury statute; and an intention to violate the usury statute.

5. Several states have exempted lenders from usury limits when making loans secured by real property mortgages. *See:*

California — Cal. Const. Art. 20 § 22 (1947). Banks and savings and loans.

Connecticut — Conn. Gen. Stat. § 37-9 (1978). Savings and loans, banks, and credit unions exempt.

Florida — Fla. Stat. Ann. § 687.10 (West 1966). All lending institutions.

Illinois — Ill. Ann. Stat. ch. 32, § 800 (1978). Savings and loans only.

Massachusetts — Mass. Gen. Laws Ann. ch., 140 § 90A (West 1974). Over $40,000 assessed value then exemption applies.

Minnesota — Minn. Stat. § 334.06 (1977). Savings and loans only.

New Hampshire — N.H. Rev. Stat. Ann. v. 3, § 336.1. No usury law.

Ohio — Ohio Rev. Code Ann. § 1151.21 (1968). Savings and loans only.

South Dakota — S.D. Comp. Laws Ann. § 54-3-12 (1977). Savings and loans only.

West Virginia — W. Va. Code § 31-6-17 (1975). Savings and loans exempt.

Wisconsin — Wis. Stat. Ann. § 219.03 (West 1957). State savings and loans only.

6. In 1980, the United States Congress enacted legislation abolishing usury limits on residential mortgage loans. *See* 12 U.S.C. § 1735f-7.

D. COVENANTS IN A MORTGAGE

The following are covenants which may be found in the typical mortgage. They are for the purpose of assuring the lender that the borrower will keep the property in such a condition that the value is not allowed to decline. Failure to comply with any of these covenants might be cause for the lender to seek return of its money through foreclosure.

1. The Mortgagor shall keep the mortgaged property in good and tenantable condition and repair.

2. The Mortgagor shall not commit waster or suffer waste to be committed on the mortgaged property, or do any act which impairs or diminishes the value of the mortgaged property.

3. The Mortgagor shall comply with all laws, ordinances, regulations and requirements of any governmental body applicable to the Property.

4. The Mortgagor shall keep the Mortgaged Property insured for fire and extended coverage in an amount equal to at least 80% of the full insurable value thereof, all policies evidencing such insurance to provide that all losses thereunder are to be payable to the Mortgagor and the Mortgagee as their respective interests may appear, such policies or evidence thereof to be deposited with and held by the Mortgagee.

5. The Mortgagor shall generally manage and maintain the Property in a manner to insure maximum rentals.

6. The Mortgagor shall maintain complete and accurate books of accounts and records adequate to reflect the results of the operation of the Property and upon Mortgagee's request, Mortgagor shall furnish within 120 days after the end of the fiscal year of mortgagor, a balance sheet and statement of income and expenses certified by mortgagor or a certified public accountant.

7. Neither Mortgagor nor any tenant or other person shall remove, demolish or alter any improvements now existing or hereafter erected on the Property or any fixture, equipment, machinery or appliance in or on the Property except when incident to the replacement of fixtures, equipment, machinery and appliances with items of like kind.

8. So long as any part of all of the principal and/or interest on the Debt Instrument and any additional indebtedness arising hereunder remains outstanding and unpaid, the Mortgagor shall not, without prior written consent of the Mortgagee, pledge or otherwise encumber, create or permit to exist any mortgage or other lien or encumbrances upon any part or all of the Mortgaged Property other than the mortgage lien hereby created.

Chapter 5

FORECLOSURE AND OTHER REMEDIES

A mortgage casts a shadow on the sunniest field.

R. G. Ingersoll, *Farming in Illinois*

A. REMEDIES BEFORE FORECLOSURE

CAROLINA PORTLAND CEMENT CO. v. BAUMGARTNER

Supreme Court of Florida
99 Fla. 987, 128 So. 241 (1930)

BROWN, J.

This is an appeal by the complainant in the court below from an order of the chancellor denying the application of complainant for the appointment of a receiver in foreclosure proceedings. The bill for foreclosure, which was sworn to, was filed in October, 1928. It alleged that the defendants, Baumgartner and wife, on the 25th day of November, A. D. 1927, executed and delivered to the Hearn Construction Company their note for $25,250. To secure its payment they also contemporaneously executed and delivered their mortgage incumbering the lands described in the bill of complaint. The note and mortgage were first assigned to the Atlantic National Bank, but the bill alleged that they are now held and owned by the complainants.

The bill furthermore alleged that on the property described in the mortgage there was a large apartment house from which the principal defendant, Baumgartner, was collecting the rents. The property was subject to a first mortgage of $42,500. Baumgartner failed to pay the interest due thereon in July, 1928, and to prevent foreclosure, the complainant Carolina Portland Cement Company paid it. He likewise failed to pay the interest due August 25, 1928, on this, the second mortgage, when it matured.

The bill alleged that the second mortgage, foreclosure of which was thereby sought, contained an express pledge of the rents, etc.; the following language being used:

> Together with all and singular the tenements, hereditaments and appurtenances thereunto belong or in anywise appertaining, *and the rents, issues and profits thereof,* and also the estate, right, title, interest, homestead, dower and right of dower, separate estate, property, possession, and all claim and demand whatsoever, as well in law as in equity, of the said party of the first part, of, in and to the same, and every part thereof, with the appurtenances. (Italics supplied.)

There was also a provision for the appointment of a receiver, as follows:

> That in case any default is made by the party of the first part, as mentioned in the preceding paragraph, and a suit in equity is instituted by the party of the second part to enforce his rights, the party of the second part shall be entitled to apply to the Court having jurisdiction of such suit for the *appointment of a receiver of all and singular said property, and the rents, issues and profits thereof.* And it is further covenanted and agreed that thereupon such court shall forthwith, as a strict matter of right in the party of the second part, appoint a receiver of all such property with the usual powers and duties including the power to rent said property and to collect the rental thereof and

therefrom; the revenue derived from said property to be applied by such receiver as required by law and under the direction of said court. (Italics supplied.)

Relying on the foregoing clauses and the facts above stated, the complainants applied to the lower court for the appointment of a receiver. Several days after the date noticed for the hearing of such application, but two days prior to the making of the order, defendant Baumgartner filed his sworn answer. The application for appointment of a receiver was denied, and this appeal is from the order of denial.

The bill contained no allegation that the defendant mortgagor was insolvent or that the security afforded by the property mortgaged was inadequate.

The briefs and argument of counsel for both appellants and appellees assume that the only question in the case is whether or not the complainants, without making any showing as to the insolvency of the mortgagor or the inadequacy of the security, were entitled to the appointment of a receiver, by virtue of those clauses in the mortgage sought to be foreclosed which expressly pledged the rents, issues, and profits of the mortgaged premises as security for the debt, and providing for the appointment of a receiver.

The chancellor rendered his order without opinion, but it is assumed by counsel that the above question, and the decision reached thereon, was the sole determinative consideration upon which the order appealed from was based. This assumption may be correct, and we would hardly be warranted in adjudicating this appeal without some consideration of the above-stated question, which has been ably and earnestly argued by counsel for both sides, though, for reasons hereinafter stated, the chancellor may have been influenced in reaching his decision to deny the receiver by certain allegations in the defendant's verified answer.

. . . .

We will first consider whether a mortgagor may lawfully pledge the rents and profits of real estate in a mortgage thereof, and, if so, whether such a provision possesses any significance or efficacy.

Clauses of this character are so frequently embraced in mortgages these days, that the question becomes an important one. It is also obvious that such a clause, upon default in payments due under the mortgage, cannot generally be enforced except through the medium of a receiver. Land cannot run away, and buildings may be kept insured. Hence there is generally good reason for denying a receiver of mere real estate unless waste is being committed, or there be insolvency of the mortgagor and inadequacy of the property as security. But the mortgagors, even after default, can collect the rents, and dissipate them, and the mortgagees are powerless to prevent it, although the mortgage expressly pledges the rents as part of the security, unless a receiver be appointed to impound the rents pending the foreclosure proceedings and hold them subject to the orders of the court.

. . . .

It has also been held in a number of states that the mortgagor, when there is no prohibitory statute, may pledge the rents and profits of real estate in a mortgage thereof. Indeed, this appears to be in harmony with the weight of authority, though there are some cases to the contrary. See valuable note in 4 A. L. R. 1405 et seq., and Jones on Mortgages (8th Ed.) § 1930. Among the states so holding are New York and Illinois. Such also is the holding by the United States Supreme Court. See *Gisborn v. Charter Oak Life Insurance Co.,* 142 U. S. 326, 12 S. Ct. 277, 35 L. Ed. 1029; *Freedman's Savings & Trust Co. v. Shepherd,* 127 U. S. 494, 8 S. Ct. 1250, 32 L. Ed. 163. In the latter case it was held that such a provision does not become practically effective until a receiver is appointed or the mortgagee goes into actual possession; that as long as the mortgagor continues in possession, he can collect the rents. See also Jones Mortgages (8th Ed.) § 827; and in section 975 of that work it is said: "In the absence of a specific pledge of the rents and profits to the mortgagee as part of his security, the mortgagor, though insolvent, may, until the foreclosure sale, or until the appointment of a receiver pending the foreclosure suit, receive them to his own use, or assign them to another" — citing a New York case.

"Rents and profits are as much property as the estate out of which they arise, and as such they are equally the subject of a mortgage." 41 C. J. 375, citing a number of cases.

In *Pasco v. Gamble,* 15 Fla. 562, in an able opinion by that great jurist, Justice Westcott, it was held, in a case where there was no express provision in the mortgage pledging the rents and profits, that in spite of the Florida statute providing that a mortgage is merely a specific lien upon property and that the mortgagee could not acquire possession until after foreclosure and sale, the possession of the mortgagor was subordinate to the equitable rights of the mortgagee, and that under certain conditions, such as default in payment of interest and taxes, insolvency of the mortgagor, and inadequacy of the property as security, a receiver of the rents and profits should be appointed. That under such circumstances, as between the mortgagor and mortgagee, equity makes the mortgage a charge upon the rents and profits of the mortgaged property as well as upon the property itself, "regarding the land with all its produce as a security for the mortgage debt." *Pasco v. Gamble,* 15 Fla. 562, 568.

If the owner of real property may, as he unquestionably can, assign away the rents and profits thereof, why may he not pledge them along with the land, thus incumbering them with a contract lien, as security for a debt? We find no valid reason in the authorities why this may not be lawfully done. In fact, while many courts, perhaps a majority of them, have been extremely reluctant to give full effect to such a provision, very few deny the lawful power of a mortgagor to so stipulate. In a few of the states, such a provision, as well as one agreeing to the appointment of a receiver, are regarded as contrary to the varying statutes existing in such states. But a pledge of the rents and profits, along with the land, as security for the mortgage debt, creating as it does a mere contract lien to secure a debt, which can only be made effective and enforceable by the appointment of a receiver by the court, does not conflict with our statute any more than the lien created by the mortgage on the land itself.

The statute, section 5725, Comp. Gen. Laws, derived from an act of 1853, reads: "A mortgage shall be held to be a specific lien on the property therein described, and not a conveyance of the legal title or of the right of possession." But the lien exists in spite of the mortgagor's right of possession, and even this right of possession may be subordinated in equity to the protection of the mortgagee's equitable rights.

If, as was held in *Pasco v. Gamble,* supra, in cases of insolvency and inadequacy of the property as security, the mortgage, though containing no provision on the subject, will be held in equity to constitute a lien upon the rents and profits, as well as upon the land itself, why may not the parties, by the contract, expressly create such a lien upon the rents and profits, which shall attach, and in proper cases be enforced, regardless of the mortgagor's insolvency and in some cases perhaps regardless even of the inadequacy of the property itself as security? We see no reason why the courts should deny the right of a property owner to so create a contract lien upon the rents and profits of his property. It might well become a valuable right when he finds it necessary to borrow money. It is his property, and if he sees fit to incumber it and also its rents, with a lien to secure a debt, we know of no statutory or constitutional provision which prohibits him from so doing. Certainly section 5725, Comp. Gen. Laws, does not prohibit him from mortgaging the rents any more than the land. It was said in *Pasco v. Gamble,* quoting Chancellor Kent, that while the mortgagee's common-law rights of entry and possession were gone, the mortgage remains as a "lien by contract." If the mortgage on the realty is a mere lien by contract, and the pledging of the rents and profits of the realty is also a lien by contract, which may be created in the same instrument, why should not the latter be enforced and protected by the courts as much so as the former? And if waste of the real estate security is in proper cases considered good ground for the court to interpose and by writ of injunction to restrain the mortgagor from committing such waste, why should not the security afforded, under the terms of the contract, by the rents and profits be also protected, by appointing a receiver in proper cases, to prevent such rents from being wasted and dissipated by a mortgagor in default?

Appellees contend that the position of appellant is based upon decisions from those jurisdictions, such as Illinois and New York, in which a mortgage is regarded as passing the legal title and right of possession as at common law, whereas our statute makes it merely a lien, with the title and right of possession remaining in the mortgagor. A review of the Illinois cases in 41 C. J. 276, shows that they have departed considerably from the common-law conception, while it appears that New York, if it ever recognized the common law theory, has long since adhered to the equitable theory. And the same may be said of many of the other states which are supposed to retain the common law doctrine. In fact, in a majority of the states, partly by force of statutes and partly by the decisions of the courts, the common-law doctrine has been abrogated, and has given place to the equitable theory, similar to that obtaining with us, according to which a mortgage is nothing more than a mere lien or security for a debt, passing no title or estate, nor right of possession. 41 C. J. 279, 280. Such is the holding in New York, cases from which, as well as from other states, are cited by appellant. But this mortgagor's right of possession, as we have above seen, can be subordinated in equity when necessary for the protection of the equitable rights of the mortgagee.

This theory, that the appointment of a receiver of the rents and profits is dependent upon the recognition of the common-law doctrine that the mortgagee is entitled to possession, was shown to be untenable in *Pasco v. Gamble,* supra, wherein Justice Westcott said:

> At the outset of this investigation, controlled principally by the California decisions, our view was, that the statute, destroying all rights of possession to the mortgagee, destroyed also all his equitable rights and remedies by which a sequestration of the rents and profits of the land might be had. This view in California has been condemned in Nevada, where, notwithstanding the statute gives the right of possession to the mortgagor until foreclosure and sale, the court in such a case as this sanctions the appointment of a receiver. ([*Hyman v. Kelly*] 1 Nevada, 184.)

> . . . .

As to the argument that an express stipulation pledging the rents and profits is unnecessary, as being no more than the law writes into every mortgage of real property, it will have been observed that the constructive equitable lien on the rents and profits which courts of equity have created is only recognized where the mortgagor in default is insolvent and the security afforded by the real property inadequate. But where the mortgage expressly pledges the rents and profits in addition to the property, as security for the payment of the debt, such a provision might in many cases be properly considered by the courts as authorizing the exercise of the discretionary power of appointing a receiver where without such express agreement a receiver would be denied, such, for instance, as cases where, although the mortgagor was not shown to be insolvent, nor the security of the property clearly inadequate, yet the security afforded by the lien on the rentals might well be impounded through a receiver pending foreclosure proceedings when it appears that such action is reasonably necessary to effectively enforce the payment of the debt secured. While it is our statutory policy to leave the mortgagor in possession until after foreclosure and sale, and equity will enforce this policy until it becomes necessary to subordinate the mortgagee's possession in order to protect the equitable rights of the mortgagee, yet when the mortgage expressly gives a lien upon the rents and profits and consents to the appointment of a receiver upon default, such stipulation should be accorded considerable weight by the courts, and will in many cases afford good grounds for the appointment of a receiver where without them a receiver might not be appointed.

. . . .

Of course, the mere fact that the mortgage pledges the rents and profits, and consents in advance to the appointment of a receiver upon default or breach of conditions, does not mean that upon such a showing alone a court of equity should appoint a receiver as a matter of course. Thus, if it were made to appear that, although in default, the mortgagor was exercising reasonably good care and management of the property and applying the receipts from rentals to the payment of the taxes and the interest on the mortgage debt as far as they would go, a receiver could do no more, and no equitable ground would exist for interfering with the right of possession, which under the statute the mortgagor retains. But where, as in this case, according to the bill, the mortgagor is receiving a large amount monthly in rents, yet failing to keep down the interest on the first mortgage, thus compelling the second mortgagee to pay such interest to prevent foreclosure of the first mortgage, and also failing to pay the installments falling due on the second mortgage, which pledged such rents and profits and agreed to the appointment of a receiver on default, such bill makes out a good case for the appointment of a receiver. *Cross v. Will County Nat'l Bank,* 177 Ill. 33, 52 N. E. 322; *Keogh Mfg. Co. v. Whiston* (Sup.) 14 N. Y. S. 344; Jones on Mortgages (8th Ed.) § 1937.

. . . .

In the light of the principles above outlined, we think that in the case at bar, if the chancellor had granted the application for a receiver, his action, if appealed from, should have been affirmed; but, on the other hand, in view of the allegations of the sworn answer attacking the bona fides of the second mortgage, alleging that it had been fraudulently procured and that the complainants had taken assignments thereof with notice of such alleged infirmities, we hardly feel authorized to hold that the learned chancellor was guilty of an abuse of discretion in denying such application under these circumstances, in the absence of the production of some evidence before him which would satisfy him either as to initial validity of the mortgage or that the complainants had acquired the same as bona fide purchasers without notice of such infirmities. The rule that a party is not entitled to have a receiver appointed, unless there is strong reason to believe that he will recover, has already been alluded to. This is said without any intention of prejudging or prejudicing any action that has been or may be taken in the court below as to the sufficiency of such answer, either in form or substance. As to that question we intimate no opinion. While the answer was filed in the clerk's office two days before the order of the chancellor was rendered, the record does not show whether it was ever presented to the chancellor or considered by him. But the record fails to show that it was not so presented and considered; and if it was, whether well or illy pleaded, it makes certain charges of fraud and bad faith which may have influenced the chancellor, in the exercise of his discretion, to refuse the application of complainants for a receiver, and which charges were sufficiently grave to prevent us from holding that the chancellor clearly abused his discretion.

The order denying the appointment of a receiver will therefore be affirmed, but with directions that the chancellor permit complainants to renew their application for the appointment of a receiver, if they so desire; such new application to be considered and adjudicated in harmony with the views above enunciated.

Affirmed with directions.

TERRELL, C. J., and ELLIS, J., concur.

WHITFIELD, P.J. and STRUM and BUFORD, JJ., concur in the opinion and judgment.

The case of *Carolina Portland Cement v. Baumgartner, supra,* provides a good lead into one area that must be considered in determining the remedies available to a mortgagee before a foreclosure is commenced. That is the area of lien or title theory jurisdiction. In order to properly consider the difference, it is desirable to know some of the evolutionary process by which we arrived at the American means of foreclosure.

At common law there was not a problem of the mortgagee obtaining possession in the event of a default; the mortgagee was given possession at the time the mortgage conveyance was executed.[1] There were no installment loans at common law and no monthly payments or amortization to concern either party to the mortgage. The loan was due on one day which was designated Law Day. The entire obligation was due that day and if not paid timely, the borrower simply forfeited his property.[2] Equity later imposed foreclosure by sale in England which has become the general form used in this country.

Since the American way allows the mortgagor to retain possession of the land during the term of the mortgage, it is obvious that a borrower could continue to utilize the income from the property for his own use while allowing payments due the lender to go into default. In order to prevent this situation from arising, the mortgagee will want to obtain possession of the land and control the rents or profits generated by it. The manner in which this control is accomplished will vary depending on whether a jurisdiction is a "lien theory" state, a "title" state, or an intermediate "hybrid" state.

In a title state the theory of mortgages is that a conveyance of the property occurs with the execution of a mortgage, and the mortgagee is entitled to possession at that time.[3] Naturally, this would pose considerable problems for the typical mortgagor, for who would want the savings and loan to have possession during a loan term amortized over thirty years? Likewise, if the property is

---

[1] G. Osborne, Mortgages 8 *et seq.* (2d ed 1970).

[2] G. Osborne, G. Nelson & D. Whitman, Real Estate Finance Law § 1.2, p. 7 (1979).

[3] G. Osborne, G. Nelson & D. Whitman, Real Estate Finance Law § 4.1, p. 115 (1979).

income producing, the mortgagor needs control of the property so that income can be generated and partially used to satisfy the loan obligation. Thus, in title theory states the lenders and borrowers have a contractual arrangement whereby the borrower retains possession of the land unless there is a default in payment of the obligation, at which time the lender may take possession.[4]

In lien theory states the courts have held that a mortgage does not convey title to the land and the lender is not entitled to possession until after the foreclosure sale (at which the lender presumably buys the land). Hybrid states allow the borrower the right to possession until default, giving the parties essentially the same rights by law that they have by contract in most title theory situations.

The mortgagee may wish to take possession personally, or may prefer to have the court appoint a receiver. There are positive and negative factors to each situation. A mortgagee in possession is held to a higher standard in accounting for the rents and profits. The mortgagee must account for not only that which was taken in, but for that *which should have been taken in*. A receiver only has to account for income and expenditures.[5] A mortgagee in possession is liable in tort for latent defects the same as the owner of land would be while the receiver enjoys a reduced duty and is liable only for his negligence.[6]

1. RENTS AND PROFITS

EAST GRAND FORKS FEDERAL SAVINGS & LOAN ASS'N v. MUELLER

Supreme Court of North Dakota
198 N.W.2d 124 (1972)

STRUTZ, CHIEF JUSTICE, on reassignment.

The plaintiff, East Grand Forks Federal Savings and Loan Association, the mortgagee, appeals from a judgment dismissing its action against the mortgagors, their successors in interest, and the tenant for recovery of rents claimed under a written assignment of rents contained in a real estate mortgage, which mortgage is in default.

The property described in the mortgage was owned by Theodore E. Jarombek and Thersa A. Jarombek, the mortgagors. They executed and delivered to the mortgagee a mortgage on Lot 10, Block 2, Dacotah Place Addition to the City of Grand Forks, which mortgage contained an assignment of rents. The mortgage was duly filed and recorded in the office of the register of deeds of Grand Forks County and has been in default during all times pertinent to this action.

The mortgagors did not answer the plaintiff's complaint, were not represented by counsel at the trial of this action, and are not parties on this appeal. The claimants in this action to the rental moneys paid on the property in question, which moneys have been deposited with the clerk of the district court of Grand Forks County, are the mortgagee, which claims such moneys under the assignment-of-rents clause in the mortgage, and the defendant and respondent Red River Realty, Inc.

The property described in the mortgage has been subject to several transactions since the mortgage in question was executed and delivered by the

---

[4] G. Osborne, G. Nelson & D. Whitman, Real Estate Finance Law § 4.1, p. 118 (1979).

[5] A receiver must only account for those funds actually received. *See* Fairchild v. Gray, 242 N.Y.S. 192, 136 Misc. 704 (1930).

[6] It may be that a receiver is not held to the same standard of liability for latent defects since a receiver generally must have court approval to make repairs. *See* Women's Hosp. v. Loubern Realty Corp., 266 N.Y. 123, 194 N.E. 56 (1934).

Jarombeks, as owners, on or about the 30th day of March, 1962. One of the provisions in the mortgage reads:

5. If at any time the mortgagors shall be in default in performance of any of the agreements herein or in the said note contained, the Association shall have power and authority to remove the occupant and to take possession of the said real estate and to manage, control and lease the same even if it be a homestead, and collect all the rents, issues and profits therefrom or collect reasonable rent from the occupants if a homestead and shall then apply such income to pay all expenses of management and preservation of the property, taxes and assessments, reasonable and necessary repairs.

Some time after the mortgage was delivered to the mortgagee, the mortgagors employed Red River Realty, Inc., a real estate brokerage firm in Grand Forks, to sell the property for them. Certain buyers were found, and on November 17, 1964, the mortgagors sold the property to Walter and Adeline Beglo under a contract for deed calling for monthly installment payments. The Beglos made the monthly installment payments for a number of years, but eventually they defaulted in payment of installments due for the months of April, May, June, July, and August of 1969. It would appear from the record that on or about August 8, 1969, the Beglos assigned their interest in the contract for deed to Red River Realty, Inc.

As a result of the default in payments by the Beglos, the Jarombeks began proceedings to cancel the contract which they had executed with the Beglos. Judgment of cancellation of contract was entered on April 13, 1970, which judgment provided for a ninety-day period of redemption. No redemption was made within such period, and the mortgagors regained the right to possession of the property.

Before entry of judgment in the action to cancel the contract for deed, Red River Realty, Inc., attempted to sell the property to Allen and Donna Brownell. The new purchasers applied for financing through the appellant mortgagee, but such sale never was consummated and the Brownells occupied the property for a time only as tenants. They made payments of rent directly to East Grand Forks Federal Savings and Loan Association, the mortgagee herein.

After it became apparent that they would be unable to secure financing to purchase the property, the Brownells vacated, and the property then was rented to the defendant Arnold R. Mueller. His family occupied the premises as tenants at the time this action was commenced.

The record discloses that default was made on payments on the mortgage in March of 1969. By September of 1969, the defaults totaled $529.42. A letter from the mortgagee to the tenant Mueller in September of 1969 notified the tenant that East Grand Forks Federal Savings and Loan Association, the mortgagee, was invoking its rights to such rents under the assignment of rents contained in its mortgage. The tenant however, continued making his payments of rent to Red River Realty, which in turn deposited such rent money with the clerk of the district court pending the outcome of the action involving the cancellation of the contract for deed. The sum of $657.89, a portion of the amount claimed in this action, represents the rental payments for the period September 1969 through April 13, 1970. In addition, during the same period of time, Red River Realty collected $140 in rents from Mueller, which, through some oversight, was not deposited with the clerk of the district court. The claim for a total of $797.89, which the mortgagee is seeking to recover in this action, is based upon the theory that the mortgagee had invoked the assignment-of-rents provision of the mortgage which it held.

The trial court denied the mortgagee's claim to such rentals and ordered a dismissal of the complaint. In its memorandum decision, the trial court said:

> While East Grand Forks Federal Savings and Loan Association is the nominal plaintiff in the case at hand the real parties in interest are defendants, Theodore E. Jarombek and Theresa A. Jarombek, because any payment on the mortgage reduces their obligation as mortgagors. Under the circumstances the defense of Section 32-19-07, N.D. C.C., asserted by the Defendant, Red River Realty, Inc., is well taken.

The court then points out that the plaintiff mortgagee had made no effort to foreclose the mortgage or to gain possession of the premises, and that the plaintiff therefore had no right to the rents which were paid on the premises.

. . . .

At the outset of our consideration of this appeal, we would point out that the respondent Red River Realty, Inc., has conceded in its brief that the recent decision of this court in *Skinner v. American State Bank*, 189 N.W.2d 665, decided by this court in December of 1971, appears to overrule the trial court's decision, which was based upon the premise that a debtor in possession is at all times entitled to rents and profits from the property until after the expiration of the period of redemption. In *Skinner*, we held that an assignment-of-rents agreement given with a real estate mortgage was enforceable by the mortgagee prior to foreclosure of the mortgage, and that the provision of Section 29-24-11, North Dakota Century Code, which deals with rents and profits during the period of redemption, has no bearing upon the mortgagee's rights under the assignment-of-rents agreement prior to foreclosure.

The respondent now urges this court to re-examine its decision in *Skinner* in the light of Section 32-19-07, North Dakota Century Code. That section provides, in part:

> . . . Except as otherwise provided in sections 32-19-04 and 32-19-06, neither before nor after the rendition of a judgment for the foreclosure of a real estate mortgage or for the cancellation or foreclosure of a land contract made after July 1, 1951, shall the mortgagee or vendor, or the successor in interest of either, be authorized or permitted to bring any action in any court in this state for the recovery of any part of the debt secured by the mortgage or contract so foreclosed. It is the intent of this section that no deficiency judgment shall be rendered upon any note, mortgage, or contract given after July 1, 1951, to secure the payment of money loaned upon real estate or to secure the purchase price of real estate, and in case of default the holder of a real estate mortgage or land contract shall be entitled only to a foreclosure of the mortgage or the cancellation or foreclosure of the contract except as provided by sections 32-19-04 and 32-19-06.

The respondent correctly states that the provisions of Section 32-19-07, North Dakota Century Code, were not considered in our decision in *Skinner*. The reason that section was not considered in *Skinner* was that we deemed the section wholly inapplicable since there had been no foreclosure started. The defendant and respondent Red River Realty asserts that that section goes farther than merely preventing a deficiency judgment because its language clearly prohibits "any action for the recovery of any part of any debt secured by the mortgage." The defendant, in quoting from Section 32-19-07, omits a very important portion thereof, the words "so foreclosed." That section commences:

> Neither before nor after the rendition of a judgment for the foreclosure of a real estate mortgage or for the cancellation or foreclosure of a land contract

... [shall any action be permitted for the recovery of] any part of the debt secured by the mortgage or contract *so foreclosed*. ... [Emphasis supplied.]

The intention of the Legislative Assembly in enacting a statute must be ascertained from the language of the law, and where such language is clear and unambiguous, the court must give effect to the intention of the Legislature clearly expressed. *Brenna v. Hjelle,* 161 N.W.2d 356 (N.D.1968); *City of Fargo v. Annexation Review Commission,* 148 N.W.2d 338 (N.D.1966); *Kessler v. Board of Education of City of Fessenden,* 87 N.W.2d 743 (N.D.1958). We therefore hold that Section 32-19-07 clearly indicates that the intention of the Legislature was to prevent deficiency judgments in the event of foreclosure, except as provided by Sections 32-19-04 and 32-19-06, North Dakota Century Code.

In the case here under consideration, as was true in *Skinner,* there had been no foreclosure commenced. Upon default, the mortgagee relied entirely upon its rights under the assignment-of-rents agreement. This court has held that an assignment-of-rents agreement given by the mortgagor as additional security is lawful, and that such agreement will be enforced by the courts. *Skinner v. American State Bank, supra; Fargo Building and Loan Assn. v. Rice,* 66 N.D. 100, 262 N.W. 345 (1935).

. . . .

The trial court, in deciding this case, did not have the benefit of our decision in *Skinner v. American State Bank, supra.* That case was decided sometime after judgment had been entered in the case now before us.

For reasons stated in this opinion, we find that the plaintiff mortgagee is entitled to the rents under its assignment of rents. We reverse the judgment of the trial court, and order that the moneys in question be paid to the mortgagee under the assignment-of-rents provision of the mortgage.

ERICKSTAD and PAULSON, J., concur.

TEIGEN, JUDGE (dissenting).

MARSHALL & ILLSLEY BANK v. CADY

Supreme Court of Minnesota
76 Minn. 112, 78 N.W. 978 (1899)

MITCHELL, J. In this action to foreclose a mortgage, the court, on the motion of the plaintiff, appointed a receiver of the mortgaged premises during the pendency of the action to collect the rents, profits, and income of the property, and apply the same, as far as necessary, in payment of the taxes and assessments that were then a lien against the premises, and to bring the balance, if any, into court. In the final decree of foreclosure rendered in November, 1897, the court directed that the receivership should be continued until the further order of the court. The premises were sold under the judgment in December, 1897, and purchased by the plaintiff for a sum about $300 less than the amount due on the mortgage, for which a deficiency judgment was entered after the sale was confirmed. At the date of the sale the taxes for 1893, amounting to over $80, remained unpaid, and constituted a lien on the property. The receiver remained in possession, collecting the rents and profits of the premises, until the expiration of the time for redemption, in December, 1898. Subsequently the receiver filed in court an account of his receipts and disbursements. The court disallowed some of the items of his account for fees and disbursements, and settled the net balance in his hands at $77.66. The plaintiff asked that this balance be applied either on the deficiency judgment, or on payment of the taxes of 1893. The defendant asked that the receiver be directed to pay the amount over to him. The court granted defendant's motion, and the plaintiff appealed. The receiver has not appealed.

The further facts may be stated (although probably immaterial) that the premises were never redeemed; also, that at least a part of the balance in the hands of the receiver was derived from rents received after the foreclosure sale. The plaintiff excepts to the action of the court in disallowing some of the charges of the receiver for fees and disbursements. This is a matter personal to the receiver, and does not concern the plaintiff. If it is entitled to the balance, the disallowance of these items would make the amount coming to it the larger by the amount disallowed. The receiver being content, it does not lie in the mouth of the plaintiff to object.

To the contention that the balance in the hands of the receiver should be applied towards the payment of the taxes for 1893, the short answer is that these taxes were a paramount lien upon the premises when plaintiff purchased them; that it purchased subject to this lien, and presumably fixed the amount of its bid with reference to that fact. Hence the practical effect of applying this balance on these taxes would be to enable the plaintiff to get the property for that much less than its bid at the foreclosure sale. Neither is the plaintiff entitled to have the balance of the rents and profits in the hands of the receiver applied on the deficiency judgment. If it is, it must be on the ground that it has a lien, legal or equitable, on the rents and profits of the mortgaged premises, as security for the payment of the mortgage debt. It is unnecessary to consider when, and for what purposes, a mortgagee was entitled to a receivership of the rents and profits at common law, when the legal title, with the right of possession, was vested in him. Under our statute, a mortgage conveys no legal title to the mortgagee. It is but security for the debt. The mortgagor has the legal title, and is entitled to the possession until a sale has been made, and the title of the purchaser has become absolute at the expiration of the year for redemption. Under this state of the law, a mortgage binds only the land, and the rents and profits of the premises do not enter into, or form any part of, the security. Courts have sometimes been led into error by assuming an analogy or similarity between a receiver of the rents and profits and "a mortgagee in possession," who cannot be evicted until the mortgage debt is fully paid. But in this assumption they lose sight of the fact that a mortgagee in possession derives his right of possession, not under his mortgage, but under a subsequent and independent agreement with the mortgagor. This court has repeatedly held that this consent of the mortgagor is the very basis of the rights of a mortgagee in possession. We have no doubt of the power of a court, in a proper case, even under our statute, to appoint a receiver of the rents and profits of the mortgaged premises during foreclosure. Neither do we doubt that this might be done, at the instance of the purchaser, after sale, and during the year allowed for redemption. But the question is what, in view of the respective rights of mortgagor and mortgagee under the modern law of mortgages, would be a proper case for the appointment of a receiver, and for what purposes can such a receiver be appointed. As already suggested, no such appointment could be made on the ground that under the mortgage the rents and profits enter into, and become a part of, the security for the payment of the debt. Therefore, in our opinion, the only ground upon which a receiver of the rents and profits can be appointed in such a case is the equitable one that it is necessary to prevent waste, and protect and preserve the premises themselves; and this is the only purpose for which a receivership can be exercised, or for which the rents and profits can be used. The fact that the premises are inadequate security, or that the mortgagor is insolvent, or both combined, is, of itself alone, no ground for the appointment of a receiver, although it might be a very material consideration in passing upon the propriety or necessity of appointing a receiver for the purpose of preserving the premises. To hold otherwise would be to defeat the provisions of the statute which gives the right of possession to the mortgagor, to deprive him of those substantial rights which it was the evident intent he should have, and to allow the mortgagee to do indirectly what he cannot do directly. That this cannot be done would seem to be a necessary corollary from the doctrine of this court as announced in *Cullen v. Trust Co.,* 60 Minn. 6, 61 N. W. 818. It is unnecessary to consider at this time what state of facts would constitute a ground for appointing a receiver to prevent waste, and to preserve the property, but it will be found that, in every instance where this court has sustained such an appointment, it has been upon that ground; and we have recognized as sufficient causes waste, the loss of business good will resulting from the disuse of the property for the only purpose for which it was reasonably adapted, and the accumulation of delinquent taxes, or of interest on prior incumbrances, which jeopardized the mortgage security, and to the payment of which the mortgagor failed or refused to apply current rents and profits. It can hardly be necessary, in view of what has been said, to suggest that, even where a receiver has been properly appointed for the purpose of protecting and preserving the property, the rents and profits can only be used for that purpose, and not for the purpose of paying the mortgage debt. As sustaining our views, see *Wagar v. Stone,* 36 Mich. 365, and *Guy v. Ide,* 6 Cal. 99.

It must be conceded that the decisions of the courts, under similar statutes, on this question, seem to be somewhat conflicting. Doubtless, some of them have been influenced by preconceived ideas derived from the common law, while others, which hold that a receiver of the rents and profits may still be appointed, have failed to fully appreciate the limitations upon the right resulting from the change in the law of mortgages. The dissent from the doctrine of the Michigan and California decisions seems to be based upon the assumption that they hold that no receiver of the rents and profits can be appointed in any case, — not even for the purpose of preventing waste and preserving the property. Such seems to have been the impression of this court when referring to these cases in *Lowell v. Doe,* 44 Minn. 144, 46 N. W. 297. But we do not think that they can be fairly construed as going that far. No such question was before the court in either case. In *Schreiber v. Carey,* 48 Wis. 208, 4 N. W. 124, much relied on by the appellant, the appointment of a receiver was justifiable on the ground that it was necessary in order to protect and preserve the mortgage security against delinquent taxes, for which the premises had been already sold to the county, and the certificates of sale assigned to strangers, although in the lengthy opinion much is said by way of argument and illustration in which we cannot fully concur.

Order affirmed.

2. MORTGAGEE IN POSSESSION

BRUNDAGE v. HOME SAVINGS & LOAN ASS'N

Supreme Court of Washington
11 Wash. 277, 39 P. 666 (1895)

ANDERS, J. The appellant is a corporation organized and existing under the laws of the state of Minnesota, and was at all times hereinafter mentioned doing business in this state at the city of Spokane. The object for which the association was incorporated was, according to its charter, "to assist its members to buy real estate, and build, enlarge, or repair houses, paying for the same in weekly or monthly installments, and to accumulate funds from payments on stock subscribed by its members, and to loan such funds to its members on approved real-estate security or the paid-up stock of its members." It appears that, under its charter and the laws of Minnesota, it is empowered to loan its funds only to its members. It also appears that on or about July 28, 1892, the respondents made and signed an application for membership in this association, and subscribed for 160 shares of its "running" or installment stock, and agreed to abide by the terms and conditions of its charter and by-laws. The association thereupon issued and delivered its certificate for said shares of stock to the respondents, who thereby became members of said association. About the time respondents made their application for membership and subscribed for the stock above mentioned, they executed and delivered to the association a written application for a loan of $16,000, which they represented they desired for the purpose of paying off and discharging an incumbrance upon their property situated upon the northwest corner of Monroe street and College avenue, in the city of Spokane, and erecting thereon a one-story brick building, to cost $5,000. The association advanced the sum of $16,000 to the respondents, and also the further sum of $3,200, for the purpose aforesaid, to secure which sums the respondents, on August 19, 1892, executed and delivered to the appellant association two mortgages on the above-mentioned property, — one for $16,000, and the other for $3,200, — both of which were recorded on the following day. Instead of erecting the building mentioned in their application for a loan to the appellant, the respondents entered upon the construction of a building of an entirely different character, and of much greater cost, having two stories and a stone basement, not contemplated in the original plan for the building. When the building was partially erected, they found they had not sufficient funds to complete it; that it was open and exposed to the elements, and was being greatly damaged; and that liens to the extent of about $3,000 had been filed against the property. Being so circumstanced, the respondents urged the appellant to advance sufficient money to properly complete the building and offered to give additional security for the payment thereof. After some hesitation, the appellant agreed to advance the further sum of $7,500; and respondents, to secure this sum, executed a third mortgage, covering the property upon which the other two mortgages were given and other property known as the "Brundage Block," on Post street, and also their homestead in Spokane. This mortgage, so far as the Brundage block was concerned, was subject to a first mortgage, held by the defendant bank, in the sum of $10,000. To further secure the sums advanced and owing, the respondents executed to appellant, simultaneously with this last-mentioned mortgage, an agreement reciting that it was executed to secure the payment of the mortgages above mentioned, and in order to secure this loan, and providing that the rents and income should be collected and received by the defendant association, and applied to the reduction and payment of the mortgages above mentioned, to the expense of caring for said property, and collecting and disbursing said rents, and paying light and water rates, and making repairs which the mortgagee might deem necessary to have made, to the payment of any other liens existing against the property which the appellant might deem advisable to have paid; and, until all such sums were paid, the appellant was to "take and hold the exclusive possession of all the property herein mentioned"; to rent any of said property, upon such terms and conditions as seemed best to appellant; to make leases for such times and upon such terms as appellant might deem best for its interests; to care for the said property in such manner as appellant might deem proper; to employ such agents as it deemed proper, who were to have full power and authority, under the direction of appellant and at the expense of respondents, to do any and all things in regard to the said property which the appellant might deem proper to do; to apply the moneys received as above stated; and to return to the plaintiffs any moneys remaining in its hands after the foregoing application had been made; and at least once in every six months to render a true and itemized statement of all moneys received and disbursed. This agreement was duly acknowledged and properly recorded in the auditor's office of Spokane county. Before the expiration of the six months within which the appellant was, under the provisions of the contract, to furnish an itemized statement, the respondents instituted this action praying for the appointment of a receiver, for the restitution and possession of the property, for $5,000 damages for the withholding thereof, for $2,750, value of rents and profits, and for such other and further relief as to the court might seem just and proper.

The complaint alleges, . . . that, unless a receiver be appointed, the said property will be wholly lost to plaintiffs.

. . . Upon the hearing, the court appointed a permanent receiver, over the objection of the defendant, with power to take charge of and collect the rents of the property theretofore in the possession of the defendant.

It is contended by appellant that the court had no right or power to appoint a receiver in this instance, because the facts show that the appellant was a mortgagee, rightfully in possession of the premises which the respondents seek to obtain possession of in this action. At common law, a mortgagee in possession of real property, after condition broken, was deemed the absolute owner, and, as such, had a right to the possession of the property mortgaged. In fact, the mortgage was itself considered a conveyance of the property mortgaged, subject to being defeated upon payment of the amount due thereon. The mortgagee, even before condition broken, had a right to take possession of the mortgaged premises, and it logically followed, and the courts held, that ejectment would not lie against the mortgagee in possession. Under our statute, however, and the statutes of several other states, a mortgage is not considered a conveyance, but is deemed simply a lien, and the mortgagor is the owner of the incumbered premises, and cannot be dispossessed except by foreclosure and sale. But while he has a right to remain in possession of the mortgaged premises until sale thereof, he also has a right to place his mortgagee in possession; and if he does so for a valuable consideration, he is bound by the stipulations of his contract. In this case it appears that the appellant took possession of the premises in dispute with the direct assent and knowledge of the respondents, and, if it does not appear that such possession was obtained by fraud, it cannot be ousted in this proceeding, through the medium of a receiver or otherwise. We think the proof clearly shows that the possession of the appellant was not obtained by fraud, but that the respondents were aware of all of the conditions, as well as of the effect, of their contract. It also appears from the undisputed evidence filed on behalf of the appellant that the respondents, at the time the receiver was appointed, were indebted to the appellant in the sum of $2,500, as above stated; and there is nothing disclosed by the evidence which warranted the appointment of a receiver in this case to take the possession and control of the premises from the appellant. It seems that the main allegations relied upon as showing that the appellant obtained fraudulent possession of the premises are that the respondents did not recognize the validity and binding effect of the contract for possession after they became aware that it had not been formally signed and executed by the appellant, and that the appellant never advanced the $7,500 specified in the contract. It would appear from the allegations in the complaint, as well as from the evidence, that the respondents did recognize and act upon the contract prior to the time they discovered that it had not been signed by the appellant; and we think the fact that it was not signed is not proof of fraud on the part of appellant, nor is it, under the circumstances of the case, in any wise material. The appellant recognized the contract and took possession and control of the premises under it, and placed it upon record. It thus became binding upon the appellant, and it could not thereafter be heard to say that it was not its agreement. It was therefore a valid agreement as to both parties. *Muscatine Waterworks Co. v. Muscatine Lumber Co.* (Iowa) 52 N. W. 108; *Dows v. Morse* (Iowa) 17 N. W. 495; *Gas Co. v. Kibby* (Ind. Supp.) 35 N. E. 392. And the evidence shows, as matter of fact, that the $7,500 was advanced by appellant in accordance with the terms of the agreement, and expended by it in completing the building and in paying debts theretofore contracted. There having been no fraud practiced by the appellant in obtaining the possession of the premises in question, and it being undisputed that the respondents were indebted to the appellant, and it appearing that the appellant was rightfully in possession, the court had no right to deprive it of its possession by the appointment of a receiver. Beach, Rec. § 80; High, Rec. § 419.

Nor do we think the evidence shows that the building was injured or not properly constructed through any fault of the appellant or its agents. Nothing was done by the appellant, while in possession, that it was not clearly authorized to do by the express terms of the agreement. The action is in substance and effect an action of ejectment to recover the possession of the property rightfully, as we have said, in the possession of the defendant; and the mere allegations of fraud, mismanagement, and incompetency, without corroborative proof, do not entitle the respondents to the equitable relief demanded. Courts will not appoint a receiver except when it is necessary either to prevent fraud, protect property from injury, or preserve it from destruction, and mere allegations of these facts are not sufficient to authorize a court to appoint a receiver. The plaintiff must establish such facts, and make out a strong case for relief, before such appointment will be made. *Baker v. Backus,* 32 Ill. 79; *Roberts v. Sutherlin,* 4 Or. 220; *Phyfe v. Riley,* 15 Wend. 248; *Frink v. Leroy,* 49 Cal. 314; *Hamilton v. Transit Co.,* 3 Abb. Pr. 255. It is well settled that a mortgagee in possession, so long as there is any question whether the mortgage debt has been paid in full, cannot be dispossessed by an action in ejectment. Jones, Mortg. §§ 674, 1093; *Moulton v. Leighton,* 33 Fed. 143. If it were true that the appellant was committing waste upon the premises, that fact alone would not be sufficient to authorize the appointment of the receiver. *State v. Second Judicial District Court* (Mont.) 34 Pac. 609. In such a case the plaintiff could maintain an action at law for damages, or defendant might be restrained by injunction. There is no allegation or proof of insolvency on the part of the appellant. On the contrary, the proof shows that it is able to respond in damages for any injury it may cause to the premises, and therefore equitable relief is not necessary. Again, it appears that the respondents have acted under this contract and received benefits from it, and they are therefore estopped from denying its existence and force.

. . . .

The order of the court below is reversed.

Hoyt, C. J., and Scott, J., concur.

NEW YORK & SUBURBAN FEDERAL SAVINGS & LOAN ASS'N v. SANDERMAN

New Jersey Superior Court, Chancery Division
162 N.J. Super. 216, 392 A.2d 635 (1978)

Dwyer, J. S. C.

New York and Suburban Federal Savings and Loan Association (Association) commenced an action to foreclose a first mortgage it held against the lands and buildings which were formerly the Convalescent Hospital of the City of Newark.

In 1959 Newark declared the property surplus and sold it to Philip Tatz. Without my detailing the history of the title, Association has had a first mortgage on the subject premises since 1962. In the intervening years title was placed in various corporations and then conveyed to partnerships which included Philip Tatz and Bernard Bergman. By means of various documents the original mortgage was modified, extended and consolidated with other mortgages.

On September 22, 1975 a partnership consisting of Philip Tatz, Bernard Bergman *et al.,* conveyed the subject premises to Richard Sanderman and Louis Cesarano for $901,479.10. The deed recited that it was subject to a $301,479.10 mortgage in favor of Association and that a $600,000 purchase money second mortgage in favor of the grantors was the balance of the consideration. On that same date the grantors executed the last of the documents with Association which established the amount of its first mortgage as $301,479.10.

Thereafter, Bernard Bergman assigned his interest in the second mortgage to the Franklin National Bank as part of the collateral for a loan. In connection with the liquidation of that bank the Federal Deposit Insurance Corporation (FDIC) succeeded to the bank's interest in the second mortgage. It initially contested the validity of the first mortgage and a number of items for which Association claimed a right to be reimbursed for preserving the property as a mortgagee in possession. After a hearing all issues but one were resolved — that is, Association's claim to be reimbursed the sum of $45,360 for the cost of maintaining a guard on the premises 24 hours a day at a cost of $120 a day from February 5, 1977 to February 17, 1978.

This amount crystalized at the hearing. Supplemental affidavits were submitted by Association concerning the circumstances under which the expense was incurred and the need for it. Supplemental briefs were submitted on the question of law. Counsel for both parties waived further testimony and argument and requested that the court decide the matter.

In connection with the foreclosure of mortgages on real property in certain of the central cities, there have been requests for reimbursement of expenses, such as boarding up the windows and doors to protect the property against vandalism between the date of entry of the judgment of foreclosure and the time of sale. See *Cunningham and Tischler, 30 N.J. Practice, (Law of Mortgages,)* § 195 (particularly at 48 for other problems related to vandalism and a mortgagee in possession).

FDIC urges that the expense was unnecessary because the license to operate the nursing home had been revoked, the structures could not be economically used, and to salvage the land value the structures will have to be torn down; hence there was no need for guard service. Its counsel points out that the officers of the Association who testified at the hearing admitted that when the Association received an appraisal report from an outside appraiser pointing these facts out, the Association immediately suspended the guard service. To allow this sum as part of the amount to be raised will shift the cost to the junior lienholders in this case and in others to a mortgagor seeking to redeem; therefore, the FDIC urges that the sum be disallowed.

Association urges that under the decisions in *Zanzonico v. Zanzonico,* 2 *N.J.* 309, 66 *A.2d* 530 (1949), *cert. den.* 338 *U.S.* 868, 70 *S.Ct.* 143, 94 *L.Ed.* 532 (1949); *Newark v. Sue Corp.,* 124 *N.J.Super.* 5, 7-8, 304 *A.2d* 567 (App.Div.1973), a mortgagee in possession has a duty to protect against vandalism or to be held liable for loss or destruction of the property. It points to the following statement in *Zanzonico:*

> A mortgagee who goes into possession of the mortgaged lands assumes a grave responsibility for the management and preservation of the property. It is notorious that in Newark untenanted property is apt to be wrecked by vandals. When the tenants in the six-family house vacated the premises on the order of the public authorities [Tenement House Commission — ed.], complainant could have surrendered the house to Antonio's devisee Michael, or he could have made the necessary repairs and alterations and charged the cost against future rents. But he did neither; he allowed the house to remain empty and took inadequate means to protect it. He is liable for the resulting damage. . . . [at 316, 66 *A.2d* at 533]

A mortgagee who goes into possession is under a duty to maintain and preserve the property. The standard by which the discharge of that duty should be judged is that of a provident owner. *Essex Cleaning Contractors, Inc. v. Amato,* 127 *N.J.Super.* 364, 366, 317 *A.2d* 411 (App.Div. 1974), certif. den. 65 *N.J.* 575, 325 *A.2d* 709 (1974); *Cunningham and Tischler, op. cit.,* § 195 at 40. However, until the mortgagee has foreclosed he is not the owner and must act with due regard to the interests of the junior encumbrancers and the holder of the equity of redemption. *Shaeffer v. Chambers,* 6 *N.J.Eq.* 548 (Ch.1847); *cf. Taylor v. Morris,* 1 *N.J.Super.* 410, 61 *A.2d* 758 (Ch.Div.1948).

It is suggested in 4 *American Law of Property,* § 16.100 at 190, that there is a limit on the duty of the mortgagee in possession:

> He must, therefore, conserve its value by making repairs, and this duty is recognized on the one hand by charging him for any loss that flows from his failure to act and, on the other hand, by allowing him credit for expenditures in carrying it out. There are, however, limitations on this. One is that he is not bound to dig into his own pocket and so need not expend more than the rents and profits he receives. Another is that he does not have to make good or prevent the depreciation caused by ordinary wear and tear — "the silent effect of waste and decay from time." Indeed, in casting upon him this duty of affirmative conduct the standard for its invocation is "willful default," "gross negligence," or "recklessness and improvidence," a rather low standard of responsibility whose [sic] mildness is explained by the fact that the mortgagor, the owner, also should look after the upkeep of his own property. . . .

Whether this suggestion is a correct statement of the law of New Jersey in all circumstances is not necessary to decide. However, the suggestion that the extent of the duty of the mortgagee in possession is influenced by the amount of rents received or receivable does accord with the holding in *Zanzonico, supra.*

Judge Bigelow, who wrote the language quoted by the Supreme Court in *Zanzonico, supra,* in essence gave the mortgagee an option either to take possession, expending funds and collecting the expenditures from future rents, or not take possession but proceed quickly to foreclosure and sale of the real property. Under the first alternative the mortgagee, like a provident owner, would have to weigh the probability of collecting rents against the cost of repairs, taxes, insurance and the mortgagor redeeming the property. Under the second the mortgagee could proceed to foreclosure quickly and rely upon the right to collect any deficiency from the mortgagor. In no circumstance was the mortgagee to take possession and then allow the real property to be dissipated before foreclosure. In other words, the mortgagee was under a duty to evaluate what to do in the same manner as a provident owner would do. But as the Chancery Court pointed out in *Seacoast Real Estate Co. v. American Timber Co.,* 89 *N.J.Eq.* 293, 104 *A.* 437 (1918), rev'd on other grounds 92 *N.J.Eq.* 219, 113 *A.* 489 (E. & A.1920), it would not allow as part of the amount due on a mortgage on tidal lands sums expended to improve a dike so that the acreage would be increased, but only expenses for repairing an existing dike:

> Complainant when he made his expenditures in 1914 knew that he was not the owner of the premises, but only the mortgagee in possession. Assuming some repairs to the dike were necessary, the danger, at the time, of injury to the property and mortgage security, was neither imminent or impending. The expenditures were made without notice to the owners and without their knowledge, and these expenditures were made not merely for repairs, but as a part of a scheme to improve and develop the property. [at 305, 104 *A.* at 441]

Based on the record before the court, the court finds that there was a default under the first mortgage at least in January 1977. Association was aware that the patients at the nursing home had to be moved out and they were.

There is no evidence that Association had a copy of the list of physical deficiencies in the structure for use as a nursing home released by the Department of Health on September 23, 1975. However, Association is chargeable with knowledge that a nursing home in New Jersey is required to be licensed and that the physical plant must meet certain standards, *N.J.S.A.* 30:11-1 *et seq.* There is no dispute that the State had revoked the license to use the premises as a nursing home before January 1977.

In an affidavit submitted to the court the officer of Association in charge of real estate stated he visited the property on February 4, 1977 to inspect the premises. He talked to Richard Sanderman, who was one of the record owners. He further stated:

> 8. On my visit on February 4, 1977 and in reaching my recommendation [for guard service — ed.] ... I considered the physical structure, the neighborhood, the fact that the title owner to the property had paid 1.2 million dollars for the land and improvements in 1975, but I did not consider what would be the best use for the property or the value of the property in relationship to comparable sales in the community, etc.

He also stated that he learned during his inspection trip that the nearby Ivy Hill Nursing Home had been almost completely vandalized after it was closed and left unguarded. He reported to Association about the apartments and other structures in the neighborhood of the premises and recommended the employment of 24-hour guard service to prevent vandalism.

From what appears in the record, the Association made its decision to employ 24-hour guard service solely on this recommendation. According to the background of the officer set forth in the affidavit, he had worked for a construction firm in a responsible position. He had been employed by Association for five years.

The structure in question was built in the 1920s. The main portion is 141' x 44' with a full basement and two wings measuring 105' x 26'. It has a slate hip roof of wood construction. Each wing has a hallway which starts at the center and runs the length of each wing and off of which are the rooms formerly used for patients. There are no private bathroom facilities. There is little closet space. Without stating further detail, the court concurs with the finding of all appraisers that the building was least outmoded. The area in which the property is located is zoned residential.

FDIC employed its appraiser before June 1, 1977, the date of his rather extensive report. FDIC made a copy of it available to Association at least by October 1977. There is a suggestion that a copy was made available earlier, but there is insufficient evidence to so find. Association received a letter report from its own appraiser dated February 10, 1978. It reached the same conclusions as the FDIC report. All concur that the building will have to be demolished.

The court is not concerned with the question of how well Association monitored the mortgage or the activities on the premises such as the revocation of the license. The court is concerned with the action of Association after it went into possession and the inquiry which it then made.

There is no evidence that it inquired of the State Department of Health as to the circumstances, if any, under which the premises could be operated as a nursing home, or as to what could be done with the premises. It basically inquired whether the structure was weather tight and structurally sound.

Although tax assessment practices in Newark have been the subject of litigation in recent years, there is no evidence that it considered that the land was assessed at almost three times the value of the structure and for an aggregate amount $50,000 below the amount of its first mortgage.

The court finds that this is not a situation where Association acted in good faith on a temporary basis in order to secure time to find out what a provident owner should do. The court concludes that a provident owner would have rather promptly gathered the data on tax assessments, licensing condition, structural condition, zoning, neighborhood conditions and the probability of generating any income from the property while in possession, as well as various means to appropriately preserve the property. Based on the record the court concludes all this data could have been available within a week or ten days if the effort had been made to get it. The court finds that this was not done.

The court also finds that a mortgagee in possession, acting as a provident owner, would give notice at least to a holder of a junior encumbrance in the amount held by FDIC before incurring a *per diem* expense of $120 for which it would seek reimbursement.

The court concludes that Association did not act as a provident owner and denies the application for reimbursement for guard service. Since there is no evidence of any expenditure for boarding the premises up or installing a fire or burglar alarm even since the guard service was terminated, the court does not make any determination in respect to such matters.

3. RECEIVERS

Code of Laws of South Carolina

§ 15-65-10. Appointment of receiver.

A receiver may be appointed by a judge of the circuit court, either in or out of court:

(1) Before judgment, on the application of either party, when he establishes

an apparent right to property which is the subject of the action and which is in the possession of an adverse party and the property, or its rents and profits, are in danger of being lost or materially injured or impaired, except in cases when judgment upon failure to answer may be had without application to the court;

(2) After judgment, to carry the judgment into effect;

(3) After judgment, to dispose of the property according to the judgment or to preserve it during the pendency of an appeal or when an execution has been returned unsatisfied and the judgment debtor refuses to apply his property in satisfaction of the judgment;

(4) When a corporation has been dissolved, is insolvent or in imminent danger of insolvency or has forfeited its corporate rights, and, in like cases, of the property within this State of foreign corporations; and

(5) In such other cases as are provided by law or may be in accordance with the existing practice, except as otherwise provided in this Code.

West Virginia Code

§ 53-6-1. Special receiver — Appointment generally; bond; notice of application for appointment.

A court of equity may, in any proper case pending therein, in which funds or property of a corporation, firm or person is involved, and there is danger of the loss or misappropriation of the same or a material part thereof, appoint a special receiver of such funds or property, or of the rents, issues and profits thereof, or both, who shall give bond with good security to be approved by the court, or by the clerk thereof, for the faithful performance of his trust, and for paying over and accounting for, according to law, all such moneys that may come into his hands by virtue of his appointment. But no such receiver shall be appointed of any real estate, or of the rents, issues and profits thereof, until reasonable notice of the application therefor has been given to the owner or tenant thereof. A judge of such court in vacation may appoint such receiver of any such property, except real estate, and the rents, issues and profits thereof. (Code 1868, c. 133, § 28; 1882, c. 78, § 28; 1919, c. 122, § 28; Code 1923, c. 133, § 28.)

Colorado Revised Statutes

§ 38-39-113. Appointment of receiver to prevent waste.

(1) During the period of redemption the owner of the premises or the person in possession shall not commit waste, and the purchaser shall have such action or remedy for waste, including injunction, as he would have as owner of the premises. During such period the owner of the premises shall keep the premises in repair, shall use reasonable diligence to continue to keep the premises yielding an adequate income, and shall pay current taxes before a penalty accrues and interest due on any prior encumbrance, keep the premises insured for the protection of the holder of the certificate of purchase, and, in case of a leasehold, pay the rent and other sums due under the lease, and failure to do so shall constitute waste. In case of waste committed or danger of waste or an actual probability of the security being rendered inadequate, a receiver may be appointed to take possession and preserve the property at any time after the sale under such foreclosure. A receiver appointed before the sale shall continue after sale unless otherwise directed by the court.

(2) If the facts would justify the appointment of a receiver under this section but one is not applied for and if the premises are abandoned by the owner

thereof, the purchaser may take possession and shall be subject to the same duties and liabilities for the care of the premises and for the application of the rents and profits as would a receiver.

(3) Nothing in this article shall restrict the power of the court in the appointment of a receiver pursuant to existing law or pursuant to agreement between the parties.

NEILSEN v. HEALD

Supreme Court of Minnesota
151 Minn. 181, 186 N.W. 299 (1922)

TAYLOR, C. Plaintiff brought this action to foreclose a second mortgage on an apartment building in the city of Minneapolis, and procured the appointment of a receiver to collect the rents and profits during the pendency of the action. Defendant Forsythe appeals from the order appointing the receiver. So far as the record discloses the other defendants have not appeared or taken any part in the proceedings.

The title to the property was held by defendant Mary Heald until conveyed to defendant Forsythe as hereinafter stated. Defendant Anderson, a contractor and builder, constructed the apartment building and completed it in July, 1920. On February 5, 1920, the Healds executed a mortgage on the property to David P. Jones & Co. for $27,500, payable in installments, and bearing interest at the rate of 6 per centum per annum payable semiannually on the 5th day of January and July of each year. On April 15, 1920, the Healds executed a second mortgage on the property to defendant Anderson for $17,000, payable in monthly installments of $250 each, and bearing interest at the rate of 6 per centum per annum. On June 15, 1920, Anderson sold and transferred this second mortgage to plaintiff for the sum of $14,000. On August 12, 1920, the Healds sold the property to defendant Forsythe and conveyed it to him by warranty deed subject to the two mortgages which he assumed and agreed to pay as a part of the purchase price. For the remainder of the purchase price, he conveyed to the Healds a farm in Renville county of the value of $28,800, subject to a mortgage of $4,000, which farm the Healds sold and conveyed to third parties shortly thereafter. When Forsythe, who was a retired farmer living in Renville county, made his purchase, the Healds and Anderson stated and represented to him that all claims incurred in the construction of the building had been paid and satisfied and that no lienable claims of any kind were outstanding, and he relied thereon in making the purchase. These representations were not true, however, and between September 22 and December 29, 1920, liens were filed against the property amounting in the aggregate to the sum of $28,225. If valid they are prior and superior to plaintiff's mortgage. Their validity is not admitted by Forsythe and has not yet been determined in proceedings to enforce them, but plaintiff asserts that they are valid in the amount of, at least, $20,000. The value of the property is placed at $55,000, several thousand dollars less than the aggregate amount of the two mortgages and the liens. Both Anderson and the Healds are insolvent. Forsythe took possession of the property under his deed and thereafter maintained and operated it, and collected the rentals of $855 per month. He paid plaintiff seven installments of the second mortgage and $660 as interest, making a total of $2,410. He also paid the first installment of interest on the first mortgage. In January, 1921, $500 of principal and $825 of interest became due on the first mortgage, and $250 of principal and $76.25 of interest became due on the second mortgage, and these amounts still remain unpaid. Plaintiff's application for the appointment of a receiver is dated February 8, 1921. Plaintiff's mortgage contains a provision authorizing him to declare the entire amount due in case of default in any payment and he has declared the entire amount to be due, and asks judgment therefor, and that the property be sold to satisfy the same, and that he have a personal judgment against defendants for any deficiency in the amount realized from such sale.

The question before this court is whether the trial court overstepped the bounds of its judicial discretion in appointing a receiver to collect the rents and profits and care for the property during the pendency of the action. Ordinarily, under our law, the mortgagor or his successor in interest is entitled to the possession of the property and to the rents and profits therefrom during foreclosure proceedings and until the expiration of the period of redemption (*Marshall & Ilsley Bank v. Cady,* 76 Minn. 112, 78 N. W. 978); but, if he permits waste of a character to impair the security, and the security is inadequate and those personally liable for the debt are insolvent, a receiver may be appointed to take charge of the property and to apply the rents and profits, or so much thereof as may be necessary for that purpose, in protecting it from preventable waste. 19 R. C. L. 560, 563; *Lowell v. Doe,* 44 Minn. 144, 46 N. W. 297; *Haugan v. Netland,* 51 Minn. 552, 53 N. W. 873; *Marshall & Ilsley Bank v. Cady,* 76 Minn. 112, 78 N. W. 978; *Donnelly v. Butts,* 137 Minn. 1, 162 N. W. 674; *Justus v. Fagerstrom,* 141 Minn. 323, 170 N. W. 201.

Speaking in general terms it may be said that a mortgagor is chargeable with waste within the meaning of the rule whenever, through the fault of the mortgagor, the mortgagee loses some part of the security which he had when he took his mortgage. Failure to pay claims or charges which were not liens on the property when the mortgage was taken but which, if not paid, will become liens thereon superior to the mortgage is deemed waste within the rule. Failure to pay interest on prior mortgages or to pay taxes falls within this species of waste. *Lowell v. Doe,* 44 Minn. 144, 46 N. W. 297; *Haugen v. Netland,* 51 Minn. 552, 53 N. W. 873; *Cullen v. Minnesota L. & T. Co.,* 60 Minn. 6, 61 N. W. 818; *Farmers' Nat. Bank v. Backus,* 64 Minn. 43, 66 N. W. 5; *Marshall & Ilsley Bank v. Cady,* 75 Minn. 241, 77 N. W. 831; *Donnelly v. Butts,* 137 Minn. 1, 162 N. W. 674.

Plaintiff, having applied for the appointment of a receiver, had the burden of proving, by clear and convincing evidence, that his security had become impaired by waste caused or permitted by the defendants. *Northland Pine Co. v. Melin Bros., Inc.,* 136 Minn. 236, 161 N. W. 407, 1 A. L. R. 1463. But the order appointing the receiver was, in effect, a finding that all the facts necessary to authorize such appointment had been established. The finding that plaintiff's security was inadequate must stand, for the court could find that plaintiff's mortgage together with the valid prior incumbrances exceeded the value of the property by a substantial amount. It is conceded that Anderson and the Healds are wholly insolvent, but plaintiff's assertion that Forsythe is also insolvent is emphatically denied by the latter and plaintiff adduced no evidence to prove it. Although Forsythe asserts that he is solvent, he does not concede that he is personally liable for the payment of the mortgages. On the contrary he sets forth facts, seemingly undisputed, which are sufficient to constitute a complete defense on the ground of fraud to any action brought to enforce such liability. On this state of the record we think the court was justified in finding that plaintiff must look solely to his security for the payment of his mortgage.

The inadequacy of the security and the insolvency of those personally liable for the debt are not of themselves sufficient grounds for the appointment of a receiver, for the rents and profits are no part of the security, and the mortgagee is not entitled to them. To obtain the appointment of a receiver the mortgagee must show not only that the security is inadequate and the debtor insolvent, but also that his security is becoming impaired through the wrongful failure of the mortgagor or his successor in interest to protect the property from waste.

Plaintiff assigns the following as the grounds upon which defendants are chargeable with waste: That they permitted an installment of both principal and interest on the first mortgage to become delinquent; that they permitted mechanics' liens to become liens on the property superior to his mortgage; and that defendant Forsythe is appropriating the rents and profits to his own use instead of applying them to the payment of the liens and the interest on the first mortgage, and intends to continue to do so in the future.

Defendants are not chargeable with waste for failing to discharge claims which were liens on the property at the time plaintiff's mortgage was taken. *Marshall & Ilsley Bank v. Cady,* 76 Minn. 112, 78 N. W. 978; *National Fire Ins. Co. v. Broadbent,* 77 Minn. 175, 79 N. W. 676. The rents and profits form no part of the security acquired under the mortgage, and the mortgagee can reach them only by invoking the equitable powers of the court, and then only to the extent necessary to protect the property from deterioration and from liens arising out of claims which were suffered to accrue after the mortgage was taken but which, if not paid, will take precedence over the mortgage. In other words he has no right to have the rents and profits applied for his benefit except in so far as may be necessary to give him the same security which he had when his mortgage was taken. *Sales v. Lusk,* 60 Wis. 490, 19 N. W. 362.

The principal of the first mortgage was an existing lien when the second was taken and the failure to pay installments thereof furnished no ground for the appointment of a receiver.

Under our statute all the mechanics' liens attached and took effect at the time the first item of material or labor for the building was furnished on the premises. G. S. 1913, § 7023; *Erickson v. Ireland,* 134 Minn. 156, 158 N. W. 918. The record fails to show when these liens in fact attached, or when the material and labor which gave rise to them was actually furnished, but, as plaintiff concedes that they are prior and superior to his mortgage, they must be deemed to have existed when the mortgage was taken, at least in the absence of proof that they accrued for labor and material furnished thereafter. It follows that the failure to pay these liens furnished no ground for the appointment of a receiver. Whether the failure to pay a lien for labor and material shown to have been furnished after the mortgage was taken would constitute a ground for the appointment of a receiver is not involved in this case and is not determined, for no such showing was made and the burden of making it rested on plaintiff.

Interest in the sum of $825 became due on the first mortgage and remains unpaid. This fact furnished a ground for the appointment of a receiver, if it further appeared that Forsythe had rents and profits out of which he ought to have discharged this interest. The evidence bearing on this question is not very clear or definite, but we think is sufficient to sustain the finding of the trial court within the rule which governs this court when reviewing such findings. By appointing the receiver the court necessarily determined that plaintiff's security had become endangered to such an extent that the court ought to take control of the property for his protection. The existence of the mechanics' liens was unknown to Forsythe and apparently also to plaintiff until the statements therefor were filed. The assertion of these liens made a radical change in the situation. If they are valid — and that the major part of them are valid does not seem to be seriously questioned — Forsythe stands to lose his entire investment, and plaintiff a portion of his mortgage. In this situation there is little, if any, inducement for Forsythe to apply rents and profits received by him in reducing the incumbrances, and we cannot say that the court exceeded its discretion in taking control of the property through its receiver for the purpose of applying the rents and profits as the law directs.

Order affirmed.

DIBELL, J. I dissent. The taxes and insurance have been paid and the property is in good condition. The claim of waste rests upon the failure to pay $850 in interest which became due on the first mortgage in the early part of January, 1921. Forsythe is apparently solvent. Whether he is personally liable on the mortgage notes seems a matter of controversy. The failure to pay interest on a first mortgage is not waste as to the mortgagee in a second mortgage unless the property produces an income with which to pay it. The mortgaged property is income-bearing. There is no showing that the plaintiff has used the income for purposes other than the payment of taxes and insurance and interest and upkeep. It is a fair inference from the record that an amount equal to the income has been used in protection of the property. The appointment of a receiver is a drastic remedy. Forsythe was greatly wronged by Anderson. So was the plaintiff, though in taking the $17,000 mortgage he got a $3,000 discount and has that much margin. Forsythe is the greater sufferer. He wants to save something if he can. He seems to be acting in good faith. His efforts should not be unnecessarily forestalled. A receivership means expense and waste, and embarrassment to him in his efforts. Viewing his situation as well as that of the plaintiff there is no compelling equity calling for the appointment of a receiver. It seems to me that the appointment of a receiver, under the circumstances, is inequitable.

HALLAM, J. I agree with the above.

UNION GUARDIAN TRUST CO. v. RAU

Supreme Court of Michigan
255 Mich. 324, 238 N.W. 166 (1931)

SHARPE, J.
On August 16, 1928, the defendant Litta W. Rau executed a promissory note, payable to the plaintiff, in the sum of $100,000, secured by a mortgage on certain real estate in the city of Detroit. Default having occurred in the payment of a part of the principal and of interest and taxes, this bill was filed for the foreclosure of the mortgage. It contained a provision under which the mortgagee in case of default was entitled: "To the appointment by any competent Court or Tribunal, without notice to any party of a Receiver of the rents, issues and profits of the said premises with power to lease the said premises, or such part thereof as may not then be under lease, and with such other powers as may be deemed necessary. . . ."

Pursuant thereto, the plaintiff petitioned for the appointment of a receiver, and, after notice to the defendants and a hearing thereon, an order was entered appointing the plaintiff, the mortgagee, receiver, of which the defendants here seek review by appeal.

On August 16, 1928, the defendant Litta W. Rau conveyed the premises in question to David R. Cass, now deceased. Gerson Cass, individually and as administrator of the estate of David R. Cass, and Gertie Cass were made defendants as claimants of the interest of David R. Cass in the property.

The right of a mortgagee to dispossess a mortgagor, or one holding under him, in the event of default, was before this court in the somewhat recent case of *Nusbaum v. Shapero,* 249 Mich. 252, 228 N. W. 785, 786. The mortgage in that case ran to the plaintiff as trustee to secure the issue of first mortgage bonds. It contained a provision under which the trustee was entitled to possession in the event of default, and the bill was filed to secure specific performance of this provision. Plaintiff had decree, and on appeal to this court there was modification thereof, limiting plaintiff's rights to the recovery of sums due for taxes and insurance premiums. In that case, Mr. Justice Butzel, speaking for the court, said: "The law is well settled in this state that as a rule a mortgagee may not divest the mortgagor of possession of mortgaged premises until the title thereto shall have become absolute upon foreclosure of the mortgage."

The statute and decisions of this court on which this rule was founded were cited and quoted from at some length, and need not be here repeated. It was thereafter said: "We do not find the exact question ever passed upon by this court in a case where the facts were similar to the one at issue. We believe, however, that a court of equity should not refuse to lend its aid where defendants have taken property subject to a trust mortgage with provisions similar to the one hereinbefore described, where the public, who have bought the bonds, should be protected, where there is uncertainty in regard to the present owners of the title, where the income from the property is far in excess of the requirements for the upkeep of the property, where there is already an outstanding tax title and other taxes are not being paid, where insurance premiums are likewise unpaid, and where the mortgagee may have no financial interest in the mortgage except to carry out his duties as trustee."

As will be seen from this statement, decision was based upon the fact that, under a trust mortgage, the plaintiff, being a naked trustee, could not otherwise protect the rights of the bondholders whose interests were dependent upon their security being held intact.

It is urged that "nonpayment of taxes by mortgagor in possession constitutes waste," and that a receiver may be appointed to protect the mortgagee therefrom. Where the mortgagee is a trustee, with no financial interest in the mortgage, such protection may be deemed necessary. But in the case of a mortgagee such as we have here, and considering the time which must elapse before a tax title may be acquired, we see no reason for affording such protection by the appointment of a receiver. See *Jenks v. Horton,* 96 Mich. 13, 55 N. W. 372. In *Minnesota Building & Loan Ass'n v. Murphy,* 176 Minn. 71, 222 N. W. 516, 517, it was said: "It clearly appears that the only justification for a receiver is nonpayment of taxes. . . . It has been held that nonpayment of taxes is a species of waste, but although so denominated this sort of waste alone does not justify the appointment of a receiver of the property during the running of the year of redemption. . . . There are no exceptional circumstances connected with the only item of waste found, namely, the nonpayment of the taxes. The amount thereof is not large. If it were a case where the delinquent taxes might ripen into a title before the sale or before the year of redemption expired, a different question as to the consequence of this waste might be presented. But as it appears from this record we must hold the appointment of the receiver unwarranted."

Several cases from that court were cited in support of this holding.

The order appointing a receiver is reversed and set aside, with costs to defendants.

NOTES

1. From the cases in this section the reader can see that receivers, mortgagees in possession, and assignees of rents and profits can sometimes be considered interchangeable by the courts. In some instances the mortgagee takes possession by virtue of the law in that jurisdiction (title or intermediate hybrid states), and in others as a result of the mortgage itself (lien theory states). The receiver appointed by the court may be the mortgagee, but in most cases will be a disinterested but responsible third person. In some instances the rents and profits are not available as part of the security unless there has been an assignment of the rents and profits in the mortgage.

2. The criteria for the appointment of a receiver varies considerably from state to state. The three statutes in this section illustrate that variety. Notice that of the three examples, only the Colorado statute refers to waste as such. West Virginia refers to a loss of the property as well as the rents and profits, while South Carolina refers to the property being "materially injured or impaired." Does South Carolina really mean "if waste is being committed"? Generally waste must be shown in order to obtain the appointment of a receiver unless there is statutory authority otherwise permitting a receiver.

3. Whether the failure to pay taxes is waste will vary depending upon how stringent the waste requirement is for the appointment of a receiver. If a receiver cannot be appointed without a finding of waste, then failure to pay taxes will likely be held waste as in *Union Guardian Trust Co. v. Rau, supra*. However, for the opposite approach see *American Medical Services, Inc. v. Mutual Federal Savings & Loan Ass'n*, 52 Wis. 2d 198, 188 N.W.2d 529 (1971). There the court held " [t]he term 'waste' has been broadly construed to include not only the deterioration of property but the failure to pay interest and taxes where they were pledged as security."

B. FORECLOSURE

Having departed from the harshness of Law Day and forfeiture found at common law, the American way of foreclosure seems much more equitable. It is for the most part comparable to foreclosure by sale in England. However, there are two very different means of foreclosure, and the last remaining vestiges of a third, used in the United States. The three are, in order of usage, judicial foreclosure, power of sale foreclosure, and strict foreclosure.

Judicial foreclosure is available in all fifty states. It is accomplished by litigation commenced by the mortgagee against the mortgagor and any junior lienors on the property. If the mortgagee is successful in proving the obligation and a default, the trial will result in a judgment fixing the amount of the debt due and directing a sale of the property. The sale is conducted by the person either designated by statute or appointed by the court.[7] A public auction is held and the property sold to the highest bidder in cash.[8] The mortgagee can bid the amount of the debt without involving cash since the mortgagor owes the amount of the debt to the mortgagee already. The proceeds of the sale are used to satisfy the debt fixed by the judgment. If the sale generates less than the debt, the mortgagee may have a judgment for the difference if the jurisdiction allows deficiency judgments. If the sale generates a surplus beyond the amount of the debt owed the foreclosing mortgagee, the proceeds in excess are distributed pursuant to either statute or judgment. Generally the surplus will go to junior lienors in chronological order first, and then to the mortgagor. Senior lienors participate in the proceeds only if their debt is also due. If it is not, the purchaser at the foreclosure sale takes title subject to the senior lien.

Power of sale foreclosure, also known as non-judicial foreclosure, does not

---

[7] C.J.S. *Mortgages* § 728, p. 1322.

[8] Ohio Rev. Code Ann. § 2329.52 (Page 1954).

involve litigation but requires certain statutory procedures be followed, such as posting,[9] publication,[10] mailing of notice,[11] or recording notice.[12] No judgment is entered against the mortgagor. If the proceeds of sale are insufficient to satisfy the debt, the mortgagee must then commence litigation to obtain a deficiency judgment, where permitted.

Strict foreclosure is a procedure used in some states today to quiet the title of a purchaser at a previous foreclosure sale following a judicial foreclosure from which a junior lienor has been omitted. This process is discussed later in the section Parties Omitted from a Foreclosure *infra* p. 240. However, a procedure for strict foreclosure has been used until recently in Vermont, Illinois, and Connecticut. Its usage was limited to instances where the mortgagor was insolvent and the mortgagee was willing to accept the land as full satisfaction of the obligation. Now it appears that Connecticut is the only remaining state to utilize strict foreclosure for a mortgagee.

Statutory Authority for Foreclosure in the United States

	JUDICIAL	NON-JUDICIAL
ALABAMA	Ala. Code § 35-10-3 (1975)	§ 35-10-1
ALASKA	Alaska Stat. § 09.41.170 (1962)	§ 34.20.080
ARIZONA	Ariz. Rev. Stat. § 33-721 (1974)	
ARKANSAS	Ark. Stat. Ann. § 51-1106 (1947)	§ 51.1112
CALIFORNIA	Cal. Civ. Code §§ 725, 726 (West 1970)	§ 2931, § 2932, § 858
COLORADO	Colo. Rev. Stat. § 13-52-102 (1973)	§ 38-32-114
CONNECTICUT	Conn. Gen. Stat. Ann. (1960) §§ 49.24, 49-17	
DELAWARE	Del. Code tit. 10, § 5061 (1974)	§ 45-603
DISTRICT OF COLUMBIA	D.C. Code § 45-616 (1973)	§ 45-603
FLORIDA	Fla. Stat. § 702.01 (1973)	
GEORGIA	Ga. Code § 67-201 (1975)	§ 37-607
HAWAII	Haw. Rev. Stat. § 36-667-5 (1967)	§ 36-667-1
IDAHO	Idaho Code § 6-101 (1967)	§ 45-1503
ILLINOIS	Ill. Ann. Stat. ch. 95, § 23 (Smith-Hurd 1950)	
INDIANA	Ind. Code Ann. § 32-8-11-3 (Burns 1973)	
IOWA	Iowa Code Ann. § 654.1 (1950)	

---

[9] Cal. Civ. Code § 2924(f).
[10] Cal. Civ. Code § 2924(f).
[11] Cal. Civ. Code § 2924(b).
[12] Cal. Civ. Code § 2924.

	JUDICIAL	NON-JUDICIAL
KANSAS	Kan. Stat. Ann. § 60-2401 (1964)	§ 58-2418
KENTUCKY	Ky. Rev. Stat. § 426.005 (1970)	
LOUISIANA	La. Civ. Code Ann. art. 3398 (1950)	
MAINE	Me. Rev. Stat. tit. 14 § 6201 (1964)	
MARYLAND	Md. Real Prop. Code Ann. § 14-103 (1974)	§ 7-105
MASSACHUSETTS	Mass. Gen. Laws Ann. ch. 244, § 1 (1959)	ch. 244, § 11
MICHIGAN	Mich. Comp. Laws § 600.3101 (1970)	§ 600.3201
MINNESOTA	Minn. Stat. § 581.01 (1947)	§ 580.01
MISSISSIPPI	Miss. Code Ann. § 11-5-1 (1972) or Art. 4 § 111 (1972)	§ 89-1-55
MISSOURI	Mo. Rev. Stat. § 443.190 (1949)	§ 443.290 (mortgage) § 443.410 (trust deed)
MONTANA	Mont. Rev. Codes Ann. § 52-111 (1963)	§ 52-112
NEBRASKA	Neb. Rev. Stat. § 25-2137 (1943)	
NEVADA	Nev. Rev. Stat. § 21.150 (1973)	§ 107.080
NEW HAMPSHIRE	N.H. Rev. Stat. Ann. § 479.19 (1966)	§ 479.25
NEW JERSEY	N.J. Rev. Stat. § 25-331 (1937)	
NEW MEXICO	N.M. Stat. Ann. § 61-7-7 (1953)	
NEW YORK	N.Y. Real Prop. Acts. Law § 1351 (Consol. 1963)	§ 1401
NORTH CAROLINA	N.C. Gen. Stat. § 1-339.1 (1966)	§ 45-21.1
NORTH DAKOTA	N.D. Cent. Code § 32-19-01 (1972)	§ 35-22-01
OHIO	Ohio Rev. Code Ann. § 2329.09 (1953)	
OKLAHOMA	Okla. Stat. Ann. tit. 12, § 686 (1951)	46 § 32 (trust deed) 60 § 198 (mortgage)
OREGON	Or. Rev. Stat. § 88.010 (1971)	§ 86.735
PENNSYLVANIA	Pa. Stat. Ann. tit. 21, § 791 (1967)	
RHODE ISLAND	R.I. Gen. Laws § 34-27-1 (1956)	§ 34-11-22

	JUDICIAL	NON-JUDICIAL
SOUTH CAROLINA	S.C. Code § 29-3-650 (1976)	
SOUTH DAKOTA	S.D. Comp. Laws Ann. § 21-47-1 (1967)	§ 21-48-1
TENNESSEE	Tenn. Code Ann. § 21-1208 (1956)	
TEXAS	Tex. Civ. Pro. Rules Ann., Rule 309 (1977)	Tex. Stat. Ann. art. § 3810 (1979 Supp.)
UTAH	Utah Code Ann. § 78-37-1 (1953)	§ 57-1-23
VERMONT	Vt. Stat. Ann. tit. 12, § 4526	
VIRGINIA	Va. Code § 8.01-462 (1950)	§ 55-59
WASHINGTON	Wash. Rev. Code § 61.12.060 (1975)	§ 61.24.020 § 61.24.030
WEST VIRGINIA	W. Va. Code § 38-1-1 (1966)	§ 38-1-3
WISCONSIN	Wis. Stat. Ann. §§ 278.01, 846.01 (West 1976)	§ 297.01 § 816.51
WYOMING	Wyo. Stat. § 1-18-111 (1977)	§ 34-4-102

1. JUDICIAL FORECLOSURE

D'AGOSTINO v. WHEEL INN, INC.

Rockland County Court
65 Misc. 2d 227, 317 N.Y.S.2d 472 (1970)

JOHN A. GALLUCCI, JUDGE:

On May 8, 1963, the defendant, The Wheel Inn, Inc., executed and delivered to the plaintiff its corporate note in the principal sum of $20,000.00, together with interest thereon at the rate of six per centum per annum on the original amount of principal indebtedness. The note is payable in equal monthly installments of $266.00, commencing June 8, 1963, and continuing monthly thereafter until fully paid. The corporate note was executed by its president, Frank P. Sinopoli. He also personally guaranteed the payment of the corporate obligation. Simultaneously and as security for said note, the corporation executed and delivered its mortgage to plaintiff upon premises owned by it and located in Rockland County, New York, which mortgage was recorded in the Rockland County Clerk's Office in Liber 791 of Mortgages, at page 1181. As collateral security for said corporate obligations, plaintiff also obtained from the individual defendant Frank P. Sinopoli and his wife, Rose Sinopoli, their individual bond and mortgage in the principal sum of $10,000.00, together with interest thereon at the rate of six per centum per annum on the original amount of principal indebtedness. The individual bond and mortgage also provides for monthly installment payments of $266.00 each, commencing June 8, 1963, and continuing monthly thereafter until fully paid, and mortgages their premises at Stony Point, Rockland County, New York. The individuals' mortgage is recorded in the Rockland County Clerk's Office in Liber 792 of Mortgages, at page 328.

Plaintiff commenced an action against The Wheel Inn, Inc., and Frank P.

Sinopoli by the service of a summons and complaint dated December 28, 1967. The complaint alleged default in the payment of the monthly installments provided for by the corporate note commencing March 8, 1967, to and including December 8, 1967. The named defendants have entered a general denial to plaintiff's complaint, an affirmative defense thereto and, also, three counterclaims on behalf of the defendant Frank P. Sinopoli and two counterclaims by the defendant The Wheel Inn, Inc. The plaintiff has replied to the counterclaims and said action is presently pending before the Court.

The plaintiff has, by summons and complaint dated October 30, 1970, commenced a second action against the defendant The Wheel Inn, Inc., and others, to foreclose the hereinbefore mentioned corporate mortgage dated May 8, 1963. Plaintiff's second action alleges default in making monthly payments as provided by said mortgage commencing March 8, 1967, and continuing until October 8, 1970. It seeks judgment of foreclosure and sale and a deficiency judgment against the defendant The Wheel Inn, Inc.

The defendants, The Wheel Inn, Inc., and Scotland Hill Investors, Ltd., now move for an order pursuant to Rule 3211 CPLR dismissing plaintiff's complaint on the grounds that plaintiff's foreclosure action is barred by the prior pending action and that plaintiff has failed to obtain the consent of the Court to the commencement of its foreclosure action as required by Section 1301 Real Property Actions and Proceedings Law.

Plaintiff opposes the motion and cross-moves for an order (1) discontinuing plaintiff's first action; (2) severing the counterclaims set forth in the first action; (3) consolidating plaintiff's foreclosure action with said counterclaims; and (4) granting leave to plaintiff to maintain his present foreclosure action.

The parties do not dispute that plaintiff's first action is to recover a part of the mortgage debt secured by the mortgage now sought to be foreclosed and is still pending before this Court.

Each party relies on Section 1301 RPA&PL in support of their respective applications. The defendants contend that plaintiff has not obtained the required leave of the Court to commence its foreclosure action and the plaintiff requests that the Court grant its consent to the continuance of its foreclosure action.

The Court has carefully reviewed Section 1301 RPA&PL and finds that plaintiff's foreclosure action is not barred by its prior pending action. The Court also finds that the leave of the Court is not a necessary prerequisite to plaintiff's commencement and maintenance of its foreclosure action.

Section 1301 RPA&PL, which is entitled "Separate Action for mortgage debt" provides as follows:

1. Where final judgment for the plaintiff has been rendered in an action to recover any part of the mortgage debt, an action shall not be commenced or maintained to foreclose the mortgage, unless an execution against the property of the defendant has been issued upon the judgment to the sheriff of the county where he resides, if he resides within the state, or if he resides without the state, to the sheriff of the county where the judgment-roll is filed; and has been returned wholly or partly unsatisfied.

2. The complaint shall state whether any other action has been brought to recover any part of the mortgage debt, and, if so, whether any part has been collected.

3. While the action is pending or after final judgment for the plaintiff therein, no other action shall be commenced or maintained to recover any part of the mortgage debt, without leave of the court in which the former action was brought. Added L.1962, c. 312, § 27, eff. Sept. 1, 1963.

In the instant case, plaintiff has not obtained a final judgment in its pending action to recover a part of the mortgage debt. (Section 1301, subd. 1, RPA&PL). The complaint in plaintiff's foreclosure action alleges the pendency of plaintiff's prior action and, therefore, is not subject to dismissal for failure to comply with Section 1301, subd. 2, RPA&PL. Plaintiff's foreclosure action has been commenced subsequent to its pending action and does not require the leave of the court provided for in Section 1301, subd. 3, RPA&PL.

Section 1301 RPA&PL does clearly bar a foreclosure action where final judgment has been obtained by a plaintiff in an action to recover any part of the mortgage debt until after execution has been returned wholly or partly unsatisfied. Said section also clearly requires the leave of the court to commence an action to recover any part of the mortgage debt while a foreclosure action is pending or after final judgment has been awarded to a plaintiff therein.

Section 1301 RPA&PL does not, however, set forth the procedure to be followed where a plaintiff commences an action to recover a part of the mortgage debt, and while such action is pending and before any final judgment is obtained therein, then commences an action to foreclose the mortgage securing the debt. It also fails to make provision where, as in this case, the defendants in each action are not common defendants.

In the absence of an express statutory prohibition, "A prior pending action at law to recover on the bond is not a bar to a suit in equity to foreclose the mortgage which collaterally secures its payment. *(Gillette v. Smith,* 18 Hun 10; *Suydam v. Bartle,* 9 Paige 294; *Williamson v. Champlin,* 8 Paige 70.)" *(Sologub v. Sologub,* 200 Misc. 829, at page 831, 111 N.Y.S.2d 423 at page 425).

The Court finds that although Section 1301 RPA&PL restricts and limits the rights of a holder and owner of a bond or note and mortgage to pursue, at the same time, alternate remedies in enforcement thereof, it does not totally bar or prohibit concurrent actions by a plaintiff or require the leave of the Court in all instances of dual enforcement of remedies. Indeed, if it was the legislative intent to absolutely prohibit simultaneous actions to foreclose the mortgage and to recover on the mortgage debt secured thereby, the legislature would have so provided. It also would not have enacted subd. 3 of Section 1301 RPA&PL, which permits both actions to proceed after leave of the Court has been obtained and, further, requires leave of the Court only when a plaintiff seeks to commence an action to recover a part of the mortgage debt either during or after a prior foreclosure action.

The Court in making its decision is fully aware that Section 1301 RPA&PL and its predecessor sections, Sections 1077 and 1078 Civil Practice Act, and Rule 255 Rules of Civil Practice, indicate a general legislative policy of the State of New York that the owner and holder of a bond or note and mortgage may not, without court consent, pursue his election of remedies at the same time. *(Kamerman v. C. D. C. Furniture Manufacturing Corporation,* 5 Misc.2d 27, 162 N.Y.S.2d 999). The Court is also aware that courts of the State of New York have repeatedly ruled that although the owner and holder of a bond or note and mortgage has two remedies in enforcement thereof, namely, to recover a judgment for the debt owed, or to proceed to foreclose the mortgage secured thereby, a party may not pursue or enforce both remedies at the same time. *(White Factors, Inc. v. Friedman,* 32 Misc.2d 978, 224 N.Y.S.2d 339; *First National Bank & Trust Co. of Walton v. Eisenrod,* 263 App.Div. 227, 32 N.Y.S.2d 641; *White v. Wielandt,* 259 App.Div. 676, 20 N.Y.S.2d 560, am'd on other grounds, 260 App.Div. 871, 23 N.Y.S.2d 476, aff'd 286 N.Y. 609, 36 N.E.2d 452; *President and*

Directors of Manhattan Company v. Callister Brothers, 256 App. Div. 1097, 11 N.Y.S.2d 593; *French v. French,* 107 App.Div. 107, 94 N.Y.S. 1026; *Dudley v. Congregation Third Order of St. Francis,* 138 N.Y. 451, 34 N.E. 281). Judicial findings regarding the extent and application of the prohibitory rule have not, however, been consistent. (See *Daint-I-Way Laundry v. Suey H. Ng,* Sup., 89 N.Y.S.2d 867; *Sologub v. Sologub,* supra).

The Court's decision is based upon a strict construction of Section 1301 RPA&PL, which statute is itself in derogation of the right of a party plaintiff at common law to pursue his alternate remedies of foreclosure and an action to recover the mortgage debt at the same time.

Since Section 1301 RPA&PL as it presently exists does not expressly cover the factual situation set forth in this instant matter, and because of the apparent conflicting court rulings on said factual situation, clarification by legislation or decision of an appellate court would be appropriate.

Accordingly, defendants' motion is denied.

The Court having denied defendants' motion, plaintiff's cross-motions have become moot and are denied without prejudice.

a. Parties Omitted from a Foreclosure

MURPHY v. FARWELL

Supreme Court of Wisconsin
9 Wis. 102 (1859)

By the Court, PAINE, J. This case has once been in this court on a demurrer to the complainant's bill. It was a bill to redeem certain premises from a sale on the foreclosure of a first mortgage, the complainant claiming under a second mortgage which he had owned and foreclosed, buying, himself, at the sale. He was not made a party to the first foreclosure suit, nor did he make those interested in the first mortgage nor *Farwell* the purchaser under it, parties to his foreclosure suit. The demurrer was urged on the ground that by foreclosing and selling on the second mortgage the complainant had so changed his position as to have lost the right to redeem and that his bill was in the nature of an ejectment in equity. The case is reported in 2 Wis., 533, from which it appears that this court held that the complainant upon the facts set forth in the bill, had a right to redeem; and the demurrer was overruled.

The case was sent back to the circuit where various proceedings were had; including answers by the defendants; a change of venue to Racine county; the taking of testimony and preparation for final hearing; when the defendant *Farwell* having filed a petition claiming the right to redeem the premises, by paying the amount of the decree in the second foreclosure suit, interest and costs; paid the money into court, except the costs in this suit; and the court entered a decree adjudging *Farwell* to be the owner of the fee, and *Murphy* to have only the rights of a subsequent mortgagee; that *Farwell* had the right to pay off *Murphy's* lien, and ordered the bill to be dismissed on payment of the costs in this suit, within ten days after notice of their taxation. The costs were paid, and from that decree the complainant appeals to this court.

It was urged by the counsel for the appellant, on the argument that inasmuch as neither of these parties was bound by the proceedings in the foreclosure suit of the other, that the result of the two foreclosures and sales was to vest in each a perfect title to the premises, as against all the world except the other, and that all that was necessary for either to perfect his title was to pay off the amount paid by the other. That this right was mutual, neither having any superiority over the other, but both standing originally on a footing of entire equality; and this being the case, he urged that the complainant, by his greater diligence in first offering to redeem, had acquired a superior equity over *Farwell*, who had delayed through several years of litigation to make any offer or attempt to exercise the right on his part.

But the counsel for the respondent contended that these parties did not stand on an equal footing after their respective sales. But that, on the contrary, *Farwell* purchasing at the sale under the first mortgage, acquired the entire right of the owner of the first mortgage, and the entire equity of redemption, subject only to the second mortgage, while *Murphy* purchasing at the sale under the second mortgage, in a proceeding against *Cady* alone, acquired nothing by his purchase, so far as the lots covered by both mortgages were concerned, for the reason that *Cady's* interest had been entirely divested by the previous sale on the first mortgage. So that *Farwell* owning the entire property in fee, subject only to the second mortgage, and *Murphy* owning only the interest represented by the second mortgage, *Farwell* had an absolute right to pay the second mortgage and extinguish its lien, as he was allowed to do by the court below. The case must be decided according to the correctness of the one or the other of these theories.

And we must confess at the outset that the proposition of the appellant's counsel seems to us difficult to comprehend, or to be arrived at. We understood him to insist that the purchaser at each of these sales acquired among other rights the entire equity of redemption in those lots covered by both mortgages, as against all the world, except the other. We cannot understand how such a result could have been accomplished.

It would seem obvious that if the sale under the first mortgage was operative at all, that it would have conveyed to *Farwell*, the purchaser, the entire equity of redemption remaining in *Cady*, who was a party to that suit. If this was done, it is difficult to see how the same equity of redemption could have been conveyed to *Murphy* at the second sale. If it did remain to be conveyed to *Murphy* at that sale, it is equally difficult to understand by what process of reasoning it could still be shown to be in *Farwell*.

If such a complex condition of things could be produced at all, it must have been from one or both of the following reasons, as no others were suggested: First, because *Murphy* was not a party to the first suit; or, secondly, because the rule of *lis pendens* applied to the sale, at which *Farwell* purchased; the second foreclosure suit being pending at that time. Let us see if either of these reasons is sufficient to produce such a result.

It seems very clear that the first is not. For if *Murphy* had not commenced his foreclosure suit until after the first sale, there can be no doubt that the entire interest remaining in *Cady* would have been transferred by that sale to *Farwell*, not only as against all the world, except *Murphy*, but as against *Murphy* himself. Of course, he not being a party, his rights would not have been affected by the proceedings. *Farwell* would have taken *Cady's* interest just as *Cady* held it, that is, subject to *Murphy's* mortgage. But he would have taken it, the whole of it, as well against *Murphy* as against *Cady* himself. And it needs hardly be said, that this is not at all inconsistent with the doctrine that a person, not a party to a proceeding is not bound by it; for it is very obvious that *Murphy's* rights would have remained quite as perfect as before, only in pursuing them he would have to pursue a different party. For a subsequent foreclosure against *Cady*, and a sale under it, would, as to the lots covered by the first mortgage, have been a mere nullity. It seems very clear, therefore, that the fact that *Murphy* was not a party to the first suit, did not prevent the entire interest of *Cady* from being tansferred to *Farwell* by the sale, as well against *Murphy* as everybody else.

Would the doctrine of *lis pendens*, applied to the first sale, have produced the result contended for? It seems to us clearly not; because the entire equity of redemption being still in *Cady* at the time of commencing the second suit; then if the doctrine of *lis pendens* applied to the sale to *Farwell* in the first suit, *Murphy* at the purchase in the second suit would have taken the entire interest of *Cady,* as well against *Farwell* as against *Cady,* because such we understand to be the precise effect of the rule of *lis pendens;* that is, that a purchaser within a rule, is just as much bound by the final decree or judgment rendered, as is the party whose right he purchases. And he cannot by such a purchase prevent the one pursuing the property by litigation from obtaining his judgment or decree with the same effect it would have had if no such purchase had been made.

We think it clear, therefore, that the equity of redemption, or the entire interest remaining in *Cady* after the execution of the two mortgages, was acquired by one of these purchasers to the exclusion of the other, and not by both equally. If the rule of *lis pendens* did not apply to the sale under the first mortgage, then it was acquired by *Farwell.* If it did apply, then it was acquired by *Murphy.* The whole question, therefore, turns upon whether this rule was applicable or not; and we are very clearly of the opinion that it was not. The reason on which it rests fails entirely in such a case. That reason is to prevent parties, by voluntary conveyance after litigation commenced, from eluding the grasp of the law, and baffling justice, to prevent mere intruders from acquiring rights in property after suits begun in regard to it, and then claiming the right to litigate over again, the questions which those suits settled as against their vendors, or those whose interests they may have attached. But it would be very strange to say that this rule applied to a sale under a first mortgage, in enforcing a paramount and adverse title. Such a mortgagee, is no intruder — no volunteer to acquire a right after suit begun. On the contrary, he is only enforcing a specific right to the property which he had before the suit. And the purchaser at such sale should be regarded in the same light as the mortgagee, because it is part of the right of the mortgagee that the purchaser should be protected. To apply the rule here, would be to say that after a first mortgagee has begun his foreclosure, and obtained his decree of sale, that a second mortgagee, by beginning his suit, arrests the proceedings of the first, or subjects him to the disability of being bound, or having a purchaser at his sale, bound by a judgment in a suit to which they are neither parties. It is plain that the reason of the rule does not exist here, and that to apply it, would be to subject a prior and a paramount right to an unjust and oppressive disability. And we think the authorities fully sustain this view.

In the case of *Parks v. Jackson,* 11 Wend., 442, it was held that where a man having a contract for the purchase of land, on which he had made some payments, having also made some improvement on the land, perfected his title, and took a deed after a suit in equity brought against his vendor to set aside the vendor's title as fraudulent, that such purchaser was not within the rule of *lis pendens.* The opinion of Senator SEWARD contains a very able review of the authorities, and the reasons of the rule; and shows that these reasons did not exist in that case. And if a contract for purchase, before suit brought, will enable the party to go on and perfect his title by taking a deed afterwards without bringing him within the rule, it seems equally clear that a prior mortgagee may proceed to enforce all the rights that he had under the mortgage, without coming within it.

The same doctrine is held in *Gibler et al. v. Trimble,* 14 Ohio, 323, where the distinction is recognized between one going on, after suit, to perfect a right, or protect an interest which he had before, and one who without any prior right, acquires his whole interest after suit brought. The court, after alluding to the rule of *lis pendens,* says: "But this doctrine does not apply to persons who had an interest in the subject-matter before suit commenced, and who should have been made parties; if such persons are not made parties, they may proceed, having an equity before suit, to clothe themselves with the legal title; because, having an interest before suit commenced, and being necessary parties, and not having been made such, neither equity nor the doctrine of *lis pendens* forbids them to protect themselves by acquiring the legal title."

Clarkson et al. v. Morgan's devisees, 6 B. Mon., 441, and *Hopkins v. McLaren,* 4 Cow., 667, are authorities to the same point. The exception is based not on the mere fact that the sale is under a decree or judgment, for that might not always be sufficient; but it is founded on the existence of a prior right before suit, which the owner subsequently may protect or enforce.

We think it clear, therefore, that the rule of *lis pendens* did not apply to the sale where *Farwell* became the purchaser, and that a second mortgagee cannot, by beginning a foreclosure suit, to which the first is not a party, diminish the right of the first, who had begun a prior suit, to proceed to decree and sale with the same effect as though the second suit had not been begun. Indeed, it would seem that if the rule is applicable at all, it would be against *Murphy,* and not in his favor. For a sale of the property having already been adjudged in the first suit, when his was commenced, it might be said that he was bound to take notice that he could not, by proceeding against the property by a second suit, change the effect of the first. But we do not say that the rule would be applicable to a sale under a second mortgage; we only hold it not applicable to a sale under the first.

What, then, were the rights of these purchasers? *Farwell* acquired the interest of all the parties to the first suit, including the interest represented by the first mortgage, and the equity of redemption subject only to the second mortgage. *Murphy* having proceeded in his suit against *Cady* alone, could by a sale, after *Cady's* entire interest had been divested by the first sale, only have acquired the interest represented by the second mortgage, so far as the two lots covered by the first were concerned. *Farwell,* then, as owner of the fee, subject to the second mortgage, had the right to pay it, as he was permitted to do by the court below.

It has been urged upon us that this conclusion is contrary to the former decision of the court in this case, and that the decision settled the whole matter now presented, so that it is *res adjudicata.* We have examined it very carefully, and are unable to perceive that it had any such effect. A judgment makes only that which was in issue, *res adjudicata.* What was in issue in this suit when it was then before this court? There was a demurrer to the bill, which was urged principally for the reason that the sale to *Murphy* had so changed his rights, as to deprive him of the right to redeem. If he had the right still, of course the demurrer would have to be overruled. The court held that he had, and the demurrer was overruled, as, undoubtedly, it ought to have been. That decision, therefore, made it *res adjudicata,* that the bill was not without equity, and that *Murphy* had the right to redeem. But whether he had all the rights that he may have supposed he had, whether the effect of allowing him to redeem would have been all that the or his counsel may have thought as indicated by the bill, was not settled, because not in issue.

It may be that some language used by the court assumes that the second sale had a different effect from that we think it had. But there was nothing in the issue presented, nor in the arguments urged, to call the attention of the court to the precise effect of that sale, further than to determine whether it cut off *Murphy's* right to redeem. This they determined, and determined properly, and this, we think, was all they determined.

They say, also, though it was not strictly presented by the issue, that *Farwell* had a right to redeem from the complainant. But whether the position of one was in any respect superior to that of the other; whether *Farwell* would have the right to do as he has since done, and pay off the amount of *Murphy's* mortgage, notwithstanding the latter had first filed his bill to redeem, neither of these things did they decide, because neither of them was presented. They are presented to us by this appeal, and we have determined them as already stated, as we deem it, not at all in conflict with the former decision of the court.

The judgment of the court below must be affirmed.

COLE, J., *dissenting.* It seems to me that the question involved in this case has already been adjudicated upon and settled in this court. And after the rigid application of the doctrine of *res adjudicata,* which we have made at this term to cases already disposed of, I do not feel at liberty to make the present case an exception in the application of that doctrine; even if I did not in all respects concur in the views previously expressed in the opinion reported in 2 Wis., 539. It is unnecessary to state at length the bill filed by *Murphy.* The substance is contained in the opinion of Justice CRAWFORD just referred to. It is a bill for an account on the part of *Farwell,* of the rents and profits received by him while in possession of the premises in controversy, to pay off and redeem the *Severn* mortgage; and that *Farwell* be compelled to surrender the possession of the premises, and to execute and deliver to *Murphy* a good and sufficient conveyance of an undivided half of lots one and three. The idea, object, aim and end of the bill, if I can understand it, is to discharge an encumbrance against the property, so that *Murphy* might become the owner of an indefeasible and absolute estate in fee simple, of the premises. It is such a bill as a person having the equity of redemption in a subsisting estate has a clear right to file, to discharge the property from an incumbrance outstanding against it.

To this bill a special demurrer was interposed, assigning several causes of demurrer. If any one is curious enough to look into that demurrer, he will see that the demurrants understood this bill precisely as I do. And in resisting the object of the bill, in the eighth ground of demurrer, the point is distinctly and clearly made, that *Murphy* had shown in "his bill of complaint, that *Farwell* and *Cady* had a right to the equity of redemption in the premises prior to his own."

The circuit court overruled the demurrer, as to all the points taken in it, and that decision this court affirmed in every particular. So that whatever points were taken in that demurrer, were distinctly, squarely and fully presented to this court and held to be insufficient in law. It is suggested now that in the previous decision, this court only decided that *Murphy* might pay off or redeem the *Severn* mortgage, but did not decide that he could redeem the property and perfect the title in himself.

It is said that *Farwell* must be considered as at once a mortgagee and mortgagor, uniting in himself the rights and obligations of a mortgagee under the *Severn* mortgage, and the rights and obligations of a mortgagor by operation of law under the chancery sale. This is certainly a cast of characters not often found in the books, that the same person, at the same time, should be a mortgagor and mortgagee. But with this I have nothing to do. I do not find any such intimation, or idea, or suggestion, advanced in the opinion of the court. Besides, no such point was presented for the consideration of the court. The bill is not formed with any other aspect than to redeem the premises. That is the principal relief asked for, and as incidental to this, an account is demanded. And it is said by very high authority, that no person, except a mortgagor, his heirs or privies in estate, has a right to redeem or to call for an account, unless it can be shown that there is collusion between them and the mortgagee. *Troughton v. Binkis,* 6 Ves., 572; *White v. Parnther,* 1 Knapp, 229; 2 Story Eq. Jur., § 1023.

The demurrer raised the point distinctly, as to whether, by the bill, it did not appear that *Farwell* had a prior equity of redemption in the premises. The court overruled the demurrer thus, saying that he had not. Furthermore, the court says: "Inasmuch as the bill before us states that at the time of the prior foreclosure proceedings *Murphy* was the assignee of the second mortgage, having a claim to the equity of redemption of the first mortgage, which was known to all the parties, and was not brought in, his rights remain unimpaired by the proceedings to which he was not a party, and we think he may well insist upon redemption at any time within the period of limitation, when he has not been foreclosed," (p. 539). Again: "From the best examination of the case in all its bearings, which we have been able to give it, we cannot perceive why the present complainant is not entitled to redeem the portion of the premises purchased by *Mr. Farwell,* which was embraced in the sale, on the second foreclosure," etc., (p. 540).

If by this language the court is to be understood as saying that by the prior foreclosure proceedings, *Murphy,* who had a claim to the equity of redemption of the first mortgage, had not the right to redeem that portion of the premises purchased by *Farwell,* and had no right to disengage the property from all encumbrance and perfect the title in himself, but only had the right to buy in the *Severn* mortgage, so as to become the holder of the two mortgages, then I despair of ever ascertaining the point decided in any case. But really, if the object and purpose of the bill are looked at, if the points raised by the special demurrer, are regarded, if the questions discussed by counsel, and necessarily considered by the court, do not show that this court then really and truly held, that under the facts and circumstances of the case, and the peculiar relations of the parties, *Farwell* and *Murphy* had a mutual and reciprocal right to redeem the premises, discharge all encumbrances, and become the owner of an absolute estate in fee simple; I think it may be safely said it never decided anything. And, if it did decide this, if it be held that *Murphy* had a right to redeem the premises and perfect the title in himself, and that *Farwell* at the commencement of the suit, had the same right, then I understand my brethren to admit that *Murphy,* by his superior diligence, has acquired the stronger equity and should now be permitted to redeem the property.

As I have already said, whether the view taken of the case when before the court at the former hearing, be correct or not, I am not now disposed to discuss. Within the decisions made, at this term, that is not an open question, I therefore dismiss the case without further remark, simply adding, that in my opinion, the judgment of the circuit court was directly opposed to the previous decisions of this court, and the prior equitable rights of *Murphy,* and should be reversed.

VALENTINE v. PORTLAND TIMBER & LAND HOLDING CO.

Court of Appeals of Washington
15 Wash. App. 124, 547 P.2d 912 (1976)

SWANSON, JUDGE.

QUAERE:

If the grantee of an unrecorded and subordinate interest in real property is not joined in an action to foreclose a mortgage on that property, is he bound by the foreclosure decree? The trial court said "yes" and granted summary judgment quieting title in plaintiffs Valentine and Schaap to certain real property in which defendants Portland Timber and Land Holding Company (Portland Timber) and Verde Mining Company (Verde Mining) assert an interest.

Portland Timber is a grantee of the timber and mineral rights to the property. Plaintiffs' claim of superior title rests essentially on a sheriff's deed issued to Harry H. Olson, Inc. (Olson), the mortgagee who purchased at his foreclosure sale and subsequently conveyed the property to plaintiffs. The trial court determined on undisputed facts that the mortgage foreclosure proceeding "cut off" defendants Portland Timber's and Verde Mining's interests in the property, even though they were not parties to the foreclosure action, because Portland Timber's deed from the mortgagor Martinson is subsequent in time to Martinson's mortgage of the premises to Olson and there was no compliance with the recording statute, RCW 65.08.070. We agree and affirm.

The genesis of this controversy was E. C. Martinson's conveyance of the timber and minerals on his property to Portland Timber on October 16, 1964, after having mortgaged the premises the previous year to Olson. Olson's mortgage dated October 30, 1963, was recorded promptly on November 1, 1963, but Portland Timber failed to record its deed until February 4, 1969. On November 18, 1964, Olson commenced foreclosure of its mortgage, but did not name Portland Timber in that action. It is undisputed that Portland Timber's deed was not of record, Portland Timber was not in possession of the premises, and Olson had no actual notice of its interest. A decree of foreclosure was entered ordering the property sold. Olson was the successful bidder and received a certificate of sale. The court confirmed the sale and a sheriff's deed issued to Olson which was recorded November 25, 1965. Thereafter, Olson sold the premises, including the timber and minerals, to Boyd A. Zepp and Wilma Zepp by real estate contract which the Zepps assigned to the plaintiffs. The assignment was recorded October 15, 1968. Olson conveyed the premises on May 14, 1973, in fulfillment of the contract previously assigned to the plaintiffs.

On these undisputed facts, summary judgment was granted quieting title in plaintiffs Valentine and Schaap. In this appeal following the denial of a motion for reconsideration, defendants assign error only to the orders granting summary judgment and denying reconsideration without further specification.

. . . .

Considering first the question of joinder, we recognize the purpose of the sale under the decree of foreclosure is to pass to a purchaser the entire title to the property, both that of the mortgagor and of the mortgagee, as it was at the time the mortgage was given. G. Osborne, *Mortgages* § 319 (2d ed. 1970). Consequently, joinder of any person having an interest in the property is essential in that, if not joined, his interest will not be affected by the foreclosure. Clearly, due process requires a "day in court" before property interests can be extinguished. To that extent Portland Timber, the vendee of a deed from the mortgagor Martinson, valid between the parties, is a necessary party. That does not mean, however, that failure to join such a person nullifies the action. It only means such a person's interest is unaffected. *Spokane Savings & Loan Soc. v. Liliopoulos,* 160 Wash. 71, 294 P. 561 (1930). But plaintiffs contend that public policy demands that the failure to join a necessary party be excused by the foreclosing mortgagee's lack of notice, either actual or constructive, of such subordinate interest.

The rule regarding joinder is stated in G. Osborne, *Mortgages* § 322 (2d ed. 1970) at page 672:

> The general rule is that lack of knowledge or notice of the subordinate interest of another person in the mortgaged land does not excuse a foreclosing mortgagee from making such person a party to his suit. If he fails to do so, the subordinate interest, regardless of whether it be legal or equitable and one of ownership or lien, is not subject to the decree.

(Footnote omitted.) There are limitations upon the generality of this rule equally well established: the bona fide purchase rule as to equitable interests; provisions of recording acts; and the common law doctrine of lis pendens, or statutes to the same effect. G. Osborne, *Mortgages* § 322 (2d ed. 1970). The limiting exception applicable here is the provision of our recording act, RCW 65.08.070, which provides as follows:

> A conveyance of real property ... may be recorded in the office of the recording officer of the county where the property is situated. Every such conveyance not so recorded is void as against any subsequent purchaser or mortgagee in good faith and for a valuable consideration from the same vendor, his heirs or devisees, of the same real property or any portion thereof whose conveyance is first duly recorded. An instrument is deemed recorded the minute it is filed for record.

By its terms an unrecorded conveyance is void as against a subsequent purchaser in good faith for value from the same vendor of the same property whose conveyance is first recorded. In describing the purpose of our recording statute, the Washington Supreme Court, in *Tacoma Hotel, Inc. v. Morrison & Co.,* 193 Wash. 134, 140, 74 P.2d 1003, 1006 (1938), said,

> The purpose of the recording statute is to make the deed first recorded superior to any outstanding unrecorded conveyance of the same property unless the mortgagee or purchaser had actual knowledge of the transfer not filed of record.

Defendants argue that the recording statute is of no aid to plaintiffs because their predecessor Olson was not a bona fide purchaser for value. Defendants rely upon a line of cases, of which *Desimone v. Spence,* 51 Wash.2d 412, 318 P.2d 959 (1957), is representative, to support the proposition that a judgment creditor purchasing at his own execution sale is not a bona fide purchaser within the meaning of the recording act because he does not give value — the consideration being only his pre-existing debt. But the cases upon which defendants rely all involve a judgment creditor purchasing at an execution sale rather than a mortgagee purchasing at a mortgage foreclosure sale. Moreover, there is considerable support for a contrary view. *See* R. Patton, *Land Titles* § 17 at 92 (2d ed. 1957). This is because the consideration the purchaser pays includes something more than his pre-existing debt, namely, the legal expenses of the proceeding. In the instant case, the defendants challenge Olson's status as a good faith purchaser on the basis he failed to give value. The only facts presented to the trial court on this question are found in the affidavit of Harry Olson and the request for admissions of fact, which state,

[t]he King County Sheriff sold the premises to Harry H. Olson, Inc. as the highest bidder at public auction for the sum of $14,704.73, and issued said purchaser a certificate of sale. On April 2, 1965, the King County Superior Court confirmed the sale of the premises to Harry H. Olson, Inc.

On these admitted facts, we cannot say that the $14,704.73 paid for the premises represents a pre-existing debt, the amount of the judgment, or was not cash consideration given at the time of the sale. Neither the amount of the original debt nor the amount of the judgment is included among the admitted facts presented to the trial court.

Even assuming arguendo that the amount of Olson's bid represents the amount of his judgment, we are not persuaded that the mortgagee at a foreclosure sale cannot qualify as a bona fide purchaser for value. In *Attebery v. O'Neil,* 42 Wash. 487, 85 P. 270 (1906), the court held that a mortgagee who purchased at his foreclosure sale was a bona fide purchaser for value as against unknown and unrecorded equitable interests, cutting off the children of the mortgagor's first wife. *See Lewis v. Kujawa,* 158 Wash. 607, 291 P. 1105 (1930). Public policy reasons dictate that the recording statute should protect the foreclosing mortgagee as well as the purchaser at a foreclosure sale against unrecorded and unknown interests. This policy is well expressed in G. Osborne, *Mortgages* § 322 at 673 (2d ed. 1970):

Although there may be some argument as to the proper basis of the result, it seems highly desirable to protect both the foreclosing mortgagee as well as a purchaser on foreclosure sale against interests that are acquired but remain unrecorded prior to the beginning of a foreclosure action. That protection should extend at least far enough to cut off all such interests of which there was no actual notice before suit, or actual knowledge during the pendency of the litigation.

(Footnote omitted.) A mortgage properly recorded gives notice of its contents to parties acquiring interests subsequent to the filing and recording of the instrument. *Kendrick v. Davis,* 75 Wash.2d 456, 464, 452 P.2d 222 (1969). We stated in *Koch v. Swanson,* 4 Wash.App. 456, 459, 481 P.2d 915, 917 (1971),

one searching the index has a right to rely upon what the index and recorded document discloses and is not bound to search the record outside the chain of title of the property presently being conveyed.

. . . .

. . . It would unduly lengthen this opinion to detail the defendants' additional arguments, except to note they essentially involve a collateral attack upon the decree of foreclosure, a procedure condemned in *Globe Construction Co. v. Yost,* 169 Wash. 319, 13 P.2d 433 (1932), and discuss asserted defects in the foreclosure proceeding not presented to the trial court when considering the motion for summary judgment.

Judgment affirmed.

WILLIAMS, C. J. and CALLOW, J., concur.

STATE BANK v. AMAK ENTERPRISES, INC.

Supreme Court, Special Term, Sullivan County
77 Misc. 2d 340, 353 N.Y.S.2d 857 (1974)

George L. Cobb, Justice.

Defendant Amak Enterprises, Inc. moves "for an order dismissing the complaint herein pursuant to CPLR 3212 and directing the entry of partial summary judgment for the defendant Amak Enterprises, Inc., upon the cause of action set forth in the complaint and for a further order restraining and enjoining the plaintiff pending the determination of the issues in the action from taking any further action whatsoever in connection with cause of this action set forth in the complaint and staying, enjoining and restraining the plaintiff until the determination of the issues herein" and for such other, further and different relief as to the court shall seem just and proper.

The action is brought by the plaintiff bank to foreclose a certain mortgage given in 1966 by the defendant Amak Enterprises, Inc. (hereinafter "Amak") upon certain motel property and it is also brought to foreclose another mortgage on the same premises given by Amak on August 2, 1968 to the plaintiff bank to secure the performance by Amak of a written guaranty of payment which Amak had given to the bank on or about July 31, 1968. The latter instrument guaranteed the payment by Amak of the existing and the future indebtedness of Monis I. Brafman, Sylvia Brafman, Mollie Brafman, and Monis Brafman, d/b/a Sylvie and Me Poultry Farms, to the bank.

In 1965 and again in 1967 the Brafmans had borrowed substantial sums from the bank and such loans had been secured by mortgages on the farm properties owned by them. When the Brafmans failed to repay this indebtedness as agreed, and Amak failed to comply with the bank's demand for payment, the bank in 1969 began the foreclosure of the Brafman mortgages, but did not name Amak as a party to that foreclosure action (hereinafter referred to as the "farm foreclosure"). In the farm foreclosure action, a judgment was entered in favor of the bank for approximately $95,800 and at the foreclosure sale in 1970 the bank bid in the property for $35,000. The referee's report of sale showed a deficiency due the bank of about $63,000, but the bank did not then seek any deficiency judgment against anyone.

Thereafter, the bank sold the farm to a third party for $55,000, thereby reducing the deficiency from $63,000 to about $43,000, and, because Amak refuses to pay this $43,000 to the bank, pursuant to the 1968 guaranty agreement, the bank says it is entitled to foreclose the 1968 mortgage on the motel property, which was given to secure Amak's guaranty of the Brafman debts. Amak, on the other hand, while conceding that the bank is entitled to foreclose the 1966 mortgage, vigorously contends that, because the bank did not seek to enforce Amak's liability for the Brafman debts in the farm foreclosure action, any liability it had under the guaranty agreement has been discharged and the bank may not, therefore, foreclose the 1968 mortgage.

For some time, it has been the public policy of this State "to give the court in which the foreclosure of the mortgage was had, full jurisdiction over the whole subject . . . and to allow one court to dispose of the whole subject". The policy "is applicable to every case where the owner of the mortgage has any personal security for the mortgage debt, whether it be the bond of the mortgagor or the covenant of another person" and its purpose is "to confine all the proceedings to recover a mortgage debt to one court". (Scofield v. Doscher, 72 N.Y. 491, 493-494.) Accordingly, pursuant to section 1313 of the Real Property Actions and Proceedings Law, the bank, if it had elected to do so, could have joined Amak in the farm mortgage foreclosure action (*Weinstein v. Sinel,* 133 App.Div. 441, 442, 117 N.Y.S. 346, 347) and, pursuant to subdivision 1 of section 1371 of the Real Property Actions and Proceedings Law, could have sought a deficiency judgment against Amak as one "severally liable" (*Kerhonkson Nat. Bank v. Granite Sunshine Hotel,* 26 A.D.2d 713, 714, 271 N.Y.S.2d 376, 377).

Section 1301 (subd. 3) of the Real Property Actions and Proceedings Law says that while a mortgage foreclosure action is pending or after final judgment for the plaintiff therein, no other action shall be commenced or maintained to recover any part of the mortgage debt, without leave of the court wherein the former action was brought. If that part of the instant action which seeks foreclosure of the 1968 mortgage be an "action . . . to recover any part of the mortgage debt" on the farm, and there is some authority which would indicate that it is (see *Kings Co. Sav. Bank v. Fulton Sav. Bank Kings Co.,* 268 App.Div. 452, 454, 52 N.Y.S.2d 47, 49), then no foreclosure of the 1968 mortgage may be had herein unless the grant of such leave be pleaded and proved by plaintiff (*Scofield v. Doscher,* supra, 72 N.Y. p. 496; *Gorgoglione v. Contreras,* 41 A.D.2d 644, 340 N.Y.S.2d 845). There is, however, some authority which suggests that an action to foreclose the 1968 mortgage is not an action to recover on the debt and therefore leave of court is not required (*e. g., Reichert v. Stilwell,* 172 N.Y. 83, 64 N.E. 790). The issue need not be resolved since movant is entitled to the relief sought on other grounds.

Section 1371 (subd. 3) of the Real Property Actions and Proceedings Law says that "[i]f no motion for a deficiency judgment shall be made as herein prescribed the proceeds of the sale regardless of amount shall be deemed to be in full satisfaction of the mortgage debt and no right to recover any deficiency in any action or proceeding shall exist". Where, as here, a guarantor of a mortgage debt is not joined in the foreclosure action and no notice of an application for a deficiency judgment in such action is given to such guarantor, the proceeds of the sale in foreclosure must be "deemed to be in full satisfaction of the mortgage debt as to . . . [such guarantor] and no right to recover any deficiency in any action or proceeding exists." (*Kings Co. Sav. Bank v. Fulton Sav. Bank Kings Co.,* 268 App.Div. 452, p. 454, 52 N.Y.S.2d 47, p. 49).

The bank, in opposition to the motion, cites *Westerbeke v. Bank of Huntington & Trust Co.,* 247 App.Div. 915, mod., 248 App.Div. 632, 287 N.Y.S. 228, affd., 272 N.Y. 593, 4 N.E.2d 819. In that case, as additional security for the mortgage debt, the mortgagor and mortgagee of certain lands entered into an escrow agreement with a certain bank, which agreement provided that, if upon a mortgage foreclosure sale the mortgagee did not receive the full amount of the debt, the bank as escrow agent would sell all of the stock which had been turned over to such agent, or so much thereof as was necessary to satisfy the deficiency, and said agent would thereupon pay over the sums so realized to the mortgagee to be applied upon the debt. When the proceeds of the foreclosure sale did not fully discharge the mortgage debt, the mortgagee sought to compel the sale of the stock as provided in the agreement, or, in lieu thereof, a judgment for the amount of the deficiency. Although no motion for a deficiency judgment had been made in the foreclosure action, the court granted the requested relief.

The opinion of the court in *Westerbeke* (p. 916, supra) said that the statutory language, quoted above, concerning the effect of a failure to apply for a deficiency judgment, was not applicable when the creditor was not seeking a "deficiency judgment or a personal judgment" against the debtor, but was instead merely "resorting to the additional security which, under the agreement, was to be available for the payment of the debt in the event of a deficiency upon the sale". The same Appellate Court some years later, notwithstanding the fact that the authority of *Westerbeke* (supra) had been substantially undermined by the holding in *Matter of Williams,* 258 App.Div. 592, 17 N.Y.S.2d 335, applied the Westerbeke rule to a case where additional security for the mortgage debt had been supplied directly by the debtor to the creditor without the intervention or participation of a stakeholder or escrow agent (see *Bedcro Realty Corp. v. Title Guarantee & Trust Co.,* 265 App.Div. 7, 37 N.Y.S.2d 529), but that holding was reversed by the Court of Appeals (*Bedcro Realty Corp. v. Brooklyn Trust Co.,* 290 N.Y. 520, 49 N.E.2d 992) with the observation (p. 523, 49 N.E.2d p. 993) that "[f]ailure to move for a deficiency judgment . . . raised a conclusive presumption that the value of the property received by the mortgagee on foreclosure equaled, at least, the entire 'mortgage debt' and no right remained to enforce payment thereof, in whole or in part, from any other security".

Because the plaintiff in this case failed to timely move for a deficiency judgment in the farm foreclosure action, a conclusive presumption arose that the debt was paid (*Bedcro,* supra) and the benefits of the presumption extended not only to the principal debtor, but also to the guarantor of the mortgage debt (*Kings Co. Sav. Bank v. Fulton Sav. Bank Kings Co.,* 268 App.Div. 452, 52 N.Y.S.2d 47, supra). When the debt was extinguished, the lien of the mortgage given to collaterally secure that debt necessarily expired (*Olafsson v. Appolonio,* 28 Misc.2d 683, 685, 216 N.Y.S.2d 225, 226).

It follows that the motion should be, and it will be, granted to the extent that the court will dismiss that portion of the complaint which alleges a cause of action for the enforcement of the 1968 guaranty agreement or for the foreclosure of the 1968 mortgage.

NOTES

1. In *Murphy v. Farwell* it appears that Murphy foreclosed against the wrong individual by commencing an action against Cady, since Cady's interest had already been sold at Farwell's foreclosure sale. However, would the result have been any different if Murphy had commenced a judicial foreclosure against Farwell? As an omitted junior lienor, it seems clear that Murphy had the right to foreclose against Farwell. Could Farwell then have tendered payment in full of Murphy's lien and satisfied the debt due Murphy?

2. In *State Bank v. Amak Enterprises, Inc., supra,* was the issue the omission of the guarantor, or was it the failure to timely seek the deficiency? Would the result have been different if the deficiency had been sought earlier?

3. Omitted juniors in general are said to be unaffected by the judicial foreclosure of a senior lien, not having been a party to the action. This means that the purchaser at the foreclosure sale buys the property subject to the lien of the omitted junior. Had the junior been a party to the foreclosure, it is unlikely that a higher sale price would have been generated. However, the junior cannot be deprived of his position without his day in court. The purchaser at the foreclosure sale of the senior can commence an action in strict foreclosure naming the omitted junior as defendant. The court will then issue an order compelling the junior to buy out the purchaser's position or forfeit his interest in the subject property. At first this seems harsh, but the result is essentially the same as if the junior had been a party to the senior's foreclosure action. In that case the junior lienor would have had the choice to either satisfy the debt due the senior or forfeit his (the junior's) security interest in the property.

4. From the point of view of the omitted junior, there are two possible solutions. Since he still has a lien on the property, he can foreclose if he is not paid. However, while this may give him title to the property, assuming he buys with a "paper bid" at the foreclosure

sale, the previous purchaser at the earlier sale is now in a position of a senior lienor, that lien having been revived and now capable of being foreclosed again. So foreclosure of an omitted junior lien does not appear to be a feasible way for the junior lienor to be satisfied. The junior can compel redemption with an action in strict foreclosure which will allow the junior to pay off the purchaser at the senior's sale, and then stand in the position of owning both the senior and junior liens. Notice that the junior will have to satisfy the senior's debt in every case, or forfeit his (the junior's) interest in the property. This seems appropriate since the junior did loan on the property when there was an outstanding senior lien. One of the hazards of loaning in a junior position is having to take over the senior obligation.

2. POWER OF SALE FORECLOSURE

GARFINKLE v. SUPERIOR COURT

Supreme Court of California
21 Cal. 2d 268, 578 P.2d 925 (1978)

MANUEL, JUSTICE.

This petition for writ of mandate challenges the constitutionality of California's procedure for the nonjudicial foreclosure of deeds of trust on real property. Petitioners contend that this procedure permits the deprivation of the trustor's property without adequate notice or hearing in violation of the due process guarantees of the Fourteenth Amendment to the United States Constitution and of article I, section 7 of the California Constitution. We conclude, in agreement with the decisions which have considered this question in relation to California's nonjudicial foreclosure procedure (*Strutt v. Ontario Sav. & Loan Ass'n* (1972) 28 Cal.App.3d 866, 105 Cal.Rptr. 395; *U. S. Hertz, Inc. v. Niobrara Farms* (1974) 41 Cal.App.3d 68, 116 Cal.Rptr. 44; *Davidow v. Corporation of America* (1936) 16 Cal. App.2d 6, 60 P.2d 132; *Davidow v. Lachman Bros. Inv. Co.* (9th Cir. 1935) 76 F.2d 186; *Lawson v. Smith* (N.D.Cal.1975) 402 F.Supp. 851) and in accord with the overwhelming majority of decisions which have considered this question in relation to similar nonjudicial foreclosure procedures of other jurisdictions, that California's procedure constitutes private, not state action and is therefore exempt from the due process constraints of the federal Constitution. We also conclude that the private action herein involved does not satisfy the state action requirement of the due process clause of the state Constitution.

In January 1970, petitioners Susan and Gary Garfinkle (the Garfinkles) purchased a family residence from the Lannings, whose loan on the property was secured by a deed of trust in favor of Wells Fargo Bank (Bank). This deed of trust contained a standard due-on-sale clause which provided that the Bank could accelerate the balance due on the loan if the Lannings sold the property without the written consent of the Bank. The deed of trust also contained a power of sale clause which provided in part as follows:

> If default be made in the payment of said promissory note . . . or in case any change is made in the title to all or any part of the said property . . . all sums hereby secured shall, at the election of the Bank, forthwith become due and payable, without notice, and the Bank may cause the said property to be sold in order to accomplish the object of these trusts, and upon demand of the Bank the Trustee shall sell the whole, or such portion of the said property as the Trustee shall deem necessary to accomplish the purposes of these trusts, and such sale may be made in any manner provided by law, and if none is provided, then by first giving notice of the time and place of sale in the manner and for

a time not less than that now required by law for the sale of real property on execution. . . .

The Bank offered to let the Garfinkles assume the Lanning loan at an increased rate of interest in return for the Bank's agreement not to accelerate the balance due on that loan pursuant to the due-on-sale clause. The Garfinkles refused to assume the Lanning loan on these terms. Thereafter, the Bank notified both the Lannings and the Garfinkles that it had accelerated the Lanning loan and that the balance owing thereon was due and payable in its entirety. In June 1970 when the balance due had not been paid, the Bank recorded its notice of default as required by section 2924 of the Civil Code. The Lannings and Garfinkles received actual notice of the Bank's notice of default. The Garfinkles then brought a series of legal actions challenging both the constitutionality of California's nonjudicial foreclosure procedure and the validity of the automatic enforcement of the due-on-sale clause; and culminating in the present action seeking declaratory relief on both of these issues in respondent Contra Costa County Superior Court. The Bank filed a general demurrer to the Garfinkles' complaint. Respondent sustained the demurrer without leave to amend as to the constitutional challenge to the nonjudicial foreclosure procedure on the ground that no state action was involved.

. . . By this petition for mandate the Garfinkles seek review of the trial court's order.

The statutory provisions regulating the nonjudicial foreclosure of deeds of trust on real property are contained in Civil Code sections 2924-2924h. Basically, these provisions require that before the trustee, acting under a power of sale contained in the deed of trust, can sell the subject trust property, the trustee must first record a notice of default setting forth the nature of the default and the election to exercise the power of sale. (§ 2924.) If the trustor (borrower) has recorded a request for notice or if the deed of trust contains a request for notice, the trustee is required to mail a copy of the notice of default to the trustor at the address specified in the recorded request or in the deed of trust. (§ 2924, subd. (b).)

After the notice of default has been recorded, the trustee must allow three months to elapse, during which time, the trustor may "cure" the default and reinstate the deed of trust, where reinstatement is possible. (§ 2924c.)

Upon expiration of this 90-day period, the trustee must then post a written notice of sale in a conspicuous place on the property at least 20 days prior to the date of sale (§ 2924f), and must mail a copy of this notice of sale to the trustor if notice has been requested. The trustee can then proceed to sell the property. There is no statutory provision for a judicial determination, prior to the sale, of the validity of the alleged default.

The property must be sold by public auction to the highest bidder (§ 2924h) to whom title is transferred by a trustee's deed. Thereafter, upon recording of this deed, the purchaser is entitled to bring an unlawful detainer action against the trustor in order to get possession of the property. (Code Civ.Proc., § 1161a.)

Petitioners contend that this nonjudicial procedure violates procedural due process under both the federal and state Constitutions because it deprives real property owners of their property without adequate notice and without a judicial hearing, thus coming within the scope of the decisions in *Sniadach v. Family Finance Corp.* (1969) 395 U.S. 337, 89 S.Ct. 1820, 23 L.Ed.2d 349 and its progeny.

We first turn to petitioner's federal constitutional claim. The Fourteenth

Amendment to the United States Constitution provides in part: "No state shall make or enforce any law which shall abridge the privileges or immunities of citizens of the United States; nor shall any state deprive any person of life, liberty, or property without due process of law; . . ."

"The Fourteenth Amendment prohibits the state from depriving any person of life, liberty, or property, without due process of law; but it adds nothing to the rights of one citizen as against another." (*United States v. Cruikshank* (1875) 92 U.S. 542, 554, 23 L.Ed. 588.) The Fourteenth Amendment "erects no shield against merely private conduct, however discriminatory or wrongful." (*Shelley v. Kraemer* (1948) 334 U.S. 1, 13, 68 S.Ct. 836, 842, 92 L.Ed. 1161.) The question presented here, as in all actions challenged under the Fourteenth Amendment, is whether "there is a sufficiently close nexus between the state and the challenged action . . . so that the action . . . may be fairly treated as that of the State itself." (*Jackson v. Metropolitan Edison Co.* (1974) 419 U.S. 345, 351, 95 S.Ct. 449, 453, 42 L.Ed.2d 477.) Thus, the threshold question which we must determine is whether the state is significantly involved in the nonjudicial foreclosure procedure so as to bring that procedure within the reach of the due process clause.

Petitioners first contend that there is significant involvement by the state in nonjudicial foreclosures because these foreclosures are pervasively regulated by detailed statutory provisions. It is also argued that the nonjudicial foreclosure procedure when viewed as a whole, requires participation by a state official, the county recorder, and by the state courts. Petitioners rely primarily on our decision in *Connolly Development Inc. v. Superior Court, supra,* 17 Cal.3d 803, 132 Cal.Rptr. 477, 553 P.2d 637, in support of this contention.

In *Connolly,* we held that the mechanics' lien constitutes state action because that lien not only is governed by detailed statutory provisions but also only becomes effective upon recordation with the county recorder and can only be enforced by resort to the state courts. (17 Cal.3d 803, 815, 132 Cal.Rptr. 477, 553 P.2d 637.) We also held in *Connolly* that the stop notice procedure constitutes state action because use of that procedure, which was created by statute and is governed by comprehensive statutory regulations, is encouraged and in fact only made possible by virtue of statutory authorization for its enforcement. (17 Cal.3d 803, 815, 132 Cal.Rptr. 477, 553 P.2d 637.)

There are several significant differences, however, between the creditors' remedies involved in *Connolly* and the remedy of nonjudicial foreclosure pursuant to a power of sale that is at issue in the case at bar. Unlike the mechanics' lien or stop notice which are authorized by statute and not by the contract of the parties (see also *Adams v. Department of Motor Vehicles, supra,* 11 Cal.3d 146, 153, 113 Cal.Rptr. 145, 520 P.2d 961) the power of sale exercised by the trustee on behalf of the lender/creditor in nonjudicial foreclosures is a right authorized solely by the contract between the lender and trustor as embodied in the deed of trust. (*Davidow v. Corporation of America, supra,* 16 Cal.App.2d 6, 13, 60 P.2d 132; *U. S. Hertz, Inc. v. Niobrara Farms, supra,* 41 Cal.App.3d 68, 87, 116 Cal.Rptr. 44.) The contractual nature of the power of sale and right of the parties to include such a power in the deed of trust to be exercised in the event of a default was first recognized by this court in 1859. Noting that deeds of trust containing powers of sale were commonly utilized in this state, this court held in *Koch v. Briggs* (1859) 14 Cal. 256, that these contractual powers are valid and enforceable and that merchantable title is transferred pursuant to the exercise thereof.

In 1881, this court, again recognizing the validity of nonjudicial foreclosures of deeds of trust pursuant to powers of sale contained therein, reiterated that this remedy is created by contract and that a sale conducted in accordance with the conditions of the power would result in the transfer of good title to the purchaser. *(Bateman v. Burr* (1881) 57 Cal. 480.) In so holding, the court rejected the contention that judicial foreclosure was the proper method of enforcing the security interest embodied in the deed of trust.

In 1917, the Legislature impliedly recognized the validity of this contractual remedy when, acting under its police power, it established certain minimum standards for conducting nonjudicial foreclosures, by placing various restrictions on the creditors' exercise of the power of sale in order to protect the trustor/debtor against forfeiture. (§ 2924; *Smith v. Allen* (1968) 68 Cal.2d 93, 96, 65 Cal.Rptr. 153, 436 P.2d 65; *Strutt v. Ontario Sav. & Loan Ass'n, supra,* 28 Cal.App.3d 866, 877, 105 Cal.Rptr. 395; see also Burke & Reber, *State Action, Congressional Power and Creditors' Rights; An Essay on the Fourteenth Amendment* (1973) 47 So.Cal.L.Rev. 1, 23-28, 32.) Since that time these statutory protections have been expanded into a comprehensive statutory scheme regulating in detail all aspects of the nonjudicial foreclosure process. (See *Smith v. Allen, supra,* 68 Cal.2d 93, 96, 65 Cal.Rptr. 153, 436 P.2d 65.)

Petitioners contend that this comprehensive statutory regulation of nonjudicial foreclosures constitutes state action because it encourages and facilitates use of that remedy. This contention does not withstand examination. *The nonjudicial foreclosure statutes do not authorize or compel inclusion of a power of sale in a deed of trust or provide for such a power of sale when one has not been included by the parties. Nor do these statutes compel exercise of the power of sale.* The decision whether to exercise the power of sale is a determination to be made by the creditor. The statutes merely restrict and regulate the exercise of the power of sale once a choice has been made by the creditor to foreclose the deed of trust in that manner. [Emphasis added.]

We are also unpersuaded that the state encourages nonjudicial foreclosures by acknowledging the legal validity of the title transferred thereby. Mere recognition of the legal effect of the private arrangements of the lender and trustor is not sufficient to convert the acts of the lender or trustee into the acts of the state for Fourteenth Amendment purposes. As the court in *Barrera v. Security Building & Investment Corporation, supra,* 519 F.2d 1166, 1170, cogently stated: "Virtually all formal private arrangements assume, at some point, the supportive role of the state. To hold that the state, by recognizing the legal effect of those arrangements, converts them into state acts for constitutional purposes would effectively erase to a significant extent the constitutional line between private and state action and subject to judicial scrutiny under the Fourteenth Amendment virtually all private arrangements that purport to have binding legal effect." *(Id.* at p. 1170.)

Similarly, we are not convinced that the state has encouraged or facilitated nonjudicial foreclosure by enacting comprehensive and detailed regulations governing that process. As we stated earlier, these statutory regulations were enacted primarily for the benefit of the trustor and for the greatest part limit the creditors' otherwise unrestricted exercise of the contractual power of sale upon default by the trustor. For this reason, it cannot realistically be claimed that the state, by acting to protect the debtor, has thereby become the partner of the creditor so that the creditor's actions are converted into the actions of the state. (See *Burton v. Wilmington Pkg. Auth.* (1961) 365 U.S. 715, 81 S.Ct. 856, 6 L.Ed.2d 45; *Barrera v. Security Building & Investment Corporation, supra.)*

We also reject petitioners' contention that the nonjudicial foreclosure procedure involves significant acts of the county recorder. We agree with the decision in *Lawson v. Smith, supra,* 402 F.Supp. 851, in which it was concluded that the acts of the county recorder required by the California nonjudicial foreclosure statutes are ministerial in nature, and are thus distinguishable from the significant, discretionary acts of the county recorder under North Carolina's nonjudicial foreclosure procedure, which has been held to constitute significant state action. (See *Turner v. Blackburn* (W.D.N.C. 1975) 389 F.Supp. 1250, 1258.) Other than these ministerial acts by the county recorder, we note that there is no participation or intervention by any state official or judicial officer prior to the trustee's sale and the vesting of title in the purchaser. (See *Levine v. Stein, supra,* 560 F.2d 1175.) This absence of judicial involvement represents another significant difference between the nonjudicial foreclosure of a deed of trust and the mechanics' lien and stop notice in *Connolly,* where court action was required for the enforcement of those liens. Petitioners argue, however, that although judicial intervention may not occur prior to the transfer of title, resort to the state's courts later becomes necessary because the purchaser in order to enforce the rights previously acquired at the trustee's sale ordinarily must bring an action in unlawful detainer against a trustor who will not voluntarily relinquish possession of the property. For this reason, it is argued that when the nonjudicial foreclosure process is viewed as a whole, the state's involvement therein becomes apparent. We disagree. The fact that a purchaser who has acquired rights by virtue of a trustee's deed, like a party who has acquired rights under any other type of contract, may have a right to resort to the courts in order to enforce such previously acquired contractual rights when that becomes necessary, is not sufficient to convert the acts creating these contractual rights into state action. For to hold otherwise, would be to subject every private contract to review under the Fourteenth Amendment. (See *Federal National Mortgage Ass'n v. Howlett, supra,* 521 S.W.2d 428, 437.)

. . . .

We conclude therefore that California's nonjudicial foreclosure procedure does not constitute state action and is therefore immune from the procedural due process requirements of the federal Constitution.

. . . .

The alternative writ heretofore issued is discharged and a peremptory writ is denied.

BIRD, C. J., and TOBRINER, MOSK, CLARK, RICHARDSON and NEWMAN, JJ., concur.

Rehearing denied; NEWMAN, J., dissenting.

NOTES

1. The issue of the validity of power of sale foreclosures has been litigated in several states with results similar to that in *Garfinkle.* See *Kennebec, Inc. v. Bank of the West,* 88 Wash. 2d 718, 565 P.2d 812 (1977); *Federal National Mortgage Ass'n v. Howlett,* 521 S.W.2d 428 (Mo. 1975); *Coffey Enterprises & Co. v. Holmes,* 233 Ga. 937, 213 S.E.2d 882 (1975); *Armenta v. Nussbaum,* 519 S.W.2d 673 (Tex. Civ. App. 1975); *Levine v. Stein,* 560 F.2d 1175 (4th Cir. 1977); *Barrera v. Security Building & Investment Corp.,* 519 F.2d 1166 (5th Cir. 1975); *Northrip v. Federal National Mortgage Ass'n,* 527 F.2d 23 (6th Cir. 1975); *Bryant v. Federal Savings & Loan Ass'n,* 166 U.S. App. D.C. 178, 509 F.2d 511 (1974).

2. The *Garfinkle* case avoids reaching a conclusion on the issue of due process by

finding a lack of state action. If there had been a finding of state action do you think the California procedure would have satisfied the requirements of due process?

3. Power of sale foreclosure was the exclusive remedy in California until 1933 when the legislature enacted California Code of Civil Procedure § 725a authorizing judicial foreclosure.

FOSTER LUMBER CO. v. WESTON CONSTRUCTORS, INC.

Colorado Court of Appeals
33 Colo. App. 436, 521 P.2d 1294 (1974)

ENOCH, JUDGE.

Foster Lumber Company (Foster) appeals from a judgment dismissing both claims in its complaint: The first, a claim for the amount due on a note secured by deed of trust, and the second, an action under C.R.C.P. 106 to compel defendant Bain as public trustee to conduct a foreclosure sale pursuant to the terms of the deed of trust. We affirm the result.

In 1969 Foster conveyed real property to defendant Weston Construction in exchange for a promissory note secured by a first deed of trust on the property. It is alleged that defendants Ponton and Darpo Construction (Darpo) subsequently assumed the obligation represented by the note. Monthly installments due on August 1 and September 1, 1972, were not paid, and on September 8 Foster filed its election and demand for foreclosure with defendant Bain, the public trustee. The sale was set for October 31. At the time Foster filed its election and demand it discovered that, contrary to a covenant in the deed of trust, property taxes for 1971 had not been paid.

In order to cure the default, Darpo, through the public trustee, tendered to Foster on September 29 checks totaling $1,605.28 and receipts for the payment of past due property taxes. Foster refused to accept this tender and insisted that the property be sold by the public trustee. The trustee refused and this suit resulted.

After Foster's Complaint was filed, Bain filed a motion to dismiss for failure to state a claim, and defendants Ponton and Darpo filed motions to dismiss and motions for summary judgment. Weston Construction, the maker of the note, did not enter an appearance in the action. After a hearing on the motions judgment was entered dismissing Foster's complaint as to all defendants.

The issues in this case are governed by 1969 Perm.Supp., C.R.S.1963, 118-9-18, which provides in pertinent part:

When only default is nonpayment. — Whenever the *only default* or violation in the terms of the *note and deed of trust* or mortgage being foreclosed is nonpayment of *any sum due* thereunder, the owner or owners of the property being foreclosed or party or parties liable thereon *shall be entitled to cure* said particular default if . . . the owners or parties pay to the officer conducting the sale *all delinquent principal and interest payments* which are due as of the date of such payment exclusive of that portion of the principal which would not have been due in the absence of acceleration, plus all *costs, expenses, late charges, attorney's fees and other fees incurred by the holder of such note,* deed of trust, or mortgage as of the date of payment in connection with such proceedings for collection and foreclosure . . . . Upon payment of all withdrawal fees and costs plus an additional thirty-five dollars public trustees' costs . . . all proceedings for foreclosure *shall* terminate. (emphasis added)

This statute represents a legislative expansion of equitable principles espoused by Justice Cardozo in his dissent in *Graf v. Hope Building Corp.,* 254 N.Y. 1, 171

N.E. 884, and applied by courts to relieve debtors of the strict requirements of timely payments under the terms of a mortgage. *See Arizona Coffee Shops, Inc. v. Phoenix Downtown Parking Ass'n, Inc.,* 95 Ariz. 98, 387 P.2d 801; Rosenthal, The Role of Courts of Equity in Preventing Acceleration Predicated Upon a Mortgagor's Inadvertent Default, 22 Syracuse L.J. 897. Several other states have enacted similar legislation. *See, e. g.,* Cal.Civ.Code § 2924c (West Supp. 1973); Ore.Rev.Stat. § 86.760 (1971).

I

On appeal, Foster argues that the statute does not apply to a situation where, as here, default in the terms of the note and deed of trust consists not only of non-payment of principal and interest, but also of failure to pay real property taxes. We do not agree.

The language of the statute does not clearly indicate whether it was intended to apply to non-payment of taxes as well as default in payment of principal and interest. When describing the precise requirements of tender, the statute refers only to "principal and interest payments . . . costs, expenses, late charges, attorney's fees and other fees incurred by the holder of such note . . . ." However, the phrase "any sum due thereunder" is susceptible to an interpretation including delinquent taxes. The statute must be interpreted so as to carry out the general legislative intent, which was to permit debtors to prevent foreclosure of mortgages or deeds of trust in instances in which the creditor's interests will not be jeopardized.

If the only default is failure to pay principal and interest, the statute permits a debtor to prevent foreclosure if he is able to pay the amount in default plus expenses incurred by the holder. Upon such payment, the position of the creditor is the same as if the payments had been timely. With respect to overdue taxes, in many instances the creditor can also be made whole by the mere payment of money. *See Middlemist v. Mosier,* 151 Colo. 113, 377 P.2d 110; *Bisno v. Sax,* 175 Cal.App.2d 714, 346 P.2d 814. In this case, tax receipts evidencing payment of all taxes due were tendered prior to foreclosure by the public trustee. The lien for unpaid taxes was thereby dissolved and any impairment of the creditor's collateral resulting from overdue taxes vanished. Under these circumstances, we hold that the statute serves as a bar to prevent foreclosure.

Foster cites *Motlong v. World Savings & Loan Ass'n,* 168 Colo. 540, 452 P.2d 384, for the proposition that non-payment of taxes constitutes an independent default which will support an action for foreclosure. However, the facts in that case are significantly different from the case at hand. In addition to non-payment of taxes, the debtor (Motlong) had permitted the property to deteriorate.

> Motlong was fully aware of the several violations of the covenants in the deed of trust, and apparently made no effort to repair the premises or pay the taxes after he learned of the foreclosure proceedings. . . . After the sale, he apparently made no attempt to redeem the property.

In the case at hand, there is no allegation that the property had deteriorated. Also, Darpo moved quickly to cure the default in tax payments prior to the date scheduled for the foreclosure sale.

II

Foster does not challenge the sufficiency of the tender with respect to overdue principal, interest, and other expenses, and we must assume that it was adequate. The public trustee was therefore justified in refusing to conduct the foreclosure sale.

Foster argues that, even if foreclosure is not permitted under the deed of trust, the trial court erred in dismissing its first claim for relief requesting a money judgment on the underlying note. Foster contends that the statute only prevents foreclosure by the public trustee, and does not prohibit suit on the note. The amount sought by Foster in its first claim for relief is the entire amount due on the note pursuant to a clause which permits acceleration upon default.

In Colorado, the holder of a note secured by deed of trust or mortgage has traditionally had the right to sue on the note alone, to foreclose on the property, or to join these proceedings in one action. *Foothills Holding Corp. v. Tulsa Rig, Reel & Mfg. Co.,* 155 Colo. 232, 393 P.2d 749; *Greene v. Wilson,* 90 Colo. 562, 11 P.2d 225; *Folda Real Estate Co. v. Jacobsen,* 75 Colo. 16, 223 P. 748. Prior to enactment of the statute permitting cure of default, nothing prevented a creditor, after default, from accelerating payments under the terms of a note and deed of trust or mortgage, and the choice of remedies did not produce inconsistent results. If the creditor invoked an acceleration clause, the debtor was obligated for the entire amount due, whether the creditor brought foreclosure proceedings or a suit on the note. However, the statute has modified the common law by limiting the right of acceleration. This appeal requires us to determine precisely what those limitations are.

The statute specifically refers to defaults on "the note, deed of trust, or mortgage" and was obviously intended to permit a debtor to cure a default in the terms of either instrument. It is important to note, however, that by its terms, the statute applies only to deeds of trust or mortgages "being foreclosed" and that the statutory mechanism for tender operates through the public trustees or other officers "conducting the sale." Statutory coverage is therefore triggered by initiation of foreclosure proceedings on the mortgage or deed of trust. In this case, when Foster filed its election and demand with the public trustee and the debtor tendered the overdue sums and costs, the statute operated to cure the default.

The crucial issue, then, is whether, once the provisions of the statute have been complied with and the appropriate sums tendered by the debtor, the default is cured only for the purpose of preventing foreclosure, or whether the creditor is also precluded from maintaining an action on the note based on that default. We believe the latter interpretation is correct. Where the creditor has elected to pursue foreclosure on his security, as he did in this case, the statute controls the proceedings, and a statutory tender by the debtor not only precludes foreclosure under the deed of trust but also precludes the creditor from pursuing an independent claim on the note under its acceleration clause, since a necessary element permitting acceleration, namely default, is no longer present.

As we pointed out above, adequate tender under the statute puts the creditor in the same position he would have been in if payments had been timely. From the creditor's point of view, it is as though a default had not occurred since any harm resulting from late payment has been cured.

The construction urged by plaintiff would allow a creditor who has elected to foreclose on the property to achieve indirectly the result prohibited by 1969 Perm. Supp., C.R.S.1963, 118-9-18. Even though tender under the statute had been made, the creditor could obtain a judgment for the full amount of the note and then levy on the real property covered by the deed of trust or any other assets of the debtor. Certainly the legislature did not intend that the statute be circumvented so easily.

. . . .

As modified, the judgment is affirmed.

PIERCE and RULAND, JJ., concur.

3. STRICT FORECLOSURE

BRAND v. WOOLSON

Supreme Court of Connecticut
120 Conn. 211, 180 A. 293 (1935)

BANKS, JUDGE.

This was a foreclosure of a purchase-money mortgage given by the defendant to the plaintiff. By a judgment rendered December 20, 1934, the court found the amount of the debt due to be $9,090, and fixed the third Friday of December, 1936, as the law day for the defendant to redeem. The only question presented on this appeal is whether the court abused its discretion in fixing a law day for the defendant two years from the date of foreclosure. From the finding, which is not subject to material correction, the following facts appear: The defendant purchased the premises under foreclosure, consisting of about twenty-four acres, most of which is woodland upon which there are no buildings, from the plaintiff in October, 1929, for $21,000. He has paid $12,000 of the purchase price, leaving a balance of $9,000 on the mortgage note which became due October 15, 1934. Interest has never been in default and the taxes are paid to November, 1935. The value of the premises is approximately $14,425. The plaintiff attacks this finding of the value of the property, but it is supported by expert testimony offered by the defendant and cannot be corrected.

It also appeared that in October, 1934, the defendant tendered to the plaintiff $270 for six months' interest on the note to April, 1935, which the latter refused, that the defendant offered the plaintiff a certified check for $1,000 to apply on the note if the latter would extend the time for payment of the note for a period of five years, which offer was rejected; also that the defendant offered to include a fifty-foot strip of land adjoining the premises in a new mortgage if the plaintiff would extend the time for payment of the note, and that the wife of the defendant was the owner of a second mortgage on property in Westport, the proceeds of which the defendant was willing to give to the plaintiff. The defendant was unable to pay the note at maturity, and at the date of the judgment was unable to refinance the property under the existing conditions of the real estate market. The plaintiff is an elderly woman financially in need and owes approximately $8,000.

The plaintiff contends that the allowance of two years in which to redeem is, under the circumstances of the case, unreasonable, arbitrary, and an abuse of the court's discretion. An action to foreclose a mortgage is peculiarly an equitable action. *Beach v. Isacs*, 105 Conn. 169, 176, 134 A. 787. Courts of equity applying their established jurisdiction to relieve against penalties and forfeitures created the equity of redemption giving the mortgagor a reasonable time to cure the default arising from his failure to pay upon the day fixed in his mortgage. *Louisville Joint Stock Land Bank v. Radford*, 295 U. S. 555, 55 S. Ct. 854, 79 L. Ed. — [sic].

In most jurisdictions the foreclosure is by a sale of the property and the time for redemption is fixed by statute. In this jurisdiction, except when, upon written motion, the court in its discretion decrees a sale, a mortgage is foreclosed by strict foreclosure, and the time for redemption is fixed by the court. Though this has been characterized as a severe remedy, it has been considered "more convenient and equitable to give the party himself a reasonable time to effect the sale, which can probably be done by him at a much greater advantage than by a forced sale at auction." 2 Swift's Digest, 198.

The procedure has always been that outlined by Chief Justice Swift: "On an application for a foreclosure the court will ascertain the sum that is due on the mortgage, and enquire into the value of the mortgaged premises, and will limit a time for redemption having regard to the value of the [mortgaged] premises when compared with the debt. If the land is worth about the amount of the debt or less, they will give but a short time; if the value of the land considerably exceeds the debt, so that it is an object to redeem, they will give a proportional time according to the circumstances of the case to prevent a sacrifice of the property; but no precise period has been established." 2 Swift's Digest, 197.

The flexibility of the procedure which permits the court to exercise its discretion in fixing the law day so as to protect the rights of all parties modifies any severity that may be thought to inhere in this method of foreclosure. The discretion exercised by the court in fixing the law day in a foreclosure is a legal discretion. Its exercise will not be interfered with on appeal to this court except in a case of manifest abuse and when injustice appears to have been done. *Hayward v. Plant,* 98 Conn. 374, 382, 119 A. 341. When it appears that there is an equity in the mortgaged property so that it is an object for the mortgagor to redeem, the court in fixing the law day may properly take into consideration the probability that the necessary money can be procured within the time limited for redemption. The difficulty of raising money, under existing conditions, upon any kind of security, is a matter of common knowledge. If an "emergency may furnish the occasion for the exercise of power," as was said in *Home Building & Loan Ass'n v. Blaisdell,* 290 U. S. 398, 426, 54 S. Ct. 231, 78 L. Ed. 413, 88 A. L. R. 1481, upholding a Minnesota statute providing for an extension of the statutory time for redemption of a mortgage, it may well furnish the occasion for an exercise of discretion in fixing a law day beyond a time which the court would feel justified in granting under normal conditions.

The court has found an equity in the mortgaged premises of $5,355, which is approximately 37 per cent. of their value. The taxes and interest have been kept up. All the facts found indicate that the defendant intends in good faith to redeem, and the probability that he will be able to do so within the time limited by the court. They furnish no support for the claim of the plaintiff that the judgment of the court has deprived her of any substantial right. Clearly, they furnish no basis for a conclusion that its action was unreasonable, arbitrary, or an abuse of its legal discretion.

There is no error.

In this opinion, the other Judges concurred.

PORTLAND MORTGAGE CO. v. CREDITOR'S PROTECTIVE ASS'N

Supreme Court of Oregon
199 Or. 432, 262 P.2d 918 (1953)

BRAND, JUSTICE.

This is an appeal by the Creditors Protective Association from an order denying a motion made by it for an order requiring the sheriff of Multnomah County to accept an offer of redemption made by it for the real property described in these proceedings.

The Portland Mortgage Company, a corporation, held a first mortgage upon the real property involved in this case. Katherine M. and Byron L. Randol were the mortgagors. The appellant Creditors Protective Association, a corporation, obtained a judgment against the Randols, which became a lien against said property, subsequent in time and inferior to the lien of the plaintiff's mortgage. The judgment was entered on 21 March 1950. On 24 March 1950 the plaintiff brought suit to foreclose its mortgage, but did not join the judgment lienholder as a party. The mortgage was foreclosed by decree on 25 May 1950 and the plaintiff purchased the property at the foreclosure sale for $6,214.72, being the amount of the mortgage plus costs. On 3 July 1950 the sheriff executed and delivered to the plaintiff a certificate of sale to the property. The sale was confirmed on 20 July 1950. On 17 August 1950 the plaintiff filed a suit in equity against the defendant Creditors Protective Association, the judgment lienholder. The complaint alleged that the judgment lien of the defendant, which had not been foreclosed in the original suit, constituted a cloud upon the plaintiff's title, and that it was subsequent in time and inferior to the interest of the plaintiff as purchaser at the mortgage foreclosure sale, except for the statutory right of redemption possessed by the defendant as a judgment lien creditor. The complaint prayed for the entry of an interlocutory judgment and decree requiring that the defendant redeem from the sheriff's sale to the plaintiff "within such time as the court shall deem reasonable in the manner and mode provided by statute for the redemption by a lien creditor from a sale of real property on execution, and in the event of the failure of the defendants so to redeem said property, that a final judgment and decree be entered herein forever barring ..." the claim of the defendant in or to the real property.

On 16 July 1951, more than a year after the sale of the mortgaged property to the plaintiff, and pursuant to the foreclosure decree, the sheriff executed and delivered to the plaintiff a deed conveying the premises. On 20 August 1951 the circuit court entered an interlocutory decree reciting the entry of a default against the defendant and providing that said defendant should have a period of 60 days from the date of the decree within which to redeem the property "in the manner and mode provided by the statutes of the State of Oregon for redemption by a lien creditor from an execution sale of real property from the Sheriff's sale to plaintiff", and providing further that in the event of failure of the defendant to redeem within the time allowed, a final judgment would be entered, barring and foreclosing the right of the defendant in the property. On 20 September 1951 the defendant judgment lienholder filed with the sheriff of Multnomah County a notice addressed to the plaintiff, its attorneys, the contract purchasers from the plaintiff and the sheriff, by the terms of which the parties mentioned, were notified that the defendant claimed a judgment lien against the property, which was due and unpaid. The notice further provided:

> ... that pursuant to Chapter 6-1605, O.C.L.A.1940, you are hereby requested to account on or before the expiration of ten days of the receipt of this notice for all rents, issues and profits from the following described property ... [describing it] and you are further notified of redemption of said property, and that on the 9th day of October, 1951 at 10:00 o'clock A.M., Creditors Protective Association, an Oregon corporation, will apply to the Sheriff of Multnomah County to redeem the above described real property pursuant to Chapter 6-1607, O.C.L.A.1940.

On 8 October 1951 the plaintiff filed with the sheriff of Multnomah County an accounting which reads in part as follows:

> Pursuant to written notice served upon Portland Mortgage Co., the above

named plaintiff, purchaser at execution sale of the real property described in the above suit . . . subject to right of redemption of the property described in the above suit, the said Portland Mortgage Co. and . . . [others] hereby present their verified account of all rents, issues and profits accruing from, and all sums which they claim as a lien upon the property sought to be redeemed. . . .

Then followed a statement of the account, showing a balance, as the amount necessary to redeem on 9 October 1951, of $7,037.88. It was also stated that interest after the date of October 9, 1951 would accrue at the rate of $1.98 per day.

On 9 October 1951 at the hour of 9:30 a. m., being one-half hour before the time specified by the defendant as the time at which it would "apply to the sheriff of Multnomah County to redeem . . ." the property, the plaintiff paid to the clerk of Multnomah County the sum of $321.50 which was sufficient to constitute full satisfaction of the judgment of the defendant, and thereupon the clerk satisfied said judgment on the margin of the record. It is stipulated that said funds are still being held by the county clerk. At the hour of 10 o'clock a. m., being the time set in the so-called notice of redemption, the defendant applied to the sheriff to redeem the real property and tendered to the sheriff the sum of $7,037.88, being the amount set out in the accounting as the amount necessary to redeem the property. The plaintiff, through its attorney, then exhibited the receipt of the county clerk for the sum of $321.50, received as satisfaction of the defendant's judgment. The defendant, by its attorney, refused said sum of $321.50. The sheriff denied the application of the defendant to redeem, for the reason that the judgment records showed that the judgment held by the defendant had been satisfied in full prior to the tender of the redemption money by the defendant, basing his decision upon the provisions of O.C.L.A. §§ 6-1602, subsection (2), 6-1607, subsections (1) (b) and (1) (c). The sheriff certified that the defendant was not a lien creditor entitled to redeem.

On 22 October 1951 the defendant filed a motion for an order requiring the sheriff to accept the offer of redemption made by it. That motion was made and filed in the case which the plaintiff had instituted on 17 August 1950 for the purpose of foreclosing the interest of the defendant judgment lienholder, and in which case the defendant had defaulted. The offer was accompanied by an affidavit reciting the facts and stating that the payment of $321.50 to the clerk by the plaintiff was made without the knowledge or consent of defendant. On 12 December 1951 the court denied the motion of the defendant, from which order the defendant appeals. There is a serious question whether the defendant had any standing to seek relief in the case in which he had been adjudged in default. True, he had no wish to be relieved from the decree entered on his default. But he did seek an order from the court requiring the sheriff to accept the redemption money. It may be that the proper procedure would have been to bring mandamus against the sheriff rather than seeking an order in a case in which he had been adjudged in default, but the issue was presented to the court on the merits by both parties and the court decided it on the merits. There is no issue raised in this court concerning the procedure followed. We will therefore consider the case on its merits here.

Only one assignment of error is presented by the defendant for consideration here, namely, that the court erred in denying the motion of the defendant for an order directing the sheriff of Multnomah County to accept the tender of defendant and to allow it to redeem the subject real property. The defendant maintains that the right of a lien creditor to redeem is a valuable and absolute right granted by statute which cannot be abridged or defeated by the purchaser at a mortgage foreclosure sale without the consent of the lien creditor. He relies upon the provisions of O.C.L.A. §§ 6-1602 to 6-1607 inclusive as the basis of the asserted right.

The plaintiff relies upon the provisions of O.C.L.A. § 6-1001, the relevant parts of which read as follows:

> Any person, against whom exists a judgment for the payment of money or who is interested in any property upon which any such judgment is a lien, may pay the amount due on such judgment to the clerk of the court in which such judgment was rendered, and such clerk shall thereupon release and satisfy such judgment upon the records of said court. . . .

The defendant intimates that a lien creditor is a necessary party to a mortgage foreclosure. This is true only in a limited sense. The statute provides that any person having a lien subsequent to the plaintiff upon the same property shall be made a defendant in a suit to foreclose a mortgage. O.C.L.A. §§ 9-501, 9-502. But it is established that although junior lien claimants are necessary parties if the decree is to affect them, nevertheless the decree of foreclosure is valid as to all parties who are properly joined even though other lienors are not joined. The omitted junior lienholder is in the same position as if no foreclosure had ever taken place, and he has the same rights, no more and no less, which he had before the foreclosure suit was commenced. *Monese v. Struve,* 155 Or. 68, 62 P.2d 822; *Gaines v. Childers,* 38 Or. 200, 63 P. 487; *Koerner v. Willamette Iron Works,* 36 Or. 90, 58 P. 863; *Sellwood v. Gray,* 11 Or. 534, 5 P. 196. One of the rights available to the junior lienholder is to redeem the mortgage and thus become subrogated to the position of the senior mortgagee. *Brown v. Crawford,* D.C., 252 F. 248; *Coughanour v. Hutchinson,* 41 Or. 419, 69 P. 68. This right was therefore available to the defendant unless it was cut off by the act of the plaintiff in paying into court the amount of the judgment which was a lien on the mortgaged property. It would appear that the rights of a junior judgment lien claimant attach to him only so long as he has an unpaid judgment which alone constitutes the basis for his lien.

Just as the omitted junior lienholder retains the rights he had in the property subject to the lien, so the senior mortgagee retains rights with respect to the junior lienholder which are the equivalent of those held by him before the foreclosure of his mortgage. The purchaser at the foreclosure sale, whether he be the mortgagee or a third party, is vested with the rights of the mortgagee as against any omitted parties in the foreclosure suit, and may proceed to cut off the junior lien by suit for strict foreclosure. By the decree the junior lienor will be required to redeem or be barred of any rights in the property. This is the procedure sanctioned by the courts of this state. *Gaines v. Childers; Koerner v. Willamette Iron Works; Sellwood v. Gray,* all supra.

The defendant claims that his right to redeem in this case is granted by statute and relies on O.C.L.A. § 6-1602(2), which provides that a creditor having a lien by judgment may redeem property sold subject to redemption. It is evident from defendant's argument and brief that it has confused the equitable right of redemption or equity of redemption with the statutory right of redemption. A clear distinction must be made between these two concepts.

The difference between the equity of redemption and statutory redemption has been made clear by the decisions of this court. *Higgs v. McDuffie,* 81 Or. 256, 157 P. 794, 158 P. 953; and *Sellwood v. Gray,* supra. The classic statement is that of Mr. Justice Lord in *Sellwood v. Gray* [11 Or. 534, 5 P. 198]. We quote:

... His equity of redemption is the right to redeem from the mortgage — to pay off the mortgage debt — until this right is barred by a decree of foreclosure; but until this right is barred, his estate, in law or in equity, is just the same after as it was before default. It is a right, though, of which the law takes no cognizance, and is enforceable only in equity, and has nothing to do with our statute of redemptions. [Citing cases.] This is a valuable right, and exists not only in the mortgagor himself, but in every other person who has an interest in, or legal or equitable lien upon, the mortgaged premises, and includes judgment creditors, all of whom may insist upon a redemption of the mortgage. [Citing authorities.] Nor can one against his consent be deprived of this right without due process of law. To bar his right of redemption he must be made a party to the foreclosure, or the proceeding as to him will be a nullity. . . .

The exercise of the equitable right of redemption has the effect of discharging the lien if the redemption is by the mortgagor or his successor in interest, but if a junior lien claimant redeems, the effect is to substitute the junior for the senior lienholder. In the latter case, the aggregate of the liens will be unchanged, but the persons holding the liens will be different. A junior lien, and the right of redemption which is an incident thereof, will remain in existence unless and until the same is foreclosed by a senior lienholder. When the junior lien is foreclosed, then the statutory right of redemption as to junior lien creditors given by O.C.L.A. § 6-1602(2) comes into existence. If there has never been a foreclosure of the junior lien, then there is no statutory right of redemption, only the equitable right of redemption. Concerning the rights of an omitted junior lienholder, a learned author states:

> ... This man's rights remain as they were, because the foreclosure does not bind him; and so, as a participant in the equity of redemption which, as to him, was never foreclosed, he can redeem in equity. That, indeed, is not only his proper course, but it is the only procedure that should be open to him. He cannot resort to statutory redemption, because he is not within the terms of the statute. The latter comes into effect at and with foreclosure, as we have seen, but the statute envisages those only whom the foreclosure has barred. It follows that one who has never been foreclosed cannot resort to statutory redemption. His remedy remains where it always was, regardless of whether the particular State had provided for statutory redemption. The remedy is redemption in equity after the ancient mode. 2 Glenn on Mortgages, § 238.

It is apparent, therefore, that the defendant cannot rely on the statutory provisions as a basis for his claim of an absolute right to redeem. The obvious purpose of the statutory right of redemption is to give an additional opportunity to the mortgagor to recover his land and to the subsequent lien creditors to protect their interests. But, as has been indicated, the defendant herein can protect his interests without resort to the statutory right of redemption, and we therefore hold that the defendant does not come within the provisions of O.C.L.A. § 6-1602(2). The provisions of O.C.L.A. § 6-1603 limiting the right of a lien creditor to redeem to the period of 60 days from date of sale clearly indicates that the statutory right of redemption does not apply in cases such as the one at bar. It was provided in the interlocutory decree that the defendant "shall have a period of sixty days from the date of this decree within which to redeem in the manner and mode provided by the statutes of the State of Oregon for redemption by a lien creditor from an execution sale of real property. . . ." The quoted provision did not constitute a holding that the defendant had a statutory right of redemption. The decree only adopted the procedure of statutory redemption as that which should be followed by the defendant if it should choose to redeem.

The junior lienor, who was omitted in the foreclosure of the senior mortgage, still has the valuable right of redemption available to him, but, when such a right is exercised, the authorities are clear that the redeeming junior lienholder is not entitled to a conveyance of the property, but rather to an assignment of the security interest of the senior mortgage. *Renard v. Brown,* 7 Neb. 449; *Smith v. Shay,* 62 Iowa 119, 17 N.W. 444; *O'Brien v. Perkins,* Tex.Civ.App., 276 S.W. 308; *Shelton v. O'Brien,* Tex.Com.App., 285 S.W. 260. This rule is stated in 2 Jones, Mortgages, 8th ed, § 1376, as follows:

> A junior incumbrancer who, not having been made a party to a foreclosure of a prior mortgage, afterward redeems, redeems not the premises, strictly speaking, but the prior incumbrance; and he is entitled, not to a conveyance of the premises, but to an assignment of the security. Therefore if the prior mortgagee in such case has become the purchaser at the foreclosure sale, and has thus acquired the equity of redemption of the mortgaged premises, the junior mortgagee upon redeeming is not entitled to a conveyance of the estate, but to an assignment of the prior mortgage; whereupon the prior mortgagee, as owner of the equity of redemption, may, if he choose, pay the amount due upon the junior mortgage, redeeming that. . . .

When a junior lienholder has redeemed the senior incumbrance and steps into the shoes of the prior mortgagee, he must foreclose his lien and have the property sold, in order to realize on his security, unless the purchaser at the prior foreclosure, who has acquired the mortgagor's equity of redemption, chooses to redeem from him. The equity of redemption acquired by the purchaser at the foreclosure sale, when perfected by delivery of a sheriff's deed, constitutes the basis of his right to re-redeem from a junior lienholder who by redemption from the purchaser has acquired the rights of the senior mortgagee but has not acquired the property. We quote:

> Redemption by a junior lienor, however, means a correlative privilege on the part of the senior whose mortgage has gone through foreclosure. The junior lien, in the beginning, was subject to redemption on the part of the mortgagor. The latter, of course, lost all his rights and interest when the decree of foreclosure was entered against him. But let us remember that the junior's security consisted only of the equity of redemption, or a share in it. Hence if he redeems after a foreclosure from which he has been omitted, he is not redeeming the premises as the mortgagor would have done, but is merely acquiring the senior mortgage for the protection of his own interest. It follows that he can be met at the gate by the purchaser at the sale, whether he be the senior mortgagee or a third party, with a tender of money in payment of his debt with interest. In other words, the purchaser at the sale can dispose of the junior mortgagee by redeeming the land from his lien. 1 Glenn, Mortgages, § 86.5.

Parcells v. Nelson, 103 Mont. 412, 63 P.2d 131, 135, is a case in which an omitted junior mortgagee sought to redeem from the purchaser at the prior foreclosure sale. Concerning his right to redeem, the court said:

> The purpose of preserving to a lienholder an equity of redemption is to protect him from loss, and if such a one receives all that he is entitled to, his lien is extinguished and, with it, his equity of redemption. . . . On the other hand, these defendants [the purchasers at the foreclosure sale] acquired the legal title to the premises [citing cases], subject to the lien of plaintiff's mort-

gage, and the equity of redemption with respect to it was available to them for the purpose of clearing their title [citing cases]. . . .

The authorities cited control the decision in the pending case. Since the sheriff's deed to the plaintiff conveyed all the interests in the property except the judgment lien held by the defendant, the plaintiff acquired an owner's interest in the property entitling it to pay off the judgment of defendant and free the land of the lien. O.C.L.A. § 6-1001. No question is raised in this court as to the right of the clerk of the court to enter the satisfaction of judgment as permitted by O.C.L.A. § 6-1001. Since the purchaser, having a sheriff's deed, could redeem from the junior lienholder if the latter had redeemed from the senior mortgage, and could thereby acquire unencumbered and unclouded title, we can see no reason why such junior lienholder cannot be paid off prior to any redemption. In the view we take of this case, it therefore makes no difference whether the notice of redemption by the junior lienholder was given prior to the time plaintiff paid the judgment, or how far such proceedings had been carried.

Cases cited by the defendant to show that the holder of the certificate of sale under a foreclosure proceeding has an insufficient interest in the property in question to pay a judgment which has become a lien on that property are not in point because the plaintiff here had received a sheriff's deed.

It is also argued by the defendant that the plaintiff has come to court with unclean hands, and that it is seeking equity while it refuses to do equity. But we have shown that plaintiff was under no obligation to join the defendant in the mortgage foreclosure case and that failure to do so did not affect defendant's lien.

Defendant contends that even if we should hold that the plaintiff had a right to pay off the defendant's judgment the result would merely be to give to plaintiff a choice between paying off the judgment on the one hand or suing for strict foreclosure on the other and that by suing for strict foreclosure the plaintiff made an election of remedies from which he could not withdraw. This contention is untenable. Since the plaintiff as owner would still have had the right to pay off the defendant's judgment if the defendant had redeemed from plaintiff's mortgage, it would be useless to permit defendant to pay to plaintiff the amount of the first mortgage, only to be required to receive back the same amount from the plaintiff plus the amount of the defendant's lien. If the same result would be possible under either course of action it can hardly be said that the preliminary choice of one necessarily bars the other.

We hold that the payment by the plaintiff to the county clerk pursuant to the provisions of O.C.L.A. § 6-1001 and the entry of satisfaction on the margin of the record discharged defendant's judgment and that thereupon the defendant ceased to be a lienholder. Having been fully paid he had no right to redeem.

The order of the trial court denying defendant's motion to require the sheriff to accept defendant's offer of redemption is affirmed.

LATOURETTE, C.J., concurs in the result of this opinion.

NOTE

Note the difference between the two types of strict foreclosure dealt with in this section. The first, in *Brand v. Woolson, supra,* allows the mortgagee to become the owner of the encumbered property on Law Day by which the mortgagor must redeem or lose the property after a default. The Oregon case, *Portland Mortgage Co. v. Creditor's Protective Ass'n, supra,* demonstrates the same format whereby a junior lienor must pay or forfeit the security interest by a date certain. Notice, however, in the second case that it is not the mortgagee but the purchaser who is in the position of power, at a foreclosure sale following a judicial foreclosure, from which a junior lienor has been omitted. The junior lienor's position is comparable to that of the mortgagor in Connecticut's strict foreclosure. While strict foreclosure is available in several jurisdictions as an action to remove the cloud of an omitted junior's lien from the title, strict foreclosure as a remedy for mortgagees wishing to foreclose is available only in Connecticut.

Chapter 6

REDEMPTION

> Anticipated rents, and bills unpaid,
> Force many a shining youth into the shade,
> Not to redeem his time, but his estate,
> And play the fool, but at a cheaper rate.

Cowper, *Retirement*

The concept of redemption is simple enough: A mortgagor has the right to pay off the obligation and have the mortgage removed from the property. Statutory redemption provides this right to the mortgagor even after a foreclosure sale has taken place. Because this right appears to be repugnant to the basic law of contracts, law students frequently have a difficult time accepting the fact that several legislatures have conferred such a right on defaulting mortgagors. However, there are many exceptions to basic contract law which exist in our everyday commercial society. The "cooling-off" period under some Consumer Protection Acts is but one example of how the law allows exception to basic contract law.[1] Americans have come to expect that most department stores will, within reasonable limits, allow customers to return merchandise for a credit or refund without justifying reason; one would not expect a department store clerk to refuse a refund on the legal basis that the contract had been fully executed. Once the student realizes that there are both everyday and statutory exceptions to the fundamentals of contracts, then the concept of statutory redemption is more palatable. Legislatures can, as demonstrated by the statutes, grant a defaulting mortgagor time to pay off the mortgage and avoid losing the property even though it has already been sold at a foreclosure sale and even though the contract had no such provision.

In order to fully appreciate redemption rights it is necessary to separate equitable redemption from statutory redemption. All mortgagors have the right to pay the amount of the obligation and have the mortgage removed from their land. This is equitable redemption. Remember that at common law the mortgagor had but one day, Law Day, on which to pay the mortgage in full.[2] That rule has obviously changed today with amortized mortgages and limited rights to make payments late [3] or pay off the mortgage early.[4] However, a one-day-only time period in which to pay was the rule until Courts of Equity began to alleviate some of the harshness of such a rule. Remember also that there was no foreclosure, but rather the mortgagee simply retained the property and the mortgagor lost all rights if payment was not made on Law Day. Equity created a *right to redeem* after Law Day. Considering that title passed to the mortgagee upon execution, subject to the mortgagor performing the obligation to pay on Law Day, an

---

[1] For example, the Home Transaction Solicitation Act, Tex. Civ. Code Ann. art. 5069-13.01 (Vernon), provides that any consumer who enters into a contract that has been solicited at the consumer's home has three business days during which the contract may be revoked.

[2] "The day prescribed in a bond, mortgage, or defeasible deed for payment of the debt secured thereby, or, in default of payment, the forfeiture of the property mortgage." Black's Law Dictionary, p. 473 (Rev'd 4th ed. 1968).

[3] Late payments are dealt with in Chapter 4.

[4] 12 C.F.R. § 454.6-12.

extension of time in which to pay was a drastic step for the court to take. It also violated the terms of the contract between the borrower and lender. The next step in the evolution of mortgagor's rights was the elimination of the automatic termination of the mortgagor's rights. Equity required the mortgagee to foreclose and have the property sold in order to satisfy the debt. In fact the term "foreclosure" is but a shortened way to refer to the process of *foreclosing the borrower's equity of redemption.* It is that right to redeem and save the property that is being foreclosed.

With that background it should not be difficult to accept as a matter of course further deviation from contract law by allowing the defaulting mortgagor, by statute, the right to pay up during some specified time after the foreclosure sale has been conducted. Prior to the sale, when redemption is considered it is the borrower's equity of redemption, or equitable redemption; after the sale the borrower has no further time nor right to redeem unless the legislature creates such a right by statute. Thus after the sale any redemption right must be statutory redemption. Of course there are some minor variations in this area; one state provides by statute for redemption after a court has ordered a sale but before the sale actually takes place,[5] another simply does not allow the foreclosure deed to be executed for a year after the sale, during which time the borrower may still satisfy the debt and save the property.[6]

Neither equitable nor statutory redemption should be confused with the borrower's right to reinstate a delinquent obligation by paying the delinquent amount plus some penalty. California provides a three month period of time after a power of sale foreclosure is commenced during which the delinquent borrower may pay the arrearage plus costs and have the foreclosure rescinded.[7] This is a right to reinstate which has been created by statute. It is not redemption, since only the arrearage is paid and the remaining balance must still be paid. The mortgage still exists and the borrower must renew making installment payments or have the process begin again with a new foreclosure.

Another way to compare the difference between redemption and reinstatement is to consider that reinstatement refers to making some delinquent payments and continuing to do so consistent with the contract; redemption contemplates paying the entire balance due in one payment. Today's mortgage can be for a long period of time; residential mortgages are usually for 360 monthly payments. At common law and until the end of the 1930s American mortgages were not amortized and the principal was paid in one payment at the end of a relatively short term of interest-only payments. No need for any statutory provision for reinstatement existed since a borrower could not fall behind in principal payments. However, when only one principal payment was due and it was not timely made legislatures sought to mitigate the harsh effect by giving the mortgagor some time in which to pay and avoid loss of the land.

A. EQUITABLE REDEMPTION

Equitable redemption in its simplest form is merely completing the borrower's obligation by paying in full the debt secured by the mortgage and having the mortgage released. A dispute between the borrower and lender as to whether the borrower has the right to pay in full after the due date can be resolved by the

---

[5] Ohio Rev. Code Ann. § 2329.33 (1981).
[6] Wis. Stat. § 846.10 (1981 Supp.).
[7] Cal. Civ. Code § 2924c.

borrower bringing a Bill in Equity. In order to do so the borrower is generally required to tender payment in full. If the borrower fails to make the payment, then the court can treat the action as a foreclosure and order the property sold.

Another aspect of equitable redemption is that there is a limit placed on the borrower and lender that precludes them from agreeing at the time the mortgage is executed to any terms that would cut off the borrower's equity of redemption. To attempt to do so is called *clogging the equity of redemption*. The right to redeem is apparently not waivable at the time a mortgage is entered into but can be accomplished when a default occurs by the borrower tendering a deed in lieu of foreclosure to the lender. If accepted, the lender takes the land, the debt is satisfied and the borrower has no further redemption rights.

California Civil Code (1981 Supp.)

§ 2924c. Cure of default; payment of arrearages, costs and fees; statement

(a) Whenever all or a portion of the principal sum of any obligation secured by deed of trust or mortgage on real property hereafter executed has, prior to the maturity date fixed in such obligation, become due or been declared due by reason of default in payment of interest or of any installment of principal, or by reason of failure of trustor or mortgagor to pay, in accordance with the terms of such obligation or of such deed of trust or mortgage, taxes, assessments, premiums for insurance or advances made by beneficiary or mortgagee in accordance with the terms of such obligation or of such deed of trust or mortgage, the trustor or mortgagor or his successor in interest in the mortgaged or trust property or any part thereof, or any beneficiary under a subordinate deed of trust or any other person having a subordinate lien or encumbrance of record thereon, at any time within three months of the recording of the notice of default under such deed of trust or mortgage, if the power of sale therein is to be exercised, or, otherwise at any time prior to entry of the decree of foreclosure, may pay to the beneficiary or the mortgagee or their successors in interest, respectively, the entire amount then due under the terms of such deed of trust or mortgage and the obligation secured thereby (including costs and expenses actually incurred in enforcing the terms of such obligation, deed of trust or mortgage, and trustee's or attorney's fees actually incurred not exceeding one hundred dollars ($100) in case of a mortgage and fifty dollars ($50) in case of a deed of trust or one-half of 1 percent of the entire unpaid principal sum secured, whichever is greater) other than such portion of principal as would not then be due had no default occurred, and thereby cure the default theretofore existing, and thereupon, all proceedings theretofore had or instituted shall be dismissed or discontinued and the obligation and deed of trust or mortgage shall be reinstated and shall be and remain in force and effect, the same as if no such acceleration had occurred. The provisions of this section shall not apply to bonds or other evidences of indebtedness authorized or permitted to be issued by the Commissioner of Corporations or made by a public utility subject to the provisions of the Public Utilities Code. . . .

GRAF v. HOPE BUILDING CORP.

Court of Appeals of New York
254 N.Y. 1, 171 N.E. 884 (1930)

O'BRIEN, J. Plaintiffs, as executors of Joseph L. Graf, are the holders of two consolidated mortgages forming a single lien on real property the title to which is vested in defendant Hope Building Corporation. According to the terms of the agreement consolidating the mortgages the principal sum is made payable January 1, 1935. Nevertheless, a clause provides that the whole shall become due after default for twenty days in the payment of any installment of interest. David Herstein is the controlling stockholder and also president and treasurer of defendant. He alone was authorized to sign checks in its behalf. Early in June, 1927, he went to Europe. Before his departure a clerical assistant who was also the nominal secretary of the corporation computed the interest due July 1, and through an error in arithmetic incorrectly calculated it. Mr. Herstein signed the check for the erroneous amount, but before the date upon which the interest became due, the secretary discovered the error, notified the mortgagee of the shortage of $401.87, stated that on the president's return from Europe the balance would be paid, and on June 30 forwarded to the mortgagee the check as drawn. It was deposited by the mortgagee and paid by defendant. On July 5, Mr. Herstein returned, but, through an omission in his office, he was not informed of the default in the payment of interest. At the expiration of twenty-one days this action of foreclosure was begun. Defendant made tender of the deficiency, but the mortgagee, strictly insisting on his contract rights, refused the tender and elected to assert the power created by the acceleration clause in the consolidation agreement.

On the undisputed facts as found, we are unable to perceive any defense to the action, and are therefore constrained to reverse the judgment dismissing the complaint. Plaintiffs may be ungenerous, but generosity is a voluntary attribute and cannot be enforced even by a chancellor. Forbearance is a quality which under the circumstances of this case is likewise free from coercion. Here there is no penalty, no forfeiture (*Ferris v. Ferris,* 28 Barb. 29; *Noyes v. Anderson,* 124 N. Y. 175, 180, 26 N. E. 316, 317, 21 Am. St. Rep. 657), nothing except a covenant fair on its face to which both parties willingly consented. It is neither oppressive nor unconscionable. *Valentine v. Van Wagner,* 37 Barb. 60. In the absence of some act by the mortgagee which a court of equity would be justified in considering unconscionable he is entitled to the benefit of the covenant. The contract is definite and no reason appears for its reformation by the courts. *Abrams v. Thompson,* 251 N. Y. 79, 86, 167 N. E. 178. We are not at liberty to revise while professing to construe. *Sun Printing & Publishing Ass'n v. Remington Paper & Power Co.,* 235 N. Y. 338, 346, 139 N. E. 470. Defendant's mishap, caused by a succession of its errors and negligent omissions, is not of the nature requiring relief from its default. Rejection of plaintiffs' legal right could rest only on compassion for defendant's negligence. Such a tender emotion must be exerted, if at all, by the parties rather than by the court. Our guide must be the precedents prevailing since courts of equity were established in this state. Stability of contract obligations must not be undermined by judicial sympathy. To allow this judgment to stand would constitute an interference by this court between parties whose contract is clear. One has been unfortunately negligent, but neither has committed a wrong. If defendant's president had left some person in charge with authority to deal with affairs as they might arise, the first error could have been immediately corrected and the second would not have occurred. Even after Mr. Herstein's return on July 5, two weeks remained before the expiration of the twenty days. The secretary's forgetfulness during this time is not sufficient excuse for a court of equity to refuse to lend its aid to the prosecution of an action based upon an incontestably plain agreement. Such a refusal would set at nought the rules announced and enforced for a century in such cases as *Noyes v. Clark,* 7 Paige, 179, 180, 32 Am. Dec. 620; *Hale v. Gouverneur,* 4 Edw. Ch. 207; *Ferris v. Ferris,* supra; *Valentine v. Van Wagner,* supra; *Malcolm v. Allen,* 49 N. Y. 448; *Bennett v. Stevenson,* 53 N. Y. 508; *Hothorn v. Louis,* 52 App. Div. 218, 65 N. Y. S. 155, affirmed 170 N. Y. 576, 62 N. E. 1096. The words of Chancellor Walworth in *Noyes v. Clark,* supra, express the rule which has since prevailed in respect to the rights of a mortgagee against a defaulting mortgagor under an acceleration clause:

> The parties . . . had an unquestionable right to make the extension of credit dependent upon the punctual payment of the interest at the times fixed for that purpose. And if, from the mere negligence of the mortgagor in performing his contract, he suffers the whole debt to become due and payable, according to the terms of the mortgage, no court will interfere to relieve him from the payment thereof according to the conditions of his own agreement. . . .

. . . We feel that the interests of certainty and security in real estate transactions forbid us, in the absence of fraud, bad faith or unconscionable conduct, to recede from the doctrine that is so deeply imbedded in equity.

. . . .

The judgment of the Appellant Division and that of the Special Term should be reversed, and judgment ordered in favor of plaintiff for the relief demanded in the complaint, with costs in all courts.

CARDOZO, C. J. (dissenting). The action is one for the foreclosure of a consolidated mortgage.

[Here the dissent recites the same facts set forth in the majority opinion.]

These facts being proved, the trial judge held that there had been a mere mistake in computation, against which equity would relieve by refusing to co-operate with the plaintiff in the effort to collect the accelerated debt. The Appellate Division unanimously affirmed. Upon appeal by the plaintiff the case is now here by allowance of this court.

There is no undeviating principle that equity shall enforce the covenants of a mortgage, unmoved by an appeal ad misericordiam, however urgent or affecting. The development of the jurisdiction of the chancery is lined with historic monuments that point another course. Equity declines to treat a mortgage upon realty as a conveyance subject to a condition, but views it as a lien irrespective of its form. *Trimm v. Marsh,* 54 N. Y. 599, 13 Am. Rep. 623. Equity declines to give effect to a covenant, however formal, whereby in the making of a mortgage, the mortgagor abjures and surrenders the privilege of redemption. *Mooney v. Byrne,* 163 N. Y. 86, 93, 57 N. E. 163. Equity declines in the same spirit, to give effect to a covenant, improvident in its terms, for the sale of an inheritance, but compels the buyer to exhibit an involuntary charity if he is found to have taken advantage of the necessities of the seller. Pomeroy, Eq. Jur. vol. 2, § 953. Equity declines to give effect to a covenant for liquidated damages if it is so unconscionable in amount as to be equivalent in its substance to a provision for a penalty. *Kothe v. R. C. Taylor Trust,* 280 U. S. 224, 50 S. Ct. 142, 74 L. Ed. [382]. One could give many illustrations of the traditional and unchallenged exercise of a like dispensing power. It runs through the whole rubric of accident and mistake. Equity follows the law, but not slavishly nor always. *Hedges v. Dixon County,* 150 U. S. 182, 192, 14 S. Ct. 71, 37 L. Ed. 1044. If it did, there could never be occasion for the enforcement of equitable doctrine. 13 Halsbury, Laws of England, p. 68.

To all this, acceleration clauses in mortgages do not constitute an exception. They are not a class by themselves, removed from interference by force of something peculiar in their internal constitution. In general, it is true, they will be enforced as they are written. In particular this has been held of a covenant in a mortgage accelerating the maturity of the principal in default of punctual payment of an installment of the interest. If the quality of a penalty inheres in such a covenant at all, it is not there to such a degree as to call, in ordinary circumstances, for mitigation or repression. *Noyes v. Clark,* 7 Paige, 179, 32 Am. Dec. 620; *Ferris v. Ferris,* 28 Barb. 29; *Malcolm v. Allen,* 49 N. Y. 448; *Bennett v. Stevenson,* 53 N. Y. 508. Less favor has been shown to a provision for acceleration of a mortgage in default of punctual payment of taxes or assessments. We have held that such a provision, though not a penalty in a strict or proper sense, is yet so closely akin thereto in view of the forfeiture of credit that equity will relieve against it if default has been due to mere venial inattention and if relief can be granted without damage to the lender. *Noyes v. Anderson,* 124 N. Y. 175, 26 N. E. 316, 21 Am. St. Rep. 657; followed in *Ver Planck v. Godfrey,* 42 App. Div. 16, 58 N. Y. S. 784; *Germania Life Ins. Co. v. Potter,* 124 App. Div. 814, 109 N. Y. S. 435, and cf. *Trowbridge v. Malex Realty Corporation,* 198 App. Div. 656, 191 N. Y. S. 97. In the one case as in the other, in foreclosure for default of taxes just as in foreclosure for default of interest, the privilege of acceleration is absolute in the event of a default, if the privilege is to be measured by the language of the covenant. The distinction lies in this only, that the punctual payment of interest has an importance to the lender as affecting his way of life, perhaps the very means for his support, whereas the importance of payment of the taxes is merely as an assurance of security. The difference is not one of kind, for the provision is enforcible even as to taxes if the default is continuous or willful; it is a difference merely of degree, the purpose of the payment being referred to as a test wherewith to gauge the measure of the hardship, the extent of the oppression.

There is neither purpose nor desire to impair the stability of the rule, which is still to be enforced as one of general application, that nonpayment of interest will accelerate the debt if the mortgage so provides. The rule is well understood, and is fair to borrower and lender in its normal operation. Especially is it fair if there is a period of grace (in this case twenty days) whereby a reasonable leeway is afforded to inadvertence and improvidence. In such circumstances, with one period of grace established by the covenant, only the most appealing equity will justify a court in transcending the allotted period and substituting another. . . .

When an advantage is unconscionable depends upon the circumstances. It is not unconscionable generally to insist that payment shall be made according to the letter of a contract. It may be unconscionable to insist upon adherence to the letter where the default is limited to a trifling balance, where the failure to pay the balance is the product of mistake, and where the mortgagee indicates by his conduct that he appreciates the mistake and has attempted by silence and inaction to turn it to his own advantage. The holder of this mortgage must have understood that he could have his money for the asking. His silence, followed, as it was, by immediate suit at the first available opportunity, brings conviction to the mind that he was avoiding any act that would spur the mortgagor to payment. What he did was almost as suggestive of that purpose as if he had kept out of the way in order to avoid a tender. *Noyes v. Clark,* supra. Demand was, indeed, unnecessary to bring the debt to maturity at law. There is not a technical estoppel. *Thompson v. Simpson,* 128 N. Y. 270, 291, 28 N. E. 627; Spencer Bower on Estoppel, pp. 61, 352, 358; cf. Williston, Contracts, vol. 3, §§ 1497, 1548, 1557. The consequence does not follow that, in conditions so peculiar, the omission to make demand is without signifance in equity. Significant it may then be in helping the court to a determination whether the conduct of a suitor in taking advantage of a default, so easily averted and so plainly unintentional, is consistent with good conscience. Cf. *Retan v. Clark,* 220 Mich. 493, 190 N. W. 244. True, indeed, it is that accident and mistake will often be inadequate to supply a basis for the granting or withholding of equitable remedies where the consequences to be corrected might have been avoided if the victim of the misfortune had ordered his affairs with reasonable diligence. *United States v. Ames,* 99 U. S. 35, 47, 25 L. Ed. 295; *Grymes v. Sanders,* 93 U. S. 55, 23 L. Ed. 798; *Noyes v. Clark,* supra. The restriction, however, is not obdurate, for always the gravity of the fault must be compared with the gravity of the hardship. *Noyes v. Anderson,* supra; *Lawrence v. American Nat. Bank,* 54 N. Y. 432; *Ball v. Shepard,* 202 N. Y. 247, 253, 95 N. E. 719. Let the hardship be strong enough, and equity will find a way, though many a formula of inaction may seem to bar the path. *Griswold v. Hazard,* 141 U. S. 260, 284, 11 S. Ct. 972, 999 35 L. Ed. 678.

. . . .

In this case, the hardship is so flagrant, the misadventure so undoubted, the oppression so apparent, as to justify a holding that only through an acceptance of the tender will equity be done. The omission to pay in full had its origin in a clerical or arithmetical error that accompanied the act of payment, the very act to be performed. The error was not known to the debtor except in a constructive sense, for the secretary, a subordinate clerk, omitted to do her duty and report it to her principal. The deficiency, though not so small as to be negligible within the doctrine of de minimis, was still slight and unimportant when compared with the payment duly made. The possibility of bad faith is overcome by many circumstances, of which not the least is the one that instantly upon the discovery of the error, the deficiency was paid, and this only a single day after the term of grace was at an end. Finally, there is no pretense of damage or even inconvenience ensuing to the lender. On the contrary, and this is the vital point, the inference is inevitable that the lender appreciated the blunder and was unwilling to avert it. From his conduct on the day, immediately succeeding the default, we can infer his state of mind as it existed the day before. When all these circumstances are viewed in their cumulative significance, the enforcement of the covenant according to its letter is seen to approach in hardship the oppression of a penalty, just as truly as in *Noyes v. Anderson* there was unconscionable hardship in an insistence upon a default in the discharge of an assessment. Ninety-one per cent. of the interest had been paid when it matured. The other nine per cent. was paid as soon as the underpayment became known to an agent competent to act and only a day too late. Equity declines to intervene at the instance of a suitor who after fostering the default would make the court his ally in an endeavor to turn it to his benefit.

The judgment should be affirmed with costs.

POUND, CRANE, and HUBBS, JJ., concur with O'BRIEN, J.

CARDOZO, C. J., dissents in opinion in which LEHMAN and KELLOGG, JJ., concur.

Judgment accordingly.

HUMBLE OIL & REFINERY CO. v. DOERR

New Jersey Court of Chancery
123 N.J. Super. 530, 303 A.2d 898 (1973)

ACKERMAN, J.S.C. The ancient doctrine that a mortgagor's equity of redemption may not be "clogged" has rarely been involved in litigation in this state. This case involves a novel application of the doctrine and, so far as research by counsel and the court has disclosed, there are no precedents directly in point.

The specific point involved is whether the doctrine, which bars a mortgagee from clogging the mortgagor's equity of redemption and prohibits him from taking an option to purchase the property from the mortgagor as a part of the original mortgage transaction, also bars the mortgagor's guarantor from taking such option. In the circumstances of this case it is the conclusion of the court that it does.

I

Certain of the factual issues were hotly contested, including those relating to the value of the property at the time of the option, the alleged ignorance of the optionors as to the existence and meaning of the option, and whether or not there were fraudulent misrepresentations and concealment in the obtaining of the option. However, the case does not really turn upon the resolution of these issues and the result is the same regardless of how they are determined. The basic facts are as follows.

Defendant Josephine Venice Rokita Doerr (hereinafter referred to as "Josephine") is the owner of a piece of real property located on the northeast corner of Boulevard and Michigan Avenue in Kenilworth. The parties agree that it is now one of the choice locations for a gasoline service station in Union County. The property was acquired in about 1944 by Pat Venice, Josephine's first husband. He intended to erect a service station thereon but died in 1947 without having carried his plans into effect, and Josephine succeeded to the sole ownership of the premises as well as to other parcels of real estate in Kenilworth. A few years thereafter Josephine's family, and in particular her brother Sal Amoroso, erected a three-bay service station on the property and operated same, apparently making "rent" payments from the income of the business to Josephine. In connection with the initial construction of the station the property was mortgaged to the Union County Trust Company, which granted a $12,000 loan for ten years at 5% interest in 1952 to Josephine, her brother and his wife.

In 1953 Josephine remarried. Her second husband, Victor W. Rokita (hereinafter "Victor"), took over the management of the service station. In 1958 he took steps to add three bays to the garage in order to expand the facilities for performing automotive repair work. He went to the Union County Trust Company, which already held the mortgage on the premises, to arrange for additional financing, and that bank apparently agreed to advance approximately $20,000 secured by a first mortgage on the land and building. These plans came to the attention of plaintiff Humble Oil & Refining Company (then Esso Standard Oil Company and hereinafter referred to as "Humble") whose products were sold at the station. John Alden, the Humble representative who serviced Victor's account, approached Victor and told him that Humble could get him better terms — $35,000, rather than $20,000 at a lesser interest rate and for a longer term. Alden discussed the matter and negotiated first with Victor alone and then with both Victor and Josephine. These favorable terms were to be obtained by leasing the station to Humble at a rental equal to the amount to be paid each month by Victor and Josephine on the new mortgages, which would be granted by The National State Bank, Elizabeth, N. J., and by having Victor and Josephine assign the Humble rental payments to the bank as additional security. Humble would then lease back to them at the same rental and they would continue to operate the service station. (This arrangement is referred to as a "two-party" lease. See Point IV, *infra*.)

As the result of the negotiations it was agreed that the financing arranged by Humble would be accepted, and a lease was entered into between Victor and Josephine, as lessors, and Humble, as lessee, under date of September 5, 1958, for a 15-year term commencing on September 1, 1959 (approximately one year later) and ending on September 1, 1974, at a rental to be paid by Humble of $272.30 a month, the exact amount required to be paid each month to The National State Bank by Victor and Josephine under the comtemplated mortgage. This lease, entitled "Lease to Company," was written on a printed Humble form bearing the legend "Lessor Built S.S.," which was drafted by Humble for use as the standard lease form to be utilized in instances where Humble leased premises with stations already built thereon or being constructed thereon by owner-lessors. The provisions of this form were obviously designed to be fully protective of Humble's interest as lessee.

The provision of the lease which is directly involved here is that which granted a purchase option to Humble. The option provisions recites that the lessors, "in consideration of this lease," grant to Humble the option to purchase the property for the sum of $150,000 "at any time" during the term of lease. The price is to be paid on transfer of good and marketable title by the lessors by warranty deed free and clear of all encumbrances, and requires that title should be closed and deed delivered on the 30th day after the exercise of the option, unless extended by mutual agreement.

On May 29, 1959 Victor and Josephine entered into a $35,000 construction mortgage with The National State Bank and formally assigned their interest in the Humble lease to the bank. Thereafter the additional three bays were apparently constructed and on January 12, 1960, the 15-year permanent mortgage loan for $35,000 was entered into.... A new note agreement was also entered into on January 12, 1960 between the bank and the Rokitas which contained a formal assignment to the bank of the Humble lease. This agreement provided that as "collateral security" the Rokitas assigned their interest in the Humble lease to the bank, and they agreed that the bank should collect the "rents, issues and profits accruing out of the premises" demised to Humble until repaid the full sum of $35,000 plus interest, and further, until the bank had been repaid all sums paid by it pursuant to the loan agreement and mortgage "and not repaid to it out of the rents derived from said premises." By the note agreement, as well as the mortgage, the Rokitas agreed to pay to the bank monthly a sum equal to one-twelfth of taxes. The note agreement expressly provided that if *Humble* should fail to pay any installment of rent provided for in the lease, or the Rokitas should default in performance of any of their obligations contained in the note, mortgage *or lease,* and the default continued for ten days, the bank at its option could demand immediate payment of the entire unpaid mortgage balance. The net result of this agreement was that a default by *Humble* or a failure by the Rokitas to comply with any of the conditions of the *lease* could constitute a mortgage loan default by the Rokitas.

By an agreement dated January 12, 1960, the same date on which the permanent mortgage papers were signed for the bank, a supplement to the Humble lease was signed by the Rokitas and witnessed by the attorney for the bank, modifying the lease so that the original term thereof commenced on February 1, 1960. This supplement ratified and confirmed all other terms of the lease.

On January 18, 1960 a lease was entered into between Humble, as lessee, and Victor Rokita, trading as Mayfair Esso Servicenter, whereby Humble leased the premises to Victor for a monthly rental of $272.30 a month, the same amount which Humble was required to pay to Josephine and Victor under the lease to

Humble and the same amount which Josephine and Victor were obliged to pay each month to the bank. This lease was for a period of one year and thereafter from year to year unless cancelled by 30 days' notice directed to the end of a yearly renewal period. The lease was written on a printed Humble form, and, like the other Humble lease form, was obviously designed to fully protect Humble's interests. It required the lessee to pay all taxes, provided general indemnity to Humble arising from injuries or accidents on the premises, and provided that Humble could terminate the lease and re-enter the premises without formal demand in the event that any rent was unpaid or default made in any other covenant of the lease.

Thereafter Victor encountered personal difficulties which affected his management of the service station and his relationship with his wife. Josephine divorced him in 1965. On December 16, 1961 his lease with Humble was cancelled by mutual consent and on the same day Humble leased the premises to Mayfair Servicenter, Inc., of which Salvatore Amoroso, Josephine's brother, was president. This lease was on the same form and contained the same terms as the earlier lease to Victor. The latter lease has continued in force to date and Josephine's son has in recent years managed the station.

In May 1968 Josephine married George H. Doerr. Prior to the marriage Doerr signed an agreement waiving all right to curtesy in property owned by Josephine. He defaulted and did not participate at the trial. He has no interest in the property.

By letter dated October 7, 1968, approximately ten years after the original lease was signed and 8½ years after the 15-year term of the lease commenced to run under its terms as modified, Humble wrote to Josephine and Victor exercising the option to buy the premises, free and clear of all encumbrances, for $150,000. Humble re-exercised its option by letter dated March 3, 1979. When Josephine replied through her attorneys that the option has no legal validity, Humble started this action.

Humble sues for specific performance and, in the alternative, for damages. It claims that the value of the property in 1969 at the time of final exercise of the option was $240,000. [Here the Court discusses the various defenses Josephine raised in her Answer.]

[A]t no time in her pleadings did Josephine spell out in so many words that the option was invalid because it constituted an impermissible clog on her equity of redemption. Nor was such theory specifically mentioned in her contentions contained in the pretrial order or in the trial briefs submitted in advance of trial. It was first advanced at the end of the case after the court had referred counsel to the decision in *Barr v. Granahan,* 255 Wis. 192, 38 N.W.2d 705, 10 A.L.R.2d 227 (Sup.Ct.1949). Humble argues that the clogging doctrine may not be considered in the case because there was no notice to it that the doctrine would be relied upon. However, defendant's answer does spell out facts and contentions which give notice that the option is claimed to be invalid because, among other reasons, it is unconscionable and inequitable, unjust to the defendant, and unjustly enriches Humble at defendant's expense, and her contentions in the pretrial order, among other things, state that "the option provisions of the lease and the lease itself are so manifestly unfair, unreasonable and unjust, so as to preclude the remedy of specific performance, and to require the reformation of the lease by the elimination of the option provisions." The factual allegations and contentions in her answer and the pretrial order, and the evidence adduced in support thereof, warrant relief on any legal theory that accommodates them, including the clogging doctrine, and Humble's objection is obviously without merit. See *Wimberly v. Paterson,* 75 N.J.Super. 584, 604, 183 A.2d 691

(App.Div.1962); *Vorhies v. Cannizzaro,* 66 N.J.Super. 551, 558, 169 A.2d 702 (App.Div.1961).

. . . .

It is evident, therefore, that if it were not for the fact that the option was given in connection with a mortgage loan, Josephine would not be entitled to relief. Because it was so connected however, the option is void and unenforceable. It is a clog on Josephine's equity of redemption.

III

For centuries it has been the rule that a mortgagor's equity of redemption cannot be clogged and that he cannot, as a part of the original mortgage transaction, cut off or surrender his right to redeem. Any agreement which does so is void and unenforceable as against public policy. A classic statement of the rule appears in 4 Pomeroy, Equity Jurisprudence (5th ed. 1941), § 1193 at 568 et seq.:

§ 1193. *Once a mortgage, Always a Mortgage; Collateral Agreements and Agreements Clogging the Equity of Redemption.* — In general, all persons able to contract are permitted to determine and control their own legal relations by any agreements which are not illegal, or opposed to good morals or to public policy; but the mortgage forms a marked exception to this principle. The doctrine has been firmly established from an early day that when the character of a mortgage has attached at the commencement of the transaction, so that the instrument, whatever be its form, is regarded in equity as a mortgage, that character of mortgage must and will always continue. If the instrument is in its essence a mortgage, the parties cannot by any stipulations, however express and positive, render it anything but a mortgage, or deprive it of the essential attributes belonging to a mortgage in equity. The debtor or mortgagor cannot, in the inception of the instrument, as a part of or collateral to its execution, in any manner deprive himself of his equitable right to come in after a default in paying the money at the stipulated time, and to pay the debt and interest, and thereby to redeem the land from the lien and encumbrance of the mortgage; the equitable right of redemption, after a default is preserved, remains in full force, and will be protected and enforced by a court of equity, no matter what stipulations the parties may have made in the original transaction purporting to cut off this right.

See also 4 American Law of Property (1952), §§ 16.58-16.61 at 106 et seq.; Osborne, Handbook on the Law of Mortgages, (2nd ed. 1970), §§ 96-99 at 144 et seq.; 1 Glenn on Mortgages (1943), § 44 at 278; Jones on Mortgages (6th ed. 1904), §§ 250, 251 at 185-187; 55 Am.Jur.2d, Mortgages, § 514 at 504, and § 1220 at 1001.

As indicated by the above authorities, the doctrine is universally applied, both in the United States and England, and it has long been a firm part of the law of this State. See *Youle v. Richards,* 1 N.J.Eq. 534 (Ch.1832); *Vanderhaize v. Hughes,* 13 N.J.Eq. 244 (Ch.1861); *Griffen v. Cooper,* 73 N.J.Eq. 465, 466, 68 A. 1095 (Ch.1907); *McKlosky v. Kobylarz,* 99 N.J.Eq. 202, 132 A. 497 (Ch.1926); *Mansfield v. Hammond,* 117 N.J.Eq. 509, 511, 176 A. 354 (E. & A. 1935); *Dorman v. Fisher,* 31 N.J. 13, 155 A.2d 11 (1959); *Smith v. Shattls,* 66 N.J. Super. 430, 436, 169 A.2d 503 (App.Div.1961); see *Hardyston National Bank v. Tartamella,* 56 N.J. 508, 513, 267 A.2d 495 (1970).

. . . .

As a part of the doctrine it is well settled that an option to buy the property for a fixed sum cannot be taken contemporaneously by the mortgagee. As stated in 4 American Law of Property, § 16.59 at 108:

> ... By a parity of reasoning, an agreement allowing the mortgagee to keep any part of the mortgaged property, redemption being limited to the balance, fails. Nor is the mortgagee allowed at the time of the loan to enter into an option or contract for the purchase of the mortgaged property. This rule was established early and still continues to be the law.

In 1 Glenn on Mortgages, § 44 at 278, the author, after referring to the decision in *Howard v. Harris,* 1 Vern. 7 (1681), which originated the famous phrase "once a mortgage, always a mortgage" and struck down a restriction on redemption, said:

> ... Within the next forty years the idea was extended so as to strike down a kindred effort; it being held that an option to the mortgagee, to purchase the equity of redemption (the loan, of course, being cancelled out in the process), was void, and thus the mortgagor could redeem. This continues as the rule of today, and it is applied without regard to the presence or absence of usury laws. Here, indeed, we have a real "clog" upon the equity of redemption; and, it being incompatible with all sound ideas of loan and security, our courts, English and American, are at one in denouncing such an arrangement, no matter how it may be disguised.

Accord: *Osborne,* op. cit., § 97 at 146; *Willett v. Winnell,* 1 Vern. 488, 23 Eng.Rep. 611 (Ch.1687); *Orby v. Trigg,* 9 Mod. 2, 88 Eng.Rep. 276 (Ch.1722); *In re Edwards' Estate,* 11 Ir.Ch.R. 367 (Ch.1861); *Linnell v. Lyford,* 72 Me. 280 (Sup.Ct.1881); *Wilson v. Fisher,* 148 N.C. 535, 62 S.E. 622 (Sup.Ct.1908); see *Hyndman v. Hyndman,* 19 Vt. 9, 46 Am.Dec. 171 (Sup.Ct.1845); *Dismorr v. George,* 17 V.L.R. 626 (Victoria Sup.Ct.1891); *Samuel v. Jarrah Timber and Wood Paving Corp.* (1904) A.C. 323; *Arnold v. National Trust Co.,* 5 Alta.L.R. 214, 7 Dom.L.R. 754, 22 West L.R.693 (Alberta Sup.Ct.1912); *Lewis v. Frank Love, Ltd.* (1961) 1 All.E.R. 446, 1 W.L.R. 261; *Barr v. Granahan,* 255 Wis. 192, 38 N.W.2d 705, 10 A.L.R.2d 227 (Sup.Ct.1949); see *Bromley v. Bromley, supra;* Wyman, "The Clog on the Equity of Redemption," 21 Harv.L.R. 459, 462 (1908); Note, "Bargains between Mortgagor and Mortgagee," 136 L.T. 137-139 (1913); 59 C.J.S. Mortgages § 818 at 1561; 55 Am.Jur.2d, Mortgages, § 514 at 505.

The basic policy behind the doctrine has remained vital and unchanged over the years. As stated by our Court of Chancery in 1832 in *Youle v. Richards,* 1 N.J.Eq. 534, 538, "There would have been, without it, a door open for the imposition of every kind of restraint on the equity of redemption, and thereby the borrower, through necessity, would have been driven to embrace any terms, however unequal or cruel; which would have tended greatly to the furtherance of usury, and the conversion of the equitable jurisdiction of the court into an engine of fraud and oppression". In Jones on Mortgages, § 251 at 187, the reason for this rule favoring mortgage debtors is that "their necessities often drive them to make ruinous concessions in order to raise money." Restatement, Security, § 55 at 152, states that such agreements are held to be against public policy and void because "it has long been recognized that . . . creditors are often in the position to exact severe terms from debtors." *Pomeroy,* op. cit., § 1193 at 570, states the reason for the rule as follows:

> This doctrine is based upon the relative situation of the debtor and the creditor; it recognizes the fact that the creditor necessarily has a power over his debtor which may be exercised inequitably; that the debtor is liable to yield

to the exertion of such power; and it protects the debtor absolutely from the consequences of his inferiority, and of his own acts done through infirmity of will.

In 4 American Law of Property, § 16.59 at 109, the author summarizes the policy behind the doctrine as follows:

 . . . the decisions seem correct upon a principle which underlies relief from all penalties and forfeitures. That principle is that relief will be granted where there has been a misreliance upon the "mirage of hope." Ordinarily the courts have talked in terms of granting relief because of solicitude for the "impecunious landowner" or "necessitous men [who] are not, truly speaking, free men." But another most important factor is in the mortgagee playing upon the optimism to which all mankind is prone, the "over-confidence in one's own capacities and faith in a special providence [which] leads us to over-sanguine commitments." Equity takes this human failing into account.

So strong is the policy behind the rule that it is applied to hold such options absolutely void and unenforceable regardless of whether there is actual oppression in the specific case. In 1904, in the leading case of *Samuel v. Jarrah Timber and Wood Paving Corp., supra,* the question of whether it should continue to be so applied was squarely presented to the House of Lords for reconsideration and possible change. The House affirmed the Court of Appeals and held that an option to purchase for a fixed sum taken by a mortgagee as a part of the original transaction was void as a clog on the equity of redemption regardless of fairness. Although it acknowledged that the rule might be used as a "means of evading a fair bargain come to between persons dealing at arms length and negotiating on equal terms," it nevertheless concluded that, in view of the long line of precedents applying the doctrine as a fixed rule without deviation, there should be no change therefrom. Noting that the virtue of such a fixed rule is that it serves "to obviate the necessity of inquiry and investigation in cases where suspicion may be probable and proof difficult," Lord Macnaghten said:

 Having regard to the state of authorities binding on the Court of Appeals, if not this House, it seems to me that they could not have come to any other conclusion, although the transaction was a fair bargain between men of business without any trace or suspicion of oppression, surprise or circumvention. [(1904) A.C. 323, 325]

The same rule was applied in the recent case of *Lewis v. Frank Love, Ltd., supra,* where Judge Plowman for the English Chancery Division, holding that "an option to purchase, if exercised, indubitably does stop a mortgagor from redemption," followed the *Samuel* case and ruled:

 . . . the doctrine of a clog on the equity of redemption is a technical doctrine which is not affected by the question whether in fact there has been oppression, and which applies just as much where parties are represented, as they were here, by solicitors. [(1961) 1 All.E.R. 446, 454].

See also *Arnold v. National Trust Co.* and *In re Edwards's Estate, supra.*

Where the option is a part of the original loan transaction it is therefore absolutely void.

Moreover, it is also the law that although a mortgagor can at a later date, after the original mortgage transaction, surrender his equity of redemption to the mortgagee and enter into an option or agreement to sell, it must be a fair bargain for an independent and adequate consideration. From the earliest days courts of equity have carefully scrutinized such arrangements. This rule is universally applied, in New Jersey and elsewhere, and it applies both to mortgages of real property and pledges of personal property. Normally the burden is imposed upon the mortgagee to prove fairness. The general rule is stated in 55 Am.Jur.2d Mortgages § 1220 at 1001:

> However any contract by which the mortgagor sells or conveys his interest to the mortgagee is viewed suspiciously and is carefully scrutinized in a court of equity. The sale and conveyance of the equity of redemption to the mortgagee must be fair, frank, honest, and without fraud, undue influence, oppression, or unconscionable advantage of the mortgagor's poverty, distress, or fears of the position of the mortgagee.

The black letter rule of Restatement, Security, § 55(2) at 152 is that such agreement is "valid if the pledgee sustains the burden of showing that the bargain is free from fraud and oppression," and the comment thereto (at 153) acknowledges as the reason for the rule that "[s]ubsequent to the creation of a pledge the pledgee's ability to inflict an oppressive bargain upon the pledgor is greatly diminished although not wholly absent." See also, *Wagner v. Phillips,* 78 N.J.Eq. 33, 36, 78 A. 806 (Ch.1910); *McKlosky v. Kubylarz, supra; Smith v. Shattls, supra;* 4 American Law of Property, § 16.62 at 115.

IV

The above rules, one of which applies to options taken as a part of the original mortgage transactions and the other which applies to options taken at a subsequent time, are both clearly indicative of the jealousy with which courts guard mortgagors. Normally they are applied to conventional mortgagees. Here Humble was not a conventional mortgagee since it did not lend its own funds to the Rokitas. The question, then, is to what extent do the above rules apply to the option in Humble's hands?

First, it is my conclusion on the facts of this case that the anti-clogging rule applies fully to Humble and that the option is absolutely void in its hands, regardless of actual fairness or oppression, just as it would be in the hands of any regular mortgagee.

Although perhaps not a guarantor to the bank for the Rokitas in the technical sense, it is clear that Humble's position was closely akin to that. Without question, it was in the position here where it could and did determine exactly how it would participate in this transaction. Rather than making a direct guaranty to the bank, it chose to enter into a lease in order that the rental payments which it promised to pay thereunder to the Rokitas could be assigned to the bank. This arrangement avoided a direct obligation by it to the bank and gave it an "out" if the Rokitas failed to perform their obligations under the lease and sublease back. It also gave it full security in the leased property to recoup any payment which it might choose to make to the bank and any expenditure which it might incur in connection therewith. It had the right to repay itself such sums either by withholding rent payments or by requiring the Rokitas to pay said sums directly to it with interest, and it had the right to extend the lease so long as any sums remained outstanding. It also had the right to cancel out the sublease and enter into possession in the event of a default. In this sense the lease transaction was an equitable mortgage and Humble was itself a mortgagee. It is clear that equity looks to substance rather than to form, and that a guarantor or surety who takes property or an interest therein as security for his guaranty is a mortgagee thereof in equity. See *Martin v. Bowen,* 51 N.J.Eq. 452, 26 A. 823 (Ch.1893); *Meeker v.*

Warren, 66 N.J.Eq. 146, 57 A. 421 (Ch.1904); *Maginn v. Cashin,* 196 Mich. 221, 162 N.W. 1009 (Sup.Ct.1917); *Dubois v. Bowles,* 55 Colo. 312, 134 P. 112 (Sup.Ct.1913); *Schelling v. Thomas,* 96 Cal.App. 682, 274 P. 755 (D.Ct.App.1929); *Dudley v. Buckley,* 68 W.Va. 630, 70 S.E. 376 (Sup.Ct.App.1911); *Frazier v. Frazier,* 282 Ky. 405, 138 S.W.2d 506 (Ct.App.1940). The option was therefore a clog on the Rokitas' right to redeem from Humble as an equitable mortgagee.

Moreover, Humble had the option under the lease, in the event of a mortgage default by the Rokitas and an acceleration by the bank, to step into the bank's shoes as regular mortgagee. Because of the nature of the transaction it would have been entitled to full rights of subrogation upon payment to the bank. Restatement, Security, § 141; 83 C.J.S. Subrogation § 47a at 667. There was therefore a real possibility, in the event of a default, that it would become the regular mortgagee in the place of the bank.

In addition, as indicated above, under the note agreement executed in connection with the permanent mortgage the Rokitas expressly agreed that, in the event they failed to comply with any of the "terms, promises, covenants and agreements" contained in the lease with Humble, the bank should have the right to accelerate the entire balance due on the mortgage debt and, at its option, sue for said balance or foreclose the mortgage. One of the terms and agreements contained in the lease was the option itself. Performance of the option was therefore required by the mortgage note itself, and the bank as mortgagee, as well as Humble, had some powers of enforcement. It was Humble, not the Rokitas, which had a prior relationship with the bank and brought it into this transaction. Humble was therefore not simply an isolated guarantor, and the option was an integral part of the overall mortgage transaction in which Humble was a direct participant. *Unico v. Owen,* 50 N.J. 101, 112-113, 122-123, 232 A.2d 405 (1967).

Furthermore, it is clear that Humble was the dominant party in the transaction. Humble volunteered its participation and it was Humble's power and position which caused the loan transaction to come into being. It dictated the terms of the loan and offered them to the Rokitas on a "take it or leave it" basis. Its standard printed forms were used. It, rather than the bank, insisted upon the option. It was therefore the party which was in the position to "exact severe terms" and "concessions" from the Rokitas as debtors.

Finally, it is clear that this was strictly a loan transaction. Regardless of Humble's business motives for entering into it, *cf. Esso Petroleum Co., Ltd. v. Harpers Garage (Stoweport) Ltd.,* [1968] A.C. 269, the Rokitas were bargaining for a loan and nothing more. Humble never owned a prior interest in the property and was not a joint venturer with the Rokitas in the development of the station. The lease was what is known in the trade as a "two-party" lease rather than a "three-party" lease. It was created solely as a security device in connection with a mortgage loan and it was never intended that Humble should actually enter into possession of the property, or run the business, or invest any of its own funds in the premises. There was therefore no special reason or justification for demanding an option here — it was simply a price demanded by Humble for lending credit which permitted the loan transaction to come into being.

In these circumstances all the policy reasons behind the anti-clogging rule, applicable to mortgagees in general, apply to Humble here with full vigor. Since this is so, the option is void without necessity of inquiry as to whether or not it was unfair or oppressive.

The application of the above rule disposes of the case. . . .

. . . .

Although the result in this case is arrived at by application of ancient rules relating to mortgages, it may be noted that these rules are in harmony with modern decisions which deal with somewhat similar problems and apply the same underlying considerations of public policy. Indeed, these ancient rules provide precedents from which the modern decisions flow. See *Henningsen v. Bloomfield Motors, Inc., supra; Unico v. Owen, supra; Reste Realty Corporation v. Cooper,* 53 N.J. 444, 451-454, 251 A.2d 268 (1969); *Shell Oil Co. v. Marinello, supra,* 120 N.J.Super. 357 at 372-378, 294 A.2d 253; *Ellsworth Dobbs, Inc. v. Johnson,* 50 N.J. 528, 552-556, 236 A.2d 843 (1967). As stated by our Supreme Court in *Dobbs:*

> The perimeter of public policy is an ever increasing one. Although courts continue to recognize that persons should not be unnecessarily restricted in their freedom to contract, there is an increasing willingness to invalidate unconscionable contractual provisions which clearly tend to injure the public in some way. [at 554, 236 A.2d at 857]

In *United States v. Bethlehem Steel Corp.,* 315 U.S. 289, 62 S.Ct. 581, 599, 86 L.Ed. 855, 876 (1942), the late Mr. Justice Frankfurter said:

> . . . It is said that familiar principles would be outraged if Bethlehem were denied recovery on these contracts. But is there any principle which is more familiar or more firmly embedded in the history of Anglo-American law than the basic doctrine that the courts will not permit themselves to be used as instruments of inequity and injustice? Does any principle in our law have more universal application than the doctrine that courts will not enforce transactions in which the relative positions of the parties are such that one has unconscionably taken advantage of the necessities of the other?
>
> These principles are not foreign to the law of contracts. Fraud and physical duress are not the only grounds upon which courts refuse to enforce contracts. The law is not so primitive that it sanctions every injustice except brute force and downright fraud. More specifically, the courts generally refuse to lend themselves to the enforcement of a "bargain" in which one party has unjustly taken advantage of the economic necessities of the other. "And there is great reason and justice in this rule, for necessitous men are not, truly speaking, free men, but, to answer a present exigency, will submit to any terms that the crafty may impose upon them." *Vernon v. Bethell,* 2 Eden 110, 113, 28 Eng. Reprint 838. [315 U.S. at 326, 62 S.Ct. at 599]

The above holding has been relied upon in the modern cases which have struck down unconscionable contractual provisions, including *Henningsen* and *Unico.* Far from being a new or radical departure from existing law, as Justice Frankfurter stated in his opinion, it is drawn from and supported by the fundamental principles expressed "in an almost infinite variety of cases," including the ancient rules relating to mortgages involved here. 315 U.S. at 327-330, 62 S.Ct. at 600, 86 L.Ed. at 877-879. My decision here is supported by both the ancient and modern application of the rules.

Other contentions advanced by Humble by way of defense to Josephine's counterclaim and in reply to her affirmative defenses, including the claim that she cannot prevail because of laches, are without merit. The option is unenforceable and Humble is entitled to neither specific performance nor damages.

NOTES

1. *Graf v. Hope Building Corp., supra,* is not a redemption case. Hope Building was seeking to reinstate its delinquent loan, not exercise its equity of redemption. The cost to reinstate would have been small: simply pay the amount in arrears. The cost of exercising its equity of redemption would have been to pay off the entire principal balance. Reinstatement did not exist in New York and Hope Building is really asking the court to create a new equitable right. Cardozo obviously thinks in cases of extreme hardship the rules should be bent. Knowing that Hope Building could have avoided foreclosure by paying the entire debt, do you agree with O'Brien or Cardozo?

2. *Humble Oil & Refinery Co. v. Doerr, supra,* illustrates the point that one's equity of redemption will be protected even from one's own misadventurous attempt to give it away. While the rule is clear that one may not waive one's equity of redemption, the Humble case uses the "anti-clogging" rule in an unusual circumstance. Do you find it strange that a court in 1973 would rely on an ancient rule to avoid a harsh result?

3. In both the foregoing cases a mortgagor became involved in litigation trying to avoid the harsh consequences of his or her own inadvertence. The results are opposite but the two cases are easily reconcilable. Understanding why the two cases are not inconsistent will help you better understand the law of redemption.

4. The case of *Portland Mortgage Co. v. Creditors Protective Ass'n,* 199 Or. 432, 262 P.2d 918 (1953), well illustrates the difference between equitable redemption and statutory redemption. An omitted junior lienor was paid in full but sought to exercise a statutory right of redemption. Since the junior had been omitted from the foreclosure, the junior's equity of redemption had not been foreclosed. Since statutory redemption does not come into existence until one's equity of redemption has been foreclosed, the junior had no statutory right of redemption. Obviously, the junior wanted to redeem and obtain the property rather than have its relatively small junior lien satisfied. The value of the property must have increased so that whoever redeemed and obtained the property would do so profitably. *See also* 2 GLENN ON MORTGAGES § 238 (1943).

5. The federal government will not permit state redemption rights to be exercised when the loan has been secured by an agency of the government. *See United States v. Stadium Apartments, Inc.,* 425 F.2d 358 (9th Cir. 1970), *infra* page 410.

B. STATUTORY REDEMPTION

In all states a mortgagor has the right of equitable redemption. When that right has ended, or been foreclosed, about two thirds of the states grant an additional right of redemption by statute. This is called statutory redemption and commences at the time equitable redemption ends (if it commences at all).

Because statutory redemption is created by statute there is wide variation among the states. Four areas generally provide the opportunity for variation: (1) the time period during which statutory redemption can take place; (2) the party to whom statutory redemption rights are available; (3) the amount which must be paid in order to redeem; and (4) the effect of redemption. Of these only the last should form the basis for much intellectual discussion. However, the cases which follow demonstrate that while redemption is rarely attempted an ingenious conveyancing bar will always be able to find a basis to litigate if there is economic motivation on the part of the would-be redeemer.

Colorado Revised Statutes (1980 Supp.)

§ 38-39-102. Redemption within specified period — procedure

(1) Except as provided in this section with respect to agricultural real estate, within seventy-five days after the date of the sale of real estate by virtue of any foreclosure of a mortgage, trust deed, or other lien or by virtue of an execution

and levy, the owner of the premises or any person who might be liable upon a deficiency may redeem the premises sold by paying to the public trustee, sheriff, or other proper officer the sum for which the property was sold, with interest from the date of sale at the default rate if specified in the original instrument or if not so specified at the regular rate specified in the original instrument, together with any taxes paid or other proper charges as now provided by law, and a certificate of redemption shall be executed by the proper officer and recorded, and the public trustee, sheriff, or other proper officer shall forthwith pay said money to the holder of the certificate of purchase. If the owner of the premises fails to redeem under this section, any person who might be liable upon a deficiency who redeems under this section shall be issued a certificate of redemption only after the expiration of the proper redemption period.

. . . .

(4) In the case of a foreclosure sale by a public trustee, the public trustee, at least twenty-one days prior to the date on which the sale is originally scheduled by the public trustee, shall mail a notice to the grantor of the deed of trust being foreclosed, to any subsequent owner of record, and to any other person having the right to redeem the premises under subsection (1) of this section, informing such persons of their redemptive rights, if any, under this section.

(5) The public trustee shall mail such notice to the persons described in subsection (4) of this section only if their interest in the real estate being foreclosed was established by an instrument recorded with the county clerk and recorder of the county in which said real estate is located subsequent to the recording of the deed of trust being foreclosed and prior to the recording of the notice of election and demand for sale pursuant to section 38-37-113 (1). Said notice shall be mailed to such persons at the address given in the recorded instrument evidencing their interests. Postage costs under this section shall be part of the foreclosure costs.

(6) The sheriff or other proper officer empowered to sell real estate at a foreclosure sale or at an execution sale, but not including foreclosure sales by the public trustee, at least twenty-one days prior to the date on which the sale is originally scheduled, shall mail a notice to the owner of the premises at the street address or comparable identifying numbers of the real estate being sold, if such address or numbers are displayed on the property or any building thereon, informing the owner thereof of his rights, if any, under this section. If there is no street address or comparable identifying numbers to which said notice can be mailed, the sheriff or other proper officer shall mail said notice to the last known address of the owner according to the records of the party requesting the foreclosure or execution sale.

Wisconsin Statutes (1981 Supp.)

§ 846.10. Foreclosure

(1) If the plaintiff recovers the judgment shall describe the mortgaged premises and fix the amount of the mortgage debt then due and also the amount of each instalment thereafter to become due, and the time when it will become due, and whether the mortgaged premises can be sold in parcels and whether any part thereof is a homestead, and shall adjudge that the mortgaged premises be sold for the payment of the amount then due and of all instalments which shall become due before the sale, or so much thereof as may be sold separately without material injury to the parties interested, and be sufficient to pay such principal, interest and costs; and when demanded in the complaint, direct that judgment

shall be rendered for any deficiency against the parties personally liable and, if the sale is to be by referee, he must be named therein.

(2) Any party may become a purchaser. No sale involving a one- to 4-family residence that is owner-occupied at the commencement of the foreclosure action, a farm, a church or a tax-exempt nonprofit charitable organization may be held until the expiration of 12 months from the date when judgment is entered, except a sale under s. 846.101 or 846.102. Notice of the time and place of sale shall be given under ss. 815.31 and 846.16 and may be given within the 12-month period except that the first printing of the notice shall not be made less than 10 months after the date when judgment is entered, except that the sale of a farm shall not be made or advertised until the expiration of one year from the date when such judgment is entered. In all cases the parties may, by stipulation, filed with the clerk, consent to an earlier sale. Sales under foreclosure of mortgages given by any railroad corporation may be made immediately after the rendition of the judgment.

(3) The proceeds of every sale shall be applied to the discharge of the debt adjudged to be due and the costs awarded; and if there shall be any surplus it shall be subject to the order of the court. If any surplus remains in the court for three months, without being applied for, the court shall direct the same to be put out at interest for the benefit of the party entitled thereto to be paid to him upon the order of such court.

(4) The court may order in the judgment of foreclosure that all sums advanced by the plaintiff for insurance, necessary repairs and taxes not included in the judgment may be added to the judgment by order at any time after the entry thereof.

Ohio Revised Code Annotated (1981)

§ 2329.33. Redemption by judgment debtor

In sales of real estate on execution or order of sale, at any time before the confirmation thereof, the debtor may redeem it from sale by depositing in the hands of the clerk of the court of common pleas to which such execution or order is returnable, the amount of the judgment or decree upon which such lands were sold, with all costs, including poundage, and interest at the rate of eight per cent per annum on the purchase money from the day of sale to the time of such deposit, except where the judgment creditor is the purchaser, the interest at such rate on the excess above his claim. The court of common pleas thereupon shall make an order setting aside such sale, and apply the deposit to the payment of such judgment or decree and costs, and award such interest to the purchaser, who shall receive from the officer making the sale the purchase money paid by him, and the interest from the clerk. This section does not take away the power of the court to set aside such sale for any reason for which it might have been set aside prior to April 16, 1888.

Iowa Code Title 31 (1975)

§ 628.3. Redemption by debtor

The debtor may redeem real property at any time within one year from the day of sale, and will, in the meantime, be entitled to the possession thereof; and for the first six months after such right of redemption is exclusive. Any real property redeemed by the debtor shall thereafter be free and clear from any liability for any unpaid portion of the judgment under which said real property was sold.

PORTLAND SAVINGS BANK v. LANDRY

Supreme Judicial Court of Maine
372 A.2d 573 (1977)

ARCHIBALD, JUSTICE. On October 1, 1975, an alternative procedure for the foreclosure of real estate mortgages became effective. P.L.1975, ch. 552, §§ 6321-25 (14 M.R.S.A. §§ 6321-25). The newly adopted act provided that such mortgages could be foreclosed by instituting a civil action in either the Superior or District Courts. Section 6322 authorizes redemption "within 90 days of the date of the judgment" that a breach exists, establishing the amount of the arrearage, and authorizes the mortgagee to sell the property unless the debt is paid within ninety days. The act also requires the mortgagee to account to the mortgagor for any surplus received following the foreclosure sale.

On September 21, 1972, the defendant executed a conventional real estate mortgage, running to the plaintiff, as security for her promissory note of $17,100.00 which bore interest at 7½%. The plaintiff on *October 14, 1975*, instituted a civil action in the District Court seeking the relief authorized by the newly enacted statute. By her responsive pleading the defendant admitted that the mortgage was then in default. On a motion for summary judgment the District Court entered a "judgment of foreclosure and sale" from which the defendant seasonably appealed.

The issue is brought into sharp focus by the defendant's asserted affirmative defense, namely:

> Title 14 M.R.S.A., Sec. 6321 et seq. are unconstitutional *as applied to the Defendant,* in that said statutory provisions unlawfully abridge the statutory time of redemption in effect at the time of the giving of the mortgage by the Defendant to the Plaintiff, and *therefore impaired the obligations of the contract between the parties. (Emphasis supplied.)*

We sustain the appeal.

Public Laws of 1975, ch. 552, by reducing the basic redemption period to ninety days, broke sharply with the traditional period of redemption in the State of Maine. From 1837 until 1907 the period of redemption, by whatever method foreclosure was accomplished, remained at three years. *See* R.S.1903, ch. 92, §§ 4, 7. Public Laws of 1907, ch. 163, §§ 1, 2, reduced the period of redemption under any of the acceptable methods of foreclosure to one year, and this period was retained in all the statutory revisions thereafter and remains the same today except when foreclosure is sought under the provisions of P.L.1975, ch. 552.

As we have previously pointed out, we are concerned only with the constitutionality of the 1975 act as applied to the foreclosure of the defendant's mortgage which had been executed three years prior to the 1975 enactment.

Article I, § 10 of the United States Constitution provides in pertinent part:

> No State shall ... pass any ... Law impairing the Obligation of Contracts ....

In its Declaration of Rights the Constitution of Maine, art. I, § 11, contains a similar provision.

It is well settled that the law in effect at the time of the execution of a contract becomes part of that contract. *See, e. g., Canal National Bank v. School Admin-*

istrative District, 160 Me. 309, 203 A.2d 734, 739 (1964); *Phinney v. Phinney,* 81 Me. 450, 460 (1889). Historically, it has been held that the legislature may modify the remedies available to contracting parties but cannot, constitutionally, alter the substantive obligations of the parties. . . .

Whether a statute which *reduces* a mortgagor's period of redemption is constitutional has not been directly decided by the United States Supreme Court. However, in *Barnitz v. Beverly,* 163 U.S. 118, 16 S.Ct. 1042, 41 L.Ed. 93 (1896), the Court was confronted with a constitutional attack on a statute which *increased* the redemptive period available to mortgagors. In invalidating the statute as applied to mortgages executed prior to its effective date, the Court stated:

> [W]e hold that a statute which authorizes the redemption of property sold upon foreclosure of a mortgage, where no right of redemption previously existed, or which extends the period of redemption beyond the time formerly allowed, cannot constitutionally apply to a sale under a mortgage executed before its passage.

163 U.S. at 129, 16 S.Ct. at 1046. *Accord, Worthen Co. v. Kavanaugh,* 295 U.S. 56, 55 S.Ct. 555, 79 L.Ed. 1298 (1935); *Brine v. Insurance Co.,* 96 U.S. 627, 24 L.Ed. 858 (1877); *Howard v. Bugbee,* 65 U.S. (24 How.) 461, 16 L.Ed. 753 (1860); *Bronson v. Kinzie, supra.*

In *Phinney v. Phinney, supra,* this Court relied on *Bronson v. Kinzie, supra,* in striking down a statute which expanded the right of redemption for creditors of a mortgagor.

In *Home Building & Loan Ass'n v. Blaisdell,* 290 U.S. 398, 54 S.Ct. 231, 78 L.Ed. 413, the Court upheld a Minnesota statute which temporarily extended the period of redemption available to defaulting mortgagors. The case arose in the context of "the Great Depression" of the 1930s, and it is now recognized that the Court's holding in *Blaisdell* was based on the emergency which then existed. *See W. B. Worthen Co. v. Thomas,* 292 U.S. 426, 432-33, 54 S.Ct. 816, 78 L.Ed. 1344 (1934); *Waterville Realty Corp. v. City of Eastport, supra.*

. . . .

Several decisions from other jurisdictions have held that legislative attempts to curtail retroactively a mortgagor's right of redemption are invalid. *California Federal Sav. & Loan Ass'n v. Allen,* 112 P.2d 959, 960 (Cal.App.1941), *appeal dismissed because of mootness,* 19 Cal.2d 85, 119 P.2d 137, 138 (1941); *State ex rel. Cleveringa v. Klein,* 63 N.D. 514, 249 N.W. 118, 122 (1933). Cf. *Prideaux v. Des Moines Joint-Stock Land Bank,* 34 F.2d 308, 310 (D.C.Minn.1929). *But see State Nat. Bank of Texarkana v. Morthland,* 196 Ark. 346, 118 S.W.2d 266, 268 (1938).

Having in mind this background, we now approach the problem raised by the attempted foreclosure procedure here under review. P.L.1975, ch. 552, §§ 6321-25, established a basic redemption period of ninety days. Balanced against this reduced period of redemption from the one year allowable when the mortgage was executed, is the right to be heard in court on the issue of default and, additionally, a right for a determination of the amount then due, neither of which was possible under the other existing methods of foreclosure. The 1975 statute likewise entitled the mortgagor to any surplus received from the sale of the mortgaged property beyond the mortgage debt. Arguably, this statute granted these heretofore non-existent rights as the quid pro quo for reducing the time of redemption from one year to ninety days. Despite these arguably beneficial conditions, we are not convinced that the loss in the period of redemption is balanced by the benefits we have described.

In 1972 when this mortgage was executed the defendant had every right to believe that she would have a redemption period of one year should there be a default and a foreclosure of her mortgage. Since that was the law at that time, the one year period of redemption was as much a part of the mortgage then executed as though it had so stated in precise language.

We do not believe that it is appropriate to classify the time span in which redemption may be had as merely remedial. The right of redemption has been described as

> one of the most splendid instances, in the history of our jurisprudence, of the triumph of equitable principles over technical rules; and of the homage which those principles have received, by their adoption in the Courts of law.

Wilkins v. French, 20 Me. 111, 118 (1841). This equitable principle is well defined and firmly entrenched in the legal tradition of this State. *See Kennebec & Portland R. R. Co. v. Portland & Kennebec R. R. Co.,* 59 Me. at 29-30; *Fogg v. Twin Town Chevrolet,* 135 Me. 260, 194 A. 609 (1937).

However, granting the importance of the right of redemption, we must still face the issue of whether *one year* in which to redeem is also such a significant right that constitutionally it cannot be retrospectively reduced. We may agree that a reduction in the period of redemption is permissible retrospectively, provided that it is balanced with an equally effective remedy for exercising the right of redemption. Absent such a provision, the reduction is impermissible constitutionally. *Richmond Mortgage & Loan Corp. v. Wachovia Bank & Trust Co.,* 300 U.S. at 128-29, 57 S.Ct. 382.

In Maine, as we have indicated, a period of not less than one year in which to redeem under a real estate mortgage foreclosure can be statutorily traced from 1837. Although we are not here concerned with a question of whether it was legislative intent that the 1975 law be applied retrospectively, it is interesting to note that when the Legislature in 1963 temporarily reduced the period of redemption from one year to six months, the act was made to apply prospectively only with reference to the various methods of foreclosure then permissible.

More recently we have used language which recognizes the solemnity of statutory provisions equating the period of redemption equally with the right of redemption. In *Smith v. Varney,* 309 A.2d 229, 232 (Me. 1973), we said:

> This right of redemption, once extinguished, cannot be revived by any court, *nor can the period of redemption be abridged or enlarged by operation of law.* Courts must abide by the statutory requirements except in exceptional cases where a court of equity may provide relief. (Emphasis supplied.)

We are aware that in large part Maine is a rural state and in significant measure its economy depends upon the production, harvesting and sale of agricultural produce, such as potatoes, blueberries, corn, peas, hay and grains. A farmer who has executed a real estate mortgage would be distinctly disadvantaged if, having only one annual source of income, his ability to redeem from a mortgage foreclosure is compressed into a ninety day period. We have no way of knowing how many agricultural mortgages may be now outstanding which were executed prior to the 1975 enactment, but we have every right to assume that the number would be considerable. Certainly as to those, a critical part of the mortgage contract would have been the right to redeem from the foreclosure in one year rather than limiting such right to ninety days.

For the reasons which we have enunciated, we now hold that the redemption provisions of P.L.1975, ch. 552, §§ 6321-25, are unconstitutional when applied to mortgages which were executed prior to the effective date of that statute, unless the mortgage contained language permitting foreclosure under any legal method existing at the time the mortgage became in default. *See Rendering Co. v. Stewart,* 132 Me. 139, 168 A. 100 (1933). Such language was not included within the mortgage given by the defendant to this plaintiff and, therefore, the attempted foreclosure by the plaintiff was constitutionally impermissible.

The entry is:

Appeal sustained.

All Justices concur.
DELAHANTY, J., did not sit.

NOTES

1. *Portland Savings Bank v. Landry, supra,* points out that while statutory redemption may be a creation of the legislature, any modifications of the redemption period must be done in a manner so as not to be unconstitutional.

2. The United States Supreme Court has decided some cases which at first glance appear to hold that a state may modify a mortgagor's right of redemption without offending constitutional requirements. *Aikins v. Kingsbury,* 247 U.S. 484 (1918), involved a contract to purchase state land. After execution of the contract the legislature enacted a statute changing the purchaser's right to redeem the property in the event of default. The Court upheld that statute, stating that the state had the right to modify within certain limits, which apparently were not exceeded in that case. Later, in *City of El Paso v. Simmons,* 379 U.S. 497 (1965), the Court upheld a Texas statute which reduced the period within which a purchaser of state lands could reinstate after a forfeiture. The Court cited the "State's vital interest in administering its school lands to produce maximum revenue. . . ." 379 U.S. 497, 515. This is not identical to redemption but similar enough for comparison purposes.

3. Notice the wide variation in redemption statutes shown earlier: Wisconsin postpones the sale for a year after the foreclosure order; Iowa allows redemption for a year after the sale. What are the practical differences between these two approaches?

1. TIME FOR REDEMPTION

PURCELL v. SMITH

Supreme Court of Alabama
388 So. 2d 525 (1980)

PER CURIAM. This appeal arises from the trial court's decree granting appellee's motion for summary judgment and denying the relief sought in appellant's complaint for redemption of certain property following a foreclosure sale.

In 1975, appellant, Patricia Yost Purcell, and her husband purchased a lot and house, giving a mortgage for a portion of the purchase price. Thereafter, appellant and her husband were divorced. As a part of the divorce settlement, the parties agreed that appellant would forego possession of the property in return for her ex-husband's assuming responsibility for the mortgage, taxes, and insurance payments. Legal title to the property was not changed and remained in both appellant's and her ex-husband's name.

Subsequently, the mortgage was foreclosed because the husband defaulted in the payment of the mortgage debt, and on June 15, 1978, the property was sold pursuant to a power of sale contained in the mortgage agreement. Appellee, F. L. Smith, purchased the property at the foreclosure sale.

On June 1, 1979, a Friday, at 4:30 p. m. appellant's attorney mailed a certified letter, restricted delivery requested, to appellee notifying him of appellant's desire to redeem the property and demanding a list of all lawful charges due. The notice was mailed to the address of the subject property and was returned June 28, 1979, as unclaimed.

On June 11, 1979, ten days after the demand was mailed, with no response from appellee, appellant filed a complaint for redemption of the property and alleged the failure of appellee to respond to the demand for a statement of lawful charges. Four days later, appellant's attorney received a letter from appellee's attorney acknowledging receipt of the complaint, but not of the demand made on June 1, and requesting appellant to deliver a specified sum in certified funds, the amount paid at the foreclosure sale plus 10% interest per annum as allowed by law, and reserving the right to claim any additional amounts later determined to be lawfully chargeable.

Both parties filed motions for summary judgment with supporting documents. The court granted appellee's motion, denying appellant's, as follows:

> This cause having been submitted to the Court on Motions For Summary Judgment, and the Court finding that a written demand for the statement of debt and lawful charges having been made by the Plaintiff, by mailing the said demand at 4:30 P. M., June 1, 1979, a Friday, and the Court finding that a reasonable time for said letter to have been delivered would be no sooner than June 4, 1979, and the Court finding that the Bill of Complaint in this cause was filed on the 11th day of June, 1979 less than ten (10) days after said demand was made, and the Court further finding that there is no evidence of a tender being made by the Plaintiff to the Defendant in this cause, and the Plaintiff having failed to pay into Court any sums of money,
>
> It is therefore ORDERED, ADJUDGED and DECREED by the Court that the Motion for Summary Judgment by the Plaintiff is denied.
>
> It is further ORDERED, ADJUDGED and DECREED by the Court that the Motion for Summary Judgment by the Defendant is hereby granted, and finds and orders that the Plaintiff is entitled to no relief under her Bill of Complaint.

The sole question is at what time does the ten-day period for a response begin running when a redemptioner makes a written demand for lawful charges by mail?

Appellant contends that the ten-day period must be "triggered" by the certain event of the day on which the notice was mailed; otherwise, the commencement of the running of the period is dependent upon "happenstance" and is rendered uncertain in every case. Appellee, on the other hand, contends that the court's finding that three days is a reasonable time for delivery by mail so that the ten-day period commences to run three days after the date of mailing is reasonable and should be upheld.

Section 6-5-230 of the Alabama Code provides, "Where real estate, or any interest therein is sold . . . by virtue of any . . . power of sale in a mortgage, the same may be redeemed by the debtor . . . from the purchaser or his vendee within one year thereafter in the manner provided in this article." The steps necessary to be taken within one year to exercise the statutory right of redemption are set forth in § 6-5-234 as follows:

> Anyone desiring and entitled to redeem may make written demand of the purchaser or his vendee for a statement in writing of the debt and all lawful charges claimed by him, and such purchaser or vendee shall, *within 10 days after such written demand,* furnish such person making the demand with a written itemized statement of the debt and all lawful charges claimed by him; and failing so to do, he shall forfeit all claims or right to compensation for improvements, and the party so entitled to redeem may, on the expiration of

the 10 days, file his complaint without a tender to enforce his rights under this article. [Emphasis added.]

Ordinarily, unless a tender is excused by failure of the purchaser to respond to the demand for lawful charges within ten days, the complaint is defective if it does not show a tender of the amount due. *See, e. g., Foerster v. Swift,* 216 Ala. 228, 113 So. 31 (1927). Thus, unless the ten-day period for the purchaser's response began to run from the date of mailing of the demand, appellant's complaint was premature and was due to be dismissed, there having been neither a tender as required by the statute nor a valid excuse for the failure thereof.

The statute itself offers little guidance in the resolution of this question; it merely states that the statement of charges shall be furnished "within 10 days after such written demand."

The written demand of the purchaser for lawful charges must be made within the one-year redemptive period; it was in this case. Furthermore, the demand may be made by personal delivery to the purchaser or by mail, be it regular, certified, or registered.

Although the date of placing the demand in the mail would be the most certain and uniform date for the "triggering" of the ten-day period, the reality is that the purchaser, through no fault of either of the parties, may not receive the demand until much later after it was mailed. The statute gives the purchaser ten days in which to prepare the statement of lawful charges so that he may have time to consult with his attorney, if necessary, and to fairly and reasonably assess his proper demands. *See Foerster v. Swift,* 216 Ala. at 229, 113 So. at 31. But more importantly, the purchaser forfeits the right to claim improvements on the property if he does not respond within ten days. Code 1975, § 6-5-234. The forfeiture of such important rights cannot depend upon the vagaries of modern mail delivery. The ten-day period for response by the purchaser must begin to run from actual receipt by the purchaser of the demand. The burden is on the redemptioner to see that the purchaser receives the demand either by personal delivery or by mail within a sufficient time to effect redemption. If the period for redemption is fast running out and the redemptioner relies upon the mails to timely deliver his demand, then he so relies at his peril.

In *Foerster v. Swift, supra,* the redemptioner filed her complaint for redemption one day before the expiration of the redemptive period. There was no tender. She made the written demand upon the purchaser one day prior to filing the complaint. In reversing the trial court for failure to dismiss the complaint, this court said:

> It thus appears complainant places some reliance upon section [6-5-234] of the Code . . . , in that she avers written demand was made upon respondent for a statement in writing of the debt and lawful charges claimed, but this demand was made just one day previous to the filing of the bill, while the above-cited statute gave respondent a period of ten days within which to comply therewith. True, complainant was forced to file the bill at that time to come within the statutory period of two years [now one year], but the above-noted section was adopted primarily for the benefit of the redemptioner, and, if he delays to make the demand as therein authorized for a statement until too late for the purchaser or his vendee to have the benefit of the ten-day period allowed by the statute for a compliance, then he can claim no benefit thereunder. Any hardship resulting from a loss of the privileges therein bestowed is the result of his own lack of diligence.

In *Hale v. Kinnaird,* 200 Ala. 596, 76 So. 954 (1917), the purchaser prepared an itemized statement of lawful charges within the ten-day period, but mailed it after the expiration of the ten days. Obviously, the tardiness of the response excused tender in that case. However, the court, in dictum, stated the following in regard to when a demand or notice sent by mail is deemed made: "If she mailed the [statement of lawful charges] on said latter date [within the ten-day period], and it was delayed in transmission through the mails to April 24th [seven days after the expiration of the ten-day period], the burden of compliance resting on her, the delay must affect her right, rather than that of him who made the demand under the statute. The written demand was delivered to her in person. To insure a due reply, under the statute, she should have shown due diligence toward statutory compliance." 200 Ala. at 600, 76 So. at 958. Although this statement is dictum and speaks to the converse duty of the purchaser to timely respond, the rationale is persuasive for our holding that a demand for a statement of lawful charges, sent by mail, is deemd made when received by the purchaser. The burden of compliance rests upon the redemptioner and any delay in the making of the demand must, similarly, affect his right rather than that of the purchaser upon whom the demand is made. Since the forfeiture of important rights depends upon the timeliness of a response, the purchaser cannot be penalized by the uncertainties of the mails and the burden rests on the redemptioner to make a written demand, by whatever mode, within the statutory time limit. Of course, the purchaser may not intentionally defeat the privilege to redeem. *See Hudson v. Morton,* 231 Ala. 392, 165 So. 227 (1936).

Allowing three days for delivery by mail before the ten days start to run is not realistically related to actual delivery time — actual delivery could be sooner or much later — and therefore, is not any more satisfactory than using the date of mailing as the time when a demand by mail is made. Also, both the parties cite different provisions in the Alabama Rules of Civil Procedure as to when a notice or demand by mail is effective. However, the time for effectiveness largely depends upon the context, so the ARCP do not furnish an appropriate analogy in this case. *Compare* ARCP 4.1(c) *with* ARCP 5(b) and 6(e).

Appellant further contends that she is excused from making tender because appellee furnished her with only a partial or incomplete statement of charges. Without regard to the effect of an incomplete statement, the complaint in this case was filed without a tender before the ten-day period expired and before the incomplete statement was even given. Thus, the partial or incomplete statement of charges cannot possibly serve to excuse tender in this case.

Accordingly, this case is due to be affirmed.

Affirmed.

TORBERT, C. J., and FAULKNER, ALMON, EMBRY and BEATTY, JJ., concur.

MOLLERUP v. STORAGE SYSTEMS INTERNATIONAL

Supreme Court of Utah
569 P.2d 1122 (1977)

HALL, JUSTICE: D. Richard Moench appeals from two orders of the District Court of Salt Lake County extending the time for redemption after foreclosure on real property.

The factual sequence giving rise to this controversy is as follows: Defendants Robert T. and Ernestina M. Martin hereinafter referred to as "Martins," purchased real estate assigning their interest therein to plaintiff, J. A. Mollerup, hereinafter referred to as "Mollerup," as security for a loan. Martins defaulted on the contract and summary judgment of foreclosure was granted in favor of Mollerup who in turn assigned his interest to appellant, D. Richard Moench, hereinafter referred to as "Moench," who was the successful bidder at the sheriff's sale. Thereafter, Martins filed a petition in bankruptcy and respondent, John C. Green, hereinafter referred to as "Green," was appointed trustee.

The six month period of redemption expired on October 13, 1976, and based on an ex parte motion of Green the lower court entered an order on October 15, 1976, extending the redemption period for 45 days and Green subsequently sought and obtained a second ex parte order extending the redemption period for 45 days from the date this Court renders its opinion on appeal.

The sole question on appeal involves the power of the lower court to extend the redemption period, and if so, upon what circumstances. Title 78-37-6 U.C.A., 1953, establishes the statutory right of redemption from foreclosure sales:

> Sales of real estate under judgments of foreclosure of mortgages and liens are subject to redemption as in case of sales under executions generally. . . .

Rule 69(f)(3) U.R.C.P. establishes the time for redemption from sales on execution.

> The property may be redeemed from the purchaser within six months after the sale on paying the amount of his purchase with 6 percent thereon in addition, together with the amount of any assessment or taxes, and any reasonable sum for fire insurance and necessary maintenance, upkeep, or repair of any improvements upon the property which the purchaser may have paid thereon after the purchase, with interest on such amounts, and, if the purchaser is also a creditor having a lien prior to that of the person seeking redemption, other than the judgment under which said purchase was made, the amount of such lien, with interest. . . .

The orders of the trial court are apparently based on Rule 6(b) U.R.C.P. which reads in part as follows:

> When by these rules or by a notice given thereunder or by order of the court an act is required or allowed to be done at or within a specified time, the court *for cause shown* may at any time in its discretion (1) with or without motion or notice order the period enlarged if request therefor is made before the expiration of the period originally prescribed or as extended by a previous order . . . but it may not extend the time for taking any action under Rules 50(b), 52(b), 59(b), (d) and (e), 60(b) and 73(a) and (g), except to the extent and under the conditions stated in them. [Emphasis added.]

The provisions of said Title 78-37-6, supra, are more than procedural; they confer and define the extent of the right to redeem, as well as provide the method in which redemption shall be made.

The right of redemption has long been recognized as a substantive right to be exercised in strict accord with statutory terms. It is not an equitable right created or regulated by principles of equity but, rather, is a creature of statute and depends entirely upon the provisions of the statute creating the right.

Notwithstanding the foregoing, a court, sitting in equity, may in appropriate instances extend the period. This Court has recognized that equitable principle by setting aside a sale after the time for redemption had expired, when the sale was attended by such substantial irregularities as must have prevented a sale at a fair sum, resulting in a gross sacrifice of the judgment creditor's property. A similar case can be made to relieve a mortgagor of the consequences of fraud, accident, mistake, or waiver as was found to exist in *United States v. Loosley,* Utah, 551 P.2d 506 (1976). In that case, the mortgagor tendered payment for redemption to the purchaser's attorney one day prior to the expiration of the six month period and the same was returned eight days later with the explanation it had been tendered to the wrong person and citing additional other technical defects. The court held that the refusal to accept the tender was not justified and the failure to state objections to the tender was deemed to be a waiver of any such technical defects.

This Court has also considered the matter of bankruptcy after foreclosure and sale and has determined that such does not extend the time of redemption. If the bankrupt, or his trustee, fails to exercise the right of redemption during the period provided by law, the right is lost.

The facts and circumstances of this particular case reflect nothing as would move the conscience of the Court in favor of Green. A further brief review of the facts points this out. He readily admits that no tender was ever made since the bankrupt estate was and is entirely without assets and that the only prospect of an "asset" is the value, if any, of the right of redemption for which he is hopeful of finding a purchaser. He merely filed an affidavit alleging the redemption figures were not promptly furnished and were questionable.

It is obvious that Green is in no position to redeem and is merely attempting to sell the right of redemption. It is also obvious that because of the economic conditions which have prevailed during the some 16 months that have elapsed since the foreclosure sale, that land values have increased sharply and the prolonged redemption period has certainly worked in favor of Green.

Green asserts that equity favors his position, however, when we consider the position of Moench who expended in excess of $76,000.00 to purchase and has been prevented from perfecting title for a period of 16 months it is clear that the equities are balanced in the latter's favor. To determine otherwise would allow others similarly situated to simply appear ex parte, assert a dispute, a possible sale of the right to redeem, or some other such self-serving matter and the effect would be to abridge the rights of a purchaser at sale.

The extensions granted were not based upon adequate cause shown as required under Rule 6(b), supra, and amounted to an abuse of discretion under the facts of this case.

The orders are reversed, vacated, and set aside. Costs awarded to Moench.

ELLETT, C. J., and CROCKETT, MAUGHAN, and WILKINS, JJ., concur.

2. WHO MAY REDEEM

CALL v. THUNDERBIRD MORTGAGE CO.

Supreme Court of California
58 Cal. 2d 542, 375 P.2d 169 (1962)

McComb, Justice.

. . . .

Plaintiff, who acquired an assignment of a mechanic's lien judgment and who later purchased the property involved at the foreclosure sale on such judgment, brought a quiet title action and sought declaratory relief against defendant Thunderbird Mortgage Co., Inc. (hereinafter called "Thunderbird"). The action also named as defendants certain parties who were grantees from Thunderbird and encumbrancers from such grantees. Any reference to defendant in the singular is to defendant Thunderbird in view of the fact that the rights of all other defendants are derivative and are based upon the legal position of Thunderbird. Thunderbird based its claim of title upon a deed from the original owner (and judgment debtor) and upon a certificate of redemption issued by the marshal.

The trial court, sitting without a jury, declined to give effect to the certificate of redemption issued by the marshal to Thunderbird and rendered judgment in favor of plaintiff, and from this judgment defendants appeal.

The facts may be summarized as follows:

In 1951, Mr. and Mrs. McGinnis (hereinafter referred to as "debtors" or "judgment debtors") purchased a large lot in the Culver City area of Los Angeles from the Oswalds. The McGinnises executed two purchase money deeds of trust in favor of the sellers, a first in the sum of $4,000, and a second in the sum of $1,500. Both deeds of trust were recorded on May 22, 1951.

In connection with a work of improvement on the property, a mechanic's lien in the sum of $315 was recorded by the Colich Construction Company on July 14, 1952 (hereinafter sometimes referred to as the "mechanic's lien"). This claim was assigned to V. O. Matchett for collection; action to foreclose the lien was filed on October 10, 1952; judgment of foreclosure was entered on April 2, 1953.

In addition to the two deeds of trust and the mechanic's lien, there were numerous liens and encumbrances subsequently recorded against the property including judgments, state and federal tax liens and other mechanic's liens, none of which are in dispute here.

The debtors conveyed their land by grant deed to Thunderbird through which deed it now claims its rights as a successor in interest of such judgment debtors. This deed was dated and executed on June 2, 1955, and was recorded February 8, 1957.

The second deed of trust was in default and was assigned by the Oswalds (the original sellers) to V. O. Matchett, who brought a court action to foreclose on October 14, 1954. The defendants named in said action included, among others, the debtors and Thunderbird, who were represented by an attorney, Mr. Isenberg. On May 2, 1957, a judgment of foreclosure was entered in said 1954 action, the amount of the judgment totaling $4,568.85.

Before the foreclosure sale of the second deed of trust Thunderbird, as record owner, decided on a plan whereby it would subdivide the one large lot in question into three smaller residential lots. The plan contemplated that the funds from the proposed sale would be used to pay off all existing encumbrances totaling around $20,000. In early May 1957 plaintiff saw a "for sale" sign on the property; inquired of the realtors the asking price and found they were asking $9,000 per lot, totaling $27,000 for the three; was directed by a third party to Mr. Riskin who was in the process of foreclosing the second deed of trust for his client Matchett; and entered into an alleged agreement with Mr. Riskin whereby he would be able to obtain the property for about $20,000 by buying up the liens on said property.

On May 23, 1957, prior to the sale, Mr. Riskin obtained an assignment of the mechanic's lien judgment from his client V. O. Matchett for plaintiff. Under instructions from Mr. Riskin to Commissioner R. E. Allen, a sale under the deed of trust foreclosure decree was had on June 10, 1957. Thunderbird and plaintiff Call were the bidders at the sale with Thunderbird being the successful bidder at $6,500. Subsequent to the sale, on June 12, 1957, Mr. Riskin, for plaintiff Call, obtained an assignment of Matchett's right to the proceeds of the sale for the sum of $4,005.17. Plaintiff also took an assignment of the first deed of trust from the Oswalds.

On June 10, 1957, plaintiff through his attorney Riskin issued instructions to the marshal to levy upon and sell the parcel pursuant to the 1953 mechanic's lien judgment of foreclosure. This sale complied with the statutory requirements (notice was posted and publication had), but no notice was given to Thunderbird. On July 12, 1957, plaintiff became the purchaser at that sale of the judgment debtor's interest in the property for the sum of $475.40. It is through this sale that plaintiff asserts his status as successor in interest of the judgment debtor.

It should also be noted that the three lots were sold, one each to the defendants Elmer and Fleming for $9,500 per lot and one to Merch for $8,375. Escrows on these sales were opened in June 1957 and closed on July 31, 1957. Defendants Markworth and Lavoie each hold encumbrances issued by the new purchasers. The title company issued policies of title insurance after Thunderbird on July 5, 1957, agreed to enter into an indemnity agreement whereby Thunderbird agreed to obtain releases of all of the liens and encumbrances disclosed in the preliminary reports of title, including the mechanic's lien judgment and the first deed of trust which was subsequently assigned to plaintiff. By the time this cause was heard in the trial court, the three purchasers had built homes on these lots, which properties, defendant asserts, are now worth over $100,000.

After the escrows were closed on July 31, 1957, Mr. Riskin (on behalf of plaintiff) made demand upon R. E. Allen as commissioner for a certificate of redemption from the second trust deed foreclosure sale on the basis that plaintiff, by purchasing at the mechanic's lien foreclosure sale, was "the successor in interest of the judgment debtor." The commissioner issued the certificate of redemption upon the payment of the amount of the sale plus interest and this certificate was recorded August 14, 1957.

Prior to the time of redemption Thunderbird offered to pay plaintiff the amount of his mechanic's lien. This tender was refused. Thunderbird then attempted to effect a redemption as "successor in interest" of the judgment debtor by offering to pay plaintiff the amount paid to redeem from the first sale plus the amount of his judgment plus interest. These tenders were refused on the ground that Thunderbird was not a "successor in interest" of the judgment debtor since it did not have a deed executed *after* the sale. The marshal also refused to allow redemption on the authority of *Lawler v. Gleason* (1955) 130 Cal.App.2d 390 [279 P.2d 70], which had been called to his attention by Mr. Riskin.

Since the refusal of both Mr. Riskin and the marshal was based upon the fact that Thunderbird's deed was received in 1955, Thunderbird had obtained a quitclaim deed dated September 16, 1957, from the judgment debtors. On the basis of this new deed and other supporting documents, the marshal then allowed Thunderbird to effect a redemption from plaintiff upon payment of the sum of $7,157.79 (representing the amount paid by plaintiff on his redemption plus the amount of his mechanic's lien plus interest).

The trial court in effect concluded that the second deed received by Thunderbird was a nullity and gave it no interest in the land and as a result the redemption from plaintiff was improper. Title was quieted in plaintiff by virtue of plaintiff's certificate of sale on the mechanic's lien foreclosure.

The principal contentions made by defendants on this appeal are: (1) plaintiff had no right to redeem from the trust deed foreclosure sale at which Thunderbird was the purchaser; (2) Thunderbird, as successor in interest to the judgment debtors, had a clear right of redemption from plaintiff as the purchaser at the mechanic's lien foreclosure sale, and having deposited the full redemption price of $7,157.79 and having received the certificate of redemption, it was entitled to judgment in the trial court.

It is helpful to analyze the status of the title and the rights of the parties after the judicial foreclosure of the second deed of trust. This foreclosure sale was held

June 10, 1957, and Thunderbird was the purchaser. At this date, Thunderbird was the successor in interest of the debtors because it held a deed from the McGinnises dated June 2, 1955, recorded February 8, 1957. Thunderbird stood in the shoes of the original debtors (trustors) and when it bid in and became the purchaser, it was exactly the same legal situation as though the property had been bid in and purchased by the debtors or owners.

The instant case presents an unusual and rare situation where the record owner (and successor in interest to the debtor) purchases in at the foreclosure sale. However, as will be pointed out, there is no element of fraud involved because subsequent and junior liens are not wiped out by such sale. The ordinary rule is, of course, that the purchaser at the foreclosure or execution sale takes title as of the date the lien vested and all subsequent or junior liens are eliminated. (See *Bateman v. Kellogg,* 59 Cal.App. 464, 474 [211 P. 46].)

The rule is different where the judgment debtor is the purchaser at such foreclosure or execution sale. The legal result is that the lien levied upon or foreclosed is satisfied and discharged, the effect of the sale is terminated, and the property remains subject to subsequent and junior liens.

The situation is analogous to that where a judgment debtor redeems property after an execution sale. The redemption wipes out the effect of the execution sale and the property is still subject to junior liens. The rule and the reason therefor are clearly pointed out in *Kaiser v. Mansfield,* 160 Cal. App.2d 620 [325 P.2d 865], where the court said at page 628:

A redemption by the judgment-debtor terminates the particular sale in which *that redemption is made and restores the estate of the judgment-debtor.* Section 701 of the Code of Civil Procedure provides that redemption may be made by a creditor having a lien or by the judgment-debtor or his successor in interest. Section 703 specifically provides "if the debtor redeem, the effect of the sale is terminated, and he is restored to his estate." A redemption by the judgment-debtor's "successor in interest" has the same effect. . . . These statutes were designed to protect the redemption rights of various parties, not to relieve the judgment-debtor from the payment of his just debts. When a redemption is made by a creditor the junior lien which is wiped out does not represent a debt which is owed by the redeeming creditors. There would be no justice, however, in permitting a judgment-debtor to redeem from a first execution sale and thereby cancel and wipe out his obligation on there execution liens covering debts which he also owes. We cannot construe these statutes as having that effect and as leading to such a result. The same rule would apply where the redemption from the first sale is made by the "successor in interest" of the judgment-debtor who stands in his shoes, and is entitled only to the same rights. (Italics added.)

Thus, the legal title to the property here, following the foreclosure sale on July 10, 1957, stood in the name of Thunderbird subject, however, to certain liens, including the lien of the mechanic's lien judgment of foreclosure entered April 2, 1953.

The mechanic's lien judgment of foreclosure was not enforced until 1957; the foreclosure sale was held July 12, 1957, and plaintiff was the purchaser at such sale. By this sale, plaintiff acquired the interest of the judgment debtor in the property as it existed at the time the mechanic's lien became effective.

The question presented is whether plaintiff could thereafter legally redeem from Thunderbird as the purchaser at the trust deed forclosure sale. Ordinarily, a subsequent judgment lien creditor can redeem (Code Civ. Proc., § 701, subd. 2) from a sale on a prior lien because such sale wipes out his lien and he is given the right of protection; however, in the instant case, the subsequent judgment creditor still has his lien, it is not wiped out or eliminated and the rule of redemption is not applicable.

As applied here, plaintiff did not have to redeem from Thunderbird because his lien (and the acquisition of the rights of the judgment debtor by reason of the sale) was effective. Therefore such attempted redemption by plaintiff from the foreclosure sale on the second deed of trust may be disregarded as being ineffective and not necessary to protect plaintiff's rights as purchaser on the foreclosure sale under the mechanic's lien judgment.

Any equity in plaintiff created by the payment to redeem from the trust deed foreclosure sale is fully protected here because the full sum paid by plaintiff to redeem was later returned to plaintiff (and is now held by plaintiff's attorney) upon the later redemption made by Thunderbird from the mechanic's lien judgment forclosure sale.

We now turn to the principal issue in the case, the legal effect of the mechanic's lien judgment foreclosure sale, at which plaintiff was the purchaser, and the redemption from such sale by Thunderbird.

As previously stated, this sale was held July 12, 1957; plaintiff was the purchaser thereat and plaintiff thereby acquired all the interest of the judgment debtors in the property at the time the mechanic's lien became effective.

Previous to the execution sale, Thunderbird had obtained a deed to the property from the owners and judgment debtors (the McGinnises); the deed was dated June 2, 1955, and recorded February 8, 1957.

This clearly and without any doubt made Thunderbird the "successor in interest" of the judgment debtor (McGinnis) and under section 701, subdivision 1, Code of Civil Procedure, "Property sold subject to redemption . . . may be redeemed in the manner hereinafter provided, by . . . 1. The judgment debtor, or his successor in interest, in the whole or any part of the property." Under the statute Thunderbird had the legal right to redeem. This *right of redemption* follows as a result of the establishment of the status of being a *successor in interest* to the judgment debtor and *the date of the deed* or other conveyance is immaterial. Certainly the statute giving the right of redemption to a successor in interest of the judgment debtor specifies no requirement of the date of such succession in interest. Logically, there is no reason why the succession in interest must follow the execution sale; a judgment debtor may have conveyed the property (and all his interest therein) long before the date of the execution sale (as in the instant case) and the grantee's status as successor in interest gives him *the right of redemption* in order to protect his interest as *owner of the property* in question. A successor in interest has been defined as follows: "A successor in interest of the judgment debtor is one who has acquired (or succeeded to) the interest of the judgment debtor in the property, subject, of course, to the effect of the judgment and sale; . . . A grantee of the mortgagor-defendant, claiming under an unrecorded deed made prior to foreclosure, would be a 'successor in interest,' as would a grantee of the 'judgment debtor' taking by deed after judgment or sale." (Ogden's California Real Property Law, § 17.57, pp. 662, 663.)

To summarize, as shown by the statute, it is the *status* that is the important and determining factor, not the *date* of the deed or conveyance.

Any statements in *Lawler v. Gleason,* 130 Cal.App.2d 390 [279 P.2d 70], contrary to the rules announced in this decision are disapproved.

It is our conclusion that Thunderbird, holding the 1955 deed from the judgment debtors which was recorded February 8, 1957, was a successor in interest to the judgment debtors within the meaning of subdivision 1 of section 701 of the Code of Civil Procedure, and having such *status* it was entitled to redeem from plaintiff who purchased at the mechanic's lien judgment execution sale held on July 12, 1957. Having paid the full redemption price ($7,157.79) and having received the certificate of redemption from the marshal, defendant Thunderbird (and its grantees and their encumbrancers as the other defendants in this action) should have had judgment in the trial court.

Because of the decision made above on the effective and valid redemption made by Thunderbird it is unnecessary to pass upon the other points as to the equities of the parties, as raised on this appeal by Thunderbird.

It appears from the record that plaintiff acquired an assignment of the first deed of trust against the property and that the amount necessary to pay and discharge this encumbrance, the sum of $2,784.93, has been tendered to plaintiff by Thunderbird, and that this amount is now held by Mr. Riskin, as plaintiff's attorney. The trial court made no disposition or ruling as to this item.

The judgment is reversed, and the trial court is directed to order (1) that the sum last above mentioned, now held by plaintiff's attorney as trustee, be paid to plaintiff; (2) that plaintiff execute and deliver the proper and necessary papers to bring about a full reconveyance of the property from the first trust deed; and (3) that the sum of $7,157.79, now held by plaintiff's attorney as trustee, be paid to plaintiff, this amount being the full redemption price payable to plaintiff by Thunderbird. In all other respects the judgment should be for defendants on the quiet title and declaratory relief issues, defendants to recover their costs on appeal.

GIBSON, C. J., TRAYNOR, J., SCHAUER, J., PETERS, J., WHITE, J., and TOBRINER, J., concurred.

NOTES

1. Allowing a mortgagor time in which to save the land even after a foreclosure does not seem inappropriate. Likewise, junior lienors being extended additional time to avoid being "sold out" is consistent. However, courts have allowed a variety of people to exercise redemption rights, some likely and some not so likely. For example, a spouse in a non-community property state being allowed redemption rights appears an equitable interpretation of a statutory right vested in the mortgagor. *See Martin v. Sprague,* 29 Minn. 53, 11 N.W. 143 (1882).

2. If one accepts that long term installment contracts for the purchase and sale of land are in reality a form of disguised mortgage, then allowing the vendee under such a contract to exercise statutory redemption rights is consistent. Notice that the contract vendee has the right to redeem after the vendor has defaulted on a mortgage. This is different from allowing the contract vendee to reinstate after a default on the contract. For a case involving a vendee's right to redeem *see Pine v. Pittman, infra* page 304.

3. One recent case prevented the beneficiary under a land trust from exercising redemption rights even though it was the beneficial interest in the land which had been assigned as security for the note. The court said that the beneficial interest under a land trust was personal property and that assignment of that interest to secure a note did not convert it to a mortgage. *See Sheridan v. Park National Bank,* 422 N.E.2d 1130 (Ill. App. 1981).

3. THE PRICE OF REDEMPTION

SPRINGER CORP. v. KIRKEBY-NATUS

Supreme Court of New Mexico
80 N.M. 205, 453 P.2d 376 (1969)

NOBLE, CHIEF JUSTICE. Kirkeby-Natus (hereafter termed Kirkeby) foreclosed its first mortgage covering 403 acres of lands securing an indebtedness of $521,458.11, bidding in the land for $323,625.00, and obtained a deficiency judgment for $197,833.11. Springer Corporation (hereafter termed Springer) held a second mortgage on 94.96 acres of the land mortgaged to Kirkeby, securing an indebtedness of $77,800.00. By reason of an abstractor's error, Springer was not made a party to the Kirkeby foreclosure. Springer then brought this action to foreclose its second mortgage. Kirkeby, in this suit, by counterclaim, was granted foreclosure of its first mortgage against Springer. Springer was held entitled to redeem from the Kirkeby foreclosure, within nine months after the date of the judgment in this case, but only upon payment of the full amount paid by Kirkeby for the entire 403 acres bought at the foreclosure sale — $323,625.00, plus $13,041.07, being the unpaid balance of the deficiency judgment. Springer has appealed. The cross-complainants have likewise appealed.

The trial court found that Kirkeby had received a credit of $184,792.04 on its deficiency judgment, leaving a balance of $13,041.07. Springer appears to contend that a greater credit should have been allowed but Findings 24 and 25, so determining, have not been attacked as being unsupported by the evidence and, accordingly, are binding on this court on appeal. *Cooper v. Bank of New Mexico,* 77 N.M. 398, 423 P.2d 431; *Baca v. Gutierrez,* 77 N.M. 428, 423 P.2d 617. Also, it is clear that the findings are amply supported by the proof.

It is settled in this jurisdiction that the rights of one who is not a party to a mortgage foreclosure action are not affected by any judgment rendered therein nor by a foreclosure sale pursuant thereto. *Conway v. San Miguel County Board of Education,* 59 N.M. 242, 282 P.2d 719; *Mann v. Whitely,* 36 N.M. 1, 6 P.2d 468. See also Annot., 134 A.L.R. 1490, 1492. Thus, the failure to join Springer, a junior lien holder, left its rights, including its equity of redemption, unaffected and unimpaired.

The fact that Springer was not a party to the Kirkeby foreclosure, however, does not deprive Kirkeby of the benefit of its judgment against those parties who were before the court in its foreclosure action. *Mann v. Whitely,* supra. The counterclaim in the instant case constituted a separate and independent action to foreclose the Kirkeby mortgage against the Springer rights. Kirkeby, relying on §§ 24-2-19 and 24-2-19.1, N.M.S.A.1953, argues that Springer was only entitled to redeem within nine months from the date of sale held pursuant to the Kirkeby foreclosure.

It is clear to use that since Springer's rights, including its right of redemption, were not impaired or affected by the original Kirkeby foreclosure to which Springer was not a party, its right of redemption only accrues upon the entry of a judgment foreclosing its rights in a separate and independent action, or the judgment on the counterclaim in the instant case. *John Hancock Mut. Life Ins. Co. v. Mays,* 152 Kan. 46, 102 P.2d 984.

Relying on *Green v. Dixon,* 9 Wis. 532 (1859); 2 Wiltsie on Mortgage Foreclosure (4th Ed.) § 1071; and 2 Jones on Mortgages (8th Ed.) § 1375,

Springer argues that because it was not made a party to the Kirkeby senior mortgage foreclosure proceeding, and because Springer's junior mortgage only covers some 95 acres out of the 403 acres securing the senior mortgage, it should be permitted to redeem from the Kirkeby sale pro tanto by paying only the pro rata part of the amount for which the property sold at the Kirkeby sale. We cannot agree.

This question is one of first impression in New Mexico and appears to have been resolved by relatively few courts of other jurisdictions. It is a general rule that a mortgage is an entire thing, and must be redeemed in its entirety, and that a mortgagee cannot be required to divide either his debt or his security. 2 Jones on Mortgages (8th Ed.) § 1372; Annot., 134 A.L.R. 1490, 1511. An exception pointed out by the author, supra, at § 1375, indicating that where an owner of the land has not been made a party to the foreclosure of the senior mortgage, and the senior mortgagee is the purchaser at the sale, the owner not made a party may redeem pro tanto upon the theory that the senior mortgagee, by such purchase, voluntarily severed his right and obtained an indefeasible title to part of the land and a defeasible title to another part, affords some color for the Springer argument. See also 2 Wiltsie on Mortgage Foreclosure (4th Ed.) § 1071; *Monese v. Struve,* 155 Or. 68, 62 P.2d 822. Our research discloses that the statement in Wiltsie has support only in *Green v. Dixon,* supra. 2 Jones on Mortgages, § 1375, states a similar exception, relying only on *Green v. Dixon,* supra, and *Wilson v. Tarter,* 22 Or. 504, 30 P. 499. The basis of these decisions and the exceptions stated in Wiltsie and Jones is criticized by the author in 2 Glenn on Mortgages (1943) § 299.1, who says the rule is objectionable because of a false premise, that is, it assumes that the senior mortgagee in his second independent action to require the junior lien holder to elect whether to redeem, is asking a favor of equity, and thus can be forced to accept a partial redemption as the price of equity. Glenn argues that, in fact, the senior mortgagee is not asking a favor, and that partial redemption should not be allowed merely because the junior encumbrancer happened to be omitted as a party in the first foreclosure. The exception to the general rule is likewise critized in a note, 50 Harvard L.Rev. 990. See 25 Ill.L.Rev. 720. 2 Glenn on Mortgages, supra, at 1257, points out that the real relief of a partial encumbrancer lies in invoking the rule of marshalling by which the junior encumbrancer may require a senior mortgagee to exhaust his remedy against property other than that covered by the partial mortgage of the junior encumbrancer. That doctrine was applied in *Hinners v. Birkevaag,* 113 N.J. Eq. 413, 167 A. 209, at the instance of an omitted junior mortgagee, who established the relative values of the respective tracts in the subsequent independent action.

The Wisconsin Supreme Court, in *Buchner v. Gether Trust,* 241 Wis. 148, 5 N.W.2d 806, without reference to its earlier decision in *Green v. Dixon,* supra, appears to have rejected the reasoning of the earlier case. In *Buchner,* the court expressly said that the rights of a junior encumbrancer not made a party to the foreclosure of the senior mortgage are "unimpaired and unchanged by the defective foreclosure." The court further said:

> . . . Except for the dictum in the *Winter case,* [*Winter v. O'Neill,* 241 Wis. 280, 5 N.W.2d 809] we discover no case holding that the rights of the junior claimant are improved or increased by the defect in the foreclosure proceedings. In accordance with quite elementary principles of justice, his position is preserved and equity will not permit that he suffer any disadvantage from the failure to include him as a party. It would be utterly unfair to do more than this. . . .

The Supreme Court of Florida, in *Quinn Plumbing Co. v. New Miami Shores Corp.,* 100 Fla. 413, 129 So. 690, 73 A.L.R. 600, discussed *Green v. Dixon,* supra, and specifically rejected the reasoning by which a junior encumbrancer, who was not a party to the foreclosure of the senior mortgage, is permitted to redeem pro tanto from the senior mortgage. In *Key West Wharf & Coal Co. v. Porter,* 63 Fla. 448, 58 So. 599, 610, Am.Ann.Cas.1914A, 173, the Florida court said of the holder of a junior mortgage covering only a portion of the land held as security for a senior mortgage:

> . . . Their portions of said land, as well as all the residue of said mortgaged tract, are bound for the payment of the whole of both mortgages; and the courts have no power to release any part of the land from the lien of the mortgages by affixing thereto a sum, less than the entire sum of the mortgages, which, when paid, shall release such part from the lien of the mortgages. . . .

The only absolute right of a junior mortgagee, as against a senior mortgagee, is the right to redeem from the senior mortgagee. 3 Jones on Mortgages (8th Ed.) § 1781. The rights of an omitted junior encumbrancer remain precisely as they were before the proceedings were instituted to foreclose the first mortgage. They are neither enlarged nor diminished by the defective foreclosure. *McGough v. Sweetzer,* 97 Ala. 361, 12 So. 162, 19 L.R.A. 470.

The judgment appealed from must be reversed, however, and the cause remanded because the judgment provided that Springer should have a period of nine months from the date of the entry of the judgment in the instant case within which to redeem the property from the mortgage foreclosure sale in Cause No. A-12537 on the docket of the district court of Bernalillo County. Section 24-2-18, N.M.S.A. 1953, provides that no property shall be sold under a mortgage foreclosure proceeding until sixty days after the date of the entry of the foreclosure judgment. Section 24-2-19, N.M.S.A.1953, gives a person entitled to redemption nine months from the date of such foreclosure sale within which to redeem therefrom. Construing the two statutory provisions together, as we must, its is apparent that a person entitled to redeem is thus given at least eleven months from the date of the foreclosure judgment within which to redeem. We have said that because Springer was not a party to the first foreclosure action, it will not be permitted to suffer any disadvantage from the failure to include it as a party. It is apparent that the judgment in the instant case shortened Springer's period of redemption by sixty days. This was error.

What we have said makes it unnecessary to discuss other questions argued or briefed. It follows that the judgment appealed from should be affirmed in all respects except that the judgment must be vacated and a new judgment entered granting Springer eleven months from the date of such judgment within which to redeem from the Kirkeby foreclosure sale.

It is so ordered.

MOISE and TACKETT, JJ., concur.

4. THE EFFECT OF REDEMPTION

PINE v. PITTMAN

Supreme Court of Kansas
506 P.2d 1184 (1973)

FATZER, CHIEF JUSTICE: This was an action in forcible detainer. (K.S.A.1972 Supp. 61-2301 et seq.) At issue is the right to possession of the premises located at 6408 Larson Lane, Shawnee, Kansas, during the eighteen-month period of redemption resulting from the foreclosure of a first mortgage on the property, owned by the Prudential Insurance Company of America, a corporation.

Upon consideration of the admissions and stipulations of record; the evidence introduced by the appellees, and from documents marked as exhibits and submitted by the parties, the district court found and determined the defendants Carl L. Pittman and Carolyn L. Pittman, husband and wife, were entitled to the use and occupancy of the premises throughout the period of redemption, and that monthly payments of $100 theretofore made by them to the clerk of the district court during the pendency of the action, as hereafter detailed should be returned to them. The plaintiff timely perfected this appeal.

A summary of the facts and relevant transactions leading up to the commencement of the action out of which this appeal arises, are summarized and quoted as follows:

On March 27, 1951, one Charles R. Bruitt and his wife Betty, the owners of the fee simple title of the property in question, executed their promissory note in the principal sum of $9,850 in favor of Mission State Bank, and also executed a first mortgage in favor of the bank to secure payment of the note. The mortgage was a Veterans Administration type mortgage and was assigned by the bank to Prudential, and later foreclosed on January 21, 1970, as hereafter noted.

On October 8, 1953, the Pruitts conveyed the property by warranty deed to Lester P. Schick and his wife Harriette, as joint tenants. However, the conveyance to the Schicks was made expressly *subject* to Prudential's first mortgage with no agreement by the Schicks to assume or pay the same.

Some nine years later, and on October 26, 1962, the Schicks executed a contract for deed to the property in question to Earl L. and Norma J. Pittman, husband and wife (the first Pittmans), as purchasers. As a part of the purchase price of $10,500, the Pittmans agreed *to assume and pay* the Prudential first mortgage then in the principal amount of $6,587.73 by making payment of $67.85 each month commencing November 1, 1962, covering principal, interest and taxes, and in addition, to pay the Schicks $22 each succeeding month on the contract. The Schick deed was to be escrowed, and was to be delivered to the first Pittmans or their assigns, when the contract was paid. Among other things, the contract provided that upon default by the Pittmans of payments under the contract, their tenancy of the real estate should become a month to month tenancy at the rate of $100 per month, at the option of the seller.

On February 27, 1968, the first Pittmans assigned all of their rights and obligations in the contract for deed to Carl L. Pittman, and Carolyn, his wife (the second Pittmans), who took possession of the property. Upon default by the second Pittmans of the first mortgage payment due on April 1, 1969 — after approximately seven years of payments by both Pittmans — Prudential brought suit for foreclosure against the Pruitts, the Schicks, and the Pittmans. The second Pittmans were substituted by both parties to the contract for deed as the equitable owners and presumably were bound to pay the mortgage and did assume and agree to pay the same. Payments by the first and second Pittmans during their occupancy reduced the first mortgage balance by $2,057.92, and there was due on the first mortgage at the time of foreclosure the sum of $4,648.96. Judgment was entered in the foreclosure action on January 21, 1970, for $4,648.96, foreclosing the interests of all defendants in the real estate, and adjudging that Prudential's lien was a first, valid and prior lien upon the premises. Although Schick (whose wife was then deceased) filed an answer *pro se* in the foreclosure action, *he did not seek affirmative relief by cross-claiming under the contract for deed against either the first or second Pittmans pursuant to K.S.A. 60-213(g) to foreclose or forfeit the equitable rights they acquired under the contract.* The district court found that Schick abandoned all his rights and interest in the contract for deed in the foreclosure action.

Except for Schick's answer, which is not contained in the record, none of the defendants pleaded or appeared on January 21, 1970, and a default foreclosure judgment was entered. The district court made specific findings of fact as to the previous transactions affecting an interest in the property, and the journal entry provided, in pertinent part:

It is further by the court,
CONSIDERED, ORDERED, ADJUDGED AND DECREED, That the defendants Charles R. Pruitt and Betty Jean Pruitt, husband and wife; the defendant, Lester P. Schick; the defendants Earl L. Pittman and Norma J. Pittman, husband and wife; the defendants Carl L. Pittman and Carolyn L. Pittman, husband and wife, and each and all of them be and they *are hereby forever barred from any right, title, estate, equity or lien in and to said premises,* or any part thereof, after such sale, *except the right of redemption, as provided by law, which is hereby fixed by the court at eighteen (18) months from the date of Sheriff's Sale as herein ordered,* and the purchaser, after the expiration of said period of redemption, be put into possession of said premises by a Writ of Assistance, or other proper process of this court, and that upon the expiration of the period of redemption herein found, the Sheriff of Johnson County, Kansas, or successor in office, make, execute and deliver to the purchaser at said Sheriff's Sale, or assigns, a good and sufficient deed for the premises hereinbefore described. (Emphasis supplied.)

No appeal was taken from that judgment, nor was it modified in any manner.

Following the judgment of foreclosure, and on February 16, 1970, Schick purportedly quitclaimed any interest he had in the property to one Isaac Pine (father of the appellant), *subject to the first mortgage and its foreclosure.* On March 12, 1970, Schick also assigned and transferred all his right, title and interest in and to the contract for deed to Isaac Pine for the sum of $350, and also assigned to Isaac Pine excess proceeds, if any, derived from the foreclosure sale of the property by Prudential.

On May 13, 1970, Isaac Pine and his wife transferred their interest in the property by deed and assignment of the contract for deed to the appellant, *subject to the first mortgage and its foreclosure.*

The first Pittmans occupied and possessed the premises continuously since 1962, and until they assigned the contract for deed to the second Pittmans on February 27, 1968. The second Pittmans occupied and possessed the premises from the latter date until the foreclosure judgment was rendered, and thereafter occupied and possessed the property until the right of redemption expired on September 13, 1971. Thus, the only question presented is who is entitled to the rents and profits from June 1, 1970 — the date this action was filed — until September 13, 1971, the date redemption expired? The only defendants to be affected by the judgment are the second Pittmans, and they are hereafter referred to as the appellees.

On June 1, 1970, the appellant filed the forcible detainer action in the magistrate court of Johnson County, and alleged that the appellees defaulted on their payments under the contract for deed on October 1, 1969; that he notified them he intended to exercise his option under the contract for deed and thereafter treat them as tenants from month to month at a rental of $100 per month during the period of redemption; that he served written notice notifying them that their failure to pay the $100 rental for the month of June, 1970, terminated the tenancy for nonpayment of rent, and further that an action was about to be brought to recover possession of the property. The prayer was for immediate restitution of the premises, for judgment of $100 for rent, and his costs.

The appellees filed their answer and a counterclaim. In addition to a general denial, they alleged that in the foreclosure action the appellant's predecessor in title, Lester P. Schick, was forever barred from any right, title, estate, equity, or lien in or to the property in question prior to his quitclaim deed to appellant; that in the same action the appellees were granted the right of redemption for eighteen months, and, therefore, have an interest in said real estate paramount to that of appellant; that if appellant's predecessor in interest had any rights against the appelles by reason of the contract for deed, it was mandatory that he affirmatively assert such rights in the foreclosure action, and that the said predecessor in interest failed to assert such rights in such action, and as a result Schick abandoned all claims to the property in such proceeding, and thereafter had no interest whatsoever to convey to the appellant.

. . . .

At a pretrial conference, the district court ordered the appellees to pay to the clerk of the district court the sum of $100 on August 15, 1970, and a like sum on the 15th day of each month until determination of the action. All money paid was to be held by the clerk for the benefit of the appellant in the event it was determined the appellees had no interest in the real estate, and that the appellant was entitled to either rentals or damages from the appellees. The court also ordered that if it was determined the appellant had no right of possession, or claim to rentals or profits accruing, all sums paid by the appellees should be returned to them.

Upon final determination of the action on February 23, 1971, the district court denied the appellant recovery and entered judgment that the appellees were entitled to the use and occupancy of the premises throughout the period of redemption and that all $100 monthly payments made to the clerk of the court be returned to them.

While the appellant made nine statements of points on appeal, it is clear from the discussion in his brief he has waived points two through nine, and has elected to stand on point one, that "[t]he decision of the trial court was contrary to the laws of the state of Kansas as set forth in K.S.A. 60-2414 and K.S.A. 60-2416." In this connection, the appellant states, "[i]t is the plaintiff's contention that pursuant to K.S.A. 60-2414 that the defendant owner does have the exclusive right of redemption . . . ."

K.S.A. 60-2414 (since amended, K.S.A. 1972 Supp. 60-2414) reads in pertinent part:

(a) Right of redemption by defendant owner; junior lienholders. Except as otherwise provided by law, the defendant owner may redeem any real property sold under execution, special execution, or order of sale, at the amount sold for, together with interest, costs and taxes, at any time within twelve (12) months from the day of sale, and within six (6) months thereafter for the amount paid by the then holder of the certificate of purchase together with interest costs and taxes to the date of redemption, and shall in the meantime be entitled to the possession of the property; but where the court or judge shall find that the lands and tenements have been abandoned, or are not occupied in good faith, the period of redemption for defendant owner shall be six (6) months from the date of sale. . . .

. . . .

(l) Holder of legal title. The holder of the legal title at the time of issuance of execution or order of sale shall have the same right of redemption upon the same terms and conditions as the defendant in execution, and also shall be

entitled to the possession of the property the same as the defendant in execution.

It should here be noted, that Pine, as successor in interest, stands in Schick's shoes. He can assert no greater interest in the property than that which was conveyed to him in the chain of title from Schick to Isaac Pine, and finally to him.

We are of the opinion this case can be disposed of by answering the following questions: (1) did the appellant have a right of redemption as a lien creditor having been assigned Schick's right under the contract for deed; (2) did the appellees have a right of redemption to the premises, and (3) as between the appellant and the appellees, who had the primary right of redeption so as to be entitled to possession of the premises during the eighteen months period of redemption.

Turning to the first question, the record clearly shows that prior to the foreclosure of the first mortgage, there were only two encumbrances on the property — Prudential's first mortgage and Schick's equitable rights under the contract for deed. The equitable rights of Prudential were asserted and were foreclosed. Schick's equitable rights were not. The district court had jurisdiction of all the parties and of the subject matter, and while Schick filed an answer *pro se,* he failed to affirmatively assert his right to foreclose or forfeit the appellees' rights under the contract for deed. Schick's failure to assert his rights in that proceeding constituted a waiver. of any rights he may have had as a lien creditor in the property, and under the circumstances, as a junior equitable mortgagee, his lien was waived and he had no right of redemption thereby. (See comment, Junior Lien Holders and Mortgage Foreclosures, 10 JBK 412, 413 [1942].) In *Federal Farm Mortgage Corp. v. Crane,* 153 Kan. 114, 109 P.2d 82, it was held:

> In a foreclosure proceeding the holder of a junior mortgage on the same land was joined as a defendant. The junior mortgagee entered a general appearance in such foreclosure action but filed no answer and asked for no affirmative relief. In the circumstances stated it is held that the lien of the junior mortgagee was waived and that he has no right of redemption under the statute.

With respect to the second question whether the appellees had a right of redemption of the premises, we answer in the affirmative. As indicated, the appellees were defendant owners in the foreclosure action as assignees to the contract for deed executed by the Schicks to the first Pittmans. As contract purchasers, the appellees were the equitable owners of the premises and had an interest therein which was substantial so as to secure to them the right of redemption as guaranteed by K.S.A. 60-2414(a). Moreover, the journal entry of judgment in the foreclosure action expressly reserved the right of redemption to the appellees. That judgment was never appealed or challenged and any inquiry into its merits now would constitute an infringement of the well-recognized principle of *res judicata.* In *Mercer v. McPherson,* 70 Kan. 617, 79 P. 118, it was said:

> It is contended, however, that the right to redeem is statutory; that none except those expressly named in the statute may avail themselves of its benefits, and that under our statute only an owner holding the legal title to the land may redeem. This claim is based mainly upon a single provision of the act that:
> "The holder of the legal title at the time of issuance of the execution or order of sale shall have the same right of redemption upon the same terms and conditions as the defendant in execution, and also shall be entitled to the possession of the property the same as the defendant in execution as hereinbefore provided." (Gen.Stat.1901, § 4945.)

While the holder of the legal title is expressly mentioned in this section, it is not provided that he shall have the exclusive right of redemption, and that such was not the intention of the legislature is manifest from the language of the following section, which mentions the assigns of the defendant in execution or order of sale in a class distinct from the holders of the legal title, and places them upon an equality of right with the holders of the legal title . . . .

. . . *The theory of the act relating to redemption is that the owner of a substantial interest, whether or not he is a defendant, may redeem from an execution or mortgage-foreclosure sale,* and the like protection is also afforded to creditors, mortgagees, and other lienholders. *The owner of an interest, although he may have no formal conveyance, is more entitled to exercise the right than one holding a naked legal title: and the interest and right held by McPherson were certainly paramount to those of Mercer, who took his deed with notice of McPherson's rights.* (L.c. 619, 620, 79 P. l.c. 119.) (Emphasis supplied.)

See, also, *National Bank of America v. Barritt,* 136 Kan. 870, 18 P.2d 552.

Schick held a warranty deed to the property and was made a party defendant to the original foreclosure action, thus he secured the right of redemption to the premises as the record title holder pursuant to K.S.A. 60-2414(*l*) and a defendant owner pursuant to K.S.A. 60-2414(a). The appellant, as Schick's successor in interest, was also entitled to redeem the property as a defendant owner. It follows that the appellant enjoyed the statutory right of redemption either as the holder of legal title or as a defendant owner; however, *that right was not exclusive,* and it did not arise by virtue of the contract for deed to the Pittmans, or the unrecorded second mortgage referred to in that agreement.

With respect to the third question, this court is of the opinion that, as between the appellant and the appellees, the latter had the paramount right of redemption and were entitled to possession of the property throughout the eighteen-month redemption period. The first Pittmans, and later the appellees, had exclusive possession of, and exercised dominion over, the property for seven years — from November 1, 1962, the date the appellant's predecessor in interest expressly surrendered possession. The combined payments of the first Pittmans and the appellees reduced the principal of the first mortgage by $2,057.92, and accordingly increased their equitable ownership in the property by that amount, so as to sustain the district court's finding of their substantial interest in the property. *(Mercer v. McPherson,* supra.)

On the other hand, the appellant merely held the legal title to the premises for which his father paid only $350. The appellant was never in possession of the premises and now attempts to assert rights under the contract for deed by serving notice on the appellees that they were tenants at will and demanded rental payments of $100 per month. The appellant had no right of possession arising by virtue of the contract for deed — his status as a lien creditor having been barred by the original foreclosure. Finally, it should be noted the appellant's interest is inferior to that of the appellees — they having *assumed* the mortgage held by Prudential — he having taken title *subject* to that mortgage.

Once the appellant's status as a lien creditor was barred by the foreclosure, all the equities are in support of a conclusion the appellees had the primary right of redemption and were entitled to the undisturbed possession of the premises during the eighteen-month period of redemption.

In conclusion, we note the appellant's conduct is analogous to that of an "equiteer" as defined in *American Home Life Ins. Co. v. Heide,* 199 Kan. 652, 656, 433 P.2d 454.

The judgment of the district court is affirmed with directions to instruct the clerk of the district court to return to appellees all payments made by them pursuant to the pretrial order.

It is so ordered.

NOTES

1. In the California system of redemption there is no set order in which redeemers must redeem. *See* California Civil Procedure Code §§ 700, 701 and 702.

2. Two cases demonstrate the California system, although neither may be very good law today. *Lawler v. Gleason,* 130 Cal. App. 2d 390, 279 P.2d 70 (1955), is disapproved by the court in *Call v. Thunderbird Mortgage Co., supra* at page 296. *Corporation of America v. Eustace,* 217 Cal. 102, 17 P.2d 723 (1932), is not mentioned in *Call* but is sufficiently inconsistent as to be overruled by implication.

3. The effect of redemption in general is that it erases the foreclosure sale and reinstates the liens that existed before the foreclosure sale. However, this rule will prevent the mortgagor from redeeming after a sale by the senior-most lienor and taking the property back free of junior liens which were sold out by the foreclosure sale.

Chapter 7

DEPRESSION LEGISLATION

I see one-third of a nation ill-housed, ill-clad and ill-nourished.
Franklin D. Roosevelt, *Second Inaugural Address,* 1937

A. INTRODUCTION

The severe economic depression and prolonged drought of the 1930s made impossible demands on the average small parcel farmer. The typical mortgage of that period was not amortized over a long time as in the decades that followed; rather, mortgagors paid interest payments over a relatively short time followed by payment of the principal balance in full (what today would be called a "balloon" payment). Obviously, the depression-era farmer could neither pay the principal nor find alternative financing, and national alarm rose at the growing number of foreclosures until, as part of increasing overall government involvement in the lives of the public, efforts were made by both state and federal legislatures to assist those with mortgages. Some states enacted legislation to put a moratorium on foreclosure, legislation which was tested in the courts and upheld. *See Home Building & Loan Ass'n v. Blaisdell,* 290 U.S. 398 (1934). Although by the 1940s and the boom economy of World War II, moratorium legislation was no longer needed, there were other forms of statutory assistance to borrowers in financial difficulty, and three forms of those statutes — anti-deficiency legislation, one form of action rules, and fair market value laws — remain today in approximately one-third of the states.

HONEYMAN v. JACOBS

United States Supreme Court
306 U.S. 539 (1938)

MR. CHIEF JUSTICE HUGHES delivered the opinion of the Court.

This case, coming here on appeal from the state court, presents the question of the validity under the contract clause of the Federal Constitution of § 1083-a of the Civil Practice Act of New York (Chapter 794 of the Laws of 1933) [1] under

---

[1] Section 1083-a, provides:

1083-a. *Limitation Upon Deficiency Judgments During Emergency Period.* — No judgment shall be granted for any residue of the debt remaining unsatisfied as prescribed by the preceding section where the mortgaged property shall be sold during the emergency, except as herein provided. Simultaneously with the making of a motion for an order confirming the sale or in any event within ninety days after the date of the sale, the party to whom such residue shall be owing may make a motion in the action for leave to enter a deficiency judgment upon notice to the party against whom such judgment is sought or the attorney who shall have appeared for such party in such action. Such notice shall be served personally or in such other manner as the court may direct. Upon such motion the court, whether or not the respondent appears, shall determine, upon affidavit or otherwise as it shall direct, the fair and reasonable market value of the mortgaged premises as of the date of sale or such nearest earlier date as there shall have been any market value thereof and shall make an order directing the entry of a deficiency judgment. Such deficiency judgment shall be for an amount equal to the sum of the amount owing by the party liable as determined by the judgment with interest, plus the amount owing on all prior liens and encumbrances with interest, plus costs and disbursements of the action including the referee's fee and disbursements, less the market value as determined by the court or the sale price of the property whichever shall be the higher. If no motion for a deficiency judgment shall be made as herein prescribed the proceeds of the sale regardless of amount shall be deemed to be in full satisfaction of the mortgage debt and no right to recover any deficiency in any action or proceeding shall exist.

which the appellant, a mortgagee of real property, was denied a deficiency judgment in a foreclosure suit, where the state court found that the value of the property purchased by the mortgagee at the foreclosure sale was equal to the debt secured by the mortgage.

The mortgage was executed in February, 1928, that is, prior to the legislation in question, to secure a bond for $15,000, with interest, payable in February, 1931. On default in payment, appellant, the holder of the bond and mortgage, brought suit for foreclosure and judgment for foreclosure and sale was entered in April, 1938. The property was then sold to appellant for the sum of $7500. In the referee's report of sale the amount due on the bond and mortgage was stated to be $15,771.17, and the taxes, fees and expenses amounted to $1319.03, leaving a deficiency of $9590.20.

Section 1083-a of the Civil Practice Act required that the right to a deficiency judgment should be determined in the foreclosure suit. *Honeyman v. Hanan,* 275 N. Y. 382; 9 N. E. 2d 970; 302 U. S. 375, 378. Accordingly, appellant made his motion in that suit to confirm the sale and for deficiency judgment. Proof was submitted to the court that the present value of the property was $25,318. It does not appear that the correctness of this valuation was contested. The court thereupon confirmed the sale and denied the motion for deficiency judgment upon the ground "that the value of the property is equal to the debt of the plaintiff." Appellant's contention that § 1083-a as thus applied violated the contract clause of the Constitution was overruled and this ruling was sustained by the Court of Appeals. 278 N. Y. 467; 17 N. E. 2d 131. The court followed its earlier decisions, citing *Honeyman v. Hanan,* 275 N. Y. 382; 9 N. E. 2d 970; *Klinke v. Samuels,* 264 N. Y. 144; 190 N. E. 324; *City Bank Farmers Trust Co. v. Ardlea Corporation,* 267 N. Y. 224; 196 N. E. 34.

Appellant invokes the principle that the obligation of a contact is impaired by subsequent legislation which under the form of modifying the remedy impairs substantial rights. See *Sturges v. Crowninshield,* 4 Wheat. 122, 200; *Von Hoffman v. City of Quincy,* 4 Wall. 535, 553, 554; *Antoni v. Greenhow,* 107 U. S. 769, 775; *Home Building & Loan Assn. v. Blaisdell,* 290 U. S. 398, 430, 434, and cases cited, note 13; *W. B. Worthen Co. v. Thomas,* 292 U. S. 426, 433; *W. B. Worthen Co. v. Kavanaugh,* 295 U. S. 56, 60. As we said in *Richmond Mortgage Corp. v. Wachovia Bank,* 300 U. S. 124, 128, "The legislature may modify, limit or alter the remedy for enforcement of a contract without impairing its obligation, but in so doing, it may not deny all remedy or so circumscribe the existing remedy with conditions and restrictions as seriously to impair the value of the right."

We have heretofore decided that the requirement of § 1083-a that the right to a deficiency judgment must be determined in the foreclosure suit raises no substantial question under the contract clause. *Honeyman v. Hanan,* 302 U. S. at p. 378. The question is whether in the instant case the denial of a deficiency judgment substantially impaired appellant's contract right. The bond provided for the payment to him of $15,000 with the stipulated interest. The mortgage was executed to secure payment of that indebtedness. The contract contemplated that the mortgagee should make himself whole, if necessary, out of the security but not that he should be enriched at the expense of the debtor or realize more than what would repay the debt with the costs and expenses of the suit. Having a total debt of $15,771.17, with expenses, etc., of $1319.03, appellant has obtained through his foreclosure suit the property of the debtor found without question to be worth over $25,000. He has that in hand. We know of no principle which entitles him to receive anything more. Assuming that the statute before its amendment permitted a recovery of an additional amount through a so-called deficiency judgment, we cannot say that there was any constitutional sanction for such a provision which precluded the legislature from changing it so as to confine the creditor to securing the satisfaction of his entire debt.

Section 1083-a in substance assured to the court the exercise of its appropriate equitable powers. By the normal exercise of these powers, a court of equity in a foreclosure suit would have full authority to fix the terms and time of the foreclosure sale and to refuse to confirm sales upon equitable grounds where they were found to be unfair or the price bid was inadequate. *Home Building & Loan Assn. v. Blaisdell, supra,* at pp. 446, 447, and cases cited, note 18. *Richmond Mortgage Corp. v. Wachovia Bank, supra,* at p. 129. In this control over the foreclosure sale under its decree, the court could consider and determine the value of the property sold to the mortgagee and what the mortgagee would thus realize upon the mortgage debt if the sale were confirmed. See *Monaghan v. May,* 242 App. Div. 64, 67; 273 N. Y. S. 475; *Guaranteed Title & Mortgage Co. v. Scheffres,* 247 App. Div. 294; 285 N. Y. S. 464.

The reasoning of this Court in *Richmond Mortgage Corp. v. Wachovia Bank, supra,* is applicable and governs our decision. There, a statute of North Carolina, enacted after the execution of notes secured by a deed of trust, provided that where a mortgagee caused the sale of mortgaged property by a trustee and, becoming the purchaser for a sum less than the amount of the debt, thereafter brought an action for a deficiency, the defendant was entitled to show, by way of defense and set-off, that the property sold was fairly worth the amount of the debt or that sum bid was substantially less than the true value of the property, and thus defeat the claim in whole or in part. Under the former law of that State, when the mortgagee became the purchaser at the trustee's sale under a power in the deed of trust, he might thereafter in an action at law recover the difference between the price he had bid and the amount of the indebtedness. We found that the other remedy by bill in equity to foreclose the mortgage was still available. And that in such a proceeding the chancellor could set aside the sale if the price bid was inadequate, and, in addition, he might award a money decree for the amount by which the avails of the sale fell below the amount of the indebtness but that "his decree in that behalf would be governed by well-understood principles of equity." The Court was of the opinion that the statute modifying one of the existing remedies for realizing the value of the security could not "fairly be said to do more than restrict the mortgagee to that for which he contracted, namely, payment in full." The act recognized the obligation of his contract and his right to its full enforcement but limited that right "so as to prevent his obtaining more than his due. By the old and well known remedy of foreclosure, a mortgagee was so limited because of the chancellor's control of the proceeding." That "classical method" of realization upon a mortgage security through a foreclosure suit had always been understood "to be fair to both parties to the contract and to afford an adequate remedy to the mortgagee." In that view it appeared that the new law as to proceedings for a deficiency judgment after the exercise of a power of sale "merely restricted the exercise of the contractual remedy to provide a procedure which, to some extent, renders the remedy by a trustee's sale of consistent with that in equity." And that did "not impair the obligation of the contract."

We reach a similar result here upon the same ground — that under the finding of the state court the mortgagee has obtained satisfaction of his debt and that the denial by the statute of a further recovery does not violate the constitutional provision.

The judgment is

Affirmed.

GENTRY v. HIBBLER-BARNES CO.

Court of Appeals of Georgia
113 Ga. App. 1, 147 S.E.2d 31 (1966)

DEEN, JUDGE. 1. A litigant may, either consecutively or concurrently, pursue any number of consistent remedies to enforce the payment of a debt until it is satisfied. "Obtaining a judgment on the note and foreclosure of the security device are consistent remedies, and the utilization of one will not constitute either an election or abandonment of the other." *Hopkins v. West Publishing Co.*, 106 Ga.App. 596(2), 127 S.E.2d 849. See *Pioneer Investments, Inc. v. Adrine,* 97 Ga.App. 520(2), 103 S.E.2d 686.

2. Black's Law Dictionary defines *deficiency* as "that part of a debt secured by mortgage not realized from sale of mortgaged property," citing *Harrow v. Metropolitan Life Ins. Co.*, 285 Mich. 349, 280 N.W. 785, and continues: "A judgment or decree for the amount of such deficiency is called a 'deficiency judgment' or 'decree'. *Phillips v. Union Central Life Ins. Co.,* C.C.A.Minn., 88 F.2d 188, 189." Ga.L.1935, p. 381, codified as Code Ann. §§ 37-608 — 37-611, is entitled, "Foreclosure sales; deficiency judgments", and the caption of the Act recites that its purposes are (1) to provide for confirmation of sales under foreclosure proceedings; (2) to limit and abate deficiency judgments on secured debts, and (3) to provide for the advertisement of foreclosure sales. Code Ann. § 37-608 lays down a condition precedent to obtaining a deficiency judgment in cases where "any real estate is sold on foreclosure, without legal process, under powers contained in security deeds," and the sale does not cover the amount of the debt. On its face, therefore, it refers only to the foreclosure procedure. Code Ann. § 37-611 requires advertisement of the time and place of sale; this section and the Act generally were held unconstitutional in *Atlantic Loan Co. v. Peterson,* 181 Ga. 266, 182 S.E. 15 as to pre-existing contracts where the security deed contained contradictory provisions as to sale on default. The court in its explication pointed out that the Act was remedial in nature, adding: "In this case we have the promise to pay the debt as the primary obligation, and the power of sale as a remedy." P. 270, 182 S.E. p. 17. The method of exercising the power of sale, and the legal consequences of the sale itself, constitute the subject matter of the Act, and the remedy by sale will be taken to have satisfied the primary obligation unless the creditor conforms to the law by making a proper showing that the security in fact brought in its true market value, which is then credited against the primary obligation. There is nothing in this or any other law which says that the creditor may not, if he chooses, obtain satisfaction of the debt by reducing it to judgment and levying it on whatever property he chooses, whether or not it has been pledged as security for the particular debt evidenced by the note. The only defense to the actions on certain promissory notes sued on here attempted to be raised by the answers and pleas in abatement was that Code Ann §§ 37-608 to 37-611 precluded the plaintiff from bringing the suit and seeking a general judgment until the secured property had been foreclosed on and this sale confirmed. Indubitably the position is untenable, and the trial court did not

err in sustaining general demurrers to these defenses and thereafter entering up a default judgment in favor of the plaintiff.

Judgment affirmed.

Nichols, P. J., and Hall, J., concur.

B. ANTI-DEFICIENCY LEGISLATION

If a property is sold at a foreclosure sale for less than the balance due on the debt, then the mortgagee in most cases will obtain a judgment for the difference between the cash raised at the foreclosure sale and the balance due. This is called a deficiency judgment. With no restrictions on the amount bid at the foreclosure sale by the mortgagee, it was possible to purposely bid less than the principal balance of the debt and obtain both the land and a judgment for a portion of the debt. Since cash was in short supply during the 1930s, few people had any money to bid against the mortgagee in a foreclosure sale and, being the sold bidder, the mortgagee could bid as low as it wanted, acquire the property with its low "paper bid," and still have a judgment for a substantial portion of the debt. There is probably no record of the number of instances in which this situation arose but some banks were still collecting on depression judgments twenty years later, in the 1950s. It was this practice that prompted some state legislatures to enact anti-deficiency statutes so that the lender was restricted to either obtaining the land by being the high bidder at the foreclosure sale or obtaining the cash bid at the sale by another. Anti-deficiency legislation did exactly what its name implies: It prohibited a money judgment in favor of the lender after a foreclosure sale. Of the three forms of depression legislation, it is the most stringent in existence today.

Some anti-deficiency legislation is limited to a particular type of property securing the loan, *i.e.,* single family residential.[1] Other forms simply prohibit a deficiency judgment following a foreclosure of a purchase money mortgage.[2] Some statutes bar a deficiency following a non-judicial or power of sale foreclosure but do not bar a money judgment following a judicial foreclosure.[3] There is no particular consistency to this sort of legislation, for some states permit the filing of a lawsuit for the deficiency following a non-judicial sale.[4] Lawyers newly arrived at the bar would do well to learn of the limits or prohibitions on such suits in their jurisdiction, for it is a likely area for malpractice by the inexperienced.

California Code of Civil Procedure (1976)

§ 580d. Foreclosure under power of sale; no deficiency judgment; exceptions

No judgment shall be rendered for any deficiency upon a note secured by a deed of trust or mortgage upon real property hereafter executed in any case in which the real property has been sold by the mortgagee or trustee under power of sale contained in such mortgage or deed of trust.

The provisions of this section shall not apply to any deed of trust, mortgage or

---

[1] Cal. Civ. Proc. Code § 580b (1976).

[2] *Id.*

[3] Cal. Civ. Proc. Code § 580d (1976).

[4] For example, if land is sold at a non-judicial sale in Nevada, a hearing must be conducted to determine the fair market value of the land before a deficiency judgment is allowed. Nev. Rev. Stats. § 40.455 (1957).

other lien given to secure the payment of bonds or other evidences of indebtedness authorized or permitted to be issued by the Commissioner of Corporations, or which is made by a public utility subject to the provisions of the Public Utilities Act.

NORTH END BANK & TRUST CO. v. MANDELL

Supreme Court of Errors of Connecticut
113 Conn. 241, 155 A. 80 (1931)

Avery, J. August 6, 1920, the plaintiff loaned to the Hibernian Building Association of Bridgeport, Inc., $15,000, taking its note, secured by a mortgage on its property in Bridgeport, for that amount. There was also received, as further security, the written several guaranty of payment of the note, signed by Daniel J. O'Connor, Frank J. Brady, James J. Rawley, William Clifford, Patrick McCarthy, James F. Whelan, James J. Small, and John F. McCarthy. December 10, 1927, the building association, by warranty deed, conveyed the mortgaged premises to Abraham H. Mandell, who, in the deed, assumed and agreed to pay the mortgage note held by the plaintiff. Between the date of the note and July 1, 1930, $5,000 was paid to the plaintiff on account, leaving an unpaid balance of $10,000. By writ returnable the first Tuesday of September, 1930, the plaintiff brought an action to foreclose the mortgage, asking for a deficiency judgment against Mandell and the guarantors who were made parties defendant. Mandell and two of the guarantors, Frank J. Brady and William Clifford, made default of appearance. The remaining guarantors filed appearances. September 5, 1930, the plaintiff filed a motion for foreclosure by sale. September 19, 1930, judgment of foreclosure by sale was entered. October 2, 1930, the appraisers appointed by the court, filed their report, appraising the premises at $12,500. Thereafter, October 15, 1930, the premises were sold, pursuant to the judgment, for $5,000. December 15, 1930, the plaintiff claimed a deficiency judgment against Mandell and the guarantors in the amount of $5,524.42, which sum represented the full amount of the plaintiff's claim with expenses and costs, less the sale price of the premises. The appearing guarantors, at the hearing, claimed there should be a further credit on their debt of $3,750, being one-half the difference between the value of the premises as found by the appraisers and the sales price as of the date of sale, and that the deficiency judgment should be reduced by deduction of the latter amount to $1,774.42. The court entered a deficiency judgment for $5,524.42, and the guarantors who had appeared duly appealed to this court.

Two questions are presented in this case: (1) Whether the provision for a further credit of one-half the difference between the appraised value and the sales price of real estate under foreclosure must be allowed before any deficiency judgment may be entered as provided in section 5116, Gen. St. (1930), when the foreclosing plaintiff makes a motion for foreclosure by sale; and (2) whether the guarantors of payment of the mortgage can require such credit when they have been made parties defendant in a foreclosure action by the plaintiff who asks a deficiency judgment against them. The statute is appended in the margin.[1] It

---

[1] Sec. 5116. [Revision 1930]. *When proceeds of sale will not pay in full.* If the proceeds of such sale are not sufficient to pay in full the amount secured by any mortgage or lien thereby foreclosed, the deficiency shall be determined, and thereupon judgment may be rendered in such cause for such deficiency against any party liable to pay the same who is a party to the cause and has been duly served with process or has appeared therein, and all persons liable to pay the debt secured by such mortgage

provides that all persons "liable to pay the debt secured by such mortgage or lien may be made parties"; and, further, ". . . no judgment shall be rendered in such suit or in any other for the unpaid portion of the debt or debts of the party or parties upon whose motion the sale was ordered, nor shall the same be collected by any other means than from the proceeds of such sale until one-half of the difference between such appraised value and such selling price shall have been credited upon such debt or debts as of the date of sale; and, when there shall be two or more debts to which it is to be applied, it shall be apportioned between them." This statute was before us for consideration in *Staples v. Hendrick,* 89 Conn. 100, 103, 106, 93 A. 5, and *Acampora v. Warner,* 91 Conn. 586, 588, 101 A. 332. In these cases, the history of the legislation and the object to be accomplished thereby is discussed. In the *Staples Case,* we said (page 103 of 89 Conn., 93 A. 5, 6): "The plain object of these provisions is to require a mortgage creditor, who appropriates the property in part payment only of his debt, to apply the actual value of the security to the debt before collecting any claimed deficiency." And further, in the same case: "The apparent object of section 4146 [5116] is to attach a condition under certain circumstances to the allowance of a deficiency judgment, or to the collection in any other manner of the unpaid portion of the debt or debts secured by the mortgage or lien thereby foreclosed. There is good reason for such a condition, for as it is reasonable and in accordance with established practice in cases of strict foreclosure to require (in case any party desires it) a foreclosing plaintiff, who appropriates the property in just satisfaction only of his debt, to apply the appraised value of the property on the debt before claiming a deficiency judgment for the amount of any alleged deficiency; so it is reasonable to require a foreclosing plaintiff, who asks for a foreclosure by sale, with a view to the possibility of obtaining a deficiency judgment in the same action, to bear a moiety of any shrinkage in the appraised value resulting from such a sale."

In view of the interpretation placed upon it in these cases and the language of the statute itself, when thoughtfully considered in its entirety, we think the "unpaid portion of the debt or debts of the party or parties upon whose motion the sale was ordered" employs the word "debt" in the sense of the sum due to a creditor and not in the sense of an obligation payable by a debtor. A foreclosure by sale is not a matter of right, but rests in the discretion of the court before which the foreclosure proceedings are pending. *Bradford Realty Corp. v. Beetz,* 108 Conn. 26, 31, 142 A. 395. When a foreclosing plaintiff asks and obtains an order of sale instead of taking over the property by a strict foreclosure, he causes, in many instances, a sacrifice of its value. It is just and equitable that, if he seeks a deficiency judgment, part of the loss in value sacrificed by the forced sale should fall on him.

The mortgagee is entitled to no more than the satisfaction of his debt, and if that has been paid in full, either in cash or by the appropriation of the property to its payment, there is nothing further due him. *Bergin v. Robbins,* 109 Conn. 329, 334, 146 A. 724. "When collateral security is given, or property assigned,

---

or lien may be made parties; but all other proceedings for the collection of the debt shall be stayed during the pendency of the foreclosure suit, and, if a deficiency judgment shall be finally rendered therein, such other proceedings shall forthwith abate. If the property shall have sold for less than the appraisal provided for in section 5113, no judgment shall be rendered in such suit or in any other for the unpaid portion of the debt or debts of the party or parties upon whose motion the sale was ordered, nor shall the same be collected by any other means than from the proceeds of such sale until one-half of the difference between such appraised value and such selling price shall have been credited upon such debt or debts as of the date of sale; and, when there shall be two or more debts to which it is to be applied, it shall be apportioned between them.

for the better protection or payment of a debt, it shall be made effectual for that purpose, — and that not only to the immediate party to the security, but to others, who are entitled to the debt. And to make them thus effectual, a court of chancery will lend its aid." *Homer v. Savings Bank*, 7 Conn. 478, 484; *New London Bank v. Lee*, 11 Conn. 112, 118, 27 Am. Dec. 713; *Stearns v. Bates*, 46 Conn. 306, 312. In the absence of statute a guarantor of a mortgage debt is not a proper party to a foreclosure suit. 3 Jones Mortgages (8th Ed.) §§ 1821, 1822. "Authority is sometimes given by statute to join such obligors in foreclosure and obtain a deficiency judgment against them." 3 Jones Mortgages (8th Ed.) § 1823. Our law, Gen. Stat. 1930, § 5080, provides: "The foreclosure of a mortgage shall be a bar to any further action upon a mortgage debt, note or obligation, unless the person or persons who are liable for the payment thereof are made parties to such foreclosure." "If the mortgagee is not willing to take the property mortgaged as full payment for his debt, he has only to make all the persons to whom he may wish to resort for further payment parties to his foreclosure suit." *Ansonia Bank's Appeal from Commissioners*, 58 Conn. 257, 259, 18 A. 1030, 1031, 20 A. 394. Having been brought in by the plaintiff as defendants in the foreclosure action, the guarantors are entitled to have the value of the security as ascertained by law applied pro tanto to the satisfaction of the debt; and in computing the deficiency to be paid by them, the statutory credit is to be allowed to the same extent as if claimed by the mortgage debtor. It follows that the appearing guarantors were entitled to a credit of one-half the difference between the sales price and the appraised price.

There is error; the deficiency judgment is set aside as to the appellants, and the cause remanded to the superior court, with directions to enter a deficiency judgment against them as of December 15, 1930, in the amount of $1,774.42.

All the Judges concur.

BERGIN v. ROBBINS

Supreme Court of Errors of Connecticut
109 Conn. 329, 146 A. 724 (1929)

Banks, J. The plaintiff brought this action to foreclose a fourth mortgage, which he had upon property owned by one Swirsky. A receiver of the rents of the mortgaged premises was appointed by the court on July 18, 1928, who collected a part of the rents for the month of July and all of the rents for the months of August, September, October, and November. The receiver filed an account showing a balance, after the payment of certain expenditures for the upkeep of the premises, of $2,169.36. This fund was claimed by the plaintiff, and also by Frank, a prior incumbrancer, and was awarded by the court to plaintiff, from which decree Frank appeals.

The plaintiff filed a plea in abatement in this court, alleging that the appellant, Frank, was not a party to this action in the superior court, and that he had never been made a party. From a stipulation of facts filed, and other facts found in the record, it appears that Frank, whose mortgage was an incumbrance upon the property prior to that of the plaintiff, was not a party defendant to the original complaint and has made no formal written motion to be made a party. His attorney did enter an appearance on his behalf in the superior court, and there made claim to this fund in the hands of the receiver. He was treated by the trial court and by the plaintiff's attorney, in the proceedings in the superior court, as a party defendant, and, had the plaintiff raised the objection in that court, undoubtedly proper steps would have been taken to make him a party of record.

This should be done on the retrial. He filed a request for a finding, upon which the court made a finding in which he is referred to as one of the defendants. It appears that he has an interest in the disposition of the fund here in dispute. It is rather late for the plaintiff for the first time in this court to contend that the appellant, Frank, is not a party defendant in this action. The plea in abatement is overruled.

Subsequent to the commencement of this action the appellant, Frank, brought an action to foreclose a second mortgage upon these premises, and on October 12, 1928, procured a judgment of strict foreclosure against the owner of the equity of redemption and all subsequent incumbrancers, including the plaintiff herein, under which title to the property vested in him on December 1, 1928. The finding recites that the receiver has not paid, or reserved money to pay, any of the interest on the first mortgage, and that he has not paid any insurance premiums, water rates, or any part of the taxes due on this property during the time that he had possession of it as receiver. The amount of these items which were due and payable during the term of the receivership is not found. One of the claims of the appellant appears to be that he is entitled to reimbursement out of this fund for payments which he claims to have made on account of these items of interest on the first mortgage, insurance premiums, water rates, and taxes. This claim cannot receive consideration, since there is no finding that such payments were made by him. His claim to the fund as against the plaintiff must rest upon his position as a prior incumbrancer. Ordinarily it would make no practical pecuniary difference whether rents in the hands of a receiver were paid to a prior or to a subsequent incumbrancer, provided the mortgage of the prior incumbrancer was amply secured. If paid to the prior incumbrancer, they would reduce the amount of incumbrances upon the property, and increase pro tanto the equity of the junior incumbrancer. If paid to the latter, he would still be obliged to take care of all prior incumbrances.

Here the appellant, Frank, has foreclosed his mortgage, which was prior to that of the plaintiff, in an action in which the latter was made a party, with an opportunity to redeem, but failed to do so. The plaintiff in this action might have moved for a foreclosure by sale in that action, in which case he would have been entitled to have any sum remaining from the proceeds of the sale, after the satisfaction of incumbrances prior to his own, applied to the satisfaction of his mortgage. He failed to do this, or to redeem, and the decree in that action, which was entered while this action was still pending, rendered its further prosecution ineffectual, and foreclosed thus plaintiff's right to look to the property as security for the payment of his debt.

The court reached the conclusion that the appellant was not entitled to the fund in the hands of the receiver because, having failed to procure a deficiency judgment, he is presumed to take the property foreclosed by him in full discharge of all sums due him under his note and mortgage. This conclusion involved an erroneous conception of the legal effect of the decree granting a strict foreclosure of a mortgage.

Prior to 1833 the foreclosure of a mortgage operated as a bar to any subsequent action upon the mortgage debt. Since that time the right of a mortgagee to a deficiency judgment has been recognized, if the property acquired on foreclosure fails to satisfy the mortgage debt, and the foreclosure is not a bar to further action upon the debt, provided the person or persons who are liable for the payment of it are made parties to the foreclosure. General Statutes, §§ 5196, 5197. But the procedure provided in section 5197 for procuring a deficiency judgment does not furnish an exclusive remedy. Where the person or persons liable upon the mortgage debt are made parties to the foreclosure action, the mortgagee may bring a separate action against them to recover the unpaid balance of the debt, although he has not asked for a deficiency judgment in his foreclosure action. *Acampora v. Warner,* 91 Conn. 586, 101 A. 332; *German v. Gallo,* 100 Conn. 708, 124 A. 837. In the foreclosure of the Frank mortgage the maker of the note was made a party to the action, and the foreclosure decree was not, therefore, a bar to any further action upon the mortgage debt, and the failure of the plaintiff in that action to procure a deficiency judgment did not operate as a discharge of the sums due him upon his note and mortgage. If that debt was not discharged, he was entitled to the fund in the hands of the receiver as against the plaintiff, whose mortgage was subsequent to his.

The mortgagee is, of course, entitled to no more than satisfaction of his debt. If that has been paid in full, either in cash or by the appropriation of the property to its payment, there is nothing further due him. The trial court has found that title to the property vested in Frank under the foreclosure decree in his favor on December 1, 1928. That fact alone did not constitute an appropriation of the property to the payment of the debt. A foreclosure decree, aside from such provision as may be made in it to put the mortgagee in possession of the property, merely cuts off the outstanding rights of redemption, and the statement in the certificate of foreclosure that title has become absolute in the plaintiff adds nothing to its legal effect. *Cion v. Schupack,* 102 Conn. 644, 649, 129 A. 854.

If, however, the plaintiff in the foreclosure action actually takes possession of the property by virtue of his foreclosure decree, and the property is of greater value than the amount of the debt, that act constitutes an appropriation of the property to the payment of the debt in full, and the debt is discharged in the same way as it would be if paid in money. *Loomis v. Knox,* 60 Conn. 343, 351, 22 A. 771. In *Cion v. Schupack,* supra, title had vested in the plaintiff under his decree of foreclosure, but he had never taken possession of the property, because a receiver appointed in a suit to foreclose a subsequent mortgage upon the premises had been in charge of them.

It appears from the finding in the present case that the receivership ceased on the last day of November, 1928, the day before that on which the title became vested in the appellant. It might be inferred that the appellant thereupon took possession of the premises, but there is no finding that he did so, and in the absence of such a finding we cannot assume that he did. Nor does it appear that the property was of greater value than the debt of the appellant. If it was not, his act in taking possession would not discharge his debt. The fund here in dispute, except for a small interest item, came from the rents from this property during the period covered by the receivership. It has been held in some jurisdictions that a junior mortgagee, who brings a foreclosure suit and secures the appointment of a receiver of the rents, acquires a lien upon them superior to that of the claims of prior mortgagees who were not made parties to such foreclosure action. Under these decisions, if the prior mortgagee sees fit to assert his rights, he may have the receivership extended to his mortgage, and then has a prior right to the rents thereafter accruing.

Under our practice a receiver is an officer of the court, appointed on behalf of all who may establish an interest in the property. The funds which come into his hands are disbursed by him under the orders of the court to those who may establish their right to them in the order of the priority of their respective claims, and it is not of importance upon whose application the appointment of the receiver is made. The court should have ordered the receiver to pay the interest upon the first mortgage, insurance premiums, water rents, and taxes which accrued during the time that he was in possession as receiver. So far as appears, the only claimants to the balance in the hands of the receiver were the plaintiff, who was the fourth mortgagee, and the appellant, Frank, a second mortgagee, who had entered his appearance as a party to the action and made claim to the fund as the holder of an incumbrance prior to that of the plaintiff. As such prior incumbrancer he was entitled to the fund in preference to the plaintiff, unless, as we have said, it should appear that the property was of greater value than his debt and that his claim had already been discharged by his taking possession of the property and thereby appropriating it to the payment of his debt.

There is error, and the case is remanded to be proceeded with according to law.

In this opinion the other Judges concurred.

BROWN v. JENSEN

Supreme Court of California
41 Cal. 2d 193, 259 P.2d 425 (1953)

CARTER, JUSTICE. Defendants appeal from a judgment for plaintiff on a promissory note.

Plaintiff was the owner of real property which, on April 26, 1950, she sold to defendants, Rose Jensen and Leota Triplett. As a part of the purchase price and on the same day, defendants executed in favor of Glendale Federal Savings & Loan Association (hereafter called Federal) a note for $11,300, secured by a first trust deed on the property. At the same time, and also as a part of the purchase price, a second note was executed by them in favor of plaintiff for $7,200, secured by a second trust deed on the property. Hence both trust deeds were purchase money trust deeds.

It does not appear from the pleadings or findings how the first trust deed was "foreclosed," that is, whether by court action or by the exercise of the power of sale thereunder. While it is stated simply that the property was "sold under foreclosure," it appears from the affidavits on motion for a summary judgment that the sale was under the power of sale in the trust deed. Neither of the notes had been paid and Federal had the property sold pursuant to the power of sale and bid it in for $11,896.63, and a trustees' deed was thereupon delivered to Federal. Plaintiff made no attempt to buy the property at the sale so as to protect her second trust deed.

Plaintiff's complaint stated a cause of action on her note, and to meet the claim that but one action could be brought on a debt secured by a trust deed, namely, one for foreclosure, Code Civ.Proc. § 726, alleged that her security (her second trust deed) had become valueless because it had become exhausted by the sale under the first trust deed. Under section 726 of the Code of Civil Procedure, there may be only one action for the recovery of a debt secured by a trust deed, which action is one of foreclosure. In addition compliance must be had with the conditions of the chapter in which section 726 appears. One of these conditions is that any deficiency judgment is limited to the difference between the fair market value of the property and the amount for which the property was sold. It has been held under that section that where the security has been exhausted or rendered valueless through no fault of the mortgagee, or beneficiary under a trust deed, an action may be brought on the debt on the theory that the limitation to the single action of foreclosure refers to the time the action is brought rather than when the trust deed was made, and that if the security is lost or has become valueless at the time the action is commenced, the debt is no longer secured. *Security-First Nat. Bank v. Chapman,* 31 Cal.App.2d 182, 87 P.2d 724; *Hellman Com. T. & S. Bank v. Maurice,* 105 Cal.App. 653, 288 P. 683; *Ferry v. Fisk,* 54 Cal.App. 763, 202 P. 964; *Crescent Lumber Co. v. Larson,* 166 Cal. 168, 135 P. 502; *Otto v. Long,* 127 Cal. 471, 59 P. 895; *Savings Bank v. Central Market Co.,* 122 Cal. 28, 54 P. 273; *Commercial Bank v. Kershner,* 120 Cal. 495, 52 P. 848; *Merced Security v. Casaccia,* 103 Cal. 641, 37 P. 648; *Salter v. Ulrich,* 22 Cal.2d 263, 138 P.2d 7, 146 A.L.R. 1344; *Republic Truck Sales Corp. v. Peak,* 194 Cal. 492, 229 P. 331. That rule has been applied in favor of a second mortgagee, the security being considered lost or valueless as to him, where a first mortgagee forecloses his mortgage and the property is sold for no more than the senior debt and a deed has been given. *Savings Bank v. Central Market Co.,* supra, 122 Cal. 28, 54 P. 273; *Giandeini v. Ramirez,* 11 Cal.App.2d 469, 54 P.2d 91.

It would appear from the facts here presented that plaintiff has brought herself within those rules and hence section 726 is not an obstacle to her action on the promissory note. There are, however, additional restrictions on deficiency judgments on secured debts. Defendants pleaded section 580b of the Code of Civil Procedure,[1] and as seen the facts here show that plaintiff's second trust deed is clearly a purchase money trust deed. It is urged, however, that inasmuch as there has not been a sale by plaintiff under her trust deed within the wording of section 580b, supra, it does not apply. It is further urged that it does not apply because the security has become valueless by reason of the sale under Federal's first trust deed, and the case is not one involving a "deficiency" as there cannot be a deficiency if there is no security to sell because it presupposes a partial satisfaction of the debt by a sale which exhausts the security.

In order to solve this question there must be a further examination of the Code sections. There are other restrictions besides section 726, supra, and 580b, supra. Section 580a applies the fair market value test of section 726 to sales made without court assistance under a power of sale contained in a trust deed. Section 580d goes further and provides that no judgment shall be rendered for any deficiency on a note secured by a trust deed where the property has been sold under the power of sale (as distinguished from a sale in a foreclosure action) contained in the trust deed. These provisions indicate a considered course on the part of the Legislature to limit strictly the right to recover deficiency judgments, that is, to recover on the debt more than the value of the security. Next comes section 580b, supra, here involved, which deals with a special type of security transaction, a trust deed, given to secure to the vendor of property the purchase price agreed to be paid by the vendee. That section is necessarily intended to provide a protection for the trustor because if it were intended to cover only the situation where there has been an actual sale of the security under the power of sale in the trust deed, it would be superfluous. Section 580d covers precisely that situation in *all* trust deeds, whether purchase money or otherwise. The broad protection provision, Code Civ. Proc. § 580b, for purchase money trust deeds stands on a reasonable footing. A purchase money trust deed is not like an ordinary trust deed and note upon which only one action may be brought under section 726. Under section 726, as above stated, it is held that whether there is

---

[1] "No deficiency judgment shall lie in any event after any sale of real property for failure of the purchaser to complete his contract of sale, or under a deed of trust, or mortgage, given to secure payment of the balance of the purchase price of real property.

"Where both a chattel mortgage and a deed or [*sic*] trust or mortgage have been given to secure payment of the balance of the combined purchase price of both real and personal property, no deficiency judgment shall lie at any time under any one thereof." Code Civ.Proc. § 580b.

a security is determined as of the time the action is commenced and if the security is lost or has become valueless, an action on the note will lie because the events which caused it to become valueless were beyond the control of the trustor and were not contemplated at the time the money was loaned and the trust deed given. With purchase money trust deeds, however, the character of the transaction must necessarily be determined at the time the trust deed is executed. Its nature is then fixed for all time and as so fixed no deficiency judgment may be obtained regardless of whether the security later becomes valueless.

The question is, therefore, did plaintiff take a purchase money trust deed on the property when it was purchased? If she did, then section 580b is applicable and she may look only to the security. That is the clear import of the wording of section 580b. The one taking such a trust deed knows the value of his security and assumes the risk that it may become inadequate. Especially does he know the risk where he takes, as was done here, a second trust deed. It is true that the section speaks of a deficiency judgment after sale of the security but that means after an actual sale or a situation where a sale would be an idle act, where, as here, the security has been exhausted. The deficiency judgment which cannot be obtained is still a deficiency judgment even though it may consist of the whole debt because a deficiency is nothing more than the difference between the security and the debt, or, as was said in *Carr v. Cleveland Trust Co.,* Ohio App., 74 N.E.2d 124, 128 (in dealing with a case where the sale under the first mortgage produced only enough to pay it and the effect of a two-year limitation period for obtaining a deficiency judgment on a mortgage secured debt against the holder of a note secured by a second mortgage): "But in whatever light we view the proceedings which took place, either by way of foreclosure or by separate personal judgment on the note, one fact stands out in bold relief and that is that a deficiency judgment resulted from the entire proceedings by reason whereof the plaintiffs are entitled to whatever benefits accrue from the provisions of the deficiency judgment act so-called." Indeed the purpose of section 580b is that "... for a purchase money mortgage or deed of trust the security alone can be looked to for recovery of the debt." *Mortgage Guarantee Co. v. Sampsell,* 51 Cal.App.2d 180, 185, 124 P.2d 353, 355. The section states that in *no event* shall there be a deficiency judgment, that is, whether there is a sale under the power of sale or sale under foreclosure, or no sale because the security has become valueless or is exhausted. The purpose of the "after sale" reference in the section is that the security be exhausted and that result follows after a sale under the first trust deed.

The foregoing construction of section 580b is further fortified by the last paragraph thereof, supra, for it provides that where a chattel and real property mortgage are given to secure the purchase price of real and personal property, no deficiency judgment shall be given at *any time* under either of them.

Plaintiff relies on *Hillen v. Soule,* 7 Cal.App.2d 45, 45 P.2d 349, involving an action on a promissory note secured by a purchase money trust deed which was inferior to a first trust deed which was foreclosed and the security thereby exhausted. It was held that section 580b was not applicable because plaintiff's action was not for a deficiency judgment as the security was exhausted and plaintiff had not sold under his trust deed. That conclusion is out of harmony with the foregoing discussion. Evidently the factors above discussed were not called to the court's attention. In the later case of *Mortgage Guarantee Co. v. Sampsell,* supra, 51 Cal.App.2d 180, 185, 124 P.2d 353, the court states that the security alone may be looked to for payment of a debt secured by a purchase money trust deed. However, the result reached in the *Hillen* case was correct because the trust deeds there were given in 1927 before the adoption of section

580b (section 580b was added to the Code of Civil Procedure in 1933, Stats.1933, p. 1673) and hence that section could not have been applicable there.

The judgment is reversed and the court directed to enter judgment for defendants.

GIBSON, C. J., and SHENK, EDMONDS, TRAYNOR and SCHAUER, JJ., concur.

SPENCE, JUSTICE. I dissent.

The majority opinion declares that "section 726 is not an obstacle" to plaintiff's action on her promissory note, but it holds that plaintiff's action is one for a "deficiency judgment" within the meaning of section 580b of the Code of Civil Procedure and is therefore barred by the terms of that section. I cannot agree with this last mentioned conclusion. The security afforded by plaintiff's *second* deed of trust was extinguished by the sale held under the power of sale in the first deed of trust. Therefore there never had been a sale under the power of sale contained in plaintiff's second deed of trust.

A reading of sections 580a, 580b, 580c and 580d of the Code of Civil Procedure makes it entirely clear that the words "deficiency judgment" are consistently used therein in their ordinary meaning. They refer to a judgment sought for the balance allegedly due upon the personal obligation imposed by a written instrument secured by a deed of trust or mortgage "following the exercise of the power of sale in *such* deed of trust or mortgage . . . ." Code Civ.Proc. § 580a; emphasis added, and where "the real property has been sold by the mortgagee or trustee under power of sale contained in *such* a mortgage or deed of trust", Code Civ.Proc. § 580d; emphasis added.

The decisions in this state show that this is the meaning which has been heretofore given to the words "deficiency judgment," as used in section 580a. *Hatch v. Security-First Nat. Bank,* 19 Cal.2d 254, 258, 120 P.2d 869; *Bank of America etc. Ass'n v. Gillett,* 36 Cal.App.2d 453, 456, 97 P.2d 875; see *Bank of America etc. Ass'n v. Hunter,* 8 Cal.2d 592, 597-598, 67 P.2d 99; *Everts v. Matteson,* 21 Cal.2d 437, 448, 132 P.2d 476. It is also the common meaning attached to the term in other jurisdictions. *Phillips v. Union Central Life Ins. Co.,* 8 Cir., 88 F.2d 188, 189; *Bank of Douglas v. Neel,* 30 Ariz. 375, 247 P. 132, 133; *Cragin v. Ocean & Lake Realty Co.,* 101 Fla. 1324, 133 So. 569, 135 So. 795, 797; *Harrow v. Metropolitan Life Ins. Co.,* 285 Mich. 349, 280 N.W. 785, 788; *Tiedeman v. Dorn,* 137 Misc. 136, 241 N.Y.S. 490, 492-493; *Stretch v. Murphy,* Or. 439, Or.439, 112 P.2d 1018, 1021; *Bailey v. Block,* 104 Tex. 101, 134 S.W. 323, 325; 59 C.J.S., Mortgages, § 777, p. 1474.

Section 580b was originally enacted with section 580a in 1933, Stats. 1933, pp. 1672, 1673, and the meaning of "deficiency judgment" was undoubtedly intended to be the same for both sections. When section 580d was added in 1940, Stats. 1st Ex.Sess.1940, ch. 29, § 2, it was again made clear that "deficiency judgment" referred to a judgment sought for the balance allegedly due a person whose obligation had been secured by a deed of trust or mortgage and where the real property had been sold "under power of sale contained in *such* a mortgage or deed of trust." While sections 580b and 580d do overlap to some extent, section 580b cannot be properly characterized as "superfluous."

In 1935 and shortly after the enactment of section 580b, it was construed with relation to similar facts in *Hillen v. Soule,* 7 Cal.App.2d 45, 45 P.2d 349. It was there said: "Appellant first contends that this is an action for a deficiency judgment after a sale under a deed of trust given to secure the balance of the purchase price of real property, and that such action cannot be maintained by reason of the provisions of section 580b of the Code of Civil Procedure. It is a sufficient answer to state that this is not an action for a deficiency judgment. The security was exhausted by the sale under the first deed of trust and no sale was had under respondent's deed of trust. We are therefore of the opinion that the provisions of said section are inapplicable." 7 Cal.App.2d at page 47, 45 P.2d at page 349.

The Legislature has twice amended section 580b since this construction was placed upon the words "deficiency judgment." Stats.1935, pp. 1806, 1869; Stats.1949, ch. 1599, § 1. As no change was made by these amendments in the phrase "deficiency judgment," it may be assumed that the Legislature approved the construction placed on that term in *Hillen v. Soule,* 7 Cal.App.2d 45, 45 P.2d 349, supra. Furthermore, the wording of section 580d as enacted in 1940 also indicates such legislative approval.

The evil motivating the Legislature in enacting these sections was that "creditors were frequently able to bid in the debtor's real property at a nominal figure and also to hold the debtor personally liable for a large proportion of the original debt." *Hatch v. Security-First Nat. Bank,* supra, 19 Cal.2d 254, 259, 120 P.2d 869, 872; see 22 Cal.L.Rev. 170, 180. The purpose was not to prevent any recovery where the security had become completely valueless or a senior mortgagee had foreclosed, leaving no security for the junior debt.

Thus, it appears to me that the majority opinion has stretched the meaning of section 580b far beyond its terms. Both sections 580b and 580d prevent the holder of a purchase money deed of trust from having a "deficiency judgment" after a sale under *such* a deed of trust. They do not cover the situation where no sale has been held under *such* deed of trust and no "deficiency judgment" is sought. To so construe these sections results in placing the holder of a purchase money note secured by a second deed of trust in a less favorable position than the holder of an unsecured note given for such purchase money. The Legislature has not so declared. Until it does so, the courts should not enter the legislative field by broadening the terms of statutes beyond their common meaning and contrary to the judicial interpretation which had been placed thereon prior to the time that the parties entered into their contractual relations.

The majority opinion relies on *Mortgage Guarantee Co. v. Sampsell,* 51 Cal.App.2d 180, 124 P.2d 353. It is sufficient to state that that case did not present the question here involved. The broad language quoted by the majority opinion is mere dictum, unnecessary to the decision of that case.

I would affirm the judgment.

Rehearing denied; SPENCE, J., dissents.

THOMAS v. VALLEY BANK

Supreme Court of Nevada
629 P.2d 1205 (1981)

MOWBRAY, JUSTICE. The issue presented on this appeal is whether the protections of the anti-deficiency legislation, NRS 40.451 *et seq.,* apply to guarantors. Appellant asks us to reconsider our decision in *Manufacturers & Traders Trust v. Dist. Ct.,* 94 Nev. 551, 583 P.2d 444 (1978) in which we held that they do not.

The Facts

Respondent, Valley Bank of Nevada (Bank) loaned C. H. Thomas Investments Inc. (Corporation) $165,000.00 for the purchase and development of certain real property. Corporation gave Bank its note for the amount of the loan, secured by a trust deed covering the property. Appellant, Charles H. Thomas, (Guarantor) signed a separate agreement with Bank guaranteeing payment of the note.[1]

Corporation defaulted and Bank foreclosed on the security, purchasing the property at the foreclosure sale for $100,000.00.

Bank then sought a deficiency judgment against Corporation for approximately $34,000.00, the difference between Bank's bid for the security and the amount of the principal debt. In the same action Bank sued Thomas on his contract of guaranty for the same amount.

The district court, relying upon our decision in *Manufacturers & Traders Trust v. Dist. Ct., supra,* ruled that Thomas, as guarantor, was not entitled to the protection of the anti-deficiency statutes. The district court entered judgment against Thomas for the difference between the price paid for the security at the foreclosure sale and the total amount of the debt. The court refused to enter judgment against the principal obligor, the Corporation.[2] Thomas, the guarantor, appeals.

The Anti-Deficiency Statutes

We hold that the anti-deficiency statutes, NRS 40.451 *et seq.,* do not apply to the obligations of guarantors. The language of the statutes in question confines their applicability to debts "secured by a mortgage or deed of trust," NRS 40.451. The guarantor's contract is not a secured obligation, and the protection of NRS 40.459, which limits the amount of a deficiency judgment to the difference between the fair market value of the security at the time of sale and the total amount of the debt, does not apply to the contract of guaranty. *First National Bank of Nevada v. Barengo,* 91 Nev. 396, 536 P.2d 487 (1975); *Randono v. Turk,* 86 Nev. 123, 466 P.2d 218 (1970); *Short v. Sinai,* 50 Nev. 346, 259 P. 417 (1927); *see also Coombs v. Heers,* 366 F.Supp. 851 (D.Nev.1973).

The definition of a debt in NRS 40.451 [3] declares that only the principal

---

[1] The terms of said guaranty provide in pertinent part:

For value received the undersigned, jointly and severally, guarantee and promise to pay the note on the reverse hereof and all extensions and renewals thereof, which extensions and renewals may be made without notice to or consent of the undersigned and all taxes and insurance premiums and other sums that may become due and payable under and by virtue of the provisions of any Deed of Trust, Security Agreement, or other instrument of security, securing the aforesaid note and hereby waive . . . (b) the right, if any, to the benefit of, or to direct the application of any security hypothecated to the holder until all indebtedness of the maker to the holder, howsoever arising, shall have been paid; (c) the right to require the holder to proceed against any person, or to pursue any other remedy in the holder's power; *and agree that the holder may proceed against the undersigned directly and independently of any person, and that the cessation of the liability of the maker for any reason other than full payment, or any extension, renewal, forbearance, change of rate of interest, or acceptance, release or substitution of security, of any impairment or suspension of the holder's remedies or rights against any person shall not in any way affect the liability of the undersigned hereunder.* (Emphasis added.)

[2] Although the district court refused to enter a deficiency judgment against the primary obligor, the corporate defendant below, its findings indicate that the property which secured the primary obligation, upon which the respondent foreclosed, was sold at its fair market value.

The Court in its conclusions of law ruled:

4. That the sole bid made at the foreclosure sale was $100,000.00 by Valley Bank of Nevada. That said bid encompassed all nine parcels of land. That the bid was fair and equitable as an estimation of the fair market value as of April 22, 1976 [sic], of all nine properties.

5. That $100,000.00 is the proper amount to be deducted from the $132,809.64 due and owing on the promissory note on the date of foreclosure.

[3] NRS 40.451 provides, in pertinent part, that " 'indebtedness' means the principal balance of the obligation secured by a *mortgage or deed of trust*" (emphasis added).

obligation, which is secured by the property mortgaged or subject to a deed of trust, is covered by the anti-deficiency statute. It has always been the law of this state that a contract of guaranty is not a secured obligation, even if the primary obligation is secured. *Randono v. Turk, supra.* The anti-deficiency statute is designed to protect obligors who give security as collateral. Since the guarantor has no interest in the security, there is no need to seek a deficiency judgment, under the statute, against him; his liability as guarantor is defined by his independent contract with the creditor.

The consistent law of this state, that a contract of guaranty is an obligation quite separate from the primary debt, does not leave the guarantor without protection in a case of this sort. The measure of the guarantor's liability is determined by his own contract of guaranty. If the primary debt is secured, we discern no impediment to a guaranty providing for liability only to the extent that a deficiency judgment would be obtainable against the primary debtor. The most obvious protection for the guarantor would be to attend the foreclosure sale of the security and bid up the price to its fair market value: by that means he would ensure that his liability under the contract of guaranty would be precisely coextensive with the potential liability of the primary debtor under the anti-deficiency statute.

Considerable confusion is apparent in the agruments of the parties which rely upon California law. The fundamental principle of the guaranty law of Nevada is the distinction between guarantors, whose obligations are wholly separate from the principal obligation guaranteed, and sureties, who are co-obligors with the principal debtor. This distinction between guarantors and sureties has been abolished by statute in California, Cal.Civ.Code § 2787, but it remains in force in Nevada. *Short v. Sinai, supra.* Although a surety's liability is measured by that of the principal, this Court has never held that a guarantor's liability must be thus limited. *See Bank of Nevada v. Friedman,* 82 Nev. 417, 420 P.2d 1 (1966) (guarantor held liable even though statute of limitations had run against principal obligor).

Accordingly, we reaffirm our holding in *Manufacturers & Traders Trust v. Dist. Ct., supra,* and we therefore affirm.

Manoukian, J., and Griffin, District Judge, concur.

Gunderson, Chief Justice, with whom Batjer, Justice, concurs, dissenting:

The sole issue raised by appellant is whether the district court erred by concluding that appellant, as an individual guarantor of the note sued upon, was not entitled to the protection of NRS 40.451 to 40.459 inclusive.[1] In concluding

---

[1] The pertinent language in these provisions for purposes of this appeal is the following:

40.453

1. It is hereby declared by the legislature to be against public policy for any document relating to the sale of real property to contain any provision whereby a mortgagor or trustor waives any right secured to him by the laws of this state.

2. No court shall enforce any such provision.

40.455

Upon application of the judgment creditor or the beneficiary of the deed of trust within 3 months from the date of the foreclosure sale or the trustee's sale held pursuant to NRS 107.080, respectively, and after the hearing conducted under NRS 40.457, the court may award a deficiency judgment to the judgment creditor or the beneficiary of the deed of trust if it appears from the sheriff's return or the recital of consideration in the trustee's deed that there is a deficiency of sale proceeds and a balance remaining due to the judgment creditor or the beneficiary of the deed of trust, respectively.

that the appellant was not entitled to the protection of these provisions, the district court relied on this court's opinion in *Manufacturers & Traders Trust v. Dist. Ct.,* 94 Nev. 551, 583 P.2d 444 (1978). The appellant asks us to reconsider our decision in *Manufacturers* and either to distinguish that case from the instant matter or to overrule that decision.

Justice Batjer and I believe that, as a matter of law, the appellant, as an individual guarantor of the note sued upon, is protected by NRS 40.451 to 40.459 inclusive. Accordingly, we would overrule that portion of this court's decision in *Manufacturers* which holds that the protections of NRS 40.451, *et seq.,* are afforded only to principal obligors and do not apply to guarantors.

Properly interpreted, we believe the language adopted by the Legislature to describe the parties in NRS 40.451 *et seq.* should be read to protect all "defendants" who are potentially liable (including guarantors), and not simply mortgagors and trustors. NRS 40.453 declares that it is against public policy for a document to contain a waiver of a right secured to a "mortgagor or trustor." However, the statutory provisions dealing directly with deficiencies refer to "*defendants* personally liable for the debt." NRS 40.459. (Emphasis added.) *See also* NRS 40.457(1). It therefore is inconsistent with that express language to protect only the principal obligors.

In *Manufacturers,* this court relied in part on the fact that, "California courts have consistently refused to extend the deficiency judgment statutes to guarantors." *See* fn. 2 in *Manufacturers* at 556. However, examination of the California statutes in question, *i. e.,* West's Ann.C.C.P. § 580(a)-(d), discloses that they contain no language comparable to that found in NRS 40.457(1) concerning the right of "*all defendants*" to receive notice of the hearing which must be held prior to the award of a deficiency judgment. Nor do the California statutes contain language like that found in NRS 40.459 concerning the court's capacity to "*award a money judgment against the defendant or defendants personally liable for the debt.*" (Emphasis added.) The comparable California statutory provisions speak exclusively about "mortgagees or trustees" whenever they mention parties.

Moreover, it is an elementary tenet of law that once a guarantor pays the alleged deficiency under the note, he is then subrogated to the rights of the creditor to pursue the maker of the note (and the principal obligor) for any amounts paid on the maker's behalf. *Cf. Union Bank v. Gradsky,* 265 Cal.App.2d 40, 71 Cal.Rptr. 64 (Cal. App.1968). Under generally accepted principles, the maker-obligor can therefore be subjected by indirection to a debt which could not be recovered directly. Furthermore, if we attempt to avoid this result, by allowing the maker-obligor to assert a defense against the guarantor under the deficiency statute — a defense created solely by the creditor's failure to act — then the result will be to subject the guarantor to a defense which he never contemplated, and which results not from his own actions, but from the creditor's neglect.

40.457

1. Before awarding a deficiency judgment under NRS 40.455, the court shall hold a hearing and shall take evidence presented by either party concerning the fair market value of the property sold as of the date of foreclosure sale or trustee's sale. Notice of such hearing shall be served upon all defendants who have appeared in the action and against whom a deficiency judgment is sought, or upon their attorneys of record, at least 15 days before the date set for hearing.

2. Upon application of any party made at least 10 days before the date set for the hearing the court shall, or upon its own motion the court may, appoint an appraiser to appraise the property sold as of the date of foreclosure sale or trustee's sale.... Any appraiser so appointed may be called and examined as a witness by any party or by the court....

40.459

After the hearing under NRS 40.457, the court may award a money judgment against the defendant or defendants personally liable for the debt....

We therefore respectfully submit that the court's ruling in *Manufacturers* is untenable and should be overruled.

BATJER, JUSTICE, concurs.

NOTES

1. Note that some anti-deficiency statutes allow for a deficiency judgment in the event the lender's security has become impaired. However, a full credit bid conclusively establishes that there has been no impairment of the security and precludes recovery of other damages possibly incurred which might have been recoverable if less than a full paper bid had been made. *See Brown v. Critchfield,* 100 Cal. App. 3d 858 (1980).

2. In *Cook v. Farmers & Merchants Bank,* 279 S.E.2d 199 (Ga. 1981), a judgment creditor obtained an assignment of a note secured by a mortgage. The judgment creditor caused the property to be sold at a foreclosure sale which generated more than the debt on the secured note. The judgment creditor kept the excess proceeds and applied them to the outstanding prior existing judgment. The court held that the judgment and the debt on the note did not tack together and become one obligation. Therefore, there was no deficiency. Had the two obligations tacked and become one, the judgment creditor would have been limited to recovering the value of the property. However, treating the two obligations as distinctly separate from one another, the judgment creditor was able to foreclose and apply first enough of the funds to completely satisfy the secured debt with the excess being applied to the judgment.

C. PURCHASE MONEY MORTGAGES

While it may seem straightforward to state that there can be no judgment for a deficiency following the foreclosure sale when the mortgage has been a purchase money mortgage, it is somewhat more difficult to define exactly what a purchase money mortgage is. The simplest form of a purchase money mortgage comes into being when a purchaser of land executes a note payable to the seller for a portion of the purchase price and that note is secured by a mortgage on the subject property. It is truly a purchase money mortgage for it is a mortgage used to secure the payment of a part of the purchase price. However, it is less clear when the transaction between the purchaser and seller is an "all cash" transaction but the funds are furnished by a lender, typically a bank or a savings and loan association. It has been held that if a lender provides all or a part of the funds used to pay the seller in cash, that the mortgage held by the lender is a purchase money mortgage.[5] The question of what is purchase money becomes even more confused when the land has been purchased for cash but the improvements paid for with borrowed money [6] or later improvements are added to the land with borrowed money.[7] The debate over the status of the mortgage as purchase money or otherwise will usually occur when the lender seeks a deficiency or the borrower anticipates such action by the lender. Obviously, the borrower will assert that the loan was purchase money if there is a bar on purchase money deficiency judgments.

California Code of Civil Procedure (1976)

§ 580b. Purchase money mortgages, etc.; no deficiency judgment

No deficiency judgment shall lie in any event after any sale of real property for failure of the purchaser to complete his contract of sale, or under a deed of

---

[5] Bargioni v. Hill, 59 Cal. 2d 121, 378 P.2d 593 (1963).
[6] *See* Prunty v. Bank of America, *infra* page 330.
[7] *See* Allstate Sav. & Loan Ass'n v. Murphy, *infra* page 336.

trust, or mortgage, given to the vendor to secure payment of the balance of the purchase price of real property, or under a deed of trust, or mortgage, on a dwelling for not more than four families given to a lender to secure repayment of a loan which was in fact used to pay all or part of the purchase price of such dwelling occupied, entirely or in part, by the purchaser.

Where both a chattel mortgage and a deed of trust or mortgage have been given to secure payment of the balance of the combined purchase price of both real and personal property, no deficiency judgment shall lie at any time under any one thereof if no deficiency judgment would lie under the deed of trust or mortgage on real property.

Oregon Revised Statutes (1979)

§ 88.070. Decree foreclosing purchase money mortgage on real property

When a decree is given for the foreclosure of any mortgage given to secure payment of the balance of the purchase price of real property, the decree shall provide for the sale of the real property covered by such mortgage for the satisfaction of the decree given therein, but the mortgagee shall not be entitled to a deficiency judgment on account of the mortgage or note or obligation secured by the same.

PRUNTY v. BANK OF AMERICA

California District Court of Appeal
37 Cal. App. 3d 430, 112 Cal. Rptr. 370 (1974)

RATTIGAN, ACTING PRESIDING JUSTICE. The question presented on this appeal (apparently as a matter of first impression) is whether Code of Civil Procedure section 580b[1] bars a deficiency judgment, against a borrower and in favor of a lender, after judicial foreclosure and sale of real property under a deed of trust executed by the borrower to secure payment of a "construction loan" (1) which was used to finance construction of his personal residence on land already owned by him in fee, but (2) which was not used to finance his purchase of the land itself. We hold that the statute bars a deficiency judgment under the circumstances presented here.

---

[1] We hereinafter refer to the cited statute as "section 580b" or as "the statute." The language thereof which controls the present case appears in its text as amended in 1963 (Stats. 1963, ch. 2158, § 1, p. 4500) to provide in pertinent part as follows (with the 1963 amendment shown by italics):

No deficiency judgment shall lie in any event after any sale of real property for failure of the purchaser to complete his contract of sale, or under a deed of trust, or mortgage, given *to the vendor* to secure payment of the balance of the purchase price of real property, *or under a deed of trust, or mortgage, on a dwelling for not more than four families given to a lender to secure repayment of a loan which was in fact used to pay all or part of the purchase price of such dwelling occupied, entirely or in part, by the purchaser.*
Where both a chattel mortgage and a deed of trust or mortgage have been given to secure payment of the balance of the combined purchase price of both real and personal property, no deficiency judgment shall lie at any time under any one thereof *if no deficiency judgment would lie under the deed of trust or mortgage on real property.*

As originally enacted in 1933, and as reenacted without change in 1935, the statute contained this language only: "No deficiency judgment shall lie in any event after any sale under a deed of trust or mortgage given to secure payment of the balance of the purchase price of real property." (Stats.1933, ch. 642, § 5, p. 1673; stats.1935, ch. 650, §§ 5 [p. 1806], 9 [p. 1807].)

The statute's present language relative to a sale of real property after default under a "contract of sale" was added in 1935 (stats.1935, ch. 680, § 1, pp. 1868-1869); its second paragraph was added in 1949. (Stats.1949, ch. 1599, § 1, p. 2846.) Neither of these provisions is involved in the present case.

Plaintiffs are the owners in fee of certain real property upon which they executed a deed of trust, in favor of defendant Bank of America as beneficiary, to secure payment of a construction loan made by the bank to them for the purpose of financing the erection of a residence on the property. The residence was built and completed with the proceeds of the construction loan, but was demolished as the result of a natural disaster. In this action, thereafter commenced against the bank and the trustee under the deed of trust (defendant Continental Auxiliary Company), plaintiffs sought a declaratory judgment to the effect that Code of Civil Procedure section 580b barred the bank from recovering a deficiency judgment in the event of their default and a *judicial* foreclosure and sale under the deed of trust.

After a nonjury trial, the court found in favor of plaintiffs and entered a declaratory judgment substantially as prayed. Defendants appeal from the declaratory judgment.

Facts

Including those just summarized, most of the material facts appear in the trial court's findings. For this reason, and because they are undisputed, we quote the findings (with insignificant editorial changes, and with footnoted references to some evidence not specifically mentioned therein) as follows:

FINDINGS OF FACT

1. In 1964, plaintiffs purchased with their own funds certain unimproved real property generally known and described as 6163 Chelton Drive, Oakland, California, intending to build their own home thereon. 2. In 1965, while the property was still unimproved, plaintiffs applied to defendant Bank of America for a loan in the sum of $40,000. 3. On June 23, 1965, defendant Bank of America loaned $40,000 to plaintiffs and the plaintiffs gave defendant their note in the sum of $40,000 and a deed of trust against said real property. . . .

. . . .

9. All the proceeds of said loan were used by plaintiffs to pay the purchase price of labor and materials which were used in constructing a single family residence on the property. . . .

12. Said land, without the improvements [constructed] thereon, had a value of $7,500. 13. After the construction of said improvements, said land had a fair market value of $96,000. 14. Upon completion of the construction of the dwelling, it was occupied by plaintiffs and used by them as their place of residence. 15. In April, 1967, a major landslide occurred in the area of the residence. As a result of the damage done to the residence and to the real property itself, the residence was torn down and demolished.

16. Defendant Bank of America required that plaintiffs have a policy of insurance on the land and improvements with a lender's loss payable endorsement. 17. Plaintiffs obtained said policy of insurance but it did not cover them or defendant Bank of America against the risk of a landslide. 18. No insurance which would cover said risk was available to the parties. 19. To the extent of the unpaid balance of its loan to plaintiffs, . . . [defendant bank] . . . is subrogated to plaintiffs' claims against any other party for damages suffered by reason of the destruction of their residence.

In the declaratory judgment entered pursuant to the above-quoted findings, the trial court ordered that defendant bank was *not* entitled to recover a deficiency judgment from plaintiffs. The court unmistakably determined that a deficiency judgment was barred, under the facts as found by the provisions of section 580b. Upon examination of the facts in light of the language of the statute as amended in 1963 (see fn. 1, *ante*), we agree: for the reasons next stated, we affirm the declaratory judgment.

On their appeal from the declaratory judgment, defendants first contend that section 580b does not bar a deficiency judgment in this case because the deed of trust given by plaintiffs was not a "purchase money" instrument "within the meaning" of the statute. (See fn. 1, *ante*.) The contention rests upon the premises (1) that section 580b operates to bar a deficiency judgment after the sale of real property under a "purchase money" mortgage or trust deed only, and (2) that plaintiffs' trust deed was not a "purchase money" instrument because it was given to secure payment of a construction loan whose proceeds financed the residential improvement of their property but not its "purchase."

Defendants' first premise is undeniably correct: section 580b has consistently been interpreted as barring "any deficiency judgment after sale under a purchase money mortgage or trust deed" only. (*Roseleaf Corp. v. Chierighino* (1963), 59 Cal.2d 35, 41, 27 Cal.Rptr. 873, 876, 378 P.2d 97, 100. Cf. Riesenfeld, California Legislation Curbing Deficiency Judgments (1960) 48 Cal.L.Rev. 705, 711; California Land Security and Development (Cont.Ed.Bar 1960) § 16.8, p. 395; Hetland, California Real Estate Secured Transactions (Cont.Ed.Bar 1970) [hereinafter cited as "Hetland"] § 6.21, p. 265.)

The validity of defendants' second premise — that plaintiffs' trust deed is not a purchase money instrument within the meaning of section 580b because it was given to secure payment of a construction loan only — requires analysis of the language of the 1963 amendment of the statute (see fn. 1, *ante*) according to the conventional canons of statutory construction. " 'The fundamental rule of statutory construction is that the court should ascertain the intent of the Legislature so as to effectuate the purpose of the law.' ..." ...

    . . . .

Because the Legislature's "purpose" in adopting the 1963 amendment of section 580b is the paramount consideration in our construction of the language employed in it, we first resort to the history of the statute which preceded it. At all times prior to the amendment (and without reference to the language which was added to the statute by earlier amendments and which is not relevant here), section 580b expressly barred a deficiency judgment only after a sale under a mortgage or trust deed "given ... to secure payment of the balance of the purchase price of real property." (See fn. 1, *ante*.) The just-quoted language clearly limited the definition of a "purchase money instrument," a sale under which would bar a deficiency judgment according to the statute's terms, to a mortgage or trust deed given by a *vendee* of the affected real property, for the security purpose expressly stated, because a vendee is ordinarily the person who is obligated to pay "the balance of the purchase price of [the affected] real property." Because a landowner who borrows construction money is not obligating himself to pay any part of "the purchase price of [his] real property," the same language imported that a mortgage or trust deed given to secure payment of the loan was not a "purchase money instrument" which would invoke the anti-deficiency protection of the statute.

By reason of the pre-1963 language mentioned, the principal decisions which dealt with it involved trust deeds which had been given by *vendees* "to secure payment of the balance of the purchase price of real property." (See, e. g., *Stockton Sav. & Loan Bank v. Massanet* (1941), 18 Cal.2d 200, 207-209, 114 P.2d

592; *Brown v. Jensen* (1953), 41 Cal.2d 193, 194-196, 197-198, 259 P.2d 425; *Roseleaf Corp. v. Chierighino, supra,* 59 Cal.2d 35 at p. 41, 27 Cal.Rptr. 873, 378 P.2d 97; *Bargioni v. Hill* (1963), 59 Cal.2d 121, 122-124, 28 Cal.Rptr. 321, 378 P.2d 593.) In the one decision cited herein which involved a sale of property under an instrument given to secure payment of a "construction loan," by persons who owned the property but were not its vendees (and at a time when the same pre-1963 language of section 580b controlled the transaction), it was held that the statute did not bar a deficiency judgment against their successors because the construction borrowers had not been "purchase money trustors" when the transaction was executed. (*Paramount Sav. & Loan Ass'n v. Barber* (1968), 263 Cal.App.2d 166, 167-169, 69 Cal.Rptr. 390.)

In the *Roseleaf* case (*Roseleaf Corp. v. Chierighino, supra,* 59 Cal.2d 35, 27 Cal.Rptr. 873, 378 P.2d 97), the question was whether certain trust deeds which had been given by one of several vendees of a hotel, for the literal purpose of securing "payment of the balance of the purchase price" thereof, were purchase money instruments which entitled him to the anti-deficiency protection of section 580b as it read prior to the 1963 amendment. The Supreme Court first held that whether a given mortgage or trust deed was a purchase money instrument within the meaning of the statute depended upon whether it comported with the statute's purpose, stating: "Section 580b was apparently drafted in contemplation of the standard purchase money transaction, in which the *vendor* of real property retains an interest in the land sold to secure payment of part of the purchase price. *Variations on the standard are subject to section 580b only if they come within the purpose of that section.*" (*Roseleaf Corp. v. Chierighino, supra,* 59 Cal.2d 35 at p. 41, 27 Cal.Rptr. 873 at p. 876, 378 P.2d 97 at p. 100 [italics added].)

After summarizing and discarding "[v]arious purposes ... [which had] ... been ascribed to section 580b," the *Roseleaf* court next defined the statute's purposes in this language: "*Section 580b places the risk of inadequate security on the purchase money mortgagee. A vendor is thus discouraged from overvaluing the security.* Precarious land promotion schemes are discouraged, for the security value of the land gives purchasers a clue as to its true market value. (Citation.) *If inadequacy of the security results, not from overvaluing, but from a decline in property values during a general or local depression, section 580b prevents the aggravation of the downturn that would result if defaulting purchasers were burdened with large personal liability. Section 580b thus serves as a stabilizing factor in land sales.*" (*Roseleaf Corp. v. Chierighino, supra,* 59 Cal.2d 35 at p. 42, 27 Cal.Rptr. 873 at p. 877, 378 P.2d 97 at p. 101 [italics added].) The court concluded by holding that the trust deeds before it were not purchase money instruments within the meaning of the pre-1963 statute, and that the latter did not protect the trustor-vendee against a deficiency judgment, because there was no evidence that the hotel had been overvalued when he bought it and executed the instruments to secure payment of its purchase price. (*Id.,* at pp. 42-43, 27 Cal.Rptr. 873, 378 P.2d 97.)

In the *Bargioni* case (*Bargioni v. Hill, supra,* 59 Cal.2d 121, 28 Cal.Rptr. 321, 378 P.2d 593), the Supreme Court reiterated its *Roseleaf* reasoning as the basis for holding, for the first time since the original enactment of section 580b (see Hetland, *op. cit. supra,* § 6.24, p. 271), that a mortgage or trust deed given by a vendee of real property, but to a third party lender rather than to the property's vendor, was a purchase money instrument which operated to bar a deficiency judgment under the pre-1963 statute. The court stated: *"This section compels a purchase money mortgagee to assume the risk that the security is inadequate. The purposes are to discourage land sales that are unsound because the land is overvalued and, in the event of a depression in land values, to prevent the aggravation of the downturn that would result if defaulting purchasers lost the land and were burdened with personal liability.* (See *Roseleaf Corp. v. Chierighino, ante,* 59 Cal.2d pp. 35, 42, 27 Cal.Rptr. 873, 378 P.2d 97.) These purposes are served by relieving the purchaser of personal liability to any person who finances the purchase and takes as security a trust deed or mortgage on the property purchased, provided the financier intended the loan to be used to pay all or part of the purchase price. (Citation.)" (*Bargioni v. Hill, supra,* at p. 123, 28 Cal.Rptr. at p. 322, 378 P.2d at p. 594 [italics added].)

In the 1963 amendment of section 580b, the Legislature first provided that a deficiency judgment would not lie after a sale under a deed of trust or mortgage given *to a vendor* "to secure payment of the balance of the purchase price of real property." (See fn. 1, *ante.*) This wording reiterated the narrow language of the pre-1963 statute which necessarily limited the definition of a "purchase money instrument," which would invoke the statutory bar, to one given for the quoted purpose if it had been given to the *vendor* of the affected property. According to this portion of the amendment, the statute remains within the *Roseleaf* court's concept that it was "drafted in contemplation of the standard purchase money transaction, in which the vendor of real property retains an interest in the land sold to secure payment of part of the purchase price." (*Roseleaf Corp. v. Chierighino,* quoted *supra,* 59 Cal.2d 35 at p. 41, 27 Cal.Rptr. 873 at p. 876, 378 P.2d 97 at p. 100.)

The second portion of the 1963 amendment provides that a deficiency judgment is barred, after sale under a deed of trust or mortgage given "on a dwelling," if the "dwelling" meets a specific description and if the instrument had been given to a "lender" (as distinguished from a "vendor") "to secure repayment of a loan which was in fact used to pay all or part of the *purchase price* of such dwelling occupied . . . by the *purchaser."* (Italics added.) Because this language refers to a "lender," and departs from the pre-1963 wording of the statute by referring to the "purchase price of . . . [a] . . . dwelling," instead of the "purchase price of real property," the anti-deficiency protection of the amended statute is no longer limited to the narrow bounds of the "standard purchase money transaction," and the retention of a security interest by the *vendor* of "land sold," as discussed in the *Roseleaf* decision. (*Roseleaf Corp. v. Chierighino, supra,* 59 Cal.2d 35 at p. 41, 27 Cal.Rptr. 873, 378 P.2d 97.) On the other hand, it appears that the broader language of the second portion of the amendment bars a deficiency judgment in contemplation of another "standard" transaction in which a third party lender finances the "purchase price" of a described "dwelling" and receives from the "purchaser" a mortgage or trust deed to secure payment of his loan. The final question in the present case is whether the broader language should be interpreted to bar a deficiency judgment after a sale "under a deed of trust [plaintiffs'] . . . given to a lender [defendant bank] to secure repayment of a loan which was in fact used to pay all or part" of the *cost of constructing* plaintiffs' "dwelling occupied . . ." by the borrower(s) (plaintiffs).

. . . .

Despite the operation of the 1963 amendment to eliminate the anti-deficiency protection previously afforded the purchaser of commercial property against a third party lender . . . under the pre-1963 language of the statute and under the *Bargioni* decision (*Bargioni v. Hill, supra,* 59 Cal.2d 121 at p. 123, 28 Cal.Rptr. 321, 378 P.2d 593), it appears that the amendment was adopted in direct response to *Bargioni* (Hetland, *op. cit. supra,* § 6.24, p. 272), and that the

Legislature thereby codified that decision to the extent of continuing the protection extended, against third party lenders, to the limited class of residential purchaser-borrowers described in the amendment. Although decided upon in apposite facts, at least one recent decision already indicates that the *Roseleaf-Bargioni* definition of the statute's purposes survived the 1963 amendment. (*Spangler v. Memel, supra,* 7 Cal.3d 603 at p. 610, 102 Cal.Rptr. 807, 498 P.2d 1055.)

As stated in *Bargioni,* "[t]he purposes [of section 580b] are [1] to discourage land sales that are unsound because the land is overvalued and [2], in the event of a depression in land values, to prevent the aggravation of the downturn that would result if defaulting purchasers lost the land and were burdened with personal liability." (*Bargioni v. Hill, supra,* 59 Cal.2d 121 at p. 123, 28 Cal.Rptr. 321 at p. 322, 378 P.2d 593 at p. 594 [citing *Roseleaf Corp. v. Chierighino, supra,* 59 Cal.2d 35 at p. 42], 27 Cal.Rptr. 873, 378 P.2d 97.) The first purpose is served by application of the amended statute's anti-deficiency protection to residential construction borrowers who fall within its terms . . .: it thus tends to discourage construction borrowing which is "unsound" because the financed construction is overvalued.

The amended statute's application to residential construction borrowers also serves its second purpose, which contemplates "depression in land values" and "aggravation of the downturn that would result if defaulting purchasers lost the land and were burdened with personal liability." We perceive no real distinction between the present situation, where the value of the security has been diminished by a natural disaster, and a case where the same result has occurred by reason of cyclical economic decline: the spirit of the statute is to protect the borrower against the "aggravation" of any such "downturn," and the *Roseleaf* and *Bargioni* courts both held that its effect is to impose the "risk" of inadequate security upon the secured lender rather than upon the borrower. (*Roseleaf Corp. v. Chierighino, supra,* 59 Cal.2d 35 at p. 42, 27 Cal.Rptr. 873, 378 P.2d 97; *Bargioni v. Hill, supra,* 59 Cal.2d 121 at p. 123, 28 Cal.Rptr. 321, 378 P.2d 593.)

In the present case, it seems particularly appropriate that the "risk," and the ensuing loss in consequence, be borne by defendant bank because of the opportunities it had — and utilized — to protect its security interest against the landslide loss which actually occurred. These opportunities included the control exercised by the bank over the plans, specifications and construction of plaintiffs' residence in contemplation of landslide and other physical risks . . ., and the requirement in plaintiffs' trust deed that they furnish insurance whose coverage protected the bank against loss and which was "satisfactory" to it. (See . . . the trial court's findings 16, 17 and 18, quoted *supra.*) We may reasonably assume that such protective measures are readily available to lenders who finance residential construction, that the Legislature was aware of this when it amended section 580b in 1963, and that its protection of residential construction borrowers, against deficiency judgments, was continued (under the 1963 amendment) in recognition of the fact that the lenders involved are able to protect themselves against loss of [*sic*] devaluation of their security which might be caused by physical catastrophe. Under these and all the circumstances previously discussed, we hold that section 580b bars a deficiency judgment in the present case.

. . . .

The judgment is affirmed.

Devine and Bray, JJ., concur.
Hearing denied; Burke and Clark, JJ., dissenting.

ALLSTATE SAVING & LOAN ASS'N v. MURPHY

California District Court of Appeal
98 Cal. App. 3d 761 (1980)

Beach, Associate Justice.

Facts:

Following a foreclosure sale of defendant borrowers' single-family dwelling by the holder of the first trust deed on the property, plaintiff lender sued defendants for the unpaid amount on two promissory notes, which were secured by trust deeds on the same property and whose proceeds were used for the construction of a swimming pool and a concrete block wall at the property. Plaintiff alleged in its complaint that as a result of the senior creditor's foreclosure sale, which did not provide funds to satisfy defendants' indebtedness to plaintiff, plaintiff's deeds of trust were rendered valueless. Defendants interposed the defense of the anti-deficiency provision of Code of Civil Procedure section 580, subdivision (b) (hereafter referred to as "section 580b" or "the statute"). After the trial court granted plaintiff's motion for summary judgment on the ground that section 580b applies only to loans to finance the purchase of a dwelling and not to loans for the construction of a swimming pool, defendants appealed.

Issue on Appeal and Holding:

The question presented on appeal is whether section 580b bars a deficiency judgment against a lender who loaned a borrower money for the purpose of constructing a swimming pool. We hold it does not, as we shall explain below.

Discussion:

Section 580b provides in pertinent part: "No deficiency judgment shall lie in any event . . . under a deed of trust, or mortgage . . . on a dwelling for not more than four families given to a lender to secure repayment of a loan which was in fact used to pay all or part of the purchase price of such dwelling occupied, entirely or in part, by the purchaser." A statute which has a single meaning apparent on its face requires no interpretation. (*Friends of Mammoth v. Board of Supervisors*, 8 Cal.3d 247, 256, 104 Cal.Rptr. 761, 502 P.2d 1049; *Benor v. Board of Medical Examiners*, 8 Cal.App.3d 542, 546-547, 87 Cal.Rptr. 415). Here, the statute clearly contemplates protection of the borrower who takes out a loan to finance the purchase of a dwelling. In the case at bench, however, plaintiff loaned defendants money not to finance the purchase of a dwelling but to finance the construction of a swimming pool some 17 months after they had bought the dwelling and moved in. *Prunty v. Bank of America,* 37 Cal.App.3d 430, 112 Cal.Rptr. 370, relied on by defendants, is factually distinguishable. In *Prunty,* the purpose of the loan was to build a *dwelling* on land already owned by the borrower. We hold that construction loans for improvements or repairs of the type involved in this case are not within the description of loans protected by the purchase-money deficiency prohibition of section 580b. (See Hetland, Cal.

Real Estate Secured Transactions (Cont.Ed.Bar 1974) § 9.27, p. 218: construction loans do not fall under section 580b's anti-deficiency provision unless used by the borrower to finance his personal residence.)

The judgment is affirmed.

ROTH, P. J., and FLEMING, J., concur.

NOTES

1. Funds supplied from a third party lender have been held to be purchase money. *See Bargioni v. Hill,* 59 Cal. 2d 121, 378 P.2d 593 (1963).

2. A purchaser who assumes a non-purchase money obligation of the vendor as part of the purchase price should logically have the protection of anti-deficiency legislation enacted for purchase money mortgages. However, the California Court of Appeals has held that for purposes of anti-deficiency statutes this assumption of debt as part of the purchase price is not considered purchase money. *See Banta v. Rosasco,* 12 Cal. App. 2d 420, 55 P.2d 601 (1936).

3. If the security is exhausted by a senior lienor's foreclosure sale, a junior lienor may not seek a personal judgment against the debtor even if the junior received none of the proceeds from the senior's sale. The theory operating here is that the entire amount of the junior lien is a deficiency beyond the value of the property. Deficiency judgments being barred, the holder of the junior lien cannot sue. This is the rule in *Brown v. Jensen, supra* at page 321. However, *Brown v. Jensen* has been subsequently eroded by *Spangler v. Memel,* 7 Cal. 3d 603, 498 P.2d 1055 (1972), which carefully avoids overruling *Brown v. Jensen* but which allows the holder of a sold out junior lien to sue because the junior had originally subordinated to the senior lien which ultimately foreclosed. This case weakens the holding of *Brown v. Jensen* without overruling it.

D. ONE FORM OF ACTION

The one form of action rule exists in few states and in some of those it is used in connection with other forms of depression legislation. The basic import of the one form of action rule is that it allows the mortgagor to force the mortgagee to resort to the property first. It also provides that the mortgagee is protected from a multiplicity of actions.

In the event the lender files suit on the debt before seeking any funds from the property the borrower has two alternative choices: (1) he can allow the suit to go to judgment and later enjoin any attempted foreclosure on the subject property; or, (2) he can force the borrower to foreclose on the property before pursuing his suit on the debt. If the lender commences a foreclosure action in which he seeks a deficiency judgment in the event the property does not generate sufficient funds at the foreclosure sale to satisfy the debt, the property can be sold, a judgment entered for the deficiency and other property of the debtor sought in order to obtain satisfaction. However, the one form of action rule has forced the lender to resort to the property and the borrower has only been subjected to one lawsuit. This is the way the rule is supposed to work.

The one form of action rule must be pleaded affirmatively in the event a suit is filed prior to foreclosure. If the defense of the rule is not pleaded judgment may be entered against the borrower. However, the borrower could later resist an effort to foreclose the mortgage on the basis of the rule: the borrower has already had the one action. Further, if the lender reduces the debt to a judgment rather than foreclose, as a judgment creditor the judgment lien will achieve priority junior to the mortgage which could have been foreclosed. The effect is that a purchaser at a sheriff's sale to satisfy a judgment will take title subject to the encumbrances senior to the judgment. Of course the mortgage which was security for the debt sued on will be extinguished, since once the debt is satisfied the mortgage ceases to exist.

Utah Code Annotated (1977)

§ 78-37-1. Form of action — Judgment — Special execution

There can be one action for the recovery of any debt or the enforcement of any right secured solely by mortgage upon real estate which action must be in accordance with the provisions of this chapter. Judgment shall be given adjudging the amount due, with costs and disbursements, and the sale of mortgaged property, or some part thereof, to satisfy said amount and accruing costs, and directing the sheriff to proceed and sell the same according to the provisions of law relating to sales on execution, and a special execution or order of sale shall be issued for that purpose.

ROSELEAF CORP. v. CHIERIGHINO

Supreme Court of California
59 Cal. 2d 35, 378 P.2d 97 (1963)

TRAYNOR, J. — Roseleaf Corporation sold its hotel to Willy Chierighino and his family. The consideration given by the Chierighinos included a note (not involved in this action) secured by a first trust deed and chattel mortgage on the hotel and its furnishings and three notes each secured by a second trust deed on real property owned by Willy.[1] The first trust deeds on these three parcels were owned by strangers to this action.[2] After the sale of the hotel, those owners caused the three parcels to be sold under powers of sale contained in the first trust deeds. The second trust deeds held by Roseleaf were not protected at the sales and were rendered valueless thereby. Thereafter Roseleaf brought this action to recover the full amount unpaid on the three notes secured by the second trust deeds. The trial court entered judgment for Roseleaf. Defendant Willy Chierighino appeals, contending that Roseleaf's action is limited by section 580a and barred by sections 580b and 580d of the Code of Civil Procedure.

In the absence of a statute to the contrary, a creditor secured by a trust deed or mortgage on real property may recover the full amount of the debt upon default. He may realize the security or sue on the obligation or both; the obligation is an independent undertaking by the debtor to pay. (See 2 Glenn, Mortgages (1943) § 140, p. 811). In most states now, however, the creditor's right to enforce such a debt is restricted by statute. Thus, in California the creditor must rely upon his security before enforcing the debt. (Code Civ. Proc., §§ 580a, 725a, 726.) If the security is insufficient, his right to a judgment against the debtor for

---

[1] Two of the trust deeds were on property originally owned by Willy's relatives, the third was on property owned by Willy. Under the escrow instructions the three parcels were conveyed to Roseleaf, then reconveyed to Willy. The trial court found on substantial evidence that these conveyances were not intended to be bona fide sales to Roseleaf. There is no merit in defendant's contention that extrinsic evidence was improperly admitted to show the facts and circumstances surrounding the transaction. (Barham v. Barham, 33 Cal.2d 416, 423 [202 P.2d 289]; see Imbach v. Schultz, 58 Cal.2d 858 [27 Cal.Rptr. 160, 377 P.2d 272.]

[2] Two of the trust deeds were apparently executed to the owners thereof by Willy. The third was executed by Willy to Roseleaf, which in turn assigned it to the ultimate owner. These transactions took place while the hotel was in escrow, the purpose being to raise the cash that Roseleaf demanded as a condition to the sale.

the deficiency may be limited or barred by sections 580a, 580b, 580d, or 726 of the Code of Civil Procedure.

Under sections 580a and 726, proceedings for a deficiency must be initiated within three months after either a private sale under a power of sale or a judicial sale, and the recovery may not exceed the difference between the amount of the indebtedness and the fair market value of the property at the time of the sale.[3] The "one form of action" rule of section 726 does not apply to a sold-out junior lienor (*Savings Bank v. Central Market Co.,* 122 Cal. 28, 33-36 [54 P. 273]; *see Brown v. Jensen,* 41 Cal. 2d 193, 196 [259 P.2d 425]), nor does the three-months limitation of section 580a. (*Hillen v. Soule,* 7 Cal.App.2d 45, 47 [45 P.2d 349] [holding that section 580b did not apply disapproved in *Brown v. Jensen,* 41 Cal.2d 193, 198 [259 P.2d 425]].) There is no reason to compel a junior lienor to go through foreclosure and sale when there is nothing left to sell. Moreover, to compel a junior lienor to sue for a deficiency within three months of the senior's sale would unnecessarily compel acceleration of the junior obligation, to the detriment of the debtor.

The fair-value limitations of sections 580a and 726 likewise do not apply to a junior lienor, such as Roseleaf, whose security has been rendered valueless by a senior sale. Section 726 provides that the decree of foreclosure "shall determine the personal liability of any defendant for the payment of the debt secured by *such* mortgage or deed of trust," (italics added) referring to the mortgage or deed of trust foreclosed by the same decree. Section 580a refers to a suit for the balance due on an obligation secured by a mortgage or deed of trust "following the exercise of the power of sale in *such* deed of trust or mortgage." (Italics added.) (See Riesenfeld, *California Legislation Curbing Deficiency Judgments* (1960) 48 Cal. L. Rev. 705, 726.)

The purpose of the fair-value limitations in sections 580a and 726 does not extend to sold-out junior lienors. Many states enacted fair-value statutes similar to sections 580a and 726 during the 1930's when it was felt that real property could not be sold for its "true" value. (See Glenn, Mortgages (1943) § 156, pp. 857-861; Poteat, *State Legislative Relief for the Mortgage Debtor During the Depression* (1938) 5 Law & Contemp. Prob. 517, 529-544.) Fair value provisions are designed to prevent creditors from buying in at their own sales at deflated prices and realizing double recoveries by holding debtors for large deficiencies. (See *Hatch v. Security-First Nat. Bank,* 19 Cal.2d 254, 259 [120 P.2d 869]; *Sivade*

---

[3] Section 580a provides in part: "Whenever a money judgment is sought for the balance due upon an obligation for the payment of which a deed of trust or mortgage with power of sale upon real property or any interest therein was given as security, following the exercise of the power of sale in such deed of trust or mortgage. . . .

"The court may render judgment for not more than the amount by which the entire amount of indebtedness due at the time of sale exceeded the fair market value of the real property or interest therein sold at the time of sale. . . .

"Any such action must be brought within three months of the time of sale under such deed of trust or mortgage.

"No judgment shall be rendered in any such action until the real property or interest therein has first been sold pursuant to the terms of such deed of trust or mortgage, unless such real property or interest therein has become valueless."

Section 726 provides in part: "The decree for the foreclosure of a mortgage or deed of trust secured by real property or any interest therein shall declare the amount of the indebtedness or right so secured and . . . shall determine the personal liability of any defendant for the payment of the debt secured by such mortgage or deed of trust. . . . [U]pon application of the plaintiff filed at any time within three months of the date of the foreclosure sale . . . the court shall render a money judgment . . . for the amount by which the amount of the indebtedness . . . exceeds the fair value of the property or interest therein sold as of the date of sale. . . ."

v. Smith, 104 N.J. Eq. 528 [146 A. 364]; *Wheeler v. Ellis,* 56 N.J.L. 28 [27 A. 911]; *Culliford v. Weingrad,* 196 Misc. 86 [91 N.Y.S.2d 333, 335-336]; *Continental Bank & Trust Co. v. Gedex Realty Corp.,* 60 N.Y.S.2d 710, 712; *Northwestern Loan & Trust Co. v. Bidinger,* 226 Wis. 239, 245 [276 N.W. 645]; 22 Cal.L.Rev. 180, 181.) Thus some fair-value statutes apply only if the creditor purchases at the sale. Mich. Laws Comp. § 692.51; Mo. Stat. Ann. (Vernon's) § 443.410; N.C. Gen. Stats. 45-21.36 (Supp. 1961).

Some courts have limited deficiency judgments to prevent double recoveries in the absence of statute (see *Investors Mortgage & Realty Co. v. Preakness Hills Realty Co.,* 133 N.J. Eq. 258 [31 A.2d 830]; *Suring State Bank v. Giese,* 210 Wis. 489 [246 N.W. 556, 85 A.L.R. 1477]), but they have not limited such judgments when sought by nonselling junior lienors. (*Hillside Nat. Bank v. Silverman,* 116 N.J.Eq. 463 [173 A. 326].) Fair-value statutes no more precisely worded than sections 580a and 726 have been held inapplicable to the nonselling junior lienor (*Alabama Mortgage & Securities Corp. v. Chinery,* 237 Ala. 198 [186 So. 136]; *Realty Associates Securities Corp. v. Hoblin,* 288 N.Y.S. 875; *Weisel v. Hagdahl Realty Co.,* 241 App.Div. 314 [271 N.Y.S. 629, 633-635]), as have other similar deficiency judgment restrictions. (*Cronin v. Gager-Crawford Co.,* 128 Conn. 688 [25 A.2d 652]; *Smith v. Mangin,* 161 Misc. 288 [292 N.Y.S. 265, 271]; *Sivade v. Smith,* 104 N.J.Eq. 528 [146 A. 364]; *Wheeler v. Ellis,* 56 N.J.L. 28 [27 A. 911]; *Carr v. Home Owners Loan Corp.,* 148 Ohio St. 533 [76 N.E.2d 389].)

The position of a junior lienor whose security is lost through a senior sale is different from that of a selling senior lienor. A selling senior can make certain that the security brings an amount equal to his claim against the debtor or the fair market value, whichever is less, simply by bidding in for that amount. He need not invest any additional funds. The junior lienor, however, is in no better position to protect himself than is the debtor. Either would have to invest additional funds to redeem or buy in at the sale. Equitable considerations favor placing this burden on the debtor, not only because it is his default that provokes the senior sale, but also because he has the benefit of his bargain with the junior lienor who, unlike the selling senior, might otherwise end up with nothing.

Nor is Roseleaf's action barred by section 580b. That section bars any deficiency judgment after sale under a purchase money mortgage or trust deed.[4] Roseleaf would clearly be barred by section 580b from suing on the note secured by the first trust deed and chattel mortgage on the hotel and its furnishings. That note, however, is not involved in this case, and the record discloses no default under it. The issue here is whether the three second trust deeds on land other than that purchased are purchase money trust deeds because they were "given to secure payment of the balance of the purchase price of real property."

Section 580b was apparently drafted in contemplation of the standard purchase money mortgage transaction, in which the vendor of real property retains an interest in the land sold to secure payment of part of the purchase price. Variations on the standard are subject to section 580b only if they come within the purpose of that section.

---

[4] Section 580b provides: "No deficiency judgment shall lie in any event after any sale of real property for failure of the purchaser to complete his contract of sale, or under a deed of trust, or mortgage, given to secure payment of the balance of the purchase price of real property.

"Where both a chattel mortgage and a deed of trust or mortgage have been given to secure payment of the balance of the combined purchase price of both real and personal property, no deficiency judgment shall lie at any time under either one thereof."

Dobias v. White, 239 N.C. 409, 412 [80 S.E.2d 23], held that a trust deed on land owned by the purchaser, given to secure payment of part of the purchase price of real property, is not a purchase money trust deed within the meaning of an antideficiency statute like section 580b. In that case, however, there was no analysis of the purpose of the applicable statute. Various purposes have been ascribed to section 580b. It has been said that it was designed to prevent creditors from buying in property for a nominal sum, after a debtor has defaulted, and then holding the debtor for the deficiency. (See *Kerrigan v. Maloof,* 98 Cal.App.2d 605, 616 [221 P.2d 153]; *Brown v. Jensen,* 41 Cal.2d 193, 201 [259 P.2d 425] [dissent].) This purpose, however, is accomplished by the fair-value sections, and does not explain for what purpose purchase money mortgages were singled out for special treatment. It has also been said that the purpose of section 580b is to make certain that in the case of "a purchase money mortgage or deed of trust the security alone can be looked to for recovery of the debt." (*Brown v. Jensen,* 41 Cal.2d 193, 198 [259 P.2d 425], quoting from *Mortgage Guarantee Co. v. Sampsell,* 51 Cal.App.2d 180, 185 [124 P.2d 353]. This conclusion states the effect of the statute after assuming that it applies, but offers no rationale for deciding whether or not it applies. In *Brown v. Jensen,* 41 Cal.2d 193, 197 [259 P.2d 425], it was stated that one reason for section 580b is that the one taking a purchase money trust deed knows the value of his security and assumes the risk that it may become inadequate. Perhaps the average vendor or financier in real estate transactions is more astute as to the value of his land that the average vendee, but it is doubtful whether that was the reason for barring deficiency judgments in purchase-money security transactions.

Section 580b places the risk of inadequate security on the purchase money mortgagee. A vendor is thus discouraged from overvaluing the security. Precarious land promotion schemes are discouraged, for the security value of the land gives purchasers a clue as to its true market value. (See Currie & Lieberman, *Purchase-Money Mortgages and State Lines: A Study in Conflict-of-Laws Methods,* 1960 Duke L.J. 1, 33-34, 39-40.) If inadequacy of the security results, not from overvaluing, but from a decline in property values during a general or local depression, section 580b prevents the aggravation of the downturn that would result if defaulting purchasers were burdened with large personal liability. Section 580b thus serves as a stabilizing factor in land sales.

There is no indication in the present case that the hotel was overvalued. The purchaser will not lose the property he purchased yet remain liable for the purchase price. To apply section 580b here would mean that the Chierighinos would acquire the hotel at less than the agreed price. Furthermore, if there is any merit in the theory that "the vendor knows the value of his security and assumes the risk of its inadequacy," that theory does not apply here. There is no reason to assume that Roseleaf had any greater knowledge of the value of the Chierighinos' land than did the Chierighinos.

Section 580d does not bar Roseleaf's action. That section provides that "No judgment shall be rendered for any deficiency upon a note secured by a deed of trust or mortage upon real property hereafter executed in any case in which the real property has been sold by the mortgagee or trustee under power of sale contained in such mortgage or deed of trust." This language is similar to that in sections 580a and 726. "[S]uch mortgage or deed of trust" refers to the instrument securing the note sued upon. Thus section 580d does not appear to extend to a junior lienor whose security has been sold out in a senior sale.

The purpose of section 580d is apparent from the fact that it applies if the property is sold under a power of sale, but not if the property is foreclosed and sold by judicial action. Before the section was enacted in 1939 (Stats. 1939, ch. 586, p. 1991), it was to the creditor's advantage to exercise a power of sale rather than to foreclose by judicial action. His right to a deficiency judgment after either was the same (Code Civ. Proc., §§ 580a, 726), but judicial foreclosure was subject to the debtor's statutory right of redemption (Code Civ. Proc., § 725a), whereas the debtor had no right to redeem from a sale under the power. (Code Civ. Proc., §§ 700a, 701; *Roberts v. True,* 7 Cal.App. 379, 381 [94 P. 392].) It seems clear, as Professor Hetland, amicus curiae herein, contends, that section 580d was enacted to put judicial enforcement on a parity with private enforcement. This result could be accomplished by giving the debtor a right to redeem after a sale under the power. The right to redeem, like proscription of a deficiency judgment, has the effect of making the security satisfy a realistic share of the debt. (See *Salsbery v. Ritter,* 48 Cal.2d 1, 11 [306 P.2d 897].) By choosing instead to bar a deficiency judgment after private sale, the Legislature achieved its purpose without denying the creditor his election of remedies. If the creditor wishes a deficiency judgment, his sale is subject to statutory redemption rights. If he wishes a sale resulting in nonredeemable title, he must forego the right to a deficiency judgment. In either case the debtor is protected.

The purpose of achieving a parity of remedies would not be served by applying section 580d against a nonselling junior lienor. Even without the section the junior has fewer rights after a senior private sale than after a senior judicial sale. He may redeem from a senior judicial sale (Code Civ. Proc., § 701), or he may obtain a deficiency judgment. (*Savings Bank v. Central Market Co.,* 122 Cal. 28 [54 P. 273]; *Giandeini v. Ramirez,* 11 Cal.App.2d 469 [54 P.2d 91]; see *Brown v. Jensen,* 41 Cal.2d 193, 196 [259 P.2d 425].) After a senior private sale, the junior has no right to redeem. This disparity of rights would be aggravated were he also denied a right to a deficiency judgment by section 580d. There is no purpose in denying the junior his single remedy after a senior private sale while leaving him with two alternative remedies after a senior judicial sale. The junior's right to recover should not be controlled by the whim of the senior, and there is no reason to extend the language of section 580d to reach that result.

The judgment is affirmed.

GIBSON, C. J., SCHAUER, J., McCOMB, J., PETERS, J., TOBRINER, J., and PEEK, J., concurred.

PARAMOUNT INSURANCE, INC. v. RAYSON & SMITLEY

Supreme Court of Nevada
86 Nev. 644, 472 P.2d 530 (1970)

COLLINS, CHIEF JUSTICE. This is an appeal from an order of the lower court discharging an attachment the issuance of which was obtained by appellants and levied upon property of respondent Smitley. We affirm that order.

Appellants, hereinafter referred to as Paramount, filed a complaint for judicial foreclosure and waste May 25, 1967. In their complaint they sought judicial foreclosure of 14 deeds of trust securing 14 promissory notes totaling $490,000, of which there remained unpaid $475,245 plus moneys paid by Paramount for fire insurance and taxes in the amount of $39,464.90, interest, costs, and attorney fees. Damages for waste were left open for later determination.

January 8, 1968, Paramount petitioned for the appointment of a receiver, alleging that the respondents had committed permissive waste by allowing the property secured by the trust deeds to deteriorate. The property was apartments, and some were said to be condemned as unfit for human occupation.

An order appointing a receiver was entered January 18, 1968, in which a lower court judge said that it appeared the mortgaged premises were inadequate security for the mortgage debt and the premises were continuing to deteriorate.

February 28, 1968, the receiver was granted an order permitting him to obtain appraisement and bids for repair of the property and to employ security personnel. On May 13, 1968, Paramount was authorized by the court to enter a cost-reimbursement contract to repair the premises.

October 6, 1969, Paramount filed an affidavit of attachment and directed the sheriff to levy on property of Smitley. October 9, 1969, Smitley moved to discharge the attachment on the grounds that it was improperly and irregularly issued. The grounds alleged were that Paramount's claim against Smitley was secured by a mortgage on real property; that the affidavit was insufficient to establish the security was valueless or of insufficient value; that the security had to first be exhausted before the value could be determined; and that the stay by the federal court relating to Rayson, a partner, applied also to actions concerning Smitley.

The trial judge granted Smitley's motion to discharge the attachment November 14, 1969.

The issues thus presented for our determination are these:

I. Whether the attachment provisions of NRS 31.010 apply in an action for judicial foreclosure of a trust deed on real property?

II. Whether an affidavit of a party's counsel is sufficient to establish that the security has become of insufficient value?

1. We are faced in this appeal with the problem of reconciling, if we can, and giving effect to two Nevada statutes, NRS 31.010 and NRS 40.430 as construed by an earlier decision of this court in *McMillan v. United Mortgage Co.,* 82 Nev. 117, 412 P.2d 604 (1966).

2. In *McMillan,* this court held that a trust deed fell within the intendment of the "one-action rule" (NRS 40.430); that the attachment statute, NRS 31.010, applied only when the security was "valueless"; that the mode of determining value of the security is first to exhaust the security by sale pursuant to the trust deed; and, finally, that, "Once the security has been sold and the debt not satisfied, an action on the note with ancillary attachment is permissible." *Id.* at 121 and 122, 412 P.2d at 606. Accordingly, the issuance of a writ of attachment pursuant to NRS 31.010 by the lower court was reversed on the ground the conclusory affidavit of the creditor was not acceptable to show the security property had become valueless, but instead sale of the security was first required.

3. We are now faced with the problem of attempting to reconcile that decision with the apparently conflicting rights granted by NRS 31.010 and NRS 40.430, where in a judicial foreclosure proceeding, as distinguished from the sale of security property under a trust deed, the security property is not valueless, but strong evidence is presented to show it is of insufficient value to secure the sum due. We conclude that the rule of *McMillan v. United Mortgage Co.,* supra, should be limited in its application to sale of security property under trust deed and not to judicial foreclosure proceedings.

4. In deciding *McMillan,* [the] court relied heavily upon *Barbieri v. Ramelli,* 84 Cal. 154, 23 P. 1086 (1890), which construed a California statute, C.C.P. § 537, from which NRS 31.010 was taken. The Nevada legislature, however, added a significant factor not found in the California statute. The California statute refers only to security which has become valueless, and does not contain the additonal words found in the Nevada statute which allows attachment to issue when the security has become insufficient in value.

5. It is apparent the one-action rule was legislatively adopted to change the common law rule which permitted a creditor to pursue either the remedy of sale of the land or suit on the note, or both at once. See *McMillan v. United Mortgage Co.,* supra, 82 Nev. at 119, 412 P.2d 604, and *Bank of Italy v. Bentley,* 217 Cal. 644, 20 P.2d 940 (1933). That purpose is accomplished in a judicial foreclosure proceeding. There is but one judicial action in which the sale of the security is first accomplished, and if any deficiency results in satisfying the debt owed, judgment for the deficient sum is rendered in the same action, which when docketed permits execution to issue.

Unless in that "one-action," attachment might be resorted to upon a proper showing the security has "become . . . insufficient in value to secure the sum due plaintiff" statutory rights of creditor-plaintiffs conferred by NRS 31.010 are effectively denied. In that regard, we must give due consideration to rules of statutory construction previously adopted by this court. In *Torreyson v. Board of Examiners,* 7 Nev. 19, 22 (1871), cited with approval in *Ex parte Smith,* 33 Nev. 466, 480, 111 P. 930, 935 (1910), this court said: "[N]o part of a statute should be rendered nugatory, nor any language turned to mere surplusage, if such consequences can properly be avoided." "Laws are also to be construed according to their spirit and meaning, and not merely according to their letter." *Lynip v. Buckner,* 22 Nev. 426, 439, 41 P. 762, 765 (1895). We see no other way to give simultaneous effect to NRS 31.010 and NRS 40.430.

By so holding, we do not overrule *McMillan.* Language in *McMillan* to the effect that NRS 31.010 applies only when the security is valueless was only dictum. That statute applies only in an "action." Thus, by its terms it is not available when a power of sale under a trust deed by the trustee is exercised. *McMillan* held that the action brought in that case on the note was improper because there had been no waiver of the security. We continue to approve that holding. It was unnecessary to the decision in that case to decide the applicability of NRS 31.010 to "actions" under the "one-action" rule. Subsequent to *McMillan,* this court recognized the alternative of proceeding by judicial foreclosure or trustee's sale was available to the beneficiary of a deed of trust. *Nevada Land & Mtge. Co. v. Hidden Wells Ranch, Inc.,* 83 Nev. 501, 435 P.2d 198 (1967). This decision points out and sharpens the distinctions between those alternatives.

6. In a foreclosure proceeding under NRS 40.430, all the steps required or permitted must be done under judicial scrutiny and supervision. If, in a foreclosure proceeding under that statute, a plaintiff seeks attachment where the security has become insufficient in value to secure the sum due, defendant has opportunity to seek discharge of that attachment by application to the very court in which the foreclosure proceeding is pending. See NRS 31.200.

7. The affidavit by counsel for Paramount, upon which the attachment was issued, stated only the sum by which the affiant believed the indebtedness exceeded the value of the security. It is a conclusory affidavit which affords no basis for a court to conclude that the security has in fact diminished in value from what it had when accepted by the plaintiff as security, and, as directed by NRS 31.010, has "become valueless or insufficient in value to secure the sum due the plaintiff." See *Barbieri v. Ramelli,* 84 Cal. 154, 23 P. 1086 (1890). We hold that an affidavit seeking issuance of a writ of attachment in a judicial foreclosure proceeding must not be merely conclusory and must contain an opinion of value by a witness qualified to express such an opinion. Furthermore, the affidavit must show that the security has decreased in value from the time the security interest attached. The affidavit relied upon in this case does not meet that test. Accordingly, the ruling of the lower court is affirmed.

8. Because of our affirmance of the lower court's ruling on the foregoing basis, it becomes unnecessary to decide whether the federal court stay relating to Rayson applied also to actions concerning Smitley.

Ruling affirmed.

ZENOFF, BATJER and MOWBRAY, JJ., concur.

THOMPSON, JUSTICE (concurring). The court holds that the affidavit supporting the attachment is insufficient and on this basis affirms the order below discharging the attachment. To this extent I agree with the opinion. However, I do not agree that the ancillary remedy of attachment is available in a judicial foreclosure proceeding. Attachment is ancillary to an action "upon a contract, express or implied, for the direct payment of money." NRS 30.010. The majority erroneously assume that judicial foreclosure, NRS 40.430, is such an action. I view judicial foreclosure as a separate statutory proceeding distinct from and not within the contract actions contemplated by the attachment statute. The very purpose of the "one action" rule, 40.430, is to preclude an action upon the secured note with its ancillary aids, unless the security is waived or has become valueless. *McMillan v. United Mortgage Co.*, 82 Nev. 117, 412 P.2d 604 (1966). This purpose prevents harassment and accommodates the implied understanding between the parties that the land shall constitute the primary fund to secure the debt. Respectfully, I suggest that the opinion today subverts the underlying purpose of the one action rule. Although *McMillan v. United Mortgage,* supra, did not concern judicial foreclosure, its reasoning applies with even greater force to a judicial foreclosure proceeding.

UTAH MORTGAGE & LOAN CO. v. BLACK

Supreme Court of Utah
618 P.2d 43 (1980)

CROCKETT, CHIEF JUSTICE: Plaintiff Utah Mortgage Loan Corporation sued to recover the unpaid balance of $36,760.01 on a $675,715.00 subdivision loan which it had advanced to defendants Don J. Black (since deceased), Betty J. Black and Don J. Black Realty, Inc., and for which defendants had executed a promissory note, and a trust deed of real property.

On the basis of the submissions, the defendants moved for summary judgment on the ground that the plaintiff had released all of the lots and, under the so-called "one-action rule," could not then recover a deficiency against the defendants. From the granting of that motion, plaintiffs appeal.

The plaintiff argues that because defendants themselves agreed to the release of the security (the lots as they were sold), the proceeds from which were not sufficient to pay the debt, they are not released from paying the balance, but should be held to pay the debt according to the note.

As opposed to the above, the position essayed by the defendants is: that the plaintiff had within its control the entire subdivision, which was sufficient security to pay off the defendants' note, that plaintiff also had discretion as to whether, and for what amounts, it would release the lots; and that having released them without satisfying defendants' debt, it should not be permitted to recover any deficiency from the defendants.

It will be seen from what has been said that the positions stated by the parties are mutually contradictory. Therefore, unless upon the basis of the submission it appears for a certainty that either one or the other is correct, and therefore entitled to prevail, it is necessary that there be a trial and resolution of this dispute between them.

Insofar as presently shown by the record, the essential facts appear to be: On June 26, 1975, the defendants executed and delivered to the plaintiff a promissory note for the above-described loan. Payment was secured by a trust deed on property located in Salt Lake County which the defendants desired to subdivide and develop. The land, which had an appraised value of $894,000, was conveyed to the plaintiff's trustee, McGhie Land Title Company. The trust deed provided that upon the plaintiff's written request, the trustee could reconvey "all or any part" of the property.

The affidavit of John D. Fry, mortgage officer for the plaintiff, states that:

> Mr. and Mrs. Black requested that Utah Mortgage agree to release single lots from the trust deed upon payment of the sum of $5,200. This Utah Mortgage agreed to do.

The affidavit of Craig D. Anderson states that:

> Utah Mortgage agreed with the Blacks and Black Realty that it would give a release on individual lots upon payment of $5,200 per lot . . . the release price was later raised to $5,500.

It further appears that all of the lots were released in that manner and that the plaintiff executed a general release to the entire subdivision.

Thereafter, the plaintiff brought this action alleging that, after applying the total proceeds from the release of the lots, there remained a balance on defendants' note of $36,760.01.

The statutory provision which creates the "one-action rule," relied upon by the defendants, is Section 78-37-1, which provides that:

> There can be one action for the recovery of any debt or the enforcement of any right secured solely by mortgage upon real estate which action must be in accordance with the provisions of this chapter. Judgment shall be given adjudging the amount due, with costs and disbursements, and the sale of mortgaged property, or some part thereof, to satisfy said amount and accruing costs, and directing the sheriff to proceed and sell the same . . . .

(All emphasis herein added.)

In view of our conclusion that it is necessary that there be a trial of the dispute as to material facts, it is appropriate that we comment on certain principles concerning the application of that statute.

The purpose of the statute was to eliminate harassment of debtors and multiple litigation which sometimes occurred under the common-law rule which allowed a creditor to foreclose and sell the land, and to sue on the note. The statute limits the creditor to one remedy in exhausting his security before having recourse to the debtor for a deficiency. Consequently, if the creditor (plaintiff here) fails to comply with the statute in not applying the security to the defendants' obligation in accordance with their agreement, that would preclude its recovery of any deficiency against them.

We proceed upon the premise, accepted by the parties and the trial court, that the so-called "one-action rule" is also a "one-remedy rule"; and that when a creditor uses up the security which it was agreed would stand good for his debt, he may not look to the debtor personally for any deficiency. In any event, that principle would not apply when the security has been lost or disposed of without any fault or blameworthy conduct on the part of the creditor (plaintiff here). In such instance, an action may be brought upon the note without going through a fruitless procedure of foreclosure on non-existent security. However, if the security is lost or disposed of because of any failure or neglect of the creditor, he deprives himself both of the right to foreclose on the security and to seek a deficiency from the debtor.

It is further true that the creditor cannot waive the application of the statute without the consent of the debtor (defendants here) by releasing the mortgage for the purpose of bringing an action on the note. But it is also true that if the debtor (defendants here) requests or consents to the disposition of the security, and it does not satisfy his full debt, he is precluded from complaining about the disposition of the security, and is still liable for the obligation on his note.

The critical question here is whether, as defendants contend, the plaintiff had "sole discretion" as to whether, and for what amounts, it would release the lots; or, as the plaintiff contends, the defendants both agreed to and requested that the lots be released on payments of the amounts of $5,200, or later for $5,500 each, which did not aggregate enough to pay for the defendants' debt.

From the facts thus far revealed in the record by the submissions and averments of the parties, the dispute between them as to their mutual obligations and performance of their duties cannot be resolved with any degree of certainty. On remand, if it appears that the defendants are correct in their assertion that the plaintiff could "at its sole discretion," without let or hindrance from the defendants, either release the lots or not, or could itself require whatever lot release price it desired, then the plaintiff should be held responsible for permitting the security to be disposed of, and should not be able to look to the defendants for a deficiency. On the other hand, if it is determined to be the fact that the defendants requested and agreed that the lots be released, first for the $5,200 and later for the $5,500 each, they should not be heard to complain that the plaintiff acted in accordance with their agreement, and they should be held liable for remaining indebtedness on the note.

Inasmuch as there is dispute as to material facts, it is necessary that the summary judgment be vacated and that this case be remanded to the district court for further proceedings consistent with this opinion. The parties to bear their own costs.

MAUGHAN, WILKINS and STEWART, JJ., concur.

HALL, J., concurs in result.

NOTES

1. Five states currently have one form of action rules in effect: California, Idaho, Montana, Nevada and Utah.

2. Some states combine various forms of statutory protection for the mortgagor. California employs all three forms: anti-deficiency, found in California Code of Civil Procedure §§ 580b and 580d; the one form of action rule, California Code of Civil Procedure § 726; and the fair value statutes, found in California Code of Civil Procedure §§ 726 and 580a. North Dakota has a statute that allows three alternatives: foreclose without seeking a deficiency, foreclose and seek a deficiency, or sue for the difference between the debt and the fair value of the property without having first foreclosed. *See First State Bank v. Ihringer,* 217 N.W.2d 857 (N.D. 1974).

3. The one form of action rule provides the debtor with an election in the event the mortgagee sues first without seeking foreclosure. The mortgagor can either allow the suit to go to judgment, knowing that it will be a later bar to a foreclosure, or can defend the suit by forcing the mortgagee to foreclose first. If a power of sale foreclosure is used, then a later suit for money damages would be barred. *See* California Civil Procedure Code § 580d.

4. The problems attendant to using combined security of realty and personalty are demonstrated in *Walker v. Community Bank,* 10 Cal. 3d 729, 518 P.2d 329 (1974). It would appear that suit on the note would bar a subsequent foreclosure on the realty under

the one form of action rule. Likewise a prior foreclosure on the realty would bar a later suit. The only possible remedy would be a judicial action seeking foreclosure on both the realty and the personalty. This would appear to preclude for practical reasons using a non-judicial foreclosure when combined security is utilized.

5. For an interesting Utah case in which the court granted a deficiency judgment *see* *Bullington v. Mize,* 25 Utah 173, 478 P.2d 500 (1970). However, it is basically a conflict of laws case, since the property in question, and obviously the foreclosure, were in the state of Texas. What is interesting is the court's consideration of the public policy behind the anti-deficiency laws. The court held that while a deficiency judgment could not be obtained in Utah after the foreclosure sale of Utah land, it was not against the public policy of Utah to enforce the laws of Texas including the right to a deficiency judgment.

E. FAIR MARKET VALUE STATUTES

Some jurisdictions require that a deficiency can only be entered as the difference between the fair market value of the mortgaged property and the debt. This all but eliminates the problem of underbidding at a foreclosure sale. Without a fair value statute a mortgagee could bid less than the value of the property and obtain a judgment for the difference. The net effect of such underbidding is that the mortgagee is unjustly enriched. This, of course, assumes that the mortgagee is the sole bidder at the foreclosure sale, which is usually the case.

During the depression of the 1930s it was not uncommon for lenders to underbid the value of the property, take back the property, and at the same time obtain a judgment for the difference between their bid and the debt. If collectable, the judgment put into the lender's hands cash plus the property at a total value of more than the debt foreclosed. To stop this practice, state legislatures enacted statutes which either prevented deficiency judgments altogether or limited them by the fair market value rule.

Oklahoma Statutes, Title 12 (1960)

§ 686. Judgment in foreclosure suit — Sale of real estate — Lands in different counties — Application of proceeds — Attorney's fees and expenses, taxation of — Putting purchaser in possession — Deficiency judgments

In actions to enforce a mortgage, deed of trust, or other lien or charge, a personal judgment or judgment or judgments shall be rendered for the amount or amounts due as well to the plaintiff as other parties to the action having liens upon the mortgaged premises by mortgage or otherwise, with interest thereon, and for sale of the property charged and the application of the proceeds; or such application may be reserved for the future order of the court, and the court shall tax the costs, attorney's fees and expenses which may accrue in the action, and apportion the same among the parties according to their respective interests, to be collected on the order of sale or sales issued thereon; when the same mortgage embraces separate tracts of land situated in two or more counties, the sheriff of each county shall make sale of the lands situated in the county of which he is sheriff. No real estate shall be sold for the payment of any money or the performance of any contract or agreement in writing, in security for which it may have been pledged or assigned, except in pursuance of a judgment of a court of competent jurisdiction ordering such sale. The court may, in the order confirming a sale of land under order of sale on foreclosure or upon execution, award or order the issuance of a writ of assistance by the clerk of the court to the sheriff of the county where the land is situated, to place the purchaser in full possession of such land, and any resistance of the service of such writ of assistance shall constitute an indirect contempt of the process of such court, and if any person who has been removed from any lands by process of law or writ of assistance or who has removed from any lands pursuant to law or adjudication or direction of any court, tribunal or officer, afterwards, without authority of law, returns to settle or reside upon such land, he shall be guilty of an indirect contempt of court, and may be proceeded against and punished for such contempt. Notwithstanding the above provisions no judgment shall be enforced for any residue of the debt remaining unsatisfied as prescribed by this Act after the mortgaged property shall have been sold, except as herein provided. Simultaneously with the making of a motion for an order confirming the sale or in any event within ninety days after the date of the sale, the party to whom such residue shall be owing may make a motion in the action for leave to enter a deficiency judgment upon notice to the party against whom such judgment is sought or the attorney who shall have appeared for such party in such action. Such notice shall be served personally or in such other manner as the court may direct. Upon such motion the court, whether or not the respondent appears, shall determine, upon affidavit or otherwise as it shall direct, the fair and reasonable market value of the mortgaged premises as of the date of sale or such nearest earlier date as there shall have been any market value thereof and shall make an order directing the entry of a deficiency judgment. Such deficiency judgment shall be for an amount equal to the sum of the amount owing by the party liable as determined by the judgment with interest, plus costs and disbursements of the action plus the amount owing on all prior liens and encumbrances with interest, less the market value as determined by the court or the sale price of the property whichever shall be the higher. If no motion for a deficiency judgment shall be made as herein prescribed the proceeds of the sale regardless of amount shall be deemed to be in full satisfaction of the mortgage debt and no right to recover any deficiency in any action or proceeding shall exist.

In any action pending at the time this Act becomes effective or thereafter commenced, other than an action to foreclose a mortgage, to recover a judgment for any indebtedness secured by a mortgage on real property and which originated simultaneously with such mortgage and which is secured solely by such mortgage, against any person or corporation directly or indirectly or contingently liable therefor, any party against whom a money judgment is demanded, shall be entitled to set off the fair and reasonable market value of the mortgaged property less the amounts owing on prior liens and encumbrances. Provided that nothing in this Section shall limit or reduce any deficiency judgment in favor of or in behalf of the State for any debts, obligations or taxes due the State, now or hereafter.

Washington Revised Code (1961)

§ 61.12.060. Judgment — Order of sale — Satisfaction — Upset price

In rendering judgment of foreclosure, the court shall order the mortgaged premises, or so much thereof as may be necessary, to be sold to satisfy the mortgage and costs of the action. The payment of the mortgage debt, with interest and costs, at any time before sale, shall satisfy the judgment. The court, in ordering the sale, may in its discretion, take judicial notice of economic conditions, and after a proper hearing, fix a minimum or upset price to which the mortgaged premises must be bid or sold before confirmation of the sale.

The court may, upon application for the confirmation of a sale, if it has not theretofore fixed an upset price, conduct a hearing, establish the value of the property, and, as a condition to confirmation, require that the fair value of the property be credited upon the foreclosure judgement. If an upset price has been established, the plaintiff may be required to credit this amount upon the judgment as a condition to confirmation. If the fair value as found by the court, when applied to the mortgage debt, discharges it, no deficiency judgment shall be granted.

North Dakota Century Code (1976)

§ 32-19-03. Who subject to deficiency judgment

If the mortgage debt is secured by the obligation, or other evidence of debt, of any person other than the mortgagor, the plaintiff may make such other person a party to the action and the court may render judgment for the balance of the debt remaining unsatisfied after a sale of the mortgaged premises as against such other person and may enforce such judgment as in other cases by execution or other process. Nothing elsewhere contained in this chapter shall be construed to postpone or affect any remedies the creditor may have against any person personally liable for the debt, other than the mortgagor or purchaser and the successors in interest of either.

§ 32-19-04. What complaint shall state

In an action for the foreclosure or satisfaction of a mortgage, the complaint shall state whether any proceedings have been had at law or otherwise for the recovery of the debt secured by such mortgage, or any part thereof, and if there have been, whether any and what part thereof has been collected. The plaintiff shall also state in his complaint whether he will in a later and separate action demand judgment for any deficiency which may remain due to him after sale of the mortgaged premises against every party who is personally liable for the debt secured by the mortgage.

§ 32-19-05. When judgment at law obtained

If it appears that any judgment has been obtained in an action at law for the moneys demanded by the complaint, or any part thereof, no proceedings shall be had in the foreclosure action, unless an execution against the property of the defendant in such judgment has been issued and the sheriff shall have made return that the execution is unsatisfied in whole or in part and that the defendant has no property out of which to satisfy such execution.

§ 32-19-06. What judgment shall contain — Deficiency judgments and other suits prohibited in excess of amount by which debt exceeds fair value of mortgaged premises — Determination of fair value of mortgaged real property

In any action for the foreclosure of a real estate mortgage or the cancellation or the foreclosure of a land contract, the court shall have the power to render judgment for the amount found to be due at the time of the rendition of said judgment, and the costs of the action, and to order and decree a sale of the premises in such mortgage or contract described, or such part thereof as may be sufficient to pay the amount adjudged to be due and the costs of the action. The court shall have power to order and compel delivery of the possession of the premises to the purchaser at such sale, but in no case shall the possession of the premises so sold be delivered until after the expiration of one year from such sale, and the court shall direct, and the judgment shall provide, that during such one-year period the debtor or owner of the premises shall be entitled to the possession, rents, use, and benefit of the real property sold. The court under no circumstances shall have power to render a deficiency judgment for any sum whatever against the mortgagor or purchaser, or the successor in interest of either, except as hereinafter provided. Where a note or other obligation and a mortgage upon real property have been given to secure a debt contracted subsequent to July 1, 1951, and the sale of the mortgaged premises has failed to satisfy in full the sum adjudged to be due and the costs of the action, the plaintiff may, in a separate action, ask for a deficiency judgment, if he has so indicated in his complaint, against the party or parties personally liable for that part of the debt and costs of the action remaining unsatisfied after the sale of the mortgaged premises. Such separate action for a deficiency judgment must be brought within ninety days after the sale of the mortgaged premises. The court, in such separate action, may render a deficiency judgment against the party or parties personally liable, but such deficiency judgment shall not be in excess of the amount by which the sum adjudged to be due and the costs of the action exceed the fair value of the mortgaged premises. In case the mortgaged premises sell for less than the amount due and to become due on the mortgage debt and costs of sale, there shall be no presumption that such premises sold for their fair value. In all actions brought for a deficiency judgment and before any judgment can be rendered therein, the determination of the fair value of the mortgaged premises shall first be submitted to a jury at a regular term or to a jury impaneled for that purpose, and no deficiency judgment can be rendered against the party or parties personally liable unless the fair value of the mortgaged premises is determined by such jury to be less than the sum adjudged to be due and the costs of the action. Fifteen days' notice of the time and place when or where such fair value of the mortgaged premises shall be so determined shall, in all cases, be given, as the court may direct, to the party or parties against whom personal judgment is sought. At such time and place such party or parties may offer evidence to show the fair value of the mortgaged premises even though they may not have otherwise appeared in the action for a deficiency judgment. Any deficiency judgment so obtained shall be enforced by execution as provided by law, except that no execution shall be enforced after three years from the date of the rendition of such deficiency judgment. The mortgagee or vendor or the successor in interest of either shall not be permitted or authorized either before or after the rendition of a judgment for the foreclosure of a real estate mortgage or the cancellation or the foreclosure of a land contract, if such mortgage or contract was made after July 1, 1951, to bring any action in any court in this state for the recovery of any part of the debt secured by the mortgage or contract so foreclosed or canceled in excess of the amount by which such debt and the costs of the action exceed the fair value of the mortgaged premises. Such fair value shall be determined by a jury in the same manner as the fair value is determined in cases where a deficiency judgment is sought in an action to foreclose the mortgage and such judgment shall be enforced by execution as provided by law except that no such execution shall be enforced after three years after the date of the rendition of such judgment.

§ 32-19-07. Other suits prohibited

Neither before nor after the rendition of a judgment for the foreclosure of a real estate mortgage or for the cancellation or foreclosure of a land contract made between July 1, 1937, and July 1, 1951, shall the mortgagee or vendor, or the successor in interest of either, be authorized or permitted to bring any action in any court in this state for the recovery of any part of the debt secured by the mortgage or contract so foreclosed. It is the intent of this section that no deficiency judgment shall be rendered upon any note, mortgage, or contract given between July 1, 1937, and July 1, 1951, to secure the payment of money loaned upon real estate or to secure the purchase price of real estate, and in case of default the holder of a real estate mortgage or land contract shall be entitled only to a foreclosure of the mortgage or the cancellation or foreclosure of the contract. Except as otherwise provided in sections 32-19-04 and 32-19-06, neither before nor after the rendition of a judgment for the foreclosure of a real estate mortgage or for the cancellation or foreclosure of a land contract made after July 1, 1951, shall the mortgagee or vendor, or the successor in interest of either, be authorized or permitted to bring any action in any court in this state for the recovery of any part of the debt secured by the mortgage or contract so foreclosed. It is the intent of this section that no deficiency judgment shall be rendered upon any note, mortgage, or contract given after July 1, 1951, to secure the payment of money loaned upon real estate or to secure the purchase price of real estate, and in case of default the holder of a real estate mortgage or land contract shall be entitled only to a foreclosure of the mortgage or the cancellation or foreclosure of the contract except as provided by sections 32-19-04 and 32-19-06.

SIMSBURY BANK & TRUST CO. v. RAY CARLSON LUMBER CO.

Supreme Court of Connecticut
154 Conn. 216, 224 A.2d 544 (1966)

HOUSE, ASSOCIATE JUSTICE. This appeal arises out of a mortgage foreclosure action. On April 29, 1965, the plaintiff obtained a judgment of strict foreclosure on a second mortgage. The last law day was set as June 22, 1965. None of the defendants redeemed, and title to the mortgaged premises became absolute in the plaintiff on June 23, 1965. The plaintiff sold the premises on August 27, 1965, and after paying all prior encumbrances, taxes and costs, claimed that it had sustained a net loss of $14,413.68. On September 10, 1965, it filed a motion for deficiency judgment, although prior to this application neither it nor any other party to the foreclosure had moved for the appointment of appraisers pursuant to § 49-14 of the General Statutes.

Section 49-14 concerning the rendition of deficiency judgments provides that, upon the motion of any party to a foreclosure action, the court shall appoint three appraisers who shall, within ten days after the time limited for redemption has expired, appraise the property and report their appraisal to the clerk of the court, and that the court in which the action is pending may, by supplemental judgment, at any time within ninety days after the time limited for redemption has expired, if the appraisal and report thereof have been made, render judgment for the plaintiff for the difference between the appraisal and the plaintiff's claim.

In *People's Holding Co. v. Bray,* 118 Conn. 568, 173 A. 233, we had occasion to consider this statutory provision and held that a strict compliance with its provisions was a condition precedent to the entry of a deficiency judgment. "We incline to the view that the words of the statute are not ambiguous as to the time during which they require the appraisal to be made — the ten days after the expiration of the limitation to redeem — but, be that as it may, this construction is amply confirmed by the object of the provision and the practical considerations which commend it and indicate the legislative intent. The necessity of a definite rule of general application and, as well, an unvarying adherence to it, is manifest. Departures from it, if permitted, 'might lead to grave abuses.' *Congress Bank & Trust Co. v. Brockett,* 111 Conn. 490, 493, 150 Atl. 742, 743. We may not contenance and justify violations of the rule, although they be productive of no actual prejudice; the statute leaves no room for such indulgences. *Wilcox v. Bliss,* 116 Conn. 329, 333, 164 Atl. 659." Id., 573.

While, of necessity, admitting that "the court has consistently held that the appointment of three appraisers, under what is now § 49-14 of the General Statutes, was compulsory in a deficiency judgment action and must be strictly complied with; and, if there was no appointment of the appraisers according to the statute, there could be no deficiency judgment," the plaintiff nevertheless now contends that "such action should be optional."

Briefly stated, it is the plaintiff's contention that the 1957 action of the General Assembly in repealing, by Public Act No. 443, § 7191 of the 1949 Revision of the General Statutes and in enacting what is now § 49-1 of the 1958 Revision justifies, if it does not require, a reversal of the decision in *People's Holding Co. v. Bray,* supra. Prior to 1957, a foreclosing mortgagee could recover the difference between the value of the foreclosed property and the debt either by proceeding for a deficiency judgment under what is now § 49-14 or by a separate suit on the mortgage debt, note or obligation against anyone liable thereon who had been made a party to the foreclosure action. Rev.1949, § 7191; *Bugg v. Guilford-Chester Water Co.,* 141 Conn. 179, 182, 104 A.2d 543; *Cronin v. Gager-Crawford Co.,* 128 Conn. 688, 695, 25 A.2d 652; *Cion v. Schupack,* 102 Conn. 644, 649, 129 A. 854; *German v. Gallo,* 100 Conn. 708, 711, 124 A. 837; *Acampora v. Warner,* 91 Conn. 586, 588, 101 A. 332; 32 Conn.B.J. 200. Public Act No. 443 of the 1957 Session (now General Statutes, § 49-1) drastically changed the rights of a foreclosing mortgagee proceeding under the second alternative by prohibiting any further action on the mortgage obligation against a person liable thereon except against those upon whom in personam service could not have been made at the commencement of the foreclosure action. We find nothing, however, in either the language or the legislative history of § 49-1 to support the plaintiff's contention that the repeal of § 7191 and the enactment of § 49-1 render the appraisal provisions of § 49-14 optional rather than mandatory. The requirements of § 49-14 providing for deficiency judgments are explicit and unambiguous. Since there was no compliance with its requirements as to appraisal and report, the plaintiff was not entitled to, and the court properly denied its motion for, a deficiency judgment.

There is no error.

In this opinion the other judges concurred.

MORELAND v. MARWICH, LTD.

Colorado Court of Appeals

629 P.2d 1095 (1981)

VAN CISE, JUDGE. Defendant Marwich, Ltd., appeals an order setting aside public trustee deeds and dismissing Marwich's forcible entry and detainer action (FED) against plaintiffs Bobbie L. and Elizabeth K. Moreland. We reverse.

The Morelands executed two deeds of trust on their residential property to secure promissory notes payable to Platte Valley Bank (the bank). The notes became in default. In July 1979, the bank commenced foreclosure proceedings by filing with the defendant public trustee notices of election and demand for sale of the property and, pursuant to C.R.C.P. 120, filed with the district court motions for authorization for public trustees sales.

The Morelands filed timely responses to the motions, setting forth, as a defense, that the bank's action in initiating foreclosure was in violation of its agreement with them to refinance or to obtain for the Morelands from other lenders long-term financing in lieu of the present short-term loans held by the bank. At the hearing on August 16, 1979, the court refused to consider the defense raised in the responses, ruling that the only issues to be determined were whether the owners were in the military service and whether the debts were in default. Since there was no dispute that the money had not been paid and no claim of military service had been made, orders authorizing sale were entered. However, they were stayed for ten days to permit the Morelands to file an independent action if they so desired and, in such action, to ask the court to enjoin the sale.

The Morelands did not file a separate action at that time, and the public trustee sold the properties on September 12 to the bank for the amount owing on the notes, plus interest, costs, and attorney's fees, a total of $20,302.58. The owners did not redeem within the 75 day redemption period expiring November 26. Marwich, a junior lienholder, redeemed from the bank, paying the bank's purchase price plus accrued interest, and, on December 7, received public trustee's deeds to the property.

On December 12, Marwich initiated an FED proceeding in the county court against the Morelands to obtain possession of the property occupied by them as a residence. In response, the Morelands commenced the present action in the district court. The FED action was certified to the district court and the two cases were consolidated.

The plaintiffs' complaint raised a number of issues, but, because of a pre-trial stipulation, the only ones remaining for determination were whether they had been denied due process in the C.R.C.P. 120 proceedings and whether the amount bid for the property was unconscionably low, the property being stipulated to be worth $100,000, subject to a first deed of trust in the amount of about $5,000 that was not in default. The Morelands asked for the public trustee sale to be declared null and void, the redemption and the deeds to be set aside, and for an order granting the Morelands a reasonable time within which to cure or redeem.

After trial, the court, on March 17, 1980, found that the grounds claimed had been established and were sufficient to warrant the exercise of the court's equity jurisdiction to provide a reasonable extension of the period of redemption. *See Arnold v. Gebhardt,* Colo.App., 604 P.2d 1192 (1979). It reasoned that the grant of that relief would not affect (1) the public trustee, (2) the bank, since it had been fully paid, or (3) Marwich, since on redemption it would receive back its full payment with statutory interest. What would be affected is Marwich's potential for a large unearned windfall profit arising from the disparity between what Marwich paid and the actual value of the property. The court then granted the Morelands 30 days from the date its order became a final judgment within which to redeem. On April 8, after the Morelands had deposited the redemption amount with the public trustee, the court directed the redemption money to be paid over to Marwich, dismissed the FED action, and set aside the public trustee deeds. Marwich appeals the March 17 and April 8 orders.

I

In the C.R.C.P. 120 hearing on the bank's motions for orders authorizing sale, the court should have allowed the Morelands to be heard on the issue raised in their responses. This went to the question of whether, under the circumstances, there was any default and, therefore, was within the scope of inquiry specified in C.R.C.P. 120(d). Had the court, without more, ordered the sale, it would have been a denial of due process as contended by the Morelands and held by the trial court in the instant case (through a different judge). *See Valley Development at Vail, Inc. v. Warder,* 192 Colo. 316, 557 P.2d 1180 (1976); *Princeville Corp. v. Brooks,* 188 Colo. 37, 533 P.2d 916 (1975).

However, the court in the C.R.C.P. 120 hearing granted the Morelands a ten-day stay of execution to permit them to file an independent action if they wished to do so. Also, the court indicated it would listen, at that time, if they wished to ask for a restraining order extending it further. In view of this, we see no denial of due process. The Morelands were given the opportunity to be heard on their contention before the sale, but did not take advantage of it.

II

At least 60 days prior to the expiration of the redemption period, the Morelands were informed of the proper amount required to redeem the property from the sale. They did not redeem.

Only after the sale had been held, the redemption period had expired, and the public trustee deeds had been issued, and after service of summons in the FED action brought by the grantees of those deeds, did the Morelands take action to protect their property. There was no claim of fraud or irregularity in connection with the foreclosure proceedings. Their main contention for relief was that the property, bid in at sale for the amount owing thereon, was worth three times as much as the price paid.

There is nothing improper in a foreclosing creditor bidding in the amount of its debt. *Rowe v. Tucker,* 38 Colo.App. 532, 560 P.2d 843 (1977). And, when he is not seeking a deficiency judgment, and bids the full amount of the debt, he is not required to bid the fair market value of the property. *Hawthorne v. Assured Premiums Corp.,* 472 P.2d 715 (Colo.App.1970) (not selected for official publication). *Cf. Chew v. Acacia Mutual Life Insurance Co.,* 165 Colo. 43, 437 P.2d 339 (1968); *Handy v. Rogers,* 143 Colo. 1, 351 P.2d 819 (1960).

In considering the exercise of equity jurisdiction, the court may take into account a disparity between the market value and the purchase price paid at the foreclosure sale. However, that element is not controlling and, standing alone, is not sufficient cause for setting aside a sale. *Chew v. Acacia Mutual Life Insurance Co., supra; Arnold v. Gebhardt, supra.* Equity aids one who has been vigilant, not one who has slept on his rights. *People v. District Court,* 87 Colo.

316, 287 P. 849 (1930). *See Fitzwater v. Norcross,* 95 Colo. 527, 37 P.2d 522 (1934). Under the circumstances here, where the Morelands could have redeemed but did not, where the bid was for the full amount due to the creditor, and where no deficiency judgment was sought, there was no justification for the additional relief granted.

The orders are reversed and the cause is remanded with directions (1) to dismiss the Morelands' complaint, (2) to order the return to the Morelands of all the money previously paid by them to redeem the property from Marwich, (3) to enter an order granting Marwich possession as sought in the FED action, and (4) to consider and rule on any claim of Marwich against the Morelands for use and occupancy of the subject property.

PIERCE and KELLY, JJ., concur.

NOTE

There is nothing improper in a foreclosing mortgagee entering a "paper bid" for the entire balance of the debt, notwithstanding that the debt is less than the fair market value of the property. So long as a deficiency judgment is not sought and the full amount of the debt is bid, the mortgagee is not required to bid the fair market value. *See Moreland v. Marwich, Ltd.,* 629 P.2d 1095 (Colo. App. 1981).

Chapter 8

TRANSFERS

> Put not your trust in money, but put your money in trust.
>
> O.W. Holmes, *The Autocrat of the Breakfast Table*

In today's economy it is necessary that the lender be able to transfer the right to collect the debt, if for no other reason than to recoup some of the funds in its portfolio so that the money can be loaned again at a higher interest rate. Institutional lenders indulge in transfers for this purpose and in fact large organizations exist for the sole purpose of creating a market to buy portions of lenders' portfolios.[1] This area is treated in Chapter 9 in the section which deals with the Federal National Mortgage Association, the Government National Mortgage Association and the Federal Home Loan Mortgage Corporation. These organizations, commonly known as "Fanny May," "Ginnie May," and "Freddie Mac" make up a large part of the secondary market for institutional lenders. That such transactions which occur between lenders and these three are vital to the mortgage industry is unquestionable.

One does not make a monthly trip to make one's home mortgage payment to ascertain whether the savings and loan has sold the note to Fanny May. However, for less institutionalised transactions such a trip might be necessary. If a private lender sells the note, presumably at a discount in order to get immediate cash, the borrower could conceivably pay the wrong person. This is the principal area of concern for borrowers in the area of transfers by lenders.

Likewise, the status of the borrower's liability is of concern to lenders after the borrower transfers the property that is subject to the mortgage. It is primarily with these two areas of concern that this chapter deals.

A. TRANSFERS BY THE MORTGAGEE

Commercial necessity dictates that lenders have the ability to transfer the right to payment on a mortgage note. How this transfer occurs is of some importance, for it may affect the borrower's liability for paying more than one person. First, it is important to remember that a mortgage cannot exist without a debt or obligation; a note can exist without a mortgage but a mortgage cannot exist without an underlying debt or obligation.[2] If a lender wishes to transfer the mortgage and its underlying debt to a person for immediate cash it can be accomplished by a simple assignment of the note. The mortgage is said to follow the debt.[3] However, the converse will not be effective. An attempt to assign the mortgage without also assigning the debt will be a nullity; the mortgage could not exist without the debt so the attempted transfer is void. It is also possible for a lender in some states to transfer its rights by a transfer or conveyance of the lender's interest in the subject real property. However, such a conveyance would

---

[1] *See* Chapter 9, *infra,* at page 409.

[2] *See* Tyler v. Wright, *supra,* at page 4.

[3] At common law the mortgage did not follow the transfer of a debt. However, today the transfer of a negotiable instrument secured by a mortgage does also affect a transfer of the mortgage. Jones on Mortgages § 834, p. 693 (3d ed. 1882). Some states have made this the law by statute. *See* Cal. Civ. Code § 2936.

be of no effect in lien theory states and actually is of limited use in title theory states.[4]

What is critical from the borrower's perspective is that ultimately payment is made to the correct person or entity so that when the principal balance is paid in full, the borrower can expect to receive the note marked "paid" and have the mortgage released. If the lender has transferred the note and mortgage to another and the borrower pays the original lender, the borrower may have to pay the lender's assignee in order to avoid suit and to have the mortgage released from the land. Naturally, if the borrower pays the original lender who is not entitled to be paid, having sold the note, the borrower has a right to sue the original lender for the return of the improper payment. This right becomes academic if the original lender is insolvent, has fled the jurisdiction, or is incarcerated presumably for similar activities. Therefore, for practical purposes, if the borrower pays the wrong person first, the borrower will likely have to pay the right person also. The law appears very harsh in this area. The basic rule is that borrowers must ascertain that they are paying the right person; otherwise, the borrower pays at his peril.[5]

---

[4] There is a split of authority in title theory states as to whether transfer of an interest in the land will transfer the mortgagee's security interest. In lien states it is universally held to be an ineffective attempt at transferring the mortgage. However, if a mortgage is disguised in a form such as a deed absolute then conveyance of the land will transfer the "mortgagee's" interest. *See generally* Osborne, Mortgages § 225, p. 444 (2d ed. 1970).

[5] American Law of Property § 16.109 (1952). *See also* Jones on Mortgages § 956 (3d ed. 1882).

DOCUMENT NO.

ASSIGNMENT OF MORTGAGE
STATE OF WISCONSIN—FORM 43

THIS SPACE RESERVED FOR RECORDING DATA

For and in consideration of..
....Dollars,

to.................... in hand paid, ...

of..., County of......................................,

State of....................................., do.......... hereby grant, bargain, sell,
assign, transfer, convey and set over unto..

a certain Indenture of Mortgage, executed by...

of..., County of......................................,

State of Wisconsin, and dated the.................... day of.., A. D., 19.........

to ....

RETURN TO

on certain lands in the County of.. and State of Wisconsin, together with
the.. there in referred to and all the right, title and interest conveyed by said
Mortgage, in and to said lands, which Mortgage was duly recorded in the office of the Register of Deeds in and for
the County of.., in the State of Wisconsin, on the.................................. day
of.................................., A. D., 19........, at.................... o'clock .... M., in Volume .... of
Mortgages, on page...................................., Document No. ....

To have and to hold the said.. and Mortgage, and the debt
thereby secured, and all right, title and interest conveyed by said Mortgage, in and to the lands therein described,
to the said ....

heirs, executors, administrators and assigns forever, for.................... and their use and benefit.

And.................... hereby covenant..... that there is now owing and unpaid on the said..................................
and Mortgage, as principal, a sum not less than..Dollars,
and also interest..
and that.................... ha.......... good right to assign the same.

In Witness Whereof, ... have hereunto set.................... hand..... and seal.... this................................
day of...................................., A. D., 19..........

....(SEAL)

SIGNED AND SEALED IN PRESENCE OF

....(SEAL)

....(SEAL)

....(SEAL)

STATE OF WISCONSIN } ss.
.... County.

Personally came before me, this.................... day of...................................., A. D., 19........,
the above named ....

to me known to be the person...... who executed the foregoing instrument and acknowledged the same.

THIS INSTRUMENT WAS DRAFTED BY

NOTARY
SEAL

Notary Public, ... County, Wis.

My commission (expires) (is)....................................

(Section 59.51 (1) of the Wisconsin Statutes provides that all instruments to be recorded shall have plainly printed or typewritten thereon
the names of the grantors, grantees, witnesses and notary. Section 59.513 similarly requires that the name of the person who, or governmental agency which, drafted such instrument, shall be printed, typewritten, stamped or written thereon in a legible manner.)

ASSIGNMENT OF REAL ESTATE MORTGAGE   STATE OF WISCONSIN   Wisconsin Legal Blank Company
FORM No. 43   Milwaukee, Wis. (Job 31011)

Illustration 6
Assignment of Mortgage

1. PAYMENT TO THE ASSIGNOR

CULBERTSON STATE BANK v. DAHL

Supreme Court of Montana
617 P.2d 1295 (1980)

HASWELL, CHIEF JUSTICE. Plaintiff-respondent, Culbertson State Bank (Bank) brought this action to foreclose a real estate mortgage in the Richland County District Court. The District Court, sitting without a jury, entered judgment in favor of the Bank and a decree of foreclosure, and Harold and Geneva Dahl appealed.

Harold and Geneva Dahl, as makers, executed a $20,000 promissory note to Maurice Sythe, the payee, on February 14, 1974. The Dahls also executed a real estate mortgage in Sythe's favor which was recorded on the same date. The terms of the note specify that it is to be paid in equal annual installments of $4,000 plus 7% interest, payments to commence on February 14, 1975. The note also designates the Culbertson State Bank as the place where payment is to be made. The note was placed in an escrow account with the Bank. The escrow account was opened by Maurice Sythe on May 10, 1974.

Maurice Sythe obtained a $10,000 note from the Bank on November 6, 1974. The note stated that the Bank's security consisted of an "Assignment of Harold Dahl Note." Consistent with this provision, the "Dahl note" was endorsed by Sythe, payable to the Bank.

On March 27, 1975, Bank notified Harold Dahl that the February 14, 1975, payment had not been received on the promissory note held in escrow. Mr. Dahl made a payment of $5,572.50 ($4,000 on the principal) on March 31, 1975, which was to be applied to the note held in escrow. He testified that on March 31, 1975, he told Alan Peterson, Bank's executive vice-president, that he had already paid the $20,000 owing to Sythe. Peterson testified that Dahl had said something about Sythe owing him money but that Dahl had not said anything concerning a belief that nothing was owed to the Bank or Sythe.

$5,000 on principal and $382.64 in interest was credited to Sythe's $10,000 note on March 31, 1975. Sythe obtained a $5,000 note from Bank on April 23, 1975, at which time he told Alan Peterson that he did not owe Harold Dahl any money. Bank took a written assignment of the Dahl real estate mortgage on this date. The assignment was recorded on January 27, 1976. Bank sent a letter to Harold Dahl on April 23, 1975, informing him that a written assignment of the mortgage was taken. Another letter was sent on January 26, 1976, which informed Dahl that the assignment had been recorded and that a payment was due February 14, 1976.

Bank did not receive any payments from Maurice Sythe on his two $5,000 notes. Harold Dahl also refused to make any further payments on the note which had been assigned to the Bank. The Bank filed a complaint on October 3, 1977, against Harold and Geneva Dahl and Maurice Sythe. Bank was never able to make service of process upon Maurice Sythe. This action came on for trial against Harold and Geneva Dahl on December 19, 1979.

Harold Dahl's defense at trial was that he had paid the note and was discharged from liability. He attempted to show that payments on the $20,000 promissory note had been made directly to Maurice Sythe. He introduced several exhibits in this regard including: a check to Sythe for $9,520 dated March 4, 1975; and $11,800 promissory note from Sythe to himself dated January 1, 1975; and an unnegotiated check dated April 23, 1975, made out by himself and allegedly signed by Sythe for $5,572.50, containing a notation that it was a refund of the payment made by Dahl.

The appellant expended considerable effort at trial in attempting to prove that direct payments had been made to Maurice Sythe, and the respondent devoted a similar effort in attempting to rebut these allegations.

The District Court found that: the $20,000 note was executed on February 14, 1974; a real estate mortgage was executed and recorded on the same date; one of the terms of the promissory note which was incorporated in the mortgage specified the place of payment as the Culbertson State Bank; Maurice Sythe endorsed the promissory note payable to the Bank and delivered it to the Bank on May 10, 1974; the Bank, for the consideration of the assignment of the note and delivery of the assignment of the mortgage, loaned Maurice Sythe $10,000 on November 6, 1974 and $5,000 on April 23, 1975; the Bank is the lawful "owner and holder" of all the notes and the mortgage; Harold and Geneva Dahl have paid only $4,000 on the note assigned to the Bank; $11,000 with interest from March 31, 1975 is now due and owing from Harold and Geneva Dahl to the Bank; and the Bank has incurred attorney fees in enforcing the collection of the note. The District Court concluded that all of the terms and conditions of the note had been broken by the makers and that the Bank was entitled to have the mortgage enforced and foreclosed and to receive attorney fees.

On appeal, the appellant contends that . . . there is insufficient evidence to support the judgment.

With regard to appellant's contention that there is insufficient evidence to support the judgment, we find the Uniform Commercial Code controlling. The District Court properly found that the Bank was a "holder" of the promissory note, since it was in possession of the note which was endorsed by Maurice Sythe. Section 30-1-201(20), MCA. As a result of Bank's status as a "holder" and its production of the instrument, it is entitled to recover unless the defendant establishes a defense. Section 30-3-307(2), MCA.

As previously stated, appellant's sole defense was his assertion that liability had been discharged by payments allegedly made directly to Maurice Sythe. However, the affirmative defense of payment only discharges the maker's liability on the instrument under section 30-3-603, MCA, if payment is made to the "holder." The appellant never attempted to prove that payment was made to the "holder." He instead attempted to prove that payments were made to Maurice Sythe, the original payee. Thus, even had the court determined that payments had been made to Sythe, the appellant would not have been discharged from liability on the instrument. In short, the appellant failed to establish a valid defense and the Bank was entitled to recover under section 30-3-307(2), MCA.

Since the Bank is the holder of the note and a valid assignee of the mortgage which secures the note, it is entitled to a decree of foreclosure to the extent of the debt due and owing on the date of commencement.

DALY, HARRISON, SHEA and SHEEHY, JJ., concur.

PHILLIPS v. LATHAM

Court of Civil Appeals of Texas
523 S.W.2d 19 (1975)

GUITTARD, JUSTICE. This suit arose out of an allegedly wrongful trustee's sale of a residence owned and occupied by plaintiffs C. T. Latham and wife. They sued C. R. Smith (or Carolyn R. Smith), who had held a second-lien note secured by the deed of trust under which the property was sold, Charles Ben Howell, an attorney, who acted as substitute trustee, and Durwood Phillips, who bought the property at the sale. Plaintiffs' petition includes a count in trespass to try title and also a count for actual and exemplary damages for "illness and many hours of worry," and loss of time from their work, caused by an alleged conspiracy between the defendants to deprive plaintiffs of their home. After a jury trial, judgment was rendered in plaintiffs' favor against all defendants for title to the property, and against defendants Phillips and Howell for damages, and these defendants appeal.

We hold that the judgment for title was correct, but that the recovery of damages is without support in the evidence.

Title

Defendant Phillips asserts that he purchased the property at a valid trustee's sale on September 2, 1969. Alternatively, he claims under a second trustee's sale on March 2, 1971. Plaintiffs contend that neither of these sales passed title to the property because the indebtedness was not in default when either sale was made. We conclude that the verdict establishes that the indebtedness was not in default at the time of either sale.

The verdict must be construed in the light of the evidence. The promissory note in question was payable in twenty-dollar installments, due on the twentieth day of each month. C. R. Smith acquired the note in June 1969. Shortly afterward, defendant Howell, acting for her, wrote plaintiffs a letter notifying them of her acquisition of the note and advising: "Payments may be made by personal check as long as a valid check is actually received before the due date." The letter states further: "[P]ayment must be in the hands of the undersigned owner before the due date." Howell's law-office address appears on the letter, apparently as the address to which payments should be sent.

Default in payment of the monthly installments was a sharply contested issue. Admittedly, the installment due June 20, 1969, was duly received and acknowledged. Howell testified that no payments were received after that time. Plaintiffs testified that they mailed the checks every month to C. R. Smith at the address given. Although the court's charge did not expressly submit the issue of "default," the jury found in response to issues submitted that after plaintiffs were advised that C. R. Smith has acquired title to the second-lien note, plaintiffs mailed twenty-dollar checks to C. R. Smith for twenty-one months beginning July 20, 1969, on or before the due date of each installment, and that if each of the checks had been presented to the bank monthly in due course of business, all would have been paid. The last of the twenty-one monthly payments so found by the jury would have been on March 20, 1971. Under these circumstances, the jury's findings established that no default occurred because of failure to pay any of the monthly installments due before the dates of either the trustee's sale on September 2, 1969, or the sale on March 2, 1971.

Defendant Phillips contends that even though the verdict may establish that the monthly payments were not in default at the time of the first trustee's sale in September 1969, it does not establish that all payments were properly made before the second trustee's sale in March 1971. He argues that after September 1969, all payments were made to the wrong party because, even if the first sale was void, it nevertheless operated as an equitable assignment to him of the note and lien.

This argument is without merit because plaintiffs had no notice that anyone other than C. R. Smith was the holder of the note. The jury found, on sufficient evidence, that the first notice to plaintiffs that the property had been sold to Phillips was after the second trustee's sale, when they received a notice to vacate preliminary to a forcible detainer suit, which Phillips later filed. Payment to the original creditor is effective as against an assignee if made in good faith, without notice of the assignment. *Olshan Lumber Co. v. Bullard,* 395 S.W.2d 670, 672 (Tex.Civ.App., Houston 1965, no writ).

. . . .

[T]he cause is remanded with instructions in accordance with the procedure prescribed in *Jasper State Bank v. Braswell,* 130 Tex. 549, 111 S.W.2d 1079, 1086 (1938). . . .

Reversed and remanded with instructions.

NOTES

1. The general rule is that the mortgagor pays at his peril and must bear the responsibility for ascertaining that the person to whom payment is made is the correct person. If the mortgagor pays the original mortgagee-assignor in error, the mortgagor will likely end up paying twice. It will be small consolation that there is a cause of action against the mortgagee-assignor if that person has become insolvent or fled the jurisdiction.

2. "Where a negotiable instrument is secured by a mortgage, the latter will not be discharged by payment to the record holder if as a matter of fact the note and mortgage has already been transferred to a bona fide holder for value before maturity, even though no assignment has been recorded. Such is the general rule by the very definite weight of authority. This flows from the general rule that in such cases the mortgage follows the rules applicable to the negotiable instrument it secures. Nor will the result be different if the mortgagor asked for the note and was given a plausible but false explanation for its nonproduction. The risk is absolute." 4 AMERICAN LAW OF PROPERTY § 16.117 (1952).

3. This rule came about at a time when most mortgages required interest-only payment for a short term, with the entire principal due in what would today be called a "balloon" payment. In those circumstances it would be reasonable for a borrower to ask for production of the note and mortgage at the time the one principal payment was due. How feasible would it be with today's amortized mortgages for the borrower to ask for production of the loan documents each time a principal payment became due?

2. MERGER

In a world where commercial necessity dictates that transfers be freely accomplished there is always the possibility that in doing so the mortgage may be affected or even eliminated. The concept of merger is simple: if the same person owns both the land subject to the mortgage and the mortgage itself, the two rights (or collection of rights) merge into one. The land owner would then own the land free and clear of the mortgage which has disappeared as a result of the merger. However, as we shall see, it is not always that simple.

HARRIS v. ALASKA TITLE GUARANTY CO.

Supreme Court of Alaska
510 P.2d 501 (1973)

ERWIN, JUSTICE. On July 16, 1961, Allen conveyed property by warranty deed to Jackson. Concurrently, a deed of trust was executed by Jackson as trustor, Alaska Title Guaranty Company as trustee, and Allen as beneficiary.

On August 16, 1963, Jackson conveyed her interest in the property to Bradley by warranty deed dated August 16, 1963. Concurrently, a deed of trust was executed by Bradley as trustor, Alaska Title Guaranty Company as trustee, and

Jackson as beneficiary. The Jackson deed of trust was specifically made subject to the Allen deed of trust, and the underlying obligation was, pursuant to the agreement between Jackson and Bradley, assumed by Bradley. The debt secured by the Allen deed of trust was $15,500.00. The debt secured by the Jackson deed of trust was $2,757.42.

On November 29, 1964, Bradley executed a deed of trust conveying the same property, subject to the Allen and Jackson deeds of trust, to Alaska Title Guaranty Company as Trustee and Harris as beneficiary to secure performance of an agreement.

Sometime in 1967, Bradley became delinquent in his payments to Allen and Jackson. Jackson wished to keep the Allen payments current, but she was advised that any payments she made to Allen on behalf of Bradley would not be secured by her (Jackson) deed of trust. On the advice of the title company, and unaware of the existence of the Harris deed of trust due to an error in preparing the title report, she accepted a new deed of trust from Bradley securing the entire amount ($15,168.88) then owed by Bradley to her and Allen. The new deed of trust and a reconveyance under the original Jackson deed of trust were recorded on February 9, 1967.

In the spring of 1967, 3000 Spenard Corporation became interested in acquiring the property. The corporation agreed to pay $25,500 for the property, provided Bradley could convey clear title. A title search disclosed the Allen, Jackson and Harris trust deeds. Contact with the encumbrancers indicated that the $25,500 would be sufficient to enable Bradley to secure releases of the trust deed and convey clear title. Accordingly the corporation deposited that amount in escrow with the title company and Bradley conveyed the property to 3000 Spenard Corporation.

Harris, however, refused to authorize the reconveyance of his deed of trust. On August 8, 1967, the title company then purchased the Allen and Jackson trust deeds for the purpose of clearing title by foreclosure using the 3000 Spenard Corporation's deposit to do so. Allen and Jackson executed assignments of their interests to 3000 Spenard Corporation. On October 10, 1967, the corporation reassigned the Allen and Jackson trust deeds to the title company.

Bradley owed the title company, as assignee of Allen and Jackson, a total of $15,509.87, plus interest from July 17, 1967. However, only $12,613.10 of the $15,509.87 was attributable to the Allen deed of trust while the balance was from the Jackson deed of trust. On December 22, 1967, the company recorded a notice of default. The notice declared that the Allen deed of trust was in default and that $15,509.87 plus interest was then owing on it.

The trustee's sale was held, pursuant to the notice of default and notice of sale, on March 28, 1968, at 10:15 a. m. Harris did not attend and sent no representative. The title company was the highest bidder and purchased the property for an offset bid of $13,649.66. The property was conveyed to the title company by trustee's deed on April 2, 1968. On the same date, the title company conveyed the property to 3000 Spenard Corporation.

Five days prior to the sale Harris, through his attorney, sent a letter to the title company's attorney. The letter expressed the opinion that the notice could not conceivably state the correct amount of the obligation and that, in any event, the deed of trust to be foreclosed may have been extinguished as a consequence of merger when the Allen and Jackson deeds of trust were transferred to 3000 Spenard Corporation. The letter asked that the March 28th sale be postponed. The title company did not agree.

Harris initiated an action on March 27, 1968 praying for judgment declaring that the Allen deed of trust was "extinct, void and an annullity" and that his deed of trust was "a first deed of trust". He also asked that the company be "enjoined from continuing" the sale scheduled for the next day.

An order enjoining the company from further proceedings until the date of hearing was signed by the court. On April 16, 1968, the judge declined to issue a preliminary injunction thus permitting the title company to proceed with the sale.

The title company filed its motion for summary judgment on June 18, 1971. Pursuant to notice, the motion was heard on June 28th. Harris filed no opposition and did not appear. The court took argument and granted the motion.

On July 8, 1971, Harris moved for relief from judgment. His motion was supported by counsel's affidavit explaining Harris' failure to oppose the summary judgment motion and a memorandum detailing substantive objections to summary judgment. Harris submitted no affidavit or other evidence to controvert the showing made by the title company. By reply the title company joined issue on Harris' substantive arguments. The motion was heard on July 27th on the merits of Harris' opposition to judgment. The court again granted the title company's motion for judgment. Judgment dismissing the complaint with prejudice and awarding costs to the title company was entered on August 2, 1971.

In attacking the summary judgment below, Harris raises three major issues:

a. In a complex case which turns upon questions of motivation and intent, summary judgment is inappropriate.

b. The doctrine of merger of estates should have been applied in this instance.

. . . .

Since the first two issues are closely inter-related in this particular case, they will be discussed together.

Generally, the question of intent is essentially one of credibility. The United States Supreme Court has recognized this and urged that summary judgment be used sparingly where intent is the main issue.

[W]here motive and intent play leading roles, the proof is largely in the hands of the alleged conspirators, and hostile witnesses thicken the plot. It is only when the witnesses are present and subject to cross-examination that their credibility and the weight to be given their testimony can be appraised. Trial by affidavit is no substitute for trial by jury. . . .

As recently as 1971, this court said, "The most difficult determinations lie in the area of credibility. The question of when summary judgment should be denied because of credibility is difficult to determine."

Harris is quite correct when he states that the question of merger inevitably involves the issue of intent. The doctrine of merger "is frequently applied to mortgages, but generally only when it accords with the actual or presumed intention of the parties."

The mere fact that there are issues of credibility, does not preclude summary judgment. In *Braund,* this court said that:

the party seeking the judgment must not only prove his own case but also disprove the affirmative defenses of his opponent . . . . [But t]he respondent must present *factual* material to avoid summary judgment, and he may not rely on general allegations. 486 P.2d at 54 n.5 (emphasis added.)

The title company offered proof before the court below that there was never any intention of a merger by initial transfer of the Allen and Jackson deeds of trust to 3000 Spenard Corporation. Harris, on the other hand, offered nothing more than general allegations. Given this, it does not seem unreasonable for the superior court to find that no triable issue of fact existed.

However, even if this court were to take the position that there was an issue of fact which should have gone to trial, the resulting error of the superior court in granting summary judgment is rendered harmless because, as a matter of *law,* "[t]he presence of an intermediate estate [i. e. the Harris deed of trust] prevents a merger." As one court has put it:

> Equity will not declare a merger under circumstances which will give the holder of an intervening incumbrance [sic] a greater lien and priority than he had.

On the facts presented to the superior court, we agree there was no merger of estates, and that summary judgment was properly entered.

. . . .

The decision of the trial court is hereby affirmed.

FITZGERALD, J., not participating.

NOTE

Harris v. Alaska Title Guaranty Co., supra, appears to make merger a matter of the intent of the parties. However, it is possible for merger to occur without the parties having any intent to have such a result. In *Cook v. American States Insurance Co.,* 275 N.E.2d 832 (Ind. 1971), an insurance company paid a fire loss by paying the lender who held the mortgage on the fire-damaged property in exchange for an assignment of the mortgage rights held by the lender. The original mortgagor had transferred title to the property to a third person. That third person executed a quitclaim deed in favor of the insurance company in return for a dismissal of its suit on the debt. The court later held that acceptance of the quitclaim deed by the insurance company created a merger that barred subsequent suit against the original mortgagor-maker of the note. Justice Sullivan in a concurring opinion disagrees with the majority, taking the position that merger requires the intent of the parties, either express or implied. He further states: "[I]f a merger would be disadvantageous to the party acquiring both interests, then no merger will take place." 275 N.E.2d 832, 844 (Ind. 1971).

B. TRANSFERS BY THE MORTGAGOR

If one assumes in real property that the greatest of all goods is good and marketable title, then it is imperative that landowners be able to freely alienate their lands with as little restriction as possible. In fact, any restriction on one's right to alienate one's property is repugnant to the concept of fee simple absolute.[6] In Chapter 4 we dealt with the problems of the "due-on sale" clause and its restricting effect on one's right to alienate one's property. That portion could have easily been included in this chapter as it deals with transfers, or attempted transfers, by the mortgagor. A mortgagee's ability to restrict a mortgagor's right to transfer the subject property is one of the two principal problems in the area of transfers by the mortgagor.

The other problem which gives rise to litigation is the status of liability of both the mortgagor and his transferee. Whether the mortgagor remains liable after

---

[6] Since the passage of the Statute Quia Emptores in 1290 A.D., the concept of fee simple absolute includes the right to freely alienate one's lands. Any rule limiting the right to such free alienation is contrary to the concept of fee simple absolute. *See* Coast Bank v. Minderhout, *supra,* at page 38.

the transfer is of concern to the lender and borrower alike. Whether the mortgagor's transferee becomes liable, either also or instead of the mortgagor, is of importance to all the parties in such a transaction.

1. CONSENT OF THE MORTGAGEE

SILVER v. ROCHESTER SAVINGS BANK

New York Supreme Court, Appellate Division
73 A.D. 81, 424 N.Y.S.2d 945 (1980)

WITMER, JUSTICE. This appeal turns on the right of a lending institute to withhold its consent to the sale of real property on which it holds a mortgage lien and to declare it due unless the purchaser agrees to pay an increased rate of interest on the unpaid balance of the mortgage. No appellate authority in New York on this subject has come to our attention; but in several other States the problem has been presented, with divergent results. Because of the special facts in this case we do not need to explore all the ramifications of this subject, but we shall advert to some of them.

In 1973 plaintiff owned unimproved real property in the Town of Sweden, Monroe County and desired to sell it. Defendant, Rochester Savings Bank (the bank), wished to establish a branch bank on the site; but for its own financial reasons it preferred to rent rather than to own such facility. It entered into an agreement with plaintiff wherein she granted to the bank an option to lease the property for 20 years for use as a branch bank and plaintiff agreed to (and did) construct on the property a building in accordance with plans furnished by the bank, aided by a loan made to her by the bank. The loan was made payable over the 20-year period, with monthly payments to be made by plaintiff from monthly rents to be paid to her by defendant in an amount sufficient to cover all costs of construction together wtih an amount to allow plaintiff a reasonable return on the value of her land, plus 8½% interest per annum payable to the bank on the mortgage. The total principal amount was ultimately fixed at $191,000, and plaintiff's monthly payment thereon to the bank was fixed at $1469 for the 20-year period. In return, the bank agreed to pay to plaintiff a net-net rent [1] of $2304.16 per month for 20 years, with the right to renew the lease for an additional 10 years at the rental of $2649.41 per month; and the bank was given the right of first refusal to purchase the property in case another party should offer to buy it. At the end of the lease the bank could buy the land and building for the sum of $85,000 above the construction costs.

The building was completed and the bank entered and still occupies it. In 1979 plaintiff received an offer for the property which the bank chose not to meet. The offer was conditioned on the buyer being permitted by the bank to assume the mortgage without an increase in the interest rate. The bank refused to agree to such terms, although it acknowledged that the proposed buyer's credit is impeccable and better than plaintiff's. The bank demanded that the rate of interest on the mortgage be increased 2% per annum, and plaintiff's buyer refused to complete the purchase on that basis unless the bank would agree to increase its monthly rental payments by an amount sufficient to repay the 2% increase in the mortgage interest rate. The bank declined to do that and stated that it would declare the unpaid balance of the mortgage due and payable if the plaintiff sold the property to such purchaser without the latter agreeing to increase the interest rate to 10.5% per annum.

---

[1] The bank also agreed to pay the taxes, insurance and maintenance expenses of the property.

The mortgage between plaintiff and defendant provided (¶ 13) that "[s]hould Mortgagor transfer title to mortgaged premises . . . without first obtaining the written consent of Mortgagee . . . , Mortgagee shall have the option to declare the whole of the unpaid principal sum . . . due and payable." It also provided (¶ 12) that "where any of the terms . . . of this mortgage require the approval . . . or consent of Mortgagee . . . [it] shall not be unreasonably withheld . . . by Mortgagee." In light of the latter provision in the mortgage and the basic agreement of the parties in this transaction, plaintiff instituted this action for judgment declaring that defendant was unreasonably withholding its consent to plaintiff's proposed sale of the property.

Defendant acknowledges that the proposed purchaser is financially sound and, in effect, that its only reason for refusing to consent to the sale is that the money market has soared so much that, in its own business interest, it is seizing the opportunity to upgrade the interest on this mortgage to current mortgage interest rates. Special Term held that the bank has the right to do this. With much sympathy for the bank's position, we conclude that as a matter of law it cannot use the approval clause as a weapon to protect itself against the changed interest-market conditions.[2]

The rights of the parties under the above quoted terms of the mortgage depend upon their intention in placing such provisions therein. Some States have interpreted a provision that the sale of the mortgaged premises is subject to the mortgagee's right to declare the mortgage due and payable as giving to the mortgagee absolute authority to refuse to agree to a continuance of the mortgage loan except upon such terms as the mortgagee shall determine and accept (see *Crockett v. Sav. & Loan Assn.*, 289 N.C. 620, 224 S.E.2d 580 [1976]; *Mutual Fed. Sav. & Loan Assn. v. Wisconsin Wire Works,* 71 Wis.2d 531, 239 N.W.2d 20 [1976]; *Malouf v. Midland Fed. Sav. & Loan Assn.,* 181 Colo. 294, 509 P.2d 1240 [1973]; *Century Fed. Sav. and Loan Assn. v. Van Glahn,* 144 N.J.Super. 48, 364 A.2d 558 [1976]; see also *Mutual Real Estate Inv. Trust v. Buffalo Sav. Bank,* 90 Misc.2d 675, 395 N.Y.S.2d 583; *Stith v. Hudson City Sav. Inst.,* 63 Misc.2d 863, 313 N.Y.S.2d 804). Some other States have interpreted such a provision as requiring the lender to show that it has reason to believe that its security may be impaired if the transfer is made (see *Wellenkamp v. Bank of America,* 21 Cal.3d 943, 148 Cal.Rptr. 379, 582 P.2d 970 [1978]; *Patton v. First Fed. Sav. and Loan Assn. of Phoenix-Ariz.,* 118 Ariz. 473, 578 P.2d 152 [1978]; *Tucker v. Pulaski Fed. Sav. & Loan Assn.,* 252 Ark. 849, 481 S.W.2d 725 [1972]; *Nichols v. Ann Arbor Fed. Sav. and Loan Assn.,* 73 Mich.App. 163, 250 N.W.2d 804 [1977]; *First So. Fed. Sav. and Loan Assn. of Mobile v. Britton,* 345 So.2d 300 [Ala.Civ.App.1977]). At best, such a clause in the mortgage, standing alone, is ambiguous and misleading to the mortgagor. The normal inference to be drawn from it is that the lender is concerned about the security of the mortgage upon the transfer of ownership of the property. To construe it as granting to the lender an unlimited right to decline to accept a grantee for any reason, including the lender's refusal to consent to a change of the mortgage contract by increasing the rate of interest, is a giant step, which, as shown above, many States have,

---

[2] Had the bank expressly provided in the mortgage that upon sale of the property it reserved the right to increase the rate of interest thereon, a different question would be presented. Then, at least, the mortgagor would have had clear notice of the bank's asserted right, and there is authority that the provision, exercised in good faith, would be valid. (See Miller v. Pacific First Fed. Sav. and Loan Assn., 86 Wash.2d 401, 545 P.2d 546 [1976]; Tidwell v. Wittmeier, 150 Ala. 253, 43 So. 782 [1907]; and see Graf v. Hope Building Corp., 254 N.Y. 1, 171 N.E. 884). It appears, however, that under some circumstances in California such a provision would be held to be unconstitutional, as in restraint of the right of alienation (Wellenkamp v. Bank of America, 21 Cal.3d 943, 148 Cal. Rptr. 379, 582 P.2d 970 [1978]).

nevertheless taken. Even in California, one intermediate court gave that interpretation to such a clause in respect of commercial properties, such as we have here (*Medovoi v. American Sav. and Loan Assn.,* 152 Cal.Rptr. 572, 581 [Cal.App.1979]). It should be noted, however, that in denying appeal in that case the Supreme Court of California ordered that the opinion therein be not officially published, as that court is authorized to direct under Rule 976 of California Rules of Court. That suggests that the *Wellenkamp* case, supra, continues without limitation in California. We do not need, however, to reach that question on this appeal, because of the history of the underlying transaction herein and because of the inclusion in the mortgage of the clause that the mortgagee will not unreasonably withhold its consent to a sale of the property by the mortgagor.

In lieu of buying the land on which this branch bank building was erected, the bank arranged for construction of the building for its use under a 20-year lease, the monthly rental of $2304 being based upon plaintiff's costs. Included as an item of such costs was the 8½% interest rate which it was agreed that plaintiff would pay to defendant for the morgage money. It was agreed that at the termination of the lease, the bank could buy our [sic] plaintiff's interest for $85,000 above the construction costs. Under such agreement plaintiff cannot increase the rent, and at the termination of the lease the purchase price by the bank is fixed. As part of the agreement the bank granted to plaintiff the right to sell the property subject to the mortgage, upon condition that the bank approve of the purchaser, and the bank agreed not unreasonably to withhold such approval.

To permit the bank to condition its approval of the sale upon the purchaser agreeing to increase the interest rate on the mortgage by two per cent per annum, amounts to reducing plaintiff's equity in the property and it would constitute an intrinsic breach of the bank's contract with the plaintiff. This is true because by the bank refusing to increase its rental payments to cover the increase in the interest charged, the property will not be as good an investment unless the purchase price is lowered so that the reduced net income on the investment, resulting from the higher mortgage interest rate, will produce the same rate of return on the purchase price as the purchaser expected when he originally made his offer. This analysis shows that it was not the intent of the parties in this case to permit the bank to interpret the clause requiring its approval of the buyer as authorizing it to increase the interest rate as a condition thereof.

Apart from the implications of the special contract arrangement between the parties as above discussed, it seems clear in this case that on the sale of the property by the plaintiff to one whose economic status is completely unobjectionable to the bank, the clause requiring the bank's approval of the purchaser may not be interpreted as permitting it to condition that approval on an increase in the mortgage interest rate. The reason is that the bank expressly agreed that it would not unreasonably withhold its consent to a sale by plaintiff. If no case where courts have interpreted the so-called "due on sale" clause as authorizing the lender to condition its approval on an increase in the mortgage interest rate, was there a clause that the lender would not unreasonably withhold its consent to the sale by the mortgagor. Indeed, in some cases the significance of this point has been observed and the courts refused to imply such a clause in the mortgage where the parties had not expressly provided for it (see *Mutual Real Estate Inv. Trust v. Buffalo Sav. Bank,* 90 Misc.2d 675, supra, at 676 and 679, 395 N.Y.S.2d 583, at 584 and 586; *Stith v. Hudson City Sav. Inst.,* 63 Misc.2d 863, supra, at 865, 313 N.Y.S.2d 804, at 807). On the contrary, all of the courts, above cited, which hold that consent may not be withheld solely to obtain a higher rate of interest have found an implied duty on the part of the lender to act reasonably.

Finally, in this case the bank prepared the documents in issue and, if there is ambiguity therein, it is only proper that such ambiguity be resolved against it and in favor of plaintiff (*67 Wall St. Co. v. Franklin Nat. Bank,* 37 N.Y.2d 245, 249, 371 N.Y.S.2d 915, 918, 333 N.E.2d 184, 187; 4 Williston Contracts [3d ed.] § 621; 10 N.Y.Jur., Contracts, § 223).

We conclude that in this case the parties intended the clause, requiring the bank's approval of the purchaser, to grant to the bank only the right to approve of the character and financial ability of the buyer and not to authorize it to alter the terms of the mortgage by raising the interest rate therein as a condition of approval.

The judgment should, therefore, be reversed, defendant's cross-motion for summary judgment should be denied and plaintiff's motion for summary judgment should be granted, declaring that it is unreasonable for defendant to withhold its consent to plaintiff's proposed sale of her property unless the buyer agrees to pay a higher rate of interest on the mortgage to be assumed.

Judgment unanimously reversed with costs, defendant's motion denied and plaintiff's motion for summary judgment granted.

HANCOCK, J. P., and SCHNEPP, CALLAHAN and DOERR, JJ., concur.

LANE v. BISCEGLIA

Court of Appeals of Arizona
15 Ariz. App. 269, 488 P.2d 474 (1971)

CASE, JUDGE. This is an appeal by appellants (hereinafter referred to as purchasers) from a judgment for appellees (hereinafter referred to as vendors). The action was tried to the court which made findings of fact and conclusions of law.

Briefly, the facts are that during the first week in March, 1969, vendors and purchasers discussed the sale of certain property located on North Central Avenue, Phoenix, Arizona. At that time the vendors mentioned that the property was encumbered by a 6% mortgage, payments on which amounted to $226.00 per month. There was no discussion at that time regarding whether the mortgagee could increase this rate, since both parties were ignorant of such a possibility. On April 15, 1969, the parties signed escrow instructions which delineated the terms of their agreement to buy and sell the property. As part of the consideration, the purchasers were to assume the mortgage which was described in the following terms:

MORTGAGE of record, due SOUTHWEST SAVINGS AND LOAN ASSOCIATION 110 02667 with a principal sum remaining unpaid of approximately $31,000.00 with interest as therein specified . . . .

Approximately one week after the signing of the instructions, the purchasers, during a conversation with a representative of Southwest Savings and Loan, discovered that the mortgagee would not be agreeable to the assumption of the mortgage at the rate of 6%, but would only approve the assumption at the rate of 6¾%. The representative of Southwest Savings and Loan also stated that if the transfer of property was made without their approval, the indebtedness could become immediately due and payable at their option. Under these conditions the purchasers told Southwest they would not complete the transaction.

Thereafter, on or about May 6, 1969, vendors executed the final papers and on being told that the purchasers would not sign any instruments, followed the procedure outlined in the escrow instructions for the forfeiture of the $5,000.00 earnest money on deposit. This lawsuit was brought to prevent the title company from paying the vendor the earnest money, to rescind the contract and restore the parties to the *status quo ante,* i. e., return the $5,000.00 to the purchasers.

After a trial to the court, the following findings of fact and conclusions of law were reached:

FINDINGS OF FACT

1. That a binding written contract was entered into between the plaintiffs and the defendants for the purchase of a piece of property located in Phoenix, Arizona.

2. The contract provided that the plaintiffs would assume the existing mortgage loan at 6% interest but the mortgage company, Southwest Savings & Loan Association would not consent to the assumption unless the interest rate was increased to 6¾%.

3. The plaintiffs refused to complete the purchase and stated that the ¾% interest increase was the reason. The defendants had forfeiture notice sent out and claimed the $5,000.00 earnest money which was deposited in escrow.

4. The ¾% interest increase resulted in an additional $3.00 a month to be paid to the mortgage company which meant a payment of $229.00 rather than $226.00. The increase would have meant that the plaintiff would have paid an amount of approximately $690.00 over the remaining 19 years of the mortgage.

5. The plaintiffs intended to add additional rental units on the property as soon as they were able to acquire the necessary refinancing to pay for the additions.

6. The mortgage interest increase was not the reason that the plaintiffs refused to complete the purchase of the property.

7. That the defendants at all times acted in good faith and substantially complied with the terms and conditions of the purchase agreement.

CONCLUSIONS OF LAW

1. That the escrow instructions constituted a valid purchase agreement between the parties.

2. That the defendants substantially complied with the terms of the purchase agreement and the plaintiffs failed to act in good faith when they refused to complete the purchase as agreed to.

3. That the defendants gave the proper cancellation notice as required by the purchase agreement and therefore are entitled to the $5,000.00 earnest money.

4. That the plaintiffs are not entitled to the preliminary injunction and restraining order as heretofore granted.

In reviewing this decision we must view the evidence in a light most favorable to sustaining the judgment and must accept the trial court's findings of fact unless they are clearly erroneous. Rule 52(a) Ariz.R.Civ.P., 16 A.R.S.; *Bass Investment Co. v. Banner Realty, Inc.,* 103 Ariz. 75, 436 P.2d 894 (1968). To the contrary, we are free to draw our own conclusions of law from the facts determined. *Cantlay & Tanzola, Inc. v. Senner,* 92 Ariz. 63, 373 P.2d 370 (1962); *Tuab Mineral Corp. v. Anderson,* 3 Ariz.App. 512, 415 P.2d 910 (1966).

The purchasers question the correctness of findings of fact numbers 5, 6 and 7 while agreeing with numbers 1 through 4. The vendors question none of the findings. Though the burden is great, we are compelled to disregard a portion of finding of fact number 7.

The portion of that finding which states that the vendors substantially complied with the terms and conditions of the purchase agreement is improper for two reasons. First, the finding conflicts with the court's previous findings which indicate that the mortgage agreed upon was a 6% mortgage. Second, the finding is actually not one of fact, but a legal conclusion, which goes to the very core of the instant dispute.

The Arizona Supreme Court in *Baker v. Leight,* 91 Ariz. 112, 370 P.2d 268 (1962), discussed various problems present when a lending company has the apparent power to accelerate the obligation assumed following an unapproved transfer of the property. The Court therein implied that if the land purchase contract contained language referring generally to the mortgage, the buyer was charged with knowledge of the clause in the mortgage and subject to it. But, when the contract provided for the assumption of an identified mortgage of a specified amount, at a given specific rate of interest, with stated monthly payments, the buyer would not be charged with knowledge of the various clauses in the mortgage and would be entitled to rely on the representations made in the contract regarding the mortgage. In the instant case, the finding by the court indicates the contract specified the interest rate on the loan was 6% and the balance due was approximately $31,000.00. We find it unimportant to decide whether the purchasers under these facts would be charged with knowledge of the various clauses in the mortgage, since we find that the mortgage company only had the apparent right, *Baltimore Life Insurance Co. v. Harn,* 15 Ariz.App. 78, 486 P.2d 190 (1971), to approve or reject the assumption and had no right to conditionally approve the assumption at a greater rate of interest.

This conclusion is reached by examining the wording of the mortgage. Clause 5 thereof specifically entitled the lender to alter the interest rate of the note when further advances are made to the borrower. Such language is not present in clause 13. Thus, clause 13 merely permits the lender to approve or disapprove the transfer and contains no authority entitling the mortgagee to vary the interest rate.

The vendors did not fulfill their part of the contract by providing the purchaser with a mortgage to assume at 6%. When the vendors materially breached the contract by requiring the purchaser to assume a note and mortgage at a higher interest rate, *Kammert Bros. Enter., Inc. v. Tanque Verde Plaza Co.,* 102 Ariz. 301, 428 P.2d 678 (1967), the purchasers had a right to rescind and recover their earnest money. See, *Mahurin v. Schmeck,* 95 Ariz. 333, 390 P.2d 576 (1964); *Allen v. Pockwitz,* 103 Cal. 85, 36 P. 1039 (1894); *Nelson v. Jardine,* 46 Idaho 82, 267 P. 447 (1928).

Vendors attempt to support the trial court's decision by relying on *Cracchiolo v. Carlucci,* 62 Ariz. 284, 157 P.2d 352 (1945), wherein the doctrine of part performance was enunciated. In that case, the court specifically conditioned the application of this doctrine to situations where "a contract has been partly performed by one party and the other has derived a substantial benefit therefrom . . . ." Id. at 292, 157 P.2d at 355. Obviously, such doctrine does not apply to a wholly executory land contract where restoration of the parties to the *status quo ante* is easily accomplished by rescission.

It should be noted that the court's finding of fact number 6, regarding the purchasers' motive for rescinding is irrelevant since the actual motive of a purchaser is immaterial where there has been a material breach. *Crim v. Umbsen,* Cal. Cla. 597, 103 P. 178 (1909).

The vendors' argument that the difference between 6¾% and 6% is insignificant, i. e., $3.00 per month and $690.00 over the life of the loan, leads us to inquire why they did not offer to assume the difference in the interest rates through negotiations with Southwest Savings and Loan or with the purchasers and elect to make a counter offer to the purchasers instead of seeking default under the escrow instructions. Such action probably would have been performance by the vendors and required the purchasers to go through with the deal or default.

The issuance of the mandate in this cause shall constitute directions to the trial court to enter judgment in favor of appellants.

STEVENS, P. J., and JACOBSON, J., concur.

2. TRANSFERS "SUBJECT TO" THE MORTGAGE

One often hears reference to a loan as "assumable." In a tight money market with high interest rates the properties most likely to sell are those which a purchaser can buy and take over the vendor-mortgagor's payments on an old loan with a relatively low interest rate. The question usually asked is "Is the loan assumable?" when shopping for a home. While the question has come to communicate a meaning in the industry, a more appropriate phrasing would be "Can the property be purchased 'subject to' the existing loan without the lender increasing the interest rate?"

Any mortgage loan might be said to be assumable since the lender would in most cases welcome a new debtor taking up the burden of the monthly payments if the lender was able to increase the interest rate on an old loan to the current market rate. If a mortgage contains a due-on sale clause, the lender has the option of accelerating the maturity date of the principal balance upon a sale by the mortgagor. The buyer of the property must then find new financing. The alternative is for the buyer to continue with the old loan but at an increase in the interest rate, which will increase the monthly payments. If the mortgage does not have a due-on sale clause, then the mortgagor can transfer the property to a new owner "subject to" the mortgage. In most cases this will not result in the new owner becoming personally liable on the debt. However, if the new owner fails to make the payments the lender will foreclose and the owner "subject to" will lose the land at a foreclosure sale.

DEL RIO LAND, INC. v. HAUMONT

Supreme Court of Arizona
110 Ariz. 7, 514 P.2d 1003 (1973)

HOLOHAN, JUSTICE. By this appeal appellant seeks to set aside the judgment of the superior court ordering specific performance. The Court of appeals granted the motion of appellees to dismiss the appeal as moot. 18 Ariz. App. 348, 501 P.2d 1189 (1972). We granted review. The decision of the Court of Appeals is vacated, and the judgment of the superior court is reversed.

The appellant corporation is a family corporation owned by the Carr family. The corporation ceased its business activity in 1968, and two years later the decision was made to sell the real property and equipment of the corporation. It was decided that the sale should be by auction. The auction was arranged and an agreement between appellant and the auctioneer provided that the land would be sold "subject only to the existing mortgage." A similar provision was contained in the advertising brochure sent out to interested persons including appellee Pierre Haumont.

It was the contention of the officers of appellant that the original listing with the auctioneer was for not less than $4,500 per acre "at the discretion of the owners," but the auctioneer secured a second listing, claiming to have lost the first, and he had the listing signed in blank promising to fill it out in the same terms as the original. The listing was filled out to read that the sale was "subject to the approval of the auctioneers."

There is a dispute in the facts as to whether the auctioneer announced the sale as subject to a mortgage of some $55,000 on the land or whether he announced the sale for a bid price as the full purchase price of the property with the mortgage to be paid from the proceeds of the sale. Appellee Pierre Haumont took the position in his deposition that the sale was under the latter conditions, which would have required the appellant to pay off the mortgage from the proceeds of the sale.

Appellant refused to accept the appellees' bid of $2,600 per acre. Haumont brought action for specific performance, and, after discovery by both parties had been completed, Haumont moved for, and was granted, summary judgment for specific performance.

It is axiomatic that a motion for summary judgment may not be granted if there is a material dispute in the facts. Viewing the facts in the light most favorable to the party opposing the motion for summary judgment [*Hall v. Motorists Insurance Corporation,* 109 Ariz. 334, 509 P. 2d 604 (1973)] it appears that there are disputed fact issues which must be tried.

The trial court may have taken the position that there was not a material dispute in the facts, at least insofar as a resolution of the dispute between the corporation and Haumont. Apparently the trial court concluded that the term "subject to the mortgage" meant that the seller would be required to use the proceeds of the sale to pay off the mortgage. This was the position advocated by the auctioneer and Haumont. We cannot agree with this interpretation of the words used.

The term "subject to" has a variety of definitions depending upon the subject matter in which it is used. 83 C.J.S. p. 555. When the subject matter is real property and mortgages, the term "subject to" has generally meant "burdened with." Thus, a sale of real property subject to a mortgage means that the buyer acquires the property subject to the burden of the mortgage. The buyer, by taking subject to the mortgage, does not necessarily assume a personal obligation to pay it. *Seale v. Berryman,* 46 Ariz. 233, 49 P.2d 997 (1935); *S. L. Nusbaum & Co. v. Atlantic Virginia Realty Corp.,* 206 Va. 673, 146 S.E.2d 205 (1966). A purchaser who buys real property subject to a mortgage pays the consideration required by the seller and takes the land subject to the encumbrances without a personal obligation to pay the mortgage, but subjects himself to loss of the property if the mortgage debt is not paid. *Shepherd v. May,* 115 U.S. 505, 6 S.Ct. 119, 29 L.Ed. 456 (1885).

A sale or auction subject to a mortgage means that the seller receives the purchase price and the buyer takes the property subject to the unpaid mortgage; while the buyer is not under a personal obligation to pay the mortgage, he must do so if he desires to retain the ownership of the property, for the seller is not required to use the funds paid him to pay off the mortgage. The terms of a sale which include a provision, "subject to the mortgage" indicates that the actual or true purchase price of the property is in actuality the amount paid to the seller plus the amount of the mortgage.

. . . .

Judgment reversed.

HAYS, C. J., CAMERON, V. C. J. and STRUCKMEYER, J., concur.

BEST FERTILIZERS v. BURNS

Court of Appeals of Arizona
117 Ariz. 178, 571 P.2d 675 (1977)

HATHAWAY, JUDGE. This is an appeal involving two mortgages. The trial court found that appellee's mortgage was senior to that of appellant and entered judgment foreclosing appellee's mortgage. Appellant challenges the foreclosure contending that the senior note has been discharged and the mortgage thereby released.

Appellee's note and mortgage originated when Marcus Vanderslice gave them as a purchase money note and mortgage to Mr. and Mrs. Dees in exchange for title to real property. Mr. Vanderslice later sold the property to McFaddin Ranches subject to the Dees mortgage. McFaddin Ranches did not assume the mortgage but made payments on it. In 1970, McFaddin Ranches ceased making payments. Marcus Vanderslice then, in order to avoid default, paid the balance of the money owed to the Dees who then endorsed and assigned the note and mortgage to Mr. Vanderslice. Appellant contends that this transaction resulted in discharge of the note and release of the mortgage. Mr. Vanderslice, in consideration of the payment of $35,000, endorsed the note and assigned the mortgage to Burns, the appellee. Burns filed an action seeking judgment on the note and foreclosure of the mortgage. Best Fertilizers, holder of a note and mortgage given to it by McFaddin Ranches and encumbering the same property as appellee's mortgage, counterclaimed for judgment on the note and foreclosure of its mortgage. The trial court granted Burns' motion for summary judgment and Best Fertilizers appealed.

We have concluded that the trial court's judgment in favor of appellee must be reversed. Appellee's mortgage was released when the Dees transferred it back to Vanderslice, the original mortgagor. The note signed by Vanderslice was a negotiable instrument within A.R.S. § 44-2504(A). It was discharged when Mr. Vanderslice reacquired it. A.R.S. § 44-2568(C)(1). Appellee argues that these statutes, part of the Uniform Commercial Code as enacted in Arizona, are inapplicable to his note because the note is secured by a real estate mortgage. Albeit the Code does not apply to security interests in realty, the promissory note is not a security interest in realty. Under A.R.S. § 44-2505(A)(5), a note does not cease to be negotiable even though it is secured by a mortgage. Furthermore, A.R.S. § 44-2512(A) states that "[t]he negotiability of an instrument is not affected by: . . . 2. A statement that collateral has been given to secure obligations . . . ."

In *Capital Investors Co. v. Executors of Estate of Morrison*, 484 F.2d 1157, 1160 (4th Cir. 1973), the court held:

. . . the transferability of such notes, as well as the rights flowing from such transfers, are to be determined by the legal principles unique to negotiable instruments. This is so, though the notes are secured by a real estate mortgage.

When Mr. Vanderslice purchased the note and mortgage from the Dees he became the holder of his own note and mortgage bringing the transaction within A.R.S. § 44-2568(C)(1). "The liability of all parties is discharged when any party who has himself no right of action or recourse on the instrument: 1. Reacquires the instrument in his own right." Mr. Vanderslice had no right of action or recourse on the instrument. He was the only person liable for payment. McFaddin Ranches, his grantee, had been making payments but had not assumed the mortgage. Mr. Vanderslice therefore had no right to demand payment from McFaddin Ranches. This result is in accord with pre-existing common law relating to mortgages. Osborne, Handbook on the Law of Mortgages 554 (2d Ed. 1979).

Once the note is discharged, the mortgage is released. The mortgage ceases to be a lien upon the property because there can be no mortgage unless there is a debt. Our Supreme Court has held that "The very essence of a mortgage is a subsisting obligation to pay. It matters not whether the debt existed before or was created by the transaction in question. But debt there must be." *Merryweather v. Pendleton,* 90 Ariz. 219, 367 P.2d 251 (1961); *Charter Gas Engine Co. v. Entrekin,* 30 Ariz. 341, 246 P. 1038 (1926). Also, a mortgage has been found to be "incident to the note and inseparable therefrom" so that " 'A mortgage, as distinct from the debt it secures, is not a thing of value nor a fit subject of transfer. . . .' " *Hill v. Favour,* 52 Ariz. 561, 567, 84 P.2d 575, 578 (1938). Among the "gems" and "free" offerings of the late Professor Chester Smith of the University of Arizona College of Law was the following analogy. The note is the cow and the mortgage the tail. The cow can survive without a tail, but the tail cannot survive without the cow.

Reversed and remanded for proceedings consistent with our holding that appellee's note was discharged and the accompanying mortgage released.

HOWARD, C. J., concurs.

SCHROEDER, JUDGE, dissenting: The majority reaches a harsh result which is not in accordance with what I believe to be the principles of law applicable to this case. Mr. Vanderslice as the original mortgagor sold the property to McFaddin Ranches and McFaddin was to make the payments on the mortgage to Dees. McFaddin did make the payments for a time but then defaulted. Because Vanderslice remained liable on the mortgage, he paid off the underlying debt in an effort to protect the property and his position. The majority holds that having paid the mortgage, he accomplished neither objective and was legally entitled to nothing.

In my opinion, when Vanderslice sold the property to McFaddin, he in effect became a surety and ceased being the primary obligor. When Vanderslice paid off the debt, he became subrogated as to the rights of the creditor, Dees. Vanderslice therefore had rights senior to the junior mortgage of appellant. As Vanderslice's successor in interest, the appellee had similar rights which were properly upheld by the trial court. Osborne states these principles as follows:

> Thus in the law of mortgages, a mortgagor who has sold the property to an assuming grantee and then has had to pay is entitled to be subrogated to all rights of the mortgage creditor, both against the assuming grantee personally and in the mortgaged property in his hands. Similarly, if the sale is subject to the mortgage and the mortgagor is forced to pay, he gets subrogation to the creditor's security interest in the property now owned by the grantee, it being regarded as the principal and the mortgagor, as to it, surety. Osborne, Mortgages, § 278, p. 563 (2nd ed. 1970).

I recognize that today's decision is based upon the fact that the underlying debt in this case was a promissory note. The majority in effect holds that the statutes applicable to negotiable instruments abrogate the suretyship principles otherwise applicable to mortgages. I recognize further that there is considerable authority for such a conclusion in cases holding that suretyship principles do not apply with respect to extension agreements of promissory notes secured by mortgages. See *e. g., Mortgage Guarantee Company v. Chotiner,* 8 Cal.2d 110, 64 P.2d 138 (1936). See also, Osborne, supra, § 271. However, Osborne states in the heading to that section that such an abrogation rule has been "universally criticized." Today's decision is contrary to the only case called to our attention by the parties involving a situation similar to that presented here. *Mueller v. Jagerson Fuel Company,* 203 Wis. 453, 233 N.W. 633 (1930).

If in fact there had never been any obligation on the part of McFaddin to pay the mortgage, and the obligation had remained solely that of Vanderslice, the principles relied on by the majority might well apply. Here, however, even though McFaddin did not formally assume the mortgage, it did take the property subject to the mortgage and did make payments on it. There is no contention that in making the sale to McFaddin, Vanderslice did anything other than rely upon McFaddin's payment of the mortgage as part of the consideration for the sale. In those circumstances, the principles of suretyship should apply in order to avoid a wholly inequitable and very substantial loss to appellee coupled with a windfall for the appellant whose security interest was from its inception undeniably junior.

NOTE

In one case the maker of a non-recourse note secured by a mortgage sold the property "subject to" the debt, which at that point no one has personal liability to pay. The improvements were destroyed by fire and the insurance carrier refused to pay the owner who had taken subject to on the basis that the policy required payment to the lender with subrogation rights to the insurance company. Since the debt was non-recourse, there were no rights to be subrogated to and the carrier did not have to pay. *See Standard Fire Insurance Co. v. Fuller,* 195 F.2d 782 (D.C. Cir. 1952).

3. ASSUMPTION OF THE MORTGAGE

There will be occasions when the owner of a property wishes to transfer it to a party who is willing to assume personal liability for the debt. This may be done with or without a release of liability of the borrower by the lender. If the borrower does not obtain a release, so that the new owner takes the borrower's place, then the borrower becomes a surety after the new owner. Actually the land is always the primary source of payment of a mortgage loan but for purposes of considering the relationship between a mortgagor-vendor and the vendee who assumes liability of the mortgage, the vendee becomes primarily liable and the vendor becomes a surety.

THIS AGREEMENT, entered into between

_____ , of _____ , Wisconsin,
hereinafter referred to as the Association,
and_____ ,
of_____ , hereinafter referred to as the Mortgagor,
and_____ ,
of_____ , hereinafter referred to as the Purchaser;

   WITNESSETH: WHEREAS, the Mortgagor did execute a note and a
mortgage to secure said note in the amount of_____
($_____) Dollars, to the Association, dated the _____ day
of _____ , 19____ , and which mortgage is recorded in the office of
the Register of Deeds of _____ County, Wisconsin, on the _____
day of _____ , 19____ , in _____ of _____ ,
                 (vol.) no.   (Mortgages) (page no.)
as Document No. _____ , and which is identified as Association
Loan No. _____ ; and

   WHEREAS, said mortgage provides that upon transfer of title to
the mortgaged premises, the entire indebtedness pursuant to the
mortgage shall be due and payable at the option of the mortgagee, and,

   WHEREAS, the Mortgagor has sold and conveyed his interest in said
Mortgaged premises to the Purchaser, and said Purchaser wishes to
assume and pay said note and mortgage:

   NOW THEREFORE, IN CONSIDERATION of the covenants herein
contained, it is agreed by and between the parties hereto as follows:

   1.   That the Association hereby consents to the transfer of the
mortgaged premises from the Mortgagor to the Purchaser;

   2.   That the Purchaser assumes and agrees to pay said note and
mortgage and further agrees that he is personally liable to the
Association for all of the terms and conditions of said note and
mortgage the same as if said Purchaser had executed said note and
mortgage in the first instance;

   3.   That the interest on the remaining principal balance of
$_____ on said indebtedness shall be at the rate of _____
percent per annum computed according to the terms of the original
note, and that the new monthly payment for principal and interest
shall be $_____ per month commencing _____ ,
plus the necessary monthly installments of taxes and insurance as
provided in the original note, subject to adjustments as provided in
said note;

   4.   That the Mortgagor hereby consents that the funds in his Tax
and Insurance Escrow Accounts be transferred to the Purchaser's
account;

   5.   That this Agreement shall relieve the Mortgagor from his
liability to the Association under the terms and conditions of said
note and mortgage and as amended by this Agreement;

Illustration 7

Assumption of Mortgage

6.   That the Purchaser hereby makes application for membership in said Association and agrees to conform to and abide by the Articles of Incorporation, Bylaws, Rules and Regulations of said Association now or hereafter in force;

7.   That in all other respects the note and mortgage above referred to shall remain in full force and effect, and are amended only by the terms and conditions of this Assumption Agreement; And, the Mortgagor further agrees to be bound by and hereby consents to any subsequent change in the time, term, manner or method of payment of said indebtedness, or any part thereof, contracted by the Association and the Purchaser or the transferees of the Purchaser.

_____

_____

_____

IN WITNESS WHEREOF, the said parties have hereunto set their hands and seal this _____ day of _____, 19____ .

Signed and Sealed in Presence of:

_____ (SEAL)
                    Mortgagor

_____ (SEAL)
                    Mortgagor

_____   _____ (SEAL)
                    Purchaser

                        _____ (SEAL)
                    Purchaser

_____   _____
    (CORPORATE SEAL)   (Association)

                    By _____
ASSUMPTION AGREEMENT   President

                        _____
                          Secretary

FIRST FEDERAL SAVINGS & LOAN ASS'N v. ARENA

Court of Appeals of Indiana
406 N.E.2d 1279 (1980)

CHIPMAN, JUDGE.

Case Summary

First Federal Savings and Loan Association of Gary, (First Federal), appeals from a grant of summary judgment in favor of Michael and Grace Arena, (Arenas), in a foreclosure action brought by First Federal against the Arenas and their grantee, Sanford G. Richardson, as well as various lienholders.

First Federal asserts it was erroneous for the trial court to hold that altering the mortgages' interest rate was a material change which discharged the Arenas from personal liability on the mortgages. According to First Federal, a reservation of rights clause contained in the supplemental agreements to the mortgages executed by the Arenas and First Federal, permitted First Federal in its dealings with Mr. Richardson to increase the rate of interest on the mortgages without first affording the Arenas notice or obtaining their consent, while still retaining the Arenas' liability on the mortgages. The trial court, however, found the reservation of rights clause did not authorize First Federal to so act and entered judgment in favor of the Arenas.

We affirm the judgment of the trial court.

Facts

On May 26, 1965, the Arenas executed a note, mortgage, and supplemental agreement with First Federal. The note provided for a loan of $32,000 at an interest rate of 5¾%, and the mortgage securing this note provided for advances of up to $6,400. March 11, 1966, the Arenas were granted an advance of $5,100, and in consideration, they executed a modification and extension agreement which provided they would owe a new balance of $36,664.81, and the interest rate would be increased to 6%. A separate note, mortgage, and supplemental agreement were also executed by the Arenas in relation to this advance.

March 10, 1969, the Arenas conveyed the real estate which was the subject of both the May 26, 1965, and March 11, 1966, mortgages to Sanford G. Richardson by warranty deed subject to the two mortgages to First Federal. The same day, without notice to or the consent of the Arenas, Mr. Richardson and First Federal entered into a modification and extension agreement, under the terms of which Richardson assumed both of the mortgages in question, and the time for payment was extended to twenty years; there was also a change in the interest rate from 6% to 7¼%. Thus, this agreement, signed only by Richardson and First Federal, was designed to be a modification of First Federal's earlier agreement with the Arenas by extending the time of payment and modifying the terms of payment to which the Arenas and First Federal had agreed.

After June 27, 1975, Richardson failed to make the payments due under the March 10, 1969, modification and extension agreement. As a result, a default on the mortgages and notes occurred and a suit in foreclosure was filed on behalf of First Federal against the Arenas, Richardson, and several lienholders.

Issue

Before setting forth the issue before us, it appears imperative we reiterate that *all* allegations of error claimed to have occurred prior to the filing of the motion to correct errors must be *specifically* set forth within that motion in order to preserve the alleged error for appellate review. In First Federal's motion to correct errors it raised one broad allegation of error. On appeal, First Federal has attempted to raise tangential issues not heretofore specifically presented. Having sown the seed to bring forth one allegation of error, First Federal can not expect to now cultivate a garden of many on appeal. We therefore, confine our review to whether the entry of summary judgment was "contrary to the great weight of authority and law which has held that in a factual situation of the type that exists in this case, there should be no discharge of personal liability as to the original mortgagors, the Arenas." Thus, the sole question which has been duly and properly preserved for our consideration is the propriety of granting the Arenas' motion for summary judgment.

Before considering the merits of the respective arguments, we note the standard of review involved in a summary judgment. It is well settled that a motion for summary judgment may be sustained only where the pleadings and other matters filed with the court reveal no genuine issue as to any material fact exists, and the moving party is entitled to judgment as a matter of law. Ind.Rules of Procedure, Trial Rule 56(C); *Randolph v. Wolff,* (1978) Ind.App., 374 N.E.2d 533; *Johnson v. Motors Dispatch, Inc.,* (1977) Ind.App., 360 N.E.2d 224; *Letson v. Lowmaster,* (1976) 168 Ind.App. 159, 341 N.E.2d 785. Moreover, in determining whether a genuine issue of material fact exists, the facts set forth by the opponent must be taken as true, and all doubts must be resolved against the proponent of the motion. *Crase v. Highland Village Value Plus Pharmacy,* (1978) Ind.App., 374 N.E.2d 58; *Levy Company, Inc. v. State Board of Tax Commissioners,* (1977) Ind. App., 365 N.E.2d 796; *Union State Bank v. Williams,* (1976) Ind.App., 348 N.E.2d 683. With this standard of review in mind, we now address First Federal's appeal.

Decision

Conclusion — By reason of an expressed provision to that effect in the supplemental agreements between the Arenas and First Federal, the Arenas were not released from liability upon extension of the mortgage in the agreement between Mr. Richardson and First Federal; however, this agreement not only extended the time for payment, but it also modified the terms of payment by increasing the interest rate. It is our opinion the trial court properly found the Arenas had not consented to such a change in interest rates and, therefore, were released from liability. Arenas' grantee and First Federal could not modify the original mortgagors' agreement without the mortgagors' consent.

The focal point in this controversy is the meaning to be accorded a reservation of rights clause which appeared in the supplemental agreement executed by the Arenas when they obtained the initial mortgage and later secured the advance. The agreement provided:

> THE UNDERSIGNED, Michael Arena and Grace Arena, Husband and Wife, . . ., hereinafter referred to as the Mortgagor, hereby executes and delivers to FIRST FEDERAL SAVINGS AND LOAN ASSOCIATION OF GARY, . . ., hereinafter referred to as the Mortgagee, this Supplemental Agreement, pursuant to a Mortgage executed and delivered concurrently

herewith, and this Supplemental Agreement is expressly made a part of said Mortgage, ...

THE MORTGAGOR COVENANTS:

. . . .

6. That in the event the ownership of said property or any part thereof becomes vested in a person other than the Mortgagor, the Mortgagee may, without notice to the Mortgagor, deal with such successor or successors in interest with reference to this mortgage and the debt hereby secured in the same manner as with the Mortgagor, and may forbear to sue or may extend time for payment of the debt, secured hereby, without discharging or in any way affecting the liability of the Mortgagor hereunder or upon the debt hereby secured. . . .

First Federal asserts the reservation of rights language set out above permitted it, in dealing with Richardson, to increase the interest rate and extend the time of payment without first obtaining the Arenas' consent while still retaining their liability. Appellant takes the position that the portion of paragraph six providing for no discharge modified forbearing to sue and extending time for payment as well as dealing in the same manner as with the mortgagor; therefore, since the interest rate was increased when the Arenas were given their additional advance, according to First Federal, raising the interest rate in its agreement with Richardson would merely be dealing with him in the same manner as it had dealt with the Arenas and, consequently, should not result in a discharge.

The Arenas, on the other hand, contend the reservation of rights clause in the Supplemental Agreement made no reference to the alteration or modification of the interest rate but rather, referred only to an extension of the time for payment or the decision to forbear to sue.

While it is true paragraph six indicates First Federal could deal with successors in interest to the mortgage in the same manner as with the mortgagor, we hold the resolution of whether this meant First Federal and the Arenas' grantee would be permitted to increase the interest rate without affecting the Arenas' liability was a question of law for the trial court since the rules applicable to construction of contracts generally apply to the construction of an agreement whereby a purchaser of mortgaged premises assumes the payment of the mortgage. 20 I.L.E. *Mortgages* § 193.

As a rule, the interpretation, construction, or legal effect of a contract is a question of law for the trial court, not a question of fact. *Kleen Leen, Inc. v. Mylcraine,* (1977) Ind.App., 369 N.E.2d 638. However, when the terms of the contract are ambiguous *and* their meaning is to be determined by extrinsic evidence, the construction of the contract is for the jury. Conversely, where the ambiguity in the contract arises by reason of the language used and not because of extrinsic facts, the construction of the contract is a question of law. *Wilson v. Kauffman,* (1973) 156 Ind. App. 307, 296 N.E.2d 432. Thus, whenever summary judgment is granted based upon the construction of a contract, the trial court has determined as a matter of law that the contract in question is not so ambiguous or uncertain that resort must be made to extrinsic evidence in order to ascertain the contract's meaning.

The essence of the appeal before us then is whether the trial court correctly concluded that as a matter of law, the scope of the reservation of rights clause found in paragraph six did not include altering or modifying the interest rate, and consequently, First Federal did not reserve the right to modify and increase the interest rate from 6% to 7¼% without the consent of the Arenas. We hold the trial court's entry of summary judgment in favor of Arenas was proper.

When the Arenas conveyed the real estate to Richardson subject to the existing mortgages to First Federal, the land became as to said parties, the primary source of funds for payment of the debt. *Mutual Ben. Life Ins. Co. v. Lindley,* (1932) 97 Ind.App. 575, 183 N.E. 127. No technical relation of principal and surety arose between the Arenas and their grantee from this conveyance, but an equity did arise which bears a close resemblance to the equitable rights of a surety. As a result, the Arenas assumed a position analogous to that of a surety, and the grantee became the principal debtor to the extent of the value of the land conveyed. *Mutual Ben. Life Ins. Co. v. Lindley, supra;* Warm, *Some Aspects of the Rights and Liabilities of Mortgagee, Mortgagor and Grantee,* 10 *Temple L.Q.* 116 (1936).

While a mortgagor in such a situation may consent in advance to future modifications or agree his liability will not be discharged by subsequent agreements between his grantee and the mortgagee, such clauses are to be strictly construed against the mortgagee, *see* Friedman, *Discharge of Personal Liability on Mortgage Debts in New York,* 52 *Yale L.J.* 771, 788 (1943), since it would be unjust to subject the mortgagor to a new risk or material change to which he has not consented. Consequently, a reservation of rights clause will not prevent a discharge of liability where the modification in question exceeds the scope of the consent in the clause. This should come as no surprise since the mortgagor occupies the position of a surety, and the law of suretyship provides that a surety is entitled to stand on the strict letter of the contract upon which he is liable, and where he does not consent to a variation and a variation is made, it is fatal, *see American States Insurance Co. v. Floyd I. Staub, Inc.,* (1977) Ind.App., 370 N.E.2d 989; *White v. Household Finance Corp.,* (1973) 158 Ind.App. 394, 302 N.E.2d 828; therefore, an agreement between the principals for a higher interest than called for by the original contract will, if made without the surety's consent, release him from all liability. 74 Am.Jur.2d *Suretyship* § 47 (1974); *see also* 4 Am.Jur.2d *Alteration of Instruments* § 55 (1962).

The fact First Federal dealt with the grantee shows it knew of the Arenas' conveyance, and knowing of this conveyance, it was incumbent upon First Federal not to deal with the grantee in such a manner as would jeopardize or alter the surety-principal relationship. Warm, *Some Aspects of the Rights and Liabilities of Mortgagee, Mortgagor and Grantee,* 10 *Temple L.Q.* 116 (1936). The modification and extension agreement in question provided Mr. Richardson would personally assume the mortgage debt and thus, inured to the benefit of First Federal, but at the same time, the terms of the Arenas' earlier mortgage were changed to the detriment of the Arenas. If this increase in the interest rate was beyond the scope of the reservation of rights clause, the Arenas were thereby discharged, and the grantee became the sole debtor on the mortgages.

We hold the trial court properly rejected First Federal's argument that by increasing the interest rate it was merely dealing with Mr. Richardson in the same manner as it had dealt with the Arenas, and therefore, according to paragraph six, the Arenas should not have been discharged.

While it is true paragraph six indicated First Federal could deal with successors in interest to the mortgage in the same manner as with the mortgagor, this provision did not say First Federal could do so with impunity. We agree with the trial court that the portion of this paragraph providing for no discharge only modified forbearing to sue or extending the time for payment; consequently, the mortgagor would not be discharged from liability if the mortgagee simply extended the time for payment of the debt or opted not to bring suit, but these were the only situations where the mortgagee knew to a certainty his actions in dealing with the grantee would not discharge the mortgagor. The reservation of rights clause in paragraph six did not apply to activities which allegedly came within the ambit of dealing in the same manner as with the mortgagor. At the risk of being redundant, we again note, paragraph six stated in part:

> 6. [T]he Mortgagee may, without notice to the Mortgagor, deal with . . . successors in interest with reference to this mortgage and the debt hereby secured in the same manner as with the Mortgagor, *and* . . . . (our emphasis)

The punctuation used clearly sets this portion of paragraph six apart from the remainder of the paragraph which then goes on to provide the mortgagee

> may forbear to sue or may extend time for payment of the debt, . . . , without discharging or in any way affecting the liability of the Mortgagor hereunder or upon the debt hereby secured.

In order to give the reservation of rights clause the expanded application urged by First Federal so that it also applied to dealing in the same manner as with the mortgagor, it would be necessary to ignore the punctuation used and the maxim that such clauses should be strictly construed against the mortgagee. Further, such a construction would change the reservation of rights provision from applying in two definite situations to an open-ended invitation to argue there was no discharge because the mortgagee either could have or in fact had dealt with the mortgagor in the same manner; the possible activities which arguably could then come within this clause's application would be indefinite.

We hold the construction of the supplemental agreement between the Arenas and First Federal was a question of law for the trial court, which correctly held paragraph six did not authorize First Federal and the Arenas' grantee to alter the terms of payment on the mortgage debt by increasing the interest rate without affecting the Arenas' liability.

Judgment affirmed.

MILLER, P. J., and YOUNG, J., concur.

BRICE v. GRIFFIN

Court of Appeals of Maryland
269 Md. 558, 307 A.2d 660 (1973)

DIGGES, JUDGE. This is an appeal from the $3,380.70 portion of a judgment entered in the Circuit Court for Prince George's County in favor of the appellees, Charles and Marilyn Griffin, against appellants, Charles Brice and Charles Gaddis. The facts of this case have never been in dispute; however, the application of the law to those facts is vigorously contested. The evidence shows that the Griffins, as owners of an apartment building located on 28th Place, S. E., Washington, D. C., contracted with the appellants, on December 28, 1969, to sell them that building for a total purchase price of $64,221.23. Appellants were to take title to the property "subject to a first and second deed of trust." The sale was consummated on January 15, 1970 with the pertinent parts of the settlement sheet showing the following:

	Debit	Credit
"Price paid for property		$64,221.23
First trust note (People's Life) 12/30	$49,298.44	
Interest on first trust note 1-14 Jan.	115.02	
Second trust note (Groner) 12/14	11,922.79	
Water escrow for final bill if any due	50.00	
New trust note to sellers	2,300.00	
Balance to seller	534.98	
	$64,221.23	$64,221.23"

As may be seen from this settlement statement, in order to account for the full purchase price, the sums then due under the first and second trusts were deducted from that amount.

About eighteen months after this purchase, the second trust note holder, Erwin Groner, advised the Griffins, as the signators to that instrument, that there was a delinquency in the payments due under both the first and second trusts. This was followed three weeks later by the owner of the first trust note, People's Life Insurance Co. of Washington, D. C., advising the Griffins that, because payments for the last four months due it on the note in the amount of $3,075.54 were in arrears, it was then preparing to institute foreclosure proceedings. There is no dispute here that this amount as well as the $2,300 owed the Griffins by the appellants under the third trust were in fact then due. In order to prevent this threatened foreclosure, the Griffins paid Groner (apparently to be forwarded by him to People's Life) the amount required to satisfy the delinquency on the first trust in exchange for his promise to hold them harmless for any deficiency that may result from a default in payments under the second trust. Additionally, in connection with that payment, the Griffins reserved any rights to reimbursement they might have against the appellants for the sums advanced. Later, when they did not receive reimbursement or payment on their third trust, the Griffins filed this suit.

Here, as in the trial court, appellants' resistance to reimbursement is based principally on the theory that they did not assume the first and second deed of trust obligations and therefore are not liable to the Griffins on them. As did Judge Loveless in the trial court, we reject this hypothesis, since we conclude that as between the parties to this case the appellants had assumed the obligation of paying the outstanding indebtedness on the property which they purchased, and of protecting their vendors against any liability on account thereof.

The law is clear in this State that the mere purchase of a property subject to an existing mortgage or deed of trust does not create a personal obligation on the part of the purchaser to pay it. *McKenna v. Sachse, Executor,* 225 Md. 595, 171 A.2d 732 (1961); *Wright v. Wagner,* 182 Md. 483, 34 A.2d 441 (1943); *Rosenthal v. Heft,* 155 Md. 410, 142 A. 598 (1928). But, the law here is equally clear, if the purchaser assumes the payment of an existing mortgage or deed of trust as a part of the purchase price of the property, then, in that event, it becomes his duty to satisfy the obligation, and to protect his vendor against any demands that may be made for payment of the debt it secures. *Wright v. Wagner; Rosenthal v. Heft,* both *supra.* Whether the purchaser as between a vendor and vendee assumes the payment of such an existing obligation is a matter for agreement, which may be either express or implied, written or parol, and even separate from the deed conveying the property; but, in the absence of an express contrary agreement, an assumption will be implied when, as here, the amount then due under the trust obligation has been deducted from the purchase price. *Wright v. Wagner; Rosenthal v. Heft,* both *supra.*

In this case, the appellants contracted to take title to the apartment property "subject to the first and second deed of trust." Standing alone, and without relating it to the agreed upon purchase price, that language would mean that Brice and Gaddis acquired only the equity of redemption and thereby assumed no personal responsibility to pay the obligations created by the existing deeds of trust. But here, as the settlement sheet demonstrates, instead of paying the purchase price in full, appellants elected to deduct from that price the sums due under the two existing trusts. In these circumstances, what we said in *Rosenthal v. Heft, supra* 155 Md. at 420, 142 A. at 603, a case with a factual pattern remarkably similar to the one here, is appropriate:

> When [the purchaser] elected to "deduct" the amount due on the mortgages from the "purchase price," he must have "deducted" it to pay the mortgages, for otherwise, instead of deducting it from the purchase price, he would have bought the equity of redemption for the difference between the amount due on the mortgages, and the purchase price, but, in the absence of any evidence qualifying the language of the contract and the deed, we cannot assume that the [vendor] intended, and that [the vendee] understood, that he was to retain out of the purchase price the amount due on the mortgages, without any obligation on his part to pay the mortgages so as to exonerate the [vendor] from any liability on account thereof. A more reasonable assumption is that by that arrangement he undertook, as a part of the purchase price, to pay the mortgages when and as they became due. *See also, Wright v. Wagner, supra.*

It is reasonable to make the same assumption here.

However, appellants argue that *Rosenthal* is inapposite since here there has been no foreclosure or other judicial proceeding determining a deficiency and compelling the Griffins to make the payments they did. The answer to this contention is also found in *Rosenthal v. Heft, supra,* 155 Md. at 426, 142 A. at 605, where, after rejecting a broad approach that would hold that a vendor's right of action accrued when his vendee failed to pay, when due, the mortgage indebtedness he had assumed, we said that: "the sounder and the better rule is that no right of action accrued to the vendors until their liability had been judicially determined, *or until they had paid the mortgage debts.*" (Emphasis added.) For a case readopting this language see *Green Properties v. Livingston,* 230 Md. 193, 197-198, 186 A.2d 475 (1962).

We conclude that under the well settled law of this State, when the appellants purchased this apartment property, they assumed personal responsibility to pay the obligations of the vendors created under the existing deeds of trust as well as a duty to protect and exonerate the appellees from any demands that might be made against them for those debts. As the Griffins were called upon to satisfy and did pay an arrearage concededly due, the trial court was correct in awarding them damages in the amount of that payment, plus interest.

Judgment affirmed. Costs to be paid by appellants.

BEAVER v. LEDBETTER

Supreme Court of North Carolina
269 N.C. 142, 152 S.E.2d 165 (1967)

Plaintiff seeks to recover from defendants on their alleged assumption and agreement to pay a $12,000.00 purchase money note executed and delivered by Hagerty Realty Corporation (Hagerty) to plaintiff.

Plaintiff sold and conveyed to Hagerty a lot in Charlotte on which an 8-unit apartment is located. Hagerty executed (1) a first lien deed of trust to I. O. Brady, Trustee, as security for Hagerty's debt of $25,000.00 to Durham Life Insurance Company for money borrowed, and (2) a second lien deed of trust to Brock Barkely, Trustee, as security for Hagerty's $12,000.00 purchase money note to plaintiff. The $12,000.00 note bears interest from date (July 12, 1963) and is payable in monthly installments. Provision is made for the entire balance to become due and payable immediately if there is default in respect of any installment.

A deed dated March 22, 1965, recorded on April 16, 1965, in Book 2637, p. 127, Mecklenburg Registry, executed by Hagerty, purports to convey said property to P. L. Ledbetter and wife, Katherine H. Ledbetter. The deeds of trust in favor of Durham Life Insurance Company and plaintiff are excepted from the warranty provisions and it is set forth that "the parties of the second part" assume and agree to pay, *inter alia,* "that certain obligation due to Turner Brothers for rental and maintenance in the amount of $642.05," and "the balance due Mildred C. Beaver on the aforesaid deed of trust. . . ."

There was evidence tending to show a foreclosure of the deed of trust to Brady, Trustee, was completed on July 27, 1965. Plaintiff alleged "the property was bid in at a price sufficient only to pay the balance of the indebtedness to Durham Life Insurance Company and the expenses of the sale." Defendants' brief contains a statement to this effect.

Defendants, answering, alleged in substance: Katherine H. Ledbetter had no part in or knowledge of any transaction involving said property. In February or March 1965, a representative of Hagerty proposed a sale of said property to P. L. Ledbetter; that P. L. Ledbetter "made no down payment or any other payment on said property and never consummated the contract proposed by Hagerty Realty Corporation"; and that, notwithstanding P. L. Ledbetter had neither accepted nor rejected Hagerty's proposal, Hagerty, without instructions from P. L. Ledbetter, caused said deed dated March 22, 1965, to be prepared and recorded.

. . . .

The motion of each defendant for judgment of nonsuit was denied. With reference to each of the three issues, the court gave a peremptory instruction in favor of plaintiff.

The issues submitted, and the jury's answers, are as follows: "1. Did the defendant P. L. Ledbetter assume and agree to pay the indebtedness to the plaintiff referred to in the complaint? ANSWER: Yes. 2. Did the defendant Katherine H. Ledbetter assume and agree to pay the indebtedness to the plaintiff referred to in the complaint? ANSWER: Yes. 3. What amount, if any, is the plaintiff entitled to recover? ANSWER: $10,738.80, with interest from April 1, 1965."

In accordance with the verdict, the court entered judgment providing "that the plaintiff have and recover of the defendants, jointly and severally, the sum of $10,738.80 with interest thereon from the 1st day of April, 1965, and the costs of this action to be taxed by the clerk." Defendants excepted and appealed.

Bobbitt, Justice. Plaintiff bases her right to recover on this well settled legal principle: Where a purchaser of mortgaged land, by a valid and sufficient contract of assumption, agrees with the mortgagor, who is personally liable therefor, to assume and to pay the mortgage debt, such agreement inures to the benefit of the holder of the mortgage; and the holder of the mortgage can maintain an action at law on such agreement. *Baber v. Hanie,* 163 N.C. 588, 80 S.E. 57, 12 A.L.R. 1518; *First Carolinas Joint Stock Land Bank v. Page,* 206 N.C. 18, 173 S.E. 312; 4 Corbin on Contracts, § 796.

The general rule is stated in 59 C.J.S. Mortgages § 407, as follows: "A grantee who *with knowledge of its contents* accepts a conveyance which requires him to assume the payment of an existing mortgage becomes personally liable therefor even though he does not sign the deed or was not present when the grantor signed and acknowledged it, and even in the absence of an antecedent agreement to assume, and without entry of possession." (Our italics.) Accord: 37 Am.Jur., Mortgages § 994.

. . . .

Where a deed contains an assumption clause or other collateral provision purporting to impose a personal liability upon the grantee, it is our opinion, and we so hold, that the mere fact that such a deed has been executed and recorded is insufficient to raise a presumption that the grantee agreed to such collateral contractual provision. Evidence that such grantee had knowledge of such provision and expressly or impliedly assented thereto, or that she ratified such provision after acquiring knowledge thereof, is required before liability may be imposed upon such grantee under the terms thereof. There being no evidence that Katherine H. Ledbetter agreed to assume and pay Hagerty's note to plaintiff or that she ratified the assumption clause in Hagerty's deed to the Ledbetters, her motion for judgment of nonsuit should have been allowed. Hence, as to her, the judgment of the court below is reversed.

NOTES

1. Some assumption agreements are three party documents in which the mortgagee consents to the assumption by the mortgagor's grantee. However, some agreements are between the mortgagor and his grantee only. In that case the mortgagee has some alternative courses available. "As between the mortgagor and his grantee who assumes the payment of an encumbrance, the grantee becomes the principal debtor and the mortgagor becomes his surety. If the mortgagee is not a party to the agreement, its interest is not affected. Upon default, it may disregard the agreement and bring an action against the original debtor, or it may accept the promise made for its benefit and bring the action against the grantee." *Prudential Savings & Loan Ass'n v. Nadler,* 345 N.E.2d 782 (Ill. 1976). Illinois courts have held that the grantee becomes absolutely liable and that it is not necessary to prove third party beneficiary in order that the mortgagee recover from the grantee. *See LaGrange Federal Savings & Loan Ass'n v. Rock River Corp.,* 423 N.E.2d 496 (Ill. App. 1981).

2. A grantee who assumes a mortgage and pays it in full is not an assignee of the mortgagee for purposes of claiming against the mortgagee's title insurance policy for forged documents affecting title. *See Capital America, Inc. v. Industrial Discounts, Inc.,* 383 So. 2d 936 (Fla. App. 1980).

3. The basic rule on any assumption is that if the mortgagee and the mortgagor's grantee modify the terms of the debt, the mortgagor is released from liability unless the mortgagor consented to the modification. Some courts have held this release to be contingent on the mortgagee's knowledge of the relationship between the mortgagor and his grantee. For a lengthy list of citations in this area, *see Alropa Corp. v. Snyder,* 182 Ga. 305, 185 S.E. 352 (1936).

C. WRAP-AROUND MORTGAGES

If the owner of a property wishes to sell the property and carry back a purchase money mortgage for a portion of the purchase price, it is possible to increase the interest rate by utilizing a "wrap-around" mortgage, or "WA" mortgage.

A wrap-around mortgage is a mortgage encompassing an existing one and subordinate thereto. The existing mortgage remains on the property as an unsatisfied outstanding obligation with the wrap-around mortgage becoming a secondary mortgage. The face amount of the wrap-around mortgage is the present remaining principal balance on the existing first mortgage, plus the amount being advanced by the wrap-around lender. The interest payable on the wrap-around is always greater than on the first mortgage. The annual debt service is, however, figured on the face amount of the wrap-around. Therefore, the wrap-around lender actually receives a substantial interest bonus, insofar as it collects the higher rate on the full outstanding amount, but only remits to the first mortgagee the interest rate specified on the first mortgage. The wrap-around lender either agrees to assume the existing debt or on receipt of the debt service on the wrap-around mortgage, to deduct therefrom and remit directly to the first mortgagee, the required debt service on the first mortgage. The wrap-around mortgage contains covenants by the borrower identical with those in the first mortgage, including the escrow of taxes and insurance premiums which, on receipt by wrap-around lender, will be remitted to the first mortgagee. The first mortgage must not contain covenants personal to the borrower and which cannot be cured or complied with by the wrap-around mortgagee. The wrap-around borrower agrees to comply with all nonmoney covenants in the first mortgage and a default in the first mortgage is a default in the wrap-around mortgage.

A wrap-around mortgage can be utilized in the following situations:

1. When additional financing is desired, but the present mortgage holder is unwilling or unreasonable in his demands, and the mortgage permits no pre-payment, or pre-payment only with an exorbitant penalty; at the same time, conventional secondary financing is too costly in rate and too heavy in debt service.

2. When the existing first mortgage interest rate is very low and terms are otherwise quite favorable, but the borrower desires additional financing which the first mortgagee will not advance at a favorable rate. Conventional secondary financing would not meet these requirements.

Situations (1) and (2) are usually referred to as "additional-funds WA mortgage."

3. When the existing first mortgage is satisfactory in amount but the borrower desires to obtain debt-service relief to improve his return on equity. This situation is commonly known as the "extended term WA mortgage."

4. When a commitment for permanent financing is inadequate, although the lender has agreed to lend its statutory maximum, so that additional financing is required but conventional secondary financing would be too expensive and burdensome. This situation is commonly known as the "simultaneous WA mortgage."

See Gunning, *The Wrap-Around Mortgage — Friend or U.F.O.?*, Shopping Center Reports No. 22 (1969).

5. Other advantages of the wrap-around mortgage include:

a. Simplicity of structuring tailor-made financing which has great flexibility

b. Higher yield than a second mortgage

c. Higher return without violating usury laws

d. Purchaser can secure a better loan than could be obtained from a new money lender

e. Flexible financing without disturbing existing mortgages

Example: Additional Funds WA Mortgage

Debtor has an existing first mortgage with an outstanding balance of $64,500. The first mortgage had an original balance of $100,000, a 20 year term, at 6% interest and an annual debt service of $8,600. The first mortgage is now 10 years old. Debtor seeks additional financing from the wrap-around in the amount of $85,500, to be secured by the wrap-around mortgage with a face amount of $150,000 at 7% interest, for a term of 20 years and 1 month, with an annual debt service of $13,950. In the first year $6,630 is the interest earned. To determine the effective rate of interest earned, divide the differential interest by the net investment ($6,630 divided by $85,500) or 7¾% (1% of $64,500 = $645 plus 7% of $85,500 = $5,985, totalling $6,630). The effective rate of interest computed over the life of the wrap-around mortgage will be less than the effective rate of interest during the first year.

The following chart shows the application of the debt service on the two mortgages, according to their respective amortization schedules, during the first year and the amount of interest earned, the amount of interest deferred, and the effective rate of interest on the amount advanced.

Chart: Application of Debt Service—First Year

	1st Mtge.	WA Mtge.	Differential
Interest	$3,870	$10,500	$6,630
			(Interest Earned)
Principal	4,730	3,450	1,280
D/S	$8,600	$13,950	$5,350
Interest	$6,630		
D/S Retained	$5,350		
Interest Earned but not retained (*i.e.*, deferred)	$1,280		
Effective Rate of	$6,630	7¾% or equal to 1% x	
Interest Earned	$85,500	$64,000 + 7% x $85,500	

This chart also illustrates the mechanics of the agreement by the WA lender to remit, directly to the first mortgagee, the debt service on the first mortgage. The amount retained, $5,350, is less than the interest, $1,280, has been deferred and added to the WA lender's original advance and represents his net investment. Examples taken from Gunning, *The Wrap-Around Mortgage — Friend or U.F.O.?*, Shopping Center Reports No. 22 (1969).

However, there are some potential problems in using a wrap-around mortgage. The lien of the WA mortgage is inferior to that of the existing first mortgage and therefore suffers from many of the infirmities of a subordinate lien. Not all lenders would be permitted to make a WA mortgage because conventional mortgage financing is oftentimes conditioned upon the security of a first mortgage. It would appear, however, to a limited extent, that insurance companies do have the right to make "basket" or "leeway" loans to the extent of 2 or 3 percent of their assets, which loans are subject to no restrictions. Banks may make loans based on the general credit standing of a borrower and thus may make wrap-around loans. The contract rate of the WA mortgage does not exceed the permitted maximum rate but it is computed and paid on loan proceeds never advanced to borrower. The aggregate amount of interest so paid is, therefore, attributable to the funds actually advanced and, when so calculated, may exceed the maximum rate. It might be argued that the borrower paid only at the legal rate and by coincidence the lender received interest above the permitted maximum. Then the question would seem to be: does usury depend upon the interest rate the borrower pays on the WA mortgage or the interest rate actually received by the lender because of the leveraging effect of the WA mortgage? *See Mindlin v. Davis,* 74 So. 2d 789 (1954). The laws in several states prohibit the recording of a mortgage in an amount greater than the amount actually to be disbursed. Some also require certification in the mortgage that the stated indebtedness is bona fide. A WA mortgagor might have serious reservations about executing such a certificate. Aside from maximum interest laws, a number of states preclude the collection of interest payable on interest as a matter of declared public policy. In WA financing the deferred interest also accrues interest at the contract rate in the payout of the WA mortgage following the payoff of the first mortgage. A restriction of this type would, therefore, preclude the results the parties intended. Finally, a WA mortgage is not possible if there is a due-on sale clause in the mortgage. If the lender has the right to increase the interest rate or call the loan, then a wrap-around is no more feasible than an ordinary purchase money second mortgage.

MINDLIN v. DAVIS

Supreme Court of Florida
74 So. 2d 789 (1954)

PATTERSON, ASSOCIATE JUSTICE. This is an appeal by the mortgagees, defendants below, from a decree of the Circuit Court of Dade County declaring the mortgagees' note and mortgage usurious and imposing the forfeitures provided in Sec. 687.04, Florida Statutes, F.S.A.

The facts from which this litigation arose are set out in extensive findings by the master which are sufficiently supported by the evidence. The Peoples Mortgage Corporation, mortgage brokers, persuaded the mortgagors, plaintiffs below, to apply through them for a ten per cent mortgage loan in the principal amount of $3,300 for the purpose of consolidating their various obligations including an existing five per cent first mortgage on their home in favor of Chase Federal Savings and Loan Association, which is referred to as the Chase mortgage. Before the loan applied for was closed, Peoples Mortgage Corporation had sold the mortgage to appellants and informed appellees that the loan would be closed directly with appellants as mortgagees. Appellees' loan application to Peoples Mortgage Corporation provided that the applied for mortgage should be a first mortgage, for the placing of which appellees agreed to pay Peoples Mortgage Corporation a commission of $263.40, such commission expressly to include "all costs incidental to the closing of the transaction." Implicit in the terms of the application and the negotiations for the new mortgage was the agreement that the Chase mortgage should be discharged out of the proceeds of the new mortgage.

The mortgage application was signed December 3rd. The note and mortgage were dated December 9th but for reasons not entirely clear in the evidence, closing of the loan was not accomplished until December 15th. Closing statement indicated that the proceeds of the loan were applied $263.40 to expenses of the loan, $1,488.02 to pay in full the Chase mortgage, and $1,548.58 in cash to appellees. To close the loan appellants furnished their attorney sufficient funds to pay the expense item and to make the cash disbursement to appellees, but retained the amount of $1,488.02 to be applied in payment and discharge of the Chase mortgage. At the closing, appellant's attorney made the cash disbursement to appellees and paid out the $263.40 as expenses of the loan, including $185 to Peoples Mortgage Corporation as brokerage, and $50 to himself as attorney fee for attending closing and examining abstract. The payment of the Chase mortgage was not handled by appellants' attorney in closing the loan, but instead appellants merely continued the monthly installments on that mortgage in the name of the appellees until, after having made eight such payments, the remaining balance was paid and mortgage satisfied on August 6, 1953, after the commencement of this suit. It is not disputed that the appellants intended, contrary to the implicit requirement of the mortgage contract, and without the knowledge of the appellees, to pay off the Chase mortgage by installments rather than immediate payment in full, standing ready, so it is claimed, to make full payment at any time if demanded by either party to that mortgage.

The new mortgage required payments of principal and interest of $60 per month for five years, with final payment of $843.37 on December 9, 1957. The borrowers had made seven such monthly payments of $60 at the time this suit was commenced. No interest credit was allowed for the six days' delay between the date of the mortgage note and the date of closing.

Upon the facts here set out, the Master concluded that the transaction was rendered usurious in three particulars: first, the failure to credit appellees with interest in the amount of $5.60 accruing between December 9 and December 15; second, the charge of $50 as fee for appellants' attorney; and third, the failure of appellants to pay off the Chase mortgage with the proceeds retained for that purpose. Upon a detailed calculation of the actual interest involved in the transaction, the Master recommended the forfeiture of the total interest contracted and the additional amount of $546.18, being twice the amount of interest actually exacted and received, according to his calculation. The Master's conclusions were approved in the final decree and the mortgage was reformed by reducing the monthly payments to an amount sufficient to pay out the principal, less forfeitures, by the end of the term of the mortgage. The findings of usury, as well as the manner of imposing the forfeiture, are challenged on this appeal.

Manifestly, if the transaction presented here, in any of the particulars charged, constitutes a device or contrivance for the exaction of additional interest over that provided in the mortgage note itself, then the whole transaction is rendered usurious inasmuch as ten per cent interest contracted in the note is the maximum allowable under the law. The controlling statutes, Sec. 687.03 and 687.04, Florida Statutes, F.S.A., provide:

> 687.03 It shall be usury and unlawful for any person, or for any agent, officer or other representative of any person, to reserve, charge or take for any loan, or for any advance of money, or for any forbearance to enforce the collection

of any sum of money, a rate of interest greater than ten per cent per annum, either directly or indirectly, by way of commission for advances, discounts, exchange, or by any contract, contrivance or device whatever, whereby the debtor is required or obligated to pay a sum of money greater than the actual principal sum received, together with interest at the rate of ten per cent, as aforesaid. . . .

687.04 Any person, or any agent, officer or other representative of any person, willfully violating the provisions of § 687.03 shall forfeit the entire interest so charged, or contracted to be charged or reserved, and only the actual principal sum of such usurious contract can be enforced in any court in this state, either at law or in equity; and when said usurious interest is taken or reserved, or has been paid, then and in that event the person, who has taken or reserved, or has been paid, either directly or indirectly, such usurious interest, shall forfeit to the party from whom such usurious interest has been reserved, taken or exacted in any way, double the amount of interest so reserved, taken or exacted; . . . .

We cannot agree that either the failure to credit interest for the delay in closing or the charge of the fee for appellants' attorney is a violation of the statute under the facts before us. With respect to the interest credit, there is no suggestion in the evidence that the note was predated or that the delay in closing was contrived with any intent to circumvent the statute. Nor do we think such usurious intent may reasonably be imputed to the appellants from the other aspects of the transaction. In the absence of any reasonable basis for imputing such an intent, it is our view that the failure to abate interest until the actual closing was an error in closing and should be adjusted as such rather than an usurious exaction. *Maule v. Eckis,* 156 Fla. 790, 24 So.2d 576; *Chandler et ux. v. Kendrick, Fla.,* 108 Fla. 450, 146 So. 551.

The attorney's fee charged the borrowers in this case was included as part of the expenses of the loan as agreed in the loan application. It is settled in this state that the borrower may legitimately agree with the lender to pay actual reasonable expenses of examining and appraising security offered for a loan as well as the costs of closing the transaction, even though such payments, when added to the interest contracted for, exceed the maximum interest allowed by law. *Pushee v. Johnson,* 123 Fla. 305, 166 So. 847, 105 A.L.R. 789. Examining title of the loan security and handling the closing of a loan are services traditionally rendered by attorneys at law and involve an actual expense to the lender which he may pass on to the borrower under the rule quoted. The holding below, and the contention here, is that the fee in this case is ruled by the holding of this Court in *Stoutamire v. North Florida Loan Association,* 152 Fla. 321, 11 So.2d 570. We do not agree with such contention. From the particular facts of the *Stoutamire* case, the Court found that a pretended attorney's fee was in reality a bonus paid to the lenders' agent and attorney in fact rather than a legitimate expense of the loan. Under the facts peculiar to that case the Court applied the rule of *Richter Jewelry Co. v. Schweinert,* 125 Fla. 199, 169 So. 750, that our statute reaches the acts of the lender's agent as well as the lender himself and that such agent cannot under our statute be the employed agent of the lender and at the same time make a profit for himself by exacting a bonus or commission from the borrower if the commission, together with the interest, exceeds the legal limits and amounts to usury. The situation of that case is expressed in the language [152 Fla. 321, 11 So.2d 571]: "In the transaction his status as an attorney in fact was definitely fixed and in that capacity he dealt with the appellant. He could not then adopt the position of attorney at law for the purpose of receiving compensation as a legitimate item in the expenses of the loan. For practical purposes, in making the loan he *was* the lender." Nothing in the case now before us justifies the application of that rule. The attorney's participation in the transaction involved here goes no further than the rendering of a legitimate legal service and his fee is legally chargeable to the borrowers under the general rule of *Pushee v. Johnson,* supra.

We must next decide whether appellants' method of discharging the Chase mortgage renders this transaction usurious. To decide that question we must consider the fact that the payment by appellants of the Chase mortgage on behalf of the borrowers, appellees, is in legal effect only a disbursal of the proceeds to the borrowers, but elected to be made directly by lenders to the mortgagee as a precaution to assure to the lenders the discharge of that mortgage constituting a lien prior to their own. Thus a delay in making that payment amounts to a delay in the advancement of a substantial portion of the loan. Since time as well as amount of principal is a factor in the calculation of interest, it is evident that retention of a substantial portion of the loan without a corresponding abatement of interest on the amount retained has the effect of substantially increasing the per centum of interest on the actual amount advanced by the lenders and received by the borrowers, which is the significant amount contemplated by the statute. It is undisputed in the evidence that the retention by the lenders of that portion of the principal earmarked for the Chase mortgage was by their original intention and design, that it continued for over seven months, and although gradually reduced by installments, would have continued throughout the term of the loan except for the compulsion of this litigation. It is not difficult to appreciate the effect of such a scheme and to recognize it as a device or contrivance for the exaction of usurious interest condemned by the statute. The statute recognizes that usurers are necessarily driven to various schemes and devices to cover their evasions of the law, and the Courts have always been alert to recognize the substance of their transactions and to impose the prescribed penalties. 55 Am.Jur., Usury, Sec. 14, page 332; *Wicker v. Trust Co. of Florida,* 109 Fla. 411, 147 So. 586; *Beacham v. Carr,* 122 Fla. 736, 166 So. 456; *Grider v. Calfee,* 242 Ala. 50, 4 So.2d 474.

We hold, therefore, that the scheme resorted to in this case constitutes a violation of the usury statute and invokes the forfeiture of the entire interest contracted. In addition, the evidence shows that of the seven monthly installments paid by appellees, a total of $186.73 was charged to interest by appellants, for which they must forfeit twice that amount as usurious interest actually paid and exacted.

The final decree accomplishes the forfeitures against appellants by reducing the amount of the monthly installments of the mortgage note. We think that the forfeitures imposed do not require or justify altering the fixed provision of the note that it shall be repaid in monthly installments of $60 each. The total obligation of the note has been reduced in these proceedings, but the effect is that each such agreed installment shall henceforth be applied entirely to principal until the face of the note, less credit for forfeitures, shall have been fully paid.

The final question presented here by appellants concerns the amount of the fee allowed the special Master. Upon a consideration of the evidence we do not consider the fee allowed to be so excessive that we should disturb it.

The decree appealed from is affirmed in part and reversed in part and remanded for the entry of final decree in conformity with this opinion.

ROBERTS, C. J., and SEBRING and HOBSON, JJ., concur.

NOTE, WRAP-AROUND FINANCING: A TECHNIQUE FOR SKIRTING THE USURY LAWS?, 1972 Duke Law Journal 785*

In recent years the inflationary spiral and the tight money market have forced interest rates to increase at an accelerated rate. As the lender is able to command a higher return on his money, he becomes increasingly aware of the limitations placed upon him by the usury laws. In the field of real property financing, lenders have employed several techniques to secure a higher rate of return while avoiding the limitations of the usury laws. Devices such as the sale-leaseback [1] and sale-buyback [2] have taken their place alongside contingent interest [3] and "front money" loans [4] as the basic trade tools of the lending institution in its efforts to construct a shield from the pitfalls created by the usury statutes.[5]

A new tool, the "wrap-around" loan, has recently appeared in the lender's repertory. This "new" contrivance, which has actually been in existence since the 1930's,[6] has recently become the subject of considerable interest among lenders, realtors, escrow personnel and attorneys. Although theoretically applicable to most loan transactions, the technique has primarily been utilized in real property financing, where it has been referred to variously as the "wrap-around," "all-inclusive," "hold-harmless" or "overriding" mortgage or deed of trust.[7]

---

* Copyright 1972, Duke Law Journal. Reprinted by Permission.

[1] A sale-leaseback involves a sale and transfer of property followed by a lease of the same property from the transferee to the transferor. Thomas, Leasebacks in Commercial and Family Transactions, 28 Mont. L. Rev. 25 (1966).

The following hereinafter Citations will be used in this Note:

Benfield, Money, Mortgages, and Migraine, The Usury Headache, 19 Case W. Res. L. Rev. 819 (1968) [hereinafter cited as Benfield];

Hershman, Usury and "New Look" in Real Estate Financing, 4 Real Prop., Prob. & Tr. J. 315 (1969) [hereinafter cited as Hershman].

[2] In a sale-buyback, the investor purchases the property and immediately resells it to the former owner at the same price on a long-term installment contract. Hershman 321.

[3] The contingent interest method involves participation by the mortgagee in income from the mortgaged property above a fixed interest on the loan. It takes several forms:

percentage of gross income, percentage of gross income in excess of a specified dollar amount . . . percentage of overages, percentage of net income before taxes and depreciation or before depreciation and a percentage of a defined net income under which certain items of expense are limited for the purpose of the computation. Hershman 315.

[4] The front money loan is a recently developed technique in which an investor normally contributes

up to 100 percent of the required cash investment in a project. The developer contributes his time and entrepreneurship to the undertaking. Sometimes he is the owner or has an option on the land to be developed and the deal involves sale of one-half of it to the investor for a price which gives the developer the cash needed to contribute his part to the undertaking.

The investor and the developer enter into a joint venture or partnership, or form a corporation in which the two share in the stock. The division of ownership and profits is negotiated and, in many instances, where the investor is putting up all of the cash, there is provision for the investor getting all of his money out first with an appropriate return on the investment before any split of the net income takes place. Hershman 324.

[5] For a detailed description and analysis of these techniques *see* P.L.I., Real Estate Financing: Business and Legal Considerations (1968); Anderson, Tight-Money Real Estate Financing and the Florida Usury Statute, 24 U. Miami L. Rev. 642 (1970); Hershman.

[6] Healey, A "New" Security Instrument, 41 J. State B. Calif. 681 (1966).

[7] *Id.* at 681. Although there are differences in the operation and legal effects of the mortage and the deed of trust when used as security devices for real property financing, these distinctions are inconsequential for purposes of the usury discussion in this Note. Consequently, the term "wrap-around mortgage" will be used hereinafter to describe the lending and security instrument applicable to wrap-around financing. Nevertheless, the principles to which this Note is addressed are equally applicable in jurisdictions which favor utilization of the trust deed, rather than the mortgage instrument, as a real property financing device.

While it has been the subject of considerable legal commentary,[8] the wrap-around technique has, to date, been utilized only sparingly and with a great deal of caution in the United States.[9] The usury threat is undoubtedly among the reasons for the reluctance on the part of lenders to enter into wrap-around transactions, especially because the technique apparently has not yet been examined under the usury laws by an American court.[10] It is the purpose of this Note to identify and resolve the issues which will arise when a wrap-around loan is challenged as being usurious.

The Wrap-Around Technique

The "wrap-around" mortgage is a subsequent and subordinate mortgage secured by real property upon which there exists a first mortgage which remains outstanding and unsatisfied. The wrap-around mortgage differs from a conventional second mortgage in that it entails a special agreement between the parties for payment of the first mortgage obligation by the lender, and consequently, the principal of the wrap-around loan is the sum of the outstanding indebtedness on the first mortgage and the new funds advanced.[11] When the wrap-around mortgage is executed at an interest rate which exceeds the contractual rate of the first mortgage, it becomes possible for the lender to increase his effective interest yield from the overall transaction. The benefits to be derived from the use of wrap-around financing, therefore, can be realized primarily in a period of rising interest rates.

Although wrap-around financing has been employed primarily through real estate investment trusts in transactions involving large commercial loans, the technique can perhaps best be illustrated by a simplified refinancing transaction. Assume that X owns Blackacre subject to a $10,000 first mortgage bearing five percent interest with a remaining life of two years and an outstanding principal due in the amount of $5,000 in one year and the remaining $5,000 at maturity. Blackacre has a fair market value of $30,000, and X, in order to procure additional capital, desires to refinance his real property by securing a loan on his equity. X approaches L, requesting a loan of $10,000 to be secured by his equity in Blackacre. Instead of consummating the loan through the issuance of a conventional $10,000 second mortgage, L offers to grant X the requested loan on the condition that X permit L to "wrap-around" the existing first mortgage through the use of a wrap-around loan. Under this proposal, X will execute and convey a new mortgage to L in a face amount of $20,000, and L in return will

---

[8] See, e.g., P.L.I., supra note 5, at 1.13, 10.20-.24; Gunning, The Wrap-Around Mortgage — Friend or U.F.O., in International Council of Shopping Centers (Rep. No. 22) (1969); A Panel on Wrap-Around Mortgages, in Proceedings of the American Life Convention 151 (1966); Gunning & Roegge, Contemporary Real Estate Financing Techniques: A Dialogue on Vanishing Simplicity, 3 Real Prop., Prob. & Tr. J. 325, 337-39 (1968); Healey, supra note 6; Hershman 323-24; Lowell, A Current Analysis of the Usury Laws — A National View, 8 San Diego L. Rev. 193, 213-14 (1971); Wainberg, All-Inclusive Deed of Trust Is Good Tool, Calif. Real Estate Ass'n Mag., July 1966, at 25; Healey, A Legal View of 'Wrap-Around' Mortgage, New York Law Journal, Oct. 14, 1970, at S5, col. 1.

[9] Although the wrap-around is a relatively new form of instrument in the United States, it has been widely utilized in Canada where it is referred to as a "blanket mortgage." Gunning, supra note 8, at 1. In Canada, the lenders need not contend with the usury problem "since there are no usury laws, as such," other than a limitation against the exaction of unconscionable interest. Id. at 10.

[10] See Lowell, supra note 8, at 214.

[11] Gunning, supra note 8, at 2.

advance the desired $10,000 cash and agree to make payments of interest and outstanding principal under the first mortgage as they become due.

If, in the above example, the full $20,000 principal of the wrap-around mortgage is to be paid at the end of ten years and bear nine percent annual interest, L, the lender, will receive $1,800 interest per annum. During the first year, L will pay the five percent interest due under the $10,000 first mortgage ($500) and will net $1,300, an effective interest rate of thirteen percent on the $10,000 he has advanced to X. At the beginning of the second year, L will pay the $5,000 principal due under the first mortgage. During the course of the second year, L will receive $1,800 interest from X and will pay the five percent interest due on the remaining $5,000 principal of the first mortgage ($250), thereby netting $1,550 on the $15,000 he has dispersed, an effective interest rate of 10.33 percent. At the beginning of the third year, L will then pay the final $5,000 principal due under the first mortgage, and will thereafter receive nine percent on $20,000 for the remaining life of the wrap-around mortgage.

In the above transaction, L, the lender, will receive an effective interest rate of thirteen percent during the first year, 10.33 percent during the second year, and nine percent, the contractual interest rate of the wrap-around mortgage, thereafter. The aggregate rate of return, or effective yield, to L over the ten year maturity of the loan would, therefore, be 9.324 percent. Here, as in any typical wrap-around transaction, the lender receives a higher interest return during the earlier years. The reason for this increment is twofold: (1) the lender has not advanced the full principal of the loan during the early years but nevertheless draws interest on the full amount, and (2) the lender receives the benefit of the interest differential between the low rate of the first mortgage and the high rate of the wrap-around mortgage during the remaining life of the first mortgage.

Since the return to the lender in the above example fluctuates between nine and thirteen percent, potential usury violations are present in all jurisdictions which set a statutory ceiling below thirteen percent. If the interest ceiling is below nine percent — the contractual interest rate specified on the face of the wrap-around loan — the transaction is obviously usurious. The real problems arise in those jurisdictions where maximum lawful rates fall between the nine percent contractual rate and thirteen percent, the highest annual return received by the lender. On the one hand, it could be argued that the wrap-around loan is usurious whenever the statutory maximum is below the highest annual interest return to the lender (thirteen percent). On the other hand, it could be contended that, since the mortgage recites an interest rate of nine percent, the loan is usurious only when the statutory ceiling is below nine percent. Between these two extremes, it might be asserted that since the effective interest yield to the lender is 9.324 percent, the loan would be usurious in a jurisdiction which sets the permitted maximum at nine percent but non-usurious where the ceiling is ten percent.

In addition to its application in a *refinancing* transaction analogous to the one in the above example, the wrap-around loan can be employed in two basic types of *sales* transactions: (1) where a vendor wraps around his existing first mortgage obligation and finances a sale of his own real estate under a purchase money wrap-around mortgage, or (2) where a third-party lender wraps-around a vendor's prior mortgage obligation in order to finance the purchase of real property. In each of these contexts different considerations are present. As will be discussed later, a loan which would be usurious in one context may not violate the usury laws in another context.

. . . .

The Refinancing Wrap-Around Mortgage

When one examines the substance of a refinancing agreement which employs the wrap-around technique, violation of the usury laws becomes apparent. In the illustrative transaction previously set forth, *L,* the lender, has, in lieu of issuing a conventional second mortgage, persuaded *X,* his borrower, to give up the advantageous low-interest first mortgage as a condition to granting the loan. The fact that the borrower has been required to give up the benefits of an advantageous agreement may in itself be enough to taint the transaction as usurious. A loan which stipulates interest at the highest lawful rate may be rendered usurious when the creditor, as a condition to making the loan, requires the debtor to enter into an additional agreement with him.[60] While a few jurisdictions may permit a lender to condition a loan upon the borrower's granting some collateral advantage in addition to the lawful rate of interest,[61] it is universally held that contracts which give the lender a collateral benefit resulting in the exaction of usurious interest are usurious when the stipulation is made purely to evade the usury laws.[62]

As a general rule, therefore, any benefit or advantage exacted by the lender from the borrower, whatever its name or form, which when added to the interest taken or received would yield a greater return than is allowed by law, renders the transaction usurious. In holding usurious a complex real estate financing scheme, the Supreme Court of Vermont in *Farnsworth v. Cochran*[63] noted:

> A contract is usurious when any premium, profit, bonus, or charge is exacted or required by the lender in excess of the money actually loaned, which, in addition to the interest stipulated, renders the return to the lender greater than the lawful rate of interest.[64]

When these principles are applied to a case in which real property is refinanced pursuant to a wrap-around transaction, the differential between the interest called for in the first mortgage and that specified in the wrap-around mortgage can be viewed as an exaction of additional interest and will contribute, therefore, to the aggregate interest return of the loan for usury purposes. It thus appears that even when the interest rate paid by the borrower on the face of the loan is valid, the refinancing wrap-around loan will be usurious whenever the aggregate interest return, or effective yield, to the lender computed over the entire term of the obligation exceeds the maximum interest rate embodied in the applicable usury statute.

In addition to being considered usurious because of the exaction from the borrower of an extra interest benefit through the assumption by the lender of the payment obligation under the low-interest first mortgage, the refinancing wrap-around loan with a valid contractual interest rate could have an excess effective yield due to the presence of a second element. As previously indicated, the lender derives a twofold benefit from the wrap-around transaction in that (1)

---

[60] *See, e.g., In re* Perry, 272 F. Supp. 73 (D. Me. 1967); Equitable Life Assur. Soc'y v. Kerpel, 38 Misc. 2d 856, 238 N.Y.S.2d 1016 (Sup. Ct. 1963); Richeson v. Wood, 158 Va. 269, 163 S.E. 339 (1932).

[61] *See, e.g.,* Commercial Credit Plan, Inc. v. Chandler, 218 Ark. 966, 239 S.W.2d 1009 (1951); Hatridge v. Home Life & Accident Ins. Co., 246 S.W.2d 666 (Tex. Civ. App. 1951).

[62] *See, e.g.,* Klett v. Security Acceptance Co., 38 Cal. 2d 770, 242 P.2d 873 (1952); Virginia Hotel Co. v. Dusenberry, 218 S.C. 524, 63 S.E.2d 483 (1951). *See also* Ferdon v. Zarriello Bros. Inc., 87 N.J. Super. 124, 208 A.2d 186 (1965).

[63] 125 Vt. 174, 212 A.2d 818 (1965).

[64] *Id.* at 181, 212 A.2d at 824.

he receives an additional yield from the differential in interest rates while (2) retaining the use of a portion of the interest-bearing principal of the loan during the period in which the earlier, "wrapped-around" obligation is left outstanding. This second factor is equally capable of rendering the wrap-around transaction usurious since the interest rate in any loan must be computed on the actual amount advanced from the actual date of advancement.[65] The rule is set forth in *Penziner v. West American Finance Co.*:[66]

> In testing a transaction for usury, interest must be computed on the actual sum advanced from date of advancement.... "While the mere fact that the whole sum loaned is not drawn promptly by the borrower does not render the loan usurious, provided the whole sum was held subject to the borrower's order, yet when such a result is in accordance with an agreement made at the time of the loan, the transaction is obviously usurious" .... If the agreement contemplates that the entire loan shall be available to the borrower, mere delay in its payment to him, in the absence of intent to evade the Usury Law, does not make the loan usurious, but if, as an condition of the loan, the borrower is required to leave part with the lender, interest in excess of the legal rate on [the] sum actually advanced in usurious.[67]

Applying this rule to the hypothetical refinancing transaction, it can be observed that during the first year *L,* the lender, will receive interest on the full $20,000 at a time in which he has advanced only $10,000. Futhermore, *L* will not actually disburse the full $20,000 until two years following the execution of the wrap-around mortgage when the principal amount remaining under the first trust deed becomes due. Hence the wrap-around lender in the early stages of the loan period has advanced a sum less than the full principal on which he is drawing interest. Since the interest return must be calculated on the basis of the principal actually advanced, the net effect of the above delay in advancement of principal will be an increase in the aggregate interest return of the loan. When the face interest rate of the wrap-around refinancing loan is already at or near the statutory maximum, the aggregate interest return, therefore, will undoubtedly be usurious.[68]

The fact that a mortgage corporation had collected interest on funds which it had not actually advanced was determinative to a holding by the Florida

---

[65] *See, e.g.,* American Acceptance Corp. v. Schoenthaler, 391 F.2d 64 (5th Cir.), *cert. denied,* 392 U.S. 928 (1968) (interest may not be charged on portions of principal not disbursed to borrower); Penziner v. West Am. Fin. Co., 133 Cal. App. 578, 24 P.2d 501 (Dist. Ct. App. 1933); Mindlin v. Davis, 74 So. 2d 789 (Fla. 1954); Barr's Adm'rx v. African M.E. Mt. Pisgah Church, 10 A. 287 (N.J. Ch. 1887).

[66] 133 Cal. App. 578, 24 P.2d 501 (Dist. Ct. App. 1933).

[67] *Id.* at 590, 24 P.2d at 506.

[68] The refinancing wrap-around loan with a face interest rate at the statutory maximum would probably be considered usurious even under the unlikely circumstance that a lender voluntarily and promptly prepays the attractive first mortgage obligation despite his contractual right to make payments only as they become due. Whether or not such a voluntary prepayment would be a valid defense to a usury charge would depend, first of all, on whether a court will look at the course of performance of the loan contract in determining its validity, or will look exclusively at the contract as it was made. However, even if a court were willing to accept the former approach and consider that for usury purposes the full amount of the loan principal had in fact been advanced, the lender would still be confronted with the fact that the low-interest benefit of the first mortgage had been exacted from the borrower as a condition or integral part of the wrap-around loan. Hence the wrap-around loan would still be usurious because of the presence of this second element. See notes 60-64 *supra* and accompanying text.

Supreme Court in *Mindlin v. Davis*[69] that a certain refinancing transaction analogous to a wrap-around loan was usurious. In this case the maximum lawful interest rate in Florida was ten percent, and a mortgage corporation had persuaded certain borrowers to apply for a ten percent mortgage loan in the principal amount of $3,300 for the purpose of consolidating borrower's various prior obligations, including an existing five percent first mortgage on their home. The mortgage corporation then sold the $3,300 mortgage to other lenders and informed the borrowers that the loan would be closed directly with the assignee lenders as mortgagees. Implicit in the terms of the application and the negotiations for this mortgage was an agreement that the first mortgage should be discharged out of the proceeds of the new mortgage. The lenders paid the cash portion of the principal to the borrowers and retained the remaining principal to be applied in payment and discharge of the first mortgage. In lieu of immediately discharging the first mortgage pursuant to the implied understanding among the parties, however, the lenders merely paid the monthly installments thereon in the name of the borrowers as they became due.

The borrowers then brought an action for forfeiture of interest as provided under the Florida usury statute,[70] alleging that the note and mortgage were usurious. Although the loan recited an interest rate of ten percent, the maximum lawful rate, the Florida Supreme Court held that retention by lenders of part of the loan principal without a corresponding abatement of interest constituted a scheme designed to exact excess interest over that provided in the note and, therefore, rendered the whole transaction usurious.[71] The court noted:

> Since time as well as amount of principal is a factor in the claculation of interest, it is evident that retention of a substantial portion of the loan without a corresponding abatement of interest on the amount retained has the effect of substantially increasing the per centum of interest on the actual amount advanced by the lenders and received by the borrowers, which is the significant amount contemplated by the statute. It is undisputed in the evidence that the retention by the lenders of that portion of the principal earmarked for the [first] mortgage was by their original intention and design. . . . It is not difficult to appreciate the effect of such a scheme and to recognize it as a device or contrivance for the exaction of usurious interest condemned by the statute.[72]

Although there apparently are no reported decisions which have dealt with the usury issue in a wrap-around transaction,[73] the Florida Supreme Court in *Mindlin* held usurious a loan which, in effect, gave the lender the same dual advantages which he would have received had the transaction been consummated by employing a wrap-around mortgage. It should be noted, however, that the loan which was held usurious, while having the same effects as a wrap-around transaction, did not have the additional element of an *exaction* of an advantageous first mortgage as a condition to the granting of the loan. The lenders in *Mindlin* retained the benefit of the low-interest first mortgage not as a condition, or requirement, of the second loan, but rather as a unilateral action in violation of an implied understanding that the prior loan be extinguished immediately.

---

[69] 74 So. 2d 789 (Fla. 1954).
[70] Fla. Stat. Ann. § 687.03 (Supp. 1972).
[71] 74 So. 2d at 793.
[72] *Id.*
[73] See note 10 *supra* and accompanying text.

On the basis of the foregoing discussion, it would appear that a wrap-around *refinancing* agreement with a valid contractual interest rate would be usurious if the loan renders an effective interest yield in excess of the statutory ceiling due to the existence of either, or both, of two factors: (1) the lender receives interest on a full loan principal which exceeds the total funds he has actually advanced,[74] or (2) the lender exacts additional interest in the form of reaping the benefits of the low interest rate in the prior obligation which is "wrapped around." [75]

The Purchase Money Wrap-Around Mortgage

The legal consequences of wrap-around financing vary when viewed in the context of a sales transaction. This can be illustrated by altering the facts of the example previously used as follows: X owns Blackacre, real property valued at $30,000, subject to an outstanding $10,000 first mortgage bearing five percent interest, with $5,000 of the principal due in one year and the remaining $5,000 principal due in two years. P desires to purchase Blackacre, but offers only $10,000 as a down payment. X agrees to sell the real property to P under the following terms: P will make the $10,000 down payment to X and will execute a wrap-around mortgage for $20,000 bearing nine percent interest, naming X as the mortgagee thereunder. X in return will convey the property to P and will covenant to continue discharging the remaining obligations under the outstanding first mortgage as they mature.

When viewed in the above context of a sales transaction, the wrap-around loan differs from the refinancing loan in two basic ways which diminish the usury implications of the overall transaction. First, in the purchase money loan, unlike the refinancing loan, the lender does not *exact* from the borrower the interest benefit of an advantageous contract. Whereas the benefits of a low interest first mortgage are transferred from borrower to lender as an integral part of the refinancing loan, the wrap-around lender in the sales transaction merely remains personally liable under a prior obligation [76] for which the purchaser-borrower was never personally obligated. A second difference between the two types of wrap-around loans lies in the extent to which the lender actually advances the full principal of the loan upon which he is drawing interest. In the hypothetical refinancing transaction, the borrower becomes obligated under a $20,000 wrap-around mortgage and in exchange receives $10,000 cash plus the lender's promise to pay the borrower's outstanding $10,000 debt obligation on the first mortgage. During the early stages of the loan period before the first mortgage is satisfied, the lender receives interest on the full $20,000 principal; but, he has actually advanced only $10,000 of that amount. On the other hand, the purchaser-borrower in the sales transaction appears to receive a loan for the full $20,000 because he has purchased property valued at $30,000 for a down payment of $10,000, and because the $10,000 first mortgage, although theoretically encumbering the purchased property, is the personal obligation of the seller-lender.

At first glance, therefore, the two elements which tainted the effective interest yield in the refinancing wrap-around loan — the exaction of an extra interest

---

[74] See notes 65-72 *supra* and accompanying text.

[75] See notes 60-64 *supra* and accompanying text.

[76] Since a person may loan or sell his credit without violating the usury laws, the extra return to the lender under the purchase money wrap-around mortgage may be viewed as nonusurious compensation for his loan of credit. *See generally* Annot., 104 A.L.R. 245 (1936).

benefit and the retention of part of the interest-bearing principal [77] — appear
to be absent for the basic purchase money wrap-around loan. Yet, although the
purchaser is paying only nine percent on the amount of his indebtedness in the
above illustration, the overall profit to the seller-lender from the entire
transaction, due to the fact that the lender possesses the low-interest first mortgage obligation, is 9.324 percent. If the lawful interest maximum were set at nine
percent, the same as the contractual rate of the loan, any refinancing
wrap-around loan showing the above performance figure would be usurious.
However, a distinction must be drawn in the case of the purchase money
wrap-around mortgage in that the seller-lender has not agreed to pay the debts
of another, but has continued to be responsible for a debt under which he was
always personally obligated. In essence, what might otherwise appear to be an
extra interest return exacted by the lender as an integral part of the purchase
money wrap-around loan is actually only an independent profit resulting from
the fact that the lender is merely re-lending at a high interest rate a sum of money
which he has personally borrowed at a lower rate. If one borrows a sum of
money, the fact that the lender himself had previously borrowed the principal
amount at a lower rate gives the borrower no cause to complain.[78]
Consequently, the fact that the seller-lender in the purchase money wrap-around
transaction has procured a portion of the principal amount which he is lending
to the purchaser at an interest rate below that which he has charged to the
purchaser-borrower should not permit the latter to successfully challenge the
loan as usurious. In fact, it is the use of this "leverage" which enables most
institutional lenders to operate at a profit.

It follows, then, that the interest differential, or "leverage," inherent in the
purchase money wrap-around loan is an independent profit, and there is no
"exaction" of interest element which can give rise to an excess effective yield for
usury purposes. The purchase money wrap-around transaction can be attacked,
therefore, only on the remaining ground that the vendor is receiving interest on
a principal amount which is greater than that which he has actually advanced.
This attack will probably fail because the seller-lender continues to be the sole
obligor under the first mortgage obligation, which, when added to the lender's
remaining equity in the property, will be equal to the full principal of the
wrap-around loan.

The problem of determining the amount which should be treated as the
principal in computing the allowable rate of interest in a loan was recognized by
the California District Court of Appeals in *Orlando v. Berns*.[79] In this case, a
borrower had fallen deeply in debt, had encountered difficulty in obtaining a
loan to liquidate his debts, and was in imminent danger of losing his property.
As a result of negotiations, certain lenders promised to liquidate borrower's
outstanding indebtedness, in exchange for which the borrower conveyed his real
property to the lenders and received back a written option to repurchase. In
order to extinguish the borrower's prior debts, the lenders, in turn, obtained an
independent loan of $145,000 upon a substantial portion of the property, evi-
denced by their own promissory note and secured by a deed of trust on the
property. The lenders then used the $145,000 proceeds of their independent
loan and an additional sum of $30,874.20 cash to pay the borrower's prior debts
as agreed. The lenders agreed to pay the monthly installments of principal and

---

[77] See text accompanying notes 74-75 *supra*.
[78] *Cf.* note 82 *infra* and accompanying text.
[79] 154 Cal. App. 2d 753, 316 P.2d 705 (Dist. Ct. App. 1957).

interest on the $145,000 loan until the borrower exercised his option, at which time the borrower would buy the property back subject to the outstanding indebtedness of this loan. Thereafter, the borrower exercised his option to repurchase at the agreed price of $200,000 less the amount of the principal balance remaining due on the $145,000 loan.[80]

The borrower subsequently brought an action alleging that the agreement constituted a usurious loan. The trial court found, first of all, that the transaction was in fact a loan to the borrower and not a sale with an option to repurchase. The trial court then held the loan to be usurious by calculating the interest rate based on a principal of only $30,874.20, the amount of cash advanced by the lenders towards liquidating the borrower's debts.[81] On appeal, however, the California District Court of Appeals concluded that the loan was not usurious and held that the principal of the loan should include not only the amount the lenders had advanced in cash, but the $145,000 which they had borrowed independently on their own promissory note and used toward extinguishing the borrower's original indebtedness. As stated by the *Orlando* court:

> The $145,000 was an integral part of the transaction. The defendants [lenders] hired it from the insurance company upon their own promissory note as makers. The fact that some of plaintiff's [borrower's] property was used as security does not detract from the fact that defendants obtained the money (which plaintiff was unable to do) and made it available to liquidate his debts and refinance his undertaking. Defendants continued as obligors to the insurance company and will continue so until plaintiff completes his repurchase and assumes the payment of the unpaid balance of $145,000. Indeed, they will continue obligated until the entire amount is paid unless and until the insurance company lender accepts the plaintiff as sole debtor in lieu of the defendants.[82]

In holding that the amount borrowed independently by the lenders in order to pay off their borrower's prior indebtedness, even though their borrower's property was used as security for the loan, should be considered as principal in determining whether the usury laws had been violated, the court in *Orlando* recognized that a loan could be predicated upon funds obtained through exercise of a lender's credit. Pursuant to this principle, it would seem that the amount loaned to the purchaser of property by a vendor who has wrapped around a prior loan obligation obtained by him on his own credit should be computed in the same fashion, thus permitting the vendor to charge the maximum statutory interest rate on the full principal amount of the wrap-around loan without incurring an excess effective yield for usury purposes.[83]

The legitimacy of the wrap-around loan in a sale of real property is further enhanced by the fact that where there is a bona fide sales transaction, the seller

---

[80] *Id.* at 754, 316 P.2d at 706.

[81] By deducting the $30,874.20 from $60,509.20, the repurchase price of $200,000 minus the unpaid residue of the $145,000 loan at the time the repurchase option was exercised, the lower court held that the lenders had exacted $29,635 from the borrower. "The latter sum, treated as interest upon $30,874.20 obviously exceeded . . . the maximum rate allowable under the California usury laws." *Id.* at 758, 316 P.2d at 708.

[82] *Id.*

[83] It should be noted, however, that the refinancing transaction which was deemed nonusurious in *Orlando* is distinguishable from the refinancing wrap-around technique deemed usurious in the previous section of this Note. Contrary to the typical wrap-around refinancing loan, the deed of trust in *Orlando* was procured by the lenders on their own credit so as to make them personally obligated thereunder, and there existed no prior advantageous loan to be "exacted" from the borrower.

may designate a lower cash price and a higher term price without violating the usury laws.[84] If the vendor is free to set a higher price for a credit sale, he should also be able to condition a credit sale upon retention of the benefits of his first mortgage by insisting that the wrap-around technique be employed.

It would appear, therefore, that when a vendor of real property wraps around his prior loan obligation in order to finance a sale of his own property and imposes the maximum statutory interest rate on the face of the resultant purchase money wrap-around mortgage, the usury laws have not been violated. The dual elements which taint wrap-around loans in the refinancing context — (1) the exaction from the borrower of his prior advantageous loan and (2) the fact that the lender has advanced less than the principal amount of the wrap-around mortgage — are not present in a sales transaction where the vendor extends a purchase money wrap-around loan to his purchaser.

The Purchase Money Wrap-Around Mortgage with Third Party Financing

The wrap-around loan must be viewed in still another context which incorporates some of the elements of the refinancing and sales transactions described above. The wrap-around loan could conceivably be employed in a case where a vendor and purchaser look to a third person for aid in financing the purchase of real property. The transaction in this context may be illustrated as follows: X owns Blackacre, real property valued at $30,000, subject to a $10,000 first mortgage which bears five percent interest and will mature in two years. P desires to purchase Blackacre, but only offers $10,000 as a down payment. X and P approach L to secure financing of the sale. L agrees to finance the transaction if P will execute and convey to L a wrap-around mortgage bearing nine percent interest on a principal amount of $20,000 and if X agrees to permit L to assume the obligations under the outstanding first mortgage. If the agreement is consummated, P will receive title to Blackacre, pay the $10,000 down payment to X and pay to L the amounts which become due under the $20,000 wrap-around mortgage. L in return will pay X $10,000 cash, representing X's remaining equity in Blackacre, and will pay the obligations under the first mortgage as they mature.

As previously discussed, the wrap-around loan will be usurious whenever the effective interest yield to the lender exceeds the lawful maximum. When the interest specified on the face of the wrap-around mortgage is within the statutory ceiling, the effective yield will nevertheless be excessive and the loan will, therefore, be usurious if the lender's return is enhanced through the presence of either of two elements: (1) the receipt of interest on a principal amount in excess of that which the lender has advanced or borrowed on his own credit; or (2) the receipt of an interest differential between the high rate of the wrap-around loan and the low rate embodied in a prior obligation which is exacted by the lender as a condition to granting the loan.[85]

---

[84] *See, e.g.,* Mid-State Homes, Inc. v. Staines, 161 So. 2d 569 (Fla. Dist. Ct. App. 1964); Plastics Dev. Corp. v. Flexible Prods. Co., 112 Ga. App. 460, 145 S.E.2d 655 (1965); Falcone v. Palmer Ford, Inc., 242 Md. 487, 219 A.2d 808 (1966); Aglio v. Carousel, Inc., 34 Misc. 2d 79, 228 N.Y.S.2d 350 (Sup. Ct. 1962); Lamb v. Ed Maher, Inc., 368 S.W.2d 255 (Tex. Civ. App. 1963). *See also* Annot., 14 A.L.R.3d 1065 (1967). The existence of the "time price differential" exception prompted the New York Court of Appeals to declare that the purchase money mortgage was not a "loan" which could be governed by the New York usury statute. *See* Mandelino v. Fribourg, 23 N.Y.2d 145, 242 N.E.2d 823, 295 N.Y.S.2d 654 (1968).

[85] See notes 60-64, 65-72 *supra* and accompanying text.

In the above example, if *L,* as lender under this "tripartite" purchase money wrap-around mortgage, merely covenants to pay the obligations under the first mortgage as they become due, he will be receiving interest on an amount above that which he has advanced or borrowed on his own credit; hence, the first element of the above test will be present. Whenever the contractual interest rate is near the statutory ceiling, therefore, the aggregate return to *L* will exceed the lawful maximum, and the transaction will be usurious. Following the rule that interest must be computed on the actual sum advanced from the date of advancement, it appears that the fact that the lender is collecting interest on funds which he has not actually advanced would taint the transaction with usury pursuant to the *Mindlin* holding discussed previously.[86]

If the lender, however, rather than merely covenanting to pay the obligations under the first mortgage, could validly assume the prior mortgage, he might under some circumstances be deemed to have advanced, in cash or borrowed funds, the full principal amount of the wrap-around loan. Under such circumstances the tripartite wrap-around sales transaction with a contractual interest rate at the maximum statutory level might not be usurious. The propriety of including as principal in one loan funds which were independently borrowed by the lender in another loan, even when the lender has pledged the borrower's property as security thereon, was established in the *Orlando* case.[87] It should be noted, however, that an assumption of a first mortgage does not ordinarily release the original mortgagor from his obligations thereunder, but merely makes him a surety for the assuming party who becomes the principal obligor.[88] This fact may serve to distinguish and invalidate the tripartite loan of borrowed funds from the basic purchase money wrap-around mortgage and the analogous loan transaction upheld in *Orlando.* By emphasizing the fact that the *Orlando* lenders had obtained and made available funds "upon their own promissory notes as makers," [89] the court in *Orlando* was perhaps inferring that only those funds obtained by a party as *sole* obligor in one loan could be made the proper subject of the principal extended by the same party as a lender in another loan.

Of course, the mortgagee of the first mortgage could expressly agree to accept the assuming wrap-around lender as his sole debtor and release the vendor of the encumbered property from all liability for the debt.[90] If this were the case, a stronger argument could be made for including the amount remaining due on the prior loan as principal of the wrap-around loan, since the wrap-around lender would be the sole obligor under the first mortgage and, therefore, would fall more closely within the factual situation declared nonusurious in *Orlando.*[91]

---

[86] See notes 65-67, 69-72 *supra* and accompanying text.

[87] See note 82 *supra* and accompanying text.

[88] *See, e.g.,* Layton v. West, 271 Cal. App. 2d 508, 76 Cal. Rptr. 507 (Dist. Ct. App. 1969); Betts v. Brown, 219 Ga. 782, 136 S.E.2d 365 (1964); Smith v. General Inv., Inc., 246 Miss. 765, 150 So. 2d 862 (1963). *See also* G. OSBORNE, HANDBOOK ON THE LAW OF MORTGAGES § 247 (2d ed. 1970).

[89] 154 Cal. App. 758, 316 P.2d at 708. See note 82 *supra* and accompanying text.

[90] *See, e.g.,* Seale v. Berryman, 46 Ariz. 233, 49 P.2d 997 (1935); Chatterley v. Safe Deposit & Trust Co., 168 Md. 656, 178 A. 854 (1935); State *ex rel.* Comm'rs of the Land Office v. Pitts, 197 Okla. 644, 173 P.2d 923 (1946). *See also* G. OSBORNE, HANDBOOK ON THE LAW OF MORTGAGES § 247 (2d ed. 1970).

[91] A similar argument could be made by the wrap-around lender in the *refinancing* wrap-around transaction discussed previously. However, in the unlikely event that the lender in the refinancing loan was able to assume the prior loan and secure a release of the original obligor thereon, and then persuade a court that he has in fact advanced the full principal amount in cash or funds borrowed on his own credit, the validity of the wrap-around loan would by no means be established because the second usurious element in the refinancing loan would still be present. Specifically, the fact that

Even if the lender could establish that he has in fact made a bona fide loan of funds borrowed on his credit, the tripartite purchase money wrap-around transaction might still be deemed usurious if the benefits of the first mortgage were viewed as additional interest exacted as a condition of granting the loan.[92] Of course, the difference here from the simple refinancing transaction discussed earlier is that the benefits of the prior obligation could not be exacted from the *borrower* in the tripartite transaction because he never had any claim or right to them. Rather, the low-interest obligation under the first mortgage has been held by the vendor, who is not a borrower in the tripartite purchase money wrap-around transaction and is essentially, therefore, a stranger to the basic debtor-creditor relationship of that loan. To pursue this line of attack, then, one would have to argue that since the vendor was forced to permit the lender to assume the advantageous first mortgage as a condition to financing the sales transaction, even though the vendor is essentially a third party to the basic wrap-around loan, the benefits derived therefrom should still be deemed additional interest which renders the transaction usurious. However, since nothing is exacted from the *borrower,* and since the bonus derived from the assumption of the first mortgage is given, rather, by the vendor for his own purpose to induce the making of the loan, a court would probably reject the above argument. Such a court would then hold that the exaction of the beneficial loan from the vendor in the tripartite sales transaction is not to be viewed as additional interest capable of inflating the effective yield of the loan for usury purposes. This would be in accord with numerous decisions which have held that a bonus given or paid to a lender by a *third party,* for his own purpose or reasons, to induce the making of a loan, does not taint the transaction as usurious.[93]

Evaluation of the usurious or non-usurious nature of the wrap-around loan in this tripartite context is not as clear cut as it was in the two-party refinancing and purchase money transactions. While it can safely be assumed that no exaction of extra interest from the borrower is present, it appears that the lender is receiving interest on a principal amount which is greater than that which he has advanced. If the lender merely covenants to make payments on the prior loan or simply assumes that obligation, a transaction with a contractual interest rate at or near the statutory maximum would probably be usurious because the lender has not actually borrowed the amount of the prior loan as sole obligor thereunder. The difficult case is where there has been a total assumption by a lender of the prior indebtedness which completely releases the original mortgagor. Here, a strong argument could be made for including the amount of the prior obligation as principal advanced by the lender since he has assumed sole liability for the prior indebtedness. If this theory were accepted by the courts, the loan with a contractual interest rate at the statutory maximum would not be usurious. However, it is perhaps more likely that a court would hold that borrowed funds can be viewed as principal only when the initial loan was procured by the lender on his own credit and not through coerced assumption of an outstanding loan. If the latter viewpoint were adopted, the transaction would be usurious.

In conclusion, the tripartite sales financing transaction employing the

---

the lender has exacted from the borrower the benefits derived through the interest differential between the first and wrap-around mortgages would in itself be sufficient to taint the transaction as usurious. See notes 60-64 *supra* and accompanying text.

[92] See notes 60-64 *supra* and accompanying text.

[93] *See, e.g.,* Fred G. Clark Co. v. E.C. Warner Co., 188 Minn. 277, 247 N.W. 225 (1933); Goodman v. Seely, 243 S.W.2d 858 (Tex. Civ. App. 1951); Greenberg v. Manganese Prods., Inc., 39 Wash. 2d 79, 238 P.2d 1194 (1951).

wrap-around technique would probably be deemed usurious whenever the lender charges an interest rate at or near the statutory maximum because the additional factors of delayed principal advancement and interest benefit exaction would probably be deemed to inflate the effective interest yield in excess of the statutory limit. However, the lender's chances of eliminating the effect of these factors for usury purposes and of successfully defending a usury charge are greatest in cases where the lender assumes exclusive liability for the first mortgage and, contemporaneously, procures the release of the original obligor from any obligation thereunder.

Conclusion

The prudent lender will investigate the potential effects of the usury laws before entering into a loan employing the wrap-around technique. The first inquiry should focus on the applicable statute to determine whether the contemplated loan is exempted from coverage. If the usury law does govern the transaction, the interest return of the loan must be tested for usury by computing the interest over the entire period of the loan. Consequently, any wrap-around transaction will be non-usurious if the effective yield to the lender computed over the entire period of the obligation does not exceed the maximum interest rate permitted by statute.

Where the wrap-around borrower is paying an interest rate at or near the statutory maximum, a refinancing transaction employing the wrap-around technique will produce an effective yield to the lender in excess of this lawful limit and will, therefore, be usurious. This is because the lender is receiving interest on a greater amount than he has advanced and because the exaction of the advantageous prior obligation from the borrower as a condition to granting the refinancing loan will be viewed as additional interest. In a sales transaction, on the other hand, a vendor may wrap-around his prior obligation, charge a contractual interest rate which is at or near the statutory ceiling, and receive an overall profit from the entire transaction in excess of the statutory maximum without violating the usury laws. Such a basic purchase money wrap-around is not usurious because there is no element of exaction when the vendor wraps around his personal debt and because the seller-lender has actually advanced equity and borrowed funds equal to the full principal of the loan. Finally, when a third party finances a sales transaction by wrapping around an existing obligation, charges a contractual interest rate at or near the statutory ceiling, and thereby receives an overall profit in excess of the statutory maximum, the loan is usurious if the lender has not assumed the prior obligation in such a manner as to become the sole obligor thereunder. Even if there was such an exclusive assumption, the transaction might still be deemed usurious because the bona fides of the loan of borrowed funds in this context are questionable.

As a result of these conclusions, the wrap-around lender participating in refinancing or tripartite loans should charge a contractual interest rate sufficiently below the statutory ceiling to limit his effective interest yield over the entire term of the loan to the statutory maximum and thereby ensure the legality of the transaction. The wrap-around loan may prove most beneficial to lenders in the form of the purchase money loan, where the seller-lender should be able to charge the statutory maximum to his borrower and receive an overall profit in excess of the lawful rate without violating the usury laws.

It must be recognized that the complex usury issues discussed in this Note have yet to meet judicial scrutiny.[94] This Note has attempted to speculate as to the probable judicial resolution of such issues by examining traditional usury principles and previous judicial treatment of analogous financing schemes. If lenders are able to understand the impact of the usury laws upon the wrap-around loan, they should have no fear of entering into transactions employing the wrap-around technique. However, lenders should be aware that the wrap-around loan may also require special treatment in relation to several other factors such as the application of "first lien" requirements for certain institutional lenders,[95] Securities Exchange Commission and Blue Sky Law disclosure requirements for corporate lenders, and problems created by the presence of acceleration clauses in pre-existing loan obligations.[96] In spite of the precautions which must be taken prior to its use, the wrap-around loan should prove to be of great value to the lender who utilizes the technique judiciously.

---

[94] See note 10 *supra* and accompanying text.
[95] *See generally* P.L.I., *supra* note 5.
[96] *See generally* Healey, *supra* note 6.

Chapter 9

FEDERAL GOVERNMENT INVOLVEMENT

> There are two things that can disrupt business in this country. One is
> war and the other is a meeting of the Federal Reserve Bank.
>
> Will Rogers, *Daily Telegram,* April 2, 1929

While one would expect state legislatures and courts to be concerned with the
law of real property and the attendant law of secured transactions involving real
estate, one might not consider the extent to which the federal government of the
United States is involved in various aspects of real estate finance. With most
residential financing available from federally chartered savings and loan associations and to a lesser degree from national banks, it is understandable that the
federal government is involved. Further, the programs of the government to
allow a wider range of buyers in the home market through VA and FHA insured
residential financing extend the government's involvement. The secondary
money market is a great control factor in the availability of money for real estate
finance and this is almost exclusively in the province of the federal government.
Consider such statutory restrictions as the Truth in Lending Act, 15 U.S.C.
§ 1600 et seq., and the Real Estate Settlement Procedures Act, 12 U.S.C. § 2601
et seq., or the Bankruptcy Act, 11 U.S.C. § 1 et seq., and the Soldiers' and Sailors'
Relief Act, 50 U.S.C. App. § 525, which limit foreclosure, and it is apparent that
the federal government is concerned with real estate finance from the very
beginning to the very end of a mortgage. So great is this involvement that federal
preemption now appears as a basis for limiting state courts' ability to handle
matters long thought to be entirely within their province. It is with these several
areas of federal involvement that this chapter is concerned.

A. VA AND FHA FINANCING

Two administrative agencies of the federal government have for several
decades been greatly involved in residential real estate finance: the Veterans
Administration and the Federal Housing Administration. These two agencies
provide potential buyers entry into the housing market through low down
payment financing by insuring loans made by institutional lenders. FHA loans
enable buyers to obtain financing with less cash down payment than the conventional twenty percent. FHA insured loans are made on a sliding scale down
payment, depending on the size of the loan, up to a statutory limit. 24 C.F.R.
§ 203.18; 38 C.F.R. § 36.4302. VA financing enables qualified veterans to
become homeowners with virtually no cash down payment. These two agencies
require a certain minimal quality in homes before insuring such loans, 24 C.F.R.
§§ 200.925-200.935.

VA and FHA insured financing limits the amount of interest rate lenders can
charge, 24 C.F.R. § 203.20; 38 C.F.R. § 36.4311, and to some degree sets a
standard in the industry. However, government insured financing may involve
the payment of more loan origination fee "points" [1] than conventional financing.

---

[1] "Points" refers to a percentage of the loan sought, *i.e.,* one point is one percent of the principal
so that "two points on a $100,000 loan would be a loan fee of $2,000" which typically the borrower

These federal agencies may also come in conflict with rules of state law when, after paying the insured amount to the lenders, they commence foreclosure.

UNITED STATES v. STADIUM APARTMENTS, INC.

United States Court of Appeals
425 F.2d 358 (9th Cir. 1970)

Duniway, Circuit Judge: This case presents the question whether state redemption statutes should apply when the Federal Housing Authority (FHA) forecloses a mortgage which it has guaranteed. We hold that such statutes do not apply.

The federal statute here involved is Title VI of the National Housing Act, 12 U.S.C. §§ 1736-1746a. The stated objective of Title VI is "to assist in relieving the acute shortage of housing . . . available to veterans of World War II at prices within their reasonable ability to pay. . . ." 12 U.S.C. § 1738(a). The statute confers authority upon the Secretary (formerly the Commissioner) "to make such rules and regulations as may be necessary to carry out the provisions of this subchapter." 12 U.S.C. § 1742. Such regulations were promulgated, and those that were in force in November 1949, when the mortgage here in question was executed and insured appear in the 1947 Supplement to the Code of Federal Regulations. (24 C.F.R. § 580 (1947 Supp.).) Citations to C.F.R. in this opinion are to the 1947 supplement.

The way in which the Act and regulations operated are [sic] well illustrated in this case. In 1949, appellee Stadium Apartments, Inc., desired to construct, under Title VI, an apartment house in Caldwell, Idaho. It applied to Prudential Insurance Company for a loan. Such a loan was eligible for insurance under 12 U.S.C. § 1743(a). The conditions for eligibility are set out in 12 U.S.C. § 1743(b). The mortgagor must be approved by the Secretary, who can impose certain regulations upon both the mortgagor and the property mortgaged. Certain terms of the mortgage are also prescribed. Application for approval was made, as required by 24 C.F.R. §§ 580.1-580.7. The FHA then issued a commitment of insurance, as required by 24 C.F.R. § 580.8. The mortgage was executed upon a form prescribed by FHA, and accepted for insurance. 24 C.F.R. §§ 580.10-580.37. The amount of the insured loan was $130,000. The mortgage contained this provision:

> The Mortgagor, to the extent permitted by law, hereby waives the benefit of any and all homestead and exemption laws and of any right to a stay or redemption and the benefit of any moratorium law or laws.

Stadium Apartments defaulted in 1966, and Prudential assigned the mortgage to the Secretary of Housing and Urban Development, pursuant to 12 U.S.C. § 1743(c). The Secretary paid Prudential the amount then due, as required by 12 U.S.C. § 1743(c). The United States then obtained a default judgment foreclosing the mortgage, 12 U.S.C. §§ 1713(k), 1743(f). The district judge, in spite of the foregoing provision, framed the foreclosure decree to allow for a one-year period of redemption, as provided by 2 Idaho Code § 11-402. The question is whether this was error.

Stadium Apartments, Inc., having defaulted, is not represented here. Because

---

would pay. However, in an FHA loan the borrower is not permitted to pay points, which the seller must pay. The limit set on the interest rates which FHA-insured lenders can charge also dictates the amount of points paid. 12 U.S.C. § 1425.

the question is of some importance, we were disturbed that the government had chosen to appeal this uncontested case, when hitherto the FHA has at times consented to decrees providing for post-sale redemption rights as required by state laws. We therefore determined, following the initial oral argument in which only government counsel appeared, that the Attorneys General of the states within our circuit and of the Territory of Guam should be invited to submit amicus curiae briefs. The State of California has done so, taking a position opposed to that advocated by the government. . . .

. . . .

Finally, we come to the third question: should the federal courts adopt the local law granting a post-foreclosure sale right of redemption in those states where it exists? Here, both authority and policy convince us that they should not.

Every federal appellate case dealing with the government's foreclosure remedy under insured mortgages applies federal law to assure the protection of the federal program against loss, state law to the contrary notwithstanding. Most of the cases cite and apply the principles of View Crest. Many cases rely upon express provisions in the mortgage that are in conflict with local law, but frequently couch the decision in broader terms. Several of these cases involve appointment of a receiver pending foreclosure: *United States v. Chester Park Apts.*, 8 Cir., 1964, 332 F.2d 1; *United States v. Sylacauga Properties, Inc.*, 5 Cir., 1963, 323 F.2d 487, 491; *United States v. Queen's Court Apts., Inc.*, 9 Cir., 1961, 296 F.2d 534, 539; *United States v. View Crest Garden Apts., Inc., supra*, cf. *Director of Revenue, State of Colo. v. United States*, 10 Cir., 1968, 392 F.2d 307, 311 (Small Business Administration mortgage). One such case holds that the government can collect and retain the rents during the period of redemption (consented to by the government), contrary to local Idaho law. *Clark Investment Co. v. United States*, [364 F.2d 7 (9th Cir. 1966)]. In *United States v. Queen's Court Apts., Inc., supra*, we also held, relying on 24 C.F.R. 280.30(d) (1949 ed.) and on a comparable provision in the articles of incorporation of the mortgagor, that pending foreclosure the United States could retain a "replacement reserve fund" and need not, upon foreclosure, apply it to reduce the mortgage debt.

Other cases rely on the applicable federal regulation as controlling over local law. See *United States v. Shimer*, 1961, 367 U.S. 374, 81 S.Ct. 1554, 6 L.Ed.2d 908; *United States v. Rossi*, 9 Cir., 1965, 342 F.2d 505; *McKnight v. United States*, 9 Cir., 1958, 259 F.2d 540, 543-544, all dealing with loans guaranteed by the Veterans Administration. Each holds that the federal regulation is controlling, state anti-deficiency judgment statutes to the contrary notwithstanding, because the applicable law is federal. See also *Penagaricano v. Allen Corp.*, 1 Cir., 1959, 267 F.2d 550, dealing with the duty to make repairs.

Many cases simply rely on principles of federal law, in the absence of directly applicable federal statutes or regulations. *United States v. Wells*, 5 Cir., 1968, 403 F.2d 596; *United States v. Walker Park Realty, Inc.*, 2 Cir., 1967, 383 F.2d 732; *Herlong-Sierra Homes, Inc. v. United States*, 9 Cir., 1966, 358 F.2d 300; and *United States v. Flower Manor, Inc.*, 3 Cir., 1965, 344 F.2d 958. Each holds that the United States is entitled to a deficiency judgment upon foreclosure, although in each case the local law was to the contrary. *United States v. Helz*, 6 Cir., 1963, 314 F.2d 301, upholds a personal judgment in favor of the United States against a wife who signed a note guaranteed by FHA in spite of the contrary Michigan law of coverture. See also *Director of Revenue v. United States, supra*, 392 F.2d at 312, holding that the lien of a first mortgage to the Small Business Administration prevails over a subsequent state tax lien, in spite of local state law, and *United States v. Carson*, 6 Cir., 1967, 372 F.2d 429, applying federal rather than local law to sustain liability to the United States for conversion of property subject to a chattel mortgage to the United States under the Bankhead-Jones Farm Tenant Act. 7 U.S.C. § 1941 *ff.*

Through all of these cases there runs a dominant rationale, that stated by us in *View Crest, supra,* — "Now [after default] the federal policy to protect the treasury and to promote the security of federal investment which in turn promotes the prime purpose of the Act — to facilitate the building of homes by the use of federal credit — becomes predominant. *Local rules limiting the effectiveness of the remedies available to the United States for breach of a federal duty can not be adopted."* (268 F.2d at 383, emphasis added.)

California relies heavily upon two cases, *United States v. Yazell,* 1966, 382 U.S. 341, 86 S.Ct. 500, 15 L.Ed.2d 404, and *Bumb v. United States,* 9 Cir., 1960, 276 F.2d 729. We are convinced that the facts of these two cases are distinguishable.

Yazell involved a Small Business Administration disaster loan which was individually negotiated "in painfully particularized detail." The loan contract referred to Texas law in several respects, and nowhere indicated that the Texas law of coverture would not apply. The Texas law, since repealed, provided that a married woman could not bind her separate property without court order. The Supreme Court held that the SBA could not

> voluntarily and deliberately make a negotiated contract with knowledge of the limited capacity and liability of the persons with whom it contracts, and thereafter insist, in disregard of such limitation, upon collecting (a) despite state law to the contrary relating to family property rights and liabilities, and (b) in the absence of federal statute, regulation or even any contract provision indicating that the state law would be disregarded. 382 U.S. at 350-351, 86 S.Ct. at 506.

The court contrasted the individually negotiated *Yazell* loan with the mortgage in *United States v. Helz, supra.* In *Helz,* the court refused to apply the Michigan law of coverture to a mortgage under the National Housing Act, foreclosed by an agency "which issues separate forms for each State but does not negotiate with individual applicants." *United States v. View Crest Garden Apts., Inc., supra,* is also cited in *Yazell,* 382 U.S. at 348 n. 15, 86 S.Ct. with apparent approval. The *Yazell* Court also emphasized that the *Yazell* loan involved the "intensely local interests of family property and the protection (whether or not it is up-to-date or even welcome) of married women." 382 U.S. at 349, 86 S.Ct. at 505.

In *Bumb* this court held that the Small Business Administration should have complied with a California "bulk sales" statute in perfecting its chattel mortgage, but noted that:

> it must be kept in mind that Section 3440.1 [the California Act] regulates only the manner of acquisition of a valid security interest, and does not purport to regulate the remedy of the mortgagee after default by the mortgagor . . . . This distinction was clearly recognized in *United States v. View Crest Garden Apartments, Inc., supra.* . . . 276 F.2d at 737.

Here, too, we deal with the remedy, and as we have seen, in every such case involving federally insured mortgages, the courts have applied federal law "for the protection of the treasury and to promote the security of the federal investment."

Reasons of policy dictate the same result. In the first place, only 26 of the states provide for post-foreclosure redemption. The periods of redemption vary widely.[4] So do other conditions to redemption and the rules governing right to possession, right to rents, making repairs, and other matters arising during the redemption period. See, *e.g., Clark Investment Co. v. United States, supra, . . .* right to rents. There is a split of authority as to whether the right of redemption can be waived. Similarly, there is split of authority as to the right of the mortgagee to recover the value of improvements made during the redemption period. It would be contrary to the teaching of every case that we have cited to hold that there is a different federal policy in each state, thus making FHA "subject to the vagaries of the laws of the several states." *Clearfield Trust Co. v. United States,* 1943, 318 U.S. 363, 367, 63 S.Ct. 573, 575, 87 L.Ed. 838. Which policy is to be the federal policy, that of the states which do not provide for a period of redemption, or that of those which do? And if the policy is to be the latter, is it to embrace, in each state, all of the special rules applicable in that state alone? Is it to be expanded to establish a federal right of redemption in each state where none exists under local law?

In response to our request, the government has informed us of the views of federal agencies involved in the lending or insuring of funds for private housing purposes. These include, in addition to the Federal Housing Administration, the Farmers Home Administration of the Department of Agriculture, acting under 42 U.S.C. § 1471 *ff.,* and the Veterans Administration, acting under 38 U.S.C. § 1800 *ff.* We quote the government's response:

> The Farmers Home Administration, the Federal Housing Administration, and the Veterans Administration have informed us that their experience has indicated that the imposition of post-foreclosure-sale redemption periods makes the foreclosure remedy more costly and administratively time-consuming in those states whose local law so provides. Generally, the reasons given in support of this conclusion are . . . that existence of a post-sale period for redemption chills bidding at the foreclosure sale, forcing the United States to buy the property at the sale and to hold it (paying meanwhile the costs of maintenance) until the expiration of the period, when it finally can give good title to a purchaser. . . .

We do not find the policy arguments presented by California convincing. First, it is argued that the purpose of the redemption statutes is to force the mortgagee and others to bid the full market price at the sale. We assume that this is the purpose; we are not convinced that the statutes accomplish it. What third party would bid and pay the full market value, knowing that he cannot have the property to do with as he wishes until a set period has gone by, and that at the end of the period he may not get it, but instead may be forced to accept a payment which may or may not fully reimburse him for his outlays? In some states he cannot get possession. *E.g.,* California Code Civ.Proc. § 703; *Mau,*

---

[4] The following is a list, supplied by the government, of the state laws imposing post-foreclosure redemption periods, other than Idaho, and the periods prescribed:

7 Alabama Code (Recomp.1958) 727 (2 years); Alaska Statutes 09.45.190, 09.35.250 (1 year); 4 Ariz.Rev.Stat. 12-1282 (6 months); 3A Ark.Stat.1947 Ann. 30-440 (1 year); Cal.Code Civ.Proc. 725a (1 year); Colorado Rev.Stat. (1963) 118-9-2 (6 months); 77 Ill.Ann.Stat. 18c (1 year); 4 Kan.Stat.Ann. 60-2414 (6 to 18 months); Kentucky Rev.Stat. 426.220 (1 year); 14 Maine Rev.Stat.Ann. 6204 (1 year); Mich.Stat.Ann. 27A.3140, M.C.L.A. § 600.3140 (6 months); Minn.Stat.Ann. 580.23 (6 months); 29 Vernon's Ann.Mo.Stat. 443.410 (1 year); 7 Rev.Code Mont. 93-5836(2) (1 year); 1 Rev.Stat. 21.210 (1 year); 5 N.Mex.Stat.Ann. 24-2-19, 24-2-19.1 (9 months); 6 N.Dak.Cent.Code 32-19-18 (1 year); 1 Or.Rev.Stat. 23.560 (1 year); S.D.Comp.Laws (1967) 21-52-1 et seq. (1 year); Tenn.Code Ann. 64-801 (2 years); Utah Rules Civ.Proc., Rule 69 (f) (3) (6 months); 4 Vermont Stat.Ann. Title 12, App. III, Rule 39 (1 year); Rev.Code Wash.Ann. 6.24.140 (8 months or a year); Wyoming Stat. 1-480 (6 months).

Wisconsin postpones the foreclosure sale until a one year period for redemption after judgment has expired. Wisconsin Stat.Ann. 278.10(2).

Sadler & Co. v. Kearney, 143 Cal. 506, 77 P. 411; *Haynes v. Tredway,* 133 Cal. 400, 65 P. 892. In some states if he does get possession and collects rents, they will be deducted from his reimbursement, *e.g.,* Idaho, *Clark Investment Co. v. United States, supra.* In some states, if he makes repairs, he will not be repaid for his outlays. These are precisely the problems which the federal government should not have to face. It is not in the real estate business. It should not have to hold and manage properties for any period longer than is absolutely necessary for it to get back its money. It should not be subjected to the risk that the property will deteriorate, and it should not be left with no means to protect itself against such losses.

Our doubts as to whether the statutes accomplish the purpose is reinforced by the fact that in many states, partly because of those statutes, real estate financing is almost exclusively secured by trust deeds with power of sale. This is certainly true in California, and the statutory right of redemption does not apply to such sales. *Py v. Pleitner,* 1945, 70 Cal.App.2d 576, 161 P.2d 393; *Roberts v. True,* 1908, 7 Cal.App. 379, 94 P. 392. . . . One is tempted to inquire why, if public policy so strongly favors a post-sale period of redemption, the legislature has not applied it to sales under trust deeds? Perhaps it is because the redemption statute has, in some states, made the use of mortgages almost a dead letter.

Moreover, the policy of FHA is to bid the fair market value at the foreclosure sale. For this purpose, it has the property carefully appraised before bidding. See Book 2, Volume VII, Sec. 72926 of the FHA Manual. It is authorized by 12 U.S.C. § 1713(k) to "bid any sum up to but not in excess of the total unpaid indebtedness secured by the mortgage, plus taxes, insurance, foreclosure costs, fees, and other expenses. . . ." It bids fair market value for its own protection as well as that of the mortgagor and other lienors. It is limited to the amount specified because the objective is to recover its loss on the mortgage insurance, not to put the government in the business of buying and speculating in real property. Presumably, if the property is worth more, others will increase the bid, the government will be paid in full, and the excess will go to junior lien holders and, if there be sufficient funds, to the mortgagor.

It is also suggested that a purpose of the redemption statutes is to protect junior lienors. Perhaps. But if the objective of the statutes is to obtain bids equal to market value, and if as is argued, the bidding would be lower in the absence of the statutes, then junior lienors could more easily protect themselves in the latter situation. They could buy the property at the sale for less. It is always open to the junior lienors to protect themselves by bidding. They take with notice of the senior lien. Here, the government's judgment was for $93,804.97; its bid was $55,100. The court found the value of the property to be $58,000. The deficiency judgment is for $37,728.88. This is a singularly inappropriate case in which to be concerned about junior lien holders. They simply have no equity in the property. There is no evidence that second mortgagees or contractors are less willing to extend credit on the security of junior liens in the states that have no redemption statutes than they are in the states that do, or in California when the first lien is almost always secured by a trust deed rather than by a mortgage.

Nor is it accurate to say that the application of state redemption rights does not tie up government funds; as this case illustrates, it does do so. Under 12 U.S.C. § 1743(c) the mortgagee has the option of assigning the mortgage to the Secretary and being paid the full amount of the guarantee, instead of itself foreclosing. As might be expected, that is what Prudential did in this case. Why would any mortgagee do otherwise, when by so assigning it can receive the full benefit of the insurance without having to incur the expense and risk attendant upon foreclosure? Under the statute, Prudential received the full benefit of the insurance — government obligations equal to the then total value of the mortgage, in this case more than $90,000. If the redemption period applies, the government must wait a year to get its money back — and it may not then get it all, or even as much as it bid.

We conclude that the Idaho statute providing for right of redemption is not here applicable.

Finally, we note that the district court's decision did not purport to balance state and federal policies in allowing the period of redemption. Instead, it reasoned that Prudential (the original mortgagee) would have been subject to the redemption rights provided by state law, and that the United States could have no more rights than Prudential. Even assuming *arguendo* that Prudential would have been subject to state law, it does not follow that the federal government is limited to the remedies of the private mortgagee. *Cf. Small Business Administration v. McClellan,* 1960, 364 U.S. 446, 451-453, 81 S.Ct. 191, 5 L.Ed.2d 200; *United States v. Summerlin,* 1940, 310 U.S. 414, 416, 60 S.Ct. 1019, 84 L.Ed. 1283; *United States v. Anderson,* 5 Cir., 1964, 334 F.2d 111; *Korman v. Federal Housing Administrator,* D.C.Cir., 1940, 72 App.D.C. 245, 113 F.2d 743; *Wagner v. McDonald,* 8 Cir., 1938, 96 F.2d 273. In none of the federal mortgage cases cited in this opinion was it suggested that state law might control the rights of the United States because it was the assignee of a private insured lender.

That portion of the judgment providing for a right and period of redemption is reversed and the matter is remanded to the district court with directions to modify the judgment in a manner consistent with this opinion.

ELY, CIRCUIT JUDGE (dissenting): I respectfully dissent. The majority, with broad strokes, erases highly significant redemptive rights created by statute in the Territory of Guam and eight of the states comprising our Circuit as well as equitable rights of redemption hitherto applied by the courts of Hawaii. These rights are deeply rooted in history, founded on an equitable principle applied through centuries to protect the temporarily disadvantaged without working significant prejudice against his creditor. The approach which I take is made, not only in the interests of local mortgagors involved in the federal housing program, but also in the interests of the federal program itself. I do not dispute the fact that federal abrogation of state-created rights is often necessary for the protection of federal programs, but I have been unable to accept the majority's proposition that its dramatic result is here warranted by any overpowering motive of federal self defense. Time after time, the Congress of the United States has created programs through which private loans are guaranteed by the federal government. In not one of those programs has Congress ever prescribed that, in connection with those programs, state redemptive rights, either statutory or equitable, are eliminated. To me it is inconceivable that the members of Congress, when they enacted the many federal lending programs now extant, were either ignorant of, or blind to, the existence of state redemptive rights in foreclosure proceedings. When the Country's legislators have apparently deemed it unnecessary, in protecting the interests of the federal government, to strike down the states' rights in question, I think it presumptuous that a federal court should substitute its policy judgment to the contrary. My Brother Duniway's opinion, while written with his characteristic scholarship and technical precision, does not, insofar as I can see, demonstrate the existence of any controlling precedent requiring the conclusion which is reached. In this light, as well as in that of other considerations which I shall discuss, I respectfully submit that the majority's opinion constitutes an unnecessary intrusion into the legitimate local affairs of nine western states, and of the Territory of Guam, and moreover, represents an unwarranted judicial usurpation of federal legislative power.

[W]e should first reach an understanding of the purpose and effects of state redemption statutes.

The statutes can best be understood through a brief review of their historical development. The original method of mortgage foreclosure was known as strict foreclosure, a method whereby, on default, the mortgagee obtained a court decree awarding the mortgagor's interest in the security to the mortgagee. This offensive procedure was subject to severe defects, the most obvious of which was that the mortgagor faced the possibility of forfeiting all his equity in the property in the event that the property was worth more than the unpaid balance on the debt.

The harshness of strict foreclosure led to the concept of foreclosure by sale. Theoretically, the property was to be sold to the highest bidder with the mortgagee having first claim to the proceeds and the mortgagor obtaining his equity in the form of whatever surplus remained. This approach was expected to yield more even results by allowing the competitive market to set the value of the land instead of the "value" being set at the amount of the unpaid debt as was the fact under strict foreclosure. Unfortunately, this expectation was frustrated by reason of the immense advantages favoring the mortgagee at the sale. First, it was unnecessary for the mortgagee to raise and expend any cash up to the amount of the unpaid debt. Secondly, there would not often be an interested outside buyer, or junior lienholder with cash, at the precise time of the sale. Thus, the senior mortgagee was assured of being almost always the only bidder at the sale. The junior lienors, in particular, suffered under this method since their interests were cut off by the judicial sale. Since they had no weapons with which to force the sale price above the amount of the senior's claim, they often realized nothing on their claims.

The response of many jurisdictions to the unsatisfactory results of the foreclosure-by-sale procedure was the adoption of a statutory redemption period. The basic design of statutory redemption consists of giving the mortgagor and those claiming under him (including junior lienors) the right to redeem the property from the purchaser at the sale within a specified period by paying, *not* the balance of the debt secured, but the price paid at the sale. The objective of the redemption right is that the mortgagee or other bidders, if any, shall bid not less than the fair market value of the land, since otherwise the purchaser risks being divested of the land by redemption at less than its market value.

The key to understanding the statutory redemption right lies in the proposition that the statute's operation is in the nature of a threat. When redemption is exercised, it is thereby evidenced that the mortgagee has not bid adequately at the sale and the statute has not had its intended effect. On the other hand, if the threat functions successfully and the mortgagee does bid adequately, then the mortgagor and junior lienors, if any, will have been satisfied to the full value of the property and there will be no reason for exercising the redemption right. If he bids the full market value of the property, then the mortgagee may rest secure in the knowledge that it will not be redeemed. *See generally* Durfee & Doddridge, Redemption From Foreclosure Sale, 23 Mich.L.Rev. 825, 827-834 (1925); Note, Redemption From Judicial Sales, 5 U.Chi.L.Rev. 625, 626 (1938).

With the foregoing as background, the relation of redemption statutes to the federal housing policies can be more clearly analyzed. The particular program involved here, War Housing Insurance, is only one of many administered under various Acts of Congress. This program, as the majority notes, is designed to stimulate housing for veterans; other programs are designed for rural housing, poverty relief, urban renewal, etc. All of the programs have as their basic goal the stimulation of construction by guaranteeing that lenders, contractors, and suppliers will not suffer losses on extending credit to builders and owners. Of course, some programs are more concerned with the owners and their need for housing than they are with the market for mortgages. This would be true, for instance, of a program designed to supply single-family housing while it would not be as crucial a consideration in the construction of multiple dwelling units. Thus, protection of the mortgagor's interests takes on greater or less significance depending on the type of program involved. It seems crystal clear to me, however, that the type of balancing involved in deciding what rights the mortgagor should have requires legislative attention to the entire scope of housing programs. I will deal with the Congress' role in this question later.

It seems no less clear to me that, disregarding the question of protection of the individual mortgagor, the goals of *any* federal housing program could not be served by the majority's decision. From the viewpoint of a mortgagor in a state with redemption provisions, and in the light of the majority's decision, it would be more desirable to finance privately than to finance through an FHA guaranteed mortgage. Even more important, potential junior lienors, such as contractors and suppliers, will be less willing to extend credit under these circumstances. Nor can junior lienors protect themselves, as the majority suggests, by bidding at the foreclosure sale. I have already explained that one reason for the existence of the redemption statutes is that the enormous leverage of the foreclosing mortgagee is not matched by junior lienors, who typically have very small cash reserves and never have the first "paid up" interest.

Thus one effect of the majority's decision will be to lower the attractiveness of FHA financing in states that have enacted redemption statutes. Other states have other methods of protecting both mortgagors and junior lienors that will not be matched in the redemption states. Therefore, the uniformity among the states for which the Government argues cannot possibly be furthered by the majority's decision. Instead, uniformity would be furthered by conforming federal programs with state law.

The Government, and also the majority, make several arguments designed to show that redemption statutes are neither important nor necessary. The first is that the statutes do not work because no third party will bid at the sale, knowing that he will be subject to redemption. The statutes, as I have tried to explain, are not the least bit concerned with the actions of third parties since they were necessitated by the observation that third parties do not ordinarily bid at foreclosure sales in any event. Instead of trying to stimulate bidding at the sale, they set up the more realistic possibility that the property will be redeemed if the mortgagee's bid is inadequate.

The majority also asserts that redemption rights are unimportant because most financing in modern times is accomplished through the use of trust deeds, which do not provide for redemption rights. There may be valid reasons for the distinction, but we need not be concerned with them here. What is important is that the legislatures of the states have allocated certain rights to each method of financing with the result that a choice is available depending on the nature of the transaction and the needs of the parties. Once the parties have selected either method, they should accept all its consequences. Moreover, if redemption rights truly are of negligible importance, then it could be said that the Government has wasted much valuable time in pursuing a frivolous appeal!

The Government argues at one point that the policies of the redemption right are satisfied by the alleged practice of the FHA carefully to appraise the fair market value of the property and to make its bid accordingly at the foreclosure sale. It is interesting to note that the Government argues elsewhere that the effect of redemption statutes is to *depress* bidding at the sale. But it is even more interesting, and remarkable, that a federal statute expressly prohibits the agency from bidding more than the unpaid balance on the debt! 12 U.S.C. § 1713(k), as incorporated by 12 U.S.C. § 1743(f).

Even if we assumed that the FHA contravened the prohibitory statute and was in some way bound to continue its asserted practice, such unilateral action of the FHA could not satisfy the premise of the redemption statutes. That premise is that the fair market value is realizable only through the interplay of competing economic forces. This premise is not satisfied by judicial sale because of the demonstrated falsity of the assumption, made by the majority, that a third party will come in to force the price up to market value at the sale. The fact that competing economic forces are necessary is amply shown in the case at bar, since the value of the land was set by the court according to the testimony of one Government witness. This value was less than one-half the original purchase price and far below the unpaid balance on the debt. The Government obtained a deficiency judgment for the difference between the set value and the unpaid debt. The Government then proceeded to buy in the property at the sale for an amount *less than the market value set by the court.*

. . . .

Finally, I come to the Government's lame contention that the failure of Congress to provide for redemption rights is the equivalent of an express provision that state redemption laws should not be recognized. The logical absurdity of this argument is, of itself, sufficient to subvert the contention. But the abundant statutory and regulatory language apparently adopting state law in this context should not be overlooked. For example, the statutory definition of the rights of the United States itself provides that "the term 'first mortgage' means such classes of first liens as are commonly given to secure advances on, or the unpaid purchase price of, real estate, *under the laws of the State, in which the real estate is located,* . . . ." 12 U.S.C. § 1707(a) (emphasis added). The regulations provide, "The mortgage must contain a provision or provisions, satisfactory to the Commissioner, giving to the mortgagee, in the event of default or foreclosure of the mortgage, such rights and remedies for the protection and preservation of the property covered by the mortgage and the income therefrom, *as are available under the law or custom of the jurisdiction."* 24 C.F.R. § 580.18 (1968) (emphasis added). Even the waiver in the present mortgage, on which the Government relied so stongly in the court below, provides that it is effective "to the extent permitted by law." Surely, we must presume that this language refers to the law of Idaho, for the federal law contains no such corresponding provisions to be waived or to which the waiver could be applicable.

At the very least, it seems unusual for the Government to argue that congressional silence can be equated with express abrogation of state-created rights. It is especially significant that, as we were informed on oral argument, the FHA has introduced several bills to achieve the result reached here, but Congress has consistently refused to adopt this approach. The Supreme Court has stated on more than one occasion that rights should not be displaced or eliminated without the clearest legislative mandate. *United States v. Shimer,* 367 U.S. 374, 81 S.Ct. 1554, 6 L.Ed.2d 908 (1961); *Mitchell v. Robert De Mario Jewelry, Inc.,* 361 U.S. 288, 80 S.Ct. 332, 4 L.Ed.2d 323 (1960). I could not hold that silence on the part of Congress can be taken to effect an abrogation of time-honored state rights, derived from the most exalted principles of equity and so carefully designed, not only for the protection of debtors and creditors alike, but also for the promotion of the general economic welfare of the public at large.

I would affirm.

UNITED STATES v. STEWART

United States Court of Appeals
523 F.2d 1070 (9th Cir. 1975)

PER CURIAM: The appellee, United States of America, brought this action against appellants, William Lee and Shirley Stewart, husband and wife, for a claimed deficiency on a direct loan made by the Veterans Administration (VA) to the Stewarts in the State of California. The money received from the loan, in the amount of $17,500.00, was used by the Stewarts to purchase a home in California, which loan was evidenced by a Trust Deed Note which was secured by a Deed of Trust.

The Stewarts defaulted on the payment of the loan and the VA elected to sell the home at a non-judicial sale on September 27, 1967, under and pursuant to the Deed of Trust. After the sale there remained a deficiency on the loan of $1,041.26. This action was commenced on January 10, 1973 for the deficiency, together with interest, in the State of Washington where the Stewarts were then residing.

The issue in regard to the liability of the Stewarts for the claimed deficiency was submitted to the trial court on motions for summary judgment filed by the parties, which motions were based on a stipulation of pertinent facts. The district court, relying on the decision of this court in *Branden v. Driver,* 441 F.2d 1171 (1971), granted the motion of the United States and awarded a judgment against the Stewarts for the deficiency together with interest, attorneys fees and costs in the aggregate amount of $1,412.38. The Stewarts have appealed from this judgment and we reverse.

The issue presented is whether in the posture of this case the law of the State of California, C.C.P. §§ 580a, 580b, prohibiting a deficiency judgment in such an action, should be applicable or whether the government may obtain a deficiency judgment notwithstanding the law of California.

In this case, the Note and Deed of Trust, executed by the Stewarts, each specifically provides that it is to be construed according to the laws of the State of California. It is significant that paragraph 34 of the Deed was stricken therefrom before or at the time it was executed. The stricken paragraph provides:

Title 38, United States Code and the Regulations issued thereunder shall govern the rights, duties and liabilities of the parties hereto, and any provisions of this or other instruments executed in connection with said indebtedness which are inconsistent with said Title or Regulations are hereby amended and supplemented to conform thereto.

It is abundantly clear that by striking this standard paragraph and the retaining of paragraph 35 which provides "[t]his Deed shall be construed according to the laws of the State of California", the parties intended that the laws of California should be applicable. This was an individually negotiated contract which departed from the usual form employed by the VA.

In *United States v. Yazell,* 382 U.S. 341, 86 S.Ct. 500, 15 L.Ed.2d 404 (1966), the Supreme Court stated:

> None of the cases in which this Court has devised and applied a federal principle of law superseding state law involved an issue arising from an individually negotiated contract. [382 U.S. at 353, 86 S.Ct. at 507]

In *United States v. MacKenzie,* 510 F.2d 39 (Jan. 13, 1975), this Court in an en banc decision held that congressional purpose in enacting SBA legislation was not impaired by federal deference to state laws protecting debtors by limiting deficiency judgments and by providing for redemption rights, nor did any other federal interest justify refusal to respect state interests in regard to such protection of debtors, and therefore debtors, upon foreclosure of mortgages were entitled to protection of state law of Nevada in regard to limitation of deficiency judgment based on fair market value, and law of Arizona in regard to redemption rights.

Although the loan in question was not made by the SBA as in *Yazell* and *MacKenzie,* the same principle shaould apply to a VA loan in the circumstances of this case. We believe that *Yazell* and *MacKenzie* are controlling in the disposition of this case. The government's reliance on *United States v. Stadium Apartments, Inc.,* 425 F.2d 358 (9th Cir. 1970) and *Branden v. Driver,* supra, in support of its contention that the law of California should not be applied in this case, is unavailing.

It is our opinion that there is no justifiable cause or reason why the government should not be bound by the precise terms of the negotiated loan instruments and no reason why the Stewarts should not have the protection of the California law afforded them under the terms of said instruments.

As to the remaining issue raised by appellant, we agree with the trial court that under 28 U.S.C. § 2415, the government was not barred from filing its action.

Reversed and remanded.

NOTES

1. In addition to VA and FHA financing there are other agencies of the federal government which are involved in mortgage financing. The Farmers Home Administration operates a direct loan program for persons ineligible for conventional financing who live in rural areas. Funds are raised by the sale of Farmers Home Administration (FMHA) securities which are backed by a pool of mortgages.

2. Also in the area of farm lending is the Federal Land Bank, which was established by the Federal Farm Loan Act of 1916 and which now operates under the Federal Credit Act of 1971. This agency makes direct loans on farms and farm related businesses through local associations of the Federal Land Bank.

B. THE SECONDARY MARKET: FNMA, GNMA, AND FHLMC

In the past half century the money market involving lenders of funds for real estate secured loans has been greatly enhanced by the existence of three entities, each of which is neither purely governmental nor private. These are: the Federal National Mortgage Association, the Government National Mortgage Association, and the Federal Home Loan Mortgage Corporation, commonly referred to as "Fanny May," "Ginnie May," and "Freddie Mac." These three operate in tandem with other agencies by buying from private institutional lenders so as to provide more funds for loans when lenders have reached their limits and have no more money to lend. A brief history and explanation of these three is set forth below in a reprint of a publication by the Department of Housing and Urban Development.

DEPARTMENT OF HOUSING & URBAN DEVELOPMENT, HOUSING IN THE SEVENTIES 3-42 — 3-48 (1973)

Federal National Mortgage Association

The Federal National Mortgage Association (FNMA) was chartered and organized in 1938 by the Federal Housing Administration to provide secondary market support for the new FHA mortgages. During its first decade of operation the FNMA bought FHA mortgages when mortgage funds were scarce and sold mortgages when wartime conditions led to an abundance of loanable funds while investment outlets were restricted. In 1948, the FNMA was authorized to purchase VA mortgages. Although the Emergency Home Finance Act of 1970 gave the FNMA the authority to purchase conventional mortgages, actual purchases did not begin until February, 1972, and virtually all of its activity has been in the area of Government-insured or -guaranteed mortgages. Conventional mortgages accounted for only 1 percent of its mortgage portfolio at the end of 1972. However, the FNMA has recently increased its purchases of conventional mortgages.

Over the years, the FNMA has used its resources to support a variety of Government housing programs. This was changed by the Housing and Urban Development Act of 1968 which divided the "old" FNMA into two corporate entities: The "new" FNMA, privately owned and retaining the secondary market function and, the Government National Mortgage Association, within the Department of Housing and Urban Development, and taking over the special assistance and management and liquidation functions.

Although the FNMA is now privately owned, the President of the United States appoints five of its fifteen directors. The Secretary of HUD has general regulatory responsibility over the corporation. Within statutory guidelines, the Secretary of HUD (1) sets FNMA's debt ceiling and the ratio of debt to capital, (2) sets the maximum rate for cash dividends, and (3) approves the issuance of all stock, obligations, and other securities. The Secretary of the Treasury must approve all debt issues, including the terms and conditions of sale, in order to assure coordination with Treasury debt operations.

The FNMA's basic function is to maintain a secondary market facility for residential mortgages. It fulfills this function by buying and selling mortgages. The price at which FNMA issues commitments to purchase mortgages is determined by the Free Market System auction procedure. Under the auction, commitments for the purchase of mortgages are offered on a competitive basis.

The sellers of mortgages to the FNMA include mortgage companies, commercial banks, savings and loan associations, mutual savings banks and others. During 1972 mortgage companies accounted for 76 percent of the mortgages purchased by the FNMA, banks and trusts accounted for 14 percent and the remainder was purchased from savings and loan associations, life insurance companies, the GNMA and other lenders. Sellers must meet and maintain

FNMA standards, most of them also have FHA approval. Normally, FNMA sellers will retain the servicing of the loans.

Funds for mortgage purchases and operations are obtained from mortgage repayments, sale of debentures, notes and other obligations, commitment fees, proceeds from mortgage sales and the differential between interest income and borrowing costs. All sellers of mortgages to the FNMA are required by law to hold common stock of an amount equal to ¼ of 1 percent of the unpaid principal amount of mortgages and loans purchased or to be purchased by the FNMA from such sellers. All services of one-to-four-family home mortgages for the FNMA are required to hold common stock in varying percentages of the unpaid principal amount of mortgages serviced by the FNMA.

. . . .

Government National Mortgage Association

The Government National Mortgage Association (GNMA) was created in 1968 to assume responsibility for the special assistance and management and liquidation functions of the "old" FNMA. The GNMA is a wholly-owned corporate instrumentality of the U.S. Government, operating within HUD, with the Secretary of HUD determining general GNMA policies and appointing GNMA officers.

The special assistance functions are operated exclusively for the account of the Federal Government with funds provided by the Secretary of the Treasury under authorization of Congress for the purchase of mortgages for designated Government housing programs. Programs under special authorization include housing in Guam and Alaska; housing in disaster and urban renewal areas; housing under the Sections 235 and 236 single and multi-family programs; and housing for the elderly, armed forces, and other low- and moderate-income families. Many of the mortgages obtained under these programs have been later sold to private lenders, particularly under the procedure known as the "Tandem Plan" described below.

The management and liquidation functions provide for the GNMA to manage and liquidate the portfolio of mortgages acquired for the account of the Government between February 1938 and November 1954. This includes the pre-Charter mortgage portfolio and commitments outstanding of the "old" FNMA. Also included in the management and liquidation functions were mortgages that other departments and agencies of the Government had directly acquired — for example, mortgages held by the Reconstruction Finance Corporation, the Defense Home Loan Corporation, and in later years, mortgages received from the Public Housing Administration. This function represented the centralization of Government mortgage liquidation programs. The GNMA acts as fiduciary with respect to participations in these mortgages which were sold to private investors prior to August 1968 and of which $4.4 billion are currently outstanding. During fiscal year 1973 over $1 billion of mortgages in the GNMA portfolio were sold directly to lenders during periodic auctions.

The GNMA's authorization to purchase mortgages is limited (the present limit is $7.75 billion), but its authorization can be replenished by resale of the mortgages it buys. For example, in certain of GNMA's Tandem Plans, the GNMA purchases the mortgages insured under subsidized housing programs from private lenders and then resells them to the FNMA or other investors at the lower prevailing market price. In an effort to encourage private lenders to hold these mortgages, the GNMA held the first auction of interest subsidy mortgages in the amount of $229 million in June 1972. In fiscal year 1973, the GNMA sold in auctions a total of $1.1 billion of mortgages purchased under the Tandem Plan. The funds to cover the losses on the Tandem Plan, which totaled $65 million in fiscal year 1973, are charged against operations of GNMA's revolving funds.

In addition to its special assistance and management and liquidation functions, the GNMA has developed a number of instruments that are sold by private lenders to attract more funds into housing. These instruments are the pass-through mortgage-backed security and the mortgage-backed bond, both of which are fully guaranteed by GNMA as to the timely payment of principal and interest.

The pass-through securities are issued in denominations of $25,000 and are fully amortized with the investor receiving monthly payments of principal and interest as well as any prepayments of the mortgages backing the pass-throughs. Almost all of the pass-throughs have been issued by mortgage companies as an alternative to selling the mortgages they originate directly to institutional investors. The issuer of the pass-throughs must pay the GNMA an application fee of $500 per pool of mortgages to obtain a commitment from the GNMA to guarantee the pass-through plus a fee of 6 basis points (.006 percent) on the unpaid principal balance on the pass-through securities.

As of June 30, 1973, a total of $7.8 billion of pass-throughs had been sold. During the first 3 years of the program, savings and loan associations and mutual savings banks purchased over 60 percent of these securities. However, since March 1973 over 80 percent of the pass-throughs issued have been sold to pension funds, life insurance companies and other institutions.

Federal Home Loan Mortgage Corporation

The Emergency Home Finance Act of 1970 created the Federal Home Loan Mortgage Corporation the principal purpose of which is to serve as a central credit facility and secondary market for conventional mortgages. The Federal Home Loan Mortgage Corporation is a private corporation and is a member of the Federal Home Loan Bank System. The three Presidentially-appointed directors of the Federal Home Loan Bank Board also serve as the directors of the Corporation. The Federal Home Loan Mortgage Corporation was initially financed by the sale of $100 million in nonvoting stock with a no-call provision to the twelve Federal Home Loan District Banks. Additional funds have been acquired through the sale of bonds and participation certificates.

Since the majority of mortgages originated by lenders are of the conventional type, the absence of a central credit facility for these mortgages limited the ability of public agencies to moderate fluctuations in housing starts and to insure that mortgage lenders have adequate funds and liquidity.

The Federal Home Loan Mortgage Corporation plays two primary roles as a mortgage market support agency. First, it acts as a financial intermediary and mortgage broker by purchasing mortgages for its own portfolio or for sale to other investors. Second, it is working to develop a private secondary market for mortgages that will exist independently of Government-sponsored mortgage market support institution.

Although the Federal Home Loan Mortgage Corporation was established to support the conventional market, most of its initial purchases have been Government-insured or -guaranteed mortgages. Conventional mortgages accounted for about 12 percent of its total purchases during 1972. However, the Federal

Home Loan Mortgage Corporation anticipates that in 1973 more than 80 percent of its volume will be in the conventional mortgage sector. As a new organization, the scope of its activities is small relative to the size of the market. The Federal Home Loan Mortgage Corporation's purchases of FHA/VA mortgages in 1972 accounted for only 4.9 percent of the FHA/VA mortgages originated that year.

The sales participation certificates represent a participation in groups of conventional mortgages acquired by the Federal Home Loan Mortgage Corporation. The Federal Home Loan Mortgage Corporation acquires a participation interest by providing a portion of the funds for a group of mortgages originated by a private lender. The Federal Home Loan Mortgage Corporation then separates this acquired participation into certificates in amounts designed for easy marketability and sells them to investors at a yield slightly below the yield on the pool of mortgages. The Federal Home Loan Mortgage Corporation guarantees the timely payment of interest and principal. Approximately $550 million of these certificates had been sold by the end of 1972, mostly to savings and loan associations.

. . . .

HEARINGS BEFORE THE SUBCOMMITTEE ON HOUSING OF THE SENATE COMMITTEE ON BANKING AND CURRENCY, 89th CONGRESS, 1st SESSION 172-78 (1965)

Statement of J. Stanley Baughman, President, Federal National Mortgage Association

The Federal National Mortgage Association (FNMA) is a corporation chartered under the laws of the United States. It is engaged in purchasing, managing, and selling mortgages; and for financing purposes it is empowered to serve as a fiduciary with respect to certain mortgages held by it or in which the Federal Government has an interest. FNMA is also empowered to make short-term loans on the security of mortgages. All such mortgages are ordinarily underwritten by the Government — either insured by the Federal Housing Commissioner or guaranteed by the Administrator of Veterans' Affairs.

In 1954 FNMA was rechartered by the Congress as a mixed ownership corporation. In its operations since then it has used both private and Government capital funds and operating funds. All of the common stock of FNMA, of which there is now more than $91 million outstanding, is owned by some 9,000 private shareholders. FNMA preferred stock in the amount of $50 million is held by the Secretary of the Treasury; and $109 million of such preferred stock is held by the corporation as FNMA treasury stock. Corporate obligations outstanding with private investors on December 31, 1964, aggregated $1.6 billion. On that date, under all operations, the aggregate amount owed to the U. S. Treasury was $2.2 billion. . . .

Under an arrangement entered into in March 1962 between FNMA and the Federal Housing Commissioner, FNMA acquires, under its three functions or operations, FHA-owned mortgages in exchange for FHA debentures owned by the corporation. FNMA is also authorized to acquire FHA-owned mortgages for cash under its management and liquidating functions (sec. 306(e) of the Federal National Mortgage Association Charter Act), and can acquire them similarly under its investment powers (sec. 310). Such acquisitions and purchases by FNMA have relieved the FHA of the burden of managing and servicing 45,917 home mortgages aggregating some $424 million in unpaid principal amounts. . . .

The dollar volume of FNMA's mortgage financing activities is not a true measure of FNMA's effect or impact on the availability of mortgage funds in the United States. Although FNMA funds constitute only a small percentage of the total funds participating in the general secondary mortgage market, it is significant that FNMA has remained in the mortgage market as a purchaser without interruption since 1954. It has thereby provided assurance for mortgage investors, and stability for mortgage investments, to the encouragement of all concerned. FNMA has also played a significant role in establishing purchase standards and mortgage servicing procedures and methods that are used effectively on a nationwide basis. . . .

Secondary Market Operations

FNMA's regular privately financed secondary market operations, in time to become privately owned, have the corporate charter objective of furnishing supplementary assistance to the general secondary mortgage market "by providing a degree of liquidity for mortgage investments, thereby improving the distribution of investment capital available for home mortgage financing." FNMA's capitalization relates to these operations.

Since July 1, 1961, FNMA has entered into mortgage purchase contracts under the secondary market operations totaling $1,415 million, and has completed purchases in the amount of $1,376 million. Sales of mortgages have amounted to $1,274 million. . . .

At the present time mortgage purchases under the secondary market operations are reflecting an increasingly greater degree of support for low- and moderate-income groups in need of mortgage financing. In spite of the steady increase in construction costs and the elimination of the aforementioned $20,000-mortgage-amount ceiling, the average size of mortgages purchased in these operations since 1962 has decreased from $13,100 to $10,900. Mortgages of such lower amounts are not normally attractive to private investors except at maximum discounts. During the last 3½ years under its secondary market operations, FNMA purchased $36 million of FHA-insured, section 221(d)(2) mortgages — the category usually associated with housing for low- and moderate-income families — and, at the end of 1964, outstanding contracts provided for the future purchase of $6 million more of this type of mortgage.

Special Assistance Functions

FNMA's special assistance functions are conducted for the account of the Government with Treasury money (excepting the interests of, and funds of, investors in FNMA participation certificates) to accomplish various broad national policies and objectives, as determined by the Congress or the President. FNMA carries on these functions under several special assistance programs. The various programs have the common purpose of assisting in the financing, as stated in the corporate charter, of "selected types of home mortgages (pending the establishment of their marketability) originated under special housing programs. . . ." Under the charter, special assistance may also be provided for the financing of home mortgages generally as a means of retarding or stopping a decline in mortgage lending and home building activities which threatens materially the stability of a high level economy. It should be noted that FNMA's special assistance programs originated in either of two ways — at the direction of the President of the United States pursuant to his authority in section 305 of the Federal National Mortgage Association Charter Act, or at the instance of the Congress by its enactment of express legislation. . . .

A major feature of Public Law 87-70 was its provision for an FHA mortgage insurance program for below-market-interest rate mortgages on housing for low and moderate income families. FNMA was specially empowered to purchase such mortgages insured under section 221(d)(3) of the National Housing Act and, under Presidential direction, special assistance program No. 11 was thereupon established for these mortgages. . . .

C. THE FEDERAL CREDIT ACTS

Credit has become the American way of life. Prior to 1945, the American consumer owed less than $6 billion dollars, but by 1969 the consumer debt had grown to $116 billion. For a majority of Americans in these inflationary times, credit is more than a convenience; it is a necessity. Families purchase on credit not only gasoline, household goods, and clothes, but also higher education, drugs, and food.

The increasing dependence on credit has been paralleled by a phenomenal growth of the credit information industry. *See* Note, *The Fair Credit Reporting Act: Are Business Credit Reports Regulated?,* 1971 DUKE L.J. 1229. Credit information bureaus provide businesses with current data on individual consumers who are seeking credit approval. The information acquired is both objective, in listing a person's loan, bills and employment, and subjective, in depicting his reputation and character. *See* S. Rep. No. 517, 91st Cong., 1st Sess. 2 (1969). Before 1970, there were few, if any, safeguards to prevent error or abuse in an applicant's credit report, but congressional hearings held in 1969 resulted in the passage of the Fair Credit Reporting Act. FCRA regulates consumer reporting agencies to ensure privacy and accuracy in the gathering of credit information. 15 U.S.C. §§ 1681a-1681t (1970).

In 1974, Congress passed the Equal Credit Opportunity Act, 15 U.S.C. § 1691(b), which prohibits discrimination on the basis of sex or marital status in the granting of credit.

1. THE FAIR CREDIT REPORTING ACT

In drafting FCRA, Congress stated that the banking system required accurate credit reporting. 15 U.S.C. § 1681(a)(1) (1970). The purpose of FCRA is to "insure that consumer reporting agencies exercise their grave responsibilities with fairness, impartiality and a respect for the consumer's right to privacy" and "adopt reasonable procedures for meeting the needs of commerce for consumer credit, personnel insurance, and other information in a manner which is fair and equitable to the consumer with regard to the confidentiality, accuracy, relevancy and proper utilization of such information." 15 U.S.C. § 1681(a)(4)(b). To assure this end, FCRA specifies procedures which restrict the agencies' use of the credit information, 15 U.S.C. § 1681b(d), and provide the consumer access to his or her own file, 15 U.S.C. § 1681g.

A consumer reporting agency may furnish a consumer report *only* if: (1) a court orders it to do so; (2) the consumer authorizes it in writing; or (3) the agency believes the person receiving the information is using it for credit extension, employment purposes, underwriting insurance, government licensing, or other legitimate business needs. *See* 15 U.S.C. § 1681b (1970). The procedures apply only to the reporting of objective information. In furnishing an investigative consumer report, the agency must disclose to the consumer that such investigation as to his character and reputation is being made and notify the consumer of the right to request further disclosure of the exact nature and scope of the investigation. *See* 15 U.S.C. § 1681d (1970).

FCRA provides that upon the request of a consumer, the agency must disclose the nature and substance of all its files and the sources of its information. *See* 15 U.S.C. § 1681g (1970) (the substance of a medical report need not be disclosed. Sources of investigative reports used only for that purpose need not be disclosed). When a consumer disputes the accuracy of a report, the agency must reinvestigate the information. 15 U.S.C. § 1681i(a) (1970). If the reinvestigation does not resolve the dispute the consumer may file a brief statement on the issue which will be included in any subsequent report containing the disputed information. 15 U.S.C. § 1681i(b) & (c) (1970).

An agency found guilty of willful noncompliance with FCRA may be liable for damages both actual and punitive, as well as reasonable attorney's fees. 15 U.S.C. § 1681n (1970). There is no willful noncompliance if any agency shows by a preponderance of the evidence that at the time of the violation it maintained reasonable procedures to assure compliance. *See Mirakel v. General Motors Acceptance Corp.,* 537 F.2d 871 (7th Cir. 1976). Negligent noncompliance limits liability to actual damages plus attorney's fees. 15 U.S.C. § 1681o (1970).

But these restrictions and penalties apply only to the use of a consumer report. A consumer report is limited to one establishing eligibility in (1) credit or insurance for primarily personal uses, (2) employment purposes, or (3) other as authorized. 15 U.S.C. § 1681a(d) (1970). However, information collected for a consumer report but not used to establish eligibility may still be within the protective provisions of FCRA. For a discussion of FCRA, *see The Fair Credit Reporting Act, supra,* at 1244-48. But FCRA does not extend to business credit reports or business insurance reports. *See* S. Rep. No. 589, 94th Cong., 2d Sess. 2 (1976).

PORTER v. TALBOT PERKINS CHILDREN'S SERVICES

United States District Court
355 F. Supp. 174 (S.D.N.Y. 1973)

POLLACK, DISTRICT JUDGE. The defendants, child adoption agencies, have separately moved for dismissal of the complaint herein on the ground that plaintiff has failed to state a claim upon which relief may be granted, Fed.R.Civ.P. 12(b)(6), or, alternatively, for summary judgment in their favor, pursuant to Fed.R.Civ.P. 56 and General Rule 9(g) of this Court. At issue is the question of first impression whether the Fair Credit Reporting Act, 15 U.S.C. §§ 1681-1681t, which became effective April 26, 1971, ("the Act" hereafter) applies to the activities and to the confidential information and reports of an adoption agency.

The background facts of this suit are not contested. Porter and his wife have three children and have attempted on several occasions to adopt a fourth child. Among the adoption agencies to which they applied were the four named defendants. The applications for adoption were filed with defendant Talbot in December 1969; defendant Sheltering Arms in August-November of 1970; defendant Windham in August 1970; and defendant Brookwood in August 1971. In each instance, the application was denied, as was the subsequent request addressed to each defendant for all information collected or used by the agency with respect to plaintiff and his wife. Plaintiff wrote to each of these agencies in November of 1971 for copies of any and all reports relating to his application.

Plaintiff seeks both actual and punitive damages claiming to be entitled thereto on the ground that the defendants willfully and wrongfully refused to make the requested disclosures to him in violation of the Act.

I

The purpose of the Fair Credit Reporting Act is to protect an individual from inaccurate or arbitrary information about himself in a consumer report that is being used as a factor in determining the individual's eligibility for credit, insurance or employment. 116 Cong.Rec. 36572 (1970). Congress ascertained a "need to insure that consumer reporting agencies exercise their grave responsibilities with fairness, impartiality, and a respect for the consumer's right to privacy." 15 U.S.C. § 1681(a)(4). The Act was designed to require consumer reporting agencies to

> adopt reasonable procedures for meeting the needs of *commerce* for consumer credit, personnel, insurance, and other information in a manner which is fair and equitable to the consumer, with regard to the confidentiality, accuracy, relevancy, and proper utilization of such information in accordance with the requirements of this [Act]. § 1681(b). (Emphasis supplied).

For the most part, the consumer reporting industry is comprised of credit bureaus, investigative reporting companies and other organizations whose business is the gathering and reporting of information about consumers for use by others in making a decision concerning whether to grant credit, underwrite insurance or employ the subject of such reports. F.T.C., Compliance with the Fair Credit Reporting Act, 4 CCH Consumer Credit Guide ¶ 11,302 (1971).

To advance this design, the Act provides a mechanism with which a consumer can determine what information has been gathered about him for submission to those engaged in commerce and can have the opportunity to correct any inaccuracies in that information. §§ 1681g-1681i; 116 Cong.Rec. 35941. The term "consumer" is broadly defined in the Act as an individual. § 1681a(c). Limitations are imposed on the uses to which the accumulated information may be put. § 1681f. The Act sets a time after which details must be deleted from the files. § 1681c. Willful failure to comply with the provisions of the Act, including those which specifically allow the consumer to examine and correct his file, exposes the credit reporting agency or user of information to civil liability, including actual and punitive damages. § 1681n. Negligent failure to comply may result in actual damages and the imposition of Court costs. § 1681o.

The consumer reporting agency, to which the Act is directed, is defined as follows:

> The term "consumer reporting agency" means any person which, for monetary fees, dues, or on a cooperative nonprofit basis, regularly engages in whole or in part in the practice of assembling or evaluating consumer credit information or other information on consumers *for the purpose of* furnishing consumer *reports to third parties,* and which uses any means or facility of interstate commerce for the purpose of preparing or furnishing consumer reports. § 1681a(f). (Emphasis added).

A finding that a prospective defendant fits within these definitional boundaries is requisite to the imposition of procedural requirements and possible liabilities contained in the Act.

Essentially, this definition contains four links. (1) The consumer reporting agency must act for monetary fees, dues, or on a cooperative non-profit basis; (2) it must regularly engage in whole or in part in gathering or evaluating information on consumers; (3) the purpose of such activity must be the distribution of information to third parties engaged in commerce; and (4) the agency must use a facility of interstate commerce to prepare or distribute the reports.

The Federal Trade Commission, which is vested with enforcement powers under the Act, § 1681s, has provided some preliminary interpretations of the Act, 4 CCH Consumer Credit Guide ¶ 11,301 et seq., to which the Court may refer for guidance. *Fernandez v. Retail Credit Co.,* 349 F.Supp. 652 (E.D.La.1972).

The Federal Trade Commission guidelines have interpreted the coverage of the phrase "consumer credit agencies":

> Obviously, this covers all credit bureaus and others whose business is to create and disseminate such [consumer] reports. However, there are many others who may from time to time function as consumer reporting agencies and, to the extent they issue consumer reports, they will be covered by the Act. For example, some banks and finance companies have engaged in the practice of giving out credit information other than that which they have developed from their own ledgers. To the extent they give out information and experience gained from other creditors, such banks and finance companies would be functioning as consumer reporting agencies and would be required to comply with the terms of the Act. As indicated earlier, giving out a firm's own ledger experience does not make it a consumer reporting agency or the information a consumer report. In order to be a consumer reporting agency, the firm must engage "in whole or in part" in the practice of assembling or evaluating consumer credit information or other information on consumers for the purpose of furnishing consumer reports to third parties. When a firm gives its own credit experience on a consumer to a credit bureau, that information does not constitute a consumer report. . . . ¶ 11,305.

The balance of the Federal Trade Commission's interpretation confirms that the Agency considers that the Act is dealing with commercial purposes. The persons mentioned by the Federal Trade Commission in its full interpretation are banks and finance companies, detective agencies and others preparing employment reports, and collection agencies, all of which perform services which aid and support institutions making *economic* decisions, such as whether to give employment or whether to loan money. It was to insure accuracy in reports from such organizations, affecting an individual's eligibility for credit, insurance or employment, that the Act was passed; its aim was to impose a legislative filter on the input of the burgeoning consumer credit reporting industry to the flow of commerce. § 1681(a)(2)-(4); *Fernandez v. Retail Credit Co.,* 349 F.Supp. 652 (E.D.La.1972). Certainly where an agency regularly sells consumer reports which affect commercial eligibility, that agency would properly fall within the ambit of the Act. See ¶ 11,354 of the F.T.C. guidelines, where the following interpretation is advanced:

> It is quite common for certain businesses such as insurance companies to request reports on a prospective (or current) insured from various State Departments of Motor Vehicles. These reports are sold to such companies and generally reveal a consumer's entire driving record, including arrests for speeding, drunk driving, involuntary manslaughter, etc.
>
> It is the Commission's view that, under the circumstances in which such a State motor vehicle report contains information which bears on the "personal characteristics" of the consumer (i. e., when the report refers to an arrest for drunk driving), such reports sold by a Department of Motor Vehicles are "consumer reports" and the agency is a "consumer reporting agency" when it sells such reports.

The definition of a consumer reporting agency interlocks with the definition of a consumer report. A consumer reporting agency is an entity that, in part, issues consumer reports; a consumer report is a report that, among other things, is issued by a consumer reporting agency. § 1681a(d) and (f).

"Consumer report" is defined as follows:

The term "consumer report" means any written, oral, or other communication of any information by a consumer reporting agency bearing on a consumer's credit worthiness, credit standing, credit capacity, character, general reputation, personal characteristics, or mode of living which is used or expected to be used or collected in whole or in part for the purpose of serving as a factor in establishing the consumer's eligibility for (1) credit or insurance to be used primarily for personal, family, or household purposes, or (2) employment purposes, or (3) other purposes authorized under section 1681b of this title. The term does not include (A) any report containing information solely as to transactions or experiences between the consumer and the person making the report. . . .

Among the "other purposes authorized under section 1681b" is a report to a person who

(D) intends to use the information in connection with a determination of the consumer's eligibility for a license or other benefit granted by a governmental instrumentality required by law to consider an applicant's *financial* responsibility or status. (Emphasis added).

This definition also has four elements, each of which must be present for a report to fall within the coverage of the Act. (1) There must be a communication of information (2) by a consumer reporting agency, as defined in the Act, (3) which bears on a consumer's credit status or general reputation, and (4) which is used or is expected to be used in the determination of the consumer's eligibility for credit, employment, insurance, or other commercial benefit specified in the Act.

II

The definitions in the Act, taken together, make clear that social service agencies, such as adoption agencies, were not intended to be included in the sweep of this Act. The focus of Congress was the consumer credit industry (§ 1681) which has been exercising a growing influence in economic decision-making. Of particular concern was the effect of information compiled and forwarded by an entity not dealing directly with an individual, which information would bear on that individual's ability to secure insurance, credit, or employment. Those entities which regularly engage in the collection and dissemination of information with reference to these determinations are now subject to a legislated standard of accuracy and accountability. Entities whose function is far removed from the commercial world are not brought under this standard.

Adoption agencies perform a vital social service in which the state has a large interest, as reflected in the particularity of state law. It cannot be assumed or found that Congress intended to preempt this interest by imposing a federal disclosure law over state adoption proceedings. Nothing in the language of the Act or in the legislative history suggests this radical intention. Some members of Congress did seek a broader law requiring disclosure of all information assembled on an individual, regardless of the purpose for which the information was collected and distributed. 116 Cong.Rec. 36572 (1970). But the Fair Credit Act as enacted has a more limited purpose and effect; it is designed to check informational abuses in the commercial arena.

Plaintiff has tried to characterize the adoption process in a way that can semantically edge the activities of defendants within the structure of the Act. To meet the requirements of § 1681a(f), plaintiff asserts that adoption agencies operate on a cooperative basis; that they regularly engage in part in the assembling or evaluation of "other" than credit information; that such information then becomes a consumer report conveyed to third parties, such as other adoption services; and that means of interstate commerce are employed. The information conveyed is said to constitute a consumer report in that it is purportedly used in the determination by a governmental instrumentality of eligibility for a benefit — the adoption of a child. Plaintiff contends that a Court must approve adoptions and, in its deliberations, must consider "the occupation and appropriate income" of the prospective foster parent. New York Domestic Relations Law § 112 (McKinney's Consol.Laws, Supp.1970).

The defendants herein do not prepare consumer reports, as defined in § 1681a(d) and § 1681b(3)(D). Pursuant to § 112 of the Domestic Relations Law adoptive *parents* must submit a petition containing, *inter alia,* employment and income data. The data and information ascertained by the adoption agency from interviews with and forms completed by the applicant are not to establish eligibility for credit, insurance, employment or a governmental license or benefit grounded on financial responsibility. The collected information and the evaluation thereof does *not* affect commercial decisions. The assembled and evaluated information secured for child adoption purposes should and does fall without the "consumer reports" coverage of the Act.

Since the data assembled or used by the adoption agencies herein does not come within the definition of consumer reports, the agencies are not consumer reporting agencies under the Act. § 1681a(f).

It should also be noted that there is no evidence on which to conclude that adoption agencies work on a cooperative basis or that their purpose is to provide third parties with any of the information they have compiled. Such a purpose is a prerequisite for classification as a consumer reporting agency. § 1681a(f). Plaintiff avers that there is such a purpose here; officers of defendants by affidavit declare the opposite. In *Beal v. Lindsay,* 468 F.2d 287, 291 (2nd Cir. 1972), the Court stated:

When the movant comes forward with facts showing that his adversary's case is baseless, the opponent cannot rest on the allegations of the complaint but must adduce factual material which raises a substantial question of the veracity or completeness of the movant's showing or presents countervailing facts.

Here, plaintiff has adduced no such facts.

Since the activities of the defendants and the confidential information collected by them fall outside the terms and intended coverage of the Act, the complaint must be dismissed.

III

The Fair Credit Reporting Act became effective on April 26, 1971. There is no ground for concluding that the Act was intended to be accorded retroactive effect. *Wilson v. Retail Credit Co.,* 457 F.2d 1406 (5th Cir. 1972).

Two of the defendants herein have moved for summary dismissal of the complaint on the alternative ground that their dealings with plaintiff preceded the effective date of the Act. It appears, however, that even as to these defendants plaintiff requested and was refused information on file *after* the effective date. In view of the holding herein and of the clear applicability of the Act in terms of the effective date to at least one of the defendants, this Court need not determine what actions, if any, may be committed before April 26, 1971 and still render the actor liable under the Act.

Complaint dismissed.

So ordered.

MILLSTONE v. O'HANLON REPORTS, INC.

United States Court of Appeals
528 F.2d 829 (8th Cir. 1976)

MR. JUSTICE CLARK. This is a damage action filed by James C. Millstone, appellee, alleging violations of the Fair Credit Reporting Act, 15 U.S.C. § 1681 *et seq.,* by O'Hanlon Reports, Inc., in the furnishing of a consumer credit report on Millstone to the Firemen's Fund Insurance Company. Millstone had applied to Firemen's Fund for insurance covering his Volkswagen bus. The policy was issued in due course, but a consumer credit report was ordered from O'Hanlon by the insurance company. The report was furnished to Firemen's Fund approximately a month later.

Among other things, the report related that Millstone, while living in Washington, D.C., his former residence, was a hippie-type person, with shoulder length hair and with a beard on one occasion, who participated in many demonstrations in the Capital, carried demonstrators in his bus back and forth to his home, where he housed them in his basement and wherever else there was room. It reported that he was strongly suspected of being a drug user, that he was rumored by neighbors to have been evicted from three previous residences in Washington, D.C., and that he was very much disliked by his neighbors there. Upon receiving the report, Firemen's Fund directed the agent handling the sale of the insurance to cancel the policy and secure its return. The agent advised Firemen's Fund that Millstone was a highly respected Assistant Managing Editor of the St. Louis Post-Dispatch. For a number of years, Millstone was at the Post-Dispatch's Washington office, where he often covered the White House and Presidents Johnson and Nixon. Upon learning these facts, Firemen's Fund withdrew its cancellation order and continued the policy in effect.

Millstone, however, was disturbed over the report and demanded that O'Hanlon furnish him a copy. O'Hanlon refused, but it did, about a week later, disclose orally to Millstone what it represented as a synopsis of the report. Upon Millstone's categorical denial of all of the allegations in this disclosure, O'Hanlon ordered a recheck of its sources and found no substance to the allegations contained in the original disclosure. Still, O'Hanlon persisted in its refusal to furnish a copy to Millstone and, indeed, failed to disclose to him all of the contents of the report. This suit was then filed, after which discovery procedures uncovered additional derogatory information contained in O'Hanlon's file and still not reported to Millstone. On trial, the District Judge entered a judgment against O'Hanlon for $2,500 actual and $25,000 punitive damages plus $12,500 attorneys fees.

O'Hanlon raises three questions on appeal: (1) the constitutionality of the Act under the First Amendment; (2) the conclusion of the District Court that the facts found constituted a violation of the accuracy and disclosure sections of the Act; and (3) the recovery of any damages under the proof and, in any event, their excessiveness. We find no merit in any of the points and affirm the judgment.

1. Proceedings in the District Court

The trial court filed a memorandum decision in which it entered detailed and comprehensive findings which are not challenged here. We, therefore, see no point in burdening this opinion with the morbid details of this bizarre affair. For those interested in more factual details, reference is made to the decision of the trial judge at 383 F.Supp. 269 (1974).

2. The Constitutionality of the Act

We limit our review of O'Hanlon's constitutional claim to those provisions of the Act upon which Millstone obtained relief. As we see it, a determination that consumer credit reports are protected speech is critical to O'Hanlon's defense.

The court below ruled on O'Hanlon's broad claim of constitutional privilege with respect to the consumer credit reports by deciding that the Millstone reports were "commercial speech" and thus outside of the protections of the First Amendment. 383 F.Supp. 269, 274 (E.D.Mo.1974). In so holding, the District Court considered only whether the O'Hanlon reports concerning Millstone were protected speech. Because the reports "were distributed for commercial purposes and clearly without regard to social concerns or grievances," *id.* at 275, the court decided that the protections of the First Amendment did not extend to the activities of O'Hanlon.

The "commercial speech" doctrine, first enunciated in *Valentine v. Chrestensen,* 316 U.S. 52, 62 S.Ct. 920, 86 L.Ed. 1262 (1942), has been anything but a settled area of constitutional law. The trial judge based his ruling on *Pittsburgh Press Co. v. Pittsburgh Commission on Human Relations,* 413 U.S. 376, 93 S.Ct. 2553, 37 L.Ed.2d 669 (1973). There the Supreme Court upheld an order directing a newspaper to cease publishing help-wanted advertisements under sex-based headings. The illegality of the underlying commercial activity militated against affording the advertisement the First Amendment protection that an otherwise legal commercial proposal might receive.

It is clear that a publication sold for profit is not by that fact alone considered unprotected "commercial speech." *Ginzburg v. United States,* 383 U.S. 463, 474, 86 S.Ct. 942, 16 L.Ed.2d 31 (1966). Nor is the fact that it is an advertisement or some other commercial appeal determinative. *New York Times Co. v. Sullivan,* 376 U.S. 254, 266, 84 S.Ct. 710, 11 L.Ed.2d 686 (1964). In its most recent explication of the commercial speech doctrine, the Supreme Court has indicated that commercial speech remains in a class by itself, entitled to some First Amendment protection but treated differently from other types of communication. *Bigelow v. Virginia,* 421 U.S. 809, 825-27, 95 S.Ct. 2222, 44 L.Ed.2d 600 (1975). *Bigelow* involved the conviction of a newspaper editor for printing an advertisement for a New York abortion referral service. The Supreme Court struck down the Virginia statute in issue and reversed the conviction. In announcing the standard for review in the case, the Court stated:

> Advertising, like all public expression, may be subject to reasonable regulation that serves a legitimate public interest. See *Pittsburgh Press Co. v. Pittsburgh Comm'n on Human Relations, supra; Lehman v. City of Shaker Heights,* 418 U.S. 298 [94 S.Ct. 2714, 41 L.Ed.2d 770] (1974). To the extent that commercial activity is subject to regulation, the relationship of speech to that activity may be one factor, among others, to be considered in weighing the First Amendment interest against the governmental interest alleged. *Id.* 421 U.S. at 826, 95 S.Ct. at 2234. (Footnote omitted.)

The Court went on to note that the State of Virginia's asserted interests were "entitled to little, if any, weight under the circumstances." *Id.* 421 U.S. at 828, 95 S.Ct. at 2235. One of the factors considered was the statute's impingement on the obvious right of Virginia residents to travel to another state to receive medical services legal in that state. *Id.* 421 U.S. at 824-25, 95 S.Ct. at 2234. In other words, the Court recognized the overlay between the First Amendment protection asserted for the advertisement in the case by the editor and the right to travel.

In the instant case, a similar overlay exists but with the opposite result. For here, the challenged statute supports and protects a significant personal right, the right to privacy. See *Griswold v. Connecticut,* 381 U.S. 479, 85 S.Ct. 1678, 14 L.Ed.2d 510 (1965). In fact, this interest is one that the Court considered in *Bigelow* and it found the statute lacking: "There was no possibility that appellant's activity would invade the privacy of other citizens, *Breard v. Alexandria* [341 U.S. 622 (71 S.Ct. 920, 95 L.Ed. 1233) (1951)], or infringe on other rights." *Bigelow v. Virginia,* 421 U.S. 809, 828, 95 S.Ct. 2222, 2236, 44 L.Ed.2d 600 (1975). Unlike the Virginia legislature's purpose in enacting the statute in *Bigelow,* the Congress has enacted the Fair Credit Reporting Act, 15 U.S.C. § 1681 *et seq.,* because it found that:

> There is a need to insure that consumer [credit] reporting agencies exercise their grave responsibilites with fairness, impartiality, and a respect for the consumer's right to privacy.

15 U.S.C. § 1681(a)(4).

Whether the Congress's asserted purpose be labelled a "compelling interest" or one that simply outweighs the alleged impingement on freedom of press, it is our view that by the test enunciated in *Bigelow,* consumer credit reports are not protected speech for which under the First Amendment "Congress shall make no law . . . ." We agree with the District Court that O'Hanlon's reports are "commercial speech."

Accordingly, Congress's authority to legislate that O'Hanlon "follow reasonable procedures to assure maximum possible accuracy," § 1681e(b), and "clearly and accurately disclose to the consumer" the information in its files, § 1681g, was proper. Likewise, Congress had authority to fix liability, including punitive damages and attorney fees, for willful violations of those requirements. O'Hanlon's challenge to the constitutionality of the Act is, we submit, without merit.

3. O'Hanlon's Violations of the Act

The next contention is that O'Hanlon did not violate the accuracy or disclosure provisions of the Act, §§ 1681e(b) and g, and that even if it did, Millstone was not damaged. Given the detailed account of the facts found in the record, we believe this contention merits a short answer.

To us it seems amazing that O'Hanlon makes the claim that its agent followed reasonable procedures promulgated by it to attain the maximum possible accuracy. Everything in the record is to the contrary. It shows that O'Hanlon's agent devoted at most 30 minutes in preparing his report. His report was rife with innuendo, misstatement, and slander. Indeed, the recheck of his investigation shows that he depended solely on one biased informant; made no verification of the same despite O'Hanlon's requirement that there must be verification; and, finally, it took three days to recheck the original investigation, and every allegation therein was found untrue.

O'Hanlon further asserts that its disclosures to Millstone completely revealed the "nature" and "substance" of the derogatory matters in its report. Again, the record proves otherwise. O'Hanlon sought at every step to block Millstone in his attempt to secure the rights given to him by the Act. Not only did O'Hanlon delay and mislead Millstone on the occasion of his first request, but it even did so on a second and third occasion. Not until Millstone brought pressure to bear, through the Federal Trade Commission, and, ultimately, through this lawsuit, did O'Hanlon make the disclosure required by § 1681g.

4. Damages

Finally, O'Hanlon claims that its misconduct did not damage Millstone to the extent he recovered. O'Hanlon's argument highlights the following facts: (1) the incorrect report was made for a mere $68 insurance policy; (2) Millstone himself caused further publication of the incorrect report in news stories about his problems with O'Hanlon; (3) Firemen's Fund did not believe the report when confronted with the truth by Millstone's insurance agent; (4) Millstone was not charged for lost employment time by the Post-Dispatch; and (5) Millstone suffered only loss of sleep, nervousness, frustration and mental anguish over the report. Such injury, it says, does not warrant the award of $2,500 in actual damages, or the award of punitive damages.

The fact that the Post-Dispatch did not diminish Millstone's pay for the considerable time spent fighting O'Hanlon's grossly inaccurate reports should not inure to O'Hanlon's benefit. Any windfall from his employer's generosity and O'Hanlon's payment of damages properly should go to Millstone. *Cf. Olivas v. United States,* 506 F.2d 1158, 1163-64 (9th Cir. 1974), and *Adams v. Turner,* 238 F.Supp. 643, 644-45 (D.D.C.1965). But O'Hanlon cites the much maligned rule that there should be no recovery in tort for mere mental pain and anxiety, and directs our attention to *Southern Express Company v. John Byers,* 240 U.S. 612, 36 S.Ct. 410, 60 L.Ed. 825 (1916). Here, however, the rule is inapplicable because, unlike *Southern Express,* Millstone has an independent cause of action under the Fair Credit Reporting Act quite apart from any recovery he might have sought in tort. O'Hanlon analogizes its position to the Federal Rule of Damages for Fraud utilized in cases based upon violations of the Securities Exchange Act, 15 U.S.C. § 78a *et seq.* That rule limits award for mental anguish to actual out-of-pocket losses. It is, however, inapposite to this case, for the statute here specifically calls for punitive damages.

There can be no doubt that O'Hanlon willfully violated both the spirit and the letter of the Fair Credit Reporting Act, 15 U.S.C. § 1681 *et seq.,* by trampling recklessly upon Millstone's rights thereunder. We therefore find no abuse of discretion or other error in the award.

Affirmed.

2. THE EQUAL CREDIT OPPORTUNITY ACT

The Equal Credit Opportunity Act, 15 U.S.C. §§ 1691a-1691t (1976), was originally enacted in 1974 to make credit available to all persons regardless of sex or marital status. In 1976, amendments were added extending the prohibition against discrimination in granting credit to include race, color, religion, national origin, age (providing applicant has the ability to contract) and the receipt of public assistance benefits. 15 U.S.C. § 1691(a)(1)-(3) (1976). If an applicant is refused credit, the 1976 Act requires the creditor to issue a statement of the reasons upon the request of the applicant. 15 U.S.C. § 1691(d) (1976). Creditors are bound by the procedures in the federal regulations in determining an applicant's creditworthiness. 12 C.F.R. § 202.5 (1976). For example, a creditor may not inquire if an applicant's income is from alimony or child support unless the applicant volunteers it. 12 C.F.R. § 202.5(d)(1), (2). Notice of this must be given to the applicant. Nor may a creditor inquire into the birth control practices of an applicant. 12 C.F.R. § 202.5(d)(4). However, a creditor may ask the ages of any dependents or inquire as to any dependent-related obligations. 12 C.F.R. § 202.5(d)(4).

A creditor who violates the ECOA or its regulations is liable to the individual credit applicant for any actual damages sustained. 15 U.S.C. § 1691(e) (1976). Additionally, a creditor may be liable in an individual action for punitive damages not to exceed $10,000. In a class action, punitive damages may not exceed the lesser of $500,000 or one percent of the creditor's net worth. 15 U.S.C. § 1691(e) (1976).

3. FEDERAL REGULATION UNDER ECOA

The federal regulations set forth general rules concerning the procedures to be followed by creditors in processing credit applications. 12 C.F.R. §§ 202.5-202.13 (1979). In general, a creditor may not discourage a reasonable person from making an application. 12 C.F.R. § 202.5(a). The creditor may request any information concerning the application, such as the applicant's sex, race/national origin and marital status, to be used for monitoring purposes and may request information about a spouse who will use the account, be contractually liable on the account, or who earns the income which is the basis of repayment. The creditor may also inquire about a former spouse upon whom the applicant relies for alimony and child support on which the applicant relies for credit approval. 12 C.F.R. § 202.5(b), (c). However, the creditor may not inquire into alimony or child support unless he discloses to the applicant that the income need only be revealed if the applicant wants it considered in determining creditworthiness. Additionally, the creditor may not inquire as to the sex, birth control practices, race, color, religion or national origin of an applicant. 12 C.F.R. § 202.5(d).

In evaluating the information to determine credit standing, the creditor cannot take into account the applicant's age or the fact that his income derives from public assistance. 12 C.F.R. § 202.6(b). The credit history of the applicant must be considered including an applicant's request of any account reported in the name of the applicant's spouse or former spouse. 12 C.F.R. § 202.5(d).

As to the granting of credit, a creditor may not deny credit based on sex, marital status or any other prohibited basis. 12 C.F.R. § 202.7(a). Nor may a creditor require reapplication, change the terms of the account or terminate the account of an applicant who reaches a certain age or retires. 12 C.F.R. § 202.7(c)(i)-(iii).

After receiving a completed application, the creditor has thirty days to notify an applicant of adverse action taken. 12 C.F.R. § 202.9(a)(i). The notification of a rejection must be in writing and state the specific reason for refusal of the creditor or disclose the applicant's right to request such statement within sixty days. 12 C.F.R. § 202.9(a)(2).

The ECOA also allows married persons with joint accounts the right to have credit information included in credit reports in the name of both husband and wife. 12 C.F.R. § 202.10. This right is partly the result of legislation aimed at ensuring divorced or widowed women credit histories. 12 C.F.R. § 202.10.

The regulations provide that as a general rule, the ECOA preempts only state laws inconsistent with the Act. A state law which is more protective of the applicant is not defined as inconsistent. 12 C.F.R. § 202.11.

CARROLL v. EXXON CO.

United States District Court
434 F. Supp. 557 (E.D. La. 1977)

MITCHELL, DISTRICT JUDGE. This matter was submitted to the Court on a former date, on cross-motions for summary judgment on the issue of liability. After careful consideration of the briefs and arguments of counsel, of the applicable law, and for the entire record, the Court now rules.

In August of 1976, Kathleen Carroll, a single working woman, applied for an Exxon credit card. In response to her application, the plaintiff received correspondence from defendant, dated September 14, 1976, whereby she was informed that her application for credit was denied; but no specific reason for the denial was provided. Thereafter, by her letter of September 28, 1976, Ms. Carroll requested Exxon to furnish her with the specific reasons for the credit denial. An undated response to this request revealed that the credit bureau which was contacted in regard to plaintiff's application did not respond adversely, but was unable to furnish sufficient information regarding her established credit. However, this undated letter, like that of September 14, 1976, did not contain the name of the credit bureau used by Exxon to investigate certain aspects of plaintiff's credit application.

The instant lawsuit was filed on October 26, 1976. Subsequently, on November 2, 1976, Exxon sent another letter to the plaintiff. This correspondence did contain the name and address of the credit bureau which had been contacted with regard to plaintiff's application. Counsel for both sides hotly contest the issues of whether or not these facts constitute a violation of either the Fair Credit Reporting Act or the Equal Credit Opportunity Act. However, both sides do agree that the material facts are not in dispute, and that the liability aspects of the case are in a posture for summary judgment disposition by this Court.

As her first cause of action, the plaintiff alleges that Exxon violated the terms of the Fair Credit Reporting Act (FCRA) by failing to properly identifying the consumer reporting agency which handled her credit application. The FCRA, at 15 U.S.C. § 1681m(a), provides, in part, as follows:

> Whenever credit . . . for personal . . . purposes . . . is denied . . . either wholly or partly because of information contained in a consumer report from a consumer reporting agency, the user of the consumer report shall so advise the consumer against whom such adverse action has been taken and supply the name and address of the consumer reporting agency making the report.

Exxon's defense to this part of the complaint is threefold. The major thrust of Exxon's argument is based upon the premise that it did not deny credit to the plaintiff because of information contained in the report from the consumer reporting agency, Credit Bureau Services. Reliance upon such a defense is tenuous, at best. A mere cursory reading of Exxon's undated letter to the plaintiff reveals that the credit denial was, in fact, based on the report. The entire contents of that letter are reproduced below.[3] Counsel for Exxon does not

---

[3] Thank you for your recent inquiry regarding your application for a credit card account.

Our credit decisions consider such characteristics as maturity, occupation, size of family unit, apparent ease of contact, financial stability and credit references. *We have indicated below those item[s] that either individually or considered together are the reason[s] that influenced our decision to decline your application.*

. . . Credit Bureau . . .

The credit bureau we contacted in your case did not respond adversely, but unfortunately it could furnish little or no definitive information regarding your established credit.

Sincerely,
M. Hill
Credit Services

direct his argument to the company's letter of September 14, 1976. We assume, however, that defendant's position in this regard would be equally applicable to that initial response to the plaintiff's credit card application.

Exxon next argues that it did actually furnish the plaintiff with the information required by the FCRA in its letter of November 2, 1976, which identified the credit bureau used in plaintiff's case. Like the first, this defense can be dismissed in short order. Assuming, *arguendo,* (as defendant argues) that the FCRA does not impose a minimum time standard upon the user of a credit report for the identification of the reporting agency to the consumer, it is obvious that full compliance with the Act is impossible after two violations have already been committed. Neither Exxon's letter of September 14, 1976, nor its subsequent undated letter to the plaintiff properly identified the consumer reporting agency used by Exxon in investigating Ms. Carroll's application. Exxon's *third* letter to the plaintiff, which supplied the name and address of the credit bureau, and which was written after notification of the instant lawsuit, does not constitute compliance with the FCRA, 15 U.S.C. § 1681m(a), when viewed in the context of the events and circumstances of this action.

Defendant's third defense to this part of the action is also unacceptable to this Court. Exxon seeks to avail itself of the "reasonable procedures" defense set out in the FCRA, 15 U.S.C. § 1681m(c):

> No person shall be held liable for any violation of this section if he shows by a preponderance of the evidence that at the time of the alleged violation he maintained reasonable procedures to assure compliance with the provisions of subsections (a) and (b) of this section.

Exxon has supplied various affidavits in the hope of showing that it has established and maintained reasonable procedures to assure compliance with the FCRA. However, as counsel for the plaintiff points out, at least one of defendant's supporting affidavits actually supports the plaintiff's position. According to that affidavit:

> Exxon Company, U.S.A. has established and maintained since prior to August 19, 1976, a procedure whereby it furnishes specific reasons for denial of credit to a credit applicant *upon receipt of a request for such information.* (Emphasis added.)

The FCRA, at 15 U.S.C. § 1681m(a), compels the user of a consumer report to inform the rejected credit applicant that the denial was based in whole or in part upon information received from the designated credit bureau or consumer reporting agency. There is no requirement in the FCRA that the consumer first request the name of such agency before disclosure by a user need be made. The language of 15 U.S.C. § 1681m(a) clearly requires such disclosure contemporaneously upon notification of the denial of credit.

Exxon's second, undated response to the plaintiff's application likewise fails to meet the requirements of the "reasonable procedures" defense delineated in 15 U.S.C. § 1681m(c). That defense is quite similar to the defense provided to creditors for Truth In Lending actions, at 15 U.S.C. § 1640(c). The meaning of "reasonable procedures" within the ambit of the Truth In Lending Act was well

---

Credit report was furnished by
(Blank space)
New Orleans, Louisiana
(Emphasis added) (Parenthesis added)

defined by the Seventh circuit in *Mirabal v. General Motors Acceptance Corp.*, 537 F.2d 871 (CA7-1976). There the Court said, at page 878 of its opinion:

... Congress required more than just the maintenance of procedures which were designed to provide proper disclosure calculations. Rather, it required procedures designed to avoid and prevent errors which might slip through procedures aimed at good faith compliance. This means that the procedures which Congress had in mind were to contain an extra preventative step, a safety catch or a re-checking mechanism. Congress left the exact nature of the preventative mechanism undefined. It is clear, however, that Congress required more than just a showing that a well-trained and careful clerk made a mistake.

In the instant case, defendant has produced no evidence to show that its compliance procedures, although probably designed to provide the proper information, contained any type of preventative mechanism for catching errors.

Having found that Exxon has violated the FCRA, our next task is to determine whether or not its violation was "willful" within the meaning of 15 U.S.C. § 1681n. There is no doubt that Exxon's letter of September 14, 1976, which informed the plaintiff that her credit application had been denied, neither supplied the identity of the consumer reporting agency whose report formed part of the basis for the denial, nor even attempted to do so. In fact, as we have already mentioned, Exxon would not furnish its reasons for a denial of credit to an applicant unless it was first specifically requested to provide such information. We find that Exxon's failure to properly identify the consumer reporting agency in its letter of September 14, 1976, under the facts and circumstances of this case, constitutes willful non-compliance with the requirements of the FCRA, within the meaning of 15 U.S.C. § 1681n.

Therefore, IT IS ORDERED, ADJUDGED, AND DECREED that the motion of plaintiff, Kathleen Carroll, for summary judgment on the issue of liability under FCRA, be and the same is hereby GRANTED;

IT IS FURTHER ORDERED, ADJUDGED, AND DECREED that the motion of defendant, Exxon, for summary judgment under the FCRA, be and the same is hereby DENIED;

IT IS FURTHER ORDERED, ADJUDGED, AND DECREED that this matter be referred to a Magistrate for a determination of the amount of damages, both actual and punitive, and attorney's fees, pursuant to 15 U.S.C. § 1681n.

The plaintiff also contends that Exxon violated the terms of the Equal Credit Opportunity Act (ECOA) by failing to provide her with the specific reasons for the credit denial, and by discriminating against her on the basis of marital status in evaluating her credit application.

The ECOA provides, in pertinent part, at 15 U.S.C. § 1691(a)(1):

(a) It shall be unlawful for any creditor to discriminate against any applicant, with respect to any aspect of a credit transaction —

(1) on the basis of race, color, religion, national origin, sex or marital status, or age (provided that applicant has the capacity to contract);

....

The ECOA also provides for the promulgation of regulations by the Federal Reserve Board to carry out the purposes of the Act. One such regulation, 12 CFR 202.5(m)(2), provides that "[a] creditor shall provide each applicant who is denied credit or whose account is terminated the reasons for such action, if the applicant so requests." Ms. Carroll takes the position that Exxon's undated letter, which was sent to her as a result of her request for specific reasons for the credit denial, violated the plain terms of 12 CFR 202.5(m)(2) in failing to provide the reasons for the negative action.

Counsel for Exxon argues that Exxon's undated letter and its letter of November 2, 1976, satisfy the requirement of 12 CFR 202.5(m)(2) to provide reasons for the credit denial. The legal issue before this Court, then, is whether Exxon's responses to the plaintiff satisfy the notification requirement of 202.5(m)(2).

The ECOA, at 15 U.S.C. § 1691(d)(3) provides that "[a] statement of reasons meets the requirements of this section *only if it contains the specific reasons for the adverse action taken* (emphasis added)." Our independent examination of the record of this case reveals that a number of factors contributed to the denial of Ms. Carroll's credit card application. For example, the plaintiff did not have a major credit card, she did not list a savings account on her application, she had been employed for only one year, and she had no dependents. However, for some reason, Exxon chose only to list, as its reasons for the denial of credit, that the Credit Bureau which had been contacted could furnish little or no definitive information regarding plaintiff's established credit.

The legislative history of the 1976 amendments to the ECOA is particularly instructive in construing the congressional intent behind the passage of the Act:

The requirement that creditors give reasons for adverse action is, in the Committee's view, a strong and necessary adjunct to the antidiscrimination purpose of the legislation, for only if creditors know they must explain their decisions will they effectively be discouraged from discriminatory practices. *Yet this requirement fulfills a broader need: rejected credit applicants will now be able to learn where and how their credit status is deficient and this information should have a pervasive and valuable educational benefit. Instead of being told only that they do not meet a particular creditor's standards, consumers particularly should benefit from knowing, for example, that the reason for the denial is their short residence in the area, or their recent change of employment, or their already over-extended financial situation. In those cases where the creditor may have acted on misinformation or inadequate information, the statement of reasons gives the applicant a chance to rectify the mistake.*

Therefore, even if we view Exxon's undated response to the plaintiff to have been properly amended and corrected by the letter of November 2, 1976, it is clear that Exxon has failed to meet the requirements of 15 U.S.C. § 1691(d)(3) and 12 CFR 202.5(m)(2). Exxon's responses to plaintiff's request for specific reasons for the credit denial fail to achieve the informative purposes legislated in the ECOA.[11] We do not feel that this decision will place any heavier burden on creditors than that intended by Congress to aid the consumer in the search for reliable and informative credit information.

Exxon's reliance on the defense propounded at 12 CFR 202.11(a) is inapposite. That section provides that, if a creditor fails to comply with 202.5(m) due to a "mechanical, electronic or clerical error made in good faith," it shall not be a violation of the section if "the creditor shows by a preponderance of the evidence that at the time of the noncompliance the creditor had established and was maintaining suitable procedures to assure compliance with the section." In

[11] In fact, Exxon's initial letter to the plaintiff, dated September 14, 1976, in which it informed her that her application had been denied, contravened congressional intent by failing to notify the rejected applicant of her right to a statement of reasons on request. *See* 1976 U.S. Code Cong. & Admin.News, page 410.

the instant case, we have not found that Exxon's failure to comply with the ECOA and Regulation B resulted from its failure to initially supply plaintiff with the name of the Credit Bureau used to investigate her credit application. Rather, our decision is aimed at Exxon's failure to properly inform the plaintiff of the actual reasons for the credit denial. Therefore, the defense is inapplicable to this part of the plaintiff's argument.

Finally, Ms. Carroll contends that, in evaluating her credit application, Exxon considered the number of her dependents, which evinces a bias on the basis of marital status in violation of 12 CFR 202.5(f) and 202.5(h). Plaintiff argues that, since it is unusual for an unmarried person to have any dependents, the fact that Exxon considers the number of the applicant's dependents in its scoring system constitutes discrimination on the basis of marital status, which the ECOA condemns. We disagree. We cannot conclude that, as a matter of law, Exxon's interrogatory regarding dependency violates Regulation B or the ECOA. The regulations cited by plaintiff in this regard do not prohibit the credit grantor's investigation into this area. Dependency is not limited to one's biological descendants, and is not necessarily included in "assumptions relating to the likelihood of any group of persons bearing or rearing children" within the ambit of 12 CFR 202.5(h). Furthermore, we are aware that Congress has provided some guidance as to the allocation of the burdens of proof necessary to determine the existence of discrimination under the ECOA. The credit grantor must meet the burden of showing that any given requirement has a manifest relationship to the creditworthiness of the applicant, but *only* if the complaining party has first made out a prima facie case of discrimination, *i. e.*, has shown that the credit application's interrogatories result in the selection of credit card holders in a pattern significantly different from that of the pool of applicants. The plaintiff in this case has not made out a prima facie case of discrimination under the ECOA. Therefore, since plaintiff has failed to sustain her onus under the law, Exxon is not required to show the relationship between the subject interrogatory and the creditworthiness of the applicant.

Therefore, for these reasons, IT IS ORDERED, ADJUDGED, AND DECREED that the motion of plaintiff, Kathleen Carroll, for summary judgment on the issue of liability under 12 CFR 202.5(m)(2) of the ECOA, be and the same is hereby GRANTED, and that plaintiff's motion for summary judgment under 12 CFR 202.5(f) and 202.5(h) is hereby DENIED;

IT IS FURTHER ORDERED, ADJUDGED, AND DECREED that the motion of defendant, Exxon, for summary judgment under the ECOA, be and the same is hereby DENIED;

IT IS FURTHER ORDERED that this matter be referred to a Magistrate for a determination of the amount of damages, both actual and punitive, and attorney's fees, pursuant to 15 U.S.C. § 1691e(a), (b), and (d).

MARKHAM v. COLONIAL MORTGAGE SERVICE CO.

United States Court of Appeals
605 F.2d 566 (D.C. Cir. 1979)

Swygert, Circuit Judge. The Equal Credit Opportunity Act, 15 U.S.C. §§ 1691, *et seq.,* prohibits creditors from discriminating against applicants on the basis of sex or marital status. We are asked to decide whether this prohibition prevents creditors from refusing to aggregate the incomes of two unmarried joint mortgage applicants when determining their creditworthiness in a situation where the incomes of two similarly situated married joint applicants would have been aggregated. The plaintiffs in this action, Jerry and Marcia Markham, appeal the judgment of the district court granting defendant Illinois Federal Service Savings and Loan Association's motion for summary judgment. We reverse. The plaintiffs also appeal the judgment of the district court granting a motion for summary judgment on behalf of defendants Colonial Mortgage Service Co. Associates, Inc., Al Shoemaker, and B.W. Real Estate, Inc. As to this matter, we affirm.

I

In November 1976, plaintiffs Marcia J. Harris and Jerry Markham announced their engagement and began looking for a residence in the Capitol Hill section of Washington, D.C. One of the real estate firms which they contacted, defendant B.W. Real Estate, Inc., found suitable property for them, and in December 1976, Markham and Harris signed a contract of sale for the property.

Upon the recommendation of B.W. Real Estate, plaintiffs agreed to have defendant Colonial Mortgage Service Co. Associates, Inc. (Colonial Mortgage) conduct a credit check. Plaintiffs subsequently submitted a joint mortgage application to Colonial Mortgage, who in turn submitted it to Colonial Mortgage Service Company (Colonial-Philadelphia), a business entity located in Philadelphia and not a party to this action.

In March 1976, Colonial-Philadelphia had entered into an agreement with defendant Illinois Federal Service Savings and Loan Association (Illinois Federal), whereby Illinois Federal agreed to purchase certain mortgages and trust deeds offered it by Colonial-Philadelphia. Pursuant to this agreement, Colonial-Philadelphia offered plaintiffs' mortgage application to Illinois Federal.

Plaintiffs and B.W. Real Estate had decided that February 4, 1977 would be an appropriate closing date for the purchase of the Capitol Hill residence. Accordingly, plaintiffs arranged to terminate their current leases, change mailing addresses, and begin utility service at the new property. On February 1, the loan committee of Illinois Federal rejected the plaintiffs' application. On February 3, the eve of the settlement date, plaintiffs were informed through a B.W. Real Estate agent that their loan application had been denied because they were not married. They were advised that their application would be resubmitted to the "investor" — who was not identified — on February 8, but that approval would be contingent upon the submission of a marriage certificate.

On February 8, the Illinois Federal loan committee reconsidered the plaintiffs' application, but again denied it. A letter was sent that date from Illinois Federal to Colonial-Philadelphia, which letter stated that the application had been rejected with the statement: "Separate income not sufficient for loan and job tenure."

On February 9, 1977 plaintiffs filed this suit, alleging violation of the Equal Credit Opportunity Act. After the district court separately granted the motions of Illinois Federal and the other defendants for summary judgment on May 25, 1978, plaintiffs brought this appeal.

II

A

We address first the appeal from the district court's summary judgment entered in favor of Illinois Federal. The district court concluded as a matter of law that plaintiffs could not state a claim under the Equal Credit Opportunity Act even if they showed that Illinois Federal's refusal to aggregate their incomes resulted, in whole or in part, in the denial of their loan application. This conclusion was based on the premise that creditors need not ignore the "special legal ties created between two people by the marital bond." It was the court's conclusion that under Illinois law the mere fact of marriage provides creditors with greater rights and remedies against married applicants than are available against unmarried applicants. Presumably the district court believed that this excused Illinois Federal under 15 U.S.C. § 1691d(b), which allows a creditor to take "[s]tate property laws directly or indirectly affecting creditworthiness" into consideration in making credit decisions.

We fail to see the relevance of any special legal ties created by marriage with respect to the legal obligations of joint debtors. This was not an instance where a single person is applying for credit individually and claiming income from a third party for purposes of determining creditworthiness. In such an instance, the absence of a legal obligation requiring continuance of the income claimed by the applicant from the third party would reflect on the credit applicant's creditworthiness. Inasmuch as the Markhams applied for their mortgage jointly, they would have been jointly and severally liable on the debt. Each joint debtor would be bound to pay the full amount of the debt; he would then have a right to contribution from his joint debtor. *See* 4 A. Corbin, *Contracts* §§ 924, 928 (1951). *See also Clayman v. Goodman Properties, Inc.*, 171 U.S.App.D.C. 88, 518 F.2d 1026 (1973); *Welch v. Sherwin*, 112 U.S.App.D.C. 124, 300 F.2d 716 (1962); Ill.Ann.Stat. ch. 76, § 3 (Smith-Hurd). While it may be true that judicially-enforceable rights such as support and maintenance are legal consequences of married status, they are irrelevancies as far as the creditworthiness of joint applicants is concerned. Illinois Federal would have had no greater rights against the Markhams had they been married, nor would the Markhams have had greater rights against each other on this particular obligation. Thus, inasmuch as the state laws attaching in the event of marriage would not affect the creditworthiness of these joint applicants, section 1691d(b) may not be used to justify the refusal to aggregate the plaintiffs' incomes on the basis of marital status.

B

We turn to a consideration of whether the Equal Credit Opportunity Act's prohibition of discrimination on the basis of sex or marital status makes illegal Illinois Federal's refusal to aggregate plaintiffs' income when determining their creditworthiness. Illinois Federal contends that neither the purpose nor the language of the Act requires it to combine the incomes of unmarried joint applicants when making that determination.

We start, as we must, with the language of the statute itself. *March v. United States*, 165 U.S.App.D.C. 267, 274, 506 F.2d 1306, 1313 (1974). 15 U.S.C. § 1691(a) provides:

> It shall be unlawful for any creditor to discriminate against any applicant, with respect to any aspect of a credit transaction —
>
> (1) on the basis of . . . sex or marital status
> . . . .

This language is simple, and its meaning is not difficult to comprehend. Illinois Federal itself has correctly phrased the standard in its brief: The Act forbids discrimination "on the basis of a person's marital status, that is, to treat persons differently, all other facts being the same, because of their marital status . . . ."

Brief for Defendant Illinois Federal at 18. Illinois Federal does not contend that they would not have aggregated plaintiffs' income had they been married at the time. Indeed, Illinois Federal concedes that the law would have required it to do so. Thus, it is plain that Illinois Federal treated plaintiffs differently — that is, refused to aggregate their incomes — solely because of their marital status, which is precisely the sort of discrimination prohibited by section 1691(a)(1) on its face.

Despite the section's clarity of language, Illinois Federal seeks to avoid a finding of prohibited discrimination by arguing that it was not the Congressional purpose to require such an aggregation of the incomes of non-married applicants. It can be assumed, *arguendo,* that one, perhaps even the main, purpose of the act was to eradicate credit discrimination waged against women, especially married women whom creditors traditionally refused to consider apart from their husbands as individually worthy of credit. But granting such an assumption does not negate the clear language of the Act itself that discrimination against *any* applicant, with respect to *any* aspect of a credit transaction, which is based on marital status is outlawed. When the plain meaning of a statute appears on its face, we need not concern ourselves with legislative history, *see Caminetti v. United States,* 242 U.S. 470, 485, 37 S.Ct. 192, 61 L.Ed. 442 (1917), especially when evidence of the legislation's history as has been presented to us does not argue persuasively for a narrower meaning than that which is apparent from the statutory language. *See Boston Sand & Gravel Co. v. United States,* 278 U.S. 41, 48, 49 S.Ct. 52, 73 L.Ed. 170 (1928). We believe that the meaning of the words chosen by Congress is readily apparent.

Illinois Federal expresses the fear that a holding such as we reach today will require it to aggregate the incomes of all persons who apply for credit as a group. Lest it be misinterpreted, we note that our holding is not itself that far-reaching. It does no more than require Illinois Federal to treat plaintiffs — a couple jointly applying for credit — the same as they would be treated if married. We have not been asked to decide what the effect of the Act would have been had plaintiffs not applied for credit jointly. Nor do we have before us a question of whether the Act's marital status provision in any way applies to a situation where more than two people jointly request credit. We hold only that, under the Act Illinois Federal should have treated plaintiffs — an unmarried couple applying for credit jointly — the same as it would have treated them had they been married at the time.

C

Illinois Federal also contends that, regardless of this court's decision on the issue of income aggregation, the judgment of the district court should be affirmed. The premise of this contention is that, even had the incomes of plaintiffs' been combined, Illinois Federal would still not have extended the loan because of lack of sufficient job tenure or credit history. Due to the district court's basis for decision and the state of the record, we are not in position to pass on the validity of this separate issue.

The district court entered summary judgment for Illinois Federal on the ground that the failure to aggregate incomes was not a violation of the Act. Thus, having no need to do so, it never reached the question of whether plaintiffs were otherwise eligible for the loan. Whether Illinois Federal would have otherwise extended the loan is a question of fact that is material, given our disposition of the aggregation issue. Accordingly, if there is a genuine dispute over that issue, summary judgment is inappropriate. Fed.R.Civ.P. 56. On the record, there appears to be such a dispute. Although Illinois Federal contends that plaintiffs would remain ineligible regardless of aggregation, plaintiffs assert that they were told the loan would be forthcoming if they produced a marriage certificate. Because we remand the case to the district court, we deem it sufficient to note the appearance of a genuine issue of material fact on this state of the record. Following remand, further discovery and additional affidavits may either confirm or dispel this appearance.

III

Plaintiffs also appeal from the district court's entry of summary judgment in favor of the other defendants: Colonial Mortgage, Al Shoemaker, and B.W. Real Estate. The district court based its judgment on alternative grounds, holding first that these defendants had done nothing which could be construed as a discriminatory act, and second, that regardless of their actions they were not "creditors" as that term is used in the Act. We affirm on the first ground, thus we do not reach the second.

There is no indication that these three defendants participated in Illinois Federal's decision to discriminate or in any way benefited therefrom. At most, plaintiffs' allegations describe a course of conduct whereby these defendants acted as conduits, transferring information from plaintiffs to Illinois Federal and relaying decisions back. Inasmuch as we are unable to find on the record an instance where one of these three defendants participated in a decision to discriminate against plaintiffs on the basis of marital status, we affirm the order of the district court granting summary judgment in favor of defendants Colonial Mortgage, Al Shoemaker, and B.W. Real Estate.

IV

There remain two issues requiring our attention. Plaintiffs have appealed from the district court's order denying their motion for an interim award of attorney fees. We note simply that the Act provides:

> In the case of any successful action . . . the costs of the action, together with a reasonable attorney's fee as determined by the court, shall be added to any damages awarded by the court . . . .

15 U.S.C. § 1691e(d). Because this case has not yet come to a conclusion, not even a preliminary one, and is not yet a "successful action," we hold the district court did not abuse its discretion in denying plaintiffs an interim fee award.

Finally, plaintiffs contend that the district court abused its discretion in denying their motions to compel discovery and for sanctions for failure to comply with discovery requests. The motion for sanctions, made prior to any motion to compel discovery, was appropriately denied by the district court. The motion to compel discovery was regarded as moot by the district court after its decision to grant Illinois Federal's summary judgment motion. Because we reverse the summary judgment, we remand the question of the appropriate scope of discovery to the district court for consideration in light of our decision today.

In sum, the order of the district court granting summary judgment to defendant Illinois Federal is reversed, and the cause is remanded along with the discovery question. The order of the district court granting summary judgment to defendants Colonial Mortgage, Al Shoemaker, and B.W. Real Estate is affirmed, as are the orders denying discovery sanctions and interim attorney fees.

NOTE

See also Comment, *Fair Credit Reporting Act: The Case for Revision*, 10 Loy. U.L. Rev. 409 (1977), and Comment, *Equal Credit for All — An Analysis of the 1976 Amendment to the Equal Credit Opportunity Act*, 22 St. Louis U.L.J. 326 (1978).

D. THE FEDERAL DISCLOSURE ACTS

1. TRUTH IN LENDING

The 1969 Consumer Credit Protection Act, commonly known as "Truth-in-Lending," mandates specific disclosures in consumer credit transactions. Its provisions are applicable to residential real estate sales, loans and security interests. Consumer credit protection legislation was prompted by congressional concern over the complexity of credit transactions. Consumers frequently were unaware of charges incidental to the extension of credit — charges which were not reflected in the stated interest rate. And in instances in which consumers were apprised of additional charges, confusing financial terminology rendered such information meaningless. *See* [1968] U.S. Code Cong. & Ad. News 1962. To remedy this perceived problem Congress enacted the Consumer Credit Protection Act, subjecting lenders to comprehensive disclosure requirements in the extension of consumer credit. Pursuant to authority contained in the Act, the Federal Reserve Board has promulgated Regulation Z to implement the Act. 15 U.S.C. § 1604; 12 C.F.R. § 226.1 et seq. Other federal agencies are charged with responsibility for the financial institution's compliance, *e.g.*, the Federal Home Loan Bank Board monitors compliance with TIL and Regulation Z on the part of federal savings and loan associations. 15 U.S.C. § 1607. The thrust of the federal regulation is to mandate disclosure of various credit charges in a uniform vocabulary in order that consumers may understand the actual cost of credit and compare costs among competing lenders.

The Act is limited to consumer credit arrangements. This is evidenced by the statutory definition of "consumer," being a natural person who will use the proceeds or property "primarily for personal, family, household or agricultural purposes"; and further by the enumeration of exempted transactions. *See* 15 U.S.C. § 1602(h). The Act specifically does not apply to (1) credit transactions for business, commercial or governmental purposes, (2) securities or commodities transactions, (3) credit transaction in which the total amount financed exceeds $25,000, with the exception of non-agricultural real property transactions, and (4) public utility tariff transactions under certain circumstances. 15 U.S.C. § 1603. In addition, the Act does not purport to bring within its scope the isolated extension of credit. "Creditor" refers only to creditors who regularly extend or arrange for the extension of credit for which the payment of a finance charge is required, whether in connection with loans, sales of property or services, or otherwise. 15 U.S.C. § 1602(f). Thus a homeowner-seller taking back a mortgage from the buyer would not be required to make TIL disclosures.

The most common category of home financing is, in the terminology of the Act, "consumer loans not under open end credit plans." 15 U.S.C. § 1639. In such a transaction, the creditor must disclose: (1) the amount of credit of which the obligor will have actual use, (2) all charges which are not part of the finance charge, (3) the total amount financed (sum of 1 and 2), (4) except with a purchase money first mortgage, the amount of the finance charge, (5) finance charge expressed in terms of an annual percentage rate — APR, (6) number, amount, due dates of scheduled repayments, (7) default or delinquency charges for late payments, (8) description of security interest and clear identification of the property to which the security interest pertains. Regulation Z expands somewhat on the outline of the Act, requiring disclosure of any "balloon" payments and of prepayment arrangements and penalties. 12 C.F.R. § 226.8(b).

In "sales not under open end credit plans," the seller extends or arranges for the extension of credit to the consumer. 15 U.S.C. § 1602(g). Although the disclosures are similar, the Act requires additional items to be listed: (1) the "cash price" of the property, (2) amount credited as down payment, (3) the difference between cash price and down payment. Applicable disclosures in both instances must be made "before credit is extended." 15 U.S.C. §§ 1638(b) & 1639(b).

At the center of the disclosure statement is the determination of the "finance charge," which is broadly defined as "the sum of all charges, payable directly or indirectly by the person to whom credit is extended, and imposed directly or indirectly by the creditor as an incident to the extension of credit . . . ." 15 U.S.C. § 1605(a). These charges include: (1) the interest and amounts payable under a point system, (2) service or carrying charge, (3) loan fee or finder's fee, (4) fee for investigation or credit report, (5) various credit insurance fees unless the creditor provides a statement to the consumer detailing the cost of insurance provided by the creditor and advising that the consumer may purchase insurance elsewhere. Once determined, this finance charge must be expressed as an annual percentage rate (hereafter APR). 15 U.S.C. § 1606. Thus, many formerly "hidden" charges are added to the stated interest rate, resulting in an APR that more accurately reflects the actual cost of credit to the consumer.

Despite the all-inclusive language of the finance charge definition, the statute allows exclusions from the computation in certain circumstances. The following items need not be included in the finance charge if they are separately disclosed: (1) fees prescribed by law for perfecting, ascertaining, or releasing a security interest; (2) premiums for insurance in lieu of perfecting a security interest; (3) taxes; (4) any other type of charge which is not for credit and which is approved for exclusion by the Federal Reserve Board. Also typical real estate closing costs "provided they are bona fide, reasonable in amount and not for the purpose of circumvention or evasion" are not to be computed in the finance charge. 12 C.F.R. § 226.4(e). These enumerated costs are: (1) fees and premiums for title examination or title insurance, (2) fees for deed preparation, settlement statement or other documents, (3) escrow for future insurance and taxes, (4) notary fees, (5) appraisal fees, (6) credit reports. 15 U.S.C. § 1605(e).

The basic thrust of TIL is disclosure. However, the Act confers a substantive right upon consumers in credit transactions in which a security interest is or will be retained in any real property used as the consumer's residence. Unless the security interest is a first lien acquired in financing the acquisition of the dwelling, the consumer "shall have the right to rescind the transaction until midnight of the third business day" following the transaction. 15 U.S.C. § 1635(a). Naturally, the creditor must clearly disclose to the consumer the fact that the consumer may rescind. 15 U.S.C. § 1635(a). If a consumer elects to rescind, and notifies the creditor of this election, the consumer is not liable for any finance charge, and any security interest acquired by the creditor becomes void. 15 U.S.C. § 1635(b). This right of rescission applies not only to traditional second mortgages but to nonconsensual liens such as mechanics liens and to those created by cognovit notes. It is *not* applicable if the funds coming into the hands of the mortgagor will be used for business purposes since the transaction then would not be a "consumer" transaction despite the fact a lien may be acquired on the debtor's residence. *See* Griffith, *Truth-in-Lending and Real Estate Transactions: Some Aspects,* 2 OHIO N.L.REV. 219 (1974).

The Act provides criminal liability for willful and knowing violations. An offender may be fined a maximum of $5,000, imprisoned no more than a year, or both. 15 U.S.C. § 1611. But the basic remedy for an aggrieved consumer is a civil suit alleging failure to disclose, or inaccurate disclosure. If he prevails the consumer may recover any actual damages plus two times the finance charge (but not less than $100 or more than $1,000) and reasonable attorney's fees. 15 U.S.C. § 1640(a). In a class action, the total recovery cannot exceed the lesser of $500,000 or 1% of the creditor's net worth. 15 U.S.C. § 1640(a)(2)(B) & Supp. 1976. In case of error, the creditor will not be liable if he is able to notify the consumer and make necessary adjustments within fifteen days of discovery of the error and before institution of a suit. 15 U.S.C. § 1640(b). Once an action has been brought, the creditor may attempt to defend on the basis that the error was "unintentional and resulted from a bona fide error, notwithstanding the maintenance of procedures reasonably adapted to avoid any such error." 15 U.S.C. § 1640(c).

Finally, the creditor will not be liable if he can establish that he acted in good faith conformity with any "rule, regulation or interpretation thereof by the Board or in conformity with any interpretation or approval by an official or employee of the Federal Reserve System" authorized to make such interpretation. 15 U.S.C. § 1640(f) (1976 Supp).

For a TIL disclosure statement, see Illustration 8 at the end of this chapter.

HOUSTON v. ATLANTA FEDERAL SAVINGS & LOAN ASS'N

United States District Court
414 F. Supp. 851 (N.D. Ga. 1976)

RICHARD C. FREEMAN, DISTRICT JUDGE. This is an action brought pursuant to the Truth-in-Lending provisions of the Federal Consumer Credit Protection Act, 15 U.S.C. § 1601, et seq. (hereinafter Truth-in-Lending Act) and Regulation Z, 12 C.F.R. § 226.1, et seq., promulgated pursuant thereto. The action was referred to a Bankruptcy Judge, acting as Special Master, who recommended entering judgment for defendant. The action is presently before the court on plaintiffs' objections to this recommendation. Plaintiff argues that the Special Master erred in concluding that defendant did not violate the Truth-in-Lending Act by improper disclosure of (1) the conditions under which a "late charge" for untimely payment of loan proceeds may be imposed; (2) the components of the amount financed; (3) the identity of the property subject to the security interest; and (4) the address of the defendant. . . .

. . . .

The action sub judice involves a loan covering plaintiff's residence consisting of a "First Mortgage Real Estate Note" in the amount of $44,900.00 secured by a first mortgage on the property in favor of defendant. The "total of payments" over the thirty year term of the loan is disclosed as $113,025.60, consisting of a finance charge of $69,039.60 and an amount financed disclosed as $43,986.00. Although it is unusal for a Truth-in-Lending action to involve sums of this magnitude, actions concerning security interests on residential property are not at all unusual. Most of these actions, however, involve second mortgages and so-called "home improvement" contracts, which are subject to the rescission provisions of 15 U.S.C. § 1635. E. g., Sellers v. Wollman, 510 F.2d 119 (5th Cir. 1975); Palmer v. Wilson, 502 F.2d 860 (9th Cir. 1974); Pedro v. Pacific Plan of California, 393 F.Supp. 315 (N.D.Cal.1975). Because "the creation or retention of a first lien against a dwelling to finance the acquisition of that dwelling", 15

U.S.C. § 1635(e), is specifically excepted from the rescission provisions of the Act, the issue in the instant case is whether plaintiffs may recover statutory damages and/or attorney's fees on account of the purported violations in issue. On the other hand, first mortgages, with a few exceptions, . . . are not otherwise excluded from coverage under the Truth-in-Lending Act; and this court agrees with plaintiffs that deficiencies in a disclosure statement issued in mortgage transactions should generally be treated on an equal footing with any other consumer loan transaction. *Cf. Atchison v. The Citizens & Southern National Bank,* Civil Action No. 16568 (N.D.Ga. Dec. 13, 1972). Thus, although the courts have noted the difficulties attendant upon "effort[s] to bring order from this vertitable chaos of technical language [in the Truth-in-Lending Act]," *Jones v. Community Loan & Investment Corp.,* 526 F.2d 642, 648 n. 12 (5th Cir. 1976), it is nevertheless clear in either the normal consumer loan or the mortgage loan context that "Congress did not intend creditors to escape liability where only technical violations were involved." *Pennino v. Morris Kirschman & Co., Inc.,* 526 F.2d 367, 370 (5th Cir. 1976). *Accord Powers v. Sims and Levin Realtors,* 396 F.Supp. 12, 20 (E.D. Va. 1975) (mortgage loan).

. . . .

The next purported violation consists of failure to adequately identify the property subject to the security interest. *See* 15 U.S.C. § 1639(a)(8). The property is identified on the disclosure statement as "1071 Fielding Way"; however, neither the city nor the state in which "1071 Fielding Way" is located is listed. Of course, this is another "technical" violation of the Act; but the plain language of § 1639(a)(8) requires "*a clear identification* of the property to which the security interest relates." (emphasis added). *Compare Kenney v. Landis Financial Group, Inc., supra* at 945 ("clear identification" does not require "particularization" of consumer goods subject to a security interest). In fact, as noted by the Special Master, defendant does not contest the inadequacy of the disclosure in issue. Instead, the defendant argued and the Special Master concluded that liability for this improper disclosure should be excused under the provisions of 15 U.S.C. § 1640(c), which provide in relevant part as follows:

A creditor may not be held liable . . . for a violation of this subchapter if the creditor shows by a preponderence of the evidence that the violation was not intentional and resulted from a bona fide error *notwithstanding the maintenance of procedures reasonably adapted to avoid any such error.* (emphasis added).

The majority of courts have ruled that this so-called bona fide error defense applies solely to clerical errors rather than errors of law or legal interpretation, *e. g., Haynes v. Logan Furniture Mart, Inc.,* 503 F.2d 1161 (7th Cir. 1974); *Buford v. American Finance Co.,* 333 F.Supp. 1243, 1248 (N.D.Ga.1971). Moreover, given the fact that every error of law may also, at least in cases of omission, be construed as a clerical error, the courts refuse to recognize this defense where "[t]he omissions and misstatements were part of defendants' usual credit practice and did not occur in spite of procedures designed to avoid unintentional violations of the Act." *Palmer v. Wilson, supra* at 861; *Pedro v. Pacific Plan of California, supra* at 321. In the instant case, the defendant has submitted an affidavit from one of its officials to the effect that employees preparing Truth-in-Lending disclosure statements are instructed to describe the property subject to the mortgage by "number and street, city (if in city), and county; or lot and block, subdivision, and county." As a result, the Special Master concluded that the improper disclosure in the instant case was excused by § 1640(c): "The bona fide omission of the city *and state* when the street address is disclosed is an error falling within said defense." Special Master Report at p. 25 (emphasis added). The Special Master likewise concluded that "Plaintiffs have not offered and would be unable to offer any evidence that the omission of a complete description of the property was intentional. . . ." *Id.*

Review of the Special Master's report reveals certain inconsistencies. First, it appears that the Special Master may have erroneously placed the burden on the plaintiffs of showing an intentional violation of the act, whereas, it is clear under § 1640(c) that the burden is upon the defendant of showing that the violation is "unintentional." As noted above, the courts considering this question generally base their findings on the existence vel non of procedures designed to eliminate the specific error in question. In that regard, if the Special Master's implicit finding to the effect that defendant herein maintained procedures designed to eliminate the error is not clearly erroneous, *see* Rule 53(e)(2), Fed.R.Civ.P., the erroneous legal conclusion concerning the burden of proof would not compel rejection of the recommendation. Unfortunately, this determinative factual finding is clearly erroneous. As noted above, the Special Master concluded that failure to disclose the city *and state* where the property subject to the mortgage is located would constitute a violation of the act. This ruling is not contested by defendant. . . . Although the Special Master then concluded that this violation was excused, on review of the affidavit relied upon, there is no indication that defendant required its loan origination personnel to disclose the state, as well as the street address, city and county were the property was located. The Special Master's finding to the contrary is not supported by the evidence and is clearly erroneous. As a result, defendant's uncontested violation is not excused and the Special Master's recommendation regarding this issue must be rejected.

The final violation in issue consists of plaintiffs' contention that defendant erred in failing to disclose its address on the disclosure statement. *See Welmaker v. W. T. Grant Co.,* 365 F.Supp. 531, 539-40 (N.D.Ga.1972). In *Welmaker,* Judge Smith ruled that the identification of the seller as "store # 70" violated the Act, concluding that the "seller's place of business [street address] . . . should be fully and clearly set out in the appropriate place." *Id.* at 540. In the instant case, the Special Master distinguished *Welmaker* on the ground that the defendant herein, unlike the defendant in *Welmaker,* is not a national chain having offices and stores in many states. Instead, the Special Master found that defendant conducts business under the name Atlanta Federal Savings and Loan solely in the Atlanta Metropolitan area through some twenty-one offices, and that plaintiffs could make loan payments at any of these offices or by mail. Given these distinguishing factors, the Special Master concluded that the *Welmaker* case was not controlling; however, the Special Master also concluded that the violation, if any, was an "unintentional error" which should not subject the defendants to liability. *See id.* at 540-44.

While this court does not disagree with the Special Master's conclusions in all respects, the court does not agree that the "unintentional" nature of the violation would preclude the imposition of liability. As noted above, unintentional violations are excused only where the defendant introduces evidence showing that these violations occurred despite procedures adopted to avoid the particular error. Although the weight of authority construing § 1640(c) is not uniform, *compare id. with Buford v. American Finance Co., supra,* virtually every Court of Appeals decision has rejected the *Welmaker* "good faith" defense in favor of limiting the applicability of § 1640(c) to clerical errors. *E. g., Ives v. W. T. Grant Co.,* 522 F.2d 749, 757-58 (2d Cir. 1975), *Haynes v. Logan Furniture Mart, Inc., supra; Palmer v. Wilson, supra.* On the other hand, the *Welmaker* rule, to the extent it may be limited to the class action context, has been approved by Congress:

In determining the amount of award *in any class action,* the court shall consider, among other relevant factors, the amount of any actual damages awarded, the frequency and persistence of failures of compliance by the creditor, the resources of the creditor, the number of persons adversely affected, and the extent to which the creditor's failure of compliance was intentional.

15 U.S.C. § 1640(a) (emphasis added) (added in 1974). Of course, this provision is not applicable in the instant case. Although another amendment added in 1974 and applicable to all cases provides a defense predicated on "good faith", this defense is only applicable to an "act done or omitted in good faith in conformity with any rule, regulation, or interpretation thereof by the Board, notwithstanding that . . . such rule, regulation, or interpretation is [later] amended . . . or determined . . . to be invalid . . . ." 15 U.S.C. § 1640(f). The leading judicial interpretation of this provision has limited its applicability to situations where a disclosure statement, prepared in accordance with governing rules, regulations, and interpretations, is later determined to be in violation of the Truth-in-Lending Act because the underlying regulations are invalid or no longer in effect. *Ives v. W. T. Grant Co., supra* at 758. Defendant has not introduced any evidence whatsoever showing that it relied on a specific regulation approving omission of its address; therefore defendant is not protected by § 1640(f). On the other hand, in opposition to the Special Master's recommendation, plaintiffs have not cited any authority, other than the *Welmaker* case, requiring the disclosure of the full street address. As a result, in the circumstances of this case, the Special Master's erroneous conclusion concerning the "good faith" defense does not compel rejection of his recommendation.

As noted above, the Special Master concluded that certain circumstances distinguished the instant action from the *Welmaker* decision. Irrespective of the applicability of the *Welmaker* good faith rule in this case, it is clear that the violation in *Welmaker* was predicated on application of the "catch-all" provisions of 12 C.F.R. § 226.6(c), rather than upon any specific statutory or regulatory provision requiring disclosure of the full address of the creditor. It is one thing to impose liability for a "technical" violation of the language of an express statutory or regulatory provision, and it is another matter entirely to rule, in the circumstances presented, that omission of a non-required disclosure, without more, has rendered a disclosure statement so confusing and misleading as to constitute a violation of the Act. In considering the instant purported violation, unlike the violation predicated on the *conflicting* disclosure with respect to collection of the "late charge", and unlike the circumstances in the *Welmaker* case, there is no possibility that plaintiffs herein could be confused or misled concerning the identity of their creditor. Although better practice requires disclosure of the creditor's full address, in the circumstances presented, where the creditor is a mortgage lender located in one area of one state, full disclosure of the name of the creditor is all that is required. Plaintiffs' arguments to the contrary are without merit.

In sum, this court has concluded that the Special Master's report is erroneous, to the extent that it recommended the entry of judgment for defendant. The Special Master erred in concluding that liability should not be imposed for the technical violation predicated on the conflicting disclosure with respect to accrual of late charges, and the Special Master erred in concluding that defendant's failure to clearly identify the property subject to the mortgage should be excused as a bona fide error. Similarly, although the Special Master erred in applying a "good faith" defense to the violations in issue, the Special Master was correct in ruling that the disclosure of the creditor's address and the disclosures required by 15 U.S.C. § 1639(a)(1)-(2) were sufficient under the Act.

If this were a matter of first impression, this court would be inclined to rule for defendant; for the court does not doubt that the violations found in the instant case were unintentional and did not affect the ability of the consumer to make an informed choice of credit alternatives. This court is extremely reluctant to utilize the technical provisions in issue here to provide a "bonus" to "consumers" who, given the amount of the loan in question, were no doubt able to obtain legal counsel and fully apprise themselves of the nature of their obligation and of available alternatives in the credit market. This is not a case of unequal bargaining power normally found in a small, consumer loan transaction. In fact, it appears that the parties engaged in some negotiations concerning the terms of the loan; for, on review of the documents in the record, it appears that the standard prepayment clause penalty was deleted. Nevertheless, the enactment of the Truth-in-Lending Act has ushered in the era of "let the seller beware." Cf. *Thomas v. Myers-Dickson Furniture Co., supra.* The courts have uniformly limited the applicability of available defenses by narrowly construing the "good faith" and "bona fide" error provisions of 15 U.S.C. § 1640; and authority controlling in this jurisdiction requires the imposition of statutory liability for all violations of the Act and regulations, however technical. *Pennino v. Morris Kirschman & Co., Inc.* This court is constrained to adhere to the prevailing trends and controlling authority in this area until directed to do otherwise.

Accordingly, for the reasons hereinabove expressed, plaintiffs' motion for summary judgment is hereby GRANTED. Plaintiffs are entitled to recover $1,000.00 as statutory damages as well as reasonable attorney's fees and costs, 15 U.S.C. § 1640(a); however, the award of attorney's fees is inappropriate without some evidence to support the reasonableness thereof. Accordingly, plaintiffs are hereby ORDERED to submit affidavits and other documents, as appropriate, not later than ten (10) days following this date, specifying the amount of attorney's fees sought and setting forth evidence supporting the reasonableness of the requested amount. Defendant is GRANTED seven (7) days from receipt of plaintiffs' documents in which to file a brief or other document in opposition thereto. Entry of final judgment will be deferred pending the parties' compliance with the foregoing.

It is so ordered.

[See Appendix A and Appendix B to the case, 414 F. Supp., at 861-62.]

PALMER v. WILSON

United States Court of Appeals
502 F.2d 860 (9th Cir. 1974)

Hufstedler, Circuit Judge: Plaintiffs Austin and Helen Palmer brought this action under the Truth in Lending Act, 15 U.S.C. §§ 1601-1665, to recover the statutory penalty and attorney fees provided in section 1640 and to enforce their right of rescission pursuant to section 1635. The district court granted plaintiffs' motion for summary judgment and awarded both forms of relief requested; the defendants appeal.

The record before the district court at the time of plaintiffs' motion for summary judgment revealed that the note signed by the Palmers and the

Broker's Loan Statement with which they were supplied omitted several credit terms required to be disclosed by the Truth in Lending Act, as implemented by Federal Reserve Board Regulation Z (12 C.F.R. § 226). The documents given to the Palmers failed to state the "total of payments" due (12 C.F.R. § 226.8(b)(3)) and failed to disclose the "amount financed" (*id.* § 226.8(d)(1)). Finance charges were not described in the uniform terms required by the regulations. (See *e. g.*, *id.* § 226.8(d)(2).) The defendants also failed to disclose properly the details of plaintiffs' right to rescind.

The district court correctly held that these omissions violated the Truth in Lending Act and that plaintiffs were entitled to summary judgment. The defendants do not contest the fact that they omitted credit terms required to be disclosed by the Act, but rather argue that they are entitled to the benefits of the statutory exemption for violations that are "not intentional and resulted from a bona fide error notwithstanding the maintenance of procedures reasonably adapted to avoid any such error." (15 U.S.C. § 1640(c).) The defendants' omissions and mislabeling of terms were not the result of clerical errors, which are the only violations this section was designed to excuse. (*See Ratner v. Chemical Bank New York Trust Co.* (S.D.N.Y.1971), 329 F. Supp. 270, 281-282 & n. 17.) Both the Broker's Loan Statement and the Installment Note in issue were printed, standard form instruments. The omissions and misstatements were part of defendants' usual credit practice and did not occur in spite of procedures designed to avoid unintentional violations of the Act.

In *Eby v. Reb Realty, Inc.* (9th Cir. 1974), 495 F.2d 646, we rejected defendants' contention that plaintiffs cannot successfully pursue both damages under section 1640 and rescission under section 1635. No election of remedies is required. The liability provision of section 1640 is a "civil penalty," which, unlike section 1635, is not intended to make the borrower whole.

Defendants also argue that the district court erred in enforcing plaintiffs' right of rescission because plaintiffs failed to tender the money loaned them at the time they notified defendants of their decision to exercise their right to rescind. Although tender of consideration received is an equitable prerequisite to rescission, the requirement was abolished by the Truth in Lending Act. Section 1635(a) provides that an obligor exercises his right of rescission solely by notifying the creditor within prescribed time limits of his intention to rescind. Section 1635(b) provides that upon exercise by the debtor of his right of rescission, "any security interest given by the obligator becomes void . . . ." Within ten days after receipt of notice of rescission, "the creditor shall return to the obligor any money or property given as earnest money, downpayment, or otherwise, and shall take any action necessary or appropriate to reflect the termination of any security interest created under the transaction." Only then, "[u]pon the performance of the creditor's obligation under [section 1635]," must the obligor tender the property to the creditor. Section 1635(b) expressly provides that prior to performance of the required actions by the creditor, "[i]f the creditor has delivered any property to the obligor, the obligor may retain possession of it."

In *Eby v. Reb Realty, Inc., supra,* we recognized that interaction of the right of rescission and the civil penalty provision of section 1640 can sometimes result in an unduly harsh penalty for violations of the Truth in Lending Act. This is particularly true where, as appears to be the case here, the decree granting rescission does not condition the relief upon the debtor's restoration of consideration, the creditor is reduced to the status of an unsecured creditor, and the debtors are judgment proof. Accordingly, in *Eby* we concluded that, although "sections 1635 and 1640 do not set forth exclusive remedies, we do not say that a court must always grant both forms of relief when requested. . . . In the absence of any clear congressional statement, we think a request for both forms of relief is addressed to a court's sense of equity and may properly be denied in appropriate cases." Similarly, when an obligor seeks both to rescind and to recover statutory penalty and attorney fees, the district court has equitable power to grant both forms of relief; the court may condition the granting of rescission on the debtor's compliance with the court's order to tender to the creditor the principal of the loan that the debtor has received. The propriety of such a conditional decree of rescission, of course, will depend on the equities present in a particular case, as well as consideration of the legislative policy of full disclosure that underlies the Truth in Lending Act and the remedial-penal nature of the private enforcement provisions of the Act.

Although some district courts have conditioned rescission on tender of repayment by the debtor when both rescission and damages were sought (e. g., Ljepya v. M. L. S. C. Properties (N.D.Cal.1973), 353 F.Supp. 866), the court below apparently was unaware that it had the equitable power to condition its decree. Accordingly, we vacate the judgment and remand the case for consideration of the propriety of conditioning the grant of rescission on repayment by the Palmers. Upon remand the district court may decide to invite submission of additional affidavits or may hold an evidentiary hearing on this point. It may also require the defendants to submit a proposed plan for repayment that is consistent both with the defendants' desire to recover the amount of principal loaned to the Palmers and with the Palmers' current financial situation.

The judgment is vacated and the cause remanded for further proceedings consistent with the views herein expressed.

[The concurring opinion of Judge Thompson is omitted.]

EUGENE A. WRIGHT, CIRCUIT JUDGE (concurring in part and dissenting in part):

. . . .

Section 1635(b) provides that upon the debtor's election to rescind, the creditor's security interest in the debtor's home becomes *void*. There is no requirement that the debtor tender payment before rescission. Nor is there a provision that the security interest is merely voidable by petitioning the district court. Thus, when the plaintiffs exercised their right to rescind by notifying the defendants, the security interest automatically became void and unenforceable.

. . . .

I would hold that plaintiffs are entitled to unconditional rescission under § 1635 and a civil penalty under § 1640. I would not permit the district court to enforce defendants' right to repayment. Accordingly, I would affirm the judgment of the district court in all respects.

LITTLEFIELD v. WALT FLANAGAN & CO.

United States Court of Appeals
498 F.2d 1133 (10th Cir. 1974)

BREITENSTEIN, CIRCUIT JUDGE. The issue is whether an action for rescission under the Truth in Lending Act, 15 U.S.C. § 1635, is barred by the one-year period of limitations contained in § 1640(e). The district court held that the action was barred. We reverse.

On November 25, 1970, plaintiffs-appellants contracted with defendant-appellee Perlmutter Associates, Inc., for the purchase of real property to be used by them as a residence. As part of the purchase price, purchasers gave to Perlmutter, the seller, a note for $9,260.13 secured by a second deed of trust on the property. Perlmutter assigned these instruments to defendant-appellee Walt Flanagan and Company. Although the purchase and sale was a consumer credit transaction within the purview of the Truth in Lending Act, 15 U.S.C. § 1601 et seq., none of the disclosures required by the Act were made by the seller to the purchasers. After purchasers defaulted on payments, Flanagan threatened foreclosure. Purchasers learned of their statutory right to rescind on February 20, 1972, and on the next day notified Perlmutter, the seller, that they chose to exercise the right. Defendants ignored the notice and on March 3 notice of foreclosure was published on the demand of Flanagan. Purchasers filed this suit on April 7, 1972, and sought an injunction against foreclosure, recovery of the civil liability provided by 15 U.S.C. § 1640, and rescission under 15 U.S.C. § 1635.

The district court granted a preliminary injunction barring the foreclosure sale. The seller, Perlmutter, and its assignee, Flanagan, then filed in this court a petition for mandamus to require the vacation of the injunction and the dismissal of the district court action. The district court entered orders maintaining the status quo during the mandamus proceedings. On June 28, 1972, the petition for mandamus was denied. . . . On July 12 default was entered against all defendants. On September 28 Judge Arraj vacated the default, ordered an answer on the merits only within five days, and forbade the assertion of any counterclaim. . . .

The case was heard by Judge Finesilver who held that as to both the civil liability and rescission claim jurisdiction was dependent on § 1640 and failed because of the one-year limitation which ran from the date of the transaction. . . .

So far as pertinent here the Act provides in § 1635(a), that in a consumer credit transaction in which a security interest is retained or acquired on residence property, except a first lien to finance acquisition (see § 1635(e), the obligor has the right to rescind "until midnight of the third business day following the consummation of the transaction or the delivery of the disclosures required under this section . . . ." The creditor is required to "clearly and conspicuously" disclose to the obligor his rights under § 1635, and shall provide "an adequate opportunity to the obligor to exercise his right to rescind any transaction" subject to the section.

We have here a consumer credit transaction with an acquired security interest, a second lien on real property used as a residence. Regulation Z promulgated under the Act, 12 C.F.R. § 226.9, details rules relating to notification by the seller to the purchaser of his right to rescind. Defendants ignored these rules. When the purchasers notified the seller of their desire to rescind, the seller gave no reasonable opportunity for the exercise of that right.

The question then is whether the § 1635 claim is barred by § 1640(e). In its subsection (a), § 1640 creates a specified civil liability for failure to make the disclosures which the Act requires. Subsection (e) reads:

Any action under this section may be brought in any United States District Court, or in any other court of competent jurisdiction, within one year from the date of the occurrence of the violation.

In *Stevens v. Rock Springs National Bank*, 10 Cir., 497 F.2d 307, we said that "the disclosure requirements [of the Act] may be satisfied without penalty at any time prior to the contracting to extend credit, and no violation can occur until such a credit contract is executed," and held that an action for § 1640 liability was barred when the action was brought more than one year after the closing of the purchase transaction. The *Stevens* opinion expressly left undecided any relationship between the right of rescission under § 1635 and the § 1640(e) limitation period. *Wachtel v. West*, 6 Cir., 476 F.2d 1062, cert. denied, 414 U.S. 874, 94 S.Ct. 161, 38 L.Ed.2d 114, also enforced the one-year limitation in a § 1640 action and left open the application of that limitation to a § 1635 action.

Stevens v. Rock Springs National Bank disposes of the § 1640 claim of the purchasers because the action was brought more than one year after the consummation of the transaction. The applicability of the limitation to a § 1635 claim was not decided by either *Stevens* or *Wachtel v. West*, and is apparently a matter of first impression in federal appellate courts. There is not helpful legislative history. See *Palmer v. Wilson*, N.D.Cal., 359 F.Supp. 1099, 1103-1104.

Section 1640(e) by its express terms applies only to actions to enforce § 1640 rights. Section 1635 has no provision limiting the time for suit. The three-day provision of that section does not apply because the creditor did not disclose to the obligor his right to rescind. The Act is designed to prevent "unscrupulous and predatory creditor practices," is remedial, and must be liberally construed to effectuate the intent of Congress. *N. C. Freed Co., Inc. v. Board of Governors of the Federal Reserve System*, 2 Cir., 473 F.2d 1210, 1214, cert. denied, 414 U.S. 827, 94 S.Ct. 48, 38 L.Ed.2d 61. The purchasers brought this suit about six weeks after they learned of their right to rescind. Whatever detriment might be suffered by defendants is their own fault because they chose to flaunt the statute. The purpose of the Act is furthered by permitting, rather than barring, the suit.

The fact that the rescission notice went to Perlmutter, the assignor of second lien holder Flanagan, is immaterial. Section 1635 requires that notice of intent to rescind be given to the creditor and Perlmutter was the creditor under the definition in § 1602(f). In our opinion the § 1635 rescission claim is not barred by § 1640(e) or otherwise and may be maintained. The district court erred in dismissing it.

. . . .

Reversed and remanded for further proceedings in the light of this opinion. The mandate shall issue forthwith.

NOTES

1. One contrary conclusion to *Palmer*'s majority opinion is *Bostwich v. Cohen*, 319 F. Supp. 875 (N.D. Ohio 1970) in which the court held that civil liability and rescission are alternative remedies. Once a consumer has elected to rescind, he can no longer be an aggrieved debtor seeking damages for disclosure violation. The court found no legislative history to indicate that Congress envisioned anything other than a traditional election of remedies.

2. In *Eby v. Reb Realty, Inc.*, 495 F.2d 646 (9th Cir. 1974), cited in the *Palmer* majority opinion, the court characterized the § 1640 damages provision as a civil penalty not intended to make the borrower whole but rather to encourage private enforcement of the Truth-in-Lending Act.

3. As to the timing of disclosure, the court in *Bissette v. Colonial Mortgage Corp.*, 477 F.2d 1245 (D.C. Cir. 1973) held that Truth-in-Lending disclosures made at a real estate closing were timely. Although the plaintiff-borrowers had been given notice of the approval of their loan application a month prior to the closing date, the Truth-in-Lending disclosures were not made until the day of closing. The trial court had decided that this was too late to satisfy the Act's requirements but the Court of Appeals reversed, holding that the disclosures could be made at any time prior to the existence of an actual contractual relationship between the parties. The case was remanded to determine when such a contractual relationship did occur.

4. For further discussion of the Act's applicability to real estate finance *see* Griffith, *Truth-in-Lending and Real Estate Transactions: Some Aspects*, 2 OHIO N.L. REV. 219 (1974).

2. RESPA

The Real Estate Settlement Procedures Act — RESPA — was enacted in 1974 and amended in 1975. It requires disclosure of typical "closing costs" in connection with residential real estate transactions. Like the Truth in Lending Act, RESPA is designed to provide the consumer with information as to the cost and terms of credit and the charges for settlement in order that one might compare and make informed credit decisions.

Compared to the complexity of TIL and the swirl of litigation involving violations of that Act, RESPA is a model of clarity and apparent compliance. However, RESPA has passed through a great deal of controversy centering around its initial enactment and almost immediate amendment. The stated purpose of the Act as enunciated by Congress is "to insure that consumers throughout the nation are provided with greater and more timely information on the nature and costs of the settlement process and are protected from unnecessarily high settlement charges caused by certain abusive practices that have developed in some areas of the country." 12 U.S.C. § 2601(a). The Act attempts to achieve this purpose by required disclosure of certain settlement costs, elimination of kickbacks, referrals, reduction in amounts required to be placed in tax-insurance escrow accounts, and experimental limited reform of land parcel recordation systems. 12 U.S.C. § 2601.

Federal concern with real estate transactions was prompted by a HUD-VA joint report to Congress in 1972. *See RESPA*, 63 Minn. L. Rev. 367 (1979). This report detailed abuses such as kickbacks, costs based on unrelated factors, and set fee schedules which subjected the homebuyer to unnecessary and onerous costs. *See RESPA, supra*, at 374. Congress studied three approaches to the problem: (1) HUD regulation of charges for federally related mortgages, (2) requirement that lenders absorb all costs, (3) advance disclosure to the consumer. The third option was selected. *See RESPA, supra*, at 378. As originally passed, the Act obligated lenders to disclose settlement charges to the borrower twelve days in advance of settlement, prohibited kickbacks and unearned fees, and required lenders to quote the last arms-length purchase price of non-owner occupied property. *RESPA, supra*, at 379. Within six months Congress substituted for twelve-day advance disclosure a requirement for "good faith estimates," and delegated to HUD the promulgation of rules to govern fees, with a caveat to exempt traditional real estate broker cooperative arrangements. "Advance" disclosure of the actual settlement costs was reduced to one day and then only at the borrower's specific request.

The scope of RESPA encompasses virtually all commercial lending institutions. Disclosures are required in a "federally related mortgage loan" which is a loan "secured by a first lien on residential real property designed for occupancy of from one to four families" and "is made in whole or in part by any lender the deposits or accounts of which are insured by any agency of the Federal Government or is made in whole or in part by any lender which is regulated by any agency of the Federal Government," or is insured or assisted by instrumentalities of the federal government, or will be sold to FNMA, GNMA, or FHLMC, or is made by a "creditor" as defined by TIL who makes real estate loans aggregating more than $1,000,000 a year. 12 U.S.C. § 2602(i). The Secretary of HUD is charged with the responsibility of developing standard forms to be used by lenders in clearly itemizing "all charges imposed upon the borrower and all charges imposed upon the seller in connection with settlement." 12 U.S.C. § 2603. However, the statute grants the Secretary discretion to fashion these standard forms to take into account local laws and customs. Generally the following items must be disclosed as "settlement services": "title searches, title examinations, the provision of title certificates, title insurance, services rendered by an attorney, the preparation of documents, property surveys, the rendering of credit reports or appraisals, pest and fungus inspections, services rendered by a real estate agent or broker, the handling of the processing, and closing" plus any other service provided in connection with a closing. 12 U.S.C. § 2602(3). It should be noted that these items are specifically excluded from computation of the finance charge for purposes of TIL disclosure. Additionally, the Act instructs the Secretary of HUD to prepare special information booklets to be distributed by lenders to each person applying for a residential real estate loan. 12 U.S.C. § 2604. These booklets are intended to familiarize consumers with costs incidental to settlement by describing the nature of those costs, the function of escrow accounts, and the choices available to the consumer in selecting providers of closing services. The booklets also contain an explanation of unfair practices or unreasonable charges to be avoided by the consumer. Lenders are required to provide the booklets along with a "good faith estimate of the amount or range of charges for specific settlement services the borrower is likely to incur" at the time the consumer makes application for a loan. 12 U.S.C. § 2604. The lender may not impose a fee for the preparation of any RESPA or TIL disclosure statements. 12 U.S.C. § 2610.

Because real estate transactions have traditionally been matters of local concern, RESPA was drafted to avoid, as much as possible, infringing on this area of settled law. Thus § 2615 expressly states that RESPA shall not "affect the validity or enforceability of any sale or contract for the sale of real property or any loan, loan agreement, mortgage, or lien. . . ." 12 U.S.C. § 2615. Also RESPA does not cancel or affect state laws governing settlement practices unless such laws are inconsistent with RESPA and then only to the extent of the inconsistency. 12 U.S.C. § 2616. Such limited preemption protects long-standing state procedures and laws. Despite this deference to state law, the Act provides for the introduction on an experimental basis of a model system for land title recordation in selected areas, with a view to an eventual national uniform system of land parcel recordation. 12 U.S.C. § 2611.

RESPA's final substantive provision deals with a limitation on required advance escrow payments. 12 U.S.C. § 2609. Lenders may not require at closing a deposit into escrow for taxes, insurance, and other charges, in an amount in excess of $1/6$ the estimated total annual amount necessary to pay such charges. With each subsequent loan payment, the lender may only require an escrow deposit of $1/12$ the total estimate. However, if it appears the estimate is low, the lender can require additional payments to eliminate a deficiency in the escrow account.

RESPA and Regulation X do not contain a general liability section similar to that of TIL and Regulation Z. There is express liability for violation of the kickback provisions. 12 U.S.C. § 2607(d). Depending on the nature of the offense, the lender or referring party may be liable for a fine in the amount of $10,000, one year's imprisonment, three times the illegal charge, and attorney fees. Violation of § 2608, which prohibits lenders or sellers from requiring the buyer to purchase title insurance from any particular company, carries with it liability for an amount equal to three times all title insurance charges made. 12 U.S.C. § 2608(b). Section 2614 confers jurisdiction on federal district courts for any action to recover damages under §§ 2607 and 2608, with a one year statute of limitations, but does not expressly provide a private cause of action for failure to disclose or otherwise comply with RESPA.

For a settlement statement complying with RESPA, see Illustration 9 at the end of this chapter.

VEGA v. FIRST FEDERAL SAVINGS & LOAN ASS'N

United States District Court
433 F. Supp. 624 (E.D. Mich. 1977)

KEITH, CHIEF JUDGE. In 1975 plaintiffs in this action applied for and received a conventional mortgage from defendant for the purchase of their present residence. They bring this action as a class action alleging numerous violations by defendant of the Truth in Lending Act (15 U.S.C. § 1601 *et seq.*); of Federal Regulation Z promulgated thereunder (12 C.F.R. § 226); of the Real Estate Settlement Procedures Act (12 U.S.C. § 2601 *et seq.*); and of The Department of Housing and Urban Development Regulation X, promulgated thereunder (24 C.F.R. § 82). Jurisdiction of this Court is invoked pursuant to Title 15 U.S.C. § 1640(e), Title 12 U.S.C. § 2614 and Title 28 U.S.C. § 1337.

. . . .

With regard to the Real Estate Settlement Procedure Act (hereinafter RESPA) and The Department of Housing and Urban Development Regulation X (hereinafter Regulation X) plaintiffs allege the following violations:

(1) The Settlement Disclosure Statement provided by Defendant does not conform to the requirements of RESPA and of Regulation X.

(2) Defendant failed to confirm that the sellers or their agents had made the proper written disclosure to plaintiffs as required by RESPA and by Regulation X.

(3) Defendant required escrow deposits for taxes and insurance premiums in excess of those permitted by RESPA.

(4) Defendant has imposed a fee for the preparation and submission of the Disclosure Statement required by RESPA and TILA in violation of Title 12 U.S.C. § 2610.

Defendant here moves for summary judgment as to paragraphs 10, 11, 12, 14, 15, 16, and 17 of plaintiffs' complaint alleging that none of its procedures nor actions have violated either TILA or RESPA nor regulations promulgated thereunder.

. . . .

*Alleged Violations of the Real Estate Settlement
Procedures Act and of Regulation X*

Paragraph 14

Paragraph fourteen (14) of plaintiffs' complaint (clarified by additional pleadings) alleges that defendant's Disclosure Statement for advance disclosure of settlement costs does not conform to the Uniform Settlement Disclosure Statement required by RESPA and by Regulation X. 12 U.S.C. §§ 2603, 2605; 24 C.F.R. § 82.6 as originally enacted. Specifically, plaintiff alleges 16 instances where defendant deviated from the prescribed layout on HUD-1, appended to Regulation X, either by capitalizing line items that were not in all capital letters on the authorized form or by failing to capitalize fully certain other line items. As originally enacted Title 24 C.F.R. § 82.6(b)(5), effective May 22, 1975, read:

No changes in the size or type style of print or the layout of the first two pages of the form shall be made, except as follows:

(A) The layout of the form may only be reset in type if such type style is approximately the same size and appearance, is easily readable, and the entire form layout is identical to the format as prescribed by HUD; and,

(B) Where necessary to accommodate computer equipment, the first two pages of the form may be printed in the larger size of print and different type style and a distance between lines may be increased, but not decreased, but there shall be no other change in the layout or placement on the form . . . .

Plaintiffs argue in their brief that a strict compliance standard is necessary to effectuate the intent of Congress in passing RESPA. The Court does not agree. Congress' stated purpose in enacting RESPA was to effect changes in the settlement process for residential real estate that would result "in more effective advance disclosure to home buyers and sellers of settlement costs." 12 U.S.C. § 2601(b)(1). The Court fails to see how the violations alleged by plaintiffs fly in the face of this stated purpose.

The violations asserted by plaintiffs resulted in no actual harm to plaintiffs. Although there are variances from the prescribed lower and upper case on defendant's form, the type remains easily readable, and the format is essentially the same as that prescribed by HUD-1. Moreover, since its enactment, RESPA has been amended to more fully effectuate congressional purpose. H.R.Rep.No.667, 94th Cong., 1st Sess., *reprinted in* [1975] U.S.Code Cong. & Ad.News p. 2448. The section under which plaintiffs make these assertions of non-compliance has been repealed. Pub.L. 94-205, § 5, 89 Stat. 1158 (Jan. 2, 1976). Additionally the current corresponding section of Regulation X is more liberally stated and variations from lower to upper case type would clearly be allowed in the current version.

For the above stated reasons, primary among which is the absence of any injury to plaintiffs, the Court will not hold defendant to a standard of strict compliance and will hold that under the circumstances of this case, defendant's violations were *de minimus.*

Paragraph 15

Title 12 U.S.C. § 2606 (repealed 1976) stated:

Disclosure of Previous Selling Price of Existing Real Property
(a) No lender shall make any commitment for a federally related mortgage loan on a residence on which construction has been completed more than twelve months prior to the date of such commitment unless it has confirmed that the following information has been disclosed in writing by the seller or his agent to the buyer —

(1) the name and address of the present owner of the property being sold;

(2) the date the property was acquired by the present owner (the year only if the property was acquired more than two years previously); and

(3) if the seller has not owned the property for at least two years prior to the date of the loan application and has not used the property as a place of residence, the date and purchase price of the last arm's length transfer of the property (excluding maintenance repairs) and the cost of such improvements.

(b) The obligations imposed upon a lender by this section shall be deemed satisfied and a commitment for a federally related mortgage loan may thereafter be made if the lender receives a copy of the written statement provided by the seller to the buyer supplying the information required by subsection (a).

(c) Whoever knowingly and willfully provides false information under this section or otherwise willfully fails to comply with its requirements shall be fined not more than $10,000 or imprisoned for not more than one year, or both.

Paragraph fifteen (15) of plaintiffs' complaint alleges that defendant violated this section by failing to confirm that the sellers had made the proper written disclosures as required by RESPA and by Regulation X. In its motion for summary judgment, defendant asserts that it received a copy of the Disclosure/Settlement Statement prior to making a mortgage loan offer. An affidavit is attached supporting defendant's allegation.

Plaintiffs' response concedes defendant's argument and retracts the allegation made in their complaint, but maintains that the paragraph should still stand because plaintiffs have brought this action as a class action and other members of the class may have been affected. Plaintiffs allege no known instances where defendant has violated the section in question; rather they assert that "random spot-checking of defendant's files for the presence of this completed form in the other transactions" would reveal whether defendant has violated the statute in the past. Pl. Brief in opposition to Defendant's Motion for Summary Judgment and Motion to Dismiss at 19.

Rule 23(a)(3) of the Federal Rules of Civil Procedure states that a prerequisite for certification of an action as a class action is that "the claims or defenses of the representative parties [must be] typical of the claims or defenses of the class." It is difficult for this Court to understand how plaintiffs propose to adequately represent others on a claim in which they have no interest. Vigorous representation would be lacking where the representative plaintiffs have suffered no harm. Furthermore, this Court stands unprepared to sanction what is tantamount to a fishing expedition through defendant's files for the purpose of ascertaining the possible existence of a cause of action. Consequently, in the opinion of this Court, paragraph 15 of plaintiffs' complaint cannot stand.

Paragraph 16

In paragraph sixteen (16) of their complaint, plaintiffs allege that defendant required escrow deposits for taxes and insurance in excess of those permitted by RESPA. In their pleadings in opposition to this motion, plaintiffs make no mention of any excess insurance premiums. The Court, therefore, will not consider this portion of their allegation.

Title 12 U.S.C. § 2609 (1974) (amended 1976) is the applicable section. As originally enacted, it stated in relevant part:

Limitation on Requirement of Advance Deposits in Escrow Accounts
No lender, in connection with a federally related mortgage loan, shall require the borrower or prospective borrower —
   (1) to deposit in any escrow account which may be established in connection with such loan for the purpose of assuring payment of taxes and insurance premiums with respect to the property, prior to or upon the date of settlement, an aggregate sum (for such purpose) in excess of —
   (B) in any jurisdiction where such taxes and insurance premiums are prepaid, a pro rata portion of the estimated taxes and insurance premiums corresponding to the number of months from the last date of payment to the date of settlement.
plus one-twelfth of the estimated total amount of such taxes and insurance premiums which will become due and payable during the twelve-month period beginning on the date of settlement.

Defendant estimated plaintiffs' total city tax to be $228.00 and their county tax to be $39.00. Plaintiffs' closing occurred on September 17, 1975. City taxes had last been paid on December 1, 1974, and county taxes were last paid on July 1, 1975. The statute allows defendant to deposit in escrow "a pro rata portion of the estimated taxes ... corresponding to the number of months from the last date of payment to the date of settlement. ..." In the case of city taxes, a period of 9.6 months had passed, and in the case of county taxes, 2.6 months had elapsed. Therefore, at the time of closing, defendant was permitted to collect the following taxes:

County Taxes	9.6/12 x $ 39.00 = 9.6 x $ 3.25 =	$31.20
City Taxes	2.6/12 x $228.00 = 2.6 x $19.00 =	$49.40
	TOTAL	$80.60

In addition to the $80.60 lump sum payment defendant is allowed to collect under § 2609, the statute provides that the lender may collect "one-twelfth of the estimated total amount of such taxes ... which will become due and payable during the twelve-month period beginning on the date of settlement ...."

As stated above, defendant estimated that $39.00 in county taxes and $228.00 in city taxes would become due and payable between September 17, 1975, and September 17, 1976. This would result in the defendant being able to additionally collect the following amounts.

City Taxes	$19.00	(1/12 of $228.00)
County Taxes	$ 3.25	(1/12 of $ 39.00)
TOTAL	$22.25	

Therefore, the Court concludes that under § 2609, as applied to the facts of the case at bar, defendant was entitled to collect a total of $102.85 ($80.60 + $22.25) at the time of closing to be deposited in an escrow account for the payment of taxes. At the time of closing, however, defendant required plaintiffs to deposit only $89.50 into its escrow reserves. Consequently, the Court concludes that the allegations of paragraph 16 of plaintiffs' complaint are without merit.

Paragraph 17

Plaintiffs here allege that defendant has imposed a fee or charge for the preparation and submission of the Disclosure Statement required by RESPA and TILA in violation of Title 12 U.S.C. § 2610.

In response to this allegation defendant has submitted the affidavit of Bruce E. Ruffin, Assistant Vice President of defendant, which states that defendant charged plaintiffs $250.00 as a processing/closing fee. The affidavit further asserts that this charge has been consistently imposed by defendant since September 18, 1973, and it flatly denies having imposed any fee upon plaintiffs for preparation or submission of the Disclosure/Settlement Statement or the Disclosure Statement.

In response to defendant's assertions, plaintiffs have submitted a diatribe on the evils of the "Settlement Charge Rip-Off" with liberal references to the comments of Senator William Proxmire regarding RESPA reported in 1974 U.S.Code Cong. & Ad.News pp. 6557-68. Additionally, plaintiffs have again prevailed upon the Court to allow them to develop proof of their contentions through discovery.

On a motion for summary judgment, plaintiffs cannot rest on the mere allegations in their complaint when confronted with an affidavit of the opposing party. They must set forth specific facts showing the existence of a genuine issue for trial. Otherwise, where appropriate, summary judgment will be granted against them. *See Stevens v. Barnard*, 512 F.2d 876, 878 (10th Cir. 1975); *Garcia v. American Marine Corp.*, 432 F.2d 6, 7 (5th Cir. 1970).

Plaintiffs have failed to submit any facts to lend any support to the allegations of Paragraph 17 of their complaint. The Court must, therefore, conclude that plaintiffs' allegations are lacking in foundation.

An appropriate order will be entered.

NOTES

1. RESPA's interaction with state law is considered in *Greenwald v. First Federal Savings & Loan Ass'n*, 446 F. Supp. 620 (D.C. Mass. 1978), *infra* at p. 485. The Massachusetts Commissioner of Banks sought a declaration that a state law requiring interest payments on escrow accounts was effective against federally regulated financial institutions. The Commissioner argued that RESPA had created an exception which would allow the state to overcome the preemption problem. However, the court held that RESPA was inapplicable and the federal law preempted the state's.

2. *See RESPA*, 63 Minn L. Rev. 367 (1979).

E. THE FEDERAL TEMPORARY RELIEF ACTS

As can be seen in state redemption and anti-deficiency laws, there is a general effort by the legislatures to afford mortgagors considerable opportunity to avoid loss of their land as a result of foreclosure and to soften the harshness of that loss. The Congress has been no less compassionate. Two areas of statutory law provide certain classes of borrowers a degree of relief, albeit only temporarily: the Bankruptcy Act, found at 11 U.S.C. § 1 et seq., and the Soldiers' and Sailors' Relief Act, found at 50 U.S.C. App. § 501. The relief is temporary in nature since the alternative of payment or foreclosure is merely postponed and not avoided entirely.

1. BANKRUPTCY

In 1978 the Congress enacted the Bankruptcy Reform Act, which greatly changed the prior law. New provisions of that Act provide, in 11 U.S.C. § 362, that all actions or foreclosure proceedings are "stayed" upon the filing of a petition in the Bankruptcy Court. However, the stay is subject to being modified, conditioned, or terminated. In the event the debtor has no equity in the subject property the secured creditor can seek relief from the stay and proceed to foreclose. 11 U.S.C. § 632(d). Another basis for seeking relief from the injunctive aspects of the Bankruptcy Act is by the secured creditor making a showing that "adequate protection" of an interest has not been made. 11 U.S.C. § 362(d)(1). The concept of adequate protection is designed to effect a compromise between the rights of secured creditors and the efforts of debtors to rearrange their financial lives in a Chapter 11 bankruptcy proceeding. 11 U.S.C. § 362.

DURRETT v. WASHINGTON NATIONAL INSURANCE CO.

United States Court of Appeals
621 F.2d 201 (5th Cir. 1980)

Orma R. Smith, District Judge: This appeal concerns an action instituted in the United States District Court for the Northern District of Texas, wherein plaintiff Jack W. Durrett, Sr. (herein "Durrett"), acting as debtor in possession under Chapter XI of the Bankruptcy Act,[1] 11 U.S.C. §§ 701, et seq., seeks to set aside and vacate an alleged transfer of real property effectuated nine days prior to the filing of a Petition for an Arrangement under Chapter XI. Durrett charges that the transfer is voidable under section 67(d) of the Act, 11 U.S.C. § 107(d).[2] The district court held that the non-judicial sale involved in the litigation constituted a transfer within the meaning of section 67(d). However, the court determined that the amount paid by the purchaser at the sale conducted by a trustee in the foreclosure of a deed of trust executed by Durrett, the indebtedness which it secured being then in default, was a "fair" consideration and a "fair equivalent" within the meaning of section 67(d)(1), (e)(1) of the Act, 11 U.S.C. § 107(d)(1) (e)(1). The court denied the relief sought by Durrett and he appeals. We reverse.

A review of the record on appeal reflects the following facts. On April 7, 1969, Durrett executed a note in the amount of $180,000.00 in favor of Southern Trust and Mortgage Company (hereafter "Southern"). The note was secured by a deed of trust upon the subject real property. Southern, on April 7, 1969, assigned the trust deed and note to defendant, The Washington National Insurance Company (hereafter "Washington"). Defendant J. H. Fields, Jr. (hereafter "Fields"), was named as the trustee in the deed of trust. The deed of trust contained a provision for a public sale of the real property thereby conveyed, in case of default in payment of the indebtedness.

---

[1] The sale of the property under attack here, occurred January 4, 1977. Plaintiff filed a Petition for Arrangement Under Chapter XI of the Bankruptcy Act on January 13, 1977). Section 403(a) of Pub.L. No. 95-598. Title I (Nov. 6, 1978), 92 Stat. 2549; provides as follows:

A case commenced under the Bankruptcy Act, and all matters and proceedings in or relating to any such case, shall be conducted and determined under such Act as if this Act [Pub.L. 95-598] had not been enacted, and the substantive rights of parties in connection with any such bankruptcy case, matter, or proceeding shall continue to be governed by the law applicable to such case, matter, or proceeding as if the Act had not been enacted.

Because the acts giving rise to this litigation occurred before the effective date of the new bankruptcy act, Pub.L. 95-598, the rights of the litigants are governed by "Repealed Title 11". When reference is made herein to the "Act" or the "Bankruptcy Act" the same shall refer to "Repealed Title 11".

[2] Section 67(d) of the Act provides in pertinent part:

(1) For the purposes of, and exclusively applicable to, this subdivision: . . . (e) consideration given for the property or obligation of a debtor is "fair" (1) when, in good faith, in exchange and as a fair equivalent therefor, property is transferred . . . .

(2) Every transfer made and every obligation incurred by a debtor within one year prior to the filing of a petition initiating a proceeding under this title by or against him is fraudulent (a) as to creditors existing at the time of such transfer or obligation, if made or incurred without fair consideration by a debtor who is or will be thereby rendered insolvent, without regard to his actual intent; . . .

(6) A transfer made or an obligation incurred by a debtor adjudged a bankrupt under this title, which is fraudulent under this subdivision against creditors of such debtor having claims provable under this title, shall be null and void against the trustee, except as to a bona fide purchaser, lienor, or obligee for a present fair equivalent value: . . . *And provided further,* That such purchaser, lienor, or obligee, who without actual fraudulent intent has given a consideration less than fair, as defined in this subdivision, for such transfer, lien, or obligation, may retain the property, lien, or obligation as security for repayment. . . . (Emphasis in original).

On December 13, 1976, Fields, in his capacity of trustee, posted the property for foreclosure sale. The sale was held on January 4, 1977. Defendant Shannon Mitchell, Sr. (hereafter "Mitchell"), appeared at the sale and bid the sum of $115,400.00 for the property. This was the only bid received by the trustee at the sale. The amount of the bid was the exact amount necessary to liquidate the indebtedness secured by the deed of trust. Upon receipt of the bid price, Fields executed and delivered to Mitchell a trustee's deed to the property. The parties agree that Mitchell did not have any actual fraudulent intent when making the purchase. He responded to the notice of sale and became the successful bidder. Mitchell and Durrett are the only parties now interested in the case.

Durrett contends that the transfer of the property, pursuant to foreclosure of the deed of trust, is voidable under the provision of section 67(d).

The district court dismissed the complaint after a non-jury trial. In its findings of fact, the court held that the fair market value of the property on January 4, 1977, the date of the foreclosure sale, was the sum of $200,000.00.

The parties do not take issue with this finding. Both agree that it is not clearly erroneous. *See,* Rule 52(a), Fed.R.Civ.P.; *Kentucky Fried Chicken Corp. v. Diversified Packaging Corp.,* 549 F.2d 368, 377 (5th Cir. 1977).

Durrett asserts, on appeal, only one assignment of error, i.e., "Is $115,400.00 payment for an asset worth $200,000.00, a 'fair equivalent' "?

In consideration of the issue of "fair equivalent", we should determine by what standard we are to judge the district court's conclusion of law that the amount paid for the property, $115,400.00, is "fair" consideration and a "fair equivalent" within the meaning of section 67(d)(1), (e)(1).[3]

We have held that our review of conclusions of law by the district court in non-jury cases is not restricted by the "clearly erroneous" rule and will be reversed if incorrect. *See, Ealy v. Littlejohn,* 569 F.2d 219, 229 n. 31 (5th Cir. 1978). *See also, Buchanan v. United States Postal Service,* 508 F.2d 259, 267 n. 24 (5th Cir. 1975).

The question with which we are confronted is whether the district court's conclusion of law on the "fair equivalent" issue is incorrect, when considered in light of the record made in the district court and the applicable case law.

The parties have cited a number of cases which deal with this issue. A great percentage of these, however, involve factual situations quite different from the facts which exist in this appeal. Here, there is involved only one event, i.e., one parcel of real estate sold at a foreclosure sale for a price which is approximately 57.7 percent of the fair market value of the property. Is the price paid a "fair equivalent" for the transfer of the property? We hold that it is not.

The sale of real property was involved in one of the cases cited by Durrett, *Schafer v. Hammond,* 456 F.2d 15 (10th Cir. 1972). There the Tenth Circuit affirmed a holding by the district court that a sale of real property for approximately 50 percent of its market value was void for lack of a fair consideration. Here, Mitchell paid slightly more than 50 percent (57.7%) for the property involved. The sale, however, deprived the bankruptcy estate of an equity in the property of $84,600.00, if computed on the $200,000.00 market value fixed by the district court.

We have been unable to locate a decision of any district or appellate court dealing only with a transfer of real property as the subject of attack under section

---

[3] The district court's conclusion of law refers to Mitchell's payment as being the sum of $115,000.00. The findings of fact, however, stated the payment to be $115,400.00. The record reflects the latter to be the correct bid price.

67(d) of the Act, which has approved the transfer for less than 70 percent of the market value of the property.

Assuming, arguendo, that we should review the district court's conclusion of law as a finding of fact under the "clearly erroneous" standard, the results would be the same. We cannot affirm the district court on this issue. Our review of the entire evidence leaves us with a definite and firm conviction that the price which Mitchell paid for the property at the trustee's sale was not a "fair equivalent" for the property. Under such circumstances, it is our duty to declare the transfer voidable under section 67(d). *See, United States v. United States Gypsum Co.,* 333 U.S. 364, 395, 68 S.Ct. 525, 542, 92 L.Ed. 746, 766 (1948); *George W. B. Bryson & Co., Ltd. v. Norton Lilly & Co., Inc.,* 502 F.2d 1045, 1049 (5th Cir. 1974). *See also, Tulia Feedlot, Inc. v. United States,* 513 F.2d 800, 807 (5th Cir.), *cert. denied,* 423 U.S. 947, 96 S.Ct. 362, 46 L.Ed.2d 281 (1975); *Ealy v. Littlejohn, supra* at 229 n. 30.

The defendant-appellee Mitchell seeks to sustain the final judgment of the district court on the ground that the transfer accomplished by the trustee pursuant to the power of sale provision of the deed of trust was not a transfer *made* by the debtor in possession within the contemplation of section 67(d). We find this position to be without merit.

The word "transfer" is defined in section 1 of the Act, 11 U.S.C. § 1. Section 1 provides in pertinent part:

> The words and phrases used in this title and in proceedings pursuant hereto shall, unless the same be inconsistent with the context, be construed as follows:
> . . . .
> (30) "Transfer" shall include the sale and every other and different mode, direct or indirect, of disposing of or of parting with property or with an interest therein or with the possession thereof or of fixing a lien upon property or upon an interest therein, absolutely or conditionally, voluntarily or involuntarily, by or without judicial proceedings, as a conveyance, sale, assignment, payment, pledge, mortgage, lien, encumbrance, gift, security, or otherwise; the retention of a security title to property delivered to a debtor shall be deemed a transfer suffered by such debtor; . . . .

The comprehensive character of this definition leads us to conclude that the transfer of title to the real property of the debtor in possession pursuant to an arrangement under Chapter XI of the Act, by a trustee on foreclosure of a deed of trust, to a purchaser at the sale constitutes a "transfer" by debtor in possession within the purview of section 67(d). The actual transfer of title was made by Durrett to Fields, as trustee, via the deed of trust, executed April 7, 1969, to secure an indebtedness then owing to Southern and thereafter assigned to Washington. Possession of the property was retained by Durrett subject to the power of the trustee to sell and deliver possession of the property, on default, at a foreclosure sale. While the actual conveyance of title by Durrett was made on April 7, 1969, possession was retained until foreclosure of the deed of trust. The "transfer" within the contemplation of the Act, was not final until the day of the foreclosure sale, January 4, 1977. This was accomplished within the one-year period provided by section 67(d)(2), 11 U.S.C. § 107(d)(2). This conclusion is supported by reliable and ample authority. *See* 1 Collier on Bankruptcy, § 1.30 at 1.30.28(2)(3) (14th ed. 1967), where it is said: "[t]he present definition covers not only alienations of title but includes surrender of possession". *See also,* 4 Collier on Bankruptcy, § 67.29 at 471, et seq.

For the reasons herein given, the judgment of the district court must be vacated, and the cause reversed with directions.

Upon remand, the district court shall enter judgment for plaintiff-appellant directing the rescission of the transfer under section 67(d) of the Act, dealing with the property in such manner as will protect Mitchell's equity therein. Section 67(d)(6), 11 U.S.C. § 107(d)(6).

Judgement vacated; remanded with directions.

IN RE DEL GIZZO

United States Bankruptcy Court
5 Bankr. Rptr. 446 (R.I. 1980)

ARTHUR N. VOTOLATO, JR., BANKRUPTCY JUDGE. Heard simultaneously on the complaints of Monopearl, Inc. and Rhode Island Hospital Trust National Bank for relief from the § 362 automatic stay and for authority to foreclose their respective mortgages secured by real estate of the Debtors. In the interest of expediency, an abbreviated Order was entered on June 18, 1980, to minimize ongoing preservation expenses and deterioration of the subject property. This Memorandum Opinion constitutes the findings of fact and conclusions of law required by Bankruptcy Rule 752.

Also in the interest of saving time, the parties waived hearing and the presentation of evidence, and have submitted their respective positions in written memoranda, together with an agreed statement of facts as follows: Monopearl, Inc. is the holder of a first mortgage secured by the subject property, and has a maximum possible claim under that mortgage of approximately $110,000. Rhode Island Hospital Trust National Bank has a second mortgage on the same property in an amount in excess of $134,000. The parties agree that the value of the security probably exceeds the amount due under the first mortgage, but that the second mortgage is not fully secured. Since there is no equity, the Trustee has no interest in this controversy.

Because both parties insist on being permitted to foreclose, the question is which secured creditor should be allowed to proceed with foreclosure proceedings, and this presents the specific issue whether this Court has the authority and/or discretion to allow a second mortgagee to foreclose in such circumstances.

In Monopearl's view, this court is without authority to allow a second mortgagee to foreclose on its junior mortgage ahead of a first mortgagee. Such action, Monopearl argues, would disturb the status and relative priority of secured creditors as fixed at the time of the filing of a bankruptcy petition. Moreover, Monopearl argues, established case law mandates that first lienholders be satisfied before junior lienholders are entitled to distribution. Because neither the Bankruptcy Reform Act of 1978, nor case law allows such action, Monopearl requests court permission to immediately be allowed to foreclose upon its first mortgage.

The Bank's position is that the court has the authority, in its discretion, to allow foreclosure of property by a second mortgagee. The equities in this case, in the Bank's view, favor foreclosure by the second mortgagee, since such foreclosure would not impair any rights of the first mortgagee. Allowing Monopearl to foreclose, on the other hand, would cut off any interest of the Bank in the property. The Bank argues that a foreclosure by Monopearl would force the Bank to satisfy its secured claim out of the surplus of such sale, if any, and to look to the estate as a general creditor, for any deficiency. This, in the Bank's view, would have a detrimental effect on general creditors, as well as on the Bank's ability to protect its own interest in the property.

We must also consider, as Monopearl argues, whether granting the action request by the Bank would disrupt the distributional scheme of the Bankruptcy Code or violate other "cardinal principle(s)" of bankruptcy. Monopearl's position is that the rule "first in time, first in right" must be applied here because it would be a violation of the traditional scheme of distribution of assets to secured creditors to allow a junior mortgagee to foreclose ahead of a senior mortgagee. *See In re Freeze-In Manuf. Corp.*, 128 F.Supp. 259 (E.D. Mich. 1955). We disagree.

The provisions of the Bankruptcy Reform Act of 1978 governing relief from automatic stay are found in § 362(d), 11 U.S.C. § 362(d), which provides:

> (d) on request of a party in interest and after notice and a hearing, the court shall grant relief from the stay provided under subsection (a) of this section, such as by terminating, annulling, modifying, or conditioning such stay—...
> (2) with respect to a stay of an act against property, if—
> (A) the debtor does not have an equity in such property; and
> (B) such property is not necessary to an effective reorganization.

Being parties in interest, both Monopearl and the Bank are entitled to relief under this section, since the debtor has no equity in the property, and because this is a Chapter 7 liquidation proceeding, with no conversion and/or reorganization contemplated.

The question, therefore, as stated above, is the extent of the court's authority, in granting relief from automatic stay, to allow a junior mortgagee to foreclose on real property over the objection of the first mortgagee.

Section 362(d) indicates that the court may grant several types of relief in this kind of situation. Relief can take the form of "terminating, annulling, modifying, or conditioning" the automatic stay provisions of the Bankruptcy Code. It appears, therefore, that where two mortgagees seek to foreclose on the same property at the same time, § 362(d) gives the court discretion to tailor the relief to the facts, provided such action does not conflict with any provision of the Bankruptcy Code or other principle of law governing the relationship between secured creditors.

Unlike the situation where the trustee sells property free of all tax and statutory liens, and distributes the proceeds among several competing lienholders, *see United States v. New Britian [sic]*, 347 U.S. 81, 74 S.Ct. 367, 98 L.Ed. 520 (1954); *In re Freeze-In Manuf. Corp., supra; see also United States v. Speers,* 382 U.S. 266, 86 S.Ct. 411, 15 L.Ed.2d 314 (1965), a foreclosure sale by a junior mortgagee has no effect on the rights of senior lienholders, *see Brunette v. Myette,* 40 R.I. 546, 102 A. 520 (1918), because the purchaser of a junior mortgage takes subject to the rights of all senior liens and encumbrances. As the Rhode Island Supreme Court stated in *Armand's Engineering, Inc. v. Town and Country Club, Inc.,* 113 R.I. 515, 324 A.2d 334 (1974).

> In a foreclosure of a junior mortgage, the senior mortgage remains on the land and the buyer takes the property, subject to this mortgage which remains on the land, and therefore no rights or claims of senior mortgages are affected. *Supra,* 324 A.2d at 338. *See also Wartell v. Novograd,* 49 R.I. 191, 141 A. 461 (1928).

Similarly here, allowing the Bank to foreclose first can have no effect on the rights of Monopearl under its first mortgage, and we conclude, therefore, that the question whether a junior lienholder can be allowed to foreclose is within the discretion of the court.

Since it is agreed that the value of the property is in excess of the balance due on Monopearl's first mortgage, Monopearl's interest is relatively secure no matter which lienholder is allowed to conduct the foreclosure sale. On the other hand, the Bank's junior mortgage would be wiped out at a foreclosure sale by Monopearl, and although any excess from such sale would go to the Bank, the Bank, based on reason and experience, believes that it is better able to protect its obviously precarious position by handling the disposition of the property in whatever manner it deems most commercially sound.

The equitable consideration here is one of weighing the convenience to Monopearl (that is, its ability to be taken out of this situation and probably paid off immediately if it is allowed to foreclose), as against the right of the Bank to attempt to effectuate maximum realization from the disposition of the security, which, of course, is directly connected to what its deficiency will be.

We see less risk of harm to all interested parties, including general creditors, by allowing the Bank the opportunity to foreclose on its mortgage first, particularly since the deficiency resulting from such sale will become a general claim against the estate.

That the Bank has deeper pockets than Monopearl, a fact frequently alluded to by the first mortgagee, is not a consideration which this Court feels can or should influence its decision in this case.

Accordingly, Rhode Island Hospital Trust National Bank is authorized to foreclose its second mortgage, with dispatch, in compliance with the terms of the Order dated June 18, 1980. Said foreclosure shall be subject to the first mortgage of record held by Monopearl, Inc., and the purchaser shall take title subject to said first mortgage. A hearing shall be held within two weeks after the sale to determine the apportionment of expenses incurred in preserving the property and to review and determine reasonable expenses for attorney fees in connection with these proceedings.

The Monopearl complaint for relief from automatic stay is denied, without prejudice to the right of Monopearl to renew said action in the event that a foreclosure sale is not held by the Rhode Island Hospital Trust National Bank within a reasonable time.

NOTES

1. The Bankruptcy Court sitting in Kentucky held that a sale-leaseback transaction was actually a device to finance a purchase. *In re Velasco,* 13 B.R. 872 (1981). *See also In re Berez,* 646 F.2d 420 (9th Cir. 1981) in which the court held that a sale-leaseback of property which never left the bankrupt's possession was a secured loan. See generally the discussion and cases on disguised mortgages in Chapter 2, *supra.*

2. The Bankruptcy Court sitting in Illinois has held that the automatic stay during bankruptcy operates as a toll on the redemption period under Illinois law. *Matter of Dohm,* 14 B.R. 701 (1981).

3. Notwithstanding an assignment of rents clause in a deed of trust, the beneficiary was not allowed to collect those rents during the period of time that the property was subject to the Bankruptcy Court's jurisdiction. After the subject property was abandoned by the trustee in Bankruptcy, the beneficiary foreclosed. Even though the deed of trust granted an assignment of rents and the property was abandoned by the trustee, the Bankruptcy Court would not allow the beneficiary to recover the rents collected during the bankruptcy proceedings. *In re Charles D. Stapp of Nevada, Inc.,* 641 F.2d 737 (9th Cir. 1981).

4. The "adequate protection" basis for continuing or granting relief from the stay apparently can be given broad interpretation. In the case *In re Grundstrom,* 14 B.R. 791 (1981) the debtor had an equity of twenty-three percent in the real property covered by a mortgage. However the mortgagee was granted relief from the stay and allowed to proceed with foreclosure when it was demonstrated that the house had been on the market for six months and remained unsold and that being vacant it generated no rental

income. Could it be argued that the mortgagee still had "adequate protection" in spite of these adverse economic conditions? Would the lack of insurance coverage on the house influence a court in deciding that there was not "adequate protection"?

Further, it is clear that where the debtor has no equity in the subject property the automatic stay cannot be used as a means to cure a prior default; relief from the stay will be granted and foreclosure permitted. *In re Branch,* 10 B.R. 227 (1981).

5. The changes in the Bankruptcy Act have prompted many articles in this area. For example, see Moller, *Chapter 11 of the 1978 Bankruptcy Code or Whatever Happened to Good Old Chapter XI?,* 11 St. Mary's L.J. 437 (1979); King, *Chapter 11 of the 1978 Bankruptcy Code,* 53 Am. Bank. L.J. 107 (1979); and Trost, *Business Reorganization Under Chapter 11 of the New Bankruptcy Code,* 34 Bus. Law. 1309 (1979).

2. THE SOLDIERS' AND SAILORS' RELIEF ACT

In order to provide protection to the men and women in the armed forces, shortly before the entry of the United States into World War II Congress enacted the Soldiers' and Sailors' Relief Act, 50 U.S.C. App. §§ 501-48. The Act provides a postponement of deadlines during the time one is on active military duty, as is seen in the case which follows. The Act also invokes criminal penalties in the event a secured creditor attempts a foreclosure while the debtor is on active military duty and for three months following discharge from the service. 50 U.S.C. § 532. As with the stay in bankruptcy the relief is only temporary. Eventually military service will not protect the debtor and payment must be made or foreclosure will occur. 50 U.S.C. § 700.

STEVAHN v. MEIDINGER

Supreme Court of North Dakota
79 N.D. 323, 57 N.W.2d 1 (1952)

CHRISTIANSON, JUDGE. Plaintiff brought this action to recover the rental of certain lands in McIntosh County in this state for the farming season of 1947. The trial court held that the plaintiff was entitled to recover only one-twelfth of the rental of the land in question for the farming season of 1947. The plaintiff has appealed and contends that he is entitled to recover all of such rental and that the trial court erred in rendering judgment in his favor for only one-twelfth thereof.

. . . .

. . . The material facts in the case as so found are as follows: Andreas Stevahn, the father of the plaintiff, died intestate on April 9, 1941, possessed of certain real property in McIntosh County in this state. There survived him as his next of kin and heirs at law; his wife, Christina Stevahn, his daughters, Lydia Ketterling, Christine Bier and Amanda Stevahn, and his sons, A. P. Stevahn, Ernest Stevahn, Arthur Stevahn, A. G. Stevahn and Alvin Stevahn, the plaintiff in this action. In due time proceedings for the administration of the estate of said Andreas Stevahn, deceased, were had in the County Court of McIntosh County in this state. Christina Stevahn, the surviving widow of said decedent, was duly appointed and qualified as administratrix of the estate of Andreas Stevahn, deceased, and letters of administration issued to her on May 26, 1941. At the time of the death of said decedent the real property involved in this action was encumbered by two mortgages each bearing date November 1, 1933. There was a first mortgage to the Federal Land Bank of St. Paul, Minnesota, and a second mortgage to the Land Bank Commissioner. On April 14, 1945, Christina Stevahn, the widow of the decedent, A. P. Stevahn, a son, and Lydia Ketterling,

Amanda Stevahn and Christine Bier, daughters of said Andreas Stevahn, deceased, and Christ Bier, Jr., the husband of Christine Bier, for a good and valuable consideration conveyed to the Federal Farm Mortgage Corporation all the right, title and interest that each of them had in the real property in question. Default having been made in the terms and conditions of such first mortgage action for the foreclosure of such mortgage was duly brought in the District Court of McIntosh County. In such action all the above mentioned next of kin and heirs of said Andreas Stevahn were named defendants. Such proceedings were had in such action that judgment of foreclosure was duly rendered and entered in said action on August 31, 1945. Thereafter special execution issued upon such judgment and the premises described in the said mortgage to the Federal Land Bank and in such judgment of foreclosure were duly sold to the Federal Land Bank of St. Paul, Minnesota, the plaintiff in such action on October 3, 1945, and sheriff's certificate of sale was duly issued to the said Federal Land Bank on that same day.

The laws of the State provide that property sold subject to redemption "may be redeemed . . . by . . . [t]he judgment debtor, or his successors in interest" in the manner provided by law, and that "The judgment debtor or redemptioner may redeem the property from the purchaser within one year after the sale". NDRC 1943, 28-2401, 28-2402.

No redemption was made within the period of one year as provided by NDRC 1943, 28-2402 or at all. The statutory time for redemption expired on October 3rd, 1946. At that time the right of redemption of all the above mentioned next of kin and heirs of said decedent had expired with the exception of the plaintiff in this action who was inducted into the military service of the United States on November 23, 1945, and continued in such service until he was honorably discharged therefrom on February 10, 1947. His right to redeem was extended under the provisions of the Soldiers' and Sailors' Civil Relief Act of 1940, as amended, 50 U.S.C.A.Appendix, § 525. On October 7, 1946, there was executed and delivered to the Federal Land Bank of St. Paul a sheriff's deed for the premises in question. . . .

On November 7, 1946, the Federal Land Bank sold the real property in question to the defendant Ferdinand C. Meidinger under a contract for deed. Under such contract the said defendant agreed to pay the Federal Land Bank of St. Paul for such premises the sum of $11,000 with a down payment of $6000 and the balance of the purchase price payable in annual installments of $500 each. The contract for deed provided that in case of inability to furnish marketable title the Federal Land Bank might refund all amounts paid thereunder and terminate the contract. The contract provided that the purchaser should be entitled to take possession of the premises on November 15, 1946. The purchaser paid to the Federal Land Bank the sum of $6000 as provided in the contract for deed and entered into possession of the premises in November, 1946, pursuant to the provisions of the contract. The defendant Meidinger produced a crop on said premises in 1947 and the rental for the premises for the farming season of 1947 based upon the crops harvested and sold according to the computations of the trial court amounted to $2021.81. The defendant Meidinger remained in possession of the premises until December 16, 1947, when he conveyed all right, title and interest in such premises to the Federal Land Bank by quitclaim deed, and the Federal Land Bank of St. Paul paid to the said defendant the sum of $6735, the total amount that had been paid by the defendant to said Federal Land Bank of St. Paul under said contract for deed.

The plaintiff Alvin Stevahn was inducted into the military service of the United States on November 23, 1945, and remained in such service until he was honorably discharged therefrom on February 10, 1947.

The Soldiers' and Sailors' Civil Relief Act of 1940, as amended by Congress on October 6, 1942, 50 U.S.C.A.Appendix, § 525, provided:

> The period of military service shall not be included in computing any period now or hereafter to be limited by any law, regulation, or order . . . nor shall any part of such period which occurs after the date of enactment of the Soldiers' and Sailors' Civil Relief Act Amendments of 1942 (Oct. 6, 1942) be included in computing any period now or hereafter provided by any law for the redemption of real property sold or forfeited to enforce any obligation, tax, or assessment.

It is stated in the findings of fact that in the negotiations with the Federal Land Bank of St. Paul for the purchase of the premises the defendant was informed and knew that the plaintiff "because of his being in the military service had an extended right of redemption upon his discharge therefrom." On December 5, 1947, the plaintiff tendered to the Federal Land Bank of St. Paul the sum of $11,505.15, the calculated amount necessary to effect redemption from said foreclosure sale. The Federal Land Bank accepted the amount tendered and on December 9, 1947, the said Bank made, executed, and delivered to the plaintiff a deed of conveyance of said premises.

The appellant contends that under the facts found by the trial court he was entitled to redeem, that he has effected a redemption and as a result became and is entitled to all the rental for the year 1947 measured by the market value for each fourth bushel of the grain produced, the customary rental in 1947 in that locality. In support of his contention he cites NDRC 1943, 28-2411, which provides:

> The debtor under an execution or foreclosure sale of his property shall be entitled to the possession, rents, use, and benefit of the property sold from the date of such sale until the expiration of the period of redemption.

He asserts that after the expiration of the period provided for redemption on October 3, 1946, he alone occupied the position of a redemptioner, that the rights of the other heirs "to redeem had expired" and that "after October 3, 1946, they were no longer even cotenants and that possession belonged to him alone."

. . . .

Upon the foreclosure of the mortgage held by the Federal Land Bank of St. Paul the heirs of Andreas Stevahn and the grantees of the heirs that had conveyed their interests were cotenants and each of the cotenants including the plaintiff had a right to enter upon the common estate subject to the equal rights of his companions in interest with whose possession he might not interfere. 14 Am.Juris., Cotenancy, Sec. 23, pp. 93-94. Each cotenant had the right of possession and to his proportionate share of the rental for the land until the expiration of the period of redemption. NDRC 1943, 28-2411. The appellant was entitled to possession as a cotenant and to his share of the rental of the land as measured by his interest in the premises, but his cotenant or cotenants [sic] had equal rights and he had no right to interfere with their lawful possession or to any part of the proportionate share of the rental belonging to such cotenants. Any cotenant desiring to redeem must do so within a year after the sale. NDRC 1943, 32-1918, 28-2402. None of the cotenants redeemed and all right to redeem ceased on October 3, 1946, except as to the appellant Alvin Stevahn, and as to him the period of redemption had been extended until December 20, 1947, by the Soldiers' and Sailors' Civil Relief Act of 1940, 50 U.S.C.A.Appendix, § 525.

After the period allowed by the statute for redemption had expired sheriff's deed was issued to the Federal Land Bank of St. Paul which deed vested in such bank eleven-twelfths of all the right, title, interest and estate of said Andreas Stevahn in the land at the time the mortgage was executed and subsequently acquired by him and was "a bar to all claim, right or equity of redemption in or to the property" by all the heirs at law of said Andreas Stevahn (except Alvin Stevahn) and their personal representatives and against all persons claiming under them or any of them subsequent to the commencement of the action in which the judgment was rendered pursuant to which the premises were sold. NDRC 1943, 32-1909. After such deed was executed and delivered all the heirs of Andreas Stevahn (with the sole exception of the plaintiff Alvin Stevahn) had no more interest in the premises than they would have had in case each of them had voluntarily conveyed their respective shares in the premises to another for a consideration. *Barker v. More Bros.,* 18 N.D. 82, 87, 118 N.W. 823, 825.

The result of the sale and the conveyance to the Federal Land Bank of St. Paul by the sheriff's deed was to vest the Federal Land Bank with fee simple title to eleven-twelfths interest in the premises, to discharge the indebtedness and lien of the mortgage and certificate of sale on the eleven-twelfths interest in the land so conveyed to the Federal Land Bank, and to reduce the amount of the indebtedness and lien of the mortgage and certificate of sale upon the remaining one-twelfth interest in the land still owned by the appellant Alvin Stevahn to one-twelfth of the amount that would have been required to redeem the whole of the premises from the foreclosure sale if the whole of the premises had been subject to redemption. The appellant Alvin Stevahn still owned a one-twelfth interest in the land which interest was subject to the lien of the mortgage and certificate of foreclosure sale for the amount remaining due thereon after giving credit thereon for the amount which had been discharged by the conveyance to the Federal Land Bank of the eleven-twelfth interest in the land. From the time the sheriff's deed was executed and delivered to the Federal Land Bank on October 7, 1946, until December 9, 1947, when the Federal Land Bank sold and conveyed all its interest in the premises to the appellant Alvin Stevahn, he was the owner of a one-twelfth interest which was subject to the lien of the mortgage and the certificate of foreclosure sale, as Alvin Stevahn's right to redeem had been extended by the Soldiers' and Sailors' Civil Relief Act of 1940 until December 20, 1947. This was the only interest and estate in the premises that was subject to redemption. The interests in the land of all the heirs of Andreas Stevahn, other than the appellant, had been conveyed to and vested in the Federal Land Bank of St. Paul. The bank was the owner of eleven-twelfths interest in the premises and the appellant Stevahn continued to own a one-twelfth interest. That condition continued until in November 1946 when the Federal Land Bank sold the premises to the defendant Meidinger under a contract for deed which specifically authorized the defendant Meidinger to enter into possession of the premises on November 15, 1946. Under this contract for deed the Federal Land Bank continued to hold the legal title to the eleven-twelfths interest in the land in trust for Meidinger, the vendee in the contract, to the extent of his payments and he became the beneficial owner to the extent of the payments made by him. *Woodward v. McCollum,* 16 N.D. 42, 49-50, 111 N.W. 623, 626; *Salzer Lumber Co. v. Claflin,* 16 N.D. 601, 605, 113 N.W. 1036, 1037; 55 Am.Juris., Vendor and Purchaser, Sections 355 and 356, pp. 781-783.

The appellant was a successor in interest of Andreas Stevahn to the real property owned by him at the time of his death, but he was not the only successor in interest. He succeeded to a one-twelfth interest only and his mother and brothers and sisters succeeded to the other eleven-twelfths interest. The heirs of Andreas Stevahn became tenants in common, and each of the cotenants had the right to the use, benefit and possession of the common property subject, however, to the equal rights of each of his companions in interest with whose rights he might not interfere. 14 Am.Juris., Cotenancy, Sec. 23, pp. 93-94; 62 C.J. p. 421. At all times from the death of Andreas Stevahn until the conveyance by the Federal Land Bank of St. Paul of all its right, title and interest in the premises to the appellant Stevahn on December 9, 1947, the appellant owned only a one-twelfth interest in the premises; and during all this time his cotenant and contenants each had equal right to the possession and use of the premises.

The defendant Meidinger entered into possession of the premises under the contract for deed with the Federal Land Bank and planted, harvested and threshed a crop on the lands in question during the farming season of 1947. During all the time that the crop was planted, harvested, threshed and marketed the plaintiff owned a one-twelfth interest in the land and no more; the Federal Land Bank was the legal owner of eleven-twelfths interest therein and the defendant Meidinger under the contract for deed had the right to enter upon the land and plant, harvest, thresh and market the crop as was done. On December 9, 1947, the Federal Land Bank for a valuable consideration made, executed and delivered to the appellant Alvin Stevahn a deed of conveyance to the premises. As a result the tenancy in common was terminated, 62 C.J., Sec. 18, p. 418, and the appellant Alvin Stevahn became the owner of the entire tract in fee simple. Prior to the conveyance to him by the Federal Land Bank of St. Paul of all its interest, right and title in the eleven-twelfths interest in the land the appellant Stevahn owned only a one-twelfth interest in the premises.

Plaintiff's share in the rental for the land during the farming season of 1947 was proportionate to and measured by his interest in the land. In other words, plaintiff was not entitled to more than a one-twelfth share of such rental, and that is what the trial court awarded to him. The judgment appealed from is affirmed.

Morris, C. J., and Christianson, Grimson, Sathre and Burke, JJ., concur.

On Petition for Rehearing

Christianson, Judge. The plaintiff has petitioned for a rehearing. In the petition it is said that the Court erred in the following statements in the opinion: . . . .

. . . .

2. It is said that the second statement "is contrary to the decision of this Court in *Sailer v. Mercer County* [75 N.D. 123], 26 N.W.2d 137, and contrary to the express words of the Soldiers' and Sailors' Civil Relief Act of 1940 as amended October 6, 1942."

. . . .

The property was sold subject to redemption. . . .

. . . .

No redemption was made and the statutory period for redemption expired on October 3, 1946, At that time the right of redemption of the Federal Farm Mortgage Corporation and of all the heirs at law of Andreas Stevahn, with the single exception of the plaintiff Alvin Stevahn, expired. The plaintiff Alvin Stevahn had been inducted into the military service of the United States on November 23,

1945, and continued in such service until he was honorably discharged therefrom on February 10, 1947. The period of time within which to exercise his right to redeem was extended under the provisions of the Soldiers' and Sailors' Civil Relief Act of 1940, as amended, 50 U.S.C.A.Appendix, § 525. Such act provided that the period of military service shall not be included in computing "any period now or hereafter provided by any law for the redemption of real property sold or forfeited to enforce any obligation, tax, or assessment." This provision speaks for itself. It excludes the period of military service in computing the period allowed by law for redemption of real property sold at the foreclosure sale and thus gives the person engaged in military service the additional time in which to redeem. The benefit afforded by the statute is for persons engaged in military service only. The statute does not operate in favor of other persons who are not so engaged. The statute does not purport to create a right of redemption, it merely purports to extend the time within which the right of redemption as created and existing by law may be exercised. The statute does not purport to enlarge the interest or estate which a person in military service has in the property which may be redeemed. *Tolmas v. Streiffer,* La.App., 21 So.2d 387. It merely grants him the additional time in which to make redeemption.

A rehearing is denied.

Morris, C. J., and Sathre, Burke, and Grimson, concur.

F. FEDERAL PREEMPTION

As the federal government grows, so does its involvement in the everyday life of its citizens. A century ago, the federal role in such local matters as regulation of real property and its use as security was minimal. Today, however, with the federal involvement in VA and FHA financing as well as in the secondary market—FMNA, GNMA and FHLMC — not to mention other government agencies dealing with real estate finance, it is not unusual to have federal preemption raised as an issue in litigation.

Federal government involvement, having steadily increased in the past century, is unlikely to decrease. At the present time, lobbyists for institutional lenders are increasing their efforts to have federal, to the exclusion of state, regulation of mortgages, and attorneys should be increasingly aware of the criteria for assessing federal preemption: (1) Does federal legislation or administrative law clearly show an intent to exclusively occupy the field so as to exclude state regulation? or, (2) Is there sufficient conflict between state and federal law as to require resolution of the conflict in favor of the supremacy of the federal government? If either of these is satisfied, federal preemption is established.

GLENDALE FEDERAL SAVINGS & LOAN ASS'N v. FOX

United States District Court
459 F. Supp. 903 (C.D. Cal. 1978)

Wm. Matthew Byrne, Jr., District Judge. The question presented by this motion for partial summary judgment is whether state regulation of the validity and exercisability of "due-on-sale" clauses contained in loan instruments of federal savings and loan associations executed on or after June 8, 1976, is preempted by federal law. A "due-on-sale" clause provides the lender an option to declare immediately due and payable all of the sums owed to the lender if all or any part of the real property securing the loan is sold or otherwise transferred by the borrower without the lender's prior consent.

I. Background

Glendale Federal, the plaintiff, is a federally chartered savings and loan association organized and operating under the Home Owners' Loan Act of 1933, as amended, 12 U.S.C. Section 1461, *et seq.* (hereinafter "HOLA"). The Federal Home Loan Bank Board (hereinafter "the Bank Board"), defendant and cross-claimant, is an independent agency of the United States in the Executive Branch, 12 U.S.C. § 1437(b), which, under authority delegated by Congress through Section 5(a) of the HOLA, is responsible for the chartering, examining, supervision, and regulation of federal savings and loan associations. 12 U.S.C. § 1464(a).[1]

The Bank Board has promulgated specific regulations regarding provisions which a federal savings and loan association shall and may include in its loan contracts. 12 C.F.R. § 545.6-11. With respect to the use of due-on-sale clauses by federal savings and loan associations the Bank Board, in April, 1976, adopted certain amendments specifically authorizing the use of such clauses and prescribing certain limitations on their exercise. 12 C.F.R. § 545.6-11(f) and (g). These regulations, which became effective June 8, 1976, state in pertinent part:

> A federal association continues to have the power to include, as a matter of contract between it and the borrower, a provision in its loan instruments whereby the association may, at its option, declare immediately due and payable all of the sums secured by the association's security instrument if all or any part of the real property securing the loan is sold or transferred by the borrower without the association's prior written consent. Except as provided in paragraph (g) of this section . . . exercise by an association of such an acceleration option (hereafter called a due-on-sale clause) shall be governed exclusively by the terms of the contract between the association and the borrower . . . . 12 C.F.R. § 545.6-11(f).[2]

---

[1] Section 1464(a) of Title 12, United States Code, provides:

In order to provide local mutual thrift institutions in which people may invest their funds and in order to provide for the financing of homes, the Board is authorized, under such rules and regulations as it may prescribe, to provide for the organization, incorporation, examination, operation, and regulation of associations to be known as "Federal Savings and Loan Associations", and to issue charters therefor, giving primary consideration to the best practices of local mutual thrift and home-financing institutions in the United States.

[2] 12 C.F.R. § 545.6-11(g) provides:

(1) With respect to any loan made after July 31, 1976, on the security of a home occupied or to be occupied by the borrower, a Federal association may not exercise a due-on-sale clause based on any of the following:
  (a) Creation of a lien or other encumbrance subordinate to the association's security instrument;
  (b) Creation of a purchase money security interest for household appliances;
  (c) Transfer by devise, descent, or by operation of law upon the death of a joint tenant;
  (d) Grant of any leasehold interest of three years or less not containing an option to purchase.
(2) With respect to any loan made after July 31, 1976, on the security of a home occupied or to be occupied by the borrower, no Federal association shall impose a prepayment charge or equivalent fee in connection with the acceleration of the loan pursuant to the exercise of a due-on-sale clause.
(3) With respect to any loan made after July 31, 1976, on the security of a home occupied or to be occupied by the borrower, a Federal association shall have waived its option to exercise a due-on-sale clause as to a specific transfer if, prior to that transfer the association and the person to whom the property is to be sold or transferred (the existing borrower's successor in interest) reach written agreement that the credit of such person is satisfactory to the association and that the interest payable to the association on sums secured by its security instrument shall be at such rate as the association shall request. Upon such written agreement and resultant waiver, the association shall release such existing borrower from all obligations under the loan instruments, and for purposes of § 541.14(a), the association shall be deemed to have made a new loan to such existing borrower's successor in interest.

Defendants Fox, DeClercq, and Silberman are, respectively, the Real Estate Commissioner of the State of California, a Deputy Real Estate Commissioner of the State of California, and the Secretary of the Business and Transportation Agency of the State of California. California real estate law requires that the Commissioner of Real Estate examine any proposed "subdivision,"[3] and, unless there are grounds for denial, issue to the subdivider a public report authorizing the sale or lease in California of the lots or parcels within the "subdivision."[4] The sale or lease, or offer for sale or lease, of any lots or parcels contained in a "subdivision" without first obtaining such a public report is prohibited.[5] In connection with the examination of proposed subdivisions, the Real Estate Department requires that the developer of such subdivision identify any lender that will be providing take-out loans to prospective purchasers and submit to the Department sample copies of the lender's notes, deeds of trust, mortgages or other security instruments to be executed in connection with such take-out loans.[6]

In late June or early July, 1977, Glendale Federal agreed with the developer of a partially constructed forty unit condominium project located in California (the "Casa del Rey Project") to provide take-out loans to prospective purchasers of the units. Shortly thereafter, the developer of the Casa del Rey Project notified defendant DeClercq of the Department of Real Estate that Glendale Federal would be providing take-out loans to purchasers of units in the project and provided to DeClercq sample forms of Glendale Federal's standardized notes and deeds of trust.

In early August, 1977, Glendale Federal was contacted by a representative of the Casa del Rey Project and advised that the Department of Real Estate had determined that the standardized note and deed of trust forms of Glendale Federal were "illegal" and that Glendale Federal could not serve as the take-out lender on the project unless its note and deed of trust were revised. Thereafter, Glendale Federal was provided by the developer with a letter authored by DeClercq stating that "the sample form note and deed of trust do not conform to California Civil Code Section 2924.6," which limits the exercisability of the due-on-sale clause.[7] Concurrent with Glendale Federal's receipt of DeClercq's

---

[3] California Business and Professions Code § 11000.

[4] California Business and Professions Code § 11018 provides, in pertinent part:

The Real Estate Commissioner shall make an examination of any subdivision, and shall, unless there are grounds for denial, issue to the subdivider a public report authorizing the sale or lease in this State of the lots or parcels within the subdivision.

[5] California Business and Professions Code § 11018.2.

[6] See Regulations of the Real Estate Commissioner, Title 10 California Administrative Code, § 2792.6

[7] California Civil Code § 2924.6 provides:

(a) An obligee may not accelerate the maturity date of the principal and accrued interest on any loan secured by a mortgage or deed of trust on residential real property solely by reason of any one or more of the following transfers in the title to the real property:

(1) A transfer resulting from the death of an obligor where the transfer is to the spouse who is also an obligor.

(2) A transfer by an obligor where the spouse becomes a co-owner of the property.

(3) A transfer resulting for [sic] a decree of dissolution of the marriage or legal separation or from a property settlement agreement incidental to such a decree which requires the obligor to continue to make the loan payments by which a spouse who is an obligor becomes the sole owner of the property.

(4) A transfer by an obligor or obligors into an inter vivos trust in which the obligor or obligors are beneficiaries.

(5) Such real property or any portion thereof is made subject to a junior encumbrance or lien.

letter, the association received written notice from the developer that in light of the position taken by the Department of Real Estate it would be unable to use Glendale Federal as the take-out lender on the Casa del Rey Project or on another project planned by the same developer.

Plaintiff Glendale Federal brought this action for declaratory and injunctive relief on August 30, 1977. Glendale Federal alleges that defendants failed to issue a public report in several instances because the sample notes and deeds of trust provided to the developer by Glendale Federal did not conform to California Civil Code § 2924.6. Plaintiff seeks a judgment declaring that federal law exclusively governs the validity and exercisability of the "due-on-sale" clause utilized by Glendale Federal in its loan instruments, and an injunction restraining defendants from refusing to issue a public report under the Subdivided Lands Act, or refusing to act on an application for such a public report, on the ground that the notes or deeds of trust of Glendale Federal do not conform to California Civil Code § 2924.6.

The crux of plaintiff's and cross-claimant's argument is that regulation of due-on-sale clauses in the loan instruments of federal savings and loan associations is preempted by federal law, and that defendants therefore may not refuse to issue a public report under the Subdivided Lands Act on the ground that the notes and deeds of trust of Glendale Federal do not comply with provisions of California law governing due-on-sale clauses. Defendants contend that the laws of the State of California pertaining to exercise of the due-on-sale clause apply to federal as well as state-chartered savings and loan associations located in California.[8]

Prior to June 8, 1976, the Bank Board had no regulation which specifically mentioned due-on-sale clauses. The Bank Board did have a regulation in effect from 1948 which specifically required that each "loan contract" of a federal savings and loan association "shall provide for full protection to the Federal association." 12 C.F.R. § 545.6-11 (1975). The Bank Board construed that version of 12 C.F.R. § 545.6-11 as authorizing due-on-sale clauses. *See* Advisory Opinion of Federal Home Loan Bank Board, Resolution No. 75-647, *In The Matter of Schott v. Mission Federal Savings and Loan Association.* Glendale Federal and the Bank Board contend in this action that this regulation and the scheme of regulation by the Board prior to June 8, 1976, precluded the application of California law to limit the exercisability of due-on-sale clauses in loan instruments of federal associations. This contention is not before the court on this motion, and the court expresses no view as to its merit. This motion seeks only a declaration that the Bank Board's present regulation respecting

---

(b) Any waiver of the provisions of this section by an obligor is void and unenforceable and is contrary to public policy.

(c) For the purposes of this section, "residential real property" means any real property which contains at least one but not more than four housing units.

(d) This act applies only to loans executed or refinanced on or after January 1, 1976.

[8] California Civil Code § 2924.6, *supra* note 8 [*sic*], specifically limits the exercisability of due-on-sale clauses. The California Supreme Court recently addressed the question whether enforcement of a due-on-sale clause, contained in a deed of trust securing real property, upon an outright sale of that property, constitutes an unreasonable restraint on alienation in violation of California Civil Code § 711. Wellenkamp v. Bank of America, Cal., 148 Cal.Rptr. 379 (1978). The court held that "a due-on clause contained in a promissory note or deed of trust cannot be enforced upon the occurrence of an outright sale unless the lender can demonstrate that enforcement is reasonably necessary to protect against impairment to its security or the risk of default." Id. at 385-86.

due-on-sale clauses, 12 C.F.R. § 545.6-11(f) and (g), exclusively governs the validity and exercisability of those clauses contained in loan instruments executed by federal associations on or after June 8, 1976. The court, for the reasons set forth below, concludes that 12 C.F.R. § 545.6-11(f) and (g) have, since June 8, 1976, preempted state regulation of due-on-sale clauses in the loan instruments of federal associations.

II. The Doctrine of Preemption

The doctrine of federal preemption stems from the Supremacy Clause of the Constitution: "This Constitution, and the Laws of the United States which shall be made in Pursuance thereof . . . shall be the supreme Law of the Land . . ." U.S.Const. art. VI, cl. 2. Under that clause, "[o]ccupation of a legislative 'field' by Congress in the exercise of a granted power is a familiar example of its constitutional power to suspend state laws." *Parker v. Brown,* 317 U.S. 341, 350, 63 S.Ct. 307, 313, 87 L.Ed. 315 (1942). When such preemption occurs, any state law is inapplicable to an issue which arises in that "field." *Meyers v. Beverly Hills Federal Savings and Loan Ass'n,* 499 F.2d 1145, 1146 (9th Cir. 1974).

The Supreme Court has indicated that when a State's exercise of its police power is challenged under the Supremacy Clause, "we start with the assumption that the historic police powers of the States were not to be superseded by the Federal Act unless that was the clear and manifest purpose of Congress." *Rice v. Santa Fe Elevator Corp.,* 331 U.S. 218, 230, 67 S.Ct. 1146, 1152, 91 L.Ed. 1447 (1947); *Jones v. Rath Packing Co.,* 430 U.S. 519, 525, 97 S.Ct. 1305, 1309, 51 L.Ed.2d 604 (1977); *Ray v. Atlantic Richfield Co.,* 435 U.S. 151, 157, 98 S.Ct. 988, 994, 55 L.Ed.2d 179 (1978). The relevant inquiry is whether Congress has either explicitly or implicitly declared that the States are prohibited from regulating the loan instruments of federal savings and loan associations chartered by the Federal Home Loan Bank Board. *See Ray v. Atlantic Richfield Co., supra,* 98 S.Ct. at 994. As the Court stated in *Rice, supra,* 67 S.Ct. at 1152:

[The Congressional] purpose may be evidenced in several ways. The scheme of federal regulation may be so pervasive as to make reasonable the inference that Congress left no room for the States to supplement it. . . . Or the Act of Congress may touch a field in which the federal interest is so dominant that the federal system will be assumed to preclude enforcement of state laws of the same subject. . . . Likewise, the object sought to be obtained by the federal law and the character of obligations imposed by it may reveal the same purpose. . . . *Accord, Ray v. Atlantic Richfield Co., supra,* 98 S.Ct. at 994; *City of Burbank v. Lockheed Air Terminal, Inc.,* 411 U.S. 624, 633, 93 S.Ct. 1854, 1859, 36 L.Ed.2d 547 (1973).

Even if Congress has not entirely foreclosed state legislation in a particular area, a state statute is void to the extent that it actually conflicts with a valid federal statute. *Ray v. Atlantic Richfield Co., supra,* 98 S.Ct. at 994. A conflict exists "where compliance with both federal and state regulation is a physical impossibility . . . ," *Florida Lime & Avocado Growers, Inc. v. Paul,* 373 U.S. 132, 142-43, 83 S.Ct. 1210, 1217, 10 L.Ed.2d 248 (1963), or where the state "law stands as an obstacle to the accomplishment and execution of the full purposes and objectives of Congress." *Hines v. Davidowitz,* 312 U.S. 52, 67, 61 S.Ct. 399, 404, 85 L.Ed. 581 (1941); *Jones v. Rath Packing Co., supra,* 97 S.Ct. at 1310, 1316-17; *Ray v. Atlantic Richfield Co., supra,* 98 S.Ct. at 994-95.

With this framework in mind, the court turns to the legislative history of the Home Owner's Loan Act and the regulatory scheme established by Congress under that Act.

III. The HOLA and Congressional Intent

In 1932, Congress enacted the Federal Home Loan Bank Act in an effort to ameliorate the prevailing emergency in home financing. It created a new federal administrative agency, the Federal Home Loan Bank Board, and directed that agency to charter a series of twelve Federal Home Loan Banks that would serve as wholesale banks for member financial institutions and make mortgage loans directly to members of the public. 47 Stat. 725 (1932), *codified at* 12 U.S.C. § 1421 *et seq.*

In spite of this legislation, the nation's home financing system continued to deteriorate. By 1933, it was estimated that 40% of all home loans in the United States were in default.[9] In response to this crisis, Congress enacted the Home Owners' Loan Act of 1933, the purposes of which were:

> To provide emergency relief with respect to home mortgage indebtedness, to refinance home mortgages, to extend relief to the owners of homes occupied by them and who are unable to amortize their debt elsewhere, to amend the Federal Home Loan Bank Act, to increase the market for obligations of the United States and for other purposes. Preamble to HOLA, 48 Stat. 128 (1933).

It appears that the crisis to which Congress addressed itself in the HOLA was at least in part a result of ill-advised state practices in home financing.[10] One commentator has stated that "the states had developed a hodgepodge of savings and loan laws and regulations, and Congress hoped that [Bank Board] rules would set an example for uniform and sound savings and loan regulations." T. Marvell, *The Federal Home Loan Bank Board,* p. 26 (1969). Congressional concern that pernicious state savings and loan practices be suppressed, and that the Bank Board be given broad discretion to establish uniform and sound practices, is reflected in the language of the statute and its legislative history.

The HOLA had basically three components. First, it repealed § 4(a) of the Bank Act, thereby eliminating direct loans to homeowners by the Federal Home Loan Banks. 48 Stat. 128, c. 64, § 4 (1933). Second, a new corporation, the Home Owners' Loan Corporation, was created and authorized to exchange its bonds for mortgages held by various financial intermediaries including state-chartered building and loan associations. 48 Stat. 128, c. 64, § 4 (1933) (repealed 80 Stat. 648, § 8(a) (1966)). The only mortgages eligible for such exchange were those which called for direct payment in equal monthly installments. Loans which called for balloon payments, rollover of principal at specified intervals, or repayment by sinking funds were ineligible, despite the fact that such loans were in widespread use throughout the United States at the time by state-chartered savings and loan associations. The mortgage exchange program thus had, as one

---

[9] Federal Home Loan Bank Board, The Federal Home Loan Bank System, p. 17 (1971); *see* Thomas B. Marvell, The Federal Home Loan Bank Board, pp. 18-19 (1969).

[10] These practices included the use of "sinking fund" loans. Under the terms of these loans, "principal payments were first accumulated in a compulsory savings account until the balance, together with any dividends which had been credited to the account, equalled the amount of the loan, at which time the loan was paid off. Among the disadvantages of this plan were that the loan took longer to mature than expected if dividend rates were reduced, share values could be written down in case of reorganization, and entire share accounts could be sacrificed in case of liquidation, including those required by borrowers. The borrower, however, still owed the full amount of the mortgage." Stanford Research Institute, The Savings and Loan Industry in California, Section III-37 (1960).

of its effects, the discouragement of state practices concerning the form of mortgage loan contracts and their replacement with contracts conforming to a uniform federal standard.

Third, and most significantly to this motion, the HOLA created a system of federal savings and loan associations. In creating that system, Congress could have elected to subject the operation of federal associations to state law. Instead, Congress, in section 5(a) of the HOLA, gave the Bank Board plenary authority over the creation and operation of federal associations:

> In order to provide local mutual thrift institutions in which people may invest their funds and in order to provide for the financing of homes, the Board is authorized, under such rules and regulations as it may prescribe, to provide for the organization, incorporation, examination, operation, and regulation of associations to be known as "Federal Savings and Loan Associations", and to issue charters therefor, giving primary consideration to the best practices of local mutual thrift and home-financing institutions in the United States. 12 U.S.C. section 1464(a).

Federal savings and loan associations were not to be operated and regulated by what a particular state conceived to be the "best practices." Rather, the Bank Board was delegated by Congress the authority to select from the prevailing practices in all the states what it deemed the best practices and to prescribe a nationwide system of operation, supervision, and regulation which would apply to all federal associations.[11]

In *Central Savings and Loan Ass'n of Chariton, Iowa v. Federal Home Loan Bank Board*, 293 F.Supp. 617 (S.D.Iowa 1968), *aff'd*, 422 F.2d 504 (8th Cir. 1970), the district court sustained the Bank Board's authority to authorize a federal association's use of mobile facilities, even though such practices were prohibited by state law. 293 F.Supp. at 621-22. The Eighth Circuit affirmed, stating that:

> Certainly that statutory language [in 12 U.S.C. section 1464(a)] does not bind the Board inexorably to existing and past practices of local mutual thrift and home-financing institutions. 422 F.2d at 506.

In *Lyons Savings and Loan Ass'n v. Federal Home Loan Bank Board*, 377 F.Supp. 11, 17-18 (N.D.Ill.1974), the court gave a similarly broad construction to section 5(a):

> [T]he HOLA directs the Board to give "primary consideration to the best practices of local mutual thrift and home-financing institutions in the United States." . . . [T]he courts have construed this language as vesting discretion in

---

[11] This conclusion is supported by statements made in conjunction with passage of the HOLA. Testifying at hearings on HOLA held by the U. S. House Committee of Banking and Currency, April 20, 1933, the Chairman of the Bank Board, William F. Stevenson, elaborated on the Board's authority to prescribe regulations:

> A good many people think we ought to put all the state regulations, what they ought to do and all that kind of thing, in here. But that is left to regulation by the board, who will put the most expert building and loan authorities on it to provide those regulations, so that the regulations can be varied. In some states you have to deal with them one way and in other states another way, and we want the latitude allowed to fit the regulations of the board and the associations to the state law and the different needs. Hearings on HOLA, H.R. 4980, before House Comm. on Banking and Currency, 73rd Cong., 1st Sess. 7 (April 20, 1933) (Statement of William F. Stevenson, Chairman, Federal Home Loan Bank Board).

Representative Luce, one of the managers of the bill, noted in his testimony that "we give the [Bank Board] great power to administer the act." 77 Cong.Rec. 2480, 2573-74 (April 27, 1933).

the Board to determine first, what the "best practices" are, and second, to implement them on a *nationally uniform basis*. The fact that any particular state has not adopted for its own institutions what the Board deems to be a "best practice" cannot limit the Board's authority without undermining this fundamental purpose of the statute. (emphasis in original)

Congress gave the Bank Board wide discretion to select or reject any state practices as it deemed necessary or desirable in arriving at a uniform federal savings and loan system. Nothing in the Act or its legislative history suggests the Bank Board was to be bound by or subject to any particular state practice or regulation.

Beyond the express delegation of authority contained in Section 5(a) of the HOLA, the creation in the HOLA of a comprehensive and pervasive scheme of federal regulation of federal savings and loan associations reinforces the conclusion that Congress intended to give the Bank Board complete authority to regulate the area. With limited exceptions, a federal association's operations are totally subject to the rules and regulations of the Bank Board. *See* 12 U.S.C. section 1464. The Bank Board prescribes the manner in which capital may be raised, earnings may be distributed, and withdrawals may be effectuated by a federal association. 12 U.S.C. Section 1464(b)(1). The powers of a federal savings and loan association to borrow, give security, insure notes, bonds, debentures or obligations are wholly prescribed by the Bank Board, 12 U.S.C. Section 1464(b)(2). The Bank Board also regulates the authority of a federal association to make and purchase loans and otherwise invest in real estate. 12 U.S.C. Section 1464(c). Congress granted the Bank Board authority to examine the books and records of all federal associations; to institute cease-and-desist proceedings for a violation of any law, rule, or regulation, or for engaging in an unsafe or unsound practice; and to bring charges against an officer or director of a federal association in order to remove the person from office. 12 U.S.C. Sections 1464(a), (d)(2)(A), and (d)(4)(A). The Bank Board is further authorized to appoint a conservator or receiver to manage the affairs of a federal association; to bring an action to terminate an association's insurance of accounts; and to reorganize, consolidate, liquidate, dissolve or merge federal associations. 12 U.S.C. Sections 1464(d)(6)(A), (d)(11) and 1730. It would have been difficult for Congress to give the Bank Board a broader mandate. As the Court of Appeals for the Ninth Circuit has stated,

[P]ursuant to its valid statutory authority, the Federal Home Loan Bank Board has promulgated comprehensive regulations covering all aspects of every federal savings and loan association "from its cradle to its corporate grave." *People of State of California v. Coast Federal Savings and Loan Ass'n*, S.D.Cal., 1951, 98 F.Supp. 311, 316. *Meyers v. Beverly Hills Federal Savings and Loan Ass'n*, 499 F.2d 1145, 1147 (9th Cir. 1974).

The language, history, structure, and purpose of the Home Owners' Loan Act evidence a clear Congressional intent to delegate to the Bank Board complete authority to regulate federal savings and loan associations and to preempt state regulation. Whenever the Bank Board, pursuant to that plenary authority, promulgates a regulation governing an aspect of the operation of federal savings and loan associations, that regulation governs exclusively and preempts any attempt by a state to regulate in that area.

This conclusion is in accordance with the clear preponderance of authority in this and other circuits. *See Meyers v. Beverly Hills Federal Savings and Loan Ass'n, supra*, 499 F.2d 1145, 1147 (9th Cir. 1974); *Kupiec v. Republic Federal Savings and Loan Ass'n*, 512 F.2d 147, 150 (7th Cir. 1975); *Rettig v. Arlington*

Heights Federal Savings and Loan Ass'n, 405 F.Supp. 819, 823 (N.D.Ill.1975); *City Federal Savings and Loan Ass'n v. Crowley,* 393 F.Supp. 644, 655 (E.D.Wis.1974); *Lyons Savings and Loan Ass'n v. Federal Home Loan Bank Board, supra,* 377 F.Supp. 11, 17 (N.D.Ill.1974); *Elwert v. Pacific First Federal Savings and Loan Ass'n,* 138 F.Supp. 395, 399-400 (D.Or.1956); *People of California v. Coast Federal Savings and Loan Ass'n,* 98 F.Supp. 311 (S.D.Cal.1951).

In *People v. Coast Federal, supra,* the California Attorney General sought an injunction and recovery of statutory penalties against a federal savings and loan association for violation of state banking laws on advertising. 98 F.Supp. at 315. The court found that the HOLA established a uniform national system and that state law could not be applied to the federal association:

> Not only does the act of Congress [HOLA] which authorized the creation, operation and supervision of federal savings and loan associations by the Home Loan Bank Board, embrace the entire field, but the comprehensive rules and regulations adopted by the Board clearly meet the test of covering the subject matter of the [state] statute.... It seems clear that Congress has preempted the field, making invalid the state statutes plaintiffs rely upon ... when attempted to be invoked against a Federal savings and loan association.
>
> ....
>
> [A]s to federal savings and loan associations, Congress made plenary, preemptive delegation to the Board to organize, incorporate, supervise and regulate, leaving no field for state supervision. 98 F.Supp. at 318-19; *accord Meyers v. Beverly Hills Federal Savings and Loan Ass'n, supra,* 499 F.2d at 1147.

This language of *People v. Coast Federal* has been echoed in decisions regarding federal preemption of state regulation of federal savings and loan associations.[12]

The Ninth Circuit has taken the position that Congress, in the HOLA, delegated to the Bank Board the authority to regulate the operations of federal savings and loan associations to the exclusion of state regulation. In *Meyers,* the court addressed the issue whether a Bank Board regulation specifically covering the area of prepayments of real estate loans, 12 C.F.R. Section 545.6-12(b), exempted federal associations from California law dealing with prepayment penalties. The court held that "federal law preempts the field ..., so that any California law in the area is inapplicable to federal savings and loan associations operating within California." 499 F.2d at 1147.

---

[12] *See, e. g.,* City Federal Savings and Loan Ass'n v. Crowley, *supra,* 393 F.Supp. at 655 ("The Act [HOLA] and the regulations promulgated by the [Bank Board] have been held to establish federal pre-emption over the regulation of federal savings and loan associations and thereby preclude any state legislation from applying."); Lyons Savings and Loan Ass'n v. Federal Home Loan Bank Board, *supra,* 377 F.Supp. at 17 ("[T]he plenary powers given to the Board in the HOLA clearly evidence a Congressional intention to preempt the field, thus precluding any regulation of federal associations by state law.").

The language of these cases suggests that Congress occupied the field so that, even in the absence of Bank Board regulation, the states are precluded from regulating in any way the operations of federal associations. That issue is not before the court on this motion and the court expresses no view as to its merits. However, the breadth of the position taken by these courts lends further support to the more limited conclusion reached in this opinion.

IV. Bank Board's Exercise of Its Authority

Pursuant to the plenary authority delegated to it by Congress, the Bank Board has promulgated specific regulations regarding the provisions which a federal association shall and may include in their loan contracts. 12 C.F.R. § 545.6-11. In particular, the Bank Board has promulgated a regulation specifically confirming the validity of due-on-sale clauses in mortgage loan contracts executed by federal associations. 12 C.F.R. § 545.6-11(f). Further, the Bank Board has specifically provided that the only non-contractual limitations on the exercisability of such clauses are those enumerated in 12 C.F.R. § 545.6-11(g).[13] 12 C.F.R. § 545.6-11(f). The regulations on their face indicate the Bank Board's intent to exercise the authority to preempt delegated to it by Congress and to govern exclusively the validity and exercisability of due-on-sale clauses in the lending instruments of federal associations.

The Bank Board expressed its intentions with regard to the preemptive effect of the due-on-sale regulations in the preamble thereto:

[i]t was and is the Board's intent to have . . . due-on-sale practices of Federal associations governed exclusively by Federal law. Therefore, . . . exercise of due-on-sale clauses by Federal associations shall be governed and controlled solely by § 545.6-11 and the Board's new Statement of Policy. [12 C.F.R. § 556.9]. Federal associations shall not be bound by or subject to any conflicting State law which imposes different . . . due-on-sale requirements, nor shall Federal associations attempt to . . . avoid the limitations on the exercise of due-on-sale clauses delineated in § 545.6-11(g) on the ground that such . . . avoidance of limitations is permissible under State law. Preamble to Bank Board Resolution No. 76-296, dated April 28, 1976.

The Bank Board, in promulgating these regulations, was responding to attempts by states to impose state limitations on federal associations' exercise of due-on-sale clauses. The Board deemed such limitations not to be the "best practices," and therefore specifically authorized due-on-sale clauses and preempted state regulation. In doing so, the Bank Board exercised precisely the kind of discretion that Congress intended to delegate to it in HOLA. State regulation of due-on-sale clauses, contained in the lending instruments of federal associations executed on or after June 8, 1976, is therefore preempted.

V. Conclusion

Plaintiff's and cross-claimant's motion for partial summary judgment is granted. Federal law, including specifically 12 C.F.R. § 545.6-11(f) and (g), exclusively governs the validity and exercisability of due-on-sale clauses included in Glendale Federal's loan instruments executed on and after June 8, 1976. California law on the validity and exercisability of due-on-sale clauses is inapplicable to Glendale Federal's loan instruments executed on and after June 8, 1976.

---

[13] *See* note 3 *supra*. Section 545.6-11(g) contains the only express limitations on the exercise of due-on-sale clauses by federal associations. However, the Bank Board's Statement of Policy with respect to the use of due-on-sale clauses expresses the Bank Board's view that there may be circumstances other than those described in 12 C.F.R. § 545.6-11(g)(1) where a federal association should consider waiving its contractual right to accelerate. 12 C.F.R. § 556.9.

GREENWALD v. FIRST FEDERAL SAVINGS & LOAN ASS'N

United States District Court
446 F. Supp. 620 (D.C. Mass. 1978)

CAFFREY, CHIEF JUDGE.

These consolidated civil actions challenge the applicability to Federal savings and loan associations of a Massachusetts law requiring interest payments on certain real estate tax deposits. In No. 76-3931-C, Massachusetts Commissioner of Banks Carol S. Greenwald (Commissioner), seeks declaratory and injunctive relief, specifically an order of the Court mandating defendants' compliance with the above-mentioned Massachusetts statute. Defendants in that action include the First Federal Savings and Loan Association of Boston (First Federal) and every other federal savings and loan association with its principal place of business in the Commonwealth.

No. 76-3931-C was originally filed in the Massachusetts Supreme Judicial Court. Pursuant to 28 U.S.C.A. § 1441(b), First Federal removed the matter to this Court, invoking federal question jurisdiction under 28 U.S.C.A. §§ 1331 and 1337. First Federal counterclaimed against the Commissioner and the Federal Home Loan Bank Board (Board) on the ground that any Massachusetts law requiring interest payments by federally-chartered savings and loan associations is unconstitutional. In 77-76-C, commenced in this Court, First Federal and all other federally-chartered savings and loan associations doing business in Massachusetts seek a declaration that ch. 183, § 61 does not apply to federal savings and loan associations because such associations are subject only to federal regulation. Both the Board and the Commissioner are named as defendants.

These cases are currently before the Court on the parties' cross-motions for summary judgment under Fed.R.Civ.P. 56. All parties concede there is no genuine issue of material fact. On the basis of the pleadings, a hearing on the cross-motions as well as the memoranda submitted by the parties, I rule as follows:

The basic issue raised by these cases is whether ch. 183, § 61 violates the Supremacy Clause, U.S.Const. Art. VI, cl. 2, when applied to federal savings and loan associations. First Federal contends that the Massachusetts statute is preempted by 12 C.F.R. § 545.6-11, a Board regulation. The Commissioner, on the other hand, argues that § 61 is a valid exercise of state authority in light of the Real Estate Settlement Procedures Act of 1974, *as amended,* 12 U.S.C.A. § 2601 et seq. (West Supp.1977) (RESPA).

It is familiar learning that a statute [*sic*] statute contravenes the Supremacy Clause when it obstructs "the accomplishment and the execution of the full purposes and objectives of an Act of Congress." *Hines v. Davidowitz,* 312 U.S. 52, 67, 61 S.Ct. 399, 404, 85 L.Ed. 581 (1941). Under traditional doctrine, the state statute is invalid either (1) if it appears that Congress either expressly or impliedly intended federal law to preempt the area, or (2) if the state statute conflicts irreconcilably with federal law. *Florida Lime & Avocado Growers, Inc. v. Paul,* 373 U.S. 132, 141, 83 S.Ct. 1210, 10 L.Ed.2d 248 (1963).

In urging the Court to find preemption on an implied intent theory, First Federal contends that state laws governing mortgage lending have never applied to federal savings and loan associations, but rather such associations have traditionally been governed solely by federal law. A review of the history of the federal savings and loan system demonstrates the factuality and validity of this argument. The Federal Savings and Loan system was created by Congress to provide, *inter alia,* uniform national home financing. The program began in

1932 with passage of the Federal Home Loan Bank Act, 12 U.S.C.A. §§ 1421-1449. Under that Act, the Board was created and directed to charter 12 regional federal home loan banks to serve as reservoirs of credit for member financial institutions and to make home mortgage loans directly to the public. The following year, Congress enacted the Home Owners' Loan Act (HOLA), 12 U.S.C.A. §§ 1461-1468, which withdrew from the Federal Home Loan Banks the power to make direct loans to the public and authorized creation of federally-chartered savings and loan associations.

Under power delegated by Congress through § 5(a) of HOLA, the Board was authorized to "provide for the organization, incorporation, examination, operation and regulation" of federal savings & loan associations. 12 U.S.C.A. § 1464(a). Pursuant to its statutory mandate, the Board has promulgated comprehensive regulations governing "the powers and operations of every federal savings and loan association 'from its cradle to its corporate grave'." *Kupiec v. Republic Federal Savings & Loan Ass'n,* 512 F.2d 147, 150 (7th Cir. 1975), citing *Meyers v. Beverly Hills Federal Savings & Loan Ass'n,* 499 F.2d 1145, 1147 (9th Cir. 1974).

Pursuant to its statutory authority, the Board on May 14, 1975, effective June 16, 1975, issued the previously-mentioned regulation governing interest payment on escrow accounts by all federal savings and loan associations, 12 C.F.R. § 545.6-11. In pertinent part, the regulation provides:

> (c) *Payment of interest on escrow accounts.* A Federal association which makes a loan on or after June 16, 1975 on the security of a single-family dwelling occupied or to be occupied by the borrower (except such a loan for which a bona fide commitment was made before that date) shall pay interest on any escrow account maintained in connection with such a loan (1) if there is in effect a specific statutory provision or provisions of the State in which such dwelling is located by or under which State-chartered savings & loan associations, mutual savings banks and similar institutions are generally required to pay interest on such escrow accounts, and (2) at not less than the rate required to be paid by such State-chartered institutions but not to exceed the rate being paid by the Federal association on its regular accounts. . . . *Except as provided by contract, a Federal association shall have no obligation to pay interest on escrow accounts apart from the duties imposed by this paragraph.* [Emphasis added]

Essentially, the regulation requires a Federal association to pay interest on any escrow account maintained after June 16, 1975, if the state where such dwelling is located has a specific statutory provision under which state-chartered savings and loan associations, mutual savings banks and similar thrift institutions are required to pay such interest.

The above-quoted Board regulation has the force and effect of a statute. *Milberg v. Lawrence Cedarhurst Federal Savings and Loan Ass'n,* 496 F.2d 523 (2d Cir. 1974); *Community Federal Savings and Loan Ass'n v. Fields,* 128 F.2d 705 (8th Cir. 1942). Every Federal Court which has addressed preemption questions involving HOLA has held that Congress impliedly intended that federal law should govern the regulation of federal savings and loan associations. *See, e. g., Rettig v. Arlington Heights Federal Savings and Loan Ass'n,* 405 F.Supp. 819 (N.D.Ill.1975). Such holdings establish the impropriety of any state regulation in the area. *Meyers v. Beverly Hills Savings & Loan Ass'n,* 499 F.2d 1145 (9th Cir. 1974); *Murphy v. Colonial Federal Savings & Loan Ass'n,* 388 F.2d 609 (2d Cir. 1967). Consequently, I rule that federal law and federal regulations issued thereunder preempt the field of interest payments by federally-chartered savings and loan associations.

Moreover, in litigation involving the same regulation at issue here, albeit another of its provisions, the Supreme Court of Wisconsin held that 12 C.F.R. § 545.6-11 preempted state law, stating "it is apparent that Congress has substantially occupied the field in regard to the regulation of federal savings and loan associations, particularly in the area of the regulation of lending practices. This scheme of federal regulations is pervasive." *Kaski v. First Federal Savings & Loan Ass'n of Madison*, 72 Wis.2d 132, 240 N.W.2d 367, 372 (1976).

It should be noted that exclusive Federal authority over federal savings and loan associations has been recognized legislatively by Massachusetts. Gen.Laws ch. 168, § 73B provides in pertinent part:

... Upon the grant to any association of a charter by the federal home loan bank board, the savings bank receiving such charter shall cease to be a savings bank incorporated under this chapter and shall no longer be subject to the supervision and control of the commissioner.

The Supreme Judicial Court has also ruled that local officials cannot control federal banking practices. *Springfield Institution for Savings v. Worcester Federal Savings & Loan Ass'n*, 329 Mass. 184, 107 N.E.2d 315 (1952), *cert. denied*, 344 U.S. 844, 73 S.Ct. 184, 97 L.Ed. 684.

Not only do I rule that preemption occurs under the congressional intent test enunciated in *Florida Lime and Avocado Growers, Inc. v. Paul, supra*, but also I find contravention of the Supremacy Clause because the Massachusetts statute conflicts directly with federal law in that the federal regulation applies only to loans made after June 16, 1975, while the state law requires interest payments on tax assessments based on outstanding loans made prior to that date. Another conflict lies in the fact that the federal regulation applies only to loans made on the security of single-family dwellings, whereas the Massachusetts statute requires interest payments on loans secured by other types of dwellings. Further conflict consists of the fact that the federal regulation limits the maximum rate of interest which a federal association must pay on its escrow accounts to the rate paid on its regular savings accounts, while under state law a higher interest rate could be required. Because of these direct conflicts between the federal regulation and the State statute, I rule that the federal regulation prevails insofar as federal savings and loan association mortgage-lending practices are concerned.

Having decided that federal regulation in this area preempts state law, the next question before the Court is whether Congress in enacting the RESPA intended to carve out an exception to its grant of plenary regulatory authority to the Board. The Commissioner contends that Section 18 of the RESPA permits the operation of State law. The Commissioner relies exclusively on the following provision, entitled *"State laws unaffected; inconsistent Federal and State provisions"* which provides:

This chapter does not annul, alter, or affect, or exempt any person subject to the provisions of this chapter from complying with, the laws of any State with respect to settlement practices, except to the extent that those laws are inconsistent with any provision of this chapter, and then only to the extent of the inconsistency. The Secretary is authorized to determine whether such inconsistencies exist. The Secretary may not determine that any State law is inconsistent with any provision of this chapter if the Secretary determines that such law gives greater protection to the consumer. In making these determinations the Secretary shall consult with the appropriate Federal agencies. 12 U.S.C.A. § 2616.

I rule that § 2616 of the RESPA is inapplicable to the case at bar. The clear language of § 2616 indicates that compliance with State law is permitted only when (1) the Secretary of Housing and Urban Development determines that such state law gives greater protection to a consumer than does federal law, and (2) the relevant State law covers "settlement practices." In this case there has been no Federal agency determination that Massachusetts law gives greater consumer protection than 12 C.F.R. § 545.6-11(c). Moreover, the payment of interest on escrow accounts is not a settlement practice. 12 U.S.C.A. § 2602 defines the term "settlement services" as

> including, but not limited to the following: title searches, title examinations, the provision of title certificates, title insurance, services rendered by an attorney, the preparation of documents, property surveys, the rendering of credit reports or appraisals, pest and fungus inspections, services rendered by a real estate agent or broker, and the handling of the processing, and closing or settlement.

I rule that interest payment on tax escrow accounts, which can continue long after the closing of the mortgage transaction and which can continue to occur during the entire life of the mortgage, is obviously not a settlement practice within the meaning of the statute. Therefore the Commissioner's position is not sustained.

Order accordingly.

NOTES

1. Does the *Greenwald* case render academic the *Derenco* case, *supra* at p. 157?

2. At least one state court has held that federal law does not preempt state law in the area of due-on-sale clauses notwithstanding the provisions of 12 C.F.R. § 545.8-3(f). The court in *Panko v. Pan American Federal Savings & Loan Ass'n,* 174 Cal. Rptr. 240 (Cal. App. 1981), held that there was not a conflict between the state and federal law on the basis that while due-on clauses were authorized the use of them was not compelled. The court also noted the language on the FNMA/FHLMC mortgage form which requires the mortgage (or in this case a deed of trust) to be governed by the law of the jurisdiction in which the land is located.

3. An argument can be made that while the regulations in the Code of Federal Regulations permit the inclusion of due-on's in mortgage forms, the *Wellenkamp* case merely defines or limits the use of a restraint on alienation which is real property law. On this basis there is no conflict between state and federal law.

4. There have been reported efforts to introduce legislation which would clearly establish the federal government's preemption in the area of due-on's. However, unless Congress does enact such legislation it will be up to the courts to decide, which may result in differing law in several circuits until a case reaches the United States Supreme Court.

DISCLOSURE STATEMENT REQUIRED BY FEDERAL TRUTH IN LENDING ACT
REGULATION Z

REAL PROPERTY TRANSACTION -
SECURED BY FIRST LIEN ON A DWELLING   LOAN NO.

The interest rate on this mortgage Loan is

The **FINANCE CHARGE** on this transaction will begin to accrue on

The institutions security in this transaction is a   mortgage on property located at

also specifically described in the documents furnished for this loan. The documents executed in connection with this transaction cover all after-acquired property and also stand as security for future advances, the terms for which are described in the documents.

I The AMOUNT OF THE LOAN in this transaction is
   Less PREPAID FINANCE CHARGE:
     Interest from   to
     Closing Costs

Total **PREPAID FINANCE CHARGE:**
AMOUNT FINANCED:

II OTHER NON FINANCE CHARGES:

☐ Not Included   ☐ Included in AMOUNT FINANCED

   Title Charges
   Appraisal
   Prep. of Documents
   Credit Report
   Recording Mortgage
   Notary Fee
   1st year Mtg. Ins. Prem.
   Title Insurance

Total **NON FINANCE CHARGES:**
NET PROCEEDS:

FINANCE CHARGE - Required on ADDITIONAL ADVANCE and REFINANCE only.
The finance charge on this transaction totals $ _____. This amount includes all items represented in Part I as shown above.

The **TOTAL OF PAYMENTS** on this transaction will be $ _____.
ANNUAL PERCENTAGE RATE _____ %

PAYMENT TERMS: Payments for principal and interest on this transaction shall be   monthly installments of $ beginning on   and due on the   day of each month thereafter.

LATE CHARGE: In the event of default of any   payment   the contract interest rate may be increased up to 1% during the period of default.

MISC. CLAUSE:

PREPAYMENT CHARGES:
☐ Conventional - Association shall be entitled to a minimum of 90 days interest on the original amount of the Loan.
☐ Additional

INSURANCE
PROPERTY INSURANCE
   Property insurance, if written in connection with this loan, may be obtained by borrower through any person of his choice, provided however, the creditor reserves the right to refuse, for reasonable cause, to accept an insurer offered by the borrower.
OTHER INSURANCE
   Credit Life, accident, health or loss of income insurance is not required to obtain this loan. No charge is made for such insurance and no such insurance is provided unless the borrower signs the appropriate statement below.
   is available at cost of $ per month for the   year term of the initial policy.
   is available at cost of $ est. per month for the   year term of the initial policy.

I desire   coverage.   I DO NOT desire such insurance coverage.

_____ DATE   _____ SIGNATURE   _____ DATE   _____ SIGNATURE

_____ INSTITUTION   I do hereby acknowledge receipt of the disclosure made in this notice.

Illustration 8
TIL Disclosure Statement

HUD-1 Rev. 5/76   Page 1   Form Approved
                                                                                          OMB No. 63 R-1501

W.B.A. (RESPA)—240 A (Rev. 5/76)	B. TYPE OF LOAN:
A. U.S. DEPARTMENT OF HOUSING & URBAN DEVELOPMENT SETTLEMENT STATEMENT	1. [ ] FHA 2. [ ] FMHA 3. [ ] CONV. UNINS. 4. [ ] VA 5. [ ] CONV. INS. 6. File Number: 7. Loan Number: 8. Mortgage Insurance Case Number:

C. NOTE: This form is furnished to give you a statement of actual settlement costs. Amounts paid to and by the settlement agent are shown. Items marked "(p.o.c.)" were paid outside the closing; they are shown here for informational purposes and are not included in totals.

D. NAME OF BORROWER:	E. NAME OF SELLER:	F. NAME OF LENDER:

G. PROPERTY LOCATION:	H. SETTLEMENT AGENT:	I. SETTLEMENT DATE:
	PLACE OF SETTLEMENT:	

J. SUMMARY OF BORROWER'S TRANSACTION		K. SUMMARY OF SELLER'S TRANSACTION	
100. GROSS AMOUNT DUE FROM BORROWER:		**400. GROSS AMOUNT DUE TO SELLER:**	
101. Contract sales price		401. Contract sales price	
102. Personal property		402. Personal property	
103. Settlement charges to borrower (line 1400)		403.	
104.		404.	
105.		405.	
Adjustments for items paid by seller in advance:		Adjustments for items paid by seller in advance:	
106. City/town taxes to		406. City/town taxes to	
107. County taxes to		407. County taxes to	
108. Assessments to		408. Assessments to	
109. to		409. to	
110. to		410. to	
111. to		411. to	
112. to		412. to	
120. GROSS AMOUNT DUE FROM BORROWER:		**420. GROSS AMOUNT DUE TO SELLER:**	
200. AMOUNTS PAID BY OR IN BEHALF OF BORROWER:		**500. REDUCTIONS IN AMOUNT DUE TO SELLER:**	
201. Deposit or earnest money		501. Excess deposit (see instructions)	
202. Principal amount of new loan(s)		502. Settlement charges to seller (line 1400)	
203. Existing loan(s) taken subject to		503. Existing loan(s) taken subject to	
204.		504. Payoff of first mortgage loan	
205.		505. Payoff of second mortgage loan	
206.		506.	
207.		507.	
208.		508.	
209.		509.	
Adjustments for items unpaid by seller:		Adjustments for items unpaid by seller:	
210. City/town taxes to		510. City/town taxes to	
211. County taxes to		511. County taxes to	
212. Assessments to		512. Assessments to	
213. to		513.	
214. to		514.	
215. to		515.	
216. to		516.	
217. to		517.	
218. to		518.	
219. to		519.	
220. TOTAL PAID BY/FOR BORROWER		**520. TOTAL REDUCTION AMOUNT DUE SELLER**	
300. CASH AT SETTLEMENT FROM/TO BORROWER:		**600. CASH AT SETTLEMENT TO/FROM SELLER:**	
301. Gross amount due from borrower (line 120)		601. Gross amount due to seller (line 420)	
302. Less amounts paid by/for borrower (line 220)	( )	602. Less reductions in amount due seller (line 520)	( )
303. CASH [ ] FROM [ ] TO BORROWER		603. CASH [ ] TO [ ] FROM SELLER	

Illustration 9

RESPA Disclosure/Settlement Statement

W.B.A. (RESPA)–240 B (Rev. 5/76)

DISCLOSURE/SETTLEMENT STATEMENT

L. SETTLEMENT CHARGES	PAID FROM BORROWER'S FUNDS AT SETTLEMENT	PAID FROM SELLER'S FUNDS AT SETTLEMENT
700. TOTAL SALES/BROKER'S COMMISSION based on price $ @ % =		
DIVISION OF COMMISSION (line 700) as follows:		
701. $ to		
702. $ to		
703. Commission paid at settlement		
704.		
800. ITEMS PAYABLE IN CONNECTION WITH LOAN:		
801. Loan Origination fee %		
802. Loan Discount %		
803. Appraisal Fee to		
804. Credit Report to		
805. Lender's Inspection Fee		
806. Mortgage Insurance Application Fee to		
807. Assumption Fee		
808.		
809.		
810.		
811.		
900. ITEMS REQUIRED BY LENDER TO BE PAID IN ADVANCE:		
901. Interest from to @ $ / day		
902. Mortgage insurance premium for months to		
903. Hazard insurance premium for years to		
904. years to		
905.		
1000. RESERVES DEPOSITED WITH LENDER:		
1001. Hazard insurance months @ $ per month		
1002. Mortgage insurance months @ $ per month		
1003. City property taxes months @ $ per month		
1004. County property taxes months @ $ per month		
1005. Annual assessments months @ $ per month		
1006. months @ $ per month		
1007. months @ $ per month		
1008. months @ $ per month		
1100. TITLE CHARGES:		
1101. Settlement or closing fee to		
1102. Abstract or title search to		
1103. Title examination to		
1104. Title insurance binder to		
1105. Document preparation to		
1106. Notary fees to		
1107. Attorney's Fees to		
(includes above items numbers:)		
1108. Title insurance to		
(includes above items numbers:)		
1109. Lender's coverage $		
1110. Owner's coverage $		
1111.		
1112.		
1113.		
1200. GOVERNMENT RECORDING AND TRANSFER CHARGES:		
1201. Recording fees: Deed $; Mortgage $ Releases $		
1202. City/county tax/stamps: Deed $; Mortgage $		
1203. State tax/stamps: Deed $; Mortgage $		
1204.		
1205.		
1300. ADDITIONAL SETTLEMENT CHARGES:		
1301. Survey to		
1302. Pest inspection to		
1303.		
1304.		
1305.		
1400. TOTAL SETTLEMENT CHARGES *(enter on lines 103, Section J and 502, Section K)*		

*ACKNOWLEDGMENT OF RECEIPT

HUD-1 (Rev. 5/76)

Receipt of a completed copy of this statement is acknowledged.

Seller _____   Borrower _____

Seller _____   Borrower _____

*Signatures not required, but recommended to evidence receipt.

Illustration 9

Chapter 10

OBTAINING A MORTGAGE LOAN

> If you would know the value of money, go and try to borrow some.
>
> Franklin, *Poor Richard's Almanack*

The information contained in this chapter will discuss the steps and procedures involved in obtaining a mortgage loan. The emphasis will be primarily on residential, rather than commercial, mortgage procurement. However, the legal aspects of residential and commercial mortgage procurement are closely related. The main difference is essentially that residential mortgages are made by banks and savings and loans, while commercial mortgages for office buildings, hotels, shopping centers, and the like are made primarily by pension funds and insurance companies.

The information contained in this chapter will assist one in understanding the day-to-day practice of obtaining a mortgage loan, including: (1) The steps that need to be undertaken in order to obtain a loan; (2) The considerations and analysis undertaken by the lender; (3) The economics of financing; and (4) Some of the documentation that the lawyer and his clients will encounter in this process.

The forms contained in this chapter are merely representative of the types of forms that a lawyer and/or his client will use in obtaining a mortgage loan. The contents and the provisions of said forms and documents are not deemed to be perfect and/or guaranteed not to be the subject of future legal challenge.

A. THE MORTGAGE APPLICATION

One of the first steps in obtaining a mortgage loan is to make an application to a financial institution. At the time of application, the loan officer will normally take a Residential Loan Application. At this time, the loan officer will make the necessary Truth in Lending and Real Estate Settlement Procedure Act disclosures as required by law. The Truth in Lending form is shown in Illustration No. 8, *supra,* and a RESPA Settlement Statement is shown in Illustration No. 9, *supra.* Also, the loan officer will require a copy of the accepted Offer to Purchase and/or binder contract. In some instances, the loan officer will request a Confidential Personal Financial Statement and an executed Request for Verification of Employment and Deposits from the borrower.

Pursuant to the requirements of the Real Estate Settlement Procedures Act, the loan officer will give a copy of "Settlement Costs and You" to a prospective applicant. Portions of this booklet, a guide for homeowners published by the Department of Housing and Urban Development, appear in this chapter. In most instances, the loan officer will require some tendering of a loan application fee to cover the appraisal of the property and the various credit reports on the prospective borrowers.

A typical real estate mortgage checklist and processing sheet follows, which gives, in preparation form, a checklist to the mortgage loan officer for purposes of initiating the application and for taking the loan to ultimate fruition, *i.e.,* the mortgage closing.

In some instances, the loan officer will require a non-refundable commitment fee. Normally, the amount of this fee is one percent of the amount of the loan sought. In the event the loan actually closes, the fee is applied to the costs; if it fails to close, the fee is forfeited to the lender. The following pages contain illustrations of several items a typical borrower can expect to encounter in the application process.

U.S. DEPARTMENT OF HOUSING AND URBAN DEVELOPMENT, SETTLEMENT COSTS AND YOU: A HUD GUIDE FOR HOME BUYERS (1977)

Introduction

For many people, buying a home is the single most significant financial step of a lifetime. The Real Estate Settlement Procedures Act (RESPA), a Federal statute, helps to protect you at this step.

Settlement is the formal process by which ownership of real property passes from seller to buyer. It is the end of the home buying process, the time when title to the property is transferred from the seller to the buyer.

RESPA covers most residential mortgage loans used to finance the purchase of one to four family properties, such as a house, a condominium or cooperative apartment unit, a lot with a mobile home, or a lot on which you will build a house or place a mobile home using the proceeds of the loan.

RESPA was not designed to set the prices of settlement services. Instead, it provides you with information to take the mystery out of the settlement process, so that you can shop for settlement services and make informed decisions.

This information booklet was prepared as provided in RESPA by the Office of Consumer Affairs and Regulatory Functions of the U.S. Department of Housing and Urban Development.

Part One of this booklet describes the settlement process and nature of charges and suggests questions you might ask of lenders, attorneys and others to clarify what services they will provide you for the charges quoted. It also contains information on your rights and remedies available under RESPA, and alerts you to unfair or illegal practices.

Part Two of this booklet is an item-by-item explanation of settlement services and costs . . . . Remember that terminology varies by locality so that terminology used here may not exactly match that used in your area. For example, settlement is sometimes called closing and settlement charges are frequently referred to as closing costs.

Part I

What Happens and When

Suppose you have just found a home you would like to buy. In a typical situation, when you reach an agreement with the seller on the price, you then sign a sales contract. The terms of the sales contract can be negotiated to your benefit, as the booklet explains below.

Next you will probably seek a mortgage to finance the purchase. This booklet suggests questions you should raise as you shop for a lender.

When you file your application for a loan, the lender is required by RESPA to provide a good faith estimate of the costs of settlement services and a copy of this booklet. The lender has three business days, after written loan application, to mail these materials to you.

Between loan application time and settlement, you usually have a chance to shop for settlement services, to ensure that you will obtain good value for your money.

Finally, one business day before settlement, if you so request, the person conducting the settlement must allow you an opportunity to see a Uniform Settlement Statement that shows whatever figures are available at that time for settlement charges you will be required to pay. At settlement, the completed Uniform Settlement Statement will be given to you.

Note: In some parts of the country where there is no actual settlement meeting, or in cases where neither you nor your authorized agent attends the closing meeting, the person conducting settlement has the obligation to deliver the Uniform Settlement Statement to you by mail.

There is no standard settlement process followed in all localities; therefore, what you experience, involving many of the same services, will probably vary from the description in this booklet.

Shopping for Services

When settlement arrives, you are committed to the purchase of the property and may have made a partial payment, sometimes called earnest money, to the seller or his agent. Services may have been performed for which you are obligated to pay. Unless a seller fails to perform a legally binding promise or has acted in a fraudulent fashion, you are normally obligated to complete your part of the contract and pay settlement costs. Thus the time to decide the terms of sale, raise questions, and establish fair fees is not at time of settlement, but earlier, when you negotiate with the seller and providers of settlement services. By the time of settlement, any changes in settlement costs and purchase terms may be difficult to negotiate.

You can also negotiate with the seller of the house about who pays various settlement fees and other charges. There are generally no fixed rules about which party pays which fees, although in many cases this is largely controlled by local custom.

Among the many factors that determine the amount you will pay for settlement costs are the location of your new home, the type of sales contract you negotiate, the arrangements made with the real estate broker, the lender you select, and your decisions in selecting the various firms that provide required settlement services. If the chosen house is located in a "special flood hazard area," identified as such by HUD on a flood insurance map, the lender may require you to purchase flood insurance pursuant to Federal law (See page 24). Information on flood insurance availability, limits of coverage and copies of maps can be obtained through the National Flood Insurers Association servicing company for your State or by calling HUD toll free numbers 800-424-8872 or 73.

ROLE OF THE BROKER

Although real estate brokers provide helpful advice on many aspects of home buying, and may in some areas supervise the settlement, they normally serve the interest of the seller, not the buyer. The broker's basic objective is to obtain a signed contract of sale which properly expresses the agreement of the parties, and to complete the sale. However, as state licensing laws require that the broker be fair in his dealings with all parties to the transaction, you should feel free to point this out to the broker if you feel you are being treated unfairly.

A broker may recommend that you deal with a particular lender, title company, attorney, or other provider of settlement services. Ask brokers why they recommend a particular company or firm in preference to others. Advise them that while you welcome their suggestions (and, indeed, they probably have good contacts), you reserve the right to pick your own providers of services.

Negotiating a Sales Contract

If you have obtained this booklet before you have signed a sales contract with the seller of the property, here are some important points to consider regarding that contract.

The sales agreement you and the seller sign can expressly state which settlement costs you will pay and which will be paid by the seller although some may be negotiable up to time of settlement. Buyers can and do negotiate with sellers as to which party is to pay for specific settlement costs. The success of such negotiations depends upon factors such as how eager the seller is to sell and you are to buy, the quality of the house itself, how long the house has been on the market, whether other potential buyers are interested, and how willing you are to negotiate for lower costs. If the contract is silent on these costs, they are still open to negotiation.

There is no standard sales contract which you are required to sign. You are entitled to make any modifications or additions in any standard form contract to which the seller will agree. You should consider including the following clauses:

• The seller provides title, free and clear of all liens and encumbrances except those which you specifically agree to in the contract or approve when the results of the title search are reported to you. You may negotiate as to who will pay for the title search service to determine whether the title is "clear."

• A refund of your deposit (earnest money) be made by the seller or escrow agent, and cancellation of the sale if you are unable to secure from a lending institution a first mortgage or deed-of-trust loan with an amount, interest rate, and length of term, as set forth in the contract, within a stated time period.

• A certificate be provided at time of settlement, stating that the house is free from termites or termite damage.

• A certificate that the plumbing, heating, electrical systems and appliances are in working order, and that the house is structurally sound. Negotiate who pays for any necessary inspections. There is no uniform custom in most areas. Many buyers prefer to pay for these inspections because they want to know that the inspector is conducting the service for them, not for the seller. (You can also purchase a warranty to back up the inspection, if you wish.)

• An agreement be reached on how taxes, water and sewer charges, premiums on existing transferable insurance policies, utility bills, interest on mortgages, and rent (if there are tenants) are to be divided between buyer and seller as of the date of the settlement.

Before you sign the sales contract, make sure that it correctly expresses your agreement with the seller on such important details as the sales price of the home, method of payment, the time set for your taking possession, what fixtures, appliances, and personal property are to be sold with the home, and the other items described above.

The above list is not complete, but does illustrate the importance of the sales agreement and its terms. Before you sign a sales contract you may want to ask an attorney to review the proposed agreement and determine if it protects your interest for once signed, the contract is binding on you and the seller. If you do not know of an attorney you may wish to consult the local bar association referral service or neighborhood legal service office.

Selecting an Attorney

If you seek the aid of an attorney, first ask what services will be performed for what fee. If the fee seems too high, shop for another lawyer. Does the attorney have substantial experience in real estate? The U.S. Supreme Court has said that it is illegal for bar associations to fix minimum fee schedules for attorneys, so do not be bashful about discussing and shopping for legal fees you can afford. Your attorney will understand.

Questions you may wish to ask the attorney include: What is the charge for reading documents and giving advice concerning them? For being present at settlement? Will the attorney represent any other party in the transaction in addition to you? In some areas attorneys act as closing agents handling the mechanical aspects of the settlement. A lawyer who does this may not fully represent your interests since as closing agent, he would be representing the seller and other interests as well.

Selecting a Lender

Your choice of lender will influence not only your settlement costs, but also the monthly cost of your mortgage loan.

Lending institutions require certain settlement services, such as a new survey or title insurance, or they may charge you for other settlement-related services, such as the appraisal or credit report. You may find, in shopping for a lender, that other institutions may not have such requirements. . . .

Many lending institutions deal regularly with certain title companies, attorneys, appraisers, surveyors, and others in whom they have confidence. They may want to arrange for settlement services to be provided through these parties. This booklet discusses your rights in such a situation under the section below on Homebuyer's Rights.

If you choose a lending institution which allows you a choice of settlement service providers, you should shop and compare among the providers in your area, to find the best service for the best price. Where the lender designates the use of particular firms, check with other firms to see if the lender's stated charges are competitive.

Questions you may want to ask the lender should include these:

• Are you required to carry life or disability insurance? Must you obtain it from a particular company? (You may prefer no insurance or may wish to obtain it at a better premium rate elsewhere.)

• Is there a late payment charge? How much? How late may your payment be before the charge is imposed? You should be aware that late payments may harm your credit rating.

• If you wish to pay off the loan in advance of maturity (for example, if you move and sell the house), must you pay a prepayment penalty? How much? If so, for how long a period will it apply?

• Will the lender release you from personal liability if your loan is assumed by someone else when you sell your house?

• If you sell the house and the buyer assumes your loan, will the lender have the right to charge an assumption fee, raise the rate of interest, or require payment in full of the mortgage?

• If you have a financial emergency, will the terms of the loan include a future advances clause, permitting you to borrow additional money on the mortgage after you have paid off part of the original loan?

• Will you be required to pay monies into a special reserve (escrow or impound) account to cover taxes or insurance? If so, how large a deposit will be required at the closing of the sale? The amount of reserve deposits required is limited under RESPA. Some recent state laws have required that these accounts bear interest for the benefit of the borrower (buyer). If reserve requirements can be waived, you will be responsible for paying the particular charges for taxes or insurance directly to the tax collector or insurance company. . . .

• In looking for the best mortgage to fit your particular financial needs, you may wish to check the terms and requirements of a private conventional loan versus a loan insured through the Federal Housing Administration or Farmers Home Administration or guaranteed by the Veterans Administration. The FHA, VA, and Farmers Home Administration loans involve Federal ceilings on permissible charges for some settlement services, which may be of interest to you. Ask lenders about these programs. Another source of information about the federally insured or guaranteed programs is from public documents some of which are listed in the bibliography of this booklet.

• If you are dealing with the lender who holds the existing mortgage, you might be able to take over the prior loan, in a transaction called "assumption". Assumption usually saves money in settlement costs if the interest rate on the prior loan is lower than that being asked in the market. In times of inflation in the housing market, a higher downpayment might be required than if you had obtained a new loan. You may want to ask the seller whether he would be willing to take back a second mortgage to finance part of the difference between the assumed loan and the sales price.

SELECTING A SETTLEMENT AGENT

Settlement practices vary from locality to locality, and even within the same county or city. In various areas settlements are conducted by lending institutions, title insurance companies, escrow companies, real estate brokers, and attorneys for the buyer or seller. By investigating and comparing practices and rates, you may find that the first suggested settlement agent may not be the least expensive. You might save money by taking the initiative in arranging for settlement and selecting the firm and location which meets your needs.

SECURING TITLE SERVICES

A title search may take the form of an abstract, a compilation of pertinent legal documents which provides a condensed history of the property ownership and related matters. In many areas title searches are performed by extracting information from the public record without assembling abstracts. In either situation, an expert examination is necessary to determine the status of title and this is normally made by attorneys or title company employees. In areas where both title insurance companies and attorneys perform these and other settlement services, compare fees for services (such as title certification, document preparation, notary fee, closing fee, etc.), provided by each to determine the better source for these services.

In many jurisdictions a few days or weeks prior to settlement the title insurance company will issue a binder (sometimes called a Commitment to Insure) or preliminary report, a summary of findings based on the search or abstract. It is usually sent to the lender for use until the title insurance policy is issued after the settlement. The binder lists all the defects in and liens against the title identified by the search. You should arrange to have a copy sent to you (or to an attorney who represents you) so that you can raise an objection if there are matters affecting the title which you did not agree to except when you signed the contract of sale.

Title insurance is often required to protect the lender against loss if a flaw in title is not found by the title search made when the house is purchased. You may also get an owner's title policy to protect yourself. In some states, attorneys provide bar-related title insurance as part of their services in examining title and providing a title opinion. In these states the attorney's fee may include the title insurance premium, although the total title-related charges in the transaction should be taken into account in determining whether you will realize any savings.

Bear in mind that a title insurance policy issued only to the lender does not protect you. Similarly, the policy issued to a prior owner, such as the person from whom you are buying the house, does not protect you. To protect yourself from loss because of a mistake made by the title searcher, or because of a legal defect of a type which does not appear on the public records, you will need an owner's policy. Such a mistake rarely occurs but, when it does, it can be financially devastating to the uninsured. If you buy an owner's policy it is usually much less expensive if purchased simultaneously with a lender's policy.

To reduce title insurance costs, be sure to compare rates among various title insurance companies, and ask what services and limitations on coverage are provided by each policy so that you can decide whether a higher rate is consistent with your needs.

Depending upon practice in your jurisdiction, there may be no need for a full historical title search each time title to a home is transferred. If you are buying a home which has changed hands within the last several years, inquire at the title company that issued the previous title insurance policy about a "reissue rate," which would be a lower charge than for a new policy. If the title insurance policy of the previous owner is available, take it to the title insurer or lawyer whom you have selected to do your search.

To mark the boundaries of the property as set out in the title, lenders may require a survey. A homebuyer may be able to avoid the cost of a repetitive complete survey of the property if he can locate the surveyor who previously surveyed the project which he can update. However, the requirements of investors who buy loans originated by your lender may limit the lender's discretion to negotiate this point. Check with the lender or title company on this.

Homebuyer's Rights

INFORMATION BOOKLET

When you submit or the lender prepares your written application for a loan, the lender is legally required, under RESPA to give you a copy of this booklet. If the lender does not give it to you in person on the day of your loan application, he must put it in the mail to you no later than three business days after your application is filed.

GOOD FAITH ESTIMATES

When you file your application for a loan, the lender must also, under the terms of RESPA, provide you with good faith estimates of settlement services charges you will likely incur. If he does not give it to you, he has three business days in which to put it in the mail.

. . . .

The lender is required to give you his good faith estimate, based upon his experience in the locality in which the property is located, for each settlement charge in Section L that he anticipates you will pay, except for paid in advance hazard insurance premium (line 903) and reserves deposited with the lender (all Section 1000 items). The estimate may be stated as either a dollar amount or range for each charge. Where the lender designates the use of a particular firm, the lender must make its good faith estimate based upon the lender's knowledge of the amounts charged by the firm. The form used for this good faith estimate must be concise and clear, and the estimates must bear a reasonable relationship to the costs you will likely incur. If the lender provides you good faith estimates in the form of ranges, ask the lender what the total settlement costs will most likely be. While the lender is not obligated to provide this information under RESPA, it is important for you to know as you evaluate the different mortgage packages being offered you.

Lenders were not required to give good faith estimates for reserves deposited with them or for the prepaid hazard insurance premium because these charges require information not normally known to the lender at time of loan application. It is important for you to make these calculations because they can represent a sizeable cash payment you may have to make at settlement. . . . Ask the lender what his policies are in terms of reserve accounts, for what items the lender requires reserves and for what period of time. You may want to ask the lender to run through a hypothetical calculation for you based upon the date you will most likely close on the house. Other assumptions may be necessary, for example, the assessed value of the property for determining property taxes. The lender can probably be more specific on hazard insurance premiums, particularly for those coverages which a lender requires.

Once you have obtained these estimates from the lender be aware that they are only estimates. The final cost may not be the same. Estimates are subject to changing market conditions, and fees may change. Changes in the date of settlement may result in change in escrow and proration requirements. In certain cases, it may not be possible for the lender to anticipate exactly the pricing policies of settlement firms. Moreover, your own careful choice of settlement firms might result in lower costs, just as hasty decisions might result in higher costs. Remember that the lender's estimate is not a guarantee.

LENDER DESIGNATION OF SETTLEMENT SERVICE PROVIDERS

Some lending institutions follow the practice of designating specific settlement service providers to be used for legal services, title examination services, title insurance, or the conduct of settlement.

Where this occurs the lender, under RESPA, is required to provide you as part of the good faith estimates a statement in which the lender sets forth:

(1) The name, address and telephone number of each provider he has designated. This must include a statement of the specific services each designated firm is to provide for you, as well as an estimate of the amount the lender anticipates you will have to pay for the service, based on the lender's experience as to what the designated provider usually charges. If the services or charges are not clear to you, ask further questions.

(2) Whether each designated firm has a business relationship with the lender.

While designated firms often provide the services needed, a conflict of interest may exist. Take for example the situation where the provider must choose between your interests and those of the lender. Where legal services are involved, it is wise to employ your own attorney to ensure that your interests are properly protected. It is wise for you to contact other firms to determine whether their costs are competitive and their services are comparable.

Disclosure of Settlement Costs One Day Before Closing and Delivery

One business day before settlement, you have the right to inspect the form, called the Uniform Settlement Statement, on which are itemized the services provided to you and fees charged to you. This form (developed by the U.S. Department of Housing and Urban Development) is filled out by the person who will conduct the settlement meeting. Be sure you have the name, address and telephone number of the settlement agent if you wish to inspect this form or if you have any questions.

The settlement agent may not have all costs available the day before closing, but is obligated to show you, upon request, what is available.

The Uniform Settlement Statement must be delivered or mailed to you (while another statement goes to the seller) at or before settlement. If, however, you waive your right to delivery of the completed statement at settlement, it will then be mailed at the earliest practicable date.

In parts of the country where the settlement agent does not require a meeting, or in cases where you or your agent do not attend the settlement, the statement will be mailed as soon as practicable after settlement and no advance inspection is required.

The Uniform Settlement Statement is not used in situations where: (1) there are no settlement fees charged to the buyer (because the seller has assumed all settlement-related expenses), or (2) the total amount the borrower is required to pay for all charges imposed at settlement is determined by a fixed amount and the borrower is informed of this fixed amount at the time of loan application. In the latter case, the lender is required to provide the borrower, within three business days of application, an itemized list of services rendered.

Escrow Closing

Settlement practices differ from state to state. In some parts of the country, settlement may be conducted by an escrow agent, which may be a lender, real estate agent, title company representative, attorney, or an escrow company. After entering into a contract of sale, the parties sign an escrow agreement which requires them to deposit specified documents and funds with the agent. Unlike other types of closing, the parties do not meet around a table to sign and exchange documents. The agent may request a title report and policy; draft a deed or other documents; obtain rent statements; pay off existing loans; adjust taxes, rents, and insurance between the buyer and seller; compute interest on loans; and acquire hazard insurance. All this may be authorized in the escrow agreement. If all the papers and monies are deposited with the agent within the agreed time, the escrow is "closed."

The escrow agent then records the appropriate documents and gives each party the documents and money each is entitled to receive, including the completed Uniform Settlement Statement. If one party has failed to fulfill his agreement, the escrow is not closed and legal complications may follow.

Truth-in-Lending

The lender is required to provide you a Truth-in-Lending statement by the time of loan consummation which disclosed the annual percentage rate or effective interest rate which you will pay on your mortgage loan. This rate may be higher than the contract interest rate because the latter includes only interest, while the annual percentage rate includes discount points, fees, and financing charges and certain other charges besides on the loan. The Truth-in-Lending statement will also disclose any additional charges for prepayment should you pay off the remaining balance of the mortgage before it is due.

Lenders are not required to provide you a Truth-in-Lending disclosure at the time of loan application, when the good faith estimate of settlement of costs and this informational booklet are given to you. However, since the annual percentage rate the lender will be charging you is an important item of information which you can use as you shop for services, you may want to request its disclosure at time of loan application.

PROTECTION AGAINST UNFAIR PRACTICES

A principal finding of Congress of the Real Estate Settlement Procedures Acts of 1974 is that consumers need protection from "... unnecessarily high settlement charges caused by certain abusive practices that have developed in some areas of the country." The potential problems discussed below may not be applicable to most loan settlements, and the discussion is not intended to deter you from buying a home. Most professionals in the settlement business will give you good service. Nevertheless, you may save yourself money and worry by keeping the following considerations in mind:

Kickbacks. Kickbacks and referrals of business for gain are often tied together. The law prohibits anyone from giving or taking a fee, kickback, or anything of value under an agreement that business will be referred to a specific person or organization. It is also illegal to charge or accept a fee or part of a fee where no service has actually been performed. This requirement does not prevent agents for lenders and title companies, attorneys, or others actually performing a service in connection with the mortgage loan or settlement transaction, from receiving compensation for their work. It also does not prohibit payments pursuant to cooperative brokerage, such as a multiple listing service, and referral arrangements or agreements between real estate agents and brokers.

The prohibition is aimed primarily at eliminating the kind of arrangement in which one party agrees to return part of his fee in order to obtain business from the referring party. The danger is that some settlement fees can be inflated to cover payments to this additional party, resulting in a higher total cost to you. There are criminal penalties of both fine and imprisonment for any violation of these provisions of law. There are also provisions for you to recover three times the amount of the kickback, rebate, or referral fee involved, through a private lawsuit. In any successful action to enforce your right, the court may award you court costs together with a fee for your attorney.

Title Companies. Under the law, the seller may not require, as a condition of sale, that title insurance be purchased by the buyer from any particular title company. A violation of this will make the seller liable to you in an amount equal to three times all charges made for the title insurance.

Fair Credit Reporting. There are credit reporting agencies around the nation which are in the business of compiling credit reports on citizens, covering data such as how you pay your bills, if you have been sued, arrested, filed for bankruptcy, etc. In addition, this file may include your neighbors' and friends' views of your character, general reputation, or manner of living. This latter information is referred to as an "investigative consumer report."

The Fair Credit Reporting Act does not give you the right to inspect or physically handle your actual report at the credit reporting agency, nor to receive an exact copy of the report. But you are entitled to a summary of the report, showing the nature, substance, and sources of the information it contains.

If the terms of your financing have been adversely affected by the credit report, you have the right to inspect the summary of that report free of charge (there may otherwise be a small fee). The accuracy of the report can also be challenged, and corrections required to be made. For more detailed information on your credit report rights, contact the Federal Trade Commission (FTC) in Washington, D.C. or the nearest FTC regional office. *The FTC Buyers Guide No. 7: Fair Credit Reporting Act* is a good summary of this Act.

EQUAL CREDIT OPPORTUNITY

The Equal Credit Opportunity Act prohibits lenders from discriminating against credit applicants on the basis of race, color, religion, national origin, sex, marital status, age (provided that the applicant has the capacity to enter into a binding contract), because all or part of the applicant's income derives from any public assistance program, or because the applicant has in good faith exercised any right under the Consumer Credit Protection Act. If you feel you have been discriminated against by any lender, you may have a private right of legal action against that lender and you may wish to consult an attorney; or you may wish to consult the Federal agency that administers complaince with this law concerning the lender you suspect has violated your rights thereunder. Inquire of the lender regarding the identity of that agency. You may also contact your regional Federal Reserve Bank about your rights under this Act.

THE RIGHT TO FILE COMPLAINTS

As with any consumer problems, the place to start if you have a complaint is back at the source of the problem (the lender, settlement agent, broker, etc.). If that initial effort brings no satisfaction and you think you have suffered damages through violations of the Real Estate Settlement Procedures Act of 1974, as amended, you may be entitled to bring a civil action in the U.S. District Court for the District in which the property involved is located, or in any other court of competent jurisdiction. This is a matter best determined by your lawyer. Any suit you file under RESPA must be brought within one year from the date of the occurrence of the alleged violation. You may have legal remedies under other State or Federal laws in addition to RESPA.

You should note that RESPA provides for specific legal sanctions only under the provisions which prohibit kickbacks and unearned fees, and which prohibit the seller from requiring the buyer to use a particular title insurer. If you feel you should recover damages for violations of any provision of RESPA, you should consult your lawyer.

Most settlement service providers, particularly lenders, are supervised by some governmental agency at the local, State and/or Federal level. Others are subject to the control of self-policing associations. If you feel a provider of settlement services has violated RESPA, you can address your complaint to the agency or association which has supervisory responsibility over the provider. The supervisory agency for the lending institution is provided on the back cover of this booklet. If the lender has given you this information elsewhere, he is not required to provide it here. For the names of agencies supervising other providers, you will have to check with local and State consumer agencies. You are also encouraged to forward a copy of complaints regarding RESPA violations to the HUD Office of Consumer Affairs and Regulatory Functions, which has the primary responsibility for administering the RESPA program. Your complaints can lay the foundation for future legislative or administrative actions.

Send copies of complaints, and inquiries, to:

Assistant Secretary for Consumer Affairs and Regulatory Functions
Attention: RESPA Office
U.S. Department of Housing and Urban Development
451 7th Street, S.W.
Room 4100
Washington, D.C. 20410

The Homebuyer's Obligations (Repayment of Loan and Maintenance of Home)

At settlement you will sign papers legally obligating you to pay the mortgage loan financing the purchase of your home. You must pay according to the terms of the loan — interest rate, amount and due date of each monthly payment, repayment period — specified in the documents signed by you. You will probably sign at settlement a note or bond which is your promise to repay the loan for the unpaid balance of the purchase price. You will also sign a mortgage or deed of trust which pledges your home as security for repayment of the loan.

Failure to make monthly mortgage payments on time may lead to a late payment charge, if provided for in the documents. If you default on the loan by missing payments altogether and do not make them up within a period of time usually set by State law, the documents also specify certain actions which the lender may take to recover the amount owed. Ultimately, after required notice to you, a default could lead to foreclosure and sale of the home which secures your loan.

You should also be careful to maintain your home in a proper state of repair, both for your own satisfaction and comfort as the occupant and because the home is security for your loan. The mortgage or deed of trust may in fact specifically obligate you to keep the property in good repair and not allow deterioration.

Read the documents carefully at or before settlement, and be aware of your obligations as a homeowner.

. . . .

Part II

SPECIFIC SETTLEMENT SERVICES

The following defines and discusses each specific settlement service. The numbers correspond to the items listed in Section L of the Uniform Settlement Statement form.

700. SALES/BROKER'S COMMISSION

This is the total dollar amount of sales commission, usually paid by the seller. Fees are usually a percentage of the selling price of the house, and are intended to compensate brokers or salesmen for their services. Custom and/or the negotiated agreement between the seller and the broker determine the amount of the commission.

701-702. Division of Commission

If several brokers or salesmen work together to sell the house, the commission may be split among them. If they are paid from funds collected for settlement, this is shown on lines 701-702.

703. Commission Paid at Settlement

Sometimes the broker will retain the earnest money deposit to apply towards his commission. In this case, line 703 will show only the remainder of the commission which will be paid at settlement.

800. ITEMS PAYABLE IN CONNECTION WITH LOAN

These are the fees which lenders charge to process, approve and make the mortgage loan.

801. Loan Origination

This fee covers the lender's administrative costs in processing the loan. Often expressed as a percentage of the loan, the fee will vary among lenders and from locality to locality. Generally the buyer pays the fee unless another arrangement has been made with the seller and written into the sales contract.

802. Loan Discount

Often called "points," a loan discount is a one-time charge used to adjust the yield on the loan to what market conditions demand. It is used to offset constraints placed on the yield by state or federal regulations. Each "point" is equal to one percent of the mortgage amount. For example, if a lender charges four points on a $30,000 loan this amounts to a charge of $1,200.

803. Appraisal Fee

This charge, which may vary significantly from transaction to transaction, pays for a statement of property value for the lender, made by an independent appraiser or by a member of the lender's staff. The lender needs to know if the value of the property is sufficient to secure the loan if you fail to repay the loan according to the provision of your mortgage contract, and the lender must foreclose and take title to the house. The appraiser inspects the house and the neighborhood, and considers sales prices of comparable houses and other factors in determining the value. The appraisal report may contain photos and other information of value to you. It will provide the factual data upon which the appraiser based the appraised value. Ask the lender for a copy of the appraisal report or review the original.

The appraisal fee may be paid by either the buyer or the seller, as agreed in the sales contract. In some cases this fee is included in the Mortgage Insurance Application Fee. See line 806.

804. Credit Report Fee

This fee covers the cost of the credit report, which shows how you have handled other credit transactions. The lender uses this report in conjunction with information you submitted with the application reguarding your income, outstanding bills, and employment, to determine whether you are an acceptable credit risk and to help determine how much money to lend you.

Where you encounter credit reporting problems you have protections under the Fair Credit laws as summarized under "Homebuyer's Rights" in this booklet.

805. Lender's Inspection Fee

This charge covers inspections, often of newly constructed housing, made by personnel of the lending institution or an outside inspector. (Pest or other inspections made by companies other than the lender are discussed in connection with line 1302).

806. Mortgage Insurance Application Fee

This fee covers processing the application for private mortgage insurance which may be required on certain loans. It may cover both the appraisal and application fee.

807. Assumption Fee

This fee is charged for processing papers for cases in which the buyer takes over payments on the prior loan of the seller.

900. ITEMS REQUIRED BY LENDER TO BE PAID IN ADVANCE

You may be required to prepay certain items, such as interest, mortgage insurance premium and hazard insurance premium, at the time of settlement.

901. Interest

Lenders usually require that borrowers pay at settlement the interest that accrues on the mortgage from the date of settlement to the beginning of the period covered by the first monthly payment. For example, suppose your settlement takes place on April 16, and your first regular monthly payment will be due June 1, to cover interest charges for the month of May. On the settlement date, the lender will collect interest for the period from April 16 to May 1. If you borrowed $30,000 at 9% interest, the interest item would be $112.50. This amount will be entered on line 901.

902. Mortgage Insurance Premium

Mortgage insurance protects the lender from loss due to payment default by the homeowner. The lender may require you to pay your first premium in advance, on the day of settlement. The premium may cover a specific number of months or a year in advance. With this insurance protection, the lender is willing to make a larger loan, thus reducing your downpayment requirements. This type of insurance should not be confused with mortgage life, credit life, or disability insurance designed to pay off a mortgage in the event of physical disability or death of the borrower.

903. Hazard Insurance Premium

This premium prepayment is for insurance protection for you and the lender against loss due to fire, windstorm, and natural hazards. This coverage may be included in a Homeowners Policy which insures against additional risks which may include personal liability and theft. Lenders often require payment of the first year's premium at settlement.

A hazard insurance or homeowner's policy may not protect you against loss caused by flooding. In special flood-prone areas identified by HUD, you may be required by federal law to carry flood insurance on your home. Such insurance may be purchased at low federally subsidized rates in participating communities under the National Flood Insurance Act.

1000. RESERVES DEPOSITED WITH LENDERS

Reserves (sometimes called "escrow" or "impound" accounts) are funds held in an account by the lender to assure future payment for such recurring items as real estate taxes and hazard insurance.

You will probably have to pay an initial amount for each of these items to start the reserve account at the time of settlement. A portion of your regular monthly payments will be added to the reserve account. RESPA places limitations on the amount of reserve funds which may be required by the lender. Read "Reserve Accounts" in this booklet for reserve calculation procedures. Do not hesitate to ask the lender to explain any variance between your own calculations and the figure presented to you.

1001. Hazard Insurance

The lender determines the amount of money that must be placed in the reserve in order to pay the next insurance premium when due.

1002. Mortgage Insurance

The lender may require that part of the total annual premium be placed in the reserve account at settlement. The portion to be received in reserve may be negotiable.

1003-1004. City/County Property Taxes

The lender may require a regular monthly payment to the reserve account for property taxes.

1005. Annual Assessments

This reserve item covers assessments that may be imposed by subdivisions or municipalities for special improvements (such as sidewalks, sewers or paving) or fees (such as homeowners association fees).

1100. TITLE CHARGES

Title charges may cover a variety of services performed by the lender or others for handling and supervising the settlement transaction and services related thereto. The specific charges discussed in connection with lines 1101 through 1109 are those most frequently incurred at settlement. Due to the great diversity in practice from area to area, your particular settlement may not include all these items or may include others not listed. Ask your settlement agent to explain how these fees relate to services performed on your behalf. An extended discusssion is presented on "Securing Title Services" earlier in this booklet.

1101. Settlement or Closing Fee

This fee is paid to the settlement agent. Responsibility for payment of this fee should be negotiated between the seller and buyer, at the time the sales contract is signed.

1102-1104. Abstract or Title Search, Title Examination, Title Insurance Binder

These charges cover the costs of the search and examination of records of previous ownership, transfers, etc., to determine whether the seller can convey clear title to the property, and to disclose any matters on record that could adversely affect the buyer or the lender. Examples of title problems are unpaid mortgages, judgment or tax liens, conveyances of mineral rights, leases, and power line easements or road right-of-ways that could limit use and enjoyment of the real estate. In some areas, a title insurance binder is called a commitment to insure.

1105. Document Preparation

There may be a separate document fee that covers preparation of final legal papers, such as a mortgage, deed of trust, note, or deed. You should check to see that these services, if charged for, are not also covered under some other service fees, ask the settlement agent.

1106. Notary Fee

This fee is charged for the cost of having a licensed person affix his or her name and seal to various documents authenticating the execution of these documents by the parties.

1107. Attorney's Fees

You may be required to pay for legal services provided to the lender in connection with the settlement, such as examination of the title binder or sales contract. Occasionally this fee can be shared with the seller, if so stipulated in the sales contract. If a lawyer's involvement is required by the lender, the fee will appear on this part of the form. The buyer and seller may each retain an attorney to check the various documents and to represent them at all stages of the transaction including settlement. Where this service is not required and is paid for outside of closing, the person conducting settlement is not obligated to record the fee on the settlement form.

1108. Title Insurance

The total cost of owner's and lender's title insurance is shown here. The borrower may pay all, a part or none of this cost depending on the terms of the sales contract or local custom.

1109. Lender's Title Insurance

A one-time premium may be charged at settlement for a lender's title policy which protects the lender against loss due to problems or defects in connection with the title. The insurance is usually written for the amount of the mortgage loan and covers losses due to defects or problems not identified by title search and examination. In most areas this is customarily paid by the borrower unless the seller agrees in the sales contract to pay part or all of it.

1110. Owner's Title Insurance

This charge is for owner's title insurance protection and protects you against losses due to title defects. In some areas it is customary for the seller to provide the buyer with an owner's policy and for the seller to pay for this policy. In other areas, if the buyer desires an owner's policy he must pay for it.

1200. GOVERNMENT RECORDING AND TRANSFER CHARGES

These fees may be paid either by borrower or seller, depending upon your contract when you buy the house or accept the loan commitment. The borrower usually pays the fees for legally recording the new deed and mortgage (item 1201). These fees, collected when property changes hands or when a mortgage loan is made, may be quite large and are set by state and/or local governments. City, county and/or state tax stamps may have to be purchased as well (item 1201 and 1203).

1300. ADDITIONAL SETTLEMENT CHARGES

1301. Survey

The lender or the title insurance company may require that a surveyor conduct a property survey to determine the exact location of the house and the lot line, as well as easements and rights of way. This is a protection to the buyer as well. Usually the buyer pays the surveyor's fees, but sometimes this may be handled by the seller.

1302. Pest and Other Inspections

This fee is to cover inspections for termite or other pest infestation of the house. This may be important if the sales contract included a promise by the seller to transfer the property free from pests or pest-caused damage. Be sure that the inspection shows that the property complies with the sales contract before you complete the settlement. If it does not you may wish to require a bond or other financial assurance that the work will be completed. This fee can be paid either by the borrower or seller depending upon the terms of the sales contract. Lenders vary in their requirements as to such an inspection.

Fees for other inspections, such as for structural soundness, are entered on line 1303.

1400. TOTAL SETTLEMENT CHARGES

All the fees in the borrower's column entitled "Paid from Borrower's Funds at Settlement" are totaled here and transferred to line 103 of Section J, "Settlement charges to borrower" in the *Summary of Borrower's Transaction* on page 1 of the Uniform Settlement Statement. All the settlement fees paid by the seller are transferred to line 502 of Section K, *Summary of Seller's Transaction* on page 1 of the Uniform Settlement Statement.

COMPARING LENDER COSTS

If a lender is willing to reduce his fees for such items as loan origination, discount points and other one-time settlement charges, he may gain it back if he charges a higher mortgage interest rate.

Here is one rule of thumb which you can use to calculate the combined effect of the interest rate on your loan and the one-time settlement charges (paid by you) such as "points." While not perfectly accurate, it is usually close enough for meaningful comparisons between lenders. The rule is, that one-time settlement charges equalling one percent of the loan amount increase the interest charge by one-eighth ($^1/_8$) of one percent. The $^1/_8$ factor corresponds to pay a back period of approximately 15 years. If you intend instead to hold the property for only five years and pay off the loan at that time, the factor increases to $^1/_4$.

Here is an example of the rule. Consider only those charges that differ between lenders. Suppose you wish to borrow $30,000. Lender A will make the loan at 8.5 percent interest, but charges a two percent origination fee, a $150.00 application fee, and requires that you use a lawyer, for title work, selected by the lender at a fee of $300.

Lender B will make the loan at 9 percent interest, but has no additional requirements or charges. As part of that nine percent interest, though, Lender B will not charge an application fee and will absorb the lawyer's fee. What are the actual charges for each case?

Begin by relating all of Lender A's one-time charges to percentages of the $30,000 loan amount:

2 percent origination fee	= 2 percent of loan amount
$150 application fee	= 0.5 percent of loan amount
$300 lawyer's fee	= 1 percent of loan amount
Total	= 3.5 percent of loan amount

Since each 1 percent of the loan amount in charges is the equivalent of $^1/_8$ percent increase in interest, the effective interest rate from Lender A is the quoted or "contract" interest rate, 8.5 percent plus .44 percent (3.5 times $^1/_8$), or a total of 8.94 percent interest. Since Lender B has offered a nine percent interest rate, Lender A has made a more attractive offer. Of course, it is more attractive only if you have sufficient cash to pay Lender A's one-time charges and still cover your downpayment, moving expenses, and other settlement costs. This is simply a method to compare diverse costs on an equal basis. In the above illustration, Lender A does not receive the $300 lawyer fee.

The calculation is sensitive to your assumption about the period of time you plan to own the house before paying off the mortgage. As indicated above, the factor increases to $^1/_4$ if you expect to pay off the mortgage in five years. Applying this new factor to the above illustration, the effective interest rate for Lender A would be 8.5 percent plus .87 (3.5 x $^1/_4$) for a total of 9.37 percent interest. Lender A's offer is no longer more attractive than Lender B's which was 9.0 percent.

In doing these calculations you should also be careful as to which one time fees you place into the calculation. For example, if Lender B in the above illustration did not include in his charge a legal fee but told you that you had to secure legal services in order to obtain the loan from him, you would have to add to Lender B's interest rate the legal fee that you had to incur.

You can use this method to compare the effective interest rates of any number of lenders as you shop for a loan. If the lenders have provided Truth-in-Lending disclosures, these are even a better comparative tool. You should question lenders carefully to make sure you have learned of all the charges they intend to make. The good faith estimate you receive when you make a loan application is a good checklist for this information, but it is not precise. Thus, you should ask the lender how the charges and fees are computed.

B. CREDIT EVALUATION

JOHNSON, SIX C'S OF CREDIT RISK EVALUATION, Speech Delivered to the Wisconsin Bankers' Association, November 1974*

In the evaluation of a credit risk all of us may have our own approach to screening and eventually deciding that a credit, either secured or unsecured, is proper. Under this heading are a number of statements which should be read together in terms of approving loans.

The most traditional approach to the initial credit decision evolves from the six "C's" of credit and "P" for purpose. Any loan decision may be analyzed and reached through these:

1. CHARACTER — This is the most important ingredient in a credit decision. Does the applicant have good character? A synonym for character is reputation. You can imagine all of the things that help determine a person's character; such as being a community leader or in a position of trust, the lack of a criminal record, absence of judgments, apparent absence of marital difficulties, etc., etc. J. P. Morgan, the New York financier, once said, "I wouldn't loan a dollar to a man with all the bonds in Christendom as collateral if he didn't have good character."

2. CAPACITY — Capacity refers to the ability of an individual to repay a loan — out of income or profits. If the capacity to make payments on the agreed upon method is missing, a loan should be rejected even though the collateral might be excellent. So-called "money safe" or collateral loans without a source of repayment are best avoided. Better the prospective borrower liquidate his own assets and raise his own funds.

3. CAPITAL — A major ingredient of lending is the resources available to an individual (his net worth) to meet his obligations if for any reason his source of payment (capacity) fails. People with many debts and few assets lack capital which should raise warning flags in a loan officer's mind.

4. COLLATERAL — While character, capacity, and capital are the most important ingredients in a credit decision, prudent lenders frequently require collateral to back up their judgment of a credit risk. Borrowers with assets should not be reluctant to pledge them as collateral, for a failure to willingly do so may indicate that the Borrower, given hard times, might dissipate those assets in some other way. An analogy to collateral is the use of guarantees, principally in the business borrowing field, placing an owner's personal confidence in his business activities alongside of the Bank's credit judgment.

5. CONDITIONS — Any Banker who makes loans without an eye on the condition of the economy, conditions or place of a loan applicant's employment, or what have you, is making a terrible mistake. Lending during conditions of recession or depression must be restricted as employment rates lessen and times become more difficult.

6. COMPLIANCE — Bankers must now live with, among others: Truth-in-Lending Act, Wisconsin Consumer Act, Equal Credit Opportunity Act, Fair Housing Act, Fair Credit Reporting Act, Community Reinvestment Act, and Real Estate Settlement Procedures Act. A compliance failure could

---

* The material in Mr. O. K. Johnson's speech was used before the Wisconsin Bankers' Association in a seminar on problem loans in November 1974 and later used in a speech to Marquette University Law School. Mr. Johnson is Senior Vice President of the Milwaukee Western Bank, Milwaukee, Wisconsin. He claims no originality in these materials for they are standard in the credit investigation fields in several different forms.

not only affect the collectibility of a loan, but a bank's expansion or branching plans.

7. PURPOSE — The purpose for borrowing is most important. An individual who wishes to borrow money to take an ocean cruise is perhaps not borrowing for as wise a purpose as someone who might decide to buy a second car so that his wife may drive to and from a job. An individual who wishes to borrow money to take Judo lessons may not be borrowing for as good a purpose as improving a home which shelters his family. In other words, look at the purpose for borrowing in terms of all you know about life and the sensibilities of certain actions.

Not mentioned above is the use of GOOD JUDGMENT and COMMON SENSE. Put yourself in the position of the borrower and use your brains and experience to determine if, under the circumstances, the loan really serves a useful purpose, and whether making it flies in the face of common sense and reason. Or to put it another way — if the loan goes sour can I defend my judgment in making it, or were the danger signs there all the time?

There are some specific do's and don'ts which past experience has proven correct for credit evaluation. Loans to be considered must also qualify according to these standards:

1. Those applicants with a poor paying history are not to be considered either with a co-signer or collateral. These are not loans — they are collection problems as soon as they are made. We are not a cashiering office for collateral and should not want to ask a guarantor to pay for an obligation from which he never benefited.

2. The motivation for prompt repayment is directly related to equity in a given product and/or moral responsibility of the individual and his ability to repay.

3. *It is the responsibility of the bank officer considering the loan request, not the applicant, to determine the applicant's financial ability to repay.* Many customers are impulse buyers who think in terms of meeting payments for several months, but have no real sense of financial planning into the future. We are not a social service agency and must learn to give a prompt honest NO to poor credits.

The Following Fundamentals Can Be Related to Any Loan:

1. Extend credit only to borrowers with unquestioned integrity.

2. There are men in business today, even borrowers, whose word is as good as their bond.

3. Be sure that there is a primary source of payment for every bank credit; then see that there is an alternative source of payment.

4. Avoid money-good loans that do not have a program for payment. They are not liquid. Time spent in collection nullifies the profit and is time lost from development of worthwhile business.

5. A formal loan agreement does not collect the term loan. Keep such documents as simple and as effective as possible. Depend basically on standard banking forms and procedures. The purpose of such documents is to permit renegotiation or even acceleration in the event credit conditions deteriorate during the term of the loan. A *profits recapture clause over and above instalment payments is very desirable.*

6. In extending bank credit, exert skill and knowledge. See the borrower's side; know every feature of the bank lender's side.

7. In judging a credit, reduce it to its simplest factors. Get at the fundamentals of the transaction, no matter how complex.

8. The minimum 30 days annual cleanup (without recourse to other lenders or the extension of accounts payable) is still a good test of liquidity. Longer than 30 days is even more desirable.

9. Never finance a transaction 100%. The borrower must have some of his own capital at risk.

10. We must have the best possible deposit account. Commensurate balances are vital; activity review gives clues to business health of the borrower; and there is possibility of offset if necessary.

11. Be thoroughly prepared for interest rate discussions.

12. Let's set and record our objectives in every case; then we must not permit the objectives to get buried in the credit file and lost at the time of renewal.

13. We should consider carefully what our competition could or would do, but we must not let the competitive threat lead us into low-quality loans.

1. FINANCIAL ANALYSIS

Obtaining mortgage financing may be the key to investment packaging. An understanding by the investor of the lender's psychology in the evaluation procedure is essential in selling the loan package to the lender.

In determining whether the real estate investment is saleable to the lender for mortgage financing, the investor should consider:

1. Location of Subject Property
   a. Protection against inharmonious uses
   b. Demand generators
   c. Accessibility of public transportation
   d. Neighborhood patterns
   e. Physical and social attractiveness
   f. Relative marketability
2. Property Characteristics
   a. Visual appearance
   b. Age and structural quality of improvements
   c. Livability — amenities
   d. Suitability of mechanical components
   e. Deferred maintenance, obsolescence and/or replacement potential
   f. Adjustment for non-conformity
3. Rentability-Income Expectancy of Project
   a. Renter profile
   b. Stability, durability and quality of income
   c. Survey of competition
      i.   Rent level comparables
      ii. Vacancy rates
      iii. New projects planned
4. The investor's credit history
5. The investor's stake in ownership
6. Stability of investor's earned income
7. The investor's assets-liabilities (financial statement)
8. The ratio of the debt service, *i.e.*, mortgage, to the net operating income of the subject property

Lenders who finance investment real estate projects are concerned with the relationship between Net Operating Income (NOI) and Annual Debt Service (ADS). This first line of protection for a loan is the income stream, for it is from the income stream that the lender will receive both interest on the loan and periodic principal payments. Lenders typically specify coverage ratios for Annual Debt Service. Such factor can be expressed as follows:

$$\text{Debt Coverage Ratio} = \frac{\text{Net Operating Income (NOI)}}{\text{Annual Debt Service (ADS)}}$$

Lenders will commonly require debt coverage factors in the range of 1.2 to 1.4 as a safety margin in case NOI fails to meet expectations. For example, the lender may require that NOI be 1.25 x ADS. Alternatively stated, the lender is requiring a 20% margin between NOI and ADS. For example, a property valued at $100,000 produces an NOI of $10,000. If the lender requires that there must be a 12% margin (ADS cannot exceed 88% of NOI), the coverage ratio would be expressed:

$$\frac{100}{88} = 1.14 \text{ debt coverage ratio}$$

In either case, the margin of safety is found by the extent to which NOI could drop (in this example, by 12%) and still have adequate coverage to meet the ADS requirements. If the NOI is highly stable and can be forecast with a high degree of accuracy with respect to the size, timing and duration of the NOI, the lender should require a smaller margin between NOI and ADS.

2. RESIDENTIAL INCOME-EXPENSE RATIOS

When the lending community speaks of a housing expense to income ratio, in essence it is analyzing the ratio between the monthly out-of-pocket costs for continued ownership of the home in comparison to the income generated by the prospective homeowner. Many lenders as a rule require that the monthly housing payment be no greater than 25% to 35% of the prospective homeowner's monthly income. For example, an applicant wishes to purchase a home and requests a loan of $65,000 for 30 years. The mortgage rate is 14% and the taxes are $1,800 per year. The fire (homeowners) insurance is $120 per year.

Monthly Principal & Interest	$ 770.17
Property Taxes ($1800 ÷ 12)	150.00
Fire Insurance ($120.00 ÷ 12)	10.00
Monthly payment	$ 930.17

$930.17 x 4 = $3,720.63 Monthly income requirement
$3720.63 x 12 = $44,648.16 Annual income requirement

To simplify the calculation you can use a factor. You may multiply the monthly loan payment by the factors below to arrive at the annual income requirement.

20 percent ratio factor is 60
25 percent income ratio factor is 48
30 percent income ratio factor is 40

With the factor, you would multiply $930.17 by 48 and arrive at the same figure or $44,648.16.

An FHA Income Qualifying Statement and the formula therefor follows.

First Bank of Anytown

FHA Income Qualifying Statement

GROSS FAMILY INCOME: _____

Less Federal Withholding   _____

NET EFFECTIVE INCOME: _____

Proposed payment (princi-
pal interest, taxes and
insurance)   _____

Maintenance   _____
Utilities   _____

TOTAL HOUSING EXPENSE: _____

Divide net effective income
into housing expense. (should
not exceed 35%)   _____

Housing Expense   _____
Installment Account
 Payments   _____
Life Insurance   _____
State Withholding   _____
Social Security   _____

TOTAL FIXED PAYMENT: _____

Divide net effective income
into total fixed payment.
(Should not exceed 50%)   _____

NET EFFECTIVE INCOME: _____

LESS TOTAL FIXED PAYMENTS: _____

NET REMAINING INCOME: _____

C. LOAN COMMITMENT

A loan commitment is a promise by a lender to make a loan at some future date. The loan commitment may contain some or all of the conditions and pre-close requirements as listed below:

a. An appraisal of the present fair market value of the property to be encumbered

b. A certified survey of the property to be encumbered showing all structures and improvements, roads, easements, encroachments and boundary lines

c. A statement of the financial condition showing assets, liabilities, net worth of each borrower and guarantor of the loan

d. Credit report

e. Verification of employment of Borrower

f. Title insurance binder or preliminary report

g. An insurance binder or policy naming lender as an additional insured as its interest may appear (standard mortgage clause)

h. An affidavit from an officer of the municipality in which the real estate is located as to the existence of outstanding taxes, special assessments, planned improvements, installment improvement bonds, real estate taxes, deferred water and sewer charges, health department orders and building code violations

i. Acceptance of transmatic plan or pre-authorized payment plan

j. Truth in Lending Disclosures

k. Information obtained from form UCC-11 given by Secretary of State and Register of Deeds as to financing statement filed affecting personalty located on the real estate to be encumbered

l. A certified, true and complete copy of each easement, encumbrance, limitation or restriction of record affecting the real estate to be encumbered

m. A certified copy from applicable government authority of ordinance establishing zoning classification of property and uses permitted under said zoning classification

n. A copy of all licenses and other permits issued to borrower including a permanent certificate of occupancy confirming that all improvements and their use comply fully with applicable zoning, building and all other governmental laws, rules, regulations and requirements

o. A written opinion of counsel for borrower to the effect that the loan is not usurious or otherwise illegal under applicable law, and that all loan documents are valid and binding upon the borrower and are enforceable in accordance with their terms

p. A written opinion from a registered professional engineer stating that all necessary utilities are available at the property to permit use as contemplated

q. An estoppel certificate and/or pay-off letter from every individual and entity holding a lien on the property to be encumbered

r. A copy of all leases affecting the subject real estate and acceptance by borrower of an assignment of such leases as additional security for the loan

s. A warranty from the borrower that he is presently in full compliance with the provisions of the law prohibiting discrimination in housing on the basis of race, color, creed or national origin, including but not limited to the requirements of Title VIII of the 1968 Civil Rights Act. The mortgage document shall include a covenant to future compliance with such laws during the term of the loan

t. The mortgage will contain a provision requiring the furnishing to the mortgagee of annual operating statements of the mortgaged property, containing reasonable detail as to all forms of income and expense

u. Non-refundable commitment fee

v. Borrower shall pay all expenses in connection with the loan contemplated hereby, including, but not limited to, origination fee, appraisal and survey expense, recording fees and the fees of Lender's counsel

w. The commitment shall not be assignable by Borrower without Lender's written consent

The terms and conditions of a commitment to make a loan are lengthy and might be expected in a large scale development. However, for the usual single family residential purchaser a loan commitment might be as brief as that which follows.

Dear Borrower:

We hereby commit to make you a mortgage loan on the property located at ____(address)____. Said loan shall be in the amount of $_____ amortized over a term of thirty years at an interest rate of ____% (subject to the terms of the interest adjustment provision in the mortgage note) and shall be closed on our Association's documents and governed by the provisions contained therein.

This commitment is also granted subject to satisfactory evidence of title and other related items required for the closing of this transaction and there being no substantial change in the collateral or in your credit status.

This commitment will expire if: (a) the loan to be granted under the terms of this commitment is not closed for any reason whatsoever, within ____ days of the date of this letter, or (b) the loan to be granted under this commitment is closed whereby the terms and conditions of the mortgage and the mortgage note will supersede this commitment.

Thank you for the opportunity of permitting (Name of Lender) to be of service to you.

Sincerely,

_____ Savings and Loan Ass'n

1. FAILURE TO FUND COMMITMENT BY LENDER

PIPKIN v. THOMAS & HILL, INC.

Court of Appeals of North Carolina
33 N.C. App. 710, 236 S.E.2d 725 (1977)

The gravamen of this action is an alleged breach by the defendant, Thomas & Hill, Inc., of its contract to make a permanent loan to the plaintiffs, P.W.D. & W. and its general partners, for the purpose of paying off a construction loan from Central Carolina Bank (CCB) which the plaintiffs had used to build a motel. The trial court, sitting by consent without a jury, found that the defendant made and breached a contract with the plaintiffs. The court entered judgment accordingly, but did not award all the damages which the plaintiffs requested.

In 1972 the plaintiffs, who are experienced businessmen but not experienced real estate developers, undertook to build a motel south of Raleigh. They located a possible site, obtained a satisfactory feasibility study, and then signed a franchise contract with Happy Inns of America. The franchiser introduced the plaintiffs to O. Larry Ward, Assistant Vice President and manager of the North Carolina office of Thomas & Hill, Inc., a mortgage banking company with headquarters in Charleston, West Virginia. As a mortgage banking firm the defendant customarily arranged so-called "permanent" financing for builders by placing the builder's request for a loan with a large lending institution. In other words, the defendant was a broker or "go-between" for builders requiring permanent financing. These permanent loans, if obtained, are used to "take-out"; i. e., pay off, the construction loan which the builder usually obtains from a local lending institution, such as a bank or savings and loan company, for the limited purpose of obtaining labor and materials and building a building. One customary condition of a contract for a construction loan is that the builder obtain a permanent loan "commitment" prior to approval of the construction loan.

Defendant was a mortgage broker and did not make permanent commercial construction loans. It was capitalized for something in excess of one million dollars and had lines-of-credit with lending institutions for several millions more.

The plaintiffs knew of these lines of credit; they did not know that they were limited to use in financing residential construction.

O. Larry Ward had no actual authority to make a permanent loan. In fact, Ward only had the actual authority to solicit loan applications. The defendant's firm policy even prevented Ward from committing his company, defendant, to try to place a permanent loan with a lender. However, the plaintiffs did not know about these restrictions on Ward's authority.

On 19 April 1973 the plaintiffs executed the defendant's application form for a permanent loan of $1,162,500 repayable over twenty-five years at nine and one-half percent interest. The application was signed by each of the individual plaintiffs, and nothing on the application indicated that if the application were accepted the defendant would not be the actual permanent lender. The application said:

Applicant . . . agrees:
18. This application and your [the lender's] written approval of it, when given and accepted, shall constitute the entire agreement for loan. . . .

The application was accompanied by a check for $500 as the agreed upon application fee. This check was not cashed. The application was also accompanied by a letter promising to pay a fee in consideration for the loan in the event a loan commitment was made. O. Larry Ward transmitted this application to the defendant's home office in Charleston. Personnel there attempted to place it with a lender, but they failed. The officers and executives at the defendant's home office were unaware of the events which subsequently transpired in North Carolina between the plaintiffs, their banker at CCB, and O. Larry Ward.

The plaintiffs began negotiations with CCB for a construction loan. They dealt with Scott Edwards, the credit manager at CCB's home office in Durham. On behalf of the plaintiffs, Edwards investigated the defendant's financial position and concluded that defendant was a reputable company and financially capable of making plaintiffs' permanent loan.

On 7 June 1973 O. Larry Ward received word from the defendant that it had not placed the plaintiffs' loan application. Nevertheless, on 11 June 1973, in response to a request from Edwards at CCB for a permanent loan commitment, Ward wrote to Edwards, saying:

Thomas & Hill, Inc., is processing an application for a permanent loan for Mr. P. M. Williams, Mr. D. J. Dudley, Mr. Thomas A. Pipkin, and Mr. MacDonald [sic] Weeks, on the above property.

Please accept this letter as our commitment to fund the permanent loan on or before September 1, 1974, in an amount of $1,162,500.00, as outlined in the loan submission mailed to you May 24, 1973.

Copies of this letter were sent to each of the individual plaintiffs.

Soon thereafter Edwards sent details of the CCB construction loan to Ward and asked him to incorporate them into defendant's commitment. Ward replied in a letter apparently signed by his secretary, saying:

Please accept this letter as our commitment to fund the permanent loan on or before October 1, 1974, in an amount of not less than $1,162,500 as outlined in my loan package submitted to you on May 24, 1973.

Please be further advised that your commitment dated June 26, 1973, for the construction loan is hereby made a part of our commitment to the borrowers and is attached as Exhibit A.

Again, each plaintiff received a copy of this letter.

In a third letter from Ward to Edwards, concerning modifications in CCB's construction loan commitment, Ward agreed to the change and said:

[M]y only concern will be that the borrowers have the necessary fee available to pay for the permanent commitment when same is supplied to them.

In light of Ward's representations to CCB, the bank issued a construction loan to plaintiffs. Of that loan $11,625 was earmarked as the defendant's fee for its permanent loan commitment. At O. Larry Ward's direction the money was held by plaintiffs. In August 1974 an additional $11,625 was added to this amount and the entire fund of $23,250 was placed in escrow for the defendant. The money remains in that account.

In August 1974 the defendant denied any commitment to make a permanent loan. During September the plaintiffs entered negotiations with CCB for an interim loan. On 1 October 1974 CCB accepted a new demand note from the plaintiffs at a floating interest rate of prime plus 2% in replacement for the construction loan. In December 1975 the interest rate was changed to prime plus 3%. Between 1 October 1974 and the time of the trial the plaintiffs paid $184,619.49 in interest on this interim loan; they have paid nothing on the principal. The plaintiffs have been unable to find permanent financing elsewhere.

Evidence indicates that on 1 October 1974 the "going" commercial rate of interest for a long term loan was 10½%. However, little or no money was available in the country for motel financing. In their attempt to find permanent financing the plaintiffs spent $3,000 for broker's fees, $1,025 for accounting fees and $250 for appraisal fees. They also spent $1,613.12 for title insurance in connection with the interim loan from CCB.

The trial court, as the finder of fact, found that O. Larry Ward was an agent of the defendant and had the apparent authority, though not the actual authority, to bind the defendant to make a permanent loan. He further found that Ward made such a contract and that the defendant breached it. Damages were awarded to the plaintiffs equal to the total of the fees and insurance they paid plus the present value of the difference between the interest which the plaintiffs would have paid on the 9½% loan and the interest which they would have paid on 10½% loan had they been able to obtain one. With regard to this final element of damages, the court further reduced it by more than $20,000 in order to adjust for the likelihood of early payment. However, no evidence in the record shows that the plaintiffs intended to make early payment.

Both parties appeal.

ARNOLD, JUDGE.

Defendant's position is that there was no contract, but if there was, plaintiffs were only entitled to nominal damages. Plaintiffs contend that in addition to damages awarded them they were entitled to recover interest paid on the interim loan to CCB. Thus, two questions are presented in this appeal. Was there a contract, and what is the measure of damages?

Defendant contends that it made no contract with the plaintiffs. Principally, it relies on the argument that O. Larry Ward had no authority to bind it to a contract to lend money. All parties agree that Ward lacked actual authority to make such a contract. Whether he had the apparent authority to do so is, however, a question of fact to be answered by the fact finder in light of the evidence. The evidence was mixed, and we cannot say that the court erred in finding that Ward had the apparent authority to make the contract.

The scope of an agent's apparent authority is determined not by the agent's own representations but by the manifestations of authority which the principal accords to him. Restatement (2d) of Agency, § 27 (1958). In a recent decision by our Supreme Court apparent authority was defined as ". . . that authority which the principal has held the agent out as possessing or which he has permitted the agent to represent that he possesses . . . ." *Zimmerman v. Hogg & Allen,* 286 N.C. 24, 31, 209 S.E.2d 795, 799 (1974). An agent with apparent authority can bind his principal to a contract if the other party to the contract does not know that the agent's authority is less than his apparent authority.

In the present case there is evidence that Ward was held out by defendant as its agent with authority to make a loan. Ward's position as an assistant vice president and, later, vice president of the defendant is some evidence of this apparent authority. His position as the manager of the North Carolina branch is even stronger evidence. While assistant officers customarily have little authority, managers in charge of an office usually have all the authority necessary to conduct the business of that office. In a case involving an assistant bank cashier's apparent authority, it was said: "[I]t is immaterial what the person's official position may be if he is actually engaged in the *management* of the bank's interests." *Sears, Roebuck & Co. v. Banking Co.,* 191 N.C. 500, 505, 132 S.E. 468, 471 (1926) (emphasis added).

Other facts indicate that Ward had the apparent authority to bind defendant to a loan commitment. The defendant's letterhead and business cards, which were in evidence, indicated that the company was in the business of making mortgage loans. The letterhead carried the words "Mortgage Financing". The loan application form used by the defendant said nothing which indicated that the defendant limited its service to that of a broker. On the contrary, the application indicated that the defendant was committed to make a loan once it accepted the application in writing. O. Larry Ward was authorized to execute these loan applications, and nothing in the record shows that his authority in this regard was limited to that of a scrivener. This evidence, taken together, is sufficient to support the court's findings, and these findings bind this Court.

Defendant also argues that there is insufficient evidence to support the court's finding that a contract was made. This argument has no merit. The letters sent by O. Larry Ward to Scott Edwards at CCB, copies of which were sent to the individual plaintiffs, constituted written acceptance of the plaintiffs' loan application and established the contract. The contract was supported by consideration, principally, the plaintiffs' promise to pay interest, and, additionally, their payment of a $500 application fee and establishment of an escrow account containing the defendant's fee. Evidence of a contract is ample, and that part of the judgment concluding that defendant entered a contract to loan plaintiffs on or before 1 October 1974, the sum of $1,162,500, is affirmed.

The issue of damages is now examined.

We find only a limited number of decisions in American case law which consider the measure of damages for breach of a contract to lend money. In no case do we find a determination of the question presented by this appeal: what is the measure of damages for breach of a contract to make a permanent loan for a building where the borrower is unable to obtain a new loan at any interest rate to permanently finance the building, but has to continue financing by an interim loan at a fluctuating rate of interest?

The general rule of damages handed down in England in *Hadley v. Baxendale,* 9 Exch. 341 (1854), and followed ever after is that

Where two parties have made a contract which one of them has broken, the damages which the other party ought to receive in respect of such breach of contract should be such as may fairly and reasonably be considered either arising naturally; i.e., according to the usual course of things, from such breach of contract itself, or such as may reasonably be supposed to have been in the contemplation of both parties at the time they made the contract as the probable result of the breach.

In other words, the injured party may recover all of the damages which were *foreseeable* at the time of the contract as a probable result of the breach either because they were a *natural* result or because they were a *contemplated* result of the breach. 5 Corbin on Contracts, § 1007, p. 70 (1964).

Still another rule of damages is that they must be measurable with reasonable certainty, i.e., they must be more than speculative. This rule is not a rigid one, and it usually applies in the contest of a claim to recover expected but unrealized profits, which, allegedly, would have been earned but for the breach. 5 Corbin on Contracts, § 1022, p. 138 (1964). If a breach is such that in the usual course of things it leads to a substantial loss of such a character that the loss cannot be precisely measured, substantial compensatory damages will be awarded even though they cannot be precisely measured. 5 Corbin on Contracts, § 1021, p. 134 (1964). This is fair and reasonable. Damages are more than simple restitution. They are a means of making the injured party as whole as possible by the use of money. Some injuries are nothing more than the loss of a sum certain, and there the injured party is easily made whole. Other injuries involve loss of time, opportunity, special chattel, good will, prospective profits and other things which are difficult to measure in money. The contention that no injury has occurred because the measurement of damages is too difficult is not favored.

These simple rules of *Hadley v. Baxendale, supra,* are basic to the common law, and they are part of the law in North Carolina. *Perkins v. Langdon,* 237 N.C. 159, 74 S.E.2d 634 (1953); *Machine Co. v. Tobacco Co.,* 141 N.C. 284, 53 S.E. 885 (1906). To recover damages for breach of a contract the plaintiff must show that the damages were the natural and probable consequence of the breach, and that they can be calculated with reasonable certainty. *Pike v. Wachovia Bank and Trust Co.,* 274 N.C. 1, 161 S.E.2d 453 (1968). The damages are to be measured at the time of the breach. *Maxwell v. Proctor & Gamble Distributing Co.,* 204 N.C. 309, 168 S.E. 403 (1933). Special damages may also be awarded for injury which occurred after the breach if such an injury was within contemplation of the parties at the time the contract was made. *Perkins v. Langdon, supra.*

Very few decisions in North Carolina have dealt with the breach of a contract to lend money. In *Coles v. Lumber Co.,* 150 N.C. 183, 188, 63 S.E. 736, 739 (1909), it is stated:

The measure of damage for a failure [to lend money as contracted] would be any extra expense to which [the borrower] was put to obtain the money. The failure to perform an agreement to loan a man money, unless some special and consequential damages were shown to be in contemplation of the parties when the contract was made, would not subject [the lender] to speculative damage.

In accord is *Newby v. Realty Co.,* 180 N.C. 51, 103 S.E. 909 (1920), where it was held that the plaintiffs might recover both the money lost and the profits they failed to make when defendant breached the contract to lend them money to acquire an option on land. These two cases are in accord with the general rules already discussed, and they would seem to allow the injured borrower to recover any money spent to make himself whole, including the cost of negotiating a new loan and the difference, if any, between the interest in the original contract and in the new loan, if such costs are a natural or contemplated consequence of the breach.

From decisions throughout the country it can be seen that the difference between the interest at the contract rate and the rate of interest which the borrower, because of the breach, must pay to obtain money is the common measure of damages for breach of a contract to lend money. *Bank v. New Mexico v. Rice,* 78 N.M. 170, 429 P.2d 368 (1967); *Columbian Mut. Life Assur. Soc. v. Whitehead,* 193 Ark. 598, 101 S.W.2d 455 (1937); *F..B. Collins Inv. Co. v. Sallas,* 260 S.W. 261 (Tex.Civ.App., 1924); *Culp v. Western Loan & Building Co.,* 124 Wash. 326, 214 P. 145 (1923); *Shurtleff v. Occidental Building & Loan Ass'n,* 105 Neb. 557, 181 N.W. 374 (1921); *Murphy v. Hanna,* 37 N.D. 156, 164 N.W. 32 (1917); *Hedden v. Schneblin,* 126 Mo.App. 478, 104 S.W. 887 (1907); 5 Corbin on Contracts, § 1078, p. 446 (1964); Restatement of Contracts § 343.

In addition to the difference in interest rates, the injured borrower may recover any other costs of obtaining new financing, plus consequential damages which result from the breach where they were contemplated by the parties at the time of the contract. *Coles v. Lumber Co., supra; Davis v. Small Business Inv. Co. of Houston,* 535 S.W.2d 740 (Tex.Civ.App., 1976); *Bank of New Mexico v. Rice, supra; Zelazny v. Pilgrim Funding Corp.,* 41 Misc.2d 176, 244 N.Y.S.2d 810 (1963); *Dodderidge v. American Trust and Savings Bank,* 98 Ind. App. 334, 189 N.E. 165 (1934); *Hunt v. United Bank & Trust Co.,* 210 Cal. 108, 291 P. 184 (1930); *F. B. Collins Inv. Co. v. Sallas, supra; Culp v. Western Loan & Building Co., supra; Corbin, supra; Restatement of Contracts, supra.*

It has been said that an injured borrower can recover nothing but nominal damages for breach of a contract to lend money, because, in contemplation of law, there is always money available in the marketplace. *Lowe v. Turpie,* 147 Ind. 652, 44 N.E. 25, 47 N.E. 150 (1896). Not every injury resulting from a breach of contract to lend money can be made whole by money, but the holdings of such old, uncommon cases are ill-reasoned, unjust, and they should be rejected. *See* 5 Corbin on Contracts, § 1078, pp. 447-448 (1964). In the increasingly complex world of business and economics money is a commodity which not only becomes scarce but unavailable to particular would be borrowers. A lender who, with knowledge of the borrower's purpose for acquiring the loan, contracts to lend the money, and then reneges, should reasonably be able to foresee the injury caused by his breach. In the case at bar, but for the lender's commitment to lend the money the borrowers would have acquired another commitment, or else they would not have proceeded with their project. It is natural and foreseeable that the borrower may have to pay new fees and higher interest for refinancing. It is likewise within the contemplation of the lender, where the lender knew the borrower's purpose for acquiring the loan, that future loans for such purposes may become unavailable in the money market. A lender who breaches a contract to lend money is liable for all the foreseeable damages, both natural and contemplated, which proximately arise from the breach.

The plaintiffs, in the case at bar, clearly have been injured by defendant's breach. They have been forced to negotiate an interim loan with CCB at a high interest rate, and they have been forced to attempt to negotiate for a new permanent loan, incurring expenses they would not have incurred but for the breach. They were forced into a different, and unfavorable, money market where the commercial rate of interest, at the time of the breach, was 10½ percent instead of the contract rate of 9½ percent, and, more importantly, they were unable to obtain money for permanent financing of their motel.

The trial court correctly ruled that plaintiffs were entitled to recover: (1) the cost of additional title insurance; (2) the cost of additional brokers' fees; (3) the cost of additional accounting fees; (4) and the cost of additional accounting fees. All of these were foreseeable expenses which, but for the breach, plaintiffs would not have incurred.

With respect to the remaining damages the proper measure is the interest calculated at 10½% for 25 years from the date of trial, less the interest calculated at 9½% for 25 years from 1 October 1974, which but for the breach the plaintiffs would have had to pay. This difference must then be discounted to its present cash value as of the time of trial.

The basic measure of damages here is the difference between the rate of interest during the agreed time of credit (twenty-five years in the case at bar) as specified in the contract, and the rate of interest generally available to borrowers on the date of the breach. See, *Hedden v. Schneblin, supra;* 36 A.L.R. 1408, 1411 (1925). The purpose of awarding money damages for any injury is to try to put the injured party in as good a position as if the injury had not occurred. Obviously this cannot be done with mathematical certainty, but in all fairness the difficulty in measuring damages should not bar recovery.

Applying the principle that a lender who breaches a contract to lend money is liable for all the foreseeable damages, both natural and contemplated, which proximately arise from the breach, the trial court also should have allowed recovery for interest plaintiffs had to pay to CCB on the interim loan after defendant's breach. This interest was part of the cost of negotiating new financing. It was foreseeable, and but for the breach it would not have occurred.

Finally, the trial court found that there was a likelihood of prepayment of the permanent loan by plaintiffs and made an additional reduction, or discount, for the likelihood of prepayment. This portion of the judgment cannot be sustained and is stricken. While there is evidence to indicate that prepayment is common there is no evidence that plaintiffs contemplated early payment.

This case is remanded to Superior Court of Wake County for entry of judgment in accordance with this opinion.

Affirmed in part.

Modified in part and remanded.

MORRIS and HEDRICK, JJ., concur.

According to the case of *Pipkin v. Thomas & Hill, Inc.,* 236 S.E.2d 725 (N.C. App. 1977), a lender who breaches the providing of a loan commitment will be required to pay damages to the borrower to the extent of: (i) the difference between the interest at the contract rate and the rate of interest the borrower must pay on the open market; (ii) any of the costs of obtaining new financing; and (iii) any other consequential damages contemplated by the parties at the time of the loan commitment.

In the *Pipkin* case, the commitment to the borrower had been for a loan at 9.5% interest for a 25 year amortization. The Court found that the commercial interest rate at the time of the breach was 10.5%. Therefore, the Court concluded that Pipkin should receive as damages: (i) the discounted present value of 1% per year on the outstanding loan principal for 25 years; (ii) the additional interest paid to the construction lender on the interim loan following the lender's breach, presumably for a time sufficient to permit Pipkin to find permanent financing; (iii) the additional expenses for title insurance, broker's fees, accounting costs, appraisals made necessary for the need to find new financing. *See also Gonis v. New York Life Insurance Co.*, 70 Wis. 2d 950 (1975).

2. NON-REFUNDABLE COMMITMENT FEE

The lender will normally require the borrower to pay a commitment fee. The purpose of the commitment fee is to compensate the lender for the opportunity cost and administrative burden of underwriting the loan and holding the funds available for the borrower's use. What results when the borrower has paid a commitment fee which the lender deems to be non-refundable and the borrower obtains his financing elsewhere? The Courts have consistently rejected the borrower's attempt to recoup the fee and have held that the lender is entitled to the commitment fee either as liquidated damages for breach of contract or as compensation for holding money available for the loan for the borrower.

WHITE LAKES SHOPPING CENTER, INC. v. JEFFERSON STANDARD LIFE INSURANCE CO.

Supreme Court of Kansas
208 Kan. 121, 490 P.2d 609 (1971)

FROMME, JUSTICE:

White Lakes Shopping Center, Inc. (appellant) brought this action in the district court to recover $77,000 which it had paid Jefferson Standard Life Insurance Company (appellee) in connection with a $3,850,000 written loan commitment agreement. The claim was denied in the trial court and this appeal followed. A brief recitation of background facts is necessary.

White Lakes desired to build a modern shopping center in Topeka, Kansas. White Lakes approached a mortgage brokerage company, Kansas City Mortgage Company, to locate financing. The brokerage company found that Jefferson Standard was interested in making a loan for construction of the shopping center. White Lakes then submitted a loan application to Jefferson Standard asking for $4,000,000 in "end financing." (We are advised the term "end financing" denotes the long term mortgage loan to be given on completion of construction as distinguished from interim or temporary financing used to make payments as construction progresses.) After a personal investigation of the project planned, Jefferson Standard prepared and submitted to White Lakes the first written loan commitment for $3,500,000 on September 5, 1963. The commitment agreement obligated Jefferson Standard to make the $3,500,000 loan to White Lakes on completion of the project on or before May 31, 1965.

The loan for "end financing" guaranteed by the commitment agreement was to be secured by a first mortgage on the completed shopping center property. The mortgage was to extend for a term of 22 years. Interest under the mortgage was to be paid at a rate of 5.75 percent per annum. The commitment agreement contained a provision for an advance payment by White Lakes to Jefferson Standard which payment is the subject of the present action. The payment was made and the commitment agreement was accepted and signed by White Lakes. At the request of White Lakes the amount of the commitment was increased on two occasions. Separate commitment agreements covering the increases were executed. These contained a similar binder provision requiring additional advance payments.

A total of $77,000 was paid to Jefferson Standard under the provision common to all three commitment agreements. This provision for advance payment reads:

. . . Upon the loan being closed this $77,000 deposit is to be refunded promptly; but if the loan is not closed in accordance with the terms of this alternate commitment, the $77,000 deposit is to be retained permanently by the Jefferson Standard Life Insurance Company as liquidated damages. . . .

In passing, we note the trial court held that the loan commitment agreement was complete and unambiguous. We agree. Appellant fails to point to any specific provisions to the contrary.

The final commitment agreement for $3,850,000 was dated June 29, 1964, and accepted by White Lakes on July 9, 1964. Jefferson Standard refused further requests to increase the amount of the commitment. Shortly thereafter White Lakes, through the mortgage brokerage company, located another life insurance company which eventually furnished "end financing" of $4,250,000 for the shopping center. White Lakes now sues to recover the $77,000 paid to Jefferson Standard under the loan commitment agreement.

White Lakes filed the action making two claims in separate counts of the petition. The claim in count one is based upon a contention that the provision for payment of the $77,000 was a penalty provision rather than a provision for liquidated damages and that the amount paid should be returned to them. The claim in count two is based upon a contention that the $77,000 was paid under an agreement with Jefferson Standard to meet the "ultimate necessary financing as would be required" by White Lakes and that Jefferson Standard's refusal to do so entitled White Lakes to a return of the money under a theory of unjust enrichment arising from an impossibility of performance.

After the discovery of evidence had been completed by both parties Jefferson Standard filed a motion for summary judgment against count two of the petition. The motion was sustained. Error is claimed thereon.

In entering summary judgment against White Lakes on count two the trial court found, (1) there was no evidence discovered tending to support a promise to loan an amount sufficient to meet the ultimate financial needs of White Lakes to complete the project, (2) that any evidence to support such a promise would be inadmissible under the parol evidence rule as tending to change the terms of the unambiguous written agreement, (3) that there was no evidence discovered to support any legal theory of impossibility of performance, and (4) there was no genuine issue as to any material fact and that appellee was entitled to judgment as a matter of law on count two of the petition.

These findings and the judgment as to count two are supported by the record. The written loan commitment agreement is complete, unambiguous and free from uncertainty. A written contract which is complete, unambiguous and free from uncertainty cannot be varied or changed by parol evidence of prior or contemporaneous agreements or understandings in the absence of fraud. (*Williams v. Safeway Stores, Inc.,* 198 Kan. 331, 338, 424 P.2d 541.) When no fraud is alleged and a contract is complete and unambiguous, evidence of negotiations which culminated in a written contract is not admissible for the purpose of varying the terms of the written contract. (*Edwards v. Phillips Petroleum Co.,* 187 Kan. 656, 360 P.2d 23.)

Impossibility of performance, recognized in the law as a basis for relief from contractual obligations, is not of the nature contended for by appellant. When one agrees to perform an act possible in itself he will be liable for a breach thereof although contingencies not foreseen by him arise which make it difficult, or even beyond his power, to perform and which might have been foreseen and provided against in the contract.

The impossibility which will, or may, excuse the performance of a contract must exist in the nature of the thing to be done. It must not exist merely because of the inability or incapacity of the promisor or obligor to do it. (17A C.J.S. Contracts § 463(1), p. 610; 17 Am.Jur.2d, Contracts, § 506, p. 987; *State Highway Construction Contract Cases,* 161 Kan. 7, 166 P.2d 728; *Winfrey v. Galena Automobile Co.,* 113 Kan. 343, Syl. 4, 214 P. 781.)

In *Winfrey v. Galena Automobile Co.,* supra, it was said:

> Where one agrees to perform an act possible in itself, he will be liable for a breach thereof although contingencies not foreseen by him arise which make it difficult or even beyond his power to perform, and which might have been provided against in the agreement. (Syl. ¶ 4.)

The impossibility of performance in this case existed, if at all, by reason of the inability of White Lakes to complete construction at a cost within the loan commitment it had previously secured from Jefferson Standard. This is not the impossibility recognized in the law.

We turn now to count one. The issues presented therein were submitted to the court on a stipulation of the parties as a court trial on the pleadings, depositions and the briefs of both parties. A contention of the appellant to the contrary is not supported by the record.

The issues raised on appeal as to count one depend upon the nature of the provision for payment of the $77,000. Was it a penalty provision or one for liquidated damages?

The trial court, after considering the loan commitment agreement and the deposition testimony, found the provision for the advance payment by White Lakes was a valid provision for liquidated damages and that it was not a penalty provision. In addition the court found (1) that White Lakes had willfully breached the contract, (2) that it had failed to prove the $77,000 was an excessive amount for the damages resulting from the breach, (3) that there was no showing unjust enrichment would result from enforcement of the provision, and (4) that the White Lakes' claim should be denied.

Under certain circumstances provisions similar to the present one have been enforced by this court. In such cases the advance payment is determined to have been paid under a proper agreement for liquidated damages. The amount of damages has been agreed upon in advance and such agreement forecloses any need to prove the actual damages resulting from the breach. (*Gregory v. Nelson,* 147 Kan. 682, 78 P.2d 889; *Owen v. Christopher,* 144 Kan. 765, 62 P.2d 860; *Kansas City v. Industrial Gas Co.,* 138 Kan. 755, 28 P.2d 968; *City of Topeka v. Industrial Gas Co.,* 135 Kan. 646, 11 P.2d 1034, cert. den. *National Surety Co. v. City of Topeka,* 287 U.S. 658, 53 S.Ct. 121, 77 L.Ed. 568.

However, when a provision for forfeiture of the advance payment is determined by the court to be a penalty provision, a punishment for default, without regard to actual damages resulting on a breach of the contract, it is held to be unenforceable. In such cases the nondefaulting party is left to a recovery of such actual damages as he can prove. (*Heatwole v. Gorrell,* 35 Kan. 692, 12 P. 135; *Land Co. v. Barton,* 51 Kan. 554, 33 P. 317; *Evans v. Moseley,* 84 Kan. 322, 114 P. 374; *Kuter v. State Bank,* 96 Kan. 485, 152 P. 662, modified 97 Kan. 375, 154 P. 1009; *Metz v. Clay,* 101 Kan. 45, 165 P. 809.)

The rules for determining the true nature of such an advance payment provision are set forth in *Beck v. Megli,* 153 Kan. 721, 114 P.2d 305, as follows:

> In determining whether contractual agreements are to be treated as penalties or as liquidated damages, courts look behind the words used by the

contracting parties to the facts and the nature of the transaction. The use of the terms "penalty" or "liquidated damages" in the instrument is of evidentiary value only. It is given weight and is ordinarily accepted as controlling unless the facts and circumstances impel a contrary holding. . . . The instrument must be considered as a whole, and the situation of the parties, the nature of the subject matter and the circumstances surrounding its execution taken into account. There are two considerations which are given special weight in support of a holding that a contractual provision is for liquidated damages rather than a penalty — the first is that the amount stipulated is conscionable, that it is reasonable in view of the value of the subject matter of the contract and of the probable or presumptive loss in case of breach; and the second is that the nature of the transaction is such that the amount of actual damage resulting from default would not be easily and readily determinable. . . . (p. 726, 114 P. 2d p. 308.)

Let us apply these rules to the present case. The provision in the present contract employed the term "liquidated damages." Although not conclusive this should be given some weight. No claim is made that the amount stipulated (2% of the amount of the loan committed) was unconscionable. No contention is made that a lesser percentage is commonly required. An officer of the mortgage brokerage company testified that the percentage was within the customary percentages required, *i. e.,* one-half of one percent to three percent. In this case the original commitment was issued on September 5, 1963, and the loan was to be closed in May, 1965, a year and eight months later. The commitment provided for a locked-in interest rate of 5.75 percent per annum on the long term mortgage. There was evidence that during construction of the project Jefferson Standard could be expected to make thorough inspections of the work as it progressed to insure itself of lasting construction. Jefferson Standard had its principal place of business located in Greensboro, North Carolina, and would have substantial expenses of transportation and time spent during this construction period. It would incur substantial legal and professional services in examining evaluating and approving long term leases which would be assigned to it to assure payment of the loan. The company's financial house had to be kept in order during the period to assure that $3,850,000 would be available on completion. We need not recite all evidence introduced on this point. Suffice it to say, the court's finding that the amount was reasonable is supported by substantial evidence in the record.

It is contended this was an adhesion contract and the provision for liquidated damages was not agreed upon "at arm's length." The loan commitment was obtained by White Lakes through a mortgage brokerage company with which it chose to deal and upon which it relied. Obviously the parties to this transaction which involved approximately four million dollars were dealing at arms length. No change in the percentage required was requested. It cannot be denied that White Lakes understood and paid this amount without compulsion other than a need for a commitment. The commitment for "end financing" made it possible for White Lakes to obtain interim construction financing from other sources.

The other consideration which enters into a determination of a liquidated damages provision is whether the elements and the amount of actual damage resulting from a breach are difficult to determine. When the damages on breach are more involved and difficult to establish the situation lends itself to an agreed provision for liquidated damages which will be approved by the court. Here the elements of damage are varied in nature and the actual amount would be difficult to establish with certainty and particularity.

It is suggested that we have no Kansas cases which cover like provisions in loan commitment agreements and that the rules for determination set forth herein should not apply to loan commitment agreements. The rules set forth in *Beck v. Megli*, supra, are applicable under the general law relating to contracts. We see no reason for applying different rules to loan commitment agreements. Liquidated damage provisions in loan commitment agreements are quite generally approved. Today the commitment fee has become a fact of financial life. A commitment to make the end loan is necessary for the construction as it progresses. (See *Boston Road Shopping Center, Inc. v. Teachers Insurance and Annuity Association of America*, 13 A.D.2d 106, 213 N.Y.S.2d 522, aff'd 11 N.Y.2d 831, 227 N.Y.S.2d 444, 182 N.E.2d 116; *Goldman v. Connecticut General Life Insurance Company*, 251 Md. 575, 248 A.2d 154; and *Chambers & Co. v. Equitable Life Assurance Society*, 224 F.2d 338 [5 C.A. 1955].)

In determining whether a provision in a loan commitment agreement for payment of a stipulated amount in case of breach is to be construed and enforced as a provision for "liquidated damages" or as a "penalty", the terms used by the parties are given evidentiary weight, but are not necessarily controlling, and courts will look to all the facts and circumstances of the transaction.

Unless invalid for other reasons, advance payments to be forfeited in event of a breach between parties to a loan commitment contract should be held liquidated damages, (1) if the amount is reasonable in view of the value of the subject matter and of the probable and presumptive loss in case of breach, and (2) if the amount of actual damages in case of breach would not be easily and readily determinable.

We conclude the trial court properly held the $77,000 advance payment was made under a binding agreement for liquidated damages.

The judgment is affirmed.

D. INTEREST RATES

Interest is a charge for the use or forbearance of money. A lender will charge a borrower a certain percentage of the principal as interest for each year the debt is outstanding. The amount of interest due on any one installment payment date is calculated by computing the total yearly interest based on the unpaid balance and dividing that figure by the number of payments made each year. For example, if the current outstanding loan balance is $65,000 with interest at the rate of 14 percent per annum and constant monthly payments of $770.17, the interest and principal due on the next payment would be computed as follows:

year's interest	month's interest	month's principal
$65,000	$9,100 ÷ 12 = $758.33	$770.17
x .014		- 758.33
$ 9,100		$ 11.84

Interest is customarily due and charged at the end of each month or payment period. This is known as payment in arrears. Since mortgage loan payments are customarily made each month, the interest portion of each payment covers the charge for using the borrowed money during the previous month. Some lenders, however, specify in the note that interest is charged in advance. In practice, the distinction between the two only becomes important if the property is sold before the debt is repaid.

ANNUAL PERCENTAGE RATE

At the time the loan officer gives the Truth in Lending Disclosures to the prospective applicant all pursuant to Federal Reserve Regulation Z, the law requires the giving of the Annual Percentage Rate. The Annual Percentage Rate has always caused confusion among prospective applicants in that said percentage is always higher than the contract commitment rate on which the loan will be amortized. For example, if the loan commitment rate is 14%, the Annual Percentage Rate may be 14½% because the Annual Percentage Rate includes not only the interest to be paid upon the mortgage loan but also any prepaid finance charges made at the time of the loan closing. A formula for computing the Annual Percentage Rate follows.

Computation of Annual Percentage Rates of Loans with Equal Monthly Payments

ENTER THE FOLLOWING TOTALS FROM SECTION 1:

A. Amount of Loan .... $_____
B. Prepaid Finance Charge .... $_____
C. Amount Financed .... $_____

TO COMPUTE THE ANNUAL PERCENTAGE RATE

1. Multiply the number of payments by the principal and interest payment _____ x _____ .... $_____
2. Subtract the Loan Amount (Line A above) $_____
3. The result equals the total regular interest due on loan .... $_____
4. Add the total Prepaid Finance Charge (Line B above) .... $_____
5. The total of Lines 3 and 4 equal the total FINANCE CHARGE .... $_____
6. Multiply this result (on Line 5) by 100 .... $_____ x 100
7. Divide the result of your multiplication by the Amount Financed (Line C above) _____ $_____
8. This result is the Finance Charge Per $100 $_____

Relate the Finance Charge Per $100 (Line 8 above) to Volume i of the Annual Percentage Rate Tables to obtain the ....

ANNUAL PERCENTAGE RATE OF ...... $_____

E. AMORTIZATION

"Amortization" may be defined as the periodic reduction of principal so that the borrower, when making his last regular payment, will have reduced his mortgage balance to zero.

1. EXTENDED MATURITY IS NOT ALL TO THE BORROWER'S ADVANTAGE

Loan Term	Interest Rate	Initial Loan	Total Interest Paid
25 years	9%	$39,000	$59,000
30 years	9%	$39,000	$73,971
		Difference:	$14,784

An extended maturity is not all to the Borrower's advantage. The longer he repays the loan, the more slowly his equity builds and the larger will be his total interest charges. Wisconsin Statute §215.21(6) limits the maximum loan amortization period to 30 years.

The Texas Real Estate Research Center predicts that the maximum permissible amortizable term will be increased to 35 years by 1980, and 40 years by 1987.

2. EQUITY BUILDUP — PRINCIPAL REDUCTION A SLOW PROCESS

Principal reduction by virtue of mortgage amortization is a slow process. If a borrower procured a $100,000 mortgage at 9.25% interest, with monthly payments of $822.67 and an amortizable term of 30 years, the following chart shows the principal balance after the year specified, the aggregate principal reduction, and the percentage of payments made applicable to principal reduction.

$100,000 mortgage — 30 years — 9.25% interest — $822.67 monthly payment

Year	Principal Balance	Aggregate Principal Reduction	% of Payments Applied to Reduction of Principal
1	$99,350	$650	6.58%
5	$96,064	$3,936	7.97%
10	$89,824	$10,176	10.30%

3. STAGGERING COST OF LONG-TERM MORTGAGE FINANCING

	Purchase Price	Mortgage Amt (80%)	Interest Rate (%)	Term (Years)	Monthly Payment	Annual Payment	Mortgage Cost
Jones	$30,000	$24,000	7	20	$186.07	$2,232.84	$44,656
Smith	$35,000	$28,000	8	20	$234.20	$2,810.40	$56,208
Adams	$40,000	$32,000	8½	25	$257.67	$3,092.04	$77,301
Meyers	$57,500	$46,000	9	30	$370.12	$4,441.44	$133,243

Jones: Initial Equity — $ 6,000 + $ 44,656 = $ 50,656 (169%)
Smith: Initial Equity — $ 7,000 + $ 56,208 = $ 63,208 (181%)
Adams: Initial Equity — $ 8,000 + $ 77,301 = $ 85,301 (213%)
Meyers: Initial Equity — $11,500 + $133,243 = $144,743 (252%)

4. ANNUAL CONSTANT

The annual payments on a mortgage constitute a fixed percentage of the original mortgage amount. This percentage is known as the annual constant. For instance, a $100,000 mortgage at a 10% interest rate and a 25 year amortization has annual payments of $10,904.40 — thus, an annual constant of approximately 10.91%.

CONSTANT ANNUAL PERCENT TABLE

Interest Rate	5 Years	10 Years	15 Years	20 Years	25 Years	26 Years	27 Years	28 Years	29 Years	30 Years	35 Years	40 Years	50 Years
6	23.20	13.33	10.13	8.60	7.74	7.61	7.49	7.39	7.29	7.20	6.85	6.61	6.32
¼	23.34	13.48	10.29	8.78	7.92	7.80	7.68	7.58	7.48	7.39	7.05	6.82	6.54
½	23.48	13.63	10.46	8.95	8.11	7.98	7.87	7.77	7.68	7.59	7.25	7.03	6.77
¾	23.63	13.78	10.62	9.13	8.30	8.17	8.06	7.96	7.87	7.79	7.46	7.25	7.00
7	23.77	13.94	10.79	9.31	8.49	8.37	8.26	8.16	8.07	7.99	7.67	7.46	7.23
¼	23.91	14.09	10.96	9.49	8.68	8.56	8.46	8.36	8.27	8.19	7.88	7.68	7.46
½	24.05	14.25	11.13	9.67	8.87	8.76	8.65	8.56	8.47	8.40	8.10	7.90	7.69
¾	24.19	14.41	11.30	9.86	9.07	8.96	8.85	8.76	8.68	8.60	8.31	8.12	7.92
8	24.34	14.56	11.47	10.04	9.27	9.16	9.06	8.97	8.88	8.61	8.53	8.35	8.16
¼	24.48	14.72	11.65	10.23	9.47	9.36	9.26	9.17	9.09	9.02	8.75	8.57	8.39
½	24.62	14.88	11.82	10.42	9.67	9.56	9.47	9.38	9.30	9.23	8.97	8.80	8.63
¾	24.77	15.04	12.00	10.61	9.87	9.77	9.67	9.59	9.51	9.45	9.19	9.03	8.87
9	24.92	15.21	12.18	10.80	10.08	9.97	9.88	9.80	9.73	9.66	9.41	9.26	9.11
¼	25.06	15.37	12.36	11.00	10.28	10.18	10.09	10.01	9.94	9.88	9.64	9.49	9.35
½	25.21	15.53	12.54	11.19	10.49	10.39	10.31	10.23	10.16	10.10	9.86	9.73	9.59
¾	25.35	15.70	12.72	11.39	10.70	10.60	10.52	10.44	10.38	10.31	10.09	9.96	9.83
10	25.50	15.86	12.90	11.59	10.91	10.82	10.73	10.66	10.59	10.54	10.32	10.19	10.07
¼	25.65	16.03	13.08	11.78	11.12	11.03	10.95	10.88	10.82	10.76	10.55	10.43	10.32
½	25.80	16.20	13.27	11.99	11.34	11.25	11.17	11.10	11.04	10.98	10.78	10.67	10.56
¾	25.95	16.37	13.46	12.19	11.55	11.46	11.39	11.32	11.26	11.21	11.02	10.91	10.81
11	26.10	16.54	13.64	12.39	11.77	11.68	11.61	11.54	11.48	11.43	11.25	11.14	11.05
¼	26.25	16.71	13.83	12.60	11.98	11.90	11.83	11.77	11.71	11.66	11.48	11.38	11.30
½	26.40	16.88	14.02	12.80	12.20	12.12	12.05	11.99	11.94	11.89	11.72	11.62	11.54
¾	26.55	17.05	14.21	13.01	12.42	12.35	12.28	12.22	12.16	12.12	11.95	11.87	11.79
12	26.70	17.22	14.41	13.22	12.64	12.57	12.50	12.44	12.39	12.35	12.19	12.11	12.04

Likewise, the annual payment can be approximated, using the Constant Annual Percent Table, by multiplying the amount of the mortgage times the annual constant and dividing by 100. For example, a $40,000 mortgage over a 30 year amortization period at 10% — $40,000 x 10.98 ÷ 100 — requires a $4,392 annual payment.

MEANS OF AMORTIZATION

5. LEVEL PAYMENT DEBT SERVICE

With each successive installment, the interest component gets smaller while the amortization (principal) increases. Each payment is first applied to the payment of interest on the unpaid balance; whatever sum remains is then applied to principal reduction.

Example: $37,000 at 8½% interest over a 30 year amortization period, generating a $284.50 monthly debt service.

Balance	Rate	Payment	Interest	Principal	New Balance	
37,000.00	8.50	284.50	262.08	22.42	36,877.58	1
36,977.58	8.50	284.50	261.93	22.57	36,955.01	2
36,955.01	8.50	284.50	261.77	22.73	36,932.27	3
36,932.27	8.50	284.50	261.60	22.90	36,909.38	4
36,909.38	8.50	284.50	261.44	23.06	36,886.32	5
36,886.32	8.50	284.50	261.28	23.22	36,863.10	6
36,863.10	8.50	284.50	261.11	23.39	36,839.71	7
36,839.71	8.50	284.50	260.95	23.55	36,816.16	8
36,816.16	8.50	284.50	260.78	23.72	36,792.44	9
36,792.44	8.50	284.50	260.61	23.89	36,768.56	10
36,768.56	8.50	284.50	260.44	24.06	36,744.50	11
36,744.50	8.50	284.50	260.27	24.23	36,720.28	12
36,720.28	8.50	284.50	260.10	24.40	36,695.88	13
36,695.88	8.50	284.50	259.93	24.57	36,671.31	14
36,671.31	8.50	284.50	259.76	24.74	36,646.56	15
36,646.56	8.50	284.50	259.58	24.92	36,621.64	16
36,621.64	8.50	284.50	259.40	25.10	36,596.55	17
36,596.88	8.50	284.50	259.23	25.27	36,571.27	18
36,571.27	8.50	284.50	259.05	25.45	36,545.82	19
36,545.82	8.50	284.50	258.87	25.63	36,520.19	20
36,520.19	8.50	284.50	258.69	25.81	36,494.37	21
36,494.37	8.50	284.50	258.50	26.00	36,468.37	22
36,468.37	8.50	284.50	258.32	26.18	36,442.19	23
36,442.19	8.50	284.50	258.13	26.37	36,415.82	24
2,469.78	8.50	284.50	17.49	267.01	2,202.77	352
2,202.77	8.50	284.50	15.60	268.90	1,933.87	353
1,933.87	8.50	284.50	13.70	270.80	1,663.07	354
1,663.07	8.50	284.50	11.78	272.72	1,390.35	355
1,390.35	8.50	284.50	9.85	274.65	1,115.70	356
1,115.70	8.50	284.50	7.90	276.60	839.11	357
839.11	8.50	284.50	5.94	278.56	560.55	358
560.55	8.50	284.50	3.97	280.53	280.02	359
280.02	8.50	284.50	1.98	282.52	2.49	360

6. CONSTANT AMORTIZATION (DECLINING PAYMENT): THE SAME AMOUNT OF PRINCIPAL REDUCTION IN EACH INSTALLMENT

Example: A $20,000 mortgage at 6% over a 30 year amortization period.

Month	Installment (decreases)	Interest (decreases)	Principal (constant)	Principal Balance After Monthly Payment
1	$155.55	$100.00	$55.55	$19,944.45
2	155.27	99.72	55.55	19,888.90
3	154.99	99.44	55.55	18.833.35
. . .	. . .	. . .	. . .	. . .
360	55.83	.28	55.55	—0—

With respect to the example for constant amortization, see Axelrod, Berger, and Johnstone: *Land Transfer and Finance,* 1971.

7. BALLOON PAYMENT

a. Definition

Mortgages are not always self-amortizing. If on maturity the unpaid principal balance is not or cannot be liquidated by a regular debt service installment, the mortgage is said to have a "balloon."

Example: Seller takes back a purchase money mortgage in the amount of $22,500 at an interest rate of 7½% per annum, with monthly payments of $208.58 commencing October 1, 1976. However, the entire unpaid principal balance is due and payable on the third anniversary of such Mortgage Note. Although the monthly payments referred to above reflect a 15 year amortization, on October 1, 1979, a balloon payment for the unpaid balance of $19,766 will be due and payable.

b. Why Utilize a Balloon Payment?

The "intent to refinance" is the principal underlying motive in providing for a balloon payment provision. Where the seller agrees to take back a mortgage, or real estate is bought pursuant to a land contract, the amount of equity required to be provided by the purchaser is generally smaller than that required to secure conventional financing. Since experience shows that real estate generally increases in value over the mere passage of time, enough appreciation could occur in a relatively short period to increase the investor's equity to the point where conventional forms of financing can be obtained. Thus, financing with a balloon feature may permit the investor to "build" additional equity into his investment.

8. OTHER VARIATIONS

a. Standing Mortgage, Straight or Flat Loan, Line of Credit Mortgage

This is a mortgage loan, usually for a definite term, such as six months or one year, which is payable in full — *i.e.,* principal and accrued interest, at maturity. This type of mortgage is typically used by dealers, speculators, or rehabilitators of real estate. The lender normally will loan the purchase price of the property to the borrower and, if requested, any rehabilitation funds with respect to the property, and take as security, therefore, a mortgage on the property. On a line of credit mortgage the lender will also require additional liquid collateral as security for the line of credit. Normally a five-to-one ratio is acceptable — that is, every one dollar of pledged or secured liquid assets will generate five dollars of borrowed funds.

b. Sinking-Fund Plan

This plan is used by some savings and loan associations. The essence of such financing is that amortization payments are not credited directly to the loan, but are kept in a separate account (on which dividends are paid) until this "sinking fund" equals the amount of the loan. Since the interest on the loan (which might be 6%) is invariably more than the dividends paid on the deposit account (perhaps 4%), the Borrower ends up paying more than the stated rate of interest. The excess interest rate is approximately one-half the difference between the contract rate on the loan and the dividend rate (using the above figures, the true rate of interest would be about 7%).

F. LOAN TO EQUITY OR VALUE RATIO

The reciprocal of the downpayment is the loan to value or equity ratio, which states in percentage terms the relationship between the amount of money borrowed (mortgage debt) and the real estate's purchase price or market value (i.e., mortgage debt/purchase price).

Example: $100,000 borrowed on a $125,000 property results in a 80% loan. In such a case, the borrower is said to be in a "20% equity" position.

The ratio of loan to value is extremely important to the investor in that it determines his initial stake and equity position in the property. However, loan to value ratios may be statutorily or administratively imposed. For instance, a state chartered savings and loan association may not make a mortgage loan in excess of 80% of appraised value for a multi-unit dwelling or 75% of appraised value for a commercial type property. See Wis. Adm. Code SL§18.02. However, the maximum loan ratio may be exceeded when the excess is secured by mortgage insurance but in no event shall the mortgage loan exceed 90% of appraised value. See Wis. Adm. Code SL§18.10. In periods when mortgage money is less available, mortgage lenders may require a larger downpayment or equity position, thus reducing the loan to value ratio and decreasing the borrower's leverage.

1. LEVERAGE

The term "leverage" refers to the use of borrowed funds by the borrower to complete the purchase of an investment type property. As a general proposition, the larger the percentage or ratio of borrowed funds to the total value (or purchase price), the greater is the amount of leverage. Leverage permits the investor to increase his return by reducing the amount of his personal investment in the property. To explain how leverage works, consider an investor who purchases a $1 million apartment building which produces a return of $100,000 after expenses. On an all cash purchase, the investor will earn a 10 percent cash return on his investment. Suppose instead, that he borrows to make the purchase; first $500,000, then $900,000. If the mortgages bear 9 percent interest, and if the monthly debt service (that is, the combined amount of interest and principal reduction) is sufficient to pay off the mortgages in 30 years, the cash return changes as shown below:

a. $500,000 mortgage (9%, 30 years)

Cash return before debt service	$100,000
Less debt service	48,277
Net Cash return	51,723
Percentage cash return on $500,000 equity ($51,723/$500,000)	10.3%

b. $900,000 mortgage (9%, 30 years)

Cash return before debt service	$100,000
Less debt service	86,904
Net cash return	13,096
Percentage cash return on $100,000 equity ($13,096/$100,000)	13.17%

If we were to continue to project cash returns based on ever-shrinking cash equities, the buyer's yield would improve even more dramatically. And by investing the cash elsewhere that mortgaging replaces, the purchaser can expand and diversify this holdings and improve his yield.

The real estate investment permits the use of borrowed funds in a proportion that far exceeds the requirement of equity or capital outlay by the investor. If the cost or interest rate of those borrowed funds is lower than the overall rate of return generated from the property, the investor will enhance his equity yield (the rate of return per annum on each dollar of equity funds invested) over what such return would be without the use of borrowed funds. Therefore, leverage represents the borrowing of money, the cost of which (in the form of interest) is less than the return from the investment which is purchased with the borrowed funds (financial leverage).

Example: If a $100,000 property produces $10,000 income per year and remains stable in value over the foreseeable future (that is, no allowance for capital recapture of principal is necessary), an equity investor will earn 10% per annum per dollar invested if he invests the entire $100,000 to buy the property.

If, however, the investor can borrow $80,000 (80% mortgage) at 8% interest (assume an interest only loan with a 100% balloon payment at the time of maturity), his return each year during the period that the loan is outstanding is $3,600 on his $20,000 equity investment or 18% computed as follows:

$$\frac{\text{Income - Interest Cost}}{\text{Amount Invested}}$$

or

$$\frac{\$10,000 - \$6,400}{\$20,000}$$

$$\frac{\$3600}{\$20,000}$$

equals 18%

In this case, borrowing at a mortgage interest rate *below* the overall rate resulted in an increase in equity yield from 10% to 18% per dollar of equity capital invested. This is because, in addition to earning $1,000 on the $20,000 of equity capital invested, the equity investor also received the *excess* of earnings over cost from the borrowed funds. This amounted to $1,600 since the $80,000 borrowed earned $8,000 and only cost the equity investor $6,400.

The above example represents positive financial leverage. (Using borrowed funds to create profit since you earn more money on it than you pay (before taxes).)

Leverage can also be neutral, (where you earn what you pay on the borrowed money (before taxes)) or negative (where you pay more than you earn on the borrowed money before taxes).

2. "MORTGAGING OUT"

"Mortgaging-out" is said to occur when the amount of the mortgage on the property at the time it is made is equal to or greater than the basis (cost) of the property given as security; or when the amount of the mortgage is greater than the applicable percent loan required for such property. Total or partial "mortgaging out" usually results when the fair market value (appraised value) is greater than the mortgagor's cost.

Example 1: Developer constructs a 12 family apartment building for a cost of $204,000 (including land, improvements and closing costs). At completion of construction and upon full rental, the project has a fair market value (appraised value) of $260,000. Developer procures a first mortgage loan for 80% of the appraised value, or $208,000. In essence, the proceeds of financing are greater than the Developer's actual cost or basis for the project permitting Developer to "pocket" the difference.

Example 2: High-Flyer purchases a duplex from an elderly couple for $28,000. After rent rehabilitation, the same duplex in the surrounding area has a fair market value (appraised value) of $32,500. Presuming that Fair-Shake Savings and Loan will make a mortgage loan equal to 80% of appraised value, High-Flyer will receive a mortgage loan of $26,000 or on his part, a cash requirement of $2,000 plus closing costs. If High-Flyer received a mortgage loan based upon purchase price, his cash requirement would have been $5,600 plus closing costs. In this instance, High-Flyer partially "mortgaged out" to the extent of $3,600.

Example 3: Investor intends to purchase a building; its single useful purpose is that of a supermarket. Investor obtains a letter agreement from Stole-Foods, Inc., a company listed on the NYSE, that it will lease the premises on a fully net basis for a term of 20 years with appropriate renewals. In reviewing the package, the Lender commits to 100% financing based upon the net character of the lease, the credit rating of the tenant, and the fact that the rental payable under said lease is sufficient to amortize the loan. In essence, the Lender looks primarily to the credit of the tenant as security for the loan. Of course, Lender will require an assignment of the lease as collateral security for the loan. This type of transaction is commonly referred to as a *"bondable lease"* and in essence the investor is in fact *"banking the lease."*

G. MORTGAGE CLOSING COSTS

In addition to the closing and/or settlement between a buyer and seller, an additional settlement or closing will occur between the buyer and the mortgage lender.

At the time of that closing, the buyer-mortgagor will incur certain prepaid finance charges and other advance payments and escrows.

What follows is a listing of typical mortgage closing costs and escrows:

A. Out-of-Pocket
 1. Appraisal
 2. Credit Report
 3. Survey
 4. Mortgage Title Policy
 5. Legal Fee
 6. Inspection Fee
 7. Recording Fee
 8. Point — service charge — loan fee — origination fee
 9. Interest to date of first principal payment

b. Escrows — Advance Payments
 1. Real estate taxes
 2. Hazard insurance
 3. Mortgage insurance

ABRAMOWITZ v. BARNETT BANK

District Court of Appeal of Florida
394 So. 2d 1033 (1981)

SHARP, JUDGE.

Abramowitz appeals from a judgment denying him any relief in his suit against the Barnett Bank of West Orlando, appellee, in which he sought damages for an allegedly "usurious" loan. An earlier appeal reversed a summary judgment entered in favor of the bank because there was a fact issue concerning whether or not a $4,000 "service fee" or "point" charge made at the mortgage loan closing was "interest" or whether it was in whole or in part repayment of a legitimate expense of the lender.

After a non-jury trial, the lower court concluded that the bank had incurred at least a $300 final inspection fee, several other inspection expenses during construction of the building, and unspecified expenses in obtaining other banks to participate in the loan; and that a sufficient amount of the $4,000 charge was attributable to the lender's bona fide "expenses," so as to remove from the transaction any possible "taint" of usury. It also found the bank had no intent to claim in excess of the maximum legal rate of interest. We reverse because there is not sufficient evidence in the record to sustain the trial court's findings.

The record established that Abramowitz filed three or more loan applications with the bank from February 1973 through October 1973. Originally he sought a construction loan to build a building to be leased to Ford Motor Company on land he owned near the John Young Parkway. C. Lee Maynard, president of the bank, wanted the loan for his bank, although the $300,000 to $400,000 loan requests considerably exceeded the bank's lending limits. In anticipation of making the loan, Maynard made "inspections" of the site and building being constructed, although Ford was financing the construction itself and the bank had made no loan commitment.

When the building was completed in November of 1973, the parties rushed into a mortgage loan closing without the benefit of a written loan commitment and without a carefully prepared loan closing statement. Maynard had verbally promised Abramowitz a $400,000 loan for one year, at 9% interest, with a 1% "point" or "service fee." The $4,000 "service fee" was shown on the closing statement as a "discount," but everyone agreed no "discount" was involved because the bank was not purchasing a mortgage loan from another party at less than face value.

The $4,000 service fee was deducted in full from the loan proceeds, and it was immediately received by the bank as income. During the one year term of this loan, Abramowitz was charged and he paid $36,347.78 in "interest." If the $4,000 charge was also "interest," Abramowitz paid more than $40,000 or 10% of his $400,000 loan in total interest charges. If viewed as a "discount" loan where interest is paid in advance, the rate should be properly gauged on the amount of principal actually disbursed to the borrower plus legitimate expenses — ($396,000 or a somewhat larger figure if any part of the $4,000 were attributable to a legitimate expense of the lender.)

Maynard testified that the $4,000 charge was meant to be a "service charge" or "points." He was the only mortgage loan officer at his bank, so he made "in-house" inspections of the construction of the building and a final inspection. He reported verbally to the bank's loan committee. He admitted that part of the $4,000 went to pay the bank's normal overhead expenses, such as salaries and utilities. Another expense attributed to this loan was Maynard's contacting other Barnett banks to obtain the participation of other lenders, and the preparation of loan participation agreements.

The other banker witnesses at trial testified that their banks normally imposed "service fees" or "points" on real estate loans in addition to interest, but they were careful not to exceed the usury limits when the two amounts were combined. Sometimes inspection fees were paid to architects or engineers for which the customer was charged; sometimes the inspections were done "in-house," and the borrower was charged a small amount, or was not charged at all.

A real estate appraiser testified he would have done a "final inspection" on this building for $300. If it had been a construction loan requiring approximately 5 separate inspections, his charges would have been $800.

A lender will not be allowed to impose any miscellaneous fees or service charges on the front end of a loan when that sum, added to the interest charged, exceeds the maximum legal rate of interest allowable. *Ayvas v. Green,* 57 So.2d 30 (Fla.1952); *Richter Jewelry Co. v. Schweinert,* 125 Fla. 199, 169 So. 750 (1935); *Williamson v. Clark,* 120 So.2d 637 (Fla.2d DCA 1960). Application of such fees to pay the general overhead of a lender or the cost of participating out the loan are not sufficient to alter the characterization of these charges as interest. 91 C.J.S. *Usury* § 48 (1955).

It is also well established that a borrower can be charged the actual reasonable expenses of making a particular loan. *Financial Federal Savings & Loan Assn. v. Burleigh House, Inc.,* 305 So.2d 59 (Fla.3d DCA 1974), *cert. dismissed* 336 So.2d 1145 (Fla.1976), *cert. denied,* 492 U.S. 1042, 97 S.Ct. 742, 50 L.Ed.2d 754 (1977); *Mindlin v. Davis,* 74 So.2d 789 (1954). However "bogus" charges for services not actually rendered will not be allowed to cloak the extraction of illegal interest. *Williamson v. Clark,* 120 So.2d 637 (Fla.2d DCA 1960).

The only basis to characterize the "service fee" in this case as something other than interest, is to allocate part of it as an "inspection" fee performed "in-house" by the bank's president. Such fees are usually paid to third-parties, and are documented on the mortgage loan closing statement. We are not prepared to say, however, that in all cases the inspection must be done by a third-person or that it must be documented on the closing statement, although that obviously is the better practice. The fact that Maynard himself performed the inspection does not flaw the charges although any charge for this "service" is inconsistent with his testimony that he did the inspection "in-house" to save the borrower money.

It is fundamental that the charges must be "reasonable." *Financial Federal Savings & Loan v. Burleigh House; Abramowitz v. Barnett Bank of West Orlando,* 356 So.2d 329 (Fla. 4th DCA), *cert. denied,* 364 So.2d 880 (1978). This loan was not a "construction" loan which requires more inspections to insure the lender's construction funds are being properly used as the building progresses. Rather, it was a loan on a completed building, and similar to a "take-out" loan for a permanent lender, only a final inspection fee is required. The only testimony in the record on this point established that $300 was the maximum a third party expert would have charged.

The conclusion thus follows inescapably that Abramowitz was charged in excess of 10% interest on this one-year loan.

"Service Fee"	$ 4,000.00
Less "Reasonable Expenses"	-300.00
"Hidden Interest"	$ 3,700.00
Principal of Loan	$400,000.00
Less Prepaid Interest	-3,700.00
Actual Principal	$396,300.00
Maximum legal amount of interest collectible on this loan (10%) of actual principal	$ 39,630.00
Actual interest charged and billed	36,347.78
Plus "hidden interest"	+3,700.00
	$ 40,047.78
Amount of over-charge	$ 40,047.78
	-39,630.00
	$ 417.78

The lower court found there was no "corrupt" intent on the part of the bank to charge a usurious rate of interest because the bank did not deliberately charge more than 10%. It charged 9% on the loan plus 1% in points only. The difficulty here was that the 1% was taken up-front, resulting in a reduction in principal received, and an increase in the rate paid. *Hamm v. St. Petersburg Bank & Trust Co.,* 379 So.2d 1300 (Fla.2d DCA 1980). The "intent" to exceed the legal rate of interest need not be to consciously decide to charge a borrower greater than the legal rate, when the lender consciously intends and does in fact make the charges which add up to usury. *Ellis National Bank of Tallahassee v. Davis,* 359 So.2d 466 (Fla. 1st DCA), *cert. denied* 365 So.2d 711 (Fla.1978), *cert. denied* 440 U.S. 976, 99 S.Ct. 1547, 59 L.Ed.2d 796 (1979). *See Sailboat Apt. Corp. v. Chase Manhattan Mortgage,* 363 So.2d 564 (Fla.3d DCA 1978).

In this case, the closing statement showing a 1% point or service fee was prepared by the bank; and it calculated and billed the borrower interest throughout the year. No errors were shown to have occurred in the billing. In fact during 2 quarters, the lender billed on a 360 day year basis, which for a 10% or maximum rate loan, was usurious in and of itself. *Ellis.* We conclude the bank had the requisite intent to make the usurious charges. *Sumner v. Investment Mortgage Co. of Florida,* 332 So.2d 103 (Fla. 1st DCA 1976); *Curtiss National Bank of Miami v. Solomon,* 243 So.2d 475 (Fla.3d DCA 1971); *River Hills, Inc. v. Edwards,* 190 So.2d 415 (Fla.2d DCA 1966).

Accordingly, the judgment is reversed and this case is remanded for imposition of damages against the bank, pursuant to section 687.04 and other appropriate charges.

Reversed and Remanded.

Dauksch, C. J., concurs.

Sharp, G. Kendall, Associate Judge, dissents with opinion.

Sharp, G. Kendall, Associate Judge, dissenting.

The trial judge issued a memorandum supplementing his final judgment in which he found that after some difficulty in obtaining a loan from other lending institutions, appellant secured a loan from Barnett Bank at a total rate of 9% plus a 1% service fee. At the time, all banks were charging a similar fee. The lower court found that in many instances the service fee is nothing more than concealed interest. In this case, the trial judge found as a matter of fact the bank performed several functions other than those of a straight loan transaction. The president of the bank periodically and frequently investigated progress of the construction of the building on the property. The bank also had to find other participating banks to join in making the loan, as the loan exceeded this bank's lending authority. The court found that the bank was entitled to charge a service fee *therewith*.

Appellant contends that the $4,000.00 service fee was totally interest and was withheld from the principal loan, i. e. only $396,000.00 was disbursed, plus the fact that for approximately ½ of the term of the loan, interest was charged on a 360 day year versus 365 days. With all of these factors taken as true, the interest rate would be 10.1883%. *See Hamm v. St. Petersburg Bank & Trust Co.,* 379 So.2d 1300 (Fla.2d DCA 1980).

Accepting the computation set forth above, the transaction would be facially usurious and tainted in the amount of $717.78. Even so, the trial judge found that the bank performed services to borrower in excess of that amount and could rightfully charge for those services.

The second element of usury is intent of the lender. Again, if we give the benefit to the appellant and find that the $4,000.00 service charge was all interest, it would then be the legal intent of the lender to make a 9% loan and a 1% service charge, still within the rate allowed by law.

In *Dixon v. Sharp,* 276 So.2d 817 (Fla. 1973), the Supreme Court spoke to the requisite intent required for a usurious transaction:

. . . (4) There must exist a corrupt intent to take more than the legal rate for the use of the money loaned.

[The] court in *Dixon* stressed that usury is largely a matter of intent, and is not fully determined by the fact that the lender actually receives more than the law permits, but is determined by the existence of a corrupt purpose in the lender's mind to get more than the legal interest for the money lent. Simple mathematical computation will not in itself determine necessary intent to make the debt unenforceable.

In this case there was sufficient evidence presented to the trial court to show services rendered by the bank which could be charged against the loan at least to the extent to remove the $717.78 taint of usury. The trial court further found that the bank had no other intent at the time of making the loan than to charge the stated amount of 9% plus a 1% service charge. The majority of this court is imposing its own judgment that no more than $300.00 should be allocated for reasonable expenses. They do not take into consideration any charge for securing participating lenders. It does not appear to me that $417.78 is an unreasonable charge for all services other than inspections so as to make the transaction usurious and imposes damages under section 678.04.

1. POINTS — TAX RAMIFICATIONS

Points are a premium charged by lenders, rather than increased interest rates to obtain a loan. (State law limits the maximum interest rate that can be charged.) Each point is equal to one percent of the total amount of the loan, or of the unpaid mortgage balance if an existing mortgage is assumed.

"Points" (loan origination fees) paid by the borrower out of his own funds to a mortgage lender in order to get the loan are deductible as interest if they are solely for the use or forbearance of money and are not a charge for services. Rev. Rul. 69-188, 1969-1 C.B. 54.

26 CFR 1.163-1: Interest deduction in general.

A "loan processing fee" (points) paid by a mortgagor-borrower as compensation to a lender solely for the use or forbearance of money is considered to be interest.

REVENUE RULING 69-188

Advice has been requested whether for Federal income tax purposes, a payment made under the circumstances set forth below is considered to be interest.

A taxpayer on the cash receipts and disbursements method of accounting who wished to purchase a building, arranged with a lender to finance the transaction. A conventional mortgage loan of 1,000x dollars was negotiated, secured by a deed of trust on the building, and repayable in monthly installments over a ten-year period at a stated annual interest rate of 7.2 percent. In addition to the annual interest rate the parties agreed that the borrower would pay a "loan processing fee" of 70x dollars (sometimes referred to as "points") prior to receipt of the loan proceeds. The borrower established that this fee was not paid for any specific services that the lender had performed or had agreed to perform in connection with the borrower's account under the loan contract. The loan agreement provided for separate charges for these services. For example, separate charges were made for a preliminary title report, a title report, an escrow fee, the drawing of the deed and other papers, and insurance.

In determining the amount of this "loan processing fee" the lender considered the economic factors that usually dictate an acceptable rate of interest. That is, he considered the general availability of money, the character of the property offered as security, the degree of success that the borrower had enjoyed in his prior business activities, and the outcome of previous transactions between the borrower and his creditors.

The taxpayer tendered a check for 70x dollars drawn on a bank account owned by him, which contained a sufficient balance, in payment of the fee. The monies in this account were not originally obtained from the lender.

Section 163(a) of the Internal Revenue Code of 1954 provides that there shall be allowed as a deduction all interest paid or accrued within the taxable year on indebtedness.

Section 446(a) of the Code provides that taxable income shall be computed under the method of accounting on the basis of which the taxpayer regularly computes his income in keeping his books. Section 446(b) of the Code provides, in part, that if the method used does not clearly reflect income, the computation of taxable income shall be made under such method as, in the opinion of the Secretary of the Treasury or his delegate, does clearly reflect income.

For tax purposes, interest has been defined by the Supreme Court of the United States as the amount one has contracted to pay for the use of borrowed money, and as the compensation paid for the use or forbearance of money. See *Old Colony Railroad Co. v. Commissioner,* 284 U.S. 552 (1932), Ct. D. 456, C.B. XI-1, 274 (1932); *Deputy v. DuPont,* 308 U.S. 488 (1940), Ct. D. 1435, C.B. 1940-1, 118. The Board of Tax Appeals has stated that interest is the compensation allowed by law or fixed by the parties for the use, forbearance, or detention of money. *Fall River Electric Light Co. v. Commissioner,* 23 B.T.A. 168 (1931). A negotiated bonus or premium paid by a borrower to a lender in order to obtain a loan has been held to be interest for Federal income tax purposes. *L-R Heat Treating Co. v. Commissioner,* 28 T.C. 894 (1957).

The payment or accrual of interest for tax purposes must be incidental to an unconditional and legally enforceable obligation of the taxpayer claiming the deduction. *Paul Autenreith v. Commissioner,* 115 F. 2d 856 (1940). There need not, however, be a legally enforceable indebtedness already in existence when the payment of interest is made. It is sufficient that the payment be a "prerequisite to obtaining borrowed capital." *L-R Heat Treating Co.* The fee of 70x dollars in the instant case was paid prior to the receipt of the borrowed funds; however, this does not preclude the payment from being classified as interest.

It is not necessary that the parties to a transaction label a payment made for the use of money as interest for it to be so treated. See *L-R Heat Treating Co.* The mere fact that the parties in the instant case agreed to call the 70x dollars a "loan processing fee" does not in itself preclude this payment from being interest under section 163 (a) of the Code. Further, this conclusion would not be affected by the fact that this payment is sometimes referred to as "points." Compare Revenue Ruling 67-297, C.B. 1967-2, 87, relating to the deductibility as interest of a loan origination fee paid by the purchaser of a residence to a lending institution in connection with the acquisition of a home mortgage. Also, compare Revenue Ruling 68-650, C.B. 1968-2, 78, relating to the deductibility as interest of the payment of a loan charge paid by the seller of a residence to assist the purchaser in obtaining a mortgage loan.

The method of computation also does not control its deductibility, so long as the amount in question is an ascertainable sum contracted for the use of borrowed money. See *Kena, Inc. v. Commissioner,* 44 B.T.A. 217 (1941). The fact that the amount paid in the instant case is a flat sum paid in addition to a stated annual interest rate does not preclude a deduction under section 163 of the Code.

To qualify as interest for tax purposes, the payment, by whatever name called, must be compensation for the use or forbearance of money per se and not a payment for specific services which the lender performs in connection with the borrower's account. For example, interest would not include separate charges made for investigating the prospective borrower and his security, closing costs of the loan and papers drawn in connection therewith, or fees paid to a third party for servicing and collecting that particular loan. See *Workingmen's Loan Ass'n v. United States,* 142 F. 2d 359 (1944); Rev. Rul. 57-541, C.B. 1957-2, 319. Compare Revenue Ruling 57-540, C.B. 1957-2, 318, relating to the classification as interest of the fees imposed on borrowers by a mortgage finance company. Also, even where service charges are not stated separately on the borrower's account, interest would not include amounts attributable to such services. See Rev. Rul. 67-297; compare *Norman L. Noteman, et al., Trustees v. Welch,* 108 F. 2d 206 (1939) relating to the classification as interest of the charges paid by borrowers to a personal finance company.

Accordingly, in the instant case, because the taxpayer was able to establish that the fee of 70x dollars was paid as compensation to the lender solely for the use or forbearance of money, and because he did not initially obtain the funds to pay this fee from the lender, the 70x dollars is considered to be interest.

Points paid for services of the lender, in place of specific service charges (such as the one point charge in a V.A. insured loan for the lender's appraisal fee, the cost of preparing the mortgage note, settlement fees, etc.) are not deductible as interest. Rev. Rul. 67-297, 1967-2 C.B. 87. Nor is a "commitment fee" charged for the lender's agreement to make a future loan. Rev. Rul. 70-540, 1970-2 C.B. 101. However, a commitment fee paid by a lending bank to the Federal National Mortgage Association, and withheld from the face amount of the loan proceeds advanced to the borrower, is deductible by the borrower as interest. Rev. Rul. 74-395, 1974-2 C.B. 45.

REVENUE RULING 74-395

Advice has been requested whether, for Federal income tax purposes, the fee paid by the taxpayer under the circumstances set forth below is interest within the meaning of section 163 of the Internal Revenue Code of 1954, and, if so, over what period of time may the interest be deducted, and how should the amount of each yearly deduction be determined.

A taxpayer, who reports his income under an accrual method of accounting, proposed to construct an apartment building and negotiated a long-term loan with a lender bank for that purpose. Since the construction project qualified for assistance under section 236 of the National Housing Act, 12 U.S.C., section 1715z (1968), the lender bank entered into a commitment contract with the Federal National Mortgage Association (FNMA) pursuant to which the bank obligated itself to sell, and FNMA obligated itself to purchase, at face value, the outstanding principal amount of the loan upon completion of the construction.

In connection with the commitment contract, the bank paid to FNMA a commitment fee of one percent of the loan, and, pursuant to the loan agreement with the taxpayer, discounted such amount from the face amount of the loan proceeds advanced to taxpayer. No separate service was rendered by the bank or the FNMA in return for this fee; a separate service charge was paid by the taxpayer to the bank for title search, FHA examination, etc.

Section 163(a) of the Code provides that there shall be allowed as a deduction all interest paid or accrued within the taxable year on indebtedness.

For tax purposes, interest has been defined by the Supreme Court of the United States as the amount one has contracted to pay for the use of borrowed money and as the compensation paid for the use or forbearance of money. See *Old Colony Railroad Co. v. Commissioner,* 284 U.S. 552 (1932), XI-1 C.B. 274 (1932); *Deputy v. DuPont,* 308 U.S. 488 (1940), 1940-1 C.B. 118. A negotiated bonus or premium paid by a borrower to a lender in order to obtain a loan has been held to be interest for Federal income tax purposes. Whether the amount of the bonus or premium is withheld by the lender rather than being paid back to the lender is immaterial. *L-R Heat Treating Co.,* 28 T.C. 894 (1957).

Rev. Rul. 69-118, 1969-1 C.B. 54, holds that a loan processing fee paid by a borrower to a lender prior to the receipt of the loan proceeds, and in addition to the annual interest rate, is interest. In that case the taxpayer was able to establish that the fee was not paid for any specific services that the lender had performed, or had agreed to perform, in connection with the loan.

Rev. Rul. 56-136, 1956-1 C.B. 92, involved commitment fees or standby charges incurred by a taxpayer pursuant to a bond sale agreement, under which funds for construction purposes are made available to it in stated amounts over a specified period and which vary with the period of time during which funds are held available by the lender. The conclusion reached in Rev. Rul. 56-136 is that such commitment fees were business expenses that were deductible under section 162 of the Code and not interest. Rev. Rul. 56-136 is distinguishable from this case, since here the purpose of the deduction of the commitment fee from the construction loan proceeds is for the use of money on an existing indebtedness rather than for having money made available on a when needed basis.

In the instant case, the fee paid by the taxpayer was a prerequisite to obtaining the loan and incidental to an unconditional and legally enforceable obligation of the borrower. Furthermore, no services in addition to the lending of money were rendered as a result of the fee paid by the taxpayer. Accordingly, the fee is interest deductible under the provisions of section 163(a) of the Code.

Section 461(a) of the Code provides that the amount of credit allowed by subtitle A of the Code shall be taken for the taxable year which is the proper taxable year under the method of accounting used in computing taxable income.

Since the taxpayer employs the accrual method of accounting, and since the lending instrument is silent as to what portion of each payment is discounted interest, the deduction for the interest accrues ratably over the period of the loan. *James Bros. Coal Co.,* 41 T.C. 917 (1964). If, however, the loan instrument required that prepaid interest was subject to the "Rule of 78's," that method of determining the amount of annual deductions would be used. See Rev. Rul. 72-100, 1972-1 C.B. 122.

Since the interest rate, maturity date, and outstanding principal amount of the note remained unchanged when FNMA purchased the obligation, and since no new loan was negotiated between taxpayer and FNMA upon completion of construction, the interest fee which the bank discounted from the taxpayer's loan should be ratably deducted over the entire period of the loan, and not just over the period of construction.

Rev. Rul. 56-136 is distinguished.

2. POINTS PAID BY THE BUYER

As of January 1, 1976, points are treated as prepayment of interest and are subject to the reporting requirements for prepaid interest. Prior to 1976, the entire amount paid as points by a cash basis purchaser was deductible in the year paid. An exception to this rule applies to the deductibility of points paid on certain home purchase and improvement loans. Points are deductible in the year paid if:

1. The loan is secured by the principal residence;
2. The loan is used to buy or improve the residence;
3. The charging of points is an "established business" practice in the area in which the loan is made;
4. The points charged do not exceed the points generally charged in the area for such loans.

Example: If Jones purchases a $100,000 home and is required to pay his lender one point for his $80,000 purchase money mortgage, the point (or $800) is fully deductible in the year paid. However, if Jones purchases a four-family apartment building for investment purposes for $100,000, and is required to pay his lender one point for his $80,000 purchase money mortgage, the point (or $800) is amortized over the life of the loan.

3. POINTS PAID BY THE SELLER

Points paid by the Seller of the property (that is, where the Seller arranges for the Buyer's mortgage loan — see Rev. Rul. 67-197) are *not* deductible as interest. The Seller may treat these expenses as a selling expense, thereby reducing his gain on the sale. See Rev. Rul. 68-650.

4. PREPAYMENT PENALTY

Where a borrower incurs a penalty caused by the early repayment of his indebtedness to his mortgage lender, such penalty is considered an interest expense and is currently deductible as interest. This is true even when the purpose of the prepayment is to refinance with another lender. The penalty represents an additional charge for the use of the mortgagee's money for a short period of time rather than for a longer period as originally agreed upon when the money was borrowed. *See* Rev. Rul. 57-198; Rev. Rul. 73-137; *General American Life Insurance Co.,* 25 T.C. 1265 (1956); *12701 Shaker Boulevard Co.,* T.C. (1961), *aff'd,* 312 F.2d 749 (1963).

5. TAX EFFECT — OTHER MORTGAGE COSTS

As previously indicated, the mortgagor with respect to the mortgage closing may incur certain out-of-pocket costs, including the cost of an appraisal, credit report, survey, mortgage title policy, inspection fee, etc., all of said costs being incident to obtaining the loan.

If the subject mortgage loan is for property acquired for investment and/or trade or business purposes, said paid costs are deductible for tax purposes by amortizing them over the life of the loan. *See Anover Realty Corp.,* 33 T.C. 671 (1960). Also, any costs or fees incurred for purposes of renewing or extending an existing mortgage loan should be amortized over the term of the new loan. *See Julia Stow Lovejoy,* 18 B.T.A. 1179 (1930).

6. MORTGAGE LOAN SETTLEMENT: STATEMENT AND FORMULA

a. Statement

The Mortgage Loan Settlement Statement is one of three closing statements involved in the sale and closing of the real estate transaction. (The other two are the Seller-Buyer Closing Statement and the HUD's Uniform Settlement Statement.) This statement, and corresponding formula, indicates the amount of funds which the Buyer-Mortgagor must bring to the closing to complete the transaction.

b. Formula

Prepaid Finance Charges and Escrows:

1. Application (credit report and appraisal)
2. Service Fee
3. Mortgage Insurance
4. Interest to date of first principal payment
5. Title or abstract expenses
6. Recording fees
7. Insurance premium or escrow
8. Tax escrow
9. Transfer taxes
10. Survey
11. Legal fees
12. Property inspection fees

PLUS (+) Amount due Seller per Buyer's Closing Statement
EQUALS (=) Total funds to be disbursed
MINUS (-) Amount of loan from mortgagee
EQUALS (=) Additional amount due from mortgagor at closing

A sample of a mortgage loan settlement statement which indicates the formula as previously expressed appears in the Appendix to this chapter as Illustration No. 21.

Mortgage Closing. The consummation of the mortgage transaction is the mortgage closing. Normally the closing will take place at the offices of the lender, who is actually making the mortgage loan by virtue of the fact that said lender will be charged with the disbursements of all funds necessary to close the subject transaction. At the time of closing the borrower will be requested to sign some or all of the following documents:

1. RESPA Settlement Statement (HUD Form 1) and/or Mortgage settlement statement
2. Mortgage Note
3. Mortgage
4. Assignment of Rent and Power of Attorney

7. MODIFICATIONS AND RIDERS TO THE MORTGAGE

In addition to the standard form mortgage and note as utilized by banks and savings and loans, often additional provisions will be added to standard preprinted forms in the form of modifications and/or riders. Said riders or modifications will often change some of the terms and provisions of the preprinted form for purposes of bringing the preprinted form into conformity with that particular bank and/or savings and loan's internal practice. Copies of sample modifications and/or riders to mortgage and/or notes are Illustration Nos. 25-29 in the Appendix to this chapter.

H. SECONDARY OR JUNIOR FINANCING

USES OF JUNIOR FINANCING

1. Tax Free Cash. A second mortgage is a means of obtaining equity funds to liquify one's investment without tax consequence, in essence, trading cash flow dollars for instant dollars.

Suppose an investor acquires real estate and finances the purchase with a 25-year first mortgage loan. After five years, the property increases in value by 20 percent. The first mortgage may either bar prepayment altogether or impose a substantial prepayment penalty. To pull out the appreciation or equity in cash, the investor can resort to a three- or five-year second mortgage. While the *rate* on the second mortgage will be higher than on the existing first, the total interest *cost* will still be far less than if the entire first mortgage were refinanced at a higher rate. Since only a small portion of the second mortgage will be amortized during its life, the investor must be prepared to refinance the loan at its maturity. This, of course, creates a risk that a higher interest rate may have to be paid at that time.

2. Bootstrap Funds. When one partner in a real estate business wants to buy out the other, he can raise the cash he needs by a "bootstrap second mortgage." The proceeds of the loan provide the cash for an immediate buy-out. The amount can be repaid from anticipated future income that will belong solely to the remaining partner.

3. Renovation or Rehabilitation Dollars — "Mezzanine Financing." Often, an investor will require additional funds to rehabilitate or renovate an existing property. Such funds can be obtained through the use of junior financing.

4. Purchase Money. The most common type of junior financing is the purchase money mortgage. That is, the Seller is willing to assist the Buyer's purchase by taking back a second mortgage.

DOCUMENTATION

The documentation of a second mortgage transaction necessarily contains the same features as a first mortgage and the closing requirements are usually similar with certain covenants customarily added.

1. A junior mortgage may be subordinate to specific existing mortgages, but only to the present outstanding balance of such mortgages; to specific existing mortgages and future extensions, replacements, or renewals thereof, but with specified dollar amounts; or to any mortgages, present or future, that the borrower may wish to put on the property. Clearly, the second mortgagee should seek to restrict the subordination as much as possible. A common technique is to permit the borrower to refinance the existing senior lien in a higher amount (to reflect increased value of the property), but a part or all of the excess funds from refinancing must be used to reduce the balance of the second mortgage.

2. A default on the first mortgage is an event of default under the second mortgage.

3. The owner shall immediately notify the second mortgagee of any notice of default received from the first mortgagee.

4. The second mortgagee will reserve the right to satisfy a default under the first mortgage and add the payment or cost incurred to the balance of the second mortgage.

5. To insure that debt service on the senior mortgage is actually paid, the second mortgage may require the property owner to deposit first-mortgage payments in escrow with the secondary lender, who in turn pays them to the senior lender.

6. The second mortgagee often insists on security in addition to the second mortgage itself, in view of the increased risks involved in junior financing. The additional security can include personal guarantees by the borrower or his associates; assignment of leases and rents from the property (if the senior lender has not obtained the assignment); subordination of claims by other creditors of the borrower (for example, those about to receive partial payment from the proceeds of the secondary loan); and pledge of stock or other collateral, whether of the borrowing company or otherwise.

I. MORTGAGE INSURANCE

INTRODUCTION

The greatest financial risk and exposure involved in any real estate transaction is that which is normally incurred by the lender. In most instances, the buyer will leverage his financing whereby the lender advances loans totalling 80% to 95% of the fair market value and/or purchase price of the respective property. Ultimately, the risk of loss will increase proportionately to the loan to value ratio. For example, if a lender were to make an 80% mortgage on a particular property whose value is $100,000, such mortgage would be in the principal sum of $80,000. Should the mortgagor (purchaser-borrower) default in the payment of the mortgage or commit some other breach of the mortgage agreement which would accelerate the payment of the outstanding principal balance of the mortgage and thereby cause the lender to foreclose, the chances of the lender recovering the original $80,000 plus any accrued interest and other expenses are extremely good. The reasons are that:

1. Over time the value of the premises used to secure the loan will most likely increase due to inflation and other factors.

2. The mortgagor-borrower has himself made a particularly large cash investment in the property (e.g., $20,000) which he will be reluctant to forfeit.

3. Over time the principal sum outstanding on the mortgage is reduced through amortization.

The risk of loss, however, increases significantly as the loan to value ratio increases beyond the 80% range. For instance, if a lender made a loan in the amount of 95% of the value of the same property as in the example above, this would be the principal sum of $95,000. The lender is now faced with the prospect of recovering less than the $95,000, as well as all other costs, should he be forced to foreclose the loan. It should be noted here that in cases of loans where the loan to value ratio is in excess of 80%, the lender normally increases the interest rate charged from one to two percent. Because of these factors, one can imagine the veritable reluctance of lenders to make loans in excess of 80%, which prevents many potential purchasers in the marketplace from obtaining the requisite down payment required to purchase such property.

In 1957, Mortgage Guaranty Insurance Corporation (MGIC), which is headquartered in Milwaukee, Wisconsin, was formed. MGIC, like other private mortgage insurers, provides insurance for the lender's benefit in instances where the lender makes mortgages in excess of 80% loan to value ratio. Such insurance reimburses the lender in the event of foreclosure for any amounts the lender should lose, up to 20% of the original mortgage amount. The cost of the premiums of the insurance are incurred by the mortgagor (purchaser-borrower), and the formulas for calculating such premium can be obtained through the lender. In Wisconsin, for example, all state chartered savings and loans are required to secure mortgage guaranty insurance on all mortgage loans where the loan amount exceeds 80% of the appraised value, or sales price, whichever is less, of a property. Federally chartered savings and loans, on the other hand, are required to secure MGIC insurance on all mortgage loans exceeding 90% of the appraised value or sales price, whichever is less.

MORTGAGE GUARANTY INSURANCE CORPORATION OPERATING MANUAL (1980)

Types of Loans Insurable and Equity Requirements

MGIC insurance coverage is limited to loans secured by first liens on improved residential property. These loans must provide for amortization over the term of the loan in generally regular and substantially equal monthly payments and, except where otherwise permitted, include accruals for taxes and insurance. MGIC will also consider alternative recognized mortgage payment plans. Where applicable, ground rent and common area assessments are to be included in the regular monthly payments. Where the loan to value is 80% or less, or where otherwise permitted, the accruals for taxes and insurance may be waived. "Value" is defined as the lesser of the sale price or appraised value. A property is "owner occupied" if the borrower, or a member of the borrower's immediate family, occupies the property.

MGIC will insure a maximum loan to value ratio in each category below:

A. Primary residence - (1-4 family dwelling) not to exceed 95% of value.

B. Second or leisure home - (1 family dwelling) not to exceed 90% of value.

C. One investment property - (1-4 family dwelling) generally not to exceed 80% of value.

Loans on One Through Four Family Dwellings and One Condominium Unit, Owner Occupied.

MGIC will insure loans on one through four family owner occupied dwellings and one owner occupied condominium units if the mortgage loan does not exceed 95% of the lower of appraised value or sale price and the term does not exceed 30 years.

Loans on Second or Leisure Dwellings

MGIC will insure loans on second or leisure dwellings which are owner occupied, that is, which are intended for the exclusive use and enjoyment of the primary homeowner, and which are neither part of any mandatory rental-management pool nor primarily income producing in nature.

Second or leisure dwellings not meeting the owner occupied standard may be insurable if the mortgage meets acceptable underwriting eligibility requirements and the term does not exceed 30 years.

Second homes purchased for investment or rental purposes are considered to be non-owner occupied.

Loans on One-to-Four Family Dwellings, Non-Owner Occupied

MGIC will insure loans on one-to-four family non-owner occupied dwellings if the mortgage meets acceptable underwriting eligibility requirements. For premium determination, loans on non-owner occupied properties will be classified in the next higher loan-to-value category, i.e., a mortgage not exceeding 80% loan to value will be rated as an 81-85% loan to value.

Loans on Mobile Homes Deemed to Be Real Estate

Mobile Homes that are permanently secured at a given location and deemed to be real estate by state law or lender regulatory agencies are insurable. MGIC realizes that there are many well-conceived and well-executed developments incorporating mobile type housing on permanent foundations.

MGIC will insure higher ratio loans in prior-approved projects. To obtain prior project approval for mobile home projects, contact the MGIC Appraisal Department, MGIC Plaza, Milwaukee, Wisconsin 53202.

The minimum width of insurable mobile homes is 12 feet.

I. In prior approved projects with new and existing units:

A. Double wide - Maximum term 30 years and maximum loan-to-value 90%

B. Single wide - Maximum term 20 years and maximum loan-to value 90%

II. Mobile homes located on scattered sites and **not** previously occupied:

A. Double wide - Maximum term 20 years and maximum loan-to-value 80%

B. Single wide - Maximum term 15 years and maximum loan-to-value 80%

III. Mobile homes previously occupied:

All mobile home loans underwritten in this category may have a maximum term of 10 years and a maximum loan-to-value of 70%.

IV. Unapproved project with new units:

A. Double wide - Maximum term 15 years and maximum loan-to-value 80%

B. Single wide - Maximum term 12 years and maximum loan-to-value 80%

Existing written residential underwriting guidelines for credit and property will be strictly enforced on all applications. In addition, the following requirements must be met.

1. Minimum required physical characteristics:

a. pitched roof with asphalt shingles
b. 8 inch exterior lap siding
c. attached carport of matching design

    d. if unit is basementless, a storage shed of matching design is required

    e. minimum unit size: 1,000 square feet

    f. unit must be permanently attached to land

  2. Unit must meet the HUD Mobile Home Code and be classified as above standard or deluxe by MGIC's Appraisal Department.

  3. Furniture will not be included in the property value.

  4. No applications will be approved in a "condominium" project at terms and loan-to-values for "approved" projects until after the project has been approved by MGIC Appraisal Department. Refer to Section 302.3 for Mobile Home Condominium projects.

  5. Required appraisal forms for individual units:

    a. for condominium projects - FHLMC #465 or FNMA #1073

    b. for fee simple projects - FHLMC #70 or FNMA #1004

Modular Home Policy

For MGIC to approve any modular unit, written evidence from the appropriate agency must be presented. This evidence may take the form of research reports or letters. The following list identifies the items that **must** be stated:

  1. The **manufacturer** must be certified that he is presently building the modular to the minimum standards stated below.

  2. The **modular unit** must have been evaluated and approved for design, construction and supportive systems (light and ventilation, electrical, plumbing and heating, etc.).

  3. The name of manufacturer, model identification, code being certified to and date of evaluation must be shown.

It is the responsibility of the manufacturer to furnish the following data which certify compliance with the requirements of MGIC. The minimum standard shall be certification with one of the following three national code authorities:

BOCA - Building Officials and Code Administrators International

ICBO - International Conference of Building Officials

SBCC - Southern Building Code Congress

In the event that these "codes" are superseded by various state codes, said state codes shall become the minimum standards.

In lieu of a research report or letter on the modular unit, a set of plans and specification bearing the seal of the appropriate agency, on **each** page, is acceptable. The manufacturer still must present evidence that this operation is in compliance with the inspection authority.

In the event the above requirements are certified by a third party agency, MGIC shall require additional correspondence which **specifically states** the functions performed by the third parties are **accepted** by the code or state agencies.

It is requested that appropriate brochures and price lists be submitted to the Appraisal Department with documentation.

Participation Loan Policy (PLP)

MGIC provides insurance for the investor's portion of a previously uninsured package of loans. Each loan is individually underwritten on the same basis as a new submission provided that the loan to value is 95% or less. The seller of the participation must retain at least 5% of each sold loan. Rates under this program are contained in the Premium Rates Section of this manual.

Blanket Mortgages

Blanket mortgages are generally limited to no more than two detached single family dwellings; however, MGIC will not insure more than four dwelling units on a blanket mortgage. A separate appraisal must be submitted for each dwelling unit. The maximum insurable amounts are 95% for the home that will be owner occupied and 80% for the non-owner occupied properties.

Seasoned Loan Insurance

MGIC provides insurance on loans seasoned a minimum of twelve months where no contractual delinquencies exist. No payments may have been received after a thirty day grace period. Each loan must meet MGIC's standard underwriting guidelines. Rates under this program are contained in the Premium Rates Section of this manual, if applicable in your state.

Minimum Borrower Equity

MGIC requires a borrower to provide a minimum of 5% equity in every loan for which insurance coverage is desired. This minimum equity must either be in the form of cash or its equivalent (home exchange or land value). Prepaid items and work equity are not acceptable as part of the required 5% minimum equity.

Work Equity

Equity in the form of work-to-be-done by the borrower presents an added risk and is acceptable only:

A. In addition to the minimum 5% equity
B. To a maximum of 5% of value
C. When it consists of minor items that are clearly within the borrower's abilities

In addition to the above, MGIC suggest the lender retain sufficient funds in escrow to complete the improvements. It is important to remember that the policy stipulates that in the event of a claim the title can only be tendered to MGIC on a completed property.

Secondary Financing

Secondary financing is acceptable on a loan for which insurance coverage is desired when the borrower has at least 10% equity in the property. The insured amount is the amount of the first mortgage and the premium is based upon this amount. When secondary financing is utilized, the borrower's income must be sufficient to meet the additional payment.

Collateral Pledge

Pledged collateral is acceptable on a loan: (1) if the borrower has a minimum of 5% equity in the property or (2) if the appropriate regulatory authorities have permitted lenders to consider pledge collateral as equity. However, in no event may the insured amount exceed 95% of appraised value or sales price, whichever is less.

The insured amount is the mortgage loan balance minus the amount of the collateral pledge. The premium is computed on the insured amount. When the terms and conditions of the pledge have been satisfied and the pledge has been released, lenders desiring to increase coverage to insure the entire loan amount should notify MGIC, utilizing the MGIC Application for Additional Advance. A sample of this form is in the Forms Appendix.

Lenders may desire coverage on the entire loan amount even though a collateral pledge is involved. This avoids the necessity of applying for additional coverage as the collateral pledge is released. In the event of a claim, the collateral pledge is deducted from the principal balance.

Graduated Payment Mortgages With Collateral Pledge

When there is pledged collateral and when the net mortgage balance and the insured amount are scheduled to increase under the terms of a graduated payment mortgage plan, the initial premium (annual or single) shall be charged on the original net mortgage balance. However, in no event may the insured amount exceed 95% of appraised value or sales price, whichever is less.

To calculate loan-to-value ratios for the purpose of determining the applicable initial premium rate, the original net mortgage balance shall be divided by the purchase price or appraised value, whichever is lower.

Renewal premium rates under the Standard Plan are charged on the net mortgage balance at the time of renewal. Renewal premium rates under the Constant Plan, where available, are charged on the same basis as the initial premium.

In the event of a claim, the collateral pledge will be deducted from the principal balance in determining loss.

Graduated Payment Mortgages Without Collateral Pledge

When the mortgage balance under the terms of a graduated payment mortgage plan is scheduled to increase before amortizing, then the initial premium (annual or single) shall be charged on the initial mortgage balance. However, in no event may the highest mortgage balance exceed 95% of appraised value or sales price, whichever is less.

To calculate loan-to-value ratios for the purpose of determining the applicable initial premium rate, the initial mortgage balance shall be divided by the purchase price of appraised value, whichever is lower.

Renewal premium rates under the Standard Plan are charged on the mortgage balance at the time of renewal. Renewal premium rates under the Constant Plan, where available, are charged on the same basis as the initial premium.

Lease/Rent Payment as Part of Equity

MGIC will consider a portion of lease or rent payments as equity provided such payments are above comparable market rents. Only that portion of the payment above market rents may be considered. Example: a three bedroom detached single family residence normally rents for $250.00 per month. The borrower agrees to pay $300.00 per month rent. In this case $50.00 per month could accumulate as equity.

Balloon Mortgages

MGIC will insure loans where the borrower's monthly payment scheduled to repay the indebtedness provides for amortization of the loan over a stated period of time, e.g. 30 years and where the note provides for a "balloon payment" of the amortized balance at the end of a shorter specified period of time, e.g. 5 years. These loans will be insured if either:

    I. The lender guarantees to renew the loan at the end of the shorter specified period of time, or,

II. The lender requests in writing and receives an endorsement to the Master Policy stating coverage does not apply to the borrower's failure to pay the balloon payment. A copy of this endorsement is included in the Forms Appendix for your review.

Wrap-Around Mortgages

MGIC will insure wrap-around mortgages. When the wrap-around mortgage is a purchase transaction where the borrower intends to occupy the property, the maximum loan-to-value ratio is 95%.

When the transaction is a non-purchase transaction, the maximum loan-to-value is 90%. Additionally, on non-purchase transactions MGIC requires a minimum of two years seasoning on the original first mortgage and no delinquencies during the past 12 months. The two years seasoning requirement will be waived on any nonpurchase transaction where the proceeds are to be used for home-improvement purposes that are evidenced by a signed contract of what is to be accomplished and the cost of the improvements.

Cost: Residential Loans

Premium Plan Rates For MGIC Loan Insurance

MGIC Coverage	Loan-to-Value	Annual Premium Plan	SINGLE PREMIUM PLAN					
			4 Years	5 Years	7 Years	10 Years	12 Years	15 Years
30%	91-95%	1.25%**	1.80%	2.00%	2.25%	2.75%		3.00%
	86-90%	.90%*	1.40%	1.65%	1.90%	2.40%		2.65%
	18-85%	.75%	1.30%	1.50%	1.75%	2.25%		2.50%
	80% and under	.60%	1.15%	1.35%	1.60%	2.10%		2.35%
25%	91-95%	1.00%*	1.45%	1.60%	2.00%	2.375%		2.50%
	86-90%	.65%	1.10%	1.30%	1.60%	2.00%		2.375%
	81-85%	.50%	1.00%	1.20%	1.40%	1.70%		
	80% and under	.35%	.75%	.90%	1.20%	1.50%		
22%	91-95%	.80%	1.35%	1.50%	1.80%	2.30%		2.40%
20%	91-95%	.75%	1.25%	1.40%	1.75%	2.20%		2.30%
	86-90%	.50%	.90%	1.10%	1.40%	1.80%		2.25%
	81-85%	.35%	.80%	1.00%	1.20%	1.50%		
	80% and under	.25%	.65%	.75%	1.00%	1.30%		
17%	86-90%	.40%	.75%	.90%	1.20%	1.50%	1.75%	2.00%
	81-85%	.30%	.60%	.70%	.90%	1.20%		
16%	91-95%	.625%	1.10%	1.25%	1.60%	2.10%		2.20%
12%	86-90%	.25%	.60%	.70%	.90%	1.20%		
	81-85%	.15%	.50%	.60%	.80%	1.00%		
	80% and under	.14%	.45%	.55%	.70%	.90%		

* Optional plan available at .50% each 1st 3 years, .25% annual renewal thereafter. An alternative option for 25% coverage on 91%-95% LTV loans is .50% the 1st year with annual renewal at .375% of the declining balance thereafter; or under the Constant plan .365% for years 2-10 or until the loan amortizes to 80%, whichever is less, and .125% thereafter.

** Optional plan available at .625% each 1st 3 years, .25% annual renewal thereafter.

TRUTH IN LENDING LAW

With regard to the federal and/or state Truth In Lending Laws, the MGIC insurance premium constitutes a "finance charge". Accordingly, MGIC has prepared informational materials and tables which indicate how to reflect the MGIC premium on the truth in lending disclosure form.

NOTES

(1) Annual renewal premium rates are .25% of the declining balance except for 12% coverage of 85% and under LTV, which are: .15% for 81%-85% LTV and .14% for 80% and under LTV. Five-year renewals are available as an option to the annual renewals in the 10 and 15 year programs. The five-year renewal rates are .50% of the principal balance.

(2) For seasoned loans on which, prior to application, (i) 12 or more monthly payments have been received; (ii) no contractual delinquencies exist; (iii) no payments have been received after the expiration of a "30 day grace period"; and (iv) company underwriting standards are met, the premium rate shall be determined by subtracting .25% from the initial premium rate. However, no annual plan may be reduced below a minimum of .25%, and no single premium may be reduced by an amount greater than that applicable to the annual premium plan in the same loan-to-value and coverage percentile grouping.

(3) Constant renewal premiums plans are available as an option to the annual renewals shown above. The constant renewal rates, based on the original loan amount, are as follows for the first 10 years: .24% on all coverages except on 12% coverage of 85% and under LTV where the rate is .14% for LTV of 81%-85% and .13% for LTV of 80% and under. For the 11th and subsequent years, the rate is .125% of the original loan amount for all coverages.

Underwriting Policies

MGIC believes in a uniform approach to underwriting. Each application submitted to MGIC is individually underwritten by an experienced staff underwriter. MGIC's underwriters apply the following guidelines to each transaction to insure that each case is considered fairly within its own context. In addition to normal, prudent underwriting practices, the investment quality of each loan is also weighted to provide uniformity of quality in the secondary market.

The MGIC underwriter considers the borrower(s) income and thrift habits in relation to the proposed housing obligation. The stability of the borrower(s) income with respect to housing and other obligations, the financial resources of the borrower(s), and the past regard for obligations, as well as the property and its location, are all considered an integral part of each risk evaluation.

Mortgage Payment as Percent of Borrower Income

The total monthly mortgage payment of the borrower, including all escrows, should not exceed 33% of the total gross monthly income.

Example: Borrower's gross monthly income = $2,000 per month. Total monthly mortgage payment = $660 per month. Ratio of income to house payment is:

$$\frac{\$\ 660}{\$2,000} = 33\%$$

Total Monthly Obligations as Percent of Borrower Income

The total fixed monthly obligations (those obligations of 10 months or more) of the borrower, including mortgage payment should not exceed 38% of the total gross monthly income.

Example: Borrower's gross monthly income = $2,000 per month. Total monthly house payment = $600 per month. Car payment $120 ($1,800 balance) per month. Furniture payment $40 ($600 balance) per month. Ratio of income to obligation is total monthly house payment ($600) + car payment ($120) + furniture payment ($40) = $760 per month divided by $2,000 gross monthly income equals 38%.

$$\frac{\$600\ +\ \$120\ +\ \$40}{\$2,000} = \frac{\$\ 760}{\$2,000}\ =\ 38\%$$

Other Income

MGIC considers income from overtime, part-time employment, and investments as other income. The amount of this income recognized by MGIC underwriters depends on the length of time this income has been received and the probability that this income will continue. This income must be substantiated by income and expense statements, Federal income tax forms or employment verification.

MGIC considers a borrower's past payment record an important factor in judging future payment performance. Therefore, a current credit report showing the borrower's employment status, credit history, credit references, including information with regard to lawsuits, judgments and bankruptcy, must be provided for each borrower. In cases where the Loan to value ratio exceeds 90% and the property is in an SMSA (Standard Metropolitan Statistical Area), a Factual Data Credit Report is required.

Military Service

In the event of active military duty by the borrower, modification to the amortization schedule will be granted by MGIC. These modifications are granted in accordance with the Soldiers and Sailors Civil Relief Act.

Co-Signor

In the event of a co-signor, one who is personally liable on the note, it is necessary for the lender to submit a separate loan application, credit report, and income verification on behalf of the co-signor.

Guidelines Pertaining to Property

The emphasis in appraising property for high-ratio lending should be placed on the comparability of the subject property with surrounding structures, the characteristics of design which contribute to convenience, livability and desirability, and the quality of the construction and equipment such as furnaces, plumbing, etc., all of which affect marketability.

Lack of functional utility as characterized by such factors as poor room arrangement, small room sizes, lack of adequate storage, etc., does have an adverse effect on the marketability of the property and should be noted in the appraisal. These factors are found in both old and new housing.

Older homes should, of course, have a remaining economic life in excess of the proposed amortization term. Particular attention should be given to possible problem areas such as neglected maintenance or obsolescence of fixtures, plumbing, heating plant, etc. If such problems are found to exist, their restoration, repair or replacement should be provided for as a condition of sale, or the buyer should have sufficient resources to accomplish such restoration, repair or replacement. The lender should establish an escrow for such restoration where applicable. A certificate of code compliance may also be required.

For loans on existing construction, the neighborhood should be characterized as having a broad appeal and good marketability. The subject property itself should be comparable in value to others in the neighborhood.

For new construction in areas where marketability has not been established, it is necessary to submit with the appraisal pertinent information concerning the distance to and the availability of transportation, schools, shopping, recreation, churches, water, sewer, gas, electricity, drainage, and any other factors affecting marketability.

Obtaining and Amending the Commitment

Applications for insurance coverage should be sent to the Regional Underwriting Office as listed on the first page of this Manual. Upon receipt and approval of the application, MGIC will issue a commitment to insure. The commitment obligates MGIC to insure the given loan, upon premium payment and fulfillment of any MGIC required special conditions. Information pertaining to obtaining and changing commitments is included in this section.

Exhibits Required

The documents listed below and described in Sections 400.01 through 400.06 are required in all cases for proper underwriting. In addition, copies of any further documentation that the lender has acquired or a cover letter from the lender explaining any unusual circumstances can often offer valuable assistance to the underwriter.

    A. MGIC Application Form

    B. Lender's Loan Application

    C. Current Credit Report or Factual Data Credit Report whichever is applicable

    D. Appraisal Report and one clear photo of subject property

    E. Income Verification

    F. Deposit Verification

    G. Sales Contract

H. Borrower's Past Payment Record (Refinance Only)

I. Buyer-Seller Affidavit when appropriate

MGIC Application Form

It is important that this form be completely filled out including the selection of the desired premium plan. If there is no premium plan requested, the commitment will be issued with the annual premium plan corresponding to the loan to value ratio indicated on the application. The lender should submit the application form as a part of his loan file. A sample of an application is included in the Appendix.

Lender's Loan Application

A copy of the lender's loan application, which should contain financial statements including detail of monthly obligations, family employment and income data, is required.

Credit Report

A current credit report is required for each borrower indicating employment status, credit history, credit references, and information with regard to lawsuits, judgments, and bankruptcy. In cases where the loan to value ratio exceeds 90% of the lower appraised value or purchase price, and the property is within a Standard Metropolitan Statistical Area (SMSA), a Factual Data Credit Report is required.

Property Appraisal

A current appraisal is required. The appraisal should include both cost and market approach to value. The appraisal must contain one clear photograph of the subject property. All appraisal on properties within a Standard Metropolitan Statistical Area (SMSA) must contain a stated value based on the market approach to value and supported by no less than three comparable properties which have been compared to the subject property. In addition to having the appraisal signed, the appraiser's name should also be typed under the signature. If the appraisal is not made at the request of the submitting MGIC approved lender this should also be noted.

Income Substantiation of Borrower

The employer's Verification of Income is required. When a borrower is self-employed or receives commission income, recent tax returns (past two years) or signed balance sheet and profit and loss statement will satisfy this requirement.

Affidavit of Purchase Price, Equity, and Occupancy

The MGIC Affidavit Form establishes the purchaser's equity in the property and his intention to occupy the property as his residence. This form is required in all cases, except refinances. Since this form requires the signatures of both the buyer and the seller, it should be obtained at closing and forwarded with the papers necessary to obtain certification. This form may be utilized in lieu of Federal Home Loan Bank Board Certification Forms one, two and three. Other forms may be acceptable provided they meet requirements of FHLBB Certification Forms one, two and three. A sample of the MGIC Affidavit is included in the Appendix. The Federal National Mortgage Association (FNMA) Affidavit of Equity is acceptable in lieu of MGIC Form.

Sales Contract/Offer to Purchase Real Estate

A signed or certified copy of the contract of sale is required with all submissions except refinances.

Commitment Terms and Extensions

MGIC commitments are issued for a period of 12 months. Extensions of up to three months will be granted at the lender's request for a total commitment term not to exceed 15 months. If more than a 15 month term is found to be necessary, a new application must be submitted with updated financial information and a new appraisal. A sample of the commitment is included in the Appendix.

Application Reply Procedure

All applications for mortgage insurance are processed immediately upon receipt by the respective regional underwriting office. If the underwriter has questions on any application, the lender will be contacted by telephone. Immediately after underwriting approval, MGIC's TELECOMMITMENT SERVICE will provide the lender with a report by telephone so that he may proceed with processing. A space is provided on the MGIC application form for both a telephone number and the name of the person to whom the reply should be directed. This space should only be completed when telephone approval is desired. Promptly after "Telecommitment" notification, and, in any case, within 24 hours of MGIC's receipt of the complete application, a printed commitment will be mailed to the lender.

Conditional Commitments

Commitments to insure are often issued subject to special conditions. If such special conditions exist, they will be printed on the face of the commitment. If further documentation is required to fulfill the commitment, it should be sent with the executed commitment and premium payment to avoid delays in processing of certificates. Failure to satisfy any special conditions could invalidate the insurance coverage.

Change of Existing Commitments

Recognizing that circumstances and situations change, MGIC will allow certain changes to be made on existing commitments without the necessity of submitting a new application. Changes are of two types: those not requiring prior approval from MGIC (See 404.01) and those requiring prior approval (See 404.02).

RESIDENTIAL LOAN APPLICATION

MORTGAGE APPLIED FOR	☐ Conventional ☐ FHA ☑ VA	Amount $	Interest Rate %	No. of Months	Monthly Payment Principal & Interest $	Escrow/Impounds (to be collected monthly) ☐ Taxes ☐ Hazard Ins. ☐ Mtg. Ins. ☐

Prepayment Option

SUBJECT PROPERTY

Property Street Address	City	County	State	Zip	No. Units

Legal Description (Attach description if necessary)				Year Built

Purpose of Loan: ☐ Purchase ☐ Construction-Permanent ☐ Construction ☐ Refinance ☐ Other (Explain)

Complete this line if Construction-Permanent or Construction Loan ☞	Lot Value Data Year Acquired $	Original Cost $	Present Value (a) $	Cost of Imps. (b) $	Total (a + b) $	ENTER TOTAL AS PURCHASE PRICE IN DETAILS OF PURCHASE.

Complete this line if a Refinance Loan		Purpose of Refinance	Describe Improvements [ ] made [ ] to be made
Year Acquired	Original Cost	Amt. Existing Liens	
$	$		Cost: $

Title Will Be Held In What Name(s)	Manner In Which Title Will Be Held

Source of Down Payment and Settlement Charges

This application is designed to be completed by the borrower(s) with the lender's assistance. The Co-Borrower Section and all other Co-Borrower questions must be completed and the appropriate box(es) checked if ☐ another person will be jointly obligated with the Borrower on the loan, or ☐ the Borrower is relying on income from alimony, child support or separate maintenance or on the income or assets of another person as a basis for repayment of the loan, or ☐ the Borrower is married and resides, or the property is located, in a community property state.

BORROWER		CO-BORROWER	
Name	Age / School Yrs	Name	Age / School Yrs
Present Address No. Years ___ ☐ Own ☐ Rent		Present Address No. Years ___ ☐ Own ☐ Rent	
Street		Street	
City/State/Zip		City/State/Zip	
Former address if less than 2 years at present address		Former address if less than 2 years at present address	
Street		Street	
City/State/Zip		City/State/Zip	
Years at former address ☐ Own ☐ Rent		Years at former address ☐ Own ☐ Rent	
Marital Status ☐ Married ☐ Separated ☐ Unmarried (incl. single, divorced, widowed)	DEPENDENTS OTHER THAN LISTED BY CO BORROWER NO. AGES	Marital Status ☐ Married ☐ Separated ☐ Unmarried (incl. single, divorced, widowed)	DEPENDENTS OTHER THAN LISTED BY BORROWER NO. AGES
Name and Address of Employer	Years employed in this line of work or profession? ___ years Years on this job ___ ☐ Self Employed*	Name and Address of Employer	Years employed in this line of work or profession? ___ years Years on this job ___ ☐ Self Employed*
Position/Title	Type of Business	Position/Title	Type of Business
Social Security Number***	Home Phone	Business Phone	Social Security Number***	Home Phone	Business Phone

GROSS MONTHLY INCOME				MONTHLY HOUSING EXPENSE**			DETAILS OF PURCHASE	
Item	Borrower	Co-Borrower	Total		PRESENT	PROPOSED	Do Not Complete If Refinance	
Base Empl. Income	$	$	$	Rent			a. Purchase Price	$
Overtime				First Mortgage (P&I)	$	$	b. Total Closing Costs (Est.)	
Bonuses				Other Financing (P&I)			c. Prepaid Escrows (Est.)	
Commissions				Hazard Insurance			d. Total (a + b + c)	$
Dividends/Interest				Real Estate Taxes			e. Amount This Mortgage	( )
Net Rental Income				Mortgage Insurance			f. Other Financing	( )
Other† (Before completing, see notice under Describe Other Income below.)				Homeowner Assn. Dues			g. Other Equity	( )
				Other:			h. Amount of Cash Deposit	( )
				Total Monthly Pmt.	$	$	i. Closing Costs Paid by Seller	( )
Total	$	$	$	Utilities			j. Cash Reqd. For Closing (Est.)	$
				Total	$	$		

DESCRIBE OTHER INCOME		
◁ B—Borrower C—Co-Borrower	NOTICE: † Alimony, child support, or separate maintenance income need not be revealed if the Borrower or Co-Borrower does not choose to have it considered as a basis for repaying this loan.	Monthly Amount $

IF EMPLOYED IN CURRENT POSITION FOR LESS THAN TWO YEARS COMPLETE THE FOLLOWING

B/C	Previous Employer/School	City/State	Type of Business	Position/Title	Dates From/To	Monthly Income
						$

THESE QUESTIONS APPLY TO BOTH BORROWER AND CO-BORROWER

If a "yes" answer is given to a question in this column, explain on an attached sheet.	Borrower Yes or No	Co-Borrower Yes or No	If applicable, explain Other Financing or Other Equity (provide addendum if more space is needed).
Have you any outstanding judgments? In the last 7 years, have you been declared bankrupt?			
Have you had property foreclosed upon or given title or deed in lieu thereof?			
Are you a co-maker or endorser on a note?			
Are you a party in a law suit?			
Are you obligated to pay alimony, child support, or separate maintenance?			
Is any part of the down payment borrowed?			

*FHLMC/FNMA require business credit report, signed Federal Income Tax returns for last two years, and, if available, audited Profit and Loss Statements plus balance sheet for same period.
**All Present Monthly Housing Expenses of Borrower and Co-Borrower should be listed on a combined basis.
***Neither FHLMC nor FNMA requires this information.

FHLMC 65 Rev. 8/78   FNMA 1003 Rev. 8/78

Illustration 10
Residential Loan Application

This Statement and any applicable supporting schedules may be completed jointly by both married and unmarried co-borrowers if their assets and liabilities are sufficiently joined so that the Statement can be meaningfully and fairly presented on a combined basis; otherwise separate Statements and Schedules are required (FHLMC 65A/FNMA 1003A). If the co-borrower section was completed about a spouse, this statement and supporting schedules must be completed about that spouse also.　　　☐ Completed Jointly　　☐ Not Completed Jointly

STATEMENT OF ASSETS AND LIABILITIES

ASSETS | LIABILITIES AND PLEDGED ASSETS

Indicate by (*) those liabilities or pledged assets which will be satisfied upon sale of real estate owned or upon refinancing of subject property

Description	Cash or Market Value	Creditors' Name, Address and Account Number	Acct. Name if Not Borrower's	Mo. Pmt. and Mos. left to pay	Unpaid Balance
Cash Deposit Toward Purchase Held By	$	Installment Debts (include "revolving" charge accts)		$ Pmt./Mos.	$
Checking and Savings Accounts (Show Names of Institutions/Acct. Nos.)				/	
				/	
				/	
Stocks and Bonds (No./Description)				/	
				/	
Life Insurance Net Cash Value Face Amount ($		Other Debts Including Stock Pledges		/	
SUBTOTAL LIQUID ASSETS	$				
Real Estate Owned (Enter Market Value from Schedule of Real Estate Owned)		Real Estate Loans			
Vested Interest in Retirement Fund					
Net Worth of Business Owned (ATTACH FINANCIAL STATEMENT)					
Automobiles (Make and Year)		Automobile Loans			
Furniture and Personal Property		Alimony, Child Support and Separate Maintenance Payments Owed To			
Other Assets (Itemize)					
		TOTAL MONTHLY PAYMENTS		$	
TOTAL ASSETS	A $	NET WORTH (A minus B) $		TOTAL LIABILITIES	B $

SCHEDULE OF REAL ESTATE OWNED (If Additional Properties Owned Attach Separate Schedule)

Address of Property (Indicate S if Sold, PS if Pending Sale or R if Rental being held for income)	Type of Property	Present Market Value	Amount of Mortgages & Liens	Gross Rental Income	Mortgage Payments	Taxes, Ins. Maintenance and Misc.	Net Rental Income
		$	$	$	$	$	$
TOTALS →		$	$	$	$	$	$

LIST PREVIOUS CREDIT REFERENCES

B - Borrower C - Co-Borrower	Creditor's Name and Address	Account Number	Purpose	Highest Balance	Date Paid
				$	

List any additional names under which credit has previously been received _____

AGREEMENT: The undersigned applies for the loan indicated in this application to be secured by a first mortgage or deed of trust on the property described herein, and represents that the property will not be used for any illegal or restricted purpose, and that all statements made in this application are true and are made for the purpose of obtaining the loan. Verification may be obtained from any source named in this application. The original or a copy of this application will be retained by the lender, even if the loan is not granted. The undersigned ☐ intend or ☐ do not intend to occupy the property as their primary residence.

I/we fully understand that it is a federal crime punishable by fine or imprisonment, or both, to knowingly make any false statements concerning any of the above facts as applicable under the provisions of Title 18, United States Code, Section 1014.

_____ Date _____　　_____ Date _____
Borrower's Signature　　　　　　　　　　Co-Borrower's Signature

INFORMATION FOR GOVERNMENT MONITORING PURPOSES

The following information is requested by the Federal Government if this loan is related to a dwelling, in order to monitor the lender's compliance with equal credit opportunity and fair housing laws. You are not required to furnish this information, but are encouraged to do so. The law provides that a lender may neither discriminate on the basis of this information, nor on whether you choose to furnish it. However, if you choose not to furnish it, under Federal regulations this lender is required to note race and sex on the basis of visual observation or surname. If you do not wish to furnish the above information, please initial below.

BORROWER: I do not wish to furnish this information (initials)_____
RACE/ ☐ American Indian, Alaskan Native ☐ Asian, Pacific Islander
NATIONAL ☐ Black ☐ Hispanic ☐ White SEX: ☐ Female
ORIGIN ☐ Other (specify) _____ ☐ Male

CO-BORROWER: I do not wish to furnish this information (initials)_____
RACE/ ☐ American Indian, Alaskan Native ☐ Asian, Pacific Islander
NATIONAL ☐ Black ☐ Hispanic ☐ White SEX ☐ Female
ORIGIN ☐ Other (specify) _____ ☐ Male

FOR LENDER'S USE ONLY

(FNMA REQUIREMENT ONLY) This application was taken by ☐ face to face interview ☐ by mail ☐ by telephone

_____ (Interviewer)　　　　　_____ Name of Employer of Interviewer

FHLMC 65 Rev. 8/78　　　　　REVERSE　　　　　FNMA 1003 Rev. 8/78

Illustration 10 (cont'd)

Confidential Personal Statement

To: MILWAUKEE WESTERN BANK, MILWAUKEE, WISCONSIN:　　　Date _____

Name _____

Home Address _____

Business Affiliation _____

Fill in all blanks - Writing "No" or "None" where appropriate - List in Dollars

ASSETS		LIABILITIES	
Cash on Hand and in Accounts	$	Notes Payable - This Bank (Sched. D) . .	$
Notes & Accts. Receivable.		Notes Payable - Other Banks (Sched. D).	
Cash Value - Life Ins. (Sched. A) . . .		Auto Loan(s)	
Stocks & Bonds (Sched. B)		. . . .	
Real Estate - Home (Sched. C)		Credit Cards	
Real Estate - Other (Sched. C)		Other Loans - To	
Automobile(s).		. . . .	
. . . .		Home Mtg. Payable (Sched. C)	
Other Assets (Itemize)		Other R/E Mtgs	
. . . .		Taxes	
. . . .		Other Liabilities (Itemize)	
. . . .			
. . . .			
. . . .			
Total Assets	$	Total Liabilities	$
		Assets minus Liabilities = Net Worth	$

ANNUAL INCOME: Salary . . . . $ _____　　Bonus . . . . $ _____

　　　　　　　Dividends and Interest . . $ _____　　Real Estate . . . . $ _____

Other Income (Describe) _____ $ _____

TOTAL ANUAL INCOME — All Sources _____ $ _____

CONTINGENT LIABILITY: - Personal Guarantees given on behalf of:

Name _____ Amount $ _____

Name _____ Amount $ _____

Are you presently involved in any lawsuits or income tax audits which could materially affect your financial status?

Yes _____ No _____ If yes, describe _____

Illustration 11
Confidential Personal Statement

LIFE INSURANCE - Sched. A Company	Face Amount of Policy	Gross Cash Surrender Value	Policy Loan	Beneficiary

STOCKS AND BONDS - Sched. B (Description)	Owned By	Market Where Traded	Present Value

REAL ESTATE OWNED AND MORTGAGES PAYABLE - Sched. C Location and Description	In Whose Name	Present Value	Mortgage Bal.
(Home)			
(Other)			

Are all taxes paid up to date? _____ If not, specify amount $ _____ For what year(s) _____

BANK LOANS - Sched. D Bank Name	Loan Amt.	Bank Name	Loan Amt.

For the purpose of obtaining credit from Bank and any future credit granted me by Bank, or to support the extension of credit already given, I represent that this statement is true and complete and authorize the Bank or its agents, to verify the information obtained in this statement and obtain additional information concerning my financial condition and furnish the same to others. This statement is the Bank's property. I understand that it is a federal crime punishable by fine or imprisonment or both to knowingly make any false statements concerning any of the following information as applicable under provisions of Title 18, United States Code Section 10141. I agree to notify Bank in writing, of any change that materially affects the accuracy of this statement.

State of Wisconsin }
Milwaukee County } S.S.

(Signature) _____

Subscribed and sworn to before me this _____ Day of _____ 19 _____

_____
Notary Public

My Commission (expires) (is) _____

Illustration 11 (cont'd)

LOAN NO. _____

REQUEST FOR VERIFICATION OF DEPOSIT

TO _____

_____

_____

APPLICANT AUTHORIZATION

I have applied for a mortgage loan and stated the information shown below. You are authorized to verify this information and to supply the lender identified above with the information requested. Your response is solely a matter of courtesy for which no responsibility is attached to your institution or any of your officers.

_____   _____
Applicant's Signature   Date

CHASE FEDERAL SAVINGS AND LOAN ASSOCIATION

RE: APPLICANT_____   LOAN NO._____

APPLICANT's STATEMENT				VERIFICATION OF BANK OR OTHER DEPOSITORY	
ACCOUNT TYPE	ACCOUNT NO.	BALANCE	DATE OPENED	CURRENT BALANCE	APPROX. AVERAGE BALANCE DURING PAST 2 MONTHS
Checking					
Checking					
Savings					
Savings					

DOES APPLICANT HAVE ANY OUT-STANDING LOANS OTHER THAN THOSE LISTED ( ) Yes ( ) NO (If YES, enter total below)

	ACCOUNT NO.	BALANCE	MONTHLY PAYMENT	CURRENT BALANCE	PAYMENT EXPERIENCE
Secured Loans					
Unsecured Loans					

	ACCOUNT NO.	AMOUNT RECEIVED	SOURCE	IS STATEMENT CORRECT?	IF NO, INDICATE AMOUNT RECEIVED
Direct Deposit Income					

_____   _____
Date   Completed By

_____   _____
Company Name   Title

Illustration 12
Request for Verification of Deposit

LOAN NO. _____

REQUEST FOR VERIFICATION OF EMPLOYMENT

_____

_____

_____

Gentlemen:

An application has been made by a current employee of your organization for a mortgage loan to be made by this institution.

CHASE FEDERAL SAVINGS AND LOAN ASSOCIATION

_____   _____
Loan Officer   Date

EMPLOYEE AUTHORIZATION

I hereby authorize my current employer to furnish the information requested on this form.

_____   _____
Employee's Signature   Date

EMPLOYER'S VERIFICATION

LOAN NO. _____

RE: BORROWER_____

The following information is furnished to Chase Federal Savings and Loan Association in strict confidence in response to the request of the borrower named above.

1. Position held: _____

2. Length of Employment: _____ Years Months _____

3. Base Salary: $_____ (Check One)
   ( ) Hour ( ) Week ( ) Month ( ) Year

4. Hours Worked Weekly: _____

5. Approximate Overtime Earnings:
   $_____ Week_____ Month_____ Year_____

6. Bonus or Commission: $_____

7. Earnings for Previous Year: $_____

8. Probability of Continued Employment: _____

9. Remarks:

_____   _____
Date   Signature of Employer

_____   _____
Company Name   Title

Illustration 13
Request for Verification of Employment

NOTICE OF COMMITMENT FEE POLICY

S and L has a policy of requiring commitment fees before agreeing to make a new mortgage loan. Our current fee is 1% of the loan amount and may change without notice. The commitment fee is not refundable. It will, however, be applied to your loan costs at the time of loan closing. This policy is applicable when the loan is being made directly to you. If you are assuming a loan made to a builder for the construction of your home, he will have paid the fee when we made the loan commitment. There is no additional commitment fee due to S and L for the assumption of the loan.

We have two methods of collecting fees and deposits, depending on your residency status.

If you are

1) A U.S. citizen currently residing outside the 50 United States
2) A citizen of Guam, American Samoa, American Virgin Islands, Puerto Rico currently residing outside the 50 United States
3) A foreign citizen without an immigrant visa (Green Card),

then paragraph "A" below applies to your application.

If you are

1) A U.S. citizen residing in the 50 United States
2) A citizen of Guam, American Samoa, American Virgin Islands, Puerto Rico currently residing in the 50 United States
3) A foreign citizen holding an immigrant visa (Green Card),

then paragraph "B" below applies to you.

A. A commitment fee deposit must accompany your application. The fee deposit is 1% of the amount of the loan you are requesting. It is payable in U.S. dollars by draft, check or money order drawn on a U.S. financial institution. This fee deposit will be refunded to you if you cancel your loan request prior to our approval or if your loan request is not approved. At approval, however, the deposit will become a commitment fee and will not be refunded unless you are approved for an amount less than you requested and we receive your Commitment Rejection Notice within 30 days of the date of the commitment letter. If the Commitment Rejection Notice is returned after 30 days, S and L will retain 1% of the amount approved as a commitment fee and refund the remaining portion of the deposit. We will send you a letter indicating the terms and conditions of our commitment. At your settlement on the loan, the fee will be applied to the current loan costs. If the loan is cancelled, there will be a charge of $100.00 to reactivate the request. This fee is in addition to all other fees, is non-refundable and must be paid before we will reinstate your request.

B. Upon approval of your loan, you will receive a letter stating the terms and conditions of our commitment. At that time a non-refundable fee of 1% of the loan amount is required. This fee must be received by us within 15 days of the date of the commitment letter. At the time of closing, the commitment fee will be applied to your loan costs. If, however, we do not receive the fee within 15 days of the date of the letter, we will assume that you have withdrawn your request for the loan, and your request will be cancelled. If the loan is cancelled, there will be a charge of $100.00 to reactivate the request. This fee is in addition to all other fees, is non-refundable and must be paid before we will reinstate your request.

CONVENIENT LOCATIONS SERVING SOUTH FLORIDA

MLOR NPF (16) (8/81)

Illustration 14
Notice of Commitment Fee Policy

H.C. Miller Company

Residential .... ☐

Commercial .... ☐ _____
Mortgagor

Farm .... ☐ _____
Approving Officer   Processing Officer

_____ ⎰ Tel. No.–Home ⎱ _____
Address of Mortgagor   ⎱ Tel. No.–Business ⎰ Address of Mortgaged Property

(New) – (Refinanced) Mortgage _____
Date

Appraisal ⎰ Land $_____
          ⎱ Improve-
            ments $_____ ⎰ $_____ $_____ Mortgage _____
                                    ⎱   Total   Amount   Maturity   Rate   Fee

Date _____ $_____ Renewed to_____
                                      Amount   Maturity   Rate   Fee

Appraised by _____ $_____ Renewed to_____
                                      Amount   Maturity   Rate   Fee

Appraised by _____ $_____ Renewed to_____
                                      Amount   Maturity   Rate   Fee

Name of Company	Amount	Kind	Mtge. Clause	Expires
I _____	$_____	_____	_____	_____
N _____	$_____	_____	_____	_____
S _____	$_____	_____	_____	_____
U _____	$_____	_____	_____	_____
R _____	$_____	_____	_____	_____
A
N
C
E

	Date "Recorded"	Date Returned To Bank	EVID. OF PAID R.E. TAXES IN FILE	
			Year	Date Received
Mortgage	_____	_____	_____	_____
Mtge. Assignment	_____	_____	_____	_____
Rent Assignment	_____	_____	_____	_____
Warranty Deed	_____	_____	_____	_____
R.E. Transfer Return	_____	_____	_____	_____
	_____	_____	_____	_____

	Date Ordered or Sent	Name and/or Source	Date Received		
Mtge. Application	X X X	_____	_____	_____	_____
Application Fee $ _____	X X X	_____	_____	_____	_____
Closing Cost Advance Disclosure & RESPA Book	_____	_____	X X X	_____	_____
Credit Report	_____	_____	_____	_____	_____
Employment Verification	_____	_____	_____	_____	_____
Appraisal	_____	_____	_____	_____	_____
Flood Plain Insurance Required ☐ Yes ☐ No, if yes _____	_____	_____	_____	_____	_____
Mtge. Approved By	X X X	_____	_____	_____	_____
F.H.A./V.A./P.M.I.	_____	_____	_____	_____	_____
Commit Letter	_____	_____	_____	_____	_____
T in L Discl. (WBA 241)	_____	_____	_____	_____	_____
TL-3 Rescission (if required)	_____	_____	_____	_____	_____
Survey ⎰ With Picture ☐ ⎱ No Picture ☐	_____	_____	_____	_____	_____
Abstract – Preliminary	_____	_____	_____	_____	_____
Atty. Opinion – Preliminary	_____	_____	_____	CENSUS TRACT # _____	
Abstract – Final	_____	_____	_____	_____	_____
Atty. Opinion – Final	_____	_____	_____	_____	_____
Mtgee. Title Policy – Prelim.	_____	_____	_____	_____	_____
Mtgee. Title Policy – Final	_____	_____	_____	_____	_____
Owner's Title Policy – In File	_____	_____	_____	_____	_____
Fire Insurance	_____	_____	_____	_____	_____
Buyer and Seller Closing Statement	X X X	_____	_____	_____	_____
RESPA Settlement Statement	_____	_____	_____	_____	_____
	_____	_____	_____	_____	_____

Mortgage Referred By _____

Proposed Closing Date _____ Where _____

Other Information _____

_____

W.B.A. 427 (1/79) REAL ESTATE MORTGAGE CHECKLIST AND PROCESSING SHEET

Illustration 15
Mortgage Checklist

Mortgage Corporation

GOOD FAITH ESTIMATES OF SETTLEMENT COSTS

LENDER:

This form does not cover all items you will be required to pay in cash at settlement, for example, deposit in escrow for real estate taxes and insurance. You may wish to inquire as to the amounts of such other items. You may be required to pay other additional amounts at settlement. The figures shown are computed, based on a sales price of $ _____, and a proposed mortgage of $ _____, as stated on your loan application. Please note that Item No. 803 Appraisal Fee and Item No. 804 are payable at time of application and that Item No. 808 Commitment Fee may be payable at the time the Association issues its commitment letter.

801.	Loan Origination Fee	$ _____
803.	Appraisal Fee	$ _____
804.	Credit Report	$ _____
805.	Lender's Inspection Fee	$ _____
808.	Commitment Fee	$ _____
809.	FNMA Application Fee	$ _____
810.	Pictures	$ _____
901.	Interest from funding date to the first day of the following month (one month prior to the first payment due date). Estimate given is 30 days, actual may be as little as 1 day depending on closing and funding dates.	$ _____
902.	Mortgage Insurance Premium	$ _____
1105.	Document Preparation	$ _____
1108.	Title Insurance	$ _____
1111.	Escrow Fee to Title Company	$ _____
1201.	Recording Fees	$ _____
1301.	Survey	$ _____
1303.	Amortization Schedule	$ _____
1304.	_____	$ _____
1400.	Total ESTIMATED SETTLEMENT COSTS	$ _____

Note: The above Good Faith Estimates are made pursuant to the requirements of the REAL ESTATE SETTLE-MENT PROCEDURES ACT (RESPA). These figures are only estimates, and the actual charges due at settlement may be different. This estimate does not represent a commitment to make the loan and only represent certain costs to be paid by borrower(s).

The undersigned applicant(s) hereby acknowledges receipt of the above notice as well as the above estimate of closing costs, and the SPECIAL INFORMATION BOOKLET.

_____   _____
Applicant   Applicant

Date _____
(Lender to retain one copy)

Illustration 16
Good Faith Estimates of Settlement Costs

Stock No. 11142

428 (12 80)

© Wisconsin Banker's Association

Prepared for and intended for use by commercial banks in transactions governed by Wisconsin Law.

REAL ESTATE MORTGAGE

(May use for (1) business purpose loan, (2) loan to an organization, (3) loan exceeding $25,000 or (4) loan of $25,000 or less if not governed by the Wisconsin Consumer Act.)

_____ ("Mortgagor",

whether one or more) mortgages, conveys and warrants to _____

_____ ("Lender")

In consideration of the sum of _____

_____ Dollars ($ _____),

loaned or to be loaned to _____

_____ ("Borrower", whether one or more),

evidenced by Borrower's note(s) dated _____

_____, the real estate described below, together with all privileges, hereditaments, easements and appurtenances, all rents, leases, issues and profits, all awards and payments made as a result of the exercise of the right of eminent domain, and all existing and future improvements and fixtures (all called the "Property").

RETURN TO

1. Description of Property. (This Property _____ the homestead of Mortgagor.) Tax Key # _____
　　　　　　　　　　　　　　　　　(is)　(is not)

☐ If checked here, description is continued on reverse side or attached sheet.

2. Title. Mortgagor warrants title to the Property, excepting only restrictions and easements of record, municipal and zoning ordinances, current taxes and assessments not yet due and _____.

3. Escrow. Interest _____ be paid on escrowed funds required under paragraph 7(a) on the reverse side.
　　　　　　　(will) (will not)

4. Additional Provisions. Mortgagor shall observe and comply with the Additional Provisions on the reverse side, which are incorporated herein, and shall not permit an event of default to occur.

The undersigned acknowledges receipt of an exact copy of this Mortgage.

Signed and Sealed this_____ day of_____, 19____.

SEE REVERSE SIDE FOR ADDITIONAL PROVISIONS

_____ (SEAL)

(NAME OF CORPORATION OR _____)

By: _____ (SEAL)

(_____ PRESIDENT OR _____)

*

Attest: _____ (SEAL)

(_____ SECRETARY OR _____)

*

[Witnesses not required]

_____ (SEAL)

_____

_____ (SEAL)

_____

_____

_____ (SEAL)

AUTHENTICATION OR **ACKNOWLEDGMENT**

Signatures of_____

_____

_____

authenticated this_____ day of_____, 19____.

*

Title: Member State Bar of Wisconsin or_____
authorized under Sec. 706.06, Wis. Stats.

┌─────────────────────────────────┐
│ This instrument was drafted by │
│   │
│ _____ │
└─────────────────────────────────┘

*Type or print name signed above.

STATE OF WISCONSIN ⎫
_____ County⎰ ss.

Personally came before me, this_____ day of_____, 19____
the above named_____
　　　　　　　　(NAMES OF INDIVIDUALS AND THEIR SPOUSAL)

_____
(RELATIONSHIP IF ANY. OR NAME OF OFFICER AND TITLE)

_____

to me known to be the person _____ who executed the foregoing instrument and acknowledged the same.

*_____

Notary Public_____ County, Wis.

My Commission (Expires) (Is)_____

H.C.Miller Company

Illustration 17
Wisconsin Real Estate Mortgage

ADDITIONAL PROVISIONS

4. Mortgage As Security. This Mortgage is given to secure prompt payment to Lender of the sum stated in the first paragraph of this Mortgage, plus interest and charges, according to the terms of a promissory note(s) of Borrower to Lender identified on the reverse side, and any extensions, renewals or modifications, and any additional sums loaned by Lender to any Mortgagor, to any Mortgagor and another or to another guaranteed or endorsed by any Mortgagor agreed to be secured by this Mortgage except credit the granting of which is subject to the Wisconsin Consumer Act, plus interest and charges (all called the "Note"), and the performance of all convenants, conditions and agreements contained in this Mortgage, and to the extent not prohibited by law costs and expenses of collection or enforcement. If the Note is paid according to its terms, and all other payments are made and all other terms, conditions, covenants, and agreements contained in this Mortgage and the Note are performed then this Mortgage ceases and is void.

5. Taxes. To the extent not paid to Lender under §7(a), Mortgagor shall pay before they become delinquent all taxes, assessments and other charges which may be levied or assessed against the Property, or against Lender upon this Mortgage or the Note or other debt secured by this Mortgage, or upon Lender's interest in the Property, and deliver to Lender receipts showing timely payment.

6. Insurance. Mortgagor shall keep the improvements on the Property insured against direct loss or damage occasioned by fire, extended coverage perils and such other hazards as Lender may require, through insurers approved by Lender, in amounts, without co-insurance, not less than the unpaid balance of the Note or the full replacement value, whichever is less, and shall pay the premiums when due. The policies shall contain the standard mortgage clause in favor of Lender and, unless Lender otherwise agrees in writing, the original of all policies covering the Property shall be deposited with Lender. Mortgagor shall promptly give notice of loss to insurance companies and Lender. All proceeds from such insurance shall be applied, at Lender's option, to the installments of the Note in the inverse order of their maturities (without penalty for prepayment) or to the restoration of the improvements on the Property. In the event of foreclosure of this Mortgage or other transfer of title to the Property, in extinguishment of the indebtedness secured hereby, all right, title, and interest of Mortgagor in and to any insurance then in force shall pass to the purchaser or grantee.

7. Mortgagor's Covenants. Mortgagor convenants:

(a) **Escrow.** To pay Lender sufficient funds at such times as Lender designates, to pay (1) the estimated annual real estate taxes and assessments on the Property, (2) all property insurance premiums when due, and (3) if payments owed under the Note are guaranteed by mortgage guaranty insurance, the premiums necessary to pay for such insurance which Lender may cancel at any time. Upon demand, Mortgagor shall pay Lender such additional sums as are necessary to pay these items in full when due. Lender shall apply these amounts against the taxes, assessments and insurance premiums when due. Escrowed funds may be commingled with Lender's general funds;

(b) **Condition and Repair.** To keep the Property in good and tenantable condition and repair, and to restore or replace damaged or destroyed improvements and fixtures;

(c) **Liens.** To keep the Property free from liens and encumbrances superior to the lien of this Mortgage;

(d) **Waste.** Not to commit waste or permit waste to be committed upon the Property;

(e) **Conveyance.** Not to sell, assign, lease, mortgage, convey or otherwise transfer any legal or equitable interest in all or part of the Property, or permit the same to occur without the prior written consent of Lender and, without notice to Mortgagor, Lender may deal with any transferee as to his interest in the same manner as with Mortgagor, without in any way discharging the liability of Mortgagor hereunder or upon the Note hereby secured;

(f) **Alteration or Removal.** Not to remove, demolish or materially alter any part of the Property, without Lender's prior written consent, except Mortgagor may remove a fixture, provided the fixture is promptly replaced with another fixture of at least equal utility;

(g) **Condemnation.** To pay to Lender all compensation received for the taking of the Property, or any part, by condemnation proceeuings (including payments in compromise of condemnation proceedings), and all compensation received as damages for injury to the Property, or any part. The compensation shall be applied in such manner as Lender determines to rebuilding of the Property or to installments of the Note in the inverse order of their maturities (without penalty for prepayment);

(h) **Ordinances; Inspection.** To comply with all laws, ordinances and regulations affecting the Property. Lender and its authorized representatives may enter the Property at reasonable times to inspect it and, at Lender's option, repair or restore it;

(i) **Subrogation.** That the Lender is hereby subrogated to the lien of any mortgage or other lien discharged, in whole or in part, by the proceeds of the Note.

8. Authority of Lender to Perform for Mortgagor. If Mortgagor fails to perform any of Mortgagor's duties set forth in this Mortgage, Lender may perform the duties or cause them to be performed, including without limitation signing Mortgagor's name or paying any amount so required, and the cost shall be due on demand and secured by this Mortgage, bearing interest at the highest rate stated in any Note but not in excess of the maximum rate permitted by law from the date of expenditure by Lender to the date of payment by Mortgagor.

9. Default; Acceleration; Remedies. If, (a) there is a failure to make a payment under the Note when due and such default continues for a period of ten days, (b) Mortgagor fails timely to observe or perform any of Mortgagor's convenants contained in this Mortgage, (c) any representation or warranty made in this Mortgage or otherwise to induce Lender to extend credit to Mortgagor is false in any material respect when made, or (d) Mortgagor or a surety for the Note dies, ceases to exist or becomes insolvent or the subject of bankruptcy or other insolvency proceedings, the Note will, at the option of Lender and without notice, which is hereby waived, be payable immediately, and Lender may collect the same in a suit at law or by foreclosure of this Mortgage by action or advertisement or by the exercise of any other remedy available at law or equity.

10. Waiver. Lender may waive any default without waiving any other subsequent or prior default by Mortgagor.

11. Power of Sale. In the event of foreclosure, Lender may sell the Property at public sale and execute and deliver to the purchasers deeds of conveyance pursuant to statute.

12. Receiver. Upon the commencement or during the pendency of an action to foreclose this Mortgage, or enforce any other remedies of Lender under it, without regard to the adequacy or inadequacy of the Property as security for the Note, the court may appoint a receiver of the Property (including homestead interest) without bond, and may empower the receiver to take possession of the Property and collect the rents, issues and profits of the Property and exercise such other powers as the court may grant until the confirmation of sale, and may order the rents, issues and profits, when so collected, to be held and applied as the court may direct.

13. Foreclosure Without Deficiency Judgment. If the Property is a one to four family residence that is owner-occupied at the commencement of a foreclosure, a farm, a church or owned by a tax exempt charitable organization, Mortgagor agrees to the provisions of sec. 846.101, Wis. Stats., and as the same may be amended or renumbered from time to time, permitting Lender, upon waiving the right to judgment for deficiency, to hold the foreclosure sale of real estate of 20 acres or less six months after a foreclosure judgment is entered. If the Property is other than a one to four family residence that is owner-occupied at the commencement of a foreclosure, a farm, a church or a tax exempt charitable organization, Mortgagor agrees to the provisions of sec. 846.103, Wis. Stats., and as the same may be amended or renumbered from time to time, permitting Lender, upon waiving the right to judgment for deficiency, to hold the foreclosure sale of real estate three months after a foreclosure judgment is entered.

14. Expenses. To the extent not prohibited by law, Mortgagor shall pay all reasonable costs and expenses, including without limitation, attorneys' fees and expenses of obtaining title evidence, incurred by Lender in foreclosing this Mortgage.

15. Severability. Invalidity or unenforceability of any provision of this Mortgage shall not affect the validity or enforceability of any other provision.

16. Successors and Assigns. The obligations of all Mortgagors are joint and several. This Mortgage benefits Lender, its successors and assigns, and binds Mortgagor(s) and their respective heirs, personal representatives, successors and assigns.

Illustration 17 (cont'd)

_____ _____, 19 ____ $_____

MAKER(S)

858 (3/80)
© Wisconsin Bankers Association 1980

MORTGAGE NOTE

Prepared and intended for use by commercial banks in transactions governed by Wisconsin Law.

(Do not use for a loan or additional advance of $25,000 or less to individual(s) for personal, family, household or agricultural purposes if this is not secured by a first mortgage.)

The undersigned ("Maker", whether one or more)

promises to pay to the order of _____ at _____

the principal sum of _____ DOLLARS

in _____ equal installments of $ _____ payable _____, 19 _____, and on the same day of each

_____month thereafter, PLUS a final payment of unpaid principal balance and accrued interest due on _____.

All payments include principal and interest. This Note bears interest on the unpaid balance before maturity at the rate of _____% per year. All unpaid

principal and accrued interest shall bear interest after maturity of this Note, whether occurring through lapse of time or acceleration, at the rate of

_____% per year until paid.

If any installment of principal and interest is not paid on or before the 10th day after its due date, holder may collect a delinquency charge at the rate of

_____% per year on the amount of the installment from the due date until paid or until maturity, whichever is earlier.

This Note is secured by a real estate mortgage dated _____, 19 _____, from _____

_____ to the payee. If Maker fails to make a payment under this Note when due, and the default continues for 10 days, or upon the occurrence of an event of default described in the mortgage or any other agreement securing this Note, the holder may declare the entire balance of principal and accrued interest to be payable immediately, without notice or demand. All payments shall be applied in such manner as the holder determines to interest, principal and payments due under the mortgage. At any time after the occurrence of an event of default, holder may apply against any credit balance or other money at anytime owing by holder to any Maker all or any part of the unpaid balance of this Note.

All Makers, indorsers, sureties and guarantors agree to pay all costs of collection, including, to the extent not prohibited by law, reasonable attorneys' fees.

* ☐ If checked here, any installment paid within _____ days (not to exceed 30) prior to or after its due date shall include interest to the due date of the installment and no delinquency charge will be imposed on that installment.

** ☐ If checked here, this Note may otherwise be prepaid in full or in part without penalty, and if prepaid in full, unearned interest, if any, will be refunded to the extent required by law.

☐ If checked here, full or partial prepayment of this Note: (Describe prepayment restrictions and penalty, if any)

Presentment, protest, demand and notice of dishonor are waived.

Without affecting the liability of any Maker, indorser, surety or guarantor, the holder may, without notice, grant renewals or extensions, accept partial payments, release or impair any collateral security for the payment of this Note or agree not to sue any party liable on it.

Maker acknowledges receipt of an exact copy of this Note.

_____ _____ (SEAL)

(ADDRESS)

_____ _____ (SEAL)

(ADDRESS)

_____ _____ (SEAL)

(ADDRESS)

FOR BANK CLERICAL USE

Disclosure Statement (W.B.A. (TL)-841) may be required .... ☐ Delivered

Rescission Notice (W.B.A. (TL)-3) may be required.................... ☐ Delivered

HUD form [W.B.A. (RESPA)-240 A & B] may be required .... ☐ Delivered

ALWAYS take or use a
W.B.A. — 428 Mortgage
with this Note.

* If interest is computed to actual date of payment, do not check this box.

** Check if loan is secured by first lien on 1-4 family dwelling which borrower uses as principal place of residence.

If interest is computed by the 365/360 day method, add this sentence: "Interest is computed for the actual number of days principal is unpaid on the basis of a 360 day year."

ORIGINAL BANK COPY

Illustration 18
Wisconsin Mortgage Note

PAYMENTS

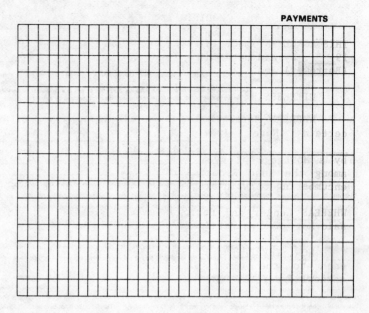

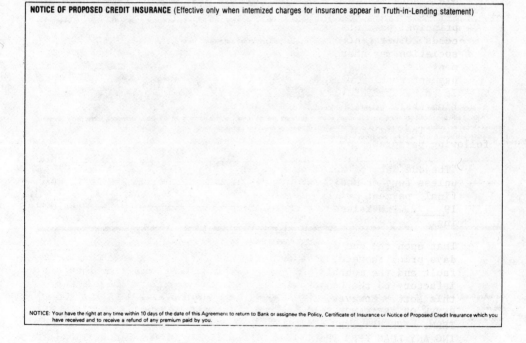

NOTICE OF PROPOSED CREDIT INSURANCE (Effective only when itemized charges for insurance appear in Truth-in-Lending statement)

NOTICE: Your have the right at any time within 10 days of the date of this Agreement to return to Bank or assignee the Policy, Certificate of Insurance or Notice of Proposed Credit Insurance which you have received and to receive a refund of any premium paid by you.

Illustration 18 (cont'd)

MODIFICATION OF NOTE AND MORTGAGE

THIS AGREEMENT made in duplicate this _____ day of _____,
19____, by and between _____
(Borrower) and _____(Lender)

WITNESSETH:

WHEREAS Borrower has this date executed in favor of Lender a
certain   Note   (the   Note)   in   the   principal   amount   of
_____ Dollars ($_____) secured
by a Mortgage of even date herewith (the Mortgage), to be recorded
among the Land Records of _____ County, Wisconsin,
encumbering certain property as described in said Mortgage; and

WHEREAS Lender and Borrower mutually desire to amend said Note and
said Mortgage as hereinafter set forth,

NOW, THEREFORE; in consideration of the sum of One Dollar ($1.00)
each to the other in hand paid, receipt of which is hereby
acknowledged, the parties hereto agree as follows:

1.   The Note is hereby modified by the elimination of the entire
paragraph dealing with prepayment and by the addition thereto of the
following:

"This Note may be prepared in part or in full at anytime with interest to date of payment, provided that when the aggregate of
principal payments made during the preceding 12 month period exceeds 20 per cent of the original amount of the loan, the Association may charge 90 days interest on that part of the prepayment which exceeds 20 per cent of said original amount. No prepayment penalty will be charged at Note Maturity. If this Note
is to be prepaid in full, 30 days written notice of such intention shall be given to the Association."

2.   The Note is hereby further modified by the addition of the
following paragraphs as integral parts thereof:

"The due date of this Note will be _____ years from this date,
unless further modified by mutual agreement of the parties; said
final payment will be due on the _____ day of _____,
19____. Provisions for renewal shall be governed by the following.

That upon the due date of the Note, or within a period of _____
days prior thereto, and provided that Borrower is not then in de-
fault and the monthly payment progress on the Note has been sat-
isfactory to the Lender, the parties may negotiate the renewal of
this Note. However, THE ASSOCIATION IS UNDER NO OBLIGATION TO
RENEW OR REFINANCE SAID LOAN UPON MATURITY OF THE INITIAL LOAN
TERM. FURTHER, THE ASSOCIATION MAKES NO REPRESENTATION REGARD-
ING ANY LOAN FEES THAT MAY BE INCURRED OR TERMS AND CONDITIONS AT
MATURITY, OR TO THE RATE OF INTEREST TO BE CHARGED, THE AMORTIZA-
TION SCHEDULE UNDER WHICH THE LOAN IS TO BE REPAID, THE AMOUNT OF
MONTHLY PAYMENTS TO BE MADE BY BORROWER FOR PRINCIPAL AND INTER-
EST, AS WELL AS ALL OF ITS OTHER PROVISIONS.

Illustration 19
Modification of Note and Mortgage

In the negotiations for the renewal of this Note, the loan-to-value ratio established at the time of the original loan shall prevail and govern all renewals granted, unless Lender in its discretion, requires a new appraisal which shall establish a new loan-to-value ratio. Upon the renewal of this Note, Lender may impose a charge covering its cost in processing such renewal, including the cost of any appraisal if required."

3.   Should the account become thirty-one days delinquent, the interest on the unpaid total of indebtedness shall be at a rate 1 1/2% per annum in excess of the rate provided by the Note not to exceed the highest rate permissible by law, until all delinquent payments have been made.

4.   If the Lender or any successor in interest as to the indebtedness transfers or assigns its total interest, or any part thereof, to the Federal Home Loan Mortgage Corporation, the Government National Mortgage Association or the Federal National Mortgage Association, it is understood and agreed that this Modification Agreement shall terminate and have no further force or effect concurrently with the recording of such transfer or assignment. In the event Lender acquires this loan, this agreement shall be treated as if it has never been terminated.

5.   All of the other terms conditions and provisions and addendums of said Note and Mortgage are hereby ratified, confirmed and reaffirmed, it being the intention of Borrower and Lender that said Note and Mortgage shall remain in full force and effect as modified hereby.

IN WITNESS WHEREOF the parties hereto have executed this instrument under seal on the day and year first above written.

BORROWER:

_____ (SEAL)

_____ (SEAL)

LENDER:

BY _____

_____ (TITLE)

STATE OF WISCONSIN
_____ COUNTY

Personally came before me this _____ day of _____ 19____, the above named _____
to me known to be the person(s) who executed the foregoing instrument and acknowledged the same as _____ their free act and deed.

_____

_____ Notary Public

_____ County, State of WI

My Commission expires _____

Illustration 19 (cont'd)

ST. FRANCIS SAVINGS & LOAN ASSOCIATION

POLICY STATEMENT

ON

SHORT TERM MORTGAGE LOANS

Loan Number:_____

St. Francis Savings & Loan Association has adopted the following
policy in regard to the short term residential mortgage loans it make
and which policy is applicable to the mortgage loan identified by the
above loan number:

A.   This mortgage loan is due and payable, in full, on
     _____, 19___. The following paragraphs out-
     line the procedure to be followed in the event that both the
     Borrower and Lender agree to enter into a new loan. How-
     ever, neither the Borrower nor the Lender is under any legal
     obligation to renew, extend or to otherwise replace this
     loan with a new loan. If this loan is not replaced with
     another loan, it shall be due and payable, in full, on the
     maturity date, without any penalty or charges except for the
     fee for recording the satisfaction of the mortgage.

B.   If Borrower so elects, the Borrower may, prior to the due
     date of this loan, make application with St. Francis Savings
     & Loan Association ("St. Francis") for a new mortgage loan.
     In considering such loan application, St. Francis shall re-
     quire that the following conditions have been met.

     1.   That there are no intervening liens against the title
          of the property, and that the borrower maintains good
          and merchantable title to the premises, except for the
          mortgage to St. Francis.

     2.   That the Borrower has maintained a record of payments
          on this note satisfactory to St. Francis.

     3.   That there has been no change in ownership of the prop-
          erty.

     4.   If the property securing this mortgage loan was to be
          occupied by the borrower at the time this mortgage loan
          was made, that it continues to be occupied by the
          borrower.

     5.   That the real estate taxes have been fully paid, when
          due, throughout the term of this mortgage loan.

The Borrower and St. Francis must agree to all terms of the new
loan and all provisions applicable to a new mortgage, including
its term, the rate of interest to be charged, the amortization
schedule under which the loan is to be repaid, the amount of the
monthly payments to be made by Borrower for principal and interest, as well as all other applicable provisions of a new mortgage
note.

Illustration 20
Policy Statement on Short Term Mortgage Loans

C.   In the negotiations for a new mortgage note, the loan to
     value ratio established at the time of the original loan
     shall prevail and govern all new loans thereafter granted,
     unless St. Francis, in its sole discretion, requires a new
     appraisal which shall estalish a revised loan to value
     ratio.

D.   In the event St. Francis grants a new mortgage loan to the
     borrower, the borrower shall be obligated to pay the costs
     of any required title insurance charges; appraisal fee, if
     required; recording fees and any other charges as may then
     be appropriate, plus a $100 loan processing fee to St. Fran-
     cis. St. Francis, in its sole discretion, may utilize any
     existing loan documents in processing any new loan applica-
     tion by the Borrower secured by a mortgage on the property
     described in the mortgage executed this date.

The undersigned acknowledged receipt of the above Policy Statement and
further acknowledge that their mortgage loan, numbered above, is due
and payable in full on _____ .

BORROWER:

_____
                              (SEAL)

_____
                              (SEAL)

_____
                              (SEAL)

_____
                              (SEAL)

LENDER:

ST. FRANCIS SAVINGS & LOAN ASSOCIATION

BY:_____

Illustration 20 (cont'd)

ADDENDUM TO NOTE
LATE CHARGE RIDER

It is mutually agreed and understood that in the event the monthly installment is more than 15 days in arrears a late charge not to exceed 1.000% per month or 12.000% per annum, not to exceed the highest rate permissible by law may be charged.

Acknowledged this _____ day of _____, 19____.

_____ (SEAL)

Mortgagor

_____ (SEAL)

Mortgagor

_____ (SEAL)

Mortgagor

_____ (SEAL)

Mortgagor

STATE OF_____)

_____ COUNTY)ss.

Personally came before me this _____ day of _____, 19____ the above named _____
_____

to me known to be the person(s) who executed the foregoing instrument and acknowledged the same.

_____

(SEAL)   Notary Public, State of _____
                                My Commission Expires_____

Illustration 21
Late Charge Rider

Addendum to Notes, Costs
Attorneys Fees & Foreclosure
Procedures

As and for further disclosure and clarification of attorney fees, etc.
relate to Paragraph 19 and 24 of the mortgage, the parties thereto
agree as follows:

"If suit is brought to collect this note, the note holder shall be
entitled to collect all reasonable costs and expenses of suit,
including, but not limited to, reasonable attorney's fees to the
extent not prohibited by Chapter 428 of the Wisconsin Statutes."

Further, it is mutually agreed and understood that said promissors and
mortgagors shall pay all costs and reasonable attorney's fees as
disclosed above, subject to such statutory limitations as may be
applicable and as incurred or paid by the Association in any suit
which it may be plaintiff or defendant by reason of being a party to
this mortgage note, or mortgage securing it, or incurred or paid by
the Association by reasons of any dispute arising from this mortgage
note or the mortgage securing same.

It is further mutually agreed and understood the mortgagor agrees that
in the event of a foreclosure of this mortgage they will be bound by
the provisions of Wisconsin Statutes Section 846.101 and Section
846.103(2) as they may be applicable to the mortgaged premise.

Date: _____

Witness: _____

_____ (SEAL)
   (Mortgagor)

_____ (SEAL)
   (Mortgagor)

_____ (SEAL)
   (Mortgagor)

_____ (SEAL)
   (Mortgagor)

STATE OF _____)
_____ COUNTY)ss.

Personally came before me this _____ day of _____,
19____ the above named _____
_____
to me known to be the person(s) who executed the foregoing instrument
and acknowledged the same.

_____

   (SEAL) ·   Notary Public
                 My Commission Expires_____

Illustration 22
Attorneys Fees and Foreclosure Procedures

<u>ADDENDUM & DISCLOSURE</u>

CHANGE OF OWNERSHIP CONSENT REQUIRED AND

NOTICE OF SPECIAL PROVISION

As and for further disclosure and clarification of Paragraph 17 of the mortgage, the parties thereto agree as follows:

It is expressly agreed and understood that this mortgage note shall become due and payable forthwith, at the option of the Association, if at any time during the terms of the mortgage loan, the promissors and mortgagors shall sell, convey, transfer, or in any manner encumber said mortgage premise, or if either legal or equitable title shall vest in any person other than the promissors and mortgagors in any manner and for any reason whatsoever, unless the consent in writing of the Association, its assessors or assignees, is first obtained. In the event of the approval by the Association of any such transfer of titles, the Association may make a commitment agreement charge based on the original amount of the mortgage loan, plus an administrative fee, which if not paid, will be added to the unpaid principal balance of the mortgage loan. This addendum shall pertain to any transfer by land contract and/or assumption.

In the event the mortgagor/s named and described herein, be an individual corporation, limited or general partnership, joint venture, co-operation, association or syndication; change the ownership of the property mortgaged hereunder in any manner whether by tranfer, assignment, equity, hypothecate equity ownership by remains of sale of stock, trade, land contract, assumption, syndication, or any other form of conveyance without explicit consent of the mortgagee; the mortgagee shall have the absolute right/option to declare the entire indebtedness described herein due and payable.

Acknowledged this _____ day of _____, 19____ .

_____ (SEAL)

_____ (SEAL)

_____ (SEAL)

_____ (SEAL)

Personally came before me this _____ day of _____, 19____ the above named _____

to me known to be the persons who executed the foregoing instrument and acknowledged the same.

(SEAL)   Notary Public, State of _____
                          My Commission Expires_____

Illustration 23
Change of Ownership Consent Required and Notice of Special Provision

MGIC **Mortgage Guaranty Insurance Corporation**
a subsidiary of MGIC Investment Corporation
MGIC Plaza, P.O. Box 488
Milwaukee, Wisconsin 53201

Application for Approval

1. Name and Address of Main Office:

2. **Telephone:**

3. **Net Worth:**
   (Not Less than $100,000)

City: State: Zip:

4. Lending Experience:

a. FHA/VA		b. Conventional Mortgages	
In Portfolio	Serviced for Others	In Portfolio	Serviced for Others
No.	No.	No.	No.
$	$	$	$

5. Originations (Last Fiscal Year):

a. FHA/VA	b. Conventionals
No.	No.
$	$

6. Examined or Supervised by:

☐ a. Federal Reserve System

☐ b. Federal Deposit Insurance Corporation

☐ c. Federal Savings & Loan Insurance Corporation

☐ d. Other Supervisory Agency —
   Describe:

7. Approved Lending Institution by:

☐ a. Federal Housing Administration

☐ b. Veteran's Administration

☐ c. Federal National Mortgage Association
   (Conventional Seller/Servicer Only)

☐ d. Federal Home Loan Mortgage Corporation

☐ e. Other Private Mortgage Insurer —
   List:

Have you been denied approval of any of the above, or has your approval ever been suspended or terminated?   Yes ☐   No ☐
If yes please explain.

8. Lending Area:
   Counties in which you normally lend: _____
   Are these located in a standard metropolitan statistical area? _____

9. a. Do you currently have a loan servicing department? ____ No ____ Yes   No. Employees _____
   b. Real estate owned or in judgment No. _____ $ _____
   c. Contracts and loans to facilitate sale No. _____ $ _____
   d. First mortgage loans in default (90 days) No. _____ $ _____

10. Attachments:
   a. Most recently published financial statement or latest independently audited financial statement.
   b. Resumes of the experience and qualifications of each loan officer, appraiser and mortgage servicer.
   c. List separately those Branch Offices that will originate only and those that will originate and service.
      Also include the name of the Managing Officer for each branch.
   d. If not supervised by 6a, 6b, 6c, submit letters from banks setting forth available lines of credit,
      and a list of current investors whose loans you service.

Date:_____   By:_____
                     Managing Officer

Form No. 01-0178 (8/77)

Illustration 24
Application for Approval

MGIC

Mortgage Guaranty Insurance Corporation

MGIC Plaza
Milwaukee, Wisconsin 53201

a subsidiary of
MGIC Investment Corporation

Commitment For Insurance

In consideration of the premium hereinafter set forth, your application has been examined, and the Company hereby issues to you a Commitment for Insurance of the loan herein described subject to the terms and conditions of your Mortgage Guaranty Policy, identified below, and subject to any special conditions that may be set forth below.

Insured
Lender's
Name
and
Mailing
Address

Lender's Identification No.	Date of Commitment	Expiration Date	This commitment shall become null and void after the expiration date
$	amount of loan insured. Amortization period	years.	
$			

ower Name:
roperty:

Special Conditions

Commitment Approved by

Underwriting Department

Instruction to Lender:

Please insert mortgage consummation date below and forward original copy of this commitment, together with premium, to Mortgage Guaranty Insurance Corporation, MGIC Plaza, Milwaukee, Wisconsin 53201, following consummation of the loan transaction.

NOTICE AND REMITTANCE

The undersigned lender hereby notifies you that the loan transaction designated above has been consummated, and requests a certificate of insurance in accordance with the terms of the commitment pertaining to said loan.

Remittance of $

in payment of premium is enclosed.

Mortgage Execution Date_____

IDER:

The effective date of the Certificate to be issued shall be the same as the Mortgage Execution Date.

By Authorized Signature of Lender

M-11086 (Rev. 12/77)   01-0034A (12/77)

Illustration 25
Commitment for Insurance

MGIC

Mortgage Guaranty Insurance Corporation

a subsidiary of MGIC Investment Corporation
MGIC Plaza, P.O. Box 488
Milwaukee, Wisconsin 53201

Certificate of Insurance

In consideration of the payment of premium or premiums set forth below, Mortgage Guaranty Insurance
Corporation hereby insures the Lender against loss on the Mortgage loan hereinafter described, subject to the terms and
conditions of the specified Policy.

Insured Lender's Name and Mailing Address

Certificate Number	Master Policy Number	Effective date of this certificate

$ amount of mortgage.   Amortization period   years.

$

Borrower Name:

Property:

In Witness Whereof,

The Company has caused its Corporate Seal to be hereto affixed and these presents to be signed
by its duly authorized officers in facsimile to become effective as its original seal and signatures and binding on the
Company.

Mortgage Guaranty Insurance Corporation

Leon T. Kendall   *John Salani*

President   Secretary

SEAL

R-311983

M-11000 (Rev. 2/76)   01-0054 (2/76)

Illustration 26
Certificate of Insurance

MGIC

Mortgage Guaranty Insurance Corporation
a subsidiary of MGIC Investment Corporation
MGIC Plaza, P.O. Box 488
Milwaukee, Wisconsin 53201

Affidavit

Lender	State of	County of

MGIC Commitment No.	Lender Loan No.

The undersigned purchaser (and, if the undersigned purchaser be more than one, each of the undersigned), having executed (or about to execute) a mortgage or other security instrument dated _____, 19_____, giving the captioned lender a lien on the real property hereinafter described, to secure a loan herein mentioned;

Now Therefore,

the undersigned, being first duly sworn, on their oaths certify that the following representations are true and correct:

A. This loan is sought

    *(1) in order that the undersigned purchasers can purchase from the undersigned vendors the

    *(2) for the purpose of having _____ (Builder or Contractor) construct a single family residence on the

    real property described as follows:

    (*Strike whichever of these statements is inapplicable.)

B. **THE TOTAL PURCHASE PRICE OF SAID PROPERTY, OR CONSTRUCTION COST PLUS LOT VALUE IS $**

C. Downpayment and Purchase Price

    (1) The items comprising the purchasers' total downpayment and purchase price consist of the following:

        (a) Cash to vendors

(i) Earnest money deposit	$	
(ii) Balance of downpayment	$	
(iii) Mortgage proceeds	$	
b Value of real estate traded in	$	
c Purchaser(s)' equity in real estate, such as lot value	$	
d Other* (if no other, so state; if other explain below)	$	
(applicable only if A (1) is stricken)		
*Explain Here: **Total**	$	

    2 The downpayment represented above is true and bona fide.

    3 The cash portion of the downpayment represented above was actually paid, or will be paid no later than the real estate closing, by the purchasers and received by the vendors. [The vendors' signature below is not applicable to (d) of subparagraph C(1).]

D. That no lien or charge upon the said real property, other than the first mortgage to be obtained from the above named lender or liens or charges which will be discharged from the proceeds of said loan, has been given or executed by the undersigned purchaser(s), or has been contracted or agreed to be given or so executed. [The vendors' signature below is applicable only with regards to liens or charges executed or agreed to be executed to the vendors by the purchasers.]

E. That the undersigned purchaser(s) intend in good faith to occupy said property as the purchaser's principal dwelling. [The vendors' signature below is not applicable to paragraph E.]

The undersigned hereby acknowledge that this affidavit is being made for the purpose of inducing an institution insured by the FSLIC to make or purchase the loan herein applied for, and that the provisions of Section 1014 of Title 18, United States Code, which provide in part: "Whoever knowingly makes any false statement or report for the purpose of influencing in any way the action . . . of a Federal Savings and Loan Association . . . upon any application . . . shall be fined not more than $5,000 or imprisoned not more than two years or both." are applicable to this transaction. The undersigned hereby further acknowledge that the lender who originated this loan has relied, and any lender who shall purchase it will rely, upon the allegations set forth by the undersigned and that Mortgage Guaranty Insurance Corporation has relied upon said allegations in insuring this loan.

In Witness Whereof the undersigned have hereunto set their hands and seals:

Purchaser	Vendor
Purchaser	Vendor

Sworn to, by the above named Purchasors	Sworn to, by the above named Vendors
on this _____ day of _____ 19____ before me a Notary Public	on this _____ day of _____ 19____ , before me a Notary Public
the County of _____ and State of _____	for the County of _____ and State of _____
Notary Public signature	Notary Public signature
Commission Expires (NOTARIAL SEAL)	Commission Expires (NOTARIAL SEAL)

MGIC Form 500 (REV. 10/78)

Illustration 27
Affidavit

MGIC   **Mortgage Guaranty Insurance Corporation**

a subsidiary of MGIC Investment Corporation
MGIC Plaza, P.O. Box 488
Milwaukee, Wisconsin 53201

Mortgage Guaranty Master Policy

MG_____

Mortgage Guaranty Insurance Corporation (a Stock Insurance Company herein called the Company) agrees to pay to

_____

_____
(HEREINAFTER CALLED THE INSURED)

in consideration of the premium or premiums to be paid by the Insured as specified in the Certificate, and in reliance upon the statements made in the Application submitted by the Insured, any loss sustained by reason of the default in payments by a Borrower as hereinafter set forth, subject to the following conditions:

CONDITIONS

1. APPLICATION AND COMMITMENT

The Insured shall furnish the Company with an Application in connection with each mortgage loan for which coverage under this policy is desired, on forms furnished and with requirements prescribed by the Company. Approval of the Application shall be at the discretion of the Company and shall be in the form of a Commitment prescribing the terms of the coverage.

2. NOTICE AND CERTIFICATE

Within five (5) days after consummation of the mortgage loan transaction the Insured shall forward notice thereof to the Company, together with the premium, and the Company shall immediately issue and forward a Certificate to the Insured or the Certificate previously issued to the Insured shall then become effective, binding the Company according to the terms and conditions of the Commitment and of this policy. The effective date of the Certificate shall become the date on which the mortgage loan transaction was consummated, which date shall precede the Commitment expiration date or an extension thereof approved in writing by the Company.

3. PAYMENT OF PREMIUMS

In the event that coverage includes renewal privileges, the renewal premiums shall be paid within 45 days following the anniversary of the effective date of the Certificate. Failure to pay any premium, initial or renewal, when due will terminate the liability of the Company with respect to the mortgage loan insured pursuant to the Certificate.

MGIC FORM NO. 4-100 (1/75)

Illustration 28
Mortgage Guaranty Master Policy

4. TERMINATION BY COMPANY

The Company shall remain liable under this policy with respect to such Commitments or Certificates issued to the Insured, as long as the terms and conditions herein contained are fully complied with. However, the Company reserves the right to terminate this policy at any time, subject to its remaining liable on such Commitments and Certificates already issued to the Insured.

5. CANCELLATION BY INSURED

The Insured shall have the privilege of canceling the coverage pursuant to any Certificate by returning such Certificate to the Company. On receipt thereof, the Company shall refund to the Insured such sum as may be determined to be due in accordance with the cancellation schedule set forth on the back cover, hereof; providing however, that no refund shall be paid in the event that a claim for loss has been filed.

6. RESTORATION OF DAMAGE

As a prerequisite for the payment of such loss as may be determined to be due herein, should there be physical loss or damage to the property from any cause, whether through accidental means or otherwise, the Insured shall cause the said property to be restored to its condition at the time of the issuance of the Certificate, reasonable wear and tear excepted.

7. OPEN-END PROVISION

The Insured may increase the mortgage loan balance by making an additional loan to the Borrower, provided that an Application is made therefor subject to approval by the Company. In the event of such approval, the prevailing premium therefor shall be paid to the Company, for the additional amount loaned to the Borrower, and the Company shall issue a Certificate insuring the additional amount.

8. COMPLETED CONSTRUCTION

In the event that the mortgaged premises consists of improvements in the process of construction, the Company shall not be liable until such construction is completed.

9. NOTICE OF DEFAULT

Within 10 days after the Borrower is four (4) months in default, notice thereof shall be given to the Company by the Insured. Monthly reports indicating the default status of the Borrower's account shall be given to the Company thereafter until such time as appropriate proceedings are commenced, title has been vested in the insured, or the Borrower is less than four (4) months in default.

10. PROCEDURE ON DEFAULT

When the Borrower's account is four (4) or more months in default, the Company may direct that the Insured commence appropriate proceedings as herein defined, which shall be commenced, in any event, when the Borrower's account is nine (9) months in default. Such proceedings, when instituted, shall be diligently pursued, and should applicable laws permit the appointment of a receiver, application therefor shall be made by the Insured, with the recommendation that an agent of the Company be appointed to so act. The Company shall be furnished, within a reasonable time, copies of all notices and pleadings required in such proceedings, and with any pertinent information requested by the Company. The Insured shall also furnish to the Company, at least fifteen days prior to the foreclosure sale, if any, a statement indicating the amount anticipated to be due, at the time of the sale, to the Insured under the terms of this policy and shall be required to bid, at the sale, the amount due to the Insured under the terms of this policy. Acceptance by the Insured at any time of a voluntary conveyance from the Borrower of his interest in the mortgaged real estate or commencement by the Insured of appropriate proceedings on default of the Borrower, even though his account is less than four (4) months in default, shall not preclude the Insured from recovery for loss under this policy.

11. COMPUTATION OF LOSS

The amount of loss payable to the Insured shall be limited to the principal balance due pursuant to the mortgage agreement, accumulated interest computed through the date of the tender of conveyance, as hereinafter set forth (penalty interest excluded), real estate taxes and hazard insurance premiums necessarily advanced by the Insured, any expenses necessarily incurred by the Insured in the preservation of the mortgaged real estate, and all other necessary expenses of the appropriate proceedings, including court costs, and reasonable attorneys' fees not exceeding three (3%) per cent of the principal and interest due as herein set forth.

12. WHEN LOSS PAYABLE

Any loss due to the Insured shall be payable within 60 days after filing a claim for such loss on a form to be furnished by the Company. The claim for loss must be accompanied by a tender to the Company of conveyance of title to the mortgaged real estate together with satisfactory evidence that such title is good and merchantable in the Insured, free and clear of all liens and encumbrances. Failure to file a claim for loss within 60 days after completion of

Illustration 28 (cont'd)

appropriate proceedings shall be deemed an election by the Insured to waive any right to claim payment under the terms of this policy.

13. OPTION OF PAYMENT

In lieu of conveyance of title to the mortgaged premises and payment as set forth in Condition 11, the Company shall have the option to pay the percentage of the amount due the insured in accordance with the amount of coverage selected and paid for as indicated on the Certificate of Insurance, or subsequent Certificate amendments which become a part of this policy, and have no claim to said real estate, such payment to be a full and final discharge of the Company's liability.

14. WHERE NOTICE IS GIVEN

All notices, pleadings, claims, tenders, reports and other data required to be given by the Insured to the Company shall be mailed postpaid to the home office of the Company.

15. NO RIGHT OF SUBROGATION AGAINST BORROWER

The Borrower shall not be liable to the Company for any loss paid to the Insured pursuant to this policy; provided, however, that the real estate shall consist of a single family dwelling occupied by the Borrower; otherwise, the Company reserves the right to make claim against the Borrower for any loss paid or deficiency suffered by the Company.

16. TO WHOM PROVISIONS APPLICABLE

The provisions of this policy shall inure to the benefit of and be binding upon the Company and the Insured, and their successors and assigns.

17. SUIT

No suit or action on this policy for recovery of any claim shall be sustained in any court of law or equity unless all the conditions of this policy have been complied with, unless specifically waived by the Company in writing, and unless commenced within two (2) years after the loss can be determined.

18. CONFLICT WITH LAWS

Any provision of this policy which is in conflict with the laws of the jurisdiction in which this policy is effective is hereby amended to conform with the minimum requirements of such laws.

19. DEFINITIONS

Four (4) months of default is defined as the failure to pay the total aggregate amount of four (4) monthly payments due under the terms of the mortgage agreement. Similarly, nine (9) months of default is defined as the failure to pay the total aggregate amount of nine (9) monthly payments due under the terms of the mortgage agreement.

Mortgage agreement is defined to include a note, mortgage, bond, deed of trust, or other instrument used in connection with the Borrower's loan.

Appropriate proceedings are defined as any practical legal remedy permissible, under the laws of the jurisdiction in which the real estate is located, to vest title in the Insured, including, but not limited to, foreclosure by public or private sale.

The term Borrower, or Insured, when used herein, shall mean the single or plural, male or female, individual, partnership, or corporation, as the case may be.

In Witness Whereof, The Company has caused its Corporate Seal to be hereto affixed and these presents to be signed by its duly authorized officers in facsimile to become effective as its original seal and signatures and binding on the Company by virtue of countersignature by its duly authorized agent.

Mortgage Guaranty Insurance Corporation

Leon T. Kendall

PRESIDENT

DATE ....

SEAL

John Halanis

SECRETARY

....
AUTHORIZED REPRESENTATIVE

Illustration 28 (cont'd)

MORTGAGE GUARANTY INSURANCE CORPORATION
SHORT RATE CANCELLATION SCHEDULE

MINIMUM RETAINED PREMIUM

Initial Coverage $50.00   Renewal of Coverage $10.00

ANNUAL PREMIUM PLAN

DAYS POLICY IN FORCE	PER CENT OF PREMIUM RETAINED	DAYS POLICY IN FORCE	PER CENT OF PREMIUM RETAINED	DAYS POLICY IN FORCE	PER CENT OF PREMIUM RETAINED	DAYS POLICY IN FORCE	PER CENT OF PREMIUM RETAINED
1	5	66- 69	29	154-156	53	256-260	77
2	6	70- 73	30	157-160	54	261-264	78
3- 4	7	74- 76	31	161-164	55	265-269	79
5- 6	8	77- 80	32	165-167	56	270-273 (9 mos.)	80
7- 8	9	81- 83	33	168-171	57	274-278	81
9- 10	10	84- 87	34	172-175	58	279-282	82
11- 12	11	88- 91 (3 mos.)	35	176-178	59	283-287	83
13- 14	12	92- 94	36	179-182 (6 mos.)	60	288-291	84
15- 16	13	95- 98	37	183-187	61	292-296	85
17- 18	14	99-102	38	188-191	62	297-301	86
19- 20	15	103-105	39	192-196	63	302-305 (10 mos.)	87
21- 22	16	106-109	40	197-200	64	306-310	88
23- 25	17	110-113	41	201-205	65	311-314	89
26- 29	18	114-116	42	206-209	66	315-319	90
30- 32 (1 mo.)	19	117-120	43	210-214 (7 mos.)	67	320-323	91
33- 36	20	121-124 (4 mos.)	44	215-218	68	324-328	92
37- 40	21	125-127	45	219-223	69	329-332	93
41- 43	22	128-131	46	224-228	70	333-337 (11 mos.)	94
44- 47	23	132-135	47	229-232	71	338-342	95
48- 51	24	136-138	48	233-237	72	343-346	96
52- 54	25	139-142	49	238-241	73	347-351	97
55- 58	26	143-146	50	242-246 (8 mos.)	74	352-355	98
59- 62 (2 mos.)	27	147-149	51	247-250	75	356-360	99
63- 65	28	150-153 (5 mos.)	52	251-255	76	361-365	100

SINGLE PREMIUM PLANS

MONTHS POLICY IN FORCE	3 YR.	4 YR.	5 YR.	7 YR.	10 YR.	12 YR.	15 YR.
1	9	8	7	6	5	3	2
2	16	13	11	9	7	5	4
3	23	18	15	11	9	8	7
4	29	23	19	15	11	10	8
5	34	28	23	17	13	11	10
6	40	33	27	20	15	13	11
7	43	37	31	23	17	15	12
8	47	40	35	25	19	16	14
9	50	42	38	29	21	18	15
10	53	45	40	31	23	20	16
11	57	47	42	35	25	22	18
12 (1 yr.)	60	50	44	37	27	23	19
13	63	52	46	39	29	24	20
14	67	55	48	40	31	26	22
15	70	57	50	41	33	28	23
16	73	60	52	43	35	30	24
17	76	62	54	44	37	31	26
18	78	65	56	46	38	33	27
19	80	67	58	47	39	35	28
20	82	70	60	49	40	36	30
21	84	72	62	50	41	37	31
22	85	75	64	51	42	38	32
23	87	76	66	53	43	39	34
24 (2 yrs.)	89	78	68	54	44	40	35
25	90	79	70	56	45	41	36
26	92	81	72	57	46	42	37
27	93	82	74	59	47	43	38
28	94	84	76	60	48	43	38
29	95	85	77	61	49	44	39
30	96	86	78	63	50	45	40

MONTHS POLICY IN FORCE	3 YR.	4 YR.	5 YR.	7 YR.	10 YR.	12 YR.	15 YR.
31	96	87	79	64	51	46	40
32	97	89	80	66	52	47	41
33	98	90	82	67	53	47	42
34	99	91	83	69	54	48	43
35	99	92	84	70	55	49	43
36 (3 yrs.)	100	93	85	71	56	50	44
37		93	86	73	57	51	45
38		94	87	74	58	52	45
39		95	88	76	59	53	46
40		96	89	76	60	53	47
41		96	90	77	61	54	47
42		97	91	78	62	55	48
43		97	91	78	63	56	49
44		98	92	80	64	57	49
45		98	93	80	65	57	50
46		99	93	82	66	58	51
47		99	94	82	67	59	51
48 (4 yrs.)		100	95	83	68	60	52
49			95	84	69	61	53
50			96	84	70	62	53
51			96	85	71	63	54
52			97	86	72	63	55
53			97	87	73	64	55
54			98	87	74	65	56
55			98	88	75	65	57
56			98	89	76	67	57
57			99	90	76	67	58
58			99	90	77	68	59
59			100	91	77	69	59
60 (5 yrs.)			100	91	78	70	60

MONTHS POLICY IN FORCE	7 YR.	10 YR.	12 YR.	15 YR.
61	92	78	71	61
62	92	79	72	61
63	93	80	73	62
64	93	80	73	63
65	94	81	74	63
66	94	82	75	64
67	95	82	76	65
68	95	83	76	65
69	95	83	77	66
70-71	96	84	77	67
72 (6 yrs.)	96	85	78	68
73	97	85	78	69
74	97	86	79	69
75	97	86	79	70
76	98	87	80	71
77	98	87	80	71
78	98	88	81	72
79	99	88	82	73
80	99	89	82	73
81	99	89	83	74
82	99	90	83	75
83	100	90	84	75
84-85 (7 yrs.)	100	91	84	76
86		91	85	77
87-88		92	86	78
89		92	86	78
90-91		93	87	78
92		93	87	79
93-94		94	88	79
95		94	89	80

MONTHS POLICY IN FORCE	10 YR.	12 YR.	15 YR.
96 (8 yrs.)	95	89	80
97-98	95	90	81
99	95	90	82
100	96	91	82
101-103	96	91	83
104-106	97	92	84
107	97	93	85
108-109 (9 yrs.)	98	93	85
110-112	98	94	86
113-115	99	95	87
116-117	99	95	88
118	100	95	88
119-121 (10 yrs.)	100	96	89
122-124		97	90
125-130		98	91
131-133 (11 yrs.)		98	92
134-139		99	93
140-142		99	94
143-148 (12 yrs.)		100	95
149-154			96
155-160 (13 yrs.)			97
161-169 (14 yrs.)			98
170-175			99
176-180 (15 yrs.)			100

Illustration 28 (cont'd)

INDEX